ALEXANDER CRUDEN, M.A.

CRUDEN'S

USEFUL

CONCORDANCE OF THE HOLY SCRIPTURES

COMPRISING
MOST OF THE REFERENCES
WHICH ARE REALLY NEEDED

A JOVE BOOK

CRUDEN'S CONCORDANCE

A Jove Book / published by arrangement with
Epworth Press

PRINTING HISTORY
Eleven previous paperback printings
Jove edition / August 1978
Second printing / October 1982

ISBN: 0-515-06741-5

Jove books are published by Jove Publications,
Inc., 200 Madison Avenue, New York, N.Y. 10016.
The words "A JOVE BOOK" and the "J" with sunburst
are trademarks belonging to Jove Publications, Inc.

PRINTED IN THE UNITED STATES OF AMERICA

INTRODUCTION

THE Compiler of this Concordance indulges
the hope that it will be found very useful to
those who love the Holy Scriptures. It
comprehends many more References than
there are in several cheap Concordances now
extant. Some of them are very deficient in
references to evangelical passages, and to
those bearing on faith and practice. To
these the Compiler has paid particular
attention, and he has included nearly the
whole of such references.

CONCORDANCE

ABASE, to make low, to humble, &c.
Job 40. 11. every one proud *a.* him
Is. 31. 4. lion will not *a.* himself
Ezek. 21. 26. exalt low and *a.* high
Dan. 4. 37. walk in pride able to *a.*
ABASED, *Matt.* 23. 12. himself shall be *a.*
Phil. 4. 12. how to be *a.* and how to
ABASING, 2 *Cor.* 11. 7. offence in *a.* myself
ABATED, *Gen.* 8. 8. After 150 days waters *a.* : 11.
Lev. 27. 18. shall be *a.* from estimation
Deut. 34. 7. nor his natural force *a.*
Judg. 8. 3. then their anger was *a.*
ABBA, *Mark* 14. 36. *a.* Father, all things are possible to thee
Rom. 8. 15. whereby we cry *a.* Father
Gal. 4. 6. sent his Spirit into your hearts crying *a.* Father
ABHOR, greatly hate and loathe
Lev. 26. 11. my soul shall not *a.* you
15. if your soul *a.* my judgments
30. my soul shall *a.* you
Deut. 7. 26. thou shalt utterly *a.* it
1 *Sam.* 27. 12. make his people to *a.* him
Job 9. 31. my own clothes shall *a.* me
Job 30. 10. they *a.* me, they flee
42. 6. I *a.* myself and repent in
Ps. 5. 6. Lord will *a.* bloody man
119. 163. I hate and *a.* lying
Prov. 24. 24. nations shall *a.* him
Jer. 14. 21. not *a.* for thy name's sake
1 *Sam.* 5. 10. they *a.* him that speaketh
6. 8. I *a.* the excellency of Jacob
Mic. 3. 9. ye that *a.* judgment
Rom. 12. 9. *a.* that which is evil
ABHORRED *Ex.* 5. 21. made our savour to be *a.*
Lev. 26. 43. their soul *a.* my statues
Deut. 32. 19. when the Lord saw it he *a.*
1 *Sam.* 2. 17. men *a.* the offering of the Lord
2 *Sam.* 16. 21. thou art *a.* of thy father
Job. 19. 19. all my inward friends *a.* me
Ps. 22. 24. nor *a.* affliction of afflicted
78. 59. wroth and greatly *a.* Israel
P . 89. 38. hast cast off and *a.* anointed
106. 40. he *a.* his own inheritance
Prov. 22. 14. *a.* of the Lord shall fall
Lam. 2. 7. L. hath *a.* his sanctuary
Ezek. 16. 25. made thy beauty *a.*
Zech. 11. 8. their soul *a.* me
ABHORREST, *Is.* 7. 16. the land that thou *a.* forsaken

Rom. 2. 22. thou that *a.* idols
ABHORRETH, *Job* 33. 20. his life *a.* bread
Ps. 10. 3. covetous whom Lord *a.*
36. 4. he *a.* not evil
107. 18. soul *a.* all manner of meat
Is. 49. 7. him whom the nation *a.*
ABHORRING *Is.* 66. 24. be *a.* to all flesh
ABIDE, continue, bear
Gen. 19. 2. will *a.* in the street all night
22. 5. *a.* you here with the ass
Gen. 29. 19. give her thee, *a.* with me
44. 33. let servant *a.* instead of lad
Ex. 16. 29. *a.* every man in place
Lev. 8. 35. *a.* at the door of the tabernacle
Num. 31. 19. *a.* without camp seven days
Num. 35. 25. *a.* in it unto the death
Ruth 2. 8. but *a.* here fast by my maidens
1 *Sam.* 1. 22. appear before the Lord *a.* for ever
5. 7. the ark of God shall not *a.* with us
22. 23. *a.* thou with me, fear not
30. 21. whom they had made to *a.* at Besor
2 *Sam.* 11. 11. ark and Israel *a.* in tents
Job 24. 13. rebel, nor *a.* in the paths of the light
38. 40. *a.* in the covert to lie in wait
39. 9. will the unicorn be willing to *a.* by thy crib
Ps. 15. 1. who shall *a.* in thy tabernacle
61. 4. I will *a.* in thy tabernacle
7. he shall *a.* before G. for ever
91. 1. *a.* under shadow of Almighty
Prov. 7. 11. her feet *a.* not in her house
19. 23. that hath it shall *a.* satisfied
Eccl. 8. 15. for that shall *a.* with him of his labour
Jer. 10. 10. nations not able to *a.* his indignation
42. 10. if ye *a.* in this land I will build
Hos. 3. 3. shall *a.* for me many days
4. Israel shall *a.* without a king
Joel 2. 11. day is terrible who can *a.* it
Nah. 1. 6. who can *a.* the fierceness of his anger
Mal. 3. 2. who may *a.* day of his coming
Matt. 10. 11. there *a.* till ye go thence
Mark 6. 10. there *a.* till ye depart
Luke 9. 4. there *a.* and thence depart
Luke 19. 5. to-day I must *a.* at thy house
24. 29. *a.* with us, for it is towards

7

evening
John 12. 46. should not *a.* in darkness
  14. 16. comforter, that he may *a.*
  15. 4. *a.* in me and I in you, ver. 7.
    10. ye shall *a.* in my love
Acts 15. 34. Silas to *a.* there still
  16. 15. come into my house and *a.* there
  20. 23. afflictions *a.* me
  27. 31. except these *a.* in ship, ye cannot be saved
1 *Cor.* 3. 14. if any man's work *a.*
  7. 8. it is good if they *a.* even as I
  20. man *a.* in the same calling
  24. is called, therein *a.* with G.
Phil. 1. 24. to *a.* in the flesh is needful
  25. know I shall *a.* with you
1 *Tim.* 1. 3. I besought thee to *a.* at Ephesus
1 *John* 2. 24. let that therefore *a.* in you
  27. 28. ye shall *a.* in him
ABIDETH, *Ps.* 49. 12. man in honour *a.* not
  55. 19. even that *a.* of old
  125. 1. like mount Zion which *a.*
Eccl. 1. 4. the earth *a.* for ever
John 3. 36. wrath of God *a.* on him
  8. 35. servant *a.* not, but the son *a.*
  12. 24. except it die it *a.* alone
  34. Christ *a.* for ever
  15. 5. *a.* in me brings forth fruit
1 *Cor.* 13. 13. now *a.* faith, hope, &c.
2 *Tim.* 2. 13. yet he *a.* faithful
Heb. 7. 3. Melchizedec *a.* a priest continually
1 *Pet.* 1. 23. word of G. *a.* for ever
1 *John* 2. 6. he that saith he *a.* in him ought to walk
  10. he that loveth his brother *a.* in the light
1 *John* 2. 17. doeth will of God *a.* ever
  3. 6. whosoever *a.* in him sinneth not
  3. 14. that loveth not his brother *a.* in death
  24. hereby we know he *a.* in us
ABIDING, 1 *Chron.* 29. 15. days are as a shadow, there is none *a.*
Luke 2. 8. there were shepherds *a.* in the field
John 5. 38. not his word *a.* in you
1 *John* 3. 15. no murderer hath eternal life *a.*
John 14. 23. make our abode with him
ABILITY, in strength, wealth, &c.
Lev. 27. 8. to his *a.* that vowed
Ezra 2. 69. they gave after their *a.* to the work
Neh. 5. 8. we after our *a.* redeemed our brethren
Dan. 1. 4. as had *a.* to stand in the king's palace
Matt. 25. 15. to every man according to his *a. Acts* 11. 29.
1 *Pet.* 4. 11. as of the *a.* G. giveth
ABJECTS, base men, *Ps.* 35. 15. Low base persons, and probably hired assassins.
ABLE, when applied to God, denotes his gracious power, and includes his love, faithfulness, and grace. It is necessary to remember this, in order to perceive the force of such expressions as *Rom.* 4. 21 ; 2 *Cor.* 9. 8 ; *Eph.* 3. 20.—Able.

Ex. 18. 21. *a.* men, such as fear God
Lev. 14. 22. such as he is *a.* to get
Num. 13. 30. go up, for we are *a.* to overcome it
Deut. 16. 17. every man give as he is *a.*
Josh. 23. 9. no man hath been *a.* to stand before
1 *Sam.* 6. 20. who is *a.* to stand before holy God
1 *Kings* 3. 9. who is *a.* to judge so great a people
2 *Chron.* 2. 6. who is *a.* to build house
  20. 6. none is *a.* to withstand
  25. 9. the Lord is *a.* to give thee much more
Job 41. 10. who is *a.* to stand before me
Prov. 27. 4. but who is *a.* to stand before envy
Ezek. 46. 11. the offering shall be as he is *a.* to give
Dan. 3. 17. God whom we serve is *a.* to deliver ; 6. 20.
  4. 37. walk in pride he is *a.* to abase
Matt. 3. 9. God is *a.* of these stones to raise up children, *Luke* 3. 8.
Matt. 9. 28. believe ye I am *a.* to do this
  10. 28. are not *a.* to kill the soul
  19. 12. *a.* to receive it let him
  20. 22. are ye *a.* to drink of cup
Mark 4. 33. as they were *a.* to hear
John 10. 29. no man *a.* to pluck
Acts 15. 10. a yoke our fathers, were not *a.* to bear
  20. 32. word of his grace *a.* to build
Rom. 4. 21. promised *a.* to perform
  14. 4. G. is *a.* to make him stand
1 *Cor.* 3. 2. neither yet now are ye *a.*
  10. 13. tempted above that ye are *a.*
2 *Cor.* 3. 6. made us *a.* ministers of N. Testament
2 *Cor.* 9. 8. *a.* to make all grace abound
Eph. 3. 20. *a.* to do exceeding abundantly
Phil. 3. 21. *a.* to subdue all things to himself
2 *Tim.* 1. 12. *a.* to keep that committed
  3. 7. never *a.* to come to the knowledge of truth
  3. 15. Scriptures *a.* to make wise
Heb. 2. 18. *a.* to succour tempted
  5. 7. *a.* to save him from death
  7. 25. *a.* to save to the uttermost
  11. 19. *a.* to raise him from the dead
James 1. 21. *a.* to save your souls
  4. 12. *a.* to save and to destroy
Jude 24. *a.* to keep from falling
Rev. 5. 3. no man was *a.* to open the book
ABLE, be able, *Lev.* 25. 20. and himself *be a.* to redeem it
Josh. 14. 12. if the Lord be with me I shall *be a.* to drive
1 *Chron.* 29. 14. that we shall *be a.* to offer willingly
Rom. 8. 39. who shall *be a.* to separate us from the love of G.
1 *Cor.* 10. 13. that ye may *be a.* to bear it
Eph. 3. 18. may *be a.* to comprehend with all saints
  6. 11. *a.* to stand against the devil
  16. faith wherewith shall *be a.* to quench

2 *Tim.* 2. 2. who shall *be a.* to teach others also

Titus 1. 9. may *be a.* by sound doctrine to exhort

2 *Pet.* 1. 15. that ye may *be a.* after my decease

Rev. 6. 17. the day of his wrath is come, and who shall *be a.* to stand ?

ABLE, not be able, *Ps.* 36. 12. cast down, and shall *not be a.* to rise

Eccl. 8. 17. ye shall *not be a.* to find it

Jer. 11. 11. *not be a.* to escape

   49. 10. *not be a.* to hide

Ezek. 7. 19. gold shall *not be a.* to deliver them

Luke 13. 24. seek, *not be a.*

   12. 15. *not be a.* to gainsay

ABLE, not able, *Num.* 13. 31. we be *not a.* to go up against the people

Num. 14. 16. because the Lord was *not a.* Deut. 9. 28.

Neh. 4. 10. so that we are *not a.* to build the wall

Ps. 40. 12. hold on me, so that I am *not a.* to look up

Luke 12. 26. if ye be *not a.* to do the thing is least

   14. 29. laid foundation, and is *not a.* to finish

Acts 6. 10. and they were *not a.* to resist the wisdom

ABOARD, *Acts* 21. 2. we went *a.* and set forth

ABODE, (noun) 2 *Kings* 19. 27 : *Isa.* 37. 28. I know thy *a.*

John 14. 23. make our *a.* with him

ABODE, (verb) *Gen.* 49. 24. but his bow *a.* in strength

Ex. 24. 16. the glory of the Lord *a.* on Sinai

Num. 9. 17. where cloud *a.* Israel pitched, 18. 21.

Judg. 21. 2. people *a.* there till even

1 *Sam.* 7. 2. while the ark *a.* in Kirjathjearim, time long

   13. 16. Saul and Jona. *a.* in Gibeah

   26. 3. David *a.* in wilderness

Ezra 8. 32. came to Jerusalem and *a.*

Matt. 17. 22. and while he *a.* in Galilee, Jesus said

   8. 27. nor *a.* in any house, but in the tombs

   8. 44. he was a murderer, and *a.* not in the truth

Luke 1. 56. Mary *a.* with Eliza. 3 months

John 1. 39. they *a.* with him that day; 32

   7. 9. said these words, he *a.* in Galilee

   11. 6. he *a.* two days where he was

Acts 1. 13. an upper room where a Peter and James

   14. 3. long time *a.* they speaking boldly in the

Acts 14. 28. there they *a.* long time

   17. 14. Silas and Timotheus *a.* there still

   18. 3. Paul *a.* with them and wrought

   21. 7. we came and *a.* with the brethren one day

   8. we entered the house of Philip and *a.* with him

Gal. 1. 18. I went and *a.* with Peter fifteen days

ABOLISH, signifies to do away, or make void. *Isa.* 2. 18. idols he shall utterly *a.*

ABOLISHED, *Isa.* 51. 6. righteousness not be *a.*

Ezek. 6. 6. your works may be *a.*

2 *Cor.* 3. 13. to the end of that *a.*

Eph. 2. 15. having *a.* in his flesh

2 *Tim.* 1. 10. J. C. who hath *a.* death

ABOMINABLE, very hateful, *Lev.* 7. 21. & 11. 43. & 18. 30. *Is.* 14. 19. & 65. 4. *Jer.* 16. 18.

1 *Chr.* 21. 6. king's word *a.* to Joab

2 *Chr.* 15. 8. Asa put away the *a.* idols from Judah

Job 15. 16. how much more *a.* is man

Ps. 14. 1. have done *a.* works. 53. 1.

Isa. 14. 19. thou art cast out like an *a.* branch

   65. 4. and broth *a.* things is in their vessels

   8. 10. I saw and behold *a.* beasts and idols

Jer. 44. 4. do not this *a.* thing I hate

Ezek. 16. 52. thy sins more *a.* than

Nah. 3. 6. I will cast *a.* filth on thee

Tit. 1. 16. in works deny him being *a.*

1 *Pet.* 4. 3. walked in *a.* idolatries

Rev. 21. 8. unbelieving and *a.*

ABOMINABLY, 1 *Kings* 21. 26. Ahab did very *a.* in following idols

ABOMINATION, what is very filthy, hateful & loathsome, as sin, *Is.* 66. 3. idols, *Ex.* 8. 26.

Deut. 7. 25. it is *a.* to the Lord thy God, 17. 1.

   13. 14. that such *a.* is wrought among you, 17. 4.

   18. 12. all that do these things are an *a.* 22. 5.

   25. 16. all that do unrighteously are an *a.* to God

Ps. 88. 8. thou hast made me an *a.* to them

Prov. 3. 32. the forward is an *a.* to the L.

   6. 16. seven things are an *a.* to the L.

   11. 1. false balance is an *a.* to the L.

   20. they of froward heart are an *a.*

   12. 22. lying lips are *a.* to the L.

   13. 19. it is an *a.* to fools to depart from evil

   15. 8. sacrifice of wicked an *a.*

   26. thoughts of wicked are *a.*

   16. 5. proud is *a.* to the L. 3. 32.

   20. 23. divers weights are *a.* to the Lord

   28. 9. his prayer shall be *a.*

   29. 27. unjust is *a.* to just, &c.

Isa. 1. 13. incense is an *a.* to me

   41. 24. an *a.* is he that chooseth you

   66. 17. eating swine's flesh, and the *a.* and mouse

Jer. 2. 7. ye entered, ye made my heritage an *a.*

   6. 15. ashamed when they committed *a.* 8. 12.

   32. 35. that they should do this *a.* to cause Judah

Dan. 11. 31. *a.* that maketh desolate, 12. 11. *Matt.* 24. 15. *Mark* 13. 14.

Luke 16. 15. is *a.* in sight of God

Rev. 21. 27. whatsoever worketh *a.*

ABOMINATIONS, *Deut.* 18. 9. not learn to do after the *a.* of nations

1 *Kings* 14. 24. did according to all *a.*

of nations
2 *Kings* 21. 2. *a.* of heathen
Ezra 9. 14. join with people of these *a.*
Prov. 26. 25. seven *a.* in his heart
Jer. 7. 10. delivered to do all these *a.*
44. 22. the Lord could not bear for the *a.*
Ezek. 8. 6. seest thou the great *a.* of Israel, but turn thee yet again, and thou shalt see greater *a.* 13. 15.
16. 2. cause Jerusalem to know her *a.* 20. 4. & 23. 36.
18. 13. done all these *a.* shall die
20. 4. cause them to know the *a.* of their father
22. 2. yea, thou shalt show her all her *a.*
36. 31. and shall loathe yourselves for all your *a.*
44. 6. O Israel, let it suffice you of all your *a.*
7. they have broken my covenant for all your *a.*
Dan. 9. 27. for overspreading of *a.*
Rev. 17. 4. mother of harlots is *a.*
ABOMINATIONS, (their) *Deut.* 20. 18. teach you not to do after all *their a.*
29. 17. and ye have seen *their a.* and their idols
Is. 66. 3. and their soul delighted in *their a.*
Jer. 7. 30. have set *their a.* in the house called 32. 34.
Ezek. 6. 9. for the evils committed in all *their a.*
12. 16. that they may declare all *their a.*
20. 30. and commit ye whoredom after *their a.*
43. 8. they have defiled my holy name by *their a.*
44. 13. they shall bear all their shame and *their a.*
ABOMINATIONS, (these) *Lev.* 18. 26. ye shall not commit any of *these a.*
27. all *these a.* have the men of the land done
29. whosoever shall commit any of *these a.*
2 *Kings* 21. 11. Manasseh had done *these a.*
Ezra 9. 14. join in affinity with people of *these a.*
ABOMINATIONS (thine or thy) *Jer.* 4. 1 if thou wilt put away *thine a.* out of sight
Jer. 13. 27. I have seen *thine a.* on the hills
Ezek. 5. 9. do what I have not, because of *thine a.*
11. thou hast defiled my sanctuary with *thy a.*
16. 51. hast multiplied *thine a.* more than they
58. thou hast borne *thine a.* saith the Lord
ABOUND, to have plenty, *Prov.* 28. 20. Grace abounds, 2 *Cor.* 9. 8. Good men abound in the work of the Lord ; 1 *Cor.* 15. 58. Bad men abound in transgression ; *Prov.* 29. 22. To become very full, large ; *Prov.* 8. 24 ; *Rom.* 3. 7.
Prov. 28. 20. faithful shall *a.* blessings

Matt. 24. 12. because iniquity shall *a.*
Rom. 5. 20. offence might *a.*, sin *a.*, grace much more *a.*
6. 1. continue in sin that grace may *a.*
2 *Cor.* 1. 5. as sufferings *a.* so consolation *a.*
7. as ye *a.* in everything, see that ye *a.*
2 *Cor.* 9. 8. able to make all grace *a.* may *a.* in every good work
Phil. 1. 9. that your love may *a.*
4. 12. I know how to *a.* and how
17. fruit that may *a.* to your account
18. I have all and *a.*
1 *Thess.* 3. 12. Lord make you *a.* in love
2 *Pet.* 1. 8. these things be in you and *a.*
ABOUNDED, eth, ing, *Prov.* 8. 24. when no fountains *a.* with water
Rom. 3. 7. for if the truth of God hath more *a.*
5. 15. grace by Jesus Christ hath *a.* to many
20. but where sin *a.* grace much more *a.*
1 *Cor.* 15. 58. always *a.* in the work of the Lord
Eph. 1. 8. he hath *a.* towards us
Col. 2. 7. *a.* therein with thanksgiving
2 *Thess.* 1. 3. the charity toward each other *a.*
ABOVE, high, *Gen.* 6. 16 ; beyond, 2 *Cor.* 1. 8 ; the dignity or excellency of a person or thing, *Ps.* 113. 4 ; *Matt.* 10. 24 ; .beyond, 2 *Cor.* 1. 8 ; more than, *Gen.* 3. 14 ; a higher state or rank, *Num.* 16. 3 ; chief in authority and power, *Deut.* 28. 13 ; heaven, or the highest state, *Job* 3. 4 ; *Rom.* 10. 6 ; things that relate to heaven, *Gal.* 4. 26 ; *Col.* 3. 1 ; God, *James* 1. 17.
Gen. 1. 7. from the waters *a.* the firmament
20. and fowl that may fly *a.* the earth
7. 17. and the ark was lifted up *a.* the earth
48. 22. given thee one portion *a.* thy brethren
49. 26. prevailed *a.* the blessings of my progenitors
Ex. 25. 22. I will commune from *a.* the mercy-seat
Lev. 11. 21. which have legs *a.* their feet to leap
Num. 16. 3. lift up yourselves *a.* the congregation
Deut. 17. 20. heart be lifted up *a.* his brethren
25. 3. lest if he should beat him *a.* these
30. 5. do thee good and multiply thee *a.* thy fathers
Josh. 3. 13. the waters that come down from *a.* 16.
Judg. 5. 24. blessed shall she be *a.* women in the tent
2 *Sam.* 22. 17. he sent from *a. Ps.* 18. 16.
Neh. 7. 2. Hananiah feared God *a.* many
Job 3. 4. let not God regard it from *a.*
Ps. 10. 5. thy judgments are *a.* out of his sight
18. 48. thou liftest me *a.* those that rise up
27. 6. now shall my head be lifted up

a. mine enemies

45. 7. the oil of gladness *a.* thy fellows, *Heb.* 1. 9.

119. 127. I love thy commandments *a.* gold

137. 6. if I prefer not Jerusalem *a.* my chief joy

Prov. 8. 28. when he established the clouds *a.*

15. 24. the way of life is *a.* to the wise

31. 10. for her price is far *a.* rubies

Eccl. 3. 19. a man hath no pre-eminence *a.* a beast

Isa. 6. 2. *a.* it stood the seraphims, each had six wings

Jer. 15. 8. their widows increased *a.* sand of the seas

Ezek. 1. 26. as appearance of a man *a.* upon it

Dan. 6. 3. Daniel was preferred *a.* the presidents

Nah. 3. 16. has multiplied thy merchants *a.* the stars

Matt. 10. 24. disciple not *a.* his master, *Luke* 6. 40.

6. 13. baskets which remained over and *a.*

John 3. 31. cometh from *a.* is *a.* all

John 8. 23. I am from *a.* ye from beneath

19. 11. power given thee from *a.*

Acts 26. 13. I saw a light *a.* the brightness of the sun

Rom. 10. 6. that is, to bring Christ down from *a.*

14. 5. one man esteemeth one day *a.* another

1 *Cor.* 4. 6. not to think of men *a.* what is written

10. 13. you to be tempted *a.* that ye are able

15. 6. was seen of *a.* 500 brethren at once

2 *Cor.* 11. 23. I am more in stripes *a.* measure

12. 2. *a.* fourteen years ago, whether

Gal. 4. 26. Jerusalem which is *a.*

Eph. 4. 6. one God who is *a.* all

Phil. 2. 9. and given him a name *a.* every name

Col. 3. 1. seek things which are *a.*

2. set your affections on things *a.*

Heb. 10. 8. *a.* when he said sacrifice and offering

James 1. 17. every perfect gift from *a.*

3. 15. wisdom from *a.* is pure

ABOVE ALL, *Gen.* 3. 14. the serpent is cursed *a. all* cattle

Num. 12. 3. Moses was very meek *a. all* the men

Deut. 7. 14. thou shalt be blessed *a. all* people

10. 15. he choose you *a. all* people, as it is this day

14. 2. chosen thee *a. all* the nations, 26. 19.

1 *Kings* 16. 30. Ahab did evil *a. all* that were before him

1 *Chron.* 29. 3. over and *a. all* I have prepared

Esth. 2. 17. king loved Esther *a. all* the women

Ps. 97. 9. thou Lord art high *a. all* the earth

138. 2. magnified thy word *a. all* thy name

Jer. 17. 9. the heart is deceitful *a. all* things

Ezek. 31. 5. his height was exalted *a. all* the trees

Luke 13. 2. these sinners *a. all* the Galileans

John 3. 31. he that cometh from heaven is *a. all*

Eph. 1. 21. far *a. all* principality and power

3. 20. *a. all* that we ask or think—4.

6. one God *a. all*

6. 16. *a. all* taking shield of faith

Col. 3. 14. *a. all* things put on charity

James 5. 12. *a. all* things my brethren swear not

1 *Pet.* 4. 8. *a. all* things have fervent charity

3 *John* 2. I wish *a. all* things, that thou prosper

ABRAM, ABRAHAM, *Gen.* 12. 1. Lord said to A. get out of thy country

Gen. 12. 10. A. went down into Egypt to sojourn there

13. 1. A. went up out of Egypt, he and his wife

12. A. dwelt in land of Canaan, and Lot in cities

18. A. came and dwelt in the plain of Mamre

14. 14. A. armed his trained servants, 3. 18.

15. 1. fear not, A. I am thy exceeding great reward

18. that day the Lord made a covenant with A.

17. 5. thy name shall be A. 1 *Chr.* 1. 27; *Neh.* 9. 7.

18. 6. A. hastened into the tent unto Sarah

17. shall I hide from A. that thing which I do?

20. 2. A. said of Sarah his wife, she is my sister

22. 1. God did tempt A. and said, take thy son

23. 2. Sarah died, and A. came to mourn for her

17. A. bought the field of Ephron, 49. 30; 50. 13.

2. A. said, put thy hand under my thigh

42. O Lord God of my master A. prosper my way

25. 5. and A. gave all that he had unto Isaac

7. these are the days of the years of A. life

24. I will multiply thy seed for A. sake

50. 24. bring to land which he sware to A. *Ex.* 33. 1; *Num.* 32. 11; *Deut.* 1. 8; 6. 10; 30. 20.

Ex. 3. 6. I am the God of A. 15. 16; 4. 5. *Matt.* 22. 32; *Mark* 12. 26; *Luke* 20. 37; *Acts* 3. 13; 17. 32.

Ps. 105. 9. which covenant he made with A.

Is. 29. 22. thus saith the Lord, who redeemed A.

63. 16. art our father, though A. be ignorant of us

Ezek. 33. 24. A. was one, and he inherited the land

Mic. 7. 20. perform the mercy promised to A.

Matt. 1. 1. Christ the son of David, the son of A.

3. 9. God is able to raise up children unto A.

8. 11. shall sit down with A. in kingdom of heaven

Luke 13. 28. when ye shall see A. in the kingdom of God

16. 23. he lifted up his eyes, and seeth A. afar off

John 8. 40. this did not A. 52. A. is dead

57. hast thou seen A ? 58. before A. was, I am

Rom. 4. 2. for if A. were justified by works, he hath

3. A. believed God, and was counted to him for righteousness, 9. *Gal.* 3. 6 ; *James* 2. 23.

Gal. 3. 7. who are of faith are the children of A.

9. they of faith are blessed with faithful A.

4. 22. A. had two sons, the one by a bond-maid

Heb. 11. 8. A. obeyed. 17. by faith A. offered up Isaac

ABRAHAM *with* father, *Gen.* 26. 3. I will perform the oath to A. thy *father*

Josh. 24. 3. I took your *father* A. from the other side

Is. 51. 2. look to A. your *father* and to Sarah

Matt. 3. 9. we have A. to our *father*, *Luke* 3. 8.

Luke 1. 73. the oath which he swore to our *father* A.

16. 24. he said, *father* A. have mercy on me

John 8. 39. they said to him, A. is our *father*

53. art thou greater than *father* A.

56. your *father* A. rejoiced to see my day, and was glad

Rom. 4. 12. in the steps of that faith of our *father* A.

James 2. 21. was not A. our *father* justified by works ?

ABRAHAM *joined with* seed, *Luke* 1. 55. as he spake to A. and his *seed* for ever

John 8. 33. we be A. *seed* and were never in bondage

Rom. 4. 13. the promise was not to A. or to his *seed*

Gal. 3. 16. to A. and his *seed* were the promises made

Heb. 2. 16. took on him the *seed* of A.

ABSALOM, 2 *Sam.* 3. 3. A. the son of Maacah, 1 *Chr.* 3. 2.

2 *Sam.* 13. 22. spake to Ammon neither good nor bad

23. A. had sheep-shearers in Baal-hazor

39. the soul of king David longed to go forth to A.

14. 25. there was none to be so much praised as A.

15. 6. so A. stole the hearts of the men of Israel

17. 4. Ahithophel's counsel pleased

A. well

24. A. passed over Jordan. 26. pitched in Gilead

18. 5. saying, deal gently for my sake with A.

10. behold, I saw A. hanged in an oak

29. is young man A. safe ? 32. 33. O my son A.

2 *Chr.* 11. 20. he took Maacah daughter of A.

ABSENCE, *Luke* 22. 6. to betray him in *a.* of multitude

Phil. 2. 12. much more in my *a.* work out

ABSENT, one from another, *Gen.* 31. 49.

1 *Cor.* 5. 3. as *a.* in body, but present

2 *Cor.* 5. 6. in body *a.* from the L.

8. rather to be *a.* from the body

9. that whether present or *a.*

10. 1. but being *a.* am bold towards you

Col. 2. 5. though I be *a.* in the flesh

ABSTAIN, *Acts* 15. 20. that they *a.* from pollutions of idols

1 *Thess.* 4. 3. *a.* from fornication

5. 22. *a.* from all appearance of evil

1 *Tim.* 4. 3. command, to *a.* from meats

1 *Pet.* 2. 11. *a.* from fleshly lusts

Abstinence from meat, *Acts* 27. 21.

ABUNDANCE, great fulness and plenty *Job.* 22. 11. & 38. 34. *Deut.* 33. 19. 1 *Chr.* 22. 3. 4. 14. 15.

Deut. 28. 47. for *a.* of all things

33. 19. they shall suck of the *a.* of the seas

1 *Sam.* 1. 16. out of the *a.* of my complaint

1 *Kings* 10. 10. came no more such *a.* of spices

2 *Chron.* 9. 9. she gave the king, of spices great *a.*

Eccl. 5. 10. loveth *a.* with increase

12. of the rich will not suffer

Is. 60. 5. the *a.* of the sea shall be converted to thee

66. 11. delighted with *a.* of her glory

Jer. 33. 6. I will reveal to them the *a.* of peace

Ezek. 16. 49. *a.* of idleness was in her and daughters

26. 10. by reason of the *a.* of his horses

Matt. 12. 34. out of *a.* of the heart the mouth speaketh, *Luke* 6. 45.

Matt. 13. 12. shall have more *a.* 25. 29.

Mark 12. 44. have cast in of their *a.*

Luke 12. 15. life consisteth not in *a.*

Rom. 5. 17. more they which receive *a.* of grace

2 *Cor.* 8. 2. *a.* of their joy abounded

14. your *a. a.* supply, their *a. a.* supply for want

12. 7. through *a.* of revelations

Rev. 18. 3. waxed rich through the *a.* of her delicacies

ABUNDANCE, (in Abundance) 2 *Sam.* 12. 30. David brought spoil of the *in a.*

1 *Chron.* 22. 3. David prepared brass *in a.* 14.

15. there are workers with thee *in a.* hewers

2 *Chron.* 2. 9. even to prepare me timber *in a.*

9. 1. Queen of Sheba brought gold *in a.*

17. 5. all Judah brought presents to Jehoshaphat, and he had riches and honour *in a.*

20. 25. Jehoshaphat found spoil *in a.*

31. 5. children of Israel brought *in a.* first-fruits

32. 5. Hezekiah made darts and shields *in a.*

Neh. 9. 25. they took vineyards and fruit-trees *in a.*

Esth. 1. 7. they gave them royal wine *in a.*

Ps. 37. 11. delight themselves *in a.* of peace

105. 30. the land brought forth frogs *in a.*

Luke 12. 15. man's life consisteth not *in a.*

2 *Cor.* 8. 20. that no man blame us *in this a.*

ABUNDANT, *a.* in goodness, and in truth, *Ex.* 34. 6.

Is. 56. 12. shall be as this day, and much more *a.*

1 *Cor.* 12. 23. on these we bestow more *a.* honour

2 *Cor.* 4. 15. that the *a.* grace might redound

7. 15. his inward affection is more *a.* toward you

9. 12. for the administration is *a.* by many

11. 23. in labours more *a.*

Phil. 1. 26. that your rejoicing be more *a.*

1 *Tim.* 1. 14. and the grace of our Lord exceeding *a.*

1 *Pet.* 1. 3. his *a.* mercy hath begotten

ABUNDANTLY, *Gen.* 1. 20. Let the waters bring forth *a.* 21.

Gen. 9. 7. multiply, bring forth *a.* in the earth

Ex. 1. 7. the children of Israel increased *a.*

Num. 20. 11. Moses smote and the water came out *a.*

Job 12. 6. God bringeth *a.*

36. 28. the clouds drop, and distil upon man *a.*

Ps. 36. 8. shall be *a.* satisfied with

132. 15. I will *a.* bless her provision

145. 7. shall *a.* utter the memory of thy goodness

Songs 5. 1. yea drink *a.* O beloved

Is. 35. 2. it shall blossom *a.* and rejoice with joy

55. 7. he will *a.* pardon

John 10. 10. might have life more *a.*

1 *Cor.* 15. 10. laboured more *a.* than all

2 *Cor.* 1. 12. conversation, and more *a.* to you-wards

2.4. might know the love I have more *a.* to you

12. 15. though the more *a.* I love you, the less

Eph. 3. 20. able to do exceeding *a.*

1 *Thess.* 2. 17. endeavoured more *a.* to see your face

Heb. 6. 17. God willing more *a.* to show to the heirs

Tit. 3. 6. shed on us *a.* through J. C.

2 *Pet.* 1. 11. entrance ministered more *a.*

ABUSE, *Judg.* 19. 25. *a.* her all night till morning

1 *Cor.* 9. 18. *a.* not my power in gospel

ABUSERS, ING, 1 *Cor.* 6. 9. nor *a.* of themselves with mankind

1 *Cor.* 7. 31. and they that use this world as not *a.* it

ACCEPT, *Gen.* 4. 7. if well, shalt thou not be *a* ?

Gen. 32. 20. peradventure he will *a.* of me

Deut. 33. 11. bless and *a.* the work of his hands

2 *Sam.* 24. 23. the Lord thy God *a.* thee

Job 13. 8. will ye *a.* his person ?

10. will reprove, if ye do secretly *a.* persons

32. 21. let not *a.* any man's person

34. 19. *a.* not persons of princes

42. 9. Lord also *a.* Job

Ps. 119. 108. *a.* I beseech thee the free-will-offerings

Prov. 18. 5. not good to *a.* person of wicked

Jer. 14. 12 ; *Amos* 5. 22. I will not *a.* them

Ezek. 43. 27. I will *a.* you, saith the Lord

20. 40. there will I *a.* them, and require

41. I will *a.* you with your sweet savour

Hosea 8. 13. sacrifice, but the Lord *a.* them not

Mal. 1. 8. will he be pleased, or *a.* thy person ?

13. should I *a.* this of your hands ?

20. 21. neither *a.* person of any

Acts 10. 35. worketh righteousness is *a.*

24. 3. we *a.* it always, and in all places

Rom. 15. 31. service may be *a.* of saints

2 *Cor.* 5. 9. absent or present may be *a.*

8. 12. *a.* according to that a man hath

Eph. 1. 6. hath made us *a.* in Beloved

ACCEPTABLE, *Ps.* 19. 14. meditation of my heart be *a.*

69. 13. my prayer to thee in *a.* time

Prov. 10. 32. lips of righteous know what is *a.*

21. 3. to do justice is more *a.*

Ecc. 12. 10. preacher sought *a.* words

Isa. 49. 8. in *a.* time heard thee : 2 *Cor.* 6. 2.

61. 2. to proclaim *a.* year of L. : *Luke* 4. 19.

Jer. 6. 20. your burnt-offerings are not *a.*

Dan. 4. 27. let my counsel be *a.* to thee

Luke 4. 19. to preach the *a.* year of the Lord

Rom. 12. 1. bodies a living sacrifice, holy *a.* to God

2. what is that good and *a.* will of God

Rom. 14. 18. *a.* to God and approved of men

Eph. 5. 10. proving what is *a.* to Lord

Phil. 4. 18. a sacrifice *a.* well-pleasing to God

1 *Tim.* 2. 3. this is *a.* in sight of G. : 1 *Pet.* 2. 20.

Heb. 12. 28. whereby we may serve God *a.*

1 *Pet.* 2. 5. sacrifices *a.* to God by Jesus Christ

ACCEPTANCE, *Is.* 60. 7. they shall come up with *a.* on mine altar

ACCEPTATION, 1 *Tim.* 1. 15. this is a

faithful saying, and worthy of all *a*.

ACCEPTED, *Gen.* 4. 7. if thou dost well, shalt thou not be *a*.

Ex. 28. 38. that they may be *a*. before the Lord

Lev. 1. 4. the offering shall be *a*. for him 22. 27.

Lev. 22. 21. an offering shall be perfect, to be *a*.

23. 11. he shall wave the sheaf to be *a*.

Esth. 10. 3. *a*. of multitude of his brethren

Job 22. 8. the *a*. for countenance dwelt in it

42. 9. the Lord also *a*. Job

Luke 1. 28. hail thou that art graciously *a*.

4. 24. no prophet is *a*. in his own country

Acts 10. 35. he that worketh righteousness is *a*.

Rom. 15. 31. service may be *a*. of saints

2 *Cor.* 5. 9. labour, absent or present, we may be *a*.

6. 2. heard thee in a time *a*. now is the *a*. time

8. 12. it is *a*. according to that a man hath

Eph. 1. 6. he hath made us *a*. in the beloved

ACCESS, *Rom.* 5. 2. by whom we have *a*. by faith

Eph. 2. 18. we both have *a*. to Father

3. 12. in whom we have boldness and *a*. by faith

ACCOMPLISH, to perform fully, to finish, *Lev.* 22. 21 ; *Job* 14. 6.

Ps. 64. 6. *a*. a diligent search

Is. 55. 11. it shall *a*. that I please

Ezek. 6. 12. thus will I *a*. my fury

20. 8. I will pour out my fury to *a*. my anger, 21.

Dan. 9. 2. would *a*. seventy years

Luke 9. 31. decease would *a*. at Jerusa

ACCOMPLISHED, 2 *Chr.* 36. 22. word of the Lord be *a*.

Esth. 2. 12. days of purification were *a*. *Luke* 2. 22.

Job 15. 32. it shall be *a*. before his time

Prov. 13. 19. the desire *a*. is sweet to the soul

Is. 40. 2. her warfare is *a*. her sin is

Jer. 25. 12. when seventy years are *a*. 29. 10.

39. 16. my words shall be *a*. before thee

Ezek. 4. 6. when hast *a*. them, lie on thy right side

5. 13. thus shall mine anger be *a*.

Dan. 11. 36. shall prosper, till the indignation be *a*.

12. 7. *a*. to scatter the power of the holy people

Luke 1. 23. the days of his ministration were *a*.

2. 6. the days were *a*. that she should be delivered

12. 50. am I straitened till it be *a*.

18. 31. concerning the Son of man shall be *a*.

Luke 22. 37. that is written, must yet be *a*. in me

John 19. 28. all things were now *a*.

Acts 21. 5. when we had *a*. those days,

we departed

Heb. 9. 6. *a*. service of God

1 *Pet.* 5. 9. same afflictions are *a*. in your brethren

ACCORD, hearty agreement, *Acts* 1. 14. continued with one *a*. in prayer

Josh. 9. 2. to fight with Israel with one *a*.

Acts 2. 1. with one *a*. in one place

46. daily with one *a*. in the temple ;

4. 24. they lifted up their voice to God with one *a*.

5. 12. were all with one *a*. in Solomon's porch

12. 10. the gate opened to them of his own *a*.

18. 12. the Jews with one *a*. made insurrection

19. 29. they rushed with one *a*. into the theatre

Phil. 2. 2. of one *a*. of one mind

ACCORDING, *Gen.* 27. 19. I have done *a*. as thou badest me

Ex. 12. 25. the Lord will give *a*. as he promised

1 *Kings* 3. 6. *a*. as he walked before thee in truth

Ps. 7. 8. judge me, O God, *a*. to my righteousness

17. I will praise the Lord *a*. to his righteousness

28. 4. give them *a*. to their deeds, and *a*. to the

62. 12. for thou renderest to every man *a*. to his work, *Prov.* 24. 12. 29.

90. 11. *a*. to thy fear, so is thy wrath

159. quicken me *a*. to thy kindness, *Is.* 63. 7.

Is. 8. 20. if they speak not *a*. to this word

Hos. 3. 1. *a*. to the love of the Lord toward Israel

Matt. 9. 29. *a*. to your faith be it unto you

16. 27. he will reward every man *a*. to his works, *Rom.* 2. 6. 2 *Tim.* 4. 14. *Rev.* 2. 23.

Luke 12. 47. nor did *a*. to his will, shall be beaten

Rom. 8. 28. who are the called *a*. to his purpose

1 *Cor.* 15. 3. Christ died *a*. to the scriptures, 4.

Eph. 1. 4. *a*. as he hath chosen us in him, before

5. *a*. to good pleasure. 7. *a*. to riches of his grace.

Phil. 3. 21. *a*. to the working whereby he is able

4. 19. *a*. to his riches in

2 *Tim.* 1. 9. who hath called us not *a*. to our works

Tit. 3. 5. but *a*. to his mercy he saved us by washing

2 *Pet.* 3. 13. we *a*. to his promise look for new heavens

Rev. 20. 12. dead were judged *a*. to their works, 13.

ACCORDING to that, *Rom.* 4. 18. *a*. to. that which was spoken, thy seed be

2 *Cor.* 5. 10. *a*. to that he hath done, good or bad

8. 12. *a*. to that a man hath, not *a*. to that he hath not

ACCOUNT, reckoning, esteem

Job 33. 13. giveth not *a.* of his matters
Ps. 144. 3. that makest *a.* of him
Eccl. 7. 27. to find out the *a.*
Dan. 6. 2. that the princes might give *a.* to them
Matt. 12. 36. give *a.* in day of judgment
   18. 23. would take *a.* of his servants
Luke 16. 2. give *a.* of thy stewardship
Rom. 14. 12. give *a.* of himself to G.
Phil. 4. 17. fruit may abound to your *a.*
Philem. 18. if he oweth thee put that on mine *a.*
Heb. 13. 17. watch for souls as give *a.*
1 *Pet.* 4. 5. shall give *a.* to him that
ACCOUNTED, *Ps.* 22. 30. *a.* to Lord for a generation
Is. 2. 22. wherein is he to be *a.* of
Luke 20. 35. *a.* worthy to obtain world
   21. 36. *a.* worthy to escape
   22. 24. which should be *a.* greatest
Gal. 3. 6. *a.* to him for righteousness
Heb. 11. 19. *a.* God was able to raise
ACCURSED, signifies, (1) Devoted to destruction, *Josh.* 6. 17. (2) Separated from the church, *Rom.* 9. 3. (3) Cursed eternally from God, 1 *Cor.* 16. 22 ; *Gal.* 1. 8, 9.
Deut. 21. 23. hanged is *a.* of God
Josh. 6. 18. keep yourself from *a.* thing
   7. 1. trespass in the *a.* thing ; Achan took of *a.*
   13. there is an *a.* thing in the midst of thee
   15. he that is taken with the *a.* thing
   22. 20. did not Achan commit trespass in *a.* thing
Is. 65. 20. sinner 100 years shall be *a.*
Rom. 9. 3. wish myself *a.* from C.
1 *Cor.* 12. 3. no man by Spirit calls Jesus *a.*
Gal. 1. 8, 9. preach other gospel be *a.*
ACCUSATION, *Ezra* 4. 6. wrote *a.* against Judah
Matt. 27. 37. set over his head his *a.*
Luke 6. 7. might find *a.* against him
John 18. 29. what *a.* bring ye against this man ?
Acts 25. 18. brought no *a.* as I supposed
1 *Tim.* 5. 19. against an elder receive not an *a.*
2 *Pet.* 2. 11. not railing *a.* against them : *Jude* 9.
ACCUSE, charge with crimes
Prov. 30. 10. *a.* not servant to master
Matt. 12. 10. that they might *a.* him, *Mark* 3. 2. *Luke* 11. 54.
Luke 3. 14. neither *a.* any falsely
   23. 2. and they began to *a.* him, saying
John 5. 45. that I will *a.* you to father
   8. 6. that they might have to *a.* him
Acts 24. 2. Tertullus began to *a.* him
   8. take knowledge of all things whereof we *a.*
   25. 5. let them go down with me and *a.* this man
   28. 19. not that I had ought to *a.* my nation of
1 *Pet.* 3. 16. falsely *a.* good conversation
ACCUSED, *Matt.* 27. 12. when he was *a.* he answered nothing
Mark 15. 3. priests *a.* him many things, *Luke* 23. 10.

Acts 22. 30. the certainty wherefore he was *a.*
   23. 28. have known the cause whereof they *a.* him
   26. 7. for which hope's sake I am *a.* of the Jews
Tit. 1. 6. not *a.* of riot
Rev. 12. 10. *a.* them before our God
ACCUSERS, *John* 8. 10. where are those thine *a.*
Acts 23. 30. I gave commandment to his *a.* also
   35. I will hear thee when thine *a.* are come
   25. 16. before he have the *a.* face to face
2 *Tim.* 3. 3. false *a.* *Tit.* 2. 3.
Rev. 12. 10. *a.* of brethren is cast down
ACCUSETH, ING, *John* 5. 45. one that *a.* you
Rom. 2. 15. thoughts *a.* or excusing
ACCUSTOMED, *Jer.* 13. 23.
ACKNOWLEDGE, ING, *Deut.* 21. 17. he shall *a.* son of hatred
Deut. 33. 9. nor did he *a.* brethren nor children
Ps. 32. 5. I *a.* my sin
   51. 3. *a.* my transgressions
Prov. 3. 6. in all thy ways *a.* him
Is. 33. 13. ye near *a.* my might
   61. 9. all that see shall *a.* them
Is. 63. 16. thou art our father, though Israel *a.* us not
Jer. 3. 13. only *a.* thine iniquity
   14. 20. we *a.* O Lord our wickedness
   24. 5. *a.* them that are carried
Dan. 11. 39. strange God whom he shall *a.*
Hos. 5. 15. I will go till they *a.* their offence
1 *Cor.* 14. 37. *a.* things that I write
2 *Cor.* 1. 13. you *a.* and I trust shall *a.*
Tit. 1. 1. *a.* truth which is after godliness
Philemon 6. *a.* every good thing in Christ
2 *Tim.* 2. 25. repentance to the *a.* of the truth
ACKNOWLEDGETH, 1 *John* 2. 23. he that *a.* the Son hath the Father
ACQUAINT thyself with him, *Job* 22. 21.
Ps. 139. 3. *a.* with all my ways
Is. 53. 3. *a.* with grief
ACQUAINTANCE, familiar friends or companions, *Job* 19. 13.
Job 42. 11. then came all that had been of his *a.*
Ps. 31. 11. I was a reproach and a fear to mine *a.*
   55. 13. it was thou, mine equal, and mine *a.*
   88. 8. thou hast put away mine *a.* far from me
   18. lower put from me, and my *a.* into darkness
Luke 2. 44. they sought him among their *a.*
   23. 49. all his *a.* stood afar off, beholding things
Acts 24. 23. he should forbid none of his *a.* to come
ACQUIT, hold innocent, *Job* 10. 14.
Nah. 1. 3. will not at all *a.* the wicked
ACRE, S. 1 *Sam.* 14. 14. men within half an *a.* of land

Is. 5. 10. ten *a.* of vineyard shall yield
    one bath
ACT, *Isa.* 28. 21. and bring to pass his
    a. his strange *a.*
    59. 6. and the *a.* of violence is in
    their hands
Joh: 8. 4. was taken in adultery, in the
    very *a.*
ACTS of the Lord, *Deut.* 11. 3.
Deut. 7. your eyes have seen the great
    a. of the Lord
Judg. 5. 11. rehearse the righteous *a.* of
    the Lord
1 *Sam.* 12. 7. reason of all righteous *a,*
    of the Lord
1 *Kings* 10. 6. it was a true report
    heard of thy *a.*
    11. 41. the *a.* of Solomon are they not.
    written in the book of the *a.* of
    Solomon ? 2 *Chr.* 9. 5.
Ps. 103. 7. his *a.* to the children of Israel
    106. 2. utter mighty *a.* of the Lord
    145. 4. speak of thy mighty *a.*
    150. 2. praise him for his mighty *a.*
ACTIONS weighed, 1 *Sam.* 2. 3.
ACTIVITY, men of, *Gen.* 47. 6.
ADAMANT, *Ezek.* 3. 9 ; *Zech.* 7. 12.
ADD fifth part, *Lev.* 5. 16, & 6. 5, & 27.
    13, 15, 19, 27, 31.
Gen. 30. 24. the Lord shall *a.* to me
Deut. 4. 2. shall not *a.* the word
    29. 19. *a.* drunkenness to thirst
1 *Kings* 12. 11. I will *a.* to your yoke
Ps. 69. 27. *a.* iniquity to their iniquity
Prov. 3. 2. long life and peace shall
    they *a.* to thee
    30. 6. *a.* not to his words
Isa. 30. 1. may *a.* sin to sin
Matt. 6. 27. can *a.* one cubit, *Luke* 12.
    25.
Phil. 1. 16. to *a.* affliction to my bonds
2 *Pet.* 1. 5. *a.* to your faith virtue
Rev. 22. 18. if any man *a.* G. shall *a.*
ADDED, *Deut.* 5. 22. he *a.* no more
1 *Sam.* 12. 19. *a.* to all our sins this
Jer. 36. 32. were *a.* many like words
    45. 3. *a.* grief to my sorrow
Matt. 6. 33. all these things shall be *a.*
Luke 12. 31. be *a.* to you
Acts 2. 41. same day were *a.* 3000
    47. Lord *a.* to the church as shall
    5. 14. believers were more *a.* to L.
    11. 24. much people was *a.* to the
    Lord
Gal. 3. 19. law was *a.* because of trans-
    gressions
ADDETH, ING, *Job* 34. 37. for he *a.* re-
    bellion to his sin
Prov. 10. 22. *a.* no sorrow with it
    16. 23. the heart of the wise *a.* learn-
    ing to his lips
Gal. 3. 15. no man disannulleth or *a.*
    thereto
ADDER, poisonous serpent, *Gen.* 49. 17.
    Ps. 58. 4. & 91. 13. & 140. 3. *Prov.*
    23. 32. *Is.* 14. 29.
ADDICTED, gave up, 1 *Cor.* 16. 15.
ADJURE, charge under pain of God's
    curse, 1 *Kings* 22. 16. 2 *Chr.* 18.
    15. *Matt.* 26. 63. *Mark* 5. 7. *Acts*
    19. 13. *Josh.* 6. 26. 1 *Sam.* 14. 24.
ADMINISTRATION, 1 *Cor.* 12. 5. 2 *Cor.*
    9. 12. & 8. 19, 20. administered
ADMIRATION, high esteem, *Jude* 16.

or, wonder and amazement, *Rev.*
    17. 6.
2 *Thess.* 1. 10. *a.* in them that believe
ADMONISH, warn, reprove
Rom. 15. 14. able to *a.* one another
1 *Thess.* 5. 12. over you and *a.* you
2 *Thess.* 3. 15. *a.* him as a brother
Eccl. 12. 12. by these be *a.*
    4. 13. foolish king will no more be *a.*
Jer. 42. 19. know that I have *a.* you
Acts 27. 9. Paul *a.* them
Heb. 8. 5. as Moses was *a.* of God
Col. 3. 16. *a.* one another
1 *Cor.* 10. 11. written for our *a.*
Eph. 6. 4. bring them in the *a.* of the L.
Tit. 3. 10. after 1st & 2nd *a.* reject
ADOPTION, putting among God's chil-
    dren, *Jer.* 3. 19. 2 *Cor.* 6. 18.
Rom. 8. 15. receive spirit of *a.*
    23. *a.* redemption of our body
    9. 4. to whom pertaineth the *a.*
Gal. 4. 5. might receive *a.* of sons
Eph. 1. 5. predestined to *a.* of children
ADORN, deck out, *Is.* 61. 10 ; *Jer.* 31.
    4 ; *Luke* 21. 5.
1 *Tim.* 2. 9. women *a.* themselves in
    modest apparel, 1 *Pet.* 3. 5.
Tit. 2. 10. *a.* doctrine of God Saviour
1 *Pet.* 3. 3. whose *a.* let it not
Rev. 21. 2. as a bride *a.* for her husband
ADULTERER, put to death, *Lev.* 20. 10.
Job 24. 15. eye of *a.* waits for twilight
Is. 57. 3. seed of *a.* and whore
Jer. 23. 10. land is full of *a.*
    9. 2. *Hos.* 7. 4. be all *a.*
Mal. 3. 5. I will be swift witness against
    a.
1 *Cor.* 6. 9. neither *a.* shall inherit king
    dom
Heb. 13. 4. whoremongers and *a.* God
    will judge
James 4. 4. ye *a.* and *a.*
Prov. 6. 26. *a.* will hunt for life
    32. commits *a.* lacks understanding
Matt. 5. 28. committeth *a.* in his heart
2 *Pet.* 2. 14. having eyes full of *a.*
Matt. 15. 19. out of the heart pro-
    ceed *a.* fornications, *Mark* 7. 21.
Prov. 30. 20. way of *a.* woman
Matt. 12. 39. *a.* generation seeketh a
    sign, 16. 4. *Mark* 8. 38.
ADVANTAGE, ED, ETH, *Job* 35. 3.
    what *a.* will it be to thee ?
Luke 9. 25. what is a man *a.* if he gain
Rom. 3. 1. what *a.* then hath Jew ?
1 *Cor.* 15. 32. what *a.* me if the dead
    rise not ; let us eat and drink
2 *Cor.* 2. 11. Satan get an *a.* over us
Jude 16. having men's persons in ad-
    miration, because of *a.*
ADVENTURE, ED, *Deut.* 28. 56. not *a.*
    to set sole of foot
Judg 9. 17. my father *a.* his life far
Acts 19. 31. not *a.* into theatre
ADVERSARY, *Ex.* 23. 22. I will be *a.*
    to thine *a.*
Num. 22. 22. angel stood for an *a.*
1 *Sam.* 1. 6. her *a.* provoked her sore
1 *Kings* 5. 4. neither *a.* nor evil occur-
    rent
    11. 14. stirred up an *a.* to Solomon :
    v. 23.
Job 31. 35. that my *a.* had written *a.*
    book

Ps. 74. 10. how long shall *a.* reproach ?
Is. 50. 8. mine *a.* let him come near
Lam. 1. 10. *a.* hath spread his hand
Amos 3. 11. *a.* round about the land
Matt. 5. 25. agree with *a.* quickly lest *a.*
Luke 12. 58. when goest with thine *a.*
  18. 3. a widow saying, avenge me of
  mine *a.*
1 *Tim.* 5. 14. give none occasion to *a.*
1 *Pet.* 5. 8. your *a.* the devil as a roaring lion, walketh about, seeking

ADVERSARIES, *Deut.* 32. 27. lest *a.*
  behave strangely
Josh. 5. 13. art thou for us or our *a.* ?
1 *Sam.* 2. 10. *a.* of Lord be broken
2 *Sam.* 19. 22. that ye should this day
  be *a.* to me
Ezra 4. 1. when *a.* of Judah and Benjamin heard
Neh. 4. 11. our *a.* said, shall not know
Ps. 38. 20. render evil for good, my *a.*
  69. 19. mine *a.* are all before thee
  81: 14. subdued their enemies, and
  turned my hand against their *a.*
  89. 42. set up right hand of his *a.*
Ps. 109. 4. for my love they are my *a.*
  20. let this be reward of my *a.*
  29. let *a.* be clothed with shame
Is. 1. 24. I will ease me of my *a.*
  9. 11. Lord shall set up *a.* of Rezin
  59. 18. he will repay fury to his *a.*
  63. 18. *a.* have trodden sanctuary
  64. 2. to make thy name known to
  thy *a.*,
Jer. 30. 16. all thine *a.* shall go into
  captivity
  46. 10. that he may avenge him of
  his *a.*
Lam. 1. 5. her *a.* are chief
  17. that his *a.* should be round
  about
Mic. 5. 9. hand lifted up upon thy *a.*
Luke 13. 17. all his *a.* were ashamed
  21. 15. *a.* not able to gainsay
1 *Cor.* 16. 9. a door is opened, and
  there are many *a.*
Phil. 1. 28. nothing terrified by *a.*
Heb. 10. 27. indignation devour *a.*

ADVERSITY, affliction, misery : it
  stands opposed to prosperity,
2 *Sam.* 4. 9. redeem my soul from *a.*
Ps. 10. 6. shall never be in *a.*
  31: 7. hast known my soul in *a.*
Ps. 35. 15. in my *a.* they rejoiced
  94. 13. give rest from days of *a.*
Prov. 17. 17. brother is born for *a.*
  24. 10. if thou faint in day of *a.*
Eccl. 7. 14. in day of *a.* consider
Is. 30. 20. give you the bread of *a.*
1 *Sam.* 10. 19. saved you out of all *a.*
2 *Chr.* 15. 6. God did vex with all *a.*

ADVICE, counsel given, *Judg.* 19. 30.
Judg. 20. 7. give here your *a.* and counsel
1 *Sam.* 25. 33. blessed be thy *a.* and
  blessed be thou
2 *Sam.* 19. 43. that our *a.* should be not
  first had
Prov. 20. 18. and with good *a.* make
  war
2 *Cor.* 8. 10. and herein I give you *a.*

ADVOCATE, denotes a comforter and
  an instructor, and is applied to the
  Holy Spirit ; *John* 14. 16 ; 15. 26 ;

1 *John* 2. 1.
AFAR At a great distance, (1) *Jer.* 31
  10. (2) Estranged in affection, *Ps.*
  38. 11. (3) Not in a state of friendship and fellowship with God, *Eph.*
  2. 17.
AFAR off, *Gen.* 22. 4. & 37. 18. *Ps.* 65. 5.
Ex. 24. 1. come up and worship ye *a.*
  off
  33. 7. pitch the tabernacle *a.* off
  from the camp
Ezra 3. 13. shouted, and the noise was
  heard *a.* off
Neh. 12. 43. the joy of Jerusalem was
  heard *a.* off
Job 36. 3. I will fetch my knowledge
  from *a.*
Ps. 138. 6. proud he knoweth *a.* off
  139. 2. understandest my thought *a.* off
Prov. 31. 14. she bringeth her food
  from *a.*
Is. 23. 7. her own feet shall carry her
  a. off
  66. 19. those that escape to the isles
  a. off
Jer. 23. 23. at hand not a God *a.* off
  30. 10. I will save thee from *a.* 46. 27.
  51. 50. go away, remember the Lord
  a. off
Matt. 26. 58. but Peter followed him *a.*
  off, and went in, *Mark* 14. 54 ; *Luke*
  22. 54.
  27. 55. women beholding *a.* off, *Mark*
  15. 40.
Mark 5. 6. but when he saw Jesus *a.*
  off, he ran
Luke 16. 23. lift up his eyes, and seeth
  Abraham *a.* off
Acts 2. 39. promise is to all *a.* off
Eph. 2. 17. preached peace to you *a.* off
Heb. 11. 18. having seen promises *a.*
2 *Pet.* 1. 9. blind, and cannot see *a.*

AFFAIRS, *Ps.* 112. 5. he will guide his
  a. with discretion
Eph. 6. 21. but that ye also may know
  my *a.*
  22. I have sent, that ye might know
  our *a.*
Phil. 1. 27. or be absent, I may hear of
  your *a.*

AFFECT, to influence the passions,
  Lam. 3. 51. Men's affections, as
  love, fear, joy, delight, &c., *Col.*
  3. 2. Vile affections, *Rom.* 1. 26 ;
  Gal. 5. 24.
Gal. 4. 17. they zealously *a.* you
  18. good to be zealously *a.*
Lam. 3. 51. mine eye *a.* my heart

AFFECTION, 1 *Chr.* 29. 3. have set my
  a. to the house of God
Rom. 1. 31. without natural *a.*
2 *Cor.* 7. 15. his inward *a.* is more
  abundant to you
Col. 3. 2. mortify inordinate *a.*
AFFECTIONS, *Rom.* 1. 26. them up to
  vile *a.*
Gal. 5. 24. crucify flesh with *a.*
Rom. 12. 10. be kindly *a.*
1 *Thess.* 2. 8. being *a.* desirous
AFFINITY, relation by marriage, on
  which subject minute instruction
  was given by Moses, *Lev.* 18 ; 1
  Kings 3. 1 ; 2 *Chr.* 18. 1 ; *Ezra*
  9. 14.

AFFIRM, (1) To maintain the truth of a thing, *Acts* 25. 19. *Tit.* 3. 8. (2) To teach, 1 *Tim.* 1. 7.

Rom. 3. 8. and as some *a.* that we say, let us do evil

1 *Tim.* 1. 7. what they say, nor whereof they *a.*

Tit. 3. 8. These things I will that thou *a.* constantly

AFFIRMED, *Luke* 22. 59. about an hour after another *a.*

Acts 12. 15. but Rhoda constantly *a.* that it was so

25. 19. and of Jesus, whom Paul *a.* to be alive

AFFLICT, *Gen.* 15. 13. shall *a.* them four hundred years

Gen. 31. 50. if thou *a.* my daughters

Ex. 1. 11. taskmasters to *a.* them

22. 23. if thou *a.* them in any wise

Lev. 16, 29; 31 ; *Nu.* 29. 7. shall *a.* your souls

Judg. 16. 6. mightest be bound to *a.* thee

1 *Kings* 11. 39. I will *a.* seed of David

2 *Chr.* 6. 26. turn when thou dost *a.*
  1 *Kings* 8. 35.

Ps. 55. 19. God shall hear and *a.* them
  94. 5. they *a.* thine heritage

Is. 51. 23. into hand of that *a.* thee

58. 5. a day for a man to *a.* his soul

64. 12. wilt thou *a.* us very sore ?

Lam. 3. 33. for the Lord doth not *a.* willingly

Amos 5. 12. they *a.* the just, they take a bribe

Amos 6. 14. shall *a.* you from Hemash

Nah. 1. 12. have afflicted, I will *a.* thee

Zeph. 3. 19. I will undo all that *a.* thee

AFFLICTED, *Ex.* 1. 12. more *a.* them more they grew.

Num. 11. 11. why hast *a.* thy servant

Deut. 26. 6. the Egyptian *a.* us and laid on us

2 *Sam.* 22. 28. *a.* people wilt save

2 *Kings* 17. 20. the Lord rejected Israel and *a.* them

Job 6. 14. to *a.* pity should be showed

Job 34. 28. and he heareth the cry of the *a.*

Ps. 18. 27. wilt save *a.* people

25. 16. have mercy on me, for I am desolate and *a.*

82. 3. do justice to the *a.* and needy

88. 7. hast *a.* me with waves

90. 15. days wherein hast *a.* us

107. 17. I am *a* very much

116. 10. I was greatly *a.* 119. 67. before I was *a.*

119. 71. it is good for me that I have been *a.*

75. and that thou in faithfulness hast *a.* me

129. 1. many time have they *a.* me from youth, 2.

Prov. 15. 15. days of *a.* are evil

Is. 53. 4. did esteem him smitten of God and *a.*

7. he was oppressed, and was *a.* yet he opened not

60. 14. the sons of them that *a.* thee shall come

63. 9. in their affliction he was *a.*

Lam. 1. 4. her priests sigh, her vir-

gins are *a.*

12. my sorrow, wherewith the Lord hath *a.* me

Nah. 1. 12. though I have *a.* thee

Zeph. 3. 12. leave in thee *a.* people

Matt. 24. 9. they shall deliver you up to be *a.*

2 *Cor.* 1. 6. whether we be *a.* it is for your

1 *Tim.* 5. 10. if she have relieved the *a.*

Heb. 11. 37. being destitute *a.* and tormented

James 4. 9. be *a.* and mourn, and weep

5. 13. is any *a.* let him pray

AFFLICTION, S. *Ex.* 3. 7 ; *Acts* 7. 34. have seen *a.* of my people : 2 *Kings* 14. 26 ; *Neh.* 9. 9.

Gen. 16. 11. because the Lord hath heard thy *a.*

Ex. 3. 7. I have seen the *a.* of my people, *Acts* 7. 34.

4. 31. that he had looked on their *a.*

Deut. 16. 3. shalt eat bread of *a.* : 1 *Kings* 22. 27 ; 2 *Chr.* 18. 26.

2 *Sam.* 16. 12. may be Lord look on my *a.*

2 *Chr.* 20. 9. cry to thee in our *a.*

33. 12. Manasseh in *a.* sought Lord

Neh. 1. 3. remnant are in great *a.*

Job 5. 6. *a.* cometh not of dust

30. 16, days of *a.* have taken hold

36. 15. delivereth poor in his *a.*

21. for this hast thou chosen rather than *a.*

Ps. 25. 18. look upon my *a.* and pain

34. 19. many are *a.* of righteous

44. 24. forgettest our *a.* and oppression

88. 9. mourneth by reason of *a.*

106. 44. he regarded their *a.* when he heard

107. 10. sit in darkness, being bound in *a.* and iron

41. yet setteth he the poor on high from *a.*

119. 50. this my comfort in my *a.*

92. have perished in mine *a.*

153. consider mine *a.* and deliver

132. 1. remember David and all his *a.*

Is. 30. 20. though the Lord give you water of *a.*

48. 10. I have chosen thee in the furnace of *a.*

63. 9. in all their *a.* he was afflicted, and the angel

Jer. 16. 19. O Lord, my refuge in the day of *a.*

Lam. 3. 1. am man that hath seen *a.*

19. remembering my *a.* and my misery

Hos. 5. 15. in their *a.* will seek me

Jonah 2. 2. cried by reason of mine *a.*

Hab. 3. 7. saw tents of Cushan in *a.*

Mark 4. 17. when *a.* ariseth for the world's sake

13. 19. in those days shall be *a.*

Acts 7. 11. there came a dearth and great *a.*

2 *Cor.* 2. 4. for out of much *a.* I write to you

4. 17. our light *a.* which is but for a moment

8. 2. how that in a great trial of *a.*

Phil. 1. 16. supposing to add *a.* to my

bonds

1 *Thess.* 1. 6. received word in much *a.*
3. 3. no man be moved by *a.*

Heb. 10. 32. endured great fight of *a.*
11. 25. choosing to suffer *a.*

AFFRIGHT, ED. *Deut.* 7. 21. shalt not
be *a.* at them

2 *Chr.* 32. 18. cried with loud voice to *a.*

Job 39. 22. mocketh at fear and not *a,*

Is. 21. 4. fearfulness *a.* me

Mark 16. 5. and they were *a. Luke* 24.
37.

6. he saith, be not *a.* ye seek Jesus
crucified

Rev. 11. 13. and remnant were *a.*

AFORE, *Rom.* 1. 2. which he had promised *a.* by his prophet

9. 23. which he had *a.* prepared unto
glory

Eph. 3. 3. the mystery, as I wrote *a.* in
few words

AFORETIME, *Is.* 52. 4. my people went
forth *a.* into Egypt

Dan. 6. 10. he prayed before his God,
as he did *a.*

John 9. 13. they brought him that *a.*
was blind

Rom. 15. 4. for whatsoever things were
written *a.*

AFRAID, *Gen.* 42. 35. saw bundles of
money, they were *a.*

Ex. 34. 30. and they were *a.* to come
nigh him

Lev. 26. 6. and none shall make you *a.*
Job 11. 19.

1 *Sam.* 4. 7. the Philistines were *a.* for
they said

18. 29. Saul was yet the more *a.* of
David

2 *Sam.* 22. 5. ungodly men made me *a.*
Ps. 18. 4.

Neh. 6. 9. for they all made us *a.* saying, their hands

Job 11. 19. shalt lie down, and none
shall make thee *a.*

15. 24. trouble and anguish shall
make him *a.*

18. 11. terrors shall make him *a.* on
every side

41. 25. he raiseth up himself, the
mighty are *a.*

Ps. 56. 3. what time I am *a.* I will trust
in thee

77. 16. the waters saw thee, and they
were *a.*

Is. 17. 2. and none shall make them *a.*
Ezek. 34. 28. *Mic.* 4. 4. *Zeph.* 3. 13.

33. 14. the sinners in Zion are *a.* fearfulness hath

Jer. 30. 10. be quiet, and none shall
make him *a.*

38. 39. Zedekiah said, I am *a.* of Jews

Dan. 4. 5. I saw a dream which made
me *a.*

Jonah 1. 5. then the mariners were *a.*
10.

Mark 5. 15. in his right mind were *a.*
Luke 8. 35.

9. 32. they understood not, and were
a. to ask him

Luke 8. 25. and they being *a.* wondered,
saying

Acts 9. 26. but they were all *a.* of Saul

Gal. 4. 11. I am *a.* of you, lest I have

bestowed

AFRAID, not be, *Ps.* 3. 6. I will *not be*
a. of ten thousand of people

Ps. 56. 11. I will *not be a.* what man can
do to me

91. 5. thou shalt *not be a.* for the terror by night

112. 7. he shall *not be a.* of evil tidings, his heart

8. his heart is established, he shall
not be a.

Prov. 3. 24. when thou liest down shalt
not be a.

Is. 12. 2. God my salvation, I will trust
and *not be a.*

AFRAID, be not, *Deut.* 20. 1. *be not a.*
of them, *Josh.* 11. 6 ; *Neh.* 4. 14 ;
Jer. 10. 5 ; *Ezek.* 2. 6 ; *Luke* 12. 4.

Ps. 49. 16. *be not a.* when one is made
rich

Jer. 1. 8. *be not a.* of their faces, for I
am with thee

Matt. 14. 27. it is I, *be not a. Mark* 6. 50.
John 6. 20.

17. 7. Jesus touched them and said,
arise, *be not a.*

28. 10. *be not a.* go tell my brethren
that they go

Acts 18. 9. *be not a.* but speak, and hold
not thy peace

1 *Pet.* 3. 14. *be not a.* of their terror,
nor be troubled

AFRAID, sore, *Ex.* 14. 10. Egyptians
marched, they were *sore a.*

1 *Sam.* 17. 24. fled from Goliath, and
were *sore a.*

28. 20. Saul fell along on the earth,
and was *sore a.*

Mark 9. 6. wist not what to say, for
they were *sore a.*

Luke 2. 9. shone about them, and they
were *sore a.*

AFRAID, was, *Gen.* 3. 10. I heard thy
voice and *was a.*

Ex. 8. 6. Moses hid his face, *was a.* to
look on God

1 *Sam.* 18. 12. Saul *was a.* of David, 15.

Job 3. 25. that which I *was a.* of, is come
to me

Dan. 8. 17. when he came *was a.* and
fell on my face

Matt. 14. 30. when he saw the wind
boisterous, *was a.*

25. 25. I *was a.* and hid thy talent in
the earth

John 19. 8. when Pilate heard, he *was*
the more *a.*

Acts 10. 4. when Cornelius looked, he
was a.

AFRESH, crucify Son of God *a., Heb.* 6.
6.

AFTER, *Deut.* 6. 14. ye shall not go *a.*
other gods

Josh. 10. 14. no day like that before it,
nor *a.* it

1 *Sam.* 24. 14. *a.* whom the king is
come out ? *a.* a dog

Job 10. 6. that thou inquirest *a.* mine
iniquity

30. 5. they cried *a.* them, as *a.* a thief

Is. 11. 3. he shall not judge *a.* the sight
of his eyes

Matt. 26. 32. *a.* I am risen again, I will
go before

Mark 16. 14. which had seen him *a.* he was risen

Luke 22. 58. and *a.* a little while another saw him

23. 26. that he might bear it *a.* Jesus

John 13. 27. *a.* the sop Satan entered into him

2 *Pet.* 2. 6. to those that *a.* should live ungodly

AFTER that, *Ex.* 3. 20. and *a. that* he will let you go

2 *Sam.* 21. 14. *a. that* God was intreated for the land

Job 21. 3. *a. that* I have spoken, mock

Jer. 31. 19. *a. that* I was turned, I repented

Luke 12. 4. *a. that* have no more that they can do

13. 9. then *a. that* thou shalt cut it down

1 *Cor.* 15. 6. *a. that* he was seen of above 500 at once

AFTERNOON, *Judg.* 19. 8. they tarried till *a.* and did eat

AFTERWARD, S. *Ex.* 11. 1. *a.* he will let you go hence

Num. 31. 2. *a.* shalt thou be gathered to thy people

Ps. 73. 24. guide me, and *a.* receive me to glory

Joel 2. 28. *a.* I will pour out my spirit upon all

Matt. 4. 2. fasted, he was *a.* an hungered, *Luke* 4. 2.

John 5. 14. *a.* Jesus findeth him in the temple

John 13. 36. but thou shalt follow me *a.*

1 *Cor.* 15. 23. *a.* they that are Christ's at his coming

Heb. 12. 11. *a.* it yieldeth the peaceable fruit of righteousness

AGAIN, *Gen.* 8. 21. I will not *a.* curse, nor *a.* smite

Gen. 15. 16. they shall come hither *a.*

Ex. 10. 29. said, I will see *a.* thy face no more

1 *Kings* 17. 22. the soul of the child came into him *a.*

Job 14. 14. if a man die, shall he live *a.*

Ps. 85. 6. wilt thou not revive us *a.* that thy

Prov. 2. 19. none that go to her return *a.*

John 4. 13. drinketh of this water shall thirst *a.*

Rom. 8. 15. not received spirit of bondage *a.* to fear

Phil. 4. 4. rejoice in the Lord, *a.* I say, rejoice

1 *Pet.* 1. 3. hath begotten us *a.* to a lively hope

AGAINST, *Gen.* 16. 12. his hand shall be *a.* every man

Is. 40. 10. the Lord will come *a.* the strong hand

Ezek. 13. 20. behold, I am *a.* your pillows

Matt. 10. 35. to set a man *a.* his father, *Luke* 12. 53.

12. 30. he that is not with me, is *a.* me

Luke 2. 34. for a sign which shall be spoken *a.*

14. 31. that cometh *a.* him with 20,000

Acts 28. 22. this sect is every where spoken *a.*

AGE, is as nothing before thee, *Ps.* 39. 5.

Gen. 47. 28. the whole *a.* of Jacob was 147 years

1 *Sam.* 2. 33. shall die in the flower of their *a.*

1 *Kings* 14. 4. Ahijah's eyes were set by reason of *a.*

2 *Chr.* 36. 17. or on him that stooped for *a.*

Job. 5. 26. come to grave in full *a.*

8. 8. enquire, I pray thee, of the former *a.*

11. 17. thy *a.* shall be clearer than noon-day

Zech. 8. 4. every man with his staff for *a.*

Luke 3. 23. Jesus began to be about 30 years of *a.*

John 9. 21. he is of *a.* ask him, 23

Heb. 5. 14. strong meat to those of full *a.*

11. 11. Sarah when she was past *a.*

AGED, 2 *Sam.* 19. 32. Barzillai was a very *a.* man

Job 12. 20. he taketh away the understanding of *a.*

29. 8. and the *a.* arose and stood up

Philem. 9. such an one as Paul the *a.*

Tit. 2. 2. *a.* men be sober

AGES, *Eph.* 2. 7. & 3. 5. & 3. 21.

Col. 1. 26. mystery hid from *a.*

AGO, *Is.* 22. 11. respect to him that fashioned it long *a.*

Matt. 11. 21. would have repented long *a.* *Luke* 10. 13.

Acts 10. 30. 4 days *a.* I was fasting until this hour

2 *Cor.* 8. 10. but also to be forward a year *a.*

9. 2. that Achaia was ready a year *a.*

12. 2. I knew a man above fourteen years *a.*

AGONY, *Luke* 22. 24. being in an *a.* he prayed more earnestly

AGREE, ED, ETH, *Acts* 5. 9.

Amos 3. 3. walk together except *a.*

Is. 28. 15. with hell are we at *a.*

Matt. 5. 25. *a.* with adversary quickly

18. 19. if two shall *a.* on earth

20. 2. when he had *a.* with labourers for a penny

Mark 14. 56. their witness *a.* not together, 59

John 9. 22. the Jews had *a.* already if any man

Acts 5. 9. how is it that ye have *a.* to tempt

15. 15. and to this *a.* the words of the prophet

2 *Cor.* 6. 16. what *a.* has temple of God

1 *John* 5. 8. these three *a.* in one

Rev. 17. 17. *a.* to give their kingdom to the beast

AGROUND, *Acts* 27. 41. two seas met, they ran the ship *a.*

AGUE, *Lev.* 26. 16. I will appoint over you terror, consumption, and the burning *a.*

AIR, 2 *Sam.* 21. 10. nor birds of the *a.* to rest on

Job 41. 16. that no *a.* can come between them

Prov. 30. 19. the way of eagle in the *a.*

Eccl. 10. 20. a bird of the *a.* shall carry the voice

Matt. 8. 20. and the birds of *a.* have nests

13. 32. the birds of the *a.* come and lodge—*Mark* 4. 32 ; *Luke* 9. 58.

Acts 22. 23. and threw dust into the *a.*

1 *Cor.* 9. 26. so fight I, not as one that beateth the *a.*

14. 9. for ye shall speak into the *a.*

Eph. 2. 2. the prince of the power of the *a.*

1 *Thess.* 4. 17. caught up to meet the Lord in the *a.*

Rev. 9. 2. sun and the *a.* darkened

16. 17. angel poured out his vial into the *a.*

ALIEN, stranger, or a person born in another country, and not admitted to the privileges of the citizens of the country in which he resides.

Ex. 18. 3. I have been an *a.* in a strange land

Deut. 14. 21. or thou mayest sell it to an *a.*

Is. 61. 5. sons of the *a.* shall be your ploughmen

Eph. 2. 12. *a.* from commonwealth of Israel

Heb. 11. 34. who turned to flight the armies of *a.*

ALIENATED, *Ezek.* 23. 17. my mind was *a.* from her, 18.

Eph. 4. 18. *a.* from life of God

Col. 1. 21. were sometime *a.*

ALIKE, Signifies, (1) Without any difference, *Rom.* 14. 5. (2.) After one and the same manner, *Ps.* 33. 15 (3.) Equally troublesome, *Prov.* 27. 15.

Job 21. 26. they shall lie down *a.* in the dust

Ps. 33. 15. he fashioneth their hearts *a.*

139. 12. darkness and light are both *a.* to thee

Eccl. 9. 2. all things come *a.* to all ; one event

11. 6. whether they both shall be *a.* good

Rom. 14. 5. another esteemeth every day *a.*

ALIVE, *Gen.* 12. 12 ; *Num.* 22. 33.

Gen. 7. 23. Noah only remained *a.* and they in the ark

Ex. 1. 17. but saved the men-children *a.* 11.

22. and every daughter ye shall save *a.*

Num. 16. 33. went down *a.* into the pit 31. 15. saved all the women *a.* ?

Deut. 4. 4. *a.* every one of you this day

32. 39. I kill, and I make *a.*

Josh. 2. 13. that ye shall save *a.* my father

14. 10. the Lord hath kept me *a.*

1 *Sam.* 2. 6. kills and makes *a.*

15. 8. he took Agag the king of Amalek, *a.*

2 *Kings* 5. 7. am I God, to kill and make *a.*

Ps. 30. 3. Lord, thou hast kept me *a.*

Mark 16. 11. when they heard that he was *a.*

Luke 15. 24. son was dead and is *a.*

24. 23. they had seen angels who said he was *a.*

Acts 1. 3. he showed himself *a.* after his passion

25. 19. Jesus, Paul affirmed to be *a.*

Rom. 6. 11. *a.* to God through J. Christ

6. 13. as those *a.* from dead

7. 9. I was *a.* without the law once

1 *Cor.* 15. 22. C. shall all be made *a.*

1 *Thess.* 4. 15. 17. we who are *a.* and remain

2 *Tim.* 2. 26. who are taken *a.* by him at his will

Rev. 1. 18. I am *a.* for evermore

2. 8. was dead and is *a.*

19. 20. these were both cast *a.* into a lake of fire

ALIVE yet, *Gen.* 43. 7. asking us saying, is your father yet *a.*?

27. is he yet *a.*? 28. he is well, he is yet *a.*

45. 26. they told him, saying, Joseph is yet *a.* 28.

Ex. 4. 18. let me go and see whether they be yet *a.*

2 *Sam.* 12. 18. while the child was yet *a.* ver. 21. 22.

Ezek. 7. 13. which is sold, although they were yet *a.*

Matt. 27. 63. this deceiver said, while he was yet *a.*

ALL, A great number only, as *Ex.* 9. 6, 19 ; *Matt.* 3. 5 ; *Luke* 15. 1 ; *Acts* 1. 1. &c.

All men ; that is, all kinds of men ; *Matt.* 10. 22.

All the world. This meant the Roman empire ; a frequent expression in classical writers ; *Luke* 2. 1.

ALL, *Gen.* 20. 7. shalt surely die, thou and *a.*

37. 3. Jacob loved Joseph more than *a.* his children

42. 11. we are *a.* one man's sons

Ex. 20. 11. made heaven, earth, sea, and *a.*

33. 19. I will make *a.* my goodness pass before thee

Deut. 5. 3. who are *a.* of us alive ?

13. six days shalt thou labour and do *a.* thy work

1 *Sam.* 6. 4. one plague was on you *a.* and your lords

9. 19. I will tell thee *a.* that is in thy

Ezra 8. 22. wrath is against *a.* that forsake him

Job 16. 2. miserable comforts are ye *a.*

Ps. 14. 3. are *a.* gone aside, *a.* become

34. 19. the Lord delivereth him out of them *a.*

Ps. 38. 9. Lord, *a.* my desire is before thee

Prov. 1. 14. cast in thy lot, let us *a.* have one purse

22. 2. the Lord is maker of them *a.*

Eccl. 3. 20. *a.* of dust, *a.* turn to dust

Is. 64. 9. we are *a.* thy people

Ezek. 7. 16. *a.* of them mourning, every one for

Mal. 2. 10. have we not *a.* one father

Matt. 5. 18. pass from the law till *a.* be fulfilled

13. 56. and his sisters, are they not *a.* with us ?

Mark 12. 33. is more than *a.* burnt-offerings

44. she cast in *a.*, even *a.* that she
had, *Luke* 21. 4.

John 1. 16. of his fulness have *a.* we received

4. 39. he told me *a.* that ever I did

17. 21. that they *a.* may be one, as
thou art in me

Acts 4. 33. and great grace was upon
them *a.*

Rom. 1. 8. I thank God through Jesus
Christ for you *a.*

8. 32. delivered him up for us *a.*

1 *Cor.* 3. 22. *a.* are your's, and ye are
Christ's

Gal. 3. 22. the scripture hath concluded
a. under sin

Phil. 4. 18. but I have *a.* and abound,
and am full

Heb. 1. 14. are they not *a.* ministering
spirits, sent

12. 8. chastisement, whereof *a.* are
partakers

1 *John* 2. 19. manifest that they were
not *a.* of us

ALL, after, *Deut.* 20. 18. not to do *after
a.* their abominations

Ezek. 16. 23. *after a.* thy wickedness,
woe

Phil. 2. 26. for he longed *after* you *a.*

ALL, before, *Lev.* 10. 3. *before a.* the
people I will be glorified

Matt. 26. 70. he denied *before* them *a.*

Gal. 2. 14. I said to Peter *before* them
a.

1 *Tim.* 5. 20. that sin rebuke *before a.*

ALL, for, *Ps.* 10. 5. as *for a.* his enemies,
he puffeth

Eccl. 5. 9. the profit of the earth is *for
a.*

11. 9. *for a.* these God will bring thee
to judgment

Luke 8. 19. *for a.* the evils Herod hath
done

20. 38. God of the living, *for a.*
live unto him

Rom. 3. 23. *for a.* have sinned and come
short of

2 *Cor.* 5. 14. if one died *for a.* then were
a. dead

1 *Tim.* 2. 6. who gave himself a ransom
for a.

Heb. 8. 11. *for a.* shall know me from
the least

10. 10. offering of the body of Christ
once *for a.*

ALL, in, *Ps.* 10. 4. God is not *in a.* his
thoughts

Prov. 3. 6. *in a.* thy ways acknowledge
him

Acts 27. 37. we were *in a* in the ship
276 souls

Rom. 8. 37. *in a.* these more than conquerors

1 *Cor.* 12. 6. the same God worketh all
in a.

15. 28. put all under, that God may
be all *in a.*

Eph. 1. 23. the fulness of him that filleth all *in a.*

Col. 3. 11. but Christ is all *in a.*

ALL, upon, *Is.* 4. 5. for *upon a.* the
glory shall be a defence

Rom. 3. 22. unto all, and *upon a.* them
that believe

Jude 15. to execute judgment upon *a.*

ALL, over, *Ps.* 103. 19. his kingdom
ruleth *over a.*

John 17. 2. hast given him power *over a.*

Rom. 9. 5. who is *over a.* God blessed
for ever

10. 12. the same Lord *over a.* is rich
to all

ALL these, *Matt.* 6. 33. *a. these* shall be
added to you, *Luke* 12. 31.

Acts 2. 7. are not *a. these* Galileans ?

Heb. 11. 13. *a. these* died in faith, not
having received

ALL, to or unto, *Ps.* 145. 9. the Lord is
good *to a.* and his mercies

Eccl. 2. 14. one event happeneth *to a.*
them 9. 3, 11.

Acts 2. 39. the promise is *to a.* that are
afar off

Rom. 10. 12. the Lord is rich *unto a.*
that call on him

13. 7. render therefore *to a.* their dues

ALLEGING, affirming, *Acts* 17. 3.

ALLEGORY, *Gal.* 4. 24. which things
are an *a.* for these are

ALLELUIAH, *Rev.* 19. 1. I heard a
great voice saying, *a.* 3, 4, 6.

ALLIED, *Neh.* 13. 4. Eliashib the priest
was *a.* to Tobiah

ALLOW, deeds of fathers, *Luke* 11. 48.

Acts 24. 15. which themselves *a.*

Rom. 7. 15. what I do *a.* not

Rom. 14. 22. in that which he *a.*

1 *Thess.* 2. 4. as we are *a.* of God

ALLURE, *Hos.* 2. 14 ; 2 *Pet.* 2. 18.

ALMIGHTY, *Gen.* 17. 1. I am the A.
God

Gen. 43. 14. God A. give you mercy

Ex. 6. 3. I appeared to Abraham by the
name God A.

Job 5. 17. despise not thou the chastening of the A.

6. 14. but he forsaketh the fear of
the A.

11. 7. find out the A. to perfection

13. 3. I would speak to A.

15. 25. he strengtheneth himself
against the A.

21. 15. what is A. we should serve

22. 3. pleasure to A. art righteous

27. 10. will he delight in A.

29. 5. when A. was yet with me

31. 35. desire A. would answer

37. 23. touching A. we cannot find

Ps. 68. 14. when the A. scattereth kings

91. 1. abide under shadow of the A.

Ezek. 1. 24. heard as voice of A. : 10. 5.

Joel 1. 15. as destruction from A.

2 *Cor.* 6. 18. shall be my sons, saith the
Lord A.

Rev. 1. 8. which is, was, and is to come,
the A.

15. 3. Lord A. just and true are thy
ways, 16. 7.

21. 22. God A. and Lamb are the temple

ALMOND, S, *Ex.* 25. 33, 34 ; 37. 19, 20.
bowls like *a.*

Eccl. 12. 5. when *a.*-tree shall flourish

Jer. 1. 11. I see rod of *a.*-tree

ALMOST all things, *Heb.* 9. 22.

Ex. 17. 4. *a.* ready to stone me

Ps. 73. 2. my feet were *a.* gone

94. 17. soul had *a.* dwelt in silence

Prov. 5. 14. was *a.* in all evil in congregation

Acts 13. 44. came *a.* the whole city together

19. 26. only at Ephesus, but *a.* through all Asia

26. 28. *a.* persuadest me to be a Christian

Heb. 9. 22. *a.* all things by the law are purged

ALMS, bounty to the poor, *Acts* 3. 2, 3. & 2+. 17.

Matt. 6. 1. do not your *a.* before men

Luke 11. 41. give *a.* of such things

12. 33. sell that ye have give *a.*

Acts 10. 2. gave much *a.* to people

4. thy *a.* are come up for memorial

ALMS-DEEDS, *Acts* 9. 36. Dorcas full of *a.*-deeds which she did

ALONE, *Gen.* 32. 24.

Gen. 2. 18. not good for man to be *a.*

Deut. 32. 12. Lord *a.* did lead him

Num. 11. 14. I am not able to bear all this people *a. Deut.* 1. 9, 12.

23. 9. people dwell *a. Deut.* 33. 28.

2 Sam. 18. 24. behold, a man running *a.* 26.

25. if he be *a.* there is tidings in his mouth

Ps. 83. 18. thou whose name *a.* is Jehovah

102. 7. I watch and am as a sparrow *a.* on the house-top

136. 4. *a.* doeth great wonders

148. 13. for his name *a.* is excellent

Eccl. 4. 10. Woe to him that is *a.*

Is. 2. 11. Lord *a.* shall be exalted in that day, 17.

5. 8. that they may be placed *a.*

63. 3. trodden wine-press *a.*

Matt. 4. 4. a man shall not live by bread *a. Luke* 4. 4.

14. 23. evening was come, he was *a. Luke* 9. 18.

Luke 5. 21. forgive sins but God *a.*

9. 18. it came to pass, as Jesus was *a.* praying

10. 40. that my sister hath left me to serve *a.*

John 6. 15. he departed into a mountain *a.*

8. 16. for I am not *a.* but I and the Father, 16. 32.

17. 20. neither pray I for these *a.*

Gal. 6. 4. rejoicing in himself *a.*

Jam. 2. 17. faith if it hath not works is dead, being *a.*

ALONE, left, *John* 8. 9. and Jesus was *left a.* and the woman

29. the Father hath not *left* me *a.* for I do always

Rom. 11. 3. I am *left a.* and they seek my life

ALONE, let, *Ex.* 32. 10. *let* me *a.* that my wrath

Deut. 9. 14. *let* me *a.* that I may destroy them

Judg. 11. 37. *let* me *a.* two months, that I may go

Hos. 4. 17. Ephraim idols let him *a.*

Matt. 15. 14. let them *a.* they be blind

Mark 1. 24. let us *a.* what have we to do with thee, thou Jesus of Nazareth ? *Luke* 4. 34.

14. 6. Jesus said, *let* her *a.* why trouble ye her

15. 36. *let a.* let us see whether Elias will come

Luke 13. 8. Lord, *let* it *a.* this year also

ALTAR, *Ex.* 20. 24. *a.* of earth shalt

Ex. 27. 1. make *a.* of shittim wood

30. 28. anoint *a.* of burnt-offering

40. 5. set *a.* of gold before ark

Lev. 9. 7. go to *a.* and offer sin-offering

16. 18. make atonement for *a.*

Num. 18. 7. priests' office for everything of *a.*

Deut. 12. 27. offer burnt offering on *a.* of Lord

26. 4. set basket down before *a.*

1 Kings 1. 53. brought Adonijah from *a.*

13. 1. Jeroboam stood by *a.*

2 Kings 16. 10. Ahaz saw *a.* at Damascus

15. on great *a.* burn burnt-offering

23. 9. priests came not up to *a.*

1 Chro. 22. 1. this is *a.* of burnt-offering for Israel

2 Chro. 1. 5. brazen *a.* Bezaleel made

4. 1. he made *a.* of brass

6. 12. Solomon stood before *a.* of Lord

Ps. 43. 4. then will I go to *a.* of God

Is. 19. 19. *a.* to Lord in midst of Egypt

Ezek. 41. 22. *a.* of wood 3 cubits high

43. 15. *a.* 4 cubits and upwards, 4 horns

Matt. 23. 18. swear by *a.* it is nothing

Heb. 13. 10. we have *a.* whereof

Rev. 6. 9. under *a.* souls of slain

9. 13. voice from horns of golden *a.*

ALTARS, *Ex.* 34. 13 : *Deut.* 7. 5. shall destroy their *a.*

Num. 23. 1. build me here seven *a.*

2 Kings 18. 22 : *Is.* 36. 7. whose *a.* Hezekiah hath taken away ; *2 Chro.* 32. 12.

23. 12. *a.* did king beat down

2 Chro. 30. 14. took away *a.* that were

Jer. 17. 2. children remember their *a.*

Hos. 8. 11. made *a.* to sin, *a.* to him

10. 1. he hath increased *a.*

Amos 3. 14. I will visit *a.* of Bethel

ALTER, ED, ETH, *Lev.* 27. 10. not *a.* it good for bad

Ezra 6. 11. whoso shall *a.* this word

Ps. 89. 34. not *a.* thing gone out of lips

Dan. 6. 8. according to law which *a.* not

Luke 9. 29. his countenance was *a.*

ALWAY, S, *Deut.* 5. 29 : *Job* 27. 16.

Gen. 6. 3. my spirit not *a.* strive

Deut. 14. 23. learn to fear Lord *a.*

1 Chro. 16. 15. be mindful *a.* of covenant

Job 7. 16. would not live *a.*

27. 10. will he *a.* call on God

32. 9. great men are not *a.* wise

Ps. 9. 18. needy not *a.* be forgotten

16. 8. I set the Lord *a.* before me

103. 9. he will not *a.* chide

Prov. 5. 19. ravished *a.* with her love

28. 14. happy man that feareth *a.*

Is. 57. 16. neither will I be *a.* wroth

Matt. 26. 11. have poor *a.* with you

28. 20. I am with you *a.* to end

Mark 14. 7. but me ye have not *a. John* 12. 8.

Luke 18. 1. men ought *a.* to pray

John 8. 29. I do *a.* things that please

11. 42. I know thou hearest me *a.*

Acts 10. 2. Cornelius prayed to God *a.*

2 *Cor.* 2. 14. God, who *a.* causeth us to triumph

2 *Cor.* 6. 10. yet *a.* rejoicing

Eph. 6. 18. pray *a.* with all prayer

Phil. 1. 4. *a.* in every prayer of mine for you

4. 4. rejoice in the Lord *a.*, and again rejoice

Col. 4. 6. speech be *a.* with grace

2 *Pet.* 1. 15. to have these *a.* in remembrance

I AM, I AM that I AM, *Ex.* 3. 14. *I am that I am* hath sent

Num. 11. 21. the people amongst whom *I am*

Neh. 6. 11. who is there that being as *I am*

Ps. 35. 3. say to my soul, *I am* thy salvation

39. 4. that I may know how frail *I am*

50. 7. Israel, *I am* God, even thy God

Is. 44. 6. *I am* the first, *I am* the last, 48. 12 ; *Rev.* 1. 11.

47. 8. *I am*, and none else besides me, *Zeph.* 2. 15.

Matt. 16. 13. whom do men say *that I* the son of man *am* ? *Matt.* 8. 27 ; *Luke* 9. 18.

Luke 22. 70. art the Son of God, ye say that *I am*

John 8. 58. I say to you, before Abraham was, *I am*

17. 24. I will, that they may be with me where *I am*

Gal. 4. 12. brethren, be as *I am*, for I *am* as you are

Phil. 4. 11. for I have learned in what state *I am*

AMAZED, *Ex.* 15. 15. dukes of Edom shall be *a.*

Judg. 20. 41. men of Benjamin were *a.*

Job 32. 15. they were *a.* left off speaking

Ezek. 32. 10. make many people *a.*

Matt. 19. 25. disciples exceedingly *a.*

Mark 14. 33. Christ began to be sore *a.*

Luke 9. 43. all *a.* at mighty power

AMAZEMENT, 1 *Pet.* 3. 6. not afraid with any *a.*

AMBASSADOR, S 2 *Chr.* 32. 31. business of *a.* Babylon

2 *Chr.* 35. 21. Necho sent a. to Josiah,

Prov. 13. 17. a faithful *a.* is health

Is. 18. 2. sendeth *a.* by sea

30. 4. his *a.* came to Hanes

33. 7. *a.* of peace shall weep

Jer. 49. 14. *a.* is sent to heathen

Ezek. 17. 15. rebelled in sending *a.*

2 *Cor.* 5. 20. we are *a.* for Christ

Eph. 6. 20. for which I am *a.* in bonds

AMBASSAGE, *Luke* 14. 32. sendeth *a.* and desireth

AMBUSH, *Josh.* 8. 2. lay thee *a.* for city ; ver. 12, 19. *a.* rose quickly

AMBUSHMENT, 2 *Chr.* 13. 13. Jeroboam caused *a.*

AMEN, A Hebrew word which signifies true, faithful, certain, so to be, in a solemn assent. Sometimes rendered in our translation, verily ; *Num.* 5. 22 ; 1 *Kings* 1. 36 ; *Ps.* 72. 19 ; 89. 52 ; *Matt.* 6. 13.

Deut. 27. 15. all the people shall say *a.*

1 *Kings* 1. 36. Benaiah answered *a.*

1 *Cor.* 14. 16. how unlearned say' *a.* ?

2 *Cor.* 1. 20. promises in him *a.*

Rev. 3. 14. these things saith the *a.*

22. 20. *a.* even so, come, Lord Jesus

AMEND your ways, to make better, to grow better, to make restitution ; *Jer.* 7. 3. & 26. 13 ; your doings, 35. 15 ; *John* 4. 52 ; *Lev.* 5. 16.

John 4. 52. hour when he began to *a.*

AMENDS, *Lev.* 5. 16. make *a.* for harm

AMERCE, *Deut.* 22. 19. shall *a.* him in

AMIABLE thy tabernacles, *Ps.* 84. 1.

AMISS, 2 *Chr.* 6. 37 ; *Dan.* 3. 29.

Luke 23. 41. this man hath done nothing *a.*

James 4. 3. receive not because ask *a.*

ANATHEMA, 1 *Cor.* 16. 22. let him be *a.* maranatha

ANCESTORS, *Lev.* 26. 45. remember covenant of *a.*

ANCHOR, S, *Acts* 27. 29. cast four *a.* out of stern

Heb. 6. 19. which hope we have as *a.*

ANCIENT, *Deut.* 33. 15. chief things of *a.* mountains

2 *Kings* 19. 25 ; *Is.* 37. 26 ; of *a.* times I form

1 *Chr.* 4. 22. and these are *a.* things

Ezra 3. 12. *a.* men had seen first house

Job 12. 12. with *a.* is wisdom

Ps. 119. 100. I understand more than *a.*

Prov. 22. 28. remove not the *a.* landmark

Is. 3. 14. enter into judgment with *a.*

9. 15. *a.* and honourable is head

19. 11. how say ye, I am the son of *a.* king ?

23. 7. whose antiquity is of *a.* days

51. 9. awake, O arm of the Lord, as in the *a.* days

Dan. 7. 9. *A.* of days did sit

13. one like the Son of man came to *a.* of days

22. till *A.* of days came

ANGEL, *a.* who redeemed me, *Gen.* 48. 16.

Gen. 24. 7. send his *a.* before thee, 40.

Ex. 23. 23. my *a.* shall go before thee

Num. 20. 16. sent an *a.* and brought us out of Egypt

2 *Sam.* 24. 16. the *a.* stretched out his hand, the *a.* that destroyed the people, 1 *Chro.* 21. 15.

17. David spake when he saw the *a.* that smote

1 *Kings* 13. 18. *a.* spake to me by word

19. 5. an *a.* touched Elijah and said, arise and eat

1 *Chro.* 21. 15. God sent an *a.* to Jerusalem to destroy

2 *Chro.* 32. 21. the Lord sent an *a.* which he cut off

Is. 63. 9. *a.* of his presence saved

Dan. 3. 28. sent his *a.* and delivered

6. 22. sent *a.* and shut lion's mouth

Hos. 12. 4. had power over the *a.*

Zech. 1. 9. the *a.* that talked with me said, 4. 5.

2. 3. the *a.* that talked went out, and another *a.*

5. 5. the *a.* answered, these are the four spirits

13. Lord answered the *a.* that talked with me

Matt. 28. 5. the *a.* answered the woman, fear not
Luke 1. 19. the *a.* answered and said, I
am Gabriel
26. in the sixth month the *a.* Gabriel
was sent
30. the *a.* said to her, fear not, Mary
2. 10. the *a.* said to the shepherds,
fear not
13. suddenly there was with the *a.* a
multitude
22. 43. there appeared an *a.* strengthening him
John 5. 4. *a.* went down at season
Acts 6. 15. Stephen as face of an *a.*
7. 35. by hands of the *a.* that appeared in the bush
10. 7. when the *a.* which spake to
Cornelius
12. 8. the *a.* said to Peter, bind on
thy sandals
15. Rhoda affirmed, then said they,
it is his *a.*
23. 8. the Sadducees say, neither *a.*
nor spirit
2 *Cor.* 11. 14. is transformed into an *a.*
of light
Gal. 1. 8. though we or an *a.* from
heaven preach
Rev. 1. 1. and he signified it by his
a. to John
7. 2. I saw another *a.* ascending from
the east
8. 3. and another *a.* came and stood
at the altar
5. the *a.* took the censer, and filled it
with fire
8. 13. I heard an *a.* flying through
midst of heaven
10. 1. I saw another *a.* come down,
8. 1 ; 20. 1.
7. but in the days of the voice of the
seventh *a.*
8. go and take the book in the hand
of the *a.*
14. 6. *I* saw another *a.* fly in the
midst of heaven
14. 8. another *a.* followed, saying,
Babylon is
19. and the *a.* thrust in his sickle in
the earth
16. 2. *a.* poured his vial, 3, 4, 8, 10,
12, 17.
18. 21. and mighty *a.* took up a stone
like a great
19. 17. and I saw an *a.* standing in
the sun
21. 17. the measure of a man, that is
of the *a.*
22. 16. I Jesus have sent mine *a.* to
testify of you
ANGELS, *Gen.* 19. 1. there came two
a. to Sodom at even
Job 4. 18. his *a.* charged with folly
Ps. 8. 5. little lower than *a.*
68. 17. chariots of God, thousands of *a.*
78. 25. man did eat *a.* food
103. 20. his *a.* excel in strength
104. 4. maketh his *a.* spirits
Matt. 4. 11. *a.* came and ministered
13. 39. reapers are the *a.*
18. 10. their *a.* always behold
24. 36. no not the *a.* in heaven
25. 31. all holy *a.* with him. 24. 31.

Mark 12. 25. are as *a.* in heaven, 13. 32.
Luke 2. 15. as the *a.* were gone away
from them
16. 22. the beggar died, and was carried by the *a.*
Luke 20. 36. equal to the *a.*
John 20. 12. and seeth two *a.* in white,
sitting
Acts 7. 53. the law, by disposition of *a.*
1 *Cor.* 4. 9. a spectacle to the world, to
a. and men
6. 3. we shall judge *a.*
13. 1. though I speak with tongues of
men and *a.*
Gal. 3. 19. it was ordained by *a.* in the
hand
Col. 2. 18. beguile worshipping of *a.*
2 *Thess.* 1. 7. with his mighty *a.*
1 *Tim.* 3. 16. seen of *a.* preached to the
Gentiles
Heb. 2. 2. if the word spoken by *a.* was
steadfast
5. to the *a.* hath he not put in subjection
16. took not the nature of *a.*
12. 22. to an innumerable company
of *a.*
13. 2. entertained *a.* unawares
1 *Pet.* 1. 12. *a.* desire to look into
2 *Pet.* 2. 4. God spared not *a.* that sinned
2 *Pet.* 2. 11. *a.* greater in power and
might
Jude 6. *a.* who kept not their first state
Rev. 1. 20. *a.* of seven churches
Rev. 5. 11. the voice of many *a.* about
the throne
7. 1. I saw four *a.* standing on the four
corners
11. all the *a.* stood round about the
throne
14. 10. be tormented in presence of
the holy *a.*
21. 12. twelve gates, and at the gates
twelve *a.*
ANGELS, his, *Matt.* 13. 41. the Son of
man shall send forth his *a.*
16. 27. come in the glory of his Fa-
with his *a.*
24. 31. send *his a.* with a great sound,
Mark 13. 27.
25. 41. fire prepared for the devil and
his a.
Rev. 3. 5. will confess before my Father
and *his a.*
12. 7. Michael and *his a.*, the dragon
and *his a.*
Angels of God, *Gen.* 28. 12 ; 32. 1 & 15.
10 ; *John* 1. 51.
Matt. 22. 30. but as *a. of God* in heaven, *Mark* 12. 25.
Luke 12. 8. him shall the Son confess
before the *a. of God*
9. denieth me, shall be denied before
the *a. of God*
15. 10. there is joy in the presence of
the *a. of God*
Heb. 1. 6. let all the *a. of God* worship
him
Angel of the Lord, *Ps.* 34. 7 ; *Zech.* 12. 8.
Num. 22. 23. ass saw the *a. of L.* standing, 25. 27.
24. *a. of L.* stood in a path of the
vineyards, 26.
Judg. 2. 1. *a. of L.* came up, 1 *Kings*

19. 7 ; *Acts* 12. 7.

Judg. 5. 23. curse ye Meroz, said the *a.*
   of the Lord

6. 11. came an *a.* of the *L.* and sat
   under an oak

13. 3. *a.* of the *L.* appeared to the woman, and said

2 *Kings* 19. 35. *a.* of *L.* smote in camp,
   Is. 37. 36.

Zech. 1. 11. they answered the *a.* of the
   L. that stood

3. 5. *a.* of *L.* stood by Joshua. 6. *a.*
   of *L.* protested

Matt. 1. 20. *a.* of *L.* appeared in a dream,
   2. 13, 19.

28. 2. for the *a.* of the *L.* descended
   from heaven

Luke 1. 11. there appeared to Zacharias an *a.* of *L.*

2. 9. *a.* of *L.* came upon them, and
   glory of Lord

Acts 5. 19. *a.* of *L.* by night opened the
   prison-doors

ANGER of the Lord wax hot, *Ex.* 32. 22.

Deut. 29. 24. meaneth the heat of this *a.*

Josh. 7. 26. from fierceness of *a.*

Job 9. 13. if God will not withdraw *a.*

Ps. 27. 9. put not away servants in *a.*

30. 5. his *a.* endureth but a moment

37. 8. cease from *a.* and wrath

77. 9. hath he in *a.* shut up

78. 38. turned he his *a.* away

85. 4. cause *a.* toward us to cease

90. 7. we are consumed by thine *a.*

11. who knoweth the power of thine *a.*

103. 9. keep *a.* for ever, *Jer.* 3. 5, 12.

Eccl. 7. 9. *a.* rests in the bosom of fools

Is. 5. 25. for all this his anger is not
   turned away, 9. 12 ; 17. 21 & 10. 4.

Hos. 11. 9. not execute fierceness of *a.*

14. 4. my *a.* is turned away from him

Mic. 7. 18. retaineth not *a.* for ever

Nah. 1. 6. can abide fierceness of *a.*

Eph. 4. 31. let all *a.* be put away

Col. 3. 8. put off all these, *a.* wrath

Col. 3. 21. fathers, provoke not your
   children to *a.*

Slow to anger, *Neh.* 9. 17 ; *Ps.* 103. 8 ;
   Joel 2. 13 ; *Nah.* 1. 3 ; *James* 1. 19.

Ps. 106. 32. they *a.* him at waters

ANGRY, *Gen.* 18. 30. let not Lord be *a.*

Gen. 45. 5. be not *a.* with yourselves
   that ye sold me

Deut. 1. 37. Lord was *a.* with me

Deut. 9. 8. Lord was *a.* with you to
   have destroyed you

9. 20. Lord was *a.* with Aaron

1 *Kings* 11. 9. Lord was *a.* with Solomon

2 *Kings* 17. 18. therefore the Lord was
   a. with Israel

Ezra. 9. 14. wouldst not be *a.* with us

Ps. 2. 12. kiss son lest he be *a.*

Ps. 7. 11. God *a.* with wicked every day

76. 7. who may stand when thou *a.*

79. 5. how long wilt thou be *a* ? 80. 4 ;
   85. 5.

Prov. 14. 17. is soon *a.* dealeth foolish

21. 19. dwell in wilderness, than
   with an *a.* woman

22. 24. no friendship with *a.* man

29. 22. *a.* man stirreth up strife

Eccl. 7. 9. be not hasty to be *a.*

Songs 1. 6. mother's children were *a.*

Is. 12. 1. though thou wast *a.* with me

Dan. 2. 12. for this cause the king was *a.*

Jonah 4. 4. the Lord said, dost thou well
   to be *a.*

9. I do well to be *a.* even

Matt. 5. 22. whose is *a.* with his brother

Luke 14. 21. the master of the house
   being *a.*

15. 28. and he was *a.* and would not
   go in

Eph. 4. 26. be *a.* and sin not

Tit. 1. 7. bishop must not be soon *a.*

ANGUISH, *Gen.* 42. 21. in that we saw
   a. of his soul

Ex. 6. 9. hearken not to Moses for *a.*

2 *Sam.* 1. 9. *a.* is come upon me

Job 15. 24. *a.* shall make him afraid

Ps. 119. 143. trouble and *a.* have taken :
   Jer. 6. 24 ; 49. 24.

John 16. 21. rem. no more *a.* for joy

2 *Cor.* 2. 4. out of *a.* of heart I wrote

ANOINT, rub with oil, appoint to, to
   qualify for office of king, priest,
   prophet ; *Ex.* 28. 41.

Dan. 9. 24. to *a.* the most holy

Amos. 6. 6. *a.* with chief ointments

Matt. 6. 17. when fastest *a.* thy head

Rev. 3. 18. *a.* eyes with eye-salve

1 *Sam.* 26. 9. against the Lord's *a.*

Ps. 45. 7. *a.* these with oil of gladness

Is. 61. 1. Lord *a.* me to preach, *Luke*
   4. 18.

Zech. 4. 14. two *a.* ones before Lord

Acts 4. 27. Jesus, whom thou hast *a.*

10. 38. how God *a.* Jesus of Nazareth

2 *Cor.* 1. 21. which hath *a.* us is God

Ps. 2. 2. Lord and his *a.* 18. 50.

1 *Sam.* 2. 10 ; 2 *Sam.* 22. 51 ; *Ps.* 20. 6.
   & 28. 8.

1 *Chr.* 16. 22. touch not my *a. Ps.* 105.
   15. & 132. 17.

2 *Chr.* 6. 42. turn not away face of thy
   a. Ps. 132. 10. & 84. 9. & 89. 38, 51 ;
   Hab. 2. 13.

Ps. 23. 5. *a.* my head with oil

Is. 10. 27. because of *a.* of oil

1 *John* 2. 27. the *a.* teacheth all

James 5. 14. *a.* him with oil

ANSWER, *Gen.* 41. 16. give Pharoah *a.*
   of peace ; *Deut.* 20. 11.

Job 19. 16. he gave me no *a.*

Prov. 15. 1. soft *a.* turneth away wrath

16. 1. *a.* of tongue from the Lord

Songs 5. 6. he gave me no *a.*

Mich. 3. 7. there is no *a.* of God

Rom. 11. 4. what saith the *a.* of God

1 *Cor.* 9. 3. mine *a.* to them that do
   examine me is

2 *Tim.* 4. 16. at my first *a.* no man

1 *Pet.* 3. 15. ready to give an *a.*

21. the *a.* of a good conscience

ANSWER (verb) *Job* 40. 4. what shall I
   a. thee

Ps. 102. 2. *a.* me speedily

Ps. 108. 6. save with thy right hand,
   and *a.* me

143. 1. in thy faithfulness *a.* me

Prov. 26. 4, 5. *a.* a fool according to his
   folly

Is. 14. 32. what shall one then *a.* messengers

50. 2. when I called was none to *a.*

66. 4. when I called none did *a.*

Dan. 3. 16. not careful to *a.* thee

Matt. 25. 37. then shall righteous *a.* Lord

Mark 11. 30. was it from heaven or of men ? *a.* me

14. 40. neither wist they what to *a.* him

Luke 12. 11. what thing ye shall *a*

13. 25. he shall *a.* I know you not

21. 14. meditate not to *a.*

2 *Cor.* 5. 12. have somewhat to *a.* them

Col. 4. 6. know how to *a.* every man

Answer, I will, *Job* 14. 15. thou shalt call and I will a., & 13. 22 ; *Ps.* 91. 15 ; *Is.* 65. 24 ; *Jer.* 33. 3 ; *Ezek.* 14. 4, 7.

Answer, not, *Job* 9. 3. he cannot *a.* one of, 40. 5 ; *Prov.* 1. 28 ; *Is.* 36. 21. & 65. 12.

Ps. 18. 41. to Lord but he *a.* not

Answered, meant of God, *Ps.* 81. 7. I a. thee in secret place

Ps. 99. 6. called on the Lord and he *a.*

Prov. 18. 23. rich *a.* roughly

13. he that *a.* matter before heareth

27. 19. as face *a.* to face in water

Eccl. 10. 19. money *a.* all things

Gal. 4. 25. *a.* to Jerusalem that now is

Tit. 2. 9. not *a.* again

ANY, *Lev.* 4. 2. if a soul shall sin against *a.* of the commandments, 13. 22, 27 ; 5. 17.

Deut. 32. 39. nor *a.* that can deliver out of my hand

Job 33. 27. he looketh, and if *a.* say, I have sinned

Ps. 4. 6. many say, who will show us *a.* good

Is. 44. 8. there is no God, I know not *a.*

Amos 6. 10. he shall say, is there yet *a.* with thee ?

Mark 8. 26. nor go nor tell it to *a.* in the town

11. 25. forgive, if ye have aught against *a.*

1 *Cor.* 6. 12. I will not be brought under power of *a.*

Jam. 1. 5. if *a.* lack wisdom, let him ask of God

2 *Pet.* 3. 9. not willing that *a.* should

APART, *Ex.* 13. 12 ; *Lev.* 15. 9 ; 18. 19.

Ps. 4. 3. the Lord hath set *a.* godly

Zech. 12. 12. every family *a.* 14.

Matt. 14. 13. into a desert place *a.*

23. into a mountain *a.* ; 17. 1 ; *Luke* 9. 28.

17. 19. came the disciples to Jesus *a.*

Mark 6. 31. come ye yourselves *a.*

Jam. 1. 21. wherefore lay *a.* filthiness

APOSTLE, minister sent by God or Christ, infallibly to preach the gospel and found churches ; *Rom.* 1. 1 ; 1 *Cor.* 1. 1. & 12. 28.

Rom. 11. 13. I am the *a.* of Gentiles

1 *Cor.* 9. 1. am I not an *a.* free

15. 9. not meet to be called an *a.*

2 *Cor.* 12. 12. signs of an *a.* wrought

Heb. 3. 1. consider the *a.* and High Priest

Matt. 10. 2. names of the 12 *a.*

Luke 11. 49. I will send prophets and *a.*

1 *Cor.* 4. 9. God hath sent forth us *a.*

15. 9. I am least of the *a.*

2 *Cor.* 11. 13. such are false *a.*

Eph. 2. 20. built on foundation of *a.*

4. 11. gave some *a.* some prophets

Rev. 2. 2. say they are *a.* and are not,

18. 20 : holy *a.* and prophets, *Eph.* 3. 5.

21. 14. names of the 12 *a.* of the Lamb

APOSTLESHIP, *Acts* 1. 25. that he may take part of this *a.*

Rom. 1. 5. by whom we have received grace and *a.*

1 *Cor.* 9. 2. the seal of mine *a.* are in the Lord

Gal. 2. 8. wrought effectually in Peter to the *a.*

APPAREL, garments, *Gen.* 38. 14 ; *Lev.* 6. 11 ; *Deut.* 22. 5 ; 2 *Sam.* 12. 20 ; 13. 18.

1 *Kings* 10. 5. queen of Sheba had seen the attendance of his ministers, and their *a.* 2 *Chr.* 9. 4.

Is. 3. 22. the changeable suits of *a.* and mantles

4. 1. we will eat our own bread and wear our own *a.*

63. 1. who is this that is glorious in his *a.* ?

Acts 1. 10. two men stood by them in white *a.*

20. 33. I have coveted no man's silver or *a.*

1 *Tim.* 2. 9. that women adorn themselves in modest *a.*

Jam. 2. 2. if a man come in goodly *a.*

1 *Pet.* 3. not of wearing gold, or putting on *a.*

APPARELLED, 2 *Sam.* 13. 18. the king's daughters, virgins, were *a.*

Luke 7. 25. behold they which are gorgeously *a.*

APPEAL, ED, *Acts* 25. 11. no man deliver me, I *a.* unto Caesar

26. 32 been set at liberty if he had not *a.* to Caesar, 28. 19. I was constrained to *a.* to Caesar

APPEAR, *Gen.* 1. 9 ; *Heb.* 11. 3.

Ex. 23. 15. none shall *a.* before me empty, 34. 20 ; *Deut.* 16. 16.

Deut. 31. 11. when all Israel is come to *a.* before L.

1 *Sam.* 2. 27. did I *a.* to house of father

2 *Chr.* 1. 7. did God *a.* to Solomon

Ps. 42. 2. when shall I *a.* before God

90. 16. let thy work *a.* to servants

Ps. 102. 16. build up Zion, he shall *a.* in his glory

Songs 2. 22. the flowers *a.* on the earth, the time of

Is. 1. 12. when ye *a.* before me who

66. 5. shall *a.* to your joy, but they

Matt. 6. 16. may *a.* to men to fast

23. 27. *a.* beautiful outward, but

Matt. 24. 30. then shall *a.* the sign of the Son of man

Luke 19. 11. kingdom of God should *a.*

Rom. 7. 13. but sin, that it might *a.* sin, working

2 *Cor.* 5. 10. we must all *a.* before judgment-seat

Col. 3. 4. when Christ shall *a.* ye also *a.*

1 *Tim.* 4. 15. thy profiting *a.* to all

Heb. 9. 24. to *a.* in presence of God for

28. *a.* second time without sin to salvation

11. 3. were not made of things which do *a.*

1 *Pet.* 4. 18. where shall the ungodly and sinner *a.* ?

5. 4. when chief shepherd shall *a.*

1 *John* 2. 28. when he shall *a.* we may have confidence

3. 2. not yet *a.* what we shall be

Rev. 3. 18. shame of thy nakedness do not *a.*

APPEARANCE, *Dan.* 8. 15. stood before me as the *a.* of a man, 10. 18.

10. 6. his face as the *a.* of lightning, his eyes as

1 *Sam.* 16. 7. man looks at outward *a.*

John 7. 24. judge not according to the *a.* but judge

2 *Cor.* 5. 12. which glory in *a.* and not

1 *Thess.* 5. 22. abstain from all *a.* of evil

APPEARED, *Gen.* 12. 7. the Lord *a.* to Abram and said, 17. 1 ; 18. 1.

Ex. 3. 2. angel of the Lord *a.* in midst of the bush

6. 3. I *a.* to Abraham by name of God Almighty

2 *Sam.* 22. 16. and the channels of the sea *a.*

Neh. 4. 21. we laboured in the work till the stars *a.*

Matt. 2. 7. Herod inquired what time the star *a.*

13. 26. the blade sprung, then *a.* the tares also

17. 3. there *a.* to them Moses and Elias, *Mark* 9. 4.

27. 53. and went into the holy city, and *a.* to many

Mark 16. 9. Jesus *a.* first to Mary Magdalene

14. after he *a.* to the eleven as they sat at meat

Luke 1. 11. there *a.* to be an angel of the Lord

9. 31. who *a.* in glory, and spake of his decease

22. 42. there *a.* an angel to him, strengthening him

24. 34. the Lord is risen indeed, and *a.* to Simon

Acts 2. 3. there *a.* to them cloven tongues like fire

9. 17. even Jesus, that *a.* to thee in the way

27. 20. when neither sun nor stars *a.*

Tit. 2. 11. the grace of God hath *a.* to all men

Heb. 9. 26. in the end hath he *a.* to put away sin

Rev. 12. 1. there *a.* a great wonder in heaven, 3.

APPEARETH, *Ps.* 84. 7. every one of them in Zion *a.* before God

Mal. 3. 2. and who shall stand when he *a.* ?

Jam. 4. 14. your life is even as a vapour that *a.*

APPEARING, 1 *Tim.* 6. 14. keep commandment till *a.* of our Lord

2 *Tim.* 1. 10. but is now made manifest by the *a.*

4. 1. who shall judge the quick and dead at his *a.*

8. but to all them also that love his *a.*

Tit. 2. 13. looking for glorious *a.* of the great God

1 *Pet.* 1. 7. be found to praise at the *a* of Jesus

APPETITE, (1) Desire after food, *Job*

38. 39.—(2) Desire after worldly things, *Is.* 56. 11.—(3) Gluttonous, *Prov.* 23. 2.

APPLE of eye, *Deut.* 32. 10 ; *Ps.* 17. 8 ; *Prov.* 7. 2 ; *Lam.* 2. 18 ; *Zech.* 2. 8. In these passages reference is made to the keen sensibility of the ball of the eye. They denote God's most careful protection and security.

Apple-tree, *Songs* 2. 3. & 8. 5.

APPLES, *Prov.* 25. 11 ; *Songs* 2. 5. & 7. 8.

APPLY heart to wisdom, &c., *Ps.* 90. 12 ; *Prov.* 2. 2. & 22. 17. & 23. 12 ; *Eccl.* 7. 25. & 8. 9, 16 ; *Hos.* 7. 6.

APPOINT, ED, *Gen.* 18. 14. at time *a.* will I return

Gen. 24. 44. whom Lord hath *a.* for masters

30. 28. *a.* thy wages, and I will give

41. 34. let Pharaoh *a.* officers over the land

Num. 3. 10. thou shalt *a.* Aaron and his sons

9. 7. not offer an offering but at *a.* season

Josh. 20. 9. these are the cities *a.* for refuge

1 *Sam.* 20. 35. Jonathan went to field at time *a.*

25. 30. should have *a.* thee ruler over Israel ; 1 *Kings* 1. 35.

2 *Sam.* 15. 15. what my lord king sh. *a.*

1 *Kings* 12. 12. Jeroboam came as king had *a.* 20. 42. man whom I had *a.* to destruction

2 *Kings* 18. 14. king of Assyria *a.* to Hezekiah three hundred talents

2 *Chr.* 8. 14. Solomon *a.* according to the order of David

Neh. 12. 31. *a.* two comp. that give thanks

13. 30. *a.* wards of priests and Levites

Job 7. 1. is not *a.* time to man on earth

7. 3. and wearisome nights are *a.* to me

14. 13. that thou wouldst *a.* me a set time

14. 14. days of my *a.* time wait

30. 23. to death, and to the house *a.* for all living

Ps. 79. 11. preserve thou those that are *a.* to die

102. 20. to loose those that are *a.* to death

Prov. 8. 29. when he *a.* the foundations of the earth

Is. 1. 14. new-moons and your *a.* feasts

Is. 26. 1. salvation will God *a.* for walls and bulwarks

61. 3. to *a.* them that mourn in Zion

Dan. 11. 27.-end shall be at time *a.* : v. 35.

Mic. 6. 9. hear ye the rod, and who hath *a.* it

Matt. 24. 51. *a.* him his portion with the hypocrites

Matt. 26. 19. dis. did as Jesus *a.* : 28. 16.

27. 10. gave for the potter's field, as your Lord *a.*

Luke 12. 46. *a.* him his portion with unbelievers

Luke 22. 29. I *a.* you a kingdom

Acts 6. 3. seven men whom we *a.* over

this business

Acts 17. 31. hath *a.* day in which judge

22. 10. told thee of things *a.* to do

1 *Cor.* 4. 9. God hath set us apostles last
a. to death

1 *Thess.* 5. 9. God hath not *a.* us to
wrath, but obtain

2 *Tim.* 1. 11. whereunto I am *a.* a
preacher, apostle

Tit. 1. 5. and ordain elders in every
city, as I *a.*

Heb. 3. 2. who was faithful to him that
a. him

9. 27. and as it is *a.* to men once to
die, but after

1 *Pet.* 2. 8. disobedient, whereunto
they were once *a.*

APPOINTED time and times, *Ps.* 81. 3.
blow up the trumpet in the *time a.*

Jer. 8. 7. the stork in heaven knoweth
her *a. times*

Dan. 11. 29. at the *time a.* shall return,
and come south

35. time of the end, because it is yet
for a *time a.*

Hab. 2. 3. the vision is yet for an *a.
time,* wait for it

Acts 17. 26. God hath determined *times*
before *a.*

APPOINTMENT, *Num.* 4. 27. at the *a.*
of Aaron and his sons

APPREHEND, to seize, to take hold of,
1 *Kings* 18. 40 ; 2 *Cor.* 11. 32 ;
Phil. 3. 12 ; *Acts* 12. 4.

APPROACH, come near to, marry

Lev. 18. 6. *a.* none near of kin, 20. 16.

Ps. 65. 4. blessed whom thou causest
to *a.*

Jer. 30. 21. engageth heart to *a.* to me

1 *Tim.* 6. 16. light to which none can *a.*

Is. 58. 2. delight in *a.* to God

Heb. 10. 25. as ye see the day *a.*

APRONS, *Gen.* 3. 7. sewed fig-leaves
and made *a.*

APPROVE, to commend. Jesus Christ
was approved of God ; *Acts* 2. 22.
The apostles approved themselves
as the ministers of God ; 2 *Cor.* 6.
4 ; 2 *Tim.* 2. 15.

Ps. 49. 13. posterity *a.* their sayings

Lam. 3. 36. to subvert Lord *a.* not

Phil. 1. 10. may *a.* things excellent

Acts 2. 22. man *a.* of God

Rom. 14. 18. acceptable to God *a.* of
16. 10. Apelles *a.* in Christ

1 *Cor.* 11. 19. are *a.* may be manifest

2 *Tim.* 2. 15. show thy self *a.* to God

Rom. 2. 18. *a.* things excellent

2 *Cor.* 6. 4. in all things *a.* ourselves

APT to teach, 1 *Tim.* 3. 2 ; 2 *Tim.*
2. 24.

ARCHER, *Gen.* 21. 20. Ishmael became
an *a.*

49. 23. *a.* have sorely grieved

1 *Sam.* 31. 3 ; 1 *Chron.* 10. 3. *a.* hit him

1 *Chr.* 8. 40. sons of Ulam were *a.*

2 *Chr.* 35. 23. *a.* shot at king Josiah

Job 16. 13. his *a.* compass me round

Is. 22. 3. thy rulers are bound by *a.*

ARCHES, *Ezek.* 40. 16, 30. *a.* twenty-
five cubits long

Ezek. 40. 34. *a.* toward outer court

ARE, signifies (1) To be of great value
and esteem among men ; 1 *Cor.* 1.

28. (2) To have authority from ;
1 *John* 4. 1. (3) Reputed, judged,
esteemed ; 1 *Cor.* 4. 17. (4) Repre-
sent, or betoken, *Gen.* 41. 26, 27 ;
Rev. 1. 20.

Things which are not, 1 *Cor.* 1. 28.
*Which are of so small esteem, as if
they had no being.*

Gen. 18. 24. for the fifty righteous that
a. therein

42. 36. Jacob said, all these things *a.*
against me

Job 38. 35. that they may go and say to
thee, here we *a.*

Ps. 68. 26. bless ye God, ye that *a.* of
the fountain

Lam. 5. 7. our fathers have sinned,
and *a.* not

Matt. 2. 18. not be comforted, because
they *a.* not

Luke 13. 25. I know now whence you *a.*
27.

John 17. 11. give me, that they may be
one, as we *a.*

1 *Cor.* 1. 28. to bring to nought that *a.*
8. 6. of whom *a.* all things

2 *Cor.* 11. 22. *a.* they Hebrews ? *a.* they
Israelites ?

Heb. 2. 10. for and by whom *a.* all

Rev. 1. 19. write things that *a.*

4. 11. for thy pleasure they *a.* and
were created

Rev. 10. 6. created heaven and things
which therein *a.*

ARGUE, *Job* 6. 25. & 23. 4.

ARGUING, *Job* 6. 25. but what doth
your *a.* reprove ?

ARGUMENTS, *Job* 23. 4. I would fill
my mouth with *a.*

ARIGHT, set not heart, *a. Ps.* 78. 8.

Ps. 50. 23. ordereth conversation *a.*

Prov. 15. 2. useth knowledge *a.*

23. 31. the w..e, when it moveth itself *a.*

Jer. 8. 6. they spake not *a.*

ARISE for our help, *Ps.* 44. 26.

Deut. 13. 1. if there *a.* among you a
prophet

Josh. 1. 2. *a.* go over this Jordan

2 *Sam.* 2. 14. let the young men *a.* and
play before us

3. 21. I will *a.* and gather all Israel
to my Lord

1 *Kings* 3. 12. nor after thee shall any *a.*
like thee

1 *Chr.* 22. 16. *a.* be doing, the Lord be
with thee

Neh. 2. 20. therefore we his servants
will *a.* and build

Job 7. 4. when shall I *a.* and night be
gone ?

11. 17. thy age shall *a.* above noon

25. 3. and upon whom doth not his
light *a.*

Ps. 3. 7. *a.* O Lord, save me, O my God
for thou

44. 26. *a.* for our help, and redeem us
for thy mercy

68. 1. let God *a.* and enemies be
scattered

88. 10. shall the dead *a.* and praise
thee ?

89. 9. when the waves of sea *a.* thou

stillest them

102. 13. thou shalt *a.* and have mercy on Zion

Prov. 6. 9. when wilt thou *a.* out of thy sleep ?

Songs 2. 13. *a.* my love, my fair one

Is. 21. 5. *a.* ye princes, and anoint the shield

26. 19. together with my dead body shall they *a.*

60. 1. *a.* shine, for thy light is come

2. but the Lord shall *a.* upon thee, and his glory

Dan. 2. 39. after thee shall *a.* another kingdom

Amos 7. 2. by whom shall Jacob *a.* 5.

Mic. 7. 8. when I fall I shall *a.*

Mal. 4. 2. Sun of righteousness *a.* with

Matt. 9. 5. is it easier to say *a.* and walk ? *Mark* 2. 9.

Matt. 24. 24. for there shall *a.* false Christs

Mark 5. 41. damsel, I say to thee, *a. Luke* 8. 54.

Luke 7. 14. Lord said, young man, I say to thee *a.*

15. 18. I will *a.* and go to my father

John 14. 31. even so I do, *a.* let us go hence

Acts 9. 40 turning to the body, said, Tabitha, *a.*

22. 16. why tarriest thou ? *a.* and be baptized

Eph. 5. 14. *a.* from the dead, and Christ

2 *Pet.* 1. 19. till the day-star *a.* in your hearts

ARISETH, 1 *Kings* 18. 44. behold, there *a.* a little cloud

Ps. 112. 4. to the upright *a.* light in darkness

Matt. 13. 21. when persecution *a. Mark* 4. 17.

Heb. 7. 15. after the similitude of Melchizedec *a.*

ARK, signifies, (1) A chest or coffer to keep things sure or secret ; *Ex.* 2. 3. — (2) The great vessel in which Noah and his family were preserved during the flood, in length, 547 feet ; *Gen.* 6. 14. 15 ; *Heb.* 11. 7. —(3) That chest wherein the two tables of the law, Aaron's rod, and the pot of manna were kept ; *Ex.* 37. 1 ; *Heb.* 9. 4.

The Ark of thy strength, *Ps.* 132. 8. The seat of thy powerful and glorious presence, from whence thou dost put forth and manifest thy strength in behalf of thy people, when they desire and need it.

Was seen the Ark of his testament, *Rev.* 11. 19. Christ the true Ark of our covenant, more known, and the mysteries of religion made more common and familiar than formerly, either under the Old Testament dispensation, or during the reign of anti-christ.

Gen. 7. 7. Noah, sons, and wife went into *a.*

7. 18. and the *a.* went on the face of the waters

Ex. 2. 3. she took for him an *a.* of bulrushes

25. 10. make *a.* of shittim wood, 35. 12.

39. 35. brought to Moses *a.* of testimony

40. 3. put *a.* in tabernacle : ver. 21.

Num. 3. 31. their charge shall be the *a.*

Deut. 10. 5. I put tables in a *a.*

Josh. 3. 3. when ye see *a.* ye shall remove

6. take up *a.* and pass over

6. 6. seven priests bear trumpets before *a.*

1 *Sam.* 5. 8. what shall we do with *a.* of God ?

14. 18. Saul said, Bring *a.* of God

2 *Sam.* 6. 2. to bring up from thence the *a.* of God : 1 *Kings* 8. 4.

11. 11. the *a.* and Israel abide in tents

1 *Kings* 2. 26. because thou barest the *a.* of the Lord

6. 19. Solomon set *a.* in oracle : 2 *Chr.* 5. 7.

1 *Chr.* 6. 31. after that the *a.* had rest

13. 3. let us bring again *a.* of God : 15. 25.

15. 1. David prepared a place for the *a.* of God

2 *Chr.* 5. 5. priest and Levites brought *a.* and tabernacle

6. 41. thou and *a.* of thy strength, *Ps.* 132. 8.

Jer. 3. 16. shall say no more *a.* of covenant

Matt. 24. 38. till Noah entered the *a. Luke* 17. 27.

Heb. 11. 7. by faith Noah warned of God prepared an *a.*

1 *Pet.* 3. 20. God waited while the *a.* was preparing

Rev. 11. 19. and there was seen in his temple the *a.*

ARK, before the, *Ex.* 40. 5. thou shalt set altar of gold *before the a.*

Josh. 4. 7. waters of Jordan were cut off *before the a.*

7. 6. Joshua fell to the earth on his face *before the a.*

1 *Sam.* 5. 3. Dagon was fallen on his face *before the a.*

ARK, of the covenant, *Num.* 10. 33. *a. of the covenant* of the Lord went before them

Deut. 31. 26. put book of law inside of *a. of covenant*

Judg. 20. 27. *a. of covenant* of God was therein

2 *Sam.* 15. 24. Levites bearing *a. of covenant* of God

1 *Chr.* 17. 1. *a. of covenant* remained under curtains

Heb. 9. 4. tabernacle which had the *a. of the covenant*

ARK of God, 1 *Sam.* 3. 3. in the temple where the *a. of God* was

1 *Sam.* 4. 11. the *a. of God* was taken, 17. 22.

6. 3. if ye send away the *a. of God,* send it not empty

2 *Sam.* 6. 7. there he died before the *a. of God*

7. 2. but the *a. of God* dwelleth within curtains

15. 25. carry back the *a. of God* into the city

ARM, (1) that part of the body so called, *2 Sam.* 1. 10. (2) outward strength, and all the instruments of cruelty and mischief used by the wicked ; *Ps.* 10. 15. (3) God's infinite power in creating the world ; *Jer.* 27. 5 ; 32. 17. (4) The mighty power of God making the gospel of God effectual to the conversion of sinners ; *Is.* 53. 1 ; *John* 12. 38.

Ex. 15. 16. by greatness of thine *a.* they shall be

Deut. 33. 20. he teareth the *a.* with the crown of head

1 *Sam.* 2. 31. behold the days come when I will cut off thy *a.* and the *a.* of thy father's house

2 *Sam.* 1. 10. I took the bracelet that was on his *a.*

Job 26. 2. savest thou the *a.* that hath no strength

Job 40. 9. hast thou an *a.* like God

Ps. 44. 3. own *a.* did not save them

77. 15. thou hast with thy *a.* re-deemed thy people

89. 13. thou hast a mighty *a.* strong in thy hand

98. 1. his holy *a.* hath gotten him the victory

Songs 8. 6. set me as a seal on thine *a.*

Is. 33. 2. be thou their *a.* every

Is. 40. 10. God will come, and his *a.* shall rule for him

11. he shall gather the lambs with his *a.*

51. 5. mine *a.* shall judge : on my *a.*

9. put on strength *a.* of the Lord

52. 10. Lord made bare his holy *a.*

53. 1. *a.* of Lord revealed, *John* 12. 38.

59. 16. therefore his *a.* brought salva-tion

62. 8. Lord hath sworn by the *a.* of strength

63. 12. led them by his glorious *a.*

His arm, *Ps.* 98. 1 ; *Is.* 40. 10, 11. & 59. 16 ; *Jer.* 17. 5 ; *Ezek.* 31. 17 ; *Zech.* 41. 17 ; *Luke* 1. 51.

Jer. 17. 5. cursed be he that maketh flesh his *a.*

Zech. 11. 17. sword be on his *a.* his *a.* be dried up

Luke 1. 51. he hath showed strength with his *a.*

Stretched-out-arm, *Ex.* 6. 6 ; *Deut.* 4. 34. & 5. 15. & 7. 19. & 11. 2. & 26. 8 ; 2 *Chr.* 6. 32 ; *Ps.* 136. 12 ; *Jer.* 27. 5. & 32. 17, 21 ; *Ezek.* 20. 33, 34.

Gen. 49. 24. *a.* of hand made strong

Deut. 33. 27. underneath everlasting *a.*

1 *Pet.* 4. 1. *a.* yourselves with same

Luke 11. 21. strong man *a.* keepeth

ARMOUR, *Judg.* 9. 54. Abim. called his *a.*-bearer

1 *Sam.* 14. 7. *a.*-bearer said, do all in heart

16. 21. David became Saul's *a.*-bearer

17. 54. David put Goliath's *a.* in his tent

31. 4 ; 1 *Chr.* 10. 4. Saul's *a.*-bearer was afraid

2 *Kings* 3. 21. they gathered all able to put on *a.*

1 *Chr.* 10. 10. put his *a.* in house of their gods

2 *Sam.* 2. 21. turn thee aside and take thee his *a.*

Job 39. 21. he goeth on to meet the *a.*

Is. 22. 8. didst look to *a.* of house

Luke 11. 22. taketh his *a.* wherein

Rom. 13. 12. put on *a.* of light

2 *Cor.* 6. 7. by *a.* of righteousness

Eph. 6. 11. put on whole *a.* of God ; ver. 13. take to you the whole *a.* of God to withstand

ARMOURY, *Neh.* 3. 19. going up to *a.* at turning

Songs 4. 4. like the tower of David builded for an *a.*

Jer. 50. 25. Lord hath opened his *a.*

ARMY, IES, *Ex.* 7. 4. bring forth my *a.*

Num. 33. 1. went forth with their *a.* under Moses

Deut. 11. 4. what he did to *a.* of Egypt

Judg. 8. 6. that we should give bread to *a.*

1 *Sam.* 4. 12. man of Benjamin ran out of *a.*

17. 1. Philistines gathered to battle

1 *Kings* 20. 19. came out of city and *a.*

2 *Chr.* 25. 7. let not *a.* of Israel go with thee

26. 13. an *a.* 307,500 to help king

Job 25. 3. is there any number of his *a.* ?

Ps. 44. 9. thou goest not forth with our *a.*

Ps. 60. 10. O God, didst not go with *a.*

68. 12. kings of *a.* did flee apace

Songs 6. 13. as it were the company of two *a.*

Jer. 34. 21. give Zedekiah to king of Babylon's *a.* : 38. 3.

37. 11. broken for fear of Pharaoh's *a.*

Dan. 11. 13. king of north shall come with *a.*

Matt. 22. 7. he sent forth his *a.* and de-stroyed

Luke 21. 20. ye see Jerusalem compass-ed with *a.*

Heb. 11. 34. who turned to flight the *a.* of the aliens

Rev. 9. 16. the number of the *a.* of horsemen

Rev. 19. 14. *a.* in heaven followed him

19. against him that sat on horse and *a.*

AROSE, *Gen.* 19. 33. he perceived not when she *a.* 35.

37. 7. and lo! my sheaf *a.* and stood upright

Ex. 1. 8. now there *a.* up a new king over Egypt, who knew not Joseph, *Acts* 7. 18.

Judg. 2. 10. *a.* a generation that knew not the Lord

20. 8. all the people *a.* as one man, saying

2 *Kings* 23. 25. neither after him *a.* there any like

Job 29. 8. young men hid, aged *a.* and stood up

Ps. 76. 9. when God *a.* to judgment. to save the

Eccl. 1. 5. the sun hasteth to his place where he *a.*

Dan. 6. 19. the king *a.* early and went to the den

Matt. 2. 14. he *a.* and took the young child, 21.

8. 15. she *a.* and ministered to them, *Luke* 4. 39.

9. 9. and he *a.* and followed him, 19. *Mark* 2. 14.

25. he took her by the hand, and the maid *a.*

27. 52. and many bodies of saints which slept *a.*

Luke 6. 48. when the flood *a.* the stream beat

15. 20. he *a.* and came to his father, he kissed him

ARRAY, in order of battle, 2 *Sam.* 10. 9 ; *Job* 6. 4 ; *Jer.* 50. 14.

Array, to clothe, *Esth.* 6. 9 ; *Job* 40. 10 ; *Jer.* 43. 12 ; *Matt.* 6. 29 ; 1 *Tim.* 2. 9 ;

Arrayed, 2 *Chr.* 28. 15. took the captives, with spoil *a.* them

Matt. 6. 29. was not *a.* like one of these, *Luke* 12. 27.

Luke 23. 11. Herod and his men of war *a.* Christ

Acts 12. 21. Herod *a.* in royal apparel sat on his

ARRIVED, *Luke* 8. 26. they *a.* at the country of the Gadarenes

Acts 20. 15. and the next day we *a.* at Samos

ARROGANCY, presumptuous self-conceit, 1 *Sam.* 2. 3 ; *Prov.* 8. 13 ; *Is.* 13. 11.

ARROW, 1 *Sam.* 20. 36. Jonathan shot an *a.* beyond him

2 *Kings* 9. 24. and the *a.* went out at his heart

Job 34. 6. my *a.* is incurable without transgression

41. 28. the *a.* cannot make him flee, sling stones

Ps. 11. 2. they make ready their *a.* on the string

91. 5. nor afraid for the *a.* that fleeth by day

Prov. 25. 18. that beareth false witness is a sharp *a.*

ARROWS, *Num.* 24. 8. he shall pierce them through with his *a.*

Deut. 32. 23. I will spend mine *a.* upon them

42. I will make mine *a.* drunk with blood

1 *Sam.* 20. 20. I will shoot three *a.* on the side

2 *Sam.* 22. 15. the Lord thundered, and he sent out *a.*

Job 6. 4. the *a.* of the Almighty are within me

Ps. 7. 13. he ordaineth *a.* against the persecutors

38. 2. for thine *a.* stick fast in me, and thy hand

45. 5. thine *a.* are sharp in the heart of enemies

57. 4. sons of men, whose teeth are spears and *a.*

77. 17. clouds poured, thine *a.* also went abroad

Prov. 26. 18. as a mad man who casteth *a.* and death

Jer. 50. 9. their *a.* shall be as of an expert man

14. shoot at Babylon spare no *a.*

Ezek. 5. 16. I shall send the evil *a.* of famine

39. 3. I will cause thy *a.* to fall out of thy hand

9. Israel shall go forth, and burn bows and *a.*

ART, S, *Ex.* 30. 25. an ointment after the *a.* of the apothecary

2 *Chr.* 16. 14. divers spices prepared by *a.* of apothecary

Acts 17. 29. the Godhead not like stones graven by *a.*

19. 19. many also of them which used curious *a.*

ARTIFICER, *Gen.* 4. 22. Tubal-cain, an instructor of every *a.*

Is. 3. 3. take away the captain and the cunning *a.*

ARTIFICERS, 1 *Chr.* 29. 5. for all manner of works made by *a.*

2 *Chr.* 34. 11. to *a.* and builders gave they money

ARTILLERY, 1 *Sam.* 20. 40. Jonathan gave his *a.* to the lad

ASCEND, *Josh.* 6. 5I the people shall *a.* up every man straight

Ps. 24. 3. who shall *a.* into the hill of the Lord, and shall stand in his holy place ? *Rom.* 10. 6.

135. 7. he causeth vapours to *a.* *Jer.* 10. 13 ; 51. 16.

139. 8. if I *a.* up into heaven, thou art there

Is. 14. 13. thou hast said, I will *a.* to heaven, 14.

John 6. 62. if ye shall see the Son of man *a.* up

20. 17. I *a.* to my Father, your Father, my God

Rom. 10. 6. who shall *a.* to heaven

Rev. 17. 8. beast shall *a.* out of the bottomless pit

ASCENDED, *Ps.* 68. 18. thou hast *a.* on

Prov. 30. 4. who hath *a.* into heaven

John 3. 13. no man hath *a.* up to heaven

John 20. 17. I *a.* to my father and your

Acts 2. 34. David not yet *a.* to heavens

Eph. 4. 8. when he *a.* up on high

Rev. 8. 4. smoke of incense *a.* before

11. 12. *a.* up to heaven in a cloud

ASCENDETH, *Rev.* 11. 7. the beast that *a.* out of the bottomless pit

14. 11. the smoke of their torment *a.* for ever

ASCENDING, *Gen.* 28. 12. angels ascending and descending

John 1. 51. angels of God *a.* and descending on Son of man

6. 62. if see son of man *a.* up

ASCENT, 2 *Sam.* 15. 30. David went up by the *a.* of Olivet

1 *Kings* 10. 5. and his *a.* by which he went, 2 *Chr.* 9. 4.

ASCRIBE greatness to God, *Deut.* 32. 3.

Job 36. 3. I will *a.* righteousness to my Maker

Ps. 68. 34. *a.* strength to God

ASCRIBED, 1 *Sam.* 18. 8. *a.* to David 10,000, to me *a.* but 1,000

ASH, *Is.* 44. 14. he planteth an *a.*, the rain doth nourish it

ASHAMED and blush to, *Ezra* 9. 6.

Gen. 2. 25. man and wife naked not *a.*

Judg. 3. 25. and they tarried till they were *a.*

2 *Sam.* 10. 5. the men were greatly *a.*

1 *Chr.* 19. 5.

19. 3. as people being *a.* steal away
when they flee

2 *Kings* 2. 17. and when they urged him
till he was *a.*

8. 11. he settled his countenance till
he was *a.*

2 *Chr.* 30. 15. the priests and the Levites
were *a.*

Ezra 9. 6. I am *a.* and blush to lift up
my face to thee

Job 6. 20. they came hither, and were *a.*

19. 3. ye are not *a.* to make yourselves
strange to me

Ps. 34. 5. were lightened, and their
faces were not *a.*

74. 21. O let not the oppressed return
a. let poor

Prov. 12. 4. she that maketh *a.* is as
rottenness

Is. 20. 5. shall be *a.* of Ethiopia, their
expectations

24. 23. the sun shall be *a.* when the
Lord shall reign

30. 5. all *a.* of a people that could not
profit them

33. 9. earth mourns, Lebanon is *a.*
and hewn down

Jer. 2. 26. as the thief is *a.* when he is
found, so is

6. 15. were they *a.* ? they were not at
all *a.* 8. 12.

14. 4. plowmen were *a.* they covered
their heads

Ezek. 16. 27. the daughters of the Philistines are *a.*

32. 30. with terror they are *a.* of their

Luke 13. 17. all his adversaries were *a.*
and the people

16. 3. what shall I do ? I cannot dig,
to beg I am *a.*

Rom. 1. 16, I am not *a.* of gospel

5. 5. hope maketh not *a.* because

6. 21. whereof ye are now *a.*

2 *Cor.* 7. 14. if I have boasted anything,
I am not *a.*

2 *Tim.* 1. 12. I suffer, nevertheless I am
not *a.*

16. Onesiphorus was not *a.* of my
chain

Heb. 2. 11. he is not *a.* to call them
brethren

11. 16. God is not *a.* to be called their
God

ASHAMED, be, *Gen.* 38. 23. let her take
it to her, lest we be *a.*

Ps. 6. 10. let all my enemies be *a.* and
sore vexed

31. 1. in thee do I put my trust, let
me never be *a.*

17. let me not be *a.* let the wicked be
a. 35. 26.

69. 6. let not them that wait be *a.* for
my sake

Ps. 109. 28. when they arise, let them be
a. but let

Is. 1. 29. for they shall be *a.* of the oaks
which ye

26. 11. they shall see and be *a.* for
their envy

42. 17. they shall be greatly *a.* that
trust in images

65. 13. my servants rejoice, but ye
shall be *a.*

66. 5. shall appear to your joy, and
they shall be *a.*

Jer. 2. 36. thou shalt be *a.* of Egypt, as
a. of Assyria

3. 3. and hadst a whore's forehead,
refused to be *a.*

12. 13. and they shall be *a.* of your
revenues

17. 13. O Lord, all that forsake thee
shall be *a.*

48. 13. Moab shall be *a.* of Chemosh,
as Israel was

50. 12. your mother that bare you
shall be *a.*

Ezek. 16. 61. shalt remember thy ways,
and be *a.*

43. 10. show Israel, they may be *a.* of
their iniquities

Hos. 4. 19. they shall be *a.* because of
their sacrifices

Joel 1. 11. be ye *a.* O ye husbandmen,
howl for wheat

2. 26. and my people shall never be
a. 27.

Mark 8. 38. shall be *a.* of me and my

2 *Cor.* 9. 4. we (that we say not, you)
should be *a.*

Phil. 1. 20. that in nothing I shall be *a.*

2 *Thess.* 3. 14. no company with him,
that he may be *a.*

Tit. 2. 8. he that is on the contrary part
may be *a.*

1 *Pet.* 3. 16. may be *a.* that falsely accuse your good

ASHAMED, not be, or be not, *Num.* 12.
14. should she not be *a.* seven days

Ps. 25. 2. O my God, I trust in thee,
let me not be *a.*

37. 19. they shall not be *a.* in the evil

119. 6. then shall I not be *a.* when I
have respect to

46. I will speak of thy testimonies,
and not be *a.*

Is. 29. 22. saith the Lord, Jacob shall
not be *a.*

45. 17. ye shall not be *a.* world without end

49. 23. they shall not be *a.* that wait
for me

50. 7. my face like a flint, I know I
shall not be *a.*

Is. 54. 4. fear not, for thou shalt not be *a*

Zeph. 3. 11. in that day thou shalt not
be *a.*

Rom. 9. 33. who believeth on him shall
not be *a.* 10.

2 *Cor.* 10. 8. for though I boast, I should
not be *a.*

2 *Tim.* 1. 8. be not therefore *a.* of testimony of Lord

2. 15. to God, a workman that needeth not be *a.*

1 *Pet.* 4. 16. suffer as a Christian, let
him not be *a.*

1 *John* 2. 28. not be *a.* before him at his
coming

ASHES, *Lev.* 4. 12. carry bullock
where *a.*

Num. 4. 13. take *a.* from altar

19. 9. man clean shall gather *a.*

2 *Sam.* 13. 19. Tamar put *a.* on head

1 *Kings* 13. 3. altar shall be rent, and
a. poured out : ver. 5.

20. 38. the prophet disguised himself

with *a*.

Esth. 4. 1. Mordecai put on sackcloth with *a*.

3. and many lay in sackcloth and *a*.

Job 2. 8. Job sat down among the *a*.

13. 12. your remembrances are like to *a*.

30. 19. into mire, I am become like dust and *a*.

42. 6. I abhor myself, and repent in dust and *a*.

Ps. 102. 9. I have eaten *a*. like bread

147. 16. he scattereth the hoar-frost like *a*.

Is. 44. 20. he feedeth on *a*.

58. 5. and to spread sackcloth and *a*. under him

61. 3. to give them beauty for *a*. the oil of joy

Lam. 3. 16. he hath covered me with *a*.

Dan. 9. 3. I set my face to seek in sackcloth and *a*.

Jonah 3. 6. king covered in sackcloth, and sat in *a*.

Mal. 4. 3. wicked shall be *a*. under feet

Matt. 11. 21. if works were done, they would have repented long ago in sackcloth and *a*. *Luke* 10. 13.

Heb. 9. 13. if the *a*. of an heifer sanctifieth to the

2 *Pet.* 2. 6. and turning the cities of Sodom into *a*.

ASIDE, 2 *Kings* 4. 4. said, thou shalt set *a*. that which is full

Job 1. 19. came a great wind from *a*. wilderness

Mark 7. 33. he took him *a*. from the multitude

John 13. 4. he riseth and laid *a*. his garment

Heb. 12. 1. let us lay *a*. every weight, and sin that

ASK, (1) To inquire, *Gen.* 32. 29 ; *Mark* 9. 32. (2) To require, or demand, *Gen.* 34. 12 ; *Dan.* 2. 10. (3) To seek counsel, *Is.* 30. 2 ; *Hag.* 2. 11. (4) To pray, *John* 15. 7 ; *Jam.* 1. 6. (5) To expect, *Luke* 12. 48. (6) To salute, 1 *Sam.* 25. 5 ; 2 *Sam.* 8. 10. (7) To lay to one's charge, *Ps.* 35. 11.

Gen. 32. 29. wherefore dost thou *a*. after my name

34. 12. *a*. me never so much dowry

Deut. 4. 32. for *a*. now of the days that are past

13. 14. shall *a*. diligently, and if it be truth

32. 7. *a*. thy father, and he will show thee

Josh. 4. 6. when your children *a*. their fathers 21.

Judg. 18. 5. *a*. counsel, we pray thee, of God

1 *Sam.* 10. 4. they will *a*. thee of peace

12. 19. we have added this evil to *a*. us a king

1 *Kings* 3. 5. *a*. what I shall give thee, 2 *Chr.* 1. 7.

14. 5. the wife of Jeroboam cometh to *a*. thee

2 *Kings* 2. 9. Elijah said, *a*. what I shall do for thee

2 *Chr.* 20. 4. Judah gathered to *a*. help

of God

Job 12. 7. *a*. the beasts, and they shall teach thee

Ps. 2. 8. *a*. of me, and I will give thee the heathen

Is. 65. 1. sought of—*a*. not for me

Jer. 6. 16. *a*. for the old paths

38. 14. I will *a*. thee a thing, hide nothing from me

50. 5. they shall *a*. the way to Zion with their faces

Dan. 6. 7. who shall *a*. a petition of any god

Hag. 2. 11. *a*. now the priests concerning the law

Zech. 10. 1. *a*. ye of the Lord rain in time of latter

Matt. 6. 8. what ye have need of, before ye *a*. him

Matt. 7. 7. *a*. and it shall be given

11. give good things to—*a*. him

Matt. 20. 22. ye know not what ye *a*.

Luke 12. 48. of him they will *a*. more

John 1. 19. when the Jews sent priests to *a*. him

John 9. 21. we know not, he is of age, *a*. him, 23.

11. 22. whatsoever thou wilt *a*. of God, he will

13. 24. Peter beckoned to him that he should *a*.

15. 7. if ye abide in me, *a*. what ye will, it shall be

16. 19. Jesus knew that they were desirous to *a*.

16. 23. and in that day ye shall *a*. me

24. *a*. and ye shall receive, that your joy may be full

30. and needest not that any man should *a*. thee

18. 21. *a*. them which heard me what I said

1 *Cor.* 14. 35. let them *a*. their husbands at home

Eph. 3. 20. above all we can *a*. or

Jam. 1. 5. wisdom let him *a*. of God

6. let him *a*. in faith, not wavering

4. 2, 3. *a*. not : receive not : *a*. amiss

1 *John* 3. 22. whatsoever we *a*. we receive

5. 14, 15. *a*. according to his will

16. sin a sin which is not unto death, he shall *a*.

ASKED, *Gen.* 32. 29. Jacob *a*. him and said, tell me thy name

42. 7. the man *a*. us straitly of our kindred

Judg. 5. 25. he *a*. water, she gave him milk

1 *Sam.* 1. 17. God grant the petition thou hast *a*.

20. she called his name Samuel, that is *a*. of God

27. the Lord hath given me my petition I *a*.

1 *Kings* 3. 11. because thou *a*. this thing and not *a*.

Ps. 21. 4. he *a*. life of thee, thou gavest

105. 40. the people *a*. and he brought quails

Is. 30. 2. and have not *a*. at my mouth

65. 1. I am sought of them that *a*. not for me

John 4. 10. thou wouldst have *a*. of him

Rom. 10. 20. made manifest to them that *a.* not
ASKEST, *Judg.* 13. 18. why *a.* thou thus after my name
John 4. 9. *a.* drink of me, a woman of Samaria
  18. 21. why *a.* thou me, ask them which heard
ASKETH, *Matt.* 5. 42. give to him that *a.* thee, *Luke* 6. 30.
Matt. 7. 8. every one that *a.* receiveth, *Luke* 11. 10.
John 16. 5. none of you *a.* me whither goest thou ?
1 *Pet.* 3. 15. to every one that *a.* you a reason of hope
ASKING, 1 *Sam.* 12. 17. may see your wickedness in *a.* a king
Ps. 78. 18. tempted God by *a.* meat for their lust
John 8. 7. they continued *a.* he lifted up himself
1 *Cor.* 10. 25. *a.* no question for conscience, 27.
ASLEEP, *Songs* 7. 9. lips of those *a.* to speak
Judg. 4. 21. for Sisera was fast *a.* and
Jonah 1. 5. Jonah lay, and was fast *a.*
Matt. 8. 24. arose a storm, but he was *a. Mark* 3. 33.
  26. 40. he findeth the disciples *a. Mark* 14. 40.
Acts 7. 60. when Stephen had said this, he fell *a.*
1 *Cor.* 15. 6. part remain, but some are fallen *a.*
  18. then they which are fallen *a.* in Christ
1 *Thess.* 4. 13. ignorant concerning them that are *a.*
  15. we alive shall not prevent them that are *a.*
2 *Pet.* 3. 4. for since the fathers fell *a.* all things
ASP, S, *Deut.* 32. 33. their wine is the cruel venom of *a.*
Job 20. 14. his meat is the gall of *a.* within him
  16. he shall suck the poison of *a.* the viper's tongue
Is. 11. 8. the child shall play on the hole of the *a.*
Rom. 3. 13. the poison of *a.* is under
ASS, *Gen.* 22. 5. abide here with *a.*
Gen. 42. 26. laded *a.* with corn
  43. 24. gave their *a.* provender
  45. 23. ten *a.* laden with good things
  49. 14. Issachar is a strong *a.* couching between
Ex. 4. 20. Moses set wife and sons on *a.*
  13. 13. every firstling of an *a.* redeem
  22. 10. if a man deliver an *a.* to keep
  23. 4. if thou meet thy enemy's *a.* going astray
  12. shalt rest ; that thine ox and thine *a.* may rest
Num. 16. 15. not taken one *a.* from
  22. 23. *a.* saw angel standing
  31. 34. prey 61,000 *a.* : ver. 39.
Deut. 22. 3. in like manner do with his *a.*
  10. not plow with an ox and *a.* together
Judg. 15. 16. with the jaw-bone of an *a.*

1 *Sam.* 9. 3. *a.* of Kish were lost
2 *Sam.* 16. 2. *a.* be for king's household
Job 6. 5. wild *a.* bray when hath grass
  24. 3. they drive away the *a.* of the fatherless
Prov. 26. 3. a bridle for the *a.* and a rod for fools
Is. 1. 3. ox his owner, and *a.* his master's crib
Jer. 22. 19. shall be buried with the burial of an *a.*
Matt. 21. 2. find *a.* tied and colt ; ver. 5.
Luke 13. 15. doth not each loose his *a.* on Sabbath
  14. 5. which of you shall have an *a.* fallen into a pit
John 12. 14. when had found young *a.* : ver. 15.
2 *Pet.* 2. 16. dumb *a.* speaking forbade
ASS COLT, *Gen.* 49. 11. binding his *a. colt* to the choice vine
Job 11. 12. though man be born like a wild *a. colt*
John 12. 15. thy king cometh sitting on an *a. colt*
ASS, wild, *Job* 6. 5. doth the *wild a.* bray when he hath grass ?
  39. 5. who hath sent out the *wild a.* free ?
Jer. 2. 24. a *wild a.* used to the wilderness snuffeth
Hos. 8. 9. they are gone, a *wild a.* alone by himself
ASSES, *Gen.* 12. 16. Abram had he-*a.* and she-*a.* and camels
  30. 43. Jacob had much cattle, camels, and *a.*
  47. 17. Joseph gave bread in exchange for *a.*
Judg. 5. 10. ye that ride on white *a.*
Sam. 9. 3. the *a.* of Kish, Saul's father, were lost
  20. thy *a.* that were lost, they are found, 10. 2.
1 *Chr.* 27. 30. and over the *a.* was Jehdiah
Job 42. 12. for Job had sheep, and a thousand she-*a.*
Is. 21. 7. he saw a chariot of *a.* and of camels
Ezek. 23. 20. whose flesh is as the flesh of *a.*
ASSAULT, *Esth.* 8. 11. perish all that would *a.* them
Acts 14. 5. an *a.* made of Gentiles
ASSAY, ED, ING, *Deut.* 4. 34. *a.* to go and take nation
Job 4. 2. if we *a.* to commune
Acts 9. 26. Saul *a.* to join disciples
ASSEMBLE, *Num.* 10. 3. when they blow, the assembly shall *a.*
Is. 11. 12. he shall *a.* the outcasts of Israel
  45. 20. *a.* yourselves, and come, draw near together
Jer. 4. 5. *a.* yourselves, and let us go into the cities
  8. 14. why do we sit still ? *a.* yourselves, let us
Ezek. 11. 7. I will *a.* you out of the countries
Joel 2. 16. *a.* the elders, gather the children

3. 11. *a.* yourselves and come, all ye heathens

Zeph. 3. 8. I will *a.* the kingdoms to pour indignation

ASSEMBLED, *Ex.* 38. 8. women which *a.* at the door of the tabernacle

1 *Sam.* 2. 22. they lay with the women that *a.*

1 *Chr.* 15. 4 David *a.* the children of Aaron

2 *Chr.* 30. 13. *a.* much people to keep the feast

Neh. 9. 1. the children of Israel *a.* with fasting

Ps. 48. 4. lo! the kings were *a.* they passed by

Jer. 5. 7. *a.* themselves by troops in harlots' houses

Dan. 6. 11. these men *a.* and found Daniel praying

Matt. 28. 12. when they *a.* they gave large money

John 20. 19. the disciples *a.* for fear of the Jews

Acts 1. 4. being *a.* commanded them not to depart

4. 31. the place was shaken where they were *a.*

ASSEMBLY of wicked, *Ps.* 22. 16.

Gen. 49. 6. to their *a.* mine honour be not thou united

Num. 10. 2. and make 2 trumpets for calling the *a.*

20. 6. Moses and Aaron went from presence of *a.*

Deut. 9. 10. spake in the mount out of the midst of the fire, in the day of your *a.* 10. 4 ; 18. 16.

Ps. 22. 16. the *a.* of the wicked have inclosed me

Ps. 89. 7. G. feared in the *a.* of his saints

107. 32. praise him in the *a.* of the elders

111. 1. I will praise him in the *a.* of the upright

Prov. 5. 14. I was in all evil in the midst of the *a.*

Acts 19. 32. the *a.* was confused, and part knew not

39. it shall be determined in a lawful *a.*

41. he had thus spoken, he dismissed the *a.*

Heb. 12. 23. to the general *a.* of the first-born

Jam. 2. 2. if there come to your *a.* a man

ASSEMBLIES, *Ps.* 86. 14. the *a.* of violent men sought my soul

Eccl. 12. 11. as nails fastened by the masters of *a.*

Is. 1. 13: the calling of *a.* I cannot away

4. 5. God will create on her *a.* a cloud and smoke

Ezek. 44. 24. they shall keep my laws in all mine *a.*

Amos 5. 21. I will not smell in your solemn *a.*

ASSENT, *Luke* 23. 24. Pilate *a.* it should be as they required

Acts 24. 9. Jews also *a.* that these things were so

ASSIGNED, *Gen.* 47. 22. for the priests had a portion *a.* them

Josh. 20. 8. they *a.* Bezer, a city of refuge

ASSOCIATE, *Is.* 8. 9. *a.* yourselves and ye shall be broken in pieces

Dan. 11. 6. at the end of years they shall *a.*

ASSUAGE, *Gen.* 8. 1. over the earth, and the waters were *a.*

Job 16. 5. moving of my lips shall *a.* your grief

6. though I speak, yet my grief is not *a.*

ASSURANCE, *Deut.* 28. 66. thou shalt have none *a.* of thy life

Is. 32. 17. and the effect of righteousness *a.*

Acts 17. 31. whereof he hath given *a.* to all men

Col. 2. 2. to all riches of the full *a.* of understanding

1 *Thess.* 1. 5. our gospel came in much *a.*

Heb. 6. 11. to the full *a.* of hope to the end

10. 22. let us draw near in full *a.* of faith

ASSURE, 1 *John* 3. 19. and shall *a.* our hearts before him

ASSURED, *Jer.* 14. 13. I will give you *a.* peace in this place

2 *Tim.* 3. 14. continue in things thou hast been *a.*

ASSUREDLY, *Jer.* 32. 41. I will plant them in this land *a.*

Jer. 38. 17. if thou *a.* go forth to the king of Babylon

Acts 2. 36. let all the house of Israel know *a.*

16. 10. *a.* gathering that the Lord had called us

ASTONIED, *Ezra* 9. 3. plucked off the hair, and sat down *a.*

Job 17. 8. upright men shall be *a.* at this

18. 20. they that come after him shall be *a.*

Dan. 3. 24. Nebuchadnezzar was *a.* and rose in haste

4. 19. then Daniel was *a.* for one hour

ASTONISHED, *Lev.* 26. 32. and your enemies shall be *a.*

1 *Kings* 9. 8. every one that passeth by shall be *a. Jer.* 18. 16 ; 19. 8 ; 49. 17 ; 50. 13.

Job 26. 11. the pillars of heaven tremble and are *a.*

Is. 52. 14. as many were *a.* at thee his visage

Jer. 2. 12. be *a.* O ye heavens, at this

4. 9. the heart of priests shall be *a.*

Ezek. 3. 15. I remained *a.* among them seven days

28. 19. they that know thee shall be *a.* at thee

Matt. 7. 28. the people were *a.* at his doctrine 22. 33 : *Mark* 1. 22 ; 6. 2 ; 11. 18 ; *Luke* 4. 32.

Mark 5. 42. they were *a.* with great astonishment

10. 24. the disciples were *a.* at his words

Luke 2. 47. *a.* at his understanding and answers

5. 9. he was *a.* at the draught of fishes

24. 22. yea, and certain women also made us *a.*

Acts 9. 6. Saul trembling and *a*. said,
Lord, what
12. 16. had opened door and saw Peter, they were *a*.
ASTONISHMENT, *Deut.* 28. 28. the
Lord shall smite thee with *a*.
37. thou shalt become an *a*. and a
proverb
2 *Chr.* 7. 21. this house shall be an *a*.
to every one
Ps. 60. 3. hast made us to drink the
wine of *a*.
Jer. 5. 30. *a*. is committed in the land
8. 21. I am black, *a*. hath taken hold
on me
25. 9. I will make them an *a*. and a
hissing, 18.
29. 18. I will deliver them to be a
curse and an *a*.
42. 18. ye shall be an execration and
an *a*. 44. 12.
Jer. 44. 22. therefore is your land an *a*.
and a curse
51. 37. Babylon shall become heaps
and an *a*.
ASTRAY, *Ps.* 119. 176 ; *Is.* 53. 6 ; *Matt.*
18. 12 ; *Luke* 15. 4 ; 1 *Pet.* 2. 25.
ASTROLOGERS, *Is.* 47. 13. let now the
a. the star-gazers stand
Dan. 1. 20. he found them ten times
better than *a*.
2. 27. the secret cannot the *a*. show
to the king
5. 7. the king cried aloud, to bring in
the *a*.
ATE, *Ps.* 106. 28. they *a*. the sacrifices
of the dead
Rev. 10. 10. I took the little book, and
a. it up
ATHIRST, (1) Earnestly desirous of
liquor to drink ; *Judges* 15. 18.
(2) Desirous of happiness ; *Rev.* 21.
6. and 22. 17. (3) An ardent desire after deliverance from sin and
misery, and a true wish for communion with God ; *Ps.* 63. 1 ;
Matt. 5. 7 ; *John* 7, 37.
ATONEMENT, *Ex.* 29. 33. eat things
wherewith *a*. was made
Ex. 29. 36. thou shalt offer a bullock
every day for *a*.
30. 10. Aaron once in year shall make
a. upon it
Lev. 1. 4. it shall be accepted for him
to make *a*.
8. 34. so the Lord hath commanded
to make *a*.
16. 10. the scape-goat shall be presented to make *a*.
11. Aaron shall make an *a*. for himself and house
27. whose blood was brought in to
make *a*.
23. 27. tenth day of 7th month shall
be a day of *a*.
28. do no work, for it is a day of *a*. to
make *a*.
25. 9. in the day of *a*. make the
trumpets sound
2 *Sam.* 21. 3. wherewith shall I make
a.
1 *Chr.* 6. 49. Aaron and sons appointed
to make *a*.
2 *Chr.* 29. 24. the priests killed them to

make an *a*.
Rom. 5. 11. by whom we have now re-
ceived *a*.
ATTAIN to wise counsels, *Prov.* 1. 5.
Ps. 139. 6. high, I cannot *a*. to it
Ezek. 46. 7. according as hand shall *a*.
Phil. 3. 11. *a*. to resurrection of dead :
not already *a*.
ATTEND to my cry, *Ps.* 55. 2. & 61. 1.
& 66. 19, & 86. 6, & 142. 6; *Prov.*
4. 1. *a*. to know understanding
Prov. 4. 20. *a*. to my words, 7. 24.
5. 1. *a*. to my wisdom, bow ear
Acts 16. 14. she *a*. to—spoken
Attendance, 1 *Kings* 10. 5 ; 1 *Tim.* 4. 13 ;
Heb. 7. 13 ; *Rom.* 13. 6.
ATTENT, 2 *Chr.* 6. 40. let thine ears be
a. to the prayer
2 *Chr.* 7. 15. mine ears sha'l be *a*. at the
prayer made
Attentive, 2 *Chr.* 6. 40. & 7. 15 ; *Neh.* 1.
6. & 8. 3 ; *Ps.* 130. 2 ; *Luke* 19. 48.
ATTIRE, ED, *Lev.* 16. 4. with the linen
mitre shall Aaron be *a*.
Prov. 7. 10. met him a woman with *a*.
of an harlot
Jer. 2. 32. can a bride forget her *a*. ? yet
my people
Ezek. 23. 15. exceeding in dyed *a*. on
their heads
AUDIENCE, *Gen.* 23. 13. Abraham
spake to Ephron in *a*. of people
Ex. 24. 7. took book of covenant, and
read in *a*.
1 *Sam.* 25. 24. let thine handmaid speak
in thy *a*.
Neh. 13. 1. they read in the book of
Moses in the *a*.
Luke 7. 1. ended all his sayings in the
a. of the people
Acts 13. 16. Israel, and ye that fear
God, give *a*.
15. 12. then all the multitude gave *a*.
to Barnabas
AUSTERE, *Luke* 19. 21. I feared, because thou art an *a*. man
AUTHOR of confusion, 1 *Cor.* 14. 33.
Heb. 5. 9. *a*. of eternal salvation
12. 2. Jesus *a*. and finisher of our
faith
AUTHORITY, power to govern
Esth. 9. 29. Esther and Mordecai wrote
with *a*.
Prov. 29. 2. when righteous are in *a*.
people rejoice
Matt. 7. 29. taught them as one having
a. Mark 1. 22.
8. 9. for I am a man under *a*. and
say, *Luke* 7. 8.
20. 25. they that are great exercise *a*.
Mark 10. 42.
Mark 1. 27. for with *a*. commandeth he
even the unclean spirits, and they
obey him, *Luke* 4. 36.
13. 34. left his house, and gave *a*. to
his servants
Luke 9. 1. he gave them power and *a*.
over all devils
Luke 19. 17. have *a*. over ten cities
John 5. 27. hath given him *a*. to execute judgment
Acts 8. 27. eunuch of great *a*. under
Candace queen
Acts 9. 14. here he hath *a*. to bind : 26.

10, 12.

1 *Cor.* 15. 24. shall have put down all *a.*

2 *Cor.* 10. 8. should boast more of our *a.*

1 *Tim.* 2. 2. supplication for kings and all in *a.*

2. 12. not a woman to usurp *a.*

Tit. 2. 15. exhort and rebuke with all *a.*

1 *Pet.* 3. 22. *a.* made subject to him

Rev. 13. 2. the dragon gave him power and great *a.*

AVAILETH, *Esth.* 5. 13. yet all this *a.* me nothing so long as I see

Gal. 5. 6. in Christ circumcision *a.* not, 6. 15.

Jam. 5. 16. the prayer of a righteous man *a.* much

AVENGE not nor *Lev.* 19. 18.

Lev. 26. 25. shall *a.* quarrel of covenant

Num. 31. 2. *a.* Israel of the Midianites, 3.

Deut. 32. 43. he will *a.* blood of servants

1 *Sam.* 24. 12. the Lord judge and *a.* me of thee

Esth. 8. 13. Jews *a.* themselves on their enemies

Is. 1 24. I will *a.* me of my enemies

Luke 18. 7. shall not God *a.* his elect

8. he will *a.* them speedily

Rom. 12. 19. *a.* not yourselves

Rev. 6. 10. dost thou not *a.* our blood

AVENGED, *Gen.* 4. 24. if Cain should be *a.* seven-fold, Lamech

Josh. 4. 13. sun and moon stayed till people had *a.*

Judg. 15. 7. though ye have done this, yet I will be *a.*

1 *Sam.* 14. 24. that eateth any food, that I may be *a.*

2 *Sam.* 4. 8. the Lord hath *a.* my Lord the king

18. 19. how the Lord hath *a.* him of his enemies.

31. the Lord hath *a.* thee this day of them

Jer. 5. 9. 29. shall not my soul be *a.* on such a nation 9. 9.

Acts 7. 24. Moses *a.* him that was oppressed

Rev. 18. 20. rejoice, for God hath *a.* you on her

19. 2. hath *a.* blood of his servants at her hand

Avenger, *Num.* 35. 12 ; *Ps.* 8. 2. & 44. 16 ; 1 *Thess.* 4. 6.

2 *Sam.* 22. 48. it is God that *a.* me

Judg. 5. 2. Praise Lord for *a.* Israel

AVERSE, *Mic.* 2. 8. pass by securely, as men *a.* from war

AUGMENT, *Num.* 32. 14. ye are risen to *a.* the fierce anger

AUNT, *Lev.* 18. 14. nor approach to his wife, she is thy *a.*

AVOID it, pass not by it, *Prov.* 4. 15.

Rom. 16. 17. cause divisions *a.* them

Tit. 3. 9. *a.* foolish questions

AVOIDED, ING, 1 *Sam.* 18. 11. David *a.* out of his presence twice

2 *Chr.* 8. 20. *a.* this, that no man should blame us

1 *Tim.* 6. 20. *a.* profane and vain babblings

AVOUCHED, *Deut.* 26. 17, 18.

AWAKE, (1) To come out of natural sleep, *Luke* 9. 32. **(2)** To rouse up

out of spiritual sleep, by a vigorous exercise of grace, by leaving off all sinful courses, and setting about the performance of duties required ; *Rom.* 13. 11 ; *Eph.* 5. 14. **(3)** To raise from the dead ; *Job* 14. 12 ; *John* 11. 11. **(4)** To give present help after it hath long been kept from us, as though God had forgotten us ; *Ps.* 7. 6 ; *Is.* 51. 9.

Awake not my love till he please ; *Songs* 2. 7. Give my beloved Saviour no cause of offence or departure ; neither interrupt that peace I enjoy in him, so long as he is pleased to continue it.

Judg. 5. 12. *a. a.* Deborah, *a. a.* utter a song, arise

Job 8. 6. surely now he would *a.* for thee

14. 12. till heavens be no more, they shall not *a.*

Ps. 7. 6. *a.* for me to the judgment, 35. 23.

17. 15. be satisfied when I *a.* with thy likeness

44. 23. *a.* why sleepest thou, O Lord ? arise

57. 8. *a.* my glory, I myself will *a.* early, 108. 2.

139. 18. when I am *a.* I am still with

Songs 2. 7. not *a.* my love till he please, 3. 5 ; 8. 4.

4. 16. *a.* O north wind, and come thou

Is. 26. 19. *a.* and sing ye that dwell in the dust

51. 9. *a. a.* put on strength, O arm of the Lord, *a.* as in the ancient days, 52. 1.

Jer. 51. 57. sleep a perpetual sleep, and not *a.*

Dan. 12. 2. many that sleep in the dust shall *a.*

Zech. 13. 7. *a.* O sword, against my Shepherd, smite

Mark 4. 38. he was asleep, and they *a.* him

Rom. 13. 11. high time to *a.* out of sleep

1 *Cor.* 15. 34. *a.* to righteousness

Eph. 5. 14. *a.* thou that sleepest

AWAKED, *Gen.* 28. 16. Jacob *a.* out of his sleep, and said

Judg. 16. 14. Samson *a.* and went away with the pin

1 *Kings* 18. 27. peradventure he sleepeth and must be *a.*

Ps. 3. 5. I *a.* for the Lord sustained me

78. 65. then the Lord *a.* as one out of

AWAKEST, *Ps.* 73. 20. when thou *a.* shalt despise their image

Prov. 6. 22. when thou *a.* it shall talk with thee

AWAKETH, ING, *Ps.* 73. 20. as a dream when one *a.* so, O Lord

Is. 29. 8. he *a.* and his soul is empty, *a.* and is faint

Acts 16. 27. the keeper of the prison *a.* out of sleep

AWARE, *Songs* 6. 12. or ever I was *a.* my soul made me like

Jer. 50. 24. art taken, O Babylon, and thou art not *a.*

AWAY, *Gen.* 15. 11. when fowls came, Abraham drove them *a.*

Ex. 8. 28. only ye shall not go very far *a.*

2 *Chr.* 35. 23. have me *a.* for I am wounded
Is. 1. 13. calling of assemblies I cannot *a.* with
Luke 23. 18. *a.* with this man, release *Acts* 21. 36.
John 19. 15. *a.* with him, *a.* with him, *Acts* 21. 36.
Acts 22. 22. *a.* with such a fellow from the earth

AWE, stand in awe, sin not, *Ps.* 4. 4.
Ps. 33. 8. would stand in *a.* of him
119. 161. heart stands in *a.* of word

AWL, *Ex.* 21. 6. his master shall bore his ear with an *a.*
Deut. 15. 17. thou shalt take an *a.* and thrust it

AXE, (1) A carpenter's tool ; *Judg.* 9. 48. (2) A human instrument, the king of Assyria ; *Is.* 10. 15. (3) God's vengeance and judgment upon barren and incorrigible sinners ; *Matt.* 3. 10.
Deut. 19. 5. his hand fetched a stroke with the *a.*
20. 19. nor destroy the trees by forcing an *a.*
1 *Sam.* 13. 20. Israel went down to sharpen his *a.*
1 *Kings* 6. 7. neither hammer nor *a.* was heard
2 *Kings* 6. 5. the *a.*-head fell into the water
Is. 10. 15. shall the *a.* boast itself against him
Jer. 10. 3. for one cuts a tree with the *a.*
51. 20. thou art my battle-*a.* and weapons
Matt. 3. 10. the *a.* is laid to root of trees, *Luke* 3. 9.
1 *Sam.* 13. 21. yet they had a file for the *a.*
Ps. 74. 5. a man was famous as he lifted up *a.*
6. they break down the carved work with *a.*
Jer. 46. 22. and come against her with *a.* as hewers
Ezek. 26. 9. with *a.* he shall break down thy tower

AXLE-TREES, 1 *Kings* 7. 32. the *a.-t.* of the wheel join to the base
33. *a.t.* naves and felloes

BABBLER, *Eccl.* 10. 11. *Acts* 17. 18.
1 *Tim.* 6. 20. avoid vain *b.* 2 *Tim.* 2. 16 ; *Prov.* 23. 29.

BABE leaped in womb, *Luke* 1. 41.
Heb. 5. 13. unskilful in word is a *b.*
Ps. 8. 2. out of mouth of *b.*
17. 14. rest of substance to *b.*
Is. 3. 4. *b.* shall rule over them
1 *Cor.* 3. 1. as unto *b.* in Christ
1 *Pet.* 2. 2. as new-born *b.* desire

BACK, *b.* to go from Samuel ; 1 *Sam.* 10. 9.
1 *Kings* 14. 9. cast me behind *b.*
Ps. 129. 3. plowers plowed on *b.*
Prov. 10. 13. rod for fool's *b.* 26. 3.
Is. 38. 17. castest sins behind thy *b.*
50. 6. gave my *b.* to smiters
Jer. 2. 27. turned the *b.* 32. 33.
18. 17. I will show them *b.* not face

Ex. 33. 23. shall see my *b.* parts
Ps. 19. 13. keep *b.* thy servant from
53. 6. when God brings *b.* the captivity
Hos. 4. 16. Israel slideth *b.* as *b.*
Acts 20. 20. kept *b.* nothing profitable

BACKBITERS, haters of God, *Rom.* 1. 30.
Ps. 15. 3. *b.* not with tongue
Prov. 25. 23. *b.* tongue
2 *Cor.* 12. 20. strifes, *b.*

BACKS, *Neh.* 9. 26. they cast thy law behind their *b.*
Ezek. 8. 16. men with their *b.* towards the temple
10. 12. their whole body and *b.* full of

BACKSLIDER in heart, be filled with his ways, *Prov.* 14. 14.
Jer. 2. 19. thy *b.* reprove .
3. 6, 12. return, thou *b.* Israel, 6. 8. 11. 14, 22. & 31. 22. & 49. 4.
5. 6. *b.* are increased
8. 5. slidden *b.* by perpetual *b.*
14. 7. *b.* are many, we sinned
Hos. 11. 7. my people are bent to *b.*
14. 4. I will heal their *b.* love

BACKWARD, *Gen.* 9. 23. went *b.* and covered
Gen. 49. 17. Dan a serpent, so that his rider shall fall *b.*
1 *Sam.* 4. 18. Eli fell from off the seat *b.* by the gate
2 *Kings* 20. 10. let the shadow return *b.* *Is.* 38. 8.
Job 23. 8. and *b.* but I cannot perceive
Ps. 40. 14. let them be driven *b.* that wish me evil
Is. 1. 4. they are gone away *b.*
44. 25. that turneth the wise men *b.*
59. 14. judgment is turned away *b.*
Jer. 7. 24. but they went *b.* and not forward
15. 6. thou art gone *b.* therefore I will destroy
Lam. 1. 8. Jerusalem sigheth and turneth *b.*
John 18. 6. went *b.* and fell to ground

BAD, *Gen.* 24. 50. we cannot speak to thee *b.* or good
31. 24. speak not to Jacob good or *b.*
Lev. 27. 10. a good for a *b.* or a *b.* for a good
Num. 13. 19. the land they dwell in, if good or *b.*
24. 13. to do either good or *b.* of my own mind
1 *Kings* 3. 9. a heart that I may discern good and *b.*
Ezra 4. 12. building the rebellious and *b.* city
Matt. 13. 48. gathered the good but cast the *b.* away
22. 10. good and *b.* and the wedding was furnished
2 *Chr.* 5. 10. that he hath done, whether good or *b.*

BADNESS, *Gen.* 41. 19. never saw in Egypt for *b.*

BADE, *Gen.* 43. 17. man did as Joseph *b.*
Ruth 3. 6. all mother-in-law *b.* her
2 *Sam.* 1. 18. David *b.* them teach Judah
14. 19. for thy servant Joab he *b.* me
2 *Chr.* 10. 12. came third day as king *b.*
Luke 14. 9. and he that *b.* thee and him

come, 10.

16. a certain man made a supper and b. many

Acts 11. 12. and the Spirit b. me go with them

18. 21. but b. them farewell, saying, I must keep

22. 24. b. that he should be examined by scourging

BADGERS"SKINS, *Ex.* 25. 5 ; 26. 14 ; 35. 7, 23 ; 36. 19 ; *Num.* 4. 10 ; *Ezek.* 16. 10.

BAG, A sack or pouch, *Deut.* 25. 13 ; 1 *Sam.* 17. 40.

Bags which wax not old, *Luke* 12. 33. Heavenly treasures which perish not, as earthly things do.

Earneth wages to put into a bag with holes. *Hag.* 1. 6. What he gets or labours for, does him no manner of service, but a secret curse consumes it

Deut. 25. 13. not have in thy b. divers weights

1 *Sam.* 17. 40. smooth stones, and put them in a b.

Job. 14. 17. my transgression is sealed up in a b.

Prov. 16. 11. all the weights of the b. are his work

Mic. 6. 11. and with the b. of deceitful weights

John 12. 6. because he was a thief, and had the b.

13. 29. some thought, because Judas had the b.

BAGS, *Luke* 12. 33. provide yourselves b. that wax not old

BAKE, ED, *Gen.* 40. 17. all b. meats for Pharaoh

Ex. 12. 39. b. unleavened cakes of dough 16. 23. b. that you will b. to-day

Lev. 6. 17. shall not be b. with leaven 24. 5. take flour and b. twelve cakes 26. 26. ten women shall b. your bread in one oven

BAKER, *Gen.* 40. 1. the butler and b. had offended the king

20. lifted up the head of the chief butler and b.

22. he hanged the b. as Joseph interpreted

41. 10. and put in ward both me and the chief b.

Hos. 7. 4. they are as an oven heated by the b.

BAKERS, *Gen.* 40. 2. was wroth against the chief of the b.

1 *Sam.* 8. 13. he will take your daughters to be b.

Jer. 37. 21. gave Jeremiah bread out of b. street

BALANCE, *Job* 31. 6. let me be weighed in an even b.

Ps. 62. 9. laid in the b. are altogether vanity

Prov. 11. 1. a false b. is abomination, 20. 23.

16. 11. a just weight and b. are the Lord's

Is. 40. 12. who weighed the hills in a b. ?

15. nations counted as the small dust of the b.

46. 6. lavish gold, and weigh silver in the b.

BALANCES, *Job* 6. 2. and my calamity laid in the b. together

Ezek. 5. 1. take b. to weigh, and divide the hair

Dan. 5. 27. thou art weighed in the b. and wanting

Hos. 12. 7. the b. of deceit are in his hand

Amos 8. 5. and falsifying the b. by deceit

Rev. 6. 5. he that sat on them had a pair of b.

BALANCINGS, *Job* 37. 16. dost thou know the b. of the clouds ?

BALD, *Lev.* 13. 40. he is b. yet is he clean, 41.

2 *Kings* 2. 23. go up thou b. head, go up thou b. head

Jer. 16. 6. nor make themselves b. for them

48. 37. every head shall be b. and beard clipt

Ezek. 27. 34. they shall make themselves utterly b.

Mic. 1. 16. make thee b. and poll thee for children

BALDNESS, (1) Want of hair on the head ; *Lev.* 21. 5. (2) A sign of mourning ; *Is.* 15. 2 ; *Jer.* 47. 5.

Lev. 21. 5. they shall not make b. on their head

Deut. 14. 1. nor make any b. between your eyes

Is. 3. 24. and instead of well-set hair, b.

15. 2. on all their heads b. and every beard cut

22. 12. the Lord did call to weeping and to b.

Ezek. 7. 18. and b. on all their heads

Amos 8. 10.

Mic. 1. 16. poll thee, enlarge thy b. as the eagle

BALM, *Gen.* 37. 25. Ishmaelites bearing b. and myrrh

43. 11. take in your vessels a little b. and honey

Jer. 8. 22. is there no b. in Gilead ? is there no physician ?

Jer. 46. 11. go up to Gilead, and take b. O virgin

51. 8. howl for her, take b. for her pain

Ezek. 27. 17. Judah traded in honey, and oil, and b.

BAND, S, *Gen.* 32. Jacob divided the camels into two b.

Job. 38. 9. I made darkness a swaddling b. for it

31 canst bind the Pleiades, or loose the b. of Orion ?

Ps. 2. 3. let us break their b. asunder, and cast away

73. 4. for there are no b. in their death

107. 14. and he brake their b. in sunder

Eccl. 7. 26. woman whose heart snares, hands as b.

Is. 28. 22. be not mockers, lest b. be made strong

Ezek. 3. 25. son of man, they shall put

b. on thee

4. 8. and behold I will lay *b.* upon

34. 27. when I have broken the *b.* of their youth

Hos. 11. 4. I drew them with *b.* of love, and I was

Luke 8. 29. he brake *b.* and was driven of the devil

Acts 16. 26. and every one's *b.* were loosed

Col. 2. 19. the head, from which all the body by *b.*

Gen. 32. 10. I passed over, and now I am become two *b.*

1 *Sam.* 10. 26. and there went with him a *b.* of men

2 *Kings* 6. 23. so the *b.* of Syria came no more

1 *Chr.* 7. 4. with them were *b.* of soldiers for war

21. they helped David against the *b.* of the rovers

Ps. 119. 61. the *b.* of the wicked have robbed me

Prov. 30. 27. the locusts go forth all of them by *b.*

Matt. 27. 27. gathered to him whole *b.* *Mark* 15. 16.

John 18. 3. Judas having received a *b.* of men

12. the *b.* and captain and officer took Jesus

Acts 10. 1. a centurion of the *b.* called the Italian *b.*

21. 31. tidings came to the chief captain of the *b.*

BANDED, *Acts* 23. 12. certain of the Jews *b.* together

BANK, *Gen.* 41. 17. behold I stood on the *b.* of the river

2 *Sam.* 20. 15. they cast up a *b.* against the city

2 *Kings* 2. 13. Elisha stood by the *b.* of

19. 32. the king of Assyria not cast a *b. Is.* 37. 33.

Ezek. 47. 7. at the *b.* of the river were many trees

Dan. 12. 5. one on this side of the *b.* of the river, the other on that side of the *b.* of the river

Luke 19. 23. gavest not thou my money into the *b.* ?

BANKS, *Josh.* 3. 15. Jordan overfloweth all his *b.* 4. 18.

1 *Chr.* 12. 15. Jordan had overflowed his *b.*

Is. 8. 7. the king of Assyria shall go over all his *b.*

BANNER, a standard, or ensign, *Is.* 13. 2. *Thou hast given a banner to them that fear thee, Ps.* 60. 4. An army of men united under one banner, with ability to defend themselves and conquer their enemies ; a banner being a sign of victory, as well as of battle and union

Ps. 60. 4. thou hast given a *b.* to them that fear thee

Songs 2. 4. his *b.* over me was love

Is. 13. 2. lift *b.* on high mountain

BANNERS, *Ps.* 20. 5. in the name of our God we set up our *b.*

Songs 6. 4. thou art terrible as an army

with *b.*

BANISHED, 2 *Sam.* 14. 13. the king doth not fetch home his *b.*

14. he doth devise means that his *b.* be not expelled

BANQUET, ING, *Esth.* 5. 4. let king and Haman come to *b.*

Job 41. 6. shall companions make *b.* of him

Songs 2. 4. brought me into *b.* house

BAPTISM, *Matt.* 3. 7. when he saw the Pharisees come to his *b.*

20. 22. and to be baptized with the *b. Mark* 10. 38.

21. 25. the *b.* of John, whence was it, from heaven or of men ? *Mark* 11. 30 ; *Luke* 20. 4.

Luke 7. 29. publicans baptized with the *b.* of John

12. 50. I have a *b.* to be baptized with, and how am

Acts 1. 22. beginning from the *b.* of John to that day

10. 37. that word, after the *b.* which John preached

Acts 18. 25. Apollos knowing only the *b.* of John

19. 3. were ye baptized ? they said unto John's *b.*

Rom. 6. 4. we are buried with him by *b.* into death

Eph. 4. 5. there is one Lord, one faith, one *b.*

Col. 2. 12. buried with him in *b.* ye are risen with

Heb. 6. 2. of doctrine of *b.* and laying on of hands

1 *Pet.* 3. 21. the like figure whereunto even *b.* doth

BAPTIST, *Matt.* 3. 1. in those days came John *b.* preaching

11. 11. among them born of women, there hath not risen a greater than John the *b. Luke* 7. 28.

11. 12. from the days of John the *b.* till now

14. 2. this is John the *b.* he is risen from the dead

8. said, give me John the *b.* head in a charger

Mark 6. 14. John the *b.* was risen from the dead

25. give me in a charger the head of John the *b.*

Luke 7. 20. John the *b.* hath sent us to thee, saying

9. 19. they answering said, John the *b.*

BAPTIZE, *Matt.* 3. 11. I *b.* you with water, he shall *b.* you with the Holy Ghost, *Mark* 1. 8 ; *Luke* 3. 16 ; *John* 1. 26.

Mark 1. 4. John did *b.* in the wilderness, and preach

John 1. 33. he that sent me to *b.* said

1 *Cor.* 1. 17. Christ sent me not to *b.* but to preach

BAPTIZED, *Matt.* 3. 6. were *b.* of him in Jordan, *Mark* 1. 5.

13. then cometh Jesus to John to be *b.* of him

Matt. 16. Jesus, when he was *b.* went out of the water

Mark 1. 9. Jesus was *b.* of John in Jordan

10. 39. the baptism I am *b*. withal, shall ye be *b*.

16. 16. he that believeth and is *b*. shall be saved

Luke 3. 7. said to the multitude that came to be *b*.

12. then came the publicans to be *b*. 7. 29.

21. Jesus being *b*, and praying, heaven was opened

John 8. 22. there he tarried with them and *b*.

John 3. 23. much water there, and they came and were *b*.

4. 1. Jesus made and *b*. more disciples than John

2. though Jesus himself *b*. not, but his disciples

10. 40. into the place where John at first *b*.

Acts 1. 5. for John truly *b*. with water, but ye shall be *b*. with the Holy Ghost, 11. 16.

2. 38. repent, be *b*. every one of you

41. they that gladly received his word were *b*.

8. 12. they were *b*. both men and women

13. Simon believed also, and when he was *b*.

36. here is water, what doth hinder me to be *b*. ?

9. 18. Saul received sight, and arose and was *b*.

10. 47. can any forbid water that these should not be *b*. ?

Acts 16. 15. Lydia when she was *b*. and her household

33. jailer was *b*. and all his straightway

18. 8. many of the Corinthians believed and were *b*.

22. 16. arise, and be *b*. and wash away thy sins

Rom. 6. 3. were *b*. into Jesus, were *b*. into his death

1 *Cor.* 1. 13. were ye *b*. in the name of Paul

14. thank God that I *b*. none of you, but Crispus

16. I *b*. household of Stephanas, not *b*. any other

10. 2. and were all *b*. to Moses in the cloud

15. 29. else what shall they do who are *b*. for the dead, why are they *b*. for the dead ?

BAPTIZING, *Matt.* 28. 19. go ye and teach all nations *b*. them

John 1. 28. done beyond Jordan, where John was *b*.

31. therefore am I come *b*. with water

3. 23. and John was also *b*. in Enon, near to Salim

BARE you on eagles' wings, *Ex.* 19. 4.

Gen. 7. 17. *b*. the ark ; *Deut.* 31. 9, 25 ; *Josh.* 3. 15 ; 4. 10 ; 8. 33 ; 2 *Sam.* 6. 13 ; 1 *Chr.* 15. 15, 26, 27.

31. 39. that torn by beasts, I *b*. the loss of it

Deut. 1. 31. thy God *b*. thee as a man doth bear

Is. 53. 12. he *b*. the sin of many

63. 9. he *b*. them all the days of old

Matt. 8. 17. himself *b*. our sickness

Luke 7. 14. and they that *b*. him stood still

John 2. 8. the water made wine, and they *b*. it

12. 6. had the bag, and *b*. what was put therein

1 *Pet.* 2. 24. *b*. our sins in his own body

BARE, *Gen.* 25. 26. Isaac was 60 years, when she *b*. them

44, 27. ye know that my wife *b*. me two sons

Ex. 6. 20. Jochebed *b*. to Amram Moses and Aaron

Judg. 13. 2. Manoah's wife was barren, and *b*. not

1 *Chr.* 4. 9. Jabez, because I *b*. him with sorrow

Songs 6. 9. she is the choice of her that *b*. her

8. 5. there she brought thee forth that *b*. thee

Is. 51. 2. and look unto Sarah that *b*.

BARE fruit, *Luke* 8. 8. other sprang up, and *b*. *f*. an hundred fold

Rev. 22. 2. the tree of life *b*. twelve manner of *fruits*

BARE (adjective) (1) Naked or uncovered, *Lev.* 13. 45 ; *Is.* 32. 11. (2) Plain or real, 1 *Cor.* 15. 37. (3) Deprived of outward comforts, *Jer.* 49. 10. (4) Violently taken away, *Jer.* 13. 22.

Made bare his holy arm, Is. 52. 10. Hath discovered and put forth his great power, which for a long time seemed to be hid and unemployed

Is. 32. 11. strip ye, make ye *b*. and gird sackcloth

47. 2. make *b*. the leg, uncover the thigh, pass

52. 10. the Lord hath made *b*. his holy arm

Ezek. 16. 7. whereas thou wast naked and *b*.

22. when thou wast naked and *b*. and polluted

Joel 1. 7. my figtree he hath made it clean and *b*.

1 *Cor.* 15. 37. not that body that shall be, but *b*. grain

BARE witness and record, *Mark* 14. 56. many *b*. false *witness* against him

Luke 4. 22. all *b*. him witness and wondered

5. 33. John *b*. *witness* to the truth

19. 35. he that saw it *b*. *record*, and his record is true

John 1. 15. John *b*. *witness* of him, 32. 34.

12. 17. the people that was with him *b*. *record*

Acts 15. 8. knoweth the hearts, *b*. them *witness*

Rev. 1. 2. who *b*. *record* of the word of God

BAREFOOT, 2 *Sam.* 15. 30. he went *b*. and the people with him

Is. 20. 2. Isaiah did so, walking naked and *b*. 3.

4. led the Egyptians prisoners, naked and *b*.

BARK, *Is.* 56. 10. they are dumb dogs, they cannot *b.*

BARLEY, *Ex.* 9. 31. the *b.* was smitten, for *b.* was in the ear

Num. 5. 15. the tenth part of an ephah of *b.* meal

Deut. 8. 8. a land of wheat, and *b.* vines and fig-trees

Ruth 1. 22. came in the beginning of *b.* harvest

23. so she kept fast to the end of *b.* harvest

3. 2. behold Boaz winnoweth *b.* to-night

2 *Sam.* 14. 30. Joab's field is near, he hath *b.* there

21. 9. Saul's sons were hanged in *b.* harvest

2 *Chr.* 2. 10. I will give 20,000 measures of *b.*

15. wheat and *b.* the oil and wine, let him send

27. 5. Ammon gave 10,000 measures of *b.*

Job 31. 40. and let cockle grow instead of *b.*

Is. 28. 25. the principal wheat and appointed *b.*

Joel 1. 11. O husbandmen, howl for wheat and *b.*

Jonn 6. 9. a lad here which hath five *b.* loaves

6. 13. with the fragments of the five *b.* loaves

Rev. 6. 6. a voice say, 3 measures of *b.* for one penny

BARN, (1) A repository for any sort of grain, *Luke* 12. 24. (2) Heaven, *Matt.* 13. 30.

Job 39. 12. and gather thy seed into the *b.*

Matt. 13. 30. but gather the wheat into my *b.*

Luke 12. 24. which have no store-house nor *b.*

BARNS, *Deut.* 28. 8. the Lord shall command the blessing upon thee in thy *b.* and in all thou doest

Prov. 3. 10. so shall thy *b.* be filled with plenty

Matt. 6. 26. the fowls sow not, nor gather into *b.*

Luke 12. 18. I will pull down my *b.* and build

BARREL of meal, 1 *Kings* 17. 14.

BARREN, *Gen.* 11. 30. & 25. 21. & 29. 31 ; *Judg.* 13. 2 ; *Luke* 1. 7.

Ex. 23. 26. nothing shall be *b.*

Deut. 7. 14. there shall not be male or female *b.*

Judg. 13. 2. Manoah's wife was *b.* and bare not, 3.

1 *Sam.* 2. 5. *b.* hath born seven

Job 24. 21. he evil entreateth the *b.* that bear not

Ps. 113. 9. *b.* women to keep house

Songs 4. 2. none is *b.* among, 6. 6.

Is. 54. 1. sing O *b. Gal.* 4. 27.

Prov. 30. 16. the grave and *b.* womb not satisfied

Joel 2. 20. and I will drive him into a land *b.*

Luke 1. 7. had no child, because Elizabeth was *b.*

36. the sixth month with her, who

was called *b.*

Luke 23. 29. blessed are *b.* wombs

Gal. 4. 27. for it is written, rejoice thou *b.*

2 *Pet.* 1. 8. neither *b.* nor unfruitful

BARRENNESS, *Ps.* 107. 34. he turneth a fruitful land into *b.*

BASE, S, *Ps.* 104. 5. founded the earth on her *b.*

BASE (adjective) *Job* 30. 8. yea, they were children of *b.* men

2 *Sam.* 6. 22. and will be *b.* in mine own sight

Ezek. 17. 14. that the kingdom might be *b.*

29. 14. and they shall be there a *b.* kingdom

Mal. 2. 9. therefore I have made you *b.*

1 *Cor.* 1. 28. *b.* things of this world God hath chosen

2 *Cor.* 10. 1. I, Paul, who in presence am *b.* among

Acts 17. 5. Jews took lewd fellows of the *b.* sort for

BASEST, *Ezek.* 29. 15. Pathros shall be the *b.* of kingdoms

Dan. 4. 17. and setteth up over it the *b.* of men

BASKET, S, *Gen.* 40. 18. the three *b.* are three days

Ex. 29. 3. put them into one *b.* : *Deut.* 26. 2.

Lev. 8. 2. take *b.* of unleavened bread : ver. 26 ; Num. 6. 15.

Deut. 28. 5. blessed thy *b.* and store

17. cursed thy *b.* and store

2 *Kings* 10. 7. put heads into *b.*

Amos 8. 1. a *b.* of summer fruit

Matt. 14. 20 ; *Mark* 5. 23. they took up

12. *b.* full ; *Luke* 9. 17 ; *John* 6. 13.

15. 37 ; *Mark* 8. 8. took up seven *b.* full

Acts 9. 25. let Saul down in *b.* ; 2 *Cor.* 11. 33.

BASONS, *Ex.* 24. 6. Moses put half of blood in *b.*

Ezra 1. 10. thirty *b.* of gold, silver *b.*

8. 27. twenty *b.* of gold of 1,000 drams

BASTARD not enter, *Deut.* 23. 2.

Zech. 9. 6. *b.* shall dwell in Ashdod

Heb. 12. 8. without chastisement *b.* not

BATTLE, S, *Num.* 32. 27. pass before Lord to *b.*

Deut. 20. 1. when goest to *b.* against enemies

8. 13. Gideon returned to *b.*

Deut. 20. 14. Benjamin gathered to *b.* against Israel

1 *Sam.* 17. 21. Israel and Philistines put *b.* in array

26. 10. shall descend into *b.* and perish

2 *Sam.* 10. 8 ; 1 *Chr.* 19. 9. children of Ammon put *b.* in array

18. 6. *b.* was in wood of Ephraim

1 *Kings* 8. 44. if thy people go to *b.*

22. 15 ; 2 *Chr.* 18. 14. shall we go against Ramoth-Gilead to *b.*

2 *Kings* 3. 26. king of Moab saw *b.* too sore

2 *Chr.* 13. 3. Abijah set *b.* in array

13. 14. Judah saw *b.* before and behind

14. 10. Asa set *b.* in array against Zerah

Ps. 55. 18. hath delivered my soul from *b.*
Jer. 50. 22. sound of *b.* in land
BATTLEMENT, S, *Deut.* 22. 8. shalt make *b.* for roof
Jer. 5. 10. take away her *b.* are not Lord's
BEAM out of timber, *Hab.* 2. 11.
Judg. 16. 14. he went away with the pin of the *b.*
1 *Sam.* 17. 7. and the staff of his spear was like a weaver's *b.*, 1 *Chr.* 11. 53 ; 20. 5.
2 *Kings* 6. 2. let us go to Jordan, and take thence a *b.*
5. as one was felling a *b.* axe-head fell into water
Matt. 7. 3. considerest not *b.* in own eye
4. and behold, a *b.* is in thine own eye
BEAMS, 2 *Chr.* 3. 7. he overlaid the *b.* the posts, and walls
Neh. 2. 8. that he may give timber to make *b.*
Ps. 104. 3. who layeth the *b.* in the waters
Songs 1. 17. the *b.* of our house are cedar and rafters
BEANS, 2 *Sam.* 17. 28. Barzillai brought *b.* lentiles to David
Ezek. 4. 9. take unto thee wheat, *b.* lentiles, millet
BEAR, (1) To carry, *Jer.* 17. 21 ; *Matt.* 27. 33. (2) To suffer, or endure, 2 *Cor.* 11. 1 ; *Rev.* 2. 2. (3) To bring forth, *Gen.* 18. 13. (4) To produce, or yield, *Jam.* 3. 12. (5) To uphold, or support, *Ps.* 75. 3 ; 91. 12. (6) To be punished for, *Num.* 14. 33. (7) To undergo the care and fatigue of ruling a people, *Deut.* 1. 12. (8) To speak and utter, *Deut.* 5. 20. (9) To tell, or relate, 2 *Sam.* 18. 19. (10) To be answerable in payment for, 2 *Kings* 18. 14. (11) To lay a thing sadly to heart, *Ps.* 89. 50. (12) To give satisfaction for, *Is.* 52. 11 ; *Heb.* 9. 28. (13) To perform, or fully observe, *Acts* 15. 10.
BEAR, *Gen.* 49. 15 ; *Deut.* 1. 9, 31 ; *Prov.* 9. 12. & 30. 21 ; *Lam.* 3. 27.
Gen. 4. 13. punishment greater than I can *b.*
Num. 11. 14. not able to *b.* all this people
Ps. 75. 3. I *b.* upon the pillars of it
91. 12. *b.* thee up in their hands
Prov. 18. 14. a wounded spirit, who can *b.*
Amos 7. 10. land not able to *b.* words
Mic. 7. 9. I will *b.* indignation of Lord
Luke 14. 27. whosoever doth not *b.* his cross
18. 7. though he *b.* long with them
John 16. 12. ye cannot *b.* them now
Rom. 15. 1. strong *b.* infirmities of the weak
1 *Cor.* 3. 2. hitherto not able to *b.* it
10. 13. that may be able to *b.* it
Gal. 6. 2. *b.* one another's burdens
5. every man *b.* his own burden
17. I *b.* in my body marks of the Lord Jesus
Heb. 9. 28. offered to *b.* sins of many

Rev. 2. 2. canst not *b.* that are evil
BEAR fruit, *Ezek.* 17. 8 ; *Hos.* 9. 16 ; *Joel* 2. 22 ; *Matt.* 13. 23 ; *Luke* 13. 9 ; *John* 15. 2. 4. 8.
Ps. 106. 4. favour thou *b.* to
Rom. 11. 18. *b.* not root but
13. 4. *b.* not sword in vain
1 *Cor.* 13. 7. charity *b.* all things
Heb. 6. 8. *b.* thorns and briers
Ps. 126. 6. *b.* precious seed
Rom. 2. 15. conscience *b.* witness, 9. 1.
Heb. 13. 13. *b.* his reproach
Gen. 13. 6. the land was not able to *b.* them, 36. 7.
43. 9. let me *b.* the blame for ever, 44. 32.
49. 15. Issachar bowed his shoulder to *b.*
Ex. 18. 22. they shall *b.* the burden with thee
25. to *b.* the ark, 27. 7 ; 30. 4 ; 37. 5 ; *Deut.* 10. 8 ; *Josh.* 3. 8, 13, 14 ; 4. 16 ; 2 *Sam.* 15. 24.
28. 12. Aaron shall *b.* their names before the Lord
Lev. 19. 18. thou shalt not *b.* any grudge
Num. 14. 27. how long shall I *b.* this congregation
Deut. 1. 31. God bare thee as a man doth *b.* his son
Ps. 89. 50. how I do *b.* in my bosom the reproach
Is. 1. 14. your feasts, I am weary to *b.* them
46. 4. I have made and I will *b.* you, even carry
52. 11. be ye clean that *b.* the vessels of the Lord
Jer. 10. 19. truly this is a grief, and I must *b.* it
31. 19. because I did *b.* the reproach of my youth
Ezek. 12. 6. in their sight shalt thou *b.* on shoulders
14. 10. they shall *b.* punishment of their iniquity
16. 52. *b.* thou thine own shame for thy sins, 54.
Mic. 6. 16. ye shall *b.* the reproach of my people
Zech. 5. 10. whither do these *b.* the ephah ?
6. 13. he shall *b.* glory, and shall rule on his throne
Matt. 3. 11. whose shoes I am not worthy to *b.*
27. 32. they found Simon, they compelled him to *b.* his cross, *Mark* 15. 21 ; *Luke* 23. 26.
Acts 9. 15. he is a chosen vessel to *b.* my name
15. 10. a yoke, our fathers nor we are able to bear
Rom. 15. 1. we ought to *b.* infirmities of the weak
15. 49. we shall also *b.* the image of the heavenly
2 *Cor.* 11. 1. would to God ye could *b.* with me
Jam. 3. 12. can the fig-tree *b.* olive berries
BEAR iniquity, *Ex.* 28. 38. Aaron may *b. iniquity* of holy things
Lev. 5. 1. he shall *b.* his *iniquity*, 17 ; 7.

18 ; 17. 16 ; 19. 8 ; 20. 17.

Num. 5. 31. this woman shall *b.* her iniquity

14. 34: ye shall *b.* your *iniquity* even forty years

18. 1. Aaron and his sons *b. iniquity* of sanctuary

Is. 53. 11. my righteous servant shall *b.* their *iniquity*

Ezek. 4. 4. number of days, thou shalt *b.* their *iniquity*, 5. 6.

18. 19. why doth not son *b. iniquity* of the father

20. the son shall not *b.* the *iniquity* of the father

BEAR judgment, *Ex.* 28. 30. Aaron shall *b. judg.* of children of Israel

Gal. 5. 10. he that troubleth you shall *b.* his *judg.*

BEAR rule, *Esth.* 1. 22. every man shall *b. rule* in his house

Prov. 12. 24. the hand of the diligent shall *b. rule*

Jer. 5. 31. the priests *b. rule* by their

Ezek. 19. 11. had strong rods for them that *b. rule*

Dan. 2. 39. a kingdom of brass which shall *b. rule*

BEAR sin, *Lev.* 19. 17. rebuke, that thou *b.* not *sin* for him

20. 20. they shall *b.* their *sin*, they shall die

24. 15. whosoever curseth his God, shall *b.* his *sin*

Num. 9. 13. shall be cut off, that man shall *b.* his *sin*

18. 22. not come nigh, lest they *b. sin* and die

Heb. 9. 28. so Christ was once offered to *b.* the *sin*

BEAR witness, *Ex.* 20. 16. thou shalt not *b.* false *witness* against thy neighbour, *Deut.* 5. 20 ; *Matt.* 19. 18 ; *Rom.* 13. 9.

Mark 10. 19. do not *b.* false *witness*, *Luke* 18. 20.

John 1. 7. the same for a witness to *b. witness*

8. he was sent to *b. witness* of that light

3. 28. ye yourselves *b.* me *witness* that I said

5. 31. if I *b. witness* of myself, my witness is not true

36. same works that I do *b. witness* of me, 10. 25.

John 8. 18. I am one that *b. witness* of myself and the Father

15. 27. ye shall also *b. witness* because ye have been

Acts 22. 5. also the high priest doth *b.* me *witness*

23. 11. so must thou *b. witness* also at Rome

1 John 1. 2. we have seen it, and *b. witness*, and show

5. 8. and there are three that *b. witness* in earth

BEAR, to bring forth, *Gen.* 17. 17. and shall Sarah that is 90 years old *b.*

18. 13. shall I of a surety *b.* a child, who am old

Lev. 12. 5. but if she *b.* a maid child,

1 Kings 3. 21. behold, it was not my

son that I did *b.*

Is. 7. 14. a virgin shall conceive and *b.* a son, and

54. 1. sing, O barren, thou that didst not *b.*

Jer. 29. 6. that they may *b.* sons and daughters

1 Tim. 5. 15. younger women marry, *b.* children

BEAREST, *Judg.* 13. 3. behold, thou art barren, and *b.* not

Ps. 106. 4. with the favour thou *b.* to thy people

John 8. 13. thou *b.* record of thyself, thy record

Rom. 11. 18. *b.* not the root, but the root thee

Gal. 4. 27. rejoice thou barren that *b.* not

BEARETH, *Num.* 11. 12. as a nursing father *b.* the child

Deut. 25. 6. the first-born she *b.* shall succeed

23. It is not sown, nor *b.* nor grass groweth

32. 11. as an eagle *b.* her young on her wings

Matt. 13. 23. which also *b.* fruit, and bringeth forth

John 15. 2. every branch that *b.* not fruit, he taketh

Rom. 13. 4. for he *b.* not the sword in vain

1 Cor. 13. 7. charity *b.* all things, believeth all things

Heb. 6. 8. that which *b.* thorns is rejected

BEARETH rule, *Prov.* 29. 2. when the wicked *b. rule*, people mourn

BEARETH witness, *Prov.* 25. 18. a man that *b.* false *witness* is a maul

John 5. 32. there is another that *b. witness* of me

John 8. 18. and the Father that sent me, *b. witness* of me

Rom. 8. 16. the spirit *b. witness* with our spirit

1 John 5. 6. and it is the Spirit that *b. witness*

BEARING, *Gen.* 1. 29. I have given you every herb, *b.* seed

Gen. 37. 25. Ishmaelites with camels *b.* spicery

Num. 10. 17. set forward, *b.* the tabernacle

21. the Kohathites set forward, *b.* the sanctuary

1 Sam. 17. 7. one *b.* a shield went before him

Ps. 126. 6. he that goeth forth *b.* precious seed

Mark 14. 13. there shall meet you a man *b.* a pitcher of water, follow him, *Luke* 22. 10.

John 19. 17. he *b.* his cross, went forth to a place

Rom. 2. 15. their conscience also *b.* witness

9. 1. I lie not, my conscience *b.* me witness

2 Cor. 4. 10. *b.* in the body the dying of the Lord Jesus

Heb. 2. 4. God also *b.* them witness with signs

13. 13. let us go forth to him *b*. his reproach

1 *Tim.* 2. 15. she shall be saved in child-bearing

BEAR, S, 1 *Sam.* 17. 34. came a lion and a *b*. took a lamb

1 *Sam.* 17. 36. thy servant slew both the lion and the *b*.

2 *Kings* 2. 24. there came forth two she-*b*. and tear

Prov. 17. 12. a *b*. robbed of her whelps meet a man

Is. 11. 7. the cow and *b*. shall feed, their young

59. 11. we roar all like *b*. and mourn like doves

Hos. 13. 8. I will meet them as a *b*. bereaved

Amos 5. 19. as if a man did flee from a *b*.

Rev. 13. 2. his feet were as the feet of a *b*.

BEARD, S, *Lev.* 13. 29. if a man hath a plague on head or *b*.

Lev. 14. 9. shall shave all his hair off his head and *b*.

19. 27. nor shalt thou mar the corners of *b*. 21. 5.

1 *Sam.* 17. 35. I caught him by his *b*. and slew him

21. 13. David let his spittle fall on his *b*.

2 *Sam.* 10. 5. tarry at Jericho till your *b*. be grown and then return, 1 *Chr.* 19. 5.

19. 24. Mephibosheth trimmed not his *b*.

Ps. 133. 2. ran down to the *b*. even Aaron's *b*.

Is. 7. 20. it shall also consume the *b*.

15. 2. on all heads baldness, and every *b*. cut off

Jer. 41. 5. fourscore men having their *b*. shaved

48. 37. every head shall be bald, every *b*. clipt

Ezek. 5. 1. cause a razor to pass on thy head and *b*.

BEAST, (1) A brute void of reason, *Prov.* 12. 10. (2) All kinds of cattle, 1 *Kings* 4. 33 ; *Ps.* 8. 7. (3) Ministers of the gospel, who are full of liveliness and nimbleness in executing God's commands, *Rev.* 4. 6, 8 ; 7. 11. (4) Cruel and unreasonable men, who are led merely by their natural brutish inclinations, 1 *Cor.* 15. 32 ; 2 *Pet.* 2. 12. (5) Kingdoms, *Dan.* 7. 11 ; 8. 4. (6) Antichrist, *Rev.* 13. 2 ; 20. 4. (7) People of several nations, *Dan.* 4. 12, 21.

Gen. 1. 25. God made the *b*. of the earth after his kind

37. 20. some evil *b*. hath devoured him, 33.

Ex. 13. 12. every firstling that cometh of a *b*.

19. whose lieth with a *b*. shall be put to death, *Lev.* 18. 23 ; 20. 15, 16 ; *Deut.* 27. 21.

Lev. 11. 47. *b*. that may be eaten, and *b*. that may not

Deut. 4. 17. the likeness of any *b*. on the earth

Neh. 2. 12. nor any *b*. save the *b*. I rode on

Ps. 147. 9. he giveth to the *b*. his food, and to ravens

Prov. 12. 10. a righteous man regards life of his *b*.

Is. 43. 20. the *b*. of the field shall honour me

Dan. 4. 16. let a *b*. heart be given to him

Luke 10. 34. set him on his own *b*. and brought him

Acts 28. 5. Paul shook off the *b*. into the fire

Heb. 12. 20. if so much as a *b*. touch the mountain

Rev. 6. 3. I heard the second *b*. say, come and see

19. 19. I saw the *b*. and the kings of the earth

BEAST, (every) *Gen.* 1. 30. to *every b*. I have given green herb for

20. Adam gave names to *every b*. of the field

3. 14. thou art cursed above *every b*. of the field

7. 2. of *every* clean *b*. take to thee by sevens, 8.

14. they and *every b*. after his kind, and cattle

8. 19. *every b*. after their kinds went out of the ark

20. of *every* clean *b*. and clean fowl he offered

9. 2. dread of you shall be on *every b*. of the earth

Gen. 9. 5. your blood will I require at hand of *every b*.

Ps. 50. 10. for *every b*. of the forest is mine

104. 11. they give drink to *every b*. of the field

BEAST, joined with man, *Gen.* 6. 7. Lord said, I will destroy both *man* and *b*.

Ex. 8. 17. smote dust, it became lice in *man* and *b*.

11. 7. not a dog move his tongue against *man* or *b*.

13. 2. firstborn of *man* and *b*. is mine, *Num.* 8. 17.

19. 13. whether *man* or *b*. it shall not live

Lev. 27. 28. no devoted thing of *man* or *b*. shall be

Num. 3. 13. I hallowed to me first-born of *man* and *b*.

Ps. 36. 6. Lord, thou preservest *man* and *b*.

Jer. 31. 27. I will sow Judah with seed of *man* and *b*.

32. 43. ye say, it is desolate without *man* or *b*. 33. 10, 12 ; 36. 29 ; 51. 62.

BEAST, unclean, *Lev.* 5. 2. or if a soul touch any *unclean b*. 7. 21.

BEASTS, *Lev.* 11. 2. these *b*. ye shall eat, *Deut.* 14. 6.

Lev. 11. 3. and chew cud among *b*. shall ye eat, *Deut.* 14. 4.

Num. 20. 8. give the congregation and their *b*. drink

1 *Kings* 4. 28. barley for mules, or swift *b*.

33. Solomon spake of *b.* and of fowl, and fishes

18. 5. may find grass, that ye lose not all the *b.*

Job 12. 7. ask the *b.* and they shall teach thee

18. 3. wherefore are ye counted as *b.* and vile

Prov. 9. 2. wisdom hath killed her *b.*

30. 30. a lion which is strongest among *b.*

Ezek. 5. 17. I will send on you famine and evil *b.* pestilence, blood, and the sword, 14. 15.

32. 4. I will fill the *b.* of whole earth with thee

13. I will destroy all the *b.* thereof, 34. 25, 28.

Dan. 4. 14. let the *b.* get away from under it

15. let his portion be with the *b.* in the grass

7. 17. these four great *b.* are four kings

8. 4. that no *b.* might stand before him

Joel 1. 18. how do the *b.* groan, herds perplexed

Rom. 1. 23. changed into an image, made like to *b.*

1 *Cor.* 15. 32. if I have fought with *b.* at Ephesus

Jam. 3. 7. for every kind of *b.* is tamed but tongue

2 *Pet.* 2. 12. but these as natural brute *b.* speak evil

Jude 10. but what they know naturally as brute *b.*

Rev. 4. 6. four *b.* full of eyes before and behind

4. 9. when those *b.* give glory and honour to him

5. 6. in midst of the throne and four *b.* stood a Lamb

14. the four *b.* said Amen, and the 24 elders fell

6. 1. one of the four *b.* saying, come and see, 15. 7.

7. 11. angels stood about the throne and the four *b.*

14. 3. a new song before the throne and four *b.*

19. 4. the 24 elders and four *b.* fell down to worship

BEASTS of the earth, *Acts* 10. 12. all manner of four-footed *b. of earth*, 11. 6.

BEASTS of the field, *Ex.* 23. 11. what the poor leave *b. of field* may eat

Deut. 7. 22. lest the *b. of the field* increase upon thee

1 *Sam.* 17. 44. come, I will give thy flesh to *b. of field*

Job 5. 23. *b. of the field* shall be at peace with thee

Ps. 8. 7. thou hast put *b. of the field* under his feet

BEASTS wild, *Is.* 13. 21. but *wild b.* of the desert shall lie there

22. and the *wild b.* of the islands shall cry

34. 14. the *wild b.* of the desert shall also meet with *wild b.* of the island, *Jer.* 50. 39.

Mark 1. 13. Christ was there with the *wild b.* and

Acts 10. 12. sheet, wherein were all *wild b.* 11. 6.

BEAT, (1) To smite or strike, *Deut.* 25. 3 ; *Matt.* 21. 35. (2) To bruise, or bray, *Ex.* 30. 36 ; *Num.* 11. 8. (3) To batter, or demolish, *Judg.* 8. 17 ; 2 *Kings* 3. 25. (4) To get the better of, or overcome, 2 *Kings* 13. 25. (5) To thresh, *Ruth* 2. 17 ; *Is.* 28. 27. (6) To turn, or convert one thing into another, *Is.* 2. 4. *Joel* 3. 10.

Ex. 30. 36. some of the spice shalt *b.* very small

39. 3. they did *b.* the gold into thin plates

Deut. 25. 3. lest if he exceed and *b.* him above these

Judg. 8. 17. he *b.* down the tower of Penuel

19. 22. certain sons of Belial *b.* at the door

Ruth 2. 17. she *b.* out that she had gleaned

2 *Kin.* 13. 25. 3 times Joash *b.* Benhadad

Ps. 89. 23. I will *b.* down his foes before his face

Is. 2. 4. *b.* their swords into plowshares, *Mic.* 4. 3.

3. 15. what means ye, that ye *b.* my people

Joel 3. 10. *b.* your plow-shares into swords, and your

Matt. 7. 25. and *b.* on that house, 27 ; *Luke* 6. 48, 49.

Matt. 21. 35. took his servants and *b.* one : *Mark* 12. 3.

Mark 4. 37. waves *b.* into the ship, it was now full

Acts 16. 22. magistrates commanded to *b.* them

Acts 18. 17. the Greeks took Sosthenes and *b.* him

22. 19. I imprisoned and *b.* in every synagogue

BEATEN, *Ex.* 5. 14. the officers of Israel were *b.* 16.

Ex. 25. 18. cherub of *b.* work, 37. 17, 22 ; *Num.* 8. 4.

37. 7. made two cherubims *b.* out of one piece

Deut. 25. 2. if man worthy to be *b.*

Josh. 8. 15. all made as if *b.*

2 *Sam.* 2. 17. Abner was *b.* and men of Israel

2 *Chr.* 34. 7. when he had *b.* graven images to powder

Prov. 23. 35. they have *b.* me, and I felt it not

Jer. 46. 5. and their mighty ones are *b.* down

Mark 13. 9. in the synagogue ye shall be *b.*

Luke 12. 47. servant who knew and did not shall be *b.*

Acts 5. 40. when they called the apostles and *b.* them

16. 37. they have *b.* us openly, un condemned

2 *Cor.* 11. 25. thrice was I *b.* with rods, once stoned

BEATEN gold, *Ex.* 25. 36. all one *b.* work of pure gold : 37. 22.

Num. 8. 4. this work of the candlestick, was of *b.* gold

1 *Kings* 10. 17. made three hundred
shields of *b.* gold, 2 *Chr.* 9. 16.
BEATEN oil, *Ex.* 27. 20. pure *oil b.* for
the light, *Lev.* 24. 2.
29. 40. fourth part of an hin of *b.* oil,
Num. 12. 5.
BEATEST, *Prov.* 23. 13. for if thou *b.*
him with rod, shall not
BEATETH, 1 *Cor.* 9. 26. so fight I, not
as one that *b.* the air
BEAUTY, *Ex.* 28. 2. holy garment for
Aaron, for glory and *b.*
2 *Sam.* 1. 19. the *b.* of Israel is slain on
high places
14. 25. none so much praised as Absalom for *b.*
1 *Chr.* 16. 29. worship the Lord in the
b. of holiness, *Ps.* 29. 2 ; 96. 9.
Esth. 1. 11. to show the people and
princes her *b.*
Ps. 27. 4. to behold the *b.* of the Lord,
and inquire
39. 11. thou makest his *b.* to consume
45. 11. so shall the king greatly desire
thy *b.*
49. 14. their *b.* shall consume in the
grave
50. 2. out of Zion the perfection of *b.*
God shined
90. 17. let the *b.* of the Lord our God
be upon us
96. 6. strength and *b.* are in his sanctuary
Prov. 6. 25. lust not after her *b.* in thy
31. 30. favour is deceitful, and. b. is vain
Is. 4. 2. branch of the Lord shall be *b.*
and glory
13. 19. Babylon the *b.* of the Chaldees
excellency
Is. 33. 17. thine eyes shall see the king
in his *b.*
53. 2. there is no *b.* that we should
desire him
61 3. to give to them that mourn *b.*
for ashes
Lam. 1. 6. from Zion all her *b.* is departed
2. 15. is this the city men call the perfection of *b.* ?
Ezek. 7. 20. as for the *b.* of his ornament he set it.
16. 14. thy renown went among the
heathen for *b.*
27. 3. thou hast said I am of perfect
b. 28. 12.
4. thy builders have perfected thy *b.*
11.
31. 8. no tree was like the Assyrian
in his *b.*
Hos. 14. 6. Israel's *b.* shall be as the
olive-tree, his smell
Zech. 9. 17. how great is his goodness
and his *b.*
BEAUTIES, *Ps.* 110. 3 in the *b.* of holiness from the womb
BEAUTIFY, to render comely, *Ezra* 7.
27 ; *Ps.* 149. 4 ; *Is.* 60. 13.
BEAUTIFUL, *Gen.* 29. 17. Rachel was
b. and well-favoured
Deut. 21. 11. seest among the captives
a *b.* woman
1 *Sam.* 16. 12. David was of a *b.* countenance
25. 3. Abigail was of a *b.* counten-

ance
2 *Sam.* 11. 2. Bathsheba was very *b.* to
look upon
Esth. 2. 7. Esther was fair and *b.* Mordecai took for
Ps. 48. 2. *b.* for situation is mount Zion
Eccl. 3. 11. hath made every thing *b.* in
his time
Is. 4. 2. in that day shall the branch of
Lord be *b.*
62. 1. O Zion, put on thy *b.* garments
7. how *b.* the feet of them that bring,
Rom. 10. 15.
64. 11. our holy and *b.* house is burnt
up
Jer. 13. 20. where is the flock, thy *b.*
flock
Ezek. 16. 12. I put a *b.* crown upon thine
13. thou wast exceeding *b.* and didst
prosper
Matt. 23. 27. whited sepulchres will appear *b.*
Acts 3. 2. at the gate of the temple
called *b.* 10.
BECAME, *Gen.* 2. 7. the breath of life,
and man *b.* a living soul
Gen. 19. 26. Lot's wife looked back, and
b. a pillar of salt
49. 15. Issachar *b.* a servant to tribute
Ex. 4. 3. it *b.* a serpent ; 4. *b.* a rod in
his hand
1 *Sam.* 25. 37. Nabal's heart died, he *b.*
as a stone
Dan. 2. 35. the stone *b.* a great mountain and filled
1 *Cor.* 9. 20. to the Jews I *b.* a Jew, to
gain the Jews
Heb. 7. 26. such an high priest *b.* us,
who is holy
10. 33. whilst ye *b.* companions of
them so used
Rev. 16. 3. the sea *b.* as the blood of a
dead man
BECAMEST, *Ezek.* 16. 8. I sware unto
thee, and thou *b.* mine
BECAUSE, *Gen.* 3. 1. *b.* God hath said,
ye shall not eat
14. said to the serpent, *b.* thou hast
done this
2 *Sam.* 12. 6. *b.* he hath done this, *b.*
he hath not pity
Prov. 1. 24. *b.* I have called, and ye refused
Is. 7. 9. do ye not believe *b.* ye are not
stable
Ezek. 13. 10. *b.* even *b.* they seduced my
people
Matt. 26. 31. all ye shall be offended *b.*
of me
John 6. 26. ye seek me, not *b* ye saw
the miracles, but *b.* ye did eat of
the loaves, and were filled
10. 13. the hireling fleeth, *b.* he is an
hireling
14. 19. but ye see me, *b.* I live, ye
shall live also
Rom. 8. 10. the Spirit is life *b.* of
righteousness
Eph. 5. 6. *b.* of these cometh the wrath
of God
1 *John* 3. 14. from death to life, *b.* we
love brethren
4. 19. we love him *b.* he first loved us

BECKONED, *Luke* 1. 22. Zacharias *b.* and remained speechless

John 13. 24. Peter *b.* to him that should ask

Acts 19. 33. Alexander *b.* with his hand, 21. 40. Paul stood on stairs, and *b.* with the hand

34. 10. Paul, after the governor had *b.* answered

BECKONING, *Acts* 12. 17. Peter *b.* unto them with the hand

13. 16. Paul stood up, *b.* with his hand, said

BECOME, *Gen.* 3. 22. man is *b.* as one of us, to know good and

37. 20. we will see what will *b.* of his dreams

Ex. 15. 2. the Lord is my strength, and is *b.* my salvation, *Ps.* 118. 14 ; *Is.* 12. 2.

32. 1. for as for this Moses that brought us up, we wot not what is *b.* of him, 23 ; *Acts* 7. 40.

Matt. 21. 42. the same is *b.* the head of the corner, *Mark* 12. 10 · *Luke* 20. 17 ; *Acts* 4. 11.

John 1. 12. he gave power to *b.* the sons of God

2 *Cor.* 5. 17. in Christ, behold, all things are *b.* new

Rev. 11. 15. are *b.* the kingdoms of our Lord

BECOMETH, *Ps.* 93. 5. holiness *b.* thy house, O Lord, for ever

Matt. 3. 15. thus it *b.* us to fulfil all righteousness

13. 22. the deceitfulness of riches choketh the word, and he *b.* unfruitful, *Mark* 4. 19.

32. greatest among herbs, and *b.* a tree, *Mark* 4. 32.

Rom. 16. 2. that ye receive Phebe our sister as *b.* saints

Phil. 1. 27. let your conversation be as *b.* the gospel

1 *Tim.* 2. 10. as *b.* women professing godliness

Tit. 2. 3. aged women be in behaviour as *b.* holiness

BED, set for him, 2 *Kings* 4. 10.

Gen. 47. 31. bowed himself on the *b.* 1 *Kings* 1. 47.

49. 4. wentest up to thy father's *b.* 1 *Chr.* 5. 1.

1 *Sam.* 19. 13. Michal took an image and laid it in *b.*

2 *Sam.* 11. 2. in an evening-tide David arose from his *b.*

2 *Kings* 1. 4. shall not come down from that *b.* 6. 16.

4. 10. let us set there for him a *b.* and a table

Job 7. 13. when I say my *b.* shall comfort me

33. 15. God speaketh in slumberings upon the *b.*

Ps. 4. 4. commune with your own heart on your *b.*

36. 4. he deviseth mischief on his *b.*

41. 3. make all his *b.* in sickness

63. 6. when I remember thee upon my *b.* and

132. 3. nor go up into my *b.* till I find a place

Ps. 139. 8. if I make my *b.* in hell, thou art there

Prov. 7. 16. I have decked my *b.* with tapestry, 17.

22. 27. why should he take thy *b.* from under thee ?

26. 14. on hinges, so doth the slothful on his *b.*

Songs 3. 1. by night on *b.* I sought

9. Solomon made himself a *b.* of wood of Lebanon

Is. 28. 20. *b.* is shorter than

Matt. 9. 6. Jesus saith, take up thy *b.* and walk, *Mark* 2. 9, 11 ; *John* 5. 11, 12.

Mark 4. 21. a candle to be put under a *b. Luke* 8. 16.

Luke 11. 7. my children are with me in *b.* I cannot

17. 34. two men in one *b.* one taken

Heb. 13. 4. marriage *b.* undefiled

Rev. 2. 22. I will cast her on a *b.*

BED of spices, *Songs* 5. 13. his cheeks are as a *b. of spices,* as flowers

6. 2. my beloved is gone down to the *b. of spices*

BEDS, *Ps.* 149. 5. let the saints sing aloud on their *b.*

Is. 57. 2. they shall rest in their *b.* each one walking

Amos 6. 4. lie on *b.* of ivory, and stretch themselves

BEDSTEAD, *Deut.* 3. 11. king of Bashan, his *b.* was a *b.* of iron

BEFORE, in sight, *Gen.* 20. 15. & 43. 14 ; *Ex.* 22. 9 ; 1 *Kings* 17. 1. & 18. 15 ; 2 *Kings* 3. 14.—time in place ; *Gen.* 31. 2 ; *Job* 3. 24 ; *Josh.* 8. 10 ; *Luke* 22. 47 ; 2 *Chr.* 13. 14.—indignity, 2. *Sam.* 6. 21 ; *John* 1. 15, 27.

Gen. 24. 45. b. I had done speaking

31. 2. his countenance was not toward me as *b.*

48. 20. and he set Ephraim *b.* Manasseh

Ex. 16. 34. Aaron laid it up *b.* the testimony

Josh. 4. 18. Jordan flowed over his banks as *b.*

10. 14. there was no day like that *b.* it, or after it

Judg. 3. 2. at least such as *b.* knew nothing thereof

16. 20. said, I will go as *b.* and shake

2 *Sam.* 7. choose me *b.* thy father, and *b.* his house

10. 9. Joab saw the battle was against him *b.* and behind 1 *Chr.* 19. 10.

Job 3. 24. my sighing cometh *b.* I eat

10. 21. *b.* I go, whence I shall not return

Job 42. 10. Lord gave Job twice as much as he had *b.*

Ps. 31. 22. I am cut off from *b.* thine eyes

39. 13. spare me *b.* I go hence and be no more

119. 67. *b.* I was afflicted I went astray, but now

Is. 17. 14. and behold, *b.* the morning he is not

43. 13. *b.* the day was, I am he, and there is none

65. 24. that *b.* they call I will answer

and hear

Hos. 7. 2. their own doings, they are *b.* my face

Amos 4. 3. every cow at that which is *b.* her

Matt. 1. 18. *b.* they came together, she was with child

6. 8. knoweth what things ye need *b.* ye ask

8. 29. art thou come to torment us *b.* the time

John 6. 62. see the Son of man ascend where he was *b.*

7. 51. doth our law judge any man *b.* it hear him

13. 19. I tell you *b.* it come, 14. 29.

2 *Cor.* 8. 10. who have begun *b.* not only to do

Gal. 5. 21. of which I tell you *b.* as I told you

Phil. 3. 13. reaching forth to those things that are *b.*

Col. 1. 5. whereof ye heard *b.* in the word of truth

1 *Thess.* 2. 2. but even after that we had suffered *b.*

3. 4. when we were with you, we told you *b.*

1 *Tim.* 1. 13. who was *b.* a blasphemer, a persecutor

Heb. 7. 18. disannulling of the command going *b.*

10. 15. for after that he had said *b.* this is covenant

Rev. 3. 9. make them to worship *b.* thy feet

4. 6. were four beasts, full of eyes *b.* and behind

BEFORE, come, *Ps.* 100. 2. *come b.* his presence with thanksgiving

Mic. 6. 6. wherewithal shall I *come b.* the Lord

2 *Tim.* 4. 21. do thy diligence to *come b.* winter

BEFORE the people, *Gen.* 23. 12. Abraham bowed *b. the people* of the land

Josh. 8. 10. Joshua and elders went *b. the people* to Ai

1 *Sam.* 18. 13. he went out, and came in *b. the people*

Rev. 10. 11. thou must prophesy *b.* many *people*

BEFORE whom, *Gen.* 24. 40. Lord *b. whom* I walk will send his angel

Esth. 6. 13. Mordecai, *b. whom* thou hast begun to fall

Acts 26. 26. the king *b. whom* also I

BEFOREHAND, *Mark* 13. 11. take no thought *b.* what ye speak

2 *Cor.* 9. 5. go and make up *b.* your bounty

1 *Tim.* 5. 24. some men's sins are open *b.*

25. the good works of some are manifest *b.*

1 *Pet.* 1. 11. testified *b.* the sufferings of Christ

BEFORETIME, 1 *Sam.* 9. 9. *b.* in Israel when a man went ; he who is called a prophet was *b.* called a seer

2 *Sam.* 7. 10. nor afflict them any more as *b.*

2 *Kings* 13. 5. Israel dwelt in their tents as *b.*

Neh. 2. 1. I had not been *b.* sad in his

presence

Is. 41. 26. who hath declared *b.* that we may say

Acts 8. 9. called Simon, which *b.* used sorcery

BEGAN, *Gen.* 4. 26. then *b.* men to call on the name of Lord

1 *Sam.* 14. 35. that altar he *b.* to build to the Lord

2 *Kings* 10. 32. the Lord *b.* to cut Israel short

2 *Chr.* 20. 22. when they *b.* to sing, the Lord set

34. 3. while young Josiah *b.* to seek after God

Matt. 4. 17. from that time Jesus *b.* to preach and say

Mark 14. 72. he *b.* to weep when he thought

Luke 1. 70. which have been since the world *b.*

14. 30. this man *b.* to build and was not able

John 4. 52. inquired the hour when he *b.* to amend

9. 32. since the world *b. Acts* 3. 21 ; *Rom.* 16. 25.

2 *Tim.* 1. 9. in Christ before the world *b. Tit.* 1. 2.

Heb. 2. 3. salvation at first *b.* to be spoken by the Lord

BEGAT, *Prov.* 23. 22. hearken to thy father that *b.* thee

Jer. 16. 3. concerning their fathers that *b.* them

Zech. 13. 3. his father and mother that *b.* him

Jam. 1. 18. of his own will *b.* he us with the word

1 *John* 5. 1. every one that loveth him that *b.* loveth

BEGET, EST, ETH, *Gen.* 17. 20. twelve princes shall he *b.* I will make

Gen. 48. 6. issue which thou *b.* shall be thine

Deut. 4. 25. when thou shalt *b.* children

28. 41. thou shalt *b.* sons, but shalt not enjoy them

2 *Kings* 20. 18. of thy sons which thou shalt *b.* shall they take and make eunuchs, *Is.* 39. 7.

Eccl. 6. 3. if a man *b.* 100 children, and live many

Ezek. 18. 10. if he *b.* a son that is a robber

Is. 45. 10. that saith to his father what *b.* thou ?

Prov. 17. 21. he that *b.* a fool, doeth it to his sorrow

23. 24. he that *b.* a wise child shall have joy

BEG, begged, *Ps.* 109. 10. let his children be vagabonds and *b.*

Prov. 20. 4. therefore shall the sluggard *b.* in harvest

Matt. 27. 58. and *b.* the body of Jesus, *Luke* 23. 52.

Luke 16. 3. I cannot dig, to *b.* I am ashamed

John 9. 8. is not this he that sat and *b.*

BEGGAR, LY, ING, 1 *Sam.* 2. 8. he lifteth the *b.* from the dunghill

Ps. 37. 25. I have not seen his seed *b.* bread

Mark 10. 46. Bartimeus sat *b. Luke* 18. 35.

Luke 16. 20. and there was a *b*. named
    Lazarus
    22. the *b*. died, and was carried by
    the angels
Gal. 4. 9. how turn ye again to the *b*.
    elements

BEGIN, *Gen.* 11. 6. this they *b*. to do,
    and now nothing
Deut. 2. 25. this day I *b*. to put the
    dread of you
Josh. 3. 7. this day will I *b*. to magnify
    thee
1 Sam. 3. 12. when I *b*. will also make
    an end
Luke 3. 8. and *b*. not to say within
    yourselves
    13. 26. then shall ye *b*. to say, we
    have eaten
    14. 29. all that behold it, *b*. to mock
2 Cor. 3. 1. do we *b*. again to commend
    ourselves
1 Pet. 4. 17. the time is come, that
    judgment must *b*. at the house of
    God, and if it first *b*. at us

BEGINNING, (1) That which is the
    first, *Ex.* 12. 2. (2) The creation,
    Gen. 1. 1. (3) At the first, *Prov.* 20.
    21 ; *Is.* 1. 26. (4) That which is
    chief or most excellent ; *Prov.* 1.
    7 ; 9. 10.
Rev. 1. 8. I am. the *b*. and ending. I
    am the eternal God, and gave all
    things a being and *b*.
Gen. 49. 3. *b*. of strength, *Deut.* 21. 17.
Ex. 12. 2. *b*. of months
Job 8. 7. though thy *b*. was small, yet
    thy end increase
    42. 12. blessed the latter end of Job
    more than *b*.
Ps. 111. 10. fear of Lord is *b*. of wisdom,
    Prov. 1. 7. & 9. 10.
Prov. 17. 14. *b*. of strife, as when one
    letteth out water
Eccl. 7. 8. better is end than *b*.
    10. 13. the *b*. of words of his mouth
    is foolishness
Matt. 14. 30. *b*. to sink he cried, Lord,
    save me
    24. 8. these are *b*. of sorrows
    21. tribulation, such as was not since
    the *b*.
Luke 24. 47. among all nations *b*. at
    Jerusalem
John 2. 11. this *b*. of miracles did Jesus
    in Cana
    8. 9. went out, *b*. at the eldest even
    to the last
Col. 1. 18. who is *b*. and first-born
Heb. 3. 14. if we hold the *b*. of our con-
    fidence
Heb. 7. 3. neither *b*. of days nor end
2 Pet. 2. 20. latter end worse than *b*.
Rev. 1. 8. I am Alpha and Omega, *b*.
    and ending, 21. 6. & 22. 13.
    3. 14. saith *b*. of creation of God
BEGINNING, (at the) *Prov.* 20. 21. an
    inheritance gotten hastily *at the b*.
Is. 1. 26. I will restore thy counsellors
    as *at the b*.
Dan. 9. 23. *at the b*. of thy supplica-
    tions the command
John 16. 4. these things I said not to
    you *at the b*.
Acts 11. 15. Holy Ghost fell on them as

on us *at the b*.
BEGINNING (from the) *Deut.* 11. 12.
    eyes of Lord are on it *from the b*. of
    the year
Prov. 8. 23. I was set up *from b*. or
    ever the earth was
Is. 18. 2. go to a people terrible *from
    the b*. 7.
Is. 40. 21. hath it not been told you *from
    the b*.
    48. 16. I have not spoken in secret
    from the b.
John 6. 64. Jesus knew *from the b*. who
    believed not
    8. 44. was a murderer *from b*. and
    abode not in truth
Eph. 3. 9. which *from b*. of the world
    hath been hid
2 Thess. 2. 13. God hath *from b*. chosen
    you to salvation
2 Pet. 3. 4. all continue as they were
    from the b.
John 2. 7. word which we have heard
    from b. 3. 11.
    3. 8. is of the devil, for the devil sin-
    neth *from the b*.
BEGINNING, (in the) *Gen.* 1. 1. *in the
    b*. God created the heaven and
    earth
Prov. 8. 22. the Lord possessed me *in
    the b*. of his way
John 1. 1. *in the b*. was the Word, Word
    was with God
Phil. 4. 15. we know that *in the b*. of
    the gospel
Heb. 1. 10. thou Lord *in the b*. hast laid
    foundation
BEGOTTEN, drops of dew, *Job* 38. 28.
Judg. 8. 30. Gideon had 70 sons of his
    body *b*.
Ps. 2. 7. this day have I *b*. thee, *Acts*
    13. 33 ; *Heb.* 1. 5 ; 5. 5.
Is. 49. 21. thou shalt say, who hath *b*.
    me these ?
John 1. 14. only *b*. of Father, 18.
    3. 16. sent his only *b*. Son, 18.
1 Cor. 4. 15. have *b*. you through gospel
Phil. 10. I have *b*. in my bonds
1 Pet. 1. 3. *b*. us again to lively hope
1 John 4. 9. sent only *b*. Son—live
    5. 1. loveth him that is *b*.
FIRST-BEGOTTEN, *Heb.* 1. 6. when
    he bringeth in *first-b*. into world
Rev. 1. 5. from Jesus, who is the *first-b*.
    of the dead
BEGUILE, *Col.* 2. 4. lest any man *b*.
    you with enticing words
Col. 2. 18. let no man *b*. you of your re-
    ward
BEGUILED, ING, *Gen.* 3. 13. woman
    said, serpent *b*. me, and I did eat
    29. 25. wherefore then hast thou *b*.
    me ?
Num. 25. 18. they have *b*. you in the
    matter of Peor
Josh. 9. 22. saying, wherefore have ye *b*.
    us
2 Cor. 11. 8. but I fear lest as the ser-
    pent *b*. Eve
2 Pet. 2. 14. cannot cease from sin, *b*.
    unstable souls
BEGUN, *Num.* 16. 46. the plague is *b*.
    47. the plague was *b*.
Deut. 3. 24. thou hast *b*. to show thy

greatness

2 *Cor.* 8. 6. as he had *b.* so also would he finish

10. this is expedient for you who have *b.* before

Gal. 3. 3. having *b.* in spirit

Phil. 1. 6. hath *b.* a good work in

1 *Tim.* 5. 11. when they have *b.* to wax wanton

BEHALF, *Ex.* 27. 21. a statute on *b.* of the children of Israel

2 *Sam.* 3. 12. Abner sent to David on his *b.*

2 *Chr.* 16. 9. show himself strong in *b.* of them

Rom. 16. 19. I am· glad therefore on your *b.*

1 *Cor.* 1. 4. I thank my God always on your *b.*

2 *Cor.* 1. 11. thanks may be given by many on your *b.*

5. 12. but give you occasion to glory on our *b.*

Phil. 1. 29. to you it is given in *b.* of Christ, not only

1 *Pet.* 4. 16. let him glorify God on this *b.*

BEHAVE myself wisely, *Ps.* 101. 2.

Ps. 131. 2. 1 *b.* myself as a child

1 *Cor.* 13. 5. charity doth not *b.* itself unseemly

1 *Tim.* 3. 15. how thou oughtest to *b.* in the house of God

BEHAVED, 1 *Sam.* 18. 5. David *b.* himself wisely, 14. 15, 30.

Ps. 35. 14. I *b.* as though he had been my friend

131. 2. I have *b.* myself as a child that is weaned

1 *Thess.* 2. 10. how unblameably we *b.*

2 *Thess.* 3. 7. *b.* not ourselves disorderly among you

BEHAVIOUR, 1 *Sam.* 21. 13. David changed his *b.* before them

1 *Tim.* 3. 2. a bishop must be sober, of good *b.*

Tit. 2. 3. aged women in *b.* as becometh holiness

BEHEADED, 2. *Sam.* 4. 7. they smote Ish-bosheth, and *b.* him

Matt. 14. 10. *b.* John, *Mark* 6. 16, 27 ; *Luke* 9. 9.

Rev. 20. 4. I saw the souls of them that were *b.*

BEHELD not iniquity in Jacob, *Num.* 23. 21.

Ps. 119. 158. I *b.* transgressors and was grieved

Is. 41. 28. I *b.* and there was no man, *Jer.* 4. 25.

Luke 10. 18. I *b.* Satan fall like lightning

John 1. 14. we *b.* his glory as the glory

Acts 1. 9. they *b.* Jesus was taken up

17. 23. as I passed by and *b.* your devotions

Rev. 5. 6. I *b.* and lo ! in the midst of the throne a Lamb

Rev. 11. 12. their enemies *b.* them

BEHIND, *Lev.* 25. 51 ; *Judg.* 20. 40.

Ex. 10. 26. not an hoof left *b.*

1 *Sam.* 30. 9. where those that were left *b.* stayed

1 *Kings* 14. 9. hast cast me *b.* thy back,

Ezek. 23. 35.

Neh. 4. 16. the rulers were *b.* the house of Judah

9. 26. cast law *b.* their backs

Ps. 139. 5. beset me *b.* and before

Is. 38. 17. cast sins *b.* the back

Luke 2. 43. the child Jesus tarried *b.* in Jerusalem

1 *Cor.* 1. 7. ye come *b.* in no gift

2 *Cor.* 11. 5. I was not a whit *b.* the chiefest, 12. 11.

Phil. 3. 13. forgetting things *b.*

Col. 1. 24. fill up what *b.* of afflictions

BEHOLD, (1) Admiration, *Is.* 7. 14. (2) Joy and gladness, *Matt.* 21. 5. (3) Obedience, 1 *Sam.* 22. 12 ; *Is.* 6. 8. (4) Asseveration, *Gen.* 28. 15. (5) Exhortation to a provident care, *John* 19. 27. (6) Consideration or observation, *Luke* 24. 39 ; *John* 1. 29. (7) Suddenness or unexpectedness, *Rev.* 16. 15 ; 22. 7. (8) Certainty, *Matt.* 23. 38 ; *Luke* 1. 20.

Gen. 28. 15. *b.* I am with thee, and will keep thee

48. 1. *b.* thy father is sick ; 21. Israel said, *b.* I die

Ex. 3. 2. and *b.* the bush burned with

Job 28. 28. *b.* the fear of the Lord, that is

33. 12. *b.* in this thou art not just, I will answer

40. 4. *b.* I am vile, what shall I answer thee ?

Ps. 33. 18. *b.* eye of the Lord is on them that fear

51. 5. *b.* I was shapen in iniquity, and in sin did

Is. 7. 14. *b.* a virgin shall conceive, *Matt.* 1. 23.

12. 2. *b.* God is my salvation, I will trust, and not

29. 8. a hungry man dreameth, and *b.* he eateth

Is. 40. 9. say to the cities of Judah, *b.* your God

65. 1. I said, *b.* me, *b.* me, to a nation

Job 19. 27. my eyes shall *b.* and not

Ps. 11. 4. his eyes *b.* his eyelids try

7. countenance *b.* upright

17. 15. I will *b.* thy face in right

27. 4. desired to *b.* beauty of L.

37. 37. *b.* the upright man

113. 6. humbles himself to *b.*

Eccl. 11. 7. pleasant it is to *b.* sun

Lam. 1. 12. *b.* and see if any sorrow be like my sorrow

Hab. 1. 13. of purer eyes than to *b.*

Zech. 3. 8. *b.* I will bring my servant the branch

9. 9. *b.* thy King cometh, *Matt.* 21. 5. *John* 12. 15.

Mal. 3. 1. *b.* I will send my messenger, 4. 5 ; *Matt.* 11. 10 ; *Mark* 1. 2.

Matt. 7. 4. and *b.* a beam is in thine own eye

Matt. 18. 10. their angels *b.* face of

Mark 16. 6. is risen, *b.* the place where they laid him

Luke 24. 39. *b.* my hands and my feet

John 1. 29. *b.* the Lamb of God, which taketh, 36.

47. *b.* an Israelite indeed, in whom is no guile

17. 24. that may *b.* my glory

19. 5. Pilate saith unto them, *b.* the man

Acts 9. 11. Saul of Tar. for *b.* he prayeth

2 *Cor.* 6. 9. as dying, and *b.* we live as

1 *Pet.* 3. 2. *b.* your chaste conversation

1 *John* 3. 1. *b.* what manner of love the

Rev. 3. 20. *b.* I stand at the door and knock

16. 15. *b.* I come as a thief, blessed is

22. 7. *b.* I come quickly, blessed is he that keeps, 12.

BEHOLD, now, *Matt.* 26. 65. now *b.* ye have heard his blasphemy

Acts 13. 11. now *b.* the hand of the Lord is on thee

20. 22. now *b.* I go bound in the spirit to Jerusalem

2 *Cor.* 6. 2. *b.* now is the accepted time, *b.* now is day

BEHOLD, (verb) *Job* 19. 27. mine eyes shall *b.* and not another

Ps. 11. 4. his eyes *b.* his eye-lids try the children

17. 15. I will *b.* thy face in righteousness

27. 4. to *b.* the beauty of the Lord and inquire

37. 37. mark the perfect man, *b.* the

119. 18. open thou mine eyes, that I may *b.*

Eccl. 11. 7. and a pleasant thing it is to *b.* the sun

Is. 41. 23. do good or evil, that we may *b.* it together

63. 15. *b.* from the habitation of thy holiness

Lam. 1. 18. hear all people, and *b.* my sorrow

5. 1. O Lord, consider and *b.* our reproach

Matt. 18. 10. their angels alway *b.* face of my father

Luke 14. 29. all that *b.* it begin to mock

Acts 7. 31. as he drew near to *b.* it, the voice came

2 *Cor.* 3. 7. Israel could not *b.* the face of Moses

1 *Pet.* 2. 12. your good works which they shall *b.*

BEHOLDETH, *Jam.* 1. 24. for he *b.* himself and goeth his way

BEHOLDING, *Ps.* 119. 37. turn away mine eyes from *b.* vanity

Prov. 15. 3. Lord in every place *b.* the evil and good

Eccl. 5. 11. saving *b.* of them with eyes

Matt. 27. 55. many women were there *b.* *Luke* 23. 49.

Mark 10. 21. Jesus *b.* him, loved him, and said

2 *Cor.* 3. 18. with open face *b.* as in a glass the glory

Col. 2. 5. with you in spirit joying, and *b.* your order

Jam. 1. 23. a man *b.* his natural face in

BELIAL, devil, furious and obstinate in wickedness, *Deut.* 13. 13 ; *Judg.* 19. 22. & 20. 13 ; 1 *Sam.* 1. 16. & 2. 12. & 10. 27. & 25. 17, 25. & 30. 22 ; 2 *Sam.* 16. 7. & 20. 1. & 23. 6 ; 1 *Kings* 21. 10, 13 ; 2 *Chr.* 13. 7 ; 2 *Cor.* 6. 15.

BELIEVE, (1) To give credit to any thing, *Gen.* 45. 26. (2) To assent merely to gospel truths, *Acts* 8. 13. (3) To receive, depend, and rely upon Christ for life and salvation, *John* 1. 12 ; 3. 15, 16 ; *Rom.* 9. 33 ; 10. 4. (4) To be fully persuaded, *John* 6. 69. (5) To expect, or hope, *Ps.* 27. 13. (6) To put confidence in, 2 *Chr.* 20. 20. (7) To know, *John* 17. 21 ; *Jam.* 2. 19.

BELIEVE, *Ex.* 4. 5. that they may *b.* the Lord hath appeared

19. 9. that they may hear and *b.* thee for ever

2 *Chr.* 20. 20. *b.* in the Lord God, *b.* his prophets

Matt. 9. 28. *b.* ye that I am able to do this

Matt. 18. 6. but who so shall offend one of these little ones which *b.* in me, *Mark* 9. 42.

21. 32. repented not afterward that ye might *b.* him

27. 42. let him come down, and we will *b.* him

Mark 1. 15. repent ye and *b.* the gospel

5. 36. he saith, be not afraid, only *b.* *Luke* 8. 50.

9. 23. if thou canst *b.* all things are possible

24. Lord, I *b.* help mine unbelief, *John* 9. 38.

16. 17. these signs shall follow them which *b.*

Luke 8. 12. devil taketh away the word, lest they *b.*

13. these have no root, which for a while *b.*

24. 25. O fools, and slow of heart to *b.*

John 1. 7. that all men through him might *b.*

12. sons of God, even to them that *b.* on his name

5. 44. how can ye *b.* which receive honour one of

7. 39. Spirit, which they that *b.* on him should receive

9. 35. dost thou *b.* on the Son of God

11. 15. I was not there to the intent ye may *b.*

40. said I not to thee, if wouldst *b.* thou shouldst

48. if we let him alone, all men will *b.* on him

12. 36. while ye have light *b.* in the

13. 19. when it is come to pass ye may *b.* I am he

14. 1. not troubled, ye *b.* in God, *b.* also in me

16. 30. by this we *b.* thou camest forth from God

31. Jesus answered, do ye now *b.* ?

17. 20. I pray for them also which shall *b.* on me

Acts 8. 37. I *b.* that Jesus Christ is the Son of God

13. 39. by him all that *b.* are justified

15. 11. we *b.* through grace we shall be saved, as they

16. 31. *b.* on the Lord Jesus Christ, and thou shalt be saved

Rom. 3. 22. righteousness of God on all them that *b.*

4. 11. he might be father of all them that *b.*

24. to whom it shall be imputed, if we *b*. on him

10. 9. and shall *b*. in thy heart that God raised him

Rom. 10. 14. how shall they *b*. in him of whom not heard

Gal. 3. 22. promise might be given to them that *b*.

Eph. 1. 19. the greatness of his power to us who *b*.

Phil. 1. 29. to us it is given not only to *b*. or. him

1 *Thess*. 1. 7. ensamples to all that *b*. in Macedonia

     2. 10. we behaved ourselves among you that *b*.

     4. 14. if we *b*. that Jesus died and rose again

2 *Thess*. 1. 10. come to be admired in all those that *b*.

     2. 11. send delusion that they should *b*. a lie

1 *Tim*. 4. 10. Saviour of all men, especially of those that *b*.

Heb. 10. 39. but of them that *b*. to saving of the soul

     11. 6. he that cometh to God must *b*. that he is

Jam. 2. 19. the devils also *b*. and trem.

1 *Pet*. 1. 21. who by him do *b*. in God that raised him

     2. 7. to you therefore which *b*. he is

1 *John* 3. 23. is his commandment that we should *b*.

BELIEVE not or not **BELIEVE,** *Prov*. 26. 25. when he speaketh fair, *b*. him *not*

Is. 7. 9. if ye will *not b*. ye shall not be established

Jer. 12. 6. *b*. *not* them though they speak fair words

John 3. 12. if I told earthly things, and ye *b*. *not*

     4. 48. except ye see signs and wonders ye will *not b*.

     5. 38. for whom he hath sent, him ye *b*. *not*

     6. 36. I said to you, ye also have seen me and *b*. *not*

     8. 24. if ye *b*. *not* that I am he, ye shall die in sins

     12. 39. they could *not b*. because Isaiah said again

     20. 25. thrust my hand into his side, I will *not b*.

Rom. 3. 3. what if some did *not b*. shall unbelief

     15. 31. I may be delivered from them that do *not b*.

2 *Tim*. 2. 13. if we *b*. *not* he abideth faithful

1 *John* 4. 1. *b*. *not* every spirit, but try the spirits

BELIEVED, *Ps*. 27. 13. I had fainted unless I had *b*. to see

Ps. 106. 12. then *b*. they his words, they 116. 10. I *b*. therefore have I spoken, 2 *Cor*. 4. 13.

Is. 53. 1. who hath *b*. our report, to whom arm of the Lord revealed ? *John* 12. 38 ; *Rom*. 10. 16.

John 2. 11. his glory, and his disciples *b*. on him

     4. 50. the man *b*. the word that Jesus had spoken

     53. the father himself *b*. and his whole

5. 46. had ye *b*. Moses, ye would have *b*. me

     7. 48. have any of rulers or Pharisees *b*. on him

     16. 27. the Father loveth you, because you have *b*.

Acts 2. 44. all that *b*. were together

     4. 4. many which heard the word *b*.

     32. multitude of them that *b*. were of one heart

     8. 12. but when they *b*. Philip preaching things

     13. then Simon himself *b*. also and was baptized

     11. 21. a great number *b*. and turned to the Lord

     13. 48. as many as were ordained to eternal life *b*.

     18. 8. Crispus chief ruler of the synagogue *b*. on Lord

     27. helped them much which had *b*. through grace

Rom. 4. 18. who against hope *b*. in hope, might

     13. 11. our salvation is nearer than when we *b*.

1 *Cor*. 3. 5. but ministers by whom ye *b*. as the Lord

     11. whether I or they, so we preach, and so ye *b*.

Eph. 1. 13. in whom after ye *b*. ye were

1 *Tim*. 3. 16. *b*. on in the world, received up into glory

2 *Tim*. 1. 12. for I know whom I have *b*. he is able

Heb. 4. 3. we which have *b*. do enter into rest

1 *John* 4. 16. we have *b*. the love of God

BELIEVED not, or not BELIEVED, *Gen*. 45. 26. Jacob's heart fainted, he *b*. them *not*

Deut. 9. 23. rebelled, and *b*. him *not* nor hearkened

Job 29. 24. if I laughed on them, they *b*. it *not*

Ps. 78. 22. because they *b*. *not* in God,

Matt. 21. 32. John came unto you, and ye *b*. him *not*

Mark 16. 11. when they had heard he was alive, *b*. *not*

John 3. 18. condemned already, because he had *not b*.

     12. 37. had done so many miracles, yet they *b*. *not*

Acts 9. 26. afraid, and *b*. *not* that he was a disciple

     17. 5. the Jews which *b*. *not* moved with envy

Rom. 10. 14. how call on him in whom they have *not b*.

     11. 31. even so have these also now *not b*.

BELIEVERS, *Acts* 5. 14. *b*. were the more added to the Lord

1 *Tim*. 4. 12. but be thou an example of the *b*.

BELIEVEST, *Luke* 1. 20. be dumb because thou *b*. not my words

John 1. 50. I saw thee under the figtree, *b*. thou ?

     11. 26. believeth in me, never die, *b*. thou this ?

     14. 10. *b*. thou not that I am in the

Acts 8. 37. if thou *b.* with all thine heart
26. 27. *b.* thou the prophets ? I know
thou *b.*
Jam. 2. 19. thou *b.* that there is one
God, thou dost
BELIEVETH, *Is.* 28. 16. he that *b.* shall
not make haste
Mark 9. 23. all things are possible to
him that *b.*
16. 16. he that *b.* and is baptized,
shall be saved, but he that *b.* not
John 3. 15. whoso *b.* in him should not
perish, 16.
18. he that *b.* on him is not condemned, but he that *b.* not is condemned already
36. he that *b.* hath everlasting life,
6. 47.
5. 24. *b.* on him that sent me hath
everlasting life
6. 35. he that *b.* on me shall never
thirst
40. he that seeth the Son and *b.* on
him hath life
7. 38. he that *b.* on me, out of his
belly shall flow
11. 25. he that *b.* though he were
dead, yet shall he live
26. whosoever liveth and *b.* in me
shall never die
12. 46. whose *b.* on me, should not
abide in darkness
Acts 10. 43. who *b.* in him receive remission of sins
Rom. 1. 16. it is the power of God to
every one that *b.*
3. 26. and the justifier of him that *b.*
on Jesus
Rom. 4. 5. but to him that worketh not,
but *b.* on him
9. 33. whoso *b.* on him shall not be
ashamed, 10. 11.
10. 4. Christ is the end of law to every
one that *b.*
10. for with the heart man *b.* to
righteousness
14. 2. for one *b.* that he may eat all
things
1 *Cor.* 7. 12. if any brother hath a wife
that *b.* not
13. 7. love *b.* all things, hopeth all
things, endureth
14. 24. and there come in one that
b. not
2 *Cor.* 6. 15. what part hath he that *b.*
with infidel
1 *Pet.* 2. 6. he that *b.* shall not be confounded
1 *John* 5. 1. whoso *b.* Jesus is the Christ,
is of God
5. who is he that overcometh, but he
that *b.*
BELIEVING, *Matt.* 21. 22. ask in prayer, *b.* ye shall receive
John 20. 27. said to Thomas, be not
faithless but *b.*
31. that *b.* ye might have life through
his name
Acts 16. 34. rejoiced, *b.* in God with all
his house
Rom. 15. 13. fill you with all joy and
peace in *b.*
1 *Pet.* 1. 8. yet *b.* ye rejoice with joy
unspeakable

BELLOWS, *Jer.* 6. 29. the *b.* are burnt,
the lead is consumed
BELLY, (1) That part of the body
which contains the bowels, *Mat.*
15. 17. (2) The womb, *Jer.* 1. 5.
(3) The entrails, *Rev.* 10. 9, 10. (4)
The heart, *John* 7. 38. (5) The
whole man, *Tit.* 1. 12. (6) Carnal pleasure, *Rom.* 16. 18.
Gen. 3. 14. on thy *b.* shalt thou go, and
dust eat
Lev. 11. 42. goeth on the *b.* be an
abomination
Num. 5. 21. thy thigh to rot, and thy
b. to swell
Num. 25. 8. thrust man of Israel and
woman through the *b.*
Deut. 28. 11. plenteous in the fruit of
thy *b.*
Judg. 3. 21. the dagger, and he thrust
it into his *b.*
1 *Kings* 7. 20. had pomegranates over
against the *b.*
Job 3. 11. give up the ghost when I
came out of the *b.*
Job 15. 2. and fill his *b.* with the east
wind
35. bring vanity, and their *b.* pre-
pareth deceit
19. 17. intreated for children's sake
of my *b.*
20. 20. surely he shall not feel quietness in his *b.*
23. when about to fill his *b.* God
32. 18. the spirit of my *b.* constraineth me
19. my *b.* as wine hath no vent
Psal. 17. 14. whose *b.* thou fi'lest with
thy hid treasures
22. 10. thou art my God from my
mother's *b.*
44. 25. our *b.* cleaveth to earth
Prov. 13. 25. but the *b.* of the wicked
shall want
18. 8. go into innermost parts of the
b. 26. 22.
20. 27. searching all the inward parts
of the *b.*
Songs 5. 14. his *b.* is as bright ivory
overlaid with
7. 2. thy *b.* is like a heap of wheat
Is. 46. 3. borne by me from the *b.*
Jer. 1. 5. before I formed thee in the
b. I knew thee
Dan. 2. 32. this image's *b.* and thighs
of brass
Jonah 1. 17. Jonah was in *b.* of the fish,
Matt. 12. 40.
2. 2. out of the *b.* of hell cried I, and
thou heardst
Hab. 3. 16. when I heard, my *b.* trembled, my lips
Matt. 15. 17. whatsoever entereth in at
the mouth goeth into the *b.* and is
cast out, *Mark* 7. 19.
Luke 15. 16. fain have filled his *b.* with
the husks
John 7. 38. out of his *b.* shall flow rivers
Rom. 16. 18. they serve not our Lord,
but their own *b.*
1 *Cor.* 6: 13. meats for the *b.* and *b.* for
meats
Phil. 3. 9. whose God is their *b.* and
Rev. 10. 9. eat it up, and it shall make

thy *b.* bitter

BELLIES, *Tit.* 1. 12. the Cretians are always liars, slow *b.*

BELIED, *Jer.* 5. 12. they have *b.* the Lord, and said, it is not

BELONG, *Gen.* 40. 8. do not interpretations *b.* to God ?

Deut. 29. 29. secret things *b.* to God, revealed *b.*

Ps. 47. 9. for the shields of the earth *b.* to God

68. 20. to our God *b.* the issues from

Prov. 24. 23. these things also *b.* to the

Dan. 9. 9. to Lord our God *b.* mercies

Mark 9. 41. in my name, because ye *b.* to Christ

Luke 19. 42. things which *b.* to thy peace

1 *Cor.* 7. 32. careth for things that *b.* to the Lord

BELONGED, ETH, ING, *Num.* 7. 9. the service of the sanctuary *b.* to them

Deut. 32. 35. to me *b.* vengeance and recompense, *Ps.* 94. 1 ; *Heb.* 10. 30.

Ruth 2. 3. to light on a part of a field *b.* to Boaz

Ps. 3. 8. salvation *b.* unto the Lord

62. 11. twice have I heard, power *b.* unto God

12. also unto thee, O Lord, *b.* mercy

Prov. 26. 17. meddleth with strife, *b.* not to him

Dan. 9. 7. O Lord, righteousness *b.* to thee

8. to us *b.* confusion of face, to our

Luke 9. 10. he went into a desert *b.* to Bethsaida

23. 7. as he knew he *b.* to Herod's jurisdiction

Heb. 5. 14. strong meat *b.* to them of full age

BELOVED is applied, (1) To Christ, *Matt.* 3. 17 ; *Mark* 1. 11 ; 9. 7. (2) To the church, *Jer.* 11. 15 ; *Rom.* 9. 25. (3) To particular saints, *Neh.* 13. 26 ; *Dan.* 9. 23. (4) To wife and children, *Deut.* 21. 15 ; *Hos.* 9. 16, (5) To the New Jerusalem, *Rev.* 20. 9.

Deut. 21. 15. two wives, the one *b.* the other hated

33. 12. the *b.* of the Lord shall dwell in safety

Neh. 13. 26. Solomon, who was *b.* of his God

Ps. 60. 5. that thy *b.* may be delivered, 108. 6.

127. 2. for so he giveth his *b.* sleep

Prov. 4. 3. and only *b.* in the sight of my mother

Songs 5. 1. eat, O friends, drink abundantly, O *b.*

6. 1. whither is thy *b.* gone, O fairest

8. 5. who is this that cometh leaning on her *b.*

Dan. 9. 23. for thou art greatly *b.* 10. 11, 19.

Acts 15. 25. chosen men with *b.* Barnabas and Paul

Rom. 1. 7. to all that are in Rome, *b.* of God

9. 25. I will call her *b.* which was not *b.*

11. 28. they are *b.* for Father's sake

Eph. 1. 6. he hath made us accepted

the *b.*

6. 21. Tychicus a *b.* brother and minister, *Col.* 4. 7.

Col. 3. 12. put on as the elect of God, holy and *b.*

4. 9. with Onesimus, a faithful and *b.* brother

14. Luke the *b.* physician and Demas greet you

1 *Thess.* 1. 4. knowing *b.* your election of God

Philem. 16. above a servant, a brother *b.*

2 *Pet.* 3. 8. *b.* be not ignorant of this one thing

15. even as our *b.* brother Paul hath written

1 *John* 3. 2. *b.* now we the sons of God

21. *b.* if our heart condemn us not

4. 7. *b.* let us love one another, for love is of God

11. *b.* if God so loved us, we ought also to love

BELOVED, (my) *Songs* 1. 14. my *b.* is to me a cluster of camphire

16. behold thou art fair, my *b.* yea

2. 3. as the apple-tree, so is my *b.* among the sons

16. my *b.* is mine, and I am his, he feedeth, 6. 3.

4. 16. let my *b.* come into his garden and eat

5. 2. it is the voice of my *b.* that knocketh, 2. 8.

6. 2. my *b.* is gone : 3. I am my *b.* and my *b.* mine, 7. 10.

Is. 5. 1. a song of my *b.* touching his vineyard

Matt. 3. 17. this is my *b.* Son, 17. 5 ; *Mark* 1. 11 ; 9. 7 ; *Luke* 3. 22 ; 9. 35 ; 2 *Pet.* 1. 17.

12. 18. behold my *b.* in whom my soul is pleased

Luke 20. 13. I will send my *b.* son

1 *Cor.* 4. 14. as my *b.* sons I warn you

BEMOAN, ED, ING, *Job* 42. 11. they *b.* Job, and comforted him

Jer. 15. 5. who shall *b.* thee, O Jerusalem

22. 10. weep ye not for the dead, nor *b.* him

31. 18. I have surely heard Ephraim *b.* himself

Nah. 3. 7. Nineveh is laid waste, who will *b.* her

BENCHES, *Ezek.* 27. 6. the Ashurites made thy *b.* of ivory

BEND, *Ps.* 11. 2. for lo! the wicked *b.* their bow

Jer. 9. 3. they *b.* their tongue like a bow for lies

Jer. 50. 14. all ye that *b.* the bow shoot at her

51. 3. against him that bendeth, let the archer *b.*

Ezek. 17. 7. behold, this vine did *b.* her roots

BENDETH, ING, *Ps.* 58. 7. when he *b.* his bow to shoot arrows

Is. 60. 14. that afflicted thee shall come *b.* to thee

Jer. 51. 3. against him that *b.* let the archer bend

BENEATH, *Ex.* 20. 4. or that is in the earth *b.* Deut. 5. 8.

Deut. 4. 39. on the earth *b.* there is

33. 13. blessed, for the deep that coucheth b.

Job. 18. 16. his roots shall be dried up b.

Prov. 15. 24. that ye may depart from hell b.

Is. 14. 9. hell from b. is moved for thee
51. 6. lift up your eyes, look on the earth b.

Jer. 31. 37. foundations be searched b.

John 8. 23. ye are from b. I am from above

BENEFIT, S, (1) The gifts and favours of God to men, 2 *Chr.* 32. 25 ; *Ps.* 68. 19. (2) The favour of God to others, 2 *Cor.* 1. 15; *Philem.* 14. (3) God's righteous acts, 1 *Sam.* 12. 7. (4) Salvation, 1 *Tim.* 6. 2. (5) Favour, grace, or spiritual blessings, *Ps.* 103. 2. (6) To profit or do good, *Jer.* 18. 10.

2 *Chr.* 32. 25. Hezekiah rendered not according to b.

Ps. 68. 19. Lord who daily loadeth us with b.
103. 2. bless the Lord, and forget not all his b.
116. 12. what shall I render to Lord for all his b. ?

Jer. 18. 10. repent of good, wherewith I b. them

2 *Cor.* 1. 15. that you might have a second b.

1 *Tim.* 6. 2. faithful and beloved partakers of the b.

Philem. 14. that thy b. should not be of necessity

BENEVOLENCE, due, 1 *Cor.* 7. 3.

BEREAVE, *Jer.* 15. 7. I will b. them of children, 18. 21.

Ezek. 5. 17. evil beasts shall b. thee

Hos. 9. 12. bring up children, yet will I b. them

BEREAVED, *Gen.* 42. 36. Jacob said, me ye have b. of my children

Gen. 43. 14. if I be b. of my children, I am b.

Hos. 13. 8. I will meet thee as a bear b. of her whelps

BERRIES, *Is.* 17. 6. two or three b. in the top of the bough

Jam. 3. 12. can the fig-tree bear olive b. a vine figs

BERYL, *Dan.* 10. 6. his body also was like the b. and face

Rev. 21. 20. eighth foundation was b. ninth a topaz

BESEECH, *Ex.* 33. 18. he said, I b. thee show me thy glory

Ps. 80. 14. return, we b. thee, O God
118. 25. save I b. O Lord, I b. thee send prosperity

Amos. 7. 2. O Lord God, forgive I b. thee

Jonah 1. 14. they said, we b. thee O Lord, we b. thee
4. 3. O Lord, take, I b. thee, my life from me

Acts 26. 3. wherefore I b. thee to hear me patiently

Rom. 12. 1. I b. you by the mercies

2 *Cor.* 2. 8. I b. you, confirm your love
5. 20. as though God did b. you by us, we pray you
6. 1. we b. you receive not the word of God in vain
10. 1. I Paul b. you for the meekness

of Christ

Gal. 4. 12. I b. you, be as I am

Eph. 4. 1. I the prisoner b. you to walk

Phil. 10. I b. thee for my son Onesimus

1 *Pet.* 2. 11. I b. you as strangers

2 *John* 5. now I b. thee, lady

BESEECHING, *Matt.* 8. 5. there came a centurion b. him, *Luke* 7. 3.

BESET me behind and before, *Ps.* 139. 5.

Judg. 19. 22. sons of Belial b. the house around, 20. 5.

Ps. 22. 12. strong bulls of Bashan have b. me

Hos. 7. 2. own doings have b. them

Heb. 12. 1. sin doth so easily b. us

BESIDE waters, *Ps.* 23. 2 ; *Is.* 32. 20.

Judg. 11. 34. b. her Jepthah had no son

Ps. 23. 2. he leadeth me b. still waters

Songs 1. 8. feed kids b. the shepherds' tents

Is. 32. 20. blessed are ye that sow b. all waters

Is. 56. 8. others b. I have gathered

Luke 16. 26. b. all this, between us and you a gulf

Philem. 19. thou owest to me thine ownself b.

Beside self. *Mark* 3. 21 ; *Acts* 26. 24 ; 2 *Cor.* 5. 13.

BESIEGE, *Deut.* 28. 52. he shall b. thee in thy gates

Is. 21. 2. go up, O Elam, b. O Media

BESIEGED, *Eccl.* 9. 14. came a great king against it and b. it

Is. 1. 8. the daughter of Zion is left as a b. city

BESOM, *Is.* 14. 23. I will sweep it with the b. of destruction

BESOUGHT the Lord. *Deut.* 3. 23 ; 2 *Sam.* 12. 26 ; 1 *Kings* 13. 6.

2 *Kings* 13. 4 ; 2 *Chr.* 33. 12 ; *Ezra* 8. 23 ; 2 *Cor.* 12. 8.

BEST estate is vanity, *Ps.* 39. 5.

Gen. 43. 11. take of the b. fruits of the land
47. 6. b. of land make father dwell, 11.

Num. 36. 6. marry whom they think b.

Deut. 23. 16. dwell where it likes him b.

2 *Sam.* 18. 4. what seemeth you b. I will do

Ps. 39. 5. man at his b. state is vanity

Mic. 7. 4. b. of them as a brier

Luke 15. 22. bring forth b. robe

1 *Cor.* 12. 31. covet earnestly b. gift

BESTEAD, hardly, *Is.* 8. 21.

BESTIR, 2 *Sam.* 5. 24. when hearest the sound then b.

BESTOW a blessing, *Ex.* 32. 29.

Luke 12. 17. room to b. my fruits

1 *Cor.* 12. 23. we b. more abundant honour
13. 3 b. all my goods to feed the poor

John 4. 38. b. no labour

1 *Cor.* 15. 10. his grace b. on me

2 *Cor.* 1. 11. gift b. on us by means
8. 1. grace of God b. on churches

Gal. 4. 11. lest b. labour in vain

1 *John* 3. 1. love the Father hath b. on

2 *Kings* 5. 24. Gehazi b. them in the house

1 *Chr.* 29. 25. Lord b. on Solomon royal majesty

Rom. 16. 6. greet Mary, who b. much labour on us

BETIMES, seasonably, in due and con-

venient time, 2 *Chr.* 36. 15 ; *Job* 8.
5. & 24. 5 ; *Prov.* 13. 24 ; *Gen.* 26.
31.

BETRAY, 1 *Chr.* 12. 17. if ye be come
to *b.* me to enemies

Matt. 24. 10. and shall *b.* one another
26. 16. from that time he sought opportunity to *b.* him, *Mark* 14. 11 ;
Luke 22. 6.
21. I say unto you, that one of you
shall *b.* me, *Mark* 14. 18 ; *John* 13.
21.
46. behold, he is at hand that doth
b. me

Mark 13. 12. brother shall *b.* brother
to death

John 6. 64. Jesus knew who should *b.*
him, 13. 11.

John 13. 2. the devil put into the heart
of Judas to *b.* him

BETRAYED, *Matt.* 10. 4. Judas Isca-
riot who *b.* him, *Mark* 3. 19.
17. 22. Son of man shall *b.* into the
hands of men, 20. 18 ; 26. 2, 45 ;
Mark 14. 41.
26. 24. woe to that man by whom the
Son of man is *b. Mark* 14. 21 ;
Luke 22. 22.
48. he that *b.* gave them a sign, *Mark*
14. 44.
27. 4. I have sinned, in that I *b.* innocent blood

Luke 21. 16. and ye shall be *b.* both by
parents and

John 18. 2. Judas which *b.* him knew
the place

1 *Cor.* 11. 23. same night he was *b.* he
took bread

BETRAYERS, EST, ETH, *Mark* 14. 42.
let us go, lo! he that *b.* me is at

Luke 22. 21. the hand of him that *b.* me
is with me
48. Judas, *b.* thou the Son of man
with a kiss

John 21. 20. Lord, which is he that *b.*
thee ?

Acts 7. 52. just One, of whom ye have
been the *b.*

BETROTH, *Deut.* 28. 30. shalt *b.* a wife,
another shall lie with her

Hos. 2. 19. I will *b.* thee to me for ever
20. I will *b.* thee to me in faithfulness, shalt know

BETROTHED, *Ex.* 21. 8. if she please
not her master who *b.* her
22. 16. if a man entice a maid not *b.*
Deut. 22. 28.

Lev. 19. 20. whosoever lieth with a woman *b.*

Deut. 20. 7. who hath *b.* a wife, and not
taken her
22. 23. if a man find a virgin *b.* and
lie with her

BETTER, (1) More valuable, or prefer-
able, *Eccl.* 9. 4, 16, 18. (2) More
acceptable, 1 *Sam.* 15. 22. (3) More
able, *Dan.* 1. 20. (4) More convenient, 1. *Cor.* 7. 38. (5) More easy,
Matt. 18. 6. (6) More advantageous,
Phil. 1. 23. (7) More holy, 1 *Cor.*
8. 8. (8) More safe, *Ps.* 118. 8. (9)
More comfortable, *Prov.* 15. 16, 17.
(10) More precious, *Prov.* 8. 11.

Gen. 29. 19. *b.* I give her to thee than

to another

Ex. 14. 12. *b.* for us to have served the
Egyptians

Num. 14. 3. were it not *b.* for us to re
turn to Egypt

Judg. 8. 2. gleanings of Ephraim *b.* than
vintage

1 *Sam.* 1. 8. am I not *b.* to thee than
ten sons ?

1 *Kings* 1. 47. God make the name of
king Solomon *b.*
19. 4. Elijah said, I am not *b.* than
my fathers

2 *Kings* 5. 12. rivers of Damascus *b.*
than Jordan

2 *Chr.* 21. 13. hast slain brethren *b.*
than thyself

Ps. 69. 31. this shall please the Lord
b. than an ox

Eccl. 2. 24. nothing *b.* for a man than
to eat and drink
3. 22. there is nothing *b.* than to rejoice in his works
4. 9. two are *b.* than one : 6. 11. what
is man the *b* ?
7. 10. that the former days were *b.*
than these
10. 11. the serpent will bite, and a
babbler is no *b.*

Is. 56. 5. give a name *b.* than of sons
and daughters

Ezek. 36. 11. I will settle you, and do *b.*
to you

Hos. 2. 7. then was it *b.* with me than

Nah. 3. 8. art thou *b.* than populous No

Matt. 6. 26. behold the fowls of the air,
are ye not much *b.* than they ?
Luke 12. 24.
12. 12. how much then is a man *b.*
than a sheep
18. 6. it were *b* for him that a millstone
were hanged about his neck, *Mark*
9. 42 ; *Luke* 17. 2.

Rom. 3. 9. are we *b.* than they ? no. in
no wise

1 *Cor.* 7. 38. he that giveth her not in
marriage doth *b.*
9. 15. *b.* for me to die, than to make
my glorying void
11. 17. you come together not for *b.*
but for worse

Phil. 2. 3. let each esteem other *b.* than
himself

Heb. 1. 4. being made so much *b.* than
the angels

Heb. 6. 9. but beloved, we are persuaded *b.* things of you
7. 7. without contradiction, the less
is blessed of the *b.*
19. nothing perfect, but bringing in
of a *b.* hope did
22. Jesus was made a surety of a *b.*
testament
8. 6. by how much also he is the Mediator of a *b.* covenant, established
on *b.* promises

Heb. 9. 23. but heavenly things with *b.*
sacrifices
10. 34. in heaven a *b.* and enduring
substance
11. 16. they desire a *b.* country, an
heavenly
40. God having provided some *b.*
thing for us

12. 24. that speaketh b. things than that of Abel

2 Pet. 2. 21. b. for them not to have known the way

BETTER, is, *Prov.* 15. 16. b. is little with the fear of the Lord

17. b. is a dinner of herbs where love is, than a stalled ox

16. 8. b. is a little righteousness than revenue

16. how much b. is it to get wisdom than gold

17. 1. b. is a dry morsel and quietness

Eccl. 4. 6. b. is an handful with quietness than

13. b. is a poor wise child than a foolish king

7. 8. b. is the end of a thing than the beginning

Songs 4. 10. how much b. is thy love than wine

BETTER, is, or BETTER, is it, *1 Sam.* 15. 22. behold, to obey is b. than sacrifice

Ruth 4. 15. thy daughter is b. to thee than seven sons

Ps. 37. 16. a little a righteous man hath is b.

63. 3. thy loving kindness is b. than life

84. 10. a day in thy courts is b. than a thousand

119. 72. the law of thy mouth is b. to me than gold

Prov. 3. 14. for the merchandise of wisdom is b.

8. 11. wisdom is b. than rubies, and

19. my fruit is b. than gold, yea, than fine gold

16. 32. that is slow to anger is b. than the mighty

19. 22. a poor man is b. than a liar

27. 5. open rebuke is b. than secret love

Eccl. 7. 1. a good name is b. than precious ointment

3. sorrow is b. than laughter, for by the sadness of the countenance the heart is made b.

8. the patient in spirit is b. than the proud in spirit

9. 16. then said I, wisdom is b. than strength

Songs 1. 2. for thy love is b. than wine

Luke 5. 39. for he saith, the old is b.

Phil. 1. 23. and to be with Christ, which is far b.

BETTER, it is, or BETTER, is it, *Ps.* 118. 8. it is b. to trust in the Lord, than to put, 9.

Prov. 16. 19. b. it is to be of an humble spirit

21. 9. it is b. to dwell in a corner of the house, 25, 24.

19. it is b. to dwell in the wilderness than with

Eccl. 5. 5. b. it is that thou shouldst vow

7. 2. it is b. to go to the house of mourning than

Jonah 4. 3. it is b. for me to die than to live, 8.

Matt. 18. 8. t is b. for thee to enter into life halt or maimed, than to be cast, 9 ; *Mark* 9. 43, 45, 47.

1 Cor. 7. 9. for it is b. to marry than to burn

1 Pet. 3. 17. it is b. that ye suffer for well doing, than

BETTERED, *Mark* 5. 26. she was nothing b. but rather grew worse

BETWEEN thy seed and her, *Gen.* 3. 15.

Gen. 15. 17. a burning lamp passeth b. those places

Ex. 12. 6. kill it b. the two evenings, 13. 9. and it shall be for a sign to thee, and a memorial b. thine eyes, 16 ; *Deut.* 6. 8 ; 11. 18.

26. 33. the vail shall divide b. holy and most holy

Num. 11. 33. while the flesh was b. their teeth

2 Sam. 19. 35. discern b. good and evil, *1 Kings* 3. 9.

1 Kings 3. 9. discern b. good and bad

18. 21. long halt b. two opinions

Ezek. 22. 26. no difference b. holy and profane, 44. 23 ; *Lev.* 10. 10.

Ezek. 34. 17. I judge b. cattle, and cattle, b. rams

1 Cor. 7. 34. there is difference b. a wife and a virgin

1 Tim. 2. 5. there is no Mediator b. God and man

BETWIXT, *Job* 36. 32. not to shine by the cloud that cometh b.

Songs 1. 13. he shall lie all night b. my breasts

Phil. 1. 23. I am in a strait b. two

BID, *2 Kings* 5. 13. if the prophet had b. thee a great thing

Jonah 3. 2. preach the preaching I b.

Zeph. 1. 7. the Lord hath b. his guests

Matt. 14. 28. b. me come on the water

22. 9. ye shall find b. to the marriage

Luke 9. 61. let me first b. them farewell at home

10. 40. b. her that she help me

14. 12. lest they also b. thee again

BIDDEN, *Matt.* 1. 24. then Joseph did as the angel had b. him

Matt. 22. 3. to call them b. to wedding

Luke 14. 8. when thou art b. lest a more honourable man be b.

10. when b. sit in the lowest

24. none of those men b. shall taste of my supper

BIDE not in unbelief, *Rom.* 11. 23.

BILL, *Deut.* 24. 1, 3 ; *Is.* 50. 1 ; *Jer.* 3. 8 ; *Mark* 10. 4 ; *Luke* 16. 6, 7. take thy bill and write

BIND, sweet influences, *Job* 38. 31.

31. 36. I would b. it as a crown

Ps. 105. 22. to b. his princes at pleasure

118. 27. b. the sacrifice with cords

149. 8. to b. their kings in chains

Prov. 3. 3. b. them about thy neck

Is. 8. 16. b. up testimony seal the law

61. 1. b. up broken-hearted, to proclaim

Hos. 6. 1. smitten us and he will b. up

Matt. 12. 29. first b. strong man and

13. 30. b. the tares in bundles

16. 19. thou b. on earth, 18. 18.

22. 13. b. him hand and foot and cast

23. 4. b. heavy burdens and lay

Bindeth up, *Job* 5. 18. *Ps.* 147. 3.

BIRD, hasteth to snare, *Prov.* 7. 23.

Ps. 124. 7. escaped as b. out of the

Eccl. 10. 20. *b.* of air tell the matter

Is. 46. 11. ravenous *b.* from the east

Jer. 12. 9. heritage and speckled *b.*

Birds, *Gen.* 15. 16. & 40. 17 ; *Lev.* 14. 4 ; 2 *Sam.* 21. 10 ; *Ps.* 104. 17 ; *Eccl.* 9. 12 ; *Songs* 2. 12 ; *Is.* 31. 5 ; *Jer.* 5. 27. & 12. 4, 9 ; *Matt.* 8. 20.

BIRTH, *Gen.* 40. 20. third day which was 'Pharaoh's *b.* day

Is. 66. 9. shall I bring to *b.* and not ?

Matt. 14. 6 ; *Mark* 6. 21. Herod's *b.* day was kept

BIRTH-RIGHT, *Gen.* 25. 31. Jacob said, Sell me thy *b.-r.*

27. 36. he took away my *b.-r.*

43. 33. first born according to *b.-r.*

1 *Chro.* 5. 1. Reuben's *b.-r.* given to the sons of Joseph

BISHOP, (1) Spiritual overseers that have the charge of souls, to instruct and rule them by the word, 1 *Tim.* 3. 1, 2 ; *Acts* 20. 28. (2) Christ himself, 1 *Pet.* 2. 25.

Phil. 1. 1. to all saints at Philippi, with *b.* and deacons

1 *Tim.* 3. 1. if a man desire the office of a *b.*

1 *Tim.* 3. 2. a *b.* then must be blameless 1. 7.

1 *Pet.* 2. 25. now returned to the *b.* of your souls

BIT, S, 32. 9. mouth held in with *b.*

Jam. 3. 3. put *b.* in the horses' mouths

BIT, *Num.* 21. 6. Lord sent fiery serpents *b,* people

Amos 5. 19. leaned on a wall, and serpent *b.* him

BITE, *Num.* 21. 6, 8, 9 ; *Eccl.* 10. 8, 11 ; *Jer.* 8. 17 ; *Amos* 9. 3 ; *Heb.* 2. 7.

Mic. 3. 5. prophets *b.* with teeth

Gal. 5. 15. if ye *b.* and devour one another

BITETH, *Gen.* 40. 17. Dan an adder, that *b.* the horse heels

Prov. 23. 32. at the last it *b.* like a serpent

BITTEN, *Num.* 21. 8. every one that is *b.* when he looks on

9. came to pass, that if a serpent had *b.* any man

BITTER, made their lives, *Ex.* 1. 14.

Gen. 27. 34. Esau cried with an exceeding *b.* cry

Ex. 12. 8. with *b.* herbs eat it, *Num.* 9. 11.

15. 23. not drink of the waters, for they were *b.*

Deut. 32. 24. devoured with *b.* destruction

32. their grapes of gall clusters are *b.*

2 *Kings* 14. 26. affliction was very *b.*

Job 3. 20. why is life given to *b.* in soul

13. 26. writest *b.* things against me

23. 2. even to day is my complaint *b.*

Ps. 64. 3. their arrows even *b.* words

Prov. 5. 4. her end is *b.* as wormwood

Prov. 27. 7. every *b.* thing is sweet

Eccl. 7. 26. woman more *b.* than death

Is. 5. 20. woe to put *b.* for sweet

24. 9. strong drink shall be *b.* to them that drink

Jer. 2. 19. evil thing and *b.* that

6. 26. *b.* lamentation as for a son

31. 15. a voice was heard in Ramah, *b.* weeping

Amos 8. 10. and the end thereof as a *b.* day

Col. 3. 19. wives be not *b.* against them

Jam. 3. 14. have *b.* envying against

Rev. 8. 11. men died of waters because made *b.*

Rev. 10. 9. it shall make thy belly *b.*

BITTER-WATER, *Jam.* 3. 11. doth a fountain send sweet *w.* and *b.* ?

BITTERLY, *Judg.* 5. 23. curse *b.* inhabitants

Ruth 1. 20. Almighty dealt *b.* with me

Is. 22. 4. I will weep *b.* 33. 7.

33. 7. the ambassadors of peace shall weep *b.*

Ezek. 27. 30. shall cry *b. Zeph* 1. 14.

Hos. 12. 14. provoked him most *b.*

Matt. 26. 75. wept *b. Luke* 22. 62.

BITTERN, *Is.* 14. 23. make it a possession for the *b.* 34. 11.

Zeph. 2. 14. the *b.* shall lodge in the upper lintels

BITTERNESS of soul, 1 *Sam.* 1. 10.

1 *Sam.* 15. 32. *b.* of death is past

2 *Sam.* 2. 26. it will be *b.* in end

Job 7. 11. I will complain in the *b.* of my soul

10. 1. I will speak in the *b.* of my soul

21. 25. another dieth in the *b.* of his soul

Prov. 14. 10. heart knows its own *b.*

17. 25. a foolish son is *b.* to her that bare him

Is. 38. 15. go softly all my life in *b.* of my soul

17. behold, for peace I had great *b.*

Ezek. 3. 14. Spirit took me away, and I went in *b.*

21. 6. and with *b.* sigh before their eyes

27. 31. they shall weep for thee with *b.*

Zech. 12. 10. in *b.* for first-born

Acts 8. 23. in gall of *b.* and bond of

Rom. 3. 14. mouth full of cursing and *b.*

Eph. 4. 31. let all *b.* be put away

Heb. 12. 15. root of *b.* springing up

BLACK, (1) To the church, whose outward beauty is often eclipsed, by reason of infirmities, scandals, reproaches, and persecutions, *Songs* 1. 5. (2) To the Jews, whose countenance changed and turned black, like persons ready to be strangled being struck with terror at the approach of God's judgments, *Joel* 2. 6 ; *Nah.* 2. 10. (3) To hell, the place of extreme darkness, horror, and misery, *Jude* 13.

Prov. 7. 9. in the evening, in the *b.* and dark night

Songs 1. 5. I am *b.* but comely

6. look not upon me, because I am *b.*

5. 11. his locks are bushy and *b.* as a raven

Jer. 4. 28. for this the heavens be *b.*

8. 21. for the hurt of my people I am hurt, I am *b.*

14. the gates thereof languish, they are *b.*

Zech. 6. 2. in second chariot *b.* horses

6. *b.* horses go forth into the north country

Matt. 5. 36. canst not make one hair

white or *b.*

Rev. 6. 5. and I beheld, and lo ! a *b.* horse

12. the sun became *b.* as sackcloth of hair

BLACKER, *Lam.* 4. 8. their visage is *b.* than a coal

BLACKISH, *Job* 6. 16. *b.* by reason of ice

BLACKNESS, *Is.* 50. 3. I clothe heavens with *b.*

Joel 2. 6 ; *Nah.* 2. 10 all faces shall gather *b.*

Job 3. 5. let the *b.* of the day terrify it

Heb. 12. 18. ye are not come to *b.* and darkness

Jude 13. to whom is reserved *b.* of darkness

BLADE, *Judg.* 3. 22. the haft also went in after the *b.*

Job 31. 22. then let my arm fall from my shoulder *b.*

Matt. 13. 26. when the *b.* was sprung up, *Mark* 4. 28.

BLAME, *Gen.* 43. 9 ; let me bear the *b.* for ever, 44. 32.

2 *Cor.* 8. 20. avoiding that no man should *b.* us

Eph. 1. 4. holy and without *b.* before him in love

Blamed, 2 *Cor.* 6. 3 ; *Gal.* 2. 11.

Blameless, *Gen.* 44. 10 ; *Josh.* 2. 17 ; *Judg.* 15. 3 ; *Matt.* 12. 5 ; *Phil.* 3. 6 ; 1 *Tim.* 5. 7.

Luke 1. 6. in all the ordinances of the Lord *b.*

1 *Cor.* 1. 8. be *b.* in the day of our Lord

Phil. 2. 15. *b.* harmless children of God

1 *Thess.* 5. 23. spirit be preserved *b.*

1 *Tim.* 3. 2. bishop must be *b.*

Tit. 1. 6, 7. office of a deacon found *b.*

2 *Pet.* 3. 14. without spot and *b.*

BLASPHEME, (1) To speak evil of God, *Rom.* 2. 24 ; *Tit.* 2. 5. (2) To rail against and deny the work of the Holy Spirit out of malice, *Matt.* 12 31.

2 *Sam.* 12. 14. occasion the enemies o the Lord to *b.*

Ps. 74. 10. enemy *b.* thy name

Mark 3. 29. *b.* against Holy Ghost not forgiven

Acts 26. 11. compelled them to *b.*

1 *Tim.* .1. 20. might learn not to *b.*

Jam. 2. 7. do they not *b.* that name

Rev. 13. 6. to *b.* his name and his tabernacle

Blasphemed *Lev.* 24. 11. son *b.* name of Lord, 16.

2 *Kings* 19. 6. servant *b.* me, *Is.* 37. 6.

Ps. 74. 18. foolish people have *b.*

Is. 52. 5. my name continually is *b.*

Acts 18. 6. when they opposed themselves and *b.*

John 10. 36. whom the Father sanctifieth thou *b.*

Rom. 2. 24. name of God is *b.* through you

1 *Tim.* 6. 1. name of God and his doctrine not *b.*

Tit. 2. 5. word of God be not *b.*

Rev. 16. 9, 11, 21. *b.* God of heaven who

Blasphemest, eth, *Lev.* 24. 16. *b.* the name of Lord, put to death

Ps. 44. 16. for voice of him that *b.*

Matt. 9. 3. said this man *b.*

Luke 12. 10. to him that *b.* against Holy Ghost

Blasphemer, 1 *Tim.* 1. 13 ; 2 *Tim.* 3. 2.

Blasphemy, 2 *Kings* 19. 3 ; *Is.* 37. 3 ; *Matt.* 12. 31 ; *Mark* 7. 22 ; *Col.* 3. 8 ; *Rev.* 2. 9. & 13. 1, 6.

BLAST, *Ex.* 15. 8. with *b.* of thy nostrils the waters were

Josh. 6. 5. make a long *b.* with horns

2 *Kings* 19. 7. I will send a *b.* on Sennacherib, *Is.* 37. 7.

Job 4. 9. by the *b.* of God they perish

Is. 25. 4. when the *b.* of the terrible

BLASTED, *Gen.* 41. 6. thin ears *b.* with the east wind, 23. 27.

2 *Kings* 19. 26. as corn *b.* before grown, *Is.* 37. 27.

BLASTING, S, *Deut.* 28. 22. the Lord shall smite thee with *b.*

1 *Kings* 8. 37. if there be *b.* mildew, 2 *Chr.* 6. 28.

Hag. 2. 17. I smote you with *b.* and mildew

Amos 4. 9. I have smitten you with *b.*

BLAZE, *Mark* 1. 45. he began to *b.* abroad the matter

BLEATING, S, *Judg.* 5. 16. abodest in sheepfolds, to hear *b.* of flocks

1 *Sam.* 15. 14. what meaneth the *b.* of the sheep

BLEMISH without, *Ex.* 12. 5. & 29. 1 ; *Lev.* 1. 3, 10. & 4. 23.

Lev. 21. 17. he that hath *b.* shall not approach, 21. 23.

22. 20. whatsoever hath a *b.* not offer it shall not be acceptable, *Deut.* 15. 21.

24. 19. if a man cause a *b.* in his neighbour

Dan. 1. 4. children in whom no *b.*

Eph. 5. 27. holy and without *b.*

1. *Pet.* 1. 19. as a lamb without *b.*

BLEMISHES, 2 *Pet.* 2. 13. spots they are and *b.* sporting

BLESS, God being agent, *Gen.* 12. 2. the Lord said, I will *b.* thee, 26. 3, 24.

Gen. 12. 3. I will *b.* them that bless thee

Gen. 22. 17. in blessing, I will *b.* thee, *Heb.* 6. 14.

28. 3. God Almighty *b.* thee and multiply thee

32. 26. not let me go except thou *b.*

48. 16. *b.* the lads, and let my soul

49. 25. by the Almighty who shall *b.* thee

Ex. 20. 24. I will come to thee, and I will *b.* thee

23. 25. shall *b.* thy bread and water

Num. 6. 24. the Lord *b.* thee and keep

24. 1. it pleased the Lord to *b.* Israel

Deut. 15. 4. shall be no poor, for the Lord shall *b.* thee

18. the Lord thy God shall *b.* thee in all, 30. 16.

26. 15. look down and *b.* thy people

28. 12. and to *b.* all the work of thine hand

33. 11. *b.* Lord, his substance

Ruth 2. 4. saying, the Lord *b.* thee, *Jer.* 31. 23.

1 *Chr.* 4. 10. O that thou wouldst *b.* me indeed

28. 9. save thy people, *b.* thine in heritance
Ps. 5. 12. thou Lord, wilt *b.* the righteous
29. 11. Lord will *b.* people with peace
67. 1. God even our own God, shall *b.* us, 6, 7.
115. 12. the Lord will *b.* us, he will *b.* the house of Israel, he will *b.* the house of Aaron
128. 5. the Lord shall *b.* thee out of
132. 15. I will abundantly *b.* her provision
134. 3. the Lord *b.* thee out of Zion
Hag. 2. 19. from this day will I *b.* you
Acts 3. 26. sent him to *b.* you
BLESS, God being the object, *Deut.* 8. 10. art full, shalt *b.* the Lord
Judg. 5. 9. *b.* ye the Lord, *Ps.* 103. 21 ; 134. 1.
Ps. 16. 7. I will *b.* Lord, given counsel
26. 12. in the congregation will I *b.* the Lord
34. 1. *b.* the Lord at all times
63. 4. thus will I *b.* thee while I live
66. 8. O *b.* our God, make his praise
68. 26. *b.* ye God in the congregations
103. 1. *b.* the Lord, O my soul, 2. 22 ; 104. 1, 35.
20. *b.* the Lord, ye his angels
22. *b.* the Lord all his works
134. 2. lift up hands, *b.* you
135. 19. *b.* the Lord, O house of Israel
145. 1. I will *b.* thy name for ever
2. every day will I *b.* thee
10. O Lord, thy saints shall *b.* thee
Jam. 3. 9. therewith *b.* we God

BLESS, man agent and object, *Gen.* 27. 4. my soul may *b.* thee before I die, 25.
Gen. 27. 34. *b.* me, even me also, O
Num. 6. 23. this wise ye shall *b.* Israel
Deut. 10. 8. the Lord separated Levi to *b.* 21. 5.
Josh. 8. 33. Moses commanded should *b.*
2 *Sam.* 6. 20. then David returned to *b.* his household, 1 *Chr.* 16. 43.
Ps. 62. 4. they *b.* with their mouths
109. 28. let them curse, but *b.* thou
129. 8. we *b.* you in the name
Is. 65. 16. shall *b.* himself in God
Matt. 5. 44. *b.* them that curse you, *Luke* 6. 28 ; *Rom.* 12. 14.
1 *Cor.* 4. 12. being reviled we *b.*
1 *Cor.* 10. 16. the cup of blessing which we *b.*
BLESSED, *Gen.* 14. 19. Melchisedek *b.* Abram, and said, *b.* be
Gen. 27. 23. so Isaac *b.* Jacob and said
27. 33. I have *b.* him, yea, and he shall be *b.*
28.. 1. Isaac called Jacob, *b.* him and
31. 55. kissed his sons and daughters, and *b.* them
47. 7. Jacob *b.* Pharaoh, 10: 48. 15. he *b.* Joseph
48. 20. Jacob *b.* Manasseh and Ephraim, *Heb.* 11. 21.
49. 28. Jacob *b.* his sons, every one he *b.*
Ex. 39. 43. and Moses *b.* them, *Deut.* 33. 1.
Judg. 5. 24. *b.* above women shall Jael
2 *Sam.* 6. 18. David *b.* the people, I *Chr.* 16. 2.

1 *Kings* 2. 45. king Solomon shall be *b.*
8. 14. king Solomon *b.* all the congregation, 55.
Job 29. 11. when the ear heard me, it *b.* me
31. 20. if his loins have not *b.* me
Ps. 49. 18. while he lived he *b.* his soul
72. 17. men shall be *b.* in him, nations call him *b.*
118. 26. *b.* he that cometh in name of the Lord, we have *b.* you out of
Prov. 31. 28. her children arise, and call her *b.*
Mal. 3. 12. and all nations shall call you *b.*
Acts 20. 35. it is more *b.* to give than to receive
Tit. 2. 13. looking for that *b.* hope and
Heb. 7. 1. Melchisedek met Abraham and *b.* him
BLESSED, (God the agent) *Gen.* 1. 22. God *b.* them, saying, be fruitful, 28; 5. 2.
Gen. 26. 29. thou art now *b.* of the Lord
27. 27. the smell of a field which the Lord hath *b.*
Deut. 2. 7. thy God hath *b.* thee, 12. 7 ; 15. 14 ; 16. 10.
7. 14. thou shalt be *b.* above all
Deut. 28. 3. *b.* shalt thou be in the city, *b.* in the field
4. *b.* shall be fruit of thy body : 5. *b.* thy basket
33. 13. of Joseph he said, *b.* of the Lord be his
2 *Sam.* 6. 11. the Lord *b.* Obed-edom, and all his household, 12 ; 1 *Chr.* 13. 14 ; 26. 5.
Job 1. 10. thou hast *b.* the work of his hands
42. 12. the Lord *b.* the latter end of Job
Ps. 21. 6. thou hast made him most *b.*
33. 12. *b.* is the nation whose God is the Lord
Ps. 45. 2. therefore God hath *b.* thee for ever
89. 15. *b.* is the people that know the joyful sound
112. 2. the generation of the upright shall be *b.*
115. 15. you are *b.* of the Lord who made heaven
119. 1. *b.* are the undefiled in the way
128. 1. *b.* is every one that feareth the Lord
Prov. 10. 7. memory of the just is *b.*
22. 9. he that hath a bountiful eye shall be *b.*
Is. 61. 9. they are the seed the Lord hath *b.* 65. 23.
Matt. 5. 3. *b.* are the poor in spirit : 5. *b.* are the meek
7. *b.* are the merciful : 8. *b.* are the pure in heart
9. *b.* are the peace-makers : 10. *b.* are persecuted
13. 16. *b.* are your eyes, for they see, *Luke* 10. 23.
14. 19. he *b.* and brake, and gave the loaves, 26. 26 ; *Mark* 6. 41 ; 14. 22 ; *Luke* 9. 16 ; 24. 30.
16. 17. Jesus said, *b.* art thou Simon Bar-jona

24. 46. *b.* is that servant, *Luke* 12. 43.

25. 34. come, ye *b.* of my Father, inherit kingdom

Mark 10. 16. took them up in his arms and *b.* them

14. 61. thou art Christ the Son of the *b.*

Luke 1. 28. *b.* art thou among women, 42.

45. *b.* is she that believed : 6. 20. *b.* be ye poor

12. 37. *b.* are those servants whom the Lord when he cometh shall find watching, 38.

Luke 14. 14. thou shalt be *b.* they can not recompense

24. 50. he *b.* them ; 51. while he *b.*

Gal. 3. 9. they are *b.* with faithful Abraham

Eph. 1. 3. who hath *b.* us with spiritual blessings

Jam. 1. 25. this man shall be *b.* in his

Rev. 14. 13. *b.* are the dead that die in the Lord

BLESSED, God the object, 2 *Sam.* 22.

47. and *b.* be my rock, *Ps.* 18. 46.

Neh. 8. 6. and Ezra *b.* the Lord, the great God

9. 5. *b.* be thy glorious name, *Ps.* 72. 19.

Job 1. 21. *b.* the name of the Lord, *Ps.* 113. 2.

Dan. 2. 19. Daniel *b.* the God of heaven, 20.

4. 34. Nebuchadnezzar *b.* the most High

Luke 2. 28. took him in the arms and *b.* God

John 12. 13. *b.* is the king of Israel that cometh

Rom. 1. 25. than the Creator, who is *b.* for ever

9. 5. Christ, who is over all, God *b.* for ever

Eph. 1. 3. *b.* be the Father of our Lord, 1 *Pet.* 1. 3.

1 *Tim.* 1. 11. the glorious gospel of the *b.* God

6. 15. who is the *b.* and only potentate

BLESSED are they, *Ps.* 2. 12. *b.* are they that put their trust in him

Ps. 84. 4. *b.* are they that dwell in thy house

106. 3. *b.* are they that keep judgment at all times

Prov. 8. 32. for *b.* are they that keep my ways

Matt. 5. 4. *b.* are they that mourn shall be comforted

6. *b.* are they who hunger ; 10. who are persecuted

Luke 11. 28. yea, *b.* are they that hear the word

John 20. 29. *b.* are they that have not seen, believed

Rom. 4. 7. *b.* are they whose iniquities are forgiven

Rev. 19. 9. *b.* are they who are called to the marriage supper

22. 14. *b.* are they that do his commandments

BLESSED are ye, *Is.* 32. 20. *b.* are ye that sow beside all waters

Matt. 5. 11. *b.* are ye when men shall revile you

Luke 6. 21. *b.* are ye that hunger now, ye shall be filled ; *b.* are ye that weep now, for ye shall laugh

22. *b.* are ye when men shall hate you

BLESSED is he, *Ps.* 32. 1. *b.* is he whose transgression is forgiven

41. 1. *b.* is he that considereth the

Dan. 12. 12. *b.* is he that waiteth, cometh to days

Matt. 11. 6. and *b.* is he whosoever shall not be offended in me, *Luke* 7. 23.

Luke 14. 15. *b.* is he that shall eat bread in kingdom

Rev. 1. 3. *b.* is he that readeth, and they that hear

16. 15. *b.* is he that watcheth, and

20. 6. *b.* is he that hath part in the first resurrection

22. 7. *b.* is he that keepeth sayings of the prophecy

BLESSED is the man, *Ps.* 1. 1. *b.* is the man that walketh not in counsel

Ps. 32. 2. *b.* is the man to whom the Lord imputeth not iniquity, *Rom.* 4. 8.

34. 8. *b.* is man that trusteth in him, 84. 12 ; *Jer.* 17. 7.

40. 4. *b.* is the man that maketh the Lord his trust

65. 4. *b.* is the man whom thou choosest, and causest

84. 5. *b.* is the man whose strength is in thee

94. 12. *b.* is the man whom thou chastenest, O Lord

112. 1. *b.* is the man that feareth the Lord, that delights

Prov. 8. 34. *b.* is the man that heareth me, watching

Jam. 1. 12. *b.* is the man that endureth temptation

BLESSEDNESS, *Rom.* 4. 6. even as David describeth the *b.*

Rom. 4. 9. cometh this *b.* on the circumcision only

Gal. 4. 15. where is then the *b.* ye spake of ?

BLESSETH, *Deut.* 15. 6. thy God *b.* thee as he promised

Prov. 3. 33. but he *b.* the habitation of the just

Is. 65. 16. he who *b.* himself in the earth

BLESSING, *Gen.* 12. 2. I will bless thee, thou shalt be a *b.*

Gen. 27. 12. I shall bring a curse on me, and not a *b.*

Gen. 27. 35. brother hath taken away thy *b.*

39. 5. the *b.* of the Lord was on all

Lev. 25. 21. then will I command my *b.* on you

Deut. 11. 26. behold, I set before you a *b.* 30. 19.

27. a *b.* if ye obey the commandments of the Lord

29. thou shalt put the *b.* on mount Gerizim

Deut. 23. 5. the Lord turned the curse into a *b.*

33. 16. let the *b.* come upon the head of Joseph

Neh. 9. 5. which is exalted above all *b.*

13. 2. God turned the curse into a *b.*

Job 29. 13. the *b.* of him that was ready
to perish

Ps. 3. 8. thy *b.* is upon thy people

24. 5. he shall receive the *b.* from the
Lord

129. 8. the *b.* of the Lord be upon you

133. 3. their Lord commanded the *b.*
even life

Prov. 10. 22. the *b.* of the Lord maketh
rich

Is. 19. 24. even a *b.* in the midst of the
land

44. 3. and I will pour my *b.* on thy
offspring

Ezek. 34. 26. I will make them and the
places about my hill a *b.* there
shall be showers of *b.*

Joel 2. 14. if he will leave a *b.* behind

Zech. 8. 13. I will save you, and ye shall
be a *b.*

Mal. 3. 10. open heaven, and pour you
out a *b.*

Luke 24. 53. in the temple praising and
b. God

Rom. 15. 29. in the fulness of the *b.* of
the gospel

1 *Cor.* 10. 16. the cup of *b.* which we
bless

Gal. 3. 14. that the *b.* of Abraham
might come

Heb. 6. 7. for the earth receiveth *b.*

12. 17. when he would have inherited
the *b.*

Jam. 3. 10. of the same mouth proceed
b. and cursing

1 *Pet.* 3. 9. but contrariwise *b.* knowing
that ye are thereunto called, that
ye should inherit a *b.*

Rev. 5. 12. worthy to receive honour,
glory, *b.*

13. *b.* to him that sitteth on throne

7. 12. *b.* and glory to our God for ever

BLESSINGS, *Gen.* 49. 25. Almighty who
shall bless thee with *b.* of heaven above, *b.* of the deep, *b.* of the
breasts

Deut. 28. 2. all these *b.* shall come on
thee, if hearken

Josh. 8. 34. afterwards he read the *b.*
and cursings

Ps. 21. 3. preventest him with the *b.*

Prov. 10. 6. *b.* are upon the head of the
just

28. 20. a faithful man shall abound
with *b.*

Eph. 1. 3. who hath blessed us with all
spiritual *b.*

BLEW, (verb) *Josh.* 6. 8. priests passed
on before the Lord and *b.*

Judg. 3. 27. Ehud *b.* a trumpet in the
mount

2 *Sam.* 2. 28. Joab *b.* a trumpet, 18. 16 ;
20. 22.

20. 1. ·Sheba a Benjamite, *b.* a trumpet and said

1 *Kings* 1. 39. they *b.* the trumpet,
people said, God save king Solomon, 2 *Kings* 9. 13 ; 11. 14.

Matt. 7. 25. winds *b.* and beat on that
house, 27.

John 6. 18. the sea arose by a great
wind that *b.*

Acts 27. 13. the south wind *b.* 28. 13.

BLIND, (1) Such as are deprived of

natural sight, *John* 9. 1 ; *Acts* 13. 11.
(2) Such whose judgments are so
corrupted by taking gifts, that they
cannot, or will not discern between
right and wrong, *Ex.* 23. 8 ; *Deut.*
16. 19. (3) Such as are wilfully and
obstinately ignorant, in matters
that concern salvation, *Matt.* 15.
14. (4) Such as through simplicity
and ignorance are easily misled
and seduced by the pernicious
counsel of others, *Deut.* 27. 18 ;
Matt. 15. 14.

It is applied, (1) To ignorant ministers,
Is. 56. 10. (2) To deceitful teachers,
who are blinded by their own in-
terest against any conviction, *Is.*
42. 19 ; *Matt.* 23. 6. (3) To an ignorant people, *Matt.* 15. 14 ; *Rom.*
2. 19. (4) To such as reject the
knowledge and faith of Christ, not-
withstanding the clear discoveries
of the way of salvation in the gospel, 2 *Cor.* 4. 4. (5) To such as live
in hatred, 1 *John* 2. 11. (6) To such
as are self-conceited, being puffed
up with a high opinion of their
qualifications and attainments,
Rev. 3. 17.

Lev. 19. 14. not put a stumbling block
before *b.*

Lev. 21. 18. a *b.* or lame man not offer

22. 22. not offer the *b.* to the Lord,
Deut. 15. 21.

Deut. 27. 18. cursed that maketh the *b.*
to wander

Job 29. 15. I was eyes to the *b.*

Ps. 146. 8. openeth the eyes of the *b.*

Is. 29. 18. the eyes of the *b.* shall see,
35. 5.

Is. 42. 7. to open the *b.* eyes, 18.

6. I will bring the *b.* by a way they
knew not

19. who is *b.* but my servant

43. 8. *b.* people that have eyes

56. 10. his watchmen are *b.*

Lam. 4. 14. they wandered as *b.* men
in the streets

Mal. 1. 8. if ye offer the *b.* for sacrifice,
is it not evil ?

Matt. 9. 27. two *b.* men followed him,
crying, 20. 30.

Matt. 11. 5. *b.* receive sight, *Luke* 7. 22.

23. 16. woe to you *b.* guides, 24.

Mark 8. 23. and he took the *b.* man by
the hand

10. 46. *b.* Bartimeus sat by the way-
side begging

Luke 4. 18. recovery of sight to the *b.*

7. 21. to many that were *b.* he gave
sight

14. 13. when thou makest a feast, call
the *b.*

John 5. 3. in these lay a great multitude of *b.*

9. 1. he saw a man that was *b.* from
from his birth

39. that they which see might be
made *b.*

40. are we *b.* also ? 41. if ye were *b.*

10. 21. can a devil open the eyes of
the *b.* ?

Acts 13. 11. thou shalt be *b.* not seeing
the sun

2 Pet. 1. 9. lacks these things is *b.*
Rev. 3. 17. thou art *b.* and naked
BLINDED, *Ex.* 23. 8. take no gift, for a gift *b.* the wise
John 12. 40. *b.* their eyes
Rom. 11. 7. the rest were *b.*
2 Cor. 3. 14. their minds were *b.*
4. 4. God of this world hath *b.* minds
1 John 2. 11. darkness hath *b.* eyes
BLINDFOLDED, *Luke* 22. 64. when they had *b.* him, they struck
BLINDNESS, *Gen.* 19. 11. smote the men at the door with *b.*
2 Kings 6. 18. Elisha prayed, smite this people, I pray thee, with *b.* and he smote them with *b.*
Mark 3. 5. being grieved for their *b.* of heart
Rom. 11. 25. *b.* in part has happened to Israel
Eph. 4. 18. because of the *b.* of their heart
BLOOD, *Gen.* 4. 10. the voice of thy brother's *b.*
9. 4. the life which is the *b.* shall you not eat
37. 31. killed a kid, and dipped the coat in *b.*
Ex. 4. 9. water shall become *b.*
7. 17. waters shall be turned into *b.*
Lev. 10. 18. the *b.* of it was not brought
15. 19. and if the issue in her flesh shall be *b.*
17. 4. *b.* shall be imputed unto that man
Lev. 17. 11. for it is the *b.* that maketh atonement
Deut. 22. 8. make a battlement, that thou bring not *b.*
Job 16. cover thou not my *b.*
Job 39. 30. the eagle's young ones also suck up *b.*
Ps. 9. 12. maketh inquisition for *b.*
Ps. 30. 9. what profit is there in my *b.* ?
50. 13. or will I drink the *b.* of goats
58. 10. righteous wash his feet in the *b.* of wicked
68. 23. foot may be dipped in the *b.* of thy enemy
72. 14. precious shall their *b.* be in his sight
Is. 1. 15. your hands are full of *b.*
9. 5. garments rolled in *b.*
26. 21. earth shall disclose *b.*
Ezek. 3. 18. his *b.* will I require
9. 9. the land is full of *b.*
16. 6. polluted in thy own *b.*
18. 10. if he beget a son that is a shedder of *b.*
21. 32. thy *b.* shall be in the midst of the land, 22. 12.
24. 8. I have set her *b.* on the top of a rock
28. 23. for I will send *b.* into her streets
32. 6. I will also water with thy *b.* the land
Hos. 1. 4. for yet I will avenge the *b.* of Jezreel
4. 2. break out and *b.* toucheth *b.*
Mic. 3. 10. build up Zion with *b.*
Matt. 9. 20. behold a woman diseased with an issue of *b. Luke* 8. 43.
16. 17. flesh and *b.* have not revealed it to thee
23. 35. from the *b.* of righteous Abel, *Luke* 11. 51.
26. 28. *b.* of New Testament, *Mark* 14. 24 ; *Luke* 22. 20 ; *1 Cor.* 11. 25.
Matt. 27. 6. not to put into treasury, because it is price of *b.*
8. field of *b. Acts* 1. 19.
24. I am innocent of the *b.* of this just person
25. his *b.* be on us and our children
Luke 13. 1. whose *b.* Pilate mingled
Luke 22. 20. the new testament in my *b.*
22. 44. sweat great drops of *b.* falling
John 1. 13. born not of *b.* nor of flesh
6. 54, 56. and drinketh my *b.* shall
55. my *b.* is drink indeed
19. 34. of his side came *b.* and water
Acts 17. 26. made of one *b.* all nations
15. 20. that they abstain from *b.* 29 ; 21. 25.
18. 6. your *b.* be on your heads
20. 26. I am pure from *b.* of all men
28. God purchased with his own *b.*
Rom. 3. 25. through faith in his *b.*
5. 9. justified by his *b.*
1 Cor. 11. 27. guilty of body *b.* of Lord
15. 50. flesh and *b.* cannot inherit the kingdom
Eph. 1. 7. redemption through his *b.* even forgiveness of sins, *Col.* 1. 14.
Col. 1. 20. peace through *b.* of cross
Heb. 2. 14. the children are partakers of flesh and *b.*
9. 12. nor by the *b.* of goats, but by his own *b.*
13. if the *b.* of bulls and goats sanctifieth
20. this is the *b.* of the testament
22. without shedding of *b.* no remission
10. 19. into holiest by *b.* of Jesus
11. 28. he kept the passover and sprinkling of *b.*
12. 4. not resisted unto *b.* striving
24. *b.* of sprinkling—speaketh better
13. 11. whose *b.* is brought into the sanctuary
1 Pet. 1. 2. sprinkling of the *b.* of Jesus
19. with precious *b.* of Christ
1 John 1. 7. his *b.* cleanseth us from all
5. 6. came by water and *b.*
8. three in earth, the Spirit, the water, and *b.*
Rev. 1. 5. washed us in his own *b.*
5. 9. thou hast redeemed us to God by thy *b.*
6. 10. dost thou not avenge our *b.*
7. 14. white in the *b.* of the Lamb
8. 7. fire mingled with *b.*
12. 11. overcame by *b.* of the Lamb
14. 20. and *b.* came out of the wine
16. 6. given them *b.* to drink,
17. 6. drunken with the *b.* of saints
18. 24. in her was found the *b.* of the prophets
19. 13. he was clothed in a vesture dipped in *b.*
BLOOD of Christ, *1 Cor.* 10. 16. is it not communion of the *b.* of Christ
Eph. 2. 13. were far off, are made nigh by *b.* of Christ
Heb. 9. 14. how much more shall *b.* of Christ purge ?

1 *Pet.* 1. 19. but with precious *b.* of *Christ* as of a lamb

BLOOD of the Covenant, *Ex.* 24. 8. Moses said, behold the *b.* of the covenant

Zech. 9. 11. as for thee also by the *b.* of thy *covenant*

Heb. 10. 29. hath counted *b.* of covenant an unholy thing

13. 20. through the *b.* of the everlasting *covenant*

BLOOD, his, *Matt.* 27. 25. *his b.* be on us and our children

Heb. 13. 12. that he might sanctify the people with *his b.*

BLOOD, innocent, *Deut.* 19. 10. that *innocent b.* be not shed in the Land

21. 8. lay not *innocent b.* to thy people's charge

2 *Kings* 21. 16. Manasseh shed *innocent b.* 21. 9.

Ps. 94. 21. they gather and condemn *innocent b.*

Prov. 6. 17. Lord hateth hands that shed *innocent b.*

Is. 59. 7. and they make haste to shed *innocent b.*

Matt. 27. 4. I sinned in that I have betrayed *innocent b.*

BLOOD, shed, *Ps.* 79. 3. their *b.* shed like water round Jerusalem

Prov. 1. 16. they make haste to *shed b. Rom.* 3. 15.

Ezek. 22. 4. art become guilty in thy *b.* thou hast *shed*

Mark 14. 24. this is my *b.* which is *shed, Luke* 22. 20.

Luke 11. 50. *b.* of all the prophets that was *shed*

Acts 22. 20. when the *b.* of Stephen was *shed*

BLOOD, sprinkle, *Ex.* 29. 16. take the ram's *b.* and *sprinkle* it on altar

Lev. 5. 9. sprinkle *b.* of sin offering on side of the altar

Heb. 9. 21. he *sprinkled* with *b.*

BLOOD, with, *Ex.* 30. 10. Aaron shall make atonement *with b.*

Ps. 106. 38. and the land was polluted *with b.*

Is. 34. 6. sword of Lord filled *with b.* made fat *with b.*

59. 3. for your hands are defiled *with b.*

Ezek. 38. 22. I will plead against him *with b.*

Gal. 1. 16. immediately I conferred not *with b.*

Blood guiltiness, *Ps.* 51. 14. deliver me from *b. guiltiness*

BLOOD-THIRSTY, *Prov.* 29. 10. the *b -thirsty* hate the upright

BLOODY, *Ps.* 26. 9. gather not my life with *b.* men

Ezek. 24. 6. woe to the *b.* city, 9 ; *Nah.* 3. 1.

Acts 28. 8. father of Publius lay sick of a *b.* flux

BLOOMED, *Num.* 17. 8. Aaron's rod *b.* blossoms and almonds

BLOSSOM, A flower of a tree or plant, *Gen.* 40. 10. To put forth into flowers, or blossoms ; *Num.* 17. 5 ; *Hab.* 3. 17. To increase, flourish and prosper ; *Is.* 27. 6 ; 35. 1, 2.

Gen. 40. 10. her *b.* shot forth, and her clusters

Is. 5. 24. their *b.* go up as dust

27. 6. Israel shall *b.* and bud

35. 1. desert shall *b.* as the rose

2. it shall *b.* abundantly and rejoice

Ezek. 7. 10. rod hath *b.* pride budded

Hab. 3. 17. the fig tree shall not *b.*

BLOT out, *Ex.* 32. 32. and if not *b.* me *out* of thy book

Ex. 32. 33. whosoever hath sinned, him will I *b. out*

Deut. 9. 14. let me alone that I may *b. out* their name

25. 19. shall *b. out* the remembrance of Amalek

29. 20. the Lord shall *b. out* his name from under heaven

Ps. 51. 1. have mercy O God, *b. out* my transgressions

9. hide my sins and *b.* out all mine iniquities

Rev. 3. 5. I will not *b.* his name *out* of book of life

BLOTTED, *Ps.* 69. 28. let them be *b.* out of book of the living

Ps. 109. 13. posterity cut off, let their name be *b.* out

Is. 44. 22. I have *b.* out as a thick

Acts 3. 19. repent, that your sins may be *b. out*

BLOTTETH, ING, *Is.* 43. 25. I am he that *b.* out thy transgressions

Col. 2. 14. *b.* out the hand writing of ordinances

BLOW, (1) A stroke, calamity, affliction &c. ; "Remove thy stroke away from me," &c. ; *Ps.* 39. 10 ; *Jer.* 14. 17. (2) The displeasure of God in scattering his enemies ; *Ex.* 15. 10. (3) The blowing of the trumpets ; *Num.* 10. 5—9 ; *Josh.* 6. 4. (4) The gracious operations of the Spirit ; "The wind bloweth where it listeth," &c. ; *John* 3. 8 ; *Songs* 4. 16.

BLOW, *Ps.* 39. 10. I am consumed by the *b.* of thy hand

Jer. 14. 17. people is broken with a grievous *b.*

BLOW, (verb) *Ex.* 15. 10. thou didst *b.* with thy wind

Num. 10. 5. when ye *b.* an alarm, camps shall go, 6.

Judg. 7. 18. when I *b.* with a trumpet, then *b.* ye

Ps. 78. 26. he caused an east wind to *b.* in heaven

147. 18. caused his wind to *b.* and waters flow

Songs 4. 16. come, thou south, *b.* upon my garden

Is. 40. 24. he shall also *b.* upon them, shall wither

Hos. 5. 8. *b.* ye the cornet in Gibeah

Luke 12. 55. when ye see the southwind *b.*

BLOWETH, *Is.* 40. 7. because the Spirit of the Lord *b.* on it

54. 16. I have created the smith that *b.* the coals

John 3. 8. the wind *b.* where it listeth

BLOWN, *Job* 20. 26. a fire not *b.* shall consume him

Mal. 1. 13. whereas ye might have *b.* it

away

BLUE, *Ex.* 25. 4. *b.* purple, scarlet, 26.
1. 31, 36 ; 27. 16.

Ex. 28. 31. make the robe of the ephod
of *b.* 39. 22.

39. 3. they cut gold into wires to work
it in the *b.*

2 *Chr.* 2. 7. send a man cunning to work
in the *b.*

Esth. 1. 6. *b.* hangings, a pavement of
b. marble

8. 15. Mordecai went in a royal apparel of *b.*

Ezek. 23. 6. the Assyrians were clothed
with *b.*

Prov. 20. 30. *b.* of a wound cleanseth
away evil

BLUNT, *Eccl.* 10. 10. if iron be *b.* and
he do not whet it

BLUSH to lift up my face, *Ezra* 9. 6.
Jer. 6. 15. neither could they *b.* 8. 12.

BOAR, *Ps.* 80. 13. *b.* out of the wood
doth waste it

BOAST sometimes means vaunting and
insulting language ; *Ps.* 94. 4.
Sometimes confidence and triumph
in God ; *Ps.* 34. 2. The apostle
Paul said, if he must boast, it should
be in his infirmities. His enemies
had upbraided him with weakness
or cowardice. Of this weakness he
told them he would boast, because
the humbler he was, the more he
should be strengthened by Divine
power ; *Ps.* 10. 3. & 49. 6. & 52. 1 ;
Prov. 20. 14. & 25. 14 ; *Jam.* 3. 5.

1 *Kings* 20. 11. *b.* as he that puts it off

2 *Chr.* 25. 19. thine heart lifteth thee up
to *b.*

Ps. 44. 8. in God we *b.* all day long

Ps. 49. 6. and *b.* themselves in their
riches

94. 4. the workers of iniquity *b.* themselves

97. 7. confounded be they that *b.* of
idols

Prov. 27. 1. *b.* not of to-morrow

Is. 61. 6. in their glory shall ye *b.*
yourselves

Rom. 11. 18. *b.* not against branches

2 *Cor.* 9. 2. for which I *b.* to them of
Macedonia

10. 8. for though I should *b.* somewhat more

16. not to *b.* in another man's line

11. 16. receive me that I may *b.* myself a little

Eph. 2. 9. not works lest any should *b.*

BOASTERS, *Rom.* 1. 30. proud *b.* in-
ventors of evil things

2 *Tim.* 3. 2. covetous *b.* proud, blas-
phemers

BOASTEST, ETH, *Ps.* 10. 3. the wicked
b. of his heart's desire

Ps. 52. 1. why *b.* thou thyself in mischief

Jam. 3. 5. tongue a little member, and
b. great things

BOASTING, Substantive, *Rom.* 3. 27.
where is *b.* then ? it is excluded

2 *Cor.* 7. 14. even so our *b.* before Titus
is found truth

8. 24. show ye to them the proof of
our *b.*

11. 17. but as it were foolishly in this
confidence of *b.*

Jam. 4. 16. *b.* all rejoicing is evil

BODY, (1) The material part of man, 1
Cor. 15. 44. (2) The whole man,
Rom. 6. 12 ; 12. 1. (3) The substance of a shadow or ceremony,
Col. 2. 17. (4) The church of God
firmly united to Christ and among
themselves, by the Spirit, faith,
love, sacraments, word, and ministry, which, like the veins and
arteries in the body, serve to join
them with Christ, and among themselves, and also to convey influence
and nourishment from the head to
every particular member of this
mystical body, 1 *Cor.* 10. 17 ; *Eph.*
4. 16 ; *Col.* 1. 18. (5) The human
nature of Christ, *Heb.* 10. 5. (6)
The unrenewed part of man, such
as the sensitive powers, carnal affections, and sinful inclinations, 1
Cor. 9. 27.

This is my body, *Matt.* 26. 26. This
bread is a sign or representation,
and is hereafter to be a memorial
also, of my body, and of my sufferings in it ; and also a seal and
pledge, whereby I make over to
you all the benefits I have purchased thereby : *Or*, This taking
and eating is a holy rite of com-
memorating my death, and a means
of making all worthy receivers partakers of the benefits thereof.

Ex. 24. 10. *b.* of heaven,

Job 19. 26. worms destroy this *b.* yet in

Prov. 5. 11. when thy flesh and *b.* are
consumed

Is. 10. 18. consume both soul and *b.*

Ezek. 10. 12. their whole *b.* was full of
eyes

Matt. 5. 29. that thy whole *b.* be cast
into hell, 30.

Matt. 6. 22. *b.* full of light, *Luke* 11. 34.

23. thy whole *b.* shall be full of darkness

25. take no thought for your *b.* *Luke*
12. 22. and the *b.* more than raiment
Luke 12. 23.

10. 28. that kill the *b.* *Luke* 12. 4.

26. 12. he hath poured this ointment
on my *b.*

26. 26. this is my *b.* 1 *Cor.* 11. 24.

27. 58. Joseph of Arimethea went to
Pilate, and begged the *b.* of Jesus,
Mark 15. 43 ; *Luke* 23. 52.

Mark 14. 8. she is come aforehand to
anoint my *b.*

51. having a linen cloth cast about
his *b.*

15. 45. Pilate gave the *b.* to Joseph,
Matt. 27. 58.

Luke 17. 37. where the *b.* is, thither
the eagles

John 20. 12. where the *b.* of Jesus had

Rom. 6. 6. that *b.* of sin be destroyed

7. 4. dead to the law by *b.* of Christ

24. deliver me from this *b.* of death

8. 10. *b.* is dead because of sin

13. if ye through the Spirit mortify
deeds of the *b.*

18. through the spirit mortify deeds
of the *b.*

23. adoption the redemption of our *b.*

1 *Cor.* 6. 13. *b.* is not for fornication but for the Lord, and the Lord for the *b.*

18. every sin that a man doeth without the *b.*

19. your *b.* is the temple of the Holy Ghost

7. 4. wife hath not power of her own *b.*

9. 27. I keep under my *b.* lest that by

10. 16. communion of the *b.* of Christ

11. 27. guilty of the *b.* and blood of Lord

29. not discerning the Lord's *b.* 12. 14, 23.

12. 15. is it therefore not of the *b.* ? 16.

19. where were the *b.?* 20. many members, yet but one *b.*

27. ye are the *b.* of Christ

13. 3. though I give my *b.* to be burned

37. thou sowest not that *b.* that shall be

15. 35. with what *b.* do they come

44. sown a natural *b.* raised a spiritual *b.*

2 *Cor.* 5. 8. willing rather to be absent from the *b.*

Eph. 3. 6. fellow-heirs of the same *b.*

4. 12. for edifying the *b.* of Christ

5. 23. he is the Saviour of the *b.*

Phil. 3. 21. who shall change our vile *b.*

Col. 1. 18. he is the head of the *b.* church

2. 11. putting off the *b.* sins of the

17. shadow of things—but *b.* is Christ

19. from which the *b.* by joints and bands

23. neglecting of the *b.* not in honour

1 *Thess.* 5. 23. spirit, soul, and *b.* be preserved

Heb. 10. 5. a *b.* hast thou prepared me

Jam. 2. 16. give not things which are needful to the *b.*

26. as the *b.* without the spirit is dead, so faith

3. 2. and is able also to bridle the whole *b.*

3. 6. tongue defileth the whole *b.*

Jude 9. disputed about the *b.* of Moses

BODY, dead, *Lev.* 21. 11. nor shall ye go into any *dead b. Num.* 6. 6.

Num. 9. 6. certain men were defiled by a *dead b.* 7.

Is. 26. 19. with my *dead b.* shall they rise

BODY, fruit of the, *Deut.* 28. 4. blessed shall be the *fruit of thy b.*

Deut. 28. 11, 18, 53. *fruit of the b.*, & 30. 9.

Ps. 132. 11. *fruit of thy b.* will I set on thy throne

Mic. 6. 7. shall I give *fruit of my b.* for sin of my soul

BODY, his, *Dan.* 4. 33. *his b.* wet with the dew of heaven, 5. 21.

10. 6. *his b.* also was like the beryl

Luke 23. 55. the women beheld how *his b.* was laid

24. 23. when they found not *his b.* they came

John 2. 21. spake of the temple of *his b.*
    1 *Pet.* 2. 24. *his* own *b.* on the tree

Acts 19. 12. from *his b.* were brought to the sick

1 *Cor.* 6. 18. commits fornication sinneth against *his b.*

7. 4. the husband hath not power of *his* own *b.*

2 *Cor.* 5. 10. may receive the things done in *his b.*

Eph. 1. 23. which is *his b.* fulness o him that filleth

Phil. 3. 21. may be fashioned like to *his* glorious *b.*

1 *Pet.* 2. 24. who bare our sins in *his b.* on the tree

BODY, in, *Rom.* 6. 12. let not sin reign *in* your mortal *b.*

1 *Cor.* 5. 3. in the *b.* 2 *Cor.* 5. 6, 10. & 12. 2 ; *Phil.* 1. 20 ; *Heb.* 13. 3.

1 *Cor.* 6. 20. therefore glorify God *in* your *b.* and spirit

12. 18. God hath set members every one in the *b.*

25. that there should be no schism *in* the *b.*

2 *Cor.* 4. 10. bearing about *in* the *b.* the dying of our Lord, that life of Jesus might be manifest *in* our *b.*

5. 6. knowing that whilst we are at home in *b.*

Heb. 13. 3. as being yourselves also *in* the *b.*

BODY, one, *Rom.* 12. 4. as we have many members in *one b.*

1 *Cor.* 6. 16. he that is joined to an harlot is *one b.*

12. 12. as the *b.* is *one*, and hath many members

13. we are baptized into *one b.* whether Jews

Eph. 2. 16. he might reconcile both to God in *one b.*

4. 4. there is *one b.* and one Spirit, as ye are called

BODIES, *Ezek.* 1. 11. two wings covered their *b.* 23.

Dan. 3. 27. on whose *b.* the fire had no power

Matt. 27. 52. many *b.* of saints which slept, arose

Rom. 1. 24. gave them up to dishonour their own *b.*

Rom. 8. 11. quicken your mortal *b.*

Rom. 12. 1. present your *b.* a living sacrifice

1 *Cor.* 6. 15. your *b.* are members of Christ

15. 40. there are celestial *b.* and *b.* terrestrial

Eph. 5. 28. husbands love your wives as own *b.*

Heb. 10. 22. *b.* washed with pure water

BODILY, *Luke* 3. 22. Holy Ghost descended in *b.* shape

2 *Cor.* 10. 10. his *b.* presence is weak

Col. 2. 9. dwelleth the fulness of Godhead *b.*

1 *Tim.* 4. 8. *b.* exercise profiteth little

BOIL, *Job* 41. 31. he maketh the deep to *b.* like a pot

Is. 64. 2. the fire causeth the waters to *b.*

Ezek. 46. 20. the place where the priests shall *b.* 24.

BOILED, 1 *Kings* 19. 21. he took a yoke of oxen and *b.* them

2 *Kings* 6. 29. so we *b.* my son, and did eat him

BOLD as a lion, *Prov.* 28. 1. but the

righteous are b. as a lion

Acts 13. 46. Paul and Barnabas waxed b.

Rom. 10. 20. Esaias is very b. and saith

2 Cor. 10. 1. absent am b. toward you

   11. 21. if any is b. I am b. also

Phil. 1. 14. my bonds are much more
   b. to speak the word without fear

Philem. 8. though I might be much b.
   in Christ

BOLDLY, *Gen.* 34. 25. Simeon and Levi
   came on the city b.

Mark 15. 43. Joseph came, and went in
   b. to Pilate

John 7. 26. he speaketh b. and they say
   nothing

Acts 9. 27. how he preached b. at Damascus

   29. he spake b. in the name of the
   Lord Jesus

   18. 26. Apollos began to speak b. in
   the synagogue

Rom. 15. 15. I have written the more
   b. to you

Eph. 6. 19, 20. open my mouth b.

Heb. 4. 16. come b. to throne of grace

BOLDNESS, *Eccl.* 8. 1. and the b. of his
   face shall be changed

2 Cor. 7. 4. great is my b. of speech

Eph. 3. 12. in whom we have b. access

Heb. 10. 19. b. to enter into the holiest

1 John 4. 17. b. in the day of judgment

BOND, (1) an obligation or vow, *Num.*
   30. 5, 14. (2) Sufferings of Christ
   and his gospel, *Heb.* 13. 3.

Thou hast loosed my bonds, Ps. 116. 16.
   Thou hast rescued me from mine
   enemies, whose captive and vassal
   I was, and therefore hast a just
   and right title to me and to my
   service.

He looseth the bonds of kings, Job 12.
   18. He deprives them of that majesty, power, and authority, which
   should keep their subjects in awe,
   and wherewith they bind them to
   obedience.

Charity is the bond of perfectness, Col.
   3. 14. Love to our neighbour, flow-
   ing from love to God, is the chief
   means to a perfect union among
   all the members of the church, and
   to make their gifts and graces sub-
   servient to the good of one another.

Num. 30. 2. or swear to bind his soul
   with a b.

   3. if a woman vow and bind herself
   by a b. ; ver. 4.

Luke 13. 16. be loosed from his b. on
   the sabbath

Acts 8. 23. in gall and b. of iniquity

1 Cor. 12. 13. b. and free, *Gal.* 3. 28.

Eph. 4. 3. unity of spirit in b. of peace

BONDS, *Jer.* 5. 5. have broken the yoke,
   and burst the b.

Job 12. 18. he looseth b. of kings

Ps. 116. 16. hast loosed my b.

Acts 20. 23. b. and afflictions abide me

   23. 29. nothing worthy of death or b.

   26. 29. such as I am except these b.

Eph. 6. 20. I am an ambassador in b.

Phil. 1. 7. in b. ye are all partakers of
   my grace

   13. so that my b. in Christ are manifest

   14. the brethren waxing confident by
   my b.

   1. 16. to add affliction to my b.

Col. 4. 18. remember my b.

2 Tim. 2. 9. suffer trouble even unto b.

Philem. 10. whom I have begotten in my b.

Heb. 10. 34. compassion in my b.

   11. 36. trial of b. and imprisonments

   13. 3. remember them that are in b.

BONDAGE, (1) Outward slavery and
   oppression, *Ex.* 6. 5 ; *Ezra* 9. 8, 9.
   (2) Spiritual subjection to sin and
   Satan, *Heb.* 2. 15. (3) Subjection
   to the yoke of the ceremonial law,
   Gal. 2. 4 ; 4. 9. (4) Servile fear,
   Rom. 8. 15. (5) Corruption and
   death, *Rom.* 8. 21.

The one gendereth to bondage, Gal. 4.
   24. Begets children to bondage ;
   that is, They who adhered to the
   old covenant, or legal dispensation
   by Moses, were not thereby freed
   from their bondage to sin, Satan,
   and God's wrath, *Gal.* 3. 10. and
   were of a servile, mercenary disposition, doing what they did in God's
   service, not from love, but slavish
   fear, *Rom.* 8. 15, and thinking to
   merit heaven by their works

Ex. 1. 14. made their lives bitter with
   hard b.

   2. 23. sighed by reason of the b.

   6. 6. and I will rid you out of your b.

   13. 3. day in which ye came out of
   the house of b.

Rom. 8. 15. received again spirit of b.

   21. shall be delivered from the b. of
   corruption

1 Cor. 7. 15. brother or sister is not in b.

Gal. 4. 24. from mount Sinai, which
   gendereth to b.

   5. 1. be not entangled again with the
   yoke of b.

Heb. 2. 15. were all their life subject to b.

BONDAGE, in, into, or under, *John* 8.
   33. we were never in b. to any man

Acts 7. 6. and that they should bring
   them *into b.*

Gal. 2. 4. that they might bring us
   into b.

   4. 3. were *in b.* under the elements of
   the world

   25. answereth to Jerusalem which is
   in b.

2 Pet. 2. 19. of the same is he brought
   into b.

BOND-MAN, *Deut.* 15. 15. remember
   thou wast a b. in Egypt, and the
   Lord redeemed thee, 16. 12 ; 24.
   18, 22.

Rev. 6. 15: every b. hid themselves in

BOND-MAID, *Gal.* 4. 22. one by a b.
   the other by a free-woman

BOND-MEN, *Gen.* 43. 18. he may take
   us for b. and our asses

Lev. 25. 42. they shall not be sold as b.

   44. b. shall be of the heathen, of them
   buy b.

   46. they shall be your b. for ever

   26. 13. that ye should not be their b.

Deut. 7. 8. and redeemed you out of the
   house of b.

1 Kings 9. 22. but of Israel, did Solo,
   mon make no b.

Ezra 9. 9. we were *b.* yet God hath not forsaken

BOND-SERVANT, *Lev.* 25. 39. shalt not compel him to serve as a *b.*

Gen. 13. of the son of the *b.* will I make a nation

Gal. 4. 23. son of the *b.* was born after the flesh

31. we are not children of the *b.* but

Bond-women, *Gen.* 21. 10 ; *Gal.* 4. 23, 30.

BONE of *b.* and flesh of my flesh, *Gen.* 2. 23. & 29. 14 ; *Judg.* 9. 2 ; 2 *Sam.* 5. 1. & 19. 13.

Ex. 12. 46. not break a *b.* of it

John 19. 36. *b.* of him not be broken

Job 10. 11. fenced me with *b.* and sinew

Ps. 51. 8. *b.* broken may rejoice

Eccl. 11. 5. how *b.* grow in womb of

Matt. 23. 27. full of dead men's *b.*:

His bones, *Ps.* 34. 20 ; *Eph.* 5. 30 ; *Job* 20. 11 ; *Ezek.* 32. 27 ; *Prov.* 12. 4.

BONES MY, *Ps.* 6. 2. *my b.* are vexed

22. 14. all *my b.* are out of joint

31. 10. *my b.* are consumed

32. 3. *my b.* waxed old through

35. 10. all *my b.* shall say Lord, who

38. 3. there is no rest in *my b.*

102. 3. *my b.* are burnt as an hearth

5. *my b.* cleave to my skin

BOOK, *Gen.* 5. 1 ; *Esth.* 6. 1.

Ex. 32. 32. blot me out of thy *b.*

Num. 21. 14. it is said in the *b.* of the wars of the Lord

Josh. 10. 13. written in the *b.* of Jasher, 2 *Sam.* 1. 18.

1 *Kings* 11. 41. written in the *b.* of Acts of Solomon

Ezra 4. 15. search may be made in *b.* of records

Neh. 8. 5. Ezra opened the *b.* in the sight of all

Job 19. 23. O that—printed in a *b.*

31. 35. adversary had written a *b.*

Ps. 40. 7. in volume of *b.* *Heb.* 10, 7.

56. 8. tears are they not in thy *b.*

69. 28. let them be blotted out of *b.* of the living

139. 16. in thy *b.* all my members

Is. 34. 16. seek ye out of the *b.* of the Lord, and read

Ezek. 2. 9. and lo ! a roll of a *b.* was therein

Dan. 12. 1. every one found written in the *b.*

Mal. 3. 16. a *b.* of remembrance was written

Matt. 1. 1. the *b.* of the generation of Jesus

Luke 4. 17. there was delivered to Jesus the *b.* of the prophet Esaias, and when he had opened the *b.*

Acts 7. 42. it is written in the *b.* of the prophets

Heb. 9. 19. he sprinkled the *b.* and the people

Rev. 1. 11. what thou seest write in a *b.*

5. 2. who is worthy to open the *b.* and to loose seals

10. 2. and he had in his hand a little *b.* open

Rev. 20. 12. another *b.* was opened, the *b.* of life

22. 19. if any take away from the words of the *b.*

BOOK of Life, *Phil.* 4. 3. whose names are written in the *b. of life*

Rev. 3. 5. I will not blot out his name out of *b. of life*

13. 8. names are not written in the *b. of life,* 17. 8.

20. 12. another *b.* opened, which is the *b. of life*

15. was not found in the *b. of life*

21. 27. which are written in the Lamb's *b. of life*

22. 19. shall take away his part out of the *b. of life*

BOOK, this, *Gen.* 5. 1. *this* is the *b.* of the generation of Adam

Deut. 29. 20. the curses that are written in *this b.* 27.

2 *Kings* 23. 3. to perform the words written in *this b.*

John 20. 30. signs which are not written in *this b.*

Rev. 22. 7. the sayings of the prophecy of *this b.*

9. of them which keep the sayings of *this b.*

10. seal not the sayings of the prophecy of *this b.*

18. heareth the words of the prophecy of *this b.* if any add, add plagues

19. his part from the things written in *this b.*

BOOKS, *Ezra* 6. 1. search was made in the house of the *b.*

Eccl. 12. 12. of making many *b.* there is no end

Dan. 7. 10. and the *b.* were opened, *Rev.* 20. 12.

9. 2. I understood by *b.* the number of years

John 21. 25. the world could not contain the *b.*

Acts 19. 19. many brought their *b.* and burned them

2 *Tim.* 4. 13. bring the *b.* especially the parchments

Rev. 20. 12. dead judged out of things written in the *b.*

BOOTH, *Job* 27. 18. as a *b.* that the keeper maketh

Jonah 4. 5. Jonah went and made him a *b.*

BOOTHS, *Gen.* 33. 17. and Jacob made *b.* for his cattle

Lev. 23. 42. ye shall dwell in *b.* seven days

43. I made the children of Israel dwell in *b.*

BOOTY, IES, *Num.* 31. 32. *b.* the rest of the prey, 675,000 sheep

Jer. 49. 32. and their camels shall be a *b.*

Zeph. 1. 13. therefore their goods shall become a *b.*

BORDER, coast, bound, or limit, *Gen.* 10. 19 ; 49. 13. A border for fastening ; *Ex.* 25. 25. A skirt, hem, or fringe ; *Mark* 6. 56. Borders of delight ; *Is.* 54. 12. and I will make thy windows of agates . . . *borders* of precious stones

Ex. 19. 12. or touch the *b.* of the mount

Deut. 12. 20. when the Lord shall enlarge thy *b.*

2 *Kings* 3. 21. all that were able stood in the *b.*

Ps. 78. 54. brought them to the *b.* of his sanctuary

Is. 37. 24. I will enter into the height of his *b.*

Jer. 31. 17. thy children come again to their *b.*

Amos 1. 13. that they might enlarge their *b.*

Mal. 1. 5. Lord will be magnified from the *b.* of Israel

BORDERS, *Ex.* 16. 35. till they come to the *b.* of Canaan

Ps. 74. 17. thou hast set the *b.* of the earth

Songs 1. 11. we will make the *b.* of gold with studs

Is. 54. 12. I will make thy *b.* of pleasant stones

Ier. 15. 13. that for all thy sins even in all thy *b.*

Ezek. 45. 1. this shall be holy in the *b.*

Matt. 4. 13. in the *b.* of Zabulon and Nephthalim

23. 5. and enlarge the *b.* of their garments

BORE, *Ex.* 21. 6. his master shall *b.* his ear through

Job 41. 2. canst thou *b.* his jaw through with a thorn

BORED, *Judg.* 16. 21. the Philistines *b.* out his eyes

BORN, *Ps.* 58. 3. go astray as soon as *b.*

Ps. 87. 4. this man was *b.* there, 6.

5. this and that man—*b.* in her

Prov. 17. 17. brother is *b.* for adversity

Eccl. 3. 2. time to be *b.* and die

Is. 9. 6. unto us a child is *b.* a Saviour

66. 8. shall a nation be *b.* at once

Jer. 15. 10. *b.* me a man of strife

Matt. 11. 11. among them that are *b.* of women

26. 24. better if he had not been *b.*

John 3. 4. be *b.* when he is old

5. *b.* of water and of spirit

John 3. 6. *b.* of flesh is flesh, *b.* of spirit

Rom. 9. 11. children being not yet *b.*

1 *Cor.* 15. 8. one *b.* out of due time

Gal. 4. 23. *b.* after flesh, 29.

1 *Pet.* 2. 2. as new *b.* babes desire

Job 14. 1. *b.* of a woman, 15. 14. & 25.

4 ; *Matt.* 11. 11 ; *Luke* 7. 28 ; *b.* again, *John* 3. 3, 5, 7 ; 1 *Pet.* 1. 23.

BORN, for brought forth, *Gen.* 17. 17. a child *b.* to him 100 years old, 21. 5.

Gen. 21. 7. I have *b.* him a son in his old age

24. 15. Rebekah came, who was *b.* to Bethuel

Ex. 1. 22. every son *b* ye shall cast into the river

Lev. 12. 7. this is the law of her that hath *b.* a male

Ruth 4. 15. for thy daughter in law hath *b.* him

1 *Sam.* 2. 5. so that the barren hath *b.* seven

Job 3. 3. let the day perish wherein I was *b.*

5. 7. yet man is *b.* to trouble as sparks fly upward

11. 12. though man be *b.* like a wild ass's colt

Ps. 22. 31. shall declare to a people that shall be

20. 14. cursed be the day wherein I was *b.*

Ezek. 16. 4. in day thou wast *b.* thy navel not cut

Hos. 2. 3. lest I set her as in the day that she was *b.*

Matt. 2. 2. where is he that is *b.* king of the Jews

4. Herod demanded where Christ should be *b.*

26. 24. good if he had not been *b. Mark* 14. 21.

Luke 1. 35. that holy thing that shall be *b.* of thee

2. 11. to you is *b.* this day in the city of David

John 9. 2. master, who did sin, that he was *b.* blind

16. 21. for joy that a man is *b.* into the world

18. 37. to this end was I *b.* and for this cause

Acts 22. 3. I am a Jew *b.* in Tarsus ; 28. I was free *b.*

Rom. 9. 11. for the children being not yet *b.*

1 *Cor.* 15. 8. seen of me, as of one *b.* out of due time

Heb. 11. 23. by faith Moses when *b.* was

1 *Pet.* 2. 2. as new *b.* babes desire sincere milk of word

1 *John* 2. 29. that doeth righteousness, is *b.* of him

BORN of God, *John* 1. 13. which were *b.* not of blood, but *of God*

1 *John* 3. 9. *b. of God* doth not commit sin, because *b.*

4. 7. every one that loveth is *b. of God* and knoweth

5. 1. who believeth that Jesus is Christ is *b. of God*

18. whosoever is *b. of God* sinneth not

BORNE, *Gen.* 50. 23. children of Machir *b.* on Joseph's knees

Judg. 16. 29. the pillars on which the house was *b.* up

Mark 2. 3. bringing one sick of palsy, was *b.* of four

John 20. 15. if thou hast *b.* him hence tell me

1 *Cor.* 15. 49. as we have *b.* the image of the earthy

BORNE, *Job* 34. 31. to be said to God, I have *b.* chastisement

Ps. 55. 12. it was not an enemy, then I could have *b.*

69. 7. because for thy sake I have *b.* reproach

Is. 53. 4. surely he hath *b.* griefs, carried sorrows

Matt. 20. 12. which have *b.* burden and heat of day

Rev. 2. 3. hast *b.* and hast patience, and not fainted

BORROW, to ask for, and receive any thing ; *Ex.* 3. 21, 22 ; 11. 2 ; 12. 35 ; 22. 14 ; 2 *Kings* 4. 2 ; 6. 5 ; *Neh.* 5. 4.

BORROWER, *Prov.* 22. 7 ; *Is.* 24. 2.

Prov. 22. 7. *b.* is servant to the lender

Is. 24. 2. as with lender so with *b.*

Matt. 5. 42. from *b.* of thee turn not

BOSOM, (1) That part of the body which incloses the heart, *Ex.* 4. 6.
(2) The arms, *Ps.* 129. 7.

The Son which is in the bosom of the Father, *John* 1. 18 ; who is one with the Father, entirely beloved by him, and intimately acquainted with all his counsels and will.

Gen. 16. 5 ; *Ex.* 4. 6.
Num. 11. 12. carry them in *b.*
Deut. 13. 6. wife of *b.* 28. 54, 56.
Ruth 4. 16. Naomi took the child and laid it in her *b.*
1 *Kings* 1. 2. a young virgin, let her lie in thy *b.*
    3. 20. she arose and took my son, and laid it in her *b.* and laid her dead child in my *b.*
    17. 19. Elijah took him out of her *b.*
Ps. 35. 13. prayer return unto own *b.*
    74. 11. pluck thy hand out of *b.*
Ps. 79. 12. and render sevenfold into
    89. 50. how I do bear in my *b.* the reproach of all
Prov. 5. 20. embrace in *b.* of stranger
    6. 27. take fire in his *b.* and not
    17. 23. gift out of *b.* 21. 14.
    19. 24. hides hands in his *b.* 26. 15.
Eccl. 7. 9. anger rests in *b.* of fools
Is. 40. 11. carry the lambs in his *b.*
    65. 6. 7. recompense into their *b.* *Ps.* 79. 12 ; *Jer.* 32. 18.
Mic. 7. 5. her that lieth in thy *b.*
Luke 6. 38. men give into your *b.*
    16. 22. was carried by the angels into Abraham's *b.*
    16. 23. seeth Abraham, and Lazarus in his *b.*
John 1. 18. who is in the *b.* of Father
    13. 23. leaning on Jesus's *b.*
BOSSES, *Job.* 15. 26. upon the thick *b.* of his bucklers
BOTCH, *Deut.* 28. 27. Lord will smite thee with the *b.* 35.
BOTH, *Gen.* 2. 25. & 3. 7. & 9. 36.
Gen. 27. 45. why should I be deprived of *b.* of you in one day ?
1 *Sam.* 2. 34. in one day they shall die *b.* of them
Job 9. 33. any days man that might lay his hand on *b.*
Eccl. 4. 3. better than *b.* is he that hath not been
Mic. 7. 3. that they may do evil with *b.* hands
Zech. 6. 13. counsel of peace between *b.*
Matt. 15. 14. *b.* shall fall into the ditch, *Luke* 6. 39.
Luke 7. 42. nothing to pay, frankly forgave them *b.*
Acts 23. 8. nor angel nor spirit, but Pharisee confess *b.*
Eph. 2. 14. our peace made *b.* one
    16. that might reconcile *b.* to God
    18. we *b.* have access by one spirit
Rev. 19. 20. *b.* were cast alive into the lake of fire
BOTTLE, *Gen.* 21. 14, 15, 19.
Judg. 4. 19. she opened a *b.* of milk and covered him
1 *Sam.* 1. 24. Hannah took a *b.* of wine
2 *Sam.* 16. 1. Ziba brought to David a *b.* of wine
Ps. 56. 8. put my tears into thy *b.*
    119. 83. I am like a *b.* in the smoke
Jer. 13. 12. every *b.* filled with wine
    19. get a potter's earthen *b.* ; 10.

break the *b.*
BOTTLES, *Josh.* 9. 4. the Gibeonites took wine *b.* and rent
1 *Sam.* 25. 18. Abigail took two *b.* of wine, five sheep
Job 38. 37. *b.* of heaven
Matt. 9. 17. new wine into old *b.*
Mark 2. 22. new wine into new *b.*
BOTTOM, *Ex.* 15. 5. they sank into the *b.* as a stone
Job 36. 30. behold, God covereth the *b.* of the sea
Dan. 6. 24. or ever they came at the *b.* of the den
Jonah 2. 6. I went down to the *b.* of the mountains
Matt. 27. 51. vail rent from top to *b.* *Mark* 15. 38.
BOTTOMLESS, *Rev.* 9. 1. to him was given the key of the *b.* pit
Rev. 2. he opened the *b.* pit, and there arose smoke
    11. 7. the beast that ascendeth out of the *b.* pit
    20. 1. an angel having the key of the *b.* pit
    3. and cast him into the *b.* pit and shut him up
BOUGH, *Gen.* 49. 22. Joseph is a fruitful *b.* even a fruitful *b.* by a well, whose branches run over the wall
Judg. 9. 48. Abimelech cut down a *b.* from the trees
Is. 10. 33. the Lord shall lop the *b.* with terror
BOUGHS, *Lev.* 23. 40. *b.* of goodly trees, *b.* of thick trees
2 *Sam.* 18. 9. the mule went under the *b.* of an oak
Job 14. 9. and brought forth *b.* like a plant
Songs 7. 8. I will take hold of the *b.*
Is. 27. 11. when the *b.* thereof are withered
BOUGHT, that which is, or has been purchased. Joseph was bought by Potiphar ; *Gen.* 39. 1 ; *Lev.* 28. 24 ; *Mark* 16. 1. Men are *bought with a price,* even the Redeemer's blood ; (refer to and read the passages in the concordance part)
Gen. 17. 12 ; 33. 19. Jacob *b.* a parcel of a field, *Josh.* 24. 32.
    47. 20. Joseph *b.* all the land of Egypt, 23.
    49. 30. which Abraham *b.* 50. 13 ; *Acts* 7. 16.
Lev. 25. 30. shall be established for ever to him that *b.* it
    25. 51. give out of the money that he was *b.* for
Deut. 32. 6. not father that *b.* thee
Ruth 4. 9. I have *b.* all that was Elimelech's
    24. 24. so David *b.* the threshing-floor and oxen
Neh. 5. 16. I continued in work, nor *b.* we any land
Hos. 3. 2. so I *b.* her to me for 15 pieces of silver
Matt. 13. 46. sold all that he had and *b.*
    21. 12. Jesus cast out all them that sold and *b.* in the temple, *Mark* 11. 15 ; *Luke* 19. 45.

27. 7. took counsel and *b.* with then potter's field

Mark 15. 46. Joseph *b.* fine linen and took him down

Luke 14. 18. I have *b.* a piece of ground, and go see it

19. I have *b.* five yoke oxen, I go to prove them

1 *Cor.* 6. 20. *b.* with a price, 7. 23.

2 *Pet.* 2. 1. denying Lord that *b.* them

BOUND, actively, *Josh.* 2. 21. she *b.* a scarlet line in the window

Judg. 15. 13. they *b.* Samson with two new cords

16. 8. *b.* with withs ; 12. ropes ; 21. fetters

2 *Chr.* 33. 11. *b.* Manasseh ; 36. 6. *b.* Jehoiakim

Matt. 14. 3. Herod *b.* John and put in prison, *Mark* 6. 17.

27. 2. they had *b.* Jesus, *Mark* 15. 1 ; *John* 18. 12.

Luke 13. 16. this daughter whom Satan hath *b.*

Acts 22. 25. as they *b.* Paul with thongs he said, 29.

Rev. 20. 2. he *b.* Satan a thousand years

Bound, passively, *Gen.* 40. 3. into the prison where Joseph was *b.*

5. the butler and baker which were *b.* in prison

19. let one of your brethren be *b.* in prison

1 *Sam.* 25. 29. the soul of my lord shall be *b.*

Job 36. 8. if they be *b.* in fetters

Ps. 107. 10. being *b.* in affliction

Prov. 22. 15. foolishness *b.* in heart of

Is. 61. 1. opening of the prison to *b.*

Lam. 1. 14. the yoke of my transgressions is *b.*

Dan. 3. 21. *b.* in their coats ; 23. fell down *b.*

Matt. 16. 19. whatsoever ye *b.* on earth shall be *b.* in heaven, 18. 18.

John 11. 44. *b.* hand and foot, his face was *b.*

18 24. Annas had sent him *b.* to Caiaphas, 13.

12. 6. Peter *b.* with chains ; 24. 27. left Paul *b.*

Acts 20. 22. I go *b.* in the spirit

21. 13. ready not to be *b.* only

Rom. 7. 2. wife is *b.* by law to her husband

1 *Cor.* 7. 27. are *b.* to a wife seek not

2 *Thess.* 1. 3. we are *b.* to thank God always, 2. 13.

2 *Tim.* 2. 9. word of God is not *b.*

Heb. 13. 3. in bonds as *b.* with them

Rev. 9. 14. loose the angels *b.* in the river Euphrates

BOUND, in chains, *Ps.* 68. 6. God bringeth out those which are *b.* with chains

Jer. 39. 7. *b.* Zedekiah, 52. 11 ; 40. 1. Jeremiah *b.* with chains

Nah. 3. 10. all her great men were *b.* with chains

Mark 5. 4. because he had been often *b.* with chains

Luke 8. 29. he was kept *b.* with chains, in fetters

Acts 21. 33. commanded Paul to *b.* with two *chains*

28. 20. for hope of Israel I am *b.* with this *chain*

BOUND up, *Is.* 1. 6. closed nor *b.* up

Jer. 30. 13. none to plead, that thou mayest be *b.* up

Ezek. 30. 21. not *b.* up to be healed

34. 4. nor have ye *b.* up broken

Hos. 4. 19. the wind hath *b.* her *up* in her wings

Hos. 13. 12. iniquity of Ephraim is *b.* up

BOUNDS, *Ex.* 19. 12. thou shalt set *b.* to the people round

23. 31. I will set thy *b.* from the Red sea to sea of

Job 14. 5. hast appointed his *b.* that he cannot pass

Is. 10. 13. I have removed the *b.* of the

Acts 17. 26. hast determined the *b.* of their habitation

BOUNTY,-IFULLY, 1 *Kings* 10. 13 ; 2 *Cor.* 9. 5 ; *Prov.* 22. 9 ; *Is.* 32. 5. *b.*

Ps. 13. 6. dealt *b.* with me, 116. 7. & 119. 17. & 142. 7.

2 *Cor.* 9. 6. sows *b.* shall reap *b.*

BOW, *Gen.* 9. 13. set my *b.* in the cloud

14. the *b.* be seen in cloud, 16.

48. 22. I took of the Amorite with my sword and *b.*

49. 24. his *b.* abode in strength

Josh. 24. 12. but not with thy sword nor thy *b.*

2 *Sam.* 1. 18. teach Judah the use of *b.*

1 *Kings* 22. 34. drew a *b.* at a venture and smote the king of Israel, 2 *Chr.* 18. 33.

1 *Chron.* 5. 18. valiant men able to shoot with *b.*

Job 29. 20. my *b.* was renewed in my hand

Ps. 44. 6. I will not trust in my *b.* nor sword

Ps. 46. 9. breaketh the *b.* cutteth spear

78. 57. turned aside like deceitful *b.*

Is. 41. 2. he gave them as stubble to his *b.*

Ezek. 1. 28. as the appearance of the *b.* in the cloud

Hos. 1. 7. I will not save them by *b.* nor by sword

7. 16. not to most High, they are like a deceitful *b.*

Rev. 6. 2. he that sat on the white horse had a *b.*

BOW-SHOT, *Gen.* 21. 16. sat over against him as it were a *b.*

BOWS, 1 *Sam.* 2. 4. the *b.* of the mighty are broken

Neh. 4 13. set the people with their *b.*

Ps. 37. 15. their *b.* shall be broken

Is. 7. 24. with arrows and *b.* shall men come

Ezek. 39. 9. they shall burn the *b.* and the arrows

BOW, 2 *Kings* 5. 18. I *b.* myself in the house of Rimmon

Job 39. 3. *b.* themselves bring forth

Ps. 22. 29. all that go down to the dust shall *b.*

144. 5. *b.* heavens, O Lord, come down

Prov. 5. 1. and *b.* thine ear to my understanding

Hab. 3. 6. the perpetual hills did *b.* his ways everlasting

Eph. 3. 14. for this cause I *b.* my knees to Father

BOW down, *Gen.* 37. 10. shall I, thy mother, and brethren *b. down*

49. 8. father's children shall *b. down* before me

BOW down, *Ex.* 23. 24. thou shalt not *b. down* to their gods

Job 31. 10. let others *b. down* upon her

Ps. 31. 2. *b. down* thine ear to me, *Prov.* 22. 17.

95. 6. O come, let us worship and *b. down*

Is. 49. 23. kings and queens shall *b. down* to thee

58. 5. *b. down* his head as bulrush

Rom. 11. 10. *b. down* their back alway

BOW knee, *Gen.* 41. 43. and they cried before him, *b.* the *knee*

Is. 45. 23. to me every *knee* shall *b. Rom.* 14. 11.

Eph. 3. 14. I *b.* my *knee* to Father of our Lord Jesus

Phil. 2. 10. at the name of Jesus every *knee* shall *b.*

BOWED, *Gen.* 43. 26. Joseph's brethren *b.* themselves to him

Ruth 2. 10. fell on her face and *b.* herself

2 *Sam.* 22. 10. he *b.* heavens and came down, *Ps.* 18. 9.

1 *Kings* 1. 16. Bathsheba *b.* and did obeisance, 31.

Matt. 27. 29. *b.* the knee before him and mocked

Luke 13. 11. a spirit of infirmity, and was *b.*

BOWED head, 2 *Chr.* 20. 18. Jehoshaphat *b.* his *head* to the ground

29. 30. they sang praises and *b.* their *heads*

John 19. 30. Jesus *b.* his *head* and gave up the ghost

BOWED himself, *Judg.* 16. 30. Samson *b. himself* with all his might

1 *Sam.* 24. 8. David stooped to Saul and *b. himself*

BOWING, *Gen.* 24. 52. Eliezer *b.* himself to the earth

Job 4. 4. thou hast strengthened the *b.* knees

Mark 15. 19. they did spit upon him, *b.* their knees

BOWELS, 2 *Chr.* 21. 15. great sickness disease of thy *b.*

18. Lord smote him in his *b.* ; 19. his *b.* fell out

Job. 20. 14. his meat in his *b.* is turned

Ps. 22. 14. melted in the midst of my *b.*

71. 6. took me out of my mother's *b.*

Songs 5. 4. and my *b.* were moved for him

Is. 63. 15. where is the sounding of thy *b.* and mercies ?

Acts 1. 18. Judas burst, and all his *b.* gushed out

2 *Cor.* 6. 12. straitened in your own *b.*

Phil. 1. 8. I long after you in the *b.* of Christ

2. 1. if consol. in Chr. if there be any *b.* and mercies

Col. 3. 12. put on *b.* of mercies

Philem. 7. *b.* of saints refreshed by thee

20. yea, brother refresh my *b.* in the L.

1 *John* 3. 17. shutteth up his *b.* of compassion

BOWL, a hollow vessel to hold liquids, *Judg.* 6. 38 ; 1 *Kings* 7. 50. "The golden bowl broken," *Eccl.* 12. 6. By this, some say is meant, "The skin that covereth the brain, which is in colour like gold ; " *Zech.* 4. 2 ; *Amos* 6. 6.

BOWLS, *Ex.* 25. 29. thou shalt make *b.* to cover, 37. 16.

2 *Chron.* 4. 8. Solomon made an 100 *b.* of gold

Amos 6. 6. that drink wine in *b.* but not grieved for

BOX, 2 *Kings* 9. 1. take this *b.* of oil in thine hand, 3.

Matt. 26. 7. having an alabaster *b.*

Mark 14. 3. she brake the *b.* and poured, *Luke* 7. 37.

BOX-TREE, *Is.* 41. 19. I will set in the desert the pine and *b.*

60. 13. the glory of Lebanon shall come, the *b.*

BOY, S, *Gen.* 25. 27. the *b.* grew, and Esau was a hunter

Joel 3. 3. they have given a *b.* for a harlot

Zech. 8. 5. streets shall be full of *b.* and girls playing

BRACELET, *Gen.* 24. 30. when he saw *b.* on his sister's hands

38. 18. thy signet, thy *b.* and thy staff, 25.

2 *Sam.* 1. 10. the *b.* on his arm I have brought

Is. 8. 19. I will take away the chains, *b.*

Ezek. 16. 11. and I put *b.* upon thine hands

BRAKE the tables, *Ex.* 32. 19. & 34. 1 ; *Deut.* 9. 17. & 10. 2.

Judg. 7. 19. *b.* the pitchers

9. 53. *b.* his skull

16. 12. Samson *b.* the new ropes

1 *Sam.* 4. 18. Eli *b.* his neck and died

1 *Kings* 19. 11. wind *b.* in pieces rocks

2 *Kings* 11. 18. *b.* Baal's images, 10. 27. 18. 4. *b.* the brazen serpent

23. 14. *b.* images 2 *Chr.* 34. 4.

Job 29. 17. *b.* the jaws of wicked

Ps. 76. 3. *b.* he the arrows

105. 16. *b.* whole staff of bread

107. 14. *b.* their bands asunder

Jer. 31. 32. my covenant they *b. Ezek.* 17. 16.

Dan. 2. 1. his sleep *b.* from him

34. stone *b.* them to pieces, 45.

6. 24. *b.* all their bones to pieces

Matt. 14. 19. blessed and *b.* and gave, 15. 36. & 26. 26 ; *Mark* 6. 41. & 8. 6 & 14. 22 ; *Luke* 9. 16. & 22. 19. & 24. 30 ; 1 *Cor.* 11. 24.

Mark 8. 19. when I *b.* the five loaves among 5000

14. 3. *b.* box and poured ointment

Luke 5. 6. their net *b.* 8. 29. he *b.* the bands

John 19. 32. the soldiers *b.* the legs of the first

33. and saw that he was dead, they *b.* not his legs

Brake down images house altars of Baal, 2 *Kings* 10. 27. and 18. 1 ; 2 *Chr.* 14. 3. & 23. 17. & 34. 4. wall of Jerusalem, 2 *Kings* 14. 13. & 25. 10 ; 2 *Chr.* 25. 23. & 36. 19 ; *Jer.*

39. 8. & 52. 14. houses of Sodom-
ites, high places, altars, altar of
Beth-el, 2 Kings 23. 7, 8, 12, 15.
Ps. 74. 13, 14. b. heads of dragons
BRAMBLE, S, Judg. 9. 14. then said
all the trees to the b.
Is. 34. 13. nettles and b. shall come up
in fortresses
Luke 6. 44. nor of a b.-bush gather they
grapes
BRANCH, The boughs of any tree, Ps.
104. 12. To which are compared,
(1) Jesus Christ the Messiah, who
was born of the royal house of
David, at that time when it was in
an afflicted and contemptible condition, like a tree cut down, and
whereof nothing is left but a stump
or root under ground, Is. 11. 1 ;
Jer. 23. 5 ; Zech. 3. 8 ; 6. 12. (2)
True believers who are ingrafted
into Christ the true vine ; who is
the root, fountain, and head of influence, whence his people and
members derive life, grace, fruit-
fulness, and all good ; as fruitful
branches derive continual influence
from the vine, John 15. 5. (3)
Earthly kings descended of royal
ancestors, as branches spring from
the root, Ezek. 17. 3 ; Dan. 11. 7.
(4) Children of posterity, Job 8. 16.
15. 32.
BRANCH, with cluster of grapes,
Num. 13. 23 ; Is. 17. 9. & 18. 5.
Job 15. 32. his b. shall not be green
18. 16. his b. shall he cut off
Ps. 80. 15. b. thou madest strong for
thyself
Prov. 11. 28. righteous flourish as a b.
Is. 4. 2. b. of Lord be beautiful
9. 14. cut off b. and root, 19. 15.
11. 1. b. shall grow out of his roots
14. 19. cast out like abominable b.
25. 5. b. of terrible ones brought low
60. 21. b. of my planting, 61. 3.
Jer. 23. 5. to David a righteous b.
33. 15. cause b. of righteous to grow
Zech. 3. 8. bring my servant the b.
6. 12. man whose name is b.
Mal. 4. 1. leave neither root nor b.
Matt. 24. 32. when b. is tender
John 15. 2. every b. that beareth not fruit
4. as b. cannot bear fruit except
6. cast forth as a b. withered
Lev. 23. 40. take b. of palm trees, John
12. 13.
Job 15. 30. flame dry up his b.
Ps. 80. 11. her b. to the river
104. 12. sing among the b.
Is. 16. 8. her b. stretched out

Is. 17. 6. four or five in outmost b.
18. 5. shall cut down b. 27. 10.
Jer. 11. 16. b. are broken, Ezek. 17. 6,
7. & 19. 10, 14.
Dan. 11. 4. hew down trees cut off his b.
Hos. 14. 6. his b. shall spread
Zech. 4. 12. what be these two olive b.
John 15. 5. I am the vine, ye are b.
Rom. 11. 16. if root be holy so are b.
17. some b. be broken off, 19.
18. boast not against b.
21. God spared not natural b. 24.
BRANCHES, Ps. 80. 11. she sent out

her b. to the river
104, 12. the fowls which sing among
the b.
Joel 1. 7. my vine waste, b. thereof are
made white
Matt. 13. 32. the birds lodge in the b.
Luke 13. 19.
21. 8. others cut down b. Mark 11. 8.
John 12. 13.
Mark 4. 32. greater than all herbs,
shooteth out b.
BRAND, Judg. 15. 5 ; Zech. 3. 2.
BRASS, Gen. 4. 22 ; Dan. 5. 4.
Num 21. 9. made a serpent of b.
Deut. 8. 9. whose hills mayest dig b.
28. 23. heaven over head be b.
Job 6. 12. is my strength of b.
41. 27. esteems b. as rotten wood
Ps. 107. 16. broken the gates of b.
Is. 48. 4. neck iron brow b.
60. 17. for b. I will bring gold
Dan. 2. 32. belly and thighs of b.
Zech. 6. 1. mountains of b.
1 Cor. 13. 1. become as sounding b.
Rev. 1. 15. feet like fine b. 2. 18.
BRAWLER, a contentious, quarrel-
some, and litigious person, full of
strife, a wrangler, 1 Tim. 3. 3 ; Tit.
3. 2. Such persons were in the
church of Corinth, 2 Cor. 12. 20. A
brawling woman is described, Prov.
21. 9 ; 25. 24.
BRAY, Job 6. 5 ; Prov. 27. 22.
BRAZEN, Num. 16. 39 ; 2 Kings 18. 4.
& 25. 13 ; 2 Chr. 6. 13 ; Jer. 1. 18.
& 15. 20. & 52. 20 ; Mark 7. 4.
BREACH be upon thee, Gen. 38. 29.
Num. 14. 34. know my b. of promise
Judg. 21. 15. Lord made b. in the tribes
2 Sam. 6. 8. Lord made b. on Uzzah, 1
Chr. 13. 11. & 15. 13.
Job. 16. 14. breakest me b. upon b.
Ps. 106. 23. Moses stood in the b.
Is. 30. 13. this iniquity shall be as b.
Is. 30. 26. in day Lord bindeth up b. of
people
58. 12. called the repairer of the b.
Lam. 2. 13. b. is great like the sea
Ps. 60. 2. heal b. thereof
BREAD shall be fat, Gen. 49. 20.
Ex. 16. 4. I will rain b. from heaven
23. 25. he will bless thy b. and water
Lev. 21. 6. b. of their God they offer, 8.
Num. 21. 5. soul loatheth this light b.
Deut. 8. 3. not live by b. only, Matt. 4.
4 ; Luke 4. 4.
Ruth 1. 6. visited his people giving b.
1 Sam. 2. 5. hired themselves for b.
25. 11. take my b. and my water
1 Kings 18. 4. fed them with b. and
water
Neh. 5. 14. eaten the b. of governor
9. 15. gavest b. from heaven
Ps. 37. 25. nor his seed begging b.
78. 20. can he give b. also
80. 5. feedest them with b. of tears
102. 9. I have eaten ashes like b.
104. 15. b. which strengtheneth man's
heart
132. 15. satisfy her poor with b.
Prov. 9. 17. b. eaten in secret is pleasant
20. 17. b. of deceit is sweet
22. 9. giveth of his b. to the poor

31. 27. she eats not the *b.* of idleness

Eccl. 9. 11. nor yet *b.* to the wise

11. 1. cast thy *b.* upon the waters

Is. 3. 1. whole stay of *b.* 7.

30, 20. Lord gave you *b.* of adversity

33. 16. *b.* shall be given and water

55. 2. spend money for that is not *b.*

10. give seed to sower and *b.* to eater

58. 7. deal thy *b.* to the hungry

Lam. 4. 4. young children ask *b.*

Ezek. 18. 7. given his *b.* to the hungry

Hos. 2. 5. give me my *b.* and water

9. 4. sacrifices as *b.* of mourners

Amos 4. 6. want of *b.* in all your places

Mal. 1. 7. offer polluted *b.* on my altar

Matt. 4. 3. these stones be made *b.*

6. 11. day our daily *b.* Luke 11. 11.

7. 9. if his son ask *b.* give him a stone

15. 26. meet to take the children's *b.*

16. 5. forgotten to take *b.* 11. 12.

26. 26. took *b.* and blessed it

Mark 8. 4. satisfy these with *b.*

Luke 7. 33. neither eating *b.* nor drink

15. 17. servants have *b.* enough

24. 35. known in breaking of *b.*

John 6. 32. Moses gave you not that *b.*

33. *b.* of God is he that cometh

34. evermore give us this *b.*

35. I am the *b.* of life, 48. true *b.* 32.

41. I am the *b.* which came down

50. this *b.* that comes down, 58.

13. 18. that eateth *b.* with me

Acts 2. 42. breaking of *b.* and in prayer

46. breaking *b.* from house to house

20. 7. came together to break *b.*

27. 35. took *b.* and gave thanks

1 *Cor.* 10. 16. *b.* we break, is it not

17. we being many are one *b.* all partakers of that one *b.*

11. 23. night he was betrayed took *b.*

26. as often as ye eat this *b.* 27.

2 *Cor.* 9. 10. minister *b.* for your food

Deut. 16. 3. *b.* of affliction, 1 *Kings* 22.
27 ; 2 *Chr.* 18. 26 ; *Is.* 30. 20.

Gen. 3. 19. *b.* will eat, 28. 20 ; *Ps.* 14. 4.
& 127. 2 ; *Prov.* 25. 21 ; *Eccl.* 9. 7 ;
Mark 7. 5 ; *Luke* 14. 15 ; 1 *Cor.* 11.
26 ; 2 *Thess.* 3. 12.

1 *Sam.* 2. 36. piece of *b.* Prov. 6. 26. &
28. 21 ; *Jer.* 37. 21 ; *Ezek.* 13. 19.

Lev. 26. 26. break staff of *b.* Ps. 105. 16 ;
Ezek. 4. 16. & 5. 16. & 14. 13.

Gen. 19. 3. unleavened *b.* Ex. 12. 8, 15.
& 13. 6, 7. & 18. 20 ; Mark 14. 12 ;
Luke 22. 7 ; Acts 12. 3, & 20. 6 ; 1
Cor. 5. 8.

BREAD-CORN, *Is.* 28. 28. *b.-corn* is
bruised, because he will not be

BREAD, leavened, *Ex.* 12. 15. who eateth *leavened b.* that soul be cut off

Ex. 13. 3. there shall no *leavened b.* be
eaten

BREAD, unleavened *Ex.* 12. 18. eat passover with *unleavened b.* Num. 9. 11.

Ex. 12. 20. in all your habitations shall
ye eat *unleavened b.*

Num. 6. 15. wafers of *unleavened b.*
anointed with oil

Deut. 16. 8. six days thou shalt eat *unleavened b.*

Luke 22. 7. then came the days of *unleavened b.* Acts 12. 3.

1 *Cor.* 5. 8. but with the *unleavened b.*
of sincerity

BREADTH, *Judg.* 20. 16. could sling
stones at an hair's *b.*

Dan. 3. 1. the *b.* of the image was six
cubits

Zech. 2. 2. to measure Jerusalem, to see
the *b.*

Eph. 3. 18. what is the *b.* and length
and depth

Rev. 20, 9. they went up on the *b.* of
the earth

21. 16. the length of the city is as
large as the *b.*

BREAK, *Gen.* 19. 9. they came near to
b. the door

Ex. 12. 46. nor shall ye *b.* a bone, *Num.*
9. 12.

13. 13. then thou shalt *b.* his neck,
34. 20.

Num. 30. 2. if a man vow, he shall not
b. his word

1 *Sam.* 25. 10. *b.* away every man from
his master

Job 13. 25. wilt thou *b.* a leaf driven to
and fro

Ps. 2. 3. let us *b.* their bands asunder

9. thou shalt *b.* them with a rod of

10. 15. *b.* thou the arm of the wicked

141. 5. shall be an oil which shall not
b. my head

Songs 2. 17. until day *b.* and shadows
flee away, 4. 6.

Is. 42. 3. a bruised reed will he not *b.*
Matt. 12. 20.

58. 6. is not this the fast, that ye *b.*

Jer. 19. 10. *b.* the bottle, so will I *b.*
this people

28. 4. I will *b.* yoke of king Babylon,
11 ; 30. 8.

Ezek. 4. 16. I will *b.* the staff of bread,
5. 16 ; 14. 13.

Hos. 1. 5. I will *b.* the bow of Israel in
Jezreel

2. 18. I will *b.* the bow, the sword
and battle

10. 11. Judah shall plow, and Jacob
shall *b.* his clods

Amos 1. 5. will *b.* the bar of Damascus

Matt. 5. 19. *b.* one of these least commandments

9. 17. else the bottles *b.* and the wine
runneth

Acts 20. 7. the disciples came together
to *b.* bread

21. 13. what mean ye to weep and to
b. my heart

1 *Cor.* 10. 16. the bread which we *b.* is

BREAK covenant, *Deut.* 31. 16. this people will *b.* my *covenant* I made, 20.

Judg. 2. 1. I said, I will never *b.* my
covenant with you

Ps. 89. 34. my *covenant* will I not *b.*
nor alter the thing

BREAK down, *Ex.* 25. 24. quite *b. down*
their images, *Deut.* 7. 5.

Lev. 14. 45. and he shall *b. down* house

Neh. 4. 3. if a fox go up, he shall *b.
down* stone wall

Eccl. 3. 3. a time to *b. down,* and a time
to build

BREAK forth, *Is.* 14. 7. they *b. forth*
into singing, 44. 23 ; 49. 13 ; 54. 1.

Is. 52. 9. *b. forth* into joy, sing together
ye waste places

54. 3. for thou shalt *b. forth* on the

right hand

55. 12. hills shall *b. forth* before you into singing

58. 8. then shall thy light *b. forth* as the morning

Gal. 4. 27. *b. forth* and cry, thou that travailest not

BREAK in pieces, *Job* 19. 2. how long will ye *b.* me *in pieces* with words

Job 34. 24. shall *b. in pieces* mighty men without number

Ps. 72. 4. he shall *b. in pieces* the oppressor

Dan. 2. 40. shall it *b. in pieces* and 7. 23. the fourth beast shall *b. in pieces* the whole earth

BREAK through, *Ex.* 19. 21. lest they *b. through* to the Lord to gaze

Matt. 6. 19. thieves *b. through* ; 20. thieves *b.* not *through*

BREAK up, *Jer.* 4. 3. *b. up* your fallow ground, *Hos.* 10. 12

BREAKER, *Mic.* 2. 13. *b.* is come up ; *Rom.* 2. 25. if a *b.* of law

BREAKETH, *Gen.* 32. 26. he said, let me go, for the day *b.*

Job 16. 14. he *b.* me with breach upon breach

Ps. 10. 10. he *b.* himself that the poor may fall

29. 5. *b.* the cedars ; 46. 9. he *b.* the bow

Jer. 19. 11. as one *b.* a potter's vessel, not made whole

23. 29. is not my word like hammer that *b.* rock ?

BREAKING, *Gen.* 32. 24. there wrestled a man till the *b.* of day

Ps. 144. 14. that there be no *b.* in nor going out

Luke 24. 35. he was known of them in *b.* of bread

Acts 2. 42. they continued in *b.* of bread and prayers

46. in the temple, *b.* bread from house to house

Rom. 2. 23. through *b.* the law, dishonourest God

BREAST, *Ex.* 29. 26. take the *b.* of the ram of consecration

Lev. 7. 30. *b.* may be waved, the fat with the *b.*

8. 29. Moses took the *b.* and waved it for an offering

Num. 6. 20. is holy to the priest, with the wave *b.*

Is. 60. 16. thou shalt suck the *b.* of kings

Dan. 2. 32. head of gold, his *b.* and his arms of

Luke 18. 13. the publican smote upon his *b.* saying

John 13. 25. he then lying on Jesus's *b.* saith, 21. 20.

BREASTS, *Gen.* 49. 25. bless with blessings of the *b.* and womb

Job 3. 12. or why the *b.* that I should suck

21. 24. his *b.* full of milk, and his bones moistened

Prov. 5. 19. let her *b.* satisfy thee at all

Songs 4. 5. thy two *b.* are like two young roes, 7. 3.

8. 1. my brother that sucked the *b.* of my mother

8. we have a little sister, and she hath no *b.*

Is. 28. 9. are weaned from the milk drawn from *b.*

Ezek. 16. 7. thy *b.* are fashioned, and hair grown

23. 3. there were their *b.* pressed, 8. and they bruised the *b.* of her virginity

Hos. 2. 2. put away her adulteries from between her *b.*

Luke 23. 48. the people smote their *b.* and returned

Rev. 15. 6. having their *b.* girded with golden girdles

BREAST-PLATE, *Ex.* 25. 7. and the stones to be set in the *b.* 35. 9.

Ex. 28. 4. shall make a *b.* and ephod, 15 ; 39. 8.

29. Aaron shall bear the name of Israel in *b.*

30. put in *b.* of judgment the Urim, *Lev.* 8. 8.

1 *Kings* 22. 34. smote Ahab between joints and *b.*

Is. 59. 17. he put on righteousness as a *b.*

Eph. 6. 14. having on the *b.* of righteousness

1 *Thess.* 5. 8. putting on the *b.* of faith and love

Rev. 9. 9. they had *b.* as it were *b.* of iron 17. having *b.* of fire, of jacinth, and brimstone

BREATH, *Gen.* 2. 7. God breathed into his nostrils the *b.* of life

Gen. 6. 17. to destroy all flesh wherein is the *b.* of life

7. 15. entered two and two wherein is the *b.* of life

22. all in whose nostrils was *b.* of life died

Job 4. 9. by the *b.* of his nostrils are they consumed

9. 18. he will not suffer me to take my *b.*

11. 20. their hope shall be a puff of *b.*

17. 1. my *b.* is corrupt, my days are extinct

19. 17. my *b.* is strange to my wife, 33. 4. the *b.* of the Almighty hath given me life

Ps. 33. 6. made by the *b.* of his mouth

146. 4. his *b.* goeth forth, he returneth to earth

150. 6. let every thing that hath *b.* praise

Eccl. 3. 19. yea, they have all one *b.* all is vanity

Is. 2. 22. cease from man, whose *b.* is in his nostrils

33. 11. your *b.* as fire shall devour you 42. 5. he that giveth *b.* to the people upon it

Ezek. 37. 5. I will cause *b.* to enter into you, shall live

10. and the *b.* came into them and they lived

Dan. 5. 23. the God in whose hand thy *b.* is

Acts 17. 25. seeing he giveth to all life and *b.*

BREATHE, (1) To draw breath naturally, as man and beast do, *Josh.* 10. 40. (2) To infuse the soul into the body, *Gen.* 2. 7. (3) To live, breathing or respiration being a sign of life, *Josh.* 11. 11. (4) To inspire with the gifts and graces of the Holy Ghost, *John* 20. 22.

BREATHE, *Josh.* 11. 11. there was not any left to *b.* 14.

Ps. 27. 12. and such as *b.* out cruelty

Ezek. 37. 9. come, O breath, and *b.* on

BREATHED, *Gen.* 2. 7. God *b.* into man's nostrils the breath of life

John 20. 22. he *b.* on them, and saith, receive ye

BREATHETH, ING, *Lam.* 3. 56. hide not thine ear at my *b.*, at my cry

Acts 9. 1. Saul yet *b.* out threatenings and slaughter

BREECHES. The linen of the priests were emblems of modesty, humility, chastity, holiness ; *Ex.* 28. 42 ; *Lev.* 6. 10 ; 16. 4 ; *Ezek.* 44. 18.

BRETHREN, Men are so called, (1) By being the sons of one father and mother, or of either of them, *Gen.* 42. 13. (2) By community of nature, or habitation, *Gen.* 19. 7. (3) By natural affinity, or by being kinsmen, *Gen.* 13. 8. (4) By regeneration, and a profession of the same faith and religion, *Col.* 1. 2. (5) By adoption, *John* 20. 17. (6) By office, 1 *Chr.* 25.9 ; 2 *Cor.* 8.23.

Gen. 13. 8. no strife, for we be *b.*

42. 3. Joseph's ten *b.* went down to buy corn

6. *b.* came and bowed ; 13. we are twelve *b.* 32.

Deut. 25. 5. if *b.* dwell together and one of them die

Ps. 133. 1. pleasant for *b.* to dwell together in unity

Prov. 6. 19. and him that soweth discord among *b.*

Matt. 19. 29. every one that hath forsaken houses, *b.*

22. 25. there were with us seven *b.* *Mark* 12. 20.

Matt. 23. 8. one is your Master, even Christ, all ye are *b.*

Mark 10. 29. no man left house or *b.*

Luke 14. 26. if any one come, and hate not children, *b.*

16. 28. for I have five *b.* that he may testify to them

21. 16. betrayed by parents and *b*

Acts 3. 17. *b.* I wot that through ignorance ye did it

11. 12. moreover these six *b.* accompanied me

29. they determined to send relief to the *b.*

15. 22. Barsabas and Silas chief among the *b.*

16. 40. when they had seen the *b.* they comforted

20. 32. now *b.* I commend you to God and his grace

23. 5. I wist not *b.* that he was the high priest

28. 15. when the *b.* heard of us, they came to meet us

Rom. 1. 13. now I would not have you

ignorant *b.* 11. 25 ; 1 *Cor.* 10. 1 ; 12. 1 ; 1 *Thess.* 4. 13.

7. 1. know ye not *b* that the law hath dominion

8. 12. *b.* we are debtors, not to the flesh, to live

29. that he might be the first-born among many *b.*

10. 1. *b.* my heart's-desire, and prayer to God for Israel is, may be saved

12. 1. I beseech you therefore, *b.* by the mercies of God. 15. 30 ; 16. 17 ; 1 *Cor.* 1. 10 ; 16. 15 ; *Gal.* 4. 12 ; *Heb.* 13. 22.

16. 14. salute the *b.* which are with them, *Col.* 4. 15.

1 *Cor.* 1. 26. for ye see your calling *b.*

2. 1. and I, *b.* when I came to you, came not with

7. 29. but this I say *b.* the time is short, 15. 50.

11. 2. now I praise you *b.* that ye remember me

15. 6. after he was seen of above 500 *b.* at once

58. therefore my beloved *b.* be steadfast, *Jam.* 2. 5.

16. 20. all the *b.* greet you, *Phil.* 4. 21.

2 *Cor.* 11. 26. I have been in perils among false *b.*

13. 11. finally *b.* farewell, be perfect, of good comfort

Eph. 6. 23. peace be to the *b.* and love with faith

Phil. 1. 14. many of the *b.* waxing confident

Col. 1. 2. to the saints and faithful *b.* in Christ

1 *Thess* 5. 25. *b.* pray for us, 2 *Thess.* 3. 1.

26. greet all the *b.* with an holy kiss

Heb. 2. 11. he is not ashamed to call them *b.*

3. 1. holy *b.* partakers, consider the Apostle

1 *Pet.* 1. 22. unto unfeigned love of *b.*

3. 8. love as *b.* be pitiful, be courteous

1 *John* 3. 14. from death to life, because we love *b.*

16. we ought to lay down our lives for the *b.*

3 *John* 3. rejoiced greatly when *b.* testified of truth

BRETHREN, his, *Gen.* 9. 25. Canaan, a servant of servants shall he be to *his b.*

16. 12. he shall dwell in presence of *his b.* 25. 18.

37. 2. Joseph was feeding the flock with *his b.*

5. Joseph dreamed a dream and told it *his b.*

11. *his b.* envied him, his father observed the saying

30. Reuben returned to *his b.* and said, the child is not

47. 12. Joseph nourished his father and *his b.*

Ex. 1. 6. Joseph died, *his b.* and all that generation

Deut. 10. 9. Levi hath no part with *his b.*

24. 7. if a man be found stealing any of *his b.*

33. 9. nor did he acknowledge *his b.*

nor knew

Judg. 9. 5. Abimelech slew *his b.* being 70 persons

1 *Sam.* 16. 13. Samuel anointed him in midst of *his b.*

1 *Chr.* 4. 9. Jabez more honourable than *his b.*

5. 2. for Judah prevailed above *his b.*

7. 22. Ephraim mourned, *his b.* came to comfort him

25. 9. with *his b.* and sons were twelve

Esth 10. 3. Mordecai the Jew was accepted of *his b.*

Matt. 12. 46. his mother and *his b.* stood without, desiring to speak with him, *Mark* 3. 31 ; *Luke* 8. 19.

John 7. 5. for neither did *his b.* believe

Heb. 2. 17. it behoved him to be made like *his b.*

BRETHREN, my, *Gen.* 29. 4. Jacob said to them, *my b.* whence be ye

37. 16. I seek *my b.* tell me where they feed flocks

1 *Sam.* 20. 29. let me get away, I pray, and see *my b.*

30. 23. then David said, ye shall not do so, *my b.*

2 *Sam.* 19. 12. ye are *my b.* my bones, and my flesh

Job 6. 15. *my b* have dealt deceitfully

Ps. 22. 22. I will declare thy name to *my b. Heb.* 2. 12.

122. 8. for *my b.* and companions' sake, I will say

Matt. 12. 48. he said to him, who are *my b.* ? *Mark* 3. 33.

49. behold my mother and *my b. Mark* 3. 34.

25. 40. ye have done it to the least of these *my b.*

28. 10. go tell *my b.* that they go into Galilee

John 20. 17. go to *my b.* and say to them, I ascend

Rom. 9. 3. myself were accursed from Christ for *my b.*

Jam. 5. 10. take *my b.* the prophets who have spoken

BRETHREN, thy, *Gen.* 27. 29. be lord over *thy b.* let mothers' sons bow

37. 13. do not *thy b.* feed the flock in Shechem ?

48. 22. I have given to thee one portion above *thy b.*

49. 8. thou art he whom *thy b.* shall

Deut. 18. 15. I will raise up a prophet of *thy b.* like to me

Ezek. 11. 15. *thy b.* have dealt treacherously with thee

Matt. 12. 47. behold, thy mother and *thy b.* stand without, *Mark* 3. 32 ; *Luke* 8. 20.

Luke 14. 12. call not *thy b.* lest they bid thee again

22. 32. when converted strengthen *thy b.*

BRETHREN, your, *Gen.* 42. 19. let one of *your b.* be bound in prison

Gen. 42. 33. leave one of *your b.* here with me

1 *Kings* 12. 24. not fight against *your b.* 2 *Chr.* 11. 4.

Neh. 4. 14. and fight for *your b.*

5. 8. will you even sell *your b.* or

shall they be sold ?

Is. 66. 5. *your b.* that hated you, that cast you out

Matt. 5. 47. if ye salute *your b.* only

Acts 3. 22. a prophet shall Lord raise of *your b.* 7. 37.

1 *Pet.* 5. 9. same afflictions accomplished in *your b.*

BRIBES, the reward for fraudulent practices. A corrupting gift ; *Deut.* 16. 19 ; 1 *Sam.* 8. 3.

1 *Sam.* 12. 3. have I received any *b.*

Ps. 26. 10. right hand full of *b.*

Is. 33. 15. hands from holding *b.*

Job 15. 34. tabernacles of bribery

Amos 5. 12. they take a *b.*

BRICK, *Gen.* 11. 3. let us make *b.* they had *b.* for stone

Ex. 1. 14. they made their lives bitter in *b.*

5. 7. no more gave the people straw to make *b.* 16.

Is. 9. 10. the *b.* are fallen down, but we will build

BRICK-KILN, 2 *Sam.* 12. 31. and made them pass through the *b.*

Jer. 43. 9. hide great stones in the clay in the *b.*

Nah. 3. 14. tread the mortar, make strong the *b.*

BRIDE, binds her ornaments, *Is.* 49. 18.

Is. 61. 10. as a *b.* adorns herself

Jer. 2. 32. can a *b.* forget her attire

Joel 2. 16. *b.* go out of her closet

John 3. 29. he that hath *b.* is bridegroom

Rev. 21. 2. as a *b.* adorned for her husband

9. I will show thee the *b.* the Lamb's

22. 17. Spirit and *b.* say come

Matt. 9. 15. *b.* chamber, *Mark* 2. 19 ; *Luke* 5. 34.

BRIDE-CHAMBER, *Matt.* 9. 15. can the children of the *b.* mourn ?

Mark 2. 19. can the children of *b.* fast ? *Luke* 5. 34.

BRIDEGROOM, *Joel* 2. 16 ; *John* 2. 9.

Ps. 19. 5. *b.* coming out of

Is. 61. 10. as a *b.* decks himself

62. 5. as the *b.* rejoiceth over bride

Jer. 7. 34. cease the voice of *b.* & 25. 10. & 33. 11 ; *Rev.* 18. 23.

Matt. 9. 15. as long as the *b.* is with them, *Mark* 2. 19, 20 ; *Luke* 5. 34, 35.

25. 1. went forth to meet the *b.*

BRIDLE, for an ass, *Prov.* 26. 3.

Ps. 32. 9. mouth held with *b.*

39. 1. keep my mouth with a *b.*

Is. 37. 29. put my *b.* in thy lips

30. 28. 2 *Kings* 19. 18. *Rev.* 14. 20.

James 1. 26. *b.* not his tongue

3. 2. able to *b.* the whole body

BRIEFLY, *Rom.* 13. 9. it is *b.* comprehended in this saying

1 *Pet.* 5. 12. by Sylvanus a brother, I have written *b.*

BRIERS. A prickly sort of plant. Figuratively, an enemy, *Is.* 10. 17. Mischievous persons ; *Ezek.* 28. 24. A wicked unfruitful heart ; *Heb.* 6. 8 ; *Judg.* 8. 7, 16 ; *Is.* 7. 23, 24, 25. & 32. 13 ; *Heb.* 6. 8 ; *Mic.* 7. 4.

Is. 5. 6. come up *b.* and thorns

9. 18. wicked shall devour *b.*

27. 4. set *b.* against me in battle

55. 13. instead of *b.* shall come the myrtle

Ezek. 2. 6. though *b.* and thorns with thee

28. 24. no more pricking *b.* to house

BRIGANDINE, a coat of mail ; *Jer.* 46. 4.

51. 3. against him that lifteth up himself in his *b.*

BRIGHT, *Lev.* 13. 2. when a man shall have a *b.* spot, 24. 38.

Job. 37. 11. he scattered his *b.* cloud

Ezek. 1. 13. the fire was *b.* and out of fire lightning

21. 15. the sword is made *b.* it is wrapt up

21. for the king of Babylon made his arrows *b.*

27. 19. *b.* iron and cassia were in thy market

Zech. 10. 1. so the Lord shall make *b.*

Matt. 17. 5. behold a *b.* cloud overshadowed them

Luke 11. 36. as when the *b.* shining of a candle

Acts 10. 30. a man stood before me in *b.* clothing

Rev. 22. 16. I am the *b.* and morning star

BRIGHTNESS, 2 *Sam.* 22. 13. through the *b.* before him were coals of fire kindled ; *Ps.* 18. 12.

Job 31. 26. or beheld the moon walking in *b.*

Is. 59. 9. we wait for *b.* but we walk in darkness

60. 3. and kings shall come to the *b.* of thy rising

62. 1. till the righteousness thereof go forth as *b.*

66. 11. be delighted with the *b.* of her glory

Ezek. 1. 4. and a fire and a *b.* was about it, 27.

28. so was the appearance of *b.* around about

8. 2. as the appearance of *b.* as the colour of amber

10. 4. the court was full of *b.* of the Lord's glory

Dan. 2. 31. this great image, whose *b.* was excellent

Dan. 12. 3. the wise shall shine as the *b.* of the firmament

Acts 26. 13. light from heaven above *b.* of the sun

2 *Thess.* 2. 8. shall destroy with the *b.* of his coming

Heb. 1. 3. the *b.* of his glory, the express image of his person

BRIM, *Josh.* 3. 15. feet of the priest dipped in *b.* of water

John 2. 7. and they filled them up the *b.*

BRIMSTONE, *Gen.* 19. 24. rained on Gom. *b.* and fire ; *Luke* 17. 29.

Deut. 29. 23. the whole land thereof is *b.* and salt

Ps. 11. 6. upon wicked he shall rain snares, fire and *b.* and an horrible tempest ; *Ezek.* 38. 22.

Is. 30. 33. breath of Lord like stream of *b.*

Rev. 9. 17. out of their mouths issued fire and *b.*

18. third part of men were killed by the *b.*

14. 10. he shall be tormented with fire and *b.*

21. 8. all liars have their part in lake which burneth with fire and *b.*

BRING, *Gen.* 6. 17. *b.* a flood of waters on the earth

9. 14. when I *b.* a cloud over earth, the bow seen

42. 20. *b.* your youngest brother to me,

Ex. 10. 4. else to-morrow I will *b.* the locusts

Lev. 5. 7. if he be not able to *b.* a lamb, 11 ; 12. 8.

Num. 8. 9. and thou shalt *b.* the Levite, 10.

14. 24. my servant Caleb, him will I *b.* into the land

Deut. 1. 17. the cause too hard for you *b.* it to me

2 *Sam.* 3. 12. my hand with thee, to *b.* Israel to thee

1 *Kings* 3. 24. and the king said *b.* me a sword

Neh. 13. 18. did not our God *b.* this evil on us ?

Job 14. 4. who can *b.* a clean thing out of an unclean ?

18. 14. it shall *b.* him to the king of terrors

30. 23. for I know thou wilt *b.* me to death

33. 30. to *b.* back his soul from the pit

Ps. 72. 3. the mountains shall *b.* peace to the people

Is. 46. 13. I *b.* near my righteousness, it not be far off

60. 17. for brass I will *b.* gold, for iron *b.* silver

Ezek. 6. 3. I, even I, will *b.* a sword upon you

Hos. 2. 14. I will allure and *b.* her into wilderness

Matt. 2. 13. be thou there till I *b.* thee word

5. 23. therefore if thou *b.* thy gift to the altar

21. 2. ye shall find an ass and a colt, loose them and *b.* them unto me, *Mark* 11. 2 ; *Luke* 19. 30.

Luke 2. 10. for I *b.* you good tidings of great joy

John 10. 16. other sheep, them also I must *b.*

14. 26. and *b.* all things to your remembrance

Acts 5. 28. ye in end to *b.* this man's blood on us

1 *Cor.* 1. 19. I will *b.* to nothing the understanding

9. 27. keep under my body, I *b.* it into subjection

Gal. 3. 24. our schoolmaster to *b.* us to Christ

1 *Thess.* 4. 14. them that sleep with God *b.* with him

1 *Pet.* 3. 18. suffered that he might *b.* us to God

BRING again, 2 *Sam.* 12. 23. can I *b.* him back *again* ? I shall go to him

Prov. 19. 24. not so much as *b.* it to his mouth *again*

Jer. 12. 15. I will return and *b.* them *again*, 50. 19.

Matt. 2. 8. *b.* me word *again* that I may worship

BRING down, *Gen.* 42. 38. *b. down* my gray hairs, 44. 29, 31.

Ps. 18. 27. wilt save afflicted, *b. down* high looks

Is. 25. 5. thou shalt *b. down* the noise of strangers

Jer. 49. 16. I will *b.* thee *down* from thence, *Obad* 4.

Amos 3. 11. he shall *b. down* thy strength from thee

9. 2. though climb to heaven, thence will *b.* them *down*

BROAD, *Num.* 16. 38. make censers, *b.* plates for covering

Num. 16. 39. make *b.* plates for the covering of altar

Job 36. 16. out of strait into *b.* place

Ps. 119. 96. thy commandment is exceeding *b.*

Songs 3. 2. in the *b.* ways I will seek

Is. 33. 21. the Lord will be a place of *b.* rivers

Jer. 5. 1. know and seek in the *b.* places thereof

Jer. 51. 58. the *b.* walls of Babylon shall be broken

Matt. 7. 13. *b.* is the way that leadeth to destruction

23. 5. make *b.* their phylacteries

BROADER, *Job* 11. 9. measure thereof is *b.* then the sea

BROIDERED, *Ex.* 28. 4. make a robe, a *b.* coat, a mitre, a girdle

Ezek. 16. 10. I clothed thee also with *b.* work

26. 16. the princes shall put off their *b.* garments

27. 24. thy merchants in blue clothes and *b.* work

1 *Tim.* 2. 9. that women adorn, not with *b.* hair

BROILED, *Luke* 24. 42. they gave him a piece of a *b.* fish

BROKEN, *Gen.* 17. 14. he hath *b.* my covenant, *Ps.* 55. 20 ; *Is.* 24. 5 ; 33. 8 ; *Jer.* 11. 10.

1 *Sam.* 2. 4. the bows of the mighty men are *b.*

1 *Chr.* 14. 11. God hath *b.* in upon mine enemies

Job 4. 10. the teeth of the young lions are *b.*

7. 5. my skin is *b.* and become loathsome

Ps. 3. 7. the teeth of the ungodly

31. 12. I am like a *b.* vessel

34. 18. the Lord is nigh them of a *b.* heart, 51. 17.

20. he keepeth his bones not one of them is *b.*

51. 8. bones hast *b.* may rejoice

17. the sacrifices of God are as a *b.*

69. 20. reproach hath *b.* my heart

107. 16. for he hath *b.* the gates of brass and bars

147. 3. healeth the *b.* in heart

Prov. 15. 13. by sorrow of heart spirit is *b.*

17. 22. but a *b.* spirit drieth the bones

25. 19. is like a *b.* tooth and foot out of joint

Eccl. 4. 12. a threefold cord not quickly *b.*

12. 6. or the golden bowl be *b.* or pitcher be *b.*

Is. 33. 20. nor shall any of the cords thereof be *b.*

Jer. 2. 13. hewed out *b.* cisterns

48. 17. how is the strong staff *b.*

38. for I have *b.* Moab like a vessel

50. 17. this Nebuchadnezzar hath *b.* Israel's bones

28. the hammer of the whole earth cut asunder and *b.*

Jer. 51. 56. Babylon, their bows *b.*

58. the broad walls of Babylon shall be utterly *b.*

Ezek. 6. 4. your images shall be *b.*

34. 16. will bind up that which was *b.*

Dan. 11. 4. his kingdom shall be *b.* and

Matt. 21. 44. fall on this stone, shall be *b. Luke* 20. 18.

John 7. 23. that the law of Moses should not be *b.*

19. 36. scripture fulfilled, a bone of him shall not be *b.*

Acts 20. 11. had *b.* bread and talked a

27. 35. gave thanks when he had *b.*

1 *Cor.* 11. 24. this is my body which is *b.* for you

BROKEN down, *Neh.* 1. 3. the wall of Jerusalem is *b. down*, gates burnt

Eph. 2. 14. Christ hath *b. down* middle

BROKEN off, *Rom.* 11. 20. because of unbelief they were *b. off*, 19.

BROKEN up, *Matt.* 24. 43. not have suffered his house to be *b. up*

Mark 2. 4. when they had *b.* roof *up*

Acts 13. 43. when the congregation was *b. up*

BROKEN-HEARTED, *Is.* 61. 1. Lord sent me to bind up the *b.-hearted*

Luke 4. 18. to heal *b.-hearted*, to preach deliverance

BROOD, *Luke* 13. 34. as a hen gathers her *b.* under her wings

BROOK, *Gen.* 32. 23. he sent them over the *b.*

Num. 13. 23. came to *b.* Eschol and cut a branch

1 *Sam.* 17. 40. chose five smooth stones out of the *b.*

1 *Kings* 2. 6. the ravens brought bread, he drank of the *b.*

Job 6. 15. my brethren dealt deceitfully as a *b.*

Ps. 110. 7. he shall drink of the *b.* in the way, therefore

John 18. 1. went with his disciples over *b.* Kidron

BROOKS, *Deut.* 8. 7. to a land of *b.* of water and fountains

Job 6. 15. and as the stream of *b.* they pass away

Ps. 42. 1. panteth after the water-*b.*

BROTHER, *Gen.* 43. 6. why dealt you so ill with me, as to tell ye had a *b.*

Job 30. 29. I am a *b.* to dragons, a companion to owls

Prov. 17. 17. and a *b.* is born for adversity

24. there is a friend that sticketh closer than a *b*.

Jer. 9. 4. trust not in any *b*. for every *b*. will supplant

Matt. 10. 21. *b*. shall deliver up the *b*.
　Mark 13. 12.

John 11. 2. Mary, whose *b*. Lazarus was

Acts 9. 17. *b*. Saul, receive thy sight
　12. 2. killed James the *b*. of John with the sword

1 *Cor.* 6. 6. *b*. goeth to law with *b*. before unbelievers
　8. 11. through thy knowledge shall the weak *b*. perish

2 *Cor.* 8. 18. and we have sent with him the *b*.

Philem. 7. bowels of saints are refreshed by thee, *b*.

BROTHER, his, *Deut.* 15. 2. not exact it of his neighbour or his *b*.

Deut. 25. 6. the first-born shall succeed in name of his *b*.

Ps. 49. 7. none can by any means redeem his *b*.

Is. 3. 6. when a man shall take hold of his *b*.
　41. 6. every one said to his *b*. be of good courage

Jer. 34. 9. that none serve himself of a Jew his *b*.

Hos. 12. 3. Jacob took his *b*. by the heel in the womb

Matt. 5. 22. sayeth Raca to his *b*.

John 1. 41. he findeth his *b*. Simon

1 *Thess.* 4. 6. that no man defraud his *b*. in any matter

Jam. 4. 11. speaketh evil of his *b*.

1 *John* 4. 21. he who loveth God, love his *b*. also
　5. 16. if any see his *b*. sin a sin not to death

BROTHER, my, 2 *Sam.* 1. 26. distressed for thee, *my b*. Jonathan

Songs 8. 1. O that thou wert as *mv b*.

John 11. 21. if hadst been here, *my b*.

BROTHER, thy, *Matt.* 5. 23. rememberest that *thy b*. hath aught against
　24. first be reconciled to *thy b*. then offer thy gift

Matt. 7. 3. beholding mote in *thy b*.
　Luke 6. 41, 42.

John 11. 23, Jesus saith, *thy b*. shall rise again

Rom. 14. 10. why dost thou judge *thy b*.

BROTHER, your, *Gen.* 42. 34. bring *your b*. so will I deliver you *your b*.

Gen. 43. 3. not see my face, except *your b*. be with you

Rev. 1. 9. John, who also am *your b*.

BROTHERHOOD, *Zech.* 11. 14. might break *b*. between Judah and Israel

1 *Pet.* 2. 17. love the *b*. fear God, honour the king

BROTHERLY, *Rom.* 12. 10. be kindly affectioned with *b*. love

Heb. 13. 1. let *b*. love continue

2 *Pet.* 1. 7. to godliness *b*. kindness

BROUGHT, *Deut.* 5. 15. the Lord thy God *b*. thee out thence

Josh. 24. 7. Lord *b*. the sea upon them and covered them

Judg. 2. 1. I have *b*. you unto the land I sware

2 *Sam.* 7. 18. what is my house, that

thou hast *b*. me hitherto ? 1 *Chr.* 17. 16.

1 *Kings* 9. 9. Lord *b*. on them this evil, 2 *Chr.* 7. 22.

Neh. 4. 15. God hath *b*. their counsel to

Is. 53. 7. he is *b*. as a lamb to the slaughter
　59. 16. his arm *b*. salvation ; 63. 5.

Ezek. 23. 8. nor left she her whoredoms *b*. from Egypt
　47. 3. he *b*. me through the waters to the ancles, 4.

Matt. 10. 18. *b*. before kings for my sake, for a test, against them ;
　Mark 13. 9 ; *Luke* 21. 12.
　14. 11. she *b*. John Baptist's head
　18. 24. one was *b*. that owed me 10,000 talents

Luke 2. 22. *b*. him to Jerusalem to present him
　7. 37. a woman *b*. an alabaster-box of ointment

Acts 5. 21. and sent to the prison to have them *b*.
　15. 3. and being *b*. on their way to the church
　19. 12. from his body were *b*. to the sick, aprons
　27. 24. fear not Paul, thou must be *b*. before Caesar

Rom. 15. 24. to be *b*. on my way hither by you

1 *Cor.* 6. 12. I will not be *b*. under the power of any

2 *Tim.* 1. 10. hath *b*. life and immortality to light

1 *Pet.* 1. 13. for the grace that is to be *b*. to you

BROUGHT again, *Ex.* 10. 8. Moses and Aaron *b. again* to Pharaoh

2 *Chr.* 33. 13. Lord *b*. Manasseh *again* to Jerusalem

Matt. 27. 3. repented and *b. again* 30 pieces of silver

Heb. 13. 20. God of peace that *b. again* from the dead

BROUGHT forth, *Prov.* 8. 24. when there were no depths, I was *b. forth*

Is. 5. 2. he looked for grapes, and it *b. forth* wild grapes
　66. 7. before she travailed, she *b. forth* before her pain

Is. 66. 8. for as soon as Zion travailed, she *b. forth* children

Matt. 1. 25. till she had *b. forth* her nrst-born son
　13. 8. fell in good ground, and *b. forth* fruit ; *Mark* 4. 8.

Luke 2. 7. she *b. forth* her first-born son and wrapped him
　12. 16. the ground of a rich man *b. forth* plentifully

Rev. 12. 5. *b. forth* a man-child, to rule

BROUGHT into, *Ps.* 22. 15. hast *b*. me *into* the dust of death

Songs 1. 4. king hath *b*. me *into* his chambers

Acts 9. 8. they led him and *b*. him *into* Damascus

BROUGHT low, *Ps.* 79. 8. let mercies prevent us for we are *b. low*

Ps. 106. 43. and were *b. low* for their iniquity
　116. 6. I was *b. low*, and he helped

142. 6. attend to my cry, for I am *b.* very *low*

Eccl. 12. 4. all daughters of music shall be *b. low*

Luke 3. 5. every mountain and hill *b. low, Is.* 40. 4.

BROUGHT out, *Gen.* 15. 7. that *b.* thee out of Ur of the Chaldees

Ex. 13. 3. for by strength of hand the Lord *b.* you *out* from this place, 9, 14, 16 ; *Deut.* 6. 21.

Lev. 24. 43. when I *b.* them *out* of Egypt, 1 *Kings* 8. 21.

Ps. 78. 16. he *b.* streams *out* of the rock

30. 8. thou hast *b.* a vine *out* of Egypt

107. 14. he *b.* them *out* of darkness and brake

Acts 7. 43. this Moses, which *b.* us *out* of Egypt

12. 17. declared how the Lord *b.* him *out of prison*

BROUGHT to pass, *Ezek.* 21. 7. it cometh, and shall be *b. to pass*

1 *Cor.* 15. 54. then shall be *b. to pass* the saying

BROUGHT up, *Ex.* 17. 3. wherefore hast thou *b.* us *up? Num.* 21. 5.

32. 1. as for Moses, the man that *b.* us *up.* 23.

Deut. 20. 1. the Lord is with thee, which *b.* thee *up*

Josh. 24. 17. he it is that *b.* us *up* and our fathers

Judg. 6. 8. I *b.* you *up* from Egypt, 1 *Sam.* 10. 18.

1 *Sam.* 12. 6. Lord that *b.* your fathers *up* out of Egypt

Ps. 30. 3. thou hast *b. up* my soul from the grave

Prov. 8. 30. then I was by him, as one *b. up* with him

Is. 1. 2. I have nourished and *b. up* children

Luke 4. 16. to Nazareth, where he had been *b.*

Acts 22. 3. yet *b. up* in this city at the feet of Gamaliel

1 *Tim.* 5. 10. a widow, if she hath *b. up* children

BRUISE, (1) To crush, injure, or oppress, *Gen.* 3. 15 ; *Dan.* 2. 40. (2) To punish, chastise, or correct, *Is.* 53. 10. It is spoken, (1) Corporeally, of the body, *Luke* 9. 39. (2) Spiritually, of doubts and troubles, *Matt.* 12. 20. (3) Morally, of corruptions, *Is.* 1. 6. (4) Politically, of a weak decaying nation, 2 *Kings* 18. 21.

Gen. 3. 15. it shall *b.* thy head, thou shalt *b.* his heel

Is. 28. 28. or will he *b.* it with his horsemen

53. 10. yet it pleased the Lord to *b.*

Dan. 2. 40. as iron shall it break in pieces and *b.*

Rom. 16. 20. the God of peace shall *b.* Satan shortly

BRUISED. A bruised reed shall he not break, *Is.* 42. 3. Christ will not deal roughly and rigorously with those that come to him, but will use all gentleness and tenderness to them ; passing by their greatest sins, bearing with their present infirmities, cherishing, and encouraging the smallest beginnings of grace, and comforting and healing wounded consciences.

Lev. 22. 24. ye shall not offer to the Lord what is *b.*

2 *Kings* 18. 21. trusteth on the staff of this *b.* reed

Is. 42. 3. a *b.* reed shall he not break, *Matt.* 12. 20.

Is. 53. 5. he was *b.* for our iniquity and chastisement

Ezek. 23. 3. there they *b.* the teats of their virginity

8. and they *b.* the breasts of her virginity

Luke 4. 18. sent me to set at liberty them that are *b.*

BRUISING, *Ezek.* 23. 21. in *b.* thy teats by the Egyptians

Luke 9. 39. the spirit *b.* him, hardly departeth from

BRUIT, *Jer.* 10. 22. behold, the noise of the *b.* is come

Nah. 3. 19. all that hear the *b.* of thee shall clap

BRUTISH, man knows not, *Ps.* 92. 4.

Ps. 94. 8. understand ye *b.* among people

Prov. 30. 2. I am more *b.* than any

Jer. 10. 14. every man *b.* in his knowledge, 51. 17.

BUCKET, S, *Num.* 24. 7. he shall pour the water out of his *b.*

Is. 40. 15. the nations are as a drop of a *b.* and dust

BUCKLER is a piece of defensive armour, 1 *Chr.* 5. 18. God is often called the Buckler, or Shield of his people, *Ps.* 18. 2 ; *Prov.* 2. 7. He will protect and save them from that mischief and ruin which will befall all wicked men. And in *Songs* 4. 4. the faith of the church, or of believers, whereby they are united to Christ, is compared to the tower of David, whereon hang a thousand bucklers ; noting how strong and invincible faith is, which furnishes with weapons out of Christ's fulness, and abundantly defends from all spiritual enemies, *Eph.* 6. 16.

BUCKLER to all that trust, *Ps.* 18. 30.

2 *Sam.* 22. 31. a *b.* to all that trust in him

1 *Chr.* 5. 18. men able to bear *b.* sword

Ps. 18. 2. my *b.* and horn of salvation

91. 4. his truth shall be thy *b.*

Prov. 2. 7. a *b.* to that walk uprightly

BUD (substantive), *Job* 38. 27. cause the *b.* of the tender herb to spring

Is. 61. 11. for as the earth bringeth forth her *b.*

BUD (verb), *Gen.* 3. 18. thistles shall it cause to *b.* to thee

Job 14. 9. yet through the scent of water it will *b.*

Ps. 132. 17. I will make the horn of David to *b.*

Songs 7. 12. let us see if the pomegranates *b.* forth

Is. 37. 6. Israel shall blossom and *b.*

55. 10. maketh the earth to bring

forth and *b*.

Ezek. 29. 21. cause the horn of Israel to *b*.

BUDS, *Num.* 17. 8. Aaron's rod brought forth *b*. and bloomed forth

BUDDED, *Num.* 17. 8. Aaron's rod for the house of Levi *b*.

Heb. 9. 4. the ark wherein was Aaron's rod that *b*.

BUFFETED, signifies to smite with the hand, to harrass, reproach, persecute, 2 *Cor.* 12. 7 ; *Matt.* 26. 67 ; 1 *Cor.* 4. 11 : 1 *Pet.* 2. 20.

BUILD, (1) To erect, or make houses, *Deut.* 28. 30. (2) To strengthen and increase knowledge, faith, love, and all other graces, *Acts* 20. 32. (3) To cement and knit together spiritually ; thus believers are united to Christ by faith, and among themselves by love, *Eph.* 2. 22. (4) To preserve, bless, and prosper, *Ps.* 127. 1 ; *Jer.* 24. 6. (5) To settle and establish, 1 *Sam.* 2. 35.

Who did build the house of Israel, Ruth 4. 11. Who did increase his family by a numerous progeny.

I will build up thy throne, Ps. 89. 4. I will perpetuate thy kingdom to thy posterity

Shall build the old wastes, Is. 61. 4. The Gentiles, who have been long destitute of the true knowledge of God, and like a wilderness overgrown with briers and thorns, shall be brought, by the ministry of the word, to know and serve the true ever-living God

BUILD, referred to God, 1 *Sam.* 2. 35. I will raise up a priest, and will *b*. him a sure house, 2 *Sam.* 7. 27 ; 1 *Kings* 11. 38.

1 *Chr.* 17. 10. the Lord will *b*. an house

Ps. 28. 5. he shall destroy, and not *b*. them up

51. 18. *b*. the walls of Jerusalem

102. 16. when Lord shall *b*. up Zion

127. 1. except Lord *b*. house, they labour in vain

Jer. 18. 9. concerning a nation to *b*. it

Matt. 16. 18. on this rock will I *b*. my church

26. 61. I am able to *b*. it in three days *Mark* 14. 58.

BUILD, joined with house, *Deut.* 25. 9. man that will not *b*. his brother's house

2 *Sam.* 7. 5. shalt thou *b*. me an *house*

1 *Kings* 2. 36. *b*. thee an *house* in Jerusalem, and dwell

5. 3. David could not *b*. an *house* for wars about him

5. 1. purpose to *b*. an *house* to the Lord, 2 *Chr.* 2. 1.

17. it was in heart of David my father to *b*. an *house* for God of Israel, 1 *Chr.* 28. 2 ; 2 *Chr.* 6. 7.

1 *Chr.* 17. 12. he shall *b*. me an *house*, 2 *Chr.* 6. 9.

22. 8. shalt not *b*. an *house* because thou didst shed blood

Ps. 127. 1. they labour in vain that *b*. the *house*

Is. 65. 21. they shall *b. houses* and inhabit them

Acts 7. 49. what *house* will ye *b*. me

BUILD, *Gen.* 11. 4. go to, let us *b*. us a city and a tower

1 *Kings* 9. 19. cities of store, which Solomon desired to *b*. in Jerusalem, 2 *Chr.* 8. 6.

24. Pharaoh's daughter did *b*. Millo

1 *Chr.* 22. 19. *b*. the sanctuary of God

Neh. 2. 17. let us *b*. the wall ; 18. let us rise and *b*.

Is. 9. 10. the bricks are fallen, but we will *b*.

Dan. 9. 25. to restore and *b*. Jerusalem to Messiah

Amos 9. 11. I will *b*. it as in the days of old

Zech. 6. 12. he shall *b*. the temple of the Lord, 13.

Matt. 23. 29. ye *b*. tombs of prophets, *Luke* 11. 47, 48.

Luke 12. 18. I will pull down my barns and *b*. greater

14. 28. which of you intending to *b*. a tower ?

30. began to *b*. not able to finish

Acts 20. 32. to the word of his grace, able to *b*. you up

1 *Cor.* 3. 12. if any *b*. on this foundation, gold, silver

Gal. 2. 18. if I *b*. again the things which I destroyed

BUILDED, *Gen.* 2. 22. of the rib the Lord *b*. a woman

Ps. 122. 3. Jerusalem is *b*. a city that is compact

Prov. 9. 1. Wisdom hath *b*. her house, hewn out pillars

Eccl. 2. 4. I *b*. me houses, I planted me vineyards

Luke 17. 28. they bought, they sold, they planted, they *b*.

Eph. 2. 22. in whom ye are *b*. together

Heb. 3. 3. he who *b*. the house hath more honour

4. for every house is *b*. by some man,

BUILDER, S, *Ps.* 118. 22. stone which *b*. refuse become head stone, *Matt.* 21. 42 ; *Mark* 12. 10 ; *Luke* 20. 17 ; *Acts* 4. 11.

Heb. 11. 10. looked for a city whose *b*. and maker is God

1 *Pet.* 2. 7. the stone which the *b*. disallowed

BUILDEST, *Matt.* 27. 40. thou that destroyest the temple and *b*. it in three days, save thyself, *Mark* 15. 29.

BUILDETH, *Job* 27. 18. he *b*. his house as a moth. as a booth

Hos. 8. 14. Israel hath forgotten Maker, *b*. temples

Hab. 2. 12. woe to him that *b*. a town with blood

1 *Cor.* 3. 10. I laid the foundation, another *b*. thereon

BUILDING, 1 *Kings* 3. 1. till he made an end of *b*. his own house

1 *Kings* 7. 1. Solomon was *b*. his own house thirteen years

6. 7. no tool of iron heard in the house while *b*.

John 2. 20. this temple was forty-six

years in *b.*

Jude 20. *b.* up yourselves on your most holy faith

BUILDING (substantive), 1 *Chr.* 28. 2. had made ready for the *b.*

2 *Chr.* 3. 3. Solomon was instructed for the *b.*

1 *Cor.* 3. 9. husbandry, ye are God's *b.*

2 *Cor.* 5. 1. we have a *b.* of God, an house not made

Eph. 2. 21. all the *b.* fitly framed

Heb. 9. 11. an high-priest by a tabernacle not of this *b.*

Rev. 21. 18. *b.* of wall was of jasper

BUILDINGS, *Matt.* 24. 1. disciples came to show him *b.* of temple

Mark 13. 1. Master, see what *b.* are here, 2.

BUILT, *Deut.* 13. 16. it shall be an heap and not be *b.* again

2 *Chr.* 26. 9. Uzziah *b.* towers in Jerusalem, 10.

Ps. 79. 69. he *b.* his sanctuary like high palaces

89. 2. I have said, mercy shall be *b.* up for ever

Ezek. 16. 24. thou hast *b.* to thee an eminent place

26. 14. thou shalt be *b.* no more, saith the Lord God

Dan. 4. 30. is not this great Babylon I have *b.*

Matt. 21. 33. diggeth a wine-press, *b.* a tower, *Mark* 12. 1.

Luke 7. 5. the centurion hath *b.* us a

1 *Cor.* 3. 14. if work abide which he hath *b.* thereon

Eph. 2. 20. are *b.* on the foundation of the apostles

Col. 2. 7. rooted and *b.* up in him

Heb. 3. 4. that *b.* all things is God

BUILT house, or houses, *Matt.* 7. 24. wise man *b.* his *h.* on a rock, *Luke* 6. 48.

Matt. 7. 26. foolish man which *b.* his *h.* on sand, *Luke* 6. 49.

Acts 7. 47. but Solomon *b.* him an *house*

1 *Pet.* 2. 5. ye also are *b.* up a spiritual *h.* an holy

BULLOCK, *Num.* 15. 9. bring with the *b.* a meat-offering, 29. 37.

1 *Kings* 18. 23. and let them choose one *b.* 25.

Ps. 50. 9. take no *b.* out of thine house

69. 31. better than a *b.* that hath horns and hoofs

Jer. 31. 18. as a *b.* unaccustomed to yoke

BULLOCK, with sin-offering, *Ex.* 29. 36. after every day a *b.* for a *sin-offering*

BULLS compassed me, *Ps.* 22. 12.

Ps. 50. 13. will I eat the flesh of *b.*

68. 30. rebuke multitude of *b.*

Heb. 9. 13. if blood of *b.* and goats

10. 4. blood of *b.* cannot take away

Ps. 69. 31. than *b.* with horns

Jer. 31. 18. as *b.* unaccustomed to yoke

Ps. 51. 19. offer *b.* on thy altar

Is. 1. 11. delight not in the blood of *b.*

BULRUSHES, *Ex.* 2. 3 ; *Is.* 18. 2. & 58. 5.

BULWARKS. A fortification raised by an enemy besieging a city, *Deut.* 20. 20 ; *Eccl.* 9. 4. A strong frontier fort, or rampart ; 2 *Sam.* 20.

15 ; *Ps.* 48. 13. The defence of the church by almighty power, is called a bulwark ; *Ps.* 48. 11-14 ; *Is.* 26. 1.

BUNCH, ES, *Ex.* 12. 22. take a *b.* of hyssop and dip it in blood

2 *Sam.* 16. 1. Ziba meet him with 100 *b.* of raisins

Is. 30. 6. will carry their treasures upon *b.* of camels

BUNDLE, *Gen.* 42. 35 ; *Acts* 28. 3.

1 *Sam.* 25. 29. bound up in *b.* of life with Lord

Songs 1. 13. *b.* of myrrh is my well-beloved

Matt. 13. 20. bind tares in *b.* burn them

BURDEN, *Ex.* 18. 22. shall bear the *b.* with thee ; *Num.* 11. 17.

Num. 4. 19. Aaron shall appoint each to his *b.*

Deut. 1. 12. how can I myself alone bear your *b.*

Neh. 13. 19. no *b.* be brought in on the sabbath

Job 7. 20. as a mark, so that I am a *b.* to myself

Ps. 38. 4. iniquity as a *b.* they are too heavy for me

55. 22. cast thy *b.* on the Lord and he shall sustain thee

Eccl. 12. 5. and the grasshopper shall be a *b.*

Is. 9. 4. for thou hast broken the yoke of his *b.*

Jer. 17. 21. bear no *b.* on the sabbath-day, 22. 27.

Matt. 11. 30. my yoke is easy, and my *b.* is light

Matt. 20. 12. which have borne the *b.* and heat of the day

Acts 15. 28. seemed good to lay on you no greater *b.*

Rev. 2. 24. I will put upon you none other *b.*

BURDEN, *Is.* 13. 1. the *b.* of Babylon which Isaiah did see

15. 1. the *b.* of Moab, 17. 1. the *b.* of Damascus

19. 1. the *b.* of Egypt, 23. 1. the *b.* of Tyre

22. 1. the *b.* of the valley of vision, what aileth

Jer. 23. 33. what is the *b.* of the Lord ? what *b.* ?

Ezek. 12. 10. this *b.* concerneth the prince in Jerusalem

Nah. 1. 1. the *b.* of Nineveh, the book of the vision

Gal. 6. 5. for every man shall bear his own *b.*

BURDEN, ED, *Zech.* 12. 3. all that *b.* themselves be cut in pieces

2 *Cor.* 5. 4. in this tabernacle we groan being *b.*

8. 13. I mean not that others be eased, and you *b.*

12. 16. but be it so, I did not *b.* you, caught with

BURDENS, *Gen.* 49. 14. Issachar couching down between two *b.*

Ex. 1. 11. task-masters to afflict them with their *b.*

2. 11. Moses went out and looked on their *b.*

5. 4. the king of Egypt said, get you
to your b.

Neh. 4. 10. the strength of the bearers
of b. decayed

17. they that bare b. with other hand
held a weapon

Is. 58. 6. this is the fast to undo the
heavy b.

Matt. 23. 4. bind heavy b. *Luke* 11. 46.

Gal. 6. 2. bear ye one another's b.

BURDENSOME, *Zech.* 12. 3. I will
make Jerusalem a b. stone

2 *Cor.* 11. 9. I have kept myself from
being b. to you

12. 13. except it be that I myself was
not b. to you

14. third time I come, I will not be
b. to you

1 *Thess.* 2. 6. when we might have been
b. as apostles

BURN, *Gen.* 44. 18. Judah said, let not
thy anger b.

Ex. 27. 20. command that they bring
pure olive-oil to cause the lamp to
b. alway ; *Lev.* 24. 2.

29. 13. shalt take caul, liver, and
kidneys, and b. upon the altar, 18.
25 *Lev.* 1. 9, 15 ; 2. 2, 9, 16 ; 3. 5 ;
5. 12 ; 6. 15 : 9. 17 ; *Num.* 5. 26.

1 *Sam.* 2. 16. let them not fail to b. the
fat presently

Is. 1. 31. they shall both b. together,
10. 17. it shall b. and devour his
thorns and briers

40. 16. Lebanon is not sufficient to b.

Ezek. 24. 5. b. also the bones under it

Nah. 2. 13. I will b. her chariots in the

Mal. 4. 1. the day cometh that shall b.
as an oven

Matt. 13. 30. bind the tares in bundles
to b. them

Luke 3. 17. but chaff he will b. with
fire unquenchable

24. 32. they said, did not our heart b.
within us

1 *Cor.* 7. 9. for it is better to marry than
to b.

2 *Cor.* 11. 29. who is offended, and I b.

BURN, (1) To consume or destroy with
fire, *Josh.* 11. 13. (2) To be in-
flamed with just anger and indignation, *Lam.* 2. 3. (3) To be per-
petually haunted with violent,
lustful desires, 1 *Cor.* 7. 9. (4) To
be filled with an holy zeal for the
glory of God, and the good of
others, 2 *Cor.* 11. 29.

BURN joined with fire, *Ex.* 12. 10. that
which remaineth till morning
ye shall b. with *fire*, 29. 34 ; *Lev.*
8. 32.

Deut. 5. 23. for the mountain did b.
with *fire*

32. 22. a *fire* shall b. to the lowest
hell ; *Jer.* 17. 4.

Ps. 79. 5. how long shall thy jealousy
b. like *fire* ?

Is. 47. 14. shall be as stubble, the *fire*
shall b. them

Matt. 3. 12. he will gather his wheat,
but he will b. up the chaff with
unquenchable *fire*, *Luke* 3. 17.

BURN incense, *Ex.* 30. 1. thou shalt

make an altar to b. *incense* on

7. Aaron shall b. thereon sweet *incense* every morning, 8.

Jer. 7. 9. will ye steal and b. *incense* to
Baal ? 11. 13.

Hos. 4. 13. they b. *incense* upon the
hills under oaks

Hab. 1. 16. therefore they b. *incense* to
their drag

Luke 1. 9. Zacharias his lot was to b.
incense in temple

Ex. 3. 2. *The bush burned, and was
not consumed.* This represented
the condition of the church and
people of *Israel*, who were then in
the fire of affliction ; yet so as that
God was present with them, and
that they should be consumed in
it, whereof this vision was a pledge.

BURNED, *Deut.* 9. 15. I came down,
and mount b. with fire

Ps. 39. 3. while I was musing the fire b.

John 15. 6. withered branches are
gathered and b.

Acts 19. 19. many brought their books
and b. them

Rom. 1. 27. b. in their lust one towards
another

1 *Cor.* 13. 3. and though I give my body
to be b.

Heb. 6. 8. is rejected, whose end is to
be b.

Heb. 12. 18. for ye are not come to the
mount that b.

Rev. 1. 15. his feet like brass, as if b. in
a furnace

BURNETH, *Ps.* 46. 9. he breaketh the
bow and b. chariot in fire

Ps. 97. 3. a fire b. up his enemies round
about

Is. 9. 18. for wickedness b. as fire

62. 1. the salvation thereof as a lamp
that b.

Joel 2. 3. a fire before them, behind
them a flame b.

Rev. 21. 8. shall have part in lake which
b. with fire

Is. 4. 4. *The spirit of burning.* The
Holy Spirit of God, who is compared to fire, *Matt.* 3. 11. because
he doth burn up and consume the
dross which is in the church, and
in the minds and hearts of men,
and inflames the souls of believers
with love to God, and zeal for his
glory.

BURNING, *Gen.* 15. 17. a b. lamp passed between the pieces

Deut. 28. 22. Lord shall smite thee with
extreme b.

Job 41. 19. of his mouth go b. lamps,
sparks of fire

Ps. 11. 6. on wicked reign b. tempest

Jer. 20. 9. his word was in my heart as
a b. fire

Dan. 3. 6. shall be cast into the midst
of a b. furnace, 11.

17. is able to deliver us from the b.

26. Nebuchadnezzar came near the
b. furnace

7. 9. his throne like flame, his wheels
were as b. fire

Hab. 3. 5. and b. coals went forth at his

feet

Luke 12. 35. let your loins be girded, and lights *b*.

John 5. 35. John was a *b*. and a shining light

Rev. 4. 5. there were seven lamps *b*. before throne

8. 8. and as it were a great Mountain *b*. with fire

BURNT, *Deut.* 32. 24. shall be *b*. with hunger and devoured

2 *Sam.* 5. 21. David and his men *b*. their images

Job 30. 30. and my bones are *b*. with

Is. 1. 7. your cities are *b*. with fire

43. 2. when walkest through fire thou shalt not be *b*.

64. 11. our holy and beautiful house is *b*. with fire

1 *Cor.* 3. 15. if any man's work be *b*. shall suffer loss

Heb. 13. 11. those beasts are *b*. without the camp

BURNT-OFFERING, *Gen.* 22. 7. but where is the lamb for a *b.-offering*

13. he offered him for a *b.-offering* instead of Isaac

Ex. 18. 12. and Jethro took a *b.-offering* for God

Lev. 1. 4. he shall put his hand on head of *b.-offering*

6. 9. saying, this is the law of the *b.-offering*, 7. 37.

Num. 7. 15. one lamb of the first year for a *b.-offering*, 21, 27, 33, 39, 51, 57, 63, 69, 75, 81 ; *Ezek.* 45. 15.

28. 10. this is the *b.-offering* of every sabbath

13. for a *b.-offering* of a sweet savour unto the Lord

1 *Sam.* 7. 9. as Samuel was offering up a *b.-offering*

Ps. 40. 6. *b.-offering* hast thou not required

51. 16. for thou delightest not in *b.-offering*

19. shalt be pleased with *b.offering* and whole *b.offering*

BURNT-OFFERINGS, *Gen.* 8. 20. Noah offered *b.-offerings* on the altar

Num. 10. 10. blow with trumpet over your *b-offerings*

1 *Sam.* 15. 22. hath Lord as great delight in *b.-offerings*

1 *Kings* 3. 15. Solomon stood and offered *b.-offerings*

Ezra 3. 4. offered the daily *b.-offerings* by number

Ps. 50. 8. I will not reprove thee for thy *b.-offerings*

Ps. 66. 13. I will go into thy house with *b.-offerings*

Is. 1. 11. I am full of the *b. offerings* of rams

43. 23. nor brought me small cattle of thy *b. offerings*

Jer. 6. 20. your *b. offerings* are not acceptable

BURNT-SACRIFICE, *Deut.* 33. 10. shall put whole *b.-s*. on thine altar

Ps. 20. 3. remember thy offerings, accept thy *b.-s*.

66. 15. I will offer to thee *b.-s*. of fatlings

BURNT up, *Judg.* 15. 5. the foxes *b.up* the shocks and corn

Is. 3. 14. for ye have *b. up* the vineyard

64. 11. our holy and beautiful house is *b. up*

Matt. 22. 7. the king sent and *b. up* their city

2 *Pet.* 3. 10. earth, and works therein shall be *b. up*

Rev. 8. 7. were cast on the earth, and the third part of trees was *b. up* and grass was *b. up*

BURNISHED, *Ezek.* 1. 7. they sparkled like the colour of *b*. brass

BURST thy bands, *Jer.* 2. 20.

Jer. 5. 5. broken yoke *b*. bands, 30. 8.

Prov. 3. 10. presses *b*. out with wine

Mark 2. 22. new wine both *b*. the bottles, *Luke* 5. 37; *Job* 32. 19.

Acts 1. 18. *b*. asunder in midst bowels

BURY, *Gen.* 25. 4. that I may *b*. my dead out of my sight

Gen. 23. 6. in choice of our sepulchres *b*. thy dead, 11. 15.

47. 29. *b*. me not, I pray thee, in Egypt, 49. 29.

50. 5. let me go and *b*. my father

1 *Kings* 2. 31. go and fall upon Joab and *b*. him

13. 29. the old prophet came to mourn and *b*. him

31. when I am dead, *b*. me in the sepulchre

Ps. 79. 3. and there was none to *b*. them

Ezek. 39. 11. there shall they *b*. Gog and his multitude

Matt. 8. 21. suffer me to go *b*. my father, *Luke* 9. 59.

27. 7. bought the potter's field to *b*. strangers in

BURIED, *Gen.* 25. 10. there was Abraham *b*. and Sarah his wife

Gen. 49. 31. there they *b*. Abraham and Sarah his wife, Isaac and Rebekah his wife, and there I *b*. Leah

Deut. 10. 6. there Aaron died, and there he was *b*.

Josh. 24. 32. the bones of Joseph *b*. they in Shechem

Ruth 1. 17. where diest I will die, and there will be *b*.

Jer. 8. 2. not be gathered nor *b*. 16. 6 ; 20. 6 ; 25. 33.

22. 19. he shall be *b*. with the burial of an ass

Matt. 14. 12. his disciples took the body and *b*. it

Luke 16. 22. the rich man also died and was *b*.

Acts 2. 29. the patriarch David is both dead and *b*.

5. 9. the feet of them which *b*. thy husband

Rom. 6. 4. we are *b*. with him by baptism into death

1 *Cor.* 15. 4. that he was *b*. and rose again the third day

Col. 2. 12. *b*. with him in baptism wherein are risen

BURYING, *Gen.* 23. 4. a possessor of a *b*. place, 9 ; 49. 30 ; 50. 13.

2 *Kings* 13. 21. as they were *b*. a man they spied a band

Mark 14. 8. she is come to anoint my

body to the *b.*

John 12. 7. against day of my *b.* hath she kept this

BUSH is not burnt, *Ex.* 3. 2 ; 3. 4 ; *Acts* 7. 30 ; *Job* 30. 4.

Deut. 33. 16. good will dwelt in *b.*

Mark 12. 26. how in the *b.* God spake to him

Luke 6. 44. nor of a bramble *b.* gather they grapes

20. 37. that dead are raised, Moses showed at the *b.*

BUSHEL. A measure containing 8 gallons. To *put a candle under a bushel,* signifies concealing, or not using holy gifts ; *Matt.* 5. 15 ; *Luke* 11. 33. It is the will of God that the gifts and graces of his people should be consecrated to promote the good of others ; as the master of a family lights a candle to give light to the whole family ; *Luke* 8. 16 ; 19. 20.

BUSHEL, *Matt.* 5. 15. light a candle and put in under a *b.* but on a candlestick, *Mark* 4. 21 ; *Luke* 11. 33.

BUSHY, *Songs* 5. 11. his locks are *b.* and black

BUSINESS, *Gen.* 39. 11 ; *Rom.* 16. 2.

Ps. 107. 23. do *b.* in great waters

Prov. 22. 29. a man diligent in his *b.*

Eccl. 5. 3. dream cometh through multitude of *b.*

Luke 2. 49. be about my father's *b.*

Acts 6 3. to appoint over this *b.*

Rom. 12. 11. not slothful in *b.*

1 *Thess.* 4. 11. study to do your own *b.*

BUSY-BODY, IES, 2 *Thess.* 3. 11. but some of you are *b.-b.* 1 *Tim.* 5. 15.

1 *Pet.* 4. 15. none of you suffer as a *b.-body*

BUSY, IED, 1 *Kings* 20. 40. as thy servant was *b.* here and there

2 *Chr.* 35. 14. the sons of Aaron *b.* in offering

BUT, 1 *Sam.* 20. 3. there is *b.* a step between me and death

Ps. 115. 5. mouths *b.* speak not ; eyes *b.* see not

6. have ears *b.* hear not ; noses *b.* smell not

Matt. 24. 36. *b.* of that day and hour knoweth no man

1 *Cor.* 4. 19. I will know not the speech, *b.* the power

6. 11. *b.* ye are washed ; 7. 10. yet not I, *b.* the Lord

2 *Cor.* 2. 5. he hath not grieved me *b.* in part

4. 17. our light affliction, 'which is *b.* for a moment

BUTLER, S, *Gen.* 40. 1. the *b.* of the king of Egypt offended

Gen. 40. 9. the chief *b.* told his dream to

21. he restored the chief *b.* to his butlership

41. 9. the chief *b.* said, I remember my faults

BUTTER, *Gen.* 18. 8. Abraham took *b.* and milk, and the calf

Deut. 32. 14. *b.* of kine, milk of sheep,

2 *Sam.* 17. 29. Barzillai brought honey and *b.* for David

Job 20. 17. shall not see the brooks of

honey and *b.*

29. 6. when I washed my steps with *b.* rock poured

Ps. 55. 21. words of his mouth smoother than *b.*

Prov. 30. 33. churning of milk bringeth forth *b.*

Is. 7. 15. *b.* and honey shall he eat, 22.

BUTTOCKS, 2 *Sam.* 10. 4. cut off garments to their *b.* 1 *Chr.* 19. 4.

Is: 20. 4. with *b.* uncovered to the shame of Egypt

BUY, (1) To procure any commodity by price, 2 *Sam.* 24. 21. (2) To receive, by such ways and means as God has directed, those spiritual blessings which are freely offered in the gospel, even Christ and all his benefits, *Is.* 55. 1 ; *Rev.* 3. 18.

BUY, *Gen.* 42. 2. get you down to Egypt and *b.* for us

Gen. 42. 7. said, from land of Canaan to *b.* food, 43. 20.

Ex. 21. 2. if thou *b.* an Hebrew servant

Lev. 22. 11. if the priests *b.* any soul with money

Deut. 2. 6. ye shall *b.* meat of them for money

2 *Sam.* 24. 21. David said, to *b.* the threshing-floor, and build an altar to the Lord, 24 ; 1 *Chr.* 21. 24.

Neh. 10. 31. we would not *b.* it on the sabbath

Is. 55. 1. come *b.* and eat, *b.* wine and milk

Matt. 14. 15. may *b.* themselves victuals, *Mark* 6. 36.

25. 9. go to them that sell, and *b.* for yourselves

Luke 9. 13. except we *b.* meat for all this people

22. 36. let him sell his garment and *b.* one

John 4. 8. his disciples were gone to *b.* meat

6. 5. whence shall we *b.* bread that these may eat

1 *Cor.* 7. 30. they that *b.* as though they possessed not

Jam. 4. 13. and we will *b.* and sell, and

Rev. 3. 18. I counsel thee to *b.* of me gold tried in fire

BUY, truth, *Prov.* 23. 23. *b.* the *truth* and sell it not

BUYER, *Prov.* 20. 14. it is naught, saith the *b.*

BY-and-BY, *Matt.* 13. 21 ; *Mark* 6. 25 ; *Luke* 17. 7. & 21. 9.

BY-WORD, *Deut.* 28. 37. thou shalt become a *b.* among all nations

1 *Kings* 9. 7. Israel shall be a *b.* among all the people

CAGE, *Jer.* 5. 27. as a *c.* is full of birds, so are their houses full of deceit

Rev. 18. 2. Babylon is a *c.* of every unclean bird

CAIN and ABEL, *Gen.* 4. 1-17 ; *Matt.* 23. 35 ; *Heb.* 11. 4. & 12. 24 ; 1 *John* 3. 12. ; *Jude* 11.

CAKES, *Gen.* 18. 6 ; *Judg.* 6. 19.

Num. 15. 20. offer up a *c.* of the first of your dough

Judg. 7. 13. *c.* tumbled into host of

Midian

1 *Kings* 17. 12. have *c.* but handful
   13. make me a little *c.* first, and bring
   it to me
Jer. 7. 18. make *c.* to queen of heaven
   44. 19. make *c.* to worship her
Ezek. 4. 12. and thou shalt eat it as
   barley *c.*
Hos. 7. 8. Ephraim is a *c.* not turned
CALAMITY at hand, *Deut.* 32. 35.
Job 6. 2. my *c.* laid in the balance
   '30. 13. mark path set forward my *c.*
Ps. 18. 18. prevent me in day of *c.*
   57. 1. till the *c.* be overpast
   141. 5. my prayer shall be in their *c.*
Prov. 1. 26. I will laugh at your *c.*
   6. 15. his *c.* shall come suddenly
   19. 13. foolish son is *c.* of his father
   24. 22. their *c.* shall rise suddenly
   17. 5. that is glad that *c.* shall not
   27. 10. into brother's house in day of *c.*
Jer. 18. 17. thy face in day of thy *c.*
   46. 21. day of thy *c.* is come, 48. 16.
   & 49. 8, 32 ; *Ezek.* 35. 5 ; *Obad.* 13.
CALAMUS, *Ex.* 30. 23. take of sweet *c.*
   250 shekels
Songs 4. 14. spikenard, saffron *c.*
Ezek. 27. 19. *c.* was in the market of
   Tyrus
CALDRON, 1 *Sam.* 2. 14 ; *Job* 41. 20 ;
   Ezek. 11. 3 , 7, 11 ; *Mic.* 3. 3 ; *Jer.*
   52. 18.
CALEB and **JOSHUA**, *Num.* 13. 6. 30 ;
   14. 6, 24, 38 ; 26. 65 ; *Josh.* 14.
   30 ; 15. 14, 16 ; *Judg.* 1. 15.
CALF, *Gen.* 18. 7 ; *Job* 21. 10 ; *Ps.*
   29. 6 ; *Is.* 27. 10 ; *Rev.* 4. 7.
Ex. 32. 4. made a molten *c.* 20 ; *Deut.*
   9. 16 ; *Neh.* 9. 18 ; *Ps.* 106. 19.
Is. 11. 6. *c.* and young lion together
Jer. 34. 18. when cut *c.* in twain
Hos. 8. 5. thy *c.* O Samaria, hath cast
   thee off
   6. *c.* of Samaria shall be broken
Luke 15. 23. bring hither fatted *c.*
   27. killed the fatted *c.* 30.
CALKERS, *Ezek.* 27. 9. Gebal were in
   thee thy *c.*
Ezek. 27. 27. thy *c.* shall fall into seas
CALL, *Gen.* 2. 19. Adam, see what he *c.*
   them
Ex. 2. 7. *c.* a nurse of Hebrew women
Deut. 4. 7. as God is in all things, we *c.*
   on him for
   26. I *c.* heaven and earth to witness
   against you
Judg. 16. 25. *c.* for Samson that he may
   make us sport
1 *Sam.* 3. 6. here am I, for thou didst
   c. me, 8.
1 *Kings* 8. 52. hearken to them in all
   they *c.*
   17. 18. to *c.* my sin to remembrance
Job 5. 1. *c.* now if there be any that will
   answer
Ps. 4. 3. the Lord will hear when I *c.*
   unto him
   20. 9. let the king hear us when we *c*
   49. 11. they *c.* their lands after their
Ps. 145. 18. nigh all them that *c.* on him
Prov. 8. 4. to you, O men, I *c.* my voice
   31. 28. children arise, and *c.* her
   blessed
Is. 5. 20 woe to them that *c.* evil good

   22. 12. in that day did the Lord *c.* to
   weeping
   55. 6. *c.* ye upon him while he is near
   58. 13. *c.* the sabbath a delight, holy
   of the Lord
   65. 1. and *c.* his servants by another
   name
   24. that before they *c.* I will answer
Lam. 2. 15. is this city men *c.* perfection of beauty
Jonah 1. 6. O sleeper, arise, *c.* upon thy
   God
Zech. 3. 10. *c.* every man his neighbour
Mal. 3. 15. now we *c.* proud happy
Matt. 9. 13. I am not come to *c.* the
   righteous, but sinners to repentance, *Mark* 2. 17 ; *Luke* 5. 32.
   22. 3. sent servants to *c.* them that
   were bidden
   23. 9. *c.* no man your father upon
   earth
Luke 6. 46. why *c.* ye me Lord, and do
John 4. 16. go *c.* thy husband and come
   13. 13. ye *c.* me master and Lord
Acts 24. 14. that after the way *c.* heresy
Rom. 10. 12. the same Lord is rich to
   all that *c.* upon him
2 *Tim.* 1. 5. when I *c.* to remembrance
   the faith
Heb. 2. 11. he is not ashamed to *c.* them
   brethren
   10. 32. *c.* to remembrance the former
Jam. 5. 14. let him *c.* the elders of the
   church
CALL on name of the Lord, *Gen.* 4. 26.
   then began men to *c.* upon *name
   of the Lord*
Joel 2. 32. whosoever shall *c. on the
   name of the Lord*, *Acts* 2. 21.
CALL, not, *Ps.* 14. 4. they *c. not* upon
   the Lord
Luke 14. 12. *c. not* thy friends nor brethren
John 15. 15. henceforth I *c.* you *not*
Acts 10. 15. that *c. not* thou common,
   11. 9.
CALL, shall or shalt, *Job* 14. 15. *shalt c.*
   and I will answer thee
Ps. 50. 4. *shall c.* to the heavens above
   72. 17. blessed in him, all nations
   shall c. him blessed
Is. 7. 14. *shall c.* his name Immanuel
   44. 5. another *shall c.* himself by the
   name of Jacob
   60. 14. they *shall c.* thee the city of
   the Lord
Is. 60. 18. *shalt c.* thy walls salvation
   62. 12. they *shall c.* them the holy
   people, redeemed
Jer. 3. 17. they *shall c.* Jerusalem the
   throne of Lord
   6. 30. reprobate silver *shall* men *c.*
Matt. 1. 21. thou *shalt c.* his name Jesus
Luke 1. 13. and thou *shalt c.* his name
   John
Acts 2. 39, as many as the Lord our God
   shall c.
Rom. 10. 14. how then *shall* they *c.* on
   him in whom
CALL, will, 2 *Sam.* 22. 4. I *will c.* on
   the Lord, *Ps.* 18. 3.
Ps. 55. 16. I *will c.* upon God, 86. 7.
Acts 24. 25. a convenient season I *will*
   c. for thee

Rom. 9. 25. I *will* c. them my people which were not

CALL upon me, *Ps.* 50. 15. c. *upon me* in day of trouble, I will deliver

Prov. 1. 28. shall c. *upon me*, but I will not answer

CALLED, *Gen.* 11. 9. therefore is the name of it c. Babel

Gen. 35. 10. thy name shall not be c. any more. Jacob

1 *Chr.* 21. 26. David c. on the Lord, he answered him

Is. 34. 1. a multitude of shepherds is c. forth against him

61. 3. that they might be c. trees of righteousness

Matt. 1. 16. of whom was born Jesus, who is c. Christ

13. 55. is not his mother c. Mary

20. 16. for many be c. but few chosen, 22. 14.

23. 8. be ye not c. Rabbi, one is your Master, 10.

Luke 15. 19. no more worthy to be c. thy son, 21.

23. 33. come to the place c. Calvary

Acts 11. 26. disciples were c. Christians first at Antioch

23. 6. I am c. in question by you this day, 24. 21.

Rom. 1. 1. Paul c. to be an Apostle, 1 *Cor.* 1. 1.

6. among whom are ye also the c. of

7. to them that are c. to be saints, 1 *Cor.* 1. 1.

8. 28. who are the c. according to his

1 *Cor.* 1. 9. by whom ye are c. to the fellowship

26. not many mighty, noble, are c.

7. 24. let every man wherein he is c. therein abide

Eph. 2. 11. who are c. uncircumcision by that c.

Eph. 4. 1. walk worthy of vocation wherewith ye are c.

4. even as ye are c. in one hope of your calling

Col. 4. 11. Jesus, which is c. Justus, saluteth you

1 *Tim.* 6. 12. eternal life, whereto thou art c.

20. oppositions of science falsely so c.

Heb. 11. 16. God is not ashamed to be c. their God

24. Moses refused to be c. son of Pharaoh's daughter

1 *Pet.* 2. 9. hath c. you out of darkness

2 *Pet.* 1. 3. that hath c. us to glory

Rev. 17. 14. they that are with him, are c. and chosen

19. 9. blessed that are c. to the marriage supper

CALLED, joined with God or Lord, *Gen.* 1. 5. *God* c. light day, darkness he c. night

Gen. 1. 8. and *God* c. the firmament, Heaven

Is. 49. 1. the *Lord* hath c. me from the womb

54. 6. the *Lord* hath c. thee as a woman forsaken

1 *Cor.* 7. 15. but *God* hath c. us to peace

Gal. 1. 15. it pleased *God*, who c. me by his grace

1 *Thess.* 2. 12. who c. you to his kingdom and glory

2 *Tim.* 1. 9. who hath c. us with a holy

CALLED, he, *Gen.* 35. 10. thy name is Jacob, *he* c. his name Israel

Ex. 24. 16. the Lord c. to Moses out of the cloud

Matt. 10. 1. *he* c. the twelve ; 15. 10. *he* c. multitude

Mark 1. 20. *he* c. them, and they left

Rom. 8. 30. them *he* also c. whom *he* c. he justified

1 *Pet.* 1. 15. but as *he* who hath c. you is holy

CALLED I, or I have, *Ps.* 17. 6. *I have* c. on thee, for thou wilt hear

Ps. 88. 9. Lord, *I have* c. daily upon

Prov. 1. 24. because *I have* c. and ye refused

Zech. 11. 7. one *I* c. beauty, the other *I* c. bands

John 15. 15. not servants, but *I have* c. you friends

CALLED his name, *Gen.* 35. 18. she c. *his name* Benoni, but his father Benjamin

Matt. 1. 25. her first-born son, and he c. *his name* Jesus

Rev. 19. 13. and *his name* is c. the Word of God

CALLED, shall be, *Gen.* 2. 23. *shall be* c. woman, because taken out of man

Is. 9. 6. and his name *shall be* c. Wonderful

32 .5. vile person, *shall* no more *be* c. liberal

35. 8. and a way, and it *shall be* c. way of holiness

Jer .23 6. he *shall be* c. Lord our righteousness

Matt. 1. 23. and his name *shall be* c. Emmanuel

2. 23. fulfilled *shall be* c. a Nazarene

5. 9. peace-makers *shall be* c. the children of God

Luke 1. 32. and he shall *be* c. the Son of the Highest

35. also that holy thing *shall be* c. the Son of God

CALLED, shalt be, *Is.* 1. 26. thou *shalt be* c. the city of righteousness

Is. 4 7. 1. thou *shalt be* c. no more tender and delicate

5. thou *shalt* no more *be* c. lady of kingdoms

62. 4. thou *shalt be* c. Hephzibah, thy land Beulah

John 1. 42. *shalt be* c. Cephas, which is a stone

CALLED, they, *Ps.* 99. 6. *they* c. upon the Lord, and he answered

Matt. 10. 25. if *they* c. the master Beelzebub

Luke 1. 59. *they* c. him Zacharias, after his father

Acts 14. 12. *they* c. Barnabas, Jupiter ; and Paul, Mercurius

CALLEDST, CALLEST, 1 *Sam.* 3. 5. and he said, here am I, for thou c. me

Ps. 81. 7. thou c. in trouble, and I delivered thee

CALLETH, *Ps.* 42. 7. deep c. unto deep at the noise of thy

Ps. 147. 4. he *c.* them all by their names, *Is.* 40. 26.

Matt. 27. 47. this man *c.* for Elias, *Mark* 15. 35.

Mark 3. 13. *c.* to him whom he would, they came

10. 49. be of good comfort, arise, he *c.* thee

John 10. 3. and he *c.* his own sheep by name

11. 28. the master is come and *c.* for

CALLING, *Rom.* 11. 29. the *c.* of God without repentance

1 *Cor.* 7. 20. let every man abide in same *c.* wherein called

Eph. 1. 18. may know what is the hope of his *c.*

4. 4. called in one hope of your *c.*

Phil. 3. 14. for the prize of the high *c.*

2 *Thess.* 1. 11. that count you worthy of this *c.*

2 *Tim.* 1. 9. who hath called us with an holy *c.*

Heb. 3. 1. partakers of the heavenly *c.* consider

2 *Pet.* 1. 10. your *c.* and election sure

Acts 7. 59. stoned Stephen *c.* upon God

22. 16. wash away thy sins, *c.* on name of the Lord

CALM, *Ps.* 107. 29. he maketh the storm a *c.*

Jonah 1. 11. that the sea may be *c.* unto us

Matt. 8. 26. there was a great *c. Mark* 4. 39 ; *Luke* 8. 24.

CALVE, ED, ETH, *Job* 21. 10. their cow *c.* and casteth not her calf

Ps. 29. 9. the voice of the Lord maketh hinds to *c.*

Jer. 14. 5. the hind *c.* in the field, and forsook it

CALVES, 1 *Kings* 12. 28. the king made two *c.* of gold

32. sacrificing to the *c.* that he had made

Ps. 68. 30. rebuke the bulls with the *c.* of people

Hos. 10. 5. shall fear, because of the *c.* of Beth-aven

14. 2. so will we render the *c.* of our lips

Mic. 6. 6. shall I come with *c.* of a year old

Mal. 4. 2. ye shall grow up as *c.* of the

Heb. 9. 12. nor by blood of goats and *c.* but own blood

19. took blood of *c.* and sprinkled book and people

CAME, *Deut.* 1. 19. and we *c.* to Ka-desh-barnea

33. 2. the Lord *c.* from Sinai, and rose up from Seir

Ruth 2. 6. it is the Moabitish damsel that *c.* back

1 *Sam.* 2. 12. custom was, the priest's servant *c.* 15.

2 *Sam.* 2. 4. men of Judah *c.* and anointed David king

13. 30. while in the way the tidings *c.* to David

36. behold king's sons *c.* and wept, the king wept

2 *Kings* 4. 11. it fell on a day that he *c.*

8. 14. Hazael departed from Elisha, *c.* to his master

9. 11. wherefore *c.* this mad fellow to thee

Ezra 2. 2. which *c.* with Zerubbabel, Mordecai

Esth. 1. 17. Vashti to be brought in, but she *c.* not

2. 13. then thus *c.* every maiden to the king

Job 3. 25. I feared a fear, and it *c.* upon

26. I was not in safety, nor had rest, yet trouble *c.*

29. 13. the blessing of him that was ready to perish *c.* on him

Ps. 18. 6. my cry *c.* before me even to his ears

Jer. 7. 31. nor *c.* it into my mind, 19. 5; 32. 35.

8. 15. we looked for peace, but no good *c.*

Ezek. 33. 22. afore he that escaped *c.*

37. 7. the bones *c.* together, bone to his bone

Ezek. 37. 10. breath *c.* into them, they lived and stood up

Hab. 3. 3. God *c.* from Teman, and the

Matt. 2. 1. there *c.* wise men from the east to Jerusalem

3. 1. In those days *c.* John the Baptist preaching

7. 25. and the rains descended and the floods *c.* 27.

20. 28. Son of Man *c.* not to be minis-tered to

25. 10. they went to buy, the bride-groom *c.*

25. 36. in prison and ye *c.* to me

26. 49. *c.* to Jesus and kissed him

Luke 9. 34. there *c.* a cloud and over-shadowed them

15. 17. when he *c.* to himself, he said, how many

John 1. 7. the same *c.* to bear witness of the light

11. he *c.* to his own, and his own re-ceived him not

17. but grace and truth *c.* by Jesus Christ

Eph. 2. 17. and *c.* and preached peace to you afar off

1 *Thess.* 1. 5. our gospel *c.* not in word only but in power

1 *Tim.* 1. 15. that Christ *c.* into the world to save sinners

2 *Tim.* 3. 11. persecutions which *c.* to me at Antioch

1 *John* 5. 6. this is he that *c.* by water and blood

CAME down, *Luke* 10. 31. there *c. down* a certain priest that way

John 3. 13. he that *c. down* from hea-ven, Son of Man

6. 41. the bread which *c. down* from heaven, 51. 58.

I CAME, *Matt.* 10. 34. *I c.* not to send peace, but a sword ; *Luke* 5. 32.

John 12. 27. but for this cause I *c.* to this hour

18. 37. for this cause *c.* I into the world that I bear

Acts 10. 29. therefore *c.* I as soon as I

was sent for
24: 17. I *c.* to bring alms to my nation, and offerings
1 *Cor.* 2. 1. when I *c.* to you I *c.* not with excellency
CAME out, *Matt.* 8. 34. the whole city *c. out* to meet Jesus
27. 32. as they *c. out* they found Simon of Cyrene
53. and *c. out* of their graves after his
Mark 9. 7. a voice *c. out* of the cloud, saying, this is my
Luke 15. 28. therefore *c. out* his father and intreated
John 16. 27. because ye believed I *c. out* from God
19. 34. his side, forthwith *c. out* blood and water
1 *Cor.* 14. 36. *c.* word of God out from you, or to you
Rev. 7. 14. these *c. out* of great tribulation and washed
They CAME, or CAME they, *Job* 6. 20. *they c.* thither and were ashamed
30. 14. *they c.* upon me as a wide breaking in
Ps. 88. 17. *they c.* round about me like
Luke 2. 16. *they c.* with haste and found Mary
Acts 8. 36. *they c,* unto a certain water, eunuch said
Rev. 7. 13. what are these, and whence *c. they ?*
CAMEL, *Gen.* 24. 19 ; *Lev.* 11. 4.
30. 43. Jacob had much cattle, asses, and *c.*
31. 34. Rachel put them in the *c.*
37. 25. Ishmaelites came with their *c.*
1 *Sam.* 27. 9. David took away *c.*
30. 17. 400 young men rode on *c.*
Job 1. 3. his substance was also three thousand *c.*
Is. 21. 7. he saw a chariot of asses and of *c.*
30. 6. their treasures on the bunches of *c.*
Ezek. 25. 5. I will make Rabbah a stable for *c.*
Matt. 3. 4. raiment of *c.* hair ; *Mark* 1. 6.
19. 24. easier for a *c.* to go through
23. 24. strain at gnat swallow a *c.*
CAMP, *Ex.* 14. 19. the angel of the Lord went before the *c.*
Ex. 32. 17. a noise of war in the *c.*
36. 6. they caused it to be proclaimed through the *c.*
Num. 11. 26. Eldad and Medad prophesied in the *c.*
Deut. 23. 10. he shall not come within the *c.*
14. the Lord walked in the midst of thy *c.*
Josh. 6. 18. and make the *c.* of Israel a
Judg. 7. 17 when I come to the outside of the *c.*
13. 25. Spirit of God began to move in
21. 8. there came none to the *c.* from Jabesh
Judg. 21. 12. young virgins, they brought them to the *c.*
2 *Kings* 19. 35. the angel of the Lord

smote in the *c.* of Assyrians 185,000, *Is.* 37. 36.
Rev. 20. 9. compassed the *c.* of the saints about
CAMP, without the, *Ex.* 29. 14. the flesh of the bullock shalt thou burn *without the c. Lev.* 8. 17 ; 9. 11 ; 16. 27.
Lev. 6. 11. and shall carry forth ashes *without the c.*
Num. 5. 3. every leper shall be put out *without the c.*
31. 19. and do ye abide *without the c.* seven days
Josh. 6. 23. Rahab left her kindred *without the c.*
Heb. 13. 11. bodies of those beasts are burnt, *without the c.*
13. let us go forth to him *without the c.* bearing his
CANDLE shall be put out ; *Job* 18. 6. & 21. 17 ; *Prov.* 24. 20.
Job 29. 3. his *c.* shined on my head
Ps. 18. 28. Lord will light my *c.*
Prov. 20. 27. spirit of man is *c.* of the Lord
31. 18. her *c.* goeth not out by night
Matt. 5. 15. do men light a *c.* and put ; *Mark* 4. 21 ; *Luke* 8. 16. & 11. 33.
Luke 11. 36. shining of *c.* doth give
15. 8. light a *c.* and sweep the house
Rev. 18. 23. light of *c.* shine no more at all ; *Jer.* 25. 10.
22. 5. they need no *c.* neither
Zeph. 1. 12. search Jerusalem with *c.*
CANDLESTICK, *Ex.* 25. 31, 34 ; 37. 17, 20 ; *Lev.* 24. 4 ; *Num.* 8. 2 ; 2 *Kings* 4. 10 ; *Dan.* 5. 5.
Zech. 4. 2. behold a *c.* of gold
Matt. 5. 15. but on a *c.* it gives light to all ; *Mark* 4. 21 ; *Luke* 11. 33.
Heb. 9. 2. first wherein was the *c.*
Rev. 1. 20. seven *c.* seven churches
2. 5. I will remove thy *c.* out of place
CANE, *Is.* 43. 24. bought me no sweet *c.*
Jer. 6. 20. sweet *c.* from far country
CANKER, ED, 2 *Tim.* 2. 17. their word will eat as *c.*
Jam. 5. 3. your gold and silver is *c.*
CANKER-WORM, *Joel* 1. 4. eaten, and what *c.* left, 2. 25.
Nah. 3. 15. eat thee like *c.* make thyself many as the *c.*
CAPTAIN, *Gen.* 37. 36. sold Joseph to Potiphar *c.* of the guard
Gen. 40. 4. *c.* of the guard charged Joseph with them
Josh. 5. 14. but as *c.* of the host of the Lord I come
15. the *c.* of the Lord's host said to Joshua
Judg. 11. 6. said to Jephthah, be our *c.*
1 *Sam.* 9. 16. shalt anoint him *c.* over my people, 10. 1.
22. 2. and David became a *c.* over them
2 *Sam.* 5. 2. shall be *c.* over Israel
1 *Kings* 16. 16. Isr. made Omri *c.* king
2 *Kings* 1. 9. king sent a *c.* with fifty
5. 1. Naaman *c.* of the host of the king of Syria
20. 5. tell Hezekiah *c.* of my people
1 *Chr.* 11. 21. honourable, he was *c.*

2 *Chr*. 13. 12. God himself is with us for our *c.*

Is. 3. 3. Lord doth take away *c.* of fifty

Jer. 40. 5. *c.* gave Jer. victu. and a rew.

51. 23. appoint a *c.* against her

John 18. 12. then the band and the *c.* took Jesus

Acts 5. 26. then the *c.* with officers went and brought

Heb. 2. 10. to make *c.* of their salvation perfect through

CAPTAINS, *Ex*. 15. 4. his chosen *c.* also are drowned in the Red sea

Deut. 1. 15. I made wise men *c.* over thousands

1 *Sam*. 8. 12. he will appoint him *c.* over thousands

2 *Sam*. 18. 5. *c.* charge con. Absalom

1 *Kings* 2. 5. thou knowest what Joab did tb the *c.*

20. 24. take kings away, and put *c.*

22. 33. when the *c.* perceived that he was not the king of Israel

1 *Chr*. 4. 42. having for *c.* Pelatiah and Neariah

Job 39. 25. the thunder of the *c.* and

Jer. 13. 21. hast taught them to be *c.*

51. 23. I will break in pieces *c.*

57. I will make drunk her *c.*

Nah. 3. 17. thy *c.* as great grasshoppers

Dan. 3. 27. the *c.* saw these men on whose bodies

Mark 6. 21. Herod on birth-day made supper to his *c.*

Luke 22. 4. Judas communed with

Rev. 19. 18. may eat the flesh of *c.*

CAPTIVE, ITY, *Gen*. 14. 14. & 34. 29.

Ex. 12. 29. unto first-born of *c.*

Judg. 5. 12. led thy *c. c.*

2 *Kings* 5. 2. bro. away, *c.* a little maid

Is. 49. 24. or lawful *c.* be delivered

51. 14. *c.* or exile hastens to be loosed

52. 2 O *c.* daughter of Zion

Jer. 22. 12. die where led him *c.*

Amos 7. 11. Israel shall be led away *c.*

2 *Tim*. 2. 26. taken *c.* by him at will

3. 6. lead *c.* silly women laden

Deut. 30. 3. thy God will turn thy *c.*

Job 42. 10. L. turned the *c.* of Job

Ps. 14 7. Lord bringeth back the *c.*

68. 18. led *c. c. Eph*. 4. 8.

78. 61. delivered his strength into *c.*

85. 1. brought back the *c.* of Jacob

126. 1. Lord turned again the *c.* of Zion

4. turn again our *c.* as streams

Jer. 15. 2. such as for *c.* to *c.* 43. 11.

29. 14. I'll turn away your *c.*

30. 3. bring again *c.* of people

Hos. 6. 11. returned *c.* of people

Zeph. 2. 7. Lord shall turn away their *c.*

Rom. 7. 23. bringing me into *c.* to

2 *Cor*. 10. 5. bring into *c.* every thought

Rev. 13. 10. lead into *c.* go into *c.*

CARBUNCLE, S, *Ex*. 28. 17. first row a *c.* 39. 10.

Is. 54. 12. made thy gates of *c.*

CARCASE, the body of a dead animal or person ; *Lev*. 26. 30.

Lev. 5. 2. touch *c.* unc. thing is unc.

Josh. 8. 29. should take his *c.* down

1 *Kings* 13. 22. thy *c.* not come to sep-

24. a lion stood by the *c.*   (ulchre

2 *Kings* 9. 37. *c.* of Jezebel be as dung

Is. 14. 19. cast out as a *c.* trodden

Matt. 24. 28. *c.* is there will eagles be ; *Luke* 17. 37.

CARCASES, *Gen*. 15. 11. when fowls came on *c.*

Num. 14. 20. *c.* shall fall in wilderness.

1 *Sam*. 17. 46. I will give *c.* of Phil.

Is. 5. 25. their *c.* torn in streets

Nah. 3. 3. there is a great number of *c.*

Heb. 3. 17. whose *c.* fell in wilderness

CARE, thought and concern about a thing. God's providence towards his creatures, especially his people, is called his *care* for them. He considers their case, preserves their existence and powers, governs their acts, and promotes their welfare, *Matt*. 6. 26, 30 ; 1 *Cor*. 9. 9 ; 1 *Pet*. 5. 7.

CARE, *Luke* 10. 40 ; 1 *Cor*. 7. 21.

Matt. 13. 22. *c.* of this world choke ; *Mark* 4. 19 ; *Luke* 8. 14. & 21. 34.

1 *Cor*. 9. 9. doth God take *c.* for oxen

12. 25. have same *c.* one for another

2 *Cor*. 11. 28. the *c.* of all the churches

1 *Tim*. 3. 5. shall he take *c.* of church

1 *Pet*. 5. 7. casting all your *c.* on him

Ps. 142. 4. no man *c.* for my soul

John 12. 6. not that he *c.* for poor

Acts 18. 17. Gallio *c.* for none of

Matt. 22. 16. *c.* for any *Mark* 4. 38.

1 *Pet*. 5. 7. for he *c.* for you

Deut. 11. 12. land Lord thy God *c.* for

John 10. 13. hireling *c.* not sheep

1 *Cor*. 7. 32, 33, 34. unmarried *c.* for things of Lord—married *c.* for

CAREFUL, 2 *Kings* 4. 13. been *c.* for us

Jer. 17. 8. shall not be *c.* in the year of

Dan. 3. 16. not *c.* to answer thee

Luke 10. 41. art *c.* and troubled about

Phil. 4. 6. be *c.* for nothing but in every 10. *c.* but lacked opportunity

Tit. 3. 8. be *c.* to maintain good works

CAREFULLY, *Phil*. 2. 28. I sent him the more *c.*

Heb. 12. 17. tho' sought it *c.* with tears

CAREFULNESS, 1 *Cor*. 7. 32. I would have you without *c.*

2 *Cor*. 7. 11. *c.* it wrought in you

CARELESS, *Is*. 32. 9. hear, ye *c.* daughters

Is. 32. 10. ye *c.* women ; 11. ye *c.* ones

CARELESSLY, *Is*. 47. 8. hear thou that dwellest *c.*

Zeph. 2. 15. rejoice city that dwelt *c.*

CARES, *Mark* 4. 19. *c.* of this world choke

Luke 8. 14. choked with *c.* and riches

21. 34. overcharged with *c.* of life

CARNAL. The ceremonial ordinances were *carnal* ; they related immediately to the bodies of men and beasts, *Heb*. 7. 16 ; 9. 10. Wicked men are *carnal* and *carnally minded* ; are under the dominion of sinful lusts ; and habitually think of desire after, and delight in, sinful pleasures, and enjoyments, *Rom*. 8. 6, 7.

CARNAL, sold under sin, *Rom*. 7. 14.

Rom. 8. 7. *c.* mind is enmity against G.

15. 27. minister to them in *c.* things
1 *Cor.* 3. 1. not speak but as to *c.*
   3. yet *c.* are ye not *c.* and walk
   9. 11. if we reap your *c.* things
2 *Cor.* 10. 4. weapons are not *c.*
Heb. 7. 16. law of a *c.* commandment
   9. 10. *c.* ordinances imposed till
Rom. 8. 6. to be *c.* minded is death
CARPENTER, S, 2 *Sam.* 5. 11. Hiram
   sent *c.* to David, 1 *Chr.* 14. 1.
2 *Chr.* 24. 12. they hired *c.* to repair,
   Ezra 3. 7.
Is. 41. 7. so the *c.* encouraged the gold
   smith
Is. 44. 13. the *c.* stretcheth out his rule,
Jer. 24. 1. the *c.* and smiths he carried
   away, 29. 2.
Matt. 13. 55. is not this the *c.* son ?
Mark 6. 3. is not this the *c.* the son of
   Mary ?
CARRIAGE, S, 1 *Sam.* 17. 22. David
   left his *c.* with keeper
Is. 10. 28. at Michmash laid up *c.*
   46. 1. your *c.* were heavy laden
Acts 21. 15. we took up our *c.*
CARRY, *Gen.* 50. 25. *c.* up my bones,
   Ex. 13. 19.
Ex. 33. 15. *c.* us not up hence,
Num. 11. 12. *c.* them in thy bosom
Josh. 4. 3. *c.* the twelve stones over
1 *Kings* 18. 12. spirit of L. sh. *c.* thee
2 *Kings* 4. 19. *c.* him to his mother
1 *Chr.* 15. 2. none ought to *c.* ark but
Eccl. 10. 20. bird of air shall *c.* voice
Is. 40. 11. *c.* lambs in his bosom
   46. 4. *c.* and to hoar hairs I will *c.*
   you
Jer. 20. 5. and *c.* them to Babylon
Mark 6. 55. began to *c.* in beds sick
   11. 16. to *c.* a vessel through temple
Luke 10. 4. *c.* neither purse nor scrip
John 5. 10. not lawful to *c.* thy bed
   21. 18. *c.* thee whither thou wouldst
   not
CARRY away, 2 *Kings* 18. 11. king of
   Assyria did *c. a.* Israel
2 *Kings* 25. 11. fugitives did Nebuchadnezzar *c. a.*
Ps. 49. 17. dieth he shall *c.* nothing *a.*
Eccl. 5. 15. nothing which he may *c. a.*
Acts 7. 43. *c.* you *a.* beyond Babylon
CARRY out, *Gen.* 47. 30. shalt *c.* me *o.*
   of Egypt
Acts 5. 9. feet at door, shall *c.* thee *o.*
1 *Tim.* 6. 7. certain we *c.* nothing *o.*
CARRIED, 2 *Kings* 20. 17. have laid up
   in store, shall be *c.* to Babylon, *Is.*
   39. 6.
2 *Chr.* 28. 15. *c.* all the feeble on asses
   33. 11. *c.* Manasseh to Babylon
   36. 4. Necho *c.* Jehoahaz to Egypt
Ps. 46. 2. tho' mountains be *c.* into sea
Is. 49. 22. thy daugh. be *c.* on shoulders
   53. 4. he hath *c.* our sorrows
   63. 9. *c.* them all the days of old
Luke 7. 12. was a dead man *c.* out
   16. 22. beggar was *c.* by the angels
   24. 51. and was *c.* up into heaven
Acts 5. 6. young men *c.* Ananias out
   7. 16. our fathers were *c.* to Sychem
   8. 2. *c.* Stephen to his burial
Eph. 4. 14. *c.* with ev. wind of doctrine
Heb. 13. 9. *c.* about divers' doctrines

2 *Pet.* 2. 17. clouds *c.* with a tempest
Jude 12. clouds without water *c.*
CARRIED away, *Dan.* 2. 35. and wind
   c. them *a.*
Nah. 3. 10. No was *c. a.* into captivity
Mark 15. 1. *c.* Jesus *a.* to Pilate
1 *Cor.* 12. 2. Gentiles *c. a.* to dumb idols
Rev. 12. 15. cause her to be *c. a.* of flood
   17. 3. *c.* me *a.* in spirit, 21. 10.
CART, 1 *Sam.* 6. 7. make a new *c.* and
2 *Sam.* 6. 3. set ark on a new *c.*
Is. 28. 28. corn with wheel of *c.*
Amos 2. 13. as a *c.* is pressed that is
CART rope, *Is.* 5. 18. that draw sin as
   with a *c. r.*
CARVED, ING, INGS, *Ex.* 31. 5. Beza-
   leel in *c.* 35. 33.
1 *Kings* 6. 18. cedar within was *c.*
Ps. 74. 5. they break *c.* work
Prov. 7. 16. my bed with *c.* work
CASE, S, *Ex.* 5. 19. officers did see that
   they were in evil *c.*
Ps. 144. 15. happy that people that is
   in such a *c.*
Matt. 5. 20. ye shall in no *c.* enter the
   19. 10. if the *c.* of the man be so with
   his wife
John 5. 6. and had been now long time
   in that *c.*
1 *Cor.* 7. 15. is not under bondage in
   such *c.*
CASEMENT, *Prov.* 7. 6. at the window
   I looked through my *c.*
CASSIA, *Ex.* 30. 24. of *c.* 500 shekels
Ps. 45. 8. thy garments smell of *c.*
CAST, *Luke* 22. 41. about a stone's *c.*
CAST, *Ps.* 22. 10. I was *c.* upon thee
   from the womb
Prov. 16. 33. the lot is *c.* into the lap,
Is. 25. 7. the face of the covering *c.* over
   all people
Ezek. 15. 4. the vine-tree is *c.* into the
   fire for fuel
Dan. 3. 6. be *c.* into fiery furnace
   6. 7. be *c.* into the den of lions, 16.
Jonah 2. 4. I am *c.* out of thy sight
Matt. 4. 12. Jesus heard that John was
   c. into prison
   5. 25. to judge, and be *c.* into prison
   29. whole body be *c.* into hell, 30.
   6. 30. and to-morrow is *c.* into the
   oven ; *Luke* 12. 28.
   21. 21. be thou *c.* into the sea
Mark 9. 42. better he were *c.* into the
   sea ; *Luke* 17. 2.
   45. having two eyes, feet, to be, *c.*
   into hell, 47.
Luke 3. 9. hewn down, *c.* into the fire,
   Matt. 3. 10 ; 7. 19.
Acts 27. 26. howbeit, we must be *c.*
   upon a certain island
Rev. 20. 10. devil *c.* into lake
   14. death and hell *c.* into lake
   15. not found in the book of life, *c.*
   into the lake
CAST, *Gen.* 21. 15. Hagar *c.* the child
   under a shrub
   39. 7. master's wife *c.* eyes on Joseph
Ex. 1. 22. every son *c.* into river
   4. 3. he *c.* the rod on the ground
   15. 25. had *c.* tree into the waters
   32. 19. Moses *c.* tables out of hand
Judges 8. 25. *c.* every one the ear-rings

9. 53. a woman c. a piece of mill-stone ; 2 *Sam.* 11. 21.

1 *Kings* 7. 46. in plain of Jordan c. them,
14. 9. thou hast c. me behind thy back

2 *Kings* 6. 6. he c. in stick, iron swam

Neh. 9. 26. c. thy law behind their backs

Job 20. 23. God shall c. the fury of his wrath on him
30. 19. he hath c. me into the mire

Ps. 55. 3. they c. iniquity on me
22. c. thy burden on the Lord

Prov. 1. 14. c. in thy lot amongst us,

Eccl. 11. 1. c. thy bread on the waters,

Is. 2. 20. man shall c. his idols to bats
38. 17. c. all my sins behind thy back

Ezek. 7. 19. c. their silver in the streets
23. 35. hast c. me behind thy back

Mic. 7. 19. c. all their sins into the sea

Matt. 3. 10. is hewn down and c. into the fire, 7. 19.
5. 29. pluck it out and c. it from thee, 30 ; 18. 8, 9.
7. 6. nor c. your pearls before swine,
15. 26. children's bread, and c. it to dogs, *Mark* 7. 27.
22. 13. c. into outer darkness, 25. 30.
27. 44. thieves c. same in his teeth

Mark 9. 22. oft-times it hath c. him into the fire
43. widow hath c. more in than, 44.

Luke 12. 5. who hath power to c. into hell, fear him
19. 43. thy enemies shall c. a trench

John 8. 7. let him first c. a stone at her

Acts 16. 23. c. Paul and Silas into prison

Rev. 2. 10. devil should c. some of you
4. 10. the elders c. their crowns before
18. 21. mill-stone and c. it into sea

CAST away, *Ps.* 2. 3. c. a. their cords

Ps. 51. 11. c. me not *away* from thy

Ezek. 18. 31. c. *away* your transgressions

Matt. 13. 48. gather good, c. bad *away*

Luke 9. 25. man lose himself or c. *away*

Rom. 11. 1. hath God c. *away* his people

Heb. 10. 35. c. not *away* your confidence

CAST-AWAY, 1 *Cor.* 9. 27. lest that I myself should be a *cast-away*

CAST down, *Ps.* 17. 13. O Lord, disappoint him, c. him *down*

Ps. 37. 24. though he fall, he shall not utterly be c. *down*
42. 5. why art thou c. *down*, O my soul, 11 ; 43. 5.
6. O my God, my soul is c. *down*
102. 10. lifted up, and c. me *down*

Dan. 7. 9. till the thrones were c. *down*

Matt. 4. 6. if the Son of God, c. thyself *down*, *Luke* 4. 9.
27. 5. he c. *down* the pieces of silver

Luke 4. 29. might c. Jesus *down* headlong

2 *Cor.* 4. 9. c. *down*, but not destroyed
7. 6. God comforteth those c. *down*

Rev. 12. 10. the accuser of our brethren is c. *down*

CAST forth, *Hos.* 14. 5. he shall c. *forth* his roots as Lebanon

CAST off, *Ps.* 77. 7. will the Lord c. *off*

Ps. 94. 14. Lord will not c. *off* his people, *Lam.* 3. 31.

Rom. 13. 12. c. *off* the works of darkness

1 *Tim.* 5. 12. because they have c. *off* their first faith

CAST out, *Is.* 26. 19. and the earth shall

c. *out* the dead

Ezek. 16. 5. c. *out* in the open field

Matt. 5. 13. salt unsavoury to be c. *out*, *Luke* 14. 35.
7. 5. hypocrite first c. *out* the beam, *Luke* 6. 42.
8. 12. the children of the kingdom shall be c. *out*
12. 24. not c. *out* devils but by Beelzebub, *Luke* 11. 18.
17. 19. why could not we c. him *out*, *Mark* 9. 28.
21. 12. c. *out* all that sold, *Mark* 11. 15 ; *Luke* 19. 45.

Mark 16. 9. Magdalene, *out* of whom he had c. seven devils
17. in my name shall they c. *out* devils

Luke 6. 22. c. *out* your name as evil, for
11. 20. with finger of God c. *out* devils
13. 32. I c. *out* devils, and do cures

John 6. 37. him that cometh to me, I will in no wise c. *out*

Acts 7. 58. they c. Stephen *out* of city

Gal. 4. 30. c. *out* the bond-woman and

Rev. 12. 9. the great dragon was c. *out*

CAST up, *Is.* 57. 14. c. ye *up*, prepare the way, 62. 10.
20. waters c. *up* mire and dirt

CASTEST, ETH, 1 *John* 4. 18. but perfect love c. fear

Rev. 6. 13. fig-tree c. her untimely figs

CASTING, *Matt.* 27. 35. parted his garments, c. lots, *Mark* 15. 24.

Mark 9. 38. we saw one c. *out* devils, *Luke* 9. 49.

Luke 21. 1. rich men c. their gifts into

2 *Cor.* 10. 5. c. down imaginations and

1 *Pet.* 5. 7. c. all your care on him, for

CASTLE, 1 *Chr.* 11. 5. David took c. of Zion

Prov. 18. 19. contentions like bars of c.

Acts 21. 34. the chief captain commanded Paul to be carried into the c. 37 ; 22. 24 ; 23. 10.
23. 16. entered the c. and told Paul

CASTLES, *Gen.* 25. 16. names of Ishmael's sons by their c.

Num. 31. 10. they burnt their goodly c. with fire

2 *Chr.* 17. 12. Jehoshaphat built in Judah c.
27. 4. Jotham in the forest built c. and

CATCH every man his wife, *Judg.* 21. 21.

Ps. 10. 9. in wait to c. the poor
35. 8. in net, hid, c. himself
109. 11. extortioner c. all that he hath

Jer. 5. 26. set a trap they c. men

Mark 12. 13. to c. him in his words

Luke 5. 10. henceforth thou shalt c. men

CATCHETH, ING, *Matt.* 13. 19. devil c. away that sown

John 10. 12. wolf c. scattereth sheep

CATERPILLAR, 1 *Kings* 8. 37. if there be any c. 2 *Chr.* 6. 28.

Ps. 78. 46. gave increase to c.
105. 34. c. came without number

Jer. 51. 14. fill thee with men as with c.
27. the horses come up as the rough c.

Joel 2. 25. I will restore the ears the c. hath eaten

CATTLE thousand hills mine *Ps.* 50. 10.

Gen. 1. 25. God made the c. after their

Ex. 12. 29. smote all first-born of the c.

Ps. 104. 14. grass to grow for *c.*
Ezek. 34. 17. I judge between *c.* and *c.*
Luke 17. 7. having servant feeding *c.*
John 4. 12. drank thereof and his *c.*
CATTLE, much, *Ex.* 12. 38. Israel went out of Egypt with *much c.*
Jonah 4. 11. spare Nineveh, *much c.*
CATTLE, their, *Ps.* 78. 48. he gave up *their c.* also to the hail
Ps. 107. 38. not *their c.* to decrease
CAUGHT him kissed him, *Prov.* 7. 13.
Gen. 22. 13. behind him a ram *c.* by
39. 12. she *c.* him by garment, saying, lie with me
Judg. 1. 6. *c.* Adoni-Bezek, and cut off his thumbs
15. 4. Samson *c.* three hundred foxes
21. 23. wives danced, whom they *c.*
2 *Sam.* 18. 9. Absalom's head *c.* oak
Matt. 14. 31. Jesus *c.* Peter, and said
Mark 12. 3. *c.* servant and beat him
Luke 8. 29. oftentimes it *c.* him, and
John 21. 3. that night they *c.* nothing
Acts 6. 12. they came upon Stephen and *c.* him
Acts 8. 39. Spirit of Lord *c.* away Philip
26. 21. for these causes the Jews *c.* me in the temple
2 *Cor.* 12. 4. *c.* up into paradise
16. crafty I *c.* you with guile
12. 2. I know a man *c.* up
1 *Thess.* 4. 17. *c.* up together with them
Rev. 12. 5. her child was *c.* up to God
CAUL, S, *Ex.* 29. 13. the *c.* that is above the liver, 22 ; *Lev.* 3. 4, 10, 15 ; 4. 9 ; 7. 4 ; 8. 16, 25 ; 9. 10, 19.
Is. 3. 18. Lord will take away their *c.*
Hos. 13. 8. will rend the *c.* of heart
CAUSE come before judge, *Ex.* 22. 9.
Ex. 23. 2. nor speak in a *c.* to decline
3. not countenance poor man in his *c.*
6. nor wrest judgment of poor in *c.*
Deut. 1. 17. *c.* that is too hard
1 *Kings* 8. 45. maintain their *c.* 49.
Job 5. 8. to God would I commit my *c.*
13. 18. I have ordered my *c.*
23. 4. order my *c.* before him
Ps. 9. 4. hast maintained my *c.*
35. 23. awaken to my *c.* my God
27. that favour my righteous *c.*
140. 12. the Lord will maintain the *c.*
Prov. 18. 17. that is first in his own *c.*
25. 9. debate thy *c.* with neighbour
29. 7. the righteous considereth the *c.* of the poor
Eccl. 7. 10. what is *c.* that former days
Is. 41. 21. produce your *c.* saith the L.
51. 22. pleads the *c.* of his people
Jer. 5. 28. judge not *c.* of fatherless, 11. 20. to thee I revealed my *c.* 20. 12.
Jer. 22. 16. judged the *c.* of the poor
Lam. 3. 36. to subvert a man in his *c.*
Matt. 19. 3. put away wife for every *c.*
Luke 8. 47. what *c.* she touched him
23. 22. found no *c.* of death in him
Acts 10. 21. *c.* wherefore ye are come
2 *Cor.* 4. 16. for which *c.* we faint not
5. 13. if we be sober, it is for your *c.*
Phil. 2. 18. same *c.* ye joy with me
2 *Tim.* 1. 12. for which *c.* I suffer
Heb. 2. 11. *c.* he is not ashamed to call
1 *Pet.* 2. 23. committed *c.* to him that

CAUSE, plead, 1 *Sam.* 24. 15. the lord be judge, and *plead* my *c. Ps.* 35. 1 ; 43. 1 ; 119. 154.
Ps. 74. 22. arise, O God, *plead* thine own *c.*
Prov. 23. 11. he shall *plead* their *c.*
31. 9. open thy mouth, *plead* the *c.* of poor, needy
Jer. 30. 13. none to *plead* thy *c.*
Mic. 7. 9. until he *plead* my *c.*
CAUSE, for this, *Ex.* 9. 16. for this *c.* have I raised up Pharaoh
Dan. 2. 12. for this *c.* king angry
Matt. 19. 5. for *this c.* man leave mother, and cleave to wife, *Mark* 10 7 ; *Eph.* 5. 31.
John 12. 27. but for *this c.* came I unto this hour
18. 37. for *this c.* came I into world
2 *Thess.* 2. 11. for *this c.* God shall send strong delusion
1 *Tim.* 1. 16. for *this c.* obtained mercy
Heb. 9. 15. for *this c.* he is the mediator of new testament
1 *Pet.* 4. 6. for *this c.* was the gospel preached to them
CAUSE, Without, *Ps.* 119. 161. without *c. Prov.* 3. 30 ; *Matt.* 5. 22 ; *John* 15. 25.
Prov. 1. 11. lurk for the innocent *without c.*
3. 30. strive not with a man *without c.*
Matt. 5. 22. angry with his brother *w.c.*
CAUSE, verb, *Gen.* 7. 4. *c.* it rain forty days
Ex. 8. 5. *c.* frogs to come up
Deut. 1. 38. encourage him, for he shall *c.* Israel to inherit it, 3. 28 ; 31. 7 ; *Josh.* 1. 6.
12. 11. *c.* his name to dwell
24. 4. shalt not *c.* land to sin
Neh. 13. 26. outlandish women *c.* to sin
Job 6. 24. *c.* me to understand
Ps. 10. 17. wilt *c.* thine ear to hear
67. 1. *c.* his face to shine, 80. 3, 7, 29.
Ps. 76. 8. did *c.* judgment to be heard
85. 4. *c.* thine anger to cease
143. 8. *c.* me to hear, *c.* me to know the way
Is. 3. 12. lead thee *c.* thee to err, 9. 16.
58. 14. I will *c.* thee to ride on high
Is 61. 11. *c.* righteousness to spring forth
66. 9. and not *c.* to bring forth
Jer. 3. 12. not *c.* my anger to fall
7. 3. *c.* you to dwell in this place, 13. 16. give glory to the Lord before he *c.* darkness
15. 4. *c.* them to be removed into
11. *c.* the enemy to treat thee well
18. 2. *c.* thee to hear my words
32. 37. *c.* them to dwell safely
44. *c.* their captivity to return, 33. 7, 11, 26, & 34. 22, & 42. 12.
Lam. 3. 32. though he *c.* grief yet he'll
Ezek. 20. 37. *c.* you to pass under rod
36. 12. *c.* men to walk on you
36. 27. *c.* you to walk in my statutes
37. 5. *c.* breath to enter into you
Dan. 9. 17. *c.* thy face to shine on sanctuary
Amos 8. 9. *c.* sun to go down at noon

Rom. 16. 17. mark who *c.* divisions
CAUSED, *Gen.* 2. 21. God *c.* a deep sleep
Deut. 34. 4. land, I have *c.* thee to see it
Ps. 66. 12. *c.* men to ride over heads
　78. 13. divided sea, and *c.* to pass
　119. 49. word on which thou hast *c.* me to hope
Prov. 7. 21. fair speech *c.* to yield
Jer. 32. 23. hast *c.* all this evil to come
Ezek. 16. 7. I have *c..* thee to multiply as the bud
　29. 18. Nebuchadnezzar *c.* his army to serve against Cyrus
Dan. 9. 21. Gabriel being *c.* to fly swiftly, touched
Mal. 2. 8. have *c.* many to stumble
Acts 15. 3. *c.* great joy to brethren
CAUSES, *Deut.* 1. 16. hear the *c.* between your brethren
Lam. 3. 58. O Lord, thou hast pleaded the *c.* of my soul
Acts 26. 21. for these *c.* the Jews caught me in temple
CAUSETH, *Ps.* 104. 14. *c.* grass to grow for cattle
Ps. 135. 7. he *c.* vapours to ascend, *Jer.* 10. 13 ; 51. 16.
　147. 18. *c.* his wind to blow, and the waters flow
Prov. 10. 5. son *c.* shame, 17. 2. & 19. 26.
　18. 18. lot *c.* contentions to cease
　19. 27. cease to hear instruction that *c.* to err
Is. 64. 2. fire *c.* waters to boil
Matt. 5. 32. *c.* her to commit adultery
2 Cor. 2. 14. always *c.* us to triumph
Rev. 13. 12. *c.* the earth to worship the first beast
CAUSELESS, *Prov.* 26. 2. curse *c.* not come
CAVE, and stone lay on it, *John* 11. 38.
Gen. 19. 30. Lot dwelt in *c.* and two daughters
　23. 19. buried Sarah in the *c.*—
　25. 9. Abraham—49. 29. Jacob
Josh. 10. 16. hid themselves in a *c.*—
1 Kings 18. 4. hid them by fifty in a *c.*
Is. 2. 19. go into *c.* for fear of Lord
Ezek. 33. 27. die that be in the *c.*
Heb. 11. 38. wandered in *c.* of earth
CEASE, (1) To leave off, or give over, 1 *Sam.* 7. 8 ; *Is.* 33. 1. (2) To be utterly forgotten, *Deut.* 32. 26. (3) To be quiet, *Judg.* 15. 7. (4) To be wanting, *Deut.* 15. 11. (5) To be removed by death, or otherwise, *Lam.* 5. 14. (6) Not to lean to, or depend on, *Prov.* 23. 4. (7) To abstain from, *Ps.* 37. 8 ; *Is.* 1. 16.
CEASE, not day nor night ; *Gen.* 8. 22.
Num. 8. 25. age of fifty years shall *c.*
Deut. 15. 11. poor never *c.* out of land
Ezra 4. 23. to *c.* by force and power
Neh. 6. 3. why should the work *c.*
Job 3. 17. there the wicked *c.* troubling
Job 10. 20. days few, *c.,* let me alone
　14. 7. branch thereof will not *c.*
Ps. 37. 8. *c.* from anger and wrath
　46. 9. he maketh wars to *c.*
Prov. 19. 27. *c.* to hear instruction that
Prov. 20. 3. honour for man to *c.* from
　23. 4. *c.* from thine own wisdom

Eccl. 12. 3. grinders *c.* because they are few
Is. 1. 16. *c.* to do evil, learn to do well
　2. 22. *c.* ye from man whose breath
Jer. 14. let tears run down, and let them not *c.*
　17. 8. leaf green, or shall *c.* from yielding fruit
Lam. 2. 18. let not apple of eye *c.*
Ezek. 6. 6. your idols broken and *c.*
　7. 24. the pomp of the strong to *c.*
　30. 10. the multitude of Egypt to *c.*
Amos 7. 5. *c.* by whom Jacob arise
Acts 13. 10. wilt thou not *c.* to pervert
1 Cor. 13. 8. tongues they shall *c.*
Eph. 1. 16. *c.* not to—thanks for you
Col. 1. 9. *c.* not to pray for you
2 Pet. 2. 14. cannot *c.* from sin
CEASE, cause to, *Ezra* 4. 21. *cause* these men to *c.*
Neh. 4. 11. *cause* the work *to c.*
Ps. 85. 4. *cause* thine anger *to c.*
Jer. 7. 34. *cause* mirth *to c.* from the cities of Judah
Ezek. 16. 41. *cause* thee *to c.* from playing harlot
　23. 48. will I *cause* lewdness *to c.*
Dan. 9. 27. *cause* the oblation *to c.*
CEASED, *Ex.* 9. 33. thun. and hail *c.*
Josh. 5. 12. manna *c.* on the morrow
Ezra 4. 24. *c.* the work of the house
Luke 7. 45. this woman hath not *c.* to kiss my feet
Acts 4. 42. they *c.* not to teach and preach Jesus
　31. three years I *c.* not to warn
Heb. 10. 2. then would not have *c.* to be offered
1 Pet. 4. 1. who suffered in flesh, hath *c.* from sin
CEASETH, *Ps.* 12. 1. for godly man *c.*
Ps. 49. 8. redemption of soul precious and it *c.*
Prov. 26. 20. no tale-bearer strife *c.*
Is. 24. 8. the mirth of tabrets *c.* joy of the harp *c.*
　33. 8. the way-faring man *c.*
Acts 6. 13. this man *c.* not speak blasphemous words
CEASING, *Acts* 12. 5. prayer was made without *c.* for him
Rom. 1. 9. without *c.* I make mention, 1 *Thess.* 1. 3.
2 Tim. 1. 3. without *c.* I have remembrance of thee
CEDAR, a tree of great size and beauty in warm latitudes. It is an evergreen, of slow growth, and it does not decay when preserved from damp. A few yet remain on Lebanon. They were formerly abundant. Bayard Taylor visited them in 1852. He says, " we descended (from the snow-capped summit of Lebanon) over occasional beds of snow, and reached the cedars in an hour and a half . . . There are about three hundred trees in all, many of which are of last century's growth ; but at least fifty of them would be considered grand in any forest. Five of them are undoubt-

edly as old as the Christian era, if
not the age of Solomon."

CEDAR, Lev. 14. 4 ; Jer. 22. 14, 15.
2 Sam. 7. 2. I dwell in house of c. but
2 Kings 14. 9. thistle sent to c. in
Ps. 29. 5. voice of the Lord breaks the c.
  92. 12. grow like c. in Lebanon
Songs 1. 17. beams of our house are c.
Ezek. 31. 3. Assyrian a c. in Lebanon

CEDARS, 1 Kings 10. 27. c. made he to
be as sycamore-trees
1 Chr. 17. 1. I dwell in an house of c.
Songs 5. 15. countenance excellent as c.
Is. 9. 10. we will change them into c.
Is. 44. 14. he heweth him down c. and
taketh oak
Jer. 22. 7. shall cut down thy choice c.
  23. O Lebanon, that makest thy nest
in the c.
Amos 2. 9. Amorites as height of c.
Zech. 11. 1. O Lebanon, that fire may
devour thy c.

CEDARS of Lebanon, Ps. 104. 16. the c.
of Lebanon which he hath planted
Ezek. 27. 5. c. of Lebanon, to make
masts for thee

CELEBRATE, To solemnize ; Lev. 23.
41. To praise, render famous ; Is.
38. 18.

CELESTIAL, 1 Cor. 15. 40. are c.
bodies glory of the c. is one

CENSER, S, Lev. 10. 1. sons of Aaron
took either of them c.
Lev. 16. 12. a c. full of burning coals
Num. 16. 19. Eleazar took the brazen c.
1 Kings 7. 50. made c. of pure gold
Heb. 9. 4. the holiest had the golden c.
Rev. 8. 3. angel having a golden c.
  5. the angel took the c. and filled it
with fire

CENSURE, 2 Cor. 2. 6. sufficient to such
a man is this c.

CENTURION, S, Matt. 8. 5. there came
unto him a c. beseeching him
  8. c. said, Lord, I am not worthy thou
  27. 54. the c. saw the earthquake
Luke 7. 2. c. servant who was sick
Acts 10. 1. Cornelius was a c. of the
Italian band
  22. Cornelius the c. a just man that
  21. 32. who immediately took c. and
  22. 26. when the c. heard that, he went
  23. 17. then Paul called one of the c.
  23. he called to him c. saying, make
  24. 23. and he commanded a c. to keep
Paul
  28. 16. the c. delivered the prisoners to

CERTAIN, Deut. 13. 13. c. men children of Belial
Mark 12. 42. came a c. poor widow
Luke 23. 19. who for a c. sedition and
murder
  24. 22. c. women made us astonished
  24. c. of them went to the sepulchre
John 5. 4. angel went down at c. season
Acts 12. 1. Herod the king to vex c. of
the church
Heb. 10. 27. but a c. fearful looking for
of judgment

CERTAIN, 1 Kings 2. 37. know for c.
thou shalt surely die, 42.
Dan. 2. 45. the dream is c. sure

1 Cor. 4. 11. have no c. dwelling-place
1 Tim. 6. 7. c. we can carry nothing out

CERTAINLY, Ex. 3. 12. c. I will be
with thee
Lev. 24. 16. congregation shall c. stone
2 Kings 8. 10. thou mayest c. recover
Prov. 23. 5. riches c. make wings
Jer. 36. 29. king of Babylon shall c. destroy this land
  42. 19. know c. I have admonished
you this day
Luke 23. 47. c. this was a righteous man

CERTAINTY, Luke 1. 4. thou mightest
know the c. of those things

CERTIFY, IED, Ezra 4. 14. therefore
have we sent and c. the king
Gal. 1. 11. I c. you gospel I preached,
not after man

CHAFF is the refuse of winnowed corn,
which is barren, light, and apt to
be driven to and fro with the wind,
Ps. 1. 4. To which are compared,
(1) False doctrine, or men's dreams
and inventions, Jer. 23. 28. (2)
Fruitless plots and designs, Is. 33.
11. (3) Hypocrites and ungodly
persons, who are vile, barren, and
inconstant, like chaff, Matt. 3. 12.

CHAFF, wicked as, Job 21. 18 ; Ps. 1. 4.
& 35. 5 ; Is. 5. 24. & 17. 13. & 29. 5.
& 41. 15 ; Dan. 2. 35 ; Hos. 13. 3.

Is. 33. 11. ye shall conceive c.
Jer. 23. 28. what is the c. to wheat
Zeph. 2. 2. before day pass as c.
Matt. 3. 12. burn up c. in unquench-

CHAIN, [1] Links of iron, gold, or silver, one within another, which
were (1) Sacred, those made by the
command of God, for the breast-
plate worn by the high-priest, Ex.
39. 15, 17, 18. (2) Idolatrous, such
as were made for idols, or images,
Is. 40. 19. (3) Common, wherewith prisoners were chained, Acts
12. 7. (4) Bondage, or affliction,
Lam. 3. 7. (5) Severe laws for
the curbing of all open impiety,
Rev. 20. 1.

CHAIN, Gen. 41. 42 ; Dan. 5. 7 ; Ezek.
7. 23 ; Mark 5. 3, 4.
Ps. 73. 6. pride compasseth them as c.
  149. 8. to bind their kings with c. and
nobles
Prov. 1. 9. shall be c. about thy neck
Songs 1. 10. thy neck comely with c. of
gold
Acts 28. 20. for hope of Israel this c.
2 Tim. 1. 16. not ashamed of my c.
2 Pet. 2. 4. delivered into c. of darkness
Jude 6. reserved in everlasting c.

CHALDEANS, Job 1. 17 ; Is. 43. 14. &
48. 20 ; Jer. 38. 2. & 40. 9. & 50. 35 ;
Ezek. 23. 14 ; Dan. 1. 4. & 9. 1.

CHAMBER, (1) The clouds, Ps. 104. 13.
(2) An upper room, or an apartment
wherein people generally eat,
where the disciples did eat the
passover, and did partake of the
Lord's supper, and where afterwards they assembled for divine
worship, Acts 1. 13 ; 20. 8.
The chambers of the south, Job 9. 9.

Those stars and constellations which are towads the southern pole ; so called, because they are for the most part hid and shut up, as chambers commonly are, from these parts of the world, and do not rise or appear to us till the beginning of summer, when they raise winds and tempests, as astronomers observe.

The king hath brought me into his chambers, Songs 1. 4. Christ the king of his church hath vouchsafed unto me most intimate and familiar fellowship with himself in his ordinances.

Enter thou into thy chambers, Is. 26. 20. Fly to God by faith, prayer, and repentance, for protection, depend upon his providence, lay hold upon his promises, and make use of his attributes. He alludes to the common practice of men, who, when there are storms or dangers abroad, betake themselves to their own chambers or houses for safety ; or, as some think, to that history, Ex. 9. 19. 20. or to that command, of not going out of their houses, Ex. 12. 22. or to the like charge given to Rahab, Josh. 2. 19.

Gen. 43. 30. Joseph entered into his c. and wept

Judge 16. 9. there were liers in wait abiding in the c. 12.

2 Sam. 13. 10. bring meat into the c. that I may eat

2 Kings 4. 11. Elisha turned into the c. and laid there

Ps. 19. 5. as a bridegroom cometh out of his c.

Songs 1. 4. king brought me into his c.

Is. 26. 20. enter into thy c. shut

Dan. 6. 10. windows open in his c. to Jerusalem

Joel 2. 16. let the bridegroom go forth of his c.

Matt. 24. 26. he is in the secret c.

CHAMBER, inner, 1 Kings 20. 30. Benhadab fled to *inner* c.

1 Kings 22. 25. *inner* c. to hide, 2 Chr. 18. 24.

2 Kings 9. 2. carry Jehu into *inner* c. and take the box

CHAMBER little, 2 Kings 4. 10. let us make a *little* c. on the wall

CHAMBER, upper, 2 Kings 1. 2. Ahaz Ezek. 40. 7. *little* c. was one reed long fell through a lattice in his *upper* c.

Acts 9. 37. washed, and laid Dorcas in an *upper* c.

39. brought Peter, when come into the *upper* c.

20. 8. many lights in *upper* c. where were gathered

CHAMBERS, Deut. 32. 25. terror from the c.

1 Kings 6. 5. against wall he built c.

1 Chr. 9. 26. chief porters were over the c. 23. 28.

Job 9. 9. maketh the c. of the south

Ps. 104. 3. beams of c. in waters

Prov. 7. 27. going down to c. of death

Ezek. 8. 12. every man in the c. of his imagery

21. 14. the sword which entereth into the privy c.

CHAMBERING, Rom. 13. 13. not in c. and

CHAMBERLAIN, S, 2 Kings 23. 11. by chamber of Nathan-melech the c.

Esth. 1. 10. the seven c. that served the king

2. 15. but what Hegai the king's c. appointed

21. two of king's c. were wroth

Acts 12. 20. Blastus the king's c.

Rom. 16. 23. Erastus, c. of the city

CHAMOIS, Deut. 14. 5. these ye shall eat, wild ox and the c.

CHAMPAIGN, Deut. 11. 30. who dwell in the c.

Ezek. 37. 2. many bones in the open c.

CHAMPION, 1 Sam. 17. 4. went a c. out of camp

1 Sam. 17. 51. when the Philistines saw their c. was dead

CHANCE, Deut. 22. 6. if a bird's nest c. to be before thee

1 Sam. 6. 9. a c. that happened to us

2 Sam. 1. 6. as I happened by c.

Eccl. 9. 11. but time and c. happen

Luke 10. 31. by c. priest came that way

1 Cor. 16. 37. it may c. of wheat

CHANCELLOR, Ezra 4. 8. Rehum c. wrote a letter to Artaxerxes, 9.

CHANGE, Lev. 27. 33. both it and the c. thereof shall be holy

Job 14. 14. wait till my c. come

10. 17. c. and war are against me

Ps. 55. 19. they have no c. therefore

Prov. 24. 21. meddle not with given to c.

Heb. 7. 12. made of necessity c. of law

CHANGES, Judg. 14. 13. give me thirty c. of raiment, Zech. 3. 4 ; Is. 3. 22.

CHANGE, verb, Gen. 35. 2. be clean and c. your garments

Job 17. 12. they c. night into day

Ps. 102. 26. shalt thou c. them

Is. 9. 10. we will c. them into cedars

Jer. 13. 23. can Ethiopian c. his skin or

Dan. 7. 25. think to c. times and laws

Hos. 4. 7. c. their glory into shame

Mal. 3. 6. I am the Lord, I c. not

Rom. 1. 26. women did c. natural use

Gal. 4. 20. to be present, and c. voice

Phil. 3. 21. who shall c. our vile body

CHANGED, ETH, 1 Sam. 21. 13. c. behaviour before them

Ps. 15. 4. he sweareth to his hurt, and c. not

Ps. 102. 26. and they shall be c.

Is. 24. 5. c. the ordinance, broken

Jer. 2. 11. hath a nation c. their gods

Lam. 4. 1. gold dim, how is the most fine gold c.

Dan. 2. 21. he c. times and seasons

Dan. 3. 19. form of his visage was c. against Shadrach

27. nor were their coats c. nor smell of fire passed

Rom. 1. 23. c. the glory of God

25. c. the truth of God into a lie

1 Cor. 15. 51. shall all be c. 52.

2 Cor. 3. 18. c. into same image

Heb. 7. 12. for priesthood being c. a change of law

CHANGERS, Prov. 24. 21. fear Lord and king, meddle not with c.

Matt. 21. 12. Jesus went to temple and overthrew tables of money-c. Mark 11. 15 ; John 2. 14.

CHANGEST, ED, countenance, Job 14. 20. thou c. his countenance, sendest him away

Dan. 5. 6. the king's countenance was c. in him, 9.

10. nor let thy countenance be c ; 7. 28. my countenance c. in me

CHANGES, Gen. 45. 22. to each he gave c. to Benjamin five c.

2 Kings 5. 5. he took with him ten c. of raiment

Job 10. 17. c. and war against me

Ps. 55. 19. because they have no c. they fear not

CHANGING, Ruth 4. 7. this was manner in Israel concerning c.

CHANNEL, S, 2 Sam. 22. 16. c. of the sea appeared, Ps. 18. 15.

Is. 8. 7. come up over all his c.

27. 12. beat off from c. of the river

CHAPITER, S, Ex. 36. 38. he overlaid their c. with gold, 38. 28.

1 Kings 7. 16. made two c. of brass, 2 Chr. 4. 12, 13.

2 Kings 25. 17. the c. upon it was brass, Jer. 52. 22.

Zeph. 2. 14. the bittern shall lodge in the c.

CHAPMEN, 2 Chr. 9. 14. besides what c. and merchants brought

CHAPEL, Amos 7. 13. it is the king's c.

CHARGE, (1) To command, Ex. 1. 22. (2) To prohibit, or interdict, Gen. 28. 1. (3) To adjure, or bind by a solemn oath, 1 Sam. 14. 27. (4) To load, or burden, Deut. 24. 5 ; 1 Tim. 5. 16. (5) To exhort, 1 Thess. 2. 11. (6) An office, or employ, Num. 8. 26.

Deut. 21. 8. lay not innocent blood to people's c.

Neh. 7. 2. I gave Hanani c. over Jerusalem

Ps. 35. 11. they laid to my c. things I 91. 11. give his angels c. over thee

Songs 2. 7. I c. you O daughters of Jerusalem, 3. 5. & 5. 8. & 8. 4.

Ezek. 9. 1. that have c. over city

44. 8. not kept the c. of holy things

Acts 7. 60. lay not this sin to their c.

8. 27. eunuch, who had c. of treasure

16. 24. received such a c. thrust them into prison

Rom. 8. 33. anything to c. of God's elect

1 Cor. 9. 18. make gospel without c. 7. goes a warfare at his own c.

1 Tim. 1. 18. this c. I commit to thee 6. 17. c. them that are rich

2 Tim. 4. 16. not laid to their c.

CHARGE, give, Num. 27. 19. and give Joshua a c.

Deut. 31. 14. call Joshua that I may give him a c.

Ps. 91. 11. give his angels c. Matt. 4. 6 ; Luke 4. 10.

1 Tim. 5. 7. these things give in c.

6. 13. I give thee c. in sight of God

CHARGE, Deut. 3. 28. but c. Joshua and encourage him

1 Thess. 5. 27. I c. you that, this epistle be read

1 Tim. 1. 3. c. that they teach no other doctrine

5. 21. I c. thee before God and Jesus Christ, 2 Tim. 4. 1.

6. 17. c. them that are rich in this world, that they

CHARGEABLE, 2 Cor. 11. 9. I was c. to no man

1 Thess. 2. 9. would not be c. to any of you

2 Thess. 3. 8. not be c. to any of you

CHARGED, Gen. 49. 29. Jacob c. his sons, and said to them, I am

2 Sam. 18. 12. for in our hearing the king c. thee

Job 1. 22. nor c. God foolishly

Job 4. 18. c. his angels with folly

Matt. 9. 30. Jesus c. them, see that no man know it, Mark 5. 43 ; Luke 9. 21.

12. 16. Jesus c. not to make him known, Mark 3. 12.

1 Thess. 2. 11. c. every one as a father

1 Tim. 5. 16. let not church be c.

CHARGER, S, Num. 7. 84. this was the dedication of the altar, twelve c.

Num. 7. 85. each c. of silver weighing

Ezra 1. 9. this is number of them, one thousand c.

Matt. 14. 8. give John Baptist head in a c. Mark 6. 25.

CHARGES, 2 Chr. 8. 14. he appointed the Levites to their c.

Acts 21. 24. them take, and be at c. with them

1 Cor. 9. 7. who goeth a warfare at his own c.

CHARIOT, (1) Light coach, Gen. 46. 29. (2) Chariots of war, out of which some of the ancients fought, armed with javelins and scythes in several places, which tore every thing they met with to pieces, Ex. 14. 7 ; Josh. 11. 4. (3) Hosts or armies, Ps. 68. 17. (4) Human, or worldly things wherein men repose their confidence, Ps. 20. 7.

Elijah is called the chariot of Israel and horsemen thereof, 2 Kings 2. 12. that is, by his example, his counsels, his prayers, and power with God, he did more for the defence and preservation of Israel, than all their chariots and horses, and other warlike provisions.

Solomon made a chariot of the wood of Lebanon, Songs 3. 9. Christ, of whom Solomon was a type, established for the glory of his grace the new covenant, or the gospel, whereby believers are carried to heaven ; which is of an everlasting nature, Heb. 13. 20 ; Rev. 14. 6.

CHARIOT, Gen. 41. 43. & 46. 29.

Ex. 14. 25. took off their *c.* wheels
2 *Kings* 2. 11. appeared a *c.* of fire
    12. my father the *c.* of Israel, 13. 14.
    5. 21. he lighted from the *c.* to meet
      Gehazi
    28. servants carried him in a *c.* to
      Jerusalem, 23. 30.
Ps. 46. 9. he burneth the *c.* in the fire
Songs 3. 9. Solomon made himself a *c.* of
Is. 21. 7. he saw a *c.* with horsemen, a
    c. of asses
Mic. 1. 13. bind the *c.* to swift beast
Zech. 6. 2. first *c.* red horses, second *c.*
    black horses
Acts 8. 29. join thyself to his *c.*
CHARIOT, his, *Gen.* 46. 29. Joseph
    made ready *his c.* and went
Ex. 14. 6. Pharaoh made ready *his c.*
Judg. 4. 15. Sisera lighted off *his c.* and
    fled away
    5. 28. why is *his c.* so long in coming?
1 *Kings* 12. 18. king made speed to *his*
    c. 2 *Chr.* 10. 18.
    22. 34. he said to the driver of *his c.*
    turn thy hand
    35. Ahab was stayed up in *his c.* and
    died at even
2 *Kings* 5. 9. Naaman came with *his c.*
    and stood
    10. 16. so they made him to ride in
    his c.
Ps. 104. 3. maketh the clouds *his c.*
Acts 8. 28. sitting in *his c.* read Esaias
    the prophet
CHARIOT-CITIES, 2 *Chr.* 1. 14. horse-
    men which he placed in *c.-cities*
    8. 6. Solomon built *c.-cities,* and store
    cities
2 *Chr.* 9. 25. bestowed in the *c.-cities*
    and with the king
CHARIOT-HORSES, 2 *Sam.* 8. 4. David
    houghed all *c.-horses,* 1 *Chr.* 18. 4.
2 *Kings* 7. 14. took therefore two *c.-horses*
CHARIOT-MAN, 2 *Chr.* 18. 33. he said
    to the *c.-man,* turn
CHARIOTS, *Gen.* 50. 9. there went up
    with Joseph *c.* and horse
Ex. 14. 7. Pharaoh took 600 *c.* and all
    the *c.*
    28. the waters covered all the *c.* and
    all the host
    15. 4. Pharaoh's *c.* and host hath he
    cast into sea
Josh. 17. 16. have *c.* of iron, 18 ; *Judg.*
    1. 19 ; 4. 3.
2 *Sam.* 1. 6. the *c.* and horsemen fol-
    lowed after Saul
Ps. 68. 17. the *c.* of God are twenty
    thousand
Songs 6. 12. like the *c.* of Amminadib
Is. 2. 7. full of horses, nor is any end of
    their *c.*
    22. 18. *c.* of thy glory be the shame
    of thy Lord
    31. 1. woe to them that trust in *c.*
    37. 24. by the multitude of my *c.* am
    I come up
Jer. 47. 3. at rushing of his *c.* fathers
Joel 2. 5. like the noise of the *c.* shall
    they leap
Mic. 5. 10. I will destroy thy *c.*
Rev. 9. 9. the sound of the wings is as

    the sound of *c.*
CHARIOTS, with horses, 2 *Kings* 6. 17.
    mountain was full of *c.* and *horses*
Ps. 20. 7. some trust in *c.* and some in
    horses
Songs 1. 9. compared thee to *horses* in
    Pharoah's *c.*
Is. 66. 20. bring your brethren on *horses*
    and in *c.*
Nah. 3. 2. noise of prancing *horses* and
    jumping *c.*
Hab. 3. 8. didst ride on their *horses*
    and *c.* of salvation
Rev. 18. 13. no man buys their *horses*
    and *c.*
CHARITY is a principle of prevailing
    love to God, and good will to men,
    which effectually inclines one en-
    dued with it to glorify God, and to
    do good to others ; to be patient,
    slow to anger, and ready to put up
    with wrongs ; to show kindness to
    all, and seek the good of others,
    though with prejudice, to himself.
    A person endued therewith does
    not interpret doubtful things to
    the worst sense, but the best ; is
    sorry for the sins of others, but re-
    joices when any one does well, and
    is apt to bear with their failings
    and infirmities ; and lastly, this
    grace is never lost, but goes with
    us into another world, and is exer-
    cised there 1 *Cor.* 13. 1, 4, &c.
Rom. 14. 15. walkest not according *c.*
1 *Cor.* 13. 1. if I have not *c.* nothing, 2, 3,
    4. *c.* suffereth long ; 8. *c.* never fails
    13. now abideth faith, hope, *c.*
    14. 1. follow after *c.* and desire spirit-
    ual gifts
    16. 14. let all—be done with *c.*
Col. 3. 14. above all things put on *c.*
1 *Thess.* 3. 6. tidings of your *c.*
2 *Thess.* 1. 3. *c.* of every one aboundeth
1 *Tim.* 1. 5. end of commandment is *c.*
    2. 15. if they continue in faith, *c.*
    4. 12. be thou an example of believers
    in *c.*
2 *Tim.* 2. 22. follow righteousness,
    faith, *c.*
    3. 10. known my doctrine, faith, *c.*
Tit. 2. 2. sound in faith, in *c.*
1 *Pet.* 4. 8. have fervent *c.* among your-
    selves, *c.* shall cover multitude of
    5. 14. greet ye one another with a
    kiss of *c.*
2 *Pet.* 1. 7. add to brotherly kindness *c.*
3 *John* 6. borne witness of thy *c.*
Jude 12. spots in your feasts of *c.*
Rev. 2. 19. I know thy works, and *c.*
    and service
CHARMED, *Jer.* 8. 17.
Charmers, *Deut.* 18. 11 ; *Ps.* 58. 5 ;
    Is. 19. 3.
CHASE, *Lev.* 26. 7. shall *c.* your ene-
    mies, and they fall
Lev. 26. 8. and five of you shall *c.* an
    hundred
Deut. 32. 30. how should one *c.* 1000,
    Josh. 23. 10.
Ps. 35. 5. angel of the Lord *c.* them
CHASED, ETH, ING, *Judg.* 9. 40.

Abimelech c. him

Neh. 13. 28. therefore I c. him from me

Job 18. 18. be c. out of the world

20. 8. c. away as a vision of night

Lam. 3. 52. mine enemies c. me sore

CHASTE. To be chaste is to be pure from fleshly lusts, which war against the spirit, *James* 4. 1, 5. The church is to be " presented as a chaste virgin to Christ," 2 *Cor.* 11. 2. There is a chastity of speech, behaviour, and imagination, as well as of body, 1 *Pet.* 3. 2. " While they behold your chaste conversation coupled with fear : " *Tit.* 2. 5.

CHASTEN, (1) To correct in love, *Ps.* 118. 18 ; *Heb.* 12. 5, 6. (2) To punish in justice, *Lev.* 26. 28. (3) To humble one's self before God by fasting and prayer, *Dan.* 10. 12.

The chastisement of our peace was upon him, Is. 53. 5. That punishment by which our peace, that is, our reconciliation to God, and salvation or happiness, were to be purchased, was laid upon Christ by God's justice, with his own consent.

CHASTEN with rod of men, 2 *Sam.* 7. 14.

Ps. 6. 1. neither c. me in thy, 38. 1.

Prov. 19. 18. c. thy son while hope

Dan. 10. 12. to c. thyself before God

Rev. 3. 19. as many as I love I c.

CHASTENED, *Job* 33. 19. he is c. also with pain on his bed

Ps. 69. 10. I c. my soul with fasting

73. 14. been c. every morning

118. 18. Lord has c. me sore

1 *Cor.* 11. 32. we are c. of the Lord

2 *Cor.* 6. 9. as c. and not killed

Heb. 12. 10. for a few days c. us

CHASTENEST, ETH, ING, *Deut.* 8. 5. as a man c. his son so the Lord c.

Job 5. 17. despise not c. of the Lord, *Prov.* 3. 11 ; *Heb.* 12. 5.

Ps. 94. 12. blessed whom thou c.

Prov. 13. 24. loves him c. betimes

Heb. 12. 6. whom the Lord loveth he c.

7. what son whom the father c. not

Is. 26. 16. when thy c. was upon them

Heb. 12. 7. if ye endure c. whereof

11. no c. for the present is joyous

CHASTISE you 7 times, *Lev.* 26. 28.

Deut. 22. 18. elders shall c. him

1 *Kings* 12. 11. I will c. with scorpions, 14.

Hos. 7. 12. c. them as their congregation

10. 10. desire I should c. them

Luke 23. 16. c. him and release him, 22.

2 *Chr.* 10. 11. 14. father c. with whips, c. *Ps.* 94. 10.

Deut. 11. 2. not seen the c.

Job 34. 31. I have borne c. I will not

Is. 53. 5. the c. of our peace was on

Jer. 30. 14. with c. of a cruel one

Heb. 12. 8. if ye be without c.

CHANT, *Amos* 6. 5. they c. to the sound of the viol and invent

CHATTER like a crane, *Is.* 38. 14.

CHAWS, *Ezek.* 29. 4. will put hooks in thy c. 38. 4.

CHECK, *Job* 20. 3. the c. of my reproach

CHECKER-WORK, 1 *Kings* 7. 17. Hiram made nests of c.-w. and wreaths

CHEEK, 1 *Kings* 22. 24. Zedekiah smote Micaiah on c.

Job 16. 10. smitten me on the c.

Lam. 3. 30. he giveth his c. to him that smiteth him

Luke 6. 29. to him that smiteth one c. offer also the other

CHEEK, right, *Matt.* 5. 39. smite thee on thy *right* c. turn the other

CHEEK-BONE, *Ps.* 3. 7. smitten all mine enemies on c.-*bone*

CHEEKS, *Songs* 1. 10. thy c. are comely with rows of jewels

Songs 5. 13. his c. a bed of spices, as sweet

Is. 50. 6. I gave my c. to them that plucked off hair

CHEER, *Matt.* 9. 2. be of good c. thy sins are forgiven

14. 27. be of good c. it is I, *Mark* 6. 50.

John 16. 33. be of good c. I have overcome world

Acts 23. 11. stood by him and said, be of good c. Paul

27. 22. I exhort you to be of good c.

25. sirs, be of good c. for I believe God

CHEER, verb, *Deut.* 24. 5. c. up his wife he hath taken

Eccl. 11. 9. let thy heart c. thee in the days of thy youth

CHEERETH, *Judg.* 9. 13. wine, which c. God and man

CHEERFUL, *Prov.* 17. 13. merry heart maketh a c. countenance

2 *Cor.* 9. 7. for God loveth a c. giver

CHEERFULNESS, *Rom.* 12. 8. he that showeth mercy with c.

CHEERFULLY, *Acts* 24. 10. I do the more c. answer

CHERISH, to support, nourish, 1 *Kings* 1. 2 ; *Eph.* 5. 28, 29 ; 1 *Thess.* 2. 7.

CHERUB. The Hebrew signifies fulness of knowledge ; and angels are so called from their exquisite knowledge, and were therefore used for the punishment of man, who sinned by affecting divine knowledge, *Gen.* 3. 24. There is but an obscure description in scripture of these cherubims, which Moses placed upon the ark of the covenant, *Ex.* 25. 18, as well as of those which God posted at the entrance of that delightful garden out of which he drove Adam and Eve. But it is probable that both one and the other had a human figure, since it is said of those which were placed at the entrance of Paradise, that they had their station there assigned them, to guard the entrance to it, and held a flaming sword in their hands. And Ezekiel compares the king of Tyre to the cherub that covered the ark of the covenant, *Ezek.* 28. 14, that is, he was like to this cherub, glittering all over with gold and glory. Moses says, that two cherubims covered the mercy-seat with their wings extended on both sides, and looked one to another having their faces turned towards the mercy-seat, which covered the ark. God is supposed to sit on the mercy-seat, whose face the angels in heaven always behold, and upon whom their eyes are fixed to observe and receive his commands, and towards Christ, the true Propitiatory, which mystery they desire to look into, 1 *Pet.* 1. 12, not envying mankind their near and happy relation to him ; but taking pleasure in the contemplation of it. Moses likewise calls those representations which were made in embroideries upon the veils of the tabernacle, cherubims of cunning work, *Ex.* 26. 1.

Ex. 25. 19. make one *c.* on one end, and the other *c.* on the other end, 37. 8.

2 *Sam.* 22. 11. he rode upon a *c. Ps.* 18.

1 *Kings* 6. 25. and the other *c.* was ten cubits
   26. the height of one *c.* ten cubits, so of the other

Ezek. 9. 3. the glory of God was gone up from the *c.* to the threshold of the house, 10. 4.
   10. 7. and one *c.* stretched forth his hand from the
   14. first face was the face of a *c.* second of a man
   28. 14. thou art the anointed *c.* that covereth
   16. destroy thee, O covering *c.*

CHERUBIMS, *Gen.* 3. 24. at the east of the garden *c.*

Ex. 25. 18. thou shalt make two *c.* of gold
   37. 7. he made two *c.* of beaten gold of one piece

1 *Kings* 6. 23. within the oracle he made two *c.*
   28. and he overlaid the *c.* with gold
   8. 7. the *c.* covered the ark, 2 *Chr.* 5. 8 ; *Heb.* 9. 5.

Ezek. 10. 5. the sound of the *c.* wings was heard
   16. when the *c.* went, the wheels went by them
   19. *c.* lift up their wings

CHERUBIMS, between the, *Ex.* 25. 22. will meet thee from *between the* two *c.*

Num. 7. 89. from *between the* two *c.* he spake to him

Ps. 80. 1. that dwelleth *between the c.* shine forth
   99. 1. he sitteth *between the c.* let earth be moved

Ezek. 10. 2. fill with coals of fire from *between the c.*

CHESNUT-TREE, S, *Gen.* 30. 37. Jacob took rods of *c.-tree*

Ezek. 31. 8. the *c.-tree* were not like his branches

CHEST, S, 2 *Kings* 12. 9. Jehoiada took *c.* and bored hole in lid

2 *Chr.* 24. 8. at king's commandment they made *c.*

Ezek. 27. 24. thy merchants in *c.* of rich apparel

CHEW, *Lev.* 11. 4. not eat of them that *c.* the cud, *Deut.* 14. 7.

CHEWED, *Num.* 11. 33. ere the flesh was *c.* wrath

CHEWETH, *Lev.* 11. 4. because he *c.* the cud, 5. 6 ; *Deut.* 14. 6.
   7. yet the swine *c.* not the cud, *Deut* 14. 8.

CHIDE, *Ex.* 17. 2. the people did *c.*

Judg. 8. 1. Ephraim did *c.* with Gideon

Ps. 103. 9. he will not always *c.* nor

CHIDING, *Ex.* 17. 7. called Meribah, because of *c.* of Israel

CHIEF, (1) The principal person of a family, congregation, tribe, army, &c., *Num.* 3. 30 ; *Deut.* 1. 15 ; 1 *Sam.* 14. 38 ; 2 *Sam.* 5. 8. (2) The best, or most valuable, 1 *Sam.* 15. 21. (3) The highest, or uppermost, *Matt.* 23. 6. (4) The dearest, or most familiar, *Prov.* 16. 28. (5) The greatest, *Ps.* 137. 6. (6) Most in esteem and reputation, *Luke* 14. 1 ; 2 *Cor.* 12. 11. (7) Most forward and active, *Ezra.* 9. 2. (8) Most remarkable and wonderful, *Job* 40 19.

Gen. 37. 36. they sold Joseph to a *c.* marshal
   40. 9. the *c.* butler told his dream to Joseph
   22. but hanged the *c.* baker as Joseph interpreted

Num. 3. 32. Eleazar shall be *c.*

1 *Sam.* 15. 21. the people took the *c.*

2 *Sam.* 23. 18. Abishai brother of Joab *c.* among three

1 *Kings* 9. 23. these were the *c.* of the officers

1 *Chr.* 5. 2. for of Judah came the *c.* ruler
   18. 17. the sons of David were *c.* about the king
   26. 10. though not first-born, his father made him *c.*

Neh. 11. 3. are *c.* of the province

Ps. 78. 51. smote *c.* of strength
   137. 6. Jerusalem above my *c.* joy

Prov. 1. 21. Wisdom crieth in *c.* place
   16. 28. whisperer separateth *c.* friends

Jer. 13. 21. thou hast taught them as *c.*

Songs 5. 10. my beloved is the *c.* among 10,000

Ezek. 4. 2. set *c.* leaders against Jerusalem round

Dan. 2. 14. Arioch the *c.* marshal

Matt. 20. 27. will be *c.* among you

Mark 10. 44. *c.* shall be servant of all

Luke 11. 15. casteth out devils through *c.* of the devils

Luke 14. 7. chose the *c.* rooms, 20. 46.
   22. 26. that is *c.* as that serveth

John 12. 42. among *c.* rulers many believed on him

Acts 14. 12. Paul was the *c.* speaker
   17. 4. some believed, and of *c.* women not a few

2 *Cor.* 11. 5. whit behind *c.* of apostles, 12. 11.

Eph. 2. 20. Jesus Christ, the *c.* corner-stone, 1 *Pet.* 2. 6.

1 *Tim.* 1. 15. sinners of whom I am *c.*

1 *Pet.* 5. 4. when *c.* shepherd shall appear, shall receive

CHIEF, captain, 2 *Sam.* 5. 8. who smiteth shall be *c.* and *captain*

Acts 23. 17. bring young man to *c.* captain

CHIEF captains, *Rev.* 6. 15. *c. captains* hid themselves

CHIEF, man, or men, *Acts* 13. 50. Jews stirred up the *c. men*

Acts 15. 22. Judas and Silas *c. men*

CHIEF priest, 1 *Chr.* 29. 22. anointed Zadok to be *c. priest*

2 *Chr.* 19. 11. Amariah *c. p.* is over

26. 20. and Azariah the *c. p.* looked

CHIEF priests, *Ezra* 8. 24. separated twelve *c.* of *priests*

Matt. 26. 47. a multitude with staves from the *c. priests*

27. 12. when he was accused of *c. priests*, *Mark* 15. 3.

41. *c. priests* mocking with scribes *Mark* 15. 31.

Mark 14. 1. *c. priests* sought to take and put to death, 55 ; *Matt.* 26. 59 ; *Luke* 9. 22.

Luke 23. 23. voices of them and *c. priests* prevailed

John 7. 32. *c. priests* sent officers to take him, 18. 3.

19. 15. *c. priests* answered, we have no king but Caesar

Acts 9. 14. he hath authority from *c. priests*, 26. 10.

22. 30. commanded the *c. priests* and council to appear

CHIEF singer or singers, *Neh.* 12. 46. in days of David were *c.* of the *singers*

Hab. 3. 19. to the *c. singer* on my instruments

CHIEFEST, 1 *Sam.* 2. 29. to make yourselves fat with *c.* offerings

9. 22. Samuel made them sit in the *c.* place

CHIEFLY, *Rom.* 3. 2. *c. Phil.* 4. 22 ; 2 *Pet.* 2. 10.

CHILD. The descendants of a man, how remote soever they may be, are called sons, or children. For example : the children of *Edom*, the children of *Moab*, the children of *Israel.* These expressions, the children of light, the children of darkness are used to signify those who follow light, and those who remain in darkness : the children of the kingdom, those who belong to the kingdom. Persons who are almost of age, are often called children. For example : Joseph is called a child, though he was at least sixteen years old, *Gen.* 37. 30. and Benjamin of the age of above thirty, is still called a little child, *Gen.* 44. 20. Likewise men of full age have often the name of children given them, *Is.* 65. 20. The child shall die an hundred years old ; that is, men shall die at the

age of an hundred years ; there shall be no more untimely deaths

Children or sons of God. By this name angels are sometimes described as, *Job* 1. 6 ; 2. 1. There was a day when the sons of God came to present themselves before the Lord. Good men, in opposition to the wicked, are likewise called by this name ; the children of Seth's family, in opposition to the race of Cain, *Gen.* 6. 2. The sons of God saw the children of men. Judges and magistrates are likewise termed children of God, *Ps.* 82. 6. I have said, you are gods , and all of you are the daughters of the Most High.

In the New Testament, Believers are commonly called the children of God, by virtue of their adoption, and the prerogative which Christ purchased for them by the merits of his death and sufferings. *John* 1. 12. He hath given us power to become the sons of God : and elsewhere ; see *Rom.* 8. 14 ; *Gal.* 3. 26.

Gen. 37. 30. *c.* is not, and

Ex. 2. 2. she saw he was a goodly *c.*

2. 8. maid went, *c.* mother [less *c.*

22. 22. ye shall not afflict any father-

Judg. 11. 34. Jepthah's daughter was his only *c.*

13. 8. what we shall do to *c.*

1 *Sam.* 1. 25. they brought the *c.* to Eli

2 *Sam.* 12. 14. the *c.* that is born to thee shall die

2 *Sam.* 12. 16. David besought God for *c.*

2 *Kings* 4. 31. the *c.* is not awaked

35. and the *c.* opened his eyes

Prov. 23. 13. withhold not the correction from the *c.*

Is. 65. 20. the *c.* shall die an hundred years old

Eccl. 4. 8. hath neither *c.* nor brother

Is. 3. 5. *c.* behave himself proudly

Jer. 31. 20. son is he a pleasant *c.*

Matt. 10. 21. the father shall deliver the *c.* to death

17. 18. the *c.* are cursed from that very hour

23. 15. twofold more the *c.* of hell

Luke 1. 66. what manner of *c.* shall

2. 43. the *c.* Jesus tarried behind

9. 38. Master, look on my son, he is my only *c.*

John 4. 49. sir, come down ere my *c.* die

16. 21. as soon as delivered of the *c.*

Acts 4. 27. thy holy *c.* Jesus, 30.

13. 10. thou *c.* of the devil, thou

Rev. 12. 4. to devour her *c.* as

5. her *c.* was caught up to

CHILD, a, 1 *Sam.* 2. 18. Samuel, *a c.* girded with a linen ephod

Job 33. 25. flesh shall be fresher than *a c.*

Ps. 131. 2. quieted myself as *a c.*

Prov. 20. 11. even *a c.* is known by his doings

22. 6. train up *a. c.* in the way he should go

15. foolishness bound in heart of *a c.*

Prov. 29. 15. but *a c.* left to himself

Eccl. 4. 13. better is *a* wise *c.* than a

foolish king
10. 16. woe when thy king is *a c.*
Is. 9. 6. unto us *a c.* is born—a son
Jer. 1. 6. I cannot speak for I am *a c.*
Hos. 11. 1. when Israel was *a c.*
Mark 9. 36. took *a c.* and set him
1 *Cor.* 13. 11. was *a c.* I spake as *a c.*
Gal. 4. 1. heir as long as he is *a c.*
2 *Tim.* 3. 15. from *a c.* hast known scr.
CHILD, little, *Is.* 11. 6. *a little c.* shall
 lead them
Matt. 18. 2. Jesus called a *little c.*
Mark 10. 15. whosoever shall not re-
 ceive the kingdom of God as a *little
 c. Luke* 18. 17.
CHILD, sucking, *Num.* 11. 12. as a
 nursing father beareth *sucking c.*
Is. 11. 8. *sucking c.* shall play on the
 hole of the asp
49. 15. woman forget her *sucking c.*
CHILD, with, *Matt.* 1. 18. she was found
 with c. of the Holy Ghost
Matt. 1. 23. a virgin shall be *with c.*
 24. 19. woe to them that are *with c.*
 Mark 13. 17 ; *Luke* 21. 23.
1 *Thess.* 5. 3. as travail upon a woman
 with c.
CHILD, young, *Matt.* 2. 8. go and
 search diligently for the *young c.*
Matt. 2. 13. take the *young c.* and his
 mother, and flee
Childbearing, 1 *Tim.* 2. 15.
Childhood and youth, *Eccl.* 11. 10.
Childish things, 1 *Cor.* 13. 11.
Childless, *Gen.* 15. 2 ; *Jer.* 22. 30.
CHILDREN struggled, *Gen.* 25. 22.
Gen. 30. 1. give me *c.* else I die
Ex. 20. 5. a jealous God, visiting the
 iniquity of the fathers upon the *c.*
 34. 7 ; *Num.* 14. 18 ; *Deut.* 5. 9.
Num. 13. 28. saw the *c.* of Anak
Deut. 9. 2. who can stand before the *c.*
 of Anak?
 13. 13. *c.* of Belial are gone
 14. 1. the *c.* of the Lord your God
 24. 16. the fathers shall not be put
 to death for the *c.* nor the *c.*
 2 *Chr.* 25. 4.
 32. 20. *c.* in whom there is no faith
Judg. 3. 18. each one resembled the *c.*
 of a king
 20. 13. the *c.* of Belial
1 *Chr.* 16. 13. O ye *c.* of Jacob his chosen,
 Ps. 105. 6.
Job 19. 17. I intreated for the *c.* sake
 30. 8. they were *c.* of fools
Ps. 17. 14. they are full of *c.* and
Ps. 34. 11. come ye *c.* hearken to me
 72. 4. shall save *c.* of the needy
 102. 28. the *c.* of thy servant shall
 113. 9. a joyful mother of *c.*
 127. 3. *c.* are an heritage of the Lord
 137. 7. remember, O Lord, the *c.* of
 Edom
 149. 2. let the *c.* of Zion be joyful in
 their king
Prov. 17. 6. glory of *c.* are their fathers
Prov. 31. 28. *c.* arise, call her blessed
Songs 1. 6. my mother's *c.* were angry
Is. 1. 2. I brought up *c.* and they
 3. 4. give *c.* to their princes
 12. *c.* are their oppressors

8. 18. I and the *c.* whom the Lord
 hath given me, *Heb.* 2. 13.
30. 9. lying *c.* that will not hear
47. 9. come in one day the loss of *c.*
 and widowhood
54. 1. sing, O barren, for more are *c.*
 of the desolate than *c.* of the married wife, *Gal.* 4. 27.
63. 8. *c.* that will not lie, so he
Jer. 3. 14. turn, O backsliding *c.* saith
 the Lord, 22.
 19. how shall I put thee among the *c.* ?
31. 15. Rachel weeping for her *c.*
29. the *c.* teeth are set on edge
Lam. 2. 20. shall the women eat *c.* of a
 span long?
Ezek. 2. 4. they are impudent *c.*
 33. 30. the *c.* still are talking against
 thee by walls
Dan. 1. 4. *c.* in whom was no blemish,
 15. their countenances fairer and fat-
 ter than all *c.*
 12. 1. Michael shall stand for the *c.*
Hos. 2. 4. I will not have mercy on
 her *c.* for they be *c.*
 10. 14. the mother was dashed in
 pieces on her *c.*
Joel 2. 23. be glad then ye *c.* of Zion,
 and rejoice in the Lord
Mal. 4. 6. heart of fathers to *c. Luke*
 1. 17.
Matt. 2. 16. Herod slew all the *c.* in
 Bethlehem
Matt. 3. 9. of stones to raise up *c.*
 5. 45. that ye may be the *c.* of your
 Father in heaven
 8. 12. *c.* of the kingdom cast out
 11. 19. but wisdom is justified of her
 c. Luke 7. 35.
 15. 26. not meet to take the *c.* bread
 19. 29. forsaken wife or *c.* for my sake,
 Mark 10. 29.
Mark 7. 28. the dogs under the table
 eat of the *c.* crumbs
Luke 6. 35. shall be *c.* of Highest
 16. 8. *c.* of this world wiser than *c.*
Luke 20. 34. *c.* of this world many
Acts 3. 25. ye are *c.* of the prophets
Rom. 8. 17. if *c.* then heirs—of God
 9. 7. because the seed of Abraham
 are they all *c.*
 11. for *c.* being not yet born, nor done
 good or evil
1 *Cor.* 7. 14. else were your *c.* unclean
 14. 20. be not *c.* in understanding
2 *Cor.* 12. 14. *c.* ought not to lay up
Gal. 3. 7. of faith, the same are the *c.*
 of Abraham
Eph. 1. 5. having predestinated us to
 adoption of *c.*
 2. 2. the spirit that worketh in *c.* of
Eph. 2. 3. by nature *c.* of wrath
 4. 14. be no more *c.* tossed to
 5. 1. followers of God as dear *c.*
Eph. 5. 6. wrath of God upon *c.* of disobedience, *Col.* 3. 6 ; *Eph.* 2. 2.
 6. 1. *c.* obey your parents, *Col.* 3. 20.
Heb. 2. 14. as the *c.* are partakers of
 flesh and blood
Heb. 12. 5. exhortation speaking as to *c.*
1 *Pet.* 1. 14. as obedient *c.* not
2 *John* 1. the elder to elect lady and

her *c.*

13. the *c.* of thy elect sister greet the
Rev. 2. 23. kill her *c.* with death
CHILDREN'S children, *Gen.* 45. 10.
near, thou and thy *c. c.*
Ps. 103. 17. and his righteousness unto
c. c.
128. 6. shalt see thy *c. c.* and peace
on Israel
Jer. 2. 9. and with your *c. c.* will I plead
Ezek. 37. 25. their *c. c.* for ever
CHILDREN of God, *Matt.* 5. 9. peace-
makers shall be the *c. of God*
Luke 20. 36. *c. of God* being *c.* of resurrection
John 11. 52. should gather together in
one *c. of God*
Rom. 8. 16. witness we are the *c. of God*
21. glorious liberty of *c. of God*
Gal. 3. 26. ye are all *c. of God* by faith
in Christ
1 *John* 3. 10. *c. of God* manifest
CHILDREN, his, *Gen.* 18. 19. Abraham
will command his *c.*
2 *Chr.* 28. 3. burnt *his c.* in fire after the
heathen
33. 6. he caused *his c.* to pass through
the fire
Prov. 14. 26. *his c.* shall have refuge
20. 7. the just man *his c.* are blessed
after him
John 4. 12. *his c.* and cattle drank
thereof
1 *Thess.* 2. 11. we charged you as a father doth *his c.*
1 *Tim.* 3. 4. having *his c.* in subjection
CHILDREN of light, *Luke* 16. 8. *c.* of
this world are wiser than *c. of light*
John 12. 36. believe, be the *c. of light*
Eph. 5. 8. but now are light in Lord,
walk as *c. of light*
1 *Thess.* 5. 5. ye are all *c. of light*
CHILDREN, little, 2 *Kings* 2. 23. came
forth *little c.* and mocked him
Matt. 18. 3. converted, become as *l. c.*
19. 13. brought to him *little c.*
14. suffer *little c.* to come, *Mark* 10.
14 ; *Luke* 18. 16.
Gal. 4. 19. my *little c.* of whom I travail in birth
1 *John* 2. 1. my *little c.* I write to you,
12. 13.
4. 4. are of God, *little c.* overcome
5. 21. *little c.* keep from idols
CHILDREN, my, *Gen.* 31. 43. these *c.*
are *my c.*
Gen. 42. 36. Jacob said, me ye have bereaved of *my c.*
43. 14. if I be bereaved of *my c.*
Ex. 13. 15. first-born of *my c.* I redeem
21. 5. I love my master, wife, and *my
c.* I'll not go
Lam. 1. 16. *my c.* are desolate
Luke 11. 7. *my c.* are with me in bed
2 *Cor.* 6. 13. I speak as to *my c.* be ye
enlarged
3 *John* 4. joy to hear that *my c.* walk
in the truth
CHILDREN of promise, *Rom.* 9. 8. but
the *c. of p.* are counted for the seed
Gal. 4. 28. we, brethren, as Isaac was,
are *c. of p.*

CHILDREN, their, *Deut.* 4. 10. they
may teach *their c.*
31. 13. that *their c.* may learn to fear
the Lord
Neh. 9. 23. *their c.* thou multipliest as
stars of heaven
Ps. 78. 6. declare them to *their c.*
90. 16. thy glory appear to *their c.*
132. 12. *their c.* shall sit on thy throne
for ever
Is. 13. 16. *their c.* shall be dashed to
pieces before
Lam. 4. 10. women have sodden *their c.*
Joel 1. 3. let your *c.* tell *their c.* and
their c. another
Zech. 10. 7. yea, *their c.* shall see it and
be glad
Acts 13 33. God hath fulfilled the same
to us *their c.*
1 *Tim.* 3. 12. the deacons rule *their c.*
and houses well
CHILDREN, thy, *Deut.* 6. 7. thou shalt
teach them diligently to *thy c.*
Ps. 45. 16. instead of thy fathers shall
be *thy c.*
73. 15. should offend against generation of *thy c.*
128. 3. *thy c.* like olive-plants round
about thy table
Is. 49. 25. I will contend, and I will
save *thy c.*
54. 53- and all *thy c.* shall be taught
of the Lord, and great shall be the
peace of *thy c.*
Jer. 31. 17. there is hope that *thy c.*
shall come again
Matt. 23. 37. how often would I have
gathered *thy c.* as a hen gathereth
her chickens! *Luke* 13. 34.
Luke 19 44 they shall lay *thy c.* within
thee
2 *John* 4. that I found of *thy c.* walking
in truth
CHILDREN, your, *Ex.* 12. 26. when
your c. shall say unto you
Num. 14. 33. *your c.* shall wander i n
the wilderness
Deut. 1. 39. *your c.* shall go in thither
and possess
11. 19. these my words, ye shall teach
them *your c.*
Josh. 4. 6. when *your c.* ask their fathers, 21.
Matt. 7. 11. to give good gifts to *your
c.* *Luke* 11. 13.
12. 27. by whom do *your c.* cast them
out?
Luke 23. 28. but weep for yourselves
and *your c.*
Acts 2. 39. for the promise is to you and
your c.
1 *Cor.* 7. 14. else were *your c.* unclean,
but now holy
Eph. 6. 4. provoke not *your c.* to wrath,
Col. 3. 21.
CHILDREN, young, *Mark* 10. 13.
brought *young c.* to him to touch
them
Acts 7. 19. so that they cast out their
young c.
CHOKE, *Matt.* 13. 22. care of this world

and deceitfulness of riches *c.* word,
Mark 4. 19.

CHOKED, Matt. 13. 7. thorns *c.* them,
Mark 4. 7 ; Luke 8. 7.

Mark 5. 13. and were *c.* in the sea
Luke 8. 33.

Luke 8. 14. *c.* with cares and riches

CHOLER, Dan. 8. 7. an he-goat moved
with *c.*

Dan. 11. 11. king shall be moved with *c.*

CHOP, Mic. 3. 3. break their bones, and
c. them in pieces

CHOOSE, (1) To select or make choice
of, Ex. 17. 9 ; Ps. 25. 12. (2) To renew a choice, or to choose again
Is. 14. 1 ; 48. 10. (3) To follow imitate, or practise, Prov. 3. 31.

It is spoken, (1) Of persons, as, (1) Of
Christ, who was chosen and set
apart from eternity by God the Fa
ther for the office of Mediator. Is.
42. 1. (2) Of such whom God from
all eternity elected and separated
from among the children of men,
to deliver them from sin and hell,
and by his Spirit working in them
to unite them by faith to Christ,
the Head of the church, and to
sanctify and save them by him,
Mark 13. 20 ; Eph. 1. 4. (3) Of the
Jews, who were set apart as God's
peculiar people, Deut. 7. 6 ; Ps. 105.
6. (4) Of persons chosen to office,
John 6. 70. (II) Of things, Is. 58.
6. (III) Of places, 2 Chr. 6. 38.

CHOOSE, as an act of God, Num. 16. 7.
the man the Lord doth *c.* shall be
holy

Deut. 7. 7. the Lord did not *c.* you because more

  12. 5. the place which Lord shall *c.*

  11. 14, 18, 26 ; 14. 23, 24, 25 ; 15.
20 ; 16. 2, 6, 7, 15, 16 ; 17. 8, 10 ;
18. 6 ; 26. 2 ; 31. 11 ; Josh. 9. 27.

  17. 15. king, whom the Lord shall *c.*

2 Sam. 16. 18. Lord and his people *c.*

  21. 6. Gibeah, whom Lord did *c.*

1 Kings 14. 21. the city which the Lord
did *c.*

Ps. 25. 12. the way that he shall *c.*

  47. 4. our inheritance for us

Is. 14. 1. Lord will *c.* Israel

  49. 7. Holy One of Israel *c.* thee

  66. 4. I will *c.* their delusions

CHOOSE, verb, Ex. 17. 9. *c.* us out men,
fight

Josh. 24. 15. *c.* whom ye will serve

1 Sam. 17. 8. *c.* you a man for you

2 Sam. 17. 1. let me *c.* 12,000 men

2 Sam. 24. 12. *c.* one of them that I

Job 9. 14. *c.* out my words to reason
with him

Prov. 1. 29. did not *c.* fear of Lord

  3. 31. *c.* none of his ways

Is. 7. 15. *c.* the good and refuse, 16.

  56. 4. *c.* things that please me

  65. 12. *c.* that wherein I delight not

Phil. 1. 22. what I shall *c.* I wot not

CHOOSEST, ING, Ps. 65. 4. man thou
c. and causest

Heb. 11. 25. *c.* rather to suffer

CHOSE, Gen. 13. 11. Lot *c.* plain of

Jordan

Josh. 8. 3. Joshua *c.* 30,000 men

2 Sam. 6. 21. the Lord who *c.* me before thy father

1 Kings 8. 16. I *c.* no city out of tribes
of Israel to build a house for my
name, 2 Chr. 6. 5.

1 Chr. 28. 4. the Lord *c.* me before all
the house of

Job 29. 25. I *c.* out their way

Ps. 78. 68. but *c.* the tribe of Judah,
the mount Zion

  70. he *c.* David also his servant, and
took him

Luke 6. 13. he *c.* twelve apostles

Acts 6. 5. *c.* Stephen full of faith and
Holy Ghost

  13. 17. God of his people Israel *c.* our

  15. 40. Paul *c.* Silas and departed,
being recommended

CHOSEN, Num. 16. 5. him whom he
hath *c.* cause to come

Josh. 24. 22. ye have *c.* you the Lord to
serve him

1 Sam. 8. 18. because of the king ye
have *c.* 12. 13.

  20. 30. I know that thou hast *c.* the
son of Jesse

1 Chr. 16. 13. children of Jacob his *c.*
ones

Job. 36. 21. hast *c.* rather than affliction

Ps. 33. 12. *c.* for his own inheritance

  89. 3. I have made a covenant with
my *c.*

  19. I have exalted one *c.* out of the
people

  105. 6. children of Jacob, his *c.* 43.

  106. 5. that I may see the good of
thy *c.*

Prov. 16. 16. rather to be *c.* than silver

  22. 1. good name rather to be *c.* than

Is. 66. 3. have *c.* their own ways

Jer. 8. 3. death *c.* rather than life

  49. 19. who is *c.* man that, 50. 44.

Matt. 20. 16. many called, few *c.* 22. 14.

Mark 13. 20. elect whom he hath *c.*

Luke 10. 42. Mary has *c.* the good part

John 15. 16. ye have not *c.* me I *c.* you

Acts 1. 24. show whether of these two
thou hast *c.*

Acts 9. 15. he is a *c.* vessel to me

  22. 14. God hath *c.* thee that thou

Rom. 16. 13. salute Rufus *c.* in the Lord

1 Tim. 5. 9. let not a widow be *c.* into
the number

2 Tim. 2. 4. please him who hath *c.* him
to be a soldier

1 Pet. 2. 9. ye are a *c.* generation, a royal

Rev. 17. 14. called and *c.* and faithful

CHOSEN of God, Luke 23. 35. if he be
the Christ, the *c.* of God

Acts 10. 41. witnesses *c.* before of God

1 Pet. 2. 4. a living stone, *c.* of God and
precious

CHOSEN, God hath, Deut. 12. 21. God
hath *c.* to put name there, 16. 11.

Acts 22. 14. the God of our fathers hath
c. thee

1 Cor. 1. 27. God hath *c.* foolish things,
God hath *c.* weak things

  28. things despised God hath *c.* and
things that are

2 *Thess.* 2. 13. *God* from the beginning *hath* c. you

Jam. 2. 5. *hath* not *God* c. the poor of this world

CHOSEN, I have, *Is.* 41. 9 ; 43. 10. & 58. 5 ; *Matt.* 12. 18 ; *Ps.* 119. 30. way of truth—173. thy precepts—*Is.* 44

   1. 2. Israel—Jeshurun whom—48.

   10. c. thee in furnace of affliction—*John* 13. 18. I know whom 15. 16. 19. c, you out of world

1 *Kings* 11. 13. for David's sake and Jerusalem's sake, I have c. 2 *Kings* 21. 7 ; 23. 27 ; 2 *Chr.* 6. 6.

   32. the city which *I have* c. out of all the tribes

Ps. 119. 30. *I have* c. way of truth

Is. 41. 8. Jacob whom *I have* c. the seed of Abraham

   58. 5. is not this the fast that *I have* c.? 6.

Hag. 2. 23. *I have* c. thee, saith Lord

CHOSEN, Lord hath, *Deut.* 7. 6. *Lord hath* c. thee a special people, 14. 2.

1 *Chr.* 28. 5. *Lord hath* c. Solomon to sit to build an house, 10.

Ps. 105. 26. Aaron whom *he had* c.

   132. 13. *Lord hath* c. Zion ; 135. 4. *Lord hath* c. Jacob

Eph. 1. 4. according as *he hath* c. us in him

CHRIST, literally " *the anointed.*" The practice of anointing priests and kings has been common in all ages of the world. Our Saviour was emphatically " the Anointed One," and as such, in his two natures, human and divine, perfected a priestly work, which saves to the uttermost all that come unto God by him ; *Heb.* 7. 25. He never was externally anointed, or otherwise introduced into the outward priesthood. At the last day he will judge the world ; *Acts* 17. 31 ; 2 *Tim.* 4. 1.

Christ is taken for the mystical body of Christ, both himself the Head, and the church as his members, which make but one body, 1 *Cor.* 12. 12, likewise for the doctrine of Christ, or the rule of life prescribed by him, *Eph.* 4. 20. And for the Spirit, and spiritual gifts and grace of Christ, *Rom.* 8. 10.

CHRIST should be born, *Matt.* 2. 4.

Matt. 16. 16. thou art C. son of living

   23. 8. one your master, even C. 10.

   24. 5. come, saying, I am C. and shall deceive many, *Matt.* 13. 6 ; *Luke* 21. 8.

   26. 68. prophesy to us, thou C.

Mark 9. 41. because ye belong to C.

Luke 2. 26. should not die before he had seen C.

   23. 35. save himself if he be C.

Luke 24. 26. ought not C. to have suffered

   46. it behoved C. to suffer

John 4. 25. Messias called C.

   7. 26. this is the very C.

   27. when C. cometh no man knoweth, 28.

   9. 22. that if any man did confess he was C.

Acts 2. 30. he would raise up C. to sit

   36. God hath made that Jesus both Lord and C.

   8. 5. preached C. to them

   9. 20. and straightway he preached C. in synagogue

Rom. 5. 6. C. died for the ungodly

   8. yet sinners, C. died for us

   8. 9. have not the spirit of C.

   10. if C. be in you the body is dead

   9. 3. I could wish myself were accursed from C.

   9. 5. of whom C. came, who is over

   10. 4. the end of the law for righteousness

   10. 6. that is, to bring C. down from above

   7. that is, to bring up C. again from the dead

   15. 3. C. pleased not himself

1 *Cor.* 1. 23. preach C. crucified

   24. C. the power of God and

   3. 23. ye are C. and C. is God's

   5. 7. C. our passover is sacrificed

   10. 4. and that rock was C.

   15. 12. if C. be preached that he rose from the dead

   17. and if C. be not raised, your faith is vain

   23. every man in his own order, C. the first-fruits

2 *Cor.* 6. 15. what concord hath C. with Belial

   11. 2. as a chaste virgin to C.

Gal. 2. 20. C. liveth in me and life I live

   2. 21. if righteousness come by law, then C. died in vain

   3. 13. C. hath redeemed us from curse

   4. 19. till C. be formed in you

   5. 24. that are C. have crucified

Eph. 2. 12. ye were without C.

   3. 17. that C. may dwell in your hearts

   4. 20. ye have not so learned C.

   5. 2. as C. also loved us, and hath given himself for

   5. 14. C. shall give thee light

   23. as C. loved the church

   6. 5. in singleness as unto C.

Phil. 1. 15. some indeed preach C. of envy and strife

   16. preach C. of contention

   23. desire to depart and be with C.

   3. 8. that I may win C.

   4. 13. can do all things through C.

Col. 1. 27. C. in you the hope of glory

   3. 1. where C. sitteth on the right hand of God

   3. 4. when C. who is our life

   11. C. is all and in all

1 *Pet.* 2. 21. because C. also suffered for us, an example

   3. 18. C. hath once suffered for sins, just for unjust

Rev. 11. 15. the kingdoms of our Lord and his C.

CHRIST, for, 1 *Cor.* 1. 17. *for* C. sent

2 *Cor.* 5. 20. now we are ambassadors

for C. we pray

Eph. 4. 32. as God for C. sake hath forgiven you

CHRIST with Jesus, *John* 1. 17. but grace and truth came by Jesus C.

John 17. 3. know thee, and Iesus C. whom thou sent

Acts 8. 12. when they believed Philip preaching things concerning name of Jesus C. they were baptized

10. 36. preaching peace by Jesus C.

Rom. 3. 24. justified through the redemption in Jesus C.

8. 1. no condemnation to them that are in C. Jesus

2. law of the spirit of life in C. Jesus

1 *Cor.* 1. 30. of him are ye in C. Jesus

2. 2. save Jesus C. and him crucified

4. 15. for in C. Jesus have I begotten you through gospel

2 *Cor.* 4. 6. the knowledge of God in face of Jesus C.

13. 5. know ye not, how that Jesus C. is in you

Gal. 2. 16. a man is justified by the faith of Jesus C.

3. 28. ye are all one in C. Jesus 26.

5. 6. in C. Jesus neither circumcision avails

Eph. 1. 1. saints and faithful in C. Jesus

2. 6. heavenly places in C. Jesus

2. 10. created in C. Jesus unto, 1. 1.

Phil. 1. 8. I long after you in the bowels of Jesus C.

2. 5. mind which was in C. Jesus

Phil. 2. 11. confess that Jesus C. is Lord

3. 3. rejoice in C. Jesus and have no

3. 8. I count all loss for the excellency of C. Jesus

12. for which apprehended of C. Jesus

4. 19. riches in glory by C. Jesus

Col. 2. 6. received C. Jesus the Lord, 3. 24.

1 *Tim.* 1. 15. that Jesus C. came into

2. 5. one mediator the man C. Jesus

2 *Tim.* 2. 3. good soldier of Jesus C.

3. 12. will live godly in C. Jesus

Heb. 13. 8. Jesus C. the same yesterday

1 *John* 1. 7. blood of Jesus C. cleanseth

CHRIST, Lord Jesus, *Acts* 16. 31. believe on the Lord Jesus C. thou shalt be saved

Acts 20. 21. testifying faith toward our Lord Jesus C.

Rom. 5. 1. we have peace with God through Lord Jesus C.

1 *Cor.* 15. 57. victory through our Lord Jesus C.

2 *Cor.* 8. 9. know the grace of our Lord Jesus C.

1 *Thess.* 5. 23. be preserved unto coming of our Lord Jesus C.

1 *Tim.* 5. 21. I charge thee before Lord Jesus C. 2 Tim. 4. 1.

2 *Tim.* 4. 22. the Lord Jesus C. be with thy spirit, amen

2 *Pet.* 1. 11. an entrance into kingdom of Lord Jesus C.

3. 18. grow in grace and in knowledge of Lord Jesus C.

CHRIST, in, *Rom.* 9. 1. I say the truth in C.

Rom. 16. 10. Apelles approved in C. salute Aristo

Rom. 12. 5. one body in C.

16. 7. were in C. before me

1 *Cor.* 3. 1. I speak as unto babes in C.

4. 10. but ye are wise in C.

1 *Cor.* 15. 18. fallen asleep in C.

19. in this life only have hope in C.

2 *Cor.* 5. 17. if any man be in C.

19. God was in C. reconciling the

12. 2. I knew a man in C.

Gal. 1. 22. churches which were in C.

Eph. 1. 3. spiritual blessings in C.

20. wrought in C. when raised

Phil. 1. 13. my bonds in C. are manifest

2. 1. if any consolation in C.

Col. 1. 2. faithful brethren in C.

1 *Thess.* 4. 16. dead in C. shall rise first

1 *Tim.* 2. 7. I speak truth in C.

CHRIST, is, *Luke* 23. 2. saying, that he himself is C. a king

Rom. 8. 34. it is C. that died, yea

Phil. 1. 21. to me to live is C.

CHRIST, that, *John* 1. 25. that C. 7. 41.

John 12. 34. that C. abideth for ever

Matt. 16. 20. the C. 26. 63 ; *Mark* 8. 29. & 14. 61 ; *Luke* 3. 15. & 9. 20. & 22. 67 ; *John* 1. 20, 41. & 3. 28. & 4. 29. 42. & 7. 41. & 10. 24. & 11. 27. & 20 31 ; 1 *John* 2. 22. & 5. 1.

CHRIST, with, *Rom.* 6. 8. if we be dead with C.

8. 17. heirs of God joint-heirs with C.

Gal. 2. 20. I am crucified with C.

Eph. 2. 5. quickened us together with C.

Phil. 1. 23. desiring to be with C.

Col. 2. 20. if ye be dead with C.

3. 1. if ye be risen with C. set affec.

3. dead, and life is hid with C. in God

Rev. 20. 4. reigned with C. 1,000 years

CHRISTIAN, S, *Acts* 11. 26. first called C. at Antioch

26. 28. almost persuadest me to be C.

1 *Pet.* 4. 16. suffer as a C. let him

CHURCH, (1) A religious assembly selected and called out of the world by the doctrine of the gospel, to worship the true God in Christ, according to his word, 1 *Cor.* 1. 2 ; *Rev.* 2. 7. (2) All the elect of God, of what nation soever, from the beginning to the end of the world, who make but one body, whereof Jesus Christ is the Head, *Col.* 1. 18. (3) The faithful of some one family, together with such Christians as were wont to assemble with them for solemn worship, *Rom.* 16. 5 ; *Col.* 4. 15 ; *Philem.* 2. (4) The faithful of some one province, 2 *Thess.* 1. 1. (5) The governors, or representatives of the church, *Matt.* 18. 17. Tell it to the church ; that is, to such rulers, to whom the censures of the church do of right belong, that by them it may be communicated to the whole society. (6) A multitude of people assembled together, whether good or bad, *Acts* 19. 37. (7) The congregation of the Jews, which was formerly the church and the people of God, *Acts*

8. 38.

CHURCH, *Acts* 14. 27. & 15. 3 ; 1 *Cor.* 4. 17. & 14. 4, 23 ; 3 *John* 9.
Matt. 16. 18. on rock will I build my *c.*
18. 17. tell it to *c.* hear the *c.*
Acts 2. 47. Lord added to the *c.* daily
5. 11. fear came on all the *c.*
8. 1. great persecution against the *c.*
11. 26. assembled themselves with *c.*
14. 23. ordained elders in every *c.*
15. 22. pleased elders and whole *c.*
1 *Cor.* 14. 4, 5. that *c.* may receive edification
16.19. *c.* in house, *Col.* 4.15; *Philem.* 2.
Eph. 1. 22. head over all things to *c.*
3. 10. known by *c.* manifest wisdom of God
5. 24. as *c.* is subject to Christ
25. as Christ loved the *c.* and gave
27. present to himself a glorious *c.*
29. cherisheth it as the L. *c.*
Phil. 3. 6. zeal persecuting the *c.*
4. 15. no *c.* communicated with me
Col. 1. 18. head of his body the *c.*
24. for body's sake which is the *c.*
1 *Tim.* 5. 16. let not the *c.* be charged
Heb. 12. 23. general assembly *c.* of first-born
3 *John* 6. testified of charity before *c.*
CHURCH, in the, *Acts* 7. 38. *in the c.*
13. 1 ; 1 *Cor.* 6. 4. & 11. 18. & 12. 28. & 14. 19 ; 28. 35 ; *Eph.* 3. 21 ; *Col.* 4. 16.
Acts 20. 28. the *c.* of God, 1 *Cor.* 1. 2. & 10. 32. & 15. 9 ; 2 *Cor.* 1. 1 ; *Gal.* 1. 13 ; 1 *Tim.* 3. 5.
CHURCHES, *Acts* 9. 31. then had the *c.* rest
15. 41. confirming the *c.*
16. 5. so were the *c.* established in faith
Acts 19. 37. neither robbers of *c.*
Rom. 16. 16. *c.* of Christ salute you
1 *Cor.* 7. 17. ordain I in all *c.*
11. 16. no such custom nor *c.* of God
14. 33. as in all *c.* of saints
34. women keep silence in the *c.*
2 *Cor.* 8. 19. chosen of the *c.* to travel
23. the messengers of the *c.*
11. 8. I robbed other *c.*
23. cometh upon me daily, the care of all the *c.*
1 *Thess.* 2. 14. followers of the *c.*
2 *Thess.* 1. 4. glory in you in the *c.*
Rev. 1. 4. seven *c.* in Asia, 11.
20. angels of the seven *c.* and the seven candlesticks, are the seven *c.*
2. 7. hear what the Spirit saith to the *c.* 11. 17, 29. & 3. 6, 13, 22.
2. 23. that the *c.* may know
22. 16. testify these things in *c.*
CHURL, *Is.* 32. 5. nor shall the *c.* be said to be bountiful
CHURLISH, 1 *Sam.* 25. 3. man Nabal was *c.*
CIELED, 2 *Chr.* 3. 5. he *c.* house with fir-tree
Jer. 22. 14. it is *c.* with cedar
Hag. 1. 4. is it time for you to dwell in your *c.* houses
CIELING, 1 *Kings* 6. 15. built walls of

house with *c.*
CINNAMON, *Ex.* 30. 23. take of sweet *c.* half
Prov. 7. 17. perfumed my bed with *c.*
Songs 4. 14. thy plants are an orchard of calamus and *c.*
Rev. 18. 13. no man buyeth her merchandise of *c.*
CIRCLE, *Prov.* 8. 27. when he set a *c.* on face of the depth
Is. 40. 22. it is he that sitteth on the *c.* of the earth
CIRCUIT, S, *Job* 22. 14. walked in the *c.* of heaven
Ps. 19. 6. *c.* his *c.* from the ends
Eccl. 1. 6. wind returneth again according to his *c.*
CIRCUMCISE the flesh, *Gen.* 17. 11.
Deut. 10. 16. *c.* the foreskin of your heart
30. 6. Lord will *c.* your heart
Josh. 5. 2. *c.* again Israel ; 4. Joshua did *c.*
Jer. 4. 4. *c.* yourselves to the Lord
Gen. 17. 10. every male shall be *c.* 14. 23. 26 ; *Phil.* 3. 5.
~21. 4. Abraham *c.* Isaac
Josh. 5. 3. *c.* the children of Israel
Jer. 9. 25. punish *c.* with uncircumcision
Acts 15. 1. except ye be *c.* after manner
24. ye must be *c.* and keep the law
16. 3. *c.* him because of the Jews
Gal. 2. 3. neither compelled to be *c.*
5. 2. if ye be *c.* Christ profit nothing
Col. 2. 11. in whom ye are *c.*
John 7. 22. Moses gave *c.*
Acts 7. 8. God gave him covenant of *c.*
Rom. 2. 25. *c.* profits if thou know the law
29. *c.* is that of the heart, in spirit
3. 1. what profit is there of *c.*
30. justify the *c.* by faith and uncircumcision
4. 9. cometh this blessedness on *c.*
11. he received sign of *c.* a seal of
1 *Cor.* 7. 19. *c.* is nothing but the keeping
Gal. 2. 7. gospel of the *c.* was committed
5. 6. neither *c.* nor uncircumcision availeth, 6. 15 ; *Col.* 3. 11.
Phil. 3. 3. we are *c.* who worship God
Col. 2. 11. *c.* with *c.* without hands
Tit. 1. 10. especially they of *c.*
CIRCUMSPECT : to be circumspect is to be wary and watchful in our conduct, *Ex.* 23. 13. A man may ruin himself through carelessness, but he cannot save himself without great care and circumspection, *Eph.* 5. 15. "See then that ye walk circumspectly, not as fools, but as wise." Some read thus :—
See then that ye, upon whom Christ now shines, walk accurately according to his precepts : not as unwise men, provoking your heathen neighbours by imprudent rebukes. See verse 16.
CISTERN, (1) A vessel of lead to hold water for household uses, 2 *Kings* 18. 31. (2) Any thing that persons

put their trust in besides God, whether in idols, powerful neighbours, allies, friends, traditions, merits, &c., which are but broken cisterns, *Jer.* 2. 13. (3) The left ventricle of the heart, *Eccl.* 12. 6.

CISTERNS, 2 *Chr.* 26. 10. Uzziah cut out many c.

Prov. 5. 15. out of thy own c.

Eccl. 12. 6. wheel broken at the c.

Is. 36. 16. waters of his own c.

Neh. 9. 25. houses full of c.

Jer. 2. 13. hewed out broken c.

CITY, Cain built, *Gen.* 4. 17.

11. 4. build us a c. and a tower

8. 26. find fifty righteous within the c.

28. destroy all c. lack of five

Josh. 6. 3. compass c. and go

2 *Sam.* 12. 1. two men in c. one rich

15. 2. of what c. art thou?

Ps. 107. 4. found no c. to dwell in

7. might go to a c. of habitation

122. 3. as a c. that is compactly built

127. 1. except the Lord keep the c.

Prov. 16. 32. ruleth his spirit, than he that taketh a c.

Eccl. 9. 14. there was a little c. and few men in it

Songs 3. 4. I will go about the c. in streets

Is. 1. 21. faithful c. become harlot

22. 2. tumultuous c. joyous c.

23. 7. your joyous c. crowning c. 8.

26. 1. we have a strong c. salvation

33. 20. the c. of our solemnities

62. 12. sought out c. not forsaken

Jer. 3. 14. one of a c. two of family

29. 7. seek the peace of the c.

Lam. 1. 1. how doth c. sit solitary

2. 15. is this c. that men call perfection of beauty?

Ezek. 9. 4. go through the midst of c. Jerusalem set a mark

Amos 3. 6. be evil in a c. and Lord not

Zeph. 2. 15. the rejoicing c. that dwelt

3. 1. filthy, the oppressing c.

Zech. 8. 3. c. of truth and mountain

Matt. 5. 14. c. on hill cannot be hid

8. 34. whole c. came out to meet Jesus

10. 15. than for that c. *Mark* 6. 11 ; *Luke* 10. 12.

21. 10. all the c. was moved, saying, who is this ?

23. 34. and persecute them from c. to c.

Mark 5. 14. they that fed swine, told it in c. *Luke* 8. 34.

Luke 2. 3. taxed to his own c.

Luke 10. 8. into what c. ye enter

12. tolerable for Sodom than for that c.

19. 41. he beheld the c. and wept over it

Acts 8. 8. great joy in that c.

21. 30. all the c. was moved

Heb. 11. 10. he looked for a c. which

16. he hath prepared for them a c.

12. 22. to the c. of the living God

13. 14. have here no continuing c.

Rev. 3. 12. write name of c. of my God

20. 9. camp of saints beloved c.

21. 18. the c. was pure gold

23. the c. had no need of the sun nor moon

CITY of David, 2 *Sam.* 5. 9. called it the c. of David, 1 *Chr.* 11. 7.

2 *Sam.* 6. 10. the ark into c. of David

12. brought up the ark into the c. of David, 16.

1 *Kings* 2. 10. David was buried in the c. of David

3. 1. Solomon brought her into the c. of David

8. 1. bring the ark out of the c. of David, 2 *Chr.* 5. 2.

11. 43. Solomon buried in c. of David 2 *Chr.* 9. 31.

14. 31. Rehoboam buried in c. of David, 2 *Chr.* 12. 16.

22. 50. Jehoshaphat buried in c. of David, 2 *Chr.* 21. 1.

2 *Kings* 8. 24 ; 9. 28 ; 12. 21 ; 14. 20 ; 15. 38 ; 16. 20.

Is. 22. 9. seen the breaches of the c. of David

29. 1. woe to Ariel, the c. where David

Luke 2. 4. Joseph also went into the c. of David

11. to you is born in the c. of David a Saviour

CITY, elders with, *Deut.* 19. 12. the *elders* of his c. shall fetch him

Deut. 21. 20. say to the *elders* of his c. our sons are stubborn

22. 17. spread the cloth before the *elders* of the c.

25. 8. then the *elders* of his c. shall call him

Judg. 8. 16. Gideon took the *elders* of the c.

CITY every, *Matt.* 12. 25. and *every* c. divided

Acts 15. 21. hath in *every* c. them that preach him

36. let us go and visit our brethren in *every* c.

20. 23. the Holy Ghost witnesseth in *every* c. that

CITY, fenced, 2 *Kings* 10. 2. with you a *fenced* c.

2 *Kings* 17. 9. from the tower to the *fenced* c.

CITY of God, *Ps.* 46. 4. streams made glad the c. of God

Heb. 12. 22. ye are come to the c. of the living God

Rev. 3. 12. write on him the name of c. of my God

CITY, great, *Rev.* 14. 8. Babylon fallen, that *great* c. 18. 10, 16, 19, 21.

Rev. 21. 10. that *great* c. holy Jerusalem

CITY, holy, *Is.* 52. 1. put on thy beautiful garments, O *holy* c.

Dan. 9. 24. seventy weeks are determined on thy *holy* c.

Matt. 4. 5. the devil taketh him up into the *holy* c.

Rev. 11. 2. the *holy* c. shall they tread under foot

21. 2. I John saw the *holy* c. coming

CITY, in, or into the, 1 *Kings* 13. 25. and told it in the c.

1 *Kings* 14. 11. Jeroboam *in the* c. dogs

21. 24. that dieth of Ahab, *in the c.*
dogs eat

2 *Kings* 20. 20. how Hezekiah brought
water *into the c.*

Ps. 31. 21. the Lord, for he hath showed
me his marvellous kindness *in* a
strong *c.*

55. 9. violence and strife *in the c.*

Amos 3. 6. a trumpet be blown *in the c.*
shall there be evil *in* a *c.* and Lord
not done it ?

Matt. 9. 1. he passed over and came
into his own *c.*

10. 5. *into* any *c.* of the Samaritans
enter not

10. 11. and *into* whatsoever *c.* enter

Mark 14. 13. he saith, go *into the c.*
Acts 9. 6.

Luke 2. 3. taxed, every one *into* his *c.*

7. 37. a woman *in the c.* which was a
sinner

18. 2. there was *in* a *c.* a judge. who
feared not God

2 *Cor.* 11. 26. perils *in the c.* in the sea

Rev. 22. 14. enter through gates *into*
the c.

CITY of the Lord, *Is.* 60. 14. they shall
call thee the *c. of the Lord*

CITY, this, *Jer.* 19. 8. I will make *this*
c. desolate, and an hissing

Jer. 19. 11. break this people and *this c.*

26. 6. I will make *this c.* a curse

38. 17. *this c.* shall not be burnt

Ezek. 11. 3. *this c.* is the caldron, and
we be the flesh, 7.

11. *this c.* shall not be your caldron,
nor ye the flesh

Matt. 23. when they persecute you
in *this c.* flee

Acts 18. 10. for I have much people in
this c.

22. 3. I was brought up in *this c.* at
feet of Gamaliel

Heb. 11. 10. he looked for a *c.* which

16. he hath prepared for them a *c.*

12. 22. to the *c.* of the living God

13. 14. have here no continuing *c.*

Rev. 3. 12. write name of *c.* of my God

20. 9. camp of saints beloved *c.*

21. 18. the *c.* was pure gold

23. the *c.* had no need of the sun nor
moon

CITY of David, 2 *Sam.* 5. 9. called it
the *c. of David,* 1 *Chr.* 11. 7.

2 *Sam.* 6. 10. the ark into *c. of David*

12. brought up the ark into the *c. of*
David, 16.

1 *Kings* 2. 10. David was buried in the
c. of David

3. 1. Solomon brought her into the *c.*
of David

8. 1. bring the ark out of the *c. of*
David, 2 *Chr.* 5. 2.

11. 43. Solomon buried in *c. of David*
2 *Chr.* 9. 31.

14. 31. Rehoboam buried in *c. of*
David, 2 *Chr.* 12. 16.

22. 50. Jehoshaphat buried in *c. of*
David, 2 *Chr.* 21. 1.

2 *Kings* 8. 24 ; 9. 28 ; 12. 21 ; 14. 20 ;
15. 38 ; 16. 20.

Is. 22. 9. seen the breaches of the *c. of*
David

29. 1. woe to Ariel, the *c.* where *David*

Luke 2. 4. Joseph also went into the *c.*
of David

11. to you is born in the *c. of David*
a Saviour

CITY, elders with, *Deut.* 19. 12. the
elders of his *c.* shall fetch him

Deut. 21. 20. say to the *elders* of his *c.*
our sons are stubborn

22. 17. spread the cloth before the
elders of the *c.*

25. 8. then the *elders* of his *c.* shall
call him

Judg. 8. 16. Gideon took the *elders* of
the *c.*

CITY every, *Matt.* 12. 25. and *every c.*
divided

Acts 15. 21. hath in *every c.* them that
preach him

36. let us go and visit our brethren
in *every c.*

20. 23. the Holy Ghost witnesseth in
every c. that

CITY, fenced, 2 *Kings* 10. 2. with you a
fenced c.

2 *Kings* 17. 9. from the tower to the
fenced c.

CITY of God, *Ps.* 46. 4. streams made
glad the *c. of God*

Heb. 12. 22. ye are come to the *c. of*
the living *God*

Rev. 3. 12. write on him the name of *c.*
of my God

CITY, great, *Rev.* 14. 8. Babylon fallen,
that *great c.* 18. 10, 16, 19, 21.

Rev. 21. 10. that *great c.* holy Jerusalem

CITY, holy, *Is.* 52. 1. put on thy beautiful garments, O *holy c.*

Dan. 9. 24. seventy weeks are determined on thy *holy c.*

Matt. 4. 5. the devil taketh him up into
the *holy c.*

Rev. 11. 2. the *holy c.* shall they tread
under foot

21. 2. I John saw the *holy c.* coming

CITY, in, or into the, 1 *Kings* 13. 25.
and told it *in the c.*

1 *Kings* 14. 11. Jeroboam *in the c.* dogs

21. 24. that dieth of Ahab, *in the c.*
dogs eat

2 *Kings* 20. 20. how Hezekiah brought
water *into the c.*

Ps. 31. 21. the Lord, for he hath showed
me his marvellous kindness *in* a
strong *c.*

55. 9. violence and strife *in the c.*

Amos 3. 6. a trumpet be blown *in the c.*
shall there be evil *in* a *c.* and Lord
not done it ?

Matt. 9. 1. he passed over and came
into his own *c.*

10. 5. *into* any *c.* of the Samaritans
enter not

10. 11. and *into* whatsoever *c.* enter

Mark 14. 13. he saith, go *into the c.*
Acts 9. 6.

Luke 2. 3. taxed, every one *into* his *c.*

7. 37. a woman *in the c.* which was a

sinner
18. 2. there was in a c. a judge. who feared not God

2 Cor. 11. 26. perils in the c. in the sea

Rev. 22. 14. enter through gates into the c.

CITY of the Lord, Is. 60. 14. they shall call thee the c. of the Lord

CITY, this, Jer. 19. 8. I will make this c. desolate, and an hissing

Jer. 19. 11. break this people and this c.

26. 6. I will make this c. a curse

38. 17. this c. shall not be burnt

Ezek. 11. 3. this c. is the caldron, and we be the flesh, 7.

11. this c. shall not be your caldron, nor ye the flesh

Matt. 10. 23. when they persecute you in this c. flee

Acts 18. 10. for I have much people in this c.

22. 3. I was brought up in this c. at feet of Gamaliel

23. 25. for ye make c. the outside, Luke 11. 39.

John 13. 11. ye are not all c.

15. 3. now ye are c. through word

CLEAN hands, Job 9. 30. make my hands ever so c.

Ps. 24. 4. he that hath c. hands and a pure heart

CLEAN heart, Ps. 51. 10. create in me a c. heart

73. 1. God is good to Israel, and such as are of a c. heart

Prov. 20. 9. who can say, I have made my heart c.

CLEANSE, Ps. 19. 12. c. thou me from secret faults

51. 2. c. me from my sin

119. 9. shall a young man c. his way?

Ezek. 36. 25. from all your idols will I c. you

Matt. 10. 8. heal the sick, c. the lepers,

23. 26. c. first that which is within the cup

2 Cor. 7. 1. let us c. ourselves from all filthiness of flesh

Eph. 5. 26. might c. it with the washing of water

Jam. 4. 8. c. your hands, ye sinners,

1 John 1. 9. to c. us from all unrighteousness

CLEANSED, Ps. 73. 13. verily I have c. my heart in vain

Dan. 8. 14. then shall sanctuary be c.

Matt. 8. 3. immediately leprosy was c.

11. 5. the lepers are c. the deaf hear, Luke 7. 22.

Luke 4. 27. none was c. save Naaman the Syrian

17. 17. were not ten c. but where are the 9

CLEANSETH, 1 John 1. 7. blood of Jesus Christ c. us from all sin

CLEAR the guilty, Ex. 34. 7.

Ps. 51. 4. c. when thou judgest

Songs 6. 10. looks forth c. as the sun

Zech. 14. 6. light shall not be c. nor

2 Cor. 7. 11. ye have approved yourselves to be c.

Rev. 21. 11. her light was c. as crystal 22. 1.

18. the city was pure gold, like to c. glass

CLEARING, 2 Cor. 7. 11. what c. of yourselves it wrought

CLEARLY, Matt. 7. 5. see c. to pull out the mote, Luke 6. 42.

Mark 8. 25. was restored, and saw every man c.

Rom. 1. 20. things from creation are c.

CLEARNESS, Ex. 24. 10. and as the body of heaven in his c.

CLEAVE, verb, Gen. 2. 24. c. to his wife, Matt. 19. 5 ; Mark 10. 7 ; Eph. 5. 31.

Deut. 4. 4. ye did c. to the Lord, 10. 20. & 11. 22. & 13. 4. & 30. 20 : Josh. 22. 5. & 23. 8.

Ps. 44. 25. belly c. to the earth

102. 5. my bones c. to my skin

119. 25. soul c. to the dust

137. 6. tongue c. to roof of mouth—jaws, 22. 15 ;

Ezek. 3. 26. I will make thy tongue c. to the roof

Acts 11. 23. purpose of heart would c. to Lord

Rom. 12. 9. c. to that which is good

CLEAVETH, Ps. 22. 15. strength dried up, my tongue c. to jaws

Ps. 119. 25. my soul c. to the dust, quicken me

Luke 10. 11. the dust of your city which c. on us

CLEFT, Mic. 1. 4. the valley shall be c. as wax before the fire

Deut. 14. 6. that cleaveth the c. into two claws

CLEFTS, Songs 2. 14. O my dove, thou art in c. of the rocks

Jer. 49. 16. O thou that dwellest in the c. Obad. 3.

CLERK, Acts 19. 35. when town c. had appeased the people

CLIFT, Ex. 33. 22. I will put thee in a c. of the rock

CLIMB, Jer. 4. 29 ; Joel 2. 7, 9.

Amos 9. 2. though c. up to heaven

John 10. 1. c. some other way is a thief

CLIMBED, Luke 19. 4. Zaccheus up into a sycamore tree

CLIPT, Jer. 48. 37. every head be bald, every beard be c.

CLOAK, Matt. 5. 40 ; Luke 6. 29.

Is. 59. 17. clad with zeal as a c.

John 15. 22. have no c. for their sin

1 Thess. 2. 5. nor used c. of covetous-

1 Pet. 2. 16. liberty for c. of malicious-

CLODS, Job 7. 5. flesh clothed with c. of dust

21. 33. c. of valley be sweet to him

Hos. 10. 11. Judah shall plow, Jacob shall break his c.

CLOSE, Jer. 42. 16. famine follow c. after

Luke 9. 36. they kept it c. and told no

Acts 27. 13. they sailed c. by Crete

CLOSED, Gen. 2. 21. Lord c. up the flesh

20. 18. the Lord had fast c. up all the

wombs

Is. 1. 6. they have not been *c.*

CLOSET, a place of devotion in every Jewish house ; generally a small room built above the porch or entrance ; *Joel* 2. 16 ; *Matt.* 6. 6 ; *Luke* 12. 3.

CLOTH, *Deut.* 22. 17. shall spread the *c.* before the elders

Matt. 9. 16. putteth a piece of new *c. Mark* 2. 21.

27. 59. body, he wrapt it in a linen *c.*

Mark 14. 51. having a linen *c.* about his body

CLOTHE, *Matt.* 6. 30 ; *Luke* 12. 28 ; *Job* 10. 11. *c.* me with skin

Esth. 4. 4. she sent raiment to *c.* Mordecai

Prov. 23. 21. drowsiness shall *c.* a man with rags

Ezek. 26. 16. shall *c.* themselves with trembling

CLOTHED, *Ps.* 35. 26. be *c.* with shame, 132. 18.

104. 1. *c.* with honour and majesty

109. 18. he *c.* himself with cursing

132. 9. let priests be *c.* with righteousness.

16. *c.* with salvation

Is. 61. 10. *c.* me with garments of salvation

Ezek. 16. 10. I *c.* thee with broidered

Zeph. 1. 8. *c.* with strange apparel

Matt. 11. 8. *c.* in soft raiment ; *Luke* 7. 25.

25. 36. naked and ye *c.* me, 43. *c.* not

2 *Cor.* 5. 2. to be *c.* upon with our house

3. if so be that being *c.* we shall not

4. unclothed, but *c.* upon

1 *Pet.* 5. 5. be *c.* with humility

Rev. 3. 18. raiment that mayest be *c.*

11. 3. prophesy *c.* in sackcloth

12. 1. woman *c.* with the sun

15. 6. *c.* in fine linen clean and white

19. 13. *c.* in a vesture dipped in blood

CLOTHED, shall be, *Matt.* 6. 31. or wherewith *shall* we be *c.*

Rev. 3. 5. he that overcometh *shall be c.* 4. 4.

CLOTHES, *Gen.* 49. 11. he washed his *c.* in the blood of grapes

Neh. 4. 23. I nor brethren, none of us put off our *c.*

Luke 2. 7. and wrapped him in swaddling *c.* 12.

19. 36. as he went they spread their *c.* in the way

John 19. 40. took body of Jesus, and wound it in linen *c.*

Acts 7. 58. witnesses laid down their *c.* at Saul's feet

22. 23. as they cried out and cast off their *c.*

CLOTHING, *Job* 22. 6. & 24. 7 ; *Mark* 12. 38 ; *Acts* 10. 30 ; *James* 2. 3.

Ps. 45. 13. her *c.* is wrought of gold

Prov. 31. 25. strength and honour her *c.*

Is. 59. 17. garments of vengeance for *c.*

Matt. 7. 15. come in sheep's *c.*

11. 8. that wear soft *c.* are in

Acts 10. 30. a man stood before me in bright *c.*

Jam. 2. 3. respect to him that weareth the gay *c.*

CLOUD, *Gen.* 9. 13 ; *Is.* 18. 4.

Is. 44. 22. blots out as a *c.* thy transgressions

1 *Cor.* 10. 1. our fathers under the *c.* 2 baptized unto Moses in the *c.*

Heb. 12. 1. so great a *c.* of witnesses

Judg. 5. 4. *c.* dropped with water

2 *Sam.* 23. 4. as a morning without *c.*

Ps. 36. 5. faithfulness reacheth to *c.*

57. 10. truth to the *c.* 108. 4.

104. 3. who maketh the *c.* his chariot

Eccl. 11. 4. regardeth *c.* shall not reap

Matt. 24. 30. coming in *c.* of heaven, 26. 64. *Mark* 13. 26, & 14. 62.

1 *Thess.* 4. 17. *c.* carried with tempest

Jude 12. *c.* without water, carried

Rev. 1. 7. he cometh with *c.* and

CLOVEN, *Lev.* 11. 7. though the swine be *c.* footed he is unclean

COAL, 2 *Sam.* 14. 7 ; *Is.* 47. 14. & 6. 6 ; *Lam.* 4. 8 ; *Ps.* 18. 8, 12. & 120. 4. & 140. 10.

COALS, *Lev.* 16. 12. censer of burning *c.*

1 *Kings* 19. 6. cake baken on the *c.*

Prov. 6. 28. can one go on hot *c.*

25. 22. heap *c.* of fire on head ; *Rom.* 12. 20.

26. 21. as *c.* to burn *c.* so contentious

Songs 8. 6. *c.* thereof are *c.* of fire

Is. 44. 12. the smith with tongs worketh in the *c.*

54. 16. I created the smith that bloweth the *c.*

Ezek. 1. 13. their appearance was like burning *c.*

John 18. 18. servants made a fire of *c.*

21. 9. they saw a fire of *c.* and fish laid thereon

COAST, *Ex.* 10. 4. bring the locusts into thy *c.*

Deut. 19. 8. Lord thy God enlarge thy *c.*

1 *Sam.* 6. 9. if it go up by the way of his own *c.*

27. 1. to seek me any more in any *c.*

2 *Kings* 14. 25. Jeroboam restored the *c.* of Israel

Zeph. 2. 7. the *c.* shall be for the remnant of Judah

COAST, sea, *Ezek.* 25. 16. I will destroy the remnant of the *sea c.*

Zeph. 2. 5. woe to the inhabitants of the *sea c.*

6. the *sea c.* shall be dwellings for the shepherds

Matt. 4. 13. Jesus dwelt in Capernaum upon the *sea c.*

Luke 6. 17. multitude from *sea c.* came to hear

COASTS, *Ex.* 10. 14. the locusts rested in all the *c.* of Egypt

Deut. 19. 3. thou shalt divide the *c.* of thy land

Josh. 18. 5. Joseph shall abide in their *c.* on north

2 *Chr.* 11. 13. resorted to him out of all their *c.*

Ps. 105. 31. there came lice in all their *c.* 33. he smote their vines, and broke trees of their *c.*

Joel 3. 4. with me, all *c.* of Palestine

Matt. 2. 16. Herod sent and slew children in all the *c.*

8. 34. he would depart out of their *c.*
Mark 5. 17.

15. 21. then Jesus departed into *c.* of Tyre and Sidon

COAT, *Gen.* 37. 3. Jacob made Joseph a *c.* of many colours

32. they sent the *c.* of many colours, and said, this have we found, know whether it be thy son's *c.*

Ex. 28. 4. make for Aaron a robe and broidered *c.*

Lev. 16. 4. he shall put on the holy linen *c.*

1 *Sam.* 2. 19. his mother made Samuel a little *c.*

17. 5. Goliath was armed with a *c.* of mail, 38.

Songs 5. 3. I have put off my *c.* how shall I put it on?

Matt. 5. 40. if any sue thee and take away thy *c.*

Luke 6. 29. thy cloak forbid not to take thy *c.* also

John 19. 23. now the *c.* was without seam, woven

COATS, *Gen.* 3. 21. God made *c.* of skins and clothed them

Ex. 28. 40. for Aaron's sons thou shalt make *c.*

Dan. 3. 21. then these men were bound in their *c.*

Matt. 10. 10. neither provide two *c.* nor
Luke 3. 11. he hath two *c.* let him impart to him

COCKLE, a poisonous weed, supposed to be the deadly night-shade ; *Job* 31. 40.

COLD, *Gen.* 8. 22. *c.* and heat, day and night shall not cease

Job 24. 7. naked have no covering in the *c.*

37. 9. and *c.* cometh out of the north
Ps. 147. 17. who can stand before his *c.* ?

Prov. 20. 4. the sluggard will not plow by reason of *c.*

25. 13. as the *c.* of snow in harvest,

20. taketh away a garment in *c.*

Matt. 10. 42. give to little ones a cup of *c.* water

24. 12. love of many shall wax *c.*

John 18. 18. servants had made a fire, for it was *c.*

2 *Cor.* 11. 27. in fastings often, in *c.*

COL-HOZEH, Kol-ho´zeh.—A ruler in Jerusalem ; *Neh.* 3. 15.

COLLECTION. A voluntary contribution ; 1 *Cor.* 16. 1, 2.

COME not into secret, *Gen.* 49. 6.

Ex. 20. 24. I will *c.* and bless thee

1 *Sam.* 17. 45. I *c.* to thee in name of
1 *Chr.* 29. 14. all things *c.* of thee, 12.

Job 22. 21. good shall *c.* unto thee

37. 13. causeth it to *c.* for correction

38. 11. hitherto shalt thou *c.* but

Ps. 40. 7. lo I *c.* *Heb.* 7. 9.

22. 31. they shall *c.* and shall declare

65. 2. to thee shall all flesh *c.*

Eccl. 9. 2. all things *c.* alike to all

Songs 4. 16. north wind *c.* thou south

Is. 26. 20. *c.* my people enter into

35. 4. G. he will *c.* and save you

55. 1. *c.* to the waters, yea *c.* buy

3. incline your ear and *c.* to me

Ezek. 33. 31. *c.* to thee as the people *c.*

Mic. 6. 6. wherewith shall I *c.* before Lord

Hab. 2. 3. it will surely *c.* not tarry
Mal. 3. 1. suddenly *c.* to his temple

4. 6. lest I *c.* and smite the earth

Matt. 8. 1. many shall *c.* from east and west ; *Luke* 7. 19. 20.

11. 3. he that should *c. Gen.* 49. 10.

28. *c.* to me all ye that labour

16. 24. if any man will *c.* after me

22. 4. ready *c.* to the marriage
Luke 7. 8. I say *c.* and he cometh

14. 20. married a wife I cannot *c.*

John 1. 39. *c.* and see, 46. & 4. 29. *Rev.* 6. 1, 3, 5, 7 ; 17. 1 ; 21. 9.

5. 40. ye will not, *c.* to me—have life

6. 44. no man *c.* to me except Father

7. 37. if thirst let him *c.* to me and

14. 18. not leave—I will *c.* to you
Acts 16. 9. *c.* over and help us

1 *Cor.* 11. 26. Lord's death till he *c.*

2 *Cor.* 6. 17. *c.* out from among them

Heb. 4. 16. let us *c.* boldly to the throne

7. 25. save all that *c.* to God by him

10. 37. he that shall *c.* will *c.*

Rev. 18. 4. *c.* out of her my people

22. 7. I *c.* quickly, 12. 20.

17. spirit and bride say *c.*—will *c.*—

20. amen, even so *c.* Lord Jesus
Ps. 118. 26. *c.* in name of L. to

Eccl. 11. 8. all that *c.* is vanity
Matt. 3. 11. *c.* after me is mightier
Luke 6. 47. whosoever *c.* to me and
John 3. 31. that *c.* from above

6. 35. *c.* to me shall not hunger

37. *c.* to me I will in no wise cast out

45. learned of Father *c.* unto me

14. 6. no man *c.* to Father by me
Heb. 11. 6. that *c.* to God must believe
James 1. 17. gift *c.* down from Father
Heb. 10. 1. the *c.* thereunto perfect

COMING, *Ps.* 19. 5. & 37. 13.

121. 8. Lord shall preserve thy *c.*

Mal. 3. 2. who may abide the day of his *c.*

4. 5. before the *c.* of the great day
Matt. 24. 3. what be the sign of thy *c.*

27. so shall *c.* of Son of man be, 37. 39.

48. my Lord delays his *c. Luke* 12. 45.

John 1. 27. *c.* after me is preferred before

1 *Cor.* 1. 7. waiting for *c.* of our Lord Jesus

18. 32. that are Christ's at his *c.*

1 *Thess.* 2. 19. Jesus Christ at his *c.,* 3. 13. & 5. 23.

1 *Pet.* 2. 4. to whom *c.* as unto a living stone

2 *Pet.* 1. 16. power and *c.* of our Lord Jesus

3. 12. hasting unto *c.* of day of God

COMING of the Lord, 1 *Thess.* 4. 15; 2. *Thess.* 2. 1 ; *James* 5. 7, 8.

COMELY, 1 *Sam.* 16. 18 ; *Job* 41. 12.

Ps. 33. 1. praise is *c.* for upright, 147. 1.

Prov. 30. 29. yea four are *c.* going

Songs 1. 5. I am black but *c.*

10. thy cheeks are *c.* with rows

2. 14. thy countenance is *c.*
6. 4. thou art *c.* as Jerusalem
1 *Cor.* 7. 35. for that which is *c.*
  11. 13. is it *c.* that a woman pray unto
Is. 53. 2. no form nor *c.*
Ezek. 16. 14. perfect through my *c.*
COMFORT in my affliction, *Ps.* 119. 50.
Matt. 9. 22. be of good *c.*, *Mark* 10. 49 ;
  Luke 8. 48 ; 2 *Cor.* 13. 11.
Acts 9. 31. walking in *c.* of H. G.
Rom. 15. 4. and *c.* of the scriptures
1 *Cor.* 14. 3. to exhortation and *c.*
2 *Cor.* 1. 3. the God of all *c.*
  7. 4. I am filled with all *c.*
Col. 4. 11. have been a *c.* to me
Ps. 94. 19. *c. Is.* 57. 18.
Job 7. 13. my bed shall *c.* me
Ps. 23. 4. thy rod and staff *c.* me
  119. 82. when wilt thou *c.* me
Songs 2. 5. *c.* me with apples, for I am
Is. 40. 1. *c.* ye my people

  51. 3. Lord shall *c.* Zion ; *Zech.* 1. 17.
  61. 2. to *c.* all that mourn
Jer. 31. 13. I will *c.* and make them
  rejoice
Lam. 1. 2. none to *c.* her, 17. 21.
2 *Cor.* 1. 4. be able to *c.* them
Eph. 6. 22. might *c.* your hearts
1 *Thess.* 4. 18. *c.* one another with
  5. 11. *c.* yourselves together
  14. *c.* the feeble-minded support the
  weak
2 *Thess.* 2. 17. *c.* your hearts and stablish you
COMFORTABLY, *Is.* 40. 2 ; *Hos.* 2. 14.
  2 *Sam.* 19. 7 ; 2 *Chr.* 30. 22. & 32. 6.
COMFORTED, *Gen.* 24. 67, & 37. 35.
Ps. 77. 2. my soul refused to be *c.*
  119. 52. I have *c.* myself
Is. 49. 13. God hath *c.* his people
  54. 11. tossed afflicted and not *c.*
Matt. 5. 4. mourn they shall be *c.*
Luke 16. 25. now he is *c.* and thou tormented
Rom. 1. 12. I may be *c.* together with
  you
1 *Cor.* 14. 31. learn and all may be *c.*
2 *Cor.* 1. 4. wherewith we ourselves *c.*
  7. 13. we are comforted in your *c.*
Col. 2. 2. their hearts might be *c.*
1 *Thess.* 3. 7. were *c.* over you all
COMFORTER, *John* 14. 16, 26. & 15.
  26. & 16. 7.
Job 16. 2. *c. Ps.* 69. 20.
COMFORTETH, *Is.* 51. 12. I am he that
  c. you
2 *Cor.* 1. 4. *c.* us all in our tribulations
  7. 6. *c.* those that are cast down
COMFORTLESS, that is, orphan ;
  John 14. 18.
COMMAND, *Ex.* 8. 27. & 18. 23.
Gen. 18. 19. he will *c.* his children
Lev. 25. 21. I will *c.* my blessing
Deut. 28. 8. the Lord shall *c.* the bless-
  ing
Ps. 42. 8. Lord will *c.* his loving-kind-
  44. 4. *c.* deliverance for Jacob
Is. 45. 11. work of my hands *c.* ye me
Matt. 4. 3. *c.* these stones be bread
John 15. 14. whatsoever I *c.* you
2 *Thess.* 3. 4. things which we *c.* you

1 *Cor.* 7. 10. to the married I *c.*
1 *Tim.* 4. 11. these things *c.* and teach
Ps. 68. 28. God has *c.* thy strength
  111. 9. he hath *c.* his covenant
  119. 4. thou hast *c.* us to keep
  133. 3. *c.* the blessing, even life for
  148. 5. Lord he *c.* and were created
Matt. 28. 20. whatsoever I have *c.* you
Heb. 12. 20. not endure what was *c.*
Lam. 3. 37. when Lord *c.* not
Acts 17. 30. now *c.* all men everywhere

Gen. 49. 33. end of *c.* sons
1 *Tim.* 4. 3. *c.* to abstain from meats
Num. 23. 20. *c.* to bless
Ps. 119. 96. thy *c.* is exceeding broad
Prov. 6. 23. the *c.* is a lamp
Hos. 5. 11. willingly walked after the *c.*
Matt. 22. 38. first and great *c.* love the
John 10. 18. this *c.* I have received of
  12. 50. his *c.* is life everlasting
  13. 34. a new *c.* give I unto you
  14. 31. as Father gave me a *c.*
  15. 12. this is my *c.* that ye love one
Rom. 7. 8. sin taking occasion by *c.*
  9. when the *c.* came sin revived
  12. *c.* is holy, just, and good
1 *Tim.* 1. 5. end of *c.* is charity
Heb. 7. 16. law of a carnal *c.*
2 *Pet.* 2. 21. turn from holy *c.* delivered
1 *John* 2. 7. an old *c.* which you had, 8.
  3. 23. this is his *c.* which we believe
Ex. 34. 28. wrote on tables ten *c. Deut.*
  4. 13. & 10. 4.
Ps. 111. 7. all his *c.* are sure
  112. 1. delight greatly in his *c.*
  119. 6. respect unto all thy *c.*
  10. not wander from thy *c.*
  19. hide not thy *c.* from me
  21. do not err from thy *c.*
  32. I will run in the way of thy *c.*
  35. make me to go in path of thy *c.*
  47. I will delight myself in thy *c.*
  48. thy *c.* which I had loved
  66. I have believed thy *c.*
  73. give understanding—learn thy *c.*
  86. all thy *c.* are faithful
  98. thy *c.*—made me wiser
  127. I love thy *c.*
  131. I longed for thy *c.*
  143. thy *c.* are my delights
  151. all thy *c.* are truth
  166. I have done thy *c.*
  172. all thy *c.* are righteousness
  176. I do not forget thy *c.*
Matt. 15. 9. for doctrines the *c.* of men
  22. 40. on these two *c.* hang all
Mark 10. 19. thou knowest the *c. Luke*
  18. 20.
Luke 1. 6. walking in all the *c.* of the
Col. 2. 22. after the *c.* of men
1 *John* 3. 24. keepeth his *c.* dwelleth in
2 *John* 6. love that walk after his *c.*
Num. 15. 40. do all,—these,—my—his
  c. Deut. 6. 25. & 15. 5. & 28. 1.
  15. & 19. 9. & 27. 10. & 30. 8 ;
  1 *Chr.* 28. 7 ; *Neh.* 10. 29 ; *Ps.* 103.
  18, 20. & 111. 10 ; *Rev.* 22. 14.
COMMEND, *Gen.* 12. 15 ; *Rom.* 16. 1 ;
  2 *Cor.* 3. 1. & 5. 12. & 10. 12.
Luke 23. 46. into thy hands I *c.* my
  spirit

Acts 20. 32. I *c.* you to God and to word
Luke 16. 8. lord *c.* the unjust steward
Rom. 5. 8. God *c.* his love towards us
1 *Cor.* 8. 8. meat *c.* us not to God
2 *Cor.* 10. 18. not he that *c,* himself is
approved, but whom Lord *c.*
4. 2. *c.* ourselves to—conscience
6. 4. *c.* ourselves as ministers of God
Commendation, 2 *Cor.* 3. 1.

COMMENDED, *Gen.* 12. 15. the princes
c. Sarai before Pharaoh
Prov. 12. 8. a man shall be *c.* according
to his wisdom
Luke 16. 8. Lord *c.* unjust steward
Acts 14. 23. *c.* them to the Lord on
2 *Cor.* 12. 11. I ought to have been *c.* of
you

COMMISSION, a charge to a person to
manage an affair, a mandate, *Ezra*
8. 36 ; *Acts* 26. 12.

COMMIT adultery, *Ex.* 20. 14 ; *Deut.*
5. 18 ; *Matt.* 5. 27. & 19. 18 ; *Rom.*
13. 9 ; *Lev.* 5. 17.
Gen. 39. 8. *c.* all that he hath
Job 5. 8. to God would I *c.* my cause
Ps. 31. 5. into thy hands I *c.* my spirit
37. 5. *c.* thy way unto the Lord
Prov. 16. 3. *c.* thy works to the Lord
Luke 12. 48. *c.* things worthy of stripes
16. 11. who will *c.* to your trust
John 2. 24. did not *c.* himself to them
Rom. 1. 32. such things are worthy
of death
1 *Tim.* 1. 18. this charge I *c.* to thee
1 *Pet.* 4. 19. *c.* the keeping of their souls
1 *John* 3. 9. born of God doth not *c.* sin
Jer. 2. 13. people *c.* two evils
Luke 12. 48. men have *c.* much
1 *Tim.* 1. 11. gospel *c.* to my trust, 1 *Cor.*
9. 17 ; *Tit.* 1. 3 ; *Gal.* 2. 7 ; 2 *Cor.*
5. 19.
6. 20. keep that which is *c.* to thee
2 *Tim.* 1. 12. which I have *c.* to him
14. good thing *c.* to thee
1 *Pet.* 2. 23. *c.* himself to him that judgeth righteously
Jude 15. which they have ungodly *c.*

COMMITTEST, ETH, ING, 1 *Cor.* 6.
18. but he that *c.* fornication
Ps. 10. 14. poor *c.* himself to thee
John 8. 34. whosoever *c.* sin is the servant of sin
1 *John* 3. 4. *c.* sin transgresseth the law
8. he that *c.* sin is of the devil

COMMODIOUS, *Acts* 27. 12. the haven
was not *c.* to winter in

COMMON. By common, is meant that
which is ordinary, or usual · as a
common death, *Num.* 16. 29 ; a
common evil, *Eccl.* 6. 1. Sometimes that which is ceremonially
unclean, *Acts* 11. 9. To eat with
common hands, that is, without
washing one's hands, *Mark* 7. 2.
Common bread, that is, unhallowed
bread, 1 *Sam.* 21. 4. It is said,
Acts 2. 44. That such as believed
had all things common ; that is, as
to use, but not as to title. Moses
calls a vineyard common, or profane : What man is he that hath

planted a vineyard, and hath not
yet made it common? *Deut.* 20. 6. If
there be such a one, he may return to
his house ; because the first-fruits
of trees and vines were reckoned
unclean, or rather were consecrated to the Lord, and the owner was
not allowed to touch them, till after the fourth year, *Lev.* 19. 24, 25.

COMMON, *Num.* 16. 29 ; 1 *Sam.* 21. 4.
5 ; *Eccl.* 6. 1 ; *Ezek.* 23. 42.
Acts 2. 44. had all things *c.* 4. 32.
10. 15. what God cleansed call not *c.*
1 *Cor.* 10. 13. temptation *c.* to men
Tit. 1. 4. son after the *c.* faith
Jude 3. write of the *c.* salvation
Eph. 2. 12. *c.* wealth of Israel
Matt. 28. 15. *c.* 1 *Cor.* 5. 1.

COMMON people, *Lev.* 4. 27. if any of
the *c. people*
Jer. 26. 23. cast his dead body into the
graves of *c. people*
Mark 12. 37. the *c. people* heard gladly

COMMON-WEALTH, *Eph.* 2. 12. being
aliens from the *c. wealth* of Israel

COMMOTION. Tumult, disturbance,
trouble, *Jer.* 10. 22 ; *Luke* 21. 9.

COMMUNE, to impart sentiments, to
meditate, to converse
Ex. 25. 22. I will meet and *c.* with thee
1 *Sam.* 18. 22. *c.* with David secretly
Job 4. 2. if we essay to *c.* with thee
Ps. 4. 4. *c.* with your own heart
77. 6. in the night I *c.* with mine own
heart

COMMUNED, 1 *Sam.* 9. 25. Samuel *c.*
25. 39. David *c.* with Abigail
1 *Kings* 10. 2. the queen of Sheba *c.*
with Solomon all that was in her
heart, 2 *Chr.* 9. 1.
Eccl. 1. 16. I *c.* with mine own heart,
Dan. 1. 19. and king *c.* with them
Zech. 1. 14. angel *c.* with me, said
Luke 6. 11. they *c.* what they might do
to Jesus
24. 15. while they *c.* Jesus drew near
Acts 24. 26. Felix *c.* the oftener with
Paul

COMMUNICATE. To impart to him
that teacheth in all things, *Gal.*
6. 6.
Phil. 4. 14. *c.* with my affliction
1 *Tim.* 6. 18. distribute, willing to *c*
Heb. 13. 16. to *c.* forget not
Gal. 2. 2. *c.* to them the gospel
Phil. 4. 15. no church *c.* with me in

COMMUNICATION, 2 *Kings* 9. 11.
Matt. 5. 37. let your *c.* be yea, nay
Eph. 4. 29. let no corrupt *c.* proceed
Col. 3. 8. let no filthy *c.* proceed
Luke 24. 17. what manner of *c.* are
these
1 *Cor.* 15. 33. evil *c.* corrupt good man-
ners

COMMUNION, the concord of doctrines
or opinions in several persons. The
act of receiving the Lord's Supper,
that sign of our fellowship with
Christ ; 1 *Cor.* 10. 16. The communion of saints is that fellowship
which the saints have with Christ

by faith, and among themselves by
love ; 1 *John* 1. 3 ; *Acts* 4. 32 ; 34. 35.
1 *Cor.* 10. 16. *c.* of the blood of Christ
—*c.* of the body of C.
2 *Cor.* 6. 14. what *c.* hath light with
darkness, 13. 14. *c.* of the Holy
Ghost be with you all
COMPACT, regularly framed and
joined. *Ps.* 122. 3. The church is
compacted together ; every member
has his own proper station and
work, and yet all are so joined, as to
add to her general glory and
welfare ; *Eph.* 4. 16 ; *Col.* 2. 19.
COMPANION, *Ps.* 119. 63. I am a *c.* of
all that fear
Job 30. 29. I am a *c.* to owls
Prov. 13. 20. *c.* of fools shall be destroy
Mal. 2. 14. thy *c.* and wife of covenant
Phil. 2. 25. Epaphroditus *c.* in labour
Rev. 1. 9. your *c.* in tribulation
COMPANIONS, *Judg.* 14. 11. thirty *c.*
to be with him
Job 35. 4. answer thee and thy *c.*
41. 6. shall the *c.* make a banquet of
Ps. 45. 14. *c.* that follow her
Ps. 122. 8. for my *c.* sakes—peace be
Songs 1. 7. aside by flocks of thy *c.*
8. 13. *c.* hearken to thy voice
Is. 1. 23. princes *c.* of thieves
Ezek. 16. write on it for Judah and
Israel his *c.*
Dan. 2. 17. he made the thing known
to his *c.*
Acts 19. 29. caught Paul's *c.* in travel
Heb. 10. 33. became *c.* of them
COMPANY, *Gen.* 32. 8. 21.
1 *Sam.* 10. 5. meet a *c.* of prophets
Job 16. 7. made desolate all my *c.*
Ps. 55. 14. to the house of God in *c.*
68. 27. the princes of Judah with
their *c.*
Ps. 30. rebuke the *c.* of spearmen
Prov. 29. 3. keepeth *c.* with harlots
Songs 6. 13. as the *c.* of two armies
Luke 6. 17. *c.* of his disciples and
9. 14. sit down by fifties in a *c.*
Acts 4. 23. went to their own *c.*
Acts 10. 28. unlawful for a man that is
a Jew to *c.*
Rom. 15. 24. first filled with your *c.*
1 *Cor.* 5. 11. not to keep *c.* with
2 *Thess.* 3. 14. have no *c.* with him
Heb. 12. 22. an innumerable *c.* of angels
COMPANY, great, *Gen.* 50. 9. went with
Joseph a *great c.*
2 *Chr.* 9. 1. the queen of Sheba came
with a *great c.*
Ps. 68. 11. *great* was the *c.* of those
John 6. 5. saw a *great c.* come to him,
he saith
Acts 6. 7. a *great c.* of priests obedient
to the faith
COMPANY, with, 1 *Cor.* 5. 9. I wrote
not to *c. with* fornicators
COMPANIES, *Judg.* 7. 16. he divided
the 300 men in three *c.*
Judg. 7. 20. the three *c.* blew the trumpets
9. 34. they laid wait against Shechem
in four *c.*
1 *Sam.* 11. 11. Saul put the people in

three *c.*
Neh. 12. 31. two great *c.* of them gave
thanks, 40.
Job 6. 19. the *c.* of Sheba waited
Mark 6. 39. sit down by *c.* on green
grass
COMPANIED, *Acts* 1. 21. of these men
which have *c.* with us
COMPARABLE, *Lam.* 4. 2. the precious
sons of Zion to fine gold
COMPARE, to liken, to make like, to
put things together that the likeness
or difference may appear, *Is.* 40. 18.
Ps. 89. 6. who in heaven can be *c.* to
Lord
Prov. 3. 15. not to be *c.* to wisdom. 8. 11.
Songs 1. 9. I have *c.* my love to company
Rom. 8. 18. not worthy to be *c.*
1 *Cor.* 2. 13. *c.* spiritual things with
spiritual
2 *Cor.* 10. 12. *c.* ourselves—*c.* them-
selves
COMPARISON, *Judg.* 8. 2 ; *Hag.* 2. 3 ;
Mark 4. 30.
COMPASS, noun, *Ex.* 27. 5. put net
under *c.* of altar
Ex. 38. 4. grate of net-work under *c.*
2 *Sam.* 5. 23. fetch a *c.* bind them
2 *Kings* 3. 9. they fetched a *c.* of
seven days journey
Prov. 8. 27. set a *c.* on face of earth
Is. 44. 13. marketh image out with *c.*
COMPASS, verb, *Josh.* 6. 3. ye shall *c.*
the city
2 *Kings* 11. 8. *c.* the king round about
Job 16. 13. his archers *c.* me about
Ps. 5. 12. with favour *c.* him
26. 6. so I will *c.* thine altar
32. 10. mercy shall *c.* him about
Ps. 49. 5. the iniquity of my heels shall
c. me about
Prov. 4. 9. she shall *c.* thee with a
crown of glory
Is. 50. 11. *c.* yourselves with sparks
Jer. 31. 22. a woman shall *c.* a man
Hab. 1. 4. wicked doth *c.* about righte.
Matt. 23. 15. ye *c.* sea and land to make
Luke 19. 43. enemies shall *c.* thee round
COMPASSED, *Gen.* 19. 4. the men of
Sodom *c.* the house
Deut. 2. 1. and we *c.* mount Seir
Josh. 6. 11. so the ark of the Lord *c.* the
city
Judg. 11. 18. *c.* land of Edom and Moab
16. 2. they *c.* Samson in, and laid wait
1 *Sam.* 23. 26. Saul and his men *c.* D.
2 *Sam.* 22. 5. waves of death *c.* me
Ps. 18. 4. sorrows of death *c.* me, 116. 3.
Ps. 22. 12. many bulls *c.* me ; 16. for
many dogs *c.* me
40. 12. innumerable evils have *c.* me
about
118. 10, 11, 12. all nations *c.* me about
Jonah 2. 3. floods *c.* me about
Luke 21. 20. see Jerus. *c.* with armies
Heb. 5. 2. he himself is also *c.* with infirmity
COMPASSED, about, *Ps.* 40. 12. innumerable evils have *c.* me about
88. 17. they *c.* me a. together, 109. 3 ;
118. 11, 12.
Heb. 11. 30. walls of Jericho fell, after

c. about 7 days

COMPASSEST, ETH, *Gen.* 2. 11. *c.* Havilah ; 13. *c.* the land of Ethiopia

Ps. 73. 6. pride *c.* about as a chain

COMPASSION, 1 *Kings* 8. 50 ; 2 *Chr* 30. 9 ; 1 *John* 3. 17.

Matt. 9. 36. moved with *c.* 14. 14. and 18. 27.

COMPASSION, full of, *Ps.* 78. 38. *full of c.* forgave their iniquity

86. 15. thou art a God *full of c.* 111. 4 ; 112. 4 ; 145. 8.

COMPASSION, have or had, *Ex.* 2. 6. babe wept, she *had c.* on him

1 *Sam.* 23. 21. blessed be ye of Lord for ye *have c.* on me

2 *Chr.* 36. 15. because he *had c.* on his people

Is. 49. 15. that she should not *have c.* on son of womb

Lam. 3. 32. yet will he *have c.* Mic. 7. 19.

Matt. 15. 32. I *have c.* on the multitude, *Mark* 8. 2.

18. 33. also *have had c.* on thy fellowservant

Mark 9. 22. if thou canst *have c.* on us and help us

Luke 15. 20. father *had c.* and ran and fell on his neck

Heb. 5. 2. can *have c.* on the ignorant

10. 34. for ye *had c.* of me in my bond

Jude 22. of some *have c.* making a difference

COMPASSIONS, *Lam.* 3. 22. not consumed, because his *c.* fail not

Zech. 7. 9. show mercy and *c.* every man to brother

COMPEL them to come in, *Luke* 14. 23.

Esth. 1. 8. drinking none did *c.*

2 *Chr.* 21. 11. *c.* Judah thereto

Acts 26. 11. I *c.* them to blaspheme

2 *Cor.* 12. 11. I am a fool—ye *c.* me

Gal. 2. 3. not *c.* to be circumcised

14. why *c.* Gentiles to live as Jews

COMPLAIN, *Job* 7. 11. I will *c.* in the bitterness of my soul

Lam. 3. 39. why doth a living man *c.*

Ps. 144. 14. *c.* in streets

COMPLAINED, *Ps.* 77. 3. I *c.* and my spirit was overwhelmed

COMPLAINERS, *Num.* 11. 1. when people were *c.* it displeased Lord

Jude 16. these are murmurers, *c.* walking after lusts

COMPLAINT, 1 *Sam.* 1. 16. out of abundance of my *c.* have I spoken

Job 9. 27. if I say, I will forget my *c.*

10. 1. I will leave my *c.* on myself

21. 4. as for me, is my *c.* to man?

Ps. 55. 2. I mourn in my *c.* and make a noise

142. 2. I poured out my *c.* before him,

Acts 25. 7. laid *c.* against Paul, they could not prove

Col. 3. 13. if any man have a *c.* against

COMPLETE. To accomplish, *Lev.* 23. 15.—Entire salvation by union with Christ : " and ye are *complete* in him," *Col.* 2. 10.

COMPOUND, ETH, *Ex.* 30. 25. an ointment *c.* after art of apothecary

Ex. 30. 33. whosoever *c.* any thing like

it, or putteth any

COMPREHEND, *Job* 37. 5 ; *Eph.* 3. 18 ; *Is.* 40. 12 ; *John* 1. 5 ; *Rom.* 13. 9.

CONCEAL. To hide, to keep secret, *Gen.* 37. 26.

Job. 27. 11. with Almighty I will not *c.* 41. 12. I will not *c.* his parts

Ps. 40. 10. have not *c.* loving kindness

Prov. 12. 23. prudent *c.* knowledge

Prov. 25. 2. glory of God to *c.* a thing

CONCEIT, S, *Prov.* 18. 11. rich man's wealth as an high wall in *c.*

Prov. 26. 5. answer a fool, lest he be wise in his own *c.*

12. seest thou a man wise in his own *c.* ? more hope

16. sluggard is wiser in his own *c.* than seven men

28. 11. rich man wise in own *c.*

Rom. 11. 25. lest ye should be wise in your own *c.*

12. 16. be not wise in your own *c.*

CONCEIVE, *Judg.* 13. 3 ; *Luke* 1. 31.

Job 15. 35. they *c.* mischief, *Is.* 59. 4.

Ps. 51. 5. in sin mother *c.* me

Is. 7. 14. a virgin shall *c.*—a son

33. 11. ye shall *c.* chaff

59. 13. *c.* words of falsehood

Num. 11. 12. have I *c.* all this people

Ps. 7. 14. hath *c.* mischief—falsehood

Songs 3. 4. chamber of her that *c.* me

Jer. 49. 30. *c.* a purpose against you

Acts 5. 4. why hast thou *c.* in thy heart

Jam. 1. 15. lust hath *c.* bringeth forth

CONCERN, ETH, *Ezek.* 12. 10. this burden *c.* the princes

Acts 28. 31. teaching things which *c.* the Lord Jesus Christ

2 *Cor.* 11. 30. glory in things which *c.* my infirmities

CONCERNING, *Gen.* 19. 21. I have accepted thee *c.* this thing

Lev. 4. 26. priest make atonement for him *c.* sin, 5. 6.

Num. 10. 29. the Lord hath spoken good *c.* Israel

Ps. 90. 13. repent thee *c.* thy servants

Dan. 2. 18. desire mercies of God *c.*

Luke 24. 27. he expounded the things *c.* himself

Acts 13. 34. as *c.* that he raised him up from dead

Rom. 9. 5. of whom as *c.* flesh Christ came, who is God

16. 19. you wise to what is good, and simple *c.* evil

2 *Cor.* 11. 21. I speak as *c.* reproach

Eph. 5. 32. but I speak *c.* Christ and

Phil. 4. 15. *c.* giving and receiving

1 *Tim.* 6. 21. some professing have erred *c.* the faith

2 *Tim.* 2. 18. who *c.* the truth have erred, saying

3. 8. reprobates *c.* the faith

1 *Pet.* 4. 12. not strange *c.* the fiery trial

CONCISION, *Phil.* 3. 2. Beware of the concision, that is, such as under pretence of maintaining circumcision, which is now no longer a seal of God's covenant, and so is no better than a mere cutting or slashing of the flesh, do prove destroyers and renders of the church.

Joel 3. 14. multitudes in the valley of *c*.

Phil. 3. 2. beware of dogs, beware of the *c*.

CONCLUDE, *Rom.* 3. 28. we *c*. a man is justified by faith without

CONCLUSION, *Eccl.* 12. 13. *c*. of matter

CONCUBINE, *Judg.* 19. 2. his *c*. played the whore

20. 4. I came into Gibeah, I and my *c*. to lodge

2 *Sam.* 3. 7. why hast thou gone into my father's *c*.

21. 11. what Rizpah the *c*. of Saul had done

CONCUBINES, *Gen.* 25. 6. to sons of the *c*. Abraham gave gifts

2 *Sam.* 5. 13 David took him more *c*.

16. 22. Absalom went in to father's *c*.

19. 5. have saved lives of thy *c*.

1 *Kings* 11. 3. Solomon had three hundred *c*.

2 *Chr.* 11. 21. Rehoboam took three-score *c*.

Dan. 5. 3. the king and his *c*. drank in them, 23.

CONCUPISCENCE (1) The corruption of our nature, from whence all our actual sins proceeds, *Rom.* 7. 7 ; *Jam.* 1. 14. (2) Actual motions and inclinations of our heart towards sinful deeds, *Rom.* 7. 8. (3) Unchastity, *Col.* iii. 5 ; 1 *Thess.* 4. 5.

CONDEMNATION, *Luke* 23. 40. thou art in the same *c*.

John 3. 19. this is the *c*. that light

5. 24. shall not come into *c*.

Rom. 5. 16. judgment by one to *c*.

18. as by one, judgment came to *c*.

8. 1. no *c*. to them in Christ

1 *Cor.* 11. 34. come not together to *c*.

2 *Cor.* 3. 9. ministration of *c*. be glory

1 *Tim.* 3. 6. fall into *c*. of devil

Jam. 3. 1. receive the greater *c*.

5. 12. swear not lest ye fall into *c*.

Jude 4. of old ordained to this *c*.

CONDEMN, *Ex.* 22. 9. whom judges shall *c*.

Deut. 25. 1. judges shall *c*. wicked

Job 9. 20. my own mouth shall *c*. me

10. 2. I will say to God, do not *c*. me

Ps. 37. 33. not *c*. him when he is judged

94. 21. they *c*. innocent blood

Prov. 12. 2. of wicked devices will he *c*.

Is. 50. 9. Lord will help me, who shall *c*. me

·54. 17. tongue—thou shalt *c*.

Matt. 12. 41. and shall *c*. it, *Luke* 11. 32.

42. queen of south shall *c*. it

20. 18. *c*. him to death, *Mark* 10. 33.

Luke 6. 37. *c*. not and ye shall not be *c*.

John 3. 17. his Son to *c*. the world

8. 11. neither do I *c*. thee go thy way

1 *John* 3. 20. heart *c*. us 21.

CONDEMNED, *Job* 32. 3. yet had *c*. Job

Ps. 109. 7. be judged, let him be *c*.

Matt. 12. 7. not have *c*. guiltless

Matt. 12. 37. by words—*c*.

Mark 14. 64. all *c*. him to be guilty

Luke 24. 20. delivered him to be *c*.

John 3. 18. who believes is not *c*.

John 8. 10. hath no man *c*. thee?

Rom. 8. 3. for sin *c*. sin in the flesh

1 *Cor.* 11. 32. not be *c*. with the world

Tit. 2. 8. speech that cannot be *c*.

3. 11. being *c*. in himself

Heb. 11. 7. by which he *c*. world

Jam. 5. 6. *c*. and killed the just

CONDEMNEST, ETH, ING, 1 *Kings* 8. 32. *c*. wicked

Prov. 17. 15. *c*. the just

Acts 13. 27. fulfilled them in *c*. him

Rom. 2. 1. judgest, thou *c*. thyself

Rom. 8. 34. who is he that *c*.

14. 22. *c*. not himself in that

CONDESCENDED to—low degree, *Rom.* 12. 16.

CONDITION, S, 1 *Sam.* 11. 2. on this *c*. make covenant

Luke 14. 32. he desireth *c*. of peace

CONDUCT, ED, 2 *Sam.* 19. 15. *c*. king over Jordan, 31.

Acts 17. 15. that *c*. Paul brought

1 *Cor.* 16. 11. but *c*. him in peace

CONDUIT, 2 *Kings* 18. 17. stood by *c*.

Is. 36. 2.

2 *Kings* 20. 20. how he made a pool and *c*.

Is. 7. 3. to meet Ahaz end of *c*.

CONFECTION, *Ex.* 30. 35. make a *c*. after art

CONFEDERACY, *Is.* 8. 12. *c*. to whom people say *c*.

Obad. 7. men of thy *c*. brought

CONFEDERATE, *Gen.* 14. 13. these *c*. with Abram

Ps. 83. 5. they are *c*. against thee

Is. 7. 2. Syria is *c*. with Ephraim

CONFERENCE, *Gal.* 2. 6. they in *c*. added nothing

CONFERRED, 1 *Kings* 1. 7. Adonijah · *c*. with Joab

Acts 4. 15. *c*. among themselves

25. 12. Festus, when he had *c*.

Gal. 1. 16. I *c*. not with flesh and

CONFESS, *Lev.* 5. 5. he shall *c*. that he hath sinned

Lev. 16. 21. Aaron shall *c*. over live goat all the iniquities

Num. 5. 7. they shall *c*. their sins

Job 40. 14. I will *c*. that thy hand can save thee

Ps. 32. 5. I said, I will *c*. my transgressions to the Lord

Matt. 10. 32. whosoever shall *c*. before men, will I *c*. before my Father, *Luke* 12. 8.

John 9. 22. if *c*. that he was Christ

12. 42. did not *c*. him lest they

Acts 23. 8. say no resurrection, but Pharisees *c*. both

24. 14. this I *c*. that after the way they call heresy

Rom. 10. 9. shalt *c*. with thy mouth the Lord Jesus

14. 11. every tongue shall *c*. to God

Phil. 2. 11. that every tongue shall *c*. Jesus is Lord

Jam. 5. 16. *c*. your faults one to another

1 *John* 1. 9. if we *c*. our sins, he is faithful to forgive

Rev. 3. 5. but I will *c*. his name before my Father

CONFESSED, ETH, ING, *Ezra* 10. 1.

Ezra had *c.* weeping
Neh. 9. 2. stood and *c.* their sins
Prov. 28. 13. *c.* and forsaketh
Dan. 9. 20. *c.* my sin and the sin
Matt. 3. 6. baptized, *c.* their sins
John 1. 20. I. I am not the Christ
Heb. 11. 13. *c.* that they were strangers
CONFESSION, *Josh.* 7. 19. and make *c.*
Ezra 10. 11. make *c.* to the Lord
Dan. 9. 4. I prayed and made *c.*
Rom. 10. 10. *c.* is made to salvation
1 *Tim.* 6. 13. before Pilate witnessed a
     good *c.*
CONFIDENCE, *Job* 4. 6. & 31. 24.
Ps. 65. 5. *c.* of all the ends of earth
     118. 8. than to put *c.* in man
     9. than to put *c.* in princes
Prov. 3. 26. Lord shall be thy *c.*
     14. 26. in fear of Lord is strong *c.*
     21. 22. casteth down strength of *c.*
     25. 19. *c.* in unfaithful like a broken
     tooth
Is. 30. 15. in *c.* be your strength
Mic. 7. 5. put not *c.* in a guide, *Prov.*
     25. 19 ; *Ezek.* 28. 26. & 29. 16.
Acts 28. 31. preaching with all *c.*
2 *Cor.* 1. 15. in *c.* minded to come
     2. 3. *c.* that my joy is the joy
     7. 16. that I have *c.* in you in all
     10. 2. with the *c.* I think to be bold
     11. 17. as foolishly in this *c.* of
Gal. 5. 10. I have *c.* in you through L.
Phil. 1. 25. having this *c.* I shall abide
     3. 3. we have no *c.* in the flesh
Heb. 3. 6. if we hold fast *c.* to end
     14. beginning of our *c.* steadfast
     10. 35. cast not away your *c.*

1 *John* 2. 28. appear we may have *c.*
CONFIDENCES, *Jer.* 2. 37. Lord re-
     jected thy *c.*
CONFIDENT, *Ps.* 27. 3. *c.* *Prov.* 14. 16.
CONFIRM, *Is.* 35. 3. *c.* feeble knees
Dan. 9. 27. shall *c.* the covenant
Rom. 15. 8. to *c.* the promises
1 *Cor.* 1. 8. shall *c.* you to the end
2 *Cor.* 2. 8. *c.* your love toward
CONFIRMATION, *Phil.* 1. 7. in the *c.*
     of the gospel
Heb. 6. 16. an oath for *c.* is an end
CONFIRMED, *Esth.* 9. 32. Esther *c.*
     these matters of Purim
Dan. 9. 12. *c.* words he spake against us
Acts 15. 32. exhorted and *c.* them
1 *Cor.* 1. 6. testimony of C. *c.* in you
Gal. 3. 15. if *c.* no man disannuled it
     17. the covenant that was *c.* before
Heb. 2. 3. was *c.* to us by them that
     6. 17. he *c.* it by an oath
CONFIRMETH, ING, *Deut.* 27. 26.
     cursed be he *c.* not all
Is. 44. 26. *c.* word of his servant
Acts 14. 22. *c.* souls of disciples
Acts 15. 41. thro' Syria *c.* the churches
CONFISCATION, a punishment where-
     by a man's goods are taken from
     him, and appropriated to the king's
     use, *Ezra* 7. 26.
CONFLICT, (1) Warlike struggle or
     stroke, *Ps.* 39. 10. (2) Persecution,
     distress, *Phil.* 1. 30. (3) Deep con-
     cern, care, and anxiety to promote
     one's good. *Col.* 2. 1.

CONFORMABLE, *Phil.* 3. 10. made *c.*
     to his death
CONFORMED, *Rom.* 8. 29. *c.* to image
     of his son
Rom. 12. 2. be not *c.* to this world
CONFOUND, (1) To consume, *Ps.* 71.
     13. (2) To make haste, 1 *Pet.* 2. 6.
     compared with *Is.* 28. 16. (3) To put
     to silence, *Acts* 2. 6 ; 9. 22. (4) To
     make ashamed, 1 *Cor.* 1. 27.
Gen. 11. 7. *c.* language
Jer. 1. 17. lest I *c.* thee before them
1 *Cor.* 1. 27. foolish things to *c.* wise
CONFOUNDED, *Ps.* 69. 6. let not those
     that seek Lord be *c.*
Ps. 97. 7. *c.* that serve images
Is. 54. 4. shalt not be a. neither *c.*
Jer. 17. 18. let not me be *c.*
Ezek. 16. 52. *c.* and bear shame, 54.
     63. *c.* and never open mouth more
Zech. 10. 5. riders on horses be *c.*
CONFOUNDED, not, *Ps.* 22. 5. fathers
     trusted, were *not c.*
Is. 45. 17. nor *c.* world without end
     50. 7. God will help, I be *not c.*
1 *Pet.* 2. 6. believeth shall *not* be *c.*
CONFUSED, *Is.* 9. 5. battle is with *c.*
Acts 19. 32. the assembly was *c.*
CONFUSION, perplexity, shame, disor-
     der, ruin, 1 *Sam.* 20. 30 ; *Ps.* 35. 4 ;
     Is. 9. 5 ; 24. 10 ; *Jer.* 3. 25 ; *Acts*
     19. 29.
Ezra 9. 7. delivered to *c.* of face,
Ps. 44. 15. my *c.* is continually before
     71. 1. let me never be put to *c.*
Dan. 9. 7. to us belongeth *c.* of face
1 *Cor.* 14. 33. God is not the author of *c.*
Jam. 3. 16. for where envying and strife
     there is *c.*
CONGRATULATE, 1 *Chr.* 18. 10. of his
     welfare and *c.*
CONGREGATION, *Lev.* 4. 21.
Lev. 16. 33. atonement for all the *c.*
Num. 16. 47. Aaron ran into midst of *c.*
Judg. 20. 1. *c.* gathered as one man
Ezra 10. 8. himself separated from *c.*
Job 15. 34. *c.* of hypocrites desolate
     30. 28. and I cried in the *c.*
Ps. 1. 5. sinners in *c.* of righteous
     22. 22. in midst of *c.* will I praise
     26. 5. hated *c.* of evil-doers
     74. 19. forget not *c.* of thy poor
     75. 2. receive *c.* I will judge uprightly
     82. 1. God stands in *c.* of mighty
     89. 5. faithfulness in *c.* of saints
     111. 1. I will praise the Lord in *c.*
Prov. 21. 16. remain in *c.* of dead
Hos. 7. 12. chastise as *c.* hath heard
Joel 2. 16. sanctify the *c.*
CONGREGATIONS, *Ps.* 26. 12. in *c.*
     will I bless Lord
Ps. 68. 26. bless ye God in the *c.*
     74. 4. thine enemies roar in thy *c.*
CONQUER, to overcome, subdue. (1)
     To prevail against, take away the
     strength and bring down the power
     of enemies, *Dan.* 7. 14 ; *Mal.* 4. 3.
     (2) To bring into obedience and
     subjection, *Phil.* 3. 21 ; 1 *Cor.* 15.
     28. (3) To cultivate, rule over,
     Gen. 1. 28. Jesus Christ overcame
     the world

CONQUERORS, *Rom.* 8. 37. we are more than *c.*
CONSCIENCE, *John* 8. 9 ; *Acts* 23. 1.
Acts 24. 16. a *c.* void of offence
Rom. 2. 15. *c.* bear witness, 9, 1.
    13. 5. not for wrath, but for *c.* sake
2 *Cor.* 1. 12. testimony of our *c.*
1 *Tim.* 3. 9. mystery of faith in pure *c.*
    4. 2. having their *c.* seared as hot iron
Tit. 1. 15. mind and *c.* are defiled
Heb. 9. 14. purge *c.* from dead works
    10. 2. worshippers no more *c.* of sin
    22. hearts sprinkled from evil *c.*
Acts 23. 1. good *c.* 1 *Tim.* 1. 19 ; *Heb.* 13. 18 ; 1 *Pet.* 3. 21.

CONSCIENCES, 2 *Cor.* 5. 11. manifest in your *c.*
CONSECRATE, *Ex.* 32. 29. *c.* yourselves this day to Lord
1 *Chr.* 29. 5. to *c.* his service to Lord
Ezek. 43. 26. shall *c.* themselves
Mic. 4. 13. I will *c.* their gain to Lord
CONSECRATED, 1 *Kings* 13. 33. whosoever would, he *c.*
2 *Chr.* 29. 31. *c.* yourselves to Lord
Heb. 7. 28. Son, who is *c.* evermore
    10. 20. by a living way *c.* for us
CONSECRATION, S, *Ex.* 29. 22. for it is a ram of *c.*
Lev. 8. 28. *c.* for sweet savour to Lord
    33. till days of your *c.* be at an end
CONSENT, ED, ING, *Gen.* 34. 23. only let us *c.* to them
Deut. 13. 8. shalt not *c.* to him
1 *Kings* 20. 8. hearken not, nor *c.*
Ps. 50. 18. sawest thief, thou *c.*
Prov. 1. 10. entice thee, *c.* thou not
Luke 23. 51. same had not *c.* to deed
Acts 8. 1. Saul *c.* to his death, 22. 20.
    18. 20. to tarry longer, he *c.* not
Rom. 7. 16. I *c.* to law that it is good
1 *Tim.* 6. 3. *c.* not to wholesome words
CONSENTING, *Acts* 8. 1. & 22. 20.
CONSIDER, *Lev.* 13. 13 ; *Judg.* 18. 14.
Deut. 4. 39. *c.* it in thine heart
    32. 29. O that—*c.* their latter end
Ps. 8. 3. when I *c.* the heavens
    50. 22. *c.* this ye that forget God
    64. 9. wisely *c.* of his doings
    119. 95. but I will *c.* thy testimonies
    153. *c.* mine affliction,
Eccl. 5. 1. *c.* not that they do evil
    7. 13. *c.* the work of God
    14. in day of adversity *c.*
Is. 1. 3. my people doth not *c.*
    5. 12. neither *c.* operation of hands
    41. 20. may see, and know, and *c.*
    52. 15. what not heard shall *c.*
Hag. 1. 5, 7. Lord *c.* your ways, 2. 15, 18.
2 *Tim.* 2. 7. *c.* what I say and Lord give
Heb. 3. 1. *c.* apostle and high priest
    7. 4. *c.* how great this man was
    10. 24. *c.* one another to provoke
    12. 3. *c.* him that endureth such contradiction
CONSIDERED EST, *Job* 1. 8. hast thou *c.* my servant, 2. 3.
Ps. 31. 7. hast *c.* my trouble
    77. 5. have *c.* days of old
Prov. 24. 32. then I saw and *c.* it well
Matt. 7. 3. *c.* not the beam
Mark 6. 52. *c.* not miracle of loaves

Rom. 4. 19. *c.* not his own body dead
CONSIDERETH, ING, *Ps.* 41. 1. blessed *c.* the poor
Prov. 29. 7. the righteous *c.* the poor
Prov. 31. 16. she *c.* a field and buyeth it
Is. 44. 19. none *c.* in his heart
Gal. 6. 1. *c.* thyself lest be tempted
Heb. 13. 7. *c.* end of conversation
CONSIST, *Col.* 1. 17 ; *Luke* 12. 15.
CONSOLATION, *Acts* 4. 36. & 15. 31.
Luke 2. 25. waited for *c.* of Israel
    6. 24. woe rich have received your *c.*
Rom. 15. 5. God of *c.* grant you to be
2 *Cor.* 1. 5. so our *c.* aboundeth by Christ
Phil. 2. 1. if any *c.* in Christ
2 *Thess* 2. 16. give us everlasting *c.*
Heb. 6. 18. might have strong *c.*
CONSOLATIONS, *Job* 15. 11.
CONSPIRACY, (1) Of subjects against their prince ; 2 *Sam.* 15. 12. (2) Of servants against their master ; 2 *Kings* 12. 20. (3) Of a people against the Lord ; *Jer.* 11. 9. (4) Of false prophets against the people ; *Ezek.* 22. 25. (5) More than forty Jews against Paul ; *Acts* 23. 12. 13. (6) Joseph's brethren conspired against him ; *Gen.* 37. 18. " And when they saw him afar off, even before he came near unto them, they *conspired* against him to slay him."
CONSPIRATORS, 2 *Sam.* 15. 31. Ahitophel is among *c.* with Absalom
CONSPIRED, *Gen.* 37. 18. *c.* against Joseph to slay
1 *Sam.* 22. 8. you have *c.* against me
2 *Kings* 9. 14. Jehu *c.* against Joram
Amos 7. 10. Amos had *c.* against thee
CONSTANCY, required of us. (1) In our devotions ; *Luke* 18. 1 ; 1 *Thess.* 5. 17, 18. (2) Under our sufferings ; *Matt.* 5. 12, 13 ; 1 *Pet.* 4. 13, 14. (3) In our profession and character ; *Heb.* 10. 23. (4) In our beneficence ; *Gal.* 6. 9. (5) In our friendships ; *Prov.* 27. 10 ; *Tit.* 3. 8. " These things I will that thou affirm *constantly.*"
CONSTELLATIONS, 2 *Kings* 23. 25. put down those that burnt incense to *c.*
Is. 13. 10. the *c.* thereof shall not give their light
CONSTRAIN, *Gal.* 6. 12 ; *Acts* 16. 15.
2 *Cor.* 5. 14. love of Christ *c.* us
1 *Pet.* 5. 2. not by *c.*
CONSTRAINED, ETH, *Job* 32. 18. the spirit within me *c.* me
Matt. 14. 22. Jesus *c.* his disciples, *Mark* 6. 45.
Acts 16. 15. Lydia *c.* us to come into her house
    28. 19. I was *c.* to appeal to Caesar
2 *Cor.* 5. 14. for love of Christ *c.* us, because we thus judge
CONSULT, (1) To plot or advise together ; *Ps.* 62. 4. (2) Deliberately to consider ; *Luke* 14. 31.
CONSUME, *Deut.* 5. 25. & 7. 16.
Ex. 33. 3. lest I *c.* thee in the way
Ps. 37. 20. they shall *c.* into smoke
    39. 11. his beauty to *c.*

49. 14. their beauty shall *c.* in the grave

78. 33. days did he *c.* in vanity

Ezek. 4. 17. *c.* away for iniquity

21. 28. the sword is drawn, it is furbished to *c.*

Dan. 2. 44. it *c.* all these kingdoms

Hos. 11. 6. sword shall *c.* his branches

Zech. 14. 12. their flesh, eyes, tongue shall *c.* away

2 *Thess.* 2. 8. Lord shall *c.* with spirit

James 4. 3. *c.* it upon your lusts

CONSUMED, *Ex.* 3. 2. bush was not *c.*

Job 1. 16. the fire of God hath *c.* sheep and servants

4. 9. by the breath of his nostrils are they *c.*

7. 9. as the cloud is *c.* and vanisheth away

19. 27. my reins *c.* ; 33. 21. his flesh is *c.* away

Ps. 39. 10. I am *c.* by the blow of thine hand

73. 19. they are utterly *c.* with terrors

90. 7. we are *c.* by thine anger

119. 139. my zeal hath *c.* me

Prov. 5. 11. thy flesh and body are *c.*

Is. 64. 7. *c.* because of your iniquities

Lam. 3. 22. of Lord's mercy we are not *c.*

Ezek. 43. 8. wherefore I have *c.* them in mine anger

Gal. 5. 15. be not *c.* one of another

CONSUMETH, ING, *Deut.* 4. 24. Lord is *c.* fire ; *Heb.* 12. 29.

9. 3. the Lord goeth over before thee as a *c.* fire

Job 13. 28. he *c.* as a garment that is moth-eaten

22. 20. but the remnant of them the fire *c.*

31. 12. for it is a fire that *c.* to destruction

CONSUMMATION, *Dan.* 9. 27. shall make it desolate, even until the *c.*

CONSUMPTION, *Lev.* 26. 16 ; *Deut.* 28. 22 ; *Is.* 10. 22, 23. & 28. 22.

CONTAIN, *Ezek.* 23. 32. & 45. 11.

1 *Kings* 8. 27. heavens of heavens cannot *c.* thee ; 2 *Chr.* 2. 6. & 6. 18.

John 21. 25. world not *c.* the books

1 *Cor.* 7. 9. if they cannot *c.* let marry

CONTEMN to despise, scorn, neglect, or slight God,—wicked ; *Ps.* 10. 13.

Ezek. 21. 13. if sword *c.* the rod, 10.

Ps. 15. 4. a vile person is *c.*

Job 12. 21. he pours *c.* on princes ; *Ps.* 107. 40.

123. 3. filled with *c.* 4.

Dan. 12. 2. some to everlasting *c.*

CONTEMPTIBLE, *Mal.* 1. 7. table of Lord is *c.*

12. even his meat is *c.* ; 2. 9. I also made you *c.*

2 *Cor.* 10. 10. his speech is *c.*

CONTEND, (1) To strive, *Jer.* 18. 19. (2) To dispute, *Acts* 11. 2. (3) To debate, or plead, *Job* 9..3 ; 40. 2. (4) To fight, *Deut.* 2. 9. (5) To reprove sharply, *Neh.* 13. 11. (6) To endeavour to convince a person of, and reclaim him from his evil way, *Prov.* 29. 9. (7) To punish, *Amos* 7. 4.

Earnestly to contend for the faith, *Jude* 3. strenuously to maintain and defend the apostolical doctrine, by constancy in the faith, zeal for the truth, holiness of life, mutual exhortation, prayer, suffering for the gospel, &c. withstanding all such heretics as would impugn and corrupt the doctrines revealed in the gospel.

Is. 49. 25. I'll contend with them that *c.*

50. 8. who will *c.* with me

57. 16. for I will not *c.* for ever

Jer. 12. 5. how canst *c.* with horses

Amos 7. 4. L. called to *c.* by fire

Jude 3. *c.* earnestly for the faith

CONTENDED, EST, ING, *Neh.* 13. 11. then *c.* I with rulers and said, 17.

Job 10. 2. cause why thou *c.*

40. 2. *c.* with Almighty instruction

Is. 41. 12. thou shalt not find them that *c.* with thee

Prov. 29. 9. if a wise man *c.* with a foolish man

Acts 11. 2. they of the circumcision *c.* with him

Jude 9. *c.* with devil, he disputed about body of Moses

CONTENT, satisfied in mind and desire *Gen.* 37. 27 ; *Luke* 3. 14.

Josh. 7. 7. would to God we had been *c.* dwelt on other

Judg. 19. 6. be *c.* tarry all night

Mark 15. 15. Pilate willing to *c.* people released Barabbas

Phil. 4. 11. state therewith to be *c.*

1 *Tim.* 6. 8. raiment let us be *c.*

Heb. 13. 5. be *c.* with such things as ye

3 *John* 10. with malicious words not *c.*

CONTENTION, *Hab.* 1. 3 ; *Acts* 15. 39 ; *Phil.* 1. 16 ; 1 *Thess.* 2. 2.

Prov. 13. 10. by pride cometh *c.*

17. 14. leave off *c.* before it be

18. 6. fool's lips enter into *c.*

22. 10. cast out scorner and *c.* shall

Jer. 15. 10. born me a man of *c.*

CONTENTIONS, *Prov.* 18. 18, 19. and 19. 13. and 28. 29 ; 1 *Cor.* 1. 11 ; *Tit.* 3. 9.

CONTENTIOUS, *Prov.* 21. 19. and 26. 21. and 27. 15 ; *Rom.* 2. 8 ; 1 *Cor.* 11. 16.

CONTENTMENT, 1 *Tim.* 6. 6. but godliness with *c.* is great gain

CONTINUAL, LY, *Ex.* 29. 42 ; *Num.* 4. 7 ; *Prov.* 15. 15 ; *Is.* 14. 6.

Rom. 9. 2. *Gen.* 6. 5. only evil *c.*

Ps. 34. 1. his praise *c.* in my mouth

52. 1. goodness of G. endureth *c.*

71. 3. I resort *c.* praise *c.*

14. I will hope *c.* and praise more

73. 23. yet I am *c.* with thee

119. 44. keep thy law *c.* for ever

117. respect to thy statutes *c.*

Prov. 6. 21. bind them *c.* on thy heart

Is. 58. 11. L. shall guide thee *c.*

Hos. 12. 6. wait on thy God *c.*

Luke 24. 53. *c.* in the temple, praising

Acts 6. 4. we will give ourselves *c.* to prayer

Heb. 7. 3. abideth a priest *c.*

Heb. 13. 15. sacrifice of praise to God *c.*

CONTINUANCE, *Deut.* 28. 59 ; *Ps.*

139. 16 ; *Is.* 64. 5 ; *Rom.* 2. 7.
CONTINUE, *Ex.* 21. 21 ; *Lev.* 12. 4.
1 *Sam.* 12. 14. *c.* following the L.
1 *Kings* 2. 4. L. may *c.* his word
Ps. 36. 10. *c.* thy loving-kindness
102. 28. children of servants shall *c.*
119. 91. *c.* according to thy word
John 8. 31. if ye *c.* in my word
15. 9. *c.* ye in my love, 10
Acts 13. 43. to *c.* in grace of God
14. 22. to *c.* in the faith
Rom. 6. 1. shall we *c.* in sin because
11. 22. if thou *c.* in his goodness
Col. 1. 23. if ye *c.* in faith and not
4. 2. *c.* in prayer and watch
1 *Tim.* 2. 15. if they *c.* in faith
4. 16. doctrine *c.* in them
2 *Tim.* 3. 14. *c.* in things learned
Heb. 13. 1. let brotherly love *c.*
Rev. 11. 5. to *c.* forty-two months
CONTINUED, ETH, *Gen.* 40. 4 ; *Neh.*
5. 16.
Luke 6. 12. *c.* all night in prayer
22. 28. *c.* with me in temptation
Acts 1. 14. *c.* with one accord in prayer
2. 42. *c.* steadfast in the apostles
doctrine and
20. 7. *c.* his speech till midnight
Heb. 8. 9. *c.* not in my covenant
1 *John* 2. 19. would have *c.* with us
Job 14. 2. shadow and *c.* not
Gal. 3. 10. that *c.* not in all things
1 *Tim.* 5. 5. *c.* in supplication and
prayer
Heb. 7. 24. this man because *c.* ever
James 1. 25. looketh into law, and *c.*
CONTINUING, *Jer.* 30. 23 ; *Rom.* 12.
12 ; *Heb.* 13. 14.
CONTRADICTING-ION, *Acts* 13. 45 ;
Heb. 7. 7. & 12. 3.
CONTRARY, opposite, inconsistent,
Esth. 9. 1 ; *Matt.* 14. 24.
Lev. 26. 21. walk *c.* to, 23, 27, 28, 40, 41.
Acts 18. 13. *c.* to the law, 23. 3.
26. 9. many things *c.* to the name of
Rom. 11. 24. graffed *c.* to nature
16. 17. *c.* to the doctrine received
Gal. 5. 17. are *c.* one to the other
1 *Thess.* 2. 15. are *c.* to all men
1 *Tim.* 1. 10. is *c.* to sound doctrine
CONTRIBUTION, *Rom.* 15. 26. *c.* for
poor saints
CONTRITE. It means, the heart broken, bruised, deeply humbled, and
affected with a sense of guilt ; sorrow for sin committed against a
God of infinite purity and goodness.
Ps. 34. 18. he saveth such as be of a *c.*
51. 17. a *c.* heart, O God, thou wilt
not despise
Is. 57. 15. with him also that is of a *c.*
and humble sprit, to revive the
heart of the *c.* ones
66. 2. that is of a *c.* spirit and trembleth at my word
CONTROVERSY. A plea, a dispute, a
debate in writing, a protracted
contest.
Jer. 25. 31. Lord a *c.* with the nations
Hos. 4. 1. the Lord hath a *c.* with inhabitants of land
12. 2. the Lord hath also a *c.* with

Judah
Mic. 6. 2. Lord a *c.* with people
1 *Tim.* 3. 16. without *c.* great is the
mystery of godliness
CONVENIENT. (1) relating to food,
Prov. 30. 8. (2) To the time of be-
traying Christ, *Mark* 14. 11. (3) To
a future and more advantageous
season, *Acts* 24. 25.
Prov. 30. 8. feed me with food *c.*
Mark 6. 21. and when a *c.* day was come
Acts 24. 25. when I have a *c.* season I
Rom. 1. 28. to do those things not *c.*
Eph. 5. 4. talking, or jesting, not *c.*
Phile. 8. bold to enjoin that which is *c.*
CONVENIENTLY, *Mark* 14. 11. Judas
sought how he might *c.* betray
CONVERSATION, *Gal.* 1. 13 ; *Eph.* 2.
3. & 4. 22 ; *Heb.* 13. 7 ; 1 *Tim.* 4. 12.
Ps. 37. 14. such as be of upright *c.*
50. 23. orders his *c.* aright I will show
2 *Cor.* 1. 12., in sincerity had our *c.*
Phil. 1. 27. let your *c.* be as it becometh
the gospel
3. 20. our *c.* in heaven, from whence
Heb. 13. 5. let *c.* be without covetousness
Jam. 3. 13. show out of good *c.* of works
1 *Pet.* 1. 15. holy in all manner of *c.*
2. 12. having *c.* honest among Gentiles
3. 1. won by chaste *c.* of wives, 2.
16. accuse your good *c.* in Christ
2 *Pet.* 2. 7. vexed with filthy *c.* of wicked
3. 11. in all holy *c.* and godliness
CONVERSION of Gentiles, *Acts* 15. 3.
CONVERT. To turn men from their
evil courses and false systems, and
incline the heart to the service of
God ; *Is.* 60. 5. To renew the
heart, and turn from the power of
sin and Satan unto God. To recover one from a sinful fall, or from
error, *Luke* 20. 32 ; *Jam.* 5. 19, 20.
CONVERT and be healed, *Is.* 6. 10.
Jam. 5. 19. err and one *c.* him, 20.
Ps. 51. 13. sinners—*c.* to thee
Is. 60. 5. abundance of sea *c.* to thee
Matt. 13. 15. should be *c.* and I heal
them
18. 3. except ye be *c.* and become as
children
Luke 22. 32. when thou art *c.* strength
Acts 3. 19. repent and be *c.* sins blotted
Ps. 19. 7. law perfect, *c.* the soul
CONVICT, convince ; (1) To persuade
one of the truth of a thing, *Acts* 18.
28 ; 1 *Cor.* 14. 24. (2) To prove one
guilty, and thoroughly persuade
him of the truth and nature of his
faults, *Jam.* 2. 9 ; *Job* 32. 12.
The Spirit convinceth men of sin,
when by applying the precepts and
threatenings of the law to their
conscience, he gives them an affecting view of the facts, nature, ag-
gravations, and fruits of their sin,
Tit. 1. 9 ; *Jude* 15.
COOK, *Gen.* 40. 17. basket was work of
a *c.*
1 *Sam.* 8. 13. he will take your daughters to be *c.*

9. 24. *c.* took up the shoulder and set it before Saul

COOL, noun, *Gen.* 3. 8. walking in the garden in the *c.* of the day

COOL, adjective, *Prov.* 17. 27. a man of understanding is of a *c.* spirit

COOL, verb, *Luke* 16. 24. dip tip of the finger and *c.* my tongue

COPPER, *Ezra* 8. 27. two vessels of fine *c.*

COPPER-SMITH, 2 *Tim.* 4. 14. Alexander the *c.-s.* did me much evil

CORAL, *Job* 28. 18. no mention of *c.* or pearls

Ezek. 27. 16. Syria was thy merchant in *c.* and agate

CORBAN, *Mark* 7. 11. it is *c.* that is to say, a gift

CORD, *Josh.* 2. 15 ; *Mic.* 2. 5.

Job 30. 11. he hath loosed my *c.*

Eccl. 4. 12. a threefold *c.* is not broken

12. 6. or ever silver *c.* be loosed

Is. 54. 2. lengthen thy *c.* and strengthen

Job 36. 8. holden in *c.* of affliction

Ps. 2. 3. cast away their *c.* from us

129. 4. cut asunder *c.* of wicked

Prov. 5. 22. holden with *c.* of his sins

Is. 5. 18. draw iniquity with *c.* of vanity

Hos. 11. 4. drew them with *c.* of a man

CORIANDER, *Ex.* 16. 31. manna was like *c.* seed, *Num.* 11. 7.

CORMORANT, *Lev.* 11. 7. ye shall have in abomination the little owl, and the *c.* and the great owl, *Deut.* 14. 17.

Is. 34. 11. but the *c.* shall possess it, *Zeph.* 2. 14.

CORN, *Gen.* 41. 57. all countries came to Joseph to buy *c.*

Gen. 42. 2. Jacob heard there was *c.* in Egypt, *Acts* 7. 12.

Deut. 16. 9. to put the sickle to *c.*

25. 4. thou shalt not muzzle the ox when he treadeth out the *c.* 1 *Cor.* 9. 9 ; 1 *Tim.* 5. 18.

Josh. 5. 11. eat of the old *c.* of the land

Job 5. 26. as a shock of *c.* cometh in his

Ps. 65. 9. preparest them *c.*

13. valleys covered with *c.*

72. 16. handful of *c.* in the earth upon

78. 24. given them *c.* of heaven to eat

Prov. 11. 26. withholdeth *c.* people curse

Is. 62. 8. no more give *c.* to enemies

Ezek. 36. 29. call for *c.* and increase it

Hos. 2. 9. take away my *c.* in time of it

10. 11. loveth to tread out the *c.*

14. 7. shall revive as the *c.* and grow

Zech. 9. 17. *c.* make young men cheerful

Matt. 12. 1. to pluck the ears of *c.*

Mark 4. 28. the full *c.* in the ear

John 12. 24. except a *c.* of wheat fall

CORN, ears of, *Ruth* 2. 2. go and glean *ears of c.*

2 *Kings* 4. 42. brought full *ears of c.*

Matt. 12. 1. to pluck *ears of c. Mark* 2. 23 ; *Luke* 6. 1.

CORN-FIELDS, *Mark* 2. 23. came to pass, that he went through *c.-fields* on the sabbath-day, *Matt.* 12. 1 ; *Luke* 6. 1.

CORN and wine, *Gen.* 27. 28. God give thee plenty of *c. and wine*

Deut. 7. 13. bless thy *c. and wine*

11. 14. that mayest gather in thy *c. and wine* and oil

18. 4. give him first-fruit of thy *c. and wine* and oil

33. 28. Jacob shall be upon a land of *c. and wine*

2 *Chr.* 32. 28. store-houses for increase of *c. and wine*

Ps. 4. 7. their *c. and wine* increased

Hos. 2. 8. I gave her *c. wine* and oil

CORNER, *Prov.* 7. 8, 12 ; *Lev.* 21. 5.

Prov. 21. 9. better dwell in *c.* 25. 24.

Is. 30. 20. teachers removed into *c.*

Zech. 10. 4. came forth the *c.*

Matt. 21. 42. become head of *c. Acts* 4. 11 ; 1 *Pet.* 2. 7.

CORNER-STONE, *Ps.* 118. 22. the head-*stone* of the *c.*

Ps. 144. 12. daughters may be as *c.-stone*

Is. 28. 16. in Zion a precious *c.-stone*, 1 *Pet.* 2. 6.

CORNERS, *Lev.* 19. 9. shalt not reap the *c.* of your field, 23. 23.

Deut. 32. 26. I will scatter them into *c.*

Job. 1. 19. wind smote the four *c.* of the

Is. 11. 12. gather dispersed of Judah from four *c.*

Matt. 6. 5. pray in the *c.* of the streets

Acts 10. 11. a great sheet knit at four *c.* 11. 5.

Rev. 7. 1. four angels standing on four *c.* of the earth

CORNET, S, *Ex.* 19. 13. when the *c.* soundeth long, come up

1 *Chr.* 15. 28. brought up the ark with sound of *c.*

Hos. 5. 8. blow ye the *c.* in Gibeah

2 *Sam.* 6. 5. David played before the Lord on *c.*

CORPSE, S, 2 *Kings* 19. 35. behold they were all dead *c. Is.* 37. 36.

Nah. 3. 3. there is no end of *c.* they stumble on *c.*

Mark 6. 29. disciples took John's *c.* and laid it in tomb

CORPULENT, *Jer.* 50. 11. grown *c.* as a heifer

CORRECT thy son and he, *Prov.* 29. 17.

Ps. 39. 11. with rebukes dost *c.* man for

94. 10. chastiseth heathen not *c.* thee

Jer. 2. 19. own wickedness shall *c.* thee

10. 24. *c.* me but with judgment

30. 11. *c.* in measure, 46. 28.

Job 5. 17. happy the man whom God *c.*

Prov. 3. 12. whom the Lord loveth he *c.*

Job. 37. 13. whether for *c.*

Prov. 3. 11. be not weary of his *c.*

22. 15. rod of *c.* shall drive foolishness

23. 13. withhold not *c.* from the child

Jer. 2. 30. they received not *c.* 5. 3. & 7. 28 ; *Zeph.* 3. 2.

Hab. 1. 12. established them for *c.*

2 *Tim.* 3. 16. scripture profitable for *c.*

CORRUPT, *Job* 17. 1 ; *Ps.* 38. 5.

Gen. 6. 11. 12. earth *c.* before God

Ps. 14. 1. they are *c.* 53. 1. & 73. 8.

Mal. 1. 14. sacrificeth to God a *c.* thing

Matt. 7. 17. 18. *c.* tree brings—fruit

12. 33. make tree *c.* and fruit *c.*

Eph. 4. 22. old man which is *c.*

29. let no *c.* communication proceed

1 *Tim.* 6. 5. of *c.* minds, 2 *Tim.* 3. 8.

CORRUPT, verb, *Matt.* 6. 19. rust doth c. 20.
1 *Cor.* 15. 33. evil communications c. good manners
2 *Cor.* 2. 17. as many who c. word
Jude 10. those they c. themselves

CORRUPTED, ETH, *Gen.* 6. 12. all flesh had c. his way
Ex. 8. 24. the land was c.
Deut. 9. 12. thy people c. themselves, 32. 5.
Judg. 2. 19. c. themselves more than their fathers
Hos. 9. 9. have deeply c. themselves
Zeph. 3. 7. they rose early and c. all their doings
Luke 12. 33. where no thief approacheth, nor moth c.
2 *Cor.* 7. 2. we have c. no man
11. 3. lest your minds be c. from simplicity in Christ
Jam. 5. 1. 2. your riches are c.

CORRUPTERS, *Is.* 1. 4. children that are c.
Jer. 6. 28. they are all c.

CORRUPTIBLE, *Rom.* 1. 23. changed to an image, made like c.
1 *Cor.* 9. 25. to obtain a c. crown
15. 53. c. must put on incorruption
1 *Pet.* 1. 18. not redeemed with c. things
23. not of c. seed, but incorruptible

CORRUPTION, *Job* 17. 14 ; *Ps.* 16. 10. & 49. 9 ; *Is.* 38. 17 ; *Dan.* 10. 8 ; *Jonah* 2. 6 ; *Acts* 2. 27, 31. & 13. 34, 37 ; *Rom.* 8. 21 ; 1 *Cor.* 15. 42, 50 ; *Gal.* 6. 8 ; 2 *Pet.* 1. 4. & 2. 12, 19.

COST, 2 *Sam.* 19. 42 ; 24. 24 ; 1 *Chr.* 21. 24.
Luke 14. 28. sit. not down, counteth c.

COSTLY, 1 *Kings* 5. 17. they brought c. stones
1 *Kings* 7. 9. all these were of c. stones
10. foundations were of c. stones, even great stones
11. and above were c. stones
John 12. 3. Mary took a pound of spikenard very c.
1 *Tim.* 2. 9. that women adorn themselves not with c. array

COTTAGE, S, *Isa.* 1. 8. daughter of Zion is left as a c. in a vineyard
Is. 24. 20. the earth removed like a c.

COUCH, ES, *Gen.* 49. 4. Reuben went up to my c.
Job 7. 13. my c. ease my complaint
Ps. 6. 6. all night I water my c. with my tears
Amos 6. 4. stretch themselves upon their c.
Luke 5. 19. let him down through tiling with his c.
24. arise, take up thy c. and go into thy house

COUCHED, *Gen.* 49. 9. Judah c. as a lion
Num. 24. 9. he c. lay down as a lion

COUCHING, *Gen.* 49. 14. Issachar c. down between two burdens

COULTER, S, 1 *Sam.* 13. 20. to sharpen each his c.
1 *Sam.* 13. 21. they had a file for their c.

COUNCIL, *Matt.* 5. 22. Raca, shall be in danger of c.

Matt. 26. 59. the c. sought false witness, *Mark* 14. 55.
Mark 15. 1. whole c. bound Jesus and carried him away
Luke 22. 66. the elders led Jesus into their c.
Acts 5. 27. they brought and set them before the c.
41. departed from c. rejoicing
6. 12. Stephen brought him to the c.
15. all in the c. looking on him

COUNSEL, (1) Advice, *Prov.* 20. 18 ; *Dan.* 4. 27. (2) God's purpose and decree, *Acts* 4. 28. (3) The directions of his word, the motions of his spirit, and the kindness of his providence, *Ps.* 73. 24. (4) His will or doctrine concerning the way of salvation, *Luke* 7. 30 ; *Acts* 20. 27. (5) The designs, thoughts, and most secret resolutions, 1 *Cor.* 4. 5.

Christ Jesus is called Counsellor, Is. 9. 6. (1) On account of his infinite wisdom, *Col.* 2. 3. (2) On account of his willingness to instruct and give counsel to men ; as also, to plead their cause before his throne, *Rev.* 3. 18 ; 1 *John* 2. 1.

COUNSEL, *Num.* 27. 21. & 31. 16.
2 *Sam.* 16. 23 so was all the c. of Ahithophel with David
17. 14. the Lord defeated the good c. of Ahithophel
Neh. 4. 15. God hath brought their c. to nought
Job 5. 13. c. of forward carried headlong
12. 13. he hath c. and understanding
21. 16. c. of wicked far from me, 22. 18.
38. 2. who this that darkeneth c. by words without knowledge, 42. 3.
Ps. 1. 1. walketh not in c. of ungodly
16. 7. bless Lord who hath given me c.
33. 10. 11. c. of Lord stands for ever, *Prov.* 19. 21 ; *Is.* 46. 10, 11.
55. 14. we took sweet c. together
73. 24. guide me by thy c. afterwards
83. 3. taken crafty c. against people
Prov. 1. 25. set at nought all my c.
8. 14. c. is mine and sound wisdom
11. 14. where no c. is people fall
20. 18. purpose established by c.
21. 30. no wisdom nor c. against Lord
24. 6. by wise c. make war
27. 9. sweetness—by hearty c.
Is. 11. 2. spirit of c. and might
28. 29. Lord wonderful in c. and excel.
40. 14. with whom took he c.
44. 26. performs c. of his messengers
Jer. 32. 19. God great in c. mighty
Zech. 6. 13. c. of peace between them
Matt. 12. 14. the Pharisees held a c. against him
27. 7. they took c. and bought the potter's field
Luke 7. 30. rejected c. of God against
Acts 2. 23. by determinate c. 4. 28.
4. 28. thy c. determined before done
5. 33. heard, they took c. to slay them
5. 38. if this c. be of men it will
20. 27. to declare all the c. of God
Eph. 1. 11. after c. of his own will
Heb. 6. 17. the immutability of his c.

COUNSEL, my, *Ps.* 119. 24. thy testimonies are the men of *my c.*
Prov. 1. 25. set at nought all *my c.*
30. they would none of *my c.*
Is. 46. 10. *my c.* shall stand
Jer. 23. 22. if they had stood in *my c.*
Dan. 4. 27. O king, let *my c.* be acceptable to thee

COUNSEL, take, *Neh.* 6. 7. and let us *take c.* together
Ps. 2. 2. rulers *take c.* against Lord and anointed
Is. 8. 10. *take c.* and it shall come to nought

COUNSEL, ED, 2 *Sam.* 16. 23. which Ahithophel *c.*
2 *Sam.* 17. 7. Ahithophel hath *c.* is not
15. thus Ahithophel *c.* thus I *c.* 21.
Ps. 32. 8. I will *c.* thee, mine eyes
Rev. 3. 18. I *c.* thee to buy of me gold

COUNSELLORS, *Ezra* 4. 5. & 7. 14 ; *Job* 3. 14. & 12. 17 ; *Dan.* 3. 24.
Ps. 119. 24. thy testimonies are my *c.*
Prov. 11. 14. in multitude of *c.* is safety, 15. 22.
12. 20. to *c.* of peace is joy
Is. 1. 26. restore thy *c.* as at beginning
9. 6. wonderful C. mighty G.
19. 11. wise *c.* of Pharaoh—brutish

COUNSELS, *Ps.* 5. 10. let them fall by their own *c.*
Ps. 81. 12. walked in their own *c.*
Prov. 1. 5. man of understanding shall attain to wise *c.*
12. 5. *c.* of the wicked are deceit
1 *Cor.* 4. 5. manifest the *c.* of the heart

COUNT, *Ex.* 12. 4 ; *Lev.* 23. 15.
Num. 23. 10. who can *c.* the dust of Jacob
Job 31. 4. doth not he *c.* all my steps
Ps. 139. 18. if I *c.* them—more than
22. hate them I *c.* them my enemies
Acts 20. 24. neither *c.* I my life dear to
Phil. 3. 7, 8, 9. I *c.* all things loss—dung
13. I *c.* not myself to have apprehen.
Jam. 1. 2. *c.* it all joy when ye fall
5. 11. we *c.* them happy who endure

COUNTED, *Gen.* 15. 6. *c.* to him for righteousness, *Ps.* 106. 31 ; *Rom.* 4. 3.
Is. 40. 17. *c.* to him less than nothing
Hos. 8. 12. of law *c.* as a strange thing
Luke 21. 36. *c.* worthy to escape
Acts 5. 41. that *c.* worthy to suffer
2 *Thess.* 1. 5. *c.* worthy of the kingdom
1 *Tim.* 1. 12. he *c.* me faithful putting
5. 17. *c.* worthy of double honour
Heb. 3. 3. *c.* worthy of more glory
10. 29. *c.* blood of covenant unholy

COUNTENANCE, (1) The face or visage, 1 *Sam.* 16. 7. (2) Love, favour, and affection, *Gen.* 31. 5. (3) Brightness, festivity, or alacrity, *Dan.* 5. 6. (4) God's love and favour, manifested by the graces and benefits which he bestows upon his people, *Ps.* 4. 6. Because men by their countenance discover their anger, or love ; hence it is, that when it is attributed to God, who is said sometimes to lift up the light of his countenance upon his people, at other times to hide his face, or

countenance, it signifies either his grace and favour, or his anger, or displeasure.
Gen. 4. 5. Cain wrath, his *c.* fell
31. 2. Jacob beheld the *c.* of Laban
5. your father's *c.* is not toward me
Num. 6. 26. lift up his *c.* on thee
Judg. 13. 6. and *c.* was like angel
1 *Sam.* 1. 18. her *c.* no more sad
16. 7. look not on his *c.* or height
12. David was of a beautiful *c.* 17. 42
Neh. 2. 2. why is thy *c.* sad
Job 14. 20. thou changest his *c.*
29. 24. light of my *c.* cast
Ps. 4. 6. lift up light of thy *c.* 80. 3, 7.
Ps. 10. 4. the wicked, through pride of *c.*
42. 5. I shall yet praise him for the help of his *c.*
11. who is the health of my *c.*
89. 15. walk, O L. in the light of thy *c.*
90. 8. hast set our secret sins in the light of thy *c.*
Prov. 15. 13. a merry heart maketh a cheerful *c.*
27. 17. sharpeneth the *c.* of his friend
Eccl. 7. 3. by sadness of *c.* the heart is made better
Songs 2. 14. see thy *c.* comely
Matt. 6. 16. hypocrites of a sad *c.*
Matt. 28. 3. his *c.* was like lightning, *Luke* 9. 29.
Acts 2. 28. full of joy with thy *c.*
Rev. 1. 16. *c.* was as the sun shineth

COUNTRY, far, *Prov.* 25. 25. good news from a *far c.*
Jer. 8. 19. of them that dwell in a *far c.*
Matt. 21. 33. household went into a *far c. Mark* 12. 1.
25. 14. kingdom of heaven is as a man travelling into *far c.*
Luke 15. 13. younger son took his journey into *far c.*

COUNTRY, own, 1 *Kings* 22. 36. a proclamation every man to his *own c.*
Matt. 2. 12. departed into their *own c.*
Mark 6. 1. and came into his *own c.*
John 4. 44. a prophet hath no honour in his *own c.*

COUNTRYMEN, 2 *Cor.* 11. 26 ; 1 *Thess.* 2. 14.

COUPLED, 1 *Pet.* 3. 2. your chaste conversation *c.* with fear

COURAGE, *Josh.* 2. 11 ; *Acts* 28. 15. *Deut.* 7. 23 ; *Josh.* 1. 6, 7, 9, 18. & 10. 25. & 23. 6 ; 2 *Sam.* 10. 12 ; 1 *Chr.* 22. 13. & 28. 20 ; *Ezra* 10. 4 ; *Is.* 41. 6.

COURAGE, good, *Num.* 13. 20. be ye of *good c.*
Deut. 31. 6. be strong, and of *good c.*
Ps. 27. 14. wait on Lord, be of *good c.* and he shall strengthen thine heart, wait on Lord, 31. 24.

COURAGEOUS, *Josh.* 1. 7. be thou strong and *c.* 23. 6 ; 2 *Chr.* 32. 7.
2 *Sam.* 13. 28. fear not, be *c.* and be valiant
Amos 2. 16. he that is *c.* among mighty shall flee away

COURSE, *Acts* 13. 25. & 16. 11.
Acts 20. 24. finish my *c.* with joy
Eph. 2. 2. according to *c.* of this world

2 *Thess.* 3. 1. may have free *c.*

2 *Tim.* 4. 7. I have finished my *c.*

COURT, In Hebrew Chazer, is an entrance into a palace or house, *Esth.* 6. 4, 5. The great courts belonging to the temple were three ; the first called the court of the Gentiles, because the Gentiles were allowed to enter so far and no farther. The second called the court of Israel, because all the Israelites, if purified, had a right of admission. The third court was that of the Priests, where the altar of burnt-offerings stood and where the Priests and Levites exercised their ministry. It signifies the church of Christ, *Zech.* 3. 7. Also the false church, *Rev.* 11. 2.

Ex. 27. 9, thou shalt make the court of the tabernacle, shall be hangings for the *c.* 13 ; 18. length of the *c.*

2 *Chr.* 24. 21. they stoned Zechariah in *c.* of Lord's house

Esth. 5. 1. Esther stood in the inner *c.* of king's house

Is. 34. 13. habitation of dragons, and a *c.* for owls

Jer. 19. 14. Jeremiah stood in the *c.* of Lord's house

Ezek. 8. 7. brought me to the door of *c.*

   10. 3. the man went in the cloud filled the inner *c.*

   40. 17. he brought me into outward *c.* 42. 1 ; 46. 21.

   43. 5. the Spirit brought me into the inner *c.*

Amos 7. 13. Beth-el is king's *c.*

COURTS, *Ps.* 65. 4. may dwell in thy *c.*

   84. 10. day in thy *c.* is better

   92. 13. flourish in *c.* of our God

   100. 4. enter his *c.* with praise

Is. 1. 12. required to tread my *c.*

   62. 9. drink it in *c.* of my holiness

Luke 7. 25. delicate are in king's *c.*

Rev. 11. 2. *c.* without temple

COURTEOUS, 1 *Pet.* 3. 8. love as brethren, be pitiful, be *c.*

COURTEOUSLY, *Acts* 27. 3. & 28. 7.

COURTIER, *John* 4. 46. there was a certain *c.* whose son was

COUSIN, *Luke* 1. 36. thy *c.* Elisabeth hath conceived a son

COUSINS, *Luke* 1. 58. her neighbours and *c.* heard how Lord

COVENANT. An agreement to do some particular thing. The promise to Noah that the waters should no more destroy the earth, is called a covenant ; *Gen.* 9. 9, 17. God also made a covenant with Abraham, that he should have a numerous seed, &c., *Gen.* 16. 2, 9. The law given on Mount Sinai was another covenant, *Deut.* 4. 13. The covenant of redemption and salvation by grace, is called a *new* and *better* covenant, *Heb.* 8. 6, 8. in respect to its dispensation, and manner of manifestation ; its being ratified by the actual sufferings and blood of Christ, and freed from former ceremonies ; its containing

a more full revelation of religion, and being attended with a larger measure of the gifts and graces of the Spirit, while it is never to wax old, or to be abolished.

COVENANT, *Gen.* 17. 2. & 26. 28.

Gen. 9. 12. token of the *c.* 13. 17.

   17. 4. my *c.* is with thee, 7. 19.

   11. a token of the *c.* betwixt

   13. my *c.* shall be in the flesh

   14. he hath broken my *c.*

Ex. 2. 24. God remembered his *c.* with Abraham

   31. 16. sabbath for a perpetual *c.*

   34. 27. wrote words of *c.*

Lev. 26. 15. ye break my *c.*

Judg. 2. 1. never break *c.* with you

1 *Chr.* 16. 15. alway mindful of his *c.* *Ps.* 111. 5. & 105. 8.

Neh. 9. 38. we make a sure *c.*

Job 31. 1. I made a *c.* with mine eyes

Ps. 25. 14. Lord will show them his *c.*

   44. 17. nor dealt falsely in thy *c.*

   50. 5. made a *c.* by sacrifice

   55. 20. broken his *c.* *Is.* 33. 8.

   74. 20. have respect to the *c.*

   78. 37. not steadfast in his *c.* 10.

   89. 3. made a *c.* with my chosen

   132. 12. children will keep my *c.*

Prov. 2. 17. forgetteth the *c.* of her God

Is. 28. 18. your *c.* with death

   42. 6. thee for *c.* of people, 49. 8.

   54. 10. nor *c.* of my peace be removed

   56. 4. take hold of my *c.* 6.

Jer. 14. 21. break not *c.* with us

   31. 31. make a new *c.* with Israel

   50. 5. to Lord in a perpetual *c.*

Ezek. 20. 37. bring into bond of *c.*

Dan. 9. 27. confirm *c.* with many

Hos. 6. 7. have transgressed the *c.*

   10. 4. swearing falsely in making *c.*

Mal. 2. 14. the wife of thy *c.*

   3. 1. messenger of the *c.*

Acts 3. 25. the children of the *c.*

Rom. 1. 34. *c.* breakers, 2 *Tim.* 3. 3.

Heb. 8. 6. mediator of a better *c.* 7. 9.

COVENANT, Everlasting, *Gen.* 9. 16 ; 17. 7 ; 13. 19 ; *Lev.* 24. 8 ; 2 *Sam.* 23. 5 ; 1 *Chr.* 16. 17 ; *Ps.* 105. 10 ; *Is.* 24. 5. & 55. 3. & 61. 8 ; *Jer.* 32. 40 ; *Ezek.* 16. 60. & 37. 26 ; *Heb.* 13. 20.

COVENANT, Keep, keepest, keepeth, *c. Gen.* 17. 9, 10 ; *Ex.* 19. 5 ; *Deut.* 7. 9, 12. & 29. 9. & 33. 9 ; 1 *Kings* 8. 23. & 11. 11 ; 2 *Chr.* 6. 14 ; *Neh.* 1. 5. & 9. 32 ; *Ps.* 25. 10. & 103. 18. & 132. 12 ; *Dan.* 9. 4.

COVENANT, made, *Gen.* 15. 18. Lord made *c. Ex.* 34. 27 ; *Deut.* 5. 2, 3 ; 2 *Kings* 23. 3 ; *Job* 31. 1.

Jer. 31. 31. new *c. Heb.* 8. 8, 13. & 12. 24.

COVENANT, remember, *Gen.* 9. 15 ; *Ex.* 6. 5 ; *Lev.* 26. 42, 45 ; *Ps.* 105. 8. & 106. 45 ; *Ezek.* 16. 60 ; *Amos* 1. 9 ; *Luke* 1. 72.

Lev. 2. 13. *c.* of salt, *Num.* 18. 19 ; 2 *Chr.* 13. 5.

Deut. 17. 2. transgressed the *c. Josh.* 7. 11. 15. & 23. 16 ; *Judg.* 2. 20 ; 2 *Kings* 18. 12 ; *Jer.* 34. 18 ; *Hos.* 6. 7. & 8. 1.

Rom. 9. 4. and the *c. Gal.* 4. 24.
Eph. 2. 12. *c.* of promise
COVER, *Ex.* 10. 5. & 40. 3.
Ex. 21. 33. dig a pit and not *c.* it
    33. 22. *c.* thee with my hand
Deut. 33. 12. Lord shall *c.* him day
1 *Sam.* 24. 3. *c.* his feet, *Judg.* 3. 24.
Neh. 4. 5. *c.* not their iniquity
Job 16. 18. *c.* thou not my blood and
Ps. 91. 4. *c.* thee with his feathers
    139. 11. if I say, surely the darkness
        shall *c.* me
Is. 11. 9. as the waters *c.* the sea *Hab.*
    2. 14.
    58. 7. naked that thou *c.* him
    60. 2. for darkness shall *c.* the earth
Ezek. 7. 18. horror shall *c.* them
    32. 7. I will *c.* the heaven. I will *c.*
        the sun
Hos. 10. 8. say to mountains *c.* us, *Luke*
    23. 30 ; *Rev.* 6. 16.
Mark 14. 65. some began to spit on him
    and *c.* his face
1 *Cor.* 11. 7. man ought not to *c.* head
1 *Pet.* 4. 8. charity shall *c.* multitude
COVERED, *Gen.* 9. 23. they *c.* the
    nakedness of their father
    38. 14. Tamar *c.* her with a vail
Ex. 15. 10. the sea *c.* them, they sank
    as lead, *Josh.* 24. 7.
1 *Kings* 8. 7. cherubims *c.* ark, 1 *Chr.*
    28. 18 ; 2 *Chr.* 5. 8.
2 *Chr.* 3. 6. Solomon *c.* house with
    precious stones
Job 31. 33. if I *c.* my transgressions
Ps. 32. 1. whose sin is *c. Rom.* 4. 7.
Ps. 44. 19. though thou hast *c.* us with
    the shadow of death
    65. 13. the valleys *c.* with corn
    68. 13. shall be as the wings of a dove
    c. with silver
    85. 2. hast *c.* all their sin
Eccl. 6. 4. his name shall be *c.* with
    darkness
Is. 6. 2. with twain he *c.* his face, he *c.*
    his feet
    25. 7. will destroy the *c.* cast over
        all people
    61. 10. he *c.* me with the robe of
        righteousness
Lam. 3. 44. *c.* thyself with a cloud
Ezek. 37. 8. the flesh came up, and skin
    c. them above
Jonah 3. 6. the king of Nineveh *c.* with
    sackcloth
Hab. 3. 3. God came, his glory *c.* the
    heavens
Matt. 8. 24. the ship was *c.* with the
    10. 26. there is nothing *c.* that shall
        not be revealed, and hid that shall
        not be known, *Luke* 12. 2.
COVERED, sin or sins, *Ps.* 32. 1. blessed
    is he whose *sin* is *c.*
Ps. 85. 2. hast *c.* all their *sins*
COVEREST, *Ps.* 104. 2. *c.* thyself with
    light
COVERETH, *Ps.* 73. 6. violence *c.* thee
    as a garment
Prov. 10. 12. love *c.* all sins, *Jam.* 5. 20.
    28. 13. *c.* his sins—not prosper
COVERING, *Gen.* 8. 13. Noah removed
    the *c.* of the ark

2 *Sam.* 17. 19. woman spread a *c.* over
    well's mouth
Job 22. 14. thick clouds are a *c.* to him
    that seeth not
    24..7. naked have no *c.* in cold
    31. 19. if seen any poor without *c.*
Is. 4. 5. upon glory shall be a *c.*
1 *Cor.* 11. 15. glory to her, for her hair
    is given her for a *c.*
COVERING, *Ezek.* 28. 16. I will destroy
    thee, O *c.* cherub
COVERINGS, *Prov.* 7. 16. decked my
    bed with *c.* of tapestry
Prov. 31. 22. she maketh herself *c.* of
    tapestry
COVERT, (1) An umbrage, or shady
    place, 1 *Sam.* 25. 20. (2) A thicket
    for wild beasts, *Job* 38. 40. (3)
    Something made to shelter the
    people from the weather on the
    sabbath ; or some costly chair of
    state, wherein the king of Judah
    used to hear the priests expound
    the law on the sabbath, 2 *Kings* 16.
    18. (4) Christ Jesus, the saints'
    shelter, defence, or refuge, *Is.* 32. 2.
1 *Sam.* 25. 20. Abigail came down by
    c. of the hill
Job 38. 40. when lions abide in the *c.*
    to lie in wait
Ps. 61. 4. I will trust in the *c.* of thy
    wings
Is. 4. 6. a *c.* from storm and rain
    32. 2. a man shall be a *c.* from
COVET. This word is sometimes taken
    in a good sense, as in 1 *Cor.* 12. 31.
    ' Covet earnestly the best gifts.' This
    covetousness is good and commen-
    dable, when spiritual blessings are
    earnestly desired and sought after.
    But most commonly it is taken in
    a bad sense, for an eager and im-
    moderate desire after earthly
    things, *Josh.* 7. 21 ; *Prov.* 21. 26.
    Coveteousness is called idolatry,
    Col. 3. 5. because the covetous
    man places that love, delight, and
    confidence in riches, which are due
    to God alone. This sin is condemn-
    ed in all sorts of persons, and is
    expressly forbidden by the tenth
    commandment, Thou shalt not
    covet, *Ex.* 20. 17. Such as are ad-
    dicted to this sin, are hated of God,
    Ps. 10. 3. They are cruel and op-
    pressive, *Mic.* 2. 2. The riches
    they are so eager in the pursuit of,
    prove but poison to kill them, and
    thus they are miserable, *Job* 20. 15.
    16, 17 ; *Prov.* 1. 19. The inordinate
    love of wealth does likewise betray
    men to manifold sins, and exposes
    them to manifold sufferings ; both
    from themselves, in denying them-
    selves the comfort of their estates ;
    and from others, as extortioners,
    thieves, and the like, *Deut.* 16. 19 ;
    Eccl. 4. 8 ; *Matt.* 26. 15 ; 1 *Tim.* 6.
    10.
COVET, *Ex.* 20. 17 ; *Mic.* 2. 2.
1 *Cor.* 12. 3'. *c.* earnestly best
    14. 39. *c.* to prophesy and

COVETED, *Josh.* 7. 21. Achan said, then I *c.* them, took them
Acts 20. 33. *c.* no man's silver or gold
1 *Tim.* 6. 10. which while some *c.* after they heard
COVETETH, *Prov.* 21. 26 ; *Hab.* 2. 9.
COVETOUS, *Ps.* 10. 3. wicked blesseth *c.*
Luke 16. 14. Pharisees who were *c.*
1 *Cor.* 5. 10. or with the *c.* 11.
6. 10. nor *c.* shall inherit kingdom of
Eph. 5. 5. nor *c.* who is an idolater
1 *Tim.* 3. 3. bishop must not be *c.*
2 *Tim.* 3. 2. in last days *c.* boasters
2 *Pet.* 2. 14. exercised with *c.* practices
COVETOUSNESS, *Ex.* 18. 21. hating *c.*
Ps. 119. 36. to testimonies and not *c.*
Prov. 28. 16. hateth *c.* shall prolong days
Is. 57. 17. for his *c.* was I wroth
Jer. 6. 13. every one is given to *c.*
Ezek. 33. 31. heart goeth after their *c.*
Mark 7. 22. out of the heart proceedeth *c.*
Luke 12. 15. beware of *c.* for man's life
Rom. 1. 29. being filled with all *c.*
Col. 3. 5. *c.* which is idolatry
1 *Thess.* 2. 5. nor used we a cloak of *c.*
Heb. 13. 5. conversation be without *c.*
CRAFT, *Dan.* 8. 25 ; *Mark* 14. 1 ; *Acts* 18. 3. & 19. 25, 27 ; *Rev.* 18. 22.
Job 5. 12. disappointed devices of *c.*
15. 5. choosest tongue of *c.*
Ps. 83. 3. taken *c.* counsel against
2 *Cor.* 12. 16. being *c.* I caught
CRAFTINESS, *Job* 5. 13 ; 1 *Cor.* 3. 19 ; *Luke* 20. 23 ; 2 *Cor.* 4. 3 ; *Eph.* 4. 14.
CRANE, *Is.* 38. 14. like a *c.* did I chatter
Jer. 8. 7. *c.* and swallow observe the time of coming
CRAVED, *Mark* 15. 43. Joseph *c.* the body of Jesus
CREATE, (1) To make out of nothing, to bring being out of non-entity, *Gen.* 1. 1. (2) To change the form, state, and situation of matter, which is wholly indisposed for such a change, and requires as great power as to make out of nothing, *Gen.* 1. 21 ; 2. 19. (3) To give and work grace where it is not, *Eph.* 2. 10. (4) To cleanse the heart more and more from its natural corruption by the power of sanctifying grace, *Ps.* 51. 10.
CREATE, *Gen.* 1. 1 ; 21. 27. & 2. 3.
Ps. 51. 10. *c.* in me a clean heart
Is. 4. 5. *c.* upon every dwelling place
45. 7. I form light and *c.* darkness, I make peace and *c.* evil
57. 19. I *c.* the fruits of the lips peace
65. 17. I *c.* new heaven and new earth
18. rejoice in what I *c.* I *e.* Jerusalem
CREATED, *Gen.* 1. 1. in the beginning God *c.* heaven and earth
Gen. 1. 27. so God *c.* man in his own image, in the image of God, male and female *c.* he them, 5. 2.
102. 18. people which shall be *c.* shall praise Lord
104. 30. sendest thy Spirit, they are *c.*
148. 5. commanded and they were *c.*
40. 26. behold who hath *c.* these things
42. 5. saith Lord, he that *c.* the heavens
Is. 43. 7. I have *c.* him for my glory
45. 18. established it, *c.* not it in vain
54. 16. I have *c.* the smith, I have *c.* the waster
Jer. 31. 22. *c.* a new thing in earth
Mal. 2. 10. hath not one God *c.* us
1 *Cor.* 11. 9. neither was the man *c.* for the woman
Eph. 2. 10. *c.* in Christ Jesus unto good
3. 9. *c.* all things by Christ Jesus
4. 24. after God is *c.* in righteousness
Col. 1. 16. all things were *c.* by him
3. 10. image of him that *c.* him
1 *Tim.* 4. 3. which God *c.* to be received
Rev. 4. 11. hast *c.* all—are and were *c.*
10. 6. *c.* heaven and things therein
CREATETH, *Amos.* 4. 13. *c.* the wind
CREATION, *Mark* 10. 6. from the *c.* God made male
Mark 13. 19. as was not from the beginning of the *c.*
Rom. 1. 20. things of him from the *c.* are clearly seen
8. 22. the whole *c.* groaneth
2 *Pet.* 3. 4. things continue as they were from the *c.*
Rev. 3. 14. the Amen, the beginning of the *c.* of God
CREATOR, *Rom.* 1. 25. served the creature more than the Creator
Eccl. 12. 1. remember thy C. in days
Is. 40. 28. C. of ends of earth
43. 15. Lord—C. of Israel your King
1 *Pet.* 4. 19. as unto a faithful C.
CREATURE, S, *Gen.* 1. 20 ; *Lev.* 11. 46.
Mark 16. 15. preach the gospel to every *c.*
Rom. 8. 20. *c.* was subject to vanity
19. *c.* waiteth, 21. *c.* be delivered
2 *Cor.* 5. 17. man in Christ is a new *c.*
Gal. 6. 15. availeth—but a new *c.*
Col. 1. 15. first-born of every *c.*
1 *Tim.* 4. 4. every *c.* of God is good
Heb. 4. 13. nor any *c.* not manifest
CREATURES, *Is.* 13. 21 ; *James* 1. 18.
Ezek. 1. 5, 19. living *c.* 3. 13 ; *Rev.* 4. 6, 9. & 5. 6 ; 11. 14.
CREDITOR, *Deut.* 15. 2. every *c.* that lendeth
1 *Sam.* 22. 2. every one that had a *c.* went to David
Luke 7. 41. a certain *c.* who had two debtors
CREDITORS, *Is.* 50. 1. to which of my *c.* have I sold you ?
CREEK, *Acts* 27. 39. they discovered a certain *c.*
CREEP, *Lev.* 11. 31. these are unclean to you among all that *c.*
Ps. 104. 20. the beasts of the forest do *c.* forth
2 *Tim.* 3. 6. of this sort are they who *c.* into houses
Jude 4. *c.* in unawares
CREEPETH, *Gen.* 1. 25. God made every thing that *c.* on earth. 26.
Gen. 1. 30. have given to every thing *c.* herb for
7. 8. every thing that *c.* went in

Lev. 11. 41. every creeping thing that *c.* on the earth shall be an abomin-

CREEPING, *Gen.* 1. 26. let them have dominion over every *c.* thing

Gen. 7. 14. every *c.* thing after his kind went into the ark

Ps. 104. 25. in the sea are *c.* things innumerable

Ezek. 8. 10. *c.* things pourtrayed on wall

Acts 10. 12. Peter saw *c.* things and

Rom. 1. 23. into an image made like to *c.* things

CREPT, *Jude* 4. for there are certain men *c.* in unawares

CREW, *Matt.* 26. 74. I know not the man. and immediately the cock *c.*

Mark. 14. 68 ; *Luke* 22. 60.

Mark 14. 72. the second time the cock *c. John* 19. 27.

CRIB, a stall for cattle ; *Prov.* 14. 4 ; *Is.* 1. 3.

CRIME, a fault that deserves punishment ; *Job* 31. 11 ; *Ezek.* 7. 23.

CRIPPLE, *Acts* 14. 8. being a *c.* from his mother's womb

CRISPING-PINS, *Is.* 3. 22. Lord will take away the mantles and *c.*

CROOKED generation ; *Deut.* 32. 5.

Ps. 125. 5. aside to their *c.* ways

Prov. 2. 15. whose ways are *c.*

Eccl. 1. 15. that which is *c.* cannot be made straight ; 7. 13.

Is. 40. 4. *c.* shall be made straight ; 45. 2. & 42. 16 ; *Luke* 3. 5.

59. 8. made *c.* paths ; *Lam.* 3. 9.

Phil. 2. 15. in midst of *c.* generation

CROP, PED, *Lev.* 1. 16. shall pluck away his *c.* with his feathers

Ezek. 17. 22. I will *c.* off from the top of his twigs ; *Ezek.* 17. 4.

CROSS. A gibbet made of two pieces of wood put across at the top, like a T, or like an X. The cross was the punishment of the vilest slaves. The Redeemer was subjected to it. Christ says, That every one who would be his disciple, must take up his cross, and follow him ; *Matt.* 16. 24. He must submit readily to whatsoever afflictions God lays upon him, or any suffering that befalls him in the service of God, even to death itself. Cross is taken for the whole of Christ's sufferings, from his birth to his death, but especially those upon the tree, *Eph.* 2. 16 ; *Heb.* 12. 2. And for the doctrine of the gospel ; that is, of salvation through Christ crucified, *Gal.* 5. 11.

To crucify also implies the subduing and mortifying of sin ; for breaking the strength, and suppressing the motions and breakings out of corrupt nature, *Gal.* 5. 24. They that are Christ's have crucified the flesh. Christ's death on the cross has not only merited reconciliation with God, but is also made effectual to mortify and subdue the lusts of the flesh, *Gal.* 2. 20. I am crucified with Christ. It

is said of them who make a profession of religion, and afterwards turn apostates, that they crucify to themselves the Son of God afresh, *Heb.* 6. 6. that is, they show themselves to be of the same opinion with those that did crucify Christ, and would do it again, were it in their power.

The apostle tells the Galatians, that Christ Jesus had been evidently set forth, crucified among them, *Gal.* 3. 1. They had been as fully and clearly informed of the nature and design of Christ's sufferings, as if all had been transacted in their sight.

Matt. 10. 38. takes not up his *c.* and follows, *Luke* 14. 27.

16. 24. deny himself, take up his *c.* and follow me, *Mark* 8. 34 ; 10. 21 ; *Luke* 9. 23.

27. 32. they found Simon, him they compelled to bear his *c. Mark* 15. 21 ; *Luke* 23. 26.

40. saying, if thou be the Son of God, come down from the *c.* 42 ; *Mark* 15. 30, 32.

John 19. 17. he bearing the *c.* went forth

19. Pilate wrote title, put it on *c.*

25. by the *c.* of Jesus his mother

1 *Cor.* 1. 17. lest the *c.* of Christ be

18. preaching of *c.* is to them foolishness

Gal. 5. 11. then is offence of *c.* ceased

6. 12. suffer persecution for *c.* of

14. glory save in *c.* of Lord Jesus

Eph. 2. 16. reconcile both in one body by the *c.*

Phil. 2. 8. obedient to death of *c.*

3. 18. they are enemies of *c.* of Christ

Col. 1. 20. peace through blood of his *c.*

2. 14. took—nailing it to his *c.*

Heb. 12. 2. for joy—endured the *c.*

CROUCH, 1 *Sam.* 2. 36. *c.* to him for a piece

CROUCHETH, *Ps.* 10. 10. he *c.* and humbleth

CROWN. A cap of state, worn on the heads of sovereign princes, 1 *Chr.* 20. 2. Figuratively, it signifies honour, splendour, or dignity ; *Lam.* 5. 16. The crown is fallen from our head. And the apostle says of the Philippians, that they were his joy and crown, *Phil.* 4. 1. They were his honour and glory, the great ornament of his ministry, by means whereof they had been converted to Christ. It implies reward, because conquerors in the public games were crowned, 1 *Cor.* 9. 25 ; " They do it to obtain a corruptible crown, but we an incorruptible ; " that is, the wrestlers in those games which are practised among you, contend in order to obtain a wreath, or garland of flowers, of herbs, or leaves of laurel, olive and the like ; but we Christians strive for an inheritance incorruptible, undefiled, and that fadeth not away, reserved in heaven for us. St. John, speaking of Christ governing the affairs of his church, says, that on his head were many crowns, *Rev.* 19. 12. noting his absolute sovereignty, and many triumphs. A crown is a sign of victory, *Rev.* 4. 4.

The high-priest wore a crown, which was girt about his mitre, and was tied behind his head. On the forepart was a plate of gold, with these words engraven on it, Holiness to the Lord, *Ex.* 28. 36 ; 29. 6. New married men and women wore crowns on their wedding-day, *Songs* 3. 11. The spouse invites her companions to see king Solomon with the crown wherewith his mother crowned him in the day of his espousals ; and alluding to this custom, it is said, *Ezek.* 16. 12. that when God entered into covenant with the Jewish nation, he put a beautiful crown upon their head.

Lev. 8. 9. forefront he put the holy *c.*
21. 12. the *c.* of the anointing oil
Esth. 1. 11. Vashti with the *c.* royal
Job 31. 36. bind it as a *c.* to me
Ps. 89. 59. hast profaned his *c.*
Ps. 132. 18. shall his *c.* flourish
Prov. 4. 9. a *c.* of glory shall she deliver
Prov. 12. 4. virtuous woman is *c.* to her husband
14. 24. *c.* of wife is their riches
16. 31. hoary head is *c.* of glory
17. 6. children's children are *c.* of old
Songs 3. 11. behold king Solomon with *c.*
Is. 28. 5. Lord of Hosts for *c.* of glory
62. 3. thou shalt be a *c.* of glory
Ezek. 21. 26. remove the diadem, take off the *c.*
John 19. 5. Jesus wearing a *c.* of thorns
1 *Cor.* 9. 25. to obtain corruptible *c.*
Phil. 4. 1. my joy and *c.*
1 *Thess.* 2. 19. for what *c.* of rejoicing
2 *Tim.* 4. 8. laid up—a *c.* of righteous-
James 1. 12. receive a *c.* of life
1 *Pet.* 5. 4. receive a *c.* of glory
Rev. 2. 10. give thee a *c.* of life
3. 11. that no man take thy *c.*
6. 2. a *c.* given to him, conquering

CROWNED, *Ps.* 8. 5. *c.* with glory and honour ; *Heb.* 2. 7, 9 ; *Ps.* 21. 3.
Prov. 14. 18. prudent are *c.* with knowledge

CROWNEST, *Ps.* 65. 11. *c.* year with thy goodness
103. 4. *c.* with loving-kindness

CROWNS, *Zech.* 6. 11, 14 ; *Rev.* 4. 4, 10. & 9. 7. & 12. 3. & 13. 1. & 19. 12.

CRUCIFY, See *Cross. Matt.* 20. 19. & 23. 34 ; *Luke* 23. 21 ; *John* 19. 6, 15.
Acts 2. 23. *c.* and slain, 4. 10.
Rom. 6. 6. our old man is *c.* with him
1 *Cor.* 1. 13. was Paul *c.* 23. C. *c.*
2. 2. save J. C. and him *c.*
2 *Cor.* 13. 4. was *c.* through weakness
Gal. 2. 20. I am *c.* with Christ neverthe-
3. 1. Christ set forth *c.* among you
5. 24. C. have *c.* the flesh with affec-
6. 14. world is *c.* to me and I to world

Rev. 11. 8. where also our Lord was *c.*
CRUEL, *Prov.* 5. 9. & 11. 17. & 27. 4.
Gen. 49. 7. cursed wrath for it was *c.*
Job 30. 21. thou art become *c.* to me
Prov. 12. 10. tender mercies of wicked are *c.*
Songs 8. 6. jealousy is *c.* as the grave
Is. 13. 9. day of Lord cometh *c.* with
Jer. 6. 23. *c.* and have no mercy, 50. 42.
Heb. 11. 36. had trial of *c.* mockings
CRUELTY, *Gen.* 49. 5. instruments of *c.* in habitations
Ps. 27. 12. such as breathe out *c.* are risen up
74. 29. dark places are full of the habitations of *c.*
Prov. 27. 4. wrath is *c.* anger is
CRUMBS 'which fell from the rich man's table,' *Matt.* 15. 27 ; *Luke* 16. 21. At the feasts of the great, they wiped their hands, not with napkins, but with the soft and fine part of the bread, and afterwards threw it to the dogs. Hence these were the crumbs alluded to ; and we see the force of the words of the woman of Canaan ; " *the dogs eat of the crumbs that fall from their master's table.*"

CRUSE, a small vessel of glass, &c. for holding water, oil, &c., 1 *Sam.* 26. 11.

CRUSH, to bruise, *Num.* 22. 25. to tread to pieces, *Job* 39. 15. to oppress grievously, *Job* 20. 19. to ruin almost utterly, *Jer.* 51. 34.

CRY, *Ex.* 5. 8. & 3. 7, 9.
Gen. 18. 21. to the *c.* that is come up
Ex. 2. 23. their *c.* came up to God
22. 23. I will surely hear their *c.*
2 *Sam.* 22. 7. my *c.* did enter into ears
Job 34. 28. he hears *c.* of afflicted
Ps. 9. 12. he forgets not *c.* of humble
34. 15. his ears are open to their *c.*
145. 19. he will hear their *c.*
Jer. 7. 16. neither lift up *c.* nor prayer for them, 11. 11, 14.
Matt. 25. 6. at midnight a *c.* made
Ps. 34. 17. righteous *c.* and Lord hears
Is. 40. 6. voice said *c.*—what *c.*
42. 2. not *c.* nor lift up voice
58. 1. *c.* aloud, spare not, show trans-
Ezek. 9. 4. *c.* for all the abominations
Joel 1. 19. to thee will I *c.*
Jonah 3. 8. *c.* mightily to God
Matt. 12. 19. shall not strive nor *c.*
Luke 18. 7. *c.* day and night to him
19. 40. stones would *c.* out
Rom. 8. 15. Spirit of—*c.* Abba, Father
CRIED, *Ps.* 22. 5. *c.* and were delivered
Ps. 34. 6. this poor man *c.* and Lord
119. 145. I *c.* with my whole heart
138. 3. I *c.* thou answeredst me
Lam. 2. 18. their heart *c.* to Lord
Hos. 7. 14. not *c.* with their heart
CRIEST, *Prov.* 2. 3. if thou *c.* after
CRIETH, *Gen.* 4. 10. brother's blood *c.*
Prov. 1. 20. wisdom *c.* without
Is. 40. 3. voice *c.* in the wilderness
Mic. 6. 9. Lord's voice *c.* to the city
Matt. 15. 23. away, for she *c.* after us
Jam. 5. 4. the hire of the labourers *c.*

CRYING, *Prov.* 19. 18. not soul spare for his *c.*

Is. 22. 5. day of *c.* to the mountains
   65. 19. voice of *c.* no more heard

Zech. 4. 7. bring forth headstone with *c.*

Matt. 3..3. voice of *c.* in the wilderness, prepare, *Mark* 1. 3 ; *Luke* 3. 4 ; *John* 1. 23.
   21. 15. the children *c.* in the temple

Luke 4. 41. devils *c.* thou art Christ

Acts 8. 7. unclean spirits *c.* came out
   21. 15. laid hands on him, *c.* out, men
   36. multitude *c.* away with him

Gal. 4. 6. Spirit into hearts, *c.* Abba

Heb. 5. 7. up prayers with strong *c.*

Rev. 21. 4. there will be no more death nor *c.*

CRYSTAL, *Job* 28. 17. the gold and the *c.* cannot equal it

Ezek. 1. 22. firmament colour of terrible *c.*

Rev. 4. 6. sea of glass like unto *c.*
   21. 11. light of city was clear as *c.*
   22. 1. a pure river of water of life, clear as *c.*

CUCKOW, *Lev.* 11. 16. *c.* have in abomination, *Deut.* 14. 15.

CUCUMBERS, *Num.* 11. 5. we remember the *c.* and the melons

Is. 1. 8. Zion as lodge in a garden of *c.*

CUMBERED, ETH, *Luke* 10. 40. Martha was *c.* about much serving

Luke 13. 7. why *c.* it the ground

CUMBRANCE, *Deut.* 1. 12. how can I myself alone bear your *c.*

CUMMIN, *Is.* 28. 25. scatter the *c.* and cast in

Is. 28. 27. nor is a cart-wheel turned about upon the *c.* but the *c.* is beaten out with a rod

Matt. 23. 23. woe to you scribes, ye pay tithes of *c.*

CUNNING, *Gen.* 25. 27. and Esau was a *c.* hunter

Ex. 26. 1. with cherubims of *c.* work
   38. 23. Aholiab, a *c.* workman

1 Sam. 16. 16. a *c.* player on an harp
   18. a son of Jesse, *c.* in playing

Ps. 137. 5. if I forget, let my right hand forget her *c.*

Is. 3. 3. take away the *c.* artificer

Eph. 4. 14. and carried about by *c.*

CUP, signifies a material cup to drink out of, *Gen.* 40. 13. Figuratively (1) The wine in the cup, 1 *Cor.* 11. 27. (2) Those sufferings and afflictions which God sends upon a person or people : To drink of this cup, signifies to undergo and endure those sufferings : *Is.* 51. 17. Stand up, O Jerusalem, which hast drunk at the hand of the Lord the cup of his fury. *Ps.* 75. 8. in the hand of the Lord there is a cup, the dregs thereof all the wicked of the earth shall wring them out, and drink them. In those and the like passages God is compared to the master of a feast, who then used to distribute portions of meats or drinks to the several guests, as he thought fit. Our Saviour prays,

Matt. 26. 39. Let this cup pass from me. Let me be freed from these sufferings both in my soul and body : And he tells his disciples, *Matt.* 20. 23. That they should indeed drink of this cup ; that is, they should taste of inward afflictions and desertions, and have their share of outward sufferings for the gospel, as well as himself. (3) For God's blessings and favours, *Ps.* 23. 5.

Babylon is called a golden cup, *Jer.* 51. 7. because of her great riches and plenty. And it is said of the woman arrayed in purple, or of the anti-christian church, that she had a golden cup in her hand, *Rev.* 17. 4, which may denote the enticing means, and specious pretences, which she uses to allure people to idolatry, particularly by sensuality, luxury, and affluence.

I will take the cup of salvation, *Ps.* 116. 13. I will offer the sacrifice of thanksgiving unto God. It denotes joy and thanksgiving, and is a phrase taken from the common practice of the Jews in their thank-offerings, in which a feast was made of the remainder of their sacrifices, and the offerers, together with the priests, did eat and drink before the Lord ; and, among other rites, the master of the feast took a cup of wine into his hand, and solemnly blessed God for it, and for the mercy which was then acknowledged ; and then gave it to all the guests, of which every one did drink in his turn, 1 *Chr.* 16. 2, 3. To which custom it is supposed that our blessed Lord alludes in the institution of the cup, which also is called the cup of blessing, 1 *Cor.* 10. 16.

Ps. 11. 6. portion of their *c.*
   16. 5. Lord is portion of my *c.*
   23. 5. my *c.* runneth over
   73. 10. waters of full *c.* wrung out
   116. 13. take *c.* of salvation

Is. 51. 17. *c.* of trembling, 22 ; *Zech.* 12. 2.

Jer. 16. 7. nor give *c.* of consolation
   25. 15. wine *c.* of fury 17. 28 ; *Lam.* 4. 21 ; *Ezek.* 23. 31, 32.

Hab. 2. 16.- *c.* Lord's right hand ; *Ps.* 75. 8.

Matt. 10. 42. *c.* of cold water only
   20. 22. able to drink of the *c.*
   23. 25. make clean outside of *c.*
   26. 39. let this *c.* pass from me

John 18. 11. *c.* which my Father

1 Cor. 10. 16. *c.* of blessing which we
   21. drink *c.* of Lord and *c.* of devils
   11. 26. drink this *c.* 27. 28. *Luke* 22. 20.

Rev. 16. 19. *c.* of wrath, 14. 10.

CUPBEARER, *Neh.* 1. 11. I was the king's cupbearer, 1 *Kings* 10. 5 ; 2 *Chr.* 9. 4.

CURDLED, *Job* 10. 10. hast *c.* me like cheese

CURE, *Jer.* 33. 6. I will bring it health and c.

CURE, ED, *Jer.* 33. 6. c. them and will reveal peace

Jer. 46. 11. O daughter of Egypt, thou shalt not be c.

Hos. 5. 13. could not c. you of wound

Matt. 17. 16. disciples could not c. him

Luke 7. 21. in that hour he c. many
9. 1. gave them power to c. diseases

CURES, *Luke* 13. 32. I cast out devils I do c. to-day and

CURIOUS, *Ex.* 35. 32. devise c. works,

Acts 19. 19. many of them that used c. arts brought

CURIOUSLY, *Ps.* 139. 15. and c. wrought in the lowest parts

CURRENT, *Gen.* 23. 16. c. money with the merchant

CURSE, to curse, signifies to imprecate, to call down mischief upon, or to wish evil to : Noah cursed his grandson Canaan, *Gen.* 9. 25. Cursed be Canaan ; may he be hateful to God, abhorred by men, and miserable in his person and posterity. Jacob cursed the fury of his two sons Simeon and Levi, who massacred the Shechemites, and plundered their city, *Gen.* 49. 7. Moses enjoins the people of Israel to denounce curses against the violaters of the law, *Deut.* 27. 15, 16. &c. And Joshua cursed him who should undertake to build Jericho, *Josh.* 6. 26.

The language of the divine law is, ' Cursed is every one that continueth not in all things written in the book of the law to do them,' *Gal.* 3. 10 ; and as ' all have sinned ' personally, ' and come short of the glory of God,' that curse naturally belongs to each of us as our rightful portion. It is to the gospel, and to that alone, that we are indebted for a revealed way of deliverance from its awful sanction. There indeed we read that, ' Christ hath redeemed us from the curse of the law, having been made a curse for us,' *Gal.* 3. 13 ; 1 *Pet.* 3. 18 ; 2. 24 ; 2 *Cor.* 5. 20 ; *John* 1. 29. In the gospel, our Saviour pronounces those of his disciples to be blessed, who are loaded with curses, and requires them to bless those that curse them, to render blessing for cursing, *Matt.* 5. 11 ; *Luke* 6. 28 ; *Rom.* 12. 14.

CURSE them, *Num.* 5. 18, 19, 22, 24, 27.

Gen. 27. 12. bring a c. upon me
13. on me be thy c. my son

Deut. 11. 26. blessing and c. 30. 1.
23. 5. turn c. into blessing, *Neh.* 13. 2.

Prov. 3. 33. c. of Lord in house of wickedness
26. 2. c. causeless shall not come

Mal. 2. 2. send a c. upon you
3. 9. ye are cursed with a c. for ye have robbed me

Acts 23. 12. and bound themselves under a c. 14.

Gal. 3. 10. as are of the works of law, are under c.
13. Christ redeemed us from the c.

Rev. 22. 3. shall be no more c.

Is. 65. 15. for, or to be accursed, *Jer* 24. 9. & 25. 18. & 29. 18. & 42. 18. & 44. 8, 12. & 26. 6. & 49. 13.

CURSE, verb, *Gen.* 8. 21. I will not again c. ground
12. 3. c. him that c. thee

Ex. 22. 28. nor c. ruler of thy people

Lev. 19. 14. shall not c. the deaf

Num. 22. 6. c. me this people, 17.
23. 8. how shall I c. whom God hath not cursed ?

Deut. 23. 4. hired Balaam to c. *Josh.* 24. 9 ; *Neh.* 13. 2.

Judg. 5. 23. c. ye Meroz c. bitterly in-

2 *Sam.* 16. 10. him c. because Lord, 11.

Job 1. 11. he will c. to face, 2.
2. 9. c. God and die, 1. 5.

Ps. 62. 4. they bless with mouth but c. inwardly
109. 28. let them c. but bless thou

Prov. 11. 26. people shall c. him, 24. 24.

Eccl. 10. 20. c. not the king in the chamber

Jer. 15. 10. every one doth c. me

Mal. 2. 2. I will c. your blessings

Matt. 5. 44. bless them that c. you
26. 74. he began to c. and to swear, *Mark* 14. 71.

Rom. 12. 14. bless and c. not

Jam. 3. 9. therewith c. we men

CURSED, *Gen.* 49. 7. c. be their anger

Deut. 28. 16. c. shalt thou be in the city, c. in the field
17. c. shall be thy basket and thy store

Job 3. 1. after this Job c. his day, 8.

5. 3. I c. his habitation, 24. 18.
24. 18. portion is c. in the earth

Ps. 119. 21. proud are c. 37. 22.

Jer. 11. 3. c. be man that obeys not
17. 5. c. be man that trusteth in man
48. 10. c. doth work of Lord deceitfully

Matt. 25. 41. depart from me ye c.

Gal. 3. 10. c. is every one that continueth not in all
13. c. is every one that hangeth on a tree

2 *Pet.* 2. 14. c. children, who have forsaken the way

CURSEDST, *Matt.* 11. 21. the fig-tree thou c. is withered away

CURSES, *Num.* 5. 23. the priest shall write these c. in a book

Deut. 28. 15. that all these c. shall come on thee, 45.
29. 20. all the c. that are written in this book shall lie upon him, 27 ; 2 *Chr.* 34. 24.

CURSETH, *Prov.* 30. 11. a generation that c. their father

Matt. 15. 4. honour father and mother, he that c. father or mother, let him die the death, *Mark* 7. 10.

CURSING, *Deut.* 30. 19 ; *Rom.* 3. 14 ; *Heb.* 6. 8 ; *Ps.* 10. 7. & 59. 12. & 109. 17.

CURTAIN, *Ps.* 104. 2. who coverest thyself with light, who stretchest out the heavens like a *c. Is.* 40. 22.

CURTAINS, *Ex.* 26. 1. make tabernacle with ten *c.* 2 ; 36. 9.

2 *Sam.* 7. 2. ark of God dwelleth within *c.* 1 *Chr.* 17. 1.

Songs 1. 5. comely as the *c.* of Solomon

Is. 54. 2. stretch forth *c.* of habitation

CUSTOM, manner, or way, *Luke* 4. 16 ; that which has been long established, *Judg.* 11. 39 ; *John* 18. 39. A duty paid to the government of a country upon merchandise, imported, or exported, *Rom.* 13. 7. —*Gen.* 31. 35 ; *Luke* 4. 16 ; 1 *Cor.* 11. 16 ; *Jer.* 10. 3.

CUSTOMS, *Jer.* 10. 3. the *c.* of the people are vain

Acts 6. 14. shall change the *c.* Moses delivered us

16. 21. teach me *c.* which are not lawful

21. 21. ought not to walk after the *c.*

26. 3. know thee to be expert in all *c.*

CUT, *Lev.* 1. 6, 12. & 22. 24.

Zech. 11. 10. *c.* asunder ; *Matt.* 24. 51 ; *Luke* 12. 46 ; *Jer.* 48. 2. & 50. 23 ; *Ps.* 129. 4.

Luke 13. 7, 9. *c.* down, *Job* 22. 16, 20.

Job 4. 7. *c.* off, 8. 14 ; *Ps.* 31. 22. & 37. 9, 28. & 76. 12. & 90. 10. & 101. 5 ; *Prov.* 2. 22 ; *Matt.* 5. 30. & 18. 8 ; *Rom.* 11. 22 ; 2 *Cor.* 11. 12 ; *Gal.* 5. 12.

Acts 5. 33. *c.* to the heart, 7. 54.

CYMBAL, 1 *Cor.* 13. 1. I am become as sounding brass, or a tinkling *c.*

CYMBALS, 2 *Sam.* 6. 5. played on cornets and *c.* 1 *Chr.* 13. 8.

1 *Chr.* 16. 5. but Asaph made a sound with *c.*

Ps. 150. 5. praise him upon loud-sounding *c.*

CYPRESS, *Songs* 1. 14. my beloved cluster of *c.*

Is. 44. 14. he taketh the *c.* and the oak

DAGGER, *Judg.* 3. 16. Ehud made him a *d.* with two edges

Judg. 3. 21. he took the *d.* from his right thigh

22. that he could not draw the *d.* out of his belly

DAINTY, IES, *Gen.* 49. 20. Asher yield royal *d.*

33. 20. soul abhorreth *d.* meat

Ps. 141. 4. not of their *d.*

Prov. 23. 3. not desirous of his *d.*

DALE, *Gen.* 14. 17. Shaveh, which is king's *d.*

2 *Sam.* 13. 18. pillar in the king's *d.*

DAMAGE, *Dan.* 6. 2. king should have no *d.*

Acts 27. 10. voyage will be with hurt and much *d.*

2 *Cor.* 7. 9. receive *d.* by us in nothing

DAM, *Ex.* 22. 30. seven days with his *d.* on the eighth shall give it me, *Lev.* 22. 27.

Deut. 22. 6. not take the *d.* with young

DAMNABLE, 2 *Pet.* 2. 1. privily bring in *d.* heresies

DAMNATION, *Matt.* 23. 14. shall receive the greater *d. Mark* 12. 40 ; *Luke* 20. 47.

Matt. 23. 33. can ye escape *d.* of hell

Mark 3. 29. in danger of eternal *d.*

John 5. 29. have done evil, to the resurrection of *d.*

Rom. 3. 8. evil, that good may come, whose *d.* is just

DAMNED who believe not ; *Mark* 16. 16 ; 2 *Thess.* 2. 12.

Rom. 13. 2. receive to themselves *d.*

14. 23. doubteth is *d.* if he eat

1 *Cor.* 11. 29. eateth and drinketh *d.* to

1 *Tim.* 5. 12. having *d.* because cast

2 *Pet.* 2. 3. their *d.* slumbers not

DAMSEL, *Gen.* 34. 3. and he loved the *d.*

Gen. 34. 12. but give me the *d.* to wife

Deut. 22. 15. tokens of the *d.* virginity

21. they shall bring out the *d.* and stone her

Judg. 5. 30. divided to every man a *d.* or two

Ruth 2. 5. Boaz said whose *d.* is this ?

Matt. 14. 11. John Baptist's head was brought in a charger, and given to the *d. Mark* 6. 28.

26. a *d.* came to Peter, saying, *John* 18. 17.

Mark 5. 39. the *d.* is not dead

Acts 12. 13. a *d.* came to hearken, named Rhoda

16. 16. a certain *d.* possessed with a spirit

DAMSELS, *Ps.* 68. 25. amongst were the *d.* playing

DANCE. The Hebrew word translated dance in our version, generally signifies to leap for joy ; *Ps.* 30. 11 ; *Luke* 15. 25. Or it signifies to praise God by playing on a musical instrument

DANCE, *Ps.* 149. 3. praise him in the *d. Ps.* 150. 4.

Jer. 31. 13. virgins rejoice in the *d.*

Lam. 5. 15. our *d.* is turned into mourning

DANCE, ED, verb, *Judg.* 21. 21. daughters of Shiloh came to *d.*

Eccl. 3. 4. and a time to *d.*

2 *Sam.* 6. 14. David *d.* before the Lord

Matt. 11. 17. have piped, and ye have not *d. Luke* 7. 32.

14. 6. the daughter of Herodias *d. Mark* 6. 22.

DANCING, 1 *Sam.* 18. 6. the women came out singing and *d.*

2 *Sam.* 6. 16. she saw king David *d.*

Ps. 30. 11. turned my mourning into *d.*

Luke 15. 25. as he came he heard music and *d.*

DANDLED. To fondle on the knee ; *Is.* 66. 12. It denotes that the saints derive comfort and delight, and many gracious benefits in the ordinances of the church.

DANGER of the judgment

Matt. 5. 21, 22. *d.* of council—hell fire

Mark 3. 29. in *d.* of damnation

Acts 19. 27. craft in *d.* 40. we are in *d.*

DARE, 1 *Cor.* 6. 1 ; 2 *Cor.* 10. 12.

Rom. 5. 7. some would *d.* to die

15. 18. not d. to speak of any thing
1 Cor. 6. 1. d. any of you go to law
DARK, Gen. 15. 17 ; Job 18. 6. & 24. 16.
Lev. 13. 6. if plague be d. 21. 6.
Num. 12. 8. speak not in d. speeches
2 Sam. 22. 12. d. waters ; Ps. 18. 11.
Job 3. 9. let the stars be d.

Job 12. 25. grope in d. without light
18. 6. light be d. in his tabernacle
24. 16. in d. dig through houses
Ps. 35. 6. way be d. and slippery
49. 4. d. sayings, 78. 2.
74. 20. d. places of earth full of
78. 2. I will utter d. sayings of old
88. 12. wonders known in d.
Prov. 7. 9. in the black and d. night
Is. 45. 19. have not spoken in a d. place
Ezek. 8. 12. what the house of Israel do
   in the d.
34. 12. in the cloudy and d. day
Dan. 8. 23. understanding d. sentences
2 Pet. 1. 19. light shines in d. places
1 Cor. 13. 12. through a glass d.
DARKENED, Ex. 10. 15 ; Eccl. 12. 3.
Ps. 69. 23. let eyes be d. Rom. 11. 10.
Zech. 11. 17. his right eye utterly d.
Rom. 1. 21. foolish heart was d.
Eph. 4. 18. having understanding d.
DARKNESS, (1) The privation, or want
   of natural light, Matt. 27. 45. (2)
   Hell, the place of eternal misery,
   confusion, and horror, called outer
   darkness, Matt. 22. 13. (3) Ignorance and unbelief, which is the
   want of spiritual light, John 3. 19.
   (4) The minds of men, which, since
   the fall, are full of ignorance and
   error, John 1. 5. (5) A private or
   secret place, where but few persons are present, Matt. 10. 27.
   What I tell you in darkness ; that
   is, in parables, and in private between ourselves. (6) Great distress,
   perplexity, and calamity, Is. 8. 22 ;
   Joel 2. 2. (7) Sin, or impurity, 1
   John 1. 5.
The land of darkness is the grave, Job
   10. 21, 22. Such as sit in darkness
   and the shadow of death, Ps. 107.
   10. Such as are in a disconsolate
   and forlorn condition, shut up in
   prisons, or dungeons. The children of light, set in opposition to
   the children of darkness, means
   the righteous in opposition to the
   wicked ; the faithful in opposition
   to the incredulous and infidels, 2
   Cor. 6. 14. Our Saviour calls the
   exercise of Satan's power, the power
   of darkness, Luke 22. 53. But this
   is your hour, and the power of darkness ; this is the time wherein
   power is given to Satan, to execute
   his designs against me. The power
   of darkness, is also taken for the
   dominion of sin, and Satan, under
   which all unregenerated persons
   are, Col. 1. 13.
DARKNESS, Gen. 1. 2, 5, 18. & 15. 12.
Ex. 10. 22. thick d. in Egypt three days
Deut. 4. 11. the mountain burnt with
   thick d.

5. 32. Lord spake out of thick d.
2 Sam. 22. 10. d. was under his feet, Ps.
   18. 9.
2 Sam. 22. 29. Lord will lighten my d.
1 Kings 8. 12. Lord dwell in thick d.
Job 10. 22. a land of d. and d. itself
19. 8. hath set d. in my paths
28. 3. end to d. stones of d.
34. 22. no d. where workers
37. 19. we cannot order our speech
   by reason of d.
Ps. 18. 11. he made d. his secret place
88. 18. mine acquaintance into d.
97. 2. clouds and d. round about him
104. 20. makest d. and it is night
139. 12. d. and light are alike to thee
Is. 5. 20. put d. for light and light for d.
8. 22. behold trouble and d.
45. 7. I form light and create d.
60. 2. d. shall cover the earth, and
   gross d. the people, but Lord shall
   arise on thee
Matt. 6. 23. whole body is full of d.
8. 12. outer d. 22. 13. & 25. 30.
27. 45. from sixth hour there was d.
   Mark 15. 33.
Luke 22. 53. your hour and power of d.
John 1. 5. d. comprehended it not
3. 19. men loved d. rather than light
12. 35. lest d. come upon you
Acts 26. 18. turn them from d. to light
Rom. 13. 12. cast off works of d.
2 Cor. 4. 5. hidden things of d.
1 Cor. 4. 6. light to shine out of d.
Eph. 5. 8. were sometimes d. but now
11. no fellowship with works of d.
6. 12. rulers of d. of this world
Col. 1. 13. deliver from power of d.
1 Thess. 5. 5. not of night nor of d.
1 Pet. 2. 9. called you out of d.
2 Pet. 2. 4. reserved in chains of d.
1 John 1. 5. in him is no d. at all
2. 8. d. is past true light shineth
11. d. hath blinded his eyes
Jude 6. in everlasting chains under d.
Jude 13. blackness of d. for ever
DARKNESS, in, Deut. 28. 29. in d. 1.
2, 9 ; Ps. 107. 10. & 112. 4 ; Is. 9.
2. & 50. 10 ; Matt. 4. 16. & 10.
27 ; John 1. 5 ; 1 Thess. 5. 4.
Darkness, with light, Ps. 112. 4. to
   upright there ariseth light in d.
Ps. 139. 12. d. and light alike to thee
Eccl. 2. 13. wisdom excels as far as light
   excelleth d.
Is. 5. 20. that put d. for light and light
   for d.
Is. 9. 2. the people that walked in d. have
   seen a great light, upon them hath
   light shined, Matt. 4. 16.
42. 16. make d. light before them
45. 7. I form light and create d.
50. 10. walketh in d. and hath no light
Matt. 6. 23. light in thee be d. how great
   is that d.
10. 27. what I tell in d. speak in light,
   Luke 12. 3.
John 1. 5. light shineth in d. d. compre-
   hendeth it not
3. 19. men loved d. rather than light
12. 25. walk while ye have light, lest
   d. come

Rom. 13. 12. cast off works of d.
2 Cor. 4. 6. who commandeth *light* to shine out of d.
6. 14. communion *light* with d.
1 Pet. 2. 9. called you out of d. into marvellous *light*
1 John 1. 5. God is *light*, and in him is no d. at all.
2. 8. d. is past, true *light* shineth

DARLING, Ps. 22. 20. deliver my d. from dog
Ps. 35. 17. rescue my d. from the lions

DART, S, 2 Sam. 18. 14. Joab took three d.
2 Chr. 32. 5. Hezekiah made d.
Job 41. 29. d. are counted as stubble
Prov. 7. 23. till a d. strike through his liver
Eph. 6. 16. to quench the fiery d. of
Heb. 12. 20. thrust through with a d.

DASH, to break in pieces 2 Kings 8. 12.
Ex. 15. 6 ; Is. 13. 16, 18 ; Hos. 10. 14. & 13. 16 ; Ps. 137. 9 ; Jer. 13. 14.
Ps. 2. 9. d. them in pieces like a potter's vessel
91. 12. lest thou d. thy foot against a

DASHED, ETH, Ps. 137. 9. d. thy little ones against stones
Is. 13. 16. children be d. in pieces before eyes, Hos. 13. 16 ; Nah. 3. 10.

DATES, 2 Chr. 31. 5. the children of Israel brought d.

DAUB, ED, ING, Ex. 2. 3. d. the ark with slime and pitch
Ezek. 13. 10. d. with untempered mortar

DAUGHTER, Lev. 12. 6. days are fulfilled for a d.
Judg. 11. 34. Jephthah's came out to meet him
40. to lament Jephthah's d. four days in a year
2 Sam. 12. 3. little ewe-lamb was unto him as a d.
1 Kings 3. 1. Solomon took Pharaoh's d.
Ps. 45. 13. king's d is glorious within
Ezek. 16. 44. saying, as is the mother, so is her d.
Matt. 9. 22. d. be of good comfort thy faith hath made thee whole, Mark 5. 34 ; Luke 8. 48.
10. 37. he that loveth son or d. more
14. 6. the d. of Herodias danced
15. 28. her d. was made whole
Mark 7. 26. cast forth devil out of her d.
Heb. 11. 24. Moses refused to be called son of Pharaoh's d.

DAUGHTERS, Ps. 45. 9. king's d. among thy honourable women
Ps. 144. 12. that our d. may be as corner-stones
Prov. 31. 29. many d. have done virtuously
Songs 2. 2. as the lily among thorns, so is my love among the d.
Is. 60. 4. and thy d. shall be nursed at thy side

DAUGHTERS of Jerusalem, Songs 1. 5. I am black, but comely O d. of Jerusalem
Songs 2. 7. I charge you, O d. of Jeru-

salem, 3. 5 ; 5. 8 ; 8. 4.
3. 10. paved with love for the d. of Jerusalem
Luke 23. 28. d. of Jerusalem, weep not for me

DAUGHTERS of music, Eccl. 12. 4. the d. of music brought low

DAVID for Christ, Ps. 89. 3 ; Jer. 30. 9 ; Ezek. 34. 23, 24, & 37. 24. 25 ; Hos. 3. 5 ; Is. 55. 3.

DAWN, ING, Josh. 6. 15. they rose about the d. of day
Job 7. 4. I am full of tossings to the d. of the day
Matt. 28. 1. as it began to d. towards the first day
2 Pet. 1. 19. till day d. and day-star arise

DAY, a division of time, which signifies, (1) That space which intervenes between the rising and setting of the sun. (2) The period of a revolution of the earth on its axis, comprising 24 hours. The commencement of this period has been different among different nations. The Hebrews began in the evening, Lev. 23. 32. The Persians and Greeks begin at sunrise ; the Arabians at noon ; and ourselves and more modern nations at midnight. (3) A period in which any particular event is to occur, John 8. 56 ; 1 Thess. 5. 2. (4) A season of merciful opportunity, Luke 19. 47. (5) The time of a man's life, Job 3. 8 ; Ps. 37. 13. (6) A prophetic year, Ezek. 4. 5, 6 ; Dan. 9. 24 ; Rev. 11. 3. (7) Moral light, the knowledge and practice of religion, 1 Thess. 5. 5. (8) Heaven ; Rom. 13. 12.

DAY, Gen. 1. 5. & 32. 26.
Josh. 10. 13. the sun hasted not down about a whole d.
14. no d. like that before or
Job 14. 6. rest, till he shall accomplish his d.
18. 20. they shall be astonished at his d.
19. 25. stand at latter d. upon earth
Ps. 19. 2. d. unto d. utters speech and night shows knowledge
84. 10. a d. in courts is better
118. 24. d. which Lord made
119. 164. seven times a d. praise thee
Prov. 4. 18. shineth more and more to perfect d.
Prov. 27. 1. a d. may bring forth
Hos. 9. 5. what will ye do in solemn d.
Amos 6. 3. put far away evil d.
Zech. 4. 10. despised d. of small things
Mal. 3. 2. abide the d. of his coming
Matt. 6. 34. sufficient to d. is evil,
25. 13. know neither d. nor hour
Luke 17. 4. trespass seven times in a d.
John 6. 39. raise it again at the last d.
40. I will raise him up at the last d. 44. 54.
John 8. 56. rejoiced to see my d.
9. 4. work the work of him while d.
Acts 17. 31. appointed a d. in which
Rom. 2. 5. wrath against d. of wrath
1 Cor. 3. 13. the d. shall declare it

2 *Cor.* 6. 2. behold, now is the *d.* of sal-
Eph. 4. 30. sealed to *d.* of redemption
Phil. 1. 6. till *d.* of Jesus Christ, 10 ;
   2. 16 ; 2 *Thess.* 2. 2 ; 1 *Cor.* 1. 8.
1 *Thess.* 5. 5. children of the *d.*
Heb. 4. 7. limiteth a certain *d.* to-day
   10. 25. the more as ye see the *d.* ap-
   proaching
2 *Pet.* 1. 19. *d.* dawn, and day-star arise
Matt. 10. 5. *d.* of *judgment*, and 11. 22,
   24. & 12. 36 ; *Mark* 6. 11 ; 2 *Pet.*
   2. 9. & 3. 7 ; 1 *John* 4. 17.
Is. 2. 12. *d.* of the *Lord*, 13. 6, 9. & 34.
   8 ; *Jer.* 46. 10 ; *Lam.* 2. 22 ; *Ezek.*
   30. 3 ; *Joel* 1. 15. & 2. 1, 31. &
   3. 14 ; *Amos* 5. 18 ; *Obad.* 15. 11,
   8, 12, & 13 ; *Zech.* 1. 7. & 14.
   1 ; *Mal.* 4. 5 ; 1 *Cor.* 5. 5 ; *Rev.* 1.
   10 ; 2 *Cor.* 1. 14 ; 1 *Thess.* 5. 2 ; 2
   Pet. 3. 10.
DAY of trouble, *Ps.* 20. 1. Lord hear
   thee in *d.* of trouble
   50. 15. call on me in *d.* of *trouble*,
   91. 15.
Ps. 59. 16. my defence and refuge in *d.*
   of *trouble*
   77. 2. in *d. of trouble* I sought the
   Lord
   86. 7. in *d. of trouble* I call on thee
Is. 37. 3. it is a *d. of trouble* and rebuke
Ezek. 7. 7. time is come, *d. of trouble* is
   near
Nah. 1. 7. Lord is good, a strong hold
   in *d. of trouble*
Hab. 3. 16. I might rest in *d. of trouble*
Zeph. 1. 15. a *d. of trouble* and distress,
   desolation
DAY, all the, *Is.* 65. 2. I have spread
   out my hands *all the d.*
Matt. 20. 6. why stand *all the d.* idle ?
DAY, all the, long, *Ps.* 38. 6. I go
   mourning *all the d. long*
   44. 22. for thy sake we are killed *all
   the d. long*.
Prov. 23. 17. be in the fear of the Lord
   all the d. long. *Rom.* 10. 21.
DAY of death, *Gen.* 27. 2. I know not
   the *d.* of my *death*
Eccl. 7. 1. the *d. of death* better than
   d. of one's birth
   8. 8. neither power in the *d. of death*
DAY by day, *Gen.* 39. 10. she spake to
   Joseph *d. by d.*
Ex. 13. 21. Lord went before them *by d.*
   40. 38. cloud of the Lord upon the
   tabernacle *by d.* and fire by night ;
   Num. 9. 16.
Ps. 91. 5. the arrow that flieth *by d.*
   121. 6. sun shall not smite thee *by d.*
Is. 60. 19. the sun shall be no more thy
   light *by d.*
Luke 11. 3. give us *d. by d.* our daily
   bread
2 *Cor.* 4. 16. the inward man is renewed
   d. by d.
Rev. 21. 25. gates shall not be shut *by d.*
DAY every, *Ps.* 7. 11. God is angry
   with the wicked *every d.*
   145. 2. *every d.* will I bless thee
Is. 51. 13. and hast feared continually
   every d.
   52. 5. my name *every d.* is blas-

phemed
Luke 16. 19. rich man fared sumptuously *every d.*
Rom. 14. 5. another esteemeth *every d.*
   alike
DAY one, *Acts* 21. 7. we abode with
   the brethren *one d.*
Rom. 14. 5. one esteemeth *one d.* above
   another
2 *Pet.* 3. 8. *one d.* with the Lord as a
   thousand years
DAY and night, *Ps.* 32. 4. *d.* and *night*
   thy hand was heavy on me
   42. 3. my tears have been my meat *d.*
   and *night*
   139. 12. the *night* shineth as the *d.*
Is. 27. 3. I the Lord will keep it *d.* and
   night
   60. 11. gates not shut *d.* nor *night*
   62. 6. watchman never hold their
   peace *d.* nor *night*
Jer. 9. 1. weep *d.* and *night* for slain
   14. 17. eyes run down tears *d.* and
   night ; *Lam.* 2. 18.
Mark 4. 27. sleep and rise *night* and *d.*
   5. 5. *d.* and *night* he was in the
   mountains
   14. 30. this *d.* even this *night*, before
   the cock crow
Acts 9. 24. watched gates *night* and *d.*
   to kill him
   20. 31. cease not to warn every one
   night and *d.*
2 *Cor.* 11. 25. thrice I suffered shipwreck, a *d.* and *night*
1 *Thess.* 2. 9. labouring *d.* and *night*
   3. 10. *night* and *d.* praying exceedingly ; 1 *Tim.* 5. 5.
Rev. 4. 8. rest not *d.* and *night*, saying
   7. 15. and serve him *d.* and *night* in
   his temple
   20. 10. tormented *d.* and *night* for
   ever
DAY this, *Ps.* 2. 7. thou art my Son,
   this d. have I begotten thee ; *Acts*
   13. 33 ; *Heb.* 1. 5.
   118. 24. *this* is the *d.* which the Lord
   hath made
Is. 38. 19. the living praise thee, as I
   do *this d.*
   56. 12. to-morrow shall be as *this d.*
Matt. 6. 11. give us *this d.* our daily
   bread
Luke 2. 11. is born *this d.* a Saviour
   19. 9. *this d.* is salvation come to this
   house
   42. hadst known, in *this* thy *d.*
   22. 34. cock not crow *this d.* before
   thou deny me
Acts 2. 29. sepulchre with us to *this d.*
   26. 22. I continue unto *this d.* wit-
   nessing to small
DAY, to, 2 *Sam.* 6. 20. how glorious
   was the king *to d* !
Ps. 95. 7. we his pasture *to d.*
Matt. 6. 30. grass of the field, which *to
   d.* is, and to-morrow is cast into
   the oven ; *Luke* 12. 28.
   21. 28. go work *to d.* in my vineyard
Luke 23. 43. *to d.* be with me in
   paradise
   24. 21. *to d.* is the third day

Heb. 3. 13. exhort daily, while it is called *to d.*

5. 5. thou art my Son, *to d.* have I begotten thee

13. 8. Jesus Christ, same yester. *to d.*

Jam. 4. 13. *to d.* or morrow, we will go

2 *Pet.* 2. 8. Lot vexed his righteous soul from day *to d.*

DAYS, *Deut.* 4. 32. ask of the *d.* that are past

Job 7. 1. are not his *d.* also like the *d.* of an hireling ?

30. 27. the *d.* of affliction prevented

Job 8. 9. *d.* on earth as a shadow

14. 1. of few *d.* full of trouble

32. 7. *d.* should speak and multitude

Ps. 55. 23. deceitful men not live out half their *d.*

77. 5. I have considered the *d.* of old, the years

90. 9. *d.* are passed away in thy wrath

10. the *d.* of our years are threescore and ten

12. so teach to number our *d.*

14. rejoice and be glad all our *d.*

Prov. 3. 16. length of *d.* in her right

Is. 60. 20. *d.* of thy mourning be ended

65. 20. no more an infant of *d.*

Eccl. 7. 10. former *d.* better than

11. 8. remember *d.* of darkness

12. 1. while evil *d.* come not

Jer. 2. 32. forgotten me *d.* without number

Matt. 11. 12. from *d.* of John the Baptist

Matt. 24. 22. except those *d.* be short-

37. as *d.* of Noe, so shall the coming of the Son be

Gal. 4. 10. observe *d.* months, and years

Eph. 5. 16. because the *d.* are evil

1 *Pet.* 3. 10. would see good *d.*

Gen. 49. 1. last *d.* Is. 2. 2 ; *Mic.* 4. 1 ; *Acts* 2. 17 ; 2 *Tim.* 3. 1 ; *Heb.* 1. 2 ; *Jam.* 5. 3 ; 2 *Pet.* 3. 3.

Num. 24. 14. latter *d.* *Deut.* 31. 29 ; *Jer.* 23. 20. & 30. 24 ; *Dan.* 10. 14 ; *Hos.* 3. 5.

Job 10. 20. my *d.* 17. 1, 11.

7. 6. my *d.* are swifter than a shuttle

16. I loathe it, my *d.* are vanity

9. 25. *d.* swifter than a post

Ps. 39. 4. know measure of my *d.*

5. made my *d.* as a handbreadth

102. 3. my *d.* are consumed like smoke

—11. *d.* are like a shadow—23. are shortened

Is. 39. 8. peace and truth in my *d.*

Jer. 20. 18. my *d.* consumed with shame

DAILY, *Ps.* 61. 8. *d.* perform my vows

68. 19. who *d.* loadeth us with benefits

Ps. 72. 15. live and *d.* be praised

Matt. 26. 55. I sat *d.* with you teaching in the temple

Prov. 8. 34. watching *d.* at my gates

Is. 58. 2. seek me *d.* and delight in

Luke 9. 23. let him take up his cross *d.*

Acts 2. 47. added to church *d.* saved

17. 11. the noble Bereans searched the scriptures *d.*

Heb. 3. 13. exhort one another *d.*

7. 27. needeth not *d.* to offer

Jam. 2. 15. sister be destitute of *d.* food

DAY'S-MAN, A mediator, *Job* 9. 33.

neither is there any *d.* betwixt us

DAY SPRING, *Job* 38. 12. *d.* spring, *Luke* 1. 78.

DAY STAR, 2 *Pet.* 1. 19. *d.* star arise in your hearts

DEACON, S, *Phil.* 1. 1. saints with the bishops and *d.*

1 *Tim.* 3. 8. *d.* must be grave

10. them use the office of a *d.* 13.

12. *d.* the husband of one wife

DEAD, *Gen.* 20. 3. & 23. 3.

Num. 16. 48. stood between *d.* and

1 *Sam.* 24. 14. after a *d.* dog, after

Ps. 88. 10. shall *d.* praise, 115. 17.

Eccl. 9. 5. the *d.* know not any thing

10. 1. *d.* flies cause ointment to stink

Matt. 8. 22. let the *d.* bury their *d.*

22. 32. not God of *d.* but of living

Luke 8. 52. maid is not *d.* but sleepeth

John 5. 25. *d.* shall hear the voice of Son of God

11. 25. though he were *d.* yet shall he live

Rom. 6. 8. *d.* with Christ ; 11. *d.* to sin

Gal. 2. 19. I through law am *d.* to law

Eph. 2. 1. who were *d.* in trespasses

Col. 2. 13. being *d.* in your sins

3. 3. ye are *d.* and your life hid with

1 *Thess.* 4. 16. *d.* in Christ shall rise first

2 *Tim.* 2. 11. *d.* with him ye shall live

Heb. 11. 4. being *d.* yet speaketh

Rev. 14. 13. blessed are *d.*—in the Lord

DEADLY, *Ps.* 17. 9 ; *James* 3. 8 ; *Rev.* 13. 3.

DEAF, *Ex.* 4. 11 ; *Ps.* 38. 13 ; *Is.* 29. 18. & 35. 5 ; *Mic.* 7. 16.

Lev. 19. 14. shalt not curse the *d.*

Is. 42. 18. hear ye *d.* and look ye blind

19. who is as *d.* as my messenger

43. 8. *d.* people that have ears

Matt. 11. 5. *d.* hear, dead are raised

DEAL, *Ps.* 119. 124 *d.* with me according to thy mercy

Is. 26. 10. in land of uprightness *d.*

52. 13. my servant *d.* prudently

58. 7. to *d.* thy bread to hungry

DEALINGS, ETH, *John* 4. 9. no *d.* with Samaritans

Heb. 12. 7. God *d.* as with sons

DEALT, *Job* 6. 15. my brethren *d.* deceitfully

Ps. 13. 6. Lord *d.* bountifully with me

Acts 7. 19. *d.* subtilly with kindred

25. 24. mult. of Jews have *d.* with me

Rom. 12. 3. as God hath *d.* to every man

DEAR, *Acts* 20. 24. neither count I life *d.*

Eph. 5. 1. foll. of God, as *d.* children

Col. 1. 7. Epaphras our *d.* fellow-serv.

13. into kingdom of his *d.* Son

1 *Thess.* 2. 8. because ye were *d.* to us

DEARTH, *Acts* 7. 11. came a *d.* over all land

Acts 11. 28. there should be a great *d.*

DEATH, *Gen.* 21. 16 ; *Ex.* 10. 17.

Num. 23. 10. me die the *d.* of righteous

Deut. 30. 15. set before you life and *d.*

Ps. 6. 5. in *d.* no remembrance of thee

33. 19. deliver soul from *d.* 116. 8.

68. 20. Lord belong the issues from *d.*

73. 4. have no bands in their *d.*

89. 48. liveth and shall not see *d.*

116. 15. precious—is *d.* of saints

118. 18. not given me over to *d.*

Prov. 2. 18. house inclines to *d.*
8. 36. they that hate me love *d.*
18. 21. *d.* and life in power of tongue
Eccl. 7. 26. more bitter than *d.* the woman
8. 8. hath no power in day of *d.*
Is. 25. 8. swallow up *d.* in victory
28. 15. made covenant with *d.*
38. 18. *d.* cannot celebrate thee
Jer. 8. 3. *d.* chosen rather than
21. 8. way of life way of *d.*
Ezek. 18. 32. no pleasure in *d.* 33. 11.
Hos. 13. 14. O *d.* I will be thy plagues
Matt. 16. 28. not taste of *d.* Luke 9. 27.
26. 8. sorrowful even unto *d.*
John 5. 24. passed from *d.* unto,
8. 51. shall never see *d.*
12. 33. what *d.* he should die, 21. 19.
Acts 2. 24. loosed the pains of *d.*
Rom. 5. 12. sin entered and *d.* by sin
6. 3. baptized into his *d.*
4. buried by baptism into *d.*
5. planted in the likeness of his *d.*
9. *d.* hath no more dominion over
23. wages of sin is *d.* but gift
7. 5. bring forth fruit unto *d.*
8. 2. free from law of sin and *d.*
6. to be carnally minded is *d.*
38. *d.* not life shall separate
1 *Cor.* 3. 22. or life, or *d.* or present
11. 26. ye show Lord's *d.* till he come
15. 21. by man came *d.* and by
54. *d.* is swallowed up in victory
55. O *d.* where is thy sting
56. sting of *d.* is sin and strength of sin
2 *Cor.* 1. 9. had sentence of *d.* in our selves
10. delivered from so great a *d.*
2. 16. we are the savour of *d.* unto *d.*
4. 11. delivered to *d.* for Jesus' sake
12. *d.* worketh in us but life in you
Phil. 2. 8. obedient to the *d.* of cross
2 *Tim.* 1. 10. hath abolished *d.* and brought
Heb. 2. 9. tasted *d.* for every man
15. through fear of *d.* were subject to
11. 5. should not see *d.* Luke 2. 26.
James 1. 15. sin finished brings *d.*
5. 20. save a soul from *d.* and hide
1 *Pet.* 3. 18. put to *d.* in the flesh
1 *John* 3. 16. there is a sin not to *d.*
17. there is a sin unto *d.* I not say
Rev. 1. 18. I have the keys of hell and *d.*
2. 10. be faithful unto *d.* and I will
12. 11. loved not their lives unto *d.*
20. 6. second *d.* hath no power
21. 4. be no more *d.* nor sorrow
DEATH, from, *Ps.* 33. 19. to deliver their soul *from d.*
Hos. 13. 14. I will redeem them *f. d.*
John 5. 24. passed *f. d.* 1 John 3. 14.
Heb. 5. 7. to him able to save *from d.*
Jam. 5. 20. shall save a soul *from d.*
DEATH, gates of, *Ps.* 9. 13. liftest me from the *g. of d.*
Ps. 107. 18. they draw near to *g. of d.*
DEATH, shadow of, *Job* 16. 16. on eyelids is *shadow of d.*
Job 24. 17. morning is the *shad. of d.*
34. 22. no *s. of d.* sinners may hide
Ps. 23. 4. through valley of *sha. of d.*
Matt. 4. 16. people that sat in *s. of d.*

Luke 1. 79. give light to them in *s. of d.*
DEATHS, 2 *Cor.* 11. 23. in *d.* oft
DEBASE, To lessen, degrade ; *Is.* 57. 9.
DEBATE, to confer or dispute ; *Prov.* 25. 9. God debates with his people when he reproves and corrects them ; *Is.* 27. 8. "In measure, when it shooteth forth, thou wilt *debate* with it." *Rom.* 1. 9. It signifies contention. "Full of envy, murder, *debate,* deceit, malignity."
DEBATE, verb, *Prov.* 25. 9. *d.* cause with neighbour
Is. 27. 8. in measure wilt *d.*
DEBATES, *Rom.* 1. 29. full of envy *d.*
2 *Cor.* 12. 20. I fear lest there be *d.*
DEBT, *Rom.* 4. 4 ; *Matt.* 6. 12, 18, 27.
DEBTOR, *Matt.* 23. 16. swear b gold, is a *d.*
Rom. 1. 14. I am *d.* to the Greeks
Gal. 5. 3. a *d.* to the whole law
DEBTORS, *Matt.* 6. 12. as we forgive our *d.*
Luke 7. 41. a creditor had two *d.*
Rom. 8. 12. therefore we are *d.*
15. 27. and their *d.* they are
DECAY, to grow less, weaker ; *Job* 14. 11 ; *Neh.* 4. 10. Cities and houses are *decayed*, when broken down, and in a ruinous condition ; *Eccl.* 10. 18 ; *Is.* 44. 26.
DECEASE, to die a natural death ; *Matt.* 22. 25. Death ; *Luke* 9. 31.
DECEIT, *fraud, guile* (1) Villainous and unjust conduct, carried on under a fair show, *Ps.* 10. 7 ; 36. 3. (2) Vain pretences and devices, calculated to impose upon and deceive men, *Ps.* 38. 12.
DECEIT, *Jer.* 5. 27. & 9. 6, 8.
Ps. 72. 14. redeem their soul from *d.*
101. 7. worketh *d.* shall not dwell
Prov. 20. 17. bread of *d.* is sweet
Is. 53. 9. any *d.* in his mouth
Jer. 8. 5. they hold fast *d.* and refuse
Col. 2. 8. spoil you through vain *d.*
DECEITFUL, *Ps.* 35. 20. & 109. 2 ; *Prov.* 11. 18. & 14. 25. & 23. 3. & 27. 6.
Ps. 5. 6. abhor bloody and *d.* man
55. 23. *d.* men shall not live half
78. 57. turn like a *d.* bow, *Hos.* 7. 16.
120. 2. from a *d.* tongue, 52. 4 ; *Mic.* 6. 12 ; *Zeph.* 3. 13.
Prov. 31. 30. favour is *d.* and beauty
Jer. 17. 9. heart is *d.* above all things
Hos. 7. 16. they are like a *d.* bow
Eph. 4. 22. according to *d* lusts
Matt. 13. 22. through *d.* of riches
DECEITFULLY, *Ex.* 8. 29. let not Phar. deal *d.*
Job 6. 15. brethren dealt *d.* as brook
13. 7. will you talk *d.* for God
Num. 24. 4. nor sworn *d.*
Ps. 24. 4. nor sworn *d.*
2 *Cor.* 4. 2. nor handling word of God *d.*
DECEITFULNESS, *Matt.* 13. 22. and the *d.* of riches choke the word, *Mark* 4. 19.
Heb. 3. 13. hardened through *d.* of sin
DECEIVE, 2 *Kings* 4. 28. & 18. 29.
Prov. 24. 28. *d.* not with thy lips
Jer. 9. 5. *d.* every one his neighbour

37. 9. saith Lord, *d.* not yourselves
Matt. 24. 4. take heed that no man *d.*
24. if possible *d.* the very elect
Rom. 16. 18. fair speeches *d.* simple
1 *Cor.* 3. 18. let no man *d.* himself
Eph. 5. 6. let no man *d.* you, 2 *Thess.* 2.
3 ; 1 *John* 3. 7.
1 *John* 1. 8. we *d.* ourselves
Rev. 20. 3. *d.* the nations no more
DECEIVABLENESS, 2 *Thess.* 2. 10.
DECEIVED, *Deut.* 11. 16. heart be not *d.*
Job 12. 16. *d.* and deceiver are his
Is. 44. 20. a *d.* heart hath turned
Jer. 20. 7. O Lord thou hast *d.* me
Lam. 1. 19. my lovers they *d.* me
Ezek. 14. 9. I the Lord have *d.* that prophet
Obad. 3. thy pride hath *d.* thee
Luke 21. 8. take heed ye be not *d.*
John 7. 47. answered, are ye also *d.*
Rom. 7. 11. *d.* me, and by it slew me
1 *Cor.* 6. 9. be not *d.* 15. 33 ; *Gal.* 6. 7.
1 *Tim.* 2. 14. Adam was not *d.* but
2 *Tim.* 3. 13. *d.* and being *d.*
Tit. 3. 3. we were foolish, *d.*
Rev. 18. 23. all nations were *d.*
DECEIVER, *Gen.* 27. 12 ; *Mal.* 1. 14 ;
2 *John* 7 ; 2 *Cor.* 6. 8 ; *Tit.* 1. 10.
DECEIVETH, *Prov.* 26. 19 ; *Rev.* 12. 9.
Gal. 6. 3. when he is nothing *d.* himself
Jam. 1. 26. *d.* his own heart, 22.
DECENTLY, in a becoming manner, 1
Cor. 14. 40. compared with 1 *Cor.*
3. 5.
DECIDED, 1 *Kings* 20. 40. thyself hast
d. it
DECISION, *Joel* 3. 14. multitudes in
valley of *d.*
DECK, ED, *Job* 40. 10. *d.* thyself with
majesty
Prov. 7. 16. I have *d.* my bed
Ezek. 16. 11. I *d.* thee with ornaments
Rev. 17. 4. woman was *d.* with gold
18. 16. alas, city that was *d.*
DECLARE, to publish, tell, or explain,
Gen. 41. 24 ; *Is.* 42. 9.
Ps. 9. 11. *d.* among people his doings
19. 1. the heavens *d.* glory of God
Ps. 22. 22. *d.* thy name unto brethren
38. 18. I will *d.* my iniquity and
50. 16. what to do to *d.* my statutes
78. 6. may *d.* them to their children
145. 4. shall *d.* thy mighty acts
Is. 3. 9. they *d.* their sin as Sodom
41. 22. *d.* to us things to come
53. 8. who shall *d.* his generation
66. 19. *d.* my glory among Gentiles
Mic. 3. 8. to *d.* to Jacob his transgressions
Matt. 13. 36. *d.* parable of tares
15. 15. said Peter, *d.* this parable
Acts 13. 32. we *d.* glad tidings
41. though a man *d.* it to you
Acts 17. 23. worship him I *d.* unto you
20. 27. not shunned to *d.* all the counsel
Rom. 3. 25. to *d.* his righteousness for
remission
Heb. 11. 14. say such things *d.* plainly
1 *John* 1. 3. have seen *d.* we to you
DECLARED, *Ps.* 40. 10. I have *d.* thy
faithfulness
Ps. 71. 17. I *d.* thy wondrous works

Is. 41. 26. *d.* from beginning, 45. 21.
Luke 8. 47. she *d.* to him before all
John 17. 26. I have *d.* to them thy name
Acts 9. 27. he *d.* how he had seen Lord
15. 14. Simeon *d.* how God at first
Rom. 1. 4. *d.*—Son of God with power
2 *Cor.* 3. 3. manifestly to be the epistle of Christ
Rev. 10. 7. mystery finished, as he *d.*
DECLARETH, ING, *Is.* 41. 26. yea,
there is none that *d.*
Is. 46. 10. *d.* the end from beginning
Amos 4. 13. *d.* to man what his thought
Acts 15. 3. *d.* conversion of his Gentiles
12. *d.* what miracles God wrought
1 *Cor.* 2. 1. *d.* to you testimony of God
DECLINE to turn aside from the paths
of righteousness, 2 *Chr.* 34. 2 ; *Ps.*
119. 51, 157.
DECLINED, ETH, 2 *Chr.* 34. 2. *d.* neither to right
Job 23. 11. his way I kept, not *d.*
Ps. 44. 18. nor have our steps *d.*
102. 11. days as shadow that *d.*
119. 51. yet not *d.* from thy law
DECREASE, ED, *Gen.* 8. 5. the waters
d. continually
John 3. 30. he must increase, I *d.*
DECREE, to purpose or appoint, *Ezra*
5. 13, 17. & 6. 1, 12.
Ps. 2. 7. I will declare the *d.*
Prov. 8. 15. princes *d.* justice
Is. 10. 1. that *d.* unrighteous *d.*
Zeph. 2. 2. before *d.* bring forth
DECREED, *Is.* 10. 22 ; 1 *Cor.* 7. 37.
DEDICATE, *Deut.* 20. 5 ; 2 *Sam.* 8. 11 ;
1 *Chr.* 26. 20, 26, 27 ; *Ezek.* 44. 29.
DEDICATION, the solemn act of setting
apart any person or thing to a religious use. The Feast of Dedication, observed by the Jews for eight
days, was to commemorate the restoration of the temple at Jerusalem under Judas Maccabæus, after
it had been destroyed by Antiochus
Epiphanes ; *Num.* 7. 84 ; *Ezra* 6.
16, 17 ; *Neh.* 12. 27 ; *John* 10. 22.
DEED, DEEDS, *Gen.* 44. 15 ; *Judg.*
19. 30.
Rom. 15. 18. obedient in word and *d.*
Col. 3. 17. what ye do in word or *d.*
1 *John* 3. 18. love in *d.* and in truth
Neh. 13. 14. wipe not out my good *d.*
Ps. 28. 4. give them according to their
d. *Jer.* 25. 14 ; *Rom* 2. 6 ; 2 *Cor.* 5.
10.
John 3. 19. because their *d.* were evil
8. 41. ye do the *d.* of your father
Rom. 3. 20. by *d.* of law no flesh be
2 *John* 11. partaker of his evil *d.*
Jude 15. of all their ungodly *d.*
DEEP, signifies the sea ; *Gen.* 1. 2 ; *Job*
38. 30. Great danger, *Ps.* 69. 15.
Poverty sanctified to the good of
the saints, 2 *Cor.* 8. 2. Things
hidden, *Is.* 33. 19 ; *Dan.* 2. 22.
Intricate providences, *Ps.* 36. 6.
Ps. 36. 6. judgments are a great *d.*
42. 7. *d.* call unto *d.* at the noise
107. 24. see his wonders in the *d.*
Is. 44. 27. saith to the *d.* be dry
63. 13. that led them through the *d.*

Jonah 2. 3. hadst cast me into *d*.
Luke 5. 4. launch out into the *d*.
1 *Cor.* 2. 10. all, yea, *d*. things of God
2 *Cor.* 11. 25. night and day in the *d*.
DEEP, adjective, *Job* 12. 22. discovereth
   d. things
Ps. 64. 6. and the heart is *d*.
   69. 2. I sink into *d*. mire. I am com-
     ing into *d*. waters
   92. 5. thy thoughts are very *d*.
Dan. 2. 22. revealeth *d*. things
Luke 6. 48. and digged *d*. and laid
John 4. 11. and the well is *d*.
DEEPLY, *Is.* 31. 6. *d*. revolted
Hos. 9. 9. *d*. corrupted themselves
Mark 8. 12. sighed *d*. in spirit
DEER, *Deut.* 14. 5. ye shall eat fallow *d*.
1 *Kings* 4. 23. Solomon had *d*.
DEFAME, to slander, reproach wrong-
   fully, 1 *Cor.* 4. 13 ; *Jer.* 20. 10.
DEFENCE, places of refuge, 2 *Chr.* 11. 5
   the vindication of a person, *Acts*
   19. 33 ; *Is.* 19. 6.
Num. 14. 9. their *d*. is departed
Job 22. 25. the Almighty shall be thy *d*.
Ps. 7. 10. my *d*. is of God who saveth
   59. 9. God is my *d*. 17. & 62. 2, 6.
   & 89. 18. & 94. 22.
Eccl. 7. 12. wisdom is a *d*, and money is
Is. 4. 5. on all the glory shall be *d*.
   33. 16. place of *d*. the munitions
DEFEND, (1) To deliver, *Ps.* 5. 11.   (2)
   To protect, *Ps.* 20. 1 ; 59. 1 ; *Is.* 31.
   5. The promises of God to defend
   in time of danger, *Zech.* 9. 15.
DEFER, to exercise forbearance *Prov.*
   19. 11 ;   to put off, *Acts* 24. 22 ;
   Eccl. 5. 4 ; *Is.* 48. 9 ; *Dan.* 9. 19 ;
   Prov. 13. 12.
DEFILE, *Lev.* 11. 44. & 15. 31.
Songs 5. 3. how shall I *d*. them
Dan. 1. 8. would not *d*. himself
Matt. 15. 18. they *d*. the man, 20.
1 *Cor.* 3. 17. if *d*. the temple of God
Mark 7. 2. eat bread with *d*. hands
Is. 24. 5. earth is *d*. under inhabitants
Tit. 1. 15. *d*. and unbelieving their
   mind and con. is *d*.
Heb. 12. 15. thereby many be *d*.
Rev. 3. 4. not *d*. their garments
   14. 4. are not *d*. with women
   21. 27. any thing that *d*.
DEFRAUD, to injure another, 1 *Sam.*
   12. 3, 4 ; *Lev.* 19. 13 ; *Mark* 10. 19 ;
   1 *Cor.* 6. 7, 8. & 7. 5 ; 1 *Thess.* 4.
   6 ; 2 *Cor.* 7. 2.
DEFY, IED, 1 *Sam.* 17. 10. I *d*. armies
   of Israel
1 *Sam.* 17. 26. that he should *d*. the
   armies
   45. God of Israel whom hast *d*.
2 *Sam.* 21. 21. when he *d*. Israel, Jonathan slew him, 1 *Chr.* 20. 7.
DEGENERATE, *Jer.* 2. 21. turned into
   d. plant
DEGREE, S, 2 *Kings* 20. 9. or back, ten
   d. *Is.* 38. 8.
Ps. 62. 9. low *d*. vanity, of high *d*.
Luke 1. 52. exalted them of low *d*.
1 *Tim.* 3. 13. purchase a good *d*.
Jam. 1. 9. brother of low *d*. rejoice
DELAY, to defer, to procrastinate, *Ex.*

   22. 29. & 32. 1 ; *Luke* 12. 45.
Ps. 119. 60. I *d*. not to keep command-
   ments
Matt. 24. 48. my Lord *d*. his coming
DELECTABLE, comely, delightful, *Is.*
   44. 9.
DELICATE, *Deut.* 28. 56 ; *Is.* 47. 1 ;
   Jer. 6. 2 ; 51. 34 ; *Mic.* 1. 16.
DELICACIES, precious things, dainty
   meats, *Rev.* 18. 3.
DELICATELY, 1 *Sam.* 15. 32 ; *Prov.*
   29. 21 ; *Lam.* 4. 5 ; *Luke* 7. 25.
DELIGHT, *Gen.* 34. 19 ; *Num.* 14. 8.
Deut. 10. 15. Lord hath *d*. in thy fathers
1 *Sam.* 15. 22. hath Lord as great *d*.
Job 22. 26. have thy *d*. in Almighty
   27. 10. will he *d*. himself in Almighty
Ps. 1. 2. his *d*. is in the law of the Lord
   16. 3. saints in whom is all my *d*.
   37. 4. *d*. thyself in Lord, he will
   40. 8. I *d*. to do thy will, O my God
   94. 19. thy comforts *d*. my soul
   119. 24. thy testimonies are my *d*. 174.
Prov. 11. 20. upright are his *d*. 12. 22.
   15. 8. prayer of upright is his *d*.
   29. 17. he give *d*. to thy soul
Songs 2. 3. under shadow with great *d*.
Is. 58. 13. if thou call Sabbath a *d*.
DELIGHT, verb, *Num.* 14. 8. if Lord *d*.
   in us will bring
Job 27. 10. will he *d*. in Almighty
   34. 9. should *d*. himself with God
Ps. 119. 16. *d*. in thy statutes, 35.
Is. 55. 2. let your soul *d*. itself in fatness
   58. 2. *d*. to know—take *d*. in approach
Mal. 3. 1. messenger of cov. ye *d*. in
Rom. 7. 22. I *d*. in law of God after the
   inward man
DELIGHTED, 1 *Sam.* 19. 2. Jonathan
   d. in David
Ps. 22. 8. deliv. seeing he *d*. in him
   109. 17. as he *d*. not in blessing
Is. 66. 11. be *d*. with her glory
DELIGHTEST, ETH, *Esth.* 6. 6. *d*. to
   honour, 7. 9, 11.
Ps. 51. 16. *d*. not in burnt-offering
Ps. 112. 1. *d*. greatly in his command
   147. 10. *d*. not in strength of horse
Prov. 3. 12. son in whom he *d*.
Is. 42. 1. elect in whom my soul *d*.
   62. 4. Hephzi-bah, Lord *d*. in thee
Mic. 7. 18. because he *d*. in mercy
DELIGHTS, *Ps.* 119. 92. thy law hath
   been my *d*. 143 ; *Eccl.* 2. 8.
Prov. 8. 31. my *d*. with sons of men
Songs 7. 6. how pleasant O love for *d*.
Mal. 3. 12. for ye shall be a *delightsome*
   land, saith the Lord
DELIVER, *Ex.* 3. 8. & 5. 18.
Job 5. 19. *d*. thee in six troubles and in
   10. 7. none can *d*. out of thine hand
Ps. 33. 19. *d*. their soul from death
   50. 15. I will *d*. thee and thou, 91. 51.
   56. 13. wilt thou not *d*. my feet
   74. 19. *d*. not the soul of my turtle
   91. 3. *d*. from snare of fowler
Eccl. 8. 8. shall wickedness *d*. those that
Ezek. 14. 14. should *d*. but own soul
   34. 10. I will *d*. my flock from their
Dan. 3. 17. our God is able to *d*. us from
Hos. 11. 8. how shall I *d*. thee, Israel
Rom. 7. 24. who shall *d*. me from the

body of this death

1 *Cor.* 5. 5. to d. such a one to Satan
2 *Tim.* 4. 18. Lord shall d. me from evils
Heb. 2. 15. d. them who through fear of
death
2 *Pet.* 2. 9. Lord knows how to d. godly
DELIVERANCE, 2 *Kings* 5. 1. & 13. 17 ;
2 *Chr.* 12. 7 ; *Esth.* 4. 14 ; *Ps.* 32. 7.
& 44. 4 ; *Is.* 26. 18 ; *Joel* 2. 32 ;
Obad. 17 , *Luke* 4. 18 ; *Heb.* 11. 35.
Gen. 45. 7. great d. *Judg.* 15. 18 ; 1 *Chr.*
11. 14 ; *Ps.* 18. 50.
Ezra 9. 13. given us such d. as this
Heb. 11. 35. not accepting d.
DELIVERED, *Prov.* 11. 8. righteous is d.
out of trouble, wicked cometh, 9. 21.
Prov. 28. 26. walketh wisely shall be d.
Is. 38. 17. in love to soul d. it from pit
49. 24, 25. lawful captive—prey be d.
Jer. 7. 10. d. to do all these abominations
Ezek. 3. 19. hast d. thy soul, 21. & 33. 9.
Dan. 12. 1. thy people shall be d.
Joel 2. 32. call on the name of Lord—be
Mic. 4. 10. Babylon, shalt thou be d.
Matt. 11. 27. all things are d. to me of the
Father
Acts 2. 23. d. by determinate counsel
Rom. 4. 25. who was d. for our offences
7. 6. we are d. from the law that
8. 32. God d. him up for us all
2 *Cor.* 1. 10. who hath d. doth d. and
will d.
4. 11. always d. to death for Jesu's
sake
1 *Thess.* 1. 10. who d us from the wrath
1 *Tim.* 1. 20. whom I have d. to Satan
2 *Pet.* 2. 7. d. just Lot vexed with filthy
Jude 3. faith once d. to the saints
DELUSION, S, *Is.* 66. 4. I will choose
their d.
2 *Thess.* 2. 11. send them strong d.
DEMONSTRATION, 1 *Cor.* 2. 4.
DEN, a place for wild beasts, &c., *Judg.*
6. 2 ; *Job* 37. 8 ; *Heb.* 11. 38 ; *Rev.*
6. 15 ; *Ps.* 104. 22.
Ps. 10. 9. d. of lions ; *Songs* 4. 8 ; *Dan.*
6. 7, 24 ; *Amos* 3. 4 ; *Nah.* 2. 12.
Jer. 7. 11. d. of robbers—of thieves,
Matt. 21. 13 ; *Mark* 11. 17.
9. 11. d. of dragons, 10. 22.
DENY, to refuse, *Gen.* 18. 15 ; *Prov.* 30.
7. God cannot deny himself ;
cannot act unlike his nature, or
contrary to his promises, 2 *Tim.* 2.
13. Men deny God or Christ, when
they act contrary to his commands,
Acts 3. 14 ; or when they embrace
error, &c., 1 *Tim.* 5. 8. In matters
of salvation, not to trust in our
own righteousness, but in the finished work of Christ alone—to sacrifice our own ease, &c., in order
to do the work of God, 1 *Kings* 2.
16 ; *Job* 8. 18.
Prov. 30. 9. lest I be full and d. thee
Matt. 10. 33. shall d. before men
16. 24. let him d. himself and take
26. 34. before cock crow thou shalt d.
me
35. I will not d. thee ; *Mark* 14. 31.
2 *Tim.* 2. 12. if we d. him he will d. us
13. abideth faithful—cannot d. him-

self
Tit. 1. 16. in works they d. him
1 *Tim.* 5. 8. hath d. the faith
Rev. 2. 13. hast not d. my faith
2 *Tim.* 3. 5. godliness d. the power
Tit. 2. 12. d. ungodliness and worldly
lusts
2 *Pet.* 2. 1. d. the Lord that bought
them
DEPART from, *Job* 21. 14. & 22. 17.
Job 28. 28. to d. from evil is understanding
Ps. 34. 14. d. from evil, 37. 27 ; *Prov.*
3. 7. & 13. 19. & 16. 6, 17.
Hos. 9. 12. woe to when I d. from them
Matt. 7. 23. d. from me ye that work
25. 41. d. from me ye cursed, into
Luke 2. 29. lettest thy servant d. in
peace
5. 8. d. from me—a sinful man, O
Lord
Phil. 1. 23. having a desire to d.
1 *Tim.* 4. 1. some shall d. from faith
2 *Tim.* 2. 19. name of Christ d. from
iniquity
DEPARTED, *Ps.* 18. 21. wickedly d.
from my God, 119. 102 ; 2 *Sam.*
22. 22.
Is. 59. 15. d. from evil makes himself
Acts 20. 29. after my d. wolves
Heb. 3. 12. unbelief in d. from living
God
DEPARTURE, 2 *Tim.* 4. 6; *Ezek.* 26. 18.
DEPTH, *Job* 28. 14. & 38. 16 ; *Prov.* 8.
27 ; *Matt.* 18. 6 ; *Mark* 4. 5.
Rom. 8. 39. nor d. separate us
11: 33. O the d. of the riches of wis-
dom
Eph. 3. 18. d. of the love of Christ
DEPTHS, *Ex.* 15. 5, 8 ; *Ps.* 68. 22. & 71.
20. & 130. 1 ; *Prov.* 3. 20. & 9. 18.
Mic. 7. 19. cast sins into d. of sea
Rev. 2. 24. known d. of Satan
DERISION, *Job* 30. 1 ; *Ps.* 2. 4. & 44. 13.
& 59. 8. & 119. 51 ; *Jer.* 20. 7, 8.
DESCEND, *Ex.* 19. 18. & 33. 9.
Ps. 49. 17. glory shall not d. after him
Is. 5. 14. rejoiceth shall d. into it
1 *Thess.* 4. 16. Lord shall d. from heaven
DESCENDING, *Gen.* 28. 12. angels of
God ascending and d. *John* 1. 51.
Matt. 3. 16. spirit of God d. like a dove ;
Mark 1. 10 ; *John* 1. 32, 33.
Rev. 21. 10. city d. out of heaven from
God
DESCENT, a going down, a declining
path or way ; *Luke* 19. 37 ; *Heb.*
7. 3, 6.
DESCRIBE, to declare, or show the
characteristic marks of any person,
place, or thing ; *Josh.* 18. 4 ; *Judg.*
8. 14 ; *Rom.* 4. 6.
DESCRY. "The house of Joseph sent
to *descry* Bethel," means to espy,
or to view Bethel ; *Judg.* 1. 23.
DESERT, *Ex.* 3. 1. & 19. 2 ; *Num.* 20.
1 ; *Is.* 21. 1. & 35. 1. & 40. 3. & 43.
19. & 51. 3 ; *Jer.* 25. 24. & 50. 12 ;
Ezek. 47. 8 ; *Matt.* 24. 26.
DESIRE, *Deut.* 18. 6. & 21. 11.
Gen. 3. 16. thy d. shall be to thy husband
4. 7. to thee shall be his d. and

Ex. 34. 24. nor any man *d.* thy land
Deut. 18. 6. with all the *d.* of his mind
2 *Sam.* 23. 5. this is all my *d.*
2 *Chr.* 15. 15. with their whole *d.*
Neh. 1. 11. who *d.* to fear thy name
Job 14. 15. wilt have a *d.* to the work of
Ps. 19. 10. more to be *d.* than
 21. 14. we *d.* not knowledge of thy
Ps. 38. 9. all my *d.* is before thee
 73. 25. none I *d.* besides thee
145. 16. satisfiest the *d.* of them that
 fear him
Prov. 10. 24. *d.* of the righteous shall
 be granted
 11. 23. *d.* of righteous is only good
 13. 19. *d.* accomplished is sweet
 21. 25. *d.* of slothful killeth him
Eccl. 12. 5. *d.* shall fail because
Is. 26. 8. *d.* of soul is to thy name
Ezek. 24. 16. take *d.* of thy eyes
Hag. 2. 7. *d.* of all nations shall come
Luke 22. 15. with *d.* I have *d.* to eat this
 passover
Jam. 4. 2. *d.* to have and can't obtain
Rev. 9. 6. *d.* to die and death shall flee
Ps. 27. 4. one thing have I *d.* of the Lord
Is. 26. 9. with my soul have I *d.*
Jer. 17. 16. nor have I *d.* woeful
Hos. 6. 6. I *d.* mercy and not sacrifice
Zeph. 2. 1. gather O nation not *d.*
DESIRES, *Ps.* 37. 4. give the *d.* of heart
Eph. 2. 3. fulfilling the *d.* of the flesh
DESIREST, *Ps.* 51. 6. thou *d.* truth in
 the inward parts
Ps. 51. 16. thou *d.* not sacrifice, else
 would I give it
DESIRETH, *Job* 7. 2. as a servant ear-
 nestly *d.* the shadow
Ps. 34. 12. what man *d.* life
 68. 16. hill which God *d.* to dwell in
Prov. 12. 12. wicked *d.* net of evil men
 13. 4. soul of sluggard *d.* and hath not.
 21. 10. soul of wicked *d.* evil
Luke 14. 32. he *d.* conditions of peace
1 *Tim.* 3. 1. bishop *d.* a good work
DESIRING, *Matt.* 12. 46. *d.* to speak
 with him
2 *Cor.* 5. 2. *d.* to be clothed upon
1 *Thess.* 3. 6. *d.* greatly to see us
2 *Tim.* 1. 4. greatly *d.* to see thee
DESIROUS, *Luke* 23. 8. Herod was *d.*
 to see him
2 *Cor.* 11. 32. *d.* to apprehend me
Gal. 5. 26. not be *d.* of vain-glory
1 *Thess.* 2. 8. affectionately *d.* of you
DESOLATE, 2 *Sam.* 13. 20 ; *Job* 15. 28.
 & 16. 7 ; *Ps.* 25. 16 ; *Is.* 49. 21.
 & 54. 1 ; *Matt.* 23. 38 ; *Rev.* 17. 16.
DESOLATIONS, *Is.* 49. 6. & 61. 4 ; *Jer.*
 25. 9, 12 ; *Ezek.* 35. 9 ; *Dan.* 9. 2.
 18. 26.
DESPAIR, loss of hope, or confidence, 2
 Cor. 4. 8. & 1. 8 ; *Eccl.* 2. 20 ; 1
 Sam. 27. 1. i.e., to be past hope
DESPERATE, *Job* 6. 26 ; *Is.* 17. 11 ;
 Jer. 17. 9. *d.* wicked
DESPISE statutes, *Lev.* 26. 15.
1 *Sam.* 2. 30. that *d.* me shall be lightly
Job 5. 17. *d.* not chastening of Lord,
 Prov. 3. 11.
Ps. 51. 17. contrite heart, wilt not *d.*
 73. 20. thou shalt *d.* their image

Ps. 102. 17. will not *d.* their prayer
Prov. 1. 7. but fools *d.* wisdom
 6. 30. men do not *d.* a thief, if
 23. 22. *d.* not mother when she is old
Amos 5. 21. I hate, I *d.* your feast days
Matt. 6. 24. hold to one and *d.* the other
 18. 10. *d.* not one of these little
Rom. 14. 3. *d.* him that eateth not
1 *Cor.* 16. 11. let no man therefore *d.*
 him
1 *Thess.* 5. 20. *d.* not prophesyings
1 *Tim.* 4. 12. no man *d.* thy youth,
Tit. 2. 15. let no man *d.* thee
2 *Pet.* 2. 10. that *d.* government
Jude 8. *d.* dominion
DESPISED, *Gen.* 16. 4. mistress was *d.*
 in the eyes
Gen. 25. 34. Esau *d.* his birth-right
2 *Sam.* 6. 16. she *d.* him in her heart
Ps. 22. 6. I am of peo. *Is.* 53. 3.
106. 24. they *d.* pleasant land
Prov. 1. 30. they *d.* all my reproof
 5. 12. how hath my heart *d.* reproof
 12. 9. is *d.* and hath a servant
Eccl. 9. 16. poor man's wisdom is *d.*
Songs 8. 1. kiss thee I should not be *d.*
Is. 53. 3. he is *d.* and rejected *Ps.* 22. 6.
Jer. 33. 24. they have *d.* my people
Zech. 4. 10. *d.* day of small things
Luke 18. 9. righteous and *d.* others
1 *Cor.* 1. 28. things *d.* God chosen
Gal. 4. 14. my temptation ye *d.* not
Heb. 10. 28. that *d.* Moses' law died
Jam. 2. 6. but ye have *d.* the poor
DESPISERS, *Acts* 13. 41 ; 2 *Tim.* 3. 3.
DESPISEST, ETH, ING, *Rom.* 2. 4. *d.*
 thou riches of his goodness
Job 36. 5. God *d.* not any
Prov. 11. 12. void of wisdom *d.* neigh-
 13. 13. *d.* the word shall be destroyed
 14. 21. that *d.* his neighbour sinneth
 15. 32. refuseth instruction *d.* his soul
 19. 16. but he that *d.* his ways shall die
 30. 17. eye *d.* to obey his mother
Is. 33. 15. *d.* gain of oppression
 49. 7. whom man *d.* nation abhorreth
Luke 10. 16. *d.* you, *d.* me, *d.* him that
 sent me
1 *Thess.* 4. 8. *d.* not man but God
DESPISING, *Heb.* 12. 2. *d.* the shame
DESPITE, envy, malice, *Ps.* 10. 14 ;
 Ezek. 25. 6, 15 ; *Matt.* 5. 44 ; *Heb.*
 10. 29.
DESTITUTE, without help, happiness,
 or comfort, 1 *Tim.* 6. 5 ; *Heb.* 11.
 37 ; *Ps.* 102. 17 ; 141. 8.
DESTROY, to pull down, cut off, to
 kill, *Gen.* 19. 14. To take away, as
 Christ is said to destroy the works
 of the devil, *Heb.* 2. 14. To take
 away a thing entirely, absolutely
 remove it, so that it is no more ;
 thus Christ is said to destroy sin ;
 Rom. 6. 6. To run, to devastate—
 and cast one into hell ; *Mark* 1. 24.
DESTROY, *Gen.* 18. 23. & 19. 13.
Ps. 101. 8. I will *d.* all wicked on earth
Prov. 1. 32. prosperity of fools *d.* them
Eccl. 7. 16. why *d.* thyself before time
Matt. 5. 17. not come to *d.* but to fulfil
 10. 28. able to *d.* both soul and body
 12. 14. they may *d.* him, *Mark* 3. 6 ;

11. 18.

21. 41. miserably *d.* those wicked men

27. 20. ask Barabbas, and *d.* Jesus

John 2. 19. *d.* this temple and I will raise

Rom. 14. 15. *d.* not him with thy meat

20. for meat *d.* not work of God

1 *Cor.* 1. 19. I will *d.* wisdom of wise

1 *Cor.* 3. 17. if defile temple him will God *d.*

6. 13. God shall *d.* both it and them

1 *John* 3. 8. might *d.* works of devil

DESTROY, to, *Matt.* 26. 61. said, I am to *d.* temple

Luke 6. 9. lawful to save life, or *d.* it

9. 56. not come to *d.* men's lives

John 10. 10. thief cometh to *d.*

Jam. 4. 12. able to save and to *d.*

DESTROYED, *Ps.* 9. 5. thou hast *d.* the wicked

Prov. 13. 23. *d.* for want of judgment

Jer. 12. 10. many pastors have *d.*

Lam. 2. 5. *d.* his strong holds

Hos. 4. 6. my people are *d.* for lack of knowledge

13. 9. Israel thou hast *d.* thyself

Rom. 6. 6. body of sin might be *d.*

2 *Cor.* 4. 9. cast down but not *d.*

Gal. 1. 23. preacheth faith he *d.*

DESTROYED, shall be, *Ps.* 37. 38. transgressors *shall be d.*

Prov. 13. 13. despiseth word *shall be d.*

20. companion of fools *shall be d.*

29. 1. hardeneth his neck *shall be d.*

Acts 3. 23. will not hear *shall be d.*

1 *Cor.* 15. 26. last enemy that *shall be d.*

DESTROYER, *Job* 15. 21 ; *Ps.* 17. 4 ; *Prov.* 28. 24 ; *Jer.* 4. 7 ; 1 *Cor.* 10. 10.

Esth. 4. 14. shall be *d.* *Ps.* 37. 38. & 92. 7 ; *Prov.* 13. 13, 20. & 29. 1 ; *Is.* 10. 27 ; *Dan.* 2. 44 ; *Hos.* 10. 8 ; *Acts* 3. 23 ; 1 *Cor.* 15. 26.

DESTRUCTION, *Deut.* 7. 23. & 32. 24 ;

Job 5. 22. at *d.* and famine shalt laugh

18. 12. *d.* is ready at his side

26. 6. *d.* before him hath no covering

31. 23. *d.* from God was terror to me

Ps. 90. 3. thou turnest man to *d.*

91. 6. *d.* that wasteth at noon-day

Prov. 10. 29. *d.* shall be to workers of iniquity, 21. 15 ; *Job* 21. 30. & 31. 3.

Prov. 15. 11. hell and *d.* are before the L.

16. 18. pride goeth before *d.*

18. 12. before *d.* heart of man is

27. 20. hell and *d.* are never full

Jer. 4. 20. *d.* upon *d.* cried for land spoil-

Hos. 13. 14. O grave I will be thy *d.*

Matt. 7. 13. way that leads to *d.*

Rom. 3. 16. *d.* and misery are in all

9. 22. vessels of wrath fitted to, *d.*

1 *Cor.* 5. 5. to Satan, for *d.* of flesh

2 *Cor.* 10. 8. not for your *d.* 13. 10.

Phil. 3. 19. walk, whose end is *d.*

1 *Thess.* 5. 3. peace sudden *d.* cometh

2 *Thess.* 1. 9. punish, with everlasting *d.*

2 *Pet.* 2. 1. bring on themselves swift *d.*

3. 16. wrest scriptures to their own *d.*

DESTRUCTIONS, *Ps.* 9. 6. *d.* come to perpetual end

Ps. 35. 17. rescue my soul from *d.*

DETAIN. To hinder from proceeding ; *Judg.* 13. 16 ; 1 *Sam.* 21. 7.

DETERMINATE, *Acts* 2. 23. by the *d.* counsel of God

DETERMINE, D, To appoint ; *Job* 14. 5 To resolve ; *Is.* 10. 23 ; *Dan.* 9. 24. To conclude ; 2 *Chr.* 2. 1. To enact ; *Acts* 19. 39. See also 1 *Cor.* 2. 2. " I am determined not to know," &c. 2 *Chr.* 25. 16 ; *Is.* 28. 22 ; *Acts* 2. 23 ; 4. 28 ; 17. 26.

DETEST, DETESTABLE. To hate or abhor ; *Deut.* 7. 26 ; *Jer.* 16. 18 ; *Ezek.* 5. 11. & 7. 20. & 11. 18. & 37. 23.

DEVIL, *Matt.* 4. 5, 8, 11. & 9. 32.

Matt. 4. 1. to be tempted of the *d.*

11. 18. they say he hath a *d.*

13. 39. enemy that sowed is the *d.*

25. 41. fire prepared for the *d.* and his angels

John 6. 70. twelve, and one of you is a *d.*

7. 20. thou hast a *d.* 8. 48.

8. 44. of your father the *d.* 48.

13 2. *d.* having now entered, 27.

Acts 13. 10. thou child of the *d.* thou

Eph. 4. 27. neither give place to the *d.*

1 *Tim.* 3. 6. fall into condemnation of *d.*

2 *Tim.* 2. 26. recovered out of snare of *d.*

James 4. 7. resist the *d.* and he'll flee

1 *Pet.* 5. 8. your adversary the *d.* goeth

1 *John* 3. 8. to destroy the works of *d.*

10. children of God and children of *d.*

Jude 9. Michael contended with the *d.*

Rev. 2. 10. *d.* shall cast some of you into prison

Lev. 17. 7. offer sacrifices to *d.*

Deut. 32. 17. they sacrifice to *d.*

2 *Chr.* 11. 15. priests for the *d.*

Ps. 106. 37. sacrificed their sons to *d.*

Matt. 4. 24. possessed with *d.* 8. 16 ; 28. 33 ; *Luke* 4. 41. & 8. 36.

Mark 16. 9. cast out seven *d. Luke* 8. 2.

Luke 10. 17. even *d.* are subject to us

1 *Cor.* 10. 20. have fellowship with *d.* sacrifice to *d.*

21. cup of *d.*—table of *d.*

1 *Tim.* 4. 1. doctrines of *d.* lies

James 2. 19. *d.* believe and tremble

DEVISE, to contrive ; to plot something hurtful

Prov. 3. 29. *d.* not evil against

14. 22. do not err that *d.* evil

16. 9. man's heart *d.* his way but Lord

30. shutteth eyes to *d.* froward

Jer. 18. 18. come let us *d.* devices

Mic. 2. 1. woe to them that *d.* iniquity

Ps. 31. 13. *d.* to take my life

2 *Pet.* 1. 16. cunningly *d.* fables

DEVOTE, D, (1) Solemnly to set apart to the service and honour of God ; *Lev.* 27. 21. (2) To set apart for destruction ; *Josh.* 6. 17 ; *Deut.* 13. 17. See *Accursed.*

DEVOTIONS, religious observances ; *Acts* 17. 23. *Devout,* much given to religious exercise, whether lawful or not

DEVOUR, *Gen.* 49. 27 ; *Is.* 26. 11.

Matt. 23. 14. ye *d.* widows'. houses

2 *Cor.* 11. 20. if a man *d.* you

Gal. 5. 15. if ye bite and *d.* one another

Heb. 10. 27. which shall *d.* adversary

1 *Pet.* 5. 8. seeking whom he may *d.*

DEVOURED, *Is.* 1. 20. ye shall be *d.*
24. 6. hath the curse *d.* the earth
Jer. 30. 16. that *d.* thee shall be *d.*
Hos. 7. 7. *d.* their judges
9. *d.* his strength
Mal. 3. 11. I will rebuke *d.*
Ex. 24. 17. *d.* fire ; *Is.* 29. 6. & 30. 27.
30. & 33. 14.
Ps. 52. 4. lovest all *d.* words
DEVOUT, *Luke* 2. 25 ; *Acts* 2. 5. & 10.
2, 7. & 17. 4, 17. & 22. 12.
DEW, *Gen.* 27. 28 ; *Ex.* 16. 13. God give
thee of the *d.*
Deut. 32. 2. my speech distill as *d.*
33. 28. his heavens shall drop *d.*
Judg. 6. 37. if *d.* on fleece only
Job 38. 28. who hath begot drops of *d.*
Ps. 110. 3. hast the *d.* of thy youth
133. 3. as the *d.* of Hermon
Songs 5. 2. my head is filled with *d.*
Is. 26. 19. thy *d.* is as the *d.* of herbs
Dan. 4. 33. body wet with *d.*
Hos. 6. 4. goodness is as the early *d.*
14. 5. I will be as the *d.* to Israel
Mic. 5. 7. Jacob—as *d.* from Lord
DIADEM, *Job* 29. 14 ; *Is.* 28. 5. & 62.
3 ; *Ezek.* 21. 26.
DIE, *Gen.* 5. 5. & 6. 17.
Gen. 2. 17. thou shalt surely *d.* 3. 4. &
20. 7 ; 1 *Sam.* 14. 44. & 22. 16 ; 1
Kings 2. 37, 42 ; *Jer.* 26. 8 ; *Ezek.*
3. 18. & 33. 8, 14.
Job 2. 9. curse God and *d.*
12. 2. wisdom shall *d.* with you
14. 14. if a man *d.* shall he live
again
Ps. 49. 10. wise men *d.* also the fool
82. 7. ye shall *d.* like men
118 17. I shall not *d.* but live
Prov. 23. 13. with rod he shall not *d.*
Eccl. 3. 2. there is a time to *d.*
7. 17. why should *d.* before time
9. living know they shall *d.*
Is. 22. 13. to-morrow we shall *d.*
51. 12. afraid of a man that shall *d.*
Jer. 28. 16. this year thou shalt *d.*
31. 30. every one *d.* for his own
Ezek. 3. 19. *d.* in his iniquity, 33. 8.
18. 4. soul that sinneth shall *d.*
31. why will ye *d.* O house of Israel,
33. 11.
Jon. 4. 3. better for me to *d.* than live
Matt. 26. 35. though I should *d.* with
thee
Luke 20. 36. neither can *d.* any more
John 8. 21. ye shall *d.* in your sins, 24.
11.—50. expedient that one *d.* for the
people
12. 24. except a corn of wheat *d.*
Rom. 14. 8. *d.* we *d.* unto the Lord
1 *Cor.* 9. 15. better for me to *d.* than
15. 22. as in Adam all *d.* so in Christ
Phil. 1. 21. for me to live is Christ, to *d.*
is gain
Heb. 9. 27. it is appointed for men once
to *d.*
Rev. 3. 2. that are ready to *d.*
14. 13. blessed are *d.* who *d.* in the
Lord
DIE, I die, *Gen.* 30. 1. Rachel said give
me children or else *I d.*
Gen. 45. 28. go and see him before *I d.*

48. 21. Israel said to Joseph, behold,
I d.
50. 5. lo, *I d.* : Joseph said to his
brethren *I d.*
Ruth 1. 17. where thou diest will *I d.*
and be buried
Job 29. 18. then I said, *I* shall *d.* in my
nest and multiply
Prov. 30. 7. two things, deny me not
before *I d.*
Matt. 26. 35. though *I* should *d.* with
thee, *Mark* 14. 31.
1 *Cor.* 15. 31. I protest by your rejoicing
I d. daily
DIE, to die, *Gen.* 25. 32. I am at the
point to *d.*
Ps. 79. 11. preserve those that are appointed to *d.*
88. 15. I am afflicted and ready *to d.*
from youth
John 19. 7. by our law he ought *to d.*
Acts 21. 13. I am ready also *to d.* at Jer-
usalem
Rom. 5. 7. for a good man some would
dare *to d.*
DIE, we, *Is.* 22. 13. for to-morrow *we*
shall *d.*
John 11. 16. let us go that *we* may *d.*
with him
Rom. 14. 8. and whether *we d. we d.*
unto the Lord
DIE, ye, *Ps.* 82. 7. but *ye* shall *d.* like
men, and fall like one
John 8. 21. and *ye* shall *d.* in sin, 24.
Rom. 8. 13. after the flesh *ye* shall *d.*
DIED, *Luke* 16. 22. the beggar *d.* the
rich *d.*
Rom. 5. 6. Christ *d.* for the ungodly
8. while yet sinners Christ *d.* for us
6. 10. that he *d.* he *d.* to sin once
9. being raised he *d.* no more
7. 9. sin revived and I *d.* , 8. 34.
14. 7. no man *d.* to himself
9. to this end Christ *d.* for our sins
1 *Cor.* 15. 3. how Christ *d.* for our sins
2 *Cor.* 5. 14. if one *d.* for all, then were
all *d.*
2 *Cor.* 5. 15. he *d.* for all that they
1 *Thess.* 4. 14. believe that Jesus *d.* rose
1 *Thess.* 5. 10. who *d.* for us that
whether
Heb. 11. 13. these all *d.* in faith not
DIEST, *Ruth* 1. 17. where thou *d.* will
I d.
DIETH, *Job* 14. 10. man *d.* and wasteth
away
Job 21. 23. one *d.* in his full strength,
being at ease
Prov. 11. 7. when a wicked man *d.* his
expectations perish
Eccl. 3. 19. as the one *d.* so *d.* the other,
all one breath
Mark 9. 44. where their worm *d.* not,
46. 48.
Rom. 6. 9. Christ being raised from
dead *d.* no more
14. 7. none of us liveth and no man
d. to himself
DYED, *Is.* 63. 1. *d.* garments from Bozrah
Ezek. 23. 15. exceeding in *d.* attire upon
their heads

DYING, 2 *Cor.* 4. 10. & 6. 9 ; *Heb.* 11. 21.

DIFFER, to vary, who makes ; 1 *Cor.* 4.
   7. that *d. Rom.* 2. 18.

DIFFERENCE, *Acts* 15. 9. and put no
   d. between us and them

Rom. 10. 12. there is no *d.* between the
   Jew and Greek

Jude 22. of compassion making a *d.*

DIFFERENCES, 1 *Cor.* 12. 5. *d.* of administration

DIFFERETH, 1 *Cor.* 15. 41. one star *d.*
   from another

Gal. 4. 1. heir when a child *d.* nothing
   from a servant

DIFFERING, *Rom.* 12. 6. gifts *d.* according to the grace given

DIG, *Deut.* 8. 9. out of hills *d.* brass

Job 24. 16. in the dark they *d.* through
   houses marked

Ezek. 8. 8. he said, son of man, *d.* now
   in the wall

   12. 5. *d.* thou through the wall in
   their sight, 12.

Luke 13. 8. alone, till I shall *d.*

   16. 3. I cannot *d.* to beg I am ashamed

DIGGED, *Is.* 51. 1. hole of pit ye are *d.*

Jer. 18. 20. they have *d.* a pit for my
   soul, 22.

Matt. 21. 33. hedged it, and *d.* a wine-
   press in it

   25. 18. *d.* in the earth and hid

Rom. 11. 3. *d.* down thine altars

DIGNITY. Superiority, or strength ;
   Gen. 49. 3. Honour, reputation ;
   Esth. 6. 3 ; *Eccl.* 10. 6. To despise
   the government both of God and
   man ; 2 *Pet.* 2. 10.

DILIGENCE, 2 *Tim.* 4. 9, 21.

Prov. 4. 23. keep thy heart with all *d.*

Luke 12. 58. in way give *d.* that

2 *Pet.* 1. 5. giving all *d.* add to faith
   10. give *d.* to make calling and election sure

Jude 3. I give all *d.* to write unto you

DILIGENT, *Deut.* 19. 18 ; *Josh.* 22. 5.

Prov. 10. 4. hand of *d.* maketh rich
   12. 24. hand of *d.* shall bear rule
   27. substance of *d.* precious
   13. 4. soul of *d* shall be made fat
   21. 5. thoughts of *d.* tend to piety
   22. 29. man *d.* in his business he
   27. 23. be *d.* to know state of flocks

2 *Pet.* 3. 14. be *d.* to be found of him

Ex. 15. 26. wilt *d.* hearken to the voice
   of the Lord ; *Deut.* 11. 13. & 28. 1.
   Jer. 17. 24 ; *Zech.* 6. 15.

Deut. 4. 9. keep thy soul with all *d.*
   6. 7. teach them *d.* to thy children
   17. *d.* keep thy commandments, 11. 22.
   24. 8. thou that observe *d.* and do
   according

Ps. 119. 4. to keep thy precepts *d.*

Heb. 11. 6. rewarder of *d.* seek him

DIMINISH. To reduce in power,
   wealth, privilege, or number ; *Ezek.*
   5. 11 ; 29. 15 ; *Deut.* 4. 2 ; *Prov.*
   13. 11 ; *Rom.* 11. 12.

DIM, *Gen.* 27. 1. Isaac old, his eyes *d.*

Deut. 34. 7. Moses eye was not *d.* nor
   force abated

Lam. 4. 1. how is the gold become *d.*
   the fine gold changed

DIMNESS, *Is.* 8. 22. behold trouble
   darkness *d.* of anguish

DINE, D, *Gen.* 43. 16. these men shall
   d. with me

Luke 11. 37. a Pharisee besought him
   to *d.* with him

John 21. 12. Jesus saith, come and *d.*
   15. so when they had *d.* Jesus saith
   to Simon

DINNER, *Prov.* 15. 17. better is a *d.* of
   herbs where love is

Matt. 22. 4. prepared my *d.* my oxen

Luke 11. 38. not first washed before *d.*
   14. 12. when makest a *d.* or supper

DIP, *Lev.* 4. 6. the priest shall *d.* his
   finger, 17. 14, 16.

Lev. 14. 6. *d.* the cedar wood and the
   living bird, 51:

Num. 19. 18. clean person should *d.*
   hyssop

Luke 16. 24. send Lazarus that he may
   d. his finger

DIPPED, ETH, *Gen.* 37. 31. *d.* the coat
   in the blood

Josh. 3. 15. the priests' were *d.* in brim
   of water

2 *Kings* 5. 14. Naaman *d.* in Jordan
   seven times

Ps. 68. 23. foot be *d.* in blood

Matt. 26. 28. *d.* his hands with me in
   the dish the same shall betray me,
   Mark 14. 20.

DIPT, *Lev.* 9. 9. Aaron *d.* his finger in
   the blood

Rev. 19. 13. was clothed with a vesture
   d. in blood

DIRECT, *Eccl.* 10. 10 ; *Is.* 45. 13.

Ps. 5. 3. will I *d.* my prayer to thee
   119. 5. ways were *d.* to keep

Prov. 3. 6. he shall *d.* thy paths
   16. 9. man deviseth Lord *d.* his steps

Is. 40. 13. who hath *d.* the spirit of Lord
   61. 8. he will *d.* their work in truth

Jer. 10. 23. that walks to *d.* his steps

2 *Thess.* 3. 5. Lord *d.* your hearts into
   love

DISALLOW, *Num.* 30. 5 ; 1 *Pet.* 2. 4.

DISANNUL, to alter or abolish, *Job* 40.
   8 ; *Gal.* 3. 17.

DISAPPOINT, *Ps.* 17. 13 ; *Prov.* 15. 22.

DISCERN, to observe carefully *Gen.* 31.
   32 ; to distinguish one thing from
   another, 2 *Sam.* 14. 17. To *discern*
   Lord's body is to regard by faith
   the bread and wine as symbolical
   of Christ's sacrifice for us—his body
   was bruised, wounded, lacerated,
   and his blood was shed for the remission of sins ;

DISCERN, *Eccl.* 8. 5 ; 2 *Sam.* 14. 17. &
   19. 35 ; 1 *Kings* 3. 9, 11 ; 1 *Cor.* 2. 14.

Mal. 3. 18. *d.* between righteous and

Heb. 5. 14. to *d.* both good and evil
   4. 12. *d.* of thoughts

1 *Cor.* 11. 29. not *d.* Lord's body
   12. 10. to another *d.* of spirits

DISCERNED, ETH, *Prov.* 7. 7. I *d.*
   among the youth a young man

1 *Cor.* 2. 14. not know, because they
   are spiritually *d.*

DISCERNER, *Heb.* 4. 12. word is a *d.*
   of the thoughts of the heart

DISCERNING of spirits, 1 *Cor.* 12. 10.
It was a gift imparted by the Spirit
to certain persons, who were able
by the gift to discern the state of
mind, and the motives of persons—
a gift of the utmost importance,
when pretenders and false prophets
were so abundant ; 1 *John* 4. 1 ; 2
John 7 ; *Deut.* 18. 20—22.

DISCHARGE, to unload, to give up, 1
Kings 5. 9 ; to escape, *Eccl.* 8. 8.

DISCIPLE, *John* 9. 28. & 19. 38.

Matt. 10. 24. *d.* is not above master
42. in the name of a *d.*

Luke 14. 26. ye cannot be my *d.*

John 8. 31. then are ye my *d.* indeed
20. 2. other *d.* whom Jesus loved

Acts 21. 16. an old *d.* with whom

DISCOMFIT. To conquer, to overturn,
to frustrate, *Ex.* 17. 13.

DISCORD soweth, *Prov.* 6. 14, 19.

DISCOURAGE, *Num.* 32. 7. why *d.* ye
the hearts of the people

DISCOURAGED, *Num.* 21. 4. soul of
the people was *d.*

Num. 32. 9. they *d.* the heart of the
children of Israel

Deut. 1. 21. go, fear not, nor be *d.*
28. our brethren have *d.* our heart,
saying

Is. 42. 4. he shall not fail nor be *d.* till
he set

Col. 3. 21. provoke not your children
lest they be *d.*

DISCRETION, prudence, *Ps.* 112. 5 ;
Prov. 1. 4. & 2. 11. & 3. 21. & 11. 22.
& 19. 11 ; *Is.* 28. 26 ; *Jer.* 10. 12.

DISEASE, *Ps.* 38. 7. & 41. 8 ; *Eccl.* 6. 2 ;
Matt. 4. 23. & 9. 35. & 10. 1 ; *Ex.*
15. 26 ; *Deut.* 28. 60 ; 2 *Chr.* 21. 19.

Ps. 103. 3. who healeth all thy *d.*

Ezek. 34. 4. *d.* have ye not, 21.

DISFIGURE bodies, *Matt.* 6. 16.

DISGRACE not, *Jer.* 14. 27.

DISH, ES, *Judg.* 5. 25. she brought
forth butter in a lordly *d.*

2 *Kings* 21. 13. as a man wipeth a *d.*
turning it

Matt. 26. 23. dippeth with me in the *d.*
Mark 14. 20.

DISHONESTY, 2 *Cor.* 4. 2. have renounced the hidden things of *d.*

DISHONOUR, *Ps.* 35. 26 ; *Prov.* 6. 33.

Mic. 7. 6. son *dishonour* his father

Ps. 71. 13. covered with shame and *d.*

Rom. 1. 24. to *d.* their own bodies
9. 21. another to *d.* 2 *Tim.* 2. 20.

1 *Cor.* 15. 43. it is sown in *d.* raised in

2 *Cor.* 6. 8. by honour and *d.*

DISMAYED, *Is.* 21. 3. I was bowed
down, *d.* at the seeing of it

Is. 41. 10. fear not, be not *d.* *Jer.* 1. 17 ;
10. 2 ; 23. 4 ; 30. 10 ; 46. 27 ;
Ezek. 2. 6 ; 3. 9.

Jer. 8. 9. the wise men are *d.*
17. 18. let them be *d.* but let not me
be *d.*
50. 36. the mighty men of Babylon
shall be *d.*

Obad. 9. thy mighty men, O Teman,
shall be *d.*

DISOBEDIENCE. A version to the laws
of God and man, and disregard of
them ; 2 *Cor.* 10. 6 ; *Eph.* 2. 2. &
5. 6 ; *Col.* 3. 6.

Rom. 5. 19. by one man's *d.* many were
made

DISOBEDIENT, 1 *Kings* 13. 26 ; *Neh.*
9. 26.

Luke 1. 17. *d.* to wisdom of just

Rom. 1. 30. *d.* to parents, 2 *Tim.* 3. 2.
10. 21. *d.* and gainsaying people

Tit. 1. 16. abominable and *d.*
3. 3. *d.* deceived serving lusts

1 *Pet.* 2. 7, 8. stumbling being *d.*
3. 20. who sometimes were *d.*

DISORDERLY, 2 *Thess.* 3. 6 ; 7. 11.

DISPATCH, (1) To kill ; *Ezek.* 23. 47.
(2) To put an end to an affair ;
Ezra 10. 14.

DISPENSATION, 1 *Cor.* 9. 17. a *d.* of
gospel is committed

Eph. 1. 10. *d.* of. fulness of times
3. 2. heard of *d.* of grace of God

Col. 1. 25. minister acc. to *d.* of God

DISPERSE, signifies, (1) to place or dispose of ; 2 *Chr.* 11. 23. (2) To go
throughout ; 1 *Sam.* 14. 34. (3) To
scatter abroad ; *Esth.* 3. 8 ; *Is.* 11.
12 ; *John* 7. 35 ; 11. 52 ; *Ezek.* 12.
15. (4) To be bountiful and liberal
to the poor ; *Ps.* 112. 9. " He hath
dispersed ; he hath given to the
poor." 2 *Cor.* 9. 9.

DISPLAYED, *Ps.* 60. 4. hast given a
banner that it may be *d.*

DISPLEASE, signifies, (1) doing harm
to another ; *Judg.* 15. 3. (2) To be
angry ; *Gen.* 31. 35. (3) The wrath
of God against sin ; *Zech.* 1. 2 ; *Ps.*
60. 1 ; *Deut.* 9. 19 ; *Gen.* 38. 10 ; 2
Sam. 11. 27 ; 1 *Chr.* 21. 7 ; *Is.* 59.
15 ; *Mark* 10. 14 ; 1 *Kings* 1. 6.

Deut. 9. 19. hot or sore *d. Ps.* 2. 5. & 6.
1. & 38. 1.

DISPOSE, put for the inclination 1 *Cor.*
10. 27 ; *Acts* 18. 27. The providence of God ; *Job* 34. 13. " Who
hath *disposed* the whole world ?"
Prov. 16. 3. " The lot is cast into
the lap ; but the whole *disposing*
thereof is of the Lord."

DISPOSING is of Lord ; *Prov.* 16. 33.

Acts 7. 53. *d.* of angels

DISPUTE, signifies, (1) To reason or
plead ; *Job* 23. 7. (2) To debate or
confer about a thing ; *Mark* 9. 33.
(3) To use sound arguments ; *Acts*
17. 17. " Therefore *disputed* he in
the synagogue with the Jews."
19. 8, 9. (4) To quarrel ; *Phil.*
2. 14. " Do all things without
murmurings and *disputings* " ; that
is, frame yourselves to all peaceable conduct towards one another.
" Perverse disputings of men of
corrupt minds," 1 *Tim.* 6. 5 ; *Acts*
6. 9. & 9. 29 ; *Jude* 9.

Rom. 14. 1. doubtful *d.*

DISPUTINGS, *Phil.* 2. 14 ; 1 *Tim.* 6. 5.

DISQUIET, signifies (1) Not to let rest ;
1 *Sam.* 28. 15. (2) To vex or
trouble ; *Ps.* 39. 6. " Surely they
are *disquieted* in vain." (3) To rise

up against ; *Jer.* 50. 34. *Disquietness* signifies great distress of mind ; *Ps.* 38. 8 ; 42. 5 ; 42. 11 ; *Prov.* 30. 21.

DISSEMBLE, to act the hypocrite ; *Josh.* 7. 11 ; *Jer.* 42. 20 ; *Gal.* 2 13 ; *Ps.* 26. 4 ; *Prov.* 26. 24.

DISSENSION, strife, contention, *Acts* 15. 2. & 23. 7, 10.

DISSIMULATION, not sincere, pretence, *Rom.* 12. 9 ; *Gal.* 2. 13.

DISSOLVE, ED EST, *Job.* 30. 22. thou d. my substance

Ps. 75. 3. inhabitants thereof are d.

Is. 34. 4. the host of heaven be d.

Dan. 5. 16. thou canst d. doubts

2 *Cor.* 5. 1. house of this tabernacle d.

2 *Pet.* 3. 11. all these things be d.

12. heavens on fire shall be d.

DISTAFF, *Prov.* 31. 19. her hands hold d.

DISTIL, *Deut.* 32. 2. my speech d. as dew

Job 36. 28. the clouds d. on man

DISTINCTION, Difference, 1 *Cor.* 14. 7.

DISTINCTLY, plainly, *Neh.* 8. 8.

DISTRACTED, disturbed in mind, *Ps* 88. 15 ; 1 *Cor.* 7. 35.

DISTRESS ; *trouble* : whatever vexes, pains, or hurts our soul, body, outward enjoyments : as temptation, desertion, disquiet of mind, *Ps.* 143. 11 ; *Gen.* 42. 21 ; *Deut.* 2. 9, 19 ; *Neh.* 9. 37 ; *Luke* 21. 23, 25.

Gen. 35. 3. answered in day of my d.

2 *Sam.* 22. 7. in my d. I called on the Lord, *Ps.* 18. 6. & 118. 5. & 120. 1.

1 *Kings* 1. 29. redeemed my soul out of all d.

2 *Chr.* 28. 22. in his d. trespass more

Ps. 4. 1. enlarged my heart in d.

Prov. 1. 27. I will mock when d. come

Is. 25. 4. strength to needy in d.

Zeph. 1. 15. that day is a day of d. 17.

Luke 21. 23. shall be great in d. in land 25. on the earth d. of nations

Rom. 8. 35. shall d. separate from Christ

1 *Cor.* 7. 26. good for the present d.

1 *Thess.* 3. 7. comforted in your d.

DISTRESSED, 1 *Sam.* 28. 15. & 30. 6 ; 2 *Sam* .1. 26 ; 2 *Cor.* 4. 8.

2 *Cor.* 6. 4. my d. 12. 10.

Ps. 25. 17. out of my d. 107. 6, 13, 19, 28 ; *Ezek.* 30. 16 ; 2 *Cor.* 6. 4.

DISTRIBUTE, to divide among, *Josh.* 13. 22 ; 14. 1. To place in an orderly way, 2 *Chr.* 31. 14. To give freely, *Luke* 18. 22 ; 1 *Tim.* 6. 18 ; 1 *Cor.* 7. 17 ; *Job* 21. 17 ; *Rom.* 12. 13.

DISTRIBUTION, *Acts* 4. 35 ; 2 *Cor.* 9. 13.

DITCH, *Job* 9. 31 ; *Ps.* 7. 15 ; *Prov.* 23. 27.; *Is.* 22. 11 ; *Matt.* 15. 14 ; *Luke* 6. 39.

DIVERSITIES, 1 *Cor.* 12.´ 4, 6, 28.

DIVIDE, *Gen.* 1. 6, 14 ; *Job* 27. 17.

Ex. 14. 16. over the sea and d. it

Num. 31. 27. d. the prey into two

Josh. 1. 6. d. for inheritance, 18. 5.

1 *Kings* 3. 25. d. living child, 26.

Ps. 55. 9. destroy—d. their tongues

Is. 53. 12. I will d. him a portion with

Luke 12. 13. to d. inheritance with, 14.

22. 17. d. it among yourselves

DIVIDE, I will, *Gen.* 49. 7. *I will d.* them in Jacob

Is. 53. 12. will I d. him a portion

DIVIDED, 2 *Sam.* 1. 23. in death not d.

Job 38. 25. hath d. a watercourse

Ps. 68. 12. she that tarried d. spoil

78. 55. d. them an inheritance by line, *Acts* 13. 19.

Is. 34. 17. his hand d. it by line

Dan. 2. 41. kingdom shall be d.

5. 28. thy kingdom is d. and given

Hos. 10. 2. their heart is d.

Matt. 12. 25. kingdom or house d. not stand, *Mark* 3. 24 ; *Luke* 11. 17.

Luke 12. 52. be five in one house d.

1 *Cor.* 1. 13. is Christ d. was Paul crucified

DIVIDETH, *Ps.* 29. 7. voice of Lord d. flames

Matt. 25. 32. d. his sheep from goats

Luke 11. 22. and d. his spoils

DIVIDING, *Is.* 63. 12. d. water before them

1 *Cor.* 12. 11. d. to every man severally

2 *Tim.* 2. 15. rightly d. word of truth

Heb. 4. 12. to d. asunder of joints

DIVISIONS, *Judg.* 5. 15, 16 ; *Luke* 12. 51 ; *Rom.* 16. 17 ; 1 *Cor.* 1. 10. & 3. 3. & 11. 18.

DIVINE, something relating to God Divine sentence, *Prov.* 16. 10.

Heb. 9. 1. ordinance of d. service

2 *Pet.* 1. 3. his d. power hath given 4. partakers of a d. nature

Mic. 3. 11. prophets d. for money

DIVINATION, *Num.* 22. 7. & 23. 23 ; *Deut.* 18. 10 ; *Acts* 16. 16.

DIVINERS, *Deut.* 18. 14 ; *Is.* 44. 25 ; *Mic.* 3. 6, 7 ; *Zech.* 10. 2 ; *Jer.* 29. 8.

DIVORCE, *Jer.* 3. 8 ; *Lev.* 21. 14. & 22. 13 ; *Num.* 30. 9 ; *Matt.* 5. 32.

DIVORCEMENT, *Deut.* 24. 1, 3 ; *Is.* 50. 1 ; *Matt.* 5. 31. & 19. 7 ; *Mark* 10. 4.

DO, *Gen.* 16. 6. & 18. 25. & 31. 16.

Matt. 7. 12. men should d. to you d. ye

John 15. 5. without me ye can d. nothing

Rom. 7. 15. what I would not that d. I

Phil. 4. 13. I can d. all things through Christ

Heb. 4. 13. with whom we have to d.

10. 9. come to d. thy will, *Ps.* 40. 8.

Rev. 19. 10. see thou d. it not, 22. 9.

Rom. 2. 13. d. of it shall be justified

Jam. 1. 22. be ye d. of word and not

DOING, 1 *Chr.* 22. 16 ; *Ps.* 64. 9. & 66. 5. & 118. 23 ; *Prov.* 20. 11 ; *Is.* 1. 16 ; *Jer.* 7. 3, 5. & 18. 11. & 26. 13. & 32. 19 ; *Ezek.* 36. 31 ; *Zeph.* 3. 11 ; *Zech.* 1. 4 ; *Mic.* 2. 7 ; *Matt.* 24. 46.

Rom. 2. 7. well d. *Gal.* 6. 9 ; 2 *Thess.* 3. 13 ; 1 *Pet.* 2. 15. & 3. 17. & 4. 19.

DOCTRINE shall drop as rain, *Deut.* 32. 2.

Is. 28. 9. make to understand d. 29. 24.

Jer. 10. 8. stock a d. of vanities

Matt. 7. 28. astonished at his d. 22. 33 ;

Mark 1. 22. & 11. 18 ; *Luke* 4. 32.
16. 12. beware of *d.* of Pharisees
Mark 1. 27. what new *d.* is this
John 7. 17. shall know of the *d.*
Acts 2. 42. apostles' *d.* and fellowship
Rom. 6. 17. form of *d.* which was delivered you
16. 17. contrary to *d.* ye have learned
Eph. 4. 14. with every wind of *d.*
1 *Tim.* 5. 17. labour in word and *d.*
6. 3. *d.* according to godliness
2 *Tim.* 3. 16. profitable for *d.*
4. 3. will not endure sound *d.*
Tit. 2. 7. in *d.* showing incorruptness
10. may adorn *d.* of God our Saviour
Heb. 6. 1. principles of *d.* of Christ
2. *d.* of baptisms and laying hands
2 *John* 9. whose abideth not in the *d.* of Christ, abideth in *d.*
Rev. 2. 14. that hold *d.* of Balaam
15. that hold *d.* of Nicolaitans
Matt. 15. 9. teaching for *d.* commandments
Col. 2. 22. after *d.* of men
1 *Tim.* 4. 1. giving heed to *d.* of devils
Heb. 13. 9. carried about by strange *d.*
DOER, *Ps.* 31. 23. rewardeth the proud *d.*
Prov. 17. 4. a wicked *d.* giveth heed
2 *Tim.* 2. 9. I suffer as an evil *d.*
Jam. 1. 23. if any be not *d.* of word
25. not forgetful hearer, but *d.*
4 11. thou art not a *d.* of the law
1 *Pet.* 4. 15. none suffer as evil *d.*
DOERS, *Ps.* 101. 8. cut off all wicked *d.*
Rom. 2. 13. *d.* of law be justified
Jam. 1. 22. be ye *d.* of the word
DOG, *Ex.* 11. 7 ; *Deut.* 23. 18.
Judg. 7. 5. lappeth, as a *d.* lappeth
1 *Sam.* 17. 43. am I a *d.* 2 *Kings* 8. 13.
Ps. 22. 20. darling from power of *d.*
Prov. 26. 11. *d.* returneth to vomit, 2 *Pet.* 2. 22.
17. taketh a *d.* by the ears
Eccl. 9. 4. living *d.* better than lion
Is. 56. 10. all dumb *d.*
11. greedy *d.*
Matt. 7. 6. cast not that which is holy to *d.*
15. 27. *d.* eat of crumbs, *Mark* 7. 28.
Phil. 3. 2. beware of *d.* beware of evil-workers
Rev. 22. 15. without are *d.* sorcerers
DOING, *Ex.* 15. 11. *d.* wonders
1 *Chr.* 22. 16. arise and be *d.*
Ps. 64. 9. wisely consider of his *d.*
66. 5. he is terrible in his *d.*
118. 23. this is the Lord's *d.* it is marvellous, *Matt.* 21. 42 ; *Mark* 12. 11.
Matt. 24. 46. find so *d. Luke* 12. 43.
Acts 10. 38. went about *d.* good
2 *Cor.* 8. 11. perform the *d.* of it.
Eph. 6. 6. *d.* the will of God
DOING, well doing, *Gal.* 6. 9. weary in w-*d.* 2 *Thess.* 3. 1
1 *Pet.* 2. 15. with w-*d.* ye silence
3. 17. better suffer for w-*d.*
4. 19. commit souls to him in w-*d.*
DOINGS, *Ps.* 9. 11. declare his *d. Is.* 12. 4.
Prov. 20. 11. a child known by his *d.*
Is. 1. 16. put away evil of your *d.*
DOLEFUL, *Is.* 13. 21. full of *d.* creatures
Mic. 2. 4. with a *d.* lamentation

DOMINION. God's absolute right to, and authority over all his creatures, to do with them as he pleases, *Gen.* 27. 40. & 37. 8.
Num. 24. 19. he that shall have *d.* and
Job 25. 2. *d.* and fear are with him
Ps. 8. 6. have *d.* over work of thy hands
19. 13. not have *d.* over me, 119. 133.
49. 14. upright have *d.* over them
72. 8. his *d.* from sea to sea, *Zech.* 9. 10.
145. 13. thy *d.* endureth through all generations
Is. 26. 13. other lords have had *d.* over
Dan. 4. 3. his *d.* is from generation to generation
34. an everlasting *d.* 7. 14.
7. 27. all *d.* shall serve and obey him
Rom. 6. 9. death has no more *d.*
14. sin shall not have *d.* over you
7. 1. law hath *d.* over a man
2 *Cor.* 1. 24. not, we have *d.* over faith
Jude 8. despise *d.* and speak evil of dignities
25. to God *d.* 1 *Pet.* 4. 11. & 5. 11 ; *Rev.* 1. 6.
DOMINIONS, *Dan.* 7. 27. all *d.* shall serve him
Col. 1. 16. whether thrones or *d.*
DONE, *Ps.* 33. 9. he spake, and it was *d.*
Is. 44. 23. for the Lord hath *d.* it
Ezek. 39. 8. it is *d.* saith the Lord
Matt. 6. 10. thy will be done, 26. 42 ; *Luke* 11. 2 ; 22. 42.
25. 21. well *d.* good servant, 23.
40. as ye have *d.* it to one of these, ye
Mark 13. 30. shall not pass till these be *d.*
John 5. 29. they that have *d.* good
Acts 4. 28. determined before to be *d.*
1 *Cor.* 16. 14. be *d.* with charity
Col. 4. 9. make known all things *d.*
Rev. 16. 17. saying, it is *d.* 21. 6.
22. 6. which must shortly be *d.*
DOOR, *Judg.* 11. 31. & 16. 3.
Gen. 4. 7. sin lieth at the door
Ps. 84. 10. *d.* keeper in the house
141. 3. keep *d.* of my lips
Prov. 26. 14. as *d.* turneth upon hinges
Hos. 2. 15. valley of Achor for a *d.* of hope
John 10. 1. entereth not by the *d.* is a
John 10. 7. I am the *d.* of sheep
9. I am the *d.*
Acts 14. 27. opened *d.* of faith
1 *Cor.* 16. 9. great *d.* and effectual is opened
2 *Cor.* 2. 12. a *d.* was opened to me
Col. 4. 3. God opened a *d.* of utterance
Jam. 5. 9. judge standeth before *d.*
Rev. 3. 8. I set before thee an open *d.*
20. I stand at *d.* and knock if any man
DOORS, *Judg.* 16. 3. Samson took *d.* of the city
Job 31. 32. opened *d.* to traveller
Ps. 24. 7. be lifted up, ye everl. *d.* 9.
Prov. 8. 34. waiting at posts of my *d.*
Mal. 1. 10. shut ye the *d.* for nought
Matt. 24. 23. near even at the *d.*
Acts 5. 19. angel opened prison *d.*
23. keepers standing before *d.*

16. 26. all the *d.* were opened
27. keeper seeing prison *d.* open
DOUBLE, *Ex.* 22. 4 ; *Deut.* 21. 17.
2 *Kings* 2. 9. *d.* portion of thy spirit
1 *Chr.* 12. 33. not of a *d.* heart
Job 11. 6. secrets of. to that which is
Ps. 12. 2. with *d.* heart they speak
Is. 40. 2. *d.* for all her sins ; *Jer.* 16. 18.
61. 7. ye shall have *d.* *Zech.* 9. 12.
Jer. 17. 18. destroy with *d.* destruction
1 *Tim.* 3. 8. deacons grave, not *d.*
tongued
5. 17. elders counted worthy of *d.*
honour
James 1. 8. *d.* minded men, 4. 8.
Rev. 18. 6. *d.* to her fill her *d.*
DOUBT. To be uncertain what to think
or believe ; to fear, despond ; *John*
10. 24 ; *Deut.* 28. 66 ; *Gal.* 4. 20.
Matt. 14. 31. of little faith why dost *d.*
21. 21. have faith and *d.* not
Mark 11. 23. have no *d.* in his heart
Rom. 14. 23. he that *d.* is damned
DOUBTED, ETH, *Matt.* 28. 17. but
some *d.*
Acts 5. 24. *d.* whereunto would grow
25. 20. I *d.* of such questions
DOUBTFUL, *Luke* 12. 29. neither be ye
of *d.* mind
Rom. 14. 1. not to *d.* disputations
DOUBTING, *Acts* 10. 20. go, nothing *d.*
11. 12.
1 *Tim.* 2. 8. men pray without *d.*
DOUBTLESS, *Ps.* 126. 6. *d.* come again
rejoicing
Is. 63. 16. *d.* thou art our father
1 *Cor.* 9. 2. yet *d.* I am to you
Phil. 3. 8. yea *d.* I count all but loss
DOVE, *Gen.* 8. 8. Noah sent forth a *d.*
10. 12.
Gen. 8. 9. the *d.* found no rest
Ps. 55. 6. O that I had wings like a *d.*
Ps. 68. 13. ye shall be as wings of a *d.*
Songs 1. 15. thou hast *d.* eyes, 4. 1.
2. 14. my *d.* let me see thy counten.
6. 9. my *d.* my undefiled is but one
Is. 38. 14. mourn as *d.* 59. 11 ; *Ezek.* 7.
16 ; *Nah.* 2. 7.
Hos. 7. 11. Ephraim also is like a silly *d.*
DOVES, *Is.* 60. 8. flee as *d.* to their
windows
Matt. 10. 16. harmless as *d.*
21. 12. that sold *d.* *Mark* 11. 15.
John 2. 14. found those that sold *d.*
DOVES, turtle, *Lev.* 14. 22. take two
t-d. *Luke* 2. 24.
DOWN sitting, *Ps.* 139. 2.
DOWNWARD, *Is.* 37. 31 ; *Eccl.* 3. 21.
DOWRY, *Gen.* 30. 20. endued me with
good *d.*
Gen. 34. 12. ask me never so much *d.*
DRAG, S, *Hab.* 1. 15. gather them in
their *d.*
Hab. 1. 16. burn incense to their *d.*
DRAGON, *Ps.* 91. 13 ; *Is.* 27. 1. & 51. 9 ;
Jer. 51. 34 ; *Ezek.* 29. 3 ; *Rev.* 12. 3,
17. & 13. 2, 4, 11. & 16. 13. & 20. 2.
DRAGONS, *Deut.* 32. 33 ; *Job* 30. 29 ;
Ps. 44. 19. & 74. 13. & 148. 7 ; *Is.*
13. 22. & 34. 13. & 43. 20 ; *Jer.*
9. 11. & 14. 6 ; *Mic.* 1. 8 ; *Mal.* 1. 3.
DRANK, *Gen.* 9. 21. Noah *d.* of the

wine
1 *Sam.* 30. 12. nor *d.* water three days
1 *Kings* 17. 6. and he *d.* of brook
Luke 17. 27. they eat, they *d.* 28.
John 4. 12. Jacob *d.* thereof himself
1 *Cor.* 10. 4. *d.* of that spiritual rock
DRAUGHT, *Matt.* 15. 17. cast out in *d.*
Mark 7. 19.
Luke 5. 9. astonished at *d.* of fishes
DRAW, *Gen.* 24. 44 ; 2 *Sam.* 17. 13.
Job 21. 33. every man shall *d.* after him
Ps. 28. 3. *d.* me not away with wicked
Songs 1. 4. *d.* me we will run after thee
Is. 5. 18. woe unto them that *d.* iniquity
with cords
Jer. 31. 3. with loving kindness I *d.* thee
John 6. 44. except the Father *d.* him
12. 32. I will *d.* all men unto me
Heb. 10. 38. but if any man *d.* back, 39.
DRAW near, 1 *Sam.* 14. 36. let us *d.*
near to God
Ps. 73. 28. it is good to *d.* near to God
107. 18. *d.* near to gates of death
Is. 29. 13. *d.* near with their lips
Heb. 10. 22. *d.* near with a true heart
DRAW nigh, *Ps.* 69. 18. *d.* nigh to my
Eccl. 12. 1. years *d.* nigh when say
Heb. 7. 19. by the which we *d.* nigh
Jam. 4. 8. *d.* nigh to God he will *d.* nigh
DRAWN, *Ps.* 55. 21. than oil, yet *d.*
swords
Prov. 24. 11. that are *d.* to death
Is. 21. 15. fled from *d.* swords
28. 9. that are *d.* from breasts
Acts 11. 10. *d.* up again to heaven
Jam. 1. 14. *d.* away of his own lusts
DREAD, terror, fear, *Ex.* 15. 16 ; *Job*
13. 11, 21.
Deut. 1. 29. *d.* not nor be afraid
1 *Chr.* 22. 13. be strong, *d.* not, nor
Is. 8. 13. let him be your fear and *d.*
Dan. 9. 4. great and *d.* God
Gen 28. 17. how *d.* is this place
Mal. 1. 14. my name is *d.* among
4. 5. great and *d.* day of the Lord
DREAM. Those vain images formed
in the imagination while we are
asleep, *Job* 20. 8. He shall fly away
as a dream, and shall not be found ;
yea, he shall be chased away as a
vision of the night. The Eastern
people, and in particular the Jews,
had a very great regard to dreams ;
they observed them, and applied
to those who pretended to explain
them. We see the antiquity of
this custom among the Egyptians,
in the history of Pharaoh's butler
and baker, and in Pharaoh himself.
Gen. 40. 5, 8 ; 41. 15. Nebuchadnezzar is an instance of the same
among the Chaldeans, *Dan.* 2. 1, 2,
3. &c. God had very expressly forbidden his people to observe
dreams, and to consult those who
took upon them to explain them.
He condemned any one to death
who pretended to have prophetic
dreams, and to foretell what was to
come, though what he should so
foretell were to come to pass, if after this he would engage the people in idolatry, *Deut.* 13. 1, 2, 3, &c.

But they were not forbid, when they thought they had any significant dream, to address themselves to the prophets of the Lord, or to the high-priest dressed in his ephod, in order to have it explained.

DREAM, *Gen.* 37. 5. & 40. 5. & 41. 7.

Gen. 20. 3. God came to Abimelech in a *d*.

31. 11. angel spake to Jacob in a *d*.

24. *God* came to Laban in a *d*.

Num. 12. 6. speak to him in a *d*.

Judg. 7. 15. Gideon heard telling of *d*.

1 *Kings* 3. 5. Lord appeared to Solomon in a *d*.

Job 20. 8. fly away as a *d*.

33. 15. in a *d*. in a vision of night

Ps. 73. 20. as a *d*. when one waketh

126. 1. were like them that *d*.

Eccl. 5. 3. *d*. comes through multitude

Is. 29. 7. that fight—be as a *d*.

Jer. 23. 28. who hath a *d*. let him tell a *d*.

Dan. 2. 3. I *d*. a *d*.

4. 5. saw a *d*.

Matt. 1. 20. angel appeared in a *d*.

2. 12. Joseph warned of God in a *d*.

27. 19. suffered many things in a *d*.

DREAM, verb, *Ps.* 126. 1. we were like them that *d*.

Joel 2. 28. your old men *d*. dreams, *Acts* 2. 17.

DREAMED, *Gen.* 28. 12. Jacob *d* ; 37. 5. Joseph *d*. a dream

Gen. 42. 9. Joseph remembered the dreams which he *d*.

Dan. 2. 1. Nebuchadnezzar *d*. dreams, spirit was troubled

5. the king said to them, I have *d*. a dream

DREAMER, *Gen.* 37. 19 they said, behold, this *d*. cometh

Deut. 13. 1. if a *d*. of dreams arise among you

5. that prophet or *d*. of dreams shall be put to death

DREAMERS, *Jude* 8. those filthy *d*. divide flesh

DREAMS, *Gen.* 37. 8. hated Joseph for his *d*.

Gen. 37. 20. see what become of his *d*.

42. 9. Joseph remembered the *d*. he dreamed

Job 7. 14. scarest me with *d*.

Eccl. 5. 7. in multitude of *d*. and words

Jer. 23. 27. to forget my name with their *d*.

DREAMETH, *Is.* 29. 8. when a hungry man *d*. a thirsty man *d*.

DREGS, *Ps.* 75. 8. the *d*. thereof the wicked shall drink out

Is. 51. 17. thou hast drunken the *d*. of the cup, 22.

DRESS, *Gen.* 2. 15. God put the man into the garden to *d*.

Deut. 28. 39. thou shalt plant vineyards, and *d*. them

2 *Sam.* 12. 4. to *d*. of his own for the way-faring man

1 *Kings* 17. 12. that I may *d*. it for me and my son

DRESSED, *Gen.* 18. 1. Abraham took the calf which he had *d*.

Heb. 6. 7. bringeth herbs for them by whom it is *d*.

DRESSER, *Luke* 13. 7. then said he to the *d*. of the vineyard

DREW, *Gen.* 24. 20. Rebekah *d*. water for his camels, 45.

Josh. 8. 26. for Joshua *d*. not his hand back

Judg. 8. 10. there fell 120,000 men that *d*. sword

20. 2. the chief of Israel 400,000 that *d*. sword

2 *Sam.* 23. 16. the three mighty men *d*. water out of the well of Bethlehem

24. 9. there were in Israel 800,000 that *d*. sword

Matt. 13. 48. when full, they *d*. to shore, *Mark* 6. 53.

26. 51. Peter *d*. his sword, *Mark* 14. 47 ; *John* 18. 10.

Acts 16. 27. the jailer *d*. his sword, and would

DREW near, or nigh, *Luke* 15. 1. *d*. near the publicans

Luke 22. 1. now the feast of unleavened bread *d*. nigh

DRINK, *Ex.* 15. 24. & 32. 20.

Job 21. 20. *d*. of wrath of Almighty

Ps. 36. 8. *d*. of river of pleasure

60. 3. *d*. wine of astonishment

80. 5. givest them tears to *d*.

110. 7. *d*. of the brook in the

Prov. 4. 17. *d*. wine of violence

5. 15. *d*. out of own cistern

31. 4. not for kings to *d*. wine

5. lest they *d*. and forget law

7. *d*. and forget his poverty

Songs 5. 1. *d*. yea, *d*. abundantly, O beloved

Is. 22. 13. let us eat and *d*. 1 *Cor.* 15. 32.

43. 20. to give *d*. to my people

65. 13. my servants shall *d*.

Hos. 4. 18. their *d*. is sour, committed whoredom

Amos 4. 1. bring and let us *d*.

Matt. 10. 42. give to *d*. to one of little

20. 22. able to *d*. of cup, 23.

25. 35. I was thirsty ye gave me *d*.

26. 27. *d*. ye all of it, this is my blood

29. I'll not henceforth *d*. of fruit of vine

42. except I *d*. it thy will be

John 6. 55. my blood is *d*. indeed

18. 11. cup Father hath given shall I not *d*. it

Rom. 14. 17. kingdom of God is not *d*.

1 *Cor.* 10. 4. *d*. the same spiritual *d*.

21. cannot *d*. cup of Lord and of devils

11. 25. as often as ye *d*. it

12. 13. all made to *d*. into one spirit

DRINK, strong, *Lev.* 10. 9. not *d*. wine nor *strong d*.

wine or *strong d.* *Judg.* 13. 4, 7, 14 ; 1 *Sam.* 1. 15.

Prov. 20. 1. *strong d*. is raging

31. 4. not for princes to *d*. *strong d*.

6. give *strong d*. to those ready to perish

Is. 5. 11. follow *strong d*.

22. mingle *strong d*.

28. 7. prophet erred through *strong d*.

Mic. 2. 11. prophesy to them of *strong d*.

DRINKETH, *Job* 15. 16. which *d*.

iniquity like water
John 6. 54. *d.* my blood hath eternal life
  56. that *d.* my blood dwells in me
1 *Cor.* 11. 29. eateth and *d.* unworthily
Heb. 6. 7. earth which *d.* in rain that
  cometh

DROP. To fall gently like rain ; *Deut.*
  32. 2 ; *Judg.* 5. 4 ; *Ezek.* 20. 46.
  Figuratively to preach. "Drop
  thy word to the south" ; *Ezek.* 20.
  46 ; *Deut.* 33. 28.
Ps. 65. 11. thy paths *d.* fatness
Prov. 5. 3. *d.* as honey-comb ; *Songs*
  4. 11.
Songs 5. 5. my hands *d.* myrrh
Is. 40. 15. all nations as a *d.* of bucket

DROPS *Songs* 5. 2. locks with *d.* of night
Luke 22. 44. sweat as great *d.* of blood

DROSS, *Ps.* 119. 119. the wicked like *d.*
Prov. 25. 4. take *d.* from silver
Is. 1. 22. thy silver is become *d.*

DROVE, verb, *Gen.* 3. 24. so God *d.* out
  the man
Gen. 15. 11. Abram *d.* fowls away
Hab. 3. 6. *d.* asunder the nations
John 2. 15. *d.* them out of temple

DROUGHT, *Gen.* 31. 40. in day *d.* con-
  sumed me
Deut. 8. 15. fiery serpents and *d.*
Job 24. 19. *d.* consume snow-waters
Ps. 32. 4. my moisture into the *d.*
Jer. 2. 6. through a land of *d.*
Hos. 13. 5. know thee in land of *d.*

DROWN, to overwhelm, *Songs* 8. 7 ; 1
  Tim. 6. 9.

DROWSINESS clothe, *Prov.* 23. 21.

DRUNK, *Eph.* 5. 18. be not *d.* with wine
Rev. 17. 2. made *d.* with wine of fornication

DRUNKARD, *Deut.* 21. 20. glutton and *d.*
Prov. 23. 21. *d.* shall come to poverty
  26. 9. thorn goeth up into hand of *d.*
Is. 24. 20. earth shall reel like a *d.*
1 *Cor.* 5. 11. with railer and *d.* eat not

DRUNKARDS, *Ps.* 69. 12 ; *Is.* 28. 1, 3 ;
  Joel 1. 5 ; *Nah.* 1. 10 ; 1 *Cor.* 6. 10.
Job 12. 25. stagger like a *d.* man ; *Ps.*
  107. 27 ; *Jer.* 23. 9 ; *Is.* 19. 14.
Is. 29. 9. *d.* not with wine, 51. 21.
Acts 2. 15. these are not *d.* as ye suppose
1 *Cor.* 11. 21. one hungry another is *d.*
1 *Thess.* 5. 7. they that be *d.* are *d.* in
  the night

DRUNKENNESS, *Deut.* 29. 19 ; *Eccl.*
  10. 17 ; *Jer.* 13 13 ; *Ezek.* 23. 33 ;
  Luke 21. 34 ; *Rom.* 13. 13 ; *Gal.* 5. 21.

DRY, *Judg.* 6. 37, 39 ; *Job* 13. 25.
Ps. 105. 41. they ran in *d.* places
Prov. 17. 1. better is a *d.* morsel
Is. 32. 2. be as rivers in a *d.* place
  44. 27. saith to the deep, be *d.*
  56. 3. say, I am a *d.* tree
Ezek. 17. 24. made *d.* tree flourish
  37. 2. bones *d.* 4. O ye *d.* bones
Hos. 9. 14. give them *d.* breasts
  13. 15. his spring shall become *d.*
Zeph. 2. 13. make Nineveh *d.* like
Matt. 12. 43. through *d.* places, *Luke*
  11. 24.
Luke 23. 31. what be done in the *d.*

DRIED, *Ps.* 22. 15. my strength is *d.*
  like a potsherd

Jer. 23. 10. places of wilderness *d.* up
  50. 38. her waters shall be *d.* up
Mark 5. 29. foun. of her blood *d.* up

DRY-SHOD, *Is.* 11. 15. make men go
  over *d-s.*

DUE, *Lev.* 10. 13 ; *Deut.* 18. 3.
1 *Chr.* 15. 13. sought him not after *d.*
  order
  16. 29. give Lord glory *d.* to his name,
  Ps. 29. 2. & 96. 8.
Prov. 3. 27. withhold not good from
  whom is *d.*
Matt. 18. 34. pay all that was *d.*
Luke 23. 41. we receive the *d.* reward
1 *Cor.* 7. 3. render *d.* benevolence

DUE season, *Ps.* 104. 27. meat in *d.* season. 145. 15 ; *Matt.* 24. 45 ; *Luke*
  12. 42.
Prov. 15. 23. words spoken in *d.* season
Eccl. 10. 17. princes eat in *d.* season for
  strength
Gal. 6. 9. in *d.* season ye shall reap if
  faint not

DUE time, *Deut.* 32. 35. foot shall slide
  in *d.* time
Rom. 5. 6. in *d.* time Christ died for
  ungodly
1 *Cor.* 15. 8. as one born out of *d.* time
1 *Tim.* 2. 6. testified in *d.* time
Tit. 1. 3. hath in *d.* times manifested

DUES. *Rom.* 13. 7. render to all their *d.*

DULCIMER, *Dan.* 3. 5. *d.* and music,
  10. 15.

DULL, *Matt.* 13. 15. ears are *d.* Acts 28.
  27.
Heb. 5. 11. seeing ye are *d.* of hearing

DUMB, *Hab.* 2. 18 ; *Mark* 9. 17
Ex. 4. 11. who maketh *d.* or deaf
Ps. 38. 13. I was as a *d.* man
  39. 2. I was *d.* with silence, 9.
Prov. 31. 8. open thy mouth for *d.*
Is. 35. 6. tongue of *d.* to sing
  53. 7. sheep before shearers is *d.*
  56. 10. watchmen are all *d.* dogs
Matt. 9. 32. brought to him a *d.* man
  12. 22. and *d.* and he healed him
Luke 1. 20. shalt be *d.* until the day
Acts 8. 32. lamb *d.* before shearer
1 *Cor.* 12. 2. carried away to *d.* idols
2 *Pet.* 2. 16. the *d.* ass speaking

DUNG, *Phil.* 3. 8. I count all things *d.*

DUNG, verb, *Luke* 12. 8. dig about, and
  d. it

DUNGHILL, *Dan.* 2. 5. your houses
  be made a *d.*
Luke 14. 35. salt not fit for the *d.*

DUNGEON, *Gen.* 40. 15. should put me
  into *d.*
Gen. 41. 14. Joseph hastily out of *d.*
Jer. 37. 16. when Jeremiah entered *d.*
Lam. 3. 53. cut off my life in *d.*

DURABLE riches and right, *Prov.* 8. 18.
Is. 23. 18. merchandise for *d.* clothing

DURETH, *Matt.* 13. 21. but *d.* for a

DURST, *Job* 32. 6. *d.* not show my
  opinion
Matt. 22. 46. *d.* not ask more questions,
  Mark 12. 34 ; *Luke* 20. 40.
John 21. 12. none *d.* ask him
Acts 5. 13. then Moses *d.* not behold
Jude 9. *d.* not bring a railing accusa.

DUST, *Gen.* 3. 19. *d.* thou art, to *d.* shalt

return

Gen. 18. 27. who am but d. and ashes
Job 30. 19. I am become like d. and ashes
    34. 15. man shall turn again to d.
    42. 6. and repent in d. and ashes
Ps. 22. 15. brought me into d. of death
    30. 9. shall the d. praise thee
    72. 9. enemies shall lick the d.
    102. 14. servants favour the d. thereof
    103. 14. remembereth that ye are d.
    104. 29. die and return to d. Eccl. 3. 20.
    119. 25. soul cleaveth to the d.
Eccl. 12. 7. then shall d. return to earth
Matt. 10. 14. shake off d. of your feet,
    Luke 10. 11 ; Acts 13. 51.
DUST, in the, Job 4. 19. foundation is
    in the d.
Job 7. 21. now shall I sleep in the d.
    21. 26. lie down alike in the d.
Is. 26. 19. awake and sing, ye in the d.
Lam. 3. 29. putteth mouth in the d.
DUTY of marriage, Ex. 21. 10.
2 Chr. 8. 14. as d. of every day requires
Eccl. 12. 13. this is whole d. of man
Luke 17. 10. which was our d. to do
DWELL. To dwell signifies to abide
    in, to inhabit, to have a fixed resi-
    dence in a place. Num. 33. 53 ; Ps.
    78. 55. Sometimes it is taken for
    sojourning, Heb. 11. 9. where it is
    said, that Abraham dwelt in taber-
    nacles ; that is, sojourned ; for he
    had no fixed abode in the land of
    Canaan. It is spoken (1) Of God,
    who is said to dwell in the heavens
    Ps. 123. 1. He hath a certain and
    glorious place where he resideth,
    even the highest heavens, where
    he is clothed with infinite power
    and majesty, and from whence he
    beholdeth and governeth this lower
    world and all that is in it. His
    gracious presence with his people
    on earth is signified by dwelling
    with them, Ps. 9. 11 ; sing praises
    to the Lord who dwelleth in Zion :
    where the ark was, which was the
    symbol of his special and gracious
    presence. And in Isa. 57. 15 ;
    dwell with him that is of a contrite
    and humble spirit.
(2) Of Christ, signifying (1) His mani-
    festation in the flesh, John 1. 14.
    The Word was made flesh, and
    dwelt among us. (2) His spiritual
    abode in every faithful soul, Eph.
    3. 17. That Christ may dwell in
    your hearts by faith. Christ dwelt
    in his people by his merit to justify
    them ; by his grace and spirit to
    renew and purify them ; by his
    power to keep them ; by his wisdom
    to lead and instruct them ; and by
    his communion and compassion to
    share with them in all their trou-
    bles.
(3) Of the Holy Ghost, who dwells in
    the soul by his gracious operations,
    working faith, love, and other graces
    therein. Rom. 8. 9. But ye are not
    in the flesh, but in the Spirit, if so
    be that the Spirit of God dwell in

you.
(4) Of the word of God, which may be
    said to dwell in a person, when it
    is diligently studied, firmly be-
    lieved, and carefully practised.
    Col. 3. 16 ; Let the word of God
    dwell richly in you in all wisdom.
(5) Of Satan, who dwells in wicked men,
    when he fills them with farther
    degrees of error, malice, blasphe-
    my, impenitence, and blindness ;
    thereby making them highly wick-
    ed, and worse and worse daily,
    Matt. 12. 45.
(6) Of the godly, who are said to dwell
    in God, 1 John 3. 24. They have
    most intimate union and commu-
    nion with God in Christ.
Gen. 9. 27. Japhet shall d. in the tents
    of Shem
    16. 12. d. in presence of
Lev. 23. 42. ye shall d. in booths, 43 :
    Neh. 8. 14.
Num. 35. 34. I the Lord d. among the
    children of Israel
Deut. 33. 12. d. between his shoulders
2 Kings 4. 13. she answered, I d. among
    my own people
Ps. 15. 1. Lord, who shall d. in thy holy
    hill ?
Ps. 23. 6. I will d. in house of Lord for
    25. 13. their soul shall d. at ease
    27. 4. may d. in house of Lord and
    65. 4. to approach, that he may d. in
    thy courts
    68. 16. this is the hill which God de-
    sireth to d. in, yea the Lord will d.
    in it for ever and ever
    18. that the Lord might d. among
    them
    84. 10. than to d. in tents of wicked-
    ness
    120. 5. that I d. in tents of Kedar
    132. 14. rest here will I d. for desired
    133. 1. good for brethren to d.
    139. 9. if I d. in uttermost parts of
    the sea
Is. 13. 21. owls shall d. there, satyrs
    26. 19. awake and sing, ye that d. in
    33. 14. who shall d. with devouring
    fire—d. with everlasting burnings
    16. he shall d. on high—his place
    34. 11. the owl and the raven shall d.
    in it
Acts 28. 16. Paul was suffered to d. by
    himself
Rom. 8. 9. spirit of God d. in you, 11
2 Cor. 6. 16. I will d. in them, Ezek. 43.
    7, 9 ; Zech. 2. 10, 11.
Eph. 3. 17. that Christ may d. in hearts
Col. 1. 19. in him should all fulness d.
    3. 16. that Christ may d. in you richly
1 John 4. 13. that we d. in him
Rev. 7. 15. he that sitteth on the throne
    shall d.
    21. 3. he will d. with them
DWELL, with land, Gen. 45. 10. d. in
    the land of Goshen
Ps. 37. 3. do good, so shalt thou d. in
    the land
    85. 9. salvation near, that glory may
    d. in our land

Is. 9. 2. that *d.* in *land* of the shadow of death

DWELL together, *Deut.* 25. 25. if brethren *d. together,* and one die

Ps. 133. 1. for brethren to *d.* together in unity

DWELLEST, *Ps.* 123. 1. O thou that *d.* in the heavens

Ezek. 12. 2. thou *d.* in the midst of a rebellious house

John 1. 38. they said, Master, where *d.* thou

Rev. 2. 13: I know thy works, and where thou *d.*

DWELLETH, *Ps.* 26. 8. Lord, I loved the place where thine honour *d.*

Ps. 91. 1. he that *d.* in the secret place of the most High

John 6. 56. *d.* in me and I in him

14. 10. Father that *d.* in me

17. he *d.* with and shall be in you

Acts 7. 48. *d.* not in temples, 17. 24.

Rom. 7. 17. sin that *d.* in me, 20.

18. in my flesh *d.* no good thing

8. 11. by his spirit that *d.* in us

1 *Cor.* 3. 16. spirit of God *d.* in you

Col. 2. 9. in him *d.* all fulness of Godhead

2 *Tim.* 1. 14. Holy Ghost who *d.* in us

Jam. 4. 5. spirit which *d.* in us lusteth

2 *Pet.* 3. 13. wherein *d.* righteousness

1 *John* 3. 17. how *d.* love of God in him

24. that keepeth his commandments *d.* in him

4. 12. God *d.* in us, and his love is perfected

15. confess Jesus is Son of God, God *d.* in him

16. *d.* in love *d.* in God, and God in him

2 *John* 2. truth's sake which *d.* in us

DWELLING, Substantive, *Ps.* 49. 14. shall consume in the grave from their *d.*

Ps. 91. 10. nor shall any plague come nigh thy *d.*

DWELLING, *Ps.* 76. 2. in Salem his tabernacle, his *d.* place in Zion

Ps. 90. 1. Lord, thou hast been our *d.* place in Zion

1 *Tim.* 6. 16. *d.* in light

Heb. 11. 9. *d.* in tabernacles with

2 *Pet.* 2. 8. righteous man *d.* among

DWELLINGS, *Ps.* 87. 2. more than all the *d.* of Jacob

DWELT, *John* 1. 14. word made flesh and *d.* among us

Acts 13. 17. *d.* as strangers in Egypt

28. 30. Paul *d.* two years in his own hired house

DWELT in, *Ps.* 94. 17. my soul had almost *d.* in silence

2 *Tim.* 1. 5. faith *d.* first in grandmother

EAGLE, one of the principal birds of prey. It has a beak strong and hooked. Its feet have three toes before, and one behind. It is a very ravenous fowl. It sees or smells dead carcases at a prodigious distance. It breaks the bones of its prey, to come at the marrow. Every year it moults, and becomes almost naked and bald, and then renews its youth, by producing a set of new feathers. Eagles fly high and quick, have their nest in rocks, and are said to live an hundred years. All the species of eagles were unclean to the Jews, and were not eaten.

It is said that when an eagle sees its young ones so well-grown, as to venture upon flying, it hovers over their nest, flutters with its wings, and excites them to imitate it, and take their flight ; and when it sees them weary or fearful, it takes them upon its back, and carries them, so that the fowlers cannot hurt the young without piercing through the body of the old one. In allusion to this, it is said, *Ex.* 19. 4. That God delivered his people out of Egypt, and bore them upon eagles' wings ; and in *Deut.* 32. 11. That the Lord took upon himself the care of his people ; that he led them out of Egypt, and set them at liberty ; as an eagle takes its young out of the nest, to teach them how to fly, by gently fluttering about them.

EAGLE, stirs up nest, *Deut.* 32. 11.

Job 9. 26. as *e.* hasteth to prey

Prov. 23. 5. fly away as *e.* toward heaven

Jer. 49. 16. makest nest as high as *e.*

Ezek. 17. 3. great *e.* with great wings

Obad. 4. though thou exalt thyself as *e.*

Mic. 1. 16. enlarge baldness as *e.*

Rev. 12. 14. to woman given wings as *e.*

EAGLES, *Ex.* 19. 4. bear you on *e.* wings

2 *Sam.* 1. 23. swifter than *e.*

Ps. 103. 5. youth renewed like *e.*

Prov. 30. 17. young *e.* shall eat it

Is. 40. 31. mount up with wings as *e.*

Jer. 4. 18. horses swifter than *e.*

Lam. 4. 19. persecutors swifter than *e.*

Matt. 24. 28. *e.* are gathered together

EAR, *Num.* 14. 28 ; *Ex.* 9. 31.

Ex. 21. 6. bore his *e. Deut.* 15. 17.

2 *Kings* 19. 16. bow down *e. Ps.* 31. 2.

1 *Chr.* 17. 25. hast revealed the *e.* of thy servant

Neh. 1. 6. let thy *e.* be attentive, 11.

Job 12. 11. *e.* try words, 34. 3.

29. 11. when the *e.* heard me

21. to me men gave *e.* waited, and kept silence

36. 10. opens *e.* to discipline

42. 5. heard by the hearing of the *e.*

Ps. 10. 17. cause thy *e.* to hear

58. 4. adder that stoppeth the *e.*

77. 1. I cried unto God, and he gave *e.* unto me

94. 9. planted the *e.* shall he not hear

116. 2. inclined his *e.* unto me

Prov. 18. 15. *e.* of wise seek knowledge

20. 12. hearing *e.* and seeing eye

28. 9. turns away *e.* from hearing

Eccl. 1. 8. nor *e.* filled with hearing

Is. 50. 4. awakeneth my *e.* to hear

5. Lord hath opened mine *e.* and I was not rebellious

59. 1. neither his *e.* heavy

Jer. 6. 10. their *e.* is uncircumcised

9. 20. let your *e.* receive the word

Luke 5. 30. *e.* and *drink* with publicans
33. but thy disciples *e.* and *drink*
,12. 19. take thine ease, *e. drink*
17. 27. they did *e.* they *drank*, they
married, 28.

22. 30. *e.* and *drink* at my table
1 *Cor.* 9. 4. power to *e.* and to *drink*
11. 22. houses to *e.* and *drink* in
26. as oft as ye *e.* this bread and
drink this cup
27. *e.* and *drink* unworthily

EAT not, *Ezra* 2. 63. *not e.* of most holy
things, *Neh.* 7. 65.
Ps. 141. 4. *not e.* of their dainties
Mark 7. 3. Jews, except they wash,
they *e. not*, 4.
Luke 22. 16. I will *not e.* thereof, until
fulfilled
1 *Cor.* 8. 8. if we *e. not* are we the worse

EAT, to eat, *Ezek.* 3. 2. and he caused
me *to e.* that roll
Hab. 1. 8. they shall flee as eagle that
hasteth *to e.*
Matt. 12. 1. pluck ears of corn and *to e.*
26. 17. where prepare *to e.* passover
Luke 22. 15. I have desired *to e.* this
passover
John 4. 32. I have meat *to e.* that ye
know not of
33. brought him aught *to e.*
6. 52. how give us his flesh *to e.*
1 *Cor.* 11. 20. this is not *to e.* Lord's
supper
Rev. 2. 7. will I give *to e.* of the tree of
life in the midst
17 I will give *to e.* of hidden manna

EAT up, *Ps.* 27. 2. my enemies came on
me *to e. up* my flesh
Ps. 105. 35. did *e. up* all the herbs in
their land
Rev. 10. 9. angel said to me, take it,
and *e.* it *up*

ECHO, *Ezek.* 7. 7. and not the *e.* of
the mountains

EDGE, *Ex.* 13. 20. Etham in *e.* of wilderness, *Num.* 33. 6.
Luke 4. 29. they led Jesus to the *e.* of
the hill

EDIFICATION, *Rom.* 15. 2. please
neighbour to *e.*
1 *Cor.* 14. 3. speak unto men to *e.*
2 *Cor.* 10. 8. Lord hath given us for *e.*

EDIFY, *Rom.* 14. 19. things wherewith
one may *e.* another
1 *Cor.* 10. 23. all things are lawful, but
e. not
Eph. 4. 29. that which is good to *e.*
profitably
1 *Thess.* 5. 11. *e.* one another, even as
also ye do

EDIFIED, *Acts* 9. 31. the churches had
rest, and were *e.*

EDIFIETH, 1 *Cor.* 8. 10. knowledge
puffeth up, but charity *e.*
1 *Cor.* 14. 4. he that speaks in an unknown tongue *e.* himself ; but he
that prophesieth *e.* the church

EDIFYING, 1 *Cor.* 14. 12. excel to the
e. of church
26. let all things be done to *e.* 5. 12.
2 *Cor.* 12. 19. we do all things for your *e.*
Eph. 4. 12. for *e.* of the body of Christ

16. increase to *e.* itself in love
29. but what is good to use of *e.*
1 *Tim.* 1. 4. minister questions rather
than *e.*

EFFECT, 2 *Chr.* 34. 22 ; *Ezek.* 12. 23.
Is. 32. 17. *e.* of righteousness, quietness
Matt. 15. 6. commandment of God of
none *e.*
Mark 7. 13. making word of God of
none *e.*
Rom. 3. 3. make faith of God without *e.*
4. 14. the promise made of none *e.*
9. 6. not as though the word hath
none *e.*
Gal. 5. 4. Christ is become of no *e.* to you
1 *Cor.* 16. 9. door and *e.* is open
2 *Cor.* 1. 6. which is *e.* in enduring
Eph. 3. 7. the *e.* working of his power
4. 16. according to the *e.* working of
Philem. 6. faith may become *e.*
Jam. 5. 16. *e.* prayer of a righteous

EFFECTUALLY, *Gal.* 2. 8 ; 1 *Thess.*
2. 13.

EFFEMINATE, 1 *Cor.* 6. 9. nor *e.* shall
inherit the kingdom of God

EGG, *Deut.* 22. 6 ; *Job* 6. 6. & 39. 14 ;
Is. 10. 14. & 59. 5 ; *Jer.* 17. 11 ;
Luke 11. 12.

ELDER, primarily signifies one more
advanced in age, *Job* 15. 10 ; but as
such were commonly chosen to
bear rule, the word ordinarily signifies a subordinate ruler in church
or state. Even in Egypt, the Hebrews had *elders*, whom they own-
ed as chief men, that bare rule over
them. To these Moses intimated
his commission from God, to bring
the nation out of Egypt, *Ex.* 3. 16 ;
4. 29.

ELDER, *Gen.* 10. 21 ; 2 *John* 1 ; 3 *John* 1.
Gen. 25. 23. *e.* shall serve younger, *Rom.*
9. 12.
1 *Tim.* 5. 1. rebuke not an *e.* but
2. entreat *e.* women as mothers
1 *Pet.* 5, 1. *e.* I who am an *e.*
5. younger submit yourselves to *e.*

ELDERS, *Gen.* 50. 7. the *e.* of his house
went up with him
Lev. 4. 15. the *e.* of congregation shall
lay their hands
Num. 11. 25. Lord gave of the Spirit to
the seventy *e.*
Deut. 32. 7. ask thy *e.* they will tell thee
Ezra 10. 8. according to counsel of *e.*
Ps. 107. 32. praise him in the assembly
of the *e.*
Joel 1. 14. sanctify a fast, gather the *e.*
Matt. 15. 2. tradition of the *e.*
26. 59. the *e.* sought false witness
against Jesus
27. 20. chief priests and *e.* persuaded
the multitude
Mark 7. 3. the Jews holding the tradition of the *e.*
8. 31. must suffer and be rejected of
the *e. Luke* 9. 22.
14. 43. with Judas a great multitude
from the *e.*
Acts 14. 23. ordained *e.* in every church
15. 23. *e.* and brethren send greeting
20. 17. called the *e.* of the church

mine adversaries

EASED, 2 *Cor.* 8. 13. that other men be *e*.

EASIER, *Matt.* 9. 5. whether is *e*. to say, *Mark* 2. 9 ; *Luke* 5. 23.

Matt. 19. 24. *e*. for camel to go through eye, *Mark* 10. 25 ; *Luke* 18. 25.

Luke 16. 17. *e*. for heaven to pass

EASILY, 1 *Cor.* 13. 5. charity is not *e*. provoked

Heb. 12. 1. sin that doth so *e*. beset us

EASY, *Prov.* 14. 6. knowledge is *e*. unto him that understandeth

Matt. 11. 30. my yoke is *e*. and my burden is light

1 *Cor.* 14. 9. words *e*. to be understood

James 3. 17. gentle *e*. to be entreated

EAST, *Gen.* 28. 14. & 29. 1 ; *Ps.* 75. 6. & 103. 12 ; *Matt.* 2. 1, 2.

Is. 43. 5. bring thy seed from *e*.

Matt. 8. 11. many shall come from *e*. and west

Rev. 16. 12. way of kings *e*. might be

Gen. 41. 6. *e*. wind, *Ex.* 14. 21 ; *Job* 27. 21 ; *Ps.* 48. 7 ; *Is.* 27. 8 ; *Hos.* 12. 1. & 13. 15 ; *Hab.* 1. 9.

EAT, *Gen.* 3. 3, 5, 6, 12, 13. & 18. 8. & 19. 3.

Gen. 2. 16. of every tree freely *e*. of tree of knowledge shalt not *e*. in day thou *e*. thereof, thou shalt surely die

3. 14. dust shalt thou *e*. all thy days

17. in sorrow shalt thou *e*. of it

Neh. 8. 10. *e*. the fat drink the sweet

Ps. 22. 26. meek shall *e*. and be

53. 4. *e*. up my people as bread

78. 25. man did *e*. angel's food

29. they did *e*. and were filled

Prov. 1. 31. *e*. of the fruit of their own

Songs 5. 1. *e*. O friends, drink abundant.

Is. 1. 19. if obedient, ye shall *e*. the good of land

3. 10. shall *e*. fruit of doings

55. 1. come, yea, buy and *e*.

2. *e*. that which is good and let soul

65. 13. my servants shall *e*. but ye shall be hungry

Dan. 4. 33. did *e*. grass as oxen

Hos. 4. 10. shall *e*. and not have enough, *Hag.* 1. 6 ; *Mic.* 6. 14.

Mic. 3. 3. *e*. flesh of my people

Matt. 6. 25. what shall we *e*. and drink

12. 4. how David did *e*. the shew-bread

14. 20. did all *e*. and took up fragments, 15. 37 ; *Mark* 6. 42 ; 8. 8 ; *Luke* 9. 17.

15. 27. yet the dogs *e*. of the crumbs, *Mark* 7. 28.

26. 26. take *e*. this is my body, *Mark* 14. 22 ; 1 *Cor.* 11. 24, 26, 28.

Mark 2. 16. saw him *e*. with publicans

Luke 10. 8. *e*. such things as are set before you

15. 23. let us *e*. and be merry

17. 27. they did *e*. they drank, they married, 28.

John 6. 26. because ye did *e*. loaves

53. except ye *e*. flesh of Son of man

Acts 2. 46. did *e*. with gladness

1 *Cor.* 5. 11. with such an one not to *e*.

8. 8. if we *e*. are we the better

10. 3. *e*. same spiritual meat

31. whether ye *e*. or drink, do all to

2 *Thess.* 3. 10. work not, neither should he *e*.

2 *Tim.* 2. 17. *e*. as doth a canker

Jam. 5. 3. *e*. your flesh as fire

Rev. 17. 16. shall *e*. her flesh and burn

e. me up, *John* 2. 17 ; *Ps.* 119. 139.

Prov. 9. 17. bread *e*. in secret is pleasant

Songs 5. 1. *e*. my honeycomb with honey

Jer. 21. 29. fathers have *e*. sour grapes, *Ezek.* 18. 2.

Hos. 10. 13. having *e*. the fruit of lies

Matt. 14. 21. and they that had *e*. *Mark* 8. 9.

Luke 13. 26. have *e*. and drunk in thy presence

Acts 10. 10. he became hungry, and would have *e*.

14. Lord, I have never *e*. any thing common

Acts 12. 23. Herod was *e*. up of worms

20. 11. when he had broken bread and *e*. departed

Rev. 10. 10. *e*. it, my belly was bitter

EATER, *Judg.* 14. 14. out of *e*. came meat

Is. 55. 10. give bread to *e*. and seed to

Nah. 3. 12. fall into mouth of *e*.

EATETH, *Num.* 13. 32. a land that *e*. up the inhabitants

1 *Sam.* 14. 24. cursed be the man that *e*. 24.

Job 40. 15. behemoth *e*. grass as an ox

Eccl. 4. 5. *e*. his own flesh

Is. 28. 4. while it is yet in his hand he *e*. it up

Matt. 9. 11. why *e*. your master with publicans and sinners, *Luke* 15. 2.

Mark 14. 18. verily, one of you who *e*. with me, shall betray me, *John* 13. 18.

John 6. 54. whoso *e*. my flesh and drinketh my blood

57. he that *e*. me shall live by me

58. he that *e*. of this bread shall live

Rom. 14. 6. he that *e*. *e*. to the Lord

20. evil to man who *e*. with offence

1 *Cor.* 9. 7. who planteth a vineyard, and *e*. not of fruit thereof ? and *e*. not of the milk of the flock

1 *Cor.* 11. 29. *e*. and drinketh unworthily *e*. and drinketh damnation, 27.

EATING, *Job* 20. 23. and shall rain it upon him while he is *e*.

Is. 66. 17. *e*. swine's flesh and the abomination

Amos 7. 2. made an end of *e*. grass

Matt. 11. 18. John came neither *e*. nor drinking, *Luke* 7. 33.

19. Son of man came *e*. and drinking

24. 38. were *e*. and drinking, *Luke* 17. 27.

26. 26. as they were *e*. Jesus took

1 *Cor.* 8. 4. concern *e*. of those things

EAT, with drink, *Songs* 5. 1. *e*. O friends, yea, *drink* abundantly

Is. 22. 13. behold joy and gladness, let us *e*. and *drink*, for to-morrow we shall die, 1 *Cor.* 15. 32.

Matt. 6. 25. what shall *e*. or *drink* 31 ; *Luke* 12. 29.

10 ; *Deut.* 11. 6 ; *Ps.* 106. 17.
Deut. 28. 23. *e.* under thee be iron
32. 1. O *e.* hear the words of my mouth
Judg. 5. 4. *e.* trembled and heaven
1 *Sam.* 2. 8. pillars of *e.* are the Lord's
2 *Sam.* 22. 8. *e.* shook and trembled
1 *Chr.* 16. 31. let *e.* rejoice, *Ps.* 96. 11.
   33. cometh to judge the *e. Ps.* 96. 13 ;
   98. 9.
Job 9. 6. shaketh the *e.* out of his place
24. *e.* is given into the hand of wicked
   11. 9. longer than *e.* broader than sea
   16. 18. O *e.* cover not my blood
   26. 7. hangeth *e.* upon nothing
   28. 5. out of *e.* cometh bread
   30. 6. to dwell in caves of the *e.*
   30. 8. base viler than the *e.*
   38. 4. I laid the foundation of *e.*
Ps. 33. 5. the *e.* is full of the goodness of
   Lord
   46. 2. though the *e.* be removed
   48. 2. joy of whole *e.* is mount Zion
   65. 9. visitest *e.* and waterest it
   67. 6. *e.* shall yield her increase, 85. 12.
   72. 19. whole *e.* filled with his glory
   75. 3. *e.* and inhabitants dissolved, *Is.*
   24. 19.
Ps. 78. 69. like *e.* established for ever
   89. 11. heaven and *e.* are thine
   90. 2. or ever thou hadst formed *e.*
   97. 1. let the *e.* rejoice
   97. 4. *e.* saw and trembled
   104. 24. the *e.* is full of thy riches, 13.
   114. 7. tremble O *e.* at presence of Lord
   115. 16. *e.* given to children of men
   119. 64. *e.* is full of thy mercy
   139. 15. in lowest parts of the *e.*
Prov. 25. 3. *e.* for depth is unsearchable
Eccl. 1. 4. *e.* abideth for ever
Is. 6. 3. the whole *e.* is full of his glory
   11. 4. smite *e.* with rod of his mouth
   9. the *e.* full of knowledge of Lord,
   Hab. 2. 14.
   13. 13. *e.* shall remove out of her place
   24. 1. the Lord maketh the *e.* empty
   4. the *e.* mourneth and fadeth, 33. 9.
   5. the *e.* also is defiled under inhabitants
   19. the *e.* utterly broken down and
   dissolved
   20. the *e.* shall reel and stagger like
   a drunken man
   26. 19. the *e.* shall cast out her dead
   21. the *e.* shall disclose her blood and
   66. 1. *e.* is thy footstool where
Jer. 22. 29. O *e. e. e.* hear word of Lord
Ezek. 34. 27. the *e.* shall yield her increase
   43. 2. the whole *e.* shined with his
Hos. 2. 22. *e.* shall hear the corn
Hab. 2. 14. *e.* filled with knowledge
Hab. 3. 3. the *e.* was full of his praise
Matt. 5. 5. meek shall inherit *e.*
   13. 5. stony ground and not much *e.*
John 3. 31. that is of *e. e.*
Heb. 6. 7. *e.* which drinks in rain
Heb. 12. 26. whose voice shook *e.*
Jam. 5. 7. precious fruit of the *e.*
2 *Pet.* 3. 10. *e.* and works therein
Rev. 12. 16. *e.* opened and swallowed
EARTH, all the, *Gen.* 18. 25. judge of
   all the *e.* do right

Ps. 8. 1. excellent in *all the e.* 9.
Dan. 2. 39. kingdom rule over *all the e.*
Hab. 2. 20. let *all the e.* keep silence
Luke 23. 44. darkness over *all the e.*
Rom. 10. 18. sound went into *all the e.*
EARTH, in the, *Gen.* 4. 12. a vagabond
   in the *e.* 14.
Gen. 10. 8. Nimrod mighty one *in the e.*
Ps. 72. 16. a handful of corn *in the e.*
   119. 19. I am a stranger *in the e.*
Is. 62. 7. Jerusalem a praise *in the e.*
Matt. 25. 18. went and digged *in the e.*
   25. hid thy talent *in the e.*
Mark 4. 31. mustard seed sown *in the*
   e. less than all seeds *in the e.*
1 *John* 5. 8. three that witness *in the e.*
EARTH, on or **upon the,** *Gen.* 28. 12.
   ladder set *upon the e.*
Job 7. 1. time to man *on e* ?
   19. 25. stand at latter day *upon the e.*
Ps. 67. 2. way known *upon e.*
   73. 25. none *upon e.* I desire besides
   thee
Eccl. 5. 2. God is in heaven and thou
   on *e.*
   7. 20. there is not a just man *upon e.*
   10. 7. walking as servants *upon the e.*
Songs 2. 12. flowers appear *on the e.*
Jer. 9. 3. not valiant for truth *upon e.*
Matt. 6. 19. lay not up treasures *on e.*
   9. 6. son hath power *on e.* to forgive,
   Mark 2. 10 ; *Luke* 5. 24.
   10. 34. come to send peace *on e.*
   23. 9. call no man father *upon the e.*
Luke 2. 14. Glory to God *on e.* peace
Luke 5. 24. Son of man hath power
   upon *e.*
   12. 49. come to send fire *on the e.*
   51. come to give peace *on e.*
   18. 8. shall he find faith *on e.*
Col. 3. 5. mortify your members which
   are *upon e.*
Heb. 12. 25. refused him that spake *on e.*
EARTH, out of the, *Job* 28. 5. *e.* out of
   it cometh bread
Ps. 85. 11. truth sh. spring *out of the e.*
EARTH, to, or **unto,** *Ps.* 17. 11. bowing
   down *to the e.*
Ps. 50. 4. he shall call *to the e.*
Eccl. 3. 21. spirit of beast goeth *to e.*
   12. 7. dust return *to e.* spirit to G.
EARTHEN, *Lev.* 6. 28 ; *Jer.* 19. 1. &
   32. 14 ; *Lam.* 4. 2 ; 2 *Cor.* 4. 7.
EARTHLY, *John* 3. 12, 31 ; 2 *Cor.* 5. 1 ;
   Phil. 3. 19 ; *Jam.* 3. 15.
EARTHY, 1 *Cor.* 15. 47. first man of
   earth, *e.*
1 *Cor.* 15. 49. have borne image of *e.*
EARTHQUAKE, 1 *Kings* 19. 11, 12 ; *Is.*
   29. 6 ; *Amos* 1. 1. &c. ; *Zech.* 14.
   5 ; *Matt.* 24. 7, 27, 54. & 28. 2 ;
   Acts 16. 26.
Rev. 6. 12. a great *e.* & 8. 5. & 11. 19. &
   16. 18.
EASE, denotes peace, rest, *Job* 12. 5. &
   16. 12. & 21. 23 ; *Ps.* 25. 13. & 123.
   4 ; *Deut.* 28. 65 ; *Is.* 32. 9, 11 ;
   Jer. 46. 27. & 48. 11 ; *Ezek.* 23. 42 ;
   Amos 6. 1 ; *Zech.* 1. 15.
Luke 12. 19. take thine *e.* eat, drink,
   and be merry
EASE, verb, *Is.* 1. 24. I will *e.* me of

Matt. 10. 27. what ye hear in the *e.*
1 *Cor.* 2. 9. eye seen nor *e.* heard
    12. 16. if the *e.* shall say, because I
    am not the eye
Rev. 2. 7. he that hath an *e.* let h'm
    hear. 11. 17, 29. & 3. 6, 13, 22, & 13.
    9 ; *Matt.* 11. 15. & 13. 9, 43.
EAR, give *Ex.* 15. 26 ; *Deut.* 32. 1 ; *Judg.*
    5. 3 ; *Ps.* 5. 1. & 17. 1. & 39. 12. &
    49. 1. & 78. 1. & 54. 2. & 84. 8. &
    141. 1 ; *Is.* 1. 2, 10. & 8. 9. & 28. 23.
    & 32. 9. & 42. 23 ; *Jer.* 13. 15 ; *Hos.*
    5. 1 ; *Joel* 1. 2 ; *Ps.* 55. 1. & 86. 6.
Ps. 17. 6. incline to *e.* 45. 10. & 71. 2. & 88.
    2. & 102. 2. & 116. 2 ; *Is.* 37. 17 ;
    Dan. 9. 18 ; *Ps.* 49. 4. to a parable
    —78. 1. to words of my mouth ;
    Prov. 2. 2. to wisdom—4. 20. to my
    sayings—*Is.* 55. 3. and come unto
    me.
Jer. 11. 8. nor inclined their *e.* 17. 23.
    & 25. 4. & 35. 15.
Deut. 29. 4. Lord not given *e.* to bear
1 *Sam.* 3. 11. both *e.* shall tingle, 2
    Kings 21. 12 ; *Jer.* 19. 3.
2 *Sam.* 22. 7. cry did enter into his *e.*
Job 33. 16. open the *e.* of men
Ps. 34. 15. his *e.* are open to their cry
Ps. 40. 6. my *e.* hast thou opened
    44. 1. we have heard with our *e.* O God
Is. 6. 10. make their *e.* heavy lest hear
    35. 5. *e.* of deaf shall be unstopped
    43. 8. have *e.* and hear not
Matt. 13. 15. their *e.* are dull of hearing
    16. blessed are your *e.* for they hear
Luke 9. 44. sayings sink down into *e.*
2 *Tim.* 4. 4. turn away their *e.* from
2 *Chr.* 6. 40. thine *e.* be open to
Ps. 10. 17. cause thine *e.* to hear
    130. 2. let thine *e.* be attentive to the
    voice of my supplications
Prov. 23. 12. apply thine *e.* to words of
    knowledge
Is. 30. 21. thine *e.* shall hear a word
Ezek. 3. 10. hear with *e.* 40. 4. & 44. 5.
EARING, *Gen.* 45. 6 ; *Ex.* 34. 21.
1 *Sam.* 8. 12. *e.* ground, Is. 30. 24.
Ex. 9. 31. in the *e. Mark* 4. 28.
EARLY, *Gen.* 19. 2 ; *John* 18. 28. & 20.
Ps. 46. 5. God shall help her-that right *e.*
    57. 8. will awake right *e.* 108: 2.
    63. 1. my God *e.* will I seek thee
    78. 34. returned *e.* after God
    90. 14. satisfy us *e.* with mercy
    127. 2. vain to rise, *e.* or sit late to eat
    the bread of
Prov. 1. 28. seek me *e.* and not find me
    8. 17. that seek me *e.* shall find me
Is. 26. 9. with my spirit I seek thee *e.*
Jer. 7. 13. rising up *e.* 25. & 11. 7. & 25.
    3, 4. & 26. 5. & 29. 19. & 32. 33. &
    35. 14, 15. & 44. 4 ; 2 *Chr.* 36. 15.
Hos. 5. 15. in affliction will seek me *e.*
    6. 4. goodness as *e.* dew goeth away,
    13. 3.
Luke 24. 22. women who were *e.* at the
    sepulchre
John 18. 28. they led Jesus to the hall,
    and it was *e.*
    20. 1. the first day cometh Mary Mag-
    dalene *e.*
Jam. 5. 7. receive *e.* and latter rain

EAR-RINGS, *Gen.* 35. 4 ; *Ex.* 32. 2, 3 ;
    Job 42. 11. gave *e.* ring of gold
Prov. 25. 12. as an *e.* ring of gold
EARNEST, of spirit given, 2 *Cor.* 1. 22.
    & 5. 5.
Eph. 1. 14. *e.* of your inheritance
Rom. 8. 19. *e.* expectation of the crea-
    ture
2 *Cor.* 7. 7. told us of your *e.* desire
    8. 16. same *e.* care into—Titus
Phil. 1. 20. according to my *e.* expecta-
    tion
Heb. 2. 1. give more *e.* heed
Job 7. 2. servant *e.* desireth the shadow
Jer. 11. 7. I *e.* protested to your fathers
    31. 20. I do *e.* remember him still
Mic. 7. 3. may do evil with both hands *e.*
Luke 22. 44. in an agony prayed more *e.*
1 *Cor.* 12. 31. covet *e.* the best gifts
2 *Cor.* 5. 2. in this we groan *e.*
Jam. 5. 17. prayed *e.* it might not
Jude 3. *e.* contend for the faith
EARNETH wages, *Hag.* 1. 6.
EARTH. It is taken (1) for that gross
    and terrestrial element which sus-
    tains and nourishes us, *Gen.* 1. 10.
    God called the dry land, Earth. In
    this sense it is taken in those pas-
    sages, where the earth is said to
    yield fruit, to be barren, watered,
    &c. (2) For all that rude matter
    which was created in the begin-
    ning : *Gen.* 1. 1. God created the
    heaven and the earth ; that is, the
    matter of all sensible beings. (3)
    By the earth is meant the terraque-
    ous globe, the earth and all that it
    contains, men, animals, plants,
    metals, waters, fish, &c., *Ps.* 24. 1.
    The earth is the Lord's, and the
    fulness thereof. (4) The earth is
    often taken for those who inhabit
    it, *Gen.* 6. 13 ; 11. 1. The earth is
    filled with violence. The whole
    earth was of one language. *Ps.* 96.
    1. Sing unto the Lord, all the earth.
    (5) Sometimes the whole earth, or
    all the kingdoms of the earth, sig-
    nify no more than the whole em-
    pire of Chaldea and Assyria, *Ezra*
    1. 2. The Lord God of heaven hath
    given me all the kingdoms of the
    earth. Earth is taken for Canaan,
    or the land of the Jews, *Rom.* 9. 28.
    A short work will the Lord make
    upon the earth. He will bring a
    sudden destruction upon that land
    and people. And in *Matt.* 9. 26 ;
    Mark 15. 33 ; *Luke* 4. 25 ; the
    word which is translated land, is in
    the Greek, earth.
EARTH was corrupt, *Gen.* 6. 11, 12.
Gen. 6. 13. *e.* was filled with violence
    11. 1. whole *e.* of one language and of
    one speech
    18. 18. all nations of *e.* blessed in him,
    22. 18 ; 26. 4 ; 28. 14.
    41. 47. *e.* brought forth by handfuls
Ex. 9. 29. *e.* is the Lord's, *Deut.* 10. 14 ;
    Ps. 24. 1 ; 1 *Cor.* 10. 26, 28.
    15. 12. the *e.* swallowed them up
Num. 16. 32. *e.* opened her mouth, 26.

1 *Tim*. 5. 17. *e.* that rule well accounted worthy

Tit. 1. 5. ordain *e.* in every city

Heb. 11. 2. *e.* obtained good report

Jam. 5. 14. sick call for *e.* of church

Rev. 4. 4. four-and-twenty *e.* sitting, 10. & 5. 6, 8, 11, 14. & 11. 16. & 19. 4. & 7. 11, 13. & 14. 3.

ELDEST, *Gen*. 24. 2. Abraham said to his *e.* servant

1 *Sam*. 17. 13. the three *e.* sons of Jesse followed, 14.

John 8. 9. they went out one by one, beginning at *e.*

ELECT, or Chosen, is spoken (1) Of Christ, who was chosen and set apart from eternity by God the Father to the great work of redemption and mediation, *Is*. 42. 1 ; *Matt*. 12. 18. (2) Of good angels, whom God chose from among the rest to eternal life and happiness : I charge thee before the elect angels, 1 *Tim*. 5. 21. (3) Of the Israelites, who were God's chosen and peculiar people, *Is*. 65. 9, 22. (4) Of such as are chosen by God in Christ to eternal life and salvation out of all the nations upon earth, *Tit*. 1. 1. This election is, (1) An act of distinguishing love, *Deut*. 7. 8. (2) Of divine sovereignty irrespective of any goodness in the objects of it, *Rom*. 9. 11, 12, 16. (3) Eternal, *Eph*. 1. 4 ; 2 *Thess*. 2. 13. (4) Absolute, and irrevocable, *Rom*. 9. 11 ; 2 *Tim*. 2. 19. (5) Personal, that is, of a certain number of persons, *Matt*. 20. 23 ; 2 *Tim*. 2. 19. (6) Of some of the chief of sinners, 1 *Tim*. 1. 15. (7) It is in Christ, *Eph*. 1. 4. (8) It is to sanctification and holiness as the ◆means, and eternal glory as the end, *Eph*. 1. 4 ; 1 *Thess*. 5. 9.

Is. 42. 1. *e.* in whom my soul delighteth

45. 4. for Israel my *e.* I have called

65. 9. my *e.* shall inherit it

22. my *e.* shall long enjoy work

Matt. 24. 22. for *e.* sake days shortened

24. if possible, deceive very *e.*

31. gather together his *e.* from four

Luke 18. 7. God avenge his own *e.*

Rom. 8. 33. to charge of God's *e.*

Col. 3. 12. put on as the *e.* of God

1 *Tim*. 5. 21. charge thee before *e.* angel

2 *Tim*. 2. 10. endure all things for *e.*

Tit. 1. 1. according to faith of God's *e.*

1 *Pet*. 1. 2. *e.* according to fore-knowledge of God

2. 6. corner-stone *e.* precious

2 *John* 1. *e.* lady 13. *e.* sister

ELECTED, 1 *Pet*. 5. 13. church at Babylon *e.* together with you

ELECTION, *Rom*. 9. 11. purpose of God according to *e.*

11. 5. there is a remnant according to the *e.* of grace

7. *e.* hath obtained it and rest blinded

28. touching *e.* they are beloved

1 *Thess*. 1. 4. knowing your *e.* of God

2 *Pet*. 1. 10. make calling and *e.* sure

ELOQUENT, of an elegant and clear speech, penetrating, affecting, animating, &c., *Ex*. 4. 10 ; *Is*. 3. 3 ; *Acts* 18. 24.

EMBALM, *Gen*. 50. 2. Joseph commanded physicians to *e.* his father

EMBALMED, *Gen*. 50. 2. the physicians *e.* Israel

Gen. 50. 3. fulfilled days of those *e.*

26. they *e.* Joseph, put him in a coffin in Egypt

EMBOLDEN. To make daring or bold ; to inspire with courage, *Acts* 28. 13.

EMBOLDENED, 1 *Cor*. 8. 10. the conscience of him that is weak be *e.*

EMBOLDENETH, *Job* 16. 3. what *e.* thee that that thou answerest

EMBRACE, *Prov*. 5. 20. *e.* the bosom of a stranger

Eccl. 3. 5. a time to *e.* and refrain from embracing

Songs 2. 6. and his right hand doth *e.* me, 8. 3.

Lam. 4. 5. that were brought up in scarlet *e.* dunghills

EMBRACED, *Gen*. 29. 13. Laban *e.* Jacob

Gen. 33. 4. Esau *e.* Jacob.

Acts 20. 1. Paul *e.* disciples and departed to Macedonia

Heb. 11. 13. *e.* the promises

EMBROIDER, *Ex*. 28. 39. *e.* the coat of fine linen

EMBROIDERER, *Ex*. 35. 35. to work all manner of work of the *e.*

Ex. 38. 23. with him was Aholiab an *e.* in blue

EMERALD, S, *Ex*. 28. 18. the second row shall be an *e.* 39. 11.

Rev. 4. 3. there was a rainbow in sight like unto an *e.*

Rev. 21. 19. the fourth foundation of the city was an *e.*

EMERODS, *Deut*. 28. 27. smite thee with the *e.*

1 *Sam*. 5. 6. Lord smote them of Ashdod with the *e.*

EMINENT, high, honourable, *Ezek*. 16. 24, 39 ; 17. 22.

EMMANUEL, *Is*. 7. 14. and shall call his name *Em*. *Matt*. 1. 23.

Is. 8. 8. he shall fill the breadth of thy land, O *Em*.

EMPTY, *Gen*. 31. 42. & 37. 24. & 41. 27.

Ex. 23. 15. none shall appear before me *e.* 34. 20 ; *Deut*. 16. 16.

Deut. 15. 13. shalt not let him go away *e.*

Judg. 7. 16. with *e.* pitchers and lamps

Ruth 1. 21. the Lord hath brought me home *e.*

3. 17. *e.* to thy mother-in-law

1 *Sam*. 6. 3. send not the ark away *e.*

2 *Sam*. 1. 22. sword of Saul return not *e.*

Job 22. 9. sent widows away *e.*

Is. 29. 8. awaketh, his soul is *e.*

Hos. 10. 1. Israel is an *e.* vine he brings

Nah. 2. 10. Nineveh is *e.* void, waste

Mark 12. 3. they caught him and beat him, and sent him away *e. Luke* 20. 10, 11.

Luke 1. 53. rich hath he sent *e.* away

EMPTY, verb, *Eccl*. 11. 3. the clouds *e.* themselves on earth

EMPTIED, *Gen.* 24. 20. Rebekah *e.* her pitcher

Gen. 42. 35. it as they *e.* their sacks

Is. 24. 3. the land shall be utterly *e.* and

EMPTINESS, *Is.* 34. 11. he shall stretch out upon it the stones of *e.*

EMULATION, means striving to excel in what is good, *Rom.* 11. 14 ; in what is evil, *Gal.* 5. 20.

ENABLED, 1 *Tim.* 1. 12. I thank Christ Jesus who hath *e.* me

ENCAMP, *Num.* 3. 38. but those that *e.* before the tabernacle

Num. 10. 31. thou knowest how we are to *e.* in wilderness

2 *Sam.* 12. 28. *e.* against Rabbah

Job 19. 12. his troops came and *e.* about my tabernacle

Ps. 27. 3. though an host should *e.* against me

Zech. 9. 8. *e.* about mine house

ENCAMPED, *Ex.* 18. 5. where Moses *e.* at the mount of God

Josh. 4. 19. people came up and *e.* in Gilgal, 5. 10.

ENCAMPETH, *Ps.* 34. 7. angel of the Lord *e.* round about them

ENCOUNTERED, *Acts* 17. 18. certain philosophers *e.* him

ENCOURAGE, *Ps.* 64. 5. they *e.* themselves in an evil matter

ENCOURAGED, 1 *Sam.* 30. 6. David *e.* himself in the Lord his God

2 *Chr.* 17. 6. his heart was *e.* in ways of the Lord

35. 2. Josiah *e.* them to the service of the Lord

Is. 41. 7. carpenter *e.* the goldsmith

END of all flesh is come, *Gen.* 6. 13.

Deut. 32. 20. see what their *e.* shall be

Ps. 7. 9. the wickedness of the wicked come to an *e.*

9. 6. destructions are come to a perpetual *e.*

Ps. 37. 37. *e.* of that man is peace

39. 4. make me to know my *e.* and measure

73. 17. then understood I their *e.*

102. 27. thy years have no *e.*

119. 96. seen an *e.* of all perfection

Prov. 5. 4. her *e.* as bitter as wormwood

14. 12. *e.* thereof are ways of death

Eccl. 4. 8. no *e.* of all his labour

7. 2. that is the *e.* of all men

8. *e.* is better than beginning

12. 12. making many books no *e.*

Is. 9. 7. of his government shall be no *e.*

45. 17. shall not be confounded world without *e.*

Jer. 5. 31. what will ye do in *e.* thereof

17. 11. at his *e.* shall be a fool

Jer. 29. 11. to give an expected *e.*

31. 17. there is hope in thy *e.*

51. 13. O thou that dwellest, thine *e.* is come

31. his city taken at one *e.*

Lam. 4. 18. our *e.* is come, our *e.* is near, *Ezek.* 7. 2, 6, 7, 10, 12 ; *Amos* 8. 2.

Ezek. 21. 25. when iniquity shall have an *e.*

Dan. 8. 19. at time appointed *e.* shall be

12. 8. what shall be *e.* of these things

13. go thy way till the *e.* be

Hab. 2. 3. at *e.* it shall speak and not lie

Matt. 13. 39. harvest is *e.* of world

24. 3. what sign of *e.* of world

6. but *e.* is not yet, *Luke* 21. 9.

Luke 1. 33. of his kingdom there shall be no *e.*

John 18. 37. sayest I am a king, to this *e.* was I born

Rom. 6. 21. *e.* of those things is death

22. ye have the *e.* everlasting life

10. 4. Christ is *e.* of law for righteousness

14. 9. to this *e.* Christ both died and rose

Eph. 3. 21. to him be glory, world without *e.*

1 *Tim.* 1. 5. *e.* of the commandment is charity

Heb. 6. 8. whose *e.* is to be burned

16. oath—make an *e.* of all strife

7. 3. beginning—nor *e.* of life

13. 7. consider *e.* of their conversation

Jam. 5. 11. seen the *e.* of the Lord

1 *Pet.* 1. 9. receiving *e.* of your faith

4. 7. *e.* of all things is at hand

17. *e.* of those that obey not gospel

Rev. 21. 6. beginning and *e.* 22. 13. & 1. 8 ; 1 *Sam.* 3. 12.

Jer. 4. 27. make a full *e.* 5. 10, 18. & 30. 11 ; *Ezek.* 11. 13.

Num. 23. 10. last *e.* *Jer.* 12. 4 ; *Lam.* 1. 9. & 4. 18 ; *Dan.* 8. 19. & 9. 24.

Deut. 8. 16. latter *e.* 32. 29 ; *Job* 42. 12 ; *Prov.* 19. 20 ; 2 *Pet.* 2. 20.

Ps. 119. 33. unto the *e.* *Dan.* 6. 26 ; *Matt.* 24. 13. & 28. 20 ; *John* 13. 1 ; 1 *Cor.* 1. 8 ; *Heb.* 3. 6, 14. & 6. 11 ; *Rev.* 2. 26.

ENDLESS, 1 *Tim.* 1. 4. *e.* genealogies

Heb. 7. 16. after the power of an *e.* life

ENDEAVOUR, 2 *Pet.* 1. 15. I will *e.* that you may be able after

ENDEAVOURED, *Acts* 16. 10. *e.* to go into Macedonia

1 *Thess.* 2. 17. *e.* to see your face

ENDEAVOURING, *Eph.* 4. 3. *e.* to keep the unity of the Spirit in bond

ENDOW, to give a portion, *Ex.* 22. 16. *e.* her to be his wife

ENDS, 1 *Tim.* 1. 4 ; *Heb.* 7. 16.

Ps. 22. 27. all *e.* of the world remember

65. 5. confidence of all *e.* of earth

67. 7. all *e.* of earth shall fear him

98. 3. all *e.* of earth have seen salvation

Prov. 17. 24. eyes of fool in *e.* of earth

Is. 45. 22. be ye saved all ye *e.* of earth

52. 10. all *e.* of earth see salvation

Zech. 9. 10. his dominion to *e.* of earth

Acts 13. 47. for salvation to *e.* of earth

Rom. 10. 18. words to the *e.* of world

1 *Cor.* 10. 11. on whom *e.* of world come

ENDUED, to receive the Spirit, *Gen.* 30. 20. God hath *e.* me with a good dowry ; now will my husband

2 *Chr.* 2. 12. wise son, *e.* with prudence

2. 13. cunning man *e.* with understanding

Luke 24. 49. till ye be *e.* with power

Jam. 3. 13. who is wise and *e.* with knowledge

ENDURE, to last, to persevere, to be patient in adversity, to hold fast, *Job* 8. 15. & 31. 23.

Gen. 33. 14. as children are able to *e.*

Ps. 30. 5. weeping may *e.* for a night

102. 26. they perish, but thou shalt *e.*

Prov. 27. 24. doth crown *e.* to every generation

Ezek. 22. 14. can thy heart *e.* or hands

Mark 4. 17. no root and *e.* but for a time

2 *Tim.* 2. 3. *e.* hardness as good soldier

2. 10 *e.* all things for elect's sake

4. 3. they will not *e.* sound doctrine

5. watch thou, *e.* affliction, do

Heb. 12. 7. if ye *e.* chastening

Matt. 10. 22. that *e.* to end shall be saved, 24. 13 ; *Mark* 13. 13.

John 6. 27. meat which *e.* unto life

1 *Cor.* 13. 7. charity *e.* all things

Jam. 1. 12. blessed is the man that *e.*

Ps. 9. 7. the Lord shall *e.* for ever, 102, 12, 26. & 104. 31—his name, 72. 17. —his seed, 89. 29, 36. *e.* for ever.

1 *Chr.* 16. 34, 41. his mercy *e.* for ever, 2 *Chr.* 5. 13. & 7. 3, 6. & 20. 21 ; *Ezra* 3. 11 ; *Ps.* 106. 1. & 107. 1. & 118. 1..2, 3, 4, 29. & 136. 1.—26. & 138. 8 ; *Jer.* 33. 11 ; *Ps.* 111. 3. his righteousness *e.* for ever—10. praise *e.*—117. 2. truth of Lord *e.*—119. 160. every one of thy judgments *e.* —135. 13. thy name *e.*—1 *Pet.* 1. 25. word of Lord *e.*

Ps. 19. 9. fear of Lord *e.* for ever

Heb. 10. 34. in heaven *e.* substance

Jam. 5. 11. we count happy who *e.*

Ps. 81. 15. should have *e.* for ever

Rom. 9. 22. *e.* with much long-suffering

2 *Tim.* 3. 11. what persecutions I *e.*

Heb. 6. 15. had patiently *e.* he obtained

Heb. 10. 32. ye *e.* a great fight of afflictions

11. 27. he *e.* as seeing him who is invisible

12. 2. *e.* the cross

3. 2. *e.* contradiction

Ps. 30. 5. his anger *e.* but a moment

52. 1. goodness of God *e.* continually

100. 5. his truth *e.* to all generations

145. 13. and thy dominion *e.* throughout all generations

ENEMY, *Ex.* 15. 6, 9 ; *Ps.* 7. 5.

Ex. 23. 22. I will be an *e.* to thy *e.*

Deut. 32. 27. I feared wrath of the *e.*

1 *Sam.* 24. 19. find *e.* will he let him go

Job 33. 10. counteth me for his *e.*

Ps. 7. 5. let *e.* persecute my soul

8. 2. mightest still the *e.* and avenger

Prov. 27. 6. kisses of *e.* are deceitful

Is. 63. 10. he turned to be their *e.* and

1 *Cor.* 15. 26. last *e.* destroyed is death

Gal. 4. 16. am I therefore become your *e.*

2 *Thess.* 3. 15. count him not as *e.*

Jam. 4. 4. friend of world *e.* with God

ENEMY, mine, 1 *Kings* 21. 20. mine *e. Ps.* 7. 4 ; *Mic.* 7. 8, 10 ; *Job* 16. 9 ; *Lam.* 2. 22.

Job 27. 7. let *mine e.* be as wicked

Ps. 7. 4. yea, I delivered him that is *mine e.*

41. 11. because *mine e.* doth not triumph over me

ENEMIES, 2 *Sam.* 12. 14. give occasion to *e.* to blaspheme

2 *Sam.* 18. 32. the *e.* of my Lord be as that young man is

Ps. 17. 9. hide me from my deadly *e.* who compass

45. 5. thine arrows are sharp in heart of king's *e.*

Mic. 7. 6. man's *e.* are men of

Rom. 5. 10. if when *e.* were reconciled

1 *Cor.* 15. 25. put all *e.* under his feet

Phil. 3. 18. *e.* to the cross of Christ

Col. 1. 21. *e.* in your minds by wicked

Gen. 22. 17. his *e. Ps.* 68. 1, 21. & 112. 8. & 132. 18 ; *Prov.* 16. 7 ; *Is.* 59. 18. & 66. 6 ; *Heb.* 10. 13.

Deut. 32. 41. my *e. Ps.* 18. 17, 48. & 23. 5. & 119. 98. & 139. 22. & 143. 12 ; *Is.* 1. 24 ; *Luke* 19. 27.

32. 31. our *e. Luke* 1. 71, 74.

Ex. 23. 4. thy *e. Prov.* 25. 21 ; *Rom.* 12. 20 ; *Matt.* 5. 43.

Ex. 23. 22. thy *e. Num.* 10. 35 ; *Deut.* 28. 48, 53, 55. & 33. 29 ; *Judg.* 5. 31 ; *Ps.* 21. 8. & 92. 9. & 110. 1 ; *Matt.* 22. 44 ; *Heb.* 1. 13.

ENGRAFTED, *Jam.* 1. 21. receive with meekness the *e.* word

ENGRAVE, to cut or carve ; *Ex.* 28. 11. It is God's work, *Zech.* 3. 9 ; *Is.* 49. 16.

ENGRAVEN, 2 *Cor.* 3. 7. the ministration of death *e.* in stones

ENGRAVER, *Ex.* 28. 11. work of an *e.* in stone

Ex. 35. 35. to work all manner of work of the *e.*

38. 23. Aholiab, of the tribe of Dan, an *e.*

ENGRAVINGS, *Ex.* 28. 11. like *e.* of a signet, 21. 36 ; 39. 14, 30.

ENJOIN, *Esth.* 9. 31 ; *Job* 36. 23 ; *Philem.* 8 ; *Heb.* 9. 20.

ENJOY, *Num.* 36. 8 ; *Deut.* 28. 41.

Lev. 26. 34. land *e.* her sabbaths, 43.

Eccl. 2. 24. his soul *e.* good

Acts 24. 2. we *e.* great quietness

1 *Tim.* 6. 17. giveth richly all things to *e.*

Heb. 11. 25. *e.* pleasures of sin for

ENLARGE, *Ex.* 34. 24 ; *Mic.* 1. 16.

Gen. 9. 27. God shall *e.* Japheth

Deut. 33. 20. blessed be he that *e.* Gad

2 *Sam.* 22. 37. *e.* my steps, *Ps.* 18. 36.

Ps. 4. 1. *e.* me when in distress

25. 17. troubles of my heart are *e.*

119. 32. when thou shalt *e.* my heart

Is. 5. 14. hell hath *e.* herself

54. 2. *e.* the place of thy tent

60. 5. thine heart shall fear and be *e.*

Hab. 2. 5. *e.* his desire as hell

2 *Cor.* 6. 11. our desire is *e.* 13.

ENLARGEMENT, *Esth.* 4. 14.

ENLIGHTEN darkness, *Ps.* 18. 28.

Ps. 19. 8. command is pure *e.* the eyes

Eph. 1. 18. understanding being *e.*

Heb. 6. 4. impossible for those once *e.*

ENMITY, *Gen.* 3. 15. I will put *e.* between

Luke 23. 12. for before they were at *e.* between themselves

Rom. 8. 7. the carnal mind is *e.* against God

Eph. 2. 15. abolished *e.* ; 16. slain *e.*
ENOUGH I have, *Gen.* 33. 9, 11.
Gen. 45. 28. it is *e.* Joseph is yet alive
Ex. 36. 5. bring more than *e.*
2 *Sam.* 24. 16. said to angel, it is *e.*
1 *Kings* 19. 4 it is *e.* take away
Prov. 30. 15, 16. say not it is *e.*
Hos. 4. 10. eat and not *e. Hag.* 1. 6.
Matt. 10. 25. it is *e.* for disciple
Mark 14. 41. it is *e.* the hour is come
Luke 15. 17. bread *e.* and to spare
ENQUIRE, *Ps.* 27. 4. beauty of the Lord
and to *e.* in his temple
Is. 21. 12. if ye will *e. e.* ye, return,
come
2 *Cor.* 8. 23. whether any do *e.* of Titus
my partner
ENQUIRED, *Matt.* 2. 7. Herod *e.* of
wise men
2 *Cor.* 8. 23. or our brethren be *e.* of,
are messengers
1 *Pet.* 1. 10. of which salvation the prophets *e.*
ENRICHED, 1 *Cor.* 1. 5 ; 2 *Cor.* 9. 11.
Ps. 65. 9. thou *e.* it with river of God
ENSAMPLE, pattern, 1 *Cor.* 10. 11 ;
Phil. 3. 17 ; 1 *Thess.* 1. 7 ; 2 *Thess.*
3. 9 ; 1 *Pet.* 5. 3 ; 2 *Pet.* 2. 6.
ENSIGN. 'He will lift up an ensign,'
Is. 5. 26 ; 11. 10 ; referring to the
ancient practice of commanders,
who in times of imminent dangers
erected banners on the tops of emi-
nences, that the country might instantly be assembled ; *Ps.* 74. 4.
ENSNARE, *Job* 34. 30.
ENSUE, to follow after earnestly, 1 *Pet.*
3. 11.
ENTER, *Gen.* 12. 11 ; *Num.* 4. 23 ;
Judg. 18. 9 ; *Dan.* 11. 17 ; 40. 41.
Job. 22. 24. will he *e.* into judgment, 34.
23.
Ps. 100. 4. *e.* into his gates with thanks
118. 20. gate into which the righteous shall enter
Is. 2. 10. *e.* into rock and hide thyself
26. 2. open—righteous nation may *e.*
20. *e.* into thy chambers and shut thy
doors
57. 2. he shall *e.* into peace
Matt. 5. 20. in no case *e.* into the kingdom of heaven
6. 6. when prayest *e.* into thy closet
7. 13. *e.* at straight gate, *Luke* 13. 24.
21. shall *e.* into the kingdom of heaven
18. 8. better to *e.* into life halt
19. 23. rich man hardly *e.* into kingdom of heaven
24. than for a rich man to *e.* into
kingdom of heaven, *Mark* 10. 25 ;
Luke 18. 25.
25. 21. *e.* thou into the joy of thy Lord
Mark 14. 38. watch and pray lest ye
e. into temptation, *Luke* 22. 46.
Luke 13. 24. seek to *e.* but not able
Luke 11. 52. ye *e.* not yourselves
24. 26. suffered and *e.* into his glory
John 3. 4. can he *e.* the second time into
5. he cannot *e.* into kingdom of God
10. 9. by me if any man *e.* in
Acts 14. 22. through much tribulation
e. kingdom of God

Heb. 4. 3. we which believed do *e.* into
Heb. 4. 6. *e.* not in because of unbelief
10. 19. *e.* into holiest by blood of Jesus
Rev. 15. 8. none able to *e.* into temple
21. 27. *e.* into it any thing that defileth
22. 14. *e.* through the gates into city
ENTER not, *Ps.* 143. 2. *e. not* into judgment
Prov. 4. 14. *e. not* into path of wicked
23. 10. *e. not* into fields of fatherless
Matt. 26. 41. *e. not* into temptation
ENTERED, *John* 4. 38. and ye *e.* into
their labours
Rom. 5. 12. sin *e.* into world
20. law *e.* that offence might abound
Heb. 4. 10. that is *e.* into his rest he
ceased
ENTRANCE, *Ps.* 119. 130 ; 2 *Pet.* 1. 11.
ENTERETH, *John* 10. 1. that *e.* not by
door
ENTERING, *Matt.* 23. 13 ; *Luke* 11.
52 ; *Mark* 4. 19. & 7. 15 ; 1 *Thess.*
1. 9 ; *Heb.* 4. 1.
ENTERTAIN strangers, *Heb.* 13. 2.
ENTICE, *Ex.* 20. 16 ; *Deut.* 13. 6 ; 2
Chr. 18. 19, 20, 21 ; *Prov.* 1. 10.
ENTICED, *Job* 31. 27 ; *Jam.* 1. 14.
1 *Cor.* 2. 4. *e.* words, *Col.* 2. 4.
ENTIRE, whole, complete, faultless,
upright, *Amos* 1. 6 ; *Jam.* 1. 4.
ENVY slays silly one, *Job* 5. 2.
Prov. 3. 31. *e.* not the oppressor
14. 30. *e.* is rottenness of bones
23. 17. let not thine heart *e.* sinners
27. 4. who is able to stand before *e.*
Eccl. 9. 6. their *e.* is perished
Is. 11. 18. *e.* of Ephraim shall depart—
not *e.* Judah
26. 11. shall be ashamed for their *e.*
Ezek. 35. 11. do according to thine *e.*
Matt. 27. 18. for *e.* they delivered him
Acts 7. 9. moved with *e.* 17. 5.
13. 45. Jews filled with *e.* spake
Rom. 1. 29. full of *e.* murder
Phil. 1. 15. preach Christ of *e.*
1 *Tim.* 6. 4. whereof cometh *e.*
Tit. 3. 3. living in malice and *e.*
Jam. 4. 5. spirit in us lusteth to *e.*
1 *Pet.* 2. 1. laying aside all *e.*
Gen. 26. 14. Philistines *e.* him
30. 1. Rachel *e.* her sister
37. 11. his brethren *e.* him
Num. 11. 29. *e.* thou for my sake
Ps. 106. 16. they *e.* Moses in the camp
Eccl. 4. 4. man is *e.* of his neighbour
1 *Cor.* 13. 4. charity *e.* vaunteth not
Rom. 13. 13. not in strife and *e.*
1 *Cor.* 3. 3. there is among you *e.*
2 *Cor.* 12. 20. debates, *e.*
Gal. 5. 21. *e.* murders
26. *e.* one another
Jam. 3. 14. ye have bitter *e.* and
16. where *e.* is there is confusion
ENVIOUS, *Ps.* 37. 1. & 73. 2 ; *Prov.* 24.
1. 19.
EPHAH, is an Hebrew measure of the
same capacity as the Bath, con-
taining ten homers. See *Bath,* and
Homer.
Ex. 16. 36. an homer is the tenth part
of an *e.*
Is. 5. 10. the seed of an homer shall

yield an *e.*
Zech. 5. 6. he said, this is an *e.* that
  goeth forth
EPHOD, *Ex.* 39. 2; *Judg.* 8. 27. & 17.
  5; 1 *Sam.* 2. 18. & 21. 9. & 23. 9. &
  30. 7; 2 *Sam.* 6. 14; *Hos.* 3. 4.
EPISTLE, *Acts* 15. 30. & 23. 33; *Rom.*
  16. 22· 1 *Cor.* 5. 9; 2 *Cor.* 7. 8;
  Col. 4. 16; 1 *Thess.* 5. 27; 2 *Thess.*
  2. 15. & 3. 14, 17; 2 *Pet.* 3. 1.
2 *Cor.* 3. 2. our *e.* written in our hearts
  3. ye are declared the *e.* of Christ
EPISTLES, 2 *Cor.* 3. 1; 2 *Pet.* 3. 16.
EQUAL, *Job* 28. 17, 19; *Ps.* 17. 2. & 55.
  13; *Prov.* 26. 7; *Lam.* 2. 13.
Is. 40. 25. to whom shall I be *e.*
  46. 5. to whom will he make me *e.*
Ezek. 18. 25. way of Lord is not *e.*
  29. their way is not *e.* 33. 17, 20.
Matt. 20. 12. made them *e.* to us
Luke 20. 36. *e.* to the angels
John 5. 18. making himself *e.* with God
Phil. 2. 6. no robbery to be *e.* with God
Col. 4 1. give that which is just and *e.*
Rev. 21. 16. length, breadth, height, *e.*
EQUALS, *Gal.* 1. 14; *Ps.* 55. 13.
EQUALITY, 2 *Cor.* 8. 14.
EQUITY is that exact rule of right-
  eousness to be observed between
  man and man. It is fully expressed
  by the golden rule. *Matt.* 7. 12.
Ps. 99. 4. *e.* doth establish
  72. 2. judge poor with *e.* 98. 9.
Prov. 1. 3. receive the instruction of
  wisdom and *e.*
  2. 9. shall understand judgment *e.*
  17. 26. nor to strike princes for *e.*
Eccl. 2. 21. whose labour is in *e.*
Is. 11 4. reprove with *e.* for
  59. 14. truth fallen *e.* cannot enter
Mic. 3. 9. that pervert all *e.*
Mal. 2. 6. walked with me in *e.*
ERE, *Num.* 14. 11. how long will it be
  e. they believe me
Job 18· 2. *e.* make an end of words
Jer. 47. 6. O sword, how long *e.* thou be
  quiet
Hos. 8. 5. how long *e.* they attain to innocency
John 4 49. Sir, come *e.* my child die
ERECTED, *Gen.* 33. 20. Jacob *e.* there
  an altar. El-elohe-Israel
ERR, 2 *Chr.* 33. 9; *Is.* 19. 14.
Ps. 95. 10. *e.* in heart, *Heb.* 3. 10.
  119. 21. do *e.* from thy commandments
Prov. 14. 22. do they not *e.* devise evil
  19. 27. instruction that causeth to *e.*
Is. 3. 12. lead—cause to *e.* 9. 16.
  28. 7. they *e.* in vision
  30. 28. bridle causing them to *e.*
  35. 8. wayfaring men shall not *e.*
  63. 17. why made us to *e.* from way
Jer. 23. 13. prophet cause to *e.* by lies
Hos. 4. 12. whoredoms cause them to *e.*
Amos. 2. 4. lies caused them to *e.*
Mic. 3. 5. prophets make my people to *e.*
Matt. 22. 29. *e.* not knowing scriptures
Heb. 3. 10. always *e.* in their hearts
Jam. 1. 16. do not *e.* my brethren
  5. 19. if any *e.* from the truth
ERRAND, *Judg.* 3. 19; 2 *Kings* 9. 5.
ERRED, *Num.* 15. 22. if ye have *e.*

1 *Sam.* 26. 21. I have *e.* exceedingly
Job 6. 24. understand wherein I have *e.*
  19. 4. be it that I have *e.* my error
Ps. 119. 110. yet I *e.* not from precepts
Is. 28. 7. have *e.* through wine, priest
  and prophet have *e.* through strong
  drink
  29. 24. they that *e.* in spirit
1 *Tim.* 6. 10. have *e.* from faith
  21. *e.* concerning faith, 2 *Tim.* 2. 18.
ERRETH, *Prov.* 10. 17; *Ezek.* 45. 20.
ERROR, 2 *Sam.* 6. 7; *Job* 19. 4; *Eccl.*
  5. 6. & 10. 5.
Ps. 19. 12. who can understand his *e.*
Is. 32. 6. will utter *e.* against the Lord
Jer. 10. 15. are vanity and work of *e.*
Dan. 6. 4. neither was any *e.* found
Matt. 27. 64. last *e.* be worse than first
Rom. 1. 27. recompense of their *e.*
Heb. 9. 7. for the *e.* of the people
Jam. 5. 20. sinner from *e.* of his way
2 *Pet.* 2. 18. them who live in *e.*
  3. 17. led away with *e.* of the wicked
1 *John* 4. 6. know ye the spirit of *e.*
Jude 11. after the *e.* of Balaam
ESCAPE, *Gen.* 19. 17, 22. & 32. 8.
Ezra 9. 8. leave a remnant to *e.*
Esth. 4. 13. think not that thou shalt *e.*
Job 11. 20. but wicked shall not *e.*
Ps. 56. 7. shall they *e.* by iniquity
  71. 2. deliver me and cause me to *e.*
  141. 10. let the wicked fall whilst I *e.*
Prov. 19. 5. witness that speaketh lies
  shall not *e.*
Eccl. 7. 26. pleaseth God shall *e.* her
Is. 20. 6. we flee—how shall we *e.*
  37. 32. they that *e.* out of mount Zion
Jer. 1J. 11. evil—not be able to *e.*
Ezek. 17. 15. shall *e.* doth such things
Dan. 11. 41. but these shall *e.* out of
  his hand
  11. 42. land of Egypt shall not *e.*
Matt. 23. 33. how can ye *e.* damnation
  of hell
Luke 21. 36. accounted worthy to *e.*
Rom. 2. 3. *e.* the judgment of God
1 *Cor.* 10. 13. with the temptation make
  a way to *e.*
1 *Thess.* 5. 3. destruction they shall not *e.*
Heb. 2. 3. how shall we *e.* if we neglect
  12. 25. much more shall not we *e.* if
ESCAPE, *Ps.* 55. 8. I would hasten my
  e. from the storm
ESCAPED, *Ezra.* 9. 15. we remain yet *e.*
Job 1. 15, 16, 17, 19. I only am *e.* to tell
  19. 20. and I am *e.* with the skin of
  my teeth
Ps. 124. 7. soul is *e.* we are *e.*
Is. 45. 20. ye are *e.* of the nations
John 10. 39. he *e.* out of their hands
Acts 27. 44. they all *e.* safe to land
2 *Cor.* 11. 33. I was let down and *e.* his
  hands
Heb. 11. 34. through faith *e.* the edge of
  the sword
  12. 25. if they *e.* not who refused
2 *Pet.* 1. 4. *e.* corruption of world
  2. 18. those that were clean *e.*
  20. have *e.* pollutions of world
ESCHEW, ED, *Job* 1. 1. one that feared
  God and *e.* evil, 8; 2. 3.
1 *Pet.* 3. 11. let him *e.* evil and do good,

seek peace

ESPECIALLY, SPECIALLY, *Deut.* 4.
10; *Ps.* 31. 11.

Acts 25. 26. and *e.* before thee, O king
Agrippa

26. 3. *e.* because I know thee to be
expert

Gal. 6. 10. *e.* to household of faith

1 *Tim.* 4. 10. *e.* of them that believe

5. 8. *e.* for them of own house

17. *e.* those that labour in word

Tit. 1. 10. deceivers *e.* they of the circumcision

Philem. 16. brother beloved, *e.* to me

ESPOUSALS, *Songs* 3. 11; *Jer.* 2. 2.

2 *Cor.* 11. 2. *e.* to Christ

ESPY, *Ezek.* 20. 6.

ESPIED, *Gen.* 42. 27. he *e.* his money
in his sack's mouth

ESTABLISH and STABLISH, (1) To
fix, or settle, 1 *Kings* 9. 5. (2) to
confirm, *Num.* 30. 13; *Rom.* 1. 11,
(3) To perform, or make good, *Ps.*
119. 38. (4) To ordain, or appoint,
Hab. 1. 12. (5) To accomplish and
bring to a good issue, *Prov.* 20. 18.
(6) To set up one thing in the room
of another, *Rom.* 10. 3. (7) To
ratify, *Heb.* 10. 9.

The Lord shall establish thee an holy
people unto himself, *Deut.* 28. 9.
He shall confirm and establish his
covenant with thee, by which he
separated thee to himself as a
holy and peculiar people, and shall
publicly own thee for such.

Establish thou the work of our hands,
Ps. 90. 17. that is, Direct us in, and
give success to all our undertakings
and endeavours; carry them on,
by thy continual aid and blessing,
unto perfection.

ESTABLISH, *Num.* 30. 13; 1 *Kings* 15.
4; *Deut.* 28. 9; *Job* 36. 7.

Gen. 6. 18. *e.* my covenant, 9. 9. & 17.
7, 9, 21; *Lev.* 26. 9; *Deut.* 8. 18.

1 *Sam.* 1. 23. the Lord *e.* his word

2 *Sam.* 7. 12. I will *e.* his kingdom, 13.

25. *e.* the word for ever, and do as said

1 *Chr.* 17. 12. *e.* his throne for ever

2 *Chr.* 7. 18. *e.* throne of kingdom

2 *Chr.* 9. 8. God loved Israel to *e.* them

Ps. 7. 9. but *e.* the just; 48. 8. God will
e. it.

87. 5. the Highest shall *e.* her

89. 2. faithfulness shall *e.* in heaven

4. thy seed will I *e.* for ever

90. 17. *e.* work of our hands *e.* thou it

99. 4. dost *e.* equity executest judgment

119. 38. *e.* thy word unto thy servant

Prov. 15. 25. he will *e.* border of widow

Is. 9. 7., to *e.* it with judgment and

49. 8. give for covenant to *e.* earth

62. 7. no rest till he *e.* Jerusalem

Ezek. 16. 60. I will *e.* an everlasting covenant, 62.

Rom. 3. 31. yea we *e.* the law

10. 3. go about to *e.* their own righteousness

16. 25. that is of power to *e.* you

1 *Thess.* 3. 13. may *e.* your hearts un-

blamable

2 *Thess.* 2. 17. *e.* you in every good word

3. 3. Lord shall *e.* you and keep you

Jam. 5. 8. *e.* your hearts

1 *Pet.* 5. 10. God of all grace *e.* you

ESTABLISHED, STABLISHED, *Gen.*
41. 32. thing is *e.*

Ex. 6. 4. I *e.* my covenant with them

15. 17. which thy hands have *e.*

Ps. 24. 2. on rock he *e.* my goings

40. 2. rock, and *e.* my goings

78. 5. for he *e.* a testimony in Jacob

93. 1. world also is *e.* that cannot

2. thy throne is *e.* of old

112. 8. his heart is *e.* trusting

119. 90. hast *e.* the earth and it

140. 11. let not evil speaker be *e.*

148. 6. hath *e.* them for ever

Prov. 3. 19. the Lord hath *e.* the heavens

4. 26. let all thy ways be *e.*

8. 28. when he *e.* the clouds above

12. 3. man shall not be *e.* by wickedness

Prov. 16. 12. for the throne is *e.* by
righteousness

20. 1. every purpose is *e.* by counsel

30. 4. who hath *e.* all the ends of the
earth

Is. 7. 9. if believe not—be *e.*

16. 5. in mercy shall throne be *e.*

Jer. 10. 12. *e.* world for wisdom, 51. 15.

Dan. 4. 36. I was *e.* in my kingdom

Hab. 1. 12. *e.* them for correction

Matt. 18. 16. two or three witnesses *e.*

2 *Cor.* 13. 1. shall every word be *e.*

Acts 16. 5. so were the churches *e.*

Rom. 1. 11. to the'end you may be *e.*

Col. 2. 7. built up—*e.* in the faith

Heb. 8. 6. *e.* upon better promises

13. 9. good the heart be *e.* with grace

2 *Pet.* 1. 12. *e.* in the present truth

ESTABLISHED, shall be, *Lev.* 25. 30.
shall be *e.* *Deut.* 19. 15; 2 *Cor.*
13. 1; *Ps.* 89. 21.

2 *Chr.* 20. 20. believe in God so ye be *e.*

Job 22. 28. shall decree a thing and it
shall be *e.*

Ps. 102. 28. their seed *shall be e.* before
thee

Prov. 12. 19. lips of truth *be e.*

16. 3. commit to Lord thy thoughts
and they *shall be e.*

25. 5. his throne *shall be e.* in righteousness, 29. 14.

Is. 2. 2. Lord's house *be e.* *Mic.* 4. 1.

54. 14. righteousness thou *shalt be e.*

Jer. 30. 20. their congregation *be e.*

ESTABLISHETH, *Prov.* 29. 4. king by
judgment *e.* land

Hab. 2. 12. woe to him that *e.* city by
iniquity

2 *Cor.* 1. 21. who *e.* us with you

ESTATE or STATE, *Gen.* 43. 7; *Esth.*
1. 19.

Esth. 1. 7. according to *e.* of king

Ps. 39. 5. man at best *e.* is vanity

136. 23. remember us in our low *e.*

Prov. 27. 23. be diligent to know *e.* of
thy flocks

28. 2. by a man of knowledge *e.* shall
be prolonged

Matt. 12. 45. last *e.* of that man is worse

than the first, *Luke* 11. 26.

Luke 1. 48. regardeth low *e.* of handmaid

Rom. 12. 16. condescend to men of low *e.*

Phil. 2. 19. comfort when I know your *e.*

    20. naturally care for your *e.*

    4. 11. in whatsoever *e.* I am—content

Jude 6. ange's kept not first *e.*

ESTEEM, *Job* 36. 19; *Is.* 29. 16, 17.

Deut. 32. 15. lightly *e.* the Rock of salvation

1 *Sam.* 2. 30. despise me be lightly *e.*

Job 23. 12. I have *e.* words of his mouth

Ps. 119. 128. I *e.* all thy precepts right

Is. 53. 3. despised—we *e.* him not

    4. did *e.* him stricken, smitten of God

Luke 16. 15. is highly *e.* among men

Rom. 14. 5. *e.* one day above another, another *e.* every day alike

    14. to him that *e.* it to be unclean, it is

Phil. 2. 3. *e.* each other better than

1 *Thess.* 5. 13. *e.* them highly in Christ

Heb. 11. 26. *e* reproach of Christ greater

ESTRANGED, filled with dislike, rendered like strangers, *Job* 19. 13; *Jer.* 19. 4.

Ps. 58. 3. wicked are *e.* from womb, they

    78. 30. not *e.* from their lusts

Ezek. 14. 5. they are *e.* from

ETERNAL thy God refuge, *Deut.* 33. 27.

Is. 60. 15. make thee an *e.* excellency

Mark 3. 29. in danger of *e.* damnation

Rom. 1. 20. his *e.* power and Godhead

2 *Cor.* 4. 17. exceeding *e.* weight of glory

    18. things which are not seen are *e.*

    5. 1. I have house *e.* in the heavens

Eph. 3. 11. according to the *e.* purpose

1 *Tim.* 1. 17. to the king be *e.* honour

2 *Tim.* 2. 10. salvation with *e.* glory

Heb. 5. 9. author of *e.* salvation

    6. 2. baptisms and of *e.* judgment

    9. 12. obtained *e.* redemption for us

    14. through *e.* Spirit offered himself

    15. promise of *e.* inheritance

1 *Pet.* 5. 10. called us to *e.* glory

Jude 7. vengeance of *e.* fire

ETERNAL LIFE, *Matt.* 19. 16. that I may have *e.* life; *Mark* 10. 17. *Luke* 10. 25.

Matt. 25. 46. righteous shall go into *e.* life

Mark 10. 30. in world to come have *e.* life

John 3. 15. not perish, but have *e.* life

    4. 36. gather fruit to life *e.*

    5. 39. in scriptures ye think ye have *e.* life

    6. 54. hath *e.* life and I will raise him

    68. thou hast the words of *e.* life

    10. 28. I give unto them *e.* life

    12. 25. shall keep it unto *e.* life

    17. 2. should give *e.* life to as many

    3. this life *e.* to know only true God

Acts 13. 48. ordained to *e.* life believed

Rom. 2. 7. who seek for glory and *e.* life

    5. 21. grace might reign to *e.* life

    6. 23. gift of God is *e.* life through Jesus Christ

1 *Tim.* 6. 12. lay hold on *e.* life 19.

Tit. 1. 2. in hope of *e.* life which God who cannot lie, hath promised

    3. 7. heirs according to hope of *e.* life

1 *John* 1. 2. *e.* life was with Father

    2. 25. promise he promised us, *e.* life

1 *John* 3. 15. no murderer hath *e.* life

    5. 11. record God hath given to us *e.* life

    13. might know that ye have *e.* life

    20. the only true God and *e.* life

Jude 21. for mercy unto *e.* life

ETERNITY, that inhabiteth *e.* *Is.* 57. 15.

EUNUCH, 2 *Kings* 9. 32. & 20. 18.

Is. 56. 3. let not *e.* say I am a dry tree

Matt. 19. 12. some *e.* born made *e.*

Acts 8. 27. *e.* hath come to Jerusalem, 39.

EVEN balances, *Job* 31. 6.

Ps. 26. 12. foot stands in *e.* place

Songs 4. 2. flock of sheep *e.* shorn

Luke 19. 44. lay thee *e.* with ground

EVEN or EVENING, *Gen.* 19. 1. & 1. 5. 8. 31; *Ex.* 12. 6, 18.

1 *Kings* 18. 29. at *e.* sacrifice, *Ezra* 9. 4. 5; *Ps.* 141. 2; *Dan.* 9. 21.

Hab. 1. 8. *e.* wolves, *Zeph.* 3. 3.

Zech. 14. 7. at *e.* time shall be light

EVENT, *Eccl.* 2. 14. & 9. 2, 3.

EVER, a long time, constantly, eternally, *Josh.* 4. 7. & 14. 9.

Deut. 19. 9. to walk *e.* in his way

Ps. 5. 11. let them *e.* shout for joy

    25. 15. my eyes *e.* towards the Lord

    37. 26. he is *e.* merciful and lendeth

    51. 3. my sin is *e.* before me

    11. 5. will *e.* be mindful of covenant

    119. 98. thy commandments are *e.* with me

Luke 15. 31. Son thou art *e.* with me

John 8. 35. in house Son abideth *e.*

1 *Thess.* 4. 17. shall be *e.* with the Lord

    5. 15. *e.* follow that which is good

2 *Tim.* 3. 7. *e.* learning, and never

Heb. 7. 24. this man continueth *e.*

    25. he *e.* lives to make intercession

Jude 25. to God be glory now and *e.*

EVER, for, *Gen.* 3. 22. eat and live for *e.*

Deut. 32. 40. lift up hand and live for *e.*

Josh. 4. 24. fear Lord your God for *e.*

1 *Kings* 10. 9. Lord loved Israel for *e.*

    11. 39. afflict seed of David, but not for *e.*

Ps. 9. 7. Lord shall endure for *e.*

    19. 9. fear clean, enduring for *e.*

    22. 26. your hearts shall live for *e.*

    23. 6. I will dwell in house of Lord for *e.*

    29. 10. on floods Lord sitteth King for *e.*

    30. 12. I will give thanks to thee for *e.*

    33. 11. counsel of Lord standeth for *e.*

    37. 18. their inheritance shall be for *e.*

    28. saints are preserved for *e.*

    29. righteous inherit land, dwell for *e.*

    49. 8. redemp. of soul ceaseth for *e.*

    49. 9. he that should still live for *e.*

Ps. 49. 11. that houses shall continue for *e.*

    52. 9. I will praise thee for *e.*

    61. 4. I will abide in thy tabernacle for *e.*

    72. 17. his name shall endure for *e.*

    19. blessed be glorious name for *e.*

    73. 26. God is strength of my heart, and my portion for *e.*

    74. 1. why cast us off for *e.*

74. 19. forget not congregation of poor
for *e.*
81. 15. their time should endure *for e.*
85. 5. wilt be angry with us *for e.*
89. 2. mercy shall be built up *for e.*
92. 7. that they be destroyed *for e.*
102. 12. thou Lord shalt endure *for e.*
103. 9. Lord will not keep his anger
for *e.*
105. 8. remember his covenant *for e.*
111. 9. hath commanded his covenant
for *e.*
119. 111. testimonies as an heritage
for *e.*
125. 2. from henceforth even *for e.*
131. 3; *Is.* 9. 7.
132. 14. this is my rest *for e.* I have
146. 6. who keepeth *for e.* truth
Prov. 27. 24. riches are not *for e.*—crown
Eccl. 1. 4. the earth abideth *for e.*
Is. 26. 4. trust in Lord *for e.* for in Lord
32. 17. quietness and assurance *for e.*
40. 8. word of Lord shall stand *for e.*
Is. 51. 6. my salvation shall be *for e.*
8. my righteousness be *for e.*
57. 16. I will not contend *for e.*
59. 21. my words shall not depart *for e.*
64. 9. nor remember iniquity *for e.*
Jer. 3. 5. will he reserve anger *for e.* 12.
17. 4. kindled fire shall burn *for e.*
32. 39. that they may fear me *for e.*
Lam. 3. 31. Lord will not cast off *for e.*
Mic. 7. 18. retaineth not his anger *for e.*
Zech. 1. 5. prophets do they live *for e.*
John 6. 51. eateth shall live *for e.* 58.
8. 35. servant abideth not *for e.*
14. 16. Comforter abide with you *for e.*
Rom. 1. 25. Creator, who is blessed *for e.*
9. 5. over all God blessed *for e.*
11. 36. be glory *for e.* 16. 27.
2 *Cor.* 9. 9. his righteousness remaineth
for *e.*
Heb. 10. 12. *for e.* sat down on right
Heb. 13. 8. Jesus Christ same yesterday
to-day and *for e.*
1 *Pet.* 1. 23. word of God liveth and
abideth *for e.*
25. word of Lord endureth *for e. Is.*
40. 8.
1 *John* 2. 17. doeth will of God abideth
for *e.*
EVER and ever, *Ex.* 15. 18. Lord reigns
e. and e.
1 *Chr.* 16. 36. blessed be God for *e. and*
e. 29. 10; *Neh.* 9. 5; *Dan.* 2. 20.
Ps. 10. 16. the Lord is King for *e. and e.*
45. 6. thy throne O God is for *e. and e.*
Heb. 1. 8.
48. 14. this God is our God for *e. and*
~*e.* and guide
52. 8. I will trust in God for *e. and e.*
111. 8. command stand fast for *e. and e.*
119. 44. I will keep thy law for *e. and e.*
145. 1. I will bless thy name for *e. and*
e. 2. 21.
Dan. 12. 3. shine as stars for *e. and e.*
Mic. 4. 5. walk in name of God for *e.*
and e.
Gal. 1. 5. to whom be glory for *e. and e.*
Phil. 4. 20; 1 *Tim.* 1. 17; 2 *Tim.* 4.
18; *Heb.* 13. 21; 1 *Pet.* 4. 11. & 5.
11; *Rom.* 11. 36. & 16. 27; *Rev.* 1.

6. & 5. 13. & 7. 12.
Rev. 4. 9. who liveth for *e. and e.* 10. 6.
& 15. 7; *Dan.* 4. 34. & 12. 7.
22. 5. they shall reign for *e. and e.*
EVERLASTING hills, *Gen.* 40. 26.
Gen. 17. 8. Canaan an *e.* possession 48. 4.
21. 33. called on name of *e.* God
Ex. 40. 15. *e.* priesthood, *Num.* 25. 13.
Lev. 16. 34. this should be an *e.* statute
Deut. 33. 27. underneath are *e.* arms
Ps. 24. 7. be lifted up ye *e.* doors
41. 13. blessed be God from *e.* to *e.*
90. 2. thou art from *e.* to *e.* 106. 48.
100. 5. his mercy is from *e.*
103. 17. mercy of Lord from *e.* to *e.*
112. 6. righteous shall be in *e.* remembrance
119. 142. thy righteousness is *e.*
144. righteousness of thy testimonies is
e.
139. 24. lead me in the way *e.*
145. 13. an *e.* kingdom, *Dan.* 4. 3.
Prov. 10. 25. righteous is an *e.* foundation
Is. 9. 6. mighty God the *e.* Father
26. 4. in Lord Jehovah is *e.* strength
33. 14. who dwell with *e.* burnings
35. .10. shall come to Zion with songs
and *e.* joy, 51. 11. & 61. 7.
40. 28. *e.* God Creator fainteth not
45. 17. Israel saved in Lord with *e.*
salvation
54. 8. with *e.* kindness will I gather
55. 13. to Lord for a name and *e.* sign
56. 5. an *e.* name, 63. 12, 16.
60. 19. Lord shall be an *e.* light, 20.
Jer. 10. 10. true living God *e.* King
20. 11. *e.* confusion never forgotten
23. 40. I will bring *e.* reproach upon
31. 3. I loved thee with an *e.* love
Dan. 4. 34. *e.* dominion, 7. 14.
9. 24. to bring in *e.* righteousness
Mic. 5. 2. goings forth of old from *e.*
Hab. 1. 12. art thou not from *e.* my God
3. 6. *e.* mountains scattered his ways *e.*
Matt. 18. 8. cast into *e.* fire, 25. 41.
25. 46. shall go into *e.* punishment
Luke 16. 9. receive into *e.* habitation
2 *Thess.* 1. 9. punished with *e.* destruction
2. 16. God hath given us *e.* consolation
1 *Tim.* 6. 16. to whom be power *e.*
2 *Pet.* 1. 11. *e.* kingdom of our Lord Jesus
Christ
Jude 6. reserved in *e.* chains of darkness
Rev. 14. 6. having *e.* gospel to preach
EVERLASTING LIFE, *Dan.* 12. 2.
awake to *e.* life
Matt. 19. 29. shall inherit *e. life*
Luke 18. 30. in world to come *life e.*
John 3. 16. not perish but have *e. life*, 36.
4. 14. well springing u, to *e. life*
5. 24. heareth my word hath *e. life*
6. 27. meat which endureth to *e. life*
40. whoso believeth may have *e. life*
47. that believeth on me hath *e. life*
12. 50. his commandment is *e. life*
Acts 13. 46. yourselves unworthy of *e. life*
Rom. 6. 22. and the end *e. life*
Gal. 6. 8. soweth to the Spirit reap *life e.*
1 *Tim.* 1. 16. believe on him to *life e.*
EVERMORE, *Ps.* 16. 11. & 105. 4. &

133. 3; *John* 6. 34; 2 *Cor.* 11. 31; 1 *Thess.* 5. 16; *Rev.* 1. 18.

EVERY imagination evil, *Gen.* 6. 5.
Ps. 32. 6. for this *e.* one godly pray
119. 101. refrained feet from *e.* way
104. I hate *e.* false way, 128.
Prov. 2. 9. understand *e.* good path
14. 15. simple believeth *e.* word
15. 3. eyes of Lord are in *e.* place
30. 5. *e.* word of God is pure
Eccl. 3. 1. a time for *e.* purpose
Is. 45. 23. *e.* knee bow and *e.* tongue, *Rom.* 14. 11; *Phil.* 2. 11.
1 *Tim.* 4. 4. *e.* creature of God is good
2 *Tim.* 2. 21. prepared to *e.* good work
4. 18. Lord deliver from *e.* evil work
Tit. 3. 1. ready to *e.* good work
Heb. 12. 1. lay aside *e.* weight and sin
1 *John* 4. 1. believe not *e.* spirit
EVIDENCE, *Jer.* 32. 10; *Heb.* 11. 1.
EVIDENTLY *Job* 6. 28; *Acts* 10. 3; *Gal.* 3. 1, 11; *Phil.* 1. 28; *Heb.* 7. 14, 15.
EVIL, *Gen.* 2. 9, 17. & 3. 5, 22.
Deut. 29. 21. L. will separate him to *e.*
30. 15. set before thee death and *e.*
Josh. 24. 15. if it seem*e.* to you
Job 2. 10. we receive good and not *e.*
5. 19. in trouble no *e.* touch thee
30. 26. looked for good *e.* came
Ps. 23. 4. I will fear no *e.* for thou
34. 21. *e.* shall slay the wicked
51. 4. have done this *e.* in thy sight
52. 3. lovest *e.* more than good
91. 10. no *e.* shall befall thee
97. 10. ye that love the Lord hate *e.*
Prov. 5. 14. I was almost in all *e.*
12. 21. no *e.* shall happen to just
15. 3. beholding the *e.* and the good
31. 12. will do him good and not *e.*
Eccl. 2. 21: vanity and a great *e.*
5. 13. sore *e.* riches to hurt owners
9. 3. heart of man is full of *e.*
Is. 5. 20. call *e.* good and good *e.*
7. 15. know to refuse the *e.* 16.
45. 7. I make peace and create *e.*
57. 1. righteous taken from *e.* to come
59. 7; feet run to *e.* and make haste
Jer. 17. 17. art my hope in day of *e.*
18. 11. I frame *e.* against you
29. 11. thoughts of peace and not of *e.*
44. 11. set my face against you for *e.*
27. 1 will watch over them for *e.*
Lam. 3. 38. proceedeth not *e.* and good
Ezek. 7. 5. an *e.* an only *e.* is come
Dan. 9. 12. on us a great *e.* 13. 14.
Amos 3. 6. shall there be *e.* in a city
5. 14. see good and not *e.* that live
15. hate *e.* love good, *Mic.* 3. 2.
9. 4. set mine eyes on them for *e.*
Hab. 1. 13. purer eyes than to behold *e.*
Matt. 5. 11. all manner of *e.* against you
6. 34. sufficient unto the day is *e.*
Rom. 2. 9. upon every soul doth *e.*
7. 19. *e.* I would not that I do
21. I would no good *e.* is present with
12. 17. recompense to no man *e.* for *e.*
21. be not overcome of *e.* but overcome *e.*
16. 19. simple concerning *e.*
1 *Cor.* 13. 5. charity thinketh no *e.*
1 *Thess.* 5. 15. let no man render *e.* for *e.* 1 *Pet.* 3. 9.

22. abstain from all appearance of *e.*
1 *Tim.* 6. 10..love of money is root of *e.*
Tit. 3. 2. to speak *e.* of no man
Heb. 5. 14. discern both good and *e.*
Gen. 6. 5. thoughts only *e.* 8. 21.
47. 9. few and *e.* have been the days
Prov. 14. 19. *e.* bow before the good
15. 15. all days of afflicted are *e.*
Is. 1. 4. a seed of *e.* doers
Matt. 5. 45. sun to rise on *e.* and good
7. 11. if ye being *e.* know how, *Luke* 11. 13.
12. 34. how can ye being *e.* speak good
Luke 6. 35. kind to unthankful and *e.*
John 3. 19. because their deeds were *e.*
Eph. 5. 16. because days are *e.*
3 *John* 11. follow not that which is *e.*
Jude 10. speak *e.* of those things they
EWE or **EWES,** 2 *Sam.* 12. 3. poor man had nothing, save one *e.* lamb
Ps. 78. 71. he took him from following the
EXACT, to demand a right;—to practise extortion; *Deut.* 15. 2, 3; *Ps.* 89. 22; *Is.* 58. 3; *Luke* 3. 13.
EXACTOR. An officer whose business was to collect fines levied by the courts, and sometimes to gather taxes, *Job* 39. 7; *Is.* 60. 17.
EXALT, *Dan.* 11. 14, 36; *Obad.* 4.
Ex. 15. 2. my father's God I will *e.* him
1 *Sam.* 2. 10. *e.* the horn of the anointed
Ps. 34. 3. let us *e.* his name together
37. 34. *e.* thee to inherit land
99. 5. *e.* the Lord our God, for he is holy, 9.
107. 32. *e.* him in congregation of elders
118. 28. my God I will *e.* thee
Ezek. 21. 26. *e.* him that is low
1 *Pet.* 5. 6. may *e.* you in due time
Num. 24. 7. his kingdom to be *e.*
2 *Sam.* 22. 47. *e.* be God of my salvation
Neh. 9. 5. *e.* above all blessings and praise
Job 5. 11. *e.* to safety, 36. 7.
Ps. 89. 16. in righteousness shall they be *e.* 17.
Prov. 11. 11. by blessings of the upright city *e.*
Is. 2. 2. Lord's house *e.* above hills, *Mic.* 4. 1.
11. Lord alone shall be *e.* 17. & 5. 16. & 30. 18. & 33. 5, 10.
40. 4. every valley shall be *e.* and
49. 11. my highways shall be *e.*
52. 13. my servant shall be *e.*
Hos. 13. 1. Ephraim was *e.* in Israel, 6
Matt. 11. 23. Capernaum which art *e.* to heaven, *Luke* 10. 15.
23. 12. humbleth himself shall be *e.* *Luke* 14. 11. & 18. 14.
Luke 1. 52. *e.* them of low degree
Acts 2. 33. by right hand of God *e.* 5. 31.
2 *Cor.* 12. 7. lest I be *e.* above measure
Phil. 2. 9. God hath highly *e.* him
Jam. 1. 9. low rejoice that he is *e.*
Prov. 14. 34. righteousness *e.* a nation
Luke 14. 11. *e.* himself shall be abased, 18. 14.
2 *Cor.* 10. 5. casting down *e.* itself
2 *Thess.* 2. 4. *e.* himself above all God
EXAMINE, to investigate the state of the heart; to ascertain motives;

to search the heart, &c., *Ezra* 10.
16; *Luke* 23. 14; *Acts* 4. 9. & 12.
19, 22, 24, 29. & 28. 18; 1 *Cor.* 9. 3.
Ps. 26. 2. *e.* me, O Lord, prove and try
1 *Cor.* 11. 28. let a man *e.* himself and so
2 *Cor.* 13. 5. *e.* yourselves, prove yourselves
EXAMPLE, 1 *Thess.* 1. 7; *Jam.* 5. 10.
Matt. 1. 19. not willing to make her a
public *e.*
John 13. 15. for I have given you an *e.*
1 *Cor.* 10. 6. these things were our *e.*
Phil. 3. 17. ye have us for an *e.*
2 *Thess.* 3. 9. make ourselves an *e.* unto
1 *Tim.* 4. 12. an *e.* of believers
Heb. 4. 11. fall after same *e.* of unbelief
8. 5. *e.* shadow of heavenly things
1 *Pet.* 2. 21. Christ leaving us an *e.*
5. 3. not lords—but *e.* to flock
2 *Pet.* 2. 6. making them an *e.*
Jude 7. Sodom—set forth an *e.*
EXCEED, *Deut.* 25. 3; 1 *Kings* 10. 7.
Matt. 5. 20. except your righteousness
e. the righteousness
2 *Cor.* 3. 9. the ministration of righteousness *e.*
EXCEEDING, *Gen.* 17. 6. *e.* fruitful
15. 1. I am thy shield *e.* great reward
27. 34. cried with *e.* bitter cry
Num. 14. 7. land is *e.* good
1 *Sam.* 2. 3. talk no more so *e.* proudly
1 *Kings* 4. 29. wisdom *e.* much
1 *Chr.* 22. 5. house must be *e.* magnifical
Ps. 43. 4. I will go to God my *e.* joy
Matt. 5. 12. rejoice and be *e.* glad
26. 38. my soul is *e.* sorrowful unto
Rom. 7. 13. sin might become *e.* sinful
2 *Cor.* 4. 17. worketh a far more *e.* weight
7. 4. I am *e.* joyful in all tribulation
9. 14. for the *e.* grace of God in you
Eph. 1. 19. the *e.* greatness of his power
2. 7. show the *e.* riches of his grace
3. 20. able to do *e.* abundantly
1 *Tim.* 1. 14. grace of Lord was *e.* abundant
1 *Pet.* 4. 13. rejoice, be glad with *e.* joy
2 *Pet.* 1. 4. *e.* great and precious promises
Jude 24. present you faultless with *e.*
joy
EXCEEDINGLY, *Gen.* 13. 13. sinners
before the Lord *e.* 1 *Sam.* 26. 21;
2 *Sam.* 13. 15.
Ps. 68. 3. let righteous rejoice *e.*
119. 167. thy statutes I love *e.*
1 *Thess.* 3. 10. praying *e.* that
2 *Thess.* 1. 3. faith groweth *e.*
EXCEL, to be greater, more learned,
more honourable, more amiable,
more useful, &c., than another person, *Gen.* 49. 4; 1 *Kings* 4. 30.
Ps. 103. 20. his angels that *e.* in strength
Prov. 31. 29. thou *e.* them all
Eccl. 2. 13. wisdom *e.* folly as far
1 *Cor.* 14. 12. seek that ye may *e.*
2 *Cor.* 3. 10. by reason of glory that *e.*
EXCELLENCY, *Gen.* 49. 3. excellency
of dignity and *e.*
Ex. 15. 7. in greatness of thy *e.*
Deut. 33. 26. rideth in his *e.* on the sky
Job 13. 11. his *e.* make you afraid
37. 4. thunders with voice of his *e.*

40. 10. deck thyself with *e.*
Ps. 47. 4. *e.* of Jacob whom ye loved
68. 34. his *e.* over Israel and strength
Is. 35. 2. see glory and *e.* of God
Amos 6. 8. I abhor *e.* of Jacob
8. 7. Lord hath sworn by *e.* of Jacob
1 *Cor.* 2. 1. not with *e.* of speech
2 *Cor.* 4. 7. *e.* of power may be of God
Phil. 3. 8. count all loss for *e.* of Christ
EXCELLENT, *Esth.* 1. 4. *e.* majesty,
Job 37. 23.
Ps. 8. 1. how *e.* is thy name in earth, 9
16. 3. saints *e.* in whom all delight
36. 7. how *e.* is thy loving kindness
141. 5. it shall be an *e.* oil
148. 13. Lord for his name alone is *e.*
Prov. 12. 26. righteous is more *e.* than
17. 27. man of understanding is of *e.*
spirit
Is. 12. 5. Lord hath done *e.* things this
28. 29. wonderful in counsel and *e.* in
working
Ezek. 16. 17. art come to *e.* ornaments
Dan. 5. 12. an *e.* spirit in Daniel, 6. 3
Rom. 2. 18. approved things that are *e.*
1 *Cor.* 12. 31. show I unto you a more
e. way
Phil. 1. 10. approve things that are *e.*
Heb. 1. 4. obtained more *e.* name
8. 6. obtained more *e.* ministry
11. 4. offered more *e.* sacrifice
2 *Pet.* 1. 17. heard a voice from *e.* glory
EXCEPT, *Gen.* 32. 26. not let thee go,
e. thou bless me
Gen. 42. 15. *e.* your youngest brother
come, 43. 3, 5.
Esth. 4. 11. *e.* the king shall hold out
the golden sceptre
Ps. 127. 1. *e.* the Lord, build the house,
e. the Lord keep the city, the watchmen watch in vain
Matt. 5. 20. *e.* righteousness exceed
18. 3. *e.* ye be converted and become
26. 42. if this cup may not pass, *e.* I
drink it, thy will
John 3. 2. can do these miracles *e.* God
be with him
3. *e.* a man be born again he cannot
see the kingdom
27. can receive nothing *e.* it be given
from heaven
6. 44. *e.* the Father draw him
53. *e.* ye eat the flesh of the Son of
man
12. 24. *e.* a corn of wheat fall into the
ground
Acts 26. 29. such as I am *e.* these bonds,
Rom. 10. 15. how preach *e.* they be sent
Rev. 2. 5. remove candlestick, *e.* repent
EXCESS, *Matt.* 23. 25; *Eph.* 5. 18; 1
Pet. 4. 3, 4.
EXCHANGE, *Gen.* 47. 17. Joseph gave
them bread in *e.* for horses
Job 28. 17. *e.* shall not be for jewels
Ezek. 48. 14. shall not *e.* first fruits
Matt. 16. 26. if gain world and lose his
soul, what shall a man give in *e.*
for his soul, *Mark* 8. 37.
EXCHANGERS, *Matt.* 25. 27. ought to
have put my money to *e.*
EXCLUDE, *Gal.* 4. 17.
EXCLUDED, *Rom.* 3. 27. where is
boasting then ? it is *e.*

EXCUSE, to make pretences, to justify, *Rom.* 2. 15; *Luke* 14. 18, 19; *John* 15. 22; *Rom.* 1. 20; 2 *Cor.* 12. 19

EXECRATION, *Jer.* 42. 18. & 44. 12.

EXECUTE, to accomplish, 1 *Kings* 6. 12; to perform civil and ecclesiastical offices, *Jer.* 7. 5; to bring judgments upon men, *Ezek.* 5. 8; *Num.* 5. 30. & 8. 11.

Ex. 12. 12. e. judgment, *Deut.* 10. 18; *Ps.* 119. 84; *Is.* 16. 3; *Jer.* 21. 12. & 22. 3. & 23. 5; *Mic.* 7.9; *Zech.* 7. 9. & 8. 16; *John* 5. 27; *Jude* 15.

Ps. 149. 7. e. vengeance, *Mic.* 5. 15.

Hos. 11. 9. not e. fierceness of anger

Rom. 13. 4. revenger to e. wrath

EXERCISE, *Ps.* 131. 1; *Matt.* 20. 25; *Acts* 24. 16; 1 *Tim.* 4. 7, 8; *Heb.* 5. 14. & 12. 11; 2 *Pet.* 2. 14.

Jer. 9. 24. Lord e. loving-kindness

EXHORT, *Acts* 2. 40. & 11. 23. & 15. 32. & 27. 22; 2 *Cor.* 9. 5; 1 *Thess.* 2. 11. & 4. 1. & 5. 14; 1 *Tim.* .2. 1 2; *Tim.* 4. 2; *Tit.* 1. 9. & 26, 9, 15; 1 *Pet.* 5. 1, 12; *Jude* 3.

2 *Thess.* 3. 12. we command and e. by Christ

Heb. 3. 13. e. one another daily

10. 25. e. one another and so much

EXHORTATION, *Luke* 3. 18; *Acts* 13 15. & 20. 2; *Rom.* 12. 8; 1 *Cor.* 14. 3; 2 *Cor.* 8. 17; 1 *Thess.* 2. 3; 1 *Tim.* 4. 13; *Heb.* 12. 5. & 13. 22.

EXILE, 2 *Sam.* 15. 19. art a stranger and e.

Is. 51. 14. the captive e. hasteneth to be loosed

EXPECTATION, *Luke* 3. 15; *Acts* 12. 11.

Ps. 9. 18. e. of poor shall not perish 62. 5. for my e. is from him

Prov. 10. 28. e. of wicked shall perish 11. 7. dieth his e. shall perish 23. e. of the wicked is wrath 23. 18. e. shall not be cut off, 24. 14.

Is. 20. 5. be ashamed of their e. 6.

Zech. 9. 5. her e. shall be ashamed

Rom. 8. 19. e. of creature waiteth

Phil. 1. 20. according to my earnest e.

Jer. 29. 11. give you e. end

EXPECTING, *Acts* 3. 5. e. to receive something

Heb. 10. 13. e. till his enemies be made his footstool

EXPEDIENT for us that one man die for the people, *John* 11. 50. & 18. 14.

John 16. 7. e. for you that I go away

1 *Cor.* 6. 12. all things not e. 10. 23.

2 *Cor.* 8. 10. this is e. for you 12. 1. it is not e. to glory

EXPERIENCE, *Gen.* 30. 27; *Eccl.* 1. 16; *Rom.* 5. 4.

2 *Cor.* 9. 13. by the e. of

EXPERT in war, having experience, well skilled, 1 *Chr.* 12. 33, 35, 36; *Songs* 3. 8; *Jer.* 50. 9.

Acts 26. 3. know thee e. in all customs

EXPIRED, 1 *Sam.* 18. 26. the days were not e.

Acts 7. 30. and when forty years were e.

Rev. 20. 7. when 1,000 years are e. Satan be loosed

EXPLOITS, *Dan.* 11. 28. shall do e. and return

Dan. 11. 32. but the people shall be strong and do e.

EXPOUNDED riddle, *Judg.* 14. 19; *Mark* 4. 34; *Luke* 24. 27; *Acts* 11. 4. & 18. 26. & 28. 23.

EXPRESS, LY, *Heb.* 1. 3; 1 *Tim.* 4. 1.

EXTEND mercy, *Ezra* 7. 28. & 9. 9; *Ps.* 109. 12.

Ps. 16. 2. my goodness e. not to thee

Is. 66. 12. I will e. peace to her like a river

EXTINCT, *Job* 17. 1; *Is.* 43. 17.

EXTOL, *Ps.* 30. 1. & 66. 17. & 68. 4. & 145. 1; *Is.* 52. 13; *Dan.* 4. 37.

EXTORTION, *Ezek.* 22. 12; *Matt.* 23. 25.

EXTORTIONER, *Ps.* 109. 11; *Is.* 16. 4; *Luke* 18. 11; 1 *Cor.* 5. 10, 11. & 6. 10.

EXTREME, *Deut.* 28. 22; *Job* 35. 15.

EYE for eye, *Ex.* 21. 24; *Lev.* 24. 20; *Matt.* 5. 38.

Deut. 32. 10. as apple of his e. *Ps.* 17. 8.

Job 24. 15. no e. shall see me

Ps. 33. 18. e. of Lord on them that fear 94. 9. formed the e. shall he not see

Prov. 20. 12. seeing e. Lord hath made 30. 17. the e. that mocketh at his father

Eccl. 1. 8. e. not satisfied with seeing, 4. 8.

Is. 64. 4. neither hath e. seen, 1 *Cor.* 2. 9.

Matt. 6. 22. light of body e. *Luke* 11. 34. 18. 9. if thy e. offend thee, 5. 29.

1 *Cor.* 12. 17. if the whole body were an e.

1 *Cor.* 15. 52. in twinkling of an e.

Eph. 6. 6. e. service, *Col.* 3. 22.

2 *Sam.* 22. 25. e. sight, *Ps.* 18. 24.

Luke 1. 2. e. witnesses, 2 *Pet.* 1. 16.

Rev. 1. 7. every e. shall see him 3. 18. e. salve

EYE, Evil eye, *Prov.* 23. 4; 28. 22; *Matt.* 6. 23. & 10. 15; *Mark* 7. 22; *Luke* 11. 34.

EYES, *Gen.* 3. 5. your e. shall be opened

Job 10. 4. hast thou e. of flesh 29. 15. I was e. to the blind

Ps. 15. 4. in whose e. a vile person 145. 15. e. of all wait on thee

Eccl. 2. 14. wise man's e. are in his head 6. 9. better is sight of e. than wander. 11. 7. pleasant for e. to behold the sun

Is. 3. 16. walk with wanton e. 5.15. e. of lofty shall be humbled, 2. 11. 29. 18. e. of blind shall see out of 32. 3. e. of him that see shall 35. 5. e. of the blind shall be opened 42. 7. to open blind e. and give 43. 8. blind people that have e.

Jer. 5. 21. have e. and see not, *Is.* 42. 20.

Dan. 7. 20. horn that had e.

Hab. 1. 13. of purer e. than to behold

Zech. 3. 9. on one stone shall be seven e.

Matt. 13. 16. blessed are your e. for see 18. 9. having two e. to be cast into

Mark 8. 18. having e. see ye not

Luke 4. 20. e. were fastened on him 10. 23. blessed are the e. which see these things

John 9. 6. anointed e. of blind man

Rom. 11. 8. e. that they shall not see

Gal. 3. 1. before whose e. Jesus Christ has been

Eph. 1. 18. *e.* of your understanding enlightened

Heb. 4. 13. all opened to *e.* of him

2 *Pet.* 2. 14. *e.* full of adultery

1 *John* 2. 16. lust of *e.* pride of life

Rev. 1. 14. his *e.* as a flame of fire, 2. 18. & 19. 12.

  3. 18. anoint *e.*; 4. 6. full of *e.* 8.

  5. 6. Lamb having seven horns and seven *e.*

Deut. 13. 18. right in the *e.* of the Lord, 1 *Kings* 15. 5, 11, & 22. 43.

Gen. 6. 8. Noah found grace in *e.* of Lord

1 *Sam.* 26. 24. life set by in *e.* of Lord

1 *Sam.* 15. 25. find favour in *e.* of Lord

2 *Chr.* 16. 9. *e.* of the Lord run to and fro through

Ps. 34. 15. *e.* of Lord are on the righteous, 1 *Pet.* 3. 12.

Prov. 5. 21. ways of man are before *e.* of Lord

  15. 3. *e.* of Lord are in every place

  22. 12. *e.* of Lord preserve knowledge

Is. 49. 5. I shall be glorious in *e.* of Lord

Amos 9. 8. *e.* of Lord are upon sinful

Zech. 4. 10. *e.* of Lord will run to and fro

Ps. 25. 15. my *e.* are ever towards Lord

  101. 6. my *e.* shall be upon faithful

  119. 123. my *e.* fail for thy salvation

  148. my *e.* prevent night-watches

  141. 8. my *e.* are unto thee O God the Lord

Is. 1. 15. I will hide my *e.* from you

  38. 14. my *e.* fail with looking upward

  65. 12. did evil before my *e.* 66. 4.

Jer. 9. 1. O that my *e.* were a fountain of tears

  13. 17. mine *e.* shall weep sore because

  14. 17. mine *e.* run down with tears

  16. 17. my *e.* are upon all thy ways

  24. 6. mine *e.* set upon them for good

Amos 9. 4. I will set mine *e.* upon them for evil

Luke 2. 30. my *e.* have seen thy salvation

Ps. 123. 2. so our *e.* wait upon thee

Matt. 20. 33. that our *e.* may be opened

1 *John* 1. 1. we have seen with our *e.*

Deut. 12. 8. right in his own *e. Judg.* 17. 6. & 21. 25.

Neh. 6. 16. cast down in their own *e.*

Job 32. 1. righteous in his own *e.*

Ps. 139. 16. thine *e.* see my substance

Prov. 23. 5. set thine *e.* on that which is not

Songs 6. 5. turn away thine *e.* from me

Is. 30. 20. thine *e.* shall see thy teachers

Jer. 5. 3. are not thine *e.* upon the truth

Ezek. 24. 16. take away desire of the *e.* 25.

EYELIDS, *Job* 16. 16. & 41. 18; *Ps.* 11. 4. & 132. 4; *Prov.* 4. 25. & 6. 4, 25. & 30. 13; *Jer.* 9. 18.

FABLES, 1 *Tim.* 1. 4. nor give need to *f.*

1 *Tim.* 4. 7. but refuse profane and old wives' *f.*

2 *Tim.* 4. 4. shall be turned unto *f.*

Tit. 1. 14. not giving heed to Jewish *f.*

FACE, *Gen.* 3. 19. & 16. 8.

Lev. 19. 32. honour *f.* of old man

Num. 6. 25. Lord maketh his *f.* to shine

2 *Kings* 21. 13. he wipeth and turneth it on the *f.* thereof

2 *Chr.* 6. 42. turn not away his *f. Ps.* 132. 10.

  30. 9. Lord will not turn away his *f.* from you

Job 26. 9. he holdeth back the *f.* of his throne

Ps. 5. 8. make thy way straight before my *f.*

Ps. 17. 15. I will behold thy *f.* in righteousness

  31. 16. make thy *f.* shine, 119. 135.

  67. 1. cause his *f.* to shine, 80. 3, 7, 19.

Ps. 84. 9. behold the *f.* of thine anointed 132. 10.

  89. 14. mercy and truth shall go before thy *f.*

Is. 25. 7. he will destroy the *f.* of the covering

Ezek. 1. 10. *f.* of a man, a lion, *Rev.* 4. 7.

Dan. 9. 17. cause thy *f.* to shine on sanctuary

Hos. 5. 5. testify to his *f.* 7. 10.

Matt. 6. 17. anoint thine head, and wash thy *f.*

  11. 10. my messenger before thy *f. Mark* 1. 2; *Luke* 7. 27. & 9. 52.

Luke 9. 53. his *f.* was as though he would go to Jerusalem

  22. 64. they struck him on the *f.* and asked him

Acts 2. 25. set the Lord always before my *f.*

1 *Cor.* 13. 12. but then see *f.* to *f.*

2 *Cor.* 3. 18. all with open *f.* beholding

  4. 6. glory of God in *f.* of Jesus Christ

Gal. 2. 11. I withstood him to the *f.* because he was

Jam. 1. 23. his natural *f.* in a glass

FADE. To consume under Divine displeasure, *Jer.* 8. 13.—Sin and mortality, *Is.* 64. 6.—Frailty of life; decay of all things, *Jam.* 1. 11; but the heavenly inheritance cannot pass away, 1 *Pet.* 1. 4.

FAIL, *Deut.* 28. 32; *Job* 11. 20.

Deut. 31. 6. Lord will not *f.* nor forsake, 8; *Josh.* 1. 5; 1 *Chr.* 28. 20.

Ps. 12. 1. faithful *f.* from among men

  69. 3. my eyes *f.* while I wait for my God

  77. 8. doth his promise *f.* for ever

Lam. 3. 22. his compassions *f.* not

Luke 16. 9. when ye *f.* they may receive

  17. one tittle of law to *f. Matt.* 5. 18.

  22. 32. prayed that thy faith *f.* not

Heb. 12. 15. lest any *f.* of grace of God

Ps. 31. 10. my strength *f.* 38. 10. & 71. 9.

  40. 12. my heart *f.* me, 73. 26.

  143. 7. hear me, my spirit *f.*

Songs 5. 6. soul *f.* when he spake

Luke 12. 33. lay up treasure that *f.* not

1 *Cor.* 13. 8. charity never *f.*

Deut. 28. 65. and *f.* of eyes

Luke 21. 26. men's hearts *f.* them for fear

FAINT. To begreatly, weakened through exertion, 2 *Sam.* 21 15; to be much discouraged, *Is.* 13. 7; *Lam.* 1. 22; *Jer.* 8. 18; to be affected by moral evil, *Is.* 1. 5; to be overcome with joy, *Gen.* 45. 26; to be terrified, *Josh.* 2. 9; *Deut.* 25. 18; *Judg.* 8. 4. 5.

Judg. 8. 4. *f.* yet pursuing them

Is. 1. 5. head is sick, whole heart is *f.*
Is. 40. 29. he giveth power to the *f.*
    30. even youths shall be *f.* and weary
    31. wait on Lord, walk and not *f.*
Luke 18. 1. to pray always and not *f.*
2 *Cor.* 4. 1. received ministry we *f.* not,
    16.
Gal. 6. 9. due time reap if we *f.* not
Heb. 12. 5. nor *f.* when rebuked of him
Ps. 27. 13. I had *f.* unless believed
Rev. 2. 3. hast laboured and not *f.*
Ps. 84. 2. soul *f.* for courts of Lord
    119. 81. my soul *f.* for thy salvation
Is. 40. 28. everlasting God Creator *f.* not
FAIR, *Gen.* 6. 2. & 24. 16.
Prov. 7. 21. *f.* speech, *Rom.* 16. 18.
Songs 1. 15. behold thou art *f.* 4. 1, 7. &
    2. 10. & 6. 10. & 7. 6; *Gen.* 12. 11.
    4. 10. how *f.* is thy love, better
Jer. 12. 6. they speak *f.* words .
Acts 7. 20. Moses was exceedingly *f.*
Gal. 6. 12. desire make *f.* show in flesh
Ps. 45. 2. thou art *f.* than children of
Dan. 1. 15. their countenances appear *f.*
FAITH. Dependence on the truth of
an assertion. Divine faith is firm
belief in the authority of divine
revelation. It is thus we are persuaded to believe all truths relating
to God, revealed to us in the scriptures. Justifying, or saving, faith
is a grace wrought in the soul by
the Spirit of God, whereby we receive Christ, as he is revealed in
the gospel, to be our Prophet,
Priest, and King; trust in him;
and rely upon his righteousness
alone for salvation. This faith begets a sincere obedience in life and
conversation. ' Faith, which worketh by love,' *Gal.* 5. 6. is faith
which shows itself by producing in
us love to God and to our neighbour.
Faith is put for a belief and profession of the gospel, *Rom.* 1. 8.
FAITH, *Acts* 3. 16. & 13. 8.
Deut. 32. 20. children in whom there is
    no *f.*
Matt. 6. 30. O ye of little *f.* 8. 26. & 16.
    8. & 14. 31; *Luke* 12. 28.
    8. 10. not found so great *f.* no not in
    Israel
    17. 20. had *f.* as a grain of mustard
    21. 21. have *f.* and doubt not
    23. 23. omitted—mercy and *f.*
Mark 4. 40. how—that ye have no *f.*
    11. 22. Jesus said, have *f.* in God
Luke 7. 9. so great *f.* no not in Israel
    17. 5. Lord increase our *f.*
    6. if ye had *f.* might say to this
    18. 8. Son of man shall he find *f.* on
Acts 3. 16. the *f.* which is by him
Acts 6. 5. Stephen a man full of *f.* 8.
    7. company of priests obedient to *f.*
    11. 24. good man full of Holy Ghost
    and of *f.*
    14. 9. he had *f.* to be healed
    22. exhorting to continue in the *f.*
    27. God opened door of *f.* to the Gen-
    16. 5. churches established in the *f.*
    20. 21. *f.* toward our Lord Jesus Christ

Rom. 1. 5. for obedience to *f.* among all
    17. righteousness of God revealed
    from *f.* to *f.*
Rom. 3. 3. make *f.* of God without effect
    27. by law of works, law of *f.*
    4. 5. his *f.* is counted for righteousness
    11. circumcision, a seal of righteous-
    ness of *f.*
    12. in steps of that *f.* of Abraham, 16.
    13. through righteousness of *f.* 9. 30.
    & 10. 6.
    14. if they which are of the law are
    made heirs *f.* is made void
    16. of *f.* that by grace promise sure
    10. 8. the word of *f.* which we preach
    17. *f.* cometh by hearing and hearing
    12. 3. God hath dealt to man the mea-
    sure of *f.*
    6. according to proportion of *f.*
    14. 22. hast thou *f.* have it unto
    23. because eateth not of *f.* is sin
    16. 26. made known to obedience of *f.*
1 *Cor.* 12. 9. to another *f.* by same spirit
    13. 2. though I have all *f.* remove
    mountains
    13. now abideth *f.* hope, charity
2 *Cor.* 4. 13. we have the same spirit of *f.*
Gal. 1. 23. preach the *f.* which once
    3. 2. receive spirit by hearing of *f.* 5.
    7. they which are of *f.* 9.
    12. law is not of *f.* but the man that
    23. before *f.* came we were under law
    25. after that *f.* is come we are no
    longer
    5. 6. but *f.* which worketh by love
    22. the fruit of the Spirit is *f.*
    6. 10. do good to all household of *f.*
Eph. 4. 5. one Lord, one *f.* one baptism
    13. till we come in the unity of *f.*
    6. 16. above all take shield of *f.*
    23. love with *f.* from God the Father
    and Lord Jesus Christ
Phil. 1. 25. I will abide to your joy of *f.*
    27. striving together for *f.* of gospel
1 *Thess.* 1. 3. remember your work of *f.*
    5. 8. putting on breast-plate of *f.* love
2 *Thess.* 1. 4. we glory for patience and *f.*
    11. fulfil work of *f.* with power
    3. 2. for all men have not *f.*
1 *Tim.* 1. 5. charity out of *f.* unfeigned
    14. exceeding abundant with *f.* and
    love
1 *Tim.* 1. 19. holding *f.* and a good
    conscience concerning *f.* have made
    shipwreck
    3. 9. holding mystery of *f.* in pure
    conscience
    4. 1. in last days some depart from *f.*
    6. nourished up in words of *f.*
    5. 8. denied *f.*; 12. cast off first *f.*
    6. 10. erred from *f.*
    12. fight the good fight of *f.*
    21. erred concerning *f.*
2 *Tim.* 1. 5. unfeigned *f.* dwelt in thee
    2. 18. overthrow *f.* of some
    22. but follow righteousness, *f.* charity
    peace
    3. 8. corrupt reprobate concerning *f.*
    10. fully known my doctrine of *f.*
    4. 7. fought good fight, kept *f.*
Tit. 1. 1. according to *f.* of God's elect

4. my son after the common *f.*
Heb. 4 2. word not profit, not mixed with *f.*
6. 1. principles of *f.* towards God
10. 22. draw near in full assurance of *f.*
23. hold fast profession of *f.*
11. 1. *f.* is substance of things hoped
6. without *f.* impossible to please God
12. 2. Jesus author and finisher of *f.*
13. 7. whose *f.* follow considering the end
Jam. 2. 1. have not *f.* of our Lord Jesus Christ
14. say that he hath *f.* can *f.* save
17. *f.* if hath not works is dead
18. thou hast *f.* and I works; show *f.* —I will show *f.*
22. if wrought by works, *f.* perfect
5. 15. prayer of *f.* shall save him
2 *Pet.* 1. 1. like precious *f.* with
1 *John* 5. 4. overcome world even our *f.*
Jude 3. contend earnestly for *f.*
20. build yourselves on holy *f.*
Rev. 2. 13. hast not denied my *f.*
19. I know thy works and *f.*
13. 10. here is the *f.* of saints
14. 12. keep the *f.* of Jesus Christ
FAITH, By faith, *Hab.* 2. 4. just shall live by *f. Rom.* 1. 17; *Gal.* 3. 11; *Heb.* 10. 38.
Acts 15. 9. purifying their hearts *by f.*
26. 18. sanctified *by f.* that is in me
Rom. 1. 12. comforted *by* mutual *f.*
3. 22. righteousness which is *by f.* of Christ
28. conclude a man is justified *by f.*
30. justify circumcision *by f.*—uncircumcision through *f.*
5. 1. being justified *by f.* we have
2. have access *by f. Eph.* 3. 12.
9. 32. sought not *by f.* but by works
Rom. 11. 20. standest *by f.* be not highminded
2 *Cor.* 1. 24. your joy, *by f.* ye stand
5. 7. we walk *by f.* not by sight
Gal. 2. 16. justified *by f.* 3. 24.
20. I live *by f.* of the Son of God
3. 22. promise *by f.* might be given
26. ye are all children of God *by f.* in Christ Jesus
5. 5. wait for hope of righteousness *by f.*
Eph. 3. 17. Christ may dwell in your hearts *by f.*
Phil. 3. 9. righteousness through *f.* righteousness of God *by f.*
Heb. 11. 4. *by f.* Abel, &c.
5. *by f.* Enoch, &c.
7. heir of righteousness which is *by f.*
Jam. 2. 24. justified by works, not *by f.*
FAITH, In faith, *Rom.* 4. 19. not weak in *f.*
20. strong in *f.* giving glory to God
14. 1. him weak in *f.* receive ye but
1 *Cor.* 16. 13. stand fast in *f.* quit you like men
2 *Cor.* 8. 7. ye abound in *f.* in utterance
13. 5. examine whether ye be in the *f.*
Col. 1. 23. if ye continue in *f.* grounded
2. 7. built up in him established in *f.*
1 *Tim.* 1. 2. Timothy my own son in *f.*

4. godly edifying which is in *f.*
2. 7. teacher of Gentiles in *f.* & verity
15. if they continue in *f.* and charity
3. 13. purchase great boldness in *f.*
4. 12. be example in *f.* in purity
2 *Tim.* 1. 13. of sound words in *f.* and love
Tit. 1. 13. that may be sound in *f.* 2. 2.
3. 15. greet them that love us in the *f.*
Heb. 11. 13. all these died in *f.* not
Jam. 1. 6. let him ask in *f.* nothing wavering
2. 5. poor, rich in *f.* heirs of kingdom
1 *Pet.* 5. 9. resist steadfast in the *f.*
FAITH, Their, *Matt.* 9. 2. Jesus seeing their *f. Mark* 2. 5; *Luke* 5. 20.
FAITH, Through, *Acts* 3. 16. through *f.* in his Son
Rom. 3. 25. propitiation *through f.* in his blood
3. 31. do we make void law *through f.* 30.
Gal. 3. 8. God would justify heathen *through f.*
14. receive promise of spirit *through f.*
Eph. 2. 8. by grace are saved *through f.*
Col. 2. 12. *through f.* of the operation of God
2 *Tim.* 3. 15. salvation *through f.* which is in Christ Jesus
Heb. 6. 12. *through f.* and patience
Heb. 11. 3. *through f.* we understand worlds
11. *through f.* Sarah received strength to conceive
28 *through f.* Moses kept passover and sprinkling
33. *through f.* subdued kingdoms
39. obtained good report *through f.* 2.
1 *Pet.* 1. 5. by power of God *through f.*
FAITH, Thy, *Matt.* 9. 22. *thy f.* hath made thee whole, *Luke* 8. 48. & 17. 19.
15. 28. O woman great is *thy f.* be it
Luke 7. 50. *f.* hath saved thee, 18. 42.
22. 32. I prayed that *thy f.* fail not
Philem. 6. communication of *thy f.*
am. 2. 18. show *thy f.* without works
FAITH, Your, *Luke* 8. 25. where is *your f.*
Matt. 9. 29. according to *your f.* be it
Rom. 1. 8. *your f.* is spoken of throughout the world
1 *Cor.* 2. 5. *your f.* not stand in wisdom
15. 14. *your f.* is also vain, 17.
2 *Cor.* 1. 24. not dominion over *your f.*
10. 15. when *your f.* is increased
Eph. 1. 15. after I heard of *your f. Col.* 1. 4.
Phil. 2. 17. offered upon service of *your f.*
Col. 2. 5. behold steadfastness of *your f.* in Christ
1 *Thess.* 1. 8. *your f.* to God-ward is spread abroad
3. 2. to establish, comfort you concerning *your f.*
5. I sent to know *your f.* lest tempter
6. brought us good tidings of *your f.*
7. comforted in affliction by *your f.*
10. perfect what is lacking in *your f.*
2 *Thess.* 1. 3. *your f.* groweth exceeding.
Jam. 1. 3. trying of *your f.* worketh patience

1 *Pet.* 1. 7. trial of *your f.* being precious
 9. receiving end of *your f.* salvation
 21.that *your f.* and hope might be in God
2 *Pet.* 1. 5. add to *your f.* virtue, knowledge

FAITHFUL, 1 *Sam.* 2. 35. & 22. 14; 2
 Sam. 20. 19; *Neh.* 13. 13; *Dan.* 6.
 4; 1 *Tim.* 6. 2; 1 *Pet.* 5. 12.
Num. 12. 7. *f.* in all my house
Deut. 7. 9. *f.* God which keeps covenant
Neh. 7. 2. a *f.* man and feared God
 9. 8. found his heart *f.* before thee
Ps. 12. 1. the *f.* fail from among all men
 31. 23. Lord preserveth the *f.*
 89. 37. as a *f.* witness in heaven
 101. 6. my eyes be upon *f.* in land
 119. 86. thy commandments are *f.*
 138. thy testimonies are very *f.*
Prov. 11. 13. of a *f.* spirit concealeth
 13. 17. a *f.* ambassador is health
Prov. 14. 5. a *f.* witness will not lie
 20. 6. a *f.* man who can find
 25. 13. so is *f.* messenger to send him
 27. 6. *f.* are wounds of a friend
 28. 20. *f.* man abound with blessings
Is. 1. 21. how *f.* city become an harlot
 26. city of righteousness *f.* city
 8. 2. I took *f.* witnesses to record
 49. 7. Lord is *f.* and holy One of Israel
Jer. 42. 5. Lord be a true and *f.* witness
Hos. 11. 12. Judah *f.* with saints
Matt. 25. 21. well done *f.* servant, 24. 45.
 23. hast been *f.* in a few, *Luke* 19. 17.
Luke 12. 42. who is that *f.* steward
 16. 10. *f.* in least is *f.* also in much
 11. not been *f.* in unrighteous mammon
 12. not *f.* what is another man's
Acts 16. 15. judge me *f.* to the Lord
1 *Cor.* 1. 9. God is *f.* by whom called
 4. 2. required in stewards they be *f.*
 17. Timothy who is *f.* in the Lord
 7. 25. obtained mercy of Lord to be *f.*
1 *Cor.* 10. 13. God is *f.* and will not suffer
Eph. 1. 1. saints and *f.* in Christ Jesus,
 Col. 1. 2.
 6. 21. *f.* minister, *Col.* 1. 7. & 4. 7, 9.
1 *Thess.* 5. 24. *f.* is he that calleth
2 *Thess.* 3. 3. Lord is *f.* who shall establish you
1 *Tim.* 1. 12. he counted me *f.*
 15. this is a *f.* saying, and worthy of
 all, 4. 9.
 3. 11. wives grave, sober, *f.* in all thing
2 *Tim.* 2. 2. heard commit to *f.* men
 13. he abideth *f.* cannot deny himself,
 2 *Tim.* 2. 11; *Tit.* 3. 8.
Tit. 1. '6. blameless having *f.* children
 9. holding fast the *f.* word so
Heb. 2. 17. might be a *f.* high priest
 3. 2. was *f.* to him that appointed him
 10. 23. *f.* is he that promised, 11. 11.
1 *Pet.* 4. 19. as unto a *f.* Creator
1 *John* 1. 9. he is *f.* to forgive us
Rev. 1. 5. *f.* and true witness, 3. 14.
 2. 10. be *f.* to death; 13. my *f.* martyr
 17. 14. they are chosen and *f.*
 21. 5. words are true and *f.* 22. 6.
FAITHFULNESS, 1 *Sam.* 26. 23. render
 to every man his *f.*
Ps. 5. 9. no *f.* in their mouth
 36. 5. thy *f.* reacheth the clouds

 40. 10. declared thy *f.*
 88. 11. should thy *f.* be declared in
 destruction
 89. 1. make known thy *f.* to al! generations
 2. thy *f.* shalt thou establish in the
 heavens
 5. praise thy *f.* in great congregation
 8. who like thy *f.* round about thee
Ps. 89. 24. my *f.* shall be with him
 33. I will not suffer my *f.* to fail
 92. 2. to show thy *f.* every night
 119. 75. in *f.* thou hast afflicted me
 90. thy *f.* is to all generations
 143. 1. in thy *f.* answer me and
Is. 11. 5. *f.* is the girdle of his reins
 25. 1. thy counsels of old are *f.* and
 truth
Lam. 3. 23. mercies new, great thy *f.*
Hos. 2. 20. I will betroth thee to me in *f.*
FAITHLESS and perverse generation,
 destitute of belief in revealed
 truth, *Matt.* 17. 17; *Mark* 9. 19;
 Luke 9. 41.
John 20. 27. be not *f.* but believing
FALL, noun, *Prov.* 16. 18. haughty
 spirit before *f.*
Prov. 29. 16. righteous shall see their *f.*
Matt. 7. 27. and great was the *f.* of it
Luke 2. 34. child set for *f.* and rising
Rom. 11. 11. through their *f.* salvation
 is come to the Gentiles
FALL, verb, *Num.* 11. 31. & 14. 29, 32.
Gen. 45. 24. see ye *f.* not out by the way
Ruth 2. 16. let *f.* some handfuls
2 *Sam.* 24. 14. let us *f.* into hand of God
Ps. 37. 24. though he *f.* he shall not be
 45, 5. whereby they *f.* under thee
 82. 7. and *f.* like one of the princes
 91. 7. a thousand shall *f.* at thy side
 141. 10. wicked *f.* into their own nets
 145. 14. Lord upholds all that *f.*
Prov. 11. 5. wicked *f.* by own wickedness
 11. 14. where no counsel is the peo. *f.*
 24. 16. wicked shall *f.* into mischief
 26. 27. digs a pit shall *f.* in it, *Eccl.*
 10. 8.
 28. 14. hardeneth his heart shall *f.*
Eccl. 4. 10. if they *f.* one will lift up
Is. 8. 15. many shall stumble and *f.*
 40. 30. young men shall utterly *f.*
Dan. 11. 35. some shall *f.* to try them
Hos. 10. 8. mountains and hills *f.* on us
 Luke 23. 30; *Rev.* 6. 16.
Mic. 7. 8. rejoice not when I *f.*
Matt. 7. 27. great was the *f.* of it
 10. 29. sparrow not *f.* on ground
 12. 11. if it *f.* into a pit on sabbath
 15. 14. blind both *f.* into ditch
 21. 44. upon whomsoever it shall *f.*
 •*Luke* 20. 18.
Luke 2. 34. set for *f.* and rising of Israel
 10. 18. I beheld Satan as lightning *f.*
 23. 30. say to mountains *f.* on us
Rom. 11. 11. stumbled that they should
 f. through their *f.* salvation is come
 to the Gentiles
 14. 13. occasion to *f.* in his brother's
 way
1 *Cor.* 10. 12. stands take heed lest he *f.*
1 *Tim.* 3. 6. *f.* into condemnation of the

devil
6. 9. rich *f.* into temptation

Heb. 4. 11. *f.* after same example
10. 31. fearful to *f.* into hands of God

Jam. 1. 2. when ye *f.* into divers temptations

2 *Pet.* 1. 10. do these ye shall never *f.*
3. 17. lest ye *f.* from your steadfastness

FALL AWAY, *Luke* 8. 13. in time of temptation *f. away*

Heb. 6. 6. impossible if they shall *f. away* to renew

FALLEN, *Gen.* 4. 6. why is thy countenance *f.*

2 *Sam.* 3. 38. a great man *f.* this day
Ps. 20. 8. are brought down and *f.*
36. 12. are the workers of iniquity *f.*
Is. 14. 12. thou *f.* from heaven O Luci!
Hos. 14. 1. thou hast *f.* by iniquity
Luke 14. 5. have an ox *f.* into a pit
Phil. 1. 12. *f.* out to furtherance of gospel

FALLEN, are, *Is.* 9. 10. the bricks are *f.*
Ps. 16. 6. *f.* to me in pleasant places
Hos. 14. 1. hast *f.* by thine iniquity
1 *Cor.* 15. 6. some *are f.* asleep, 18.
Gal. 5. 4. ye *are f.* from grace
Rev. 2. 5. remember whence thou *art f.*

FALLEST, ETH, *Prov.* 24. 16. a just man *f.* seven times

Prov. 24. 17. rejoice not when thine enemy *f.*
Eccl. 4. 10. woe to him alone when *f.*
Luke 15. 12. portion of goods that *f.* to
Rom. 14. 4. to his own master he *f.*
Jam. 1. 11. flower thereof *f.* 1 *Pet.* 1. 24.

FALLING, *Job* 14. 18. mountain *f.* cometh to nought

Ps. 56. 13. thou hast delivered my feet from *f.* 116. 8.
Luke 8. 47. came trembling *f.* down
22. 44. great drops of blood *f.* down
2 *Thess.* 2. 3. come a *f.* away first
Jude 24. able to keep you from *f.*

FALLOW GROUND, a field uncultivated, *Jer.* 4. 3; *Hos.* 10. 12. Figuratively, it signifies an unbroken, impenitent heart

FALSE, *Jer.* 14. 14. & 37. 14.
Ex. 23. 1. not raise a *f.* report
7. keep thee far from a *f.* matter
Ps. 119. 104. hate every *f.* way, 128.
Prov. 11. 1. *f.* balance abomination, 20. 23.
Zech. 8. 17. love no *f.* oath
Mal. 3. 5. witness against *f.* swearers
Matt. 24. 24. *f.* Christs and *f.* prophets
2 *Cor.* 11. 13. 26. *f.* apostle *f.* brethren, *Gal.* 2. 4.
2 *Tim.* 3. 3. *f.* accusers, *Tit.* 2. 3.
2 *Pet.* 2. 1. *f.* prophets, *f.* teachers
Ps. 119. 118. their deceit is *f.*
144. 8. a right hand of *f.*
Is. 59. 13. from heart words of *f.*
Lev. 6. 3. sweareth *f.* 19. 12.
Ps. 44. 17. neither dealt *f.* in covenant
Zech. 5. 4. thief and that swears *f.* by my name
Matt. 5. 11. evil against you *f.* for my sake
Luke 3. 14. neither accuse any *f.*
1 *Pet.* 3. 16. *f.* accuse your good conversation

Acts 13. 6. *f.* prophet, *Rev.* 16. 13. & 19. 20. & 20. 10.

Matt. 7. 15. *f.* prophets, 24. 11, 24; *Luke* 6. 26; 2 *Pet.* 2. 1; 1 *John* 4. 1.

Ex. 20. 16. *f.* witness, *Deut.* 5. 20. & 19. 16; *Prov.* 6. 19. & 12. 17. & 14. 5. & 19. 5, 9. & 21. 28. & 25. 18; *Matt.* 19. 18. & 15. 19; *Rom.* 13. 9; 1 *Cor.* 15. 15.

FAMILIAR, intimate, *Job* 19. 14; *Ps.* 41. 9; *Lev.* 19. 31. & 20 6, 27; *Is.* 8. 19.

FAMILY, *Gen.* 10. 5; *Lev.* 20. 6.
Zech. 12. 12. mourn every *f.* apart
Eph. 3. 15. whole *f.* in heaven and earth
Ps. 68. 6. setteth solitary in *f.*
107. 41. maketh him *f.* like a flock
Amos 3. 2. known of all the *f.* of earth

FAMINE, *Gen.* 12. 10. *f.* was grievous in land

Gen. 41. 27. seven empty ears 7 years *f.*
56. *f.* was over all face of earth
2 *Sam.* 21. 1. *f.* in the days of David
2 *Kings* 25. 3. *f.* prevailed in Jer. no bread
Job 5. 20. in *f.* he shall redeem thee
Ps. 33. 19. to keep them alive in *f.*
37. 19. in days of *f.* they shall be sat
Lam. 5. 10. skin black, because of *f.*
Ex. 36. 29. I will lay no *f.* upon you
Amos 8. 11. send *f.* not of bread
Jer. 42. 17. they shall die by the *f.*

FAMISH, to starve or perish with hunger, *Gen.* 41. 55; *Prov.* 10. 3; *Is.* 5. 13; *Zeph.* 2. 11.

FAR, *Ex.* 8. 28; *Neh.* 4. 19.
Ex. 23. 7. keep thee *f.* from false matter
Ps. 22. 1. why so *f.* from helping me
.73. 27. they *f.* from thee shall perish
103. 12. as *f.* as east from west, so *f.* hath he removed
Prov. 15. 29. Lord is *f.* from the wicked
22. 15. rod of correct. shall drive it *f.*
31. 10. her price is *f.* above rubies
Amos 6. 3. put *f.* away evil day
Matt. 16. 22. be it *f.* from thee, Lord
Mark 12. 34. not *f.* from kingdom of God
Luke 22. 51. Jesus said, suffer ye thus *f.*
Phil. 1. 23. with Christ which is *f.* better
Eph' 2. 13. sometimes *f.* off, now nigh
2 *Cor.* 4. 17. ' *Far exceeding and eternal weight of glory.*'

FARE, 1 *Sam.* 17. 18; *Luke* 16. 19.

FAREWELL, to take leave, 1 *Kings* 19. 19, 20; *Luke* 9. 61. To wish persons prosperity, 2 *Cor.* 13. 11 and a phrase common at parting, *Acts* 15. 29; 18. 21.

FARTHINGS, *Matt.* 5. 26. till paid the uttermost *f.*
10. 29. are two sparrows sold for *f.*
Mark 12. 42. throw two mites a *f.*
Luke 12. 6. five sparrows for two *f.*

FASHION, denotes form, manner, *Gen.* 6. 15; *Ex.* 26. 30; *Mark* 2. 12.—The transitory nature of earthly things, *Jam.* 1. 11; 1 *Cor.* 7. 31.—Applied to the incarnation, *Phil.* 2. 8.—To the glorified body, *Phil.* 3. 21.

Job 10. 8. thy hands have *f.* me, *Ps.* 119. 73.

Ps. 139. 16. in continuance were f.
FASHIONED, Ezek. 16. 7. thy breasts
are f.
Phil. 3. 21. be f. like his glorious body
Ps. 33. 15. he f. their hearts alike
Is. 45. 9. clay say to him that f. it
1 Pet. 1. 14. not f. yourselves
FAST, 2 Sam. 12. 21; Esth. 4. 16.
Is. 58. 4. ye f. for strife; not f. as ye do
Jer. 14. 12. when they f. I will not hear
Zech. 7. 5. did ye at all f. unto me even
Matt. 6. 16. ye f. be not as hypocrites
18. appear not to men to f.
9. 14. why do we f. and thy disciples
f. not
15. can children of the bridechamber
f.—the bridegroom taken—and then
shall they f. Mark 2. 18, 19; Luke
5. 34, 35.
Luke 18. 12. I f. twice a week, I give
1 Kings 21. 9. proclaim a f. 12; 2 Chr.
20. 3; Ezra. 8. 21; Is. 58. 3, 5, 6;
Jer. 36. 9; Joel 1. 14. & 2. 15; Jonah
3. 5; Zech. 8. 19; Acts 27. 9.
Judg. 20. 26. f. that day
1 Sam. 7. 6. f. all that day
31. 13. f. seven days, 1 Chr. 10. 12.
2 Sam. 1. 12. they wept and f. till even
12. 16. David f. and lay all night in
sackcloth
1 Kings 21. 27. Ahab f. and lay in sackcloth
Ezra 8. 23. we f. and besought the Lord
Is. 58. 3. why have we f. and thou
Zech. 7. 5. when ye f. in fifth and seventh
Matt. 4. 2. when he had f. forty days
Acts 13. 2. ministered and f.
Acts 3. f. and prayed
Neh. 9. 1. assembled with f.
Esth. 4. 3. were f. and weeping, 9. 31.
Ps. 35. 13. humble soul with f. 69. 10.
109. 24. my knees are weak through f.
Jer. 36. 6. read the roll on f. day
Dan. 6. 18. the king passed the night f.
9. 3. to seek by prayer with f.
Joel 2. 12. turn ye to me with f.
Matt. 15. 32. not send them away f.
17. 21. this kind goeth not out
but by prayer and f. Mark 9.
29.
Luke 2. 37. with f. and prayers
Acts 10. 30. was f. till this hour
14. 23. ordained elders, prayed with f.
1 Cor. 7. 5. give yourselves to f.
2 Cor. 6. 5. in f. often, 11. 27.
FASTENED, Job 38. 6; Eccl. 12. 11; Is.
22. 25; Luke 4. 20.
FAT, is the Lord's, Lev. 3. 16. & 4. 8.
Prov. 11. 25. liberal shall be made f.
13. 4. soul of diligent shall be made f.
15. 30. good report maketh bones f.
28. 25. trust in Lord shall be made f.
Is. 25. 6. f. things full of marrow
FATNESS, Gen. 27. 28. God give thee
f. of earth
Job 36. 16. table should be full of f.
Ps. 36. 8. satisfied with f. of thy house
63. 5. shall be satisfied as with f.
65. 11. all thy paths drop f.
Is. 55. 2. let your soul delight itself in f.
Jer. 31. 14. I will satiate thy soul with f.
Rom. 11. 17. root and f. of olive tree

FATHER, Gen. 2. 24. & 4. 20, 21.
Gen. 17. 4. be a f. of many nations
2 Sam. 7. 14. I will be his f. Heb. 1. 5.
Job 29. 16. I was a f. to the poor
31. 18. he with me as with a f.
38. 28. hath the rain a f. and who
Ps. 68. 5. a f. of fatherless is God
103. 13. as a f. pitieth his children
Prov. 3. 12. correcteth, as f. the son
10. 1. maketh a glad f. 15. 20.
17. 21. the f. of a fool hath no joy
Is. 9. 6. everlasting F. Prince of peace
Jer. 31. 9. I am a F. to Israel and
Ezek. 18. 20. son shall not bear iniquity
of f.
Mal. 1. 6. if be a f. where is mine honour
2. 10. have we not all one f.
Matt. 10. 37. that loveth f. more than
26. even so F. Luke 10. 21; John 11. 41.
27. knoweth the Son but the F.
19. 5. leave f. and cleave to his wife
29. that hath forsaken f. for my
name's sake, Mark 10. 29.
Luke 15. 21. f. I have sinned against
heaven
16. 27. I pray thee f. send him
Luke 22. 42. F. if willing, remove cup
23. 34. F. forgive them, for they
46. F. into thy hands I commend
John 5. 19. what he seeth the F. do
20. F. loveth the Son, 3. 35.
21. F. raiseth dead and quickeneth
22. F. judgeth no man but
26. F. hath life in himself
6. 37. all the F. giveth me, shall
44. except the F. draw him
8. 18. F. bears witness of me
29. F. hath not left me alone, for I do
44. devil is a liar and f. of it
12. 27. F. save me from this hour
28. F. glorify thy name; then
14. 6. cometh to the F. but by me
8. Lord, show us the F.
15. 9. as the F. hath loved me, so
16. whatsoever ye ask F. 16. 23.
16. 3. not known the F. nor me
15. all things F. hath are mine
16. 32. I am not alone, F. is with me
17. 1. F. hour is come, glorify Son
5. O F. glorify thou me with
11. holy F. keep those given me
24. F. I will they be where I am
Acts 1. 4. promise of the F.
7. times F. hath put in his own power
Rom. 4. 11. the F. of all that believeth
12. f. of circumcision
16. f. of us all
17. might be a f. of many nations
8. 15. whereby we cry, Abba, F.
1 Cor. 8. 6. the F. of all things
2 Cor. 1. 3. God and F. of our Lord
Jesus Christ, F. of mercies and God
of comfort, Eph. 1. 3; 1 Pet. 1. 3, 17;
6. 18. I will be a F. to you and ye
Gal. 1. 3. peace from F. 2 Tim. 1. 2;
Tit. 1. 4.
Eph. 1. 17. God and F. of Lord Jesus
Christ, F. of glory
2. 18. access by one spirit to F.
3. 14. I bow my knees unto the F.
4. 6. one God and F. all, above all
5. 20. giving thanks to F. Col. 1. 3,

12; 13. 17.
Col. 1. 19. it pleased *F.* that all fulness
1 *Tim*. 5. 1. entreat him as a *f.*
Heb. 1. 5. I will be to him a *f.* and
　12. 7. what son *f.* chasteneth not
　12. 9. subjection to the *f.* of spirits
1 *Jam.* 1. 17. gift from *f.* of lights
1 *Pet.* 1. 2. foreknowledge of the *F.*
2 *Pet.* 1. 17. received from *F.* honour
1 *John* 2. 1. advocate with the *F.* Jesus
　3. 1. what manner of love the *F.*
　5. 7. three bear record, the *F.*
Jude 1. are sanctified by God the *F.*
FATHER, my, *Gen.* 27. 34. Esau cried,
　　bless me, *my f.*
Gen. 44. 24. thy servant *my f.* 27. 30
Ex. 15. 2. *my F.* God I will exalt
2 *Sam.* 16. 3. restore kingdom of *my f.*
1 *Kings* 5. 3. *my f.* could not build an
　　house
　8. 17. in heart of David *my f.* to build
2 *Kings* 2. 12. Elisha cried, *my f. my f.*
Ps. 27. 10. *my f.* and mother forsake me
　89. 26. thou art *my F.* my God
Prov. 4. 3. for I was *my f.* son
Jer. 3. 4. wilt thou not cry, *my f.* 19.
Matt. 7. 21. doeth will of *F.* 12. 50.
　8. 21. to go bury *my f. Luke* 9. 59.
　10. 32. him confess before *my F.*
　15. 13. plant *my F.* hath not planted
　18. 10. angels behold face of *my F.*
　20. 23. it is prepared of *my F.*
　25. 34. come, ye blessed of *my F.*
　26. 29. drink it new in *F.* kingdom
　39. O *my F.* let this cup pass
　42. *my F.* thy will be done
Luke 15. 18. I will arise and go to *my f.*
　22. 29. as *my F.* hath appointed
John 5. 17. *my F.* works and I work
　10. 17. doth *my F.* love me because
　30. I and *my F.* are one
　14. 26. him will *my F.* honour
　14. 28. *my F.* is greater than I
　15. 1. *my F.* is the husbandman
　8. herein is *my F.* glorified that
　20. 17. I ascend to *my F.* and your *F.*
Rev. 2. 27. as I received of *my F.*
　3. 5. confess his name before *my F.*
FATHER, our, *Is.* 63. 16. doubtless
　　thou art *our f.*
Matt. 6. 9. *our F.* which art, *Luke* 11. 2.
Luke 3. 8. have Abraham to *our f.*
Rom. 1. 7. peace from God *our F.* 1 *Cor.*
　1. 3; 2 *Cor.* 1. 2; *Eph.* 1. 2; *Phil.*
　1. 2; *Col.* 1. 2; 1 *Thess.* 1. 1; 2
　Thess. 1. 2; 1 *Tim.* 1. 2; *Philem.* 3.
FATHER, your, *Gen.* 31. 7. *your f.* hath
　　deceived me
Gen. 43. 7. is *your f.* alive ? have ye
Ezek. 16. 45. *your f.* an Amorite
Matt. 5. 16. glorify *your F.* in heaven
　45. may be children of *your F.*
　6. 8. *your F.* knoweth what things ye
　　have need of, 32; *Luke* 12. 30.
　14. if ye forgive, *your F.* will forgive
　10. 29. sparrow fall without *your F.*
　18. 14. not will of *your F.* one perish
　23. 9. call no man on earth *your f.*
Luke 12. 32. *your F.* good pleasure to
　　give you the kingdom
John 8. 41. ye do deeds of your *f.*
　44. ye are of your *f.* the devil

FATHERS, *Neh.* 9. 16. our *f.* dwelt
　　proudly
Ps. 22. 4. our *f.* trusted in thee
　39. 12. sojourner as all our *f.*
Ps. 44. 1. our *f.* have told us, 78. 3.
Is. 49. 23. kings be thy nursing *f.*
Lam. 5. 7. our *f.* have sinned
Acts 15. 10. our *f.* not able to bear
Rom. 9. 5. whose are the *f.*
1 *Cor.* 4. 15. yet have ye not many *f.*
Eph. 6. 4. *f.* provoke not, *Col.* 3. 21.
Heb. 1. 1. spake in times past to *f.*
　12. 9. we had *f.* who corrected us
2 *Pet.* 3. 4. since the *f.* fell asleep
FATHERS, his, *Acts* 13. 36. David was
　　laid to his *f.*
FATHERLESS, *Ex.* 22. 22. not afflict *f.*
Deut. 10. 18. execute judgment of *f.*
Ps. 10. 14. thou helper of the *f.*
　68. 5. a *F.* of *f.* is God in habitation
　82. 3. defend the poor and *f.* do jus-
　　tice
　146. 9. Lord relieveth *f.* and widow
Is. 1. 17. judge *f.* plead for widow
Hos. 14. 3. in thee the *f.* findeth
Jam. 1. 27. visit *f.* in affliction
FATLING *Is.* 11. 6; *Matt.* 22. 4.
FAULT, *Gen.* 41. 9; *Ex.* 5. 16.
Ps. 19. 12. cleanse from secret *f.*
Matt. 18. 15. if trespass tell him his *f.*
Luke 23. 4. I find no *f.* in him, 14; *John*
　18. 38. & 19. 4, 6.
1 *Cor.* 6. 7. there is utterly a *f.* among
Gal. 6. 1. if brethren be overtaken in *f.*
Jam. 5. 16. confess your *f.* one to
Jude 24. able to present you *f.*
FAVOUR. Abundance of good things;
　　Deut. 33. 23.—Kindness, *Job* 10.
　　12.—Comeliness, *Prov.* 31. 30.
　　—A good name, *Prov.* 22. 1.—
　　Acceptance, *Prov.* 3. 4.—Delight,
　　Ps. 44. 3.—Mercy, *Ps.* 30. 5; 106.
　　4; 5. 12; *Is.* 60. 10.—Regard and
　　esteem, *Gen.* 39. 21; *Luke* 2. 52;
　　1 *Sam.* 2. 26; *Ps.* 41. 11.
Ps. 112. 55. a good man showeth *f.*
Is. 26. 10. *f.* he showed to wicked
Dan. 1. 9. brought Daniel into *f.*
Acts 2. 47. *f.* with all the people
FAVOUR, findeth, *Prov.* 8. 35. findeth
　　me shall obtain *f.*
　18. 22. findeth a wife, obtaineth *f.*
FAVOURABLE, *Ps.* 77. 7. will Lord be
　　f. no more
FAVOURED, *Luke* 1. 28. hail, thou
　　highly *f.*
FEAR, *Gen.* 9. 2; *Ex.* 15. 16.
Ps. 53. 5. in *f.* where no *f.* was
　90. 11. according to thy *f.* so wrath
　119. 38. servant devoted to *f.*
120. flesh trembleth for *f.* of thee
Prov. 1. 26. mock when your *f.* cometh
　29. 25. *f.* of man bringeth a snare
Is. 8. 12. neither *f.* ye their *f.* nor be afraid
　13. let him be your *f. Gen.* 31. 42.
Is. 29. 13. their *f.* toward me is taught
　63. 17. hardened our heart from thy *f.*
Jer. 32. 40. put *my f.* in their hearts
Mal. 1. 6. if master where is my *f.*
Rom. 13. 7. render *f.* to whom *f.*
2 *Tim.* 1. 7. spirit of *f.* but of power
Heb. 2. 15. who through *f.* of death

12. 28. with reverence and godly *f.*
1 *Pet.* 1. 17. time of sojourning here with *f.*
1 *John* 4. 18. no *f.* in love, cast. out *f.*
Gen. 20. 11. *f.* of God not in this place
2 *Sam.* 23. 3. ruling in *f.*
Neh. 5. 15. so did not I because of the *f.*
Ps. 36. 1. no *f.* before his eyes, *Rom.* 3. 18.
2 *Cor.* 7. 1. perfecting holiness in *f.*
Job 28. 28. *f.* of Lord that is wisdom and to depart
Ps. 19. 9. *f.* of the Lord is clean enduring for ever
34. 11. children I will teach you the *f.*
111. 10. *f.* of Lord is beginning of wisdom, or knowledge, *Prov.* 1. 7. ·& 9. 10.
Prov. 1. 29. they did not choose the *f.* of the Lord
8. 13. *f.* of Lord is to hate evil
10. 27. *f.* of the Lord prolongeth days
14. 26. in the *f.* of the Lord is strong confidence
27. *f.* of the Lord is a fountain of life
15. 33. *f.* of Lord is the instruction of wisdom
16. 6. by *f.* of Lord men depart from
19. 23. *f.* of the Lord tendeth to life
22. 4. by *f.* of the Lord are riches honour
23. 17. be thou in *f.* of the Lord all day long
Is. 33. 6. *f.* of Lord is his treasure
Acts 9. 31. walking in *f.* of Lord and
Ps. 2. 11. with *f. Phil.* 2. 12.
Heb. 11. 7. save with *f. Jude* 23.
Deut. 4. 10. learn to *f.* me
5. 29. such an heart that would *f.* me
28. 58. mayest *f.* this glorious name
2 *Kings* 17. 39. Lord your God ye shall *f.*
1 *Chr.* 16. 30. *f.* before him all the earth
2 *Chr.* 6. 31. that they *f.* thee, 33.
Neh. 1. 11. servant desire to *f.* thy name
Ps. 23. 4. I will *f.* no evil, for thou art with me
31. 19. goodness laid up for those that *f.*
Ps. 61. 5. heritage of those that *f.* thy
86. 11. incline my heart to *f.* thy
Jer. 10. 7. who would not *f.* thee, O King
32. 39. heart that may *f.* me for ever
Mal. 4. 2. to you that *f.* my name Sun of
Luke 12. 5. *f.* him who can cast, *Matt.* 10. 28.
Rom. 8. 15. not spirit of bondage again to *f.*
11. 20. be not high-minded but *f.*
Heb. 4. 1. us *f.* lest a promise being left
12. 21. Moses said I exceedingly *f.* and quake
Rev. 2. 10. *f.* none of those things
11. 18. saints them that *f.* thy name
Gen. 42. 18. this do and live, for I *f.* God
Ex. 18. 21. such as *f.* God men of truth
Ps. 66. 16. come hear all ye that *f.* God
Eccl. 5. 7. dreams, vanities, *f.* thou God
8. 12. shall go well with them that *f.* God
12. 13. *f.* God and keep his command.
Job 37. 24. therefore men do *f.*
Ps. 25. 14. secret of Lord with them that *f.* him

33. 18. eye of Lord upon them that *f.* him
34. 7. angel of Lord encamps about them that *f.* him
9. there is no want to them that *f.* him
85. 9. his salvation is nigh to them that *f.* him
103. 13. as father pities, so Lord them that *f.* him
17. mercy everlasting on them that *f.*
111. 5. giveth meat to them that *f.*
145. 19. fulfil the desire of them that *f.*
147. 11. Lord takes pleasure in them that *f.* him
Matt. 10. 28. *f.* him who is able to destroy
Luke 1. 50. his mercy on them that *f.* him from generation
Deut. 6. 2. mightiest *f.* the Lord
13. thou shalt *f.* the Lord thy God, 10. 20.
24. *f.* the Lord our God for our good
10. 12. *f.* the Lord thy God, walk in his ways
14. 23. learn to *f.* the Lord thy God always, 17. 19. & 31. 12, 13.
Josh. 4. 24. that he might *f.* the Lord your God
24. 14. therefore *f.* the Lord, serve in sincerity
1 *Sam.* 12. 14. if ye will *f.* the Lord and serve him
24. only *f.* the Lord and serve him
1 *Kings* 18. 12. thy servant did *f.* the Lord, 2 *Kings* 4. 1.
2 *Kings* 17. 28. they should *f.* the Lord
Ps. 15. 4. he honoureth them that *f* the Lord
22. 23. ye that *f.* the Lord trust in him, 115. 11.
33. 8. let all the earth *f.* the Lord
34. 9. O *f.* the Lord ye saints, no want to them that *f*
Ps. 115. 13. he will bless them that *f.* the Lord
118. 4. let them that *f.* the Lord say
135. 20. ye that *f.* the Lord bless the
Prov. 3. 7. *f.* the Lord and depart from
24. 21. my son *f.* the Lord and meddle not with
Jer. 5. 24. let us now *f.* the Lord that giveth rain
26. 19. did he not *f.* the Lord and besought Lord
Hos. 3. 5. return and *f.* the Lord
Jonah 1. 9. I *f.* the Lord God of heaven
Gen. 15. 1. *f.* not, I am thy shield
26. 24. *f.* not for I am with thee
Num. 14. 9. Lord is with us *f.* not them
Deut. 1. 21. *f.* not, neither be discouraged nor dismayed, 31. 8; *Josh.* 8. 1. & 10. 25.
Ps. 56. 4. I will not *f.* what flesh can do, 118. 6; *Heb.* 13. 6.
Is. 41. 10. *f.* not I am with thee, I will help thee, 13. and 43. 5.
43. 1. *f.* not for I have redeemed thee
Jer. 5. 22. *f.* ye not me saith the Lord
30. 10. *f.* not O my servant Jacob, and be not dismayed, 46. 27, 28.
Matt. 10. 28. *f.* not them that kill body
Luke 12. 32. *f.* not little flock, for it is

FEARED, Ex. 1. 17. midwives f. God, 21.
14. 31. people f. Lord and believed
1 Sam. 12. 18. all people f. Lord greatly
1 Kings 18. 3. Obadiah f. Lord greatly,
Neh. 7. 2. Hananiah f. God above many
Job 1. 1. one that f. God and eschewed
   evil
Ps. 76. 7. thou art to be f. who
89. 7. God is greatly to be f. in assem-
   bly
96. 4. Lord is to be f. above all gods
130. 4. forgiveness that mayest be f.
Mal. 3. 16. they that f. Lord spake often
Acts 10. 2. one that f. Lord with all his
   house, 22.
Heb. 5. 7. was heard in that he f.
Gen. 22. 12. that thou f. God
Job 1. 8. that f. God, 2. 3.
Ps. 25. 12. what man is he that f. Lord
112. 1. blessed is man that f. Lord
128. 1. every one that f. the Lord
Prov. 28. 14. happy is man that f. alway
Is. 50. 10. who among you f. Lord
Acts 10. 22. one that f. God and of good
35. he that f. God and worketh right-
   eousness
13. 26. whosoever among you f. God

FEARFUL. It is given to God as the
   object of supreme reverence and
   adoration. Ex. 15. 11. f. in praises.
   —Applied to man
Matt. 8. 26. why are ye f. Mark 4. 40.
It denotes terror; Heb. 10. 27. certain
   f. looking for of judgment
Heb. 10. 31. f. thing to fall into hands
   of living God
Rev. 21. 8. f. and unbelieving shall be
   cast
Ps. 55. 5. f. and trembling
Is. 33. 14. f. hath surprised the hypo-
   crites
Ps. 139. 14. I am f. and wonderfully
FEAST, Gen. 19. 3. & 21. 8.
Prov. 15. 15. merry heart continual f.
Eccl. 10. 19. a f. is made for laughter
Is. 25. 6. Lord máke to all people a f.
Dan. 5. 1. Belshazzar made great f.
Luke 14. 13. makest a f. call the poor
23. 17. release one at the f.
Acts 18. 21. I must by all means keep
   this f.
1 Cor. 5. 8. keep f. not with old leaven
FEASTS, Matt. 23. 6. love uppermost
   rooms at f. chief seats in synagogues,
   Mark 12. 39; Luke 20. 46.
Jude 12. spots in your f. of charity
FEATHERS, Lev. 1. 16. his crop with
   his f.
Job 39. 13. gavest thou the goodly wings
   to the peacock ? or wings and f. to
   the ostrich ?
Ps. 68. 13. and her f. covered with yel-
   low gold
91. 4. shall cover thee with his f. under his wings
Dan. 4. 33. his hairs were grown like
   eagle's f.
FEEBLE, Gen. 30. 42; Deut. 25. 18.
   Spoken of as unable to defend themselves, Deut. 25. 18—Of persons
   discouraged, 2 Sam. 4. 1.—Of
   weak believers as follows :—Ps.

105. 37. not one f. person among
FEEBLE, Neh. 4. 2. and he said, what
   do these f. Jews
Job 4. 4. strengthened the f. knees
Ps. 38. 8. I am f. and sore broken
Is. 16. 14. the remnant shall be very
   small and f.
35. 3. confirm the f. knees
Zech. 12. 8. he that is f. shall be as David
1 Thess. 5. 14. comfort f. minded
Heb. 12. 12. lift up the f. knees
FEED, FED, Gen. 25. 30. & 30. 36.
Deut. 8. 3. he f. thee with manna
Ps. 28. 9. f. them and lift them up
37. 3. verily thou shalt be f.
49. 14. death shall f. on them
65. 25. the wolf and the lamb shall f.
   together
Ps. 81. 16. he should have f. them with
   finest of wheat
Prov. 10. 21. lips of righteous f. many
Is. 58. 14. f. thee with heritage of Jacob
Jer. 3. 15. pastors f. you with knowledge
Ezek. 16. 19. and my honey wherewith
   I f. thee
34. 2. woe to the shepherds that do
   f. themselves
3. ye eat the fat, but ye f. not the
   flock
Dan. 5. 21. they f. Nebuchadnezzar with
   grass, like oxen
Mic. 5. 4. f. in the strength of the Lord
Matt. 25. 37. when saw we thee hun-
   gered, and f. thee
Luke 16. 21. desiring to be f. with
   crumbs that fell
Acts 20. 28. to f. church of God which
1 Cor. 3. 2. I have f. you with milk and
13. 3. give all my goods to f. poor
Rev. 7. 17. Lamb in the midst of throne
   f. them
1 Kings 22. 27. f. him bread of affliction
Prov. 30. 8. f. me with food convenient
Songs 1. 8. f. thy kids beside shepherds
Mic. 7. 14. f. thy people with thy rod
John 21. 15. f. my lambs, sheep, 16. 17.
Rom. 12. 20. if enemy hunger f. him
1 Pet. 5. 2. f. the flock of God among you
Is. 44. 20. he f. on ashes, deceived
Songs 2. 16. he f. among lilies, 6. 3.
Hos. 12. 1. Ephraim f. on wind, east
Matt. 6. 26. heavenly Father f. them,
   Luke 2. 24.
1 Cor. 9. 7. who f. a flock and eateth not
FEEL, feelings, Gen. 27. 12; Judg. 16.
   26; Job 20. 20. To search as a blind
   man does by feeling; Acts 17. 27.
   if haply they might feel after him.
   —Wicked men are said to be ' past
   feeling;' Eph. 4. 19; Heb. 4. 15.
FEET, Gen. 18. 4. & 19. 2. & 49. 10.
Ex. 3. 5. shoes off thy f. Acts 7. 33.
1 Sam. 2. 9. keep f. of his saints
2 Sam. 4. 4. was lame of his f. 9. 3, 13.
12. cut off their hands and their f.
2 Kings 6. 32. sound of master's f. behind
13. 21. dead man stood on his f.
Neh. 9. 21. their f. swelled not
Job 12. 5. is ready to slip with his f.
29. 15. eyes to blind and f. to lame
Ps. 22. 16. pierced my hands and f.

21. 8. hast set my *f.* in a large room
66. 9. suffer not our *f.* to be moved
73. 2. my *f.* were almost gone
116. 8. delivered my *f.* from falling
119. 59. turned *f.* to thy testimonies
101. refrained my *f.* from evil
105. thy word is lamp to my *f.*
122. 2. *f.* stand within thy gates
Prov. 4. 26. ponder the path of my *f.*
5. 5. her *f.* go down to death, her
Songs 7. 1. how beautiful are thy *f.*
Is. 3. 16. a tinkling with their *f.*
6. 2. with twain he covered his *f.*
52. 7. *f.* of him bringeth good tidings
59. 7. their *f.* run to evil and make
60. 13. the place of my *f.* glorious
Nah. 1. 3. clouds are dust of his *f.* .
Zech. 14. 4. *f.* stand on mount of Olives
Matt. 10. 14. shake off the dust of your
f. Mark 6. 11: *Luke* 9. 5.
Luke 1. 79. guide our *f.* into way
7. 38. she kissed·his *f.* and anointed
15. 22. put shoes on his *f.*
24. 39. behold my hands and my *f.*
John 11. 2. and wiped his *f.* 12. 3.
Acts 13. 25. shoes of his *f.* not worthy
16. 24. their *f.* fast in the stocks
22. 3. brought up at *f.* of Gamaliel
26. 16. rise and stand upon thy *f.*
Rom. 3. 15. *f.* are swift to shed blood
10. 15. *f.* of them preach gospel
Eph. 6. 15. *f.* shod with preparation of
the gospel
Heb. 12. 13. straight paths for your *f.*
Rev. 11. 11. they stood upon their *f.*
FEET, at his, *Luke* 7. 38. she stood *at
his f.* behind
Rev. 1. 17. I fell *at his f.* as dead
19. 10. I fell *at his f.* to worship
FEET, under, *Ex.* 24. 10. *under his f.* a
sapphire
Ps. 8. 6. put all things *under* his *f.* 1
Cor. 15. 27; *Eph.* 1. 22.
Matt. 7. 6. lest trample *under* their *f.*
Rom. 16. 20. bruise Satan *under* your *f.*
1 *Cor.* 15. 25. all enemies *under* his *f.*
Rev. 12. 1. moon *under* her *f.*
FEET, wash, *Ex.* 30. 19. Aaron and his
sons shall *wash* their *f.* 21; 40. 41.
2 *Sam.* 11. 8. Uriah, go *wash* thy *f.*
Luke 7. 38. to *wash* his *f.* with tears
John 13. 6. Lord, dost thou *wash* my *f.*
10. needeth not save to *wash* his *f.*
FEIGN, to act the hypocrite *Luke* 20. 20.
FEIGNED, 1 *Sam.* 21. 13; *Ps.* 17. 1.
FEIGNEDLY, 2 *Pet.* 2. 3; *Jer.* 3. 10.
FELL, to cut down, 2 *Kings* 3. 19, 25; 6.
5.—Change of countenance; *Gen.*
4. 5.—Descent of the Spirit, *Ezek.*
2. 2; 3. 14; 8. 1.—Effect of Divine
power, *Heb.* 11. 30; *Josh.* 6. 13, 20.
Gen. 44. 14. Joseph's brethren *f.* before
1 *Sam.* 31. 4. Saul took sword and *f.* on it
2 *Kings* 2. 13. mantle that *f.* from Elijah
6. 5. axe head *f.* into the water
1 *Chr.* 21. 14. *f.* of Israel 70,000 men
Matt. 7. 25. the house *f.* not
27. house *f. Luke* 6. 49.
13. 4. seed *f.* by the way side, *Mark*
4. 4; *Luke* 8. 5.
Mark 14. 35. Jesus *f.* on the ground

Luke 15. 20. his father *f.* on his neck
16. 21. crumbs which *f.* from table
John 18. 6. went backward, and *f.*
Acts 1. 25. Judas by transgression *f.*
13. 36. David *f.* on sleep, saw corrup.
20. 10. Paul *f.* on Eutychus
Rom. 11. 22. on them *f.* severity
1 *Cor.* 10. 8. *f.* in one day 23,000
Rev. 1. 17. I *f.* at his feet as dead
6. 13. and the stars of heaven *f.*
8. 10. *f.* great star from heaven
FELLOW, *Gen.* 19. 9; *Ex.* 2. 13.
1 *Sam.* 21. 15. ye brought this *f.* to play
the madman, shall this *f.*
Eccl. 4. 10. if fall, one lift up his *f.*
Is. 34. 14. satyr shall cry to his *f.*
Zech. 13. 7. man that is my *f.*
John 9. 29. for this *f.* we know not
Acts 18. 13. *f.* persuaded to worship God
22. 22. away with such a *f.* from
24. 5. found this man a pestilent *f.*
Rom. 16. 7. my *f.* prisoner *Col.* 4. 10.
2 *Cor.* 8. 23. he is my *f.* helper, 3 *John* 8.
Eph. 2. 19. *f.* citizens; 3. 6. *f.* heirs
Col. 1. 7. *f.* servant, 4. 7; *Rev.* 6. 11. &
19. 10. & 22. 9.
Phil. 4. 3. *f.* labourers, 1 *Thess.* 3. 2.
2. 25. *f.* soldier, *Phil.* 1. 2, 24.
FELLOW-citizens, *Eph.* 2. 19. *f.-citizens*
with saints
FELLOW-heirs, *Eph.* 3. 6. Gentiles
should be *f.-heirs*
FELLOW-helper, or helpers, 2 *Cor.* 8.
23. Titus, my *f.-helper*
3 *John* 8. might be *f.-helper* to the truth
Fellow-labourer, or labourers, 1 *Thess.*
3. 2. sent Timothy our *f.-labourer*
Phil. 4. 3. with other *f.-labourers*
FELLOW-prisoner, or prisoners, *Rom.*
16. 7. Andron and Junia *f.-prisoners*
Col. 4. 10. Aristarchus *f.-p.* saluteth
Philem. 23. Epaphras my *f.-p.* in Christ
FELLOW-servant or servants, *Col.* 1. 7.
Epaphras our dear *f.-servant*
4. 7. Tychicus, who is a *f.-servant*
Rev. 19. 10. do it not, I am thy *f.-ser-
vant*, 22. 9.
FELLOW-soldier, *Phil.* 2. 25. Epaphro-
ditus my *f.-soldier*
Philem. 2 Paul to Archippus *f.-soldier*
FELLOW-workers, *Col.* 4. 11. these
only are my *f.-workers*
FELLOWS, *Ps.* 45. 7. with the oil of
gladness above thy *f. Heb.* 1. 9.
Dan. 2·13. Dan. and his *f.* to be slain
Matt. 11. 16. children calling to their *f.*
Acts 17. 5. lewd *f.* of the baser sort
FELLOWSHIP, *Ps.* 94. 20. throne of
iniquity have *f.* with thee
Acts 2. 42. continued in apostles doc-
trine and *f.*
1 *Cor.* 1. 9. God by whom called to *f.* of
Jesus Christ
10. 20. should not have *f.* with devils
2 *Cor.* 6. 14. what *f.* hath righteousness
with unrighteousness
8. 4. *f.* of ministering to saints
Gal. 2. 9. give us right hand of *f.*
Eph. 5. 11. no *f.* with unfruitful works
of darkness
Phil. 1. 5. for your *f.* in gospel

2. 1. if there be any *f.* of the Spirit
3. 10. know him and *f.* of his sufferings

1 *John* 1. 3. *f.* with us, *f.* with Father
6. we have *f.*; 7, *f.* one with another

FEMALE, *Gen.* 1. 27; 5. 2; *Gal.* 3. 28.

FENCE, *Ps.* 62. 3. ye shall be as a tottering *f.*

FENCED, 2 *Kings* 3. 19. shall smite every *f.* city

Is. 2. 15. day of Lord on every *f.* wall
5. 2. a vineyard, and he *f.* it

Ezek. 36. 35. ruined cities become *f.*

FENCED cities, 2 *Kings* 19. 25. should lay waste *f. cities*

2 *Chr.* 8. 5. Solomon built *f. cities*

Dan. 11. 15. king sh. take most *f. cities*

Hos. 8. 14. Judah hath multipli. *f. cities*

Zeph. 1. 16. a day of alarm aga. *f. cities*

FENS, *Job* 40. 21. Behemoth in covert of the *f.*

FERRET, *Lev.* 11. 30. the *f.* unclean

FERRY-boat, 2 *Sam.* 19. 18. *f.-boat* for king's house

FERVENT in spirit, *Acts* 18. 25.

Rom. 12. 11. *f.* in spirit, serving the Lord

2 *Cor.* 7. 7. your *f.* mind toward me, so

Jam. 5. 16. *f.* prayer of righteous man availeth much

1 *Pet.* 4. 8. have *f.* charity among yourselves

2 *Pet.* 3. 10. melt with *f.* heat, 12.

Col. 4. 12. Epaphras labouring *f.* for you in prayers

1 *Pet.* 1. 22. love one another *f.*

FETCH, *Num.* 20. 10. *f.* water out of rock

2 *Sam.* 5. 23. *f.* a compass behind

Job 36. 3. *f.* my knowledge from afar

Acts 16. 37. let come, and *f.* us out

FETCHED, *Acts* 28. 13. thence we *f.* a compass

FETTERS. Chains or shackles, for securing prisoners; *Judg.* 16. 21; 2 *Chr.* 33. 11; *Ps.* 105. 18; *Mark* 5. 4; *Luke* 8. 29.

FEVER, *Lev.* 26. 16; *Mark* 1. 30; *Luke* 4. 38.

FEW, *Gen.* 29. 20; *Ps.* 105. 12.

Gen. 47. 9. *f.* and evil have the days of *Job* 10. 20. are not my days *f.*
14. 1. man is of *f.* days, and full of
16. 22. when a *f.* years are come

Eccl. 5. 2. therefore let thy words be *f.*
12. 3. grinders cease, because *f.*

Matt. 7. 14. way to life *f.* find it

Matt. 9. 37. labourers are *f. Luke* 10. 2.
20. 16. called, but *f.* chosen, 22. 14.
25. 21. faithful in a *f.* things, 23.

Luke 12. 48. be beaten with *f.* stripes
13. 23. are there *f.* that be saved

Heb. 12. 10. for *f.* days chastened us

Rev. 2. 14. I have a *f.* things against
3. 4. thou hast a *f.* names in Sardis

FIDELITY, all good, *Tit.* 2. 10.

FIELD, *Gen.* 24. 63; *Ps.* 103. 15; 1 *Kings* 2. 26; *Matt.* 13. 38, 44.

FIERCE. Applied to the anger of man, *Gen.* 49. 7; *Deut.* 28. 50; 2 *Chr.* 28. 11; *Jam.* 3. 4.

FIERCENESS of anger, *Deut.* 13. 17;

Josh. 7. 26; 2 *Kings* 23. 26; *Job* 4. 10. & 10. 16. & 39. 24. & 41. 10; *Ps.* 85. 3; *Jer.* 25. 38; *Hos.* 11. 9.

FIERY law, *Deut.* 33. 2.

Num. 21. 6. *f.* serpents, *Deut.* 8. 15.

Ps. 21. 9. make them as a *f.* oven

Eph. 6. 16. quench *f.* darts of devil

Heb. 10. 27. *f.* indignation devour

1 *Pet.* 4. 12. not strange *f.* trial

FIGS, *Gen.* 3. 7; *Is.* 34. 4. & 38. 21.

Jer. 24. 2. very good *f.* naughty *f.* 29. 17.

Matt. 7. 16. do men gather *f.* of thistles

Jam. 3. 12. can *f.* tree bear olive berries or vine, *f.*

Judg. 9. 10. *f.* tree, 1 *Kings* 4. 25; *Mic* 4. 4; *Is.* 36. 16; *Hos.* 9. 10; *Nah.* 3. 12; *Hab.* 3. 17; *Zech.* 3. 10; *Matt.* 21. 19. & 24. 32; *Luke* 13. 6, 7; *John* 1. 48, 50; *Rev.* 6. 13.

FIGHT. Divine power for deliverance and for punishment, *Ex.* 14. 14; 2 *Chr.* 32. 8; *Ps.* 35. 1. 2; those who fight against God shall not prosper, 2 *Chr.* 13. 12; 1 *Sam.* 17. 20; *Ex.* 14. 14.

Acts 5. 39. found to *f.* against God
23. 9. let us not *f.* against God

1 *Cor.* 9. 26. so *f.* I not as one

1 *Tim.* 6. 12. *f.* the good *f.* of faith

2 *Tim.* 4. 7. I have *f.* a good *f.*

Heb. 10. 32. a great *f.* of affliction
11. 34. waxed valiant in *f.*

FIGHTINGS, 2 *Cor.* 7. 5. without were *f.*

Jam. 4. 1. whence come wars and *f.*

FIGURE, *Rom.* 5. 14; 1 *Cor.* 4. 6; *Heb.* 9. 9, 24. & 11. 19; 1 *Pet.* 3. 21.

FILE, 1 *Sam.* 13. 21. yet they had a *f.* for the mattocks

FILL, *Job* 23. 4. I would *f.* my mouth with arguments

Ps. 81. 10. open mouth wide I will *f.* it

Prov. 1. 13. *f.* our houses with spoil

Jer. 23. 24. I *f.* heaven and earth

Hag. 2. 7. *f.* this house with glory

Rom. 15. 13. God *f.* you with all joy

Eph. 4. 10. he ascended, that he might *f.* all things

Col. 1. 24. I *f.* up that behind of suffer.

FILLED, 1 *Kings* 8. 10. the cloud *f.* the house of the Lord
11. glory of Lord *f.* the house, 2 *Chr.* 5. 14; 7. 1, 2.

Job 16. 8. hast *f.* me with wrinkles

Ps. 71. 8. mouth be *f.* with praise
72. 19. let the whole earth be *f.* with his glory
104. 28. thou openest thine hand, are *f.* with good

Songs 5. 2. open to me, my head is *f.* with dew

Is. 6. 1. high and lifted up, and his train *f.* the temple

Dan. 2. 35. the stone cut out *f.* the whole earth

Matt. 27. 48. one of them ran and *f.* a sponge with vinegar, *Mark* 15. 36; *John* 19. 29.

Luke 1. 53. hath *f.* hungry with good
2. 40. Jesus waxed strong in spirit, *f.* with wisdom

15, 16. have *f.* his belly with husks
John 16. 6. sorrow hath *f.* your heart
Acts 2. 2. as of a rushing mighty wind
   f. the house
   9. 17. *f.* with Holy Ghost, 13. 9. &
   4. 6, 31. & 2. 4; *Luke* 1. 15.
Rom. 15. 13. *f.* with all knowledge
2 *Cor.* 7. 4. I am *f.* with comfort, I am
Eph. 3. 19. *f.* with all fulness of God
   5. 18. not with wine but *f.* with spirit
Phil. 1. 11. being *f.* with fruits of right-
   eousness
Col. 1. 9. *f.* with knowledge of his will
2 *Tim.* 1. 4. mindful of tears *f.* with joy
Jam. 2. 16. be ye warned and *f.*
FILLETH, *Ps.* 84. 6. the rain also *f.* the
Eph. 1. 23. the fulness of him that *f.* all
   in all
FILTH, FILTHY, *Is.* 4. 4; 1 *Cor.* 4. 13.
Job 15. 16. more *f.* is man
Ps. 14. 3. altogether become *f.* 53. 3.
Is. 64. 6. all our righteousness as *f.* rags
Col. 3. 8. put off *f.* communication
1 *Tim.* 3. 3. greedy of *f.* lucre, 8 ; *Tit.*
   1. 7, 11; 1 *Pet.* 5. 2.
2 *Pet.* 2. 7. vexed with *f.* conversation
Jude 8. *f.* dreamers defile flesh
Rev. 22. 11. that is *f.* let him be *f.* still
FILTHINESS, *Prov.* 30. 12. is not
   washed from their *f.*
Lam. 1. 9. her *f.* is in her skirts
Ezek. 24. 13. in thy *f.* is lewdness
  ·36. 25. from all your *f.* I will
2 *Cor.* 7. 1. cleanse from all *f.* of flesh
Eph. 5. 4. nor let *f.* be once named
   among you
Jam. 1. 21. lay apart all *f.*
FINALLY, 2 *Cor.* 13. 11; *Eph.* 6. 10;
   Phil. 3. 1. & 4. 8; 2 *Thess.* 3. 1; 1
   Pet. 3. 8.
FIND. (1) To convert, or recover a thing
   that was lost, *Luke* 15. 8, 9, 32. (2)
   To invent, or discover, 2 *Chr.* 2. 14.
   (3) To know experimentally, *Rom.*
   4. 1; *Rev.* 2. 2. (4) To obtain what
   we want and desire of God, *Matt.*
   7. 7. (5) To come to, *Job* 3. 22. (6)
   To understand thoroughly, *Job* 11.
   7. (7) To do, or perform, *Is.* 58. 13.
   (8) To seek, *Job* 33. 10. (9) To happen upon without seeking, *Gen.*
   37. 15. (10) To choose and appoint,
   Acts 13. 22. (11) To turn to, or light
   on, *Luke* 4. 17. (12) To observe,
   Matt. 8. 10.
FIND, *Gen.* 19. 11. & 38. 22.·
Num. 32. 23. your sin shall *f.* you out
Job 11. 7. who by searching *f.* out God
   23. 3. O that I knew where I might *f.*
   him
Prov. 1. 28. shall seek me and not *f.* me
Songs 5. 6. I sought but could not *f.* him
Jer. 6. 16. ye shall *f.* rest to your souls
   29. 13. shall seek me and *f.* me when
Matt. 7. 7. seek and ye shall *f.* *Luke* 11.
   9.
   14. way to life few that *f.* it
   10. 39. *f.* life, looseth life shall *f.* it,
   16. 25.
   11. 29. ye shall *f.* rest to your souls
Luke 15. 8. doth she not seek diligently
   till she *f.* it

John 7. 24. seek me and shall not *f.* me
Rom. 7. 18. to do good I *f.* not
2 *Tim.* 1. 18. *f.* mercy in that day
Heb. 4. 16. may *f.* grace to help
Rev. 9 6. seek death and shall not *f.* it
FINDETH, *Ps.* 119. 162. I rejoice at
   word, as one that *f.* spoil
Prov. 3. 13. happy man that *f.* wisdom
   8. 35. whoso *f.* me *f.* life
   18. 22. whose *f.* a wife *f.* good thing
Eccl. 9. 10. whatsoever thy hand *f.* to do,
   do it
Hos. 14. 3. the fatherless *f.* mercy
Matt. 7. 8. and he that seeketh *f.* *Luke*
   11. 10.
   10. 39. he that *f.* his life shall lose it
FINDING, *Is.* 58. 13. not *f.* own plea-
   sures
Rom. 11. 33. his ways past *f.* out
FINE. Spoken of gold; 2 *Chr.* 3. 5, 8.
   —Of linen, *Luke* 16. 19.—The
   righteousness of the saints, *Rev.*
   19. 8, 14.—Of flour, *Ezek.* 16. 13;
   Gen. 18. 6; *Job* 28. 1; *Is.* 3. 23;
   Lev. 2. 1; *Ps.* 81. 16; *Prov.* 25. 4.
FINE gold, *Ps.* 19. 10. art more to be
   desired than *f.* gold
Ps. 119. 127. love commandments above
   f. gold
Prov. 3. 14. gain of wisdom than *f.* gold
Is. 13. 12. will make a man more precious than *f.* gold
Lam. 4. 1. most *f.* gold changed
   2. the precious sons of Zion comparable to *f.* gold
FINE, linen, *Prov.* 7. 16. I have decked
   my bed with *f.* linen
Prov. 31. 24. she maketh *f.* linen, and
   selleth it
Mark 15. 46. Joseph bought *f.* linen and
   wrapped
Luke 16. 19. rich man clothed in purple
   and *f.* linen
FINGER of God, is used metaphorically
   for his infinite power and skill, *Ex.*
   8. 19; 31. 18; *Deut.* 9. 10. ' Putting
   out the finger ' is a contempt-
   ous insulting gesture, *Is.* 58. 9;
   Deut. 9. 10; *Luke* 11. 20.
1 *Kings* 12. 10. little *f.* shall be thicker
Ps. 8. 3. heaven is work of thy *f.*
   144. 1. he teacheth my *f.* to fight
Prov. 6. 13. he teacheth with his *f.*
Luke 11. 46. touch not with one of *f.*
John 20. 27. reach hither thy *f.*·
FINISH transgression, *Dan.* 9. 24.
John 17. 4. I have *f.* the work
   19. 30. it is *f.*
Acts 20. 24. *f.* my course with joy
2 *Cor.* 8. 6. would *f.* in you this grace
2 *Tim.* 4. 7. I have *f.* my course, I have
Jam. 1. 15. sin when *f.* brings forth
   death
Heb. 12. 2. author and *f.* of faith
FIRE, *Ex.* 3. 2. & 40. 38.
Gen. 19. 24. Lord rained brimstone
   and *f.*
2 *Kings*, 21. 6. Manasseh made son pass
   through *f.* 2. *Chr.* 33. 5.
Ps. 11. 6. rain *f.* and brimstone on wick.
   39. 3. while I was musing the *f.* burned
   46. 9. he burneth the chariot in the *f.*

Prov. 6. 27. can man take *f.* in bosom
25. 22. heap coals of *f.* on his head,
Rom. 12. 20.
Songs 8. 6. coals of *f.* vehement flame
Is. 9. 18. wickedness burneth as a *f.*
10. 17. light of Israel for *f.* for a flame
31. 9. Lord of hosts, whose *f.* in Zion
33. 14. who shall dwell with devouring *f.*
Is. 43. 2. walkest through *f.* not be burnt
66. 24. worm not die, neither their *f.*
Jer. 20. 9. his word was as a *f.* shut up in my bones
Jer. 23. 29. is not my word like *f.*
Amos 5. 6. lest Lord break out like *f.*
7. 4. Lord God calleth to contend by *f.*
Hab. 2. 13. labour in very *f.* for
Zech. 2. 5. I will be a wall of *f.* round
3. 2. brand plucked out of *f. Amos* 4. 11.
13. 9. I will bring the third part through the *f.*
Mal. 3. 2. he shall be as a refiner's *f.*
Matt. 3. 10. cut down and cast into *f.* 7. 19.
12. burn with unquenchable *f. Mark* 9. 43, 44, 46, 48; *Luke* 3. 17.
18. 8. rather than have two hands or two feet. to be cast into everlasting *f. Mark* 9. 43, 46.
Mark 9. 44. where the *f.* is not quenched, 45.
14. 54. Peter warmed himself at *f.*
Luke 9. 54. command *f.* to come down
12. 49. I came to send *f.* on earth
Acts 2. 3. cloven tongue like *f.*
1 *Cor.* 3. 13. revealed by *f. f.* try every, 15.
Heb. 12. 29. our God is a consuming *f.*
Jam. 3. 5. great matter little *f.* kindleth
6. tongue is a *f.* world of iniquity
1 *Pet.* 1. 7. gold, though tried with *f.*
2 *Pet.* 3. 7. reserved unto *f.* against day of judgment
Jude 7. suffering the vengeance of eternal *f.*
23. pulling them out of *f.* hating
Rev. 3. 18. gold tried in the *f.*
8. 7. *f.* mingled with blood
15. 2. sea of glass mingled with *f.*
20. 9. devil was cast into lake of *f.*
14. death and hell were cast into lake of *f.*
21. 8. have part in the lake which burneth with *f.*
Matt. 5. 22. hell *f.* 18. 9; *Mark* 9. 47.
Lev. 10. 1. strange *f. Num.* 3. 4. & 26. 61.
FIRES, *Is.* 24. 15. wherefore glorify ye the Lord in the *f.*
FIRM. Strong, *Job* 41. 23.—Sure, settled, *Josh.* 3. 17.—Unchangable, *Dan.* 6. 7.—Stable, durable, *Heb.* 3. 6.
FIRMAMENT, *Gen.* 1. 6. let there be a *f.* in midst of waters
Gen. 1. 8. and God called the *f.* Heaven
14. let there be lights in *f.* 15.
Ps. 19. 1. *f.* showeth handy-work
Ezek. 1. 22. likeness of *f.* was crystal
26. above the *f.* was the likeness of a throne

Dan. 12. 3. wise shall shine as the brightness of *f.*
FIR-TREE, *Is.* 55. 13. instead of the thorn shall spring up the *f.*
Is. 60. 13. the *f.* the pine tree, and box together
FIRST, *Matt.* 10. 2; *Esth.* 1. 14.
Is. 41. 4. I the Lord the *f.* and the last, 44. 6. & 48. 12; *Rev.* 1. 11. 17, & 2. 8; 22. 13.
Matt. 6. 33. seek *f.* the kingdom of God
7. 5. *f.* cast out the beam, *Luke* 6. 42.
19. 30. and many that be *f.* shall be last, 20. 16; *Mark* 10. 31.
22. 38. this is *f.* and great commandment
Acts 26. 23. *f.* that should rise from dead
Rom. 11. 35. who has *f.* given to him
1 *Cor.* 15. 45. *f.* Adam; *f.* man of earth
2 *Cor.* 8. 5. *f.* gave their ownselves to Lord
12. accepted if there be *f.* willing mind
1 *Pet.* 4. 17. if judgment *f.* begin at us
1 *John* 4. 19. because he *f.* loved
Rev. 2. 4. lest *f.* love; 5. do *f.* works
20. 5. this is *f.* resurrection, 6.
FIRST-BORN, *Ex.* 11. 5. all the *f.* in the land of Egypt shall die
Ex. 12. 29. the Lord smote all the *f.* in Egypt, 13. 15.
Mic. 6. 7. shall I give my *f.* for my transgression
Zech. 12. 10. in bitterness for his *f.*
Matt. 1. 25. *f.* born, *Luke* 2. 7.
Rom. 8. 29. *f.* among many brethren
Col. 1. 15. *f.* of every creature
18. *f.* from dead
Heb. 12. 23. to general assembly and church of *f.* born
FIRST-FRUIT, or fruits, *Ex.* 22. 29. to offer the *f.* ripe *fruits*
Ex. 23. 16. the *f.-fruits* of thy labour thou hast sown
Lev. 23. 10. bring a sheaf of the *f.-fruits* of harvest
Deut. 18. 4. the *f.-fruits* of thy corn, wine, and oil
Prov. 3. 9. honour Lord with *f.-fruits*
Rom. 8. 23. have *f.-fruits* of Spirit
11. 16. if *f.-fruit* be holy, the lump is
1 *Cor.* 15. 20. Christ *f.-fruits* of them that slept, 23.
Jam. 1. 18. we a kind of *f.-fruits* of creatures
Rev. 14. 4. redeemed are *f.-fruits* to God and the lamb
FISH, *Gen.* 1. 26. dominion over *f.* of sea. 28.
Jonah 1. 17. the Lord prepared a great *f.* to swallow Jonah, in belly of *f.* three days
Matt. 7. 10. if he ask a *f.* will he give him a serpent
17. 27. cast a hook, take up the *f.* that first cometh
Luke 24. 42. a piece of a broiled *f.*
John 21. 9. they saw *f.* laid thereon
10. bring *f.* ye have caught
13. Jesus taketh bread and *f.*
FISHERS, *Jer.* 16. 16; *Ezek.* 47. 10; *Matt.* 4. 18, 19; *John* 21. 7; *Is.* 19. 8.

FISHES, *Eccl.* 9. 12. *f.* taken in an evil net

Matt. 14. 17. we have here but five loaves and two *f.* Mark 6. 38; *Luke* 9. 13; *John* 6. 9.

Luke 5. 9. astonished at draught of *f.*

1 *Cor.* 15. 39. one flesh of beasts, another of *f.*

FIST, *Ex.* 21. 18; *Prov.* 30. 4; *Is.* 58. 4.

FIT, suitable, *Luke* 9. 62; becoming, proper, *Luke* 14. 35; *Col.* 3. 18.

FITLY, *Prov.* 25. 11. a word *f.* spoken is like apples of gold

Eph. 2. 21. in whom all building *f.* framed together

4. 16. from whom all body *f.* joined

FIX. To settle, to determine, *Ps.* 57. 7; 112. 7; *Luke* 16. 26.

FLAGS, *Ex.* 2. 3. she laid the ark in the *f.* by the river

FLAGON, 2 *Sam.* 6. 19. to each a *f.* of wine, 1 *Chr.* 16. 3.

FLAGONS, *Songs* 2. 5. stay me with *f.* comfort

Hos. 3. 1. love *f.* of wine

FLAME, *Ex.* 3. 2; *Judg.* 13. 20.

Ps. 104. 4. maketh ministers *f.* of fire, *Heb.* 1. 7.

106. 18. *f.* of fire burnt up wicked, *Num.* 16. 35.

Is. 10. 17. Holy One of Israel for a *f.*

43. 2. neither shall the *f.* kindle upon thee

Luke 16. 24. tormented in this *f.*

Heb. 1. 7. his ministers a *f.* of fire

Rev. 1. 14. eyes were as a *f.* of fire

2 *Thess.* 1. 8. in *f.* fire taking vengeance

FLATTER, FLATTERY. An extolling and fawning behaviour, attended with servile compliances and obsequiousness to gain a person's favour, or to decoy into sin, *Ps.* 12. 2.

Ps. 5. 9. they *f.* with their tongue

78. 36. *f.* him with their mouth

FLATTERETH, *Prov.* 36. 2. for he *f.* himself in his own eyes

Prov. 20. 19. meddle not with him that *f.* with his lips

Prov. 29. 5. a man that *f.* spreadeth a net for his feet

FLATTERING, *Job* 32. 22. I know not to give *f.* titles

Ps. 12. 2. with *f.* lips and double heart do speak, 3.

Prov. 7. 21. with the *f.* of her lips she forced him

FLATTERY, *Job* 17. 5. he that speaketh *f.* to his friends

Prov. 6. 24. keep from the *f.* of a strange woman

FLAY, *Mic.* 3. 3. *f.* their skins from off them, break bones

FLED, *Matt.* 26. 56. disciples forsook him and *f.* Mark 14. 50.

Acts 16. 27. supposing the prisoners *f.*

Heb. 6. 18. *f.* for refuge to lay hold on the hope

Rev. 20. 11. from whose face earth and heaven *f.* away

FLED, he, *Judg.* 9. 40. Abimelech chased Gaal, and he *f.*

Mark 14. 52. left linen cloth and *f.* naked

FLEECE, *Deut.* 18. 4. first of the *f.* give Levites

Judg. 6. 38. Gideon wringed the dew out of *f.*

Job 31. 20. warmed with *f.* of my sheep

FLEE, *Num.* 35. 6. six cities, that the man-slayer may *f.* thither

Neh. 6. 11. should such a man as I *f.*

Ps. 68. 12. kings of armies *f.* apace, she that tarried

139. whither *f.* from presence

Prov. 25. 1. wicked *f.* when no man pursueth

Matt. 2. 13. take young child and *f.*

3. 7. who warned you to *f.* from

24. 16. then let them which be in Judea *f.* to the mountains, *Mark* 13. 14; *Luke* 21. 21.

1 *Cor.* 6. 18. *f.* fornication

10. 14. *f.* from idolatry

1 *Tim.* 6. 11. man of God *f.* these things

2 *Tim.* 2. 22. *f.* youthful lusts

Jam. 4. 7. resist devil he will *f.* from

FLESH, *Gen.* 2. 21; 1 *Cor.* 15. 39.

Gen. 2. 24. they shall be one *f.* Matt. 19. 5; 1 Cor. 6. 16; *Eph.* 5. 31.

Job 10. 11. clothed me with skin and *f.*

Ps. 56. 4. what *f.* can do unto me

78. 39. remember that they were *f.*

Jer. 17. 5. cursed maketh *f.* his arm

Matt. 26. 41. spirit is willing but *f.* weak

John 1. 14. the word was made *f.*

6. 53. eat *f.* of Son of man, 52, 55, 58.

63. *f.* profiteth nothing, words are spirit and life

Rom. 7. 25. serve with *f.* law of sin

8. 12. debtors not to *f.* to live after *f.*

Rom. 9. 3. my kinsmen according to the *f.*

5. of whom concerning the *f.* Christ

13. 14. make not provision for *f.*

1 *Cor.* 1. 29. that no *f.* should glory

2 *Cor.* 1. 17. purpose according to *f.*

10. 2. walked according to *f.*

Gal. 5. 17. *f.* lusts against spirit and spirit against *f.*

24. Christ have crucified *f.* with affections and lusts

Eph. 6. 5. masters according to *f.*

Heb. 12. 9. we had fathers of our *f.*

Jude 7. going after strange *f.*

23. hating garment spotted by *f.*

FLESH, After the, *John* 8. 15. ye judge after the *f.*

Rom. 8. 1. walk not *after f.* but *after* spirit, 9.

5. they that *after f.* mind things of *f.*

13. if ye live *after f.* ye shall die, 12.

1 *Cor.* 1. 26. not many wise men *after* the *f.*

10. 18. Israel *after* the *f.* Rom. 9. 6; *Gal.* 6. 12.

2 *Cor.* 5. 16. know no man *after f.* known Christ *after f.*

10. 3. walk in *f.* not war *after* the *f.*

2 *Pet.* 2. 10. walk *after f.* in lust of uncleanness

FLESH, All, *Ps.* 65. 2. to thee shall *all f.* come

Is. 40. 6. *all f.* is grass, 1 Pet. 1. 24.

49. 26. *all f.* shall know that I thy

Redeemer

Jer. 32. 27. I am Lord the God of all *f.*
Joel 2. 28. I will pour my spirit on all *f.*
Luke 3. 6. all *f.* shall see salvation of
God, *Ps.* 98. 3.
John 17. 2. given him power over all *f.*
Rom. 7. 5. when we were in the *f.*
8. 8. that are in *f.* cannot please God
1 *Tim.* 3. 16. great mystery, God mani-
fest in the *f.*
1 *Pet.* 3. 18. he was put to death in the
f. 4. 1.
Gen. 2. 23. my *f.* 29. 14; *Job* 9. 26; *Ps.*
63. 1. & 119. 120; *John* 6. 51, 55, 56;
Rom. 7. 18.
John 1. 13. born not of the will of the *f.*
3. 6. that which is born of the *f.* is *f.*
Rom. 8. 5. after *f.* mind things of the *f.*
Gal. 5. 19. works of *f.* are manifest
6. 8. sows to *f.* shall of the *f.* reap
Eph. 2. 3. lusts of the *f.* desires of the *f.*
1 *Pet.* 3. 21. not putting away filth of *f.*
1 *John* 2. 16. lust of *f.* of eye, pride of
Matt. 16. 17. *f.* and blood not revealed
1 *Cor.* 15. 20. *f.* and blood cannot inherit kingdom of God

Gal. 1. 16. I conferred not with *f.* and
Eph. 5. 30. members of his *f.* and blood
and bones
6. 12. we wrestle not against *f.* and
blood but
Heb. 2. 14. children are partakers of *f.*
FLESHLY, 2 *Cor.* 1. 12. not with *f.* wis-
dom
2 *Cor.* 3. 3. not in *f.* tables of the heart
Col. 2. 18. puffed up by his *f.* mind
1 *Pet.* 2. 11. beloved, abstain from *f.*
lusts that war
FLIGHT, *Is.* 52. 12; *Amos* 2. 14; *Matt.*
24. 20; *Mark* 13. 18; *Heb.* 11. 34.
FLOCK, *Gen.* 32. 5; *Ps.* 77. 20; *Is.* 63.
11; *Jer.* 13. 17, 20.
Job 30. 1. I disdained to set with the
dogs of my *f.*
Songs 1. 7. makest thy *f.* to rest
Is. 40. 11. his *f.* like a shepherd
Jer. 23. 2. scattered my *f.*
Zech. 11. 4. feed the *f.* of the slaughter, 7.
Luke 2. 8. keeping watch over their *f.*
by night
12. 32. fear not little *f.* it is
Acts 20. 28. take heed to all the *f.* 29.
1 *Cor.* 9. 7. who feedeth a *f.* and eateth
not of milk
1 *Pet.* 5. 2. feed the *f.* of God among you
FLOOD, *Gen.* 6. 17. even I, bring a *f.* of
Gen. 7. 17. *f.* was forty days on earth
Josh. 24. 2. father on other side *f.* 3. 14,
15.
Ps. 29. 10. Lord sitteth upon the *f.*
69. 15. let not water *f.* overflow me
Ps. 90. 5. carriest th. away as with *f.*
Is. 59. 19. enemy shall come in like *f.*
Matt. 24. 38. in days before *f.* th. eating
39. knew not till all came, *Lu.* 17. 27.
FLOODS, *Ps.* 69. 2. waters where *f.*
overflow me
93. 8. *f.* have lifted up, O Lord
Is. 44. 3. I will pour *f.* on dry ground
Matt. 7. 25. the *f.* came, winds blew, 27.
FLOOR, *Matt.* 3. 12. thoroughly purge
his *f.* *Luke* 3. 17.

FLOURISH. To spring forth, or bud,
Songs 7. 12. To increase in wis-
dom, honour, or wealth, *Ps.* 90. 6;
92. 7, 12-14; *Is.* 17. 11. & 66. 14.
Ps. 72. 7. shall the righteous *f.* 16. &
92. 12, 13, 14; *Prov.* 11. 28. & 14. 11.
92. 7. when workers of iniquity *f.*
132. 18. upon himself shall crown *f.*
Is. 66. 14. your bones shall *f.*
Ezek. 17. 24. dry tree to *f.*
FLOURISHETH, *Ps.* 90. 6. in the morn-
ing it *f.* and
Ps. 103. 15. as a flower of field, so he *f.*
FLOW, *Songs* 4. 16. that the spices may
f. out
Is. 60. 5. shalt see and *f.* together
John 7. 38. out of belly sha. *f.* liv. water
FLOWER, *Job* 14. 2. forth as *f.* and is
cut down
Ps. 103. 15. as *f.* of field, so he flourish
Is. 28. 1. glorious beauty is fading *f.* 4.
40. 6. goodliness is as the *f.* of field
7. *f.* fadeth, 8; *Nah.* 1. 4; *Jam.* 1. 10,
11; 1 *Pet.* 1. 24.
FLOWERS, *Songs* 2. 12. the *f.* appear
on earth
Songs 5. 13. as a bed of spices, as sweet *f.*
FLY and **FLYING.** Spoken of riches,
Prov. 23. 5. ('make themselves
wings,' &c.)—The promptitude of
God to help, 2 *Sam.* 22. 11. (' and
did fly,')—The prosperity of the
church, *Is.* 60. 8. (' fly as a cloud,'
&c.)—The spread of the gospel,
Rev. 14. 6.—Human frailty, *Ps.*
90. 10.
Job 5. 7. to trouble as sparks *f.* upward
Ps. 18. 10. he did *f.* on wings of wind
55. 6. for then would I *f.* away
Is. 6. 2. six wings, with two he did *f.*
Rev. 14. 6. saw another angel *f.* in mid.
Zech. 5. 1. and behold a *f.* roll, 2.
Rev. 8. 13. angel *f.* thro' midst of heaven
FOAL, *Zech.* 9. 9. on colt *f.* of ass, *Matt.*
21. 5.
FOES, *Matt.* 10. 36. man's *f.* be they of
Acts 2. 35. until I make *f.* footstool
FOLD, *Heb.* 1. 12. as vesture shalt thou
f. them up
FOLD, *Matt.* 13. 8. brought forth fruit
some thirty *f.* 23; *Mark* 4. 8, 20.
19. 29. forsaken house receive 100. *f.*
John 10. 16. other sheep which not of
this *f.* one *f.* and one shepherd
FOLK, *Mark* 6. 5. laid hands on few
sick *f.*
John 5. 3. multitude of impotent *f.*
Acts 5. 16. about, bringing sick *f.*
FOLLOW, *Gen.* 44. 4; *Ex.* 14. 4.
Ex. 23. 2. thou shalt not *f.* a multitude
to do evil
Deut. 16. 20. that is just shalt thou *f.*
Ps. 38. 20. I *f.* thing that is good
Is. 51. 1. my people that *f.* after righte-
ousness
Hos. 6. 3. know if we *f.* on to know the
Lord
Matt. 8. 19. Master, I will *f.* thee, *Luke*
9. 57, 61.
John 10. 5. stranger will they not *f.*
Rom. 14. 19. *f.* things that make for
1 *Cor.* 14. 1. *f.* after charity desire gifts

Phil. 3. 12. but I *f*. after that I appre.
1 *Thess.* 5. 15. ever *f*. what is good
1 *Tim.* 6. 11. *f*. after righteousness, god-
    liness, faith
2 *Tim.* 2. 22. *f*. righteousness, faith,
    charity, peace
Heb. 12. 14. *f*. peace with all men
    13. 7. whose faith *f*. considering the
1 *Pet.* 2. 21. example should *f*. his steps
3 *John* 11. *f*. not evil but that is good
Rev. 14. 13. their works do *f*. them
Ps. 23. 6. goodness and mercy shall *f*.
Matt. 4. 19. *f*. me, 9. 9. & 19. 21; *Luke*
    5. 27. & 9. 59; *John* 1. 43. & 21. 19.
    16. 24. take up cross *f*. me
Luke 18. 22. sell that thou hast and *f*.
John 12. 26. if man serve me let him *f*.
FOLLOWED, *Num.* 14. 24. hath *f*. me
    fully
    32. 12. wholly *f*. the Lord, *Deut.* 1. 36;
    Josh. 14. 8, 9, 15.
Rom. 9. 30. *f*. not after righteousness
    31. *f*. law of righteousness
Ps. 63. 8. soul *f*. hard after thee
Matt. 10. 38. taketh up his cross and *f*.
Mark 9. 38. he *f*. not us, *Luke* 9. 49.
FOLLOWERS, 1 *Cor.* 4. 16. be *f*. of me
    11. 1; *Phil.* 3. 17.
Eph. 5. 1. be ye *f*. of God, as dear chil.
1 *Thess.* 1. 6. *f*. of us and of the Lord
Heb. 6. 12. *f*. of them who through faith
1 *Pet.* 3. 13. if ye be *f*. of that is good
FOLLY wrought in Israel, *Gen.* 34. 7;
    Deut. 22. 21; *Josh.* 7. 15; *Judg.*
    20. 6.
Job 4. 18. and angels he charged with *f*.
Ps. 49. 13. their way is their *f*.
    85. 8. let them not turn again to *f*.
Prov. 26. 4, 5. answer fool according to
    his *f*.
2 *Tim.* 3. 9. their *f*. shall be manifest
FOOD, *Gen.* 3. 6; *Deut.* 10. 18.
Job 23. 12. words more than necessary *f*.
Ps. 78. 25. man did eat angel's *f*.
    136. 25. giveth *f*. to all flesh
    146. 7. who giveth *f*. to the hungry
Prov. 30. 8. feed with *f*. convenient for
Acts 14. 17. filling our heart with *f*. and
2 *Cor.* 9. 10. ministering bread for your *f*.
1 *Tim.* 6. 8. having *f*. and raiment
FOOL, said in his heart *Ps.* 14. 1. & 53. 1.
Jer. 17. 11. at end of days shall be a *f*.
Matt. 5. 22. who shall say to his brother
    thou *f*.
Luke 12. 20. thou *f*. this night thy soul
1 *Cor.* 3. 18. let him become a *f*.
2 *Cor.* 11. 16. think me a *f*.; 23. as a *f*.
FOOLS, *Ps.* 75. 4. *f*. deal not *f*.
    94. 8. ye *f*: when will ye be wise
    107. 17. *f*. because of their transgres-
    sion
Prov. 1. 7. *f*. despise wisdom
    22. *f*. hate knowledge
    13. 20. companion of *f*. be destroyed
    14. 9. folly of *f*. is deceitful
Prov. 9. *f*. make a mock at sin
    16. 22. instruction of *f*. is folly
Eccl. 5. 4. he hath no pleasure in *f*.
Matt. 23. 17. ye *f*. and blind, 19.
Rom. 1. 22. professing to be wise be-
    came *f*.
1 *Cor.* 4. 10. we are *f*. for Christ's sake

Eph. 5. 15. walk circumspectly, not as *f*.
FOOLISH, *Deut.* 32. 6. *f*. people and
    unwise
Ps. 5. 5. *f*. shall not stand in thy sight
    73. 22. so *f*. was I and ignorant
Matt. 7. 26. on sand like to *f*. man
    25. 2. virgins, five wise and five *f*.
Rom. 1. 21. their *f*. heart was darkened
Gal. 3. 1. O *f*. Galatians who bewitched
Eph. 5. 4. filthiness nor *f*. talking
Tit. 3. 3. were sometimes *f*. disobedient
FOOLISHLY, *Gen.* 31. 28. done *f*. *Num.*
    12. 11; 1 *Sam.* 13. 13; 2 *Sam.* 24.
    10; 1 *Chr.* 21. 8; 2 *Chr.* 16. 9;
    Prov. 14. 17; 2 *Cor.* 11. 21.
Job 1. 22. Job sinned not nor charged
    God *f*.
2 *Sam.* 15. 31. turn the counsel into *f*.
Prov. 12. 23. heart of *f*. proclaims *f*.
    14. 24. *f*. of *f*. is folly, 15. 2, 14.
    22. 15. *f*. is bound in heart of child
    24. 9. thought of *f*. is sin
    27. 22. bray *f*. in mortar, will not his
    f. depart
1 *Cor.* 1. 18. preaching of cross is *f*. to
    persons
    21. God by *f*. of preaching to save
    23. Christ crucified to Greeks *f*.
    25. *f*. of God is wiser than men
    2. 14. they are *f*. to him neither
    3. 19. wisdom of world is *f*. with God
FOOT shall not stumble, *Prov.* 3. 23.
Eccl. 5. 1. keep thy *f*. when thou goest
    into the house of God
Is. 58. 13. turn away *f*. from the sabbath
Matt. 18. 8. if thy *f*. offend thee cut it off
1 *Cor.* 12. 15. if *f*. say because I am not
    the hand
Heb. 10. 29. trodden under *f*. the Son of
    God
FOOTED, *Acts* 10. 12.
FOOTSTEPS, signify a good conversa-
    tion and behaviour, *Ps.* 89. 51.—
    Miraculous operations of Divine
    Providence, *Ps.* 77. 19; *Ex.* 14. 28,
    29.
FOOTSTOOL, the earth, *Is.* 66. 1;
    Matt. 5. 35; *Acts* 7. 49.—The temple
    or ark in it, 1 *Chr.* 28. 2.—The sanc-
    tuary, *Ps.* 99. 5.—The enemies of
    Christ, *Ps.* 110. 1; *Matt.* 22. 44;
    Luke 20. 43; *Acts* 2. 35.
FORBEAR, to withhold or restrain, for
    a time, the exercise of rigorous jus-
    tice. It is applied to God who is
    said to be rich in his goodness, and
    long-suffering *f*. *Ex.* 23. 5; 1 *Cor.* 9. 6.
Rom. 2. 4. goodness *f*. 3. 25.
FORBID, *Mark* 10. 14; *Luke* 18. 16. &
    6. 29; *Acts* 24. 23. & 28. 31.
1 *Tim.* 4. 3. *f*. to marry
1 *Thess.* 2. 16. *f*. us to dseak to Gentiles
Gal. 6. 14. God *f*. that I should glory
FORCE, *Matt.* 11. 12; *Heb.* 9. 17.
Is. 60. 5. *f*. of Gentiles shall come unto
    thee, 11.
FORCES. Soldiers are so called, 2 *Chr.*
    17. 2. In the latter-day glory ' the
    forces of the Gentiles shall come
    unto Christ,' *Is.* 60. 5.
FORCIBLE, mighty, powerful, convinc-
    ing

Job 6. 25. how *f.* right words
FORD. A passage, or shallow part of a
river, *Gen.* 32. 22; *Josh.* 2. 7; *Isa.*
16. 2.
FOREHEAD, *Ex.* 28. 38; *Lev.* 13. 41.
Jer. 3. 3. thou hast a whore's *f.*
Ezek. 3. 8. thy *f.* strong against their *f.*
Rev. 7. 3. sealed in their *f.* 9. 4.
13. 16. mark in their *f.* 14. 9. & 20. 4.
14. 1. Father's name written in *f.* 22. 4.
FOREIGNER, S, *Ex.* 12. 45; *Deut.* 15.
3; *Obad.* 11; *Eph.* 2. 19.
FOREKNOWLEDGE, *Rom.* 8. 29. & 11. 2.
FOREKNOWLEDGE, *Acts* 2. 23. de-
livered by *f.* of God
1 *Pet.* 1. 2. elect according to *f.* of God
the Father
FOREORDAINED, that which has been
purposed, or appointed to be effect-
ed in future ages, 1 *Pet.* 1. 20.
FORERUNNER, *Heb.* 6. 20. whither
the *f.* is for us entered, even Jesus
FORESAW, *Acts* 2. 25. I *f.* the Lord al-
ways before my face
FORESEETH, *Prov.* 22. 3. & 27. 12.
FORESEEING, *Gal.* 3. 8; *Acts* 2. 25;
FOREWARN, *Luke* 12. 5.
FORGAVE, their iniquity, *Ps.* 78. 38.
Matt. 18. 27. *f.* him his debt. 32.
Luke 7. 42. frankly *f.* them both
43. love most to whom *f.* most
2 *Cor.* 2. 10. *f.* any thing, I *f.* also in the
person of Christ
Col. 3. 13. as Christ *f.* you so *f.* ye
Ps. 32. 5. *f.* the iniquity of
99. 8. thou wast a God that *f.* them
FORGET. To let things slip from the
memory, *Deut.* 4. 9. To cast off,
to cease to love, *Ps.* 79. 9; *Is.* 49.
15; *Judg.* 3. 7; 1 *Sam.* 12. 9.
Ps. 78. 11. *f.* his works and wonders,
106. 13.
106. 21. *f.* God their Saviour
Lam. 3. 17. I *f.* prosperity
Hos. 2. 13. *f.* me, saith the Lord
Deut. 9. 7. remember, and *f.* not how
thou provokest
Job 8. 13. paths of all that *f.* God
Ps. 45. 10. *f.* thine own people and
50. 22. consider this ye that *f.* God
59. 11. stay not lest people *f.*
103. 2. *f.* not all his benefits
119. 16. I will not *f.* thy words, 83. 93,
109, 141, 153, 176.
Prov. 3. 1. my son, *f.* not my law
Is. 49. 15. can a woman *f.* her sucking
child
Jer. 2. 32. can maid *f.* her ornaments
Heb. 6. 10. God is not unrighteous to *f.*
your work
13. 16. to do good and communicate
f. not
2. be not *f.* to entertain strangers
Ps. 44. 24. *f.* thou our affliction
9. 12. he *f.* not the cry of the humble
Prov. 2. 17. *f.* the covenant of her God
FORGETFUL, *Heb.* 13. 2. be not *f.* to
entertain strangers
Jam. 1. 25. be not a *f.* hearer
FORGETTETH, *Ps.* 9. 12. *f.* not the cry
of humble
Jam. 1. 24. he *f.* what manner of man

he was
FORGETTING, *Gen.* 41. 51. Joseph
called the first-born *f.*
Phil. 3. 13. *f.* those things which are
behind
FORGIVE, FORGIVENESS, *Gen.* 50.
17; *Ex.* 32. 32. now *f.* their sin
Ps. 86. 5. thou art good and ready to *f.*
Is. 2. 9. therefore *f.* them not
Jer. 31. 34. I will *f.* their iniquity, 36. 3.
Matt. 6. 12. *f.* us our debts as we *f.*
14. if ye *f.* men; 15. if you *f.* not
9. 6. Son of man has power on earth
to *f.* *Mark* 2. 10; *Luke* 5. 24.
Luke 6. 37. *f.* and ye shall be *f.*
17. 3. if he repent *f.* him, 4.
23. 34. Father *f.* them; they know not
1 *John* 1. 9. he is faithful to *f.* us our
Ps. 32. 1. whose transgression is *f.*
85. 2. *f.* the iniquity of thy people
Is. 33. 24. people shall be *f.* their iniquity
Matt. 9. 2. good cheer, thy sins be *f.*
12. 31. all manner sins *f.*; 32. not be *f.*
Luke 7. 47. to whom little is *f.* loveth
Rom. 4. 7. blessed whose iniquity are *f.*
Eph. 4. 32. as God hath *f.* you, *Col.* 2. 13.
Jam. 5. 15. if he have committed sins
they shall be *f.*
1 *John* 2. 12. your sins are *f.* you
FORGIVETH, *Ps.* 103. 3. who *f.* all
thine iniquities
FORGIVENESS, *Ps.* 130. 4. is *f.* with
thee
Dan. 9. 9. to our Lord belongeth mercy
and *f.*
Mark 3. 29. hath never *f.* *Luke* 12. 10.
Acts 5. 31. to give repentance and *f.* of
13. 38. through him is preached unto
you *f.* of sins
26. 18. may receive *f.* of sins by faith
Eph. 1. 7. *f.* of sins according to riches
Col. 1. 14. redemption, even *f.* of sins
FORGIVING, *Ex.* 34. 7. *f.* iniquity,
transgression and sin, *Num.* 14. 18;
Mic. 7. 18.
Eph. 4. 32. *f.* one another, *Col.* 3. 13.
FORGOT, FORGOTTEN, *Gen.* 41. 30;
Deut. 32. 18; 24. 19; *Job* 19. 14; *Ps.* 9.
18.
Ps. 10. 11. God ha+h *f.*
42. 9. why hast thou *f.* me
77. 9. hath God *f.* to be gracious
119. 61. I have not *f.* thy law
Is. 17. 10. *f.* the God of thy salvation
49. 14. Zion said, my Lord hath *f.* me
Jer. 2. 32. my people have *f.* me days
3. 21. have *f.* their God, *Deut.* 32. 18.
50. 5. covenant that shall not be *f.*
Heb. 12. 5. *f.* the exhortation
FORM, *Gen.* 1. 2; 1 *Sam.* 28. 14.
Is. 53. 2. hath no *f.* nor comeliness
Rom. 2. 20. hast *f.* of knowledge
6. 17. obeyed from heart that *f.* of
doctrine
Phil. 2. 6. being in *f.* of God thought
7. took on him the *f.* of servant
2 *Tim.* 1. 13. hold fast *f.* of sound words
3. 5. having *f.* of godliness, but deny.
Is. 45. 7. I *f.* the light and create dark.
FORMED, *Gen.* 2. 7. God *f.* man of the
Deut. 32. 18. forgotten God that *f.*

Job 33. 6. am *f*. out of the clay
Ps. 90. 2. or ever thou hadst *f*. the earth
94. 9. he that *f*. the eye
95. 5. the sea is his, and his hand *f*. the dry land
Prov. 26. 10. God that *f*. all things
Is. 27. 11. *f*. them will show no favour
43. 21. this people have I *f*. for myself
44. 2. I *f*. thee from the womb, 24.
54. 17. no weapon *f*. against thee shall prosper
Rom. 9. 20. thing *f*. say to him that *f*. it
Gal. 4. 19. till Christ be *f*. in you
Ps. 94. 9. that *f*. the eye
Zech. 12. 1. *f*. spirit of man within him
FORMER, *Job* 8. 8. inquire, I pray thee, of the *f*. age
Ps. 79. 8. O remember not against us *f*. iniquities
Eccl. 7. 10. that the *f*. days were better than these
Is. 46. 9. remember the *f*. things of old, for I am God
Jer. 10. 16. he is *f*. of all things, 51. 19.
Eph. 4. 22. put off concerning the *f*. conversation
1 *Pet.* 1. 14. not according to the *f*. lusts in ignorance
Rev. 21. 4. for the *f*. things are passed away
FORNICATION, 2 *Chr.* 21. 11; *Is.* 23. 17; *Ezek.* 16. 15, 26 ,29.
Matt. 5. 32. put away wife for cause of *f*.
19. 9. except it be for *f*.
John 8. 41. we be not born of *f*.
Acts 15. 20. abstain from *f*. 29. & 21. 25.
Rom. 1. 29. filled with all *f*. and wicked.
1 *Cor.* 5. 1. there is *f*. among you such
6. 13. body not for *f*.; 18. flee *f*.
7. 2. to avoid *f*. let every man have his own wife
10. 8. neither let us commit *f*.
2 *Cor.* 12. 21. not repented of their *f*.
Gal. 5. 19. works of the flesh are adultery, *f*.
Eph. 5. 3. but *f*. and all uncleanness
Col. 3. 5. mortify *f*. uncleanness
1 *Thess.* 4. 3. ye should abstain from *f*.
Jude 7. giving themselves to *f*.
Rev. 2. 14. taught to commit *f*. 20.
21. I gave her space to repent of her *f*.
21. neither repented their *f*.
14. 8. of wine of her *f*. 17. 2.
17. 4. abominations and filthiness of her *f*.
18. 3. commit *f*. with her, 9.
19. 2. corrupt the earth with her *f*.
FORNICATIONS, *Ezek.* 16. 15; *Matt.* 15. 99.
FORNICATORS, 1 *Cor.* 5. 9, 10, 11. & 6. 9; *Heb.* 12. 16.
FORSAKE, 2 *Chr.* 15. 2. if ye *f*. him he will *f*. you
Ps. 27. 10. father and mother *f*. me
94. 14. neither will he *f*. his inherit
Prov. 9. 6. *f*. the foolish and live
Is. 55. 7. let wicked man *f*. his way
Jer. 17. 13. that *f*. shall be ashamed
Jonah 2. 8. *f*. their own mercy
Acts 21. 21. teachest to *f*. Moses
FORSAKE not, *Deut.* 4. 31. Lord thy God will *not f*. thee, 31. 6, 8; 1 *Chr.*

28. 20; *Heb.* 13: 5.
1 *Sam.* 12. 22. Lord will not *f*. his people
1 *Kings* 6. 13. I will not *f*. my people
8. 57. let him not leave us nor *f*. us
Ps. 38. 21. *f*. me *not*, O Lord, 79. 9, 18.
Ps. 119. 8. O *f*. me *not* utterly
Prov. 27. 10. and father's friend *f*. *not*
FORSAKEN, *Is.* 54. 6. called thee as a woman *f*.
Is. 62. 4. shalt no more be termed *f*.

FORSAKEN, have, hast, hath, *Ps.* 22. 1. my God why *f*. me, *Matt.* 27. 46.
37. 25. I have not seen righteous *f*.
71. 11. God hath *f*. him
Is. 49. 14. Lord hath *f*. my Lord hath forgotten
54. 7. small moment have I *f*. thee
Jer. 2. 13. *f*. me fountain of living water 17. 13.
Matt. 19. 27. we have *f*. all; 29. *f*. house
2 *Cor.* 4. 9. persecuted but not *f*.
2 *Tim.* 4. 10. Demas *hath f*. me
2 *Pet.* 2. 15. which *hath f*. right way
FORSAKEN, not, *Is.* 62. 12. he called a city *not f*.
2 *Cor.* 4. 9. persecuted, but *not f*.
FORSAKETH, ING, *Job* 6. 14. he *f*. fear of Almighty
Ps. 37. 28. Lord *f*. not his saints
Prov. 2. 17. *f*. the guide of her
28. 13. confesseth and *f*. shall find
Luke 14. 33. whoso *f*. not all hath
Heb. 10. 25. not *f*. the assembling ourselves
FORSOOK, *Deut.* 32. 15. he *f*. God which made
Ps. 119. 87. I *f*. not thy precepts
Matt. 26. 56. disc. *f*. him, *Mark* 14. 50.
Mark 1. 18. they *f*. their nets
Luke 5. 11. *f*. all, and followed him
Heb. 11. 27. by faith Moses *f*. Egypt
2 *Tim.* 4. 16. all men *f*. me
FORSWEAR, *Matt.* 5. 33. thou shalt not *f*. thyself
FORTRESS, a place of defence, a strong hold; *Ezek.* 21. 2; *Nah.* 1. 7. The Lord is a fortress and rock, 2 *Sam.* 22. 2; *Ps.* 18. 2. & 31. 3. & 71. 3. & 91. 2. & 144. 2; *Jer.* 16. 19.
FORTY. Spoken of baths, 1 *Kings* 7. 38. Camels, 2 *Kings* 8. 9. Cubits, 1 *Kings* 6. 17. Days, *Gen.* 7. 4, 12; *Ex.* 24. 18; 1 *Kings* 19. 8; *Jonah* 3. 4; *Matt.* 4. 2. Kine, *Gen.* 32. 15. Stripes, *Deut.* 25. 3. Years, *Gen.* 5. 13; *Ex.* 16. 35. Hereunto are added one, 1 *Kings* 14. 21. Two, *Num.* 35. 6. Four, 1 *Chr.* 5. 18. Five, *Gen.* 18. 28. Six, *John* 2. 20. Seven, *Gen.* 47. 28. Eight, *Num.* 35. 7. Nine, *Lev.* 25. 8. Thousand, *Num.* 1. 33. One thousand, *Num.* 1. 41. Two thousand, *Judg.* 22. 6. Three thousand, *Num.* 26. 7. Four thousand, 1 *Chr.* 5. 18. Five thousand, *Num.* 1. 25. Six thousand, *Num.* 1. 21.
FORWARD, *Ex.* 14. 15; *Num.* 10. 35; *Job* 23. 8; *Gal.* 2. 10; 2 *Cor.* 8. 8.
FOUGHT, *Ps.* 109. 3. *f*. against me without a cause

1 *Cor.* 15. 32. I have *f.* with beasts
2 *Tim.* 4. 7. I have *f.* a good fight
Rev. 12. 7. Michael *f.* against Dragon
FOUL, *Job* 16. 16. my face is *f.* with weeping
Matt. 16. 3. it will be *f.* weather
Mark 9. 25. he rebuked the *f.* spirit
Rev. 18. 2. Bab. hold of ev. *f.* spirit
FOUND, to establish, *Ps.* 24. 2; to discover, or find out, *Gen.* 44. 12; to be solitary, *Ps.* 107. 4; *Gen.* 26, 19. & 31. 37.
Gen. 8. 9. the dove *f.* no rest for
   26. 19. Isaac's servants *f.* a well
   37. 32. said, this coat have we *f.*
Deut. 22. 14. *f.* her not a maid, 17.
   27. he *f.* her in field, damsel cried
Job. 33. 34. the pit I have *f.* a ransom
Ps. 69. 20. comforters, but *f.* none
   84. 3. sparrow hath *f.* an house
   89. 20. I have *f.* David my servant
   116. 3. I *f.* trouble and sorrow
Eccl. 7. 27. this have I *f.* 28.
   29. 1. *f.* God made man upright
   65. 1. *f.* of them sought me not
Eccl. 7. 27. this have I *f.* 28.
   28. one man among a thousand have I *f.*
   29. made man upright, but he
Songs 3. 1. I *f.* him; 4. I *f.* him
Is. 55. 6. seek the Lord while he may be *f.*
   65. I am *f.* of them that sought not
Jer. 15. 16. words *f.* and I did eat them
Ezek. 22. 30. I sought a man but *f.* none
Dan. 5. 27. art weighed and *f.* wanting
Hos. 14. 8. tree, from me is thy fruit *f.*
Matt. 2. 8. have *f.* him bring me word
   8. 10. not *f.* so great faith, *Luke* 7. 9.
   21. 19. he *f.* nothing thereon, *Mark* 11. 13; *Luke* 13. 6.
Luke 2. 16. *f.* babe lying in a manger
   23. 14. I have *f.* no fault in this man
   24. 2. *f.* the stone rolled away
   23. when they *f.* not his body
2 *Cor.* 5. 3. shall not be *f.* naked
Gal. 2. 17. we also are *f.* sinners
Phil. 2. 8. *f.* in fashion as a man
1 *Tim.* 3. 10. being *f.* blameless
Heb. 12. 17. he *f.* no place of repentance
Rev. 2. 2. and has *f.* them liars
   3. 2. not *f.* thy works perfect
   12. 8. nor their place *f.* in heaven
FOUND, be, *Job* 20. 8. shall fly away and not be *f.*
Ps. 37. 36. but he could not be *f.*
Prov. 30. 10. and thou be *f.* guilty
Is. 55. 6. seek Lord while he may be *f.*
Acts 5. 39. lest be *f.* to fight against God
1 *Cor.* 4. 2. a steward be *f.* faithful
2 *Cor.* 5. 3. we shall not be *f.* naked
Phil. 3. 9. be *f.* in him not having mine
2 *Pet.* 3. 14. may be *f.* of him in peace
FOUND, was, *Rom.* 10. 20. I *was f.* of them that
1 *Pet.* 2. 22. nor *was* guile *f.* in mouth
Rev. 5. 4. *was f.* worthy to open
   14. 5. in their mouth *was f.* no guile
   20. 11. *was f.* no place for them
FOUND, was not, *Heb.* 11. 5. Enoch *was not f.* because
FOUNDED, FOUNDATION, *Matt.* 7. 25. *f.* on a rock, *Ps.* 24. 2; *Prov.*

   3. 19; *Is.* 14. 32.
Ps. 11. 3. if *f.* be destroyed
Job 4. 19. whose *f.* is in the dust
Prov. 10. 25. righteous is an everlasting *f.*
Is. 28. 16. I lay in Zion a sure *f.*
Rom. 15. 20. not build on another man's *f.*
1 *Cor.* 3. 10. laid *f.*
   12. built on this *f.*
Eph. 2. 20. built on *f.* of prophets
1 *Tim.* 6. 19. lay up a good *f.* for time
2 *Tim.* 2. 19. the *f.* of God stands sure
Heb. 11. 10. a city which hath *f.*
Rev. 21. 14. twelve *f.* garnished with, 19.
Matt. 13. 35. *f.* of the world, 25. 34; *John* 17. 24; *Eph.* 1. 4; 1 *Pet.* 1. 20; *Rev.* 13. 8. & 17. 8; *Ps.* 104. 5; *Prov.* 8. 29; *Is.* 51. 13, 16.
FOUNTAIN, *Gen.* 7. 11; *Deut.* 8. 7.
Deut. 33. 28. *f.* of Jacob on a land of
Ps. 36. 9. with thee is *f.* of life
   68. 26. bless the Lord from *f.* of Israel
   74. 15. thou didst cleave the *f.*
Prov. 5. 18. let thy *f.* be blessed
   13. 14. law of wise is a *f.* of life
   14. 27. fear of Lord is a *f.* of life
Eccl. 12. 6. pitcher broken at the *f.*
Songs 4. 12. *f.* sealed; 15. *f.* of gardens
Jer. 2. 13. me *f.* of living waters, 17. 13.
   9. 1. that my eyes were a *f.* of tears
Joel 3. 18. a *f.* out of house of Lord,
Zech. 13. 1. be a *f.* opened for house
Jam. 3. 11. *f.* send forth sweet waters
Rev. 21. 6. give of *f.* of life freely, 22. 17.
FOUNTAINS, *Is.* 41. 18. I will open *f.* in valleys
Rev. 7. 17. lead them to living *f.*
   8. 10. star fell on the *f.* of waters
   14. 7. worship him made the *f.*
FOUR-FOLD, 2 *Sam.* 12. 6. restore the lamb *f.*
Luke 19. 8. any thing, I restore *f.*
FOWL, FOWLS, *Gen.* 1. 26. dominion over the *f.*
Gen. 7. 3. take also of *f.* by sevens
Ps. 8. 8. to have dominion over *f.*
   50. 11. I know all the *f.* of the
   148. 10. flying *f.* praise the Lord
Matt. 6. 26. the *f.* they sow not.
   13. 4. *f.* dev. seed, *Mark* 4. 4; *Luke* 8. 5.
Mark 4. 32. *f.* may lodge, *Luke* 13. 19.
Luke 12. 24. are ye better than *f.*
Acts 10. 12. sheet wherein were *f.* 11. 6.
FOWLER, S, *Ps.* 91. 3. from the snare of the *f.*
Ps. 124. 7. soul out of the snare of *f.*
FOX, ES, *Judg.* 15. 4. Samson caught 300 *f.*
Ps. 63. 10. shall be a portion for *f.*
Songs 2. 15. take the *f.* the little *f.*
Matt. 8. 20. *f.* have holes, *Luke* 9. 58.
Luke 13. 32. go tell that *f.* I cast out
FRAGMENTS, broken pieces, *Matt.* 14. 20; *Mark* 6. 43. & 8. 19, 20; *John* 6. 12, 13.
FRAIL, weak, short-lived, *Ps.* 39. 4. ' Lord, make me to know mine end, and the measure of my days, what it is; that I may know how frail I am.'

FRAME, to make, *Is.* 29. 16; to devise, *Jer.* 18. 11; to forge, *Ps.* 50. 19; 94. 20.—To join together, *Eph.* 2. 21.
See also *Judg.* 12. 6; *Ps.* 103. 14; *Ezek.* 40. 2; *Hos.* 5. 4; *Heb.* 11. 3.

FRANKINCENSE, *Ex.* 30. 34. take spices with pure *f.*
Lev. 2. 16. priest burn oil with *f.* 6. 15.
Songs 4. 6. I will get me to the hill of *f.*
14. cinnamon with trees of all *f.*
Matt. 2. 11. they presented to him *f.*

FRANKLY, *Luke* 7. 42. he *f.* forgave them both

FRAUD, *Ps.* 10. 7. his mouth is full of *f.*
Jam. 5. 4. hire kept back by *f.* crieth

FREE, *Ex.* 21. 2; *Lev.* 19. 20.
2 *Chr.* 29. 31. of a *f.* heart offered
Ps. 51. 12. uphold with thy *f.* spirit
88. 5. *f.* among the dead like slain
Is. 58. 6. let the oppressed *f.*
Matt. 17. 26. then are the children *f.*
John 8. 32. truth shall make you *f.*
36. if Son make *f.* shall be *f.* indeed
Rom. 5. 15. so also is *f.* gift, 16. 18.
6. 7. *f.* from sin, 18. 22.
20. *f.* from righteousness
7. 3. *f.* from law
8. 2. *f.* from law of sin
1 *Cor.* 7. 21. the Lord's *f.* man Christ's servant
Gal. 3. 28. neither bond nor *f. Col.* 3. 11.
5. 1. Christ hath made us *f.* not entangled
Eph. 6. 8. receive of Lord bond or *f.*
2 *Thess.* 3. 1. word may have *f.* course
1 *Pet.* 2. 16. as *f.* and not using liberty

FREED, *Rom.* 6. 7. he dead, is *f.* from

FREEDOM, *Lev.* 19. 20. woman, not *f.* given her
Acts 22. 28. with a great sum this *f.*

FREELY, *Gen.* 2. 16. of every tree *f.* eat
Ps. 54. 6. I will *f.* sacrifice to thee
Hos. 14. 4. I will love them *f.*
Matt. 10. 8. *f.* ye have received, *f.* give
Rom. 3. 24. justified *f.* by his grace
8. 32. with him *f.* give us all things
1 *Cor.* 2. 12. things *f.* given us of God
2 *Cor.* 11. 7. preached gospel of God *f.*
Rev. 21. 6. of fountain of life *f.* 22. 17
Rev. 22. 17. whoso will, let him take *f.*

FRET, *Ps.* 37. 1, 7, 8; *Prov.* 24. 19.
Prov. 19. 3. his heart *f.* against the Lord
Ezek. 16. 43. has *f.* me in all

FRIEND, *Jer.* 6. 21; *Hos.* 3. 1.
Ex. 33. 11. to Moses as a man to his *f.*
Deut. 13. 6. *f.* which is as own soul
2 *Sam.* 16. 17. is this kindness to thy *f.*
2 *Chr.* 20. 7. Abraham thy *f. Is.* 41. 8; *Jam.* 2. 23.
Job 6. 14. pity should be showed from his *f.*
Ps. 88. 18. lover and *f.* far from me
Prov. 17. 17. *f.* loveth at all times
18. 24. a *f.* that sticks closer than a brother
27. 6. faithful are wounds of a *f.*
27. 10. own *f.* and father's *f.* will forsake not
17. sharpeneth countenance of his *f.*
Songs 5. 16. this is my beloved and my *f.*
Mic. 7. 5. trust not in a *f.* keep door
Matt. 11. 19. *f.* of public, *Luke* 7. 34.

22. 12. *f.* how camest in hither
26. 50. *f.* why art thou come
Luke 14. 10. may say, *f.* go up higher
John 3. 29. *f.* of bridegroom rejoiceth
John 15. 13. lay down life for his *f.*
14. ye are my *f.* if; 15. called you *f.*
19. 12. thou art not Cesar's *f.*
Jam. 2. 23. Abraham called *f.* of God
Jam. 4. 4. *f.* of world is enmity with G.

FRIENDS, *Prov.* 14. 20. the rich hath many *f.*
16. 28. whisperer separateth chief *f.*
17. 9. repeateth a matter, separ. *f.*
19. 4. wealth maketh many *f.*
Prov. 22. 24. make no *f.* with an angry
Songs 5. 1. eat, O *f.* drink, yea
Mark 5. 19. Jesus saith, go home to thy *f.*
Luke 15. 9. she calleth her *f.* saying
29. might make merry with my *f.*
21. 16. ye shall be betrayed by *f.*
23. 12. Pilate and Herod made *f.*
John 15. 13. down his life for his *f.*
14. ye are my *f.* if ye do what I
15. but I have called *f.*

FRIENDLY, *Prov.* 18. 24. hath *f.* must show *f.*

FROST, *Gen.* 31. 40. *f.* consumed by night
Ex. 16. 14. as small as the hoar *f.*
Ps. 78. 47. destroy syca. trees with *f.*
147. 16. he scattereth the hoar *f.*

FROWARD, *Job* 5. 13; 1 *Pet.* 2. 18.
Deut. 32. 20. a very *f.* generation
Ps. 18. 26. with *f.* show thyself *f.*
101. 4. *f.* heart shall depart from
Prov. 4. 24. *f.* mouth, 6. 12. & 8. 13.
10. 31. *f.* tongue
11. 20. *f.* heart, 17. 20.
3. 32. *f.* is abomination to the Lord
Is. 57. 17. went on *f.*
Prov. 6. 14. *f.* is in his heart

FRUIT, *Gen.* 4. 3; *Lev.* 19. 24.
Gen. 30. 2. withheld *f.* of womb, *Ex.* 21. 22.
Lev. 19. 23. count *f.* uncircumcised
27. 30. the tithe of the *f.* is the Lord's
Ps. 72. 16. *f.* thereof shake like Leban.
127. 3. *f.* of the womb is his reward
Prov. 11. 30. *f.* of righteous is tree of life
Songs 2. 3. his *f.* was sweet to my taste
4. 13. pleasant *f.* 7. 13.
6. 11. *f.* of the valley
Is. 3. 10. eat the *f.* of their doings
27. 9. all the *f.* to take away
57. 19. create *f.* of the lips, peace,
Hos. 10. 1. empty vine brings *f.* to me
14. 8. fir-tree from me is thy *f.* found
Mic. 6. 7. *f.* of body for sin of my soul
Matt. 7. 17. good tree good *f.* 21. 19.
12. 33. *f.* good tree known by its *f.*
26. 29. not drink of *f.* of vine till that day; *Mark* 14. 25.
Luke 1. 42. blessed is the *f.* of thy womb
Luke 13. 6. he sought *f.* and found none
John 4. 36. gathers *f.* to eternal life
15. 2. bears not *f.* bears *f.*—purgeth—bring forth more *f.*
Rom. 6. 21. what *f.* had—ashamed
22. *f.* to holiness
Gal. 5. 22. *f.* of spirit is love joy, peace
Eph. 5. 9. *f.* of Spirit is in all goodness

Phil. 4. 17. desire *f.* that may abound
Heb. 12. 11. peaceable *f.* of righteous.
    13. 15. sacrifice of praise, *f.* of our lips
Jam. 3. 18. *f.* of righteousness is sown
Rev. 22. 2. yields *f.* every month
FRUIT, beareth, *Ezek.* 17. 8. that it
    bear f.
2 *Kings* 19. 30. bear *f.* upward, *Is.* 37. 31.
Joel 2. 22. the tree *beareth* her *f.*
Matt. 13. 23. is he who *beareth f.*
Luke 8. 8. on good ground and *bear f.*
    13. 9. if it *bear f.* well, if not, cut it
John 15. 2. every branch in me that
    beareth not *f.* that *beareth f.*
FRUIT, bring, bringeth, *Ps.* 1. 3. *bring-*
    eth forth f. in season
Ps. 92. 14. shall *bring forth f.* in old age
FRUIT, bring, bringeth, *Hos.* 10. 1.
    Israel *b. f.* to himself
Matt. 3. 10. *bringeth* not *forth* good *f.*
    7. 19; *Luke* 3. 9.
    7. 17. every good tree *b. f.* good *f.*
    18. a good tree cannot *b. f.* evil *f.*
    13. 26. when blade *brought forth f.*
Mark 4. 20. as hear word and *b. f. f.*
Luke 8. 14. *bring* no *f.* to perfection
John 12. 24. if it die, it *b. f.* much *f.*
    15. 5. abide in me, *bring f.* much *f.*
Rom. 7. 4. we should *b. f. f.* to God
Col. 1. 6. the gospel *bring f. f.* in you
Jam. 5. 18. Elij. prayed earth *b. f. f.*
FRUITFUL, *Ps.* 107. 34. *f.* land into
    barrenness
Ps. 128. 3. thy wife shall be a *f.* vine
Acts 14. 17. gave rain and *f.* seasons
Col. 1. 10. *f.* in every good work
FRUITS, *Matt.* 3. 8. *f.* meet for repent-
    ance, *Luke* 3. 8.
Matt. 7. 16. ye shall know them by *f.* 20.
Luke 12. 17. where to bestow my *f.*
2 *Cor.* 9. 10. increase *f.* of righteous
Phil. 1. 11. filled with *f.* of righteous.
2 *Tim.* 2. 6. first partaker of the *f.*
Jam. 3. 17. wisdom full of good *f.*
Rev. 22. 2. tree bear 12 manner of *f.*
FRUSTRATE. To disappoint, to render
    vain or abortive, to annul, or make
    void, *Is.* 44. 25; *Gal.* 2. 21.
FUGITIVE, *Gen.* 4. 12. a *f.* shalt thou be
Gen. 4. 14. I shall be a *f.* and a vaga-
    bond
FULFIL, *Gen.* 29. 27; *Ex.* 23. 26.
Ps. 145. 19. *f.* the desire of them that
Matt. 3. 15. it becometh us to *f.* all
    righteousness
    5. 17. not to destroy law but to *f.*
Acts 13. 22. who shall *f.* all my will
Luke 21. 24. till times of Gentiles be *f.*
Gal. 5. 14. law is *f.* in one word
    16. shall not *f.* lust of the flesh
    6. 2. bear burden, and so *f.* law of
Phil. 2. 2. *f.* ye my joy like-minded
Col. 4. 17. ministry that *f.* it in Lord
2 *Thess.* 1. 11. *f.* all the good pleasure
Jam. 2. 8. if ye *f.* the royal law
Rev. 17. 17. put in their hearts to *f.* his
FULFILLING, *Ps.* 148. 8. stormy wind
    f. his word
Rom. 13. 10. love is the *f.* of the law
Eph. 2. 3. *f.* desires of flesh and mind
FULL, *Gen.* 15. 16; *Ex.* 16. 3, 8.
Deut. 34. 9. Joshua *f.* of the Spirit of

Ruth. 1. 21. I went out *f.* and returned
Sam. 2. 5. that were *f.* hired out
Job 5. 26. come to grave in *f.* age
    14. 1. of few days and *f.* of trouble
Ps. 17. 14. they are *f.* of children
Prov. 27. 7. *f.* soul loatheth honeycomb
Prov. 30. 9. lest I be *f.* and deny the Lord
Luke 4. 1. Jesus being *f.* of the Holy
    Ghost
    6. 25. woe to you that are *f.*
John 1. 14. Son of God *f.* of grace and
    truth
1 *Cor.* 4. 8. now ye are *f.* now ye are rich
Phil. 4. 12. know both to be *f.* and
Col. 2. 2. riches of *f.* assurance
2 *Tim.* 4. 5. make *f.* proof of ministy
Heb. 6. 11. diligence to *f.* assurance of
    10. 22. near in *f.* assurance of faith
FULNESS, *Job* 20. 22. in *f.* of sufficiency
    in straits
Ps. 16. 11. in thy presence is *f.* of joy
John 1. 16. out of his *f.* have we received
Rom. 11. 25. till *f.* of Gentiles be come
    15. 29. *f.* of blessing of the gospel
Gal. 4. 4. when *f.* of time was come
Eph. 1. 10. dispensation of *f.* of times
    23. the *f.* of him who filleth all in all
    3. 19. ye may be filled with *f.* of God
    4. 13. perfect man to stature of. of
    Christ
Col. 1. 19. in him should all *f.* dwell
    2. 9. in him dwells all *f.* of Godhead
FURNISHED, *Deut.* 15. 14; *Prov.* 9. 2.
2 *Tim.* 3. 17. thoroughly *f.* to all good
    work
FURROW, *Ps.* 65. 10. thou settest *f.*
    thereof
Ps. 129. 3. plowers made long their *f.*
FURTHER, *Job* 38. 11. hitherto come,
    but no *f.*
Matt. 26. 65. what *f.* need of witnesses,
    Mark 14. 63; *Luke* 22. 71.
Luke 24. 28. as though he would gone *f.*
2 *Tim.* 3. 9. they shall proceed no *f.*
FURTHERANCE, *Phil.* 1. 12. things
    fallen rather to *f.* of the gospel
Phil. 1. 25. shall abide with you for
    your *f.*
FURY is not in me, *Is.* 27. 4.
    51. 17. Jeru. wh. has drunken cup of *f.*
    22. even dregs of cup of my *f.*
Is. 59. 18. repay *f.* to his adversaries
    63. 3. I will trample them in my *f.*
    5. my *f.* it upheld me, 6.
Jer. 6. 11. I am full of *f.* of Lord weary
    10. 25. pour out thy *f.* on heathen
Prov. 22. 24. with *f.* man not go

GADDEST, *Jer.* 2. 36. why *g.* thou to
    change
GAIN, *Job* 22. 3; *Prov.* 3. 14.
Job 27. 8. hypocrite when he hath *g.*
Prov. 1. 19. every one greedy of *g.*
    3. 14. *g.* is better than fine gold
Is. 33. 15. despiseth the *g.* of oppression
Mic. 4. 13. I will consecrate *g.* to Lord
Acts 16. 16. brought masters much *g.*
Matt. 16. 26. if should *g.* whole world
1 *Cor.* 9. 19. that I might *g.* the more
Phil. 1. 21. to live is Christ, to die is *g.*
    3. 7. what were *g.* to me I counted
1 *Tim.* 6. 5. supposing *g.* is godliness

6. godliness with contentment is g.

GAINED, Matt. 18. 15. thou hast g. thy brother

Luke 19. 15. how much every man g.

16. Lord, thy pound hath g. ten

GAINSAY, Luke 21. 15. adversaries not able to g.

GAINSAYERS, Tit. 1. 9. convince g.

GAINSAYING, to contradict, Acts 10. 29.

Rom. 10. 21. g. people

Jude 11. g. of Core

GALL, Job 16. 13. & 20. 14, 25.

Deut. 29. 18. root bears g. and wormwood

32. their grapes are grapes of g.

Ps. 69. 21. gave me g. for my meat

Jer. 8. 14. given us water of g. 9. 15.

Lam. 3. 19. remembering wormwood and g. 5.

Matt. 27. 34. him vine, mingled wi. g.

Acts 8. 23. thou art in g. of bitterness

GALLANT, Is. 33. 21. nor shall g. ship

GARDEN, Gen. 2. 15; 3. 23. and 13. 10.

Songs 4. 12. a g. enclosed my sister

16. blow on my g. 5. 1. & 6. 2, 11.

Is. 1. 8. daugh. of Zion as lodge in g.

58. 11. shalt be like a watered g.

Jer. 31. 12. soul as watered g.

Ezek. 28. 13. in Eden the g. of God

36. 35. desolate land like g. of Eden

John 18. 1. over Ced. where was a g.

26. did I not see thee in the g.

19. 41. a g. and in g. a sepulchre

GARLANDS, Acts 14. 13. the priest of Jupiter brougnt oxen and g.

GARLICK, Num. 11. 5. we remember the g. we did eat in Egypt

GARMENT, Josh. 7. 21; Ezra 9. 3.

Job 13. 28. consumeth as a g. that is moth-eaten

38. 14. it is turned as clay to the seal, they stand as a g.

Ps. 102. 26. they shall perish, all shall wax old like a g. Is. 50. 9; 51. 6; Heb. 1. 11.

104. 2. thou coverest thyself with light, as with a g.

109. 18. he clothed himself with cursing as with a g.

Is. 51. 8. the moth shall eat them up like a g.

61. 3. g. of praise for spirit of heavi-

Mal. 2. 16. covereth violence with g.

Matt. 9. 16. new cloth to old g. Mark 2. 21; Luke 5. 36.

Luke 22. 36. sell his g. and buy one

Jude 23. hating g. spotted by flesh

GARMENTS, Job 37. 17. how thy g. are warm

Ps. 22. 18. they part my g. among them, casting lots

45. 8. all thy g. smell of myrrh

Eccl. 9. 8. thy g. be always white

Songs 4. 11. smell of thy g. is like smell of Lebanon

Is. 9. 5. battle with g. rolled in blood

59. 17. put on g. of vengeance

Is. 63. 1. with dyed g. from Bozrah

Dan. 3. 21. were bound in their coats and other g.

Joel 2. 13. rend hearts and not g.

Matt. 21. 8. spread their g. in way

27. 35. they parted his g. Mark 15. 24.

Luke 24. 4. two men in shining g.

Acts 9. 39. showing g. Dorcas made

Jam. 5. 2. your g. are moth-eaten

Rev. 3. 4. which have not defiled their g.

16. 15. watcheth and keepeth his g.

GARNER, Matt. 3. 12. gather his wheat into the g. Luke 3. 17.

GARNISH, ED, Job 26. 13. by his spirit he hath g. the heavens

Matt. 12. 44. findeth it swept and g. Luke 11. 25.

Rev. 21. 19. the foundations of the wall are g.

GATE, Gen. 19. 1. & 34. 20, 24.

Gen. 22. 17. possess g. of his enemies

28. 17. this is house of God, g. of heaven

Judg. 16. 3. Samson took the g.

2 Kings 7. 17. a lord to have the charge of the g.

2 Chr. 8. 14. he appointed porters at every g.

Job 29. 7. I went to g. prepared

Ps. 118. 20. this g. of Lord into which

Is. 28. 6. to them that turn the battle to the g.

Matt. 7. 13. enter in at the strait g. wide is the g. and broad is the way, 14; Luke 13. 24.

Luke 16. 20. a beggar named Lazarus laid at his g. full of sores

Acts 10. 17. men from Cornelius stood before the g.

12. 14. Rhoda opened not the g. for gladness

Heb. 13. 12. suffered without g.

GATE, Prov. 17. 19. that exalteth the g. seeketh destruction

GATES, Ps. 9. 13. up from g. of death

24. 7. lift up your heads, O g.; Is. 26. 2.

87. 2. Lord loveth g. of Zion more

100. 4. enter his g. with thanksgiving

Ps. 118. 19. open to me the g. of righteousness

Prov. 8. 34. that heareth me, watching daily at my g.

31. 53. her husband is known in the g.

31. own works praise her in the g.

Is. 26. 2. open ye the g. that the righteous may enter

38. 10. go to the g. of the grave

45. 1. to open before him the two-leaved g.

Matt. 16. 18. g. of hell not prevail

Rev. 21. 12. the city had twelve g. at g. twelve angels

21. the twelve g. were twelve pearls

25. the g. of it shall not be shut at all by day

GATES, thy, Ps. 122. 2. our feet shall stand within thy g. O Jerusalem

Is. 54. 12. I will make thy g. of carbuncles

60. 18. call thy walls salvation and thy g. praise

GATHER thee from all nations, Deut. 30. 3; Neh. 1. 9; Jer. 29. 14.

Ex. 5. 7. let them go and g. straw; 12. g. stubble

Deut. 11. 14. I will give rain that thou mayest g.

30. 3. he will g. thee from all nations, *Ezek.* 36. 24.

Ps. 26. 9. g. not my soul with sinners

39. 6. and knoweth not who shall g.

Songs 6. 2. my beloved is gone down to g. lilies

Is. 40. 11. he shall g. the lambs—arms

Joel 3. 2. I will g. all nations

Zeph. 3. 18. g. them that are sorrowful

Matt. 3. 12. g. his wheat into the garner

7. 16. do men g. grapes of thorns

13. 28. that we g. them up

29. lest while ye g. up the tares

GATHER together, *Ps.* 50. 5. g. my saints *together*

Ps. 94. 21. they g. *together* against the righteous

Is. 11. 12. he shall g. *together* the dispersed of Judah

Matt. 13. 30. g. *together* first the tares

24. 31. g. *together* his elect, *Mark* 13. 27.

Eph. 1. 10. g. into one all things

Rev. 20. 8. to g. Gog and Magog *together* to battle

GATHERED, *Gen.* 25. 8. Abraham g. to his people

Ex. 16. 17. g. some more, some less

16. 18. he that g. much g. little no lack, 2 *Cor.* 8. 15.

Num. 20. 24. Aaron shall be g. to his people, 26.

27. 13. Moses g. to his people, *Deut.* 32. 50.

Ps. 59. 3. the mighty are g. against me

Eccl. 2. 8. I g. silver and gold

Is. 49. 5. though Israel be not g. yet shall I be glorious

Matt. 13. 40. as tares are g. and burnt

25. 32. before him shall be g. all nations

John 11. 47. then g. chief priests a council, and said

GATHERED together, 2 *Chr.* 20. 4. Judah g. *together* to ask help of L.

Matt. 18. 20. where two or three are g. *together*

23. 37. how often would I have g. thy children *together*, as a hen, *Luke* 13. 34.

24. 28. there will eagles be g. *together* *Luke* 17. 37.

Luke 24. 33. they found the eleven g. *together*

GATHERETH, *Ps.* 33. 7. he g. the waters of the sea together

Prov. 6. 8. the ant g. her food in the harvest

10. 5. he that g. in summer is a wise

Matt. 12. 30. he that g. not scattereth, *Luke* 11. 23.

Matt. 23. 37. g. thy children as hen g.

John 4. 36. he that reapeth g. fruit to life eternal

GATHERING, S, 1 *Kings* 17. 10., the widow woman was there g. sticks

Matt. 25. 24. and g. where thou hast not strawed

2 *Thess.* 2. 1. and by our g. together unto him

1 *Cor.* 16. 2. that there be no g. when I come

GAVE, *Gen.* 2. 20. Adam g. names to all cattle and to fowl

Gen. 3. 12. the woman g. me of the tree

14. 20. and he g. him tithes of all. *Heb.* 7. 2, 4.

Ex. 11. 3. the Lord g. the people favour, 12. 36.

Job 1. 21. Lord g. and Lord taketh away

42. 10. God g. Job twice as much as he had before

Ps. 69. 21. they g. me also gall

81. 12. I g. them up to their own hearts' lusts

Eccl. 12. 7. spirit return to God that g. it

Is. 42. 24. who g. Jacob for a spoil

Is. 43. 3. I g. Egypt for thy ransom, Seba for thee

50. 6. I g. my back to the smiters

Hos. 2. 8. for she did not know that I g. her corn

Matt. 14. 19. he brake and g. the loaves to his disciples, 15. 36; 26. 16; *Mark* 6. 41; 8. 6; 14. 22; *Luke* 9. 16; 22. 19.

25. 35. ye g. me meat, ye g. me drink, took me in

Luke 15. 16. with husks, and no man g. unto him

John 1. 12. he g. power to become sons

3. 16. God g. his only begotten Son

6. 31. he g. them bread from heaven to eat

Acts 2. 4. to speak as the Spirit g. them utterance

1 *Cor.* 3. 6. God g. the increase, 7.

2 *Cor.* 8. 5. first g. themselves to the Lord

Gal. 1. 4. who g. himself for our sins, 2. 20. g. himself for me, *Tit.* 2. 14.

Eph. 1. 22. and g. him to be head over all things

4. 8. g. gifts to men

11. g. some apostles

5. 25. Christ loved the church and g. himself for it

1 *Tim.* 2. 6. g. himself a ransom for all

GAVEST, *Ps.* 21. 4. asked life thou g. it

John 17. 4. work thou g. me to do

6. men thou g. me, 12.

8. words thou g. me

22. glory thou g. me

GAY, *Jam.* 2. 3. respect to him that weareth g. clothing

GAZE, to look earnestly, *Ex.* 19. 21.

GAZING, *Neh.* 3. 6. set thee as a g. stock

Acts 1. 11. why g. up into heaven

Heb. 10. 33. partly whilst ye were made a g. stock

GENDER to couple, *Lev.* 19. 19; to bring forth, *Gal.* 4. 24; to produce, as effect from cause, 2 *Tim.* 2. 23.

GENEALOGY, *Ezra* 2. 62. these sought their g. *Neh.* 7. 64.

Ezra 8. 1. g. of them that went up

GENEALOGIES, 1 *Tim.* 1. 4. give no heed to endless g.

Tit. 3. 9. avoid g. and contentions

GENERAL, *Heb.* 12. 23. g. assembly

and church

GENERATION, Gen. 7. 1. & 6. 9.
Deut. 32. 5. they are a perverse and crooked g.
20. a very froward g. in whom
Ps. 14. 5. God is in g. of righteous
22. 30. accounted to the Lord for a g.
24. 6. this is the g. of them that seek
102. 18. written for g. to come
112. 2. g. of upright shall be blessed
145. 4. one g. praise thy works to g.
Is. 53. 8. who declare his g. Acts 8. 33.
Matt. 3. 7. g. of vipers, 12. 34. & 23. 33.
Luke 16. 8. wiser in their g.
Acts 13. 36. had served his g. according
1 Pet. 2. 9. a chosen g. to show praises

GENERATIONS, Ps. 33. 11. thoughts to all g.
45. 17. name to be remembered in all g.
72. 5. fear thee throughout all g.
79. 13. show forth thy praise to all g.
85. 5. draw out anger to all g.
89. 4. build thy throne to all g.
90. 1. our dwelling place in all g.
100. 5. his truth endures to all g.
102. 24. thy years are through all g.
119. 90. thy faithfulness to all g.
135. 13. memorial throughout all g.
145. 13. dominion endureth to all g.
146. 10. thy God, O Zion, shall reign to all g.
Is. 51. 9. awake, O arm of the Lord, as in the g. of old
Luke 1. 48. behold, all g. shall call me blessed
Col. 1. 26. mystery hid from ages and g.

GENTILES, Gen. 10. 5; Jer. 4. 7.
Is. 11. 10. to it shall the g. seek
42. 6. a light to g. 49. 6; Luke 2. 32; Acts 13. 47.
Matt. 6. 32. after these do g. seek
Luke 21. 24. trodden down of g.
John 7. 35. to dispersed among the g.
Acts 13. 46. lo, we turn to the g.
14. 27. opened door of faith to g.
Rom. 2. 14. g. which have not the law
3. 29. is he not also God of g. yes of g.
11. 25. till fulness of g. be come in
15. 10. rejoice ye g. with his people
12. in his name g. trust, Matt. 12. 21.
Eph. 3. 6. g. fellow-heirs and partakers
8. preach among g. unsearchable riches of Christ
1 Tim. 2. 7. teacher of g. 2 Tim. 1. 11.
3. 16. God manifest in flesh, preached to g.

GENTLE, quiet, meek, peaceable. Gentle among you, 1 Thess. 2. 7.
2 Tim. 2. 24. servant of the Lord must be g.
Tit. 3. 2. g. showing all meekness
Jam. 3. 17. wisdom from above is g.
1 Pet. 2. 18. not only to g. but froward

GENTLENESS, Ps. 18. 35. thy g. made me great
2 Cor. 10. 1. beseech by the g. of Christ
Gal. 5. 22. fruit of love, joy, g.

GENTLY, 2 Sam. 18. 5. deal g. with the young man Absalom
Is. 40. 11. g. lead those with young

GET, Lev. 14. 21. poor and cannot g. 22.

Deut. 8. 18. power to g. wealth
1 Kings 1. 2. that king may g. heat
Ps. 119. 104. thro' precepts I g. unders.
Prov. 4. 5. g. wisdom, g. understand
Eccl. 3. 6. there is a time to g.
Lam. 3. 7. hedged me, I cannot g. out
Ezek. 22. 27. to g. dishonest gain
2 Cor. 2. 11. lest Satan g. advantage
Jam. 4. 13. buy, sell, and g. gain

GET thee, Gen. 12. 1. g. thee out of country, Acts 7. 3.
Is. 40. 9. O Zion, that g. t. to high mountain
Matt. 4. 10. Jes. saith, g. t. hence, Satan
16. 23. said to Peter, g. thee behind

GETTETH, Prov. 3. 13. happy man that g. understanding
Prov. 15. 32. th. hear. reproof g. understanding
19. 8. th. g. wisdom loveth own soul

GETTING, Prov. 4. 7. with all thy g. get understanding

GHOST, Gen. 49. 33. Jacob yielded up the g.
Job 10. 18. O that I had given up g.
14. 10. man giveth up g. and where
Matt. 27. 50. Jesus cried, yielded up g.

GIANT, 2 Sam. 21. 16. sons of g. 18; 1 Chr. 20. 4.
1 Chr. 20. 6. son of g.; 8. born to g.

GIANTS, Gen. 6. 4. there were g. in earth
Num. 13. 33. we saw g. sons of Anak
Deut. 2. 11. Emims were accounted g.
3. 11. Og of Bash. remained of remnant of g. Josh. 12. 4; 13. 12.

GIFT, 1 Cor. 1. 7. & 7. 7.
Ex. 23. 8. take no g. for the g. blinds the wise, Deut. 16. 19; 2 Chr. 19. 7.
Prov. 17. 8. a g. is a precious stone, 23.
18. 16. a man's g. maketh room for
21. 14. a g. in secret pacifieth anger
Eccl. 7. 7. a g. destroys the heart
Matt. 5. 24. leave there thy g. and be
John 4. 10. if thou knewest the g. of God
Acts 2. 38. ye shall receive g. of H. G.
8. 20. thought g. of G. may be purch.
Rom. 5. 15. not as offence, so is free g.
16. so is g., free g. of many offences
18. the free g. came on all men
6. 23. g. of God eternal life
1 Cor. 1. 7. ye come behind in no g.
13. 2. though I have g. of prophecy
2 Cor. 8. 4. that we would receive g.
9. 15. thanks to G. for unspeak. g.
Eph. 2. 8. through faith it is the g. of G.
Phil. 4. 17. not because I desire a g. but
1 Tim. 4. 14. neglect not g. in thee
2 Tim. 1. 6. stir up g. in thee given
Heb. 6. 4. tasted of heavenly g.
Jam. 1. 17. every good and perfect g.

GIFTS, Ps. 68. 18. received g. for men
72. 10 kings of Sheba shall offer g.
Matt. 2. 11. they presented to him g.
Matt. 7. 11. give good g. to your child.
Luke 21. 1. the rich casting their g.
Rom. 11. 29. g. and called of G. without
1 Cor. 12. 1. concerning spiritual g.
4. there are diversities of g.
31. covet earnestly the best g.
14. 1. and desire spiritual g.
Eph. 4. 8. led captive and gave g. to
Heb. 5. 1. he may offer g. and sacrifices

GIRD with strength, *Ps.* 18. 32.
45. 3. *g.* thy sword on thigh
Luke 12. 37. shall *g.* himself
John 21. 18. when old, another shall *g.* thee
GIRDED, *Lev.* 8. 7. he *g.* him with the girdle and clothed him
1 *Sam.* 2. 18. Samuel *g.* with a linen ephod
Ps. 30. 11. hast *g.* me with gladness
Ezek. 23. 15. images of the Chaldeans *g.* with girdles
Luke 12. 35. let you loins be *g.*
John 13. 4. a towel and *g.* himself
5. to wipe with the towel wherewith he was *g.*
Eph. 6. 14. having your loins *g.* with truth
GIRDEST, *John* 21. 18. when thou was young thou *g.* thyself
GIRDETH, *Ps.* 18. 32. God *g.* me
Prov. 31. 17. *g.* her loins with strength
GIRDLE, any thing bound round the waist. It is still necessary in the East, because of the long, loose raiment worn by both sexes. Girdles were sometimes excessively costly. All classes strove to obtain those of value. Girdles of leather were worn in token of humility, as by Elijah, 2 *Kings* 1. 8; and John the Baptist, *Matt.* 3. 4. Girdles of sackcloth were marks of humiliation, worn in times of mourning, *Is.* 3. 24. To have the loins girded, *Luke* 12. 35. is to be always prepared for any service that God may require, and be like servants who are ready to obey their master's commands.
1 *Sam.* 18. 4. Jonathan gave David his bow and *g.*
Job 12. 18. girdeth loins of king with *g.*
Is. 11. 5. righteousness shall be *g.* of his loins, and faithfulness *g.* of his reins
Matt. 3. 4. John had a leathern *g. Mark* 1. 6.
Acts 21. 11. took Paul's *g.* man that owneth this *g.*
Rev. 1. 13. girt with a golden *g.*
GIRDLES, *Ezek.* 23. 15. the images of Chaldeans girded with *g.*
Rev. 15. 6. seven angels girded with golden *g.*
GIRT, *John* 21. 7. Pet. *g.* fisher's coat
Eph. 6. 14. having loins *g.* with truth
GIVE, 1 *Kings* 3. 5. ask what I shall *g.* thee
2 *Sam.* 23. 15. oh that one would *g.* me drink of the water of Bethlehem, 1 *Chr.* 11. 17.
Ezra. 9. 8. *g.* us a nail in his holy place
Job 2. 4. all that a man hath will he *g.* for his life
Ps. 2. 8. I will *g.* thee the heathen for thine inheritance
29. 11. Lord will *g.* strength to his people
37. 4. *g.* thee the desires of thy heart
Ps. 49. 7. none can *g.* to God a ransom
51. 16. desirest not sacrifice, *g.* it

84. 11. Lord will *g.* grace and glory
91. 11. *g.* his angels charge, *Matt.* 4. 6.
104. 27. mayest *g.* them their meat
109. 4. I *g.* myself to prayer
Prov. 29. 15. rod and reproof *g.* wisdom
Is. 55. 10. *g.* seed to the sower and bread
61. 3. to *g.* unto them beauty for ashes
Jer. 17. 10. to give every man according to his ways, 32. 10; *Rev.* 22. 12.
29. 11. to *g.* you an expected end
Hos. 11. 8. how shall I *g.* thee up
Matt. 7. 9. bread, will he *g.* a stone
11. how to *g.* gifts to your children, so your Father to *g.* them that ask him, *Luke* 11. 13.
10. 42. whoso shall *g.* to drink a cup of cold water
Mark 6. 25. *g.* me the head of John
Luke 6. 38. *g.* and it shall be *g.* unto you
John 10. 28. I *g.* to them eternal life
14. ·16. *g.* you another comforter
27. peace I leave with you, my peace I *g.* to you not as world giveth *g.*
15. 16. whatsoever ye shall ask, he may *g.* it
16. 23. whatsoever ye ask he will *g.* it
Acts 3. 6. such as I have, I give thee
6. 4. will *g.* ourselves to prayer
20. 35. more blessed to *g.* than receive
Rom. 8. 32. with him also freely *g.* us all things
1 *Cor.* 7. 5. may *g.* yourselves to fasting
Eph. 4. 28. to *g.* to him that needeth
1 *Tim.* 4. 15. *g.* thyself wholly to them
2 *Tim.* 4. 8. righteous Judge shall *g.* me
Rev. 13. 15. he hath power to *g.* life to the image
22. 12. to *g.* every man according to his work
GIVE Thanks, 2 *Sam.* 22. 50. *g.* thanks,
1 *Chr.* 16. 8, 34, 35, 41; *Neh.* 12. 24; *Ps.* 35. 18. & 79. 13. & 92. 1. & 105. 1. & 107. 1. & 118. 1, 29. & 136. 1, 3.
Ps. 6. 5. in grave who *give thanks* to
30. 4. *g. thanks* at remembrance of his holiness, 97. 12.
119. 62. at midnight I will rise to *g. thanks*
Eph. 1. 16. cease not to *g. thanks*, 1 *Thess.* 1. 2; 2 *Thess.* 2. 13; *Col.* 1. 3.
1 *Thess.* 5. 18. in everything *g. thanks*, *Phil.* 4. 6.
GIVE, imperatively, 1 *Sam.* 8. 6. *g.* us a king to judge us
1 *Kings* 3. 26. *g.* her the living child, 27.
Ps. 60. 11. *g.* us help from trouble, 108. 12.
Prov. 23. 26. my son, *g.* me thine heart
25. 21. if enemy hunger, *g.* him bread, *Rom.* 12. 20.
30. 8. *g.* me neither poverty nor riches, feed me
Is. 62. 7. *g.* him no rest till he establish Jerusalem
Matt. 5. 42. *g.* to him that asketh thee
6. 11. *g.* us this day our daily bread, *Luke* 11. 3.
10. 8. *g.* freely ye received, freely *g.*
19. 21. go sell, and *g.* to the poor, *Mark* 10. 21.
25. 8. *g.* us of your oil

Luke 6. 38. *g.* and it shall be given
15. 12. said, *g.* me the portion of goods
John 6. 34. Lord, evermore *g.* us bread
Acts 8. 19. Simon said, *g.* me also this power
1 *Cor.* 10. 32. *g.* none offence
2 *Cor.* 9. 7. *g.* not grudgingly
1 *Tim.* 4. 13. *g.* attendance to reading
GIVE, I will, *Ps.* 30. 12. *I will g.* thanks to thee
Ps. 57. 7. *I will* sing and *g.* praise
Is. 42. 6. *I will g.* thee for covenant of the people, 49. 8.
49. 6. *I will g.* thee for a light to the Gentiles
Jer. 24. 7. *I will g.* them a heart to know me
32. 39. *I will g.* them one heart, *Ezek.* 11. 19.
Ezek. 21. 27. he come whose right it is, *I will g.* it him
36. 26. and *I will g.* you an heart of flesh
Matt. 11. 28. come unto me, and *I will g.* you rest
16. 19. *I will g.* thee the keys
Mark 6. 22. ask what thou wilt, *I will g.* it thee
Luke 21. 15. *I will g.* you a mouth
John 6. 51. the bread *I will g.* is my flesh, *I will g.* for the life of the world
Rev. 2. 10. *I will g.* thee a crown of life
28. *I will g.* him the morning star
GIVE, not, or not give, *Matt.* 7. 6. *g. not* that which is holy to the dogs
Eph. 4. 27. neither *g.* place to the devil
GIVEN, *Prov.* 19. 17. that which he hath *g.* will he pay him
Eccl. 12. 11. which are *g.* from one shepherd
Is. 9. 6. for to us a son is *g.*
Matt. 13. 11. *g.* to you to know the mysteries of the kingdom, *Mark* 4. 11; *Luke* 8. 10.
13. 12. to him shall be *g.*
Mark 4. 11. it is *g.* to you to know the mysteries
Luke 12. 48. to whom much is *g.*
John 6. 39. of all which he hath *g.* me
65. can come to me except it be *g.*
19. 11. except it were *g.* thee from above
Rom. 11. 35. hath first *g.* to him and it
1 *Cor.* 2. 12. know things freely *g.* us of God
2 *Cor.* 9. 7. God loveth cheerful *g.*
Eph. 8. 2. dispensation, which is *g.* me to you-ward
8. who am least is this grace *g.*
5. 2. Christ loved *g.* himself for us
1 *John* 3. 24. Spirit which he hath *g.* us
4. 13. hath *g.* us of his Spirit
Rev. 6. 11. white robes were *g.* to every one of them
GIVEN, God, our Lord hath, had, *Is.* 8. 18. I and the children *Lord hath g.* *Heb.* 2. 13.
50. 4. the *Lord hath g.* me the tongue of the learned
John 6. 23. after *Lord had g.* thanks

1 *Thess.* 4. 8. but *G.* who *hath g.* us his holy Spirit
1 *John* 5. 11. this is the record *G. hath g.* us
GIVETH, *Ps.* 37. 21. shows mercy and *g.*
119. 130. the entrance of thy words *g.* light
127. 2. so he *g.* his beloved sleep
Prov. 3. 34. he *g.* grace to the lowly, *Jam.* 4. 6; 1 *Pet.* 5. 5.
Prov. 28. 27. *g.* to poor shall not lack
Is. 40. 29. *g.* power to the faint
42. 5. *g.* breath to the people
John 3. 34. God *g.* not the Spirit by measure to him
6. 32. Father *g.* you true bread
33. and *g.* life to the world
37. all that the Father *g.* me shall come to me
10. 11. the good shepherd *g.* his life for the sheep
14. 27. not as the world *g.* give I
Acts 17. 25. he *g.* to all life, breath, and all things
Rom. 12. 8. he that *g.* let him do it with simplicity
1 *Cor.* 3. 7. but God that *g.* the increase
7. 38. he that *g.* her in marriage doth well
2 *Cor.* 3. 6. killeth, but the Spirit *g.* life
1 *Tim.* 6. 17. who *g.* us richly all things
Jam. 1. 5. *g.* to all men liberally and
4. 6. he *g.* more grace to the humble
1 *Pet.* 4. 11. of the ability that God *g.*
Rev. 22. 5. for Lord God *g.* them light
GIVING, *Matt.* 24. 38. marrying and *g.* in marriage
Rom. 4. 20. was strong in faith *g.* glory to God
9. 4. the *g.* of the law
2 *Pet.* 1. 5. *g.* all diligence, add to faith virtue
Jude 7. *g.* themselves over to fornication
GLAD my heart is, *Ps.* 16. 9.
Ps. 31. 7. I will be *g.* and rejoice in thy mercy
64. 10. righteous shall be *g.* in the L.
104. 34. sweet I will be *g.* in the Lord
122. 1. I was *g.* when they said to
Luke 1. 19. *g.* tidings, 8. 1, 15, 32; *Acts* 13. 32; *Rom.* 10. 15.
GLADLY, *Mark* 6. 20. Herod feared John and heard him *g.*
Mark 12. 37. the common people heard Christ *g.*
Luke 8. 40. people *g.* received him, for
Acts 2. 41. that *g.* received his word
2 *Cor.* 12. 9. most *g.* will I glory
18. I will very *g.* spend and be spent for you
GLADNESS, *Ps.* 4. 7. put *g.* in my heart
30. 11. hast girded me with *g.*
45. 7. anointed with oil of *g.* *Heb.* 1. 9.
51. 8. make me to hear joy and *g.*
97. 11. *g.* sown for upright in heart
100. 2. serve the Lord with *g.*
106. 5. rejoice in the *g.* of thy nation
Is. 35. 10. shall obtain joy and *g.* 51. 11.
35. 3. joy and *g.* shall be found in it
Acts 2. 46. eat their meat with *g.* and

singleness
14. 17. filling their hearts with food and g.

GLASS, we see through, 1 *Cor.* 13. 12.
2 *Cor.* 3. 18. beholding as in a g.
Jam. 1. 23. behold natural face in a g.
Rev. 4. 6. a sea of g. 15. 2.
   21. 18. city was pure gold like g.

GLEAN. To gather ears of corn, or grapes, left by the reapers or gatherers for the use of the poor and needy; *Ruth* 2. 2; *Lev.* 19. 9. 10; 23. 22; *Deut.* 24. 19—22; *Judg.* 20 45.

GLISTERING, *Luke* 9. 29. and his raiment was white and g.

GLITTER, spoken of the sword, *Deut.* 32. 41. " If I whet my glittering sword." This similitude showeth God's judgments to be swift, powerful, terrible, as in *Ezek.* 21. 10, 28. " The sword, the sword is drawn; for slaughter it is furbished, to consume because of the glittering."

GLOOMINESS, a darkening of the air, by the intervention of clouds or locusts, *Joel* 2. 2. God's judgments are likened to gloominess, *Zeph.* 1. 15. " A day of darkness and gloominess, a day of clouds and thick darkness."

GLORIFY, *Ps.* 22. 23. all seed of Jacob g. him
Ps. 50. 15. and thou shalt g. me
Is. 24. 15. g. ye Lord in the fires
   60. 7. I will g. house of my glory
Matt. 5. 16. g. your Father in heaven
John 12. 28. Father g. thy name
   16. 14. he shall g. me; for he shall
   17. 1. g. thy Son, that thy Son g.
   5. g. me with thine own self
   21. 19. by what death he shd. g. God
Rom. 15. 16. one mind and mouth g. G.
1 *Cor.* 6. 20. g. G. in body and in spiri
2 *Pet.* 2. 12. g. God in day of visitation

GLORIFIED, *Is.* 55. 5. Holy One of Israel hath g. 60. 9.
Is. 60. 21. work of hands th. 1 may be g.
   61. 3. planting of L. that he be g.
Dan. 5. 23. God hast thou not g.
Matt. 9. 8. marvelled and g. God, *Mark* 2. 12; *Luke* 5. 26.
John 11. 4. that Son of God might be g.
   12. 16. but when Jesus was g. then
   23. the Son of man was g.
   28. I have g. it and will glorify it
   15. 8. my Father g. that ye bear fruit
   17. 4. I have g. thee on earth
Acts 4. 21. men g. G. for what was done
Rom. 1. 21. they g. him not as God
   8. 17. suffer that we may be also g.
   30. whom he justified them he g.
2 *Thess.* 1. 10. when he come to be g.

GLORY, *Gen.* 31. 1. of our fathers gotten this g.
1 *Sam.* 2. 8. make inherit throne of g.
   4. 21. g. is departed from Israel, 22.
Ps. 24. 7. King of g. shall come in, 9.
   10. who is this King of g ?
Ps. 73. 24. afterward receive me to g.

145. 11. speak of g. of thy kingdom
Is. 4. 5. on all the g. shall be a defence
   13. 19. Babylon g. of king, as Sodom
   22. 24. hang on him g. of Father's ho.
   35. 2. g. of Lebanon shall be given to it
Ezek. 20. 6. is the g. of all lands, 15.
   25. 9. I will open g. of the country
   26. 20. set g. in land of the living
Hos. 4. 7. change their g. into shame
Hag. 2. 3. saw house in her first g.
   7. fill house with g. saith the Lord
   9. g. of latter house greater
Zech. 6. 13. build temple, he bear g.
Matt. 4. 8. kingdoms and g. of them
   16. 27. come in g. of Fa. *Mark* 8. 38.
   24. 30. Son coming with power and g. *Mark* 13. 26; *Luke* 21. 27.
Luke 2. 14. g. to God in highest, 19. 38.
   9. 31. in g. and spake of his decease
John 17. 5. g. which I had with thee
Rom. 4. 20. strong, giving g. to God
   6. 4. raised by the g. of the Father
   8. 18. not worthy to be comp. with g.
1 *Cor.* 2. 8. not crucified the Lord of g.
   15. 40. g. of celestial, g. of terrestrial
   43. sown in dishonour, raised in g.
2 *Cor.* 3. 10. no g. by reason of th. excel.
   18. all are changed from g. to g.
   4. 17. worketh eternal weight of g.
   8. 23. messengers, and g. of Christ
Eph. 1. 6. praise of g: of his grace
Phil. 3. 19. whose g. is in their shame
   4. 19. according to riches in his g.
1 *Tim.* 3. 16. received up into g.
2 *Tim.* 2. 10. Christ, with eternal g.
Heb. 2. 10. bringing many sons unto g
1 *Pet.* 1. 8. rejoice with joy full of g.
   21. God raised him, gave him g.
   4. 14. spirit of g. resteth on you
   5. 1. the g. that shall be revealed
2 *Pet.* 1. 17. voice from fr. excellent g.
Rev. 4. 11. worthy to receive g. and h.

GLORY, give, *Josh.* 7. 19. my son give g. to the God
1 *Sam.* 6. 5. ye shall *give* g. to God
Ps. 84. 11. Lord will *give* grace and g.
   115. 1. not to us, to thy name *give* g.
Is. 42. 12. let them *give* g. unto Lord
Rev. 14. 7. fear God, and *give* g. to him

GLORY of God, *Ps.* 19. 1. heaven declared the g. *of God*
Prov. 25. 2. the g. *of God* to conceal
John 11. 4. this sickness is for g. *of God*
   40. if believe, shouldst see g. *of God*
Acts 7. 55. Steph. looked, saw g. *of God*
Rom. 3. 23. all sinned, short of g. *of G.*
   5. 2. rejoice in hope of the g. *of God*
1 *Cor.* 10. 31. eat or drink, all to g. *of G.*
   11. 7. man is image and g. *of God*
2 *Cor.* 4. 6. light of know. of g. *of God*
Phil. 1. 11. by Christ to the g. *of God*

GLORY, his, *Deut.* 5. 24. Lord hath showed *his* g.
Ps. 21. 5. *his* g. is great in salvation
   29. 9. every one speak of *his* g.
   72. 19. let earth be filled with *his* g.
Ps. 97. 6. and all the people see *his* g.
   102. 16. build Zion, appear in *his* g.
Is. 6. 3. cried, whole earth full of *his* g.
   60. 2. *his* g. shall be seen upon thee
Dan. 5. 20. they took *his* g. from him

Matt. 6. 29. Solomon in *h. g. Luke* 12. 27.
19. 28. Son of man sit in *h. g. Lu.* 9. 26.
Luke 9. 32. when awake saw *his g.*
24. 26. suffered, to enter into *his g.*
John 1. 14. beheld *h. g., g.* of the only
Eph. 1. 12. to the praise of *his g.* 14.
3. 16. according to riches of *his g.*
Heb. 1. 3. the brightness of *his g.*
GLORY, my, *Ex.* 29. 43. tabernacle
    sanctified by *my g.*
Ex. 33. 22. while *m. g.* passeth by I will
Ps. 3. 3. thou art *m. g.* and lifter up
Is. 60. 7. I will glorify house of *my g.*
66. 18. shall come and see *my g.*
John 8. 50. I seek not *mine* own *g.*
17. 24. that they may behold *my g.*
GLORY of the Lord, *Ex.* 16. 7. ye shall
    see *g. of the Lord*
Ex. 24. 16. *g. of the Lord* abode on Sinai
Ps. 104. 31. *g. of the Lord* shall endure
Is. 40. 5. *g. of the Lord* shall be revealed
60. 1. *g. of the Lord* is risen upon thee
Ezek. 1. 28. the likeness of *g. of the L.*
2 *Cor.* 3. 18. as in a glass *g. of the Lord*
GLORY, thy, *Ex.* 33. 18. he said, show
    me *thy g.*
Ps. 90. 16. let *t. g.* appear unto children
102. 15. all kings of the earth *thy g.*
Is. 60. 19. God *t. g.*; 62. 2. kings see *t. g.*
63. 15. behold from habitation of *t. g.*
GLORIOUS, *Ex.* 15. 6. right hand, O
    Lord is become *g.*
Deut. 28. 58. mayest fear his *g.* name
1 *Chr.* 29. 13. we praise thy *g.* name
Neh. 9. 5. blessed be thy *g.* name
Ps. 45. 13. king's daughter *g.* within
72. 19. blessed be *g.* name for ever
145. 5. speak of *g.* honour of majesty
Is. 4. 2. branch of the Lord be *g.*
11. 10. be a root of Jesse, his rest *g.*
28. 1. *g.* beauty is a fading flower
60. 13. make the place of my feet *g.*
63. 1. who is this *g.* in apparel
12. that led them with his *g.* arm
Luke 13. 17. rejoiced for the *g.* things
Rom. 8. 21. into *g.* liberty of children
2 *Cor.* 3. 7. ministration engraven *g.*
3. 8. ministration of spirit rather *g.*
Eph. 5. 27. present it a *g.* church
Phil. 3. 21. fashioned like his *g.* body
Col. 1. 11. according to his *g.* power
1 *Tim.* 1. 11. according to *g.* gospel
Tit. 2. 13. looking for *g.* appearing
GLORIOUSLY, *Ex.* 15. 1. for he hath
    triumphed *g.*
Is. 24. 23. reign before ancients *g.*
GLORY, verb, *Ps.* 64. 10. the upright in
    heart shall *g.*
Ps. 106. 5. I may *g.* with thy inherita.
Jer. 4. 2. and in him shall they *g.*
9. 23. let not the wise, rich man *g.*
Rom. 4. 2. he hath whereof to *g.*
5. 3. we *g.* in tribulations also
1 *Cor.* 1. 29. no flesh *g.* in his presence
31. glorieth in *g.* L. 2 *Cor.* 10. 17.
9. 16. I have nothing to *g.* of
2 *Cor.* 11. 18. *g.* after the flesh, I will
    g. also
30. if *g.* I will *g.* of my infirmities
12. 1. it is not expedient for me to *g.*
5. will I *g.*, of myself I will not *g.*
9. will rather *g.* in my infirmities

GLORIETH, *Jer.* 9. 24. let him that *g.*
1 *Cor.* 1. 31; 2 *Cor.* 10. 17.
GLORYING, 1 *Cor.* 5. 6. your *g.* is not
    good
9. 15. than any sh. make my *g.* void
2 *Cor.* 7. 4. great is my *g.* of you
12. 11. I am become a fool in *g.*
GLUTTON. A voracious eater; one fond
    of much eating, *Deut.* 21. 20; *Prov.*
    23. 20, 21; 28. 7; *Matt.* 11. 19;
    Luke 7. 34.
GNASH, *Job* 16. 9; *Ps.* 35. 16. & 37. 12.
    & 112. 10; *Lam.* 2. 16; *Mark* 9. 18.
Matt. 8. 12. *g.* of teeth, 13. 42, 50. & 22.
    13. & 24. 51. & 25. 30; *Luke* 13. 28.
GNAT, *Matt.* 23. 24. who strained at a
    gnat
GNAW, *Zeph.* 3. 3; *Rev.* 16. 10.
GO, *Gen.* 32. 26. not let *g. Ex.* 3. 19;
    Job 27. 6; *Songs* 3. 4.
Ex. 4. 23. let *g.* 5. 1.
23. 23. shall *g.* 32. 34. & 33. 14; *Acts*
    25. 12.
Num. 22. 18. *g.* beyond, 1 *Thess.* 4. 6.
31. 23. *g.* through fire and water
Deut. 1. 33. by what way we should *g.*
4. 40. *g.* well with thee, 5. 16; 9. 13.
Judg. 6. 14; *g.* in, 2 *Sam.* 12. 21; *Matt.*
    8. 9; *Luke* 10. 37; *John* 6. 68.
Judg. 11. 35. *g.* back, *Ps.* 80. 18.
1 *Sam.* 12. 21. should *g. Prov.* 22. 6.
2 *Sam.* 12. 23. I shall *g.* to him, he shall
    not return to me
1 *Kings* 2. 2. I *g.* the way of all the
    earth, be strong
22. 4. wilt thou *g.* with me to battle,
    2 *Chr.* 18. 3.
Job 10. 21. I *g. Ps.* 39. 13. & 139. 7;
    Matt. 21. 30; *John* 7. 33. & 8. 14, 21.
Job 10. 21. before I *g.* whence shall not
    return, 16. 22.
Ps. 39. 13. before I *g.* hence, and be no
    more
84. 7. they *g.* from strength to strength
    till appear
85. 13. righteousness shall *g.* before
    him
89. 14. mercy and truth shall *g.* be-
    fore thy face
139. 7. whither *g.* from thy presence
Prov. 22. 6. train up a child in the way
    he should *g.*
Eccl. 3. 20. all *g.* unto one place, all are
    of the dust
5. 15. naked return, *g.* as he came
12. 5. mourners *g.* about the streets
Is. 3. 16. and mincing as they *g.*
6. 8. whom shall I send, and who
    will *g.* for us
Zech. 9. 14. and shall *g.* with whirlwinds
    of the south
Matt. 21. 30. I *g.* sir, and went not
26. 36. sit ye here, while I *g.* and pray
    yonder
28. 10. *g.* tell my brethren that they
    g. to Galilee
19. *g.* ye therefore and teach all na-
    tions
Luke 22. 33. I am ready to *g.* with thee
    to prison
John 6. 68. Lord, to whom shall we *g.*
8. 21. I *g.* my way, whither I *g.* ye

cannot come

14. 2. I g. to prepare a place for you

Jam. 4. 13. we will g. into such a city and buy

Gen. 45. 1. g. out, *Ps.* 60. 10; *Is.* 52. 11. & 55. 12; *Jer.* 51. 45; *Ezek.* 46. 9; *Matt.* 25. 6; *John* 10. 9; 1 *Cor.* 5. 10.

GO astray, *Ps.* 58. 3. they g. *astray* as soon as they be born

Prov. 5. 23. of his folly he shall g. *astray*

28. 10. whose causeth the righteous to g. *astray*

Jer. 50. 6. their shepherds caused them to g. *astray*

GO away, *Job* 4. 21. their excellency g. *away*

Matt. 8. 31. suffer us to g. *away* into the swine

25. 45. these g. *away* into everlasting punishment

John 6. 67. will ye also g. *away*

GO thy way, *Mark* 10. 52. g. *thy way*, faith made thee whole, *Luke* 17. 19.

John 4. 50. Jesus saith, g. *thy way*, thy son liveth

Acts 9. 15. g. *thy way*, is a chosen vessel

24. 25. Felix answered, g. *thy way* for this time

GO forward, *Ex.* 14. 15. speak to Israel that they g. *forward*

Job 23. 8. behold, I g. *forward*, but he is not there

GOING, *Matt.* 26. 46. rise, let us be g. behold, he is at hand

Rom. 10. 3. g. about to establish their righteousness

GOINGS, *Job* 34. 21. seeth all his g.

Ps. 17. 5. hold up my g. in thy way

40. 2. set my feet and establish my g.

68. 24. seen thy g. O God in sanctuary

121. 8. Lord preserve thy g. out and

Prov. 5. 21. ponders all his g.

20. 24. man's g. are of the Lord

Mic. 5. 2. whose g. are of old from

GOAD, S, 1 *Sam.* 13. 21. a file to sharpen the g.

Eccl. 12. 11. the words of the wise are as g. and nails

GOAT, *Lev.* 3. 12. his offering be a g.

16. 9. Aaron shall bring the g. on which the lot fell

22. he shall let go the g. in the wilderness

Is. 1. 11. delight not in blood of *he-g.*

Ezek. 34. 17. judge between rams and g.

Dan. 8. 5. he g. 8.; 21.

Zech. 10. 3. I punished the g.

Matt. 25. 32, 33. set g. on left hand

GOAT, Live-Goat, *Lev.* 16. 20. bring *live-g.*; 21. lay both hands on *l.-g.*

GOAT, Scape-Goat, *Lev.* 16. 8. and the other lot for the *scape-g.*

Lev. 16. 10. to let him go for a *scape-g.* into the wilderness

GOATS, *Gen.* 4. 4. Abel brought the firstling of the g.

Gen. 32. 14. two hundred *she-g.* and twenty *he-g.*

37. 21. Joseph's brethren killed a kid of the g.

Heb. 9. 12. nor entered by blood of g. and calves

13. if the blood of bulls and g. sanctifieth

10. 4. is not possible the blood of g. take away sin

GOD, *Gen.* 16. 13. Lord, thou G. seest

Gen. 31. 13. I am the G. of Bethel

45. 8. not you sent me hither, but G.

Num. 23. 23. what hath G. wrought

24. 23. who live when G. doeth this

Deut. 29. 13. that he may be to thee a G.

2 *Kings* 19. 15. thou art G. even thou

Neh. 9. 17. art a G. ready to pardon

Ps. 5. 4. not a G. hast pleasure in

Is. 12. 2. behold, G. is my salvation

44. 8. is there a G. besides me ? no

45. 22. I am G. there is none else

Hos. 11. 9. I am G. not man, Holy One

Mic. 7. 18. who is a G. like thee

Matt. 1. 23. name Emmanuel, wh. is G.

6. 24. ye cannot serve G. and mammon, *Luke* 16. 13.

19. 17. there is none good but one that is G. *Mark* 10. 18; *Luke* 18. 19.

John 1. 1. the Word was with G.

8. 41. we have one Father, even G.

Acts 10. 34. G. no respecter of persons

Rom. 3. 4. let G. be true, man a liar

15. 5. G. of patience and consolation

2 *Thess.* 2. 4. above all called G.

1 *Tim.* 3. 16. G. manifest in the flesh

Heb. 3. 4. he that built all things is G.

1 *John* 4. 12. no man hath seen G. at any time

Rev. 21. 4. G. shall wipe away all tears

GOD, against, 1 *Chr.* 5. 25. they transgressed *against* G.

Acts 5. 39. lest ye found to fight *a.* G.

6. 11. spoke blasphem, words *a.* G.

23. 9. let us not fight *against a.* G.

Rom. 8. 7. carnal mind enmity *a.* G.

9. 20. who art that repliest *a.* G.

GOD, before, *Ps.* 42. 2. when shall I appear *before* G.

Ps. 68. 3. let righteous rejoice *b.* G.

84. 7. every one in Zion appear *b.* G.

Luke 1. 6. were both righteous *b.* G.

12. 6. not one is forgotten *before* G.

Acts 7. 46. who found favour *before* G.

23. 1. lived in good conscience *b.* G.

Rom. 3. 19. world may become guilty *before* G.

2 *Cor.* 12. 19. we speak *b.* G. in Christ

1 *Tim.* 5. 4. good and acceptable *b.* G.

Jam. 1. 27. pure religion *before* G.

Rev. 20. 12. I saw dead stand *before* G.

GOD, eternal, *Deut.* 33. 27. the *eternal* G. is thy refuge

GOD, everlasting, *Gen.* 21. 33. Abraham called name of *everlasting* G.

Is. 40. 28. the *e.* G. fainteth not

Rom. 16. 26. commandment of *e.* G.

GOD, is, *Ex.* 20. 20. fear not, for G. *is*

Num. 23. 19. G. *is* not a man, that he

1 *Sam.* 28. 15. G. *is* departed from me

Job 33. 12. G. *is* greater than man

36. 26. G. *is* great, we know him not

Ps. 7. 11. G. *is* angry with the wicked

33. 12. blessed, whose G. *is* L. 144. 15.

46. 1. G. *is* our refuge and str. 62. 8.

5. G. *is* in midst of her, not moved

48. 3. G. *is* known in her palaces

54. 4. behold, G. is my helper
56. 9. this I know, for G. is for me
73. 1. truly G. is good to Israel
26. G. is the strength of my heart
118. 27. G. is Lord, that showed light
Eccl. 5. 2. G. is in hea. thou on earth
Zech. 8. 23. heard that G. is with you
Matt. 3. 9. G. is able of these stones to raise, Luke 3. 8.
22. 32. G. is not G. of dead, but living
John 4. 24. G. is a spirit; 13. 31. G. glorified
Acts 10. 34. G. is no respecter of persons
1 Cor. 1. 9. G. is faithful by wh. called
10. 13. G. is faithful, will not suffer
Eph. 2. 4. G. who is rich in mercy
Phil. 1. 8. G. is record, how I long
Heb. 11. 16. G. is not ashamed to be called their G.
12. 29. our G. is a consuming fire
13. 16. with such sacrifi. G. is pleased
GOD of Israel, Josh. 7. 19. to give glory to G. of Israel, 1 Sam. 6. 5.
1 Kings 8. 23. Lord G. of Israel, no G. is like thee, 2 Chr. 6. 14.
14. 13. good thing toward G. of Israel
1 Chr. 4. 10. Jabez called on G. of Israel
Ps. 41. 13. blessed be the Lord G. of Is. from everlasting to everlasting, 72. 18; 106. 48; Luke 1. 68.
Matt. 15. 31. multitude glorified G. of L.
GOD, living, Ps. 42. 2. my soul thirsteth for the l. G.
Matt. 16. 16. art Christ, son of l. G., John 6. 69.
Acts 14. 15. turn fr. vanities to l. G.
2 Cor. 3. 3. with the Spirit of l. G.
6. 16. ye are the temple of the l. G.
1 Thess. 1. 9. from idols to serve l. G.
1 Tim. 3. 15. the church of the l. G.
Heb. 3. 12. evil heart depart from l. G.
9. 14. purge conscience to serve l. G.
10. 31. to fall into hands of the l. G.
12. 22. come to Zion, city of l. G.
GOD, merciful, Ex. 34. 6. the Lord G. merciful, gracious
Deut. 4. 31. Lord thy God is a m. G.
Ps. 116. 5. gracious is Lord G. is m.
GOD, mighty, Ps. 50. 1. the m. G. hath spoken
132. 5. till I find an habitation for m. G.
Is. 9. 6. name shall be called the m. G.
Hab. 1. 12. O m. G. thou hast stab.
GOD, my, Ex. 15. 2. he is my G. my Father's
1 Chr. 28. 20. my G. will be with thee
Neh. 5. 19. think on me, my G. 13. 31.
13. 14. remember me, my G. 22.
Ps. 22. 1. my G. my G. why hast thou forsaken me; Matt. 27. 46.
31. 14. I said, thou art my G.
89. 26. thou art my Father, my G.
118. 28. art my G. I will praise thee
Is. 44. 17. deliver me, for thou art my G.
Dan. 6. 22. my G. hath sent his angel
Hos. 9. 2. Israel cry, my G. we know
Mic. 7. 7. I will wait. my G. will hear
John 20. 17. and say, I ascend to my G.
28. Thomas said, my L. and my G.
Phil. 4. 19. my G. supply your need
Rev. 3. 12. write on him name of my G.
GOD, no, Deut. 32. 39. is no G. with me

1 Kings 8. 23. no G. like thee, 2 Chr. 6. 14.
2 Chr. 32. 15. no G. of any nation
Ps. 14. 1. fool said, there is no G. 53. 1.
Is. 44. 6. besides me there is no G. 8; 45. 5, 14, 21.
GOD, of, Ps. 7. 10. my defence is of G.
Is. 53. 4. esteem him smitten of G.
John 1. 13. not of will of man, of G.
6. 46. he of G. hath seen the Father
7. 17. know doctrine whether of G.
Rom. 2. 29. praise not of men, of G.
1 Cor. 1. 30. who of G. is made wisdom
2 Cor. 2. 17. in sight of G. speak we
3. 5. our sufficiency is of G.
1 John 3. 10. doeth not righteousness, is not of G.
4. 1. try the spirits whether of G.
GOD, our 2 Chr. 2. 5. great is o. G. above all g.
14. 11. O Lord, thou art our G.
Ps. 40. 3. a new song, praise to o. G.
67. 6. G. our own G. shall bless us
68. 20. our G. is the G. of salvation
Is. 25. 9. this is our G. we have waited
Zech. 9. 7. remaineth be for our G.
GOD, their, Dan. 11. 32. people that know their G.
Zech. 12. 5. strength in Lord their G.
Heb. 11. 16. not ashamed to be call t. G.
GOD, thy, Ps. 42. 3. where is thy G. 10.
Ps. 45. 7. t. G. hath anointed, Heb. 1. 9.
50. 7. O Israel I am God, even thy G.
Is. 41. 10. be not dismayed, I am thy G.
52. 7. saith to Zion, thy G. reigneth
Dan. 6. 16. thy G. whom thou servest
20. is thy G. able to deliver
Amos 4. 12. prepare to meet thy G.
Jonah 1. 6. sleeper, arise, call upon t. G.
Mic. 6. 8. to walk humbly with thy G.
GOD, to, or unto, Gen. 40. 8. interpretation belong to G.
Job 22. 2. can a man be profitable to G.
34. 31. it is meet to be said unto G.
Eccl. 12. 7. spirit shall return unto G.
Matt. 22. 21. render u. G. things which are G.'s, Mark 12. 17; Luke 20. 25.
Rom. 6. 13. yield yourselves u. G. alive
14. 12. account of himself to G.
Heb. 7. 25. to save them come u. G.
11. 6. that cometh to G. must believe
1 Pet. 3. 18. Christ suffer bring us to G.
Rev. 5. 9. redeemed us to G. by blood
12. 5. child caught up unto G.
14. 4. first-fruits u. G. and Lamb
GOD, with, Gen. 5. 22. Enoch walked with G. 24.
Gen. 6. 9. Noah walked with G. 32. 28.
Job 9. 2. should man be just with G.
16. 21. might plead for a man with G.
25. 4. how can a man be just with G.
John 1. 1. the Word was with G.
5. 18. himself equal w. G. Phil. 2. 6.
Rom. 5. 1. by faith we have peace w. G.
1 Cor. 7. 24. every man therein abide with G.
2 Thess. 1. 6. a righteous thing with G.
Jam. 4. 4. friendship enmity with G.
1 Pet. 2. 20. this is acceptable with G.
GODDESS, 1 Kings 11. 5. Solomon went after the g.
Acts 19. 27. temple of g. Diana
35. Ephesians worshippers of the g.

37. nor yet blasphemies of your *g.*

GODHEAD, *Acts* 17. 29. nor think the *g.* like gold

Rom. 1. 20. his eternal power and *g.*

Col. 2. 9. in him the fulness of the *g.*

GODLY, *Ps.* 4. 3. Lord set apart him that is *g.*

Ps. 12. 1. help, for the *g.* man ceaseth

2 *Cor.* 1. 12. in *g.* sincerity our conv.

7. 9. sorry after a *g.* manner, 11.

10. for *g.* sorrow worketh repentance

11. 2. jealous over you with *g.* jeal.

2 *Tim.* 3. 12. all that live *g.* in Christ

Tit. 2. 12. that ye should live *g.*

2 *Pet.* 2. 9. how to deliver the *g.*

3 *John* 6. bring forward after *g.* sort

GODLINESS, 1 *Tim.* 2. 2. we may lead a life in *g.*

1 *Tim.* 3. 16. great is the mystery of *g.*

4. 8. *g.* is profitable unto all things

6. 5. supposing that gain is *g.*

6. but *g.* with contentment is gain

2 *Tim.* 3. 5. having a form of *g.*

2 *Pet.* 1. 3. things that pertain to *g.*

6. add to *g.* brotherly kindness, 7.

GOD-WARD, *Ex.* 18. 19. be thou for people to G.

2 *Cor.* 3. 4. have we thro. Christ to G.

1 *Thess.* 1. 8. your faith to G. is spread

GOLD, *Gen.* 2. 11. & 13. 2; *Is.* 2. 7.

Job 23. 10. I shall come forth like *g.*

28. 6. as for the earth, it hath the dust of *g.*

15. wisdom cannot be gotten for *g.* nor silver

16. it cannot be valued with the *g.* of Ophir

31. 24. if I made *g.* my hope, fine *g.*

36. 19. will he esteem thy riches ? no not *g.*

Ps. 19. 10. more desired than *g.* fine *g.*

72. 15. to him shall be given of the *g.* of Sheba

119. 127. loving commandments above *g.* fine *g.* 72.

Prov. 8. 19. my fruit is better than *g.*

11. 22. as a jewel of *g.* in a swine's snout

16. 16. much better is it to get wisdom than *g.*

Is. 13. 13. man more precious than *g.*

60. 17. for brass I will bring *g.*

Lam. 4. 1. how is the *g.* become dim

Zech. 13. 9. I will try them as *g.* is tried

1 *Tim.* 2. 9. adorn not with *g.* 1 *Pet.* 3. 3.

1 *Pet.* 1. 7. trial of faith more precious than *g.*

Rev. 3. 18. buy of me *g.* tried in the fire

17. 4. the woman was decked with *g.* and pearls

18. 16. that great city that was decked with *g.*

GOLD, pure, 2 *Chr.* 9. 17. he overlaid the throne with *pure g.*

Job 28. 19. wisdom not to be valued with *pure g.*

Ps. 21. 3. settest a crown of *pure g.* on his head

Rev. 21. 18. city was *pure g.;* 21. street of *pure g.*

GOLD with silver, 1 *Kings* 20. 3. *silver* and *g.* is mine; 5. deliver *silver*

and *g.*

Ps. 68. 13. covered with *silver* her feathers with *g.*

Prov. 17. 3. refining-pot for *silver,* furnace for *g.* 27. 21.

Songs 1. 11. make borders of *g.* with studs of *silver*

Is. 2. 7. the land also is full of *silver* and *g.*

Hos. 2. 8. did not know I multiplied her *silver* and *g.*

Hag. 2. 8. the *silver* is mine, and the *g.* is mine

Mal. 3. 3. he shall purge them as *g.* and *silver*

Matt. 10. 9. provide neither *g.* nor *silver,* nor brass

Acts 3. 6. Peter said, *silver* and *g.* have I none

17. 29. nor think Godhead is like to *silver* and *g.*

20. 33. coveted no man's *silver* or *g.*

1 *Cor.* 3. 12. if build *g.,* silver, precious stones

Jam. 5. 3. your *g.* and *silver* cankered

1 *Pet.* 1. 18. we were not redeemed with *silver* and *g.*

GOLDEN, *Esth.* 4. 11. king shall hold out a *g.* sceptre, 5. 2; 8. 4.

Eccl. 12. 6. *g.* bowl be broken

Rev. 1. 12. I saw seven *g.* condlesticks

2. 1. who walketh in midst of the *g.* candlesticks

5. 8. *g.* vials, 15. 7; 8. 3. having a *g.*

14. 14. on his head a *g.* crown; 17. 4. a *g.* cup full

21. 15. had a *g.* reed to measure the city and gates

GONE, *Job* 7. 4. when shall I rise. and the night be gone

Ps. 38. 10. light of mine eyes is *g.*

109. 23. I am *g.* like the shadow that declineth

Songs 6. 1. whither is thy beloved *g.*

John 4. 8. for his disciples were *g.* to buy meat

GONE about, *Acts* 24. 6. *g. about* to profane temple

GONE astray, *Ps.* 119. 176. *g. astray* like lost sheep

Is. 53. 6. all we like sheep have *g. astray*

Matt. 18. 12. if a man have 100 sheep, and one of them be *g. astray,* he seeketh that which is *g. astray*

GONE out, *Ps.* 19. 4. their line is *g. out* through all the earth

Is. 45. 23. th: word is *g. out* of my mouth

Matt. 25. 8. our lamps are *g. out*

Mark 5. 30. that virtue had *g. out* of him, *Luke* 8. 46.

Rom. 3. 12. all *g. out* of way

GONE up, *Gen.* 49. 9. from the prey, my son, thou art *g. up*

Ps. 47. 5. God *g. up* with shout

GOOD, *Deut.* 6. 24. & 10. 13.

Gen. 1. 31. all things were very *g.*

2. 18. not *g.* for man to be alone

32. 12. I will surely do thee *g.*

50. 20. God meant it unto *g.* 45. 5, 7.

2 *Kings* 20. 19. *g.* is word of Lord, *Is.* 39. 8.

Job 2. 10. shall we receive *g.* at the hand

of God
24. 21. doeth not *g.* to the widow
Ps. 4. 6. many say, who will show us
   any *g.*
14. 1. none doeth *g.* not one, 3.
34. 8. taste, see, Lord is *g.*
73. 1. truly God is *g.* to Israel
85. 12. I will give what is *g.* 84. 11.
86. 5. thou Lord art *g.* ready to forg.
106. 5. see the *g.* of thy chosen
119. 68. thou art *g.* Lord doest *g.*
145. 9. Lord is *g.* to all, 136. 1.
Prov. 17. 22. a merry heart doeth *g.* like
   a medicine
Eccl. 7. 20. that doeth *g.* and sinneth
   not
9. 18. one sinner destroyeth much *g.*
Matt. 19. 17. why call me *g.* none *g.* but
John 5. 29. that have done *g.* to the
   resurrection
Acts 10. 38. who went about doing *g.*
Rom. 2. 10. honour to every man that
   worketh *g.*
Rom. 3. 8. do evil that *g.* may come
7. 18. how to perform what is *g.* I find
1 *Thess.* 5. 15. follow *g.* 3 *John* 11.
1 *John* 3. 17. who hath this world's *g.*
   and shutteth up
GOOD for, *Ps.* 86. 17. show me a token
   for *g.*
Rom. 8. 28. we know all things work
   together *for g.*
13. 4. minister of God to thee *for g.*
GOOD, adjective, *Deut.* 33. 16. for *g.*
   will of him that dwelt in bush
1 *Sam.* 12. 23. I will teach you the *g.*
   and right way
25. 15. men were very *g.* to us
2 *Chr.* 19. 11. the Lord shall be with
   the *g.*
Ps. 25. 8. *g.* and upright is the Lord,
   therefore
37. 23. steps of a *g.* man are ordered
   by the Lord
Jer. 6. 16. where is the *g.* way, and walk
   therein
Matt. 7. 11. know how to give *g.* gifts,
   Luke 11. 13.
17. every *g.* tree bringeth forth *g.*
   fruit, 18.
9. 22. daughter, be of *g.* comfort,
   Luke 8. 48.
13. 24. *g.* seed; 19. 16. *g.* Master, what
   g. thing
25. 21. well done, thou *g.* and faithful
   servant
John 10. 11. I am the *g.* shepherd, the
   g. shepherd giveth
Tit. 1. 8. a bishop must be a lover of *g.*
GOOD, is, *Gen.* 2. 12. gold of that land
   is *g.*
Eccl. 6. 12. who knoweth what is *g.* for
   man in life
Lam. 3. 25. Lord is *g.* to them that wait
   for him
Mic. 6. 8. showed thee, O man, what
   is *g.*
Mark 9. 50. salt is *g.* but if the salt,
   Luke 14. 34.
1 *Thess.* 5. 21. prove all things, hold
   fast that which is *g.*
1 *Tim.* 1. 8. but we know that the law
   is *g.*

5. 4. is *g.* and acceptable before God
1 *Pet.* 3. 13. be followers of which is *g.*
GOOD, it is, *Ps.* 52. 9. I will wait on
   thy name, for it is *g.* 54. 6.
Ps. 73. 28. it is *g.* for me to draw near
   to God
92. 1. it is *g.* to give thanks
119. 71. it is *g.* for me that I have been
   afflicted
Gal. 4. 18. it is *g.* to be zealously affected always
GOOD man, *Ps.* 37. 23. steps of a *g. man*
   are ordered by the Lord
Prov. 12. 2. a *g. man* obtaineth favour
   of the Lord
14. 14. a *g. man* is satisfied from himself, 12. 14.
Matt. 12. 35. *g. man* out of good treasure, *Luke* 6. 45.
Luke 23. 50. Joseph was a *g. man*
John 7. 12. is a *g. man*, others said, nay
Acts 11. 24. Barnabas was a *g. man*, full
   of the Holy Ghost
GOOD, not, *Gen.* 2. 18. it is *not g.* that
   man should be alone
Prov. 19. 2. that the soul be without
   knowledge is *not g.*
20. 23. and a false balance is *not g.*
1 *Cor.* 5. 6. your glorifying is *not g.*
GOOD things, *Ps.* 103. 5. satisfieth
   mouth with *g. things*
Matt. 7. 11. give *g. things* to them that
   ask him
12. 34. how can ye being evil speak
   g. things
Luke 1. 53. he hath filled the hungry
   with *g. things*
16. 25. receivedst thy *g. things*
Rom. 10. 15. and bring glad tidings of
   g. things
Heb. 10. 1. the law having a shadow of
   g. things to come
GOOD tidings, 2 *Sam.* 18. 27. a good
   man, and cometh with *g. tidings*
1 *Kings* 1. 42. a valiant man, and bringest *g. tidings*
Is. 49. 9. O Zion, that bringest *g. tidings*
41. 27. I will give Jerusalem one that
   bringeth *g. tidings*
52. 7. the feet of him that bringeth *g.*
   tidings
61. 1. he hath anointed me to preach
   g. tidings
Luke 2. 10. I bring you *g. tidings* of
   great joy
1 *Thess.* 3. 6. brought us *g. tidings* of
   your faith
GOOD WORK, S, *Neh.* 2. 18. hand for
   this *g. work*
Matt. 26. 10. wrought a *g. work* on me
John 10. 33. for *g. work* stone thee not
2 *Cor.* 9. 8. abound to every *g. work*
Phil. 1. 6. begun a *g. work* will finish it
Col. 1. 10. fruitful in every *g. work*
2 *Thess.* 2. 17. establish you in every *g.*
1 *Tim.* 5. 10. followed every *g. work*
2 *Tim.* 2. 21. prepared to every *g. work*
   Tit. 3. 1.
Tit. 1. 16. to every *g. work* reprobate
Heb. 13. 21. perfect in every *g. work*
Matt. 5. 16. may see your *g. works*
John 10. 32. many *g. works* have I

Acts 9. 36. Dorcas was full of *g.* works
Rom. 13. 3. not a terror to *g.* works
Eph. 2. 10. created in Christ Jesus to *g.* works
1 *Tim.* 2. 10. but with *g. works* professing godliness
    5. 10. well reported of for *g.* works
    25. the *g. works* of some are manifest
Tit. 3. 8. be careful to maintain *g.* works, 14.
Heb. 10. 24. provoke to love and to *g.* works
1 *Pet.* 2. 12. may by your *g.* works which
GOODLY, *Gen.* 27. 15. Rebekah took *g.* raiment
Gen. 39. 6. Joseph was a *g.* person
Ex. 2. 2. she saw he was a *g.* child
Num. 24. 5. how *g.* are thy tents, O Jacob
Josh. 7. 21. I saw a *g.* Babylonish garment
Ps. 16. 6. yea, I have a *g.* heritage
Matt. 13. 45. merchant seeking *g.* pearls
Jam. 2. 2. if there come a man in *g.* apparel
GOODLINESS, *Is.* 40. 6. the *g.* thereof as the flower of the field
GOODNESS, *Ex.* 33. 19. make my *g.* pass
Ex. 34. 6. Lord God abundant in *g.* and truth
2 *Chr.* 6. 41. let saints rejoice in *g.*
Neh. 9. 25. delight themselves in thy *g.*
    9. 35. not served thee in thy great *g.*
Ps. 23. 6. *g.* and mercy shall follow me
    27. 13. believed to see *g.* of Lord in the land of the living
    31. 19. how great is thy *g.* Zech. 9. 17.
    33. 5. earth is full of *g.* of Lord, 145. 7.
    52. 1. *g.* of God endureth
    65. 4. satisfied with *g.* of thy house
    11. crownest year with thy *g.*
Is. 63. 7. great *g.* bestowed on Israel
Hos. 3. 5. fear the Lord and his *g.*
Rom. 2. 4. *g.* of God leads to repent.
    11. 22. behold the *g.* and severity of God
Gal. 5. 22. fruit of Spirit is *g. Eph.* 5. 9.
GORGEOUS, *Luke* 23. 11. Herod arrayed Jesus in a *g.* robe
GORGEOUSLY, *Ezek.* 23. 12. she doted on Assyrians clothed most *g.*
Luke 7. 25. that are *g.* apparelled in king's courts
GOSPEL, good news; a revelation of the grace of God to fallen man, through a Mediator; and a means which, by the Spirit, saves men from perdition. The word is also used to mean the narrative of our Saviour's life, death, and resurrection; and sometimes for the doctrines contained in that narrative. The term is found in ancient Greek writers. Plutarch, in his life of Pompey, says, the messenger arrived at Pontus, ' bringing the gospel,' i.e., the joyful intelligence.
GOSPEL, *Mark* 1. 1, 15. & 8. 35.
Matt. 4. 23. preaching *g.* of kingdom
Mark 16. 15. preach *g.* to every creature
Acts 20. 24. *g.* of the grace of God

Rom. 1. 1. *g.* of God, 15. 16; 1 *Tim.* 1. 11.
1 *Cor.* 1. 17. but to preach the *g.*
    4. 15. I have begotten you through *g.*
    9. 14. that preach *g.* live of *g.*
2 *Cor.* 4. 3. if our *g.* be hid
    4. glorious *g.*
    11. 4. another *g.* which ye, *Gal.* 1. 6.
Gal. 1. 8. preach any other *g.* 9.
Eph. 1. 13. *g.* of salvation
    6. 15. *g.* of peace
Phil. 1. 27. becoming *g.*—faith of *g.*
    5. fellowship in *g.*
Col. 1. 5. truth of *g. Gal.* 2. 5.
    23. hope of *g.*
1 *Thess.* 1. 5. our *g.* came in power
Heb. 4. 2. unto us was *g.* preached
1 *Pet.* 4. 6. *g.* was preached to dead
Rev. 14. 6. having everlas. *g.* to preach
GOVERN, *Ps.* 67. 4. thou shalt *g.* the nations
GOVERNMENT, S, *Is.* 9. 6. *g.* shall be upon his shoulder
Is. 9. 7. of the increase of his *g.* there shall be no end
1 *Cor.* 12. 28. *g.* diversities of tongue
2 *Pet.* 2. 10. them that despise *g.*
GOVERNOR, S, *Gen.* 42. 6. Joseph *g.* over land, 45. 26.
Ezra 5. 14. Cyrus deliv. vessels to *g.*
Hag. 2. 2. speak to Zerubbabel the son of *g.* 21.
Mal. 1. 8. offer it now to thy *g.*
John 2. 8. bear to the *g.* of the feast
2 *Cor.* 11. 32. the *g.* under Aretas
Matt. 10. 18. shall be brought before *g.*
1 *Pet.* 2. 14. submit yourselves to *g.*
GOURD, S, 2 *Kings* 4. 39. one gathered wild *g.*
Jonah 4. 6. God prepared *g.* Jona. glad
GRACE, *Ezra* 9. 8; *Esth.* 2. 17.
Ps. 84. 11. Lord will give *g.* and glory
Prov. 3. 34. giveth *g.* unto the lowly
Zech. 4. 7. with shoutings, crying, *g. g.*
    12. 10. spirit of *g.* and supplication
John 1. 14. of Father full of *g.* and truth
    16. of fulness we received *g.* for *g.*
    17. *g.* and truth came by Jesus Christ
Acts 14. 3. testimony to word of his *g.*
    18. 27. helped them who believed through *g.*
Rom. 1. 5. by whom we received *g.*
Rom. 3. 24. justified freely by his *g.*
    5. 20. *g.* did much more abound
    21. *g.* reigned through righteousness to eternal life
    6. 14. not under law but *g.*
    11. 5. according to the election of *g.*
    6. if by *g.* then not of works, otherwise *g.* is no more *g.*
1 *Cor.* 10. 30. if I by *g.* be a partaker
    15. 10. his *g.* bestowed not in vain
2 *Cor.* 4. 15. *g.* redound to glory of *G.*
    9. 8. God is able to make *g.* abound
    12. 9. my *g.* is sufficient for thee
Gal. 1. 15. God, who called me by his *g.*
Eph. 1. 6. the praise of the glory of *g.*
    7. forgiveness, accor. to riches of *g.*
Eph. 2. 5. by *g.* ye are saved, 8.
    7. show exceeding riches of his *g.*
    4. 29. minister *g.* to hearers
    6. 24. *g.* with all that love Lord Jesus
Col. 3. 16. singing with *g.* in hearts

4. 6. let speech be alway with g.

2 *Thess.* 2. 16. given us hope through g.

1 *Tim.* 1. 2. g. mercy and peace from
     G. our Father, and our Lord J.C.

2 *Tim.* 1. 2; *Tit.* 1. 4; 2 *John* 3.

Tit. 3. 7. justified by his g.

Heb. 4. 16. come boldly to throne of g.
     12. 28. let us have g. whereby
     13. 9. heart be established with g.

1 *Pet.* 3. 7. heirs of g. of life
     5. 5. he giveth g. to humble

2 *Pet.* 3. 18. grow in g. and knowledge

Rom. 1. 7. g. and peace to you, 1 *Cor.*
     1. 3; 2 *Cor.* 1. 2; *Gal.* 1. 3; *Eph.* 1.
     2; *Phil.* 1. 2; *Col.* 1. 2; 1 *Thess.*
     1; 2 *Thess.* 1. 2; *Philem.* 3; 1 *Pet.*
     1. 2; 2 *Pet.* 1. 2; *Jude* 4; *Rev.* 1. 4.

GRACE of God, *Luke* 2. 40. of God
     was upon him

Acts 11. 23. when he had seen g. of God
     20. 24. testify the gospel of g. of God

1 *Cor.* 1. 4. the g. of God given by J.C.
     3. 10. accord. to g. of God given to me
     15. 10. by g. of God I am what I am,
     yet not I, but g. of God was with me

2 *Cor.* 1. 12. by g. of God we had con-
     versation
     6. 1. receive not g. of God in vain
     8. 1. of g. of God bestowed on church.
     9. 14. for the exceeding g. of God in
     you

Gal. 2. 21. I do not frustrate g. of God

Col. 1. 6. knew g. of God in truth

1 *Pet.* 4. 10. stewards of manifold g. of
     Christ
     5. 12. this is true g. of God in which
     we stand

Jude 4. turning g. of God into lascivi-
     ousness

GRACE of our Lord Jesus Christ, *Acts*
     15. 11. g. of our Lord Jesus Christ

Rom. 16. 20, 24; 1 *Cor.* 16. 23; 2 *Cor.*
     8. 9. & 13. 14; *Gal.* 6. 18; *Phil.* 4. 23;
     1 *Thess.* 5. 28; 2 *Thess.* 3. 18;
     Philem. 25.

Rev. 22. 21. g. of our Lord Jesus Christ
     be with you all

GRACIOUS, *Gen.* 43. 29. God be g.
     unto thee

Ex. 22. 27. I will hear for I am g.
     33. 19. will be g. to whom I will be g.
     34. 6. Lord God merciful and g. 2 *Chr.*
     30. 9; *Neh.* 9. 17, 31; *Ps.* 103. 8. &
     116. 5. & 145. 8; *Joel* 2. 13.

Num. 6. 25. Lord be g. 2 *Sam.* 12. 22.

Job 33. 24. then he is g. to him, and

Ps. 77. 9. hath God forgotten to be g.
     86. 15. full of compassion and g. 111.
     4. & 112. 4.

Is. 30. 18. Lord wait that he may be g.
     19. he will be very g. to thee, 33. 2.

Amos 5. 15. may be the Lord will be g.

Jonah 4. 2. knew that thou art g. God

Mal. 1. 9. beseech God be g. *Is.* 33. 2.

1 *Pet.* 2. 3. if ye tasted that Lord is g.

GRACIOUSLY, *Gen.* 33. 5, 11; *Ps.* 119.
     29.

Hos. 14. 2. receive us g.

GRAIN, *Matt.* 13. 31. kingdom of hea-
     ven is like a g. of mustard-seed,
     Mark 4. 31; *Luke* 13. 19.

Matt. 17. 20. faith as a g. of mustard-

seed, ye shall say to this mountain
     remove, *Luke* 17. 6.

1 *Cor.* 15. 37. bare g. wheat or other g.

GRANDMOTHER, 2 *Tim.* 1. 5. faith
     dwelt in thy g. Lois

GRANT, 1 *Sam.* 1. 17. God g. thee thy
     petition

2 *Chr.* 12. 7. I will g. them deliverance

Esth. 5. 1. please the king g. my peti.

Ps. 20. 4. g. thee to thine own heart
     85. 7. O Lord, g. us salvation

Matt. 20. 21. g. my two sons may sit,
     Mark 10. 37.

Rom. 15. 5. God g. you to be like-mind.

Eph. 3. 16. g. you to be strengthened

2 *Tim.* 1. 18. Lord g. he may find mercy

Rev. 3. 21. will I g. to sit on my throne

GRANTED, *Job* 10. 12. thou hast g. life
     and favour

Acts 11. 18. God g. Gentiles repentance

GRAPE, *Deut.* 32. 14. didst drink blood
     of g.

Jer. 31. 29. fathers have eaten a sour g.

GRAPE-gatherer, *Jer.* 6. 9. turn back
     thy hand as a g.-*gatherer*

Jer. 49. 9. if g.-gatherer come, *Obad.* 5.

GRAPES, *Gen.* 40. 10. clusters brought
     ripe g.

Gen. 49. 11 washed clothes in blood
     of g.

Num. 13. 20. the time of the first ripe g.

Deut. 23. 24. thou mayest eat g. thy fill
     24. 21. when thou gatherest the g.

Songs 2. 13. tender g. 15.
     7. 7. clusters of g.

Is. 5. 2. it should bring forth g.
     4. brought forth wild g.

Jer. 25. 30. a shout, as they that tread g.

Ezek. 18. 2. sour g.

Mic. 7. 1. soul desireth the first ripe g.

Matt. 7. 16. do men ga. g. of thorns

Luke 6. 44. nor of bramble ga. they g.

Rev. 14. 18. her g. are fully ripe

GRASS, *Ps.* 37. 2. & 90. 5. & 92. 7. &
     102. 4, 11; *Is.* 44. 4. & 51. 12.

Ps. 103. 15. man's days are like g.

Is. 40. 6. all flesh is g. 7. 8; 1 *Pet.* 1. 24;
     Jam. 1. 10, 11.

Matt. 6. 30. if God so clothe the g.

Rev. 8. 7. green g.; 9. 4. hurt g.

GRAVE, *Gen.* 35. 20. Jacob set up a
     pillar upon her g. that is the pillar
     of Rachel's g.

Gen. 37. 35. I will go down to g. to my
     son, mourning
     42. 38. bring grey hairs with sorrow
     to the g. 44. 31.

1 *Sam.* 2. 6. Lord bringeth down to g.

Job 5. 26. come to thy g. in a full age
     14. 13. hide me in g. 17. 13.

Ps. 6. 5. in the g. who shall give thanks
     30. 3. Lord brought my soul from g.
     49. 15. redeem my soul from the
     power of the g.

Prov. 1. 12. swallow alive as g.

Eccl. 9. 10. no wisdom in the g. whither

Songs 8. 6. jealousy is cruel as the g.

Is. 38. 10. shall go to the gates of the g.
     18. g. cannot praise thee
     53. 9. made his g. with the wicked

Hos. 13. 14. power of g. O g. I will be
     thy destruction

1 *Cor.* 15. 55. O *g.* where is thy victory
GRAVEN, verb, *Hab.* 2. 18. the maker hath *g.* it
Is. 49. 16. I have *g.* thee upon palms
GRAVEN, *Ex.* 32. 16. writing of God *g.* on tables
Job 19. 24. *g.* with iron pen
Jer. 17. 1. sin *g.* on tables of their hearts
GRAVEN image, S, *Ex.* 20. 4. thou shalt not make unto thee any *g. i.*
Lev. 26. 1; *Deut.* 5. 8.
Deut. 7. 5. ye shall burn their *g. i.*
Ps. 97. 7. confounded all that serve *g. i.*
Is. 40. 19. the workman melteth *g. i.*
42. 17. be ashamed that trust in *g. i.*
44. 9. they that make *g. i.* are vanity
GRAVES, *Ex.* 14. 11. were no *g.* in
Matt. 27. 52. the *g.* were opened
John 5. 28. all in *g.* shall hear his voice
GRAVITY, 1 *Tim.* 3. 4. children in subjection with *g.*
Tit. 2. 7. in doctrine showing *g.*
GRAY, *Ps.* 71. 18; *Prov.* 20. 29; *Hos.* 7. 9.
GREAT. The word means rich, powerful, celebrated, magnificent, illustrious, ancient, *Gen.* 12. 2. & 30. 8.
Deut. 11. 7. have seen *g.* acts of the L.
29. 24. *g.* anger, 2 *Chr.* 34. 21.
1 *Sam.* 6. 9 *g.* evil, *Neh.* 13. 27; *Eccl.* 2. 21; *Jer.* 44. 7; *Dan.* 9. 12.
Ps. 47. 2. *g.* King, 48. 2. & 95. 3; *Mal.* 1. 14; *Matt.* 5. 35.
Job 32. 9. *g.* men, *Jer.* 5. 5.
Ex. 32. 11. *g.* power, *Neh.* 1. 10; *Job* 23. 6; *Ps.* 147. 5; *Num.* 1. 3; *Acts* 4. 33. & 8. 10; *Rev.* 11. 17.
32. 21. so *g. Deut.* 4. 7, 8; 1 *Kings* 3. 9; *Ps.* 77. 13. & 103. 11; *Matt.* 8. 10. & 15. 33; 2 *Cor.* 1. 10; *Heb.* 2. 3. & 12. 1; *Rev.* 16. 18. & 18. 17.
Job 5. 9. *g.* things, 9. 10. & 37. 5; *Jer.* 45. 5; *Hos.* 8. 12; *Luke* 1. 49.
Gen. 6. 5. *g.* wickedness, 39. 9; *Job* 22. 5; *Joel* 3. 13; 2 *Chr.* 28. 13.
Job 33. 12. God is *g.* than man
Matt. 12. 42. a *g.* than Solomon is here
John 1. 50. see *g.* things than these
4. 12. thou art *g.* than, 8. 53.
10. 29. my Father is *g.* than all
14. 28. my Father is *g.* than I
1 *Cor.* 14. 5. *g.* is he that prophesieth
1 *John* 4, 4. *g.* is he that is in you, 3. 20.
5. 9. witness of God is *g.*
1 *Sam.* 30. 6. David was *g.* distressed
2 *Sam.* 24. 10. I have sinned *g.* in that
1 *Kings* 18. 3. Obadiah feared Lord *g.*
1 *Chr.* 16. 25. *g.* is the Lord, and *g.* to be praised, *Ps.* 48. 1. & 96. 4. & 145. 3.
2 *Chr.* 33. 12. Manasseh humbled himself *g.* before God
Job 3. 25. thing I *g.* feared is come
Ps. 28. 7. my heart *g.* rejoiceth
47. 9. God he is *g.* exalted
89. 7. God is *g.* to be feared in assem-
116. 10. I spoke, I was *g.* afflicted
Dan. 9. 23. O man *g.* beloved, 10. 11, 19.
Mark 12. 27. ye do *g.* err
Ex. 15. 7. *g.* of thy excellency
Num. 14. 19. pardon according to *g.* of mercy
Deut. 32. 3. ascribe ye *g.* to our God

1 *Chr.* 29. 11. thine is *g.* 2 *Chr.* 9. 6.
Neh. 13. 22. spare according to *g.* of mercy
Ps. 66. 3. *g.* of thy power, 79. 11; *Eph.* 1. 19.
145. 3. his *g.* is unsearchable, 6.
Is. 63. 1. travelling in *g.* of his strength
GREEDY of gain, *Prov.* 1. 19. & 15. 27.
Is. 56. 11. they are *g.* dogs never enough
1 *Tim.* 3. 3. not *g.* of filthy lucre, 8
GREEDILY, *Prov.* 21. 26. he coveteth *g.* all day
Jude 11. ran *g.* after error of Balaam
GREEDINESS, *Eph.* 4. 19. given over to work all uncleanness with *g.*
GREEN, *Gen.* 1. 30. to beast *g.* herb for meat
Gen. 9. 3. as *g.* herb I have given you all
Job 15. 32. his branch shall not be *g.*
Ps. 37. 35. wicked spread like *g.* bay-tree
Hos. 14. 8. I am like a *g.* fir-tree
GREEN tree, *Luke* 23. 31. do these things in *g.* tree
GREET, *Rom.* 16. 3. *g.* Priscilla and Aquila
Rom. 16. 5. *g.* the church; 6. *g.* Mary
8. *g.* Amplias; 11. *g.* household
1 *Cor.* 16. 20. breth. *g.* you, *Phil.* 4. 21.
20. *g.* one another, 2 *Cor.* 13. 12; 1 *Pet.* 5. 14.
1 *Thess.* 5. 26. *g.* brethren with holy kiss
2 *Tim.* 4. 21. Eubulus *g.* thee, Pudens
GREETING, S, *Matt.* 23. 7. *g.* in the markets, *Luke* 11. 43; 20. 46.
Acts 15. 23. apostles, elders send *g.*
Jam. 1. 1. to the 12 tribes abroad, *g.*
GREW, *Ex.* 1. 12. more afflicted, more *g.*
1 *Sam.* 2. 21. the child Samuel *g.* 26.
2 *Sam.* 5. 10. David went on, *g.* great
Ezek. 17. 6. *g.* and became spreading
Mark 4. 7. and the thorns *g.* up
Luke 1. 80. child *g.* and waxed, 2. 40.
Acts 7. 17. people *g.* and multiplied
12. 24. the word of God *g.* and
19. 20. mightily *g.* the word of God
GRIEF, *Is.* 53. 3, 4, 10; *Heb.* 13. 17.
Gen. 6. 5. *g.* him at his heart
Judg. 10. 16. his soul was *g.* for misery
Ps. 95. 10. forty years long was I *g.* with
119. 158. I beheld transgressors and was *g.* 139. 21.
Is. 54. 6. woman forsaken and *g.* in
Jer. 5. 3. smitten they have not *g.*
Lam. 3. 33. nor *g.* children of men
Amos 6. 6. not *g.* for affliction of Joseph
Mark 3. 5. being *g.* for hardness of heart
10. 22. went away *g.* for he had great
Rom. 14. 15. if brother be *g.* at thy meat
Ps. 10. 5. his ways are always *g.*
Matt. 23. 4. burdens are *g.* to be borne
Acts 20. 29. death shall *g.* wolves enter
Phil. 3. 1. to me indeed is not *g.*
Heb. 12. 11. no chastening for the present is joyous but *g.*
1 *John* 5. 3. his commandments are not *g.*
Matt. 8. 6. *g.* tormented, 15. 22.
GRIND faces of poor, *Is.* 3. 15.
Matt. 21. 44. it will *g.* him to powder
GRINDERS, *Job* 29. 17. I brake the *g.* of the wicked

Eccl. 12. 3. the *g.* cease, because they are few

GRINDING, *Eccl.* 12. 4. sound of the *g.* is low

Matt. 24. 41. two women *g.* at the mill, *Luke* 17. 35.

GROAN, *Rom.* 8. 23. we ourselves *g.* within ourselves

2 *Cor.* 5. 2. in this we *g.* desiring
4. we in this tabernacle do *g.* being burdened

GROANED, *John* 11. 33. he *g.* in spirit and was troubled

GROANETH, *Rom.* 8. 22. the whole creation *g.* and

GROANING, S, *Ps.* 6. 6. weary with *g.*
38. 9. my *g.* is not hid from thee
102. 20. to hear the *g.* of prisoners

Rom. 8. 26. *g.* that cannot be uttered

GROSS, *Is.* 60. 2. and *g.* darkness shall cover the people

Matt. 13. 15. people's heart is waxed *g.*
Acts 28. 27.

GROUND. The earth. Sitting on the ground was the posture of mourning and deep distress, *Lam.* 2. 10.

Gen. 2. 7. formed man of dust of the *g.*
19. out of the *g.* the Lord formed
3. 17. cursed is the *g.* for thy
8. 21. not again curse the *g.*

Ex. 3. 5. standest is holy *g.*

Job 5. 6. trouble spring out of the *g.*
14. 8. stock thereof die in the *g.*

Ps. 107. 33. water-springs into dry *g.*

Is. 35. 7. parched *g.* become a pool

Jer. 4. 3. break up fallow *g.*

Matt. 13. 8. other fell into good *g.*

Mark 4. 26. as if man cast seed into *g.*

Luke 2. 16. the *g.* of a certain rich
8. 8. fell into good *g.*
13. 7. why cumbereth it the *g.*
14. 18. I have bought a piece of *g.*

John 4. 5. near the parcel of *g.*
12. 24. corn of wheat fall into *g.*

GROUND, on or upon, *Ex.* 4. 3. cast the rod on the *g.*
9. 23. fire ran along the *g.*

1 *Sam.* 14. 25. honey upon the *g.*

2 *Sam.* 14. 14. as water spilt on the *g.*

Is. 3. 26. shall sit on the *g.* 47. 1; *Jer.* 25. 33; *Lam.* 2. 10; *Matt.* 15. 35.

Matt. 10. 29. not fall to the *g.*

Mark 5. 4. some fell on stony *g. Luke* 8. 8, 15.

1 *Tim.* 3. 15. pillar and *g.* of truth

Eph. 3. 17. rooted and *g.* in love

Col. 1. 23. in the faith *g.* and settled

GROW. To vegetate. *Gen.* 2. 5; to become rich, *Gen.* 26. 13; the prevalency of the gospel, *Acts* 12. 24.

Gen. 2. 9. God made every tree to *g.*

Judg. 16. 22. the hair of the head began to *g.*

2 *Sam.* 23. 5. desire, though make it not to *g.*

Ps. 92. 12. *g.* like a cedar in Lebanon

Eccl. 11. 5. nor how the bones *g.* in the womb

Is. 11. 1. and a branch shall *g.* out of his roots
53. 2. *g.* up as a tender plant

Jer. 33. 15. the branch of righteousness

to *g.* to David

Hos. 14. 5. shall *g.* as the lily
7. *g.* as the vine

Zech. 6. 12. name is BRANCH, he shall *g.*

Mal. 4. 2. shall *g.* up as calves of stall

Matt. 6. 28. consider the lilies how they *g. Luke* 12. 27.
13. 30. *g.* together till harvest

Mark 4. 27. seed should *g.* up, he knoweth not how

Eph. 2. 21. *g.* unto holy temple
4. 15. may *g.* up into him in all things

1 *Pet.* 2. 2. milk that ye may *g.* thereby

2 *Pet.* 3. 18. *g.* in grace and knowledge

GROWN, *Ps.* 144. 12. that our sons may be as plants *g.* up

Prov. 24. 31. all *g.* over with thorns

Matt. 13. 32. when it is *g.* it is greatest among herbs

GROWETH, *Ps.* 90. 5. in the morning like grass which *g.* up, 6.

Eph. 2. 21. *g.* unto an holy temple in the Lord

2 *Thess.* 1. 3. because your faith *g.* exceedingly

GRUDGE, *Ps.* 59. 15. let them *g.* if they be not satisfied

Jam. 5. 9. *g.* not one against another, brethren

GRUDGING, 1 *Pet.* 4. 9. use hospitality without *g.*

GRUDGINGLY, 2 *Cor.* 9. 7. let him give not *g.* or of necessity

GUARD, *Gen.* 37. 36. Joseph sold to a captain of the *g.* 39. 1.

Dan. 2. 14. Daniel answered the captain of the *g.*

Acts 28. 16. delivered the prisoners to captain of the *g.*

GUEST, *Luke* 19. 7. gone to be *g.* with a sinner

GUEST-CHAMBER, *Mark* 14. 14. where is the *g.-chamber*, *Luke* 22. 11.

GUESTS, *Prov.* 9. 18. that her *g.* are in the depths of hell

Zeph. 1. 7. for the Lord hath prepared and bid *g.*

Matt. 22. 10. wedding furnished with *g.*
11. when the king came in to see the *g.* he saw

GUIDE unto death, *Ps.* 48. 14.

Matt. 23. 16. ye blind *g.* 24.

GUIDE, *Ps.* 25. 9. the meek will be *g.* in judgment

Ps. 31. 3. for thy name's sake lead me and *g.* me
32. 8. *g.* thee with mine eye
55. 13. it was thou, a man, my *g.* my acquaintance
73. 24. shalt *g.* me with thy counsel
112. 5. *g.* his affairs with discretion

Is. 58. 11. Lord shall *g.* thee continually

Jer. 3. 4. my Father, thou art the *g.* of my youth

Luke 1. 79. *g.* our feet into way of peace

John 16. 13. *g.* you into all truth

Acts 8. 31. how can I, except some man *g.* me

1 *Tim.* 5. 14. bear children *g.* the house

GUILE signifies deceit, hypocrisy, duplicity, *Ex.* 21. 14; *Ps.* 55. 11; 2 *Cor.* 12. 16; 1 *Thess.* 2. 3.

Ps. 32. 2. in whose spirit is no *g.*
34. 13. keep lips from *g.* 1 *Pet.* 3. 10.
John 1. 47. an Israelite indeed in whom
there is no *g.*
1 *Pet.* 2. 1. laying aside all malice and *g.*
22. neither was *g.* found in his mouth
GUILTY, *Gen.* 42. 21. we are verily *g.*
concerning our brother
Ex. 34. 7. by no means clear the *g. Num.*
14. 18; *Gen.* 42. 21.
Matt. 26. 66. they said, he is *g.* of death,
Mark 14. 64.
Rom. 3. 19. all the world *g.* before God
1 *Cor.* 11. 27. *g.* of body and blood of
Jam. 2. 10. offend in one point *g.* of all
GUILTINESS, *Ps.* 51. 14. deliver me
from blood-*g.* O God
Ps. 69. 5. and my *g.* is not hid from thee
GUILTLESS, *Ex.* 20. 7. not hold him *g.*
Matt. 12. 7. ye would not have con-
demned the *g.*
GULF, *Luke* 16. 26. between us and you
is a great *g.* fixed
GUSH, ED, *Ps.* 78. 20. he smote the
rock, the waters *g.* out, 105. 41.
Acts 1. 18. he burst asunder, and his
bowels *g.* out

HABITABLE parts, *Prov.* 8. 31.
HABITATION, a dwelling-place, *Ezek.*
29. 14. It denotes Divine protection, 2 *Chr.* 6. 2. & 29. 6; *Ps.* 71. 3.
Deut. 26. 15. look down from thy holy
h. Ps. 68. 5; *Jer.* 25. 30.
Ps. 26. 8. loved *h.* of thy house
71. 3. be thou my strong *h.*
74. 20. full of the *h.* of cruelty
89. 14. are *h.* of thy throne, 97. 2.
91. 9. hast made the most High thy *h.*
107. 7. led them to a city of *h.*
Prov. 3. 33. he blesseth *h.* of the just
Is. 33. 20. shall see Jerusalem a quiet *h.*
63. 15. behold from *h.* of thy holiness
Jer. 31. 23. O *h.* of justice and mountain
Luke 16. 9. receive you into everlast. *h.*
Eph. 2. 22. *h.* of God through the Spirit
Jude 6. angels left their own *h.*
Rev. 18. 2. *h.* of devils, hold, cage
HAIL, *Ex.* 9. 18. cause it to rain a very
grievous *h.*
Ex. 9. 23. the Lord sent thunder and *h.*
the fire ran along
Job 38. 22. the treasures of the *h.*
Ps. 78. 47. he destroyed their vines with
h. 105. 32; 148. 8; *Is.* 38. 2.
HAIL, *Matt.* 26. 49. *h.* master, and
kissed him
Matt. 27. 29. *h.* king of the Jews, *Mark*
15. 18; *John* 19. 3.
Luke 1. 28. the angel came to Mary,
and said, *h.*
HAIR, S, *Gen.* 42. 38. ye shall bring
down my *h.*
Ps. 40. 12. more than *h.* of my head,
69. 4.
Is. 46. 4. and even to hoar *h.* will I
carry you
Hos. 7. 9. gray *h.* are here and there
Matt. 5. 36. make one *h.* white or black
10. 30. *h.* of your head numbered,
Luke 12. 7.
Luke 7. 38. did wipe them with *h.* of

her head, 44.
1 *Cor.* 11. 14. if man have long *h.*
1 *Tim.* 2. 9. not with broidered *h.*
1 *Pet.* 3. 3. not of plaiting the *h.*
Rev. 1. 14. *h.* were white like wool
HALF, 2 *Sam.* 10. 4. Hanun shaved off
one *h.* of their beards
1 *Kings* 10. 7. and behold, the *h.* was
not told, 2 *Chr.* 9. 6.
Esth. 5. 3. to the *h.* of the kingdom, 7.
2; *Mark* 6. 23.
Ps. 55. 23. bloody men shall not live *h.*
their days
Rev. 8. 1. was silence about space of *h.*
an hour
HALL, *Matt.* 27. 27. the soldiers took
Jesus into common *h.*
Mark 15. 16. soldiers led him to the *h.*
HALLOW, *Ex.* 28. 38. which the chil-
dren of Israel shall *h.*
Lev. 22. 32. I will be *h.*
Jer. 17. 22. but *h.* ye the sabbath-day,
24. 27.
Ezek. 20. 20. and *h.* my sabbaths
HALLOWED, *Ex.* 20. 11. Lord blessed
the sabbath-day and *h.* it
Matt. 6. 9. *h.* be thy name, *Luke* 11. 2.
HALT, to be lame, *Luke* 14. 21.—De-
clension, infidelity *Jer.* 20. 10; *Mic.*
4. 6.—Discouragement *Ps.* 38. 17.
—Undecided, 1 *Kings* 18. 21.
HAND. Figuratively the *hand* denotes
power, especially Divine power.
Stretched out hand denotes a desire to show mercy or justice ;
Prov. 1. 24; *Is.* 65. 2. *Joining*
hands indicated an agreement to
fulfil a promise, 2 *Kings* 10. 15;
Prov. 11. 21. *Lifting of the hand*
was a solemn mode of *swearing,* for
it resembled an attitude of prayer;
Gen. 14. 22; *Ps.* 28. 2; 1 *Tim.* 11. 8.
To this refers *Ps.* 144. 8; *Is.* 44. 20.
condemnatory of hypocrisy. By
publicly washing the hands in water a person avowed his innocence,
Ps. 26. 6; *Matt.* 27. 24. Laying
hands on a person or animal, was a
solemn act of consecration to the
service of God; *Lev.* 16. 21; *Num.*
27. 18; *Acts* 6. 6.
HAND, *Gen.* 3. 22. & 16. 12.
Deut. 33. 3. all his saints are in thy *h.*
Ezra 7. 9. good *h.* of his God upon him
8. 22. *h.* of our God is on them for
Job 12. 6. into whose *h.* God bringeth
abundantly
Prov. 10. 4. *h.* of diligent—with slack *h.*
11. 21. though *h.* join in *h.* 16. 5.
12. 24. *h.* of diligent shall bear rule
Is. 1. 12. who required this at your *h.*
Matt. 22. 13. bind him *h.* and foot and
John 13. 3. giving all things into his *h.*
1 *Pet.* 5. 6. humble yourselves under
the mighty *h.* of God
Num. 11. 23. is Lord's *h.* waxed short
2 *Sam.* 24. 14. let us fall into *h.* of God,
Job 12. 9. *h.* of the Lord hath wrought
all this, *Is.* 41. 20.
19. 21. have pity, for *h.* of God hath
touched me
Is. 40. 2. received of *h.* of Lord double

for all
58. 1. *h.* is not shortened that it cannot save
Ps. 16. 8. he is at my right hand, I shall
11. at thy right *h.* are pleasures for evermore
18. 35. thy right *h.* hath holden me up
48. 10. thy right *h.* is full of righteousness
73. 23. hast holden me by my right *h.*
110. 5. Lord at thy right *h.* shall strike kings
Ps. 137. 5. let my right *h.* forget her cunning
139. 10. thy *h.* shall lead and hold me
Prov. 3. 16. length of days is in her right *h.*
Eccl. 10. 2. wise man's heart at right *h.*
9. 1. wise and their work are in *h.* of
Songs 2. 6. his right *h.* doth embrace me, 8. 3.
Matt. 5. 30. if right *h.* offend, cut it off
6. 3. let not thy left *h.* know what thy right *h.* doeth
20. 21. one on right *h.* and another on left
25. 33. sheep on right *h.* goats on left
Mark 14. 62. sitting on right *h.* of power
16. 19. sat on right *h.* of God, *Rom.* 8. 34; *Col.* 3. 1; *Heb.* 1. 3. & 8. 1. & 10. 12; 1 *Pet.* 3. 22; *Acts* 2. 33. & 7. 55, 56.
Ps. 31. 5. into *h.* I commend my spirit
145. 16. openest thy *h.* and satisfiest
Prov. 30. 32. lay thy *h.* upon thy mouth
Eccl. 9. 10. whatsoever thy *h.* findeth to do, do it with all thy might
Is. 26. 11. when thy *h.* is lifted up they
Matt. 18. 8. if thy *h.* or thy foot offend
Acts 4. 28. to do whatsoever thy *h.* and
Gen. 27. 22. *h.* are the *h.* of Esau
Ex. 17. 12. Moses *h.* were heavy
Job 17. 9. hath clean *h.* shall be strong
Ps. 24. 4. hath clean *h.* and pure heart
76. 5. men of might found their *h.*
119. 73. thy *h.* have made and fashioned me
Prov. 31. 20. reacheth forth *h.* to needy
31. give her of the fruit of *h.*
Is. 1. 15. spread forth your *h.* I will hide
Mic. 7. 3. do evil with both *h.* earnestly
Matt. 18. 8. having two *h.* or two feet, cast into fire
Luke 1. 74. delivered out of *h.* of our enemies
9. 44. delivered into *h.* of men
John 13. 9. but also my *h.* and my head
2 *Cor.* 5. 1. an house not made with *h.*
Eph. 4. 28. working with his *h.*
1 *Tim.* 2. 8. where lifting up holy *h.*
Heb. 9. 11. tabernacle not made with *h.*
10. 31. a fearful thing to fall into *h.* of living God
Jam. 4. 8. cleanse your *h.* ye sinners
1 *John* 1. 1. our *h.* have *h.* word
Col. 2. 14. the *h.* writing of ordinances
HANG, *Gen.* 40. 19. Pharaoh shall *h.* thee on a tree
Deut. 21. 23. *h.* is accursed, *Gal.* 3. 13.
28. 66. thy life shall *h.* in doubt
Esth. 6. 4. speak to king, to *h.* Mordecai
Is. 22. 24. they shall *h.* upon him all the glory

Matt. 22. 40. on thee *h.* all the law and the prophets
Heb. 12. 12. lift up hands which *h.* down
HANGED, *Gen.* 40. 22. but he *h.* the chief baker, 41. 13.
2 *Sam.* 17. 23. Ahithophel *h.* himself; 18. 10. Absalom *h.*
Ezra 6. 11. and being set up, let him be *h.* thereon
Esth. 7. 10. they *h.* Haman; 9. 14. they *h.* his ten sons
Ps. 137. 2. we *h.* our harps on the willows
Ezek. 27. 10. they *h.* the shield and helmet in thee
Matt. 18. 6. millstone *h.* about his neck
27. 5. Judas departed, *h.* himself
Luke 23. 39. one of the thieves who were *h.* railed on him
Acts 5. 30. whom. ye slew and *h.* on a tree, 10. 39.
HANGETH, *Job* 26. 7. he *h.* the earth upon nothing
Gal. 3. 13. cursed is every one that *h.* on a tree
HAPLY, *Acts* 5. 39. lest *h.* fight against God
Acts 17. 27. if *h.* they might feel
2 *Cor.* 9. 4. lest *h.* if they of Macedonia come with me
HAPPEN, 1 *Sam.* 28. 10; *Is.* 41. 22; *Rom.* 11. 25.
Prov. 12. 21. no evil shall *h.* to the just
HAPPENED, 1 *Sam.* 6. 9. a chance that *h.* to us
Jer. 44. 23. evil is *h.* to you this day
Luke 24. 14. talked of things that had *h.*
Rom. 11. 25. that blindness in part is *h.* to Israel
1 *Cor.* 10. 11. all these *h.* for ensamples
Phil. 1. 12. things *h.* to me have fallen
1 *Pet.* 4. 12. strange thing *h.* to you
2 *Pet.* 2. 22. it is *h.* to them according to the proverb
HAPPENETH, *Eccl.* 2. 14. that one event *h.* to them all
8. 14. *h.* according to work of
9. 11. time and chance *h.* to them all
HAPPY, I for daughters, *Gen.* 30. 13.
Deut. 33. 29. *h.* art thou, O Israel
1 *Kings* 10. 8. *h.* are thy men, happy are these thy servants
Job 5. 17. *h.* is man whom God correct.
Ps. 127. 5. *h.* is the man who hath his quiver full of
128. 2. *h.* shalt thou be and it be well
Ps. 144. 15. *h.* people whose God is Lord
146. 5. *h.* is he that hath God of Jacob
Prov. 3. 13. *h.* is the man that findeth wisdom, 18.
14. 21. that hath mercy on the poor *h.*
Prov. 16. 20. whose trusts in Lord, *h.* is he 28. 14. *h.* is man that feareth alway
29. 18. that keepeth the law, *h.* is he
Jer. 12. 1. why are they *h.* that deal treacherously
Mal. 3. 15. we call proud *h.* tempt God
John 13. 17. *h.* are ye if ye do them
Rom. 14. 22. *h.* is he that condemns not himself
Jam. 5. 11. count them *h.* which endure
1 *Pet.* 3. 14. suffer for righteousness, *h.* are ye

4. 14. reproached for name of Christ, *h.* are ye

1 *Cor.* 7. 40. *h.* if she so abide

HARD, *Gen.* 35. 16, 17; *Ex.* 1. 14. & 18. 26; 2 *Sam.* 13. 2; *Ps.* 88. 7.

Gen. 18. 14. is any thing too *h.* for Lord

2 *Sam.* 3. 39. sons of Zeruiah too *h.* for

2 *Kings* 2. 10. thou asked a *h.* thing

Ps. 60. 3. showed thy people *h.* things

Prov. 13. 15. but the way of transgressors is *h.*

Jer. 32. 17. nothing is too *h.* for thee, 27.

Matt. 25. 24. thou art a *h.* man

Mark 10. 24. how *h.* it is for them that trust in riches to enter into the kingdom of God

John 6. 60. this is a *h.* saying who hear

Acts 9. 5. *h.* for thee to kick, 26. 14.

2 *Pet.* 3. 16. things *h.* to understand

Jude 15. of all their *h.* speeches

HARDEN, *Ex.* 4. 21; *Deut.* 15. 7; *Josh.* 11. 20; *Job* 6. 10. & 39. 16.

Job 9. 4. who *h.* himself against God

Prov. 21. 29. *h.* his face

28. 14. *h.* his heart

29. 1. *h.* his neck destroyed without

Is. 63. 17. *h.* our heart from thy fear

Mark 6. 52. their heart was *h.*

Rom. 9. 18. whom he will *h.*

Heb. 3. 8. *h.* not your hearts as in the provocation, 15. & 4. 7; *Ps.* 95. 8.

3. 15. lest any be *h.* through deceitfulness of sin

Prov. 18. 19. a brother offended is *h.*

Jer. 5. 3. made faces *h.* than rock

Ezek. 3. 9. *h.* than flint thy forehead

Matt. 19. 8. because of *h.* of your hearts

Mark 3. 5. grieved for *h.* of their hearts

Rom. 2. 5. after thy *h.* and impenitent heart

2 *Tim.* 2. 3. endure *h.* as a good soldier

HARLOT, *Gen.* 34. 31; *Josh.* 2. 1; *Judg.* 11. 1; *Prov.* 7. 10; *Is.* 1. 21. & 23. 15.

Jer. 2. 20. play the *h.* 3. 1. 6, 8; *Ezek.* 16. 15, 16, 41; *Hos.* 2. 5. & 4. 15.

Matt. 21. 31. *h.* go into kingdom of God before, 32.

1 *Cor.* 6. 16. joined to *h.* is one body

Heb. 11. 31. by faith *h.* Rahab perished not

Jam. 2. 25. was not Rahab *h.* justified

Rev. 17. 5. mother of *h.* abomination

HARM, Damage, mischief, detriment; *Gen.* 31. 52; 1 *Sam.* 26. 21; *Gen.* 31. 52; *Acts* 28. 5.

1 *Chr.* 16. 22. and do my prophets no *h.* *Ps.* 105. 15; *Prov.* 3. 30; *Jer.* 39. 12.

1 *Pet.* 3. 13. who is he that will *h.* you

HARMLESS, *Matt.* 10. 16; *Phil.* 2. 15.

Heb. 7. 26. holy *h.* undefiled separate

HARNESS, *ED, Ex.* 13. 18. Israel went up *h.* out of the land of Egypt

1 *Kings* 20. 11. let not him girdeth on *h.* boast himself

HARP, *Gen.* 4. 21. Jubal was father of them that handle the *h.*

Gen. 31. 27. away with tabernacle and *h.*

1 *Sam.* 16. 16. cunning player on an *h.*

Ps. 33. 2. praise the Lord with the *h.* 150. 3.

43. 4. on *h.* will I praise thee

49. 4. I will open my dark sayings upon the *h.*

71. 22. sing with *h.* 92. 3; 98. 5; 147. 7; 149. 3.

81. 2. bring hither the pleasant *h.* with the psaltery

Is. 5. 12. the *h.* and the viol are in their

1 *Cor.* 14. 7. whether pipe or *h.*

HARPS, 2 *Sam.* 6. 5. David and all Israel played on *h.* and cornet

Ps. 137. 2. we hanged our *h.* upon the willows

Rev. 5. 8. having every one of them *h.* and viols

14. 2. harping with their *h.*; 15. 2. the *h.* of God

HARPERS, *Rev.* 14. 2. I heard the voice of *h.* harping with harps

Rev. 18: 22. *h.* shall be heard no more

HARROWS, 2 *Sam.* 12. 31. he put them under saws and *h.* of iron

1 *Chr.* 20. 3. and cut them with saws

HART, *Ps.* 42. 1. as the *h.* panteth after the water-brooks

Is. 35. 6. lame man leap as an *h.*

HARVEST, *Gen.* 8. 22. & 30. 14.

Ex. 34. 21. in *h.* thou shalt rest

Prov. 10. 5. he that sleepeth in *h.* causeth shame

Is. 9. 3. joy before thee according to the joy of *h.*

Jer. 5. 24. reserveth appointed weeks of the *h.*

8. 20. *h.* is past and summer ended and we are not saved

51. 33. *h.* shall come; *Joel* 3. 13.

Hos. 3. 13. put in the sickle, for the *h.* is ripe, come

Matt. 9. 37. *h.* plenteous

38. pray the Lord of *h.*

13. 39. *h.* end of the world

Mark 4. 29. put in the sickle because *h.* is come

Luke 10. 2. the *h.* truly is great

John 4. 35. then cometh *h.* the fields are white to *h.*

Rev. 14. 15. *h.* of earth is ripe; *Joel* 3. 13.

HARVEST-TIME, *Josh.* 3. 15. Jordan overfloweth at the *time* of *h.*

Prov. 25. 13. as the cold of snow in the *time* of *h.*

Matt. 13. 30. in the *time* of *h.* I will say to the reapers

HASTE, *Ex.* 12. 11, 33; *Is.* 52. 12.

Ps. 31. 22. I said in my *h.* 116. 11.

38. 22. make *h.* to help me, 40. 13. & 70. 1, 5. & 71. 12. & 141. 1.

119 .60. I made *h.* and delayed not to keep commandments

Songs 8. 14. make *h.* my beloved

Is. 28. 16. believeth shall not make *h.*

49. 17. thy children shall make *h.*

Ps. 16. 4. *h.* after another god

Is. 5. 19. let him *h.* his work that we

60. 22. I the Lord will *h.* it in his time

Jer. 1. 12. I will *h.* my word to perform

Prov. 14. 29. that is, *h.* of Spirit; *Eccl.* 7. 9.

21. 5. thoughts of *h.* only to want

29. 20. *h.* in words more hope of a fool

20. 21. inheritance gotten *h.* not blessed

HATE, Gen. 24. 60; Deut. 21. 15.
Lev. 19. 17. shalt not h. thy brother in
Deut. 7. 10. repay them that h. him
1 Kings 22. 8. I h. him, for he never
Ps. 68. 1. let them that h. him flee
97. 10. ye that love the Lord h. evil
119. 104. I h. every false way, 128
113. I h. vain thoughts
163. h. lying
139. 21. do not I h. them that h. thee
Prov. 8. 13. fear of Lord is to h. evil
36. all they that h. me love death
Jer. 44. 4. this abominable thing that I h.
Amos 5. 10. they h. him that rebuketh
15. h. the evil and love good
Mic. 3. 2. who h. the good and love evil
Luke 14. 26. and h. not his father and
his mother
John 7. 7. world cannot h. you but me it
15. 18. if world h. you it h. me before
Rom. 7. 15. what I h. that do I
1 John 3. 13. marvel not if world h. you
Rev. 2. 6. deeds of Nicolaitanes, which
I h. 15.
17. 16. these shall h. the whore
HATED, Gen. 27. 41. Esau h. Jacob
because of the blessing
Gen. 37. 4. his brethren h. Joseph
Ps. 26. 5. I have h. the congregation of
evil doers
Prov. 1. 29. for they h. knowledge
5. 12. and say how have I h. instruc-
14. 20. poor is h. even of neighbour
Eccl. 2. 17. therefore I h. life
Is. 66. 5. your brethren that h. you said
Mal. 1. 3. I h. Esau; Rom. 9. 13.
Matt. 10. 22. shall be h. of all men;
Mark 13. 13; Luke 21. 17.
Luke 19. 14. his citizens h. him
John 15. 24. h. me and my Father, 18.
25. they h. me without a cause
17. 14. world hath h. them
Eph. 5. 29. no man ever h. his own flesh
Heb. 1. 9. loved righteousness, h. ini-
quity
HATERS, Ps. 81. 15. the h. of the Lord
submitted
Rom. 1. 30. backbiters h. of God
HATEST, 2 Sam. 19. 6. h. friends and
Ps. 5. 5. h. all workers of iniquity
45. 7. thou h. wickedness
50. 17. seeing thou h. instruction, and
HATETH, Ex. 23. 5. ass of him that h.
thee lying
Prov. 13. 24. spareth the rod h. his son
John 12. 25. h. his life in this world
1 John 2. 9. h. his brother is in dark-
ness, 11. & 3. 15. & 4. 20.
HATING, Ex. 18. 21. h. covetousness
Tit. 3. 3. h. and h. one another
Jude 23. h. even the garment spotted
by the flesh
HATRED, Ps. 109. 3. compassed me
about with h.
Ps. 109. 5. rewarded me h. for my love
139. 22. I hate them with perfect h.
Prov. 15. 17. better than a stalled ox
and h. therewith
26. 26. whose h. is covered by deceit
Eccl. 9. 6. their h. is now perished
Gal. 5. 20. witchcraft h. works of flesh
HAUGHTY. Proud, lofty; 2 Sam. 22.

28. "Thine eyes are upon the
haughty," &c. The world describes
the disposition; Prov. 16. 18.—the
heart; Prov. 18. 12.—the daughters
of Zion; Ps. 3. 16.—the scorner;
Prov. 21. 24.—the inhabitants of
the earth; Is. 24. 4.—a righteous
person; Ps. 131. 1. See also Zeph.
3. 11; haughtiness; Is. 2. 11, 17;
13. 11; 16. 6.
Ps. 131. 1. my heart is not h.
Prov. 16. 18. h. spirit goeth before a fall
21. 24. proud and h. scorner
Is. 3. 16. daughters of Zion are h.
HAUGHTINESS, Prov. 21. 4. the h. of
eyes and a proud heart is sin
Is. 2. 11. h. of men shall be bowed down,
Lord exalted
17. h. of men shall be made low
HEAD, Gen. 2. 10. & 40. 13.
Gen. 3. 15. it shall bruise thy h.
49. 26. blessings on h. of him separate
from his brethren, Deut. 33. 16.
2 Sam. 3. 8. and said, am I a dog's h.
2 Kings 2. 3. master from h. to-day, 5.
4. 19. said to his father, my h. my h.
Ezra 9. 6. iniquity increased over our h.
Ps. 22. 7. shoot out lip, shake the h.
23. 5. thou anointest my h. with oil
27. 6. now shall my h. be lifted up
Ps. 38. 4. iniquity gone over my h.
141. 5. oil, which shall not break h.
Prov. 10. 6. blessings on h. of just
16. 31. hoary h. is crown of glory
20. 29. beauty of old men is gray h.
25. 22. coals of fire on h. Rom. 12. 20.
Eccl. 2. 14. wise man's eyes in his h.
9. 8. let h. lack no ointment
Songs 2. 6. left hand under my h.
5. 2. my h. is filled with dew
11. his h. is most fine gold locks
Is. 1. 5. whole h. is sick and heart faint
6. from sole of foot to crown of his h.
51. 11. everlasting joy on their h.
59. 17. helmet of salvation on h.
Jer. 9. 1. O that my h. were waters
48. 37. every h. shall be bald, and
Ezek. 9. 10. recompense way on h. 16. 43.
Dan. 2. 28. visions of thy h. on thy bed
38. thou art this h. of gold, 32.
Amos 2. 7. that pant after dust on h.
of the poor
Matt. 8. 20. not where to lay his h.
14. 8. give me the h. of John Baptist
Rom. 12. 20. coals of fire on h. Pr. 25. 22.
1 Cor. 11. 3. h. of man is Christ, h. of
woman is man, h. of Christ is God
4. h. covered dishonoureth h. 5.
Eph. 1. 22. gave him be h. over all
4. 15. grow up in all to h. even Christ
5. 23. husband h. of wife, Christ of the
church
Col. 1. 18. he is h. of the body, 2. 19.
Rev. 19. 12. on his h. many crowns
HEADLONG, Job 5. 13; Luke 4. 29;
Acts 1. 18.
HEAD-STONE, Ps. 118. 22. become
h.-stone of corner
Zech. 4. 7. bring h.-stone with shouting
HEAD of the corner, Matt. 21. 42. is be-
come h. of the corner, Mark 12. 10;
Luke 20. 17; Acts 4. 11; 1 Pet. 2. 7.

HEADY, 2 *Tim.* 3. 4. men be *h.* high-minded

HEADS, *Gen.* 43. 28. bowed their *h. Ex.* 4. 31.

Ps. 24. 7. lift up your *h.* O ye gates, 9.

Ps. 56. 12. cause men to ride over our *h.*

Is. 35. 10. everlasting joy on their *h.* 51. 11.

Matt. 27. 39. wagging *h. Mark* 15. 29

Luke 21. 28. lift up your *h.* for day of

Acts 18. 6. your blood be on your *h.*

Rev. 9. 7. their *h.* as it were crowns 13. 1. I saw a beast having seven *h.* 17. 9. seven *h.* are seven mountains

HEAL her now, O God, *Num.* 12. 13.

Deut. 32. 39. I wound, I *h.* and I kill

2 *Chr.* 7. 14. I will *h.* their land

Ps. 6. 2. *h.* me for my bones are vexed 41. 4. *h.* my soul for I have sinned 60. 2. *h.* breaches for the land shaketh

Is. 57. 18. I've seen way and I'll *h.* him

Jer. 3. 22. I will *h.* your backslidings, *Hos.* 14. 4.

17. 14. *h.* me and I shall be *h.*

Hos. 6. 1. hath torn and he will *h.* us

Luke 4. 18. *h.* the broken-hearted 23. ye will say to me, physician, *h.* thyself

John 12. 40. converted, and I should *h.*

Acts 4. 30. stretching thine hand to *h.*

HEALED, 2 *Chr.* 30. 20. Lord *h.* the people

Ps. 30. 2. I cried and thou hast *h.* me 107. 20. sent his word and *h.* them

Is. 6. 10. convert and be *h. Acts* 28. 27. 53. 5. with his stripes we are *h.* 1 *Pet.* 2. 24.

Jer. 6. 14. *h.* hurt of daughter, 8. 11. 15. 18. wound incurable, refuseth to be *h.*

Hos. 7. 1. when I would have *h.* Israel

Matt. 4. 24. he *h.* them, 12. 15. & 14. 14.

Heb. 12. 13. let it rather be *h.*

Jam. 5. 16. pray that ye may be *h.*

Rev. 13. 3. his deadly wound *h.*

HEALETH, *Ex.* 15. 26. I am the Lord that *h.* thee

Ps. 103. 3. who *h.* all thy diseases 147. 3. he *h.* broken in heart

Is. 30. 26. Lord *h.* stroke of their wound

HEALING, *Jer.* 14. 19. looked for a time of *h.* 30. 13. thou hast no *h.* medicine

Mal. 4. 2. with *h.* in his wings

Matt. 4. 23. *h.* all manner of sickness

1 *Cor.* 12. 9. to another gifts of *h.*

Rev. 22. 2. leaves are for *h.* of nations

HEALTH, *Gen.* 43. 28. our father is in good *h.*

2 *Sam.* 20. 9. art in *h.* my brother

Ps. 42. 11. *h.* of my countenance, 43. 5. 67. 2. thy saving *h.* among all nations

Prov. 3. 8. it shall be *h.* to thy navel 12. 18. the tongue of wise is *h.* 13. 17. a faithful ambassador is *h.*

Jer. 8. 15. looked for a time of *h.*

Prov. 16. 24. sweet to soul, *h.* to bones

Is. 58. 8. thy *h.* shall spring forth

Jer. 8. 22. not *h.* of my people recovered 30. 17. I will restore *h.* and *h.* thee

Acts 27. 34. take meat, for this is *h.*

HEAP, substantive, *Ex.* 15. 8. the floods stood as an *h. Josh.* 3. 13, 16; *Ps.* 33. 7; 78. 13.

Josh. 7. 26. over him a *h.* of stones

HEAP, *Deut.* 32. 23. I will *h.* mischiefs on them

Job 27. 16. he *h.* up silver as the dust 36. 13. hypocrites in heart *h.* up

Prov. 25. 22. *h.* coals of fire, *Rom.* 12. 20.

Ps. 39. 6. he *h.* up riches and knowledge

2 *Tim.* 4. 3. *h.* to themselves teachers

Jam. 5. 3. ye have *h.* treasures

HEAPS, *Judg.* 15. 16. *h.* on *h.* with the jaw-bone

Ps. 79. 1. they laid Jerusalem on *h.*

Jer. 9. 11. make Jerusalem *h.* 26. 18.

Mic. 3. 12. Jerusalem shall become *h.*

HEAR, *Gen.* 21. 6. & 23. 6.

Deut. 30. 17. if heart turn away not *h.*

Josh. 3. 9. *h.* the words of the Lord

Judg. 5. 3. *h.* O ye kings, give ear

1 *Kings* 4. 34. *h.* wisdom of Solomon, 10. 8, 24; 2 *Chr.* 9. 7, 23; *Matt.* 12. 42; *Luke* 11. 31.

8. 30. *h.* thou in heaven

2 *Kings* 7. 6. *h.* a noise of chariots 19. 16. bow down thy ear and *h.*

2 *Chr.* 6. 21. *h.* from thy dwelling-place

Neh. 1. 6. the prayer of servant 4. 4. *h.* O God, for we are despised

Job 5. 27. *h.* it and know it for thy good

Ps. 4. 1. *h.* my prayer, 39. 12. & 54. 2. & 84. 8. & 102. 1. & 143. 1. 4. 3. Lord will *h.* 17. 6. & 145. 19; *Zech.* 10. 6. 10. 17. wilt cause thy ear to *h.* 51. 8. cause me to *h.* joy and gladness 59. 7. who say they doth *h.* 10. 11. 66. 16. come and *h.* all ye that fear G. 102. 20. *h.* groaning of the prisoner 115. 6. ears but they *h.* not 138. 4. *h.* the words of thy mouth 143. 8. to *h.* thy loving-kindness

Prov. 1. 8. *h.* instruction of thy father 4. 1. *h.* ye children, instruction of a 8. 6. *h.* I speak of excellent things 33. *h.* instruction, and be wise 19. 27. cease to *h.* instruction that

Eccl. 5. 1. be more ready to *h.* 7. 5. better to *h.* the rebuke of wise 12. 13. *h.* conclusion of the matter

Songs 2. 14. let me *h.* thy voice. 8. 13.

Is. 1. 2. *h.* O heavens and give ear O earth 6. 10. lest they *h.* with ears 42. 18. *h.* ye deaf; 23. who will *h.*

Is. 55. 3. *h.* and your soul shall live

Matt. 10. 27. what ye *h.* in the ear that preach ye 13. 17. to *h.* those things ye *h.* 17. 5. this is my beloved Son, *h.* ye 18. 17. if he neglect to *h.* them

Mark 4. 24. take heed what ye *h.* 33. spake word as they were able to *h.*

Luke 5. 1. pressed on him to *h.* word 15. multitudes came together to *h.* 6. 17. came to *h.* him and he healed 8. 18. take heed how ye *h.* 16. 29. Moses and prophets, let them *h.* them

John 5. 25. they that *h.* shall live 30. I *h.* I judge; 6. 60. who *h.* 7. 51. law judge man before it *h.* him

9. 27. wherefore would ye *h.* it again
Acts 2. 8. *h.* every man in own tongue
Acts 10. 33. to *h.* all things commanded of God
1 *Cor.* 11. 18. I *h.* there be divisions
Phil. 1. 27. I may *h.* of your affairs
2 *Thess.* 3. 11. we *h.* that some walk
1 *Tim.* 4. 16. and them that *h.* thee
Jam. 1. 19. let every man be swift to *h.*
1 *John* 5. 15. we know that he *h.* us
3 *John* 4. *h.* children walk in truth
Rev. 1. 3. *h.* the words of prophecy
2. 7. let him *h.* what spirit saith to churches, 3. 6, 13, 22.
3. 20. if any *h.* my voice and open door
HEAR me, *Ex.* 6. 12. then shall Pharaoh *h. me*
Job 31. 35. O that one would *h. me*
Ps. 4. 1. *h. me* when I call O God
13. 3. consider, and *h. me*, O Lord
69. 13. multitude of mercy *h. me*
17. *h. me* speedily, 143. 7.
HEAR, not, or not hear, 1 *Sam.* 8. 18. Lord will *not h.* you
Job 35. 13. surely God will *not h.* vanity
Ps. 66. 18. regard iniquity, Lord *not h.*
94. 9. planted ear, shall he *not h.*
Is. 1. 15. make many prayers I will *not h. Jer.* 7. 16; 11. 14; 14. 12; *Ezek.* 8. 18; *Amos* 5. 23.
59. 1. ear heavy that it *cannot h.*
2. will not h. ; 65. 12. ye did *not h.*
Jer. 5. 21. have ears and *h. not, Ezek.* 12. 2; *Mark* 8. 18.
Mic. 3. 4. cry to L. he will *not h.* them
Matt. 10. 14. receive you *not h.* words
Luke 16. 31. if *h. not* Moses and proph.
John 9. 27. I told you, and ye did *not h.*
10. 8. but the sheep did *not h.* them
Gal. 4. 21. do ye *not h.* the law
HEAR now, *Num.* 12. 6. *h. now* my words, 20. 10.
Job 13. 6. *h. now* my reasoning
Is. 7. 13. *h. now*, O house of David
Is. 51. 21. *h. now* this, thou afflicted
Jer. 37. 20. *h. now*, I pray thee, O king
Zech. 3. 8. *h. now*, Joshua high-priest
Acts 2. 33. this which ye *n.* see and *h.*
Phil. 1. 30. saw in me, and *now h.*
HEAR, shall, *Num.* 14. 13. Egyptians *shall h.* it
Deut. 4. 6. *shall h.* all these statutes
Ps. 34. 2. humble *shall h.* thereof
Is. 30. 19. *shall h.* he will answer thee
Hos. 2. 21. heaven *shall h.* the earth
22. earth *shall h.* the corn and wine
Matt. 13. 14. hearing, ye *s. h. Acts* 28. 26.
18. 15. *shall h.* thee thou hast gained
24. 6. ye *shall h.* of wars and rumours, *Mark* 13. 7 ; *Luke* 21. 9.
John 5. 25. the dead *shall h.* voice
Acts 3. 22. him *shall* ye h. 7. 37.
Rom. 10. 14. how *shall* they h. without
HEAR, will, *Ex.* 20. 19. we *will h. Deut.* 5. 2.
2 *Chr.* 7. 14. *w. h.* fr. heaven, *Ps.* 20. 6.
20. 9. thou *w. h.* and help, *Ps.* 38. 15.
Ps. 4. 3. Lord *w. h.* ; 17. 6. *w. h.* me
85. 8. *will h.* what God will speak
Is. 65. 24. are yet speaking, I *will h.*
Ezek. 2. 5. whether *w. h.* 7; 3. 11.
Hos. 2. 21. I *will h.* the heavens

Acts 17. 32. we *will h.* thee again
HEARD, *Ex.* 2. 24. God *h.* their groaning
Job 15. 8. hast h. the secret of God
29. 11. when the ear *h.* me, it bless
Ps. 6. 9. Lord hath *h.* my supplication
10. 17. hast *h.* desire of humble, 34. 6.
34. 4. I sought the Lord and he *h.* me
61. 5. thou hast *h.* my vows, 116. 1.
66. 19. verily God hath *h.* me, 18. 6.
118. 21. I will praise for thou hast *h.*
120. 1. I cried to the Lord and he *h.*
132. 6. lo, we *h.* of it at Ephratah
Is. 40. 21. have ye not *h.* hath it not
28. hast thou not *h.* and hast thou not known
60. 18. violence no more *h.* in land
64. 4. from the beginning men have not *h.*
65. 19. weeping shall be no more *h.*
66. 8. who hath *h.* such a thing
Jer. 7. 13. rising early, but ye *h.* not
8. 6. I *h.* and but they
Ezek. 26. 13. harps shall be nor more *h.*
Jonah 2. 2. I cried to Lord and he *h.* me
Mal. 3. 16. the L. hearkened and *h.*
Matt. 6. 7. be *h.* for much speaking
Luke 1. 13. thy prayer is *h.* and thy wife
John 3. 22. what he hath seen and *h.*
6. 45. every man that hath *h.* of Fath.
8. 6. wrote as though he *h.* them not
21. 7. Simon Peter *h.* it was the Lord
Acts 2. 37. when *h.* this were pricked
4. 4. many which *h.* the word believ.
Acts 16. 14. woman worshipped God *h.* us
Rom. 10. 14. of whom they have not *h.*
18. have they not *h.* ? yes, verily
1 *Cor.* 2. 9. eye not seen nor ear *h.*
Phil. 4. 9. what *h.* and seen in me do
Heb. 4. 2. with faith in them that *h.* it
5. 7. he was *h.* in that he feared
Jam. 5. 11. ye *h.* of patience of Job
Rev. 3. 3. remember how hast *h.* and hold fast
9. 16. I *h.* the number of horsemen
18. 22. trumpet, shall be *h.* no more
23. voice of bride shall be *h.* no more
22. 8. saw these things and *h.* them
HEARD, I have, *Ex.* 3. 7. *I have h.* their cry
6. 5. *I have h.* their groaning, *Acts* 7. 34.
16. 12. *I have h.* their murmurings, *Num.* 14. 27.
1 *Kings* 9. 3. *I have h.* thy prayer and supplication; 2 *Kings* 19. 20. & 20. 5. & 22. 19.
Job 42. 5. *I have h.* of thee by the *h.*
Is. 49. 8. in acceptable time *have I h.* thee, 2 *Cor.* 6. 2.
Jer. 31. 18. *I have h.* Ephraim bemoaning himself
HEARD, we have, *Acts* 6. 14. *we have h.* him say, this Jesus
Heb. 2. 1. heed to things *we have h.*
1 *John* 1. 1. which *we have h.* 3.
HEARD, joined with word or words, 1 *Thess.* 2. 13. the *w.* which ye h. of
2 *Tim.* 1. 13. form of sound *w.* hast *h.*
Heb. 12. 19. that *h.* entreated that *w.*
1 *John* 2. 7. *w.* ye have *h.* from begin.
HEARER, S, *Rom.* 2. 13. not the *h.* of law are just

Eph. 4. 20. minister grace unto the *h.*
2 *Tim.* 2. 14. to subverting of the *h.*
Jam. 1. 22. doers of word, and not *h.*
   23. if any be a *h.* of the word
   25. he being not a forgetful *h.*
HEAREST, *Ps.* 22. 2. cry in day-time
   h. not
Ps. 65. 2. thou that *h.* prayer
Matt. 27. 13. *h.* thou not how many things
John 11. 42. knew thou *h.* me always
HEARETH, 1 *Sam.* 3. 9. speak Lord, for
   thy servant *h.*
Ps. 34. 17. righteous cry, the Lord *h.*
Prov. 8. 34. blessed is the man that *h.*
Matt. 7. 24. whoso *h.* those sayings of
   13. 20. same that *h.* the word, 22. 23.
Luke 10. 16. he that *h.* you *h.* me
John 9. 31. God *h.* not sinners but *h.*
1 *John* 5. 14. ask according to his will
   be *h.*
Rev. 22. 17. let him that *h.* say come
HEARING, *Job* 42. 5. of thee by *h.* of
Prov. 20. 12. *h.* ear and seeing eye
   28. 9. turneth his ear from *h.* of law
Matt. 13. 14. *h.* they *h.* not
Rom. 10. 17. faith comes by *h.* and *h.* by
1 *Cor.* 12. 17. where were the *h.*
Gal. 3. 2. or by the *h.* of faith, 5.
Heb. 5. 11. seeing ye are dull of *h.*
2 *Pet.* 2. 8. in seeing and *h.* vexed
HEARKEN, *Ex.* 6. 30. shall Pharaoh *h.*
   to me
Deut. 18. 15. a prophet, like unto me,
   to him ye shall *h.*
Deut. 28. 1. if thou *h.* diligently, 30. 10.
1 *Sam.* 15. 22. better to *h.* than fat of
Ps. 81. 8. if thou wilt *h.* unto me
   81. 11. my people would not *h.* to
   103. 20. angels *h.* to voice of his word
Jer. 26. 3. will *h.* and turn from evil
   29. 12. pray to me and I will *h.*
Zech. 7. 11. but they refused to *h.*
Acts 4. 19. *h.* to you more than to God
   12. 13. a damsel came to *h.*
HEARKEN, imperatively, *Job* 34. 10. *h.*
   unto me, men of understanding
Ps. 34. 11. *h.* I will teach you
Prov. 7. 24. *h.* to me, O child, 8. 32.
Is. 46. 12. *h.* unto me ye stout-hearted
   51. 1. *h.* unto me ye that follow right
   55. 2. *h.* diligently, eat that which is
   good, and delight
Acts 7. 2. men, brethren, and fathers *h.*
   15. 13. men and brethren *h.* to me
Jam. 2. 5. *h.* my beloved brethren
HEART, the seat of the affections and
   passions. God only knows it, *Jer.*
   17. 10. The Lord Jesus Christ,
   who demonstrated his Godhead on
   many occasions, by searching the
   heart, declares that from the heart
   of man proceeds every evil, *Matt.*
   15. 18. As the great evil which
   corrupts and defiles the heart is
   unbelief, so the only purifier of the
   heart mentioned in the scripture is
   faith, *Acts* 15. 9. ' With the heart
   man believeth unto righteousness ';
   that is, sincere and saving faith en-
   gages the affections, *Rom.* 10. 10.
   This is called the ' righteousness

of faith,' *Rom.* 4. 13.
HEART, *Ex.* 28. 30. & 35. 5.
1 *Sam.* 1. 13. she spake in her *h.* only
   10. 9. God gave him another heart
   16. 7. but Lord looketh on, the *h.*
   24. 5. David's *h.* smote him after he
1 *Chr.* 16. 10. let *h.* of them rejoice
   that seek the Lord; *Ps.* 105. 3.
   22. 19. set your *h.* to seek the Lord
2 *Chr.* 17. 6. his *h.* was lifted up in ways
   of the Lord
   30. 19. prepares his *h.* to seek God of
Ps. 22. 26. your *h.* shall live for ever,
   34. 18. Lord nigh to them of broken *h.*
   37. 31. the law of his God is in his *h.*
   51. 17. a broken and contrite *h.* *Is.*
   66. 2.
   64. 6. and the thought and *h.* is deep
   78. 37. their *h.* was not right with him
   112. 7. his *h.* is fixed trusting in Lord
Prov. 4. 23. keep thy *h.* with all diligence
   10. 20. *h.* of wicked is little worth
   16. 9. a man's *h.* deviseth his way but
   27. 19. *h.* of man answers to man
Eccl. 7. 4. *h.* of wise in house of mourning
   10. 2. wise man's *h.* at his right hand,
   but a fool's *h.* is at his left hand
Songs 3. 11. in day of gladness of his *h.*
Is. 6. 10. make the *h.* of this people fat
   57. 15. to revive *heart* of contrite ones
Jer. 11. 20. triest the reins and *h.* 17. 10.
   12. 11. no man layeth to *h. Is.* 42. 25.
   17. 9. *h.* is deceitful above all things
   24. 7. I will give them a *h.* to know me
   32. 29. I will give them one *h. Ezek.*
   11. 19.
Lam. 3. 41. lift up our *h.* with hands
Ezek. 11. 19. take stony *h.*—give *h.* of
   18. 31. make ye new *h.* and new spirit
   36. 26. new *h.* take stony *h.* and give
   h. of flesh
Joel 2. 13. rend your *h.* not your garments
Mal. 4. 6. turn *h.* of fathers to children
Matt. 6. 21. there will your *h.* be also
   12. 34. out of abundance of *h.* mouth
   speaketh
   35. out of treasure of *h. Luke* 6. 45.
   15. 19. out of *h.* proceedeth evil,
   Matt. 7. 21.
Luke 2. 19. pondered them in her *h.* 51.
   24. 25. O fools and slow of *h.* to believe
   32. did not our *h.* burn within us
John 14. 1. let not your *h.* be troubled,
   27.
Acts 5. 33. were cut to the *h.* 7. 54.
   11. 23. with purpose of *h.* they cleave
   to the Lord
   13. 22. found man after my own *h.*
Rom. 10. 10. with the *h.* man believeth
1 *Cor.* 2. 9. nor entered into *h.* of man
2 *Cor.* 3. 3. in fleshly tables of the *h.*
1 *Pet.* 3. 4. in hidden man of *h.*
1 *John* 3. 20. if *h.* condemn us God is
   greater than our *h.*
HEART, with all, *Deut.* 11. 13. serve
   him *with all* your *h. Josh.* 22. 5; 1
   Sam. 12. 20.
   13. 3. love Lord our God *with all* your

h. 30. 6; *Matt.* 22. 37; *Mark* 12. 30. 33; *Luke* 10. 27.

Deut. 26. 16. statutes keep and do them *with all h.*

30. 2. turn to the Lord *with all h.* and soul, 10. 2. *Kings* 23. 25; *Joel* 2. 12.

1 *Kings* 2. 4. walk before me in truth *with all h.* 8. 23.

8. 48. return to thee *with all their h.* 2 *Chr.* 6. 38.

2 *Chr.* 15. 12. seek God of Israel *with all h.*

22. 9. sought Lord *with all h.*

31. 21. did *with all h.*

Ps. 86. 12. I will praise thee *with all h.*

Prov. .3. 5. trust in Lord *with all h.* and be not

Jer. 29. 13. search for me *with all h.*

Zeph. 3. 14. sing, be glad, rejoice *with all h.*

Acts 8. 37. if thou believest *with all h.*

HEART, my or mine, *Ps.* 45. 1. *my h.* is inditing a good

108. 1. O God, *my h.* is fixed

61. 2. what time *my h.* is over-whelmed

73. 26. my flesh and *my h.* faileth, but God is

84. 2. *my h.* crieth out for the living God

109. 22. *my h.* is wounded within me

131. 1. Lord *my h.* is not haughty nor

Songs 5. 2. I sleep but *my heart* waketh

Jer. 3. 15. give pastures according to *my h.*

Hos. 11. 8. *my h.* is turned within me

HEART, one, 2 *Chr.* 30. 12. hand of God was to give them *one h.*

Jer. 32. 39. I will give them *one h. Ezek.* 11. 19.

Acts 4. 32. multitude that believed were of *one h.*

HEART, own, 1 *Kings* 8. 38. know every man plague of his *own h.*

1 *Kings* 12. 33. devised of his *own h.*

Ps. 4. 4. commune with your *own h.* on your bed

20. 4. grant according to *own h.*

77. 6. I commune with my *own h.*

Prov. 28. 26. he that trusteth in his *own h.* is a fool

Jam. 1. 26. deceiveth his *own h.*

HEART, our, *Ps.* 33. 21. *our h.* shall rejoice in him

Luke 24. 32. did not *our h.* burn within us, while he

2 *Cor.* 6. 11. mouth open, *our h.* enlarged

1 *John* 3. 20. if *our h.* condemn us, God is greater

21. if *our h.* condemn us not

HEART, perfect, 1 *Kings* 8. 61. *h. perfect* with Lord, 11. 4. & 15. 3, 14; 2 *Chr.* 15. 17.

2 *Kings* 20. 3. and with *perfect h.* 2 *Chr* 19. 9.

1 *Chr.* 28. 9. serve him with a *perfect h.* 29. 9.

2 *Chr.* 16. 9. is *perfect* whose *h.*

Ps. 101. 2. I will walk in house with *perfect h.*

HEART, pure, *Ps.* 24. 4. who shall ascend ? that hath a *pure h.*

Matt. 5. 8. blessed are *pure* in *h.*

1 *Tim.* 1. 5. charity out of *pure h.*

2 *Tim.* 2. 22. that call on the Lord out of a *pure h.*

1 *Pet.* 1. 22. love one another with a *pure h.* fervently

HEART, their, *Ps.* 10. 17. Lord, thou wilt prepare *their h.*

78. 18. they tempted God in *their h.* by asking meat

95. 10. it is a people that do err in *their h.*

Eccl. 9. 3. madness is in *their h.*

Is. 29. 13. *their h.* is far from me, *Matt.* 15. 8; *Mark* 7. 6.

Ezek. 33. 31. but *their h.* goeth after their covetousness

Hos. 10. 2. *their h.* is divided; 13. 6. *their h.* was exalted

13. 8. I will rend the caul of *their h.* and devour

Mark 6. 52. for *their h.* was hardened, *Rom.* 1. 21.

Luke 9. 47. Jesus perceiving the thought of *their h.*

Acts 2. 37. were pricked in *their h.*

HEART, thy, thine, *Gen.* 20. 6. thou didst this in the integrity of *thy h.*

Deut. 6. 5. thou shalt love the Lord with all *thine h.*

10. 12. to serve God with all *thy h.*

1 *Sam.* 9. 19. I will tell thee all that is in thine *h.*

2 *Kings* 22. 19. because *thine h.* was tender

2 *Chr.* 19. 3. hast prepared thine *h.* to seek God

Job 7. 17. set thine *h.* upon him

Ps. 27. 14. shall strengthen *thine h.*

37. 4. and he shall give thee the desire of *thine h.*

Prov. 4. 23. keep *thy h,* with all diligence, for out of it

6. 21. bind them continually upon *thine h.*

25. lust not after beauty in *thine h.*

7. 25. let not *thine h.* incline to her

23. 15. my son, if *thine h.* be wise, *my h.* rejoice

17. let not *thine h.* envy sinners, but be in fear

26. my son, give me *thine h.*

Ezek. 22. 14. can *thine h.* endure in the day I deal with thee

28. 17. *thine h.* was lifted up because of thy beauty

Dan. 5. 22. and thou hast not humbled *thine h.*

Acts 8. 21. for *thy h.* is not right in the sight of God

Rom. 10. 6. say not in *thine h.* who shall ascend

HEART, upright in, *Ps.* 7. 10. saveth *upright in h.*

Ps. 32. 11. shout for joy ye that are *upright in h.*

64. 10. and all the *upright in h.* shall glory

97. 11. gladness is sown for the *upright in h.*

HEART, uprightness of, *Ps.* 119. 7. I will praise thee with *uprightness of h.*

HEART, whole, *Ps.* 9. 1. praise him with *whole h.* 111. 1. & 138. 1.
119. 2. seek him with *whole h.* 10.
34. observe with *whole h.*
58. favour with *whole h.*
69. keep precepts with *whole h.*
145. I cried with *whole h.*
Jer. 3. 10. not turned with my *whole h.*
HEART, your, *Ps.* 22. 26. *your h.* shall live for ever
Ps. 62. 10. if riches increase, set not *your h.* upon them
69. 32. and *your h.* shall live that seek God
Joel 2. 13. and rend *your h.* and not
Mark 8. 17. have ye *your h.* yet hardened
10. 5. for the hardness of *your h.*
John 14. 1. let not *your h.* be troubled,
16. 6. sorrow hath filled *your h.*
22. I will see you again, and *your h.* shall rejoice
Eph. 6. 5. in singleness of *your h.* as unto Christ
HEARTILY, *Luke* 22. 15. I have *h.* desired to eat this passover
Col. 3. 23. what ye do, do it *h.* as to the Lord, not to
HEARTS, *Num.* 32. 9. discouraged the *h.* of Israel
Josh. 7. 5. *h.* of the people melted
1 *Sam.* 10. 26. band of men, whose *h.* God hath touched
1 *Chr.* 28. 9. Lord searcheth all *h.*
Prov. 31. 6. give wine to those that be of heavy *h.*
Luke 2. 35. that the thoughts of *h.* may be revealed
21. 26. men's *h.* failing them
Rom. 8. 27. he that searcheth the *h.* knoweth the
Rev. 2. 23. I am he that searcheth the reins and *h.*
HEARTS, our, *Acts* 14. 17. filling *our h.* with food and gladness
Rom. 5. 5. the love of God is shed abroad in *our h.*
2 *Cor.* 1. 22. earnest of Spirit in *our h.*
3. 2. epistle written in *our h.*
4. 6. God hath shined in *our h.* to give the light
7. 3. to you are in *our h.* to die and live with you
Heb. 10. 22. *our h.* sprinkled from an evil conscience
HEARTS, your, *Gen.* 18. 5. comfort ye *your h.* after that pass on
Deut. 20. 3. O Israel, let not *your h.* faint, fear not
Jer. 42. 20. ye dissembled in *your h.* when ye sent
Matt. 18. 35. if ye from *your h.* forgive not every one
Gal. 4. 6. God sent the Spirit of his Son into *your h.*
Eph. 3. 17. that Christ may dwell in *your h.* by faith
6. 22. I sent that he might comfort *your h.*
Phil. 4. 7. shall keep *your h.* and minds through Christ Jesus
Col. 3. 15. let the peace of God rule in

your h.
4. 8. might know your estate, and comfort *your h.*
1 *Thess.* 3. 13. may establish *your h.*
2 *Thess.* 2. 17. comfort *your h.* and establish you
Jam. 4. 8. and purify *your h.* ye double-minded
1 *Pet.* 3. 15. sanctify the Lord God in *your h.*
2 *Pet.* 1. 19. and day-star arise in *y. h.*
HEAT, *Gen.* 8. 22. cold, *h.* summer, winter, shall not cease
Deut. 29. 24. what meaneth the *h.* of this great anger
Is. 4. 6. a shadow in the day-time from *h.* 25. 4.
Matt. 20. 12. burden and *h.* of the day
2 *Pet.* 3. 10. the elements shall melt with fervent *h.*
HEATHEN, *Lev.* 25. 44. & 26. 45.
Ps. 2. 1. why do *h.* rage, *Acts* 4. 25.
8. give thee the *h.* or Gentiles for thine inheritance
46. 6. the *h.* raged, the kingdoms were moved
47. 8. God reigneth over *h.*
102. 15. the *h.* shall fear the name of the *h.*
Ezek. 20. 41. I will be sanctified before the *h.*
Matt. 6. 7. use not vain repetitions as the *h.* do
Matt. 18. 17. let him be as an *h.* man
Gal. 3. 8. justify the *h.* through faith
HEATHEN, among the, *Gal.* 1. 16. that I might preach him *among the h.*
HEAVEN, denotes the firmament, or aerial expansion, and the residence of God and holy beings. The latter is called by way of eminence the *third heaven*, the *heaven of heavens*, the highest in all that is great and excellent, *Gen.* 1. 8. 17; *Ps.* 19. 1; *Job* 22. 12; *Is.* 66. 1; *Matt.* 5. 34; *Rev.* 3. 12; 1 *Kings* 8. 27; 2 *Cor.* 12. 2.
Heaven, frequently means the church of God, called the kingdom of heaven. It consists of two divisions, one in the highest heaven, one on earth. In this extensive sense, the heaven of prophecy is often to be understood, *Rev.* 5. 6; 12. 1.—signifying the visible church.
HEAVEN of heavens cannot contain thee, 1 *Kings* 8. 27; 2 *Chr.* 2. 6. & 6. 18.
Ps. 103. 11. as *h.* is high above earth
115. 16. the *h.* even *h.* are the Lord's
Prov. 25. 3. the *h.* for height and earth
Is. 66. 1. *h.* is my throne, *Acts* 7. 49.
Jer. 31. 37. if *h.* above can be measured
Hag. 1. 10. *h.* over you is stayed from
Matt. 5. 18. till *h.* and earth pass, 24. 3.
Luke 15. 18. sinned against *h.* and in, 21.
John 1. 51. see *h.* open and angels ascending
Ps. 73. 25. whom have I in *h.* but thee
Eccl. 5. 2. God is in *h.* and thou on earth
Heb. 10. 34. have in *h.* a better substance
1 *Pet.* 1. 4. inheritance reserved in *h.*

for you

HEAVENS, *Gen.* 2. 1. thus the h. and the earth were finished

Deut. 31. 1. give ear, O h.

2 *Sam.* 22. 10. he bowed the h. and came, *Ps.* 18. 9.

1 *Kings* 8. 27. the heaven of h. cannot contain thee

2 *Chr.* 6. 25. then hear from the h.

Job 15. 15. the h. are not clean in his

Ps. 8. 3. consider the h. the work

19. 1. the h. declare the glory of God

50. 4. shall call to the h. from above, and to earth

89. 11. the h. are thine, the earth also

108. 4. for thy mercy is great above the h.

148. 1. praise ye the Lord, from h. praise him

Ps. 148. 4. praise him ye h. of h. and waters above the h.

Is. 44. 23. sing, O ye h. for the Lord hath done it

45. 8. drop down ye h. from above, let the skies pour

55. 9. for as the h. are higher than the earth

Is. 65. 17. I create new h. and new earth, 66. 22; *Rev.* 21. 1.

Hos. 2. 21. I will hear the h. they shall hear the earth

Hab. 3. 3. God came, his glory covered the h.

Acts 3. 21. h. must receive him till time

Acts 7. 56. behold, I see the h. opened, and Son of man

2 *Cor.* 5. 1. we have house eternal in h.

Eph. 4. 10. ascended far above all h.

Heb. 1. 10. the h. are the work of thine hands

4. 14. we have an High-Priest that is passed into h.

2 *Pet.* 3. 10. the h. shall pass away with a great noise

12. wherein the h. being on fire shall be dissolved

HEAVENS, in the, *Ps.* 2. 4. he that sitteth *in the h.* shall laugh

Ps. 18. 13. the Lord also thundered *in the h.*

103. 19. the Lord hath prepared his throne *in the h.*

Luke 12. 33. a treasure *in the h.* which faileth not

2 *Cor.* 5. 1. house not made with h. eternal *in the h.*

Heb. 8. 1. of the throne of the Majesty *in the h.*

9. 23. necessary that the patterns of things *in the h.*

HEAVENLY, *Matt.* 6. 14. h. Father, 26. 32. & 15. 13. & 18. 35; *Luke* 11. 13.

John 3. 12. believe if I tell you of h.

1 *Cor.* 15. 48. as is h. such are the h. 49.

Eph. 1. 3. in h. places, 20. & 2. 6. & 3. 10.

2 *Tim.* 4. 18. unto his h. kingdom to whom be glory

Heb. 3. 1. partakers of h. calling

HEAVY. Descriptive of the hands of Moses, *Ex.* 17. 12; and of the hand of God, 1 *Sam.* 5. 11; *Ps.* 32. 4; and the heart, *Prov.* 25. 20; the

eyes, *Matt.* 26. 43; *Num.* 11. 14; *Job* 33. 7.

Ps. 38. 4. as a h. burden too h. for me

Prov. 31. 6. to those of h. hearts

Is. 6. 10. make their ears h. and

58. 6. the fast to undo the h. burden

Matt. 11. 28. labour and are h. laden

23. 4. bind h. burdens and are grievous

Ps. 69. 20. I am full of h.

119. 28. my soul melteth for h.

Prov. 12. 25. h. in heart makes it stoop

14. 13. and the end of that mirth is h.

Is. 61. 3. garment of praise for spirit of h.

Rom. 9. 2. I have great h. and sorrow

1 *Pet.* 1. 6. are in h. through manifold temptations

HEDGE, Places of residence; 1 *Chr.* 4. 23.—The protection of God, *Job* 1. 10; *Prov.* 15. 19; *Is.* 5. 5; *Hos.* 2. 6; *Job* 3. 23; *Lam.* 3. 7.

HEED, care, attention, caution, 2 *Sam.* 20. 10; 2 *Kings* 10. 31.

Deut. 2. 4. take good h. to yours, 4. 15.

Josh. 22. 5. take diligent h. to do

Ps. 119. 9. by taking h. thereto accord.

Eccl. 12. 9. preacher gave good h. and sought out

Jer. 18. 18. not give h. to any of his ways

HEEL, *Gen.* 3. 15. shalt bruise his h.

Gen. 49. 17. Dan be an adder that biteth the horse's h.

Ps. 41. 9. hath lift up his h. against me, *John* 13. 18.

49. 5. when iniquity of my h. compass me about

HEIFER, *Gen.* 15. 9. take h. three years old

Judg. 14. 18. if ye had not plowed with my h.

Is. 15. 5. an h. of three years old

Jer. 50. 11. grown fat as an h. at grass

Hos. 10. 11. Ephraim is as an h. taught

Heb. 9. 13. the ashes of an h. sprinkling the unclean

HEIGHT, 1 *Sam.* 16. 7. look not on the h. of his stature

1 *Sam.* 17. 4. Goliath's h. was six cubits and a span

Job 22. 12. is not God in the h. of heaven? behold the h. of the stars, how high they are

Prov. 25. 3. the heaven for h. the earth for depth

Is. 7. 11. ask it in the depth, or in the h. above

Rom. 8. 39. nor h. nor depth shall be able to separate

Eph. 3. 18. what is the h. of the love of Christ

Rev. 21. 16. breadth and h. of city equal

HEINOUS, *Job* 31. 11. for this is an h. crime, yea, an iniquity

HEIR, *Gen.* 15. 4. & 21. 10.

Prov. 30. 23. handmaid h. to her mistress

Jer. 49. 1. hath Israel no sons, no h.

Matt. 21. 38. this is the h. let us kill him

Rom. 4. 13. that Abraham should be h. of world

Rom. 8. 17. if children then h. h. of God, joint h. with Christ

Gal. 3. 29. children *h*, according to
4. 7. if a son, then an *h*. of God.
Eph. 3. 6: Gentiles should be fellow *h*.
Heb. 1. 2. God hath appointed *h*. of all
6. 17. might show to the *h*. of promise
11. 7. became *h*. of the righteousness
by faith
1 *Pet.* 3. 7. *h*. together of grace of life
HELL, *Matt.* 18. 9; *Mark* 9. 43, 45, 47.
Deut. 32. 22. burn to lowest *h*.
2 *Sam.* 22. 6. sorrows of *h*. compassed me
Job 11. 8. it is deeper than *h*.
26. 6. *h*. is naked before him and
Ps. 9. 17. wicked shall be turned into *h*.
16. 10. not leave my soul in *h*. *Acts*
2. 27.
55. 15. let them go down quick into *h*.
86. 13. deliver my soul from lowest *h*.
116. 3. pains of hell gat hold upon me
139. 8. if I make my bed in *h*. thou
Prov. 5. 5. her steps take hold on *h*
7. 27. her house is way to *h*.
9. 18. her guests are in the depths of *h*.
15. 11. *h*. and destruction are before
24. he may depart from *h*. beneath
23. 14. shalt deliver his soul from *h*.
27. 20. *h*. and destruction are never
full
Is. 5. 14. therefore *h*. hath enlarged
14. 9. *h*. from beneath moved to
15. shalt be brought 'down to *h*.
28. 15. with *h*. are at agreement, 48.
57. 9. debase thyself even to *h*. *Ezek.*
31. 16, 17. & 32. 21, 27.
Amos 9. 2. though they dig into *h*.
Jonah 2. 2. out of the belly of *h*. cried
Hab. 2. 5. who enlargeth his desire as *h*.
Matt. 5. 22. be in danger of *h*. fire
29. body be cast into *h*. 30. & 18. 9;
Mark 9. 43, 45, 47.
10. 28. destroy both soul and body
in *h*.
11. 23. brought down to *h*. *Luke* 10. 15.
16. 18. gates of *h*. shall not prevail
against
23. 15. twofold more child of *h*. than
33. can ye escape damnation of *h*.
Luke 12. 5. power to cast into *h*.
16. 23. rich man died, in *h*. lifted up
his eyes
Acts 2. 31. his soul was not left in *h*. 27.
Jam. 3. 6. tongue set on fire of *h*.
2 *Pet.* 2. 4. cast them down to *h*.
Rev. 1.` 18. having the keys of *h*. and
death
6. 8. death and *h*. followed with him
20. 13. death and *h*. delivered up the
dead
14. death and *h*. were cast into lake of
HELMET, 1 *Sam.* 17. 5; 2 *Chr.* 26. 14.
Is. 59. 17. an *h*. of salvation on his head
Ezek. 23. 24. shall set against the shield
and *h*.
27. 10. they hanged the shield and *h*.
in thee
Eph. 6. 17. take the *h*. of salvation and
sword of the Spirit·
1 *Thess.* 5. 8. for an *h*. the hope of salvation
HELP meet for him, *Gen.* 2. 18.
Deut. 33. 29. Lord the shield of thy *h*.
Judg. 5. 23. came not to the *h*. of the

Lord against
Ps. 27. 9. thou hast been my *h*.
33. 20. he is our *h*. and shield
40. 17. my *h*. and deliverer, 70. 5.
46. 1. God a present *h*. in time of
trouble
60. 11. vain is the *h*. of man, 108. 12.
71. 12. make haste for my *h*.
89. 19. laid *h*. on one that is mighty
115. 9. Lord is their *h*. and shield,
10. 11.
124. 8. our *h*. is in name of the Lord
Hos. 13. 9. but in me is thy *h*.
Acts 26. 22. having obtained *h*. of God
1 *Cor.* 12. 28. *h*. governments
HELP, verb, *Gen.* 49. 25. by the G. of
thy father, who shall *h*. thee
Josh. 1. 14. pass before your brethren
and *h*. them
2 *Sam.* 10. 11. then *h*. me, will *h*. thee,
1 *Chr.* 19. 12.
2 *Chr.* 14. 11. it is nothing with thee to *h*.
25. 8. for God hath power to *h*. and
to cast down
32. 8. but with us is the Lord our God,
to *h*. us
Ps. 12. 1. *h*. Lord; 22. 11. for there is
none to *h*.
22. 19. haste thee to *h*. me, 38. 22; 40.
13; 70. 1.
37. 40. Lord shall *h*. them; 42. 5. God
shall *h*. her
Ps. 40. 13. Lord make haste to *h*. me
Is. 41. 10. I will *h*. thee, 13. 14. & 44. 2.
63. 5. I looked there was none to *h*.
Mark 9. 24. Lord, I believe, *h*. thou
mine unbelief
Acts 16. 9. come into Macedonia and *h*.
Heb. 4. 16. find grace to *h*. in time of
HELPED, 1 *Sam.* 7. 12. hitherto hath
the Lord *h*. us
Ps. 118. 13. I might fall but the Lord
h. me
Is. 49. 8. in day of salvation I *h*. thee
Zech. 1. 15. *h*. forward the afflicted
Acts 18. 27. *h*. them much which had
believed
Rev. 12. 16. the earth *h*. woman
HELPETH, *Rom.* 8. 26. the Spirit also
h. our infirmities
HELPER, *Ps.* 10. 14. art *h*. of the fa-
therless
54. 4. God is my *h*. *Heb.* 13. 6.
Job 9. 13. proud *h*. stoop under
2 *Cor.* 1. 24. we are *h*. of your joy, by
faith ye stand
3 *John* 8. fellow *h*. to the truth
Rom. 16. 3. Priscilla and Aquila my *h*.
in Christ
HELPING, *Ezra* 5. 2. were the prophets of God *h*. them
Ps. 22. 1. why art thou so far from *h*. me
2 *Cor.* 1. 11. ye also *h*. together by
prayer for us
HEM, *Matt.* 9. 20. woman touched *h*.
of his garment, 14. 36.
HEN, *Matt.* 23. 37. as a *h*. gathereth
chickens, *Luke* 13. 34.
HENCE, *Ps.* 39. 13. O spare me, before
I go *h*.
Matt. 17. 20. remove *h*. to yonder place
16. 26. they which would pass from

h. to you cannot

John 14. 31. arise, let us go *h.*

Acts 22. 21. I will send thee far *h.* unto the Gentiles

HENCEFORTH, *Ps.* 125. 2. so is Lord about his people from *h.*

Ps. 131. 3. Israel hope in Lord from *h* and for ever

Matt. 23. 39. not see me *h.* till ye say

26. 29. I will not drink *h.* of this fruit of the vine

Luke 1. 48. *h.* all generations shall call me blessed

John 14. 7. *h.* ye know him

15. 15. *h.* I call you not servants

Rom. 6. 6. *h.* should not serve sin

2 *Cor.* 5. 15. should not *h.* live unto themselves, but to

16. *h.* know ye no man, *h.* know we him no more

Eph. 4. 14. *h.* be no more children

2 *Tim.* 4. 8. *h.* there is laid up for me a crown of righteousness

Heb. 10. 13. *h.* expecting till enemies be made

Rev. 14. 13. blessed are they who die in Lord, from *h.*

HERB, *Gen.* 1. 11. bring forth the *h.* yielding seed, 12.

Gen. 1. 29. every *h.* bearing seed

2. 5. made every *h.*

Ex. 9. 22. the hail smote every *h.*

Deut. 32. 2. as the small rain upon the tender *h.*

Ps. 37. 2. wither as the green *h.*

104. 14. he causeth *h.* to grow for service of man

Is. 66. 14. your bones shall flourish like an *h.*

HERBS, *Ex.* 12. 8. and with bitter *h.* eat it, *Num.* 9. 11.

Prov. 15. 17. better is a dinner of *h.* where love is

27. 25. and *h.* of the mountains are gathered

Is. 26. 19. for thy dew is as the dew of *h.* and the earth

Matt. 13. 32. is greatest among all *h.* *Mark* 4. 32.

Luke 11. 42. tithe all manner of *h.*

Rom. 14. 2. another who is weak eateth *h.*

HEREAFTER, *Matt.* 26. 64. *h.* see Son of man sitting

Mark 11. 14. no man eat fruit of thee *h.* for ever

Luke 22. 69. *h.* shall Son of man sit on right hand

John 1. 51. *h.* see heaven opened

13. 7. thou knowest not now, thou shalt know *h.*

1 *Tim.* 1. 16. pattern to them which *h.* believe on him

Rev. 1. 19. write the things which shall be *h.*

4. 1. things which shall be *h.*

HEREIN, *John* 4. 37. *h.* saying true, one soweth

John 15. 8. *h.* is my Father glorified, that we bear fruit

Acts 24. 16. *h.* do I exercise myself to have conscience

1 *John* 4. 10. *h.* is love; 17. *h.* is love made perfect

HERESY, *Acts* 24. 14. after the way which they call *h.*

HERESIES, 1 *Cor.* 11. 19. also *h.* among you

Gal. 5. 20. the works of the flesh, wrath, strife, *h.*

2 *Pet.* 2. 1. privily bring in damnable *h.*

HERITAGE appointed by God, *Job* 20. 29.

Ps. 16. 6. I have a goodly *h.*

61. 5. given me *h.* of them that fear thee

119. 111. thy testimonies taken as *h.* for ever

127. 3. lo, children are *h.* of Lord

Is. 54. 17. this is the *h.* of servant of the Lord, 58. 14.

Jer. 3. 19. goodly *h.* of host of nations

Joel 2. 17. give not thy *h.* to reproach, 3. 2.

1 *Pet.* 5. 3. not as lords over God's *h.*

HEW tables of stone, *Ex.* 34. 1; *Deut.* 12. 3.

Jer. 2. 13. *h.* them out cisterns

Hos. 6. 5. have *h.* them by the prophets

HEWN, *Is.* 51. 1. look unto the rock whence ye are *h.*

Matt. 3. 10. *h.* down, 7. 19; *Luke* 3. 9.

Matt. 27. 60. and laid it in a sepulchre which he had *h.* out in the rock, *Matt.* 15. 46; *Luke* 23. 53.

HID themselves, Adam and his wife, *Gen.* 3. 8.

Ex. 2. 2. goodly child, she *h.*

Josh. 10. 16. the five kings *h.* themselves in a cave

Judg. 9. 5. Jotham *h.* himself

1 *Sam.* 10. 22. Saul *h.* himself; 20. 24.

1 *Kings* 18. 4. Obadiah *h.* the prophets, 13.

Job 3. 10. nor *h.* sorrow from mine eyes

10. 13. these things hast thou *h.* in thine heart

29. 8. the young men saw me and *h.* themselves

Ps. 119. 11. word have I *h.* in my heart

Is. 50. 6. I *h.* not my face from, shame and spitting

53. 3. *h.* our faces from him

54. 8. in a little wrath I *h.* my face from thee

Matt. 11. 25. *h.* these things from wise and prudent, *Luke* 10. 21.

25. 25. I went and *h.* thy talent in the earth

Luke 1. 24. Elizabeth *h.* herself five months

John 8. 59. but Jesus *h.* himself

2 *Cor.* 4. 3. if gospel be *h.* it be *h.* to lost

Col. 2. 3. in whom are *h.* all the treasures

3. 3. your life is *h.* with Christ in God

HID or HIDDEN, *Job* 3. 21. and dig for it more than for *h.* treasures

Ps. 51. 6. in *h.* part shall make me know wisdom

Prov. 2. 4. and searchest for her as for *h.* treasures

Matt. 10. 26. *h.* that shall not be known

1 *Cor.* 2. 7. even the *h.* wisdom which

God ordained
4. 5. will bring to light the *h.* things of darkness
2 *Cor.* 4. 2. *h.* things of dishonesty
Eph. 3. 9. from beginning *h.* in God
Col. 1.′ 26. mystery *h.* from ages
2. 3. in whom are *h.* all the treasures of wisdom
3. 3. and your life is *h.* with Christ in God
Heb. 11. 23. by faith Moses was *h.* three
1 *Pet.* 3. 4. *h.* man of heart not corruptible
Rev. 2. 17. I will give to eat of the *h.* manna

HID, be, *Zeph.* 2. 3. may be ye shall *be h.* in day
2 *Cor.* 4. 3. if our gospel *be h.* it is hid to the lost

HID, not be, *Matt.* 5. 14. a city that is set on an hill *cannot be h.*
Mark 7. 24. entered an house, but he could *not be h.*
1 *Tim.* 5. 25. they that otherwise *cannot be h.*

HIDE, *Gen.* 18. 17. shall I *h.* from Abraham
Job 33. 17. that he may *h.* pride from man
Ps. 17. 8. *h.* me under shadow of wings
27. 5. in time of trouble he shall *h.* me
30. 7. *h.* thy face and was troubled
31. 20. wilt *h.* them in secret of thy presence
51. 9. *h.* thy face from my sin
143. 9. I flee to thee to *h.* me, 7.
Is. 26. 20. *h.* thyself for a little moment
Jam. 5. 20. *h.* a multitude of sins, 1 *Pet.* 4. 8.
Rev. 6. 16. *h.* us from face of him

HIDEST, *Job* 13. 24. why *h.* thou thy face, *Ps.* 30. 7. & 44. 24. & 88. 14. & 143. 7.
Is. 45. 15. art God that *h.* thyself O God

HIDETH, *Job* 23. 9. he *h.* himself on the right hand, that
Job 34. 29. when he *h.* his face
42. 3. who is he that *h.* counsel without knowledge
Ps. 10. 11. he *h.* his face
Ps. 139. 12. darkness *h.* not from thee
Is. 8. 17. I will wait on Lord that *h.* his face

HIDING, *Job* 31. 33. by *h.* my iniquity in my bosom
Ps. 32. 7. thou art my *h.* place, 119. 114.
Is. 28. 17. the waters shall overflow the *h.* place
32. 2. a man shall be as *h.* place from the wind
Hab. 3. 4. and there was the *h.* of his power

HIGH, *Deut.* 3. 5. & 12. 2. & 28. 43.
Deut. 26. 19. make thee *h.* above
1 *Kings* 9. 8. at this house which is *h.*
1 *Chr.* 17. 17. state of man of *h.* degree
Job 11. 8. as *h.* as heaven what canst
Ps. 49. 2. hear low and *h.* rich and poor
89. 13. strong hand and *h.* thy right
97. 9. thou Lord art *h.* above all earth, 113. 14.

103. 11. as heaven is *h.* above earth
131. 1. not in things too *h.* for
138. 6. though Lord be *h.* yet hath he respect
Prov. 21. 4. a *h.* look and proud heart
Eccl. 12. 5. afraid of that which is *h.*
Is. 57. 15. I dwell in *h.* and holy place
Ezek. 21. 26. abase him that is *h.*
Rom. 12. 16. mind not *h.* things, but condescend
2 *Cor.* 10. 5. every *h.* thing that exalteth
Phil. 3. 14. for the prize of *h.* calling of God

HIGH, MOST, *Num.* 24. 16. *most H.*
Deut. 32. 8; 2 *Sam.* 22. 14; *Ps.* 7. 17. & 9. 2. & 21. 7. & 46. 4. & 56. 2. & 57. 2.
Ps. 47. 2. Lord *most H.* is terrible, great King
50. 14. pay thy vows to the *most H.*
73. 11. is there knowledge in *most H.*
83. 18. Jehovah art *most H.* over all earth
91. 9. thou made *m. H.* thy habitation
92. 8. thou art *most H.* for evermore
Is. 14. 14. I will ascend and be like the *most H.*
Dan. 4. 34. and I blessed the *most H.*
7. 18. saints of *most H.* take kingdom
Hos. 7. 16. they return, not to *most H.*
11. 7. called to *most H.* but none exalteth
Acts 7. 48. *most H.* dwelleth not in tem.

HIGH, on, *Deut.* 28. 1. God will set thee *on h.*
Job 5. 11. set up *on h.* those below
16. 19. witness in heaven and my record *on h.*
Ps. 68. 18. thou hast ascended *on h.*
69. 29. O God, set me up *on h.*
107. 41. poor *on h.* from afflictions
113. 5. like our God which dwells *on h.*
Is. 26. 5. bringeth down them that dwell *on h.*
Luke 1. 78. the day-spring from *on h.*
Luke 24. 49. endued with power from *on h.*
Eph. 4. 8. when he ascended up *on h.*

HIGHER, *Ps.* 61. 2. lead me to the Rock that is *h.*
Eccl. 5. 8. there he be *h.* than they
Is. 55. 9. heaven *h.* than earth my ways
Luke 14. 10. he may say, go up *h.*
Rom. 13. 1. be subject to *h.* powers
Heb. 7. 26. made *h.* than the heavens

HIGHEST, *Ps.* 18. 13. the *H.* gave his voice
87. 5. *H.* himself shall establish her
Prov. 9. 3. crieth on *h.* places of city
Eccl. 5. 8. he that is *h.* than *h.*
Matt. 21. 9. hosanna in *h.* *Mark* 11. 10.
Luke 1. 35. power of the *H.* overshadow
2. 14. glory to God in the *h.* 19. 38.
6. 35. shall be the children of the *H.*
14. 8. sit not down in *h.* room

HIGHLY, *Luke* 1. 28. art *h.* favoured
Luke 16. 15. which is *h.* esteemed among
Rom. 12. 3. not think of himself more *h.*
Phil. 2. 9. God hath *h.* exalted him
1 *Thess.* 5. 13. esteem them very *h.* in

HIGH-MINDED, Rom. 11. 20. be not h. minded, but fear
1 Tim. 6. 17. that they be not h. minded
2 Tim. 3. 4. heady, h. minded
HILL, Ex. 24. 4; Ps. 68. 15. 16.
Gen. 7. 19. all high h. under the heavens were covered
49. 26. utmost bound of everlasting h.
Num. 23. 9. from h. I behold him
Deut. 11. 11. it is a land of h. and valleys
33. 15. precious things of lasting h.
Ps. 2. 6. set king on holy h. of Zion, 3. 4. & 15. 1. & 43. 3. & 68. 15. & 99. 9.
18. 7. foundations of h. moved
42. 6. remember thee from h. Mizar
50. 10. cattle on thousand h. are mine
65. 12. little h. rejoice on every side
68. 16. why leap ye, ye high h. h. of God
95. 4. strength of the h. is his also
98. 8. let h. be joyful together
104. 13. he watereth h. from chambers
32. he toucheth h. and they smoke
114. 4. little h. skipped like lambs
121. 1. will lift mine eyes to the h.
Prov. 8. 25. before h. I brought forth
Is. 30. 17. be left as an ensign on an h.
40. 4. mountain and h. he made low
12. who weighed h. in balance
54. 10. mountains depart, h. remove
Hos. 10. 8. h. fall on us, Luke 23. 30.
Hab. 3. 6. perpetual h. did bow
Matt. 5. 14. city that is set on an h.
Luke 3. 5. every h. be brought low
4. 29. led him to the brow of the h.
23. 30. say to the h. cover us
Acts 17. 22. Paul stood in Mars h.
HILL, country, Josh. 13. 6. inhabitants of h.-country drive out
Luke 1. 39. Mary went to h.-country
65. noised through h.-c. of Judea
HINDER, ED, Gen. 24. 56. h. me not, seeing
Neh. 4. 8. and h. the building
Job 9. 12. behold, he taketh away, who can h. him
Acts 8. 36. h. me to be baptized
1 Cor. 9. 12. lest h. the gospel of Christ
Gal. 5. 7. who did h. you, that you should not obey truth
1 Thess. 2. 18. but Satan h.
1 Pet. 3. 7. as heirs together of life, that your prayers be not h.
HIRE, Deut. 24. 15. at this day thou shalt give him his h.
1 Kings 5. 6. give h. for thy servants
Is. 23. 18. her h. shall be holiness
Zech. 8. 10. no h. for man, h. for beast
Matt. 20. 8. give them their h.
Luke 10. 7. for the labourer is worthy of his h.
Jam. 5. 4. of h. labourers is kept back
HIRED, Hos. 8. 9. are gone up, Ephraim hath h. lovers
Matt. 20. 7. because no man hath h. us
Acts 28. 30. Paul dwelt two years in his own h. house
HIRED servants, Mark 1. 20. left Zebedee in the ship with h. servants
Luke 15. 17. how many h. servants have bread enough

19. make me as one of thy h. servants
HIRELING, Job 7. 1. days like days of an h.
Job 14. 6. accomplish as an h. his day
Mal. 3. 5. those that oppress the h.
John 10. 12. he that is an h. and not the shepherd
13. the h. fleeth, because he is an h. and careth not
HITHERTO Lord helped us 1 Sam. 7. 12.
Job 38. 11. h. shalt come but no
John 16. 24. h. ye asked nothing in my
1 Cor. 3. 2. h. ye were not able to bear
HOLD, Gen. 21. 18; Ex. 9. 2. & 20. 7.
Judg. 9. 46. h. of the house of the god Berith
1 Sam. 22. 4. David in h. 24. 22; 2 Sam. 5. 17; 23. 14.
5. abide not in the h. depart and get thee into land
Acts 4. 3. in h. unto next day
Rev. 18. 2. h. of every foul spirit
HOLD, Job 17. 9. righteous shall h. on his way
Ps. 17. 5. h. up my goings
117. h. thou me up and I shall be safe
139. 10. right hand shall h. me
Is. 41. 13. I will help, I will h. thy right hand
62. 1. for Zion's sake I will not h. my peace, 42. 14.
Jer. 2. 13. the cisterns can h. no water
Matt. 6. 24. h. to one and despise the
21. 26. all h. John as a prophet
Rom. 1. 18. h. truth in unrighteousness
Phil. 2. 29. h. such in reputation
2 Thess. 2. 15. h. the traditions
Heb. 3. 14. if we h. beginning of our confidence
Rev. 2. 14. h. the doctrine of Balaam
HOLD fast, Job 27. 6. my righteousness I h. fast
1 Thess. 5. 21. prove all things, h. fast that which is good
2 Tim. 1. 13. h. fast the form of sound
Heb. 3. 6. if we h. fast the confidence of hope
4. 14. us h. fast our profession, 10. 23.
Rev. 2. 13. h. fast my name and hast not denied
Rev. 2. 25. what ye have h. fast till I
3. 3. remember h. fast and repent
11. h. fast that thou hast, that no man
HOLDEST, Job 13. 24. wherefore h. thou me for thine enemy
Ps. 77. 4. h. my eyes waking
HOLDETH, Job 2. 3. still h. fast his integrity
Ps. 66. 9. which h. our soul in life, and
Prov. 17. 28. fool when he h. his peace
HOLDING, Jer. 6. 11. I am weary with h. in
Phil. 2. 16. h. forth the word of life that
Col. 2. 19. not h. the head from which
1 Tim. 1. 19. h. faith and a good conscience
3. 9. h. mystery of faith in a pure conscience
Tit. 1. 9. h. fast the faithful word
HOLY ground, Ex. 3. 5.
Ex. 16. 23. h. sabbath, 31. 14, 15.

19. 6. *h.* nation, 1 Pet. 2. 9.
28. 38. *h.* gifts; 29. 6. *h.* crown
30. 25. *h.* ointment
Lev. 16. 33. *h.* sanctuary
27. 14. house *h.*; 30. *h.* tithes
Num. 5. 17. *h.* water
31. 6. *h.* instruments
Lev. 11. 45. be ye *h.* for I am *h.* 20. 3, 7.
1 *Sam.* 2. 2. there is none *h.* as the Lord
21. 5. vessels of young men are *h.*
Ps. 22. 3. thou art *h.* that inhabitest
99. 5. worship at footstool, for he is *h.*
145. 17. the Lord is *h.* in all his works
Prov. 20. 25. snare to devour what is *h.*
Is. 6. 3. *h. h.* Lord God of hosts, *Rev.*
4. 8.
Ezek. 22. 26. difference between *h.* and
Matt. 7. 6. give not what is *h.* to dogs
Luke 1. 35. *h.* thing born of her
Acts 4. 27. thy *h.* child Jesus, 30.
Rom. 7. 12. law *h.* com. *h.* just, good
11. 16. if first fruit be *h.* lump also *h.*
12. 1. sacrifice *h.* acceptable to God
1 *Cor.* 7. 14. children unclean, but now *h.*
Eph. 1. 4. be *h.* without blame, 5. 27.
2 *Tim.* 1. 9. called us with *h.* calling
3. 15. hast known the *h.* scriptures
Tit. 1. 8. sober, just, *h.* temperate
1 *Pet.* 1. 15. be ye *h.* in all manner, 16.
2. 5. an *h.* priesthood; 9 *h.* nation
2 *Pet.* 1. 21. *h.* men of God spoke as
moved
3. 11. *h.* in all conversation and godliness
Rev. 3. 7. saith he that is *h.* and true
Rev. 4. 8. *h. h. h.* Lord God Almighty
15. 4. for thou only art *h.* all nations
20. 6. blessed and *h.* is he that hath
22. 11. he that is *h.* let him be *h.* still
Ex. 26. 33. most *h.* place, 34. & 29. 37.
& 40. 10; 1 *Kings* 6. 16. & 7. 50. &
8. 6; *Ezek.* 44. 13. & 45. 3.
Lev. 6. 25. most *h.* offering, 7. 1, 6. & 10.
17. & 14. 13; *Num.* 18. 9, 10; *Ezek.*
48. 12.
27. 28. most *h.* things, *Num.* 4. 4, 19;
1 *Chr.* 6. 49. & 23. 13; 2 *Chr.* 31. 14.
Lev. 21. 22. most *h.* bread
2 *Chr.* 3. 8. most *h.* house
Ezek. 43. 12. the whole limit shall be
made *h.*
Dan. 9. 24. seventy weeks determined
—and upon thy *h.* city, to finish
transgression
Jude 20. building up selves in most *h.*
faith
Ps. 42. 4. with multitude that kept *h.*
day, *Is.* 58. 13; *Col.* 2. 16; *Ex.* 35. 2.
HOLY *the most H. Ps.* 87. 1. *h.* mountain, *Is.* 11. 9. & 56. 7. & 57. 13. &
65. 11, 25. & 66. 20; *Dan.* 9. 16. &
11. 45; *Joel* 2. 1. & 3. 17; *Obad.* 16;
Zeph. 3. 11; *Zech.* 8. 3.
Lev. 20. 3. *H. name*, 22. 2, 32; 1 *Chr.* 16.
10, 35; *Ps.* 33. 21. & 103. 1. & 111.
9.'& 145. 21; *Is.* 57. 15; *Ezek.* 36.
20, 21.
Deut. 33. 8. *H. One*, *Job* 6. 10; *Ps.* 16. 10.
& 89. 19; *Is.* 10. 17. & 29. 23. & 40.
25. & 43. 15. & 49. 7; *Hab.* 1. 12. &
3. 3; *Mark* 1. 24; *Acts* 3. 14; 1
John 2. 20.

2 *Kings* 19. 22. *H. One of Israel, Ps.* 71.
22. & 78. 41. & 89. 18; *Is.* 1. 4. & 5.
19, 24. & 10. 20. & 12. 6. & 17. 7. &
29. 19. & 30. 11. 12. & 31. 1. & 41.
14. & 45. 11. & 47. 4. & 49. 7. & 55.
5. & 60. 9. 14; *Jer.* 50. 29. & 51. 5.
Deut. 7. 6. *h.* people, 14. 2, 21. & 26. 19.
& 28. 9; *Is.* 62. 12; *Dan.* 8. 24. &
12. 7.
Ex. 28. 29. *h.* place, *Lev.* 6. 16. & 10. 17;
Eccl. 8. 10.
Ps. 5. 7. *h.* temple, 11. 4. & 65. 4. & 79.
1. & 138. 2; *Jonah* 2. 4; *Mic.* 1. 2;
Hab. 2. 20; *Eph.* 2. 21.
HOLIER, *Is.* 65. 5. come not near, for
I am *h.* than thou
HOLIEST, *Heb.* 9. 3, 8. & 10. 19.
1 *Thess.* 2. 10. how *h.* and justly
HOLINESS, *Ex.* 15. 11. glorious in *h.*
28. 36. *h.* to the Lord 39. 30; *Is.* 23.
18.
1 *Chr.* 16. 29. in beauty of *h. Ps.* 29. 2.
& 96. 9. & 110. 3; 2 *Chr.* 20. 21.
2 *Chr.* 31. 18. sanctified themselves in *h.*
Ps. 30. 4. remembrance of his *h.* 97. 12.
47. 8. God sits on throne of *h.*
48. 1. in mountain of his *h. Jer.* 31. 23.
60. 6. God has spoken in his *h.* 108. 7.
89. 35. I have sworn by my *h.*
93. 5. *h.* becometh thine house O
Lord, for ever
Is. 23. 18. her hire shall be *h.* to the L.
35. 8. and it shall be called the way
of *h.*
62. 9. drink it in the courts of my *h.*
63. 15. habitation of thy *h.*
18. people of *h.*
Jer. 2. 3. Israel was *h.* to the Lord
23. 9. because of Lord and word of
his *h.*
Amos 4. 2. Lord hath sworn by his *h.*
Obad. 17. on mount Zion shall be *h.*
Zech. 14. 20. on horse-bells *h.* to L. 21.
Mal. 2. 11. Judah has profaned *h.* of
Lord
Luke 1. 75. in *h.* and righteousness before him
Acts 3. 12. as though by our *h.* we had
Rom. 1. 4. Son of God according to the
Spirit of *h.*
6. 19. yield members servants to
righteousness to *h.*
22. fruit unto *h.* and end everlasting
2 *Cor.* 7. 1. perfecting *h.* in fear of God
Eph. 4. 24. created in righteousness and
true *h.*
1 *Thess.* 3. 13. unblamable in *h.* before
God
4. 7. called not uncleanness but to *h.*
1 *Tim.* 2. 15. in faith, love, *h.* sobriety
Tit. 2. 3. behaviour as becometh *h.* no
Heb. 12. 10. partakers of his *h.*
14. *h.* without which no man see Lord
HOLY SPIRIT, Holy Ghost, *Matt.* 1. 18.
with child of the *H. Ghost*
Matt. 1. 20. that conceived in her is of
H. Ghost
3. 11. baptize you with the *H. Ghost
Mark* 1. 8; *John* 1. 33; *Acts* 1. 5.
& 11. 16.
12. 31. blasphemy against *H. Ghost,*

32; _Mark_ 3. 29.

Mark 12. 36. David said, by _H. Ghost_, _Acts_ 1. 16.

13. 11. not ye that speak, but _H. G._

Luke 1. 35. _H. Ghost_ shall come upon

2. 25. _H. Ghost_ was upon him

26. revealed to him by the _H. Ghost_.

3. 22. _H. Ghost_ descended in bodily shape

12. 10. blasphemeth against _H. Ghost_

12. _H. Ghost_ shall teach you in same

John 7. 39. for _H. Ghost_ was not yet

14. 26. Comforter, which is _H. Ghost_, whom the Father will send

20 22. receive ye the _H. Ghost_

Acts 1. 2. through _H. Ghost_ had given commandment

8. after that _H. Ghost_ is come upon

2. 33. promise of the _H. Ghost_

38. gift of _H. Ghost_, 10. 45.

5. 3. Satan filled heart to lie to _H. G._

32. we are his witnesses and also the _H. Ghost_

7. 51. ye do always resist _H. Ghost_ as your fathers

8. 15. receive _H. Ghost_, 17. 19.

18. _H. Ghost_ given

9. 31. walking in the fear of the Lord, and in the comfort of the _H. Ghost_

10. 38. anointed Jesus with _H. Ghost_

44. _H. Ghost_ fell on all them, 11. 15. & 15. 8.

47. received the _H. Ghost_

19. 2. be any _H. Ghost_, 6.

13. 2. _H. Ghost_ said, separate unto me, Saul

4. they being sent forth by the _H. G._

15. 28. it seemed good to _H. G._ and us

16. 6. forbidden of _H. Ghost_ to preach

20. 23. save that which the _H. Ghost_ witnesseth

28. flocks over which _H. Ghost_ made you overseers

21. 11. thus saith _H. Ghost_, so shall the Jews

28. 25. well spake the _H. G._ by Esaias

Rom. 5. 5. love of God shed abroad by the _H. G._

9. 1. conscience bearing witness in the _H. Ghost_

14. 17. righteousness, peace, and joy in the _H. Ghost_

15. 13. abound in hope through power of the _H. Ghost_

16. offering of Gentiles sanctified by the _H. Ghost_

1 _Cor._ 2. 13. in words which _H. Ghost_ teacheth

6. 19. temple of the _H. Ghost_ which is in you

12. 3. can say Jesus is Lord but by the _H. Ghost_

2 _Cor._ 6. 6. by the _H. Ghost_, by love unfeigned

13. 14. communion of _H. Ghost_ be with you

1 _Thess._ 1. 5. in _H. G._ much assurance

6. joy of _H. Ghost_

2 _Tim._ 1. 14. keep by _H. Ghost_ which dwells

Tit. 3. 5. not by works but by renewing

of _H. Ghost_

Heb. 2. 4. miracles and gifts of _H. G._

3. 7. wherefore as the _H. Ghost_ saith,

6. 4. made partakers of _H. Ghost_

Heb. 9. 8. _H. Ghost_ thus signifying that

10. 15. whereof _H. Ghost_ is a witness

1 _Pet._ 1. 12. preach with the _H. Ghost_ sent down

2 _Pet._ 1. 21. but _h._ men of God spake as they were moved by the _H. Ghost_

1 _John_ 5. 7. Father, Word, and _H. Ghost_ are one

Jude 20. building up yourselves, praying in _H. Ghost_

Luke 1. 15. filled with, or full of the _H. Ghost_, 41. 67; _Acts_ 2. 4. & 4. 8. & 6. 3. 5. & 9. 17. & 11. 24. & 13. 9, 52.

HOLY SPIRIT, _Ps._ 51. 11. take not thy _H. Spirit_ from

_Is._ 63. 10. rebelled and vexed his _H. S._

11. is he that put his _H. Spirit_ within

Luke 11. 13. give _H. Spirit_ to them that

Eph. 1. 13. ye are sealed with _H. Spirit_ of promise

4. 30. grieve not the _H. Spirit_ of God

1 _Thess._ 4. 8. who hath given us his _H. Spirit_

HOME, _Gen._ 39. 16. & 43. 16.

_Ps._ 68. 12. tarried at _h._ divided spoil

Eccl. 12. 5. man goeth to his long _h._

2 _Cor._ 5. 6. while we are at _h._ in body

Tit. 2. 5. chaste keepers at _h._

HONEST and good heart _Luke_ 8. 15.

Acts 6. 3. men of _h._ report full of Holy Ghost

Rom. 12. 17. provide things _h._ in sight

2 _Cor._ 8. 21. providing for _h._ things, not 13. 7. shall do that which is _h._

Phil. 4. 8. whatsoever things are _h._

1 _Pet._ 2. 12. have your conversation _h._ among

Rom. 13. 13. walk _h._ as in the day

1 _Thess._ 4. 12. walk _h._ towards them

Heb. 13. 18. all things willing to live _h._

1 _Tim._ 2. 2. in all godliness and _h._

HONEY, _Gen._ 43. 11; _Lev._ 2. 11; _Judg._ 14. 8, 18; 1 _Sam._ 14. 26, 29.

_Ex._ 16. 31. like wafers made with _h._

Deut. 8. 8. a land of olive-oil and _h._ 2. _Kings_ 18. 32.

32. suck _h._ out of the rock

1 _Sam._ 14. 25. _h._ upon the ground

1 _Kings_ 14. 3. take a cruise of _h._

_Ps._ 19. 10. sweeter than _h._ and _h._ comb. 119. 103.

Prov. 25. 27. not good to eat much _h._

Songs 4. 11. _h._ and milk are under thy

_Is._ 7. 15. butter and _h._ shall he eat, 22.

Matt. 3. 4. his meat was locusts and wild _h._

Rev. 10. 9. in thy mouth sweet as _h._ 10.

HONOUR be not united, _Gen._ 49. 6.

1 _Chr._ 29. 12. both riches and _h._ come

Job 14. 21. his sons come to _h._ he knoweth it not

_Ps._ 7. 5. lay my _h._ in the dust

8. 5. crowned him with glory and _h._

26. 8. the place where thy _h._ dwelleth

49. 12. man being in _h._ abideth not

20. man that is in _h._ and understandeth not

Ps. 96. 6. *h.* and majesty are before him strength and beauty
145. 5. I will speak of the *h.* of thy majesty
149. 9. this *h.* have his saints
Prov. 3. 16. in her left hand riches *h.*
8. 18. riches and *h.* with me
11. 16. a gracious woman retaineth *h.*
15. 33. before *h.* is humility, 18. 12.
20. 3. it is an *h.* for a man to cease from strife
26. 1. *h.* not seemly for a fool
29. 23. *h.* shall uphold the humble
Dan. 4. 30. built for *h.* of my majesty
Mal. 1. 6. if a father, where is my *h.*
Matt. 13. 57. prophet is not without *h.* save, *Mark* 6. 4; *John* 4. 44.
John 5. 41. I receive not *h.* from men
Rom. 2. 7. seek for glory, *h.* immortality
9. 21. make one vessel to *h.* and another to
12. 10. in *h.* preferring one another.
13. 7. give *h.* to whom *h.* is due
2 *Cor.* 6. 8. by *h.* and dishonour
1 *Tim.* 5. 17. elders, worthy of double *h.*
2 *Tim.* 2. 20. some to *h.* and some to dishonour
Heb. 5. 4. taketh his *h.* to himself, but
1 *Pet.* 1. 7. found to praise and *h.*
3. 7. giving *h.* unto the wife as the weaker vessel
2 *Pet.* 1. 17. he received from God the Father *h.*
Rev. 4. 11. thou art worthy to receive glory and *h.* 5. 12.
5. 13. *h.* power and might be to him, 7. 12; 19. 1.
19. 7. let us give *h.* to him
HONOUR, verb, *Ex.* 20. 12. *h.* thy father and mother, *Matt.* 15. 4.
1 *Sam.* 2. 30. them that *h.* me I will *h.*
Esth. 6. 6. whom the king delighteth to *h.* 7. 9, 11.
Prov. 3. 9. *h.* Lord with thy substance
Is. 29. 13. with lips they *h.* me
John 5. 23. should *h.* Son as they *h.* the Father
8. 49. but I *h.* my Father, and ye dishonour me
54. if I *h.* myself, my *h.* is nothing
12. 26. if serve me, him will my Father *h.*
1 *Tim.* 5. 3. *h.* widows that are widows indeed
1 *Pet.* 2. 17. *h.* all men love brotherhood
HONOURABLE, *Ps.* 111. 3. work *h.* and glorious
Is. 42. 21. he will magnify the law and make it *h.*
Mark 15. 43. Joseph of Arimathea an *h.* counsellor
Luke 14. 8. more *h.* man be bidden
1 *Cor.* 4. 10. ye are strong, ye are *h.*
Heb. 13. 4. marriage is *h.*
HONOURED, *Ex.* 14. 4. I will be *h.* on Pharaoh and his host
Prov. 13. 18. he that regardeth reproof shall be *h.*
Dan. 4. 34. I praised and *h.* him that liveth for ever
HONOURETH, *Ps.* 15. 4. he *h.* them

that fear the Lord
Mal. 1. 6. a son *h.* his Father
Matt. 15. 8. *h.* me with their lips, *Mark* 7. 6.
HOOK, *Ex.* 26. 32; *Ezek.* 29. 4. & 38. 4.
Is. 2. 4. pruning *h.* 18. 5; *Mic.* 4. 3.
HOPE in Israel concerning this, *Ezra* 10. 2.
Job 8. 13. hypocrite's *h.* shall perish
11. 20. their *h.* as giving up the Ghost
27. 8. what is *h.* of hypocrite when G.
41. 9. behold, the *h.* of man is in vain
Ps. 78. 7. might set their *h.* in God
146. 5. whose *h.* is in the Lord their God
Prov. 10. 28. *h.* of righteous shall be gladness
11. 7. the *h.* of unjust perisheth
13. 12. *h.* deferred maketh heart sick
14. 32. righteous hath *h.* in his death
19. 18. chasten thy son while there is *h.*
26. 12. more *h.* of a fool than, 29. 20.
Is. 57. 10. saidst there is no *h. Jer.* 2 25. & 18. 12; *Ezek.* 37. 11.
Jer. 14. 8. O the *h.* of Israel, 17. 13. & 50. 7.
17. 7. blessed man whose *h.* the Lord
Lam. 3. 29. if so there may be *h.*
Hos. 2. 15. valley of Achor, door of *h.*
Joel 3. 16. L. will be the *h.* of his people
Zech. 9. 12. turn to the strong hold, ye prisoners of *h.*
Acts 24. 15. have *h.* towards God
Rom. 5. 4. experience *h.*
5. *h.* maketh not ashamed
8. 24. we are saved by *h.* and *h.*
15. 4. comfort of the scriptures that we might have *h.*
1 *Cor.* 9. 10. husbandman partaker of his *h.*
13. 13. now abideth faith, *h.* charity
15. 19. in this life only *h.* in Christ
Gal. 5. 5. wait for *h.* of righteousness by faith
Eph. 2. 12. having no *h.* without God in the world
Col. 1. 23. not moved from *h.* of gospel
27. riches of glory of Christ in you the *h.* of glory
1 *Thess.* 4. 13. sorrow not as others who have no *h.*
5. 8. for an helmet the *h.* of salvation
1 *Tim.* 1. 1. Jesus Christ who is our *h.*
Tit. 2. 13. looking for blessed *h.*
3. 7. heirs according to *h.* of eternal life
Heb. 6. 11. to full assurance of *h.*
19. which *h.* we have as anchor
1 *Pet.* 1. 3. begotten us again to lively *h.*
21. that your faith and *h.* might be in God
3. 15. give a reason of *h.* in you
1 *John* 3. 3. he that hath this *h.* purifieth
HOPE, in, *Ps.* 16. 9. my flesh also shall rest *in h.*
Rom. 4. 18. who against *h.* believed *in h.*
5. 2. rejoice *in h.* of glory of God, 12.
12. 12. rejoicing *in h.*
15. 13. that ye may abound *in h.*
Tit. 1. 2. *h.* of eternal life which God promised

HOPE, my, *Job* 31. 24. if I have made
gold *my h.* or have said
Ps. 39. 7. *my h.* is in thee
71. 5. thou art *my h. Jer.* 17. 17.
119. 116. not be ashamed of *my h.*
HOPE, verb, *Ps.* 22. 9. make me *h.* when
I was
31. 24. all ye that *h.* in the Lord
33. 18. them that *h.* in his mercy, 22.
42. 5. *h.* thou in God for. 11. & 43. 5.
119. 81. but I *h.* in thy word, & 130. 5.
130. 7. let Israel *h.* in the Lord, for
HOPED, *Ps.* 119. 43. I have *h.* in thy
judgments
74. I have *h.* in thy word, 147.
Jer. 3. 23. in vain is salvation *h.* for
Luke 23. 8. he *h.* to have seen miracle
Acts 24. 26. he *h.* money should have
2 *Cor.* 8. 5 not as we *h.*
Heb. 11. 1. faith is the substance of
things *h.* for
HORN of my salvation, *Ps.* 18. 2.
Ps. 75. 4. lift not up the *h.* 5. 10.
92. 10. my *h.* shalt thou exalt like *h.*
148. 14. exalt the *h.* of his people
uke 1. 69. raised up an *h.* of salvation
Mic. 4. 13. I will make thy *h.* iron and
hoofs brass
Dan. 8. 20. having two *h.* kings, 21.
Hab. 3. 4. had *h.* coming out of his hand
Rev. 5. 6. Lamb having seven *h.*
13. 1. beast having ten *h.* 17. 3. 7.
11. had two *h.* like to a beast
HORRIBLE, dreadful, hateful *Ps.* 11. 6.
Jer. 5. 30. & 18. 13. & 23. 14; *Hos.*
6. 10; *Jer.* 2. 12; *Ezek.* 32. 10.
HORROR, *Gen.* 15. 12; *Job* 18. 20; *Ps.*
55. 5. & 119. 53; *Ezek.* 7. 18.
HORSE and rider thrown, *Ex.* 15. 21.
Job 39. 18. scorneth *h.* and his rider
Ps. 32. 9. be not as *h.* or mule
33. 17. *h.* is a vain thing for safety
147. 10. Lord delights not in strength
of *h.*
Prov. 21. 31. *h.* is prepared for day of
battle
26. 3. a whip for the *h.* a rod for the
Is. 63. 13. led through the deep as a *h.*
Jer. 8. 6. as *h.* rusheth into battle
51. 21. break in pieces *h.* and rider
HORSES, *Deut.* 17. 16. multiply *h.* to
himself to the end that he should
multiply *h.*
1 *Kings* 22. 4. and my *h.* are as thy *h.*
2 *Kings* 3. 7.
2 *Kings* 2. 11. appeared *h.* of fire
Eccl. 10. 7. seen servants on *h.*
Is. 31. 1. and stay on *h.* and trust in
chariots
3. and their *h.* are flesh, and not spirit
Jer. 12. 5. how counted with *h.*
Ezek. 23. 6. horsemen riding on *h.* 12.
Hos. 14. 3. we will not ride on *h.*
Zech. 1. 8. *h.* red, white, black, 6. 2, 3,
6; *Rev.* 6. 2, 4, 5, 8. & 9. 17.
Jam. 3. 3. put bits in the *h.* mouths
Rev. 19. 14. the armies followed him
upon white *h.*
HORSELEECH, *Prov.* 30. 15. the *h.*
hath two daughters, crying, give
HOSANNA is an Hebrew word, which
signifies, Save, I beseech you. It
is a form of acclamation, of blessing, or wishing one well. Thus at
the Saviour's entrance into Jerusalem, when the people cried Hosanna to the Son of David; their
meaning was, Lord, preserve this
Son of David; this : king heap
favours and blessings on him. The
word is found in *Matt.* 21. 9, 15;
Mark 11. 9, 10; *John* 12. 13.
HOSPITALITY, *Rom.* 12. 13. distributing to the saints given to *h.* 1 *Tim.*
3. 2.
Tit. 1. 8. but a lover of *h.*
1 *Pet.* 4. 9. use *h.* one to another
HOST, one who lodges and entertains
guests
Ps. 27. 3. though an *h.* should encamp
136. 15. but overthrew Pharaoh and
h. in Red Sea
Is. 40. 26. that bringeth out their *h.* by
Luke 2. 13. multitude of the heavenly
h. praising God
HOSTS, *Ps.* 103. 21. bless ye the Lord,
all ye his *h.*
Ps. 148. 2. praise ye him, all his angels.
all his *h.*
HOT, Spoken of an oven, *Ezek.* 24. 11;
Hos. 7. 7. The heart, *Deut.* 19. 6.
The displeasure of God, *Ps.* 6. 1. &
38. 1. & 39. 3; *Prov.* 6. 28; 1 *Tim.*
4. 2; *Rev.* 3. 15.
HOT, *Deut.* 9. 19. afraid of *h.* displeasure
Ps. 6. 1. neither chasten in thy *h.* displeasure, 38. 1.
39. 3. my heart was *h.* within me,
while musing
Dan. 3. 22. furnace was exceeding *h.*
1 *Tim.* 4. 2. their conscience seared
with a *h.* iron
Rev. 3. 15. I know thy work, neither
cold nor *h.* I would thou wert cold
or *h.* 16.
HOUR, *Dan.* 3. 6, 15. & 4. 33.
Matt. 10. 19. should be given you in
that same *h.*
24. 36. of that day and *h.* knoweth
44. such an *h.* as ye think not, 50;
Luke 12. 40. 46.
25. 13. ye know neither day nor *h.*
26. 45. the *h.* is at hand, the Son of
man is betrayed
27. 45. from the sixth *h.* was darkness
over the land to the ninth *h.* *Mark*
15. 33; *Luke* 23. 44.
Luke 12. 12. Holy Ghost teach you in
same *h.*
22. 53. this is your *h.* and power of
John 2. 4. my *h.* is not yet come
4. 23. *h.* cometh and now is, 5. 25.
7. 30. his *h.* was not yet come, 8. 20.
12. 27. save me from this *h.* came
I unto this *h.*
Rev. 3. 3. not know what *h.* I will come
10. I will keep thee from the *h.* of
temptation
8. 1. there was silence about the
space of half an *h.*
17. 12. power as kings one *h.* with
18. 10.in one *h.* is thy judgment come
HOUSE (1) A place to dwell in, *Gen.*

19. 3. (2) The household, or persons dwelling in the house, *Acts* 10. 2. Cornelius feared God with all his house, with all his family. So in *Heb.* 11. 7. Noah prepared an ark to the saving of his house. And in many other places. (3) Kindred, stock, or lineage, 2 *Sam.* 7. 18. What is my house, that thou hast brought me hitherto ? And *Luke* 1. 27. Gabriel was sent to a virgin espoused to Joseph, of the house of David; of the lineage or family of David. (4) Wealth, riches, or estates; *Matt.* 23. 14. ye devour widows' houses; ye consume their estates. (5) The grave, or a sepulchre. *Job* 30. 23: I know that thou wilt bring me to the house appointed for all living. And *Is.* 14. 18. Every one in his own house. (6) One's family affairs and concerns. 2 *Kings* 20. 1. Set thine house in order. (7) This frail, corruptible, mortal body, wherein the soul lodges for a time. 2 *Cor.* 5. 1. if our earthly house of this tabernacle were dissolved; if our bodily frame of nature were taken to pieces by death. (8) The church among the Jews. *Heb.* 3. 2. Moses was faithful in all his house. He ordered all things in the Jewish church according to the command of God.

HOUSE, *Ex.* 20. 17; *Lev.* 14. 36.

Ex. 12. 30. not an *h.* where not one dead
Job 21. 28. where is the *h.* of the
30. 23. to grave *h.* appointed for the
Ps. 84. 3. sparrow hath found an *h.*
Prov. 3. 33. curse of Lord is in *h.* of the wicked
7. 27. her *h.* is the way to hell going
12. 7. *h.* of the righteous shall
15. 25. Lord destroy *h.* of the proud
19. 14. *h.* and riches are inheritance of faith
21. 9. is better to dwell in corner of *h.* top, 25. 24.
Eccl. 7. 2. go to *h.* of mourning than to
12. 3. the keepers of *h.* tremble strong
Songs 1. 17. the beams of our *h.* are cedar, and rafters
Songs 2. 4. brought me to banquet *h.*
Is. 5. 8. woe to them that join *h.* to *h.*
60. 7. I will glorify *h.* of my glory
64. 11. our holy and beautiful *h.* in
Matt. 7. 25. and beat upon that *h.* 27; *Luke* 6. 48.
Matt. 10. 13. *h.* be worthy
12. 25. every *h.* divided against itself, *Mark* 3. 25.
23. 38. *h.* left desolate, *Luke* 11. 17. & 13. 35; *Jer.* 12. 7.
Luke 12. 8. proclaimed on the *h.* tops
John 14. 2. in my Father's *h.* are many mansions
Acts 2. 2. a sound from heaven filled all the *h.*
46. breaking bread from *h.* to *h.*
Rom. 16. 5. church in their *h.* 1 *Cor.* 16. 19; *Col.* 4. 16; *Philem.* 2.
1 *Cor.* 1. 11. by them which are of the

house of Chloe
2 *Cor.* 5. 1. earthly *h.* a *h.* not made with hands
2. *h.* from heaven
2 *Tim.* 1. 16. give mercy to *h.* of Onesiphorus
Heb. 3. 3. built *h.* hath more honour than *h.*
4. every *h.* built by some man
6. whose *h.* are we, if we hold
2 *John* 10. receive him not into your *h*
HOUSE, his, *Job* 1. 10. made an hedge about *his h.*
Job 7. 10. return no more to *his h.*
Ps. 105. 21. made him lord of all *his h.*
112. 3. wealth and riches shall be in *his h.*
Matt. 12. 29. then he shall spoil *his h.* *Mark* 3. 27.
24. 17. to take any thing out of *his h.* *Mark* 13. 15.
John 4. 53. *his* whole *h.* believed
Acts 10. 2. feared God with all *his h.*
Acts 16. 34. the jailer brought them into *his h.* he rejoiced, believing with all *his h.* 18. 8.
1 *Tim.* 5. 8. especially for those of *his* own *h.*
Heb. 3. 2. faithful in all *his h.* 5. 6.
11. 7. made an ark for saving *his h.*
HOUSE, my, *Gen.* 15. 2. the steward of *my h.* is this Eliezer
Gen. 15. 3. and lo, one born in *my h.* is mine heir
Josh. 24. 15. as for me and *my h.*
2 *Sam.* 23. 5. though *my h.* be not so with God
Job 17. 13. the grave is *mine h.*
Ps. 101. 2. I will walk within *my h.* with a perfect
Is. 56. 7. made them joyful in *my h.* of prayer, *Matt.* 21. 13; *Mark* 11. 7; *Luke* 19. 46.
Matt. 12. 44. return unto *my h.* *Luke* 11. 24.
Acts 16. 15. if faithful come into *my h.*
HOUSE, thy, *Gen.* 7. 1. come thou, and all *thy h.* into the ark
Deut. 6. 7. when sittest in *thy h.*
Ps. 26. 8. I loved habitation of *thy h.*
36. 8. satisfied with fatness of *thy h.*
65. 4. satisfied with goodness of *thy h.*
69. 9. the zeal of *thine h.* hath eaten me up, *John* 2. 17.
93. 5. holiness becometh *thine h.* O Lord, for ever
Is. 38. 1. set *thy h.* in order, for
Matt. 26. 18. I will keep the passover at *thy h.*
Luke 7. 44. I entered *thy h.* thou gavest me no water
19. 5. to-day I must abide at *thy h.*
Acts 11. 14. thou and all *thy h.* be saved, 16. 31.
Philem. 2. to the church in *thy h.*
Gen. 28. 17. *h.* of God or Lord, *Ps.* 42. 4. & 55. 14. & 122. 1. & 27. 4; *Eccl.* 5. 1; *Is.* 2. 3; *Mic.* 4. 2; 1 *Tim.* 3. 15; 1 *Pet.* 4. 17; *Ex.* 23. 19; *Josh.* 6. 24.
HOUSES, *Deut.* 6. 11. to give thee *h.* full of all good things
Job 4. 19. dwell in *h.* of clay

24. 16. in the dark dig through *h.*
Ps. 49. 11. *h.* shall continue for ever
Eccl. 2. 4. I builded me *h.*
Matt. 11. 8. in soft linen sit in king's *h.*
19. 29. forsaken *h.* lands, *Mark* 10. 29.
23. 14. devour widow's *h. Luke* 20. 47.
Luke 16. 4. may receive me into their *h.*
Acts 4. 34. possessors of *h.* sold
1 *Cor.* 11. 22. have ye not *h.* to eat in
1 *Tim.* 3. 12. ruling our *h.* well
2 *Tim.* 3. 6. creep into *h.* and lead
Tit. 1. 11. subvert whole *h.*
HOUSEHOLD, *Matt.* 10. 36. a man's
foes shall be they of his own *h.*
Acts 16. 15. baptized and her *h.*
1 *Cor.* 1. 16. baptized *h.* of Stephanas
Gal. 6. 10. *h.* of faith
Eph. 2. 19. *h.* of God
Phil. 4. 22. that are of Ceasar's *h.*
2 *Tim.* 1. 16. salute the *h.* of Onesiphorus
Matt. 13. 52. like *h.* 20. 1.
HOWL. To cry with bitter grief, *Is.*
13. 6. & 14. 31; *Jer.* 4. 8; *Joel* 1. 5,
11, 13; *Jam.* 5. 1; *Hos.* 7. 14;
Deut. 32. 16; *Amos* 8. 3.
HOW long *Ps.* 6. 3. & 13. 1. & 74. 9. & 79.
5. & 80. 4. & 89. 46; *Is.* 6. 11; *Jer.*
4. 14; *Dan.* 8. 13. & 12. 6; *Matt.*
17. 17; *Luke* 9. 41; *Rev.* 6. 10.
Job 15. 16. *h.* much more, *Prov.* 21. 27;
Matt. 7. 11; *Luke* 12. 24, 28; *Heb.*
9. 14.
Matt. 18. 21. & 23. 37. *h.* oft, *Luke* 13.
34; *Job* 21. 17; *Ps.* 78. 40.
HUMBLE. Lowly in mind before God,
and not proud before men; and
esteeming others better than ourselves, and not depreciating other
persons in order to exalt ourselves.
To HUMBLE signifies to afflict, to
prove, to try, *Deut.* 8. 2. God led
thee in the wilderness to humble
thee
HUMBLE person save *Job* 22. 29.
Ps. 9. 12. forgettest not cry of *h.*
10. 12. forgetteth not *h.*
17. desire of *h.*
34. 2. *h.* shall hear of it and be glad
69. 32. *h.* shall see this and be
Prov. 16. 19. be of *h.* spirit with lowly
29. 23. honour shall uphold *h.* in spirit
Is. 57. 15. of a contrite and *h.* spirit to
revive spirit of *h.* and the heart of
the contrite
Jam. 4. 6. gives grace to *h.* 1 *Pet.* 5. 5.
HUMBLE, verb, *Ex.* 10. 3. if thou refuse
to *h.* thyself
Deut. 8. 2. to *h.* thee and to prove, 16.
2 *Chr.* 7. 14. shall *h.* themselves
34. 27. because didst *h.* thyself before
Prov. 6. 3. *h.* thyself and make sure
friend
Jer. 13. 18. *h.* yourselves, sit down, for
Matt. 18. 4. whosoever *h.* himself shall
be exalted, 23. 12; *Luke* 14. 11. &
18. 14.
2 *Cor.* 12. 21. my God will *h.* me among
Jam. 4. 10. *h.* yourselves in the sight of
the Lord
1 *Pet.* 5. 6. *h.* yourselves therefore under
HUMBLED, *Lev.* 26. 41. if uncircum-

cised heart be *h.*
2 *Kings* 22. 19. hast *h.* thyself before
the Lord
2 *Chr.* 12. 6. princes and kings *h.* them.
12. he *h.* himself, 32. 26.
33. 12. 23. *h.* not himself before the
Lord, 36. 12.
Ps. 35. 13. I *h.* my soul with fasting
113. 6. Lord who *h.* himself to behold
Is. 2. 11. lofty looks shall be *h.* 9.
5. 15. mighty men shall be *h.* and eyes
of lofty shall be *h.*
10. 33. high and haughty shall be *h.*
Jer. 44. 10. they are not *h.* unto
Lam. 3. 20. my soul is *h.* in me
Dan. 5. 22. hast not *h.* thy heart
Phil. 2. 8. *h.* himself and became
obedient
HUMBLED, *Deut.* 21. 14. *h.* her, 22. 24,
29; *Ezek.* 22. 10, 11.
HUMBLENESS, *Col.* 3. 12. put on *h.* of
mind
HUMBLY, *Mic.* 6. 8. walk *h.* with thy
God
HUMILIATION, *Acts* 8. 33. in his *h.* his
judgment was taken away
HUMILITY, that grace of the Spirit
which, from a proper sense of lowliness and unworthiness, makes us
patient under trials, and contentedly submissive to the will of Providence.
Prov. 15. 33. and before honour is *h.*
18. 12.
Prov. 22. 4. by *h.* are riches, and honour
and life
Acts 20. 19. serving the Lord with all *h.*
of mind
Col. 2. 18. let no man beguile you in a
voluntary *h.*
1 *Pet.* 5. 5. be subject one to another,
clothed with *h.*
HUNDRED, *Matt.* 18. 12. if a man have
an *h.* sheep, *Luke* 15. 4.
Matt. 18. 28. owed him an *h.* pence
Luke 16. 6. an *h.* measures of oil
7. an *h.* measures of wheat
John 19. 39. myrrh, aloes, an *h.* weight
HUNGER, *Ex.* 16. 3; *Deut.* 28. 48.
Ps. 34. 10. young lions suffer *h.*
Prov. 19. 15. idle soul shall suffer *h.*
Jer. 42. 14. nor have *h.* of bread
Lam. 4. 9. better than they that be slain
with *h.*
Deut. 8. 3. suffered thee to *h.*
Is. 49. 10. shall not *h.* nor thirst, *Rev.*
7. 16.
Matt. 5. 6. blessed are they that *h.* after
Luke 6. 21. blessed are ye that *h.* now
25. woe to you that are full, for ye
shall *h.*
John 6. 35. come to me shall never *h.*
Rom. 12. 20. if enemy *h.* feed him
1 *Cor.* 4. 11. we both *h.* and thirst
11. 34. if any man *h.* let him eat at
home
HUNGRY, *Ps.* 107. 9. fills *h.* with goodness
Ps. 146. 7. giveth food to *h.* Lord looseth
Prov. 25. 21. if enemy be *h.* give him
27. 7. to *h.* every bitter is sweet
Is. 58. 7. to deal thy bread to *h.*

10. if draw out thy soul to *h*.
65. 13. shall eat, but ye shall be *h*.
Ezek. 18. 7. give his bread to the *h*. 16.
Luke 1. 53. filled *h*. with good things
Phil. 4. 12. how to be full and to be *h*.
HUNT, 1 *Sam*. 26. 20; *Job* 38. 39.
Job 10. 16. thou *h*. me as a fierce
Ps. 140. 11. evil doth *h*. violent man
Prov. 6. 26. adulterer will *h*. for precious life
12. 27. roasts not what he took *h*.
Ezek. 13. 18. ye *h*. souls of my people
HURT, *Gen*. 4. 23. & 26. 29.
Josh. 24. 20. I will turn and do you *h*.
Ps. 15. 4. swears to his *h*. and changeth
Eccl. 5. 13. riches kept to the owner's *h*.
Jer. 6. 14. healed the *h*. of the daughter, of my, 8. 11, 21.
Rev. 2. 11. not be *h*. of second death
6. 6. *h*. not oil and wine, 7. 3. & 9. 4.
HURTFUL, *Ezra* 4. 15; *Ps*. 144. 10.
1 *Tim*. 6. 9. fall into foolish and *h*. lusts
HUSBAND, *Gen*. 3. 6, 16. & 29. 32.
Ex. 4. 25. bloody *h*. art thou to me, 26.
Is. 54. 5. thy maker is thy *h*. Lord of Hosts
Jer. 31. 32. though I was an *h*. to them
Mark 10. 12. if woman put away her *h*.
John 4. 17. I have no *h*.; 18. had five *h*.
1 *Cor*. 7. 14. unbelieving *h*. is sanctified
34. careth how she may please her *h*.
14. 35. let them ask their *h*. at home
2 *Cor*. 11. 2. espoused you unto one *h*.
Eph. 5. 22. wives submit to own *h*. as unto the Lord
23. for the *h*. is the head of wife. 24.
25. *h*. love your wives as Christ, *Col*. 3. 19.
33. see that wife reverence her *h*.
Col. 3. 18. wives, submit yourselves to own *h*.
1 *Pet*. 3. 1. subject to their own *h*.
7. ye *h*. dwell with them according to
HUSBANDMAN. A tiller of the ground, it is applied to Christ, because he changes from sin to holiness, and causes the sinner to have his fruit unto holiness, *Gen*. 9. 20.
Zech. 13. 5. I am no prophet, I am a *h*.
John 15. 1. my Father is the *h*.
2 *Tim*. 2. 6. *h*. that laboureth must be
Jam. 5. 7. *h*. waits for precious fruits
HUSBANDMEN, *Matt*. 21. 33. he let it out to *h*. *Mark* 12. 2; *Luke* 20. 9.
Matt. 21. 41. he will let out his vineyard to other *h*.
Mark 12. 2. he might receive from the *h*. of the fruit
9. destroy the *h*. and give vineyard
1 *Cor*. 3. 9. ye are God's *h*.
HUSBANDRY, 2 *Chr*. 26. 10. Uzziah had husbandmen, for he loved *h*.
1 *Cor*. 3. 9. ye are God's *h*. ye are God's building
HUSK, S, *Num*. 6. 4. from the kernels even to the *h*.
Luke 15. 16. fain filled his belly with *h*.
HYMN, S, *Matt*. 26. 30. when they had sung an *h*. *Mark* 14. 26.
Col. 3. 16. admonishing—in psalms & *h*.
HYPOCRISY comes from the Greek, Hypocrisis: It is a counterfeiting

religion and virtue; an affectation of the name, joined with a disaffection to the thing; or, the having a form of godliness with denying the power of it. Thus he is a hypocrite who feigns to be what he is not, who puts on a false person, like the actors in Tragedies or Comedies. Our Saviour frequently accused the Pharisees of hypocrisy, *Matt*. 23. 13, 14; *Is*. 32. 6; *Matt*. 23. 28; *Mark* 12. 15; *Luke* 12. 1; 1 *Tim*. 4. 2; *Jam*. 3. 17; 1 *Pet*. 2. 1.
HYPOCRITE, *Matt*. 7. 5; *Luke* 6. 42. & 13. 15.
HYPOCRITES, *Matt*. 6. 2. & 15. 7. & 16. 3. & 23. 13.—29.
Job 8. 13. *h*. hope shall perish
15. 34. congregation of *h*. shall be desolate
20. 5. hope of *h*. is but for a moment
27. 8. what hope of *h*. in day when
36. 13. *h*. in heart heap up wrath
Is. 9. 17. every one is an *h*. and an evil doer
33. 14. fearfulness hath surprised *h*.
Matt. 24. 51. appoint his portion with *h*.
HYSSOP, *Ex*. 12. 22. bunch of *h*. and dip it
1 *Kings* 4. 33. from the cedar tree even unto the *h*.
Ps. 51. 7. purge me with *h*.
John 19. 29. they filled a sponge, and put it upon *h*.
Heb. 9. 19. blood with *h*. and sprinkled

IDLE. One who is slothful or lazy, *Ex*. 5. 8, 17.—One that would work, but is not employed or hired, *Matt*. 20. 3, 6.
IDLE, *Prov*. 19. 15. *i*. soul shall suffer hunger
Matt. 12. 36. of every *i*. word account
20. 3. standing *i*.; 6. why stand *i*.
Luke 24. 11. words seem *i*. tales
1 *Tim*. 5. 13. they learn to be *i*. not only *i*. but
IDLENESS, *Prov*. 31. 27; *Eccl*. 10. 18; *Ezek*. 16. 49.
IDOL, 2 *Chr*. 15. 16. & 33. 7.
Is. 66. 3. as if he blessed an *i*.
Zech. 11. 17. woe to *i*. shepherd
1 *Cor*. 8. 4. an *i*. is nothing in the world
Ps. 96. 5. gods of nations are *i*.
Is. 2. 8. land is full of *i*. they worship
Jer. 50. 38. are mad upon their *i*.
Hos. 4. 17. Ephraim is joined to *i*. let
Acts 15. 20. abstain from pollutions of *i*.
Rom. 2. 22. thou that abhorrest *i*.
1 *Cor*. 8. 1. touching things offered to *i*.
2 *Cor*. 6. 16. what agreement hath temple of God with *i*.
1 *John* 5. 21. keep yourselves from *i*.
Rev. 2. 14. to eat things sacrificed to *i*.
9. 20. worship devils *i*. of gold
IDOLATER, 1 *Cor*. 5. 10, 11. & 6. 9. & 10. 7; *Eph*. 5. 5; *Rev*. 21. 8. & 22. 15.
IDOLATRY, 1 *Sam*. 15. 23. rebellion is an iniquity and *i*.
Acts 17. 16. city wholly given to *i*.
1 *Cor*. 10. 14. dearly beloved flee from *i*.
Gal. 5. 20. *i*. witchcraft, hatred

Col. 3. 5. covetousness which is *i.*
1 *Pet.* 4. 3. walked in abominable *i.*
IGNORANCE, sin through *Lev.* 4. 2, 13, 22, 27; *Num.* 15. 25, 27; *Acts* 3. 17.
Acts 17. 30. times of this *i.* God winked
Eph. 4. 18. alienated through *i.* in them
Ps. 73. 22. so foolish was I and *i.*
Is. 63. 16. though Abraham be *i.*
Rom. 10. 3. being *i.* of God's righteousness
1 *Cor.* 14. 38. if any be *i.* let him be *i.*
Heb. 5. 2. have compassion on the *i.*
IGNORANTLY *Acts* 17. 23; 1 *Tim.* 1. 13.
IMAGE, *Lev.* 26. 1; *Dan.* 2. 31.
Gen. 1. 26. let us make man in our own *i.* 27. & 9. 6; *Col.* 3. 10.
5. 3. Adam begat a son after his *i.*
Ps. 73. 20. thou shalt despise their *i.*
Matt. 22. 20. whose *i.* is this, *Luke* 20. 24.
Rom. 8. 29. conformed to *i.* of his Son
1 *Cor.* 15. 49. have borne *i.* of earthly
2 *Cor.* 3. 18. into same *i.* from glory to glory
4. 4. Christ, who is the *i.* of God, *Col.* 1. 15.
Heb. 1. 3. express *i.* of his person
Rev. 13. 14. make an *i.* like to beast
Ex. 23. 24. break down *i.* 34. 13.
IMAGINE, *Ps.* 2. 1; *Acts* 4. 25; *Nah.* 1. 9; *Zech.* 7. 10. & 8. 17.
Gen. 6. 5. *i.* of thought evil, 8. 21; *Deut.* 29. 19; *Rom.* 1. 21; 2 *Cor.* 10. 5; *Prov.* 6. 18: *Lam.* 3. 60, 61.
IMMEDIATELY, *Mark* 4. 15; *Acts* 12. 23.
IMMORTAL. (1) One who is simply and every way incorruptible, without possibility of perishing or dying, 1 *Tim.* 1. 17. (2) That which being once dead shall rise again, never to die more, 1 *Cor.* 15. 53. (3) The consummate glory and eternal blessedness of the saints in heaven, *Rom.* 2. 7.
1 *Tim.* 1. 17. now to the King eternal, *i.* invisible
IMMORTALITY, *Rom.* 2. 7. who seek for *i.* eternal life
1 *Cor.* 15. 53. mortal must put on *i.* 54. when this mortal shall have put on *i.*
1 *Tim.* 6. 16. who only hath *i.*
2 *Tim.* 1. 10. who brought *i.* to light through the gospel
IMMUTABLE, ILITY, *Heb.* 6. 18. that by two *i.* things in which it was
Heb. 6. 17. the *i.* of his counsel confirmed it by an oath
IMPART, ED, *Luke* 3. 11. two coats, let him *i.* to him that hath none
Rom. 1. 11. that I may *i.* to you some spiritual gift
1 *Thess.* 2. 8. we were willing to have *i.* our own souls
IMPENITENT, *Rom.* 2. 5. thou, after thy *i.* heart, treasurest up wrath
IMPLACABLE, *Rom.* 1. 31. without natural affection *i.* unmerciful
IMPLEAD, *Acts* 19. 28. let them *i.* one another
IMPORTUNITY, *Luke* 11. 8. because of his *i.* he will rise and give him

IMPOSSIBLE, *Matt.* 17. 20. & 19. 26.
Luke 1. 37. with God nothing is *i.* 18. 27.
17. 1. it is *i.* but offences will come
Heb. 6. 4. it is *i.* for those once enlightened
18. in two things it is *i.* for God to lie
11. 6. without faith it is *i.* to please God
IMPOTENT, *John* 5. 3. a great multitude of *i.* folk
Acts 4. 9. good deed done to the *i.* man
14. 8. a man at Lystra *i.* in his feet
IMPRISONED, *Acts* 22. 19. they know that I *i.* and beat them
IMPRISONMENT, *Heb.* 11. 36. trial of mockings, bonds, *i.*
IMPRISONMENTS, 2 *Cor.* 6. 5. approving ourselves in stripes, in *i.*
IMPUDENT, *Prov.* 7. 13. and with an *i.* face she said to him
Ezek. 2. 4. for they are *i.* children, and stiff-hearted
3. 7. the house of Israel are *i.* and hard-hearted
IMPUTE, (1) Freely to account or ascribe to a person that which he himself hath not, nor did not, *Rom.* 4. 22. (2) To lay to one's charge, 2 *Sam.* 19. 19. (3) To be held guilty, *Lev.* 17. 4. (4) To suspect, 1 *Sam.* 22. 15.
Ps. 32. 2. to whom Lord *i.* not iniquity
Rom. 4. 6. *i.* righteousness without works
8. blessed to whom Lord will not *i.* sin
IMPUTED, *Rom.* 4. 11. righteousness might be *i.* to them
22. *i.* to him for righteousness, 4. 24.
5. 13. sin is not *i.* where there is no law
Jam. 2. 23. *i.* to him for righteousness
IMPUTING, 2 *Cor.* 5. 19. not *i.* their trespasses
IN Christ, *Acts* 24. 24; *Rom.* 12. 5. & 16. 7, 9, 10; 1 *Cor.* 1. 2, 30. & 3. 1. & 15. 18, 22; 2 *Cor.* 1. 21. & 2. 14. & 3. 14. & 5. 17, 19. & 12. 2; *Gal.* 1. 22; *Eph.* 1. 1, 3, 10, 12, 20. & 2. 6, 10, 13; *Phil.* 1. 1, 13. & 2. 1, 5. & 3. 14; *Col.* 1. 2, 4.
1 *Thess.* 1. 1. *i.* God, 4. 16; *John* 3. 21; *Col.* 3. 3.
Gen. 15. 6. *i.* the Lord, *Ps.* 4. 5. & 31. 24. & 34. 2. & 35. 9. & 37. 4, 7; *Is.* 45. 17, 24, 25; *Jer.* 3. 23; *Zech.* 12. 5; 1 *Cor.* 1. 31. & 4. 17. & 7. 22, 30; *Eph.* 2. 21. & 6. 10; *Phil.* 4. 2, 4;
Col. 3. 18. & 4. 7. 17, 1 *Thess.* 5. 12; *Philem.* 16. 20; *Rev.* 14. 13.
INASMUCH, *Matt.* 25. 40. *i.* as have done it to one of least of these
Matt. 25. 45. *i.* as ye did it not to one of the least of these
INCENSE, (1) A rich perfume used in sacrifices, *Ex.* 37. 29. (2) The merits of Christ's death, *Rev.* 8. 3.
Ex. 30. 8. shall burn a perpetual *i.*
37. 29. made pure *i.* of sweet spices
Lev. 10. 1. each took his censer, and put *i.* thereon
16. 13. he shall put *i.* on the fire before the Lord

Num. 16. 35. a fire consumed the 250 men that offered *i.*

46. Moses said to Aaron, put on *i.*

Ps. 66. 15. I will offer to thee *i.*

Ezek. 8. 11. thick cloud of *i.* went up

Mal. 1. 11. in every place *i.* offered

Luke 1. 10. people were praying without at the time of *i.*

Rev. 5. 8. harps, and golden vials full of *i.*

INCENSED, *Is.* 41. 11. all *i.* against thee be ashamed

Is. 45. 24. all *i.* against him shall be ashamed

INCHANTMENT. Magic or divination, much practised in former times. It was forbidden by Moses, *Deut.* 18. 10; *Lev.* 19. 26; *Num.* 23. 23; *Eccl.* 10. 11; *Is.* 47. 9.

INCLINE heart, *Josh.* 24. 23; *Judg.* 9. 3; 1 *Kings* 8. 58; *Ps.* 119. 36, 112. & 141. 4.

Ps. 78. 1. ear, 40. 1. & 116. 2; *Prov.* 2. 2. & 5. 13; *Jer.* 7. 24, 26. & 11. 8. & 17. 23. & 25. 4. & 34. 14. & 35. 15. & 44. 5; *Is.* 55. 3.

INCLOSE, to surround with a wall, hedge, or fence, *Ps.* 17. 10. & 22. 16; *Songs* 4. 12. & 8. 9; *Lam.* 3. 9.

INCONTINENT, not chaste; governed by fleshly lusts, 1 *Cor.* 7. 5; 2 *Tim.* 3. 3.

INCORRUPTIBLE, incapable of decay. Spoken of the word of God, as the instrument of conversion—of the resurrection of the body—of the crown of life, and the inheritance of heaven, *Rom.* 1. 23.

Rom. 1. 23. and changed the glory of the *i.* God

1 *Cor.* 9. 25. to obtain *i.* crown

15. 52. dead raised *i.*

1 *Pet.* 1. 4. begot. to an inheritance *i.*

23. not of corruptible seed, but *i.*

INCORRUPTION, 1 *Cor.* 15. 50. neither doth corruption inherit *i.*

1 *Cor.* 15. 53. for this corruptible must put on *i.*

54. so when this corruptible shall have put on *i.*

INCREASE. The produce of the earth, and of cattle, *Deut.* 7. 13; 32. 13; *Prov.* 14. 4.—To grow, advance, or improve, *Col.* 1. 10; 1 *Thess.* 3. 12.—To be of more esteem and authority, *John* 3. 30.—To swell up, *Gen.* 7. 17.—To multiply, 1 *Chr.* 27. 23.—To grow and enlarge, *Luke* 17. 5.—To make profitable and fruitful, 1 *Cor.* 3. 6, 7; *Lev.* 19. 25. & 25. 7.

Lev. 25. 36. take no usury nor *i.* 37.

Num. 32. 14. risen an *i.* of sinful men

Deut. 16. 15. bless thee in all thy *i.*

Ps. 67. 6. earth yield her *i.* 85. 12.

Prov. 3. 9. with first fruits of all thy *i.*

Is. 9. 7. of the *i.* of his government no end

Ezek. 18. 8. nor taken *i.* 13. 17.

1 *Cor.* 3. 6. planted God gave the *i.* 7.

Col. 2. 19. *i.* with *i.* of God

Ps. 62. 10. if riches *i.* set not your heart

115. 14. Lord shall *i.* you more and more

Prov. 1. 5. wise will *i.* in learning, 9. 9.

Eccl. 5. 11. when goods *i.* they

Is. 29. 19. meek shall *i.* their joy in the Lord

Luke 17. 5. Lord *i.* our faith

John 3. 30. he must *i.* but I decrease

1 *Thess.* 3. 12. Lord make you to *i.* in

2 *Tim.* 2. 16. will *i.* to more ungodliness

Ezra 9. 6. iniquities are *i.* over our heads

Is. 9. 3. multiplied nations, not *i.* the joy

26. 15. hast *i.* the nation, O Lord thou hast *i.* the nation

Luke 2. 52. Jesus *i.* in wisdom, favour

Acts 6. 7. the word of God *i.* and the

Rev. 3. 17.rich and *i.* with goods

Eccl. 1. 18. *i.* knowledge, *i.* sorrow

Is. 40. 29. to those of no might he *i.* strength

Col. 2. 19. whole body *i.* with *i.* of God

1. 10. *i.* in knowledge of God

INCREDIBLE, *Acts* 26. 8. why *i.* God should raise dead

INCURABLE wound, *Job* 34. 6; *Jer.* 15. 18; *Mic.* 1. 9.

Jer. 30. 12. bruise *i.*; 15. sorrow *i.*

INDEED, truly, verily, certainly, 1 *Kings* 8. 27; 1 *Chr.* 4. 10; *Matt.* 3. 11; *Luke* 24. 34; *John* 1. 47. & 4. 42. & 6. 55. & 8. 31, 36; 1 *Tim.* 5. 3, 5; 1 *Pet.* 2. 4.

INDIGNATION, wrath or anger, *Neh.* 4. 1; *Esth.* 5. 9. The judgments of God, *Is.* 26. 20. A person's holy displeasure against himself for sin, &c., 2 *Cor.* 7. 11; *Ps.* 69. 24. & 78. 49. & 102. 10.

Is. 10. 5. staff in their hand is my *i.* 25.

26. 20. hide thee till the *i.* be overpast

Mic. 7. 9. I will bear the *i.* of the Lord, because

Nah. 1. 6. who can stand before his *i.*

Matt. 20. 24. moved with *i.*

26. 8. had *i.*

Rom. 2. 8. *i.* and wrath, tribulation and

2 *Cor.* 7. 11. yea, what *i.* what

Heb. 10. 27. fiery *i.* which shall devour

Rev. 14. 10. poured into cup of his *i.*

INDITING, *Ps.* 45. 1. my heart is *i.* a good matter

INEXCUSABLE, O man, whosoever *Rom.* 2. 1.

INFALLIBLE, *Acts* 1. 3. to whom he showed himself alive by many *i.* proofs

INFANT, S, *Job* 3. 16. as *i.* which never saw light

Is. 65. 20. be no more *i.* of days

Hos. 13. 16. their *i.* shall be dashed in pieces

Luke 18. 15. they brought also *i.* to him

INFERIOR, *Job* 12. 3. understanding I am not *i.* to you, 13. 2.

2 *Cor.* 12. 13. what were ye *i.* to other churches

Heb. 2. 7. madest him little *i.* than the angels

INFIDEL, 2 *Cor.* 6. 15. hath he that believeth with an *i.*

1 *Tim.* 5. 8. and is worse than an *i.*

INFINITE, *Job* 22. 5. are not thine
iniquities *i.*
Ps. 147. 5. his understanding is *i.*
INFIRMITY, (1) Sickness, or feeble-
ness of body, 1 *Tim.* 5. 23. (2)
Afflictions, reproaches, and persecutions, 2 *Cor.* 12. 10. (3) Spiritual
weakness, and defects in grace,
Rom. 6. 19; 8. 26. (4) Failings and
mistakes, either through ignorance
or weakness, *Rom.* 15. 1.
INFIRMITY, *Ps.* 77. 10. this is my *i.*
Prov. 18. 14. spirit of man will sustain
his *i.*
Matt. 8. 17. himself took our *i.*
Rom. 8. 26. spirit helpeth our *i.*
15. 1. strong ought to bear *i.* of weak
2 *Cor.* 12. 9. glory in my *i.*
10. pleasure in *i.*
1 *Tim.* 5. 23. use a little wine for thine *i.*
Heb. 4. 15. with feeling of our *i.*
5. 2. himself also is compassed with *i.*
7. 28.
INFLAME wine idols, *Is.* 5. 11. & 57. 5.
INFLICTED punishment, 2 *Cor.* 2. 6.
INFLUENCES of Pleiades, *Job* 38. 41.
INGRAFTED word, receive, *Jam.* 1. 21.
INHABIT, *Prov.* 10. 30; *Is.* 65. 21, 22.
Ps. 22. 3. *i.* praises of Israel
Is. 57. 15. lofty One *i.* eternity
Zeph. 1. 13. build houses, not *i.* them
INHABITANT, *Is.* 5. 9. many houses
great and fair without *i.*
Is. 12. 6. cry out and shout, thou *i.* of
Zion
Jer. 4. 7. thy cities shall be laid waste
without an *i.* 9. 1; 26. 9; 33. 10;
34. 22.
Zeph. 2. 5. I will destroy, that there
shall be no *i.*
INHABITANTS, *Ps.* 33. 8. all the *i.* of
the world stand in awe of him
Is. 26. 9. the *i.* of the world shall learn
righteousness
40. 22. *i.* as grasshoppers
Rev. 17. 2. the *i.* of the earth have been
made drunk
INHERIT, *Gen.* 15. 8; *Ps.* 82. 8.
1 *Sam.* 2. 8. to make them *i.* the throne
Ps. 25. 13. his seed shall *i.* the earth
37. 11. meek shall *i.* the earth, *Matt.*
5. 5.
29. righteous shall *i.* land, *Is.* 60. 21.
Prov. 3. 35. wise shall *i.* glory
8. 21. love me to *i.* substance
Matt. 19. 29. the forsaken shall *i.* ever-
25. 34. *i.* the kingdom prepared
Mark 10. 17. what good do that I may
i. eternal life, *Luke* 10. 25. & 18. 18.
1 *Cor.* 6. 9. unrighteous not *i.* kingdom
of God, 10.
15. 50. flesh and blood cannot *i.* kingdom of God
Gal. 5. 21. do such things not *i.* kingdom of God
Heb. 6. 12. through faith *i.* the promises
1 *Pet.* 3. 9. that ye should *i.* a blessing
Tev. 21. 7. overcometh shall *i.* all things
INHERITANCE, *Num.* 18. 20. I Lord
am thy *i. Deut.* 10. 9. & 18. 2;
Ezek. 44. 28.
Deut. 4. 21. a people of *i.* 9. 26, 29. & 32.

9; 1 *Kings* 8. 51; *Ps.* 28. 9. & 32.
12. & 68. 9. & 74. 2. & 78. 62, 71. &
79. 1. & 94. 14. & 106. 5, 40; *Is.* 19.
25; *Jer.* 10. 16. & 51. 19.
Ps. 16. 5. Lord is portion of my *i.* and
47. 4. Lord shall choose our *i.* for us
Prov. 19. 14. riches *i.* of fathers
Eccl. 7. 11. wisdom is good with an *i.*
Acts 20. 32. *i.* among sanctified, 26. 18.
Eph. 1. 11. among whom we obtained
an *i.*
14. earnest of our *i.* and purchased
possession
5. 5. hath any *i.* in kingdom of Christ
and of God
Col. 1. 12. partakers of *i.* of saints
3. 24. shall receive reward of *i.*
Heb. 9. 15. receive promise of eternal *i.*
1 *Pet.* 1. 4. to an *i.* incorruptible undefiled
INIQUITY, *Gen.* 15. 16. & 19. 15.
Ex. 20. 5. visit *i.* of fathers on children,
34. 7; *Num.* 14. 18; *Deut.* 5. 9.
34. 7. forgiving *i.* transgression, sin,
Lev. 26. 41. accept punishment of your
i. 40.
Num. 23. 21. hath not beheld *i.* in Jacob
Deut. 32. 4. God of truth without *i.* just
Job 4. 8. that plough *i.* reap same
5. 16. *i.* stoppeth her mouth, *Ps.* 107.
42.
11. 6. less than thy *i.* deserves, *Ezra*
9. 13.
15. 16. drinks up *i.* like water
22. 23. put away *i.* far from thee
34. 32. if I have done *i.* I will do so no
Ps. 32. 5. thou forgavest *i.* of my sin
39. 11. thou rebukest a man for *i.*
49. 5. when the *i.* of my heels shall
compass me
51. 5. behold I was shapen in *i.*
66. 18. if I regard *i.* in heart
69. 27. add thou *i.* to their *i.*
119. 3. they also do no *i.* they walk in
133. let not any *i.* have dominion over
Prov. 22. 8. sows *i.* shall reap vanity
Eccl. 3. 16. place of righteousness *i.* was
Is. 1. 4. people laden with *i.* seed
5. 18. woe to them that draw *i.* with
cords
27. 9. this shall *i.* of Jacob be purged
33. 24. people shall be forgiven their *i.*
40. 2. her warfare accomplished, her
i. pardoned
53. 6. Lord laid on him the *i.* of us all
57. 17. for *i.* of his covetousness was
I wroth
Jer. 2. 5. what *i.* have your fathers found
3. 13. only acknowledge thine *i.*
31. 30. every one die for his own *i.*
50. 20. *i.* of Israel be sought for and
Ezek. 3. 18. die in his *i.* 19. & 18. 18. &
33. 8.
18. 30. so *i.* shall not be ruin
Dan. 9. 24. reconciliation for *i.*
Hos. 14. 2. take away all *i.* and receive
Mic. 7. 18. who is a God like thee that
pardoneth *i.*
Hab. 1. 13. holy One canst not look on *i.*
Matt. 7. 23. depart from me ye that
work *i.*
24. 12. because *i.* shall abound love

Acts 8. 23. in gall of bitterness and bond of *i.*
Rom. 6. 19. servants to uncleanness, and to *i.* unto *i.*
1 *Cor.* 13. 6. charity rejoiceth not in *i.*
2 *Thess.* 2. 7. mystery of *i.* doth already work
2 *Tim.* 2. 19. let him that nameth Christ depart from *i.*
Tit. 2. 14. to redeem us from *i.*
Jam. 3. 6. tongue a world of *i.*
Ps. 18. 23. my *i.* 25. 11. & 32. 5. & 38. 18. & 51. 2.
Job 34. 22. workers of *i. Ps.* 5. 5. & 6. 8. & 14. 4. & 92. 7; *Prov.* 10. 29. & 21. 15; *Luke* 13. 27.
Lev. 16. 21. confess all the *i.*
26. 39. in their *i.* and *i.* of fathers
Ezra 9. 6. our *i.* are increased
13. punished us less than *i.* deserve
Neh. 9. 2. confessed *i.* of your fathers
Job 13. 26. to possess *i.* of my youth
Ps. 38. 4. my *i.* are gone over my head
40. 12. my *i.* have taken hold of me
51. 9. hide thy face from my sins, and blot out all my *i.*
65. 3. *i.* prevail against me
79. 8. remember not former *i.*
90. 8. thou settest our *i.* before thee
103. 3. who forgiveth all thine *i.*
10. not rewarded us according to *i.*
107. 17. fools because of *i.* are afflicted
130. 3. if thou Lord shouldst mark *i.*
8. redeem Israel from all his *i.*
Prov. 5. 22. his own *i.* shall take the wicked
Is. 43. 24. wearied me with thy *i.*
53. 5. wounded, bruised for our *i.*
Jer. 14. 7. though our *i.* testify against
Dan. 4. 27. break off thy *i.* by mercy
Mic. 7. 19. he will subdue our *i.*
Acts 3. 26. bless you in turning from his *i.*
Rom. 4. 7. blessed whose *i.* are forgiven
Rev. 18. 5. God hath remembered her *i.*
Is. 53. 11. he shall bear their *i.*
Jer. 33. 8. I will pardon their *i.*
Ezek. 43. 10. may be ashamed of all *i.*
Heb. 12. their *i.* will remember no more, 10. 17.
Num. 14. 34. shall bear your *i.*
Is. 50. 1. for your *i.* have ye sold yourselves
59. 2. your *i.* have separated between you and God
65. 7. your *i.* and the *i.* of your fathers
Jer. 5. 25. your *i.* have turned away
Ezek. 24. 23. ye shall pine away for *i.*
36. 31. loathe yourselves for all your *i.*
33. I shall have cleansed you from all your *i.*
Amos 3. 2. I will punish you for all *i.*
INJURED not me, *Gal.* 4. 12.
INJURIOUS, 1 *Tim.* 1. 13. a persecutor and *i.* but I
INK, 2 *Cor.* 3. 3. written not with *i.*
2 *John* 12. would not write with *i.* 3 *John* 13.
INK-HORN, *Ezek.* 9. 2. with a writer's *i.* by his side, 3. 11.
INN, *Gen.* 42. 27. to give his ass provender in the *i.*

Gen. 43. 21. came to the *i.* opened sacks
Luke 2. 7. there was no room for them in the *i.*
10. 34. brought him to an *i.*
INNER, *Esth.* 4. 11. shall come to the king into the *i.* court
Ezek. 10. 3. cloud filled the *i.* court
42. 15. measuring the *i.* house
Acts 16. 24. thrust into the *i.* prison
Eph. 3. 16. strengthened with might in the *i.* man
INNERMOST, *Prov.* 18. 8. into the *i.* parts of the belly, 26. 22.
INNOCENT, *Ps.* 19. 13; *Prov.* 28. 20.
Gen. 20. 5. in *i.* of hands I
Ps. 26. 6. wash my hands in *i.* 73. 13.
Dan. 6. 22. before him *i.* was found in
Hos. 8. 5. how long ere they attain to *i.*
INNUMERABLE, *Job* 21. 33; *Ps.* 40. 12; *Luke* 12. 1; *Heb.* 11. 12. & 12. 22.
INORDINATE, *Ezek.* 23. 11. corrupt in *i.* love
Col. 3. 5. mortify fornication, *i.* affection
INQUIRE after mine iniquity, *Job* 10. 6.
Ps. 27. 4. to *i.* in his temple
78. 34. returned and *i.* early after G.
Eccl. 7. 10. dost not *i.* wisely
Is. 21. 12. if ye will *i.* ye
Ezek. 36. 37. for this I will be *i.* of
Zeph. 1. 6. have not *i.* for him
Matt. 2. 7. Herod *i.* of them diligently
1 *Pet.* 1. 10. of which salvation prophets have *i.*
Judg. 20. 27. *i.* of the Lord, 1 *Sam.* 23. 2, 4. & 30. 8; 2 *Sam.* 2. 1. & 5. 19, 23. & 21. 1; *Jer.* 21. 2.
Prov. 20. 25. after vows make *i.*
INQUISITION, *Deut.* 19. 18. the Judges shall make diligent *i.*
Esth. 2. 23. *i.* was made of the matter
Ps. 9. 12. when he maketh *i.* for blood
INSCRIPTION, *Acts* 17. 23. I found an altar with this *i.*
INSPIRATION, *Job* 32. 8; 2 *Tim.* 3. 16.
INSTANT, A short moment of time, *Is.* 29. 5. To be very urgent, *Luke* 23. 23. To perform any thing with care and diligence, *Acts* 26. 7. *i.* serving God day and night; *Is.* 30. 13; *Jer.* 18. 7; *Rom.* 12. 12; 2 *Tim.* 4. 2; *Acts* 12. 5.
Luke 7. 4. besought him *i.*
INSTRUCT, *Deut.* 4. 36. & 32. 10.
Neh. 9. 20. good spirit to *i.* them
Job. 40 2. shall he that contendeth with the Almighty *i.*
Ps. 2. 10. be *i.* ye judges of the earth
16. 7. my reins *i.* me in night
32. 8. I will *i.* thee and teach thee
Songs 8. 2. house,—who would *i.* me
Is. 8. 11. Lord *i.* me with strong hand
28. 26. his God doth *i.* him to discretion and doth teach him
Dan. 11. 33. understanding shall *i.*
Matt. 13. 52. every scribe *i.* to kingdom
1 *Cor.* 2. 16. of Lord that he may *i.* him
Phil. 4. 12. in all things I am *i.* both
2 *Tim.* 2. 25. *i.* those that oppose themselves
INSTRUCTOR, *Rom.* 2. 20. an *i.* of the foolish

1 *Cor.* 4. 15. have ten thousand *i.* in Christ

INSTRUCTION, *Job* 33. 16. seals their *i.*

Ps. 50. 17. hatest *i.* and castest my

Prov. 1. 2. and *i.* to perceive

  8. hear *i.* of thy Father, 4. 1.

Prov. 4. 13. take fast hold of *i.* keep her

  5. 12. how have I hated *i.* and have

  9. 9. give *i.* to a wise man and he will be wiser

  12. 1. whose loveth *i.* loveth knowledge

  13. 1. a wise son heareth his father's *i.*

  18. shame shall be to him that refuseth *i.*

  15.·32. he that refuseth *i.* hateth his own soul

  16. 22. the *i.* of fools is folly

  19. 27. cease to hear *i.* that causeth

  23. 12. apply thy heart to *i.*

2 *Tim.* 3. 16. profitable for *i.* in righteousness

INSTRUMENTS of cruelty, *Gen.* 49. 5.

1 *Chr.* 9. 29. to oversee all the *i.* of the sanctuary

2 *Chr.* 30. 21. singing with loud *i.* to the Lord

Ps. 7. 13. prepared for him *i.* of death

  68. 25. players on *i.* followed after

  87. 7. players on *i.* shall be there

  150. 4. praise him with stringed *i.*

Is. 32. 7. *i.* of the churl are evil

Amos 1. 3. threshing *i.* of iron

  6. 5. *i.* of music

Rom. 6. 13. members as *i.* of unrighteousness, *i.* righteousness

INSURRECTION, *Ps.* 64. 2. from the *i.* of the workers of iniquity

Mark 15. 7. lay bound with them that made *i.* who had committed murder in the *i.*

Acts 18. 12. Jews made *i.* with one accord

INTANGLE, to perplex, *Matt.* 22. 15; *Gal.* 5. 1; 2 *Tim.* 2. 4; 2 *Pet.* 2. 20.

INTEGRITY. Purity of mind, freedom from any undue bias of principle *Gen.* 20. 5; 1 *Kings* 9. 4; *Job* 2. 3. (1) That the guidance of integrity is the safest under which we can be placed; that the road in which it leads us, is, upon the whole, the freest from dangers, *Prov.* 3. 21. &c. (2) It is unquestionably the most honourable; for integrity is the foundation of all that is high in character among mankind, *Prov.* 4. 8. (3) It is the most conducive to felicity, *Phil.* 4. 6, 7; *Prov.* 3. 17 (4) Such a character can look forward to eternity without dismay, *Rom.* 2. 7.

Job 2. 3. still he holdeth fast *i.*

  27. 5. I will not remove my *i.* from me

Ps. 7. 8. according to my *i.* that is in me

  25. 21. let *i.* and uprightness preserve

Prov. 11. 3. *i.* of uprightness shall guide

INTENT, S, *John* 11. 15. not there to the *i.* ye may believe

John 13. 28. for what *i.* he spake this

Acts 9. 21. came hither for that *i.*

  10. 29. I ask for what *i.* ye have sent for me

Eph. 3. 10. to the *i.* that now to the principalities

Heb. 4. 12. discerner of the *i.* of heart

INTERCESSION. A pleading or entreating in behalf of another, *Jer.* 7. 16. It is spoken, (I) of the intercession of Christ, *Is.* 53. 12; *Heb.* 7. 26. Which he performs, (1) By appearing for us before the Father, *Heb.* 9. 24. (2) By presenting the merit of his sacrifice once offered, *Heb.* 10. 12, 14. (3) By declaring his will, that such and such blessings may be bestowed upon the elect, *Heb.* 10. 10. (4) By the Father's consenting and agreeing to this will of his Son, *John* 11. 42. (II) Of the Holy Spirit in God's children, *Rom.* 8. 26. (III) Of men interceding, (1) For temporal blessings, *Jer.* 7. 16. (2) For spiritual blessings, 1 *Tim.* 2. 1. (IV) Of Elias, who complained against the ten tribes, who were generally become idolators, *Rom.* 11. 2.

Is. 53. 12. and made   for the transgressors

Rom. 8. 26. but the Spirit maketh *i.* for us, 27. 34.

Heb. 7. 25. he ever liveth to make *i.* for them

INTERCESSIONS, 1 *Tim.* 2. 1. that prayers and *i.* be made for all men

INTERCESSOR, *Is.* 59. 16. he wondered that there was no *i.*

INTERMEDDLE, *Prov.* 14. 10. & 18. 1.

INTERPRET, *Gen.* 41. 8. none *i.* them to Pharaoh

1 *Cor.* 12. 30. do all *i* ? 14. 5. except he *i.*

INTERPRETATION, (1) A translation, or turning from one language into another, 1 *Cor.* 12. 10. (2) The gifts of expounding visions and dreams, *Gen.* 40. 8. (3) Exposition, or showing the sense and import of any thing, 2 *Pet.* 1. 20.

Gen. 40. 12. this is the *i.* of it, 18; *Dan.* 4. 24; 5. 26.

  16. baker saw the *i.* was good

Prov. 1. 6. to understand a proverb and the *i.*

Dan. 2. 45. being *i.* thereof sure

John 1. 42. Cephas, by *i.* a stone

1 *Cor.* 12. 10. to another the *i.* of tongues

  14. 26. every one of you hath an *i.*

Heb. 7. 2. by *i.* king of righteousness

2 *Pet.* 1. 20. no prophecy is of any private *i.*

INTERPRETED, *Gen.* 40. 22. Joseph *i.* 41. 13.

Matt. 1. 23. being *i.* is, God with us

Mark 5. 41. being *i.* damsel arise

  15. 22. being *i.* the place of a skull

  34. *i.* my God, my God, why hast thou forsaken me

John 1. 38. being *i.* master; 41. *i.* the Christ

Acts 4. 36. *i.* the son of consolation

INTREAT. To supplicate, or pray to, *Gen.* 12. 16. & 23. 8; *Ex.* 8. 8. & 9. 28. & 10. 17; *Jer.* 15. 11.

1 *Sam.* 2. 25. who shall *i.* for him

1 *Cor.* 4. 13. being defamed, we *i.* we are made

Phil. 4. 3. I *i.* thee true yoke-fellow

1 *Tim.* 5. 1. but *i.* him as a father

INTREATED, *Luke* 15. 28. then came his father out and *i.* him

Luke 20. 11. *i.* him shamefully

Acts 27. 3. Julius courteously *i.* Paul

1 *Thess.* 2. 2. after that shamefully *i.*

Heb. 12. 19. *i.* the word not be spoken

Jam. 3. 17. wisdom from above is easy to be *i.*

2 *Cor.* 8. 4. praying us with much *i.*

Prov. 18. 23. the poor useth *i.*

INTRUDING into *presuming Col.* 2. 18.

INVENT, to contrive, *Amos* 6. 5; *Rom.* 1. 30.

Ps. 99. 8. tookest vengeance on their *i.* 106. 29. provoked with their *i.* 39. went a whoring with their own *i.*

Prov. 8. 12. find knowledge of witty *i.*

Eccl. 7. 29. sought out many *i.*

INVISIBLE, *Rom.* 1. 20; *Col.* 1. 15, 16; 1 *Tim.* 1. 17; *Heb.* 11. 27. The Being and Perfections of God are called his 'invisible things,' in opposition to the Heathen deities, which, having form, were called 'things visible.'

INWARD friends, *Job* 19. 19.

Ps. 5. 9. *i.* part, 51. 6; *Prov.* 20. 27; *Jer.* 31. 33; *Luke* 11. 39.

Rom. 7. 22. *i.* man, 2 *Cor.* 4. 16.

2 *Cor.* 7. 15. *i.* affection

Ps. 62. 4. but they curse *i.*

Matt. 7. 15. *i.* wolves

Rom. 2. 29. Jew is one *i.*

IRON sharpeneth iron, *Prov.* 27. 17.

Eccl. 10. 10. if *i.* be blunt, put

Is, 48. 4. neck is an *i.* sinew and

Jer. 15. 12. shall *i.* break the northern *i.*

Dan. 2. 33. legs of *i.* feet of *i.* and clay

1 *Tim.* 4. 2. conscience seared with hot *i.*

ISSUE, substantive, *Matt.* 22. 25. havno *i.* left his wife

ISSUED, *Ezek.* 47. 1. waters *i.* from under the threshold

Dan. 7. 10. a fiery stream *i.*

Rev. 9. 17. out of their mouths *i.* fire, 18.

ISSUES, *Ps.* 68. 20. to God belong the *i.* from death

Prov. 4. 23. out of it are the *i.* of life

ITCHING ears, 2 *Tim.* 4. 3, 8.

JEALOUS God I am, *Ex.* 20. 5. & 34. 14; *Deut.* 5. 9. & 6. 15; *Josh.* 24. 19.

1 *Kings* 19. 10. I have been very *j.* for the Lord, 14.

Ezek. 39. 25. be *j.* for my holy name

Joel. 2. 18. will Lord be *j.* for land

Nah. 1. 2. God is *j.* and the Lord revengeth

Zech. 1. 14. I am *j.* for Jerusalem, 8. 2.

JEALOUSY, (1) Suspicion between married persons of their fidelity one to another, *Num.* 5. 14. (2) An earnest desire and concern for the welfare of others, joined with some degree of fear of them, 2 *Cor.* 11. 2. (3) The hot displeasure and

indignation of God, *Ps.* 79. 5.

Deut. 29. 20. *j.* shall smoke 32. 16. provoked him to *j.* with strange gods, 21; 1 *Kings* 14. 22; *Ps.* 78. 58.

Ps. 79. 5. shall *j.* burn like fire

Prov. 6. 34. *j.* is the rage of man

Songs 8. 6. *j.* is cruel as the grave

Rom. 10. 19. provoke them to *j.* 11. 11.

1 *Cor.* 10. 22. do we provoke the Lord to *j.*

2 *Cor.* 11. 2. *j.* over you with a godly *j.*

JEOPARDY, *Luke* 8. 23. ship was filled with water, they were in *j.*

1 *Cor.* 15. 30. why stand we in *j.*

JERUSALEM, *Josh.* 18. 28. Jebusi, which is J. *Judg.* 19. 10.

1 *Kings* 11. 13. for J. sake, which I have chosen, 2 *Chr.* 6. 6.

2 *Kings* 19. 31. out of J. shall go a remnant, and they *Is.* 37. 32. 24. 14. he carried away all J. and the princes 25. 9. Nebuzar-adan burnt all the houses of J.

Ps. 51. 18. build thou the walls of J. 122. 3. J. is builded as a city compact together 6. pray for the peace of J. 125. 2. mountains round about J. 137. 6. prefer J. above my chief joy

Songs 6. 4. thou art comely as J.

Is. 33. 20. thine eyes shall see J. a quiet habitation 40. 2. speak ye comfortably to J. 62. 1. for J. sake I will not rest till righteousness 7. give him no rest till he make J. a praise 64. 10. Zion is a wilderness, J. a desolation 65. 18. I create J. a rejoicing

Jer. 9. 11. I will make J. heaps

Dan. 6. 10. windows opened toward J. 9. 25. the commandment to build J.

Joel 3. 1. bring again captivity of J. 17. then shall J. be holy; 20. J. shall dwell

Mic. 3. 10. build J. with iniquity

Luke 21. 20. J. compassed with armies 24. J. trodden down of the Gentiles

Acts 20. 22. behold, I go bound in the Spirit to J.

Gal. 4. 25. Agar answereth to J. 26. but J. mother of us all

Rev. 3. 12. the new J. 21. 2; 21. 10. the holy J.

JERUSALEM, at, *Acts* 1. 19. known to all the dwellers *at* J.

Acts 21. 13. but also to die *at* J. for the name of Jesus

JERUSALEM, from, *Zech.* 14. 8. living waters go out *from* J.

Acts 8. 26. the way that goeth down *from* J. to Gaza

Rom. 15. 19. *from.* J. to Illyricum I have preached

JERUSALEM, in, *Acts* 26. 10. which thing I also did, *in* J. many saints

JERUSALEM, inhabitants of, *Zech.* 12. 10. pour upon *inhabitants of* J. the Spirit of grace

Zech. 13. 1. a fountain open to the inhabitants of *J.*

JERUSALEM, O, *Ps.* 137. 5. if I forget, *O J.*; 147. 12. praise Lord, *O J.*

Is. 52. 1. put on thy beautiful garments, *O J.*

Matt. 23. 37. *O J. J.* thou that killest the prophets and stonest them that are sent to thee, *Luke* 13. 34.

JERUSALEM, up to, *Matt.* 20. 18. behold, we go *up to J.* Son of man shall be betrayed, *Mark* 10. 33; *Luke* 18. 31.

Gal. 1. 17. neither went I *up to J.*

18. I went *up to J.* to see Peter

JESTING, *Eph.* 5. 4. nor filthiness, nor *j.*

JESUS, *Matt.* 1. 21. shalt call his name *J.* for he shall save his people from their sins, 25; *Luke* 1. 13; 2. 21.

Matt. 4. 1. *J.* led up of the Spirit

Matt. 12. 25. *J.* knew their thoughts

14. 1. Herod heard of the fame of *J.*

18. 2. *J.* called a little child to him

26. 26. *J.* took bread and blessed it, *Mark* 14. 22.

75. Peter remembered words of *J.*

27. 37. this is *J.* the king of

46. *J.* cried with a loud voice, *Mark* 15. 37.

Mark 9. 4. Elias and Moses were talking with *J.*

10. 21. *J.* beholding him, loved him

15. 1. bound *J.* and carried

John 6. 42. is not this *J.* son of Joseph

12. 21. sir, we would see *J.*

Acts 1. 1. of all that *J.* began to do and teach

2. 32. this *J.* hath God raised up

4. 2. preaching through *J.* resurrection from the dead

8. 35. Philip preached unto him *J.*

9. 5. I am *J.* whom thou persecutest, 22. 8; 26. 15.

10. 38. God anointed *J.* with the

17. 7. there is another king, one *J.*

18. *J.* and the resurrection

Rom. 3. 26. the justifier of him that believeth in *J.*

8. 11. the Spirit of him that raised up *J.* from dead

2 *Cor.* 4. 14. that he who raised *J.* shall raise up us also by *J.*

Eph. 4. 21. taught as the truth is in *J.*

Phil. 2. 10. at the name of *J.* every knee should bow

1 *Thess.* 1. 10. even *J.* who delivered us from wrath

1 *Thess.* 4. 14. so them that sleep in *J.* will God bring

Heb. 2. 9. *J.* made lower than angels

4. 14. we have a great high-priest, *J.* son of God, 6. 20.

10. 19. to enter into the holiest by the blood of *J.*

12. 24. to *J.* Mediator of new covenant

13. 12. *J.* suffered without the gate

1 *John* 4. 15. confess *J.* is Son of God

5. 5. believeth *J.* is the Son of God

Rev. 20. 24. beheaded for witness of *J.*

22. 16. I *J.* have sent my angel

JESUS, LORD, *Acts* 1. 21. the Lord *J.*

went in and out

Acts 2. 36. same *J.* both Lord and Christ

7. 59. *Lord J.* receive my spirit

8. 16. were baptized in the name of the *Lord J.*

9. 29. he spake boldly in the name of the *Lord J.*

19. 17. name of *Lord J.* magnified

1 *Cor.* 11. 23. *Lord J.* same night he was betrayed

2 *Cor.* 4. 10. always bearing about the dying of *Lord J.*

2 *Thess.* 1. 7. when the *Lord J.* shall be revealed

Heb. 13. 20. brought again from the dead our *Lord J.*

Rev. 22. 20. I come quickly, even so, come, *Lord J.*

JEWEL, (1) A precious and costly ornament, *Gen.* 24. 53. (2) God's children, *Mal.* 3. 17.

Prov. 11. 22. as a *j.* of gold in a swine's snout

20. 15. lips of knowledge precious *j.*

JEWELS, *Ex.* 3. 22. shall borrow *j.* of gold; 11. 2; 12. 35.

1 *Sam.* 6. 8. and put the *j.* of gold in a coffer, 15.

2 *Chr.* 20. 25. riches and precious *j.*

Job 28. 17. exchange not be for *j.* of

Songs 1. 10. thy cheeks are comely with rows of *j.*

Is. 61. 10. as a bride adorneth herself with her *j.*

Ezek. 16. 17. thy *j.* of my gold and silver

Mal. 3. 17. mine, when I make up my *j.*

JEWS first also *Greeks, Rom.* 1. 16. & 2. 9, 10.

Rom. 2. 28. not *J.* which is one outwardly, but one inwardly, 29.

10. 12. no difference between *J.* and Gentiles

1 *Cor.* 9. 20. to *J.* became as *J.*

Gal. 3. 28. neither *J.* nor Greek, *Col.* 3. 11.

Rev. 2. 9. say they are *J.* and are not,

JOIN, *Ex.* 1. 10; *Ezra* 9. 14.

Prov. 11. 21. hand *j.* hand, 16. 5.

Is. 5. 8. woe to them that *j.* house to house

Jer. 50. 5. let us *j.* ourselves to Lord in

Acts 5. 13. durst no man *j.* himself to them

8. 29. *j.* thyself to this chariot

9. 26. Saul assayed to *j.* himself to the disciples

JOINED, *Num.* 25. 3. Israel *j.* himself to Baal-Peor, *Ps.* 106. 28.

Eccl. 9. 4. *j.* to all living is hope

Hos. 4. 17. Ephraim is *j.* to idols

Zech. 2. 11. many nations shall be *j.* to the Lord

Matt. 19. 6. what God hath *j.* let no

Luke 15. 15. *j.* himself to a citizen

1 *Cor.* 1. 10. be perfectly *j.* together in same mind

6. 17. he that is *j.* to the Lord is one

Eph. 5. 31. shall be *j.* to wife, 30.

JOINT, S, *Ps.* 22. 14. all my bones are out of *j.*

Prov. 25. 19. confidence like foot out of *j.*

Dan. 5. 6. *j.* of his loins were loosed
Eph. 4. 16. which every *j.* supplieth
Col. 2. 19. all body by *j.* and bands
Heb. 4. 12. dividing asunder of *j.* and marrow

JOINT-HEIRS, *Rom.* 8. 17. *j.* heirs with Christ

JOURNEY, *Gen.* 24. 21. the Lord hath made his *j.* prosperous
Judg. 4. 9. the *j.* thou takest is not for thy honour
Matt. 10. 10. nor scrip for your *j.*
Luke 11. 6. a friend of mine in his *j.* is come to me
15. 13. the younger took his *j.* into a far country
John 4. 6. Jesus wearied with his *j.*
Rom. 1. 10. have a prosperous *j.* to come
15. 24. trust to see you in my *j.*

JOURNEYED, *Gen.* 11. 2. as they *j.* they found a plain
Gen. 13. 11. Lot *j.* east; 33. 17. Jacob *j.* to Succoth
Ex. 40. 36. when cloud was taken up Israel *j.*
Num. 9. 17. after that the children of Israel *j.* 18.
Acts 9. 3. as Saul *j.* he came near to Damascus

JOURNEYING, *Num.* 10. 2. trumpets for *j.* of the camps
Luke 13. 22. *j.* towards Jerusalem
2 *Cor.* 11. 26. in *j.* often, in perils of water

JOY, an agreeable affection of the soul, arising from the hope or possession of some benefit. Religious joy is the delight and satisfaction of the soul in its union with God in Christ, as the greatest and highest good.

JOY, 1 *Chr.* 12. 40; 2 *Chr.* 20. 27.
Neh. 8. 10. the *j.* of the Lord is your strength
Esth. 8. 16. the Jews had *j.* and gladness
Job 20. 5. *j.* of the hypocrite is but for a moment
29. 13. widow's heart to sing for *j.*
33. 26. and he will see his face with *j.*
41. 22. sorrow is turned into *j.*
Ps. 16. 11. in thy presence fulness of *j.*
30. 5. but *j.* cometh in morning
43. 4. I will go to God my exceeding *j.*
51. 8. make me hear *j.* and gladness
12. restore to me *j.* of thy salvation
126. 5. who sow in tears reap in *j.*
137. 6. prefer Jerusalem above chief *j.*
Prov. 17. 21. father of a fool hath no *j.*
23. 24. who begetteth a wise child shall have *j.*
Eccl. 9. 7. eat thy bread with *j.*
Is. 9. 3. increased *j.* according to *j.* in harvest
12. 3. with *j.* shall he draw water out
35. 10. obtain *j.* and gladness, everlasting *j.* on, 51. 11.
52. 9. break forth into *j.*; 55. 12. go out with *j.*
61. 3. oil of *j.* for mourning
7. everlasting *j.* shall be unto them
66. 5. the Lord shall appear to your *j.*
Zeph. 3. 17. the Lord will *j.* over thee

Matt. 13. 20. hear word and with *j.* receive
25. 21. enter into the *j.* of thy Lord 23.
Luke 1. 44. leaped in my womb for *j.*
10. 17. seventy returned with *j.*
15. 7. *j.* shall be in heaven over one sinner
24. 41. they believed not for *j.*
John 15. 11. your *j.* might be, 16. 24.
16. 20. your sorrow be turned into *j.*
22. your *j.* no man taketh
17. 13. have my *j.* fulfilled in themselves
Acts 20. 24. finish course with *j.*
Rom. 14. 17. righteousness, and peace, and *j.* in the Holy Ghost
15. 13. fill you with all *j.* and peace
2 *Cor.* 1. 24. we are helpers of your *j.*
2. 3. my *j.* is the *j.* of you all
Gal. 5. 22. fruit of the Spirit is love, *j.* peace
Phil. 4. 1. my *j.* and crown so stand fast
1 *Thess.* 1. 6. receive word with *j.* of Holy Ghost
2. 19. what is our hope or *j.*
Heb. 12. 2. who for the *j.* set before him
Heb. 13. 17. give account with *j.* not with grief
Jam. 1. 2. count it all *j.* when ye fall
1 *Pet.* 1. 8. rejoice with *j.* unspeakable
4. 13. rejoice, be glad with exceeding *j.*
1 *John* 1. 4. I write that your *j.* may be full
3 *John* 4. I have no greater *j.* than to hear that my
Jude 24. to present you faultless with exceeding *j.*

JOY, great, *Neh.* 12. 43. God hath made them rejoice with *great j.*
Matt. 2. 10. saw the star, they rejoiced with *great j.*
Luke 2. 10. good tidings of *great j.*
Acts 8. 8. was *great j.* in that city
15. 3. they caused *great j.* to all the brethren

JOY, shout for, *Ps.* 5. 11. let those that put their trust in thee rejoice: ever *shout for j.* 35. 27.

JOY, verb, *Ps.* 21. 1. the king shall *j.* in thy strength
Rom. 5. 11. but we also *j.* in God, through our Lord Jesus, by whom we have
Phil. 2. 17. yea, I *j.* and rejoice with you all

JOYFUL, *Ezra* 6. 22. Lord hath made them *j.*
Ps. 5. 11. let them that love thy name be *j.* in thee
35. 9. my soul shall be *j.* in the L.
63. 5. I will praise thee with *j.* lips
89. 15. blessed that know the *j.* sound
Ps. 149. 2. let the children of Zion be *j.* in their king
Eccl. 7. 14. in the day of prosperity be *j.*
Is. 56. 7. make them *j.* in house of prayer
61. 10. my soul shall be *j.* in my God
2 *Cor.* 7. 4. I am exceeding *j.* in all our tribulation

JOYFULLY, *Eccl.* 9. 9. live *j.* with wife
Heb. 10. 34. took *j.* the spoiling of your goods

JOYFULNESS, *Deut.* 28. 47. serve the

Lord with *j.*
Col. 1. 11. long-suffering with *j.*
JOYOUS, *Is.* 23. 7. is this your *J.* city, whose antiquity is
Heb. 12. 11 no chastening seemeth *J.*
JUDGE, noun, *Gen.* 18. 25. shall not the *J.* of earth do
Ex. 2. 14. who made thee a *j. Acts* 7. 27.
Deut. 17. 9. come to the *j.*
Judg. 11. 27. Lord the *J.* be *J.* this day, *Gen.* 16. 5.
1 *Sam.* 2. 25. the *J.* shall *j.* him
Job 9. 15. make supplication to my *J.*
Ps. 50. 6. for God is *j.* himself
Ps. 68. 5. Father of fatherless, *j.* of widows
75. 7. God is the *j.* he putteth, 50. 6.
Is. 33. 22. Lord is our *j.* Lord is our
Matt. 5. 25. adversary deliver thee to the *j.* deliver to officer, *Luke* 12. 58.
Luke 12. 14. who made me a *j.*
Acts 10. 42. to be *j.* of the quick and the 18. 15. no *j.* of such matters
2 *Tim.* 4. 8. Lord the righteous *J.* shall give me
Heb. 12. 23. to God, the *j.* of all, and
Jam. 5. 9. *J.* standeth before door
JUDGE, *Gen.* 16. 5. Lord *j.* between me and thee, 1 *Sam.* 24. 12.
Deut. 32. 36. the Lord shall *j.* his people, *Ps.* 135. 14; *Heb.* 10. 30.
Ps. 7. 8. Lord shall *j.* the people, *j.* me
9. 8. the Lord shall *j.* world in righteousness, 96. 13. & 98. 9; *Acts* 17. 31.
Mic. 3. 11. heads thereof *j.* for reward
Matt. 7. 1. *j.* not that ye be not *j.*
John 5. 30. as I hear I *j.* my judgment
12. 47. I came not to *j.* world
Acts 23. 3. sittest to *j.* me after the law
Rom. 2. 16. God shall *j.* the secrets of
3. 6. how then shall God *j.* the world
14. 10. why dost thou *j.* thy brother
1 *Cor.* 4. 3. I *j.* not my own self
5. *j.* nothing before the time until the
6. 3. know ye not that ye shall *j.* angels
11. 31. if we would *j.* ourselves shall
14. 29. prophets speak and others *j.*
Col. 2. 16. no man *j.* you in meat
2 *Tim.* 4. 1. who shall *j.* the quick and the dead, 1 *Pet.* 4. 5.
Jam. 4. 11. if ye *j.* law not doer, but *j.*
Ps. 72. 2. he shall *j.* thy people with righteousness
Matt. 7. 2. for with what judgments ye *j.*
John 7. 24. *j.* not according to appearance, but *j.* righteous judgment
51. doth our law *j.* any man before it
1 *Cor.* 5. 12. what have I to do *j.* them that are without, do ye not *j.* them that are within
6. 2. do ye not know that the saints shall *j.* the world
3. that ye shall *j.* angels
2 *Cor.* 5. 14. because we thus *j.* that if one died
JUDGED, *Jer.* 22. 16. *j.* the cause of the poor and needy
John 16. 11. prince of this world *j.*
Acts 26. 6. *j.* for hope of the promise
Rom. 2. 12. shall be *j.* by the law, *Jam.* 2. 12.

1 *Cor.* 6. 2. and if the world shall be *j.* by you
10. 29. for why is my liberty *j.* of another man's
1. *Cor.* 11. 32. when we are *j.* we are chastened of the Lord
Rev. 11. 18. time of the dead that they should be *j.*
20. 12. the dead were *j.* out of those things
13. were *j.* every man according to his works
JUDGEST, *Ps.* 51. 4; *Rom.* 14. 4; *Jam.* 4. 12.
JUDGETH, *Ps.* 7. 11. God *j.* righteous
58. 11. he is a God that *j.* in the earth
John 5. 22. the Father *j.* no man, but hath committed
1 *Cor.* 2. 15. spiritual man *j.* all things
4. 4. he that *j.* me is the Lord
Matt. 19. 28. *j.* tribes, *Luke* 22. 30.
JUDGMENT, *Deut.* 1. 17. the *j.* is God's
Deut. 32. 4. all his ways are *j.* a God of truth
Ps. 1. 5. wicked shall not stand in the *j.*
9. 16. Lord is known by the *j.* which
101. 1. I will sing of mercy and *j.*
119. 66. teach me good *j.* for I
143. 2. enter not into *j.* with thy servant
149. 9. execute upon them *j.*
Prov. 21. 15. it is joy to just to do *j.*
29. 26. every man's *j.* comes of the Lord
Eccl. 11. 9. God will bring into *j.* 12. 14.
Is. 1. 27. Zion shall be redeemed with *j.*
28. 17. *j.* also will I lay to line
30. 18. Lord is a God of *j. Job* 35. 14.
42. 1. bring forth *j.* to Gentiles
3. bring *j.* unto truth
53. 8. taken from prison and from *j.*
61. 8. I the Lord love *j.* hate robbery
Jer. 5. 1. if there be any thing executeth *j.*
8. 7. they know the *j.* of the Lord
10. 24. correct with *j.* not with anger
Dan. 4. 37. all whose ways are *j.*
7. 22. *j.* was given to saints
Hos. 12. 6. keep mercy and *j.*
Amos 5. 7. ye who turn *j.* to wormwood
24. let *j.* run down as waters
Matt. 5. 21. be in danger of *j.* 22.
12. 20. till he send forth *j.* unto victory
John 5. 22. Father committed all *j.* to Son
27. given him authority to execute *j.*
9. 39. for *j.* I am come into the world
16. 8. will reprove world of *j.*
Acts. 24. 25. reasoned of *j.* to come
Rom. 5. 18. *j.* came on all men to condemnation
14. 10. must all stand before the *j.* seat of Christ
Heb. 9. 27. it is appointed to all men to die and after death the *j.*
1 *Pet.* 4. 17. *j.* must begin at the house of God
Jude 15. to execute *j.* upon all ungodly
Rev. 17. 1. show thee *j.* of great whore
JUDGMENTS, *Ps.* 19. 9. *j.* of Lord are true and

36. 6. thy *j.* are a great deep, O Lord
119. 75. I know thy *j.* are right
108. O Lord teach me thy *j.*
120. I am afraid of thy *j.*
Is. 26. 8. in way of *j.* we waited
9. when thy *j.* are in the earth, the inhabitants
Jer. 12. 1. let me talk with thee of *j.*
Rom. 11. 33. unsearchable his *j.*
JUST man was Noah, *Gen.* 6. 9.
Lev. 19. 36. *j.* balance, *j.* weights, and a *j.* ephah, *Deut.* 25. 15; *Ezek.* 45. 10.
Deut. 16. 20. altogether *j.* shalt thou fall
32. 4. a God of truth *j.* and righteous
2 *Sam.* 23. 3. ruleth over men must be *j.*
Neh. 9. 33. *j.* in all brought on us
Job 4. 17. can man be more *j.* than God
9. 2. how should man be *j.* with God
Prov. 4. 18. path of *j.* as shining light that shineth
10. 6. blessings on head of *j.*
11. 1. *j.* weight is his delight
12. 21. no evil shall happen to *j.*
17. 26. to punish *j.* is not good
18. 17. first in his own cause seems *j.*
20. 7. a *j.* man walketh in his integrity
21. 15. it is joy to the *j.* to do judgment
24. 16. *j.* man falls seven times and rises
Eccl. 7. 15. *j.* man that perisheth in his righteousness
20. there is not a *j.* man upon earth
8. 14. be *j.* men to whom it happens
Is. 26. 7. way of the *j.* is uprightness, most upright dost weigh path of *j.*
45. 21. beside me a *j.* God and a Saviour
Ezek. 18. 9. he is *j.* he shall live
Hab. 2. 4. *j.* shall live by his faith, *Rom.* 1. 17; *Gal.* 3. 11; *Heb.* 10. 38.
Zeph. 3. 5. *j.* Lord in the midst thereof
Zech. 9. 9. King *j.* and having salvation
Matt. 1. 19. Joseph being a *j.* man
5. 45. sendeth rain on *j.* and unjust
Luke 15. 7. more than over ninety-nine *j.* persons
20. 20. who should feign themselves *j.* men
John 5. 30. my judgment is *j.* because
Acts 7. 52. coming of the *j.* One, 22. 14.
24. 15. resurrection both of *j.* and unjust
Rom. 2. 13. not hearers of law are *j.*
Rom. 3. 26. that he might be *j.* and
7. 12. commandments holy *j.* and good
Phil. 4. 8. whatsoever things are *j.*
Col. 4. 1. give that which is *j.* and equal
Heb. 2. 2. received a *j.* recompense of reward
12. 23. spirits of *j.* men made perfect
1 *Pet.* 3. 18. suffered once *j.* for unjust
1 *John* 1. 9. *j.* to forgive us our sins and
Rev. 15. 3. *j.* and true are thy ways
JUSTICE, *Gen.* 18. 19. to do *j.* and judgment
Deut. 33. 21. executed *j.* of the Lord
Job 37. 23. excellent in plenty of *j.*
Ps. 82. 3. do *j.* to the afflicted and needy
89. 14. *j.* and judgment are habitation of throne

Prov. 8. 15. by me princes decree *j.*
Is. 9. 7. establish his throne with *j.*
Jer. 31. 23. O habitation of *j.* and mountain, 50. 7.
Ezek. 45. 9. execute judgment and *j.* *Jer.* 23. 5.
JUSTIFY, (1) To absolve or declare one innocent, *Prov.* 17. 15. (2) To absolve and acquit a sinner from the guilt and punishment of sin, through the imputation of Christ's righteousness, *Rom.* 3. 28; 5. 9. (3) To declare another to be less guilty than ourselves, *Ezek.* 16. 51. (4) To acknowledge a thing or person to be just, *Matt.* 11. 19; *Luke* 7. 35. (5) To prove and manifest one's self to be in a justified state, *Jam.* 2. 21. It is fourfold, (1) Falsely and vain-gloriously, *Luke* 10. 29; 16. 15. (2) Politically, *Deut.* 25. 1; *Is.* 5. 23. (3) Legally, *Rom.* 3. 20; *Gal.* 2. 16. (4) Evangelically, *Rom.* 5. 1. This is said to be (1) By Christ *Gal.* 2. 16. (2) By grace freely, *Rom.* 3. 24; *Tit.* 3. 7. (3) By faith, *Gal.* 3. 8. (4) By his blood, *Rom.* 5. 9. (5) By his knowledge, *Is.* 53. 11.
JUSTIFY not wicked, *Ex.* 23. 7.
Deut. 25. 1. they shall *j.* righteous
Job 9. 20. if I *j.* myself my own mouth shall condemn
27. 5. that I should *j.* you till
33. 32. speak, I desire to *j.* thee
Is. 5. 23. which *j.* the wicked for reward
53. 11. my righteous servant shall *j.*
Luke 10. 29. he, willing to *j.* himself
16. 15. ye are they which *j.* yourselves
Rom. 3. 30. God shall *j.* circumcision
Gal. 3. 8. God would *j.* heathen through faith
JUSTIFIED, *Job* 13. 18. I shall be *j.*
Job 11. 2. should a man full of talk be *j.*
25. 4. how can man be *j.* with God
32. 2. because he *j.* himself rather than God
Ps. 51. 4. mightest be *j.* when thou speakest
143. 2. in sight no man living can be *j.*
Is. 43. 9. that they may be *j.* 26.
45. 25. in the Lord shall seed of Israel be *j.*
Jer. 3. 11. *j.* herself more than Judah
Ezek. 16. 51. *j.* thy sisters in all
Matt. 11. 19. wisdom is *j.* of her children, *Luke* 7. 35.
12. 37. by thy words thou shalt be *j.*
Luke 7. 29. *j.* Christ being baptized of John
18. 14. went *j.* rather than the other
Acts 13. 39. are *j.* from all things, from which could not be *j.* by law of Moses
Rom. 1. 23. the doers of the law shall be *j.*
3. 4. might be *j.* in thy sayings
20. shall no flesh be *j.* in his sight
24. being *j.* freely by his grace
28. man is *j.* by faith without deeds
4. 2. if Abraham were *j.* by works he

5. 1. being *j.* by faith we have peace
9. being now *j.* by his blood
8. 30. whom he *j.* he glorified
1 *Cor.* 4. 4. yet am I not hereby *j.*
6. 11. *j.* name of Lord Jesus, and by Spirit of God
Gal. 2. 16. not *j.* by works of the law might be *j.* by faith of Christ, 17.
3. 11. that no man is *j.* by law is evident
24. that we might be *j.* by faith
5. 4. *j.* by the law are fallen from grace
1 *Tim.* 3. 16. God manifest in flesh *j.* in Spirit
Tit. 3. 7. that being *j.* by his grace we should
Jam. 2. 21. was not Abraham *j.* by
24. by works a man is *j.* and not by faith only
25. was not Rahab *j.* by works
Prov. 17. 15. that *j.* wicked
Is. 50. 8. he is near that *j.* me
Rom. 4. 5. God that *j.* ungodly
8. 33. it is God that *j.* who is he that
3. 26. *j.* of him that believeth
1 *Kings* 8. 32. condemning the wicked and *j.* the righteous, 2 *Chr.* 6. 23.
Rom. 4. 25. raised for our *j.*
5. 16. gift many offences to *j.*
18. gift came on all men to *j.* of life
JUSTLY, *Mic.* 6. 8. Lord require but to do *j.*
Luke 23. 41. we indeed *j.* due reward
1 *Thess.* 2. 10. how holily and *j.* behaved

KEEP, *Gen.* 2. 15. & 33. 9.
Gen. 18. 19. they shall *k.* way of the L.
28. 15. I am with thee to *k.*
20. if God will be with me and *k.*
Ex. 23. 7. *k.* thee from a false matter
20. I send an angel to *k.* thee in the way
Num. 6. 24. Lord bless thee and *k.*
Deut. 23. 9. *k.* thee from every wicked thing
29. 9. *k.* words of his covenant and do
1 *Sam.* 2. 9. he will *k.* feet of saints
1 *Chr.* 4. 10. thou wouldst *k.* me from evil
Job 14. 13. O *k.* me secret till
Ps. 25. 10. to such as *k.* his covenant, 103. 18.
20. *k.* my soul
17. 8. *k.* me as apple of eye
19. 13. *k.* thy tongue from evil, and thy lips
39. 1. will *k.* my mouth that I sin not
89. 28. my mercy I *k.* for him
91. 11. angels charge to *k.* thee in all thy ways
103. 9. not chide nor *k.* anger for ever
119. 2. *k.* his testimonies
4. *k.* precepts, 17, 33, 34, 57, 69, 88, 100, 106, 129, 136, 146.
127. 1. except the Lord *k.* the city
140. 4. *k.* me O Lord
141. 3. *k.* door of lips, 9.
Prov. 4. 6. love wisdom shall *k.* thee
13. *k.* instruction, she is thy life
23. *k.* thy heart with all diligence
6. 22. sleepest, it shall *k.* thee
Eccl. 3. 6. there is a time to *k.*

5. 1. *k.* thy foot when thou goest
Is. 26. 3. Lord will *k.* him in perfect peace
27. 3. I the Lord *k.* it, I will *k.* it night and day
Jer. 3. 12. I will not *k.* anger for ever
Hos. 12. 6. *k.* mercy and judgment
Mic. 7. 5. *k.* doors of mouth from
Mal. 2. 7. priest's lips should *k.* knowledge
Luke 4. 10. angels charge to *k.* thee
11. 28. hear the word of God and *k.*
John 12. 25. hateth life shall *k.* it
14. 23. man love me will *k.* my word
17. 11. Holy Father *k.* through thy own name
15. shouldst *k.* them from evil
1 *Cor.* 5. 8. let us *k.* the feast not with old leaven
11. not *k.* company with such
9. 27. I *k.* under my body and
Eph. 4. 3. endeavour to *k.* unity of Spirit
Phil. 4. 7. peace of God shall *k.* your heart
2 *Thess.* 3. 3. the Lord shall establish and *k.* you
6. 20. *k.* trust that is committed to
1 *Tim.* 5. 22. of others' sins *k.* thyself
2 *Tim.* 1. 12. able to *k.* that which
14. good thing committed to thee *k.*
Jam. 1. 27. *k.* himself unspotted
2. 10. *k.* whole law and offend in one
Jude 21. *k.* yourselves in the love of God
24. able to *k.* you from falling
Rev. 1. 3. blessed are they that hear and *k.*
3. 10. I will *k.* thee from hour of temptation
22. 9. of them which *k.* sayings
KEEP Commandments, *Lev.* 26. 3. if ye *k. commandments*
Deut. 6. 17. diligently *k. commandments* alway, 11. 1.
13. 4. *k. commandments* and obey his voice, 11. 8.
Ps. 119. 60. I delayed not to *k. commandments*
Prov. 4. 4. *k.* my *commandments* and
Eccl. 12. 13. fear God and *k.* his *c.*
Matt. 19. 17. enter into life *k.* the *c.*
John 14. 15. if ye love me *k.* my *c.*
1 *John* 2. 3. we know him if we *k.* his *c.*
5. 3. this love of God that we *k.* his *c.*
Rev. 14. 12. here are they that *k.* the *c.*
KEEP Silence, Covenant, &c., *Judg.* 3. 19. *Ps.* 35. 22. & 50. 3, 21. & 83. 1; *Eccl.* 3. 7; *Is.* 41. 1. & 62. 6. & 65. 6; *Lam.* 2. 10; *Amos* 5. 13; *Heb.* 2. 20; 1 *Cor.* 14. 28, 34.
1 *Kings* 8. 23. who *k.* covenant and mercy, 2 *Chr.* 6. 14; *Neh.* 9. 32.
KEEPEST, KEEPETH, *Deut.* 7. 9. which *k.* covenant, *Neh.* 1. 5.
Ps. 34. 20. he *k.* all his bones
Ps. 121. 3. that *k.* thee will not slumber
146. 6. he *k.* truth for ever
Prov. 2. 8. *k.* the paths of judgment
Prov. 13. 3. that *k.* his mouth *k.* his life
28. 7. whoso *k.* the law is a wise son, but he
29. 18. but he that *k.* the law happy is he

Luke 11. 21. when a strong man armed
    k. his palace
John 7. 19. none of you *k.* the law
    14. 21. that hath my commandments
    and *k.* them
1 *John* 2. 5. whoso *k.* his word, in him is
    love, 3. 24.
1 *John* 5. 18. *k.* himself and that
Rev. 2. 26. overcometh and *k.* my works
    16. 15. blessed is he that *k.*
    22. 7. blessed that *k.* sayings of this
KEEPING, *Ex.* 34. 7. *k.* mercy for
    thousands
Ps. 19. 11. in *k.* of them is great reward
Dan. 9. 4. *k.* covenant and mercy
1 *Pet.* 4. 19. commit the *k.* of their souls
    to him
KEEPER, *Gen.* 4. 2. Abel was a *k.* of
    sheep; 9. my brother's *k.*
Ps. 121. 5. the Lord is thy *k.*
Eccl. 12. 3. when the *k.* of house shall
    tremble
Songs 1. 6. they made me the *k.* of vine-
    yards
    5. 7. *k.* took away my vail
Tit. 2. 5. chaste *k.* at home good
KEPT, *Deut.* 32. 10. *k.* them as the apple
    of his eye
Deut. 33. 9. they *k.* thy covenant
Josh. 14. 10. Lord that *k.* me alive
2 *Sam.* 22. 22. *k.* ways of Lord, *Ps.* 18. 21.
    24. *k.* myself from my iniquity
Job 23. 11. his ways I *k.*
Ps. 17. 4. *k.* me from the paths of the
    destroyer
    30. 3. thou hast *k.* me alive
Songs 1. 6. mine own vineyard have I
    not *k.*
Matt. 19. 20. these have I *k.* from my
    youth
Luke 2. 19. Mary *k.* all these things, 51.
John 15. 20. if they have *k.* my sayings
    17. 6. they have *k.* thy word
    12. all that thou gavest me I have *k.*
Rom. 16. 25. was *k.* secret since world
    began
2 *Tim.* 4. 7. I have fought—*k.* faith
Heb. 11. 28. Moses *k.* the passover
1 *Pet.* 1. 5. *k.* by power of God through
Jude. 6. the angels *k.* not first estate
Rev. 3. 8. hast *k.* my word and not
    denied my name
    10. *k.* the word of my patience
KICK, *Deut.* 32. 15; 1 *Sam.* 2. 29; *Acts*
    9. 5. & 26. 14.
KID, the young of the goat, esteemed
    a great luxury in the East, *Gen.* 27.
    9; 38. 17; *Judg.* 6. 19. They were
    occasionally offered in sacrifice;
    Num. 7. 16; *Is.* 11. 6; *Luke* 15. 29.
Songs 1. 8. feed thy *k.* beside the
    shepherd's tents
KILL, thou shalt not, *Ex.* 20. 13.
Deut. 32. 39. I *k.* I make alive
1 *Sam.* 2. 6. Lord *k.* and makes alive
1 *Kings* 21. 19. hast thou *k.* and taken
2 *Kings* 5. 7. am I God to *k.* and make
    alive
Ps. 44. 22. *k.* all day long, *Rom.* 8. 36.
Eccl. 3. 3. time to *k.* and time to
Matt. 10. 28. fear not them that *k.* body
    but not able to *k.* soul. *Luke* 12. 4.

Matt. 23. 37. thou hast *k.* the prophets,
    Luke 13. 34.
Mark 3. 4. to save life or to *k.*
Luke 12. 5. after he hath *k.* hath power
John 16. 2. who *k.* you shall
Acts 3. 15. *k.* Prince of life and desired
    10. 13. rise Peter, *k.* and eat
2 *Cor.* 3. 6. letter *k.* but Spirit giveth life
    6. 9. we are chastened not *k.*
1 *Thess.* 2. 15. both *k.* Lord and prophets
Rev. 13. 10. *k.* must be *k.* with sword
KIND, *Gen.* 1. 11; 2 *Chr.* 10. 7.
Luke 6. 35. he is *k.* to unthankful and
    to the evil
1 *Cor.* 13. 4. charity suffers long and
    is *k.*
Eph. 4. 32. be *k.* one to another, *Rom.*
    12. 10.
KINDNESS, 1 *Sam.* 20. 14. show me *k.*
    of the Lord
2 *Sam.* 9. 3. may show the *k.* of God to
    him
    16. 17. is this thy *k.* to thy friend
Neh. 9. 17. God slow to anger and of
    great *k.*
Ps. 117. 2. his merciful *k.* is great
    141. 5. righteous smite me it shall be
    a *k.* and let him reprove me
Prov. 19. 22. desire of man is *k.*
    31. 26. in tongue is law of *k.*
Is. 54. 8. with everlasting *k.* will I have
    10. my *k.* shall not depart from thee
Jer. 2. 2. I remember the *k.* of thy youth
Joel 2. 13. God of great *k. Jonah* 4. 2.
Col. 3. 12. put on the bowels of mercy *k.*
2 *Pet.* 1. 7. to godliness, brotherly *k.* and
KINDLE, *Prov.* 26. 21; *Is.* 10. 16.
2 *Sam.* 22. 9. coals were *k.* by it, *Ps.* 18. 8.
Ps. 2. 12. if his wrath is *k.* but a little
Is. 30. 33. breath of the Lord doth *k.*
    50. 11. walk in light of the sparks ye
    have *k.*
Hos. 11. 8. my repentings are *k.*
Luke 12. 49. fire what if it be already *k.*
KINDLY, *Gen.* 50. 21. Joseph spake *k.*
    to his brethren
Rom. 12. 10. be *k.* affectioned one
KINDRED, 1 *Tim.* 5. 8. provide not
    for those of his own *k.*
Rev. 5. 9. redeemed us out of every *k.*
    and people, and tongue
    14. 6. gospel to preach to every *k.*
KINDREDS, *Ps.* 22. 27. all *k.* of nations
    shall worship before thee
Acts 3. 25. all *k.* of the earth be blessed
Rev. 1. 7. all *k.* of the earth shall wail
    7. 9. a great multitude of all *k.*
KING, *Gen.* 14. 18. & 36. 31.
Job 18. 14. bring him to *k.* of terrors
    34. 18. fit to say to *k.* thou art wicked
Ps. 10. 16. Lord is *K.* for ever
Ps. 24. 7. *K.* of glory shall come in, 9. 10.
    33. 16. no *k.* saved by multitude of an
    47. 7. God is *K.* of the earth, 6.
    74. 12. God is my *K.* 5. 2, & 44. 4.
Prov. 30. 31. *k.* against whom no rising
Eccl. 5. 9. *k.* himself is served by
    8. 4. where word of *k.* is, there is power
Songs 1. 4. *k.* brought me into his
    chamber
    12. while *K.* sits at his table, my
    spikenard

7. 5. *K.* held in galleries, 3. 9, 11.

Is. 32. 1. a *K.* shall reign in righteousness

33. 22. Lord is our lawgiver our *K.*

43. 15. Creator of Israel your *K.*

Jer. 10. 10. Lord is true God and everlasting *K.*

23. 5. a *K.* shall reign and prosper

46. 18. saith the *K.* whose name is Lord of hosts, 51. 57.

Hos. 3. 5. seek Lord and David their *k.*

7. 5. in day of *k.* the princes

13. 11. I gave thee a *k.* in my anger and took

Zech. 9. 9. rejoice, O Zion, thy *K.* cometh unto thee

Matt. 25. 34. then shall *K.* say, 40.

Luke 23. 2. that he himself is Christ a *K.*

John 6. 15. would come by force to make him *k.*

19. 14. behold your *K.*

15. no *k.* but Caesar

1 *Tim.* 1. 17. to the *K.* eternal, immortal

6. 15. *K.* of *k.* and Lord of Lords, *Rev.* 17. 14. & 19. 16.

1 *Pet.* 2. 17. fear God, honour *k.* 13.

Rev. 15. 3. just and true,—*K.* of saints

KINGS, *Ps.* 76. 12. terrible to *k.* of earth, 72. 11.

102. 15. *k.* of earth see thy glory, *Is.* 62. 2.

144. 10. giveth salvation to *k.*

149. 8. to bind *k.* with chains

Prov. 8. 15. by me *k.* reign and princes

Hos. 8. 4. they set up *k.* but not

Matt. 11. 8. soft clothing are in *k.* houses

Luke 22. 25. *k.* of Gentiles exercise lordship

1 *Cor.* 4. 8. reigned as *k.* without

1 *Tim.* 2. 2. for *k.* and all in authority

Rev. 1. 6. make us *k.* and priests to God, 5. 10.

16. 12. way *k.* of east prepared

KINGDOM, *Ex.* 19. 6. be a *k.* of priests

1 *Sam.* 10. 25. Samuel told manner of *k.*

1 *Chr.* 29. 11. thine is *k.* O Lord, *Matt.* 6. 13.

Ps. 22. 28. for the *k.* is the Lord's and

Dan. 2. 44. in last day God set up a *k.*

4. 17. God rules in *k.* of men, 25. 32.

Dan. 7. 27. whose *k.* is an everlasting *k.*

Matt. 12. 25. every *k.* divided against itself

13. 19. heareth the word of *k.* and understandeth it not

38. good seed are children of *k.*

25. 34. inherit *k.* prepared for

Mark 11. 10. blessed be *k.* of our father David

Luke 12. 32. it is the Father's pleasure to give you the *k.*

19. 12. receive for himself a *k.*

22. 29. I appoint unto you a *k.*

John 18. 36. my *k.* is not of this world

1 *Cor.* 15. 24. have delivered up *k.*

Col. 1. 13. translated us into *k.* of Son

2 *Tim.* 4. 18. preserve me unto his heavenly *k.*

Heb. 12. 28. we receive a *k.* not moved

Jam. 2. 5. rich in faith heirs of *k.*

2 *Pet.* 1. 11. into everlasting *k.* of our

Rev. 1. 9. in *k.* and patience of Jesus C.

11. 15. *k.* of the world are become *k.* of our Lord

17. 17. to give *k.* to the beast

Matt. 6. 33. *k.* of God, 12. 28. & 21. 43; *Mark* 1. 15. & 10. 14, 15. & 12. 34. & 15. 43; *Luke* 4. 43. & 6. 20. & 9. 62. & 10. 9, 11. & 13. 29. & 17. 20, 21. & 18. 16, 17. 29. & 22. 16.

John 3. 3. except born again cannot see *k.* of God, 5.

Rom. 14. 17. *k.* of God is not meat and drink

1 *Cor.* 4. 20. *k.* of God not in word

6. 9. unrighteous shall not inherit *k.* of God

15. 50. flesh and blood cannot inherit *k.* of God

Eph. 5. 5. hath any inheritance in *k.* of God

2 *Thess.* 1. 5. be counted worthy of *k.* of God

Rev. 12. 10. now is come *k.* of God

Matt. 3. 2. *k.* of heaven, 4. 17. & 10. 7. & 5.3, 10, 19, 20. & 7. 21. & 8. 11. & 11. 11, 12. & 13. 11, 24, 31, 39. & 16. 19. & 18. 1, 3, 23. & 20. 1. & 22. 2. & 23. 13. & 25. 1, 14.

KISS, ES, *k.* the son lest he be angry, *Ps.* 2. 12.

Prov. 27. 6. *k.* of an enemy are deceitful

Songs 1. 2. let him *k.* me with *k.*

Luke 22. 48. betrayest thou the Son of man with a *k.*

Rom. 16. 16. salute with holy *k.*

1 *Cor.* 16. 20. greet with an holy *k.* 2. *Cor.* 13. 12.

1 *Thess.* 5. 26. greet brethren with holy *k.*

1 *Pet.* 5. 14. greet with *k.* of charity

KISS, verb, 1 *Kings* 19. 20. *k.* my father and mother

Matt. 26. 48. sign—saying, whomsoever I *k.* the same is he, hold him fast, *Mark* 14. 44.

Luke 22. 47. Judas drew near to Jesus to *k.* him

KISSED, *Gen.* 27. 27. Jacob came and *k.* him

Gen. 29. 11. and Jacob *k.* Rachel—wept

48. 10. Jacob *k.* Joseph's sons

50. 1. Joseph fell on his father's face and *k.* him

Ruth 1. 9. Naomi *k.* her daughters-in-law, they wept

14. and Orpah *k.* her mother-in-law, but Ruth ¹

Ps. 85. 10. righteous and peace *k.* each other

Matt. 26. 49. hail, Master, and *k.* him, *Mark* 14. 45.

Luke 7. 38. *k.* feet and anointed

15. 20. his father fell on his neck and *k.* him

Acts 20. 37. fell on Paul's neck, *k.* him

KNEE, S, *Gen.* 30. 3. & 41. 43.

Job 4. 4. feeble *k.* *Is.* 35. 3; *Heb.* 12. 12.

Is. 45. 23. every *k.* bow, *Rom.* 14. 11; *Phil.* 2. 10; *Matt.* 27. 29; *Eph.* 3. 14.

Nah. 2. 10. *k.* smite together, *Dan.* 5. 6.

KNEEL, *Ps.* 95. 6. *k.* before Lord our Maker

KNEELED, *Dan.* 6. 10. Daniel *k.* three

times a day on his knees·
Luke 22. 41. Jesus *k.* down and prayed
Acts 7. 60. Stephen *k.* and cried
    21. 5. *k.* down on shore and prayed
KNEW, *Gen.* 3. 7. & 4. 1. & 42. 8.
Gen. 28. 16. God is in this place, I *k.* it
    not
Deut. 34. 10. whom Lord *k.* face to face
Job 23. 3. O that I *k.* where I might
    find him
Jer. 1. 5. before I formed thee in the
    belly I *k.* thee
Matt. 7. 23. depart I never *k.* you
    12. 25. Jesus *k.* their thoughts, *Luke*
    6. 8.
John 4. 10. if thou *k.* gift of God
Rom. 1. 21. when they *k.* God they
    glorified him not
2 *Cor.* 5. 21. made him sin who *k.* no sin
    12. 2. I *k.* a man in Christ above
    fourteen years ago
Col. 1. 6. ye *k.* the grace of God in truth
Rev. 19. 12. name written that no man *k.*
KNIFE, *Prov.* 23. 2. & 30. 14.
KNIT, 1 *Sam.* 18. 1; *Col.* 2. 2, 19.
KNOCK, *Matt.* 7. 7; *Rev.* 3. 20.
KNOW, *Deut.* 8. 2. *k.* what was in heart
    whether thou
1 *Sam.* 3. 7. Samuel did not yet *k.* the
    Lord
1 *Kings* 8. 38. shall *k.* plague of his heart
1 *Chr.* 28. 9. *k.* thou the G. of thy father
Job 8. 9. are of yesterday and *k.* nothing
    22. 13. how doth God *k.* *Ps.* 73. 11.
Ps. 4. 3. *k.* that Lord hath set apart
    9. 10. that *k.* thy name trust
    39. 4. make me to *k.* my end and
    40. 10. be still and *k.* that I am God
    73. 16. when I thought to *k.* this hard
    89. 15. blessed that *k.* joyful sound
Eccl. 11. 9. *k.* thou that for all
Jer. 17. 9. heart is deceitful, who can *k.*
    22. 16. was not this to *k.* me, saith
    the Lord
    24. 7. I will give them a heart to *k.*
    31. 34. saying, *k.* the Lord, for they
    shall all *k.* me
    44. 28. *k.* whose words shall stand
Ezek. 2. 5. shall *k.* that a prophet, 33. 33.
Hos. 2. 20. I will betroth thee—thou
    shalt *k.* the Lord
Matt. 6. 3. let not thy left hand *k.* what
    thy right hand doeth
    7. 11. *k.* how to give good gifts, *Luke*
    11. 13.
Matt. 13. 11. given to you to *k.* mystery
John 4. 42. we *k.* this is indeed the C.
    7. 17. he shall *k.* the doctrine
    10. 4. sheep follow, they *k.* his voice
    14. 1. *k.* my sheep and am *k.*
    13. 7. *k.* not now but shall *k.* hereafter
    17. if ye *k.* these things happy are ye
    if ye do them
    35. by this shall men *know* ye are my
Acts 1. 7. not for you to *k.* the times
1 *Cor.* 2. 14. neither can ye *k.* them for
    8. 2. *k.* anything, *k.* nothing as he
    ought to *k.*
Eph. 3. 19. to *k.* love of Christ which
    passeth
1 *Thess.* 5. 12. to *k.* them which labour
    among
Tit. 1. 16. profess that they *k.* God

Ex. 4. 14. I *k.* Job 9. 2, 23. & 13. 18.
Gen. 18. 19. *k.* him that he will com-
    mand
Job 19. 25. I *k.* that my Redeemer liveth
Ps. 41. 11. by this I *k.* that thou favour-
    est me
Jer. 10. 23. I *k.* that the way of man is
    29. 11. *k.* the thoughts I think
Matt. 25. 12. I *k.* you not, *Luke* 13. 25, 27.
John 13. 18. I *k.* whom I have chosen
Acts 26. 27. I *k.* thou believest
Rom. 7. 18. I *k.* that in me my flesh
1 *Cor.* 4. 4. though I *k.* nothing
    13. 9. we *k.* in part
    12. I *k.* in part
Phil. 4. 12. *k.* how to be abased
2 *Tim.* 1. 12. I *k.* whom I have believed
1 *John* 2. 4. that saith I *k.* him
Rev. 2. 2. I *k.* thy works, 9. 13, 19. & 3.
    1, 8, 15.
Hos. 6. 3. we *k.* 8. 2. *John* 4. 22; 1 *Cor.*
    2. 12; 1 *John* 2. 3, 5.
John 16. 30. thou *k.* all things
    21. 17. thou *k.* all things, thou *k.* that
    I love thee
KNOWETH, *Ps.* 1. 6. L. *k.* way of
    righteous
    103. 14. he *k.* our frame that we are
    dust
    138. 6. proud he *k.* afar off
    139. 14. my soul *k.* right well
Eccl. 9. 1. man *k.* either love or hatred
Is. 1. 3. ox *k.* his owner and ass
Jer. 8. 7. stork in the heavens *k.* her
    appointed times
    9. 24. understandeth and *k.* me
Zeph. 3. 5. unjust *k.* no shame
Matt. 6. 8. *k.* what things ye need
    24. 36. day and hour *k.* no man
1 *Cor.* 8. 2. *k.* anything *k.* nothing as
2 *Tim.* 2. 19. Lord *k.* them are his
Jam. 4. 17. that *k.* to do good and doeth
    it not
2 *Pet.* 2. 9. Lord *k.* how to deliver godly
Rev. 2. 17. new name which no man *k.*
KNOWN, *Ps.* 9. 16. Lord is *k.* by
    judgment
    31. 7. *k.* my soul in adversity
    67. 2. thy way be *k.* on earth
Is. 45. 4. thou hast not *k.* me
Amos 3. 2. you only have I *k.*
Matt. 10. 26. hid that shall not be *k.*
    Luke 8. 17. & 12. 2.
Luke 19. 42. if thou hadst *k.* in thy day
Acts 15. 18. *k.* unto God are all his works
Rom. 1. 19. that which may be *k.* of G.
    7. 7. I had not *k.* sin but by the law
1 *Cor.* 8. 3. same is *k.* of him, 13. 12.
2 *Tim.* 3. 15. from a child *k.* holy
    scriptures
Rev. 2. 24. not *k.* depths of Satan
KNOWLEDGE, *Gen.* 2. 17. *k.* of good
    and evil
1 *Sam.* 2. 3. Lord is God of *k.* by him
Ps. 19. 2. unto night showeth *k.*
    73. 11. is there *k.* in Most High
    94. 10. he that teacheth men *k.*
    139. 6. such *k.* is too wonderful for me
Prov. 8. 12. I find *k.* of witty inventions
    9. 19. *k.* of the holy is understanding
    14. 6. *k.* is easy to him that under-
    standeth
    19. 2. soul be without *k.* it is not good

Eccl. 9. 10. no device nor *k.* in the grave
Is. 53. 11. by his *k.* shall my righteous
    servant justify many
Dan. 12. 4. to and fro,—*k.* be increased
Hos. 4. 6. destroyed for lack of *k.*
Hab. 2. 14. earth filled with *k.* of Lord,
    Is. 11. 9.
Mal. 2. 7. the priest's lips should keep
    k. and
Rom. 3. 20. by law is *k.* of sin
    10. 2. zeal not according to *k.*
1 *Cor.* 8. 1. all have *k. k.* puffeth
Eph. 3. 19. love of Christ which passeth
    k.
Phil. 3. 8. loss for excellency of the *k.*
    of Christ Jesus
Col. 2. 3. all the treasures of wisdom
    and *k.*
    3. 10. renewed *k.* after image
1 *Pet.* 3. 7. dwell with them according
    to *k.*
2 *Pet.* 1. 5. add to virtue *k.* to *k.* tem-
    perance
    3. 18. grow in grace and in *k.* of Jesus

LABOUR, *Gen.* 31. 42. & 35. 16.
Ps. 90. 10. their strength *l.* and
    104. 23. man goes to his *l.* till evening
Prov. 14. 23. in all *l.* is profit
Eccl. 1. 8. all things are full of *l.*
    4. 8. yet there is no end of *l.*
Is. 55. 2. spend your *l.* for that which
    satisfieth not
Hab. 3. 17. though *l.* of olive fail
1 *Cor.* 15. 58. *l.* is not in vain in the Lord
1 *Thess.* 1. 3. work of faith and *l.* of love
Heb. 6. 10. God not forget your *l.* of love
Rev. 14. 13. blessed are dead rest from *l.*
LABOUR, verb, *Ps.* 127. 1. except Lord
    build *l.* in vain
Prov. 23. 4. *l.* not to be rich, cease from
Matt. 11. 28. come unto me all ye that *l.*
John 6. 27. *l.* not for meat that perisheth
1 *Thess.* 5. 12. *l.* among and are over
    you in the Lord
1 *Tim.* 4. 10. *l.* and suffer reproach
    5. 17. honour especially who *l.*
Heb. 4. 11. *l.* to enter into rest
LABOURED, *Is.* 49. 4. I have *l.* in vain
John 4. 38. other men *l.* and ye entered
Rom. 16. 12. salute Persis, who *l.* much
    in the Lord
1 *Cor.* 15. 10. I *l.* more abundantly than
    they all
Phil. 2. 16. not run nor *l.* in vain
    4. 3. help those that *l.* with me in
    the gospel
Rev. 2. 3. hast borne, and for my name's
    sake *l.*
Prov. 16. 26. he that *l. l.* for himself
Eccl. 5. 12. sleep of *l.* man sweet
Col. 4. 12. Epaphras *l.* fervently in
    prayer
LABOURER, S, *Matt.* 20. 1. went out
    early to hire *l.* into his vineyard
Matt. 9. 37. *l.* are few, *Luke* 10. 2.
Luke 10. 7. *l.* worthy of his hire, 1 *Tim.*
    5. 18.
1 *Cor.* 3. 9. we are *l.* together with God
Jam. 5. 4. hire of the *l.* that reaped
LACK, noun, *Gen.* 18. 28. destroy all
    for *l.* of five
Hos. 4. 6. my people are destroyed for

l. of knowledge
Phil. 2. 30. supply your *l.* of service
LACK, verb, *Ps.* 34. 10. young lions *l.*
    and suffer hunger
Jam. 1. 5. if any of you *l.* wisdom, let
    him ask of God
LACKED, *Luke* 22. 35. I sent you with-
    out purse, *l.* ye any thing
Phil. 4. 10. ye *l.* opportunity
LACKEST, *Mark* 10. 21. but one thing
    thou *l. Luke* 18. 22.
LACKETH, ING, 2 *Cor.* 11. 9. what was
    l. to me the brethren supplied
1 *Thess.* 3. 10. might perfect what is *l.*
    in your faith
2 *Pet.* 1. 9. but he that *l.* these things is
    blind
LAD, *Gen.* 43. 8. send the *l.* with me,
    and we will arise and go
Gen. 44. 22. we said, the *l.* cannot leave
    his father
LADEN, *Is.* 1. 4. a people *l.* with
    iniquity
Matt. 11. 28. come all ye that labour
    and are heavy *l.*
2 *Tim.* 3. 6. silly women *l.* with sins
LAKE, *Luke* 5. 1. Jesus stood by the *l.*
    of Gennesaret
Rev. 19. 20. cast into a *l.* of fire
    20. 10. devil was cast into *l.*
    15. was not found in the book of life
    cast into *l.*
LAMB, *Gen.* 22. 7 8; *Ex.* 12. 3.
2 *Sam.* 12. 3. nothing, save one little
    ewe *l.*
Is. 11. 6. wolf dwell with the *l.*
    53. 7. he is brought as a *l.* to the
    slaughter
John 1. 29. behold *l.* of God which
    taketh away, 36.
1 *Pet.* 1. 19. a *l.* without blemish
Rev. 5. 12. worthy is the L. that was
    slain
    6. 16. hide us from face of the L.
    7. 14. white in blood of the L. 12. 11.
    17. *Lamb* in midst of throne feed them
    13. 8. L. slain from foundation of w.
LAME, *Lev.* 21. 18; *Mal.* 1. 8, 13.
Job 29. 15. eyes to blind feet to *l.*
Prov. 26. 7. legs of *l.* not equal
Is. 35. 6. *l.* leap as hart, 33. 23.
Matt. 11. 5. the *l.* walk, 15. 31; 21. 14
    Luke 7. 22.
Acts 3. 2. certain man *l.* from womb
Heb. 12. 13. lest that which is *l.* be
    turned out of
LAMP, *Gen.* 15. 17; *Ex.* 27. 20; 1 *Kings*
    15. 4; *Matt.* 25. 1, 3, 4, 7, 8.
2 *Sam.* 22. 29. thou art my *l.* O Lord,
    and the Lord
Job 12. 5. as *l.* despised in the thoughts
    of him at ease
Ps. 119. 105. thy word is a *l.* to my feet
    132. 17. have ordained a *l.* for anointed
Prov. 6. 23. commandment is a *l.* and
    law is right
    13. 9. *l.* of wicked be put out
Is. 62. 1. salvation as a *l.* that burneth
Ex. 25. 37. seven *l.* 37. 23; *Num.* 8. 2;
    Zech. 4. 2; *Rev.* 4. 5.
LAND. The whole earth, as distinguish-
    ed from sea, *Matt.* 23. 15. One
    particular country, *Matt.* 9. 26.

Arable ground, *Gen.* 26. 12. The inhabitants of a country, *Is.* 37. 11. A certain possession; 2 *Sam.* 19. 29; *Acts* 4. 37. See also *Eccl.* 10. 16, 17; *Is.* 5. 30; *Prov.* 28. 2.

LANGUAGE, *Gen.* 11. 1; *Neh.* 13. 24; *Ps.* 81. 5; *Is.* 19. 18; *Zeph.* 3. 9.

LANGUISH, *Ps.* 41. 3; *Is.* 24. 4.

LARGE, *Ex.* 3. 8. into a good and *l.*
2 *Sam.* 22. 20. he brought me into a *l.* place, *Ps.* 18. 19.
Neh. 4. 19. the work is great and *l.*
Ps. 31. 8. hast set my feet in a *l.* room
118. 5. Lord set me in a *l.* place
Jer. 22. 14. I will build *l.* chambers
Matt. 28. 12. gave *l.* money to soldiers
Mark 14. 15. and he will show you a *l.* upper room, *Luke* 22. 12.
Gal. 6. 11. how *l.* letter I have written
Rev. 21. 16. length as *l.* as breadth

LASCIVIOUSNESS. It signifies all kind of lusts; *Mark* 7. 22; 2 *Cor.* 12. 21; *Gal.* 5. 19; *Eph.* 4. 19; 1 *Pet.* 4. 3.
Jude 4. turn grace of God into *l.*

LAST end like his, *Num.* 23. 10.
Lam. 1. 9. remembered not *l.* end
Luke 11. 26. *l.* state worse than the first
1 *Pet.* 1. 5. *l.* time, 20; 1 *John* 2. 18.

LATTER day, *Job* 19. 25. *l.* end, *Prov.* 19. 20. *l.* house; *Hag.* 2. 9. *l.* time; 1 *Tim.* 4. 1; 2 *Tim.* 3. 1.

LAUGH, *Gen.* 17. 17. & 18. 12, 15.
2 *Chr.* 30. 10. but they *l.* them to scorn
Job 5. 22. at destruction and famine thou shalt *l.*
Ps. 2. 4. he that sits in heaven shall *l.*
37. 13. Lord shall *l.* at him
52. 6. righteous shall see and *l.* at him
59. 8. thou O Lord shall *l.* at them
Prov. 1. 26. I will *l.* at your calamity
Luke 6. 21. blessed that weep, ye shall *l.*
25. woe to them that *l.* now, ye shall mourn
Job. 8. 21. he filleth mouth with *l.*
Ps. 126. 2. mouth filled with *l.*
Prov. 14. 13. even in *l.* the heart is sorrowful
Eccl. 7. 3. sorrow better than *l.*
Jam. 4. 9. let your *l.* be turned to mourning

LAW, *Gen.* 47. 26; *Prov.* 28. 4.
Deut. 33. 2. from his hand went fiery *l.*
Neh. 8. 7. caused people to understand the *l.*
Job 22. 22. receive *l.* from his mouth
Ps. 1. 2. in *l.* doth he meditate
19. 7. *l.* of Lord is perfect converting
37. 31. *l.* of God is in his heart
78. 5. appointed a *l.* in Israel, 10.
119. 72. *l.* of thy mouth is better than
Prov. 6. 23. *l.* is light
7. 2. keep my *l.* as apple of eye
13. 14. *l.* of wise
28. 9. that turneth away his ear from hearing the *l.*
29. 18. keepeth *l.* happy is he
Is. 2. 3. go forth *l.* *Mic.* 4. 2.
8. 16. seal the *l.* among my disciples
20. to the *l.* and the testimony
42. 21. magnify *l.* and make it honourable
51. 7. people in whose heart is my *l.*
Jer. 18. 18. the *l.* shall not perish from

the priest
31. 33. I will put my *l.* in inward parts
Ezek. 7. 26. *l.* shall perish from priest
Hos. 8. 12. written great things of my *l.*
Mal. 2. 7. people seek *l.* at mouth
Luke 16. 16. *l.* and prophets
John 1. 17. *l.* was given by Moses
19. 7. we have a *l.* and by our *l.* he ought to die
Acts 13. 39. not justified by *l.* of Moses
Rom. 2. 12. sin without *l.* perish with *l.*
13. not hearers of *l.* but doers of the *l.*
14. having not *l.* are a *l.* to themselves
3. 20. by deeds of *l.* no flesh justified, for by *l.* is knowledge of sin
27. excluded by *l.* of works, by *l.* of faith
4. 15. *l.* works wrath, no *l.* no transgression
5. 13. sin not imputed no *l.*
7. not known sin but by *l.*
8. without the *l.* sin was dead
12. *l.* is holy, just and good
14. *l.* is spiritual, but I am carnal
22. I delight in *l.* of God
23. *l.* in member *l.* of mind, 25.
8. 2. *l.* of spirit of life, *l.* of sin and death
10. 4. Christ is the end of *l.* for righteousness
5. righteousness of *l.* 9. 31, 32; *Phil.* 3. 9.
1 *Cor.* 6. 1. dare any of you to go to *l.* 6. 7.
Gal. 2. 16. not justified by the *l.*
19. I through the *l.* am dead to *l.* that I
3. 10. works of *l.* under curse
12. *l.* is not of faith but man
13. Christ redeemed us from curse of the *l.*
5. 23. love, joy, peace, against such no *l.*
1 *Tim.* 1. 8. *l.* is good if use it *l.*
1. 9. not made for righteous man but *l.*
Heb. 7. 19. *l.* made nothing perfect, 10. 1.
Jam. 1. 25. *l.* of liberty
2. 8. royal *l.* 12.
1 *John* 3. 4. sin transgresseth *l.* sin is transgression of *l.*

LAW, Thy, *Neh.* 9. 26. cast *l.* behind back
Ps. 40. 8. *l.* is within my heart
94. 12. blessed is man, teachest him out of *thy l.*
119. 18. behold wondrous things out of *thy l.*
70. I delight in *l.* 77. 92, 174.
97. I love *thy l.* 113. 163, 165.

LAW, under the, *Rom.* 3. 19. it saith to them that are *under the l.*
6. 14. ye are not *under the l.* but
15. sin because not *under the l.*
1 *Cor.* 9. 20. to them *under the l.* as *under the l.* that I might gain them *under the l.*
21. not without law to God, but *under l.* to Christ
Gal. 5. 18. if led by Spirit not *under l.*

LAW, without, *Rom.* 2. 12. as many as sinned *without l.* perish *without l.*
Rom. 3. 21. the righteousness of God *without l.* is manifested

7. 8. for *without l.* sin was dead; 9.
I was alive *without l.* once

LAWS, *Gen.* 26. 5. Abraham kept my *l.*
Ex. 18. 20. shalt teach them *l.*
Esth. 1. 19. the *l.* of the Persians
Ps. 105. 45. might keep his *l.*
Heb. 8. 10. put my *l.* into their mind
10. 16. put my *l.* into their hearts

LAWFUL, *Is.* 49. 24. *l.* captive be
delivered
Ezek. 18. 5. do that which is *l.* and
right, 33. 14, 19.
Matt. 12. 10. asked, is it *l.* to heal on
the sabbath day, 12; *Mark* 3. 4;
Luke 6. 9; 14. 3.
14. 4. not *l.* to have her, *Mark* 6. 18.
1 *Cor.* 6. 12. all things are *l.* to me, 10. 23.

LAWGIVER, *Is.* 33. 22. Lord is our *l.*
Jam. 4. 12.

LAWLESS, 1 *Tim.* 1. 9. the *l.* and
disobedient

LAWYER, S, *Matt.* 22. 35. one that was
a *l.* asked him, *Luke* 10. 25.
Luke 7. 30. the *l.* rejected the counsel
of God
11. 45. then answered one of the *l.*
and said
46. woe unto you *l.* 52; 14. 3. Jesus
spake to *l.*
Tit. 3. 13. bring Zenas the *l.* and Apollos

LAY, *Gen.* 19. 33, 35; *Job* 29. 19.
Eccl. 7. 2. living *l.* it to heart
Is. 28. 16. I *l.* in Zion a tried stone
Mal. 2. 2. I cursed ye *l.* it not to heart
Matt. 8. 20. had not where to *l.* his head
Acts 7. 60. *l.* not this sin to their charge
15. 28. to *l.* on you no greater burden
Rom. 8. 33. who shall *l.* any thing to
1 *Tim.* 5. 22. *l.* hands, *Heb.* 6. 2.
Heb. 12. 1. *l.* aside every weight and sin
Jam. 1. 21. *l.* apart all filthiness and
superfluity of naughtiness, 1 *Pet.* 2. 6.

LAY down, hold, *John* 10. 15. *l. down*
life, 13. 37. & 15. 13; ; 1 *John* 3. 16.
1. *Tim.* 6. 12. they may *l. hold* of eternal life
Heb. 6. 18. *l. hold* on hope set before

LAY up, *Matt.* 6. 20. *l. up* for yourselves
treasure
2 *Cor.* 12. . 14. children not *l. up* for
parents but

LAID, *Ps.* 62. 9. to be *l.* in balance they
89. 19. I *l.* help on one mighty
Is. 53. 6. Lord *l.* on him iniquities of us
Matt. 3. 10. the axe *l.* unto root, *Luke*
3. 9.
1 *Cor.* 3. 10. I have *l.* the foundation, 11.
Heb. 6. 1. not *l.* again the foundation of
repentance
1 *Sam.* 21. 12. David *l.* up these words
Ps. 31. 19. how great *l.* up for them that
fear thee
Songs 7. 13. pleasant fruits *l.* for
Luke 1. 66. *l.* up in their hearts
12. 19. much goods *l.* for many years
Col. 1. 5. hope *l.* up for you in heaven
1 *Tim.* 6. 19. *l.* up in store good foundation
2 *Tim.* 4. 8. *l.* up for me a crown of
righteousness
Job 21. 19. God *l.* up his iniquity for his
children

24. 12. God *l.* not folly to them
Prov. 2. 7. *l.* up wisdom
26. 24. *l.* up deceit
Is. 56. 2. blessed that *l.* hold on
57. 1. no man *l.* to heart, 42. 25.
Jer. 12. 11. land desolate because no
man *l.* it to heart

LEAD, *Ex.* 15. 10; *Job* 19. 24; *Zech.* 5.
7, 8; *Gen.* 33. 14; *Ex.* 13. 21.
Ps. 5. 8. *l.* me in righteousness
25. 5. *l.* me in thy truth
27. 11. *l.* me in plain path
61. 2. *l.* me to rock higher than I
139. 24. *l.* me in way everlasting
143. 10. *l.* me into the land of uprightness
Songs 8. 2. I would *l.* thee into my
mother's house
Is. 11. 6. a little child shall *l.* them
40. 11. *l.* those with young
Matt. 15. 14. if blind *l.* blind, *Luke* 6. 39.
1 *Tim.* 2. 2. *l.* a quiet life in all
Rev. 7. 17. Lamb shall *l.* them unto
living fountains
Ps. 23. 2. *l.* me beside still waters
Is. 48. 17. Lord thy God which *l.* by way,
42. 16. & 49. 10. & 57. 18; *Jer.* 31. 9.
Matt. 7. 13. gate *l.* to destruction
14. which *l.* unto life
John 10. 3. calleth sheep and *l.* them
Rom. 2. 4. goodness of God *l.* to repentance
Gen. 24. 27. Lord *l.* 48; *Ex.* 13. 18. &
15. 13; *Deut.* 4. 27. & 32. 10,
12; *Neh.* 9. 12; *Ps.* 80. 1. & 78. 14,
53. & 106. 9. & 136. 16. & 107. 7; *Is.*
48. 21. & 65. 13, 14; *Jer.* 2. 6, 17.
Rom. 8. 14. *l.* by Spirit, *Gal.* 5. 18.
Is. 55. 4. *l.* to the people, 9. 16.

LEAN not to own understanding, *Prov.*
3. 5.
Job 8. 15. shall *l.* on his house
Songs 8. 5. wilderness *l.* on beloved
Mic. 3. 11. yet will they *l.* on the Lord
John 13. 23. *l.* on Jesus' bosom, 21. 20.

LEANNESS, *Job* 16. 8; *Ps.* 106. 15.
Is. 10. 16. my *l.* my *l.* 24. 16.

LEAP, *Ps.* 68. 16. why *l.* ye high hills
Is. 35. 6. lame man *l.* as a hart

LEAPED, 2 *Sam.* 22. 30. I *l.* over a wall,
Ps. 18. 29.
Acts 14. 10. and he *l.* and walked

LEAPING, 2 *Sam.* 6. 16. David *l.* and
dancing
Songs 2. 8. behold he cometh *l.* on the
mountains

LEARN to fear me, *Deut.* 4. 10. & 5. 1. &
14. 23. & 31. 12, 13.
Ps. 119. 71. might *l.* statutes, 73.
Prov. 22. 25. lest thou *l.* his ways
Is. 1. 17. cease to do evil, *l.* to do well
26. 10. yet he will not *l.* righteousness
Jer. 10. 2. *l.* not way of heathen
Matt. 9. 13. *l.* what that means
11. 29. *l.* of me, for I am meek
1 *Tim.* 2. 11. women *l.* in silence
Tit. 3. 14. let ours *l.* to maintain good
Rev. 14. 3. no man could *l.* song

LEARNED, *Ps.* 106. 35. *l.* their works
Is. 50. 4. Lord given me tongue of *l.*
John 6. 45. that *l.* of the Father cometh

unto me
Acts 7. 22. Moses was *l.* in all wisdom
Eph. 4. 20. ye have not so *l.* Christ
Phil. 4. 11. I have *l.* in whatsoever state
Heb. 5. 8. though son yet *l.* he obedience
LEARNING, *Prov.* 1. 5. wise will hear. and increase *l.* 9. 9.
Acts 26. 24. much *l.* makes mad
Rom. 15. 4. were written for our *l.* that we might hope
2 *Tim.* 3. 7. ever *l.* never come to knowledge of the truth
LEASING, *Ps.* 4. 2. how long seek after *l.*
Ps. 5. 6. destroy them that speak *l.*
LEAST, *Jer.* 31. 34. know thee from *l.* to the greatest
Matt. 11. 11. *l.* in kingdom of God is great
Luke 16. 10. faithful in *l.* faithful in great
1 *Cor.* 6. 4. who are *l.* esteemed in
15. 9. I am *l.* of all apostles
Eph. 3. 8. less than *l.* of all saints
LEAVE father and mother, and cleave to wife, *Gen.* 2. 24; *Matt.* 19. 5; *Eph.* 5. 31.
1 *Kings* 8. 57. let him not *l.* us nor forsake
Ps. 16. 10. not *l.* my soul in hell
27. 9. *l.* me not, neither forsake
Matt. 5. 24. *l.* thy gifts before the altar
23. 23. these done not to *l.* the other undone
John 14. 18. I will not *l.* you comfortless
Heb. 13. 5. I will never *l.* nor forsake you
LEAVING, *Luke* 10. 30. thieves *l.* him half dead
Heb. 6. 1. *l.* principles of doctrine
1 *Pet.* 2. 21. Christ suffered for us, *l.* us an example
LEAVEN, *Ex.* 12. 15; *Lev.* 2. 11.
Matt. 13. 33. kingdom of heaven like *l.*
16. 6. beware of *l.* of Pharisees, *Luke* 12. 1.
1 *Cor.* 5. 7. purge out the old *l.* malice, 8.
5 6. little *l.* lump. *Gal.* 5. 9.
LFD. *Ps.* 78. 14. he *l.* them with a cloud
Ps. 106. 9. so he *l.* them through the depths as through a wilderness, 136. 16; *Is.* 63. 13.
107. 7. he *l.* them forth by the right way
Prov. 4. 11. I have *l.* thee in right paths
Matt. 4. 1. Jesus *l.* of the Spirit, *Luke* 4. 1.
26. 57. they *l.* him to Caiaphas, *Mark* 14. 53; *Luke* 22. 54; *John* 18. 13.
Acts 8. 32. *l.* as a sheep to the slaughter
Rom. 8. 14. as many as are *l.* by the Spirit of God
LEES, *Is.* 25. 6. a feast of wine on the *l.*
Jer. 48. 11. Moab had settled on *l.*
Zeph. 1. 12. punish men settled on *l.*
LEFT, *Acts* 14. 17; *Rom.* 9. 29; *Heb.* 4. 1; *Jude* 6; *Rev.* 2. 4.
LEGS, *Ps.* 147. 10; *Prov.* 26. 7; *Ex.* 12. 9. Figuratively, it indicates strength; *Songs* 5. 15.
LEND, *Ex.* 22. 25; *Deut.* 23. 19, 20.
1 *Sam.* 1. 28. I have *l.* him to Lord
Ps. 37. 26. merciful and *l.* 112. 5.
Prov. 19. 17. giveth to the poor *l.* to the

Lord
22. 7. borrower is servant to *l.*
Jer. 15. 10. I neither *l.* on usury
Luke 6. 35. do good & *l.* hoping nothing
LENGTH, *Ps.* 21. 4. *l.* of days for ever
Prov. 3. 2. *l.* of days add to thee
Eph. 3. 18. comprehend *l.* of love of Christ
LENTILES, *Gen.* 25. 34. gave Esau pottage of *l.*
2 *Sam.* 23. 11. of ground full of *l.*
LEOPARD, *Songs* 4. 8; *Jer.* 5. 6. & 13. 23; *Hos.* 13. 7; *Hab.* 1. 8.
LEPER, *Lev.* 13. 45. *l.* in whom the plague is
Lev. 22. 4. what man is a *l.*
Num. 5. 2. put out of camp every *l.*
2 *Kings* 5. 1. Naaman was a *l.*; 11. recover the *l.*
27. a *l.* as white as snow
Matt. 8. 2. there came a *l. Mark* 1. 40.
26. 6. of Simon the *l. Mark* 14. 3.
LEPERS, *Luke* 4. 27. *l.* in Israel in time of Eliseus
Luke 17. 12. ten men that were *l.*
LEPROSY, *Lev.* 13. 2. in the skin like plague of *l.*
Lev. 13. 9. when *l.* is in a man he shall
2 *Kings* 5. 3. recover him of his *l.*
26. *l.* of Naaman shall cleave
Matt. 8. 3. his *l.* was cleansed, *Mark* 1. 42; *Luke* 5. 13.
Luke 5. 12. a man full of *l.* besought him
LESS, *Gen.* 32. 10. I am *l.* than least of all the mercies
Ezra 9. 13. punished us *l.* than our iniquities deserve
Job 11. 6. God exacteth *l.* than iniquity deserveth
Is. 40. 17. all nations are counted *l.*
Mark 4. 31. when sown is *l.* than all seeds
15. 40. Mary mother of James the *l.*
2 *Cor.* 12. 15. more I love, *l.* am loved
Eph. 3. 8. *l.* than the least of all saints
Heb. 7. 7. the *l.* is blessed of better
LETTER, *Ezra* 4. 7. written in Syrian
Neh. 2. 8. a *l.* to Asaph the keeper of the forest
Esth. 9. 29. wrote to confirm this *l.* of Purim
Rom. 2. 29. circumcision of the heart, not in the *l.*
7. 6. serve, not in oldness of *l.*
2 *Cor.* 3. 6. ministers not of *l.* but Spirit
Gal. 6. 11. ye see how large a *l.* I
Heb. 13. 22. written a *l.* in few words
LETTERS, *Acts* 22. 5. I received *l.* to the brethren
2 *Cor.* 3. 1. *l.* of commendation
10. 10. for his *l.* are weighty
LETTEST, *Luke* 2. 29; 2 *Thess.* 2. 7.
LIBERAL. Free, generous, openhearted; one who writes on all his possessions, " For myself and mankind; " and lives only to get and to do good, *Prov.* 11. 25; *Is.* 32. 5, 8; 2 *Cor.* 9. 13.
LIBERALITY, 1 *Cor.* 16. 3; 2 *Cor.* 8. 2.
Jam. 1. 5. gives to all *l.*
LIBERTY, *Lev.* 25. 10; *Jer.* 34. 8.

Ps. 119. 45. I will walk at *l.* for I seek

Is. 61. 1. anointed me. proclaim *l.* to the captives

Luke 4. 18. to set at *l.* bruised

Rom. 8. 21. into glorious *l.* of the sons of God

2 *Cor.* 3. 17. where Spirit of the Lord is, there is *l.*

Gal. 5. 1. stand fast in *l.* wherewith Christ made free

13. unto *l.* but use not *l.* for an occasion to flesh

Jam. 1. 25. looks not into law of *l.* 2. 12.

1 *Pet.* 2. 16. not using your *l.* for a cloak

LIE, *Lev.* 6. 3. & 19. 11; *Job* 11. 3.

Ps. 58. 3. wicked go astray speaking *l.*

62. 9. and men of high degree are *l.*

101. 7. telleth *l.* shall not tarry

Hos. 11. 12. compasseth—about with *l.*

2 *Thess.* 2. 11. should believe a *l.*

1 *Tim.* 4. 2. speaking *l.* hypocrisy

Rev. 22. 15. loveth and maketh a *l.* 21. 8, 27.

Num. 23. 19. God is not a man that he should *l.*

Is. 63. 8. children that will not *l.*

Hab. 2. 3. it shall speak and not *l.*

Col. 3. 9. *l.* not one to another, *Eph.* 4. 25.

Tit. 1. 2. God that cannot *l.* hath promised

Heb. 6. 18. impossible for God to *l.*

Ps. 116. 11. all men are *l.*

Is. 44. 25. frustrateth tokens of *l.*

John 8. 44. he is a *l.* and father

Rom. 3. 4. let God be true and every man a *l.*

Tit. 1. 12. Cretians are always *l.*

1 *John* 1. 10. we make him a *l.* and his word, 5. 10.

2. 4. keeps not commandments is a *l.* 4. 20.

Rev. 2. 2. tried and found them *l.*

21. 8. all *l.* have their part in

Ps. 119. 29. remove from me way of *l.*

163. I abhor *l.* but love thy law

Prov. 12. 19. *l.* tongue but for a

Jer. 7. 4. trust not in *l.* words, temple of the Lord

Hos. 4. 2. by swearing and *l.* they break

Jonah 2. 8. observe *l.* vanities forsake their own mercy

LIFE, (1) That space of time which passes between the birth and death of any person, *Ps.* 17. 14; *Prov.* 3. 2. (2) A power to move and do the actions of life, *Job* 3. 20; *Eccl.* 2. 17. (3) A spiritual, supernatural, and heavenly life, whereby we live to God, and enjoy peace with him, which also is the way to eternal life, *Rom.* 8. 6; *Col.* 3. 3. (4) Eternal happiness, glory, and blessedness, which the saints enjoy in heaven, *Rom.* 5. 17. (5) That quickening and strengthening power of the Spirit of Christ, which supports believers under afflictions and sufferings, so that they are not overwhelmed by them, 2 *Cor.* 4. 10. (6) Christ's resurrection and interces-

sion, *Rom.* 5. 10. (7) The appetite, *Job* 33. 20. (8) The nourishment or support of life, *Deut.* 20. 19. (9) Blessings pertaining to this life, 1 *Tim.* 4. 8. (10) This world, *Luke* 8. 14. (11) Conversation, *Acts* 26. 4. It is spoken, (1) Of Christ, who is the fountain of natural, spiritual, and eternal life, who has promised eternal life to his people, purchased and prepared it for them; and who prepares them for it, and will bestow it upon them, *John* 1. 4; 11. 25; *Col.* 3. 4. (2) Of the doctrine of the gospel, which points out the way to eternal life, *John* 6. 63.

LIFE, *Gen.* 2. 7, 9. & 42. 15. & 44. 30.

Deut. 30. 15. set before you *l.* and death, choose *l.*

32. 47. is not vain thing it is your *l.*

1 *Sam.* 25. 29. soul bound in the bundle of *l.*

Job 10. 12. granted me *l.* and favour

Ps. 16. 11. show me the path of *l.*

21. 4. he asked *l.* of thee and thou

30. 5. anger but a moment in his favour is *l.*

Ps. 36. 9. with thee is fountain of *l.*

63. 3. loving-kindness is better than *l.*

66. 9. holds our soul in *l.*

91. 16. with long *l.* I will satisfy

Prov. 8. 35. for whoso findeth me findeth *l.*

15. 24. way of *l.* above to wise

18. 21. death and *l.* in power of tongue

Is. 57. 10. found *l.* of thy hand

Matt. 6. 25. take no thought for your *l.*

Luke 12. 15. man's *l.* consisteth not in abundance

John 1. 4. in him was *l.* and the *l.* was light of men

3. 36. believe on Son hath everlasting *l.* 15. 13.

5. 40. not come that they might have *l.*

6. 35. I am the bread of *l.* 48; 40. 47, 54.

51. my flesh I give for *l.* of, 53.

63. words I speak are spirit and *l.*

8. 12. follows me shall have light of *l.*

10. 10. come they might have *l.*

11. 25. I am the resurrection and the *l.*

14. 6. I am way, truth, and *l.*

Rom. 5. 17. reign in *l.* by Jesus Christ, 18. 21.

8. 2. law of Spirit of *l.* in Christ Jesus hath made

6. to be spiritually minded is *l.* and

2 *Cor.* 2. 16. savour of *l.* unto *l.*

3. 6. letter killeth, spirit giveth *l.*

4. 10. *l.* of Jesus might be made manifest

5. 4. that mortality might be swallowed up of *l.*

Gal. 2. 20. the *l.* which I now live in the flesh

Eph. 4. 18. alienated from *l.* of God through ignorance

Col. 3. 3. and your *l.* is hid with Christ in God

4. when Christ who is our *l.* shall appear

1 *Tim.* 2. 2. lead a peaceable *l.* in

godliness

4. 8. godliness having promise of the *l.* that now is

2 *Tim.* 1. 10. brought *l.* and immortality to light

2 *Pet.* 1. 3. that pertains to *l.* and godliness

1 *John* 5. 12. hath Son hath *l.* not Son not *l.*

LIFE, his, *Job* 2. 4. all a man hath will he give for *his l.*

Prov. 13. 3. keepeth mouth keepeth *l.*

Matt. 10. 39. he that findeth *his l.* shall lose it; he that loseth *his l.* shall find it, 16. 25; *Mark* 8. 35; *Luke* 9. 24; 17. 33; *John* 12. 25.

Matt. 20. 28. to give *his. l.* a ransom for many, *Mark* 10. 45.

Luke 14. 26. hate not *his* own *l.* also

John 10. 11. good Shepherd giveth *his l.* for the sheep

Rom. 5. 10. shall be saved by *his l.*

1 *John* 3. 16. love of God, laid down *his l.*

LIFE, my, 1 *Kings* 19. 4. take away *my l.* 14.

Job 9. 21. though I were perfect, yet I would despise *my l.*

10. 1. my soul is weary of *my l.* I will leave

Ps. 23. 6. mercy shall follow me all the days of *my l.*

26. 9. gather not *my l.* with bloody men

27. 1. Lord is strength of *l.* of whom

Jonah 2. 6. brought up *my l.* from corruption

John 10. 15. I lay down *my l.* for sheep, 17. my Father loveth me because I lay down *my l.*

13. 37. Lord, I will lay down *my l.* for thy sake

Acts 20. 24. nor count I *my l.* dear to myself

Ps. 17. 14. this *l. Luke* 8. 14. & 21. 34; *Acts* 5. 20; 1 *Cor.* 6. 3; 15. 19.

Deut. 30. 20. he is thy *l.* and length

Ps. 103. 4. redeem thy *l.* from destruction

Jer. 39. 18. thy *l.* shall be for a prey, 45. 5.

Prov. 10. 16. tends to *l.* 11. 19. & 19. 23; *Matt.* 7. 14; *John* 5. 24; 1 *John* 3. 14; *Acts* 11. 18; *Rom.* 7. 10; *Heb.* 11. 35.

LIFT up his countenance on thee, *Num.* 6. 26.

1 *Sam.* 2. 7. L. brings low and *l.* up again

2 *Kings* 19. 4. *l.* up prayer for the remnant, 2. 6.

2 *Chr.* 17. 6. heart *l.* up in ways of the Lord

Ps. 3. 3. my glory and *l.* up of mine head

4. 6. Lord *l.* up the light of thy countenance on us.

7. 6. Lord *l.* up thyself because of the

24. 7. *l.* up heads ye gates, be *l.* up ye doors, 9.

25. 1. to thee I *l.* up my soul, 86. 4.

75. 4. *l.* not up the horn, 5.

83. 2. have *l.* up the head

102. 10. thou *l.* me up and castest me

down

121. 1. *l.* up mine eyes, 123. 1.

147. 6. Lord *l.* up the meek but

Prov. 2. 3. *l.* up thy voice for understanding

Eccl. 4. 10. one will *l.* up another

Is. 26. 11. Lord when thy hand is *l.* up they will not see

33. 10. now I will be exalted, now *l.* up myself

42. 2. shall not cry nor *l.* up his voice

Jer. 7. 16. nor *l.* up a prayer for them, 11. 14.

Lam. 3. 41. let us *l.* up our hearts with our hands

Hab. 2. 4. his soul which is *l.* up is not upright in him

Luke 21. 28. *l.* up heads for day

John 3. 14. so must Son of man be *l.* up, 12. 34.

8. 28. ye have *l.* up Son of man

12. 32. if I be *l.* up I will draw all men

Heb. 12. 12. *l.* up hands which hang

Jam. 4. 10. humble and he *l.* up *l.* you

Ps. 141. 2. the *l.* up of my hands, 1 *Tim.* 2. 8.

LIGHT, *Num.* 21. 5; *Deut.* 27. 16; *Judg.* 9. 4; 1 *Kings* 16. 31; *Ezek.* 8. 17. & 22. 7.

Is. 49. 6. is a *l.* thing to be my servant

Zeph. 3. 4. her prophets *l.* and

Matt. 11. 30. yoke easy burden *l.*

2 *Cor.* 4. 17. *l.* affliction which is but for a moment

Ps. 62. 9. *l.* than vanity

Jer. 3. 9. *l.* of whoredoms, 23. 32.

LIGHT, *Gen.* 1. 3, 4, 5, 16. & 44. 3.

Job 18. 5. *l.* of wicked be put out

25. 3. upon whom doth not *l.*

33. 30. enlightened with *l.* of the living

38. 19. way where *l.* dwells and darkness

Ps. 4. 6. lift up *l.* of countenance

36. 9. in thy *l.* shall we see *l.*

43. 3. O send out *l.* and truth

90. 8. set secret sins in *l.* of thy countenance

97. 11. *l.* is sown for righteous

104. 2. coverest thyself with *l.*

112. 4. to upright ariseth *l.* in darkness

119. 105. thy word is a *l.* to my path

139. 12. darkness and *l.* are both alike

Prov. 4. 18. path of the just is as shining *l.*

6. 23. law is *l.* and reproofs of

13. 9. *l.* of righteous rejoice

15. 30. the *l.* of the eyes rejoiceth heaven

Eccl. 11. 7. *l.* is sweet and pleasant

Is. 5. 20. darkness for *l.* and *l.* for darkness

30. *l.* is darkened, *Job* 10. 22.

8. 20. if speak not according to word, no *l.* in them

9. 2. walked in darkness seen great *l.*

30. 26. *l.* of moon as *l.* of sun, *l.* of seven days

42. 6. covenant of people *l.* of Gentiles, 49. 6.

45. 7. I form the *l.* and create

50. 10. walketh in darkness and hath

no *l.*
11. walk in *l.* of your fire and
58. 8. shall thy *l.* break forth
60. 1. arise, shine, for thy *l.* is come, 19. 20.

Zech. 14. 6. *l.* not clear
7. at evening-time it shall be *l.*

Matt. 5. 14. ye are *l.* of world
16. let *l.* shine before men
6. 22. *l.* of body eye single—full of *l.*

Luke 2. 32. a *l.* to *l.* the Gentiles
16. 8. children of world wiser than children of *l.*

John 1. 4. life was *l.* of men, was true *l.*
3. 19. men love darkness rather than *l.*
20. cometh not to the *l.*
21. doeth truth cometh to *l.*
5. 35. a burning and a shining *l.*
8. 12. I am the *l.* of the world the *l.* of life
12. 35. walk in *l.* while ye have *l.*

Acts 13. 47. I have set thee to be a *l.* to Gentiles
26. 18. turn them from darkness to *l.*

Rom. 13. 12. put on armour of *l.*

1 *Cor.* 4. 5. bring to *l.* things

2 *Cor.* 4. 4. lest *l.* of gospel shine
6. 14. what communion hath *l.* with darkness

Eph. 5. 8. walk as children of *l.*
14. Christ shall give thee *l.*

1 *Thess.* 5. 5. ye are children of *l.*

1 *Pet.* 2. 9. called into marvellous *l.*

1 *John* 1. 5. God is *l.* and in him no darkness

Rev. 21. 23. Lord is *l.* thereof, 11.

LIGHTEN, 2 *Sam.* 22. 29. Lord will *l.* my darkness

Ps. 13. 3. *l.* mine eyes, lest I sleep

Luke 2. 32. a light to *l.* the Gentiles

Rev. 21. 23. the glory of God did *l.* it

LIGHTETH, *John* 1. 9. that was the true light which *l.* every man

LIGHTING, *Matt.* 3. 16. like a dove *l.* on him

LIGHTENED, *Ps.* 34. 5. looked on him and were *l.*

Rev. 18. 1. earth was *l.* with his glory

LIGHTNING, 2 *Sam.* 22. 15. sent *l.* and discomfited them

Job 37. 3. he directeth his *l.* to the ends of the earth

Ps. 144. 6. cast forth *l.* and scatter them

Dan. 10. 6. and his face as the appearance of *l.*

Matt. 24. 27. as *l.* cometh out of east
28. 3. his countenance was as *l.*

Luke 10. 18. I beheld Satan as *l.* fall

LIGHTNINGS, *Ex.* 19. 16. thunders, *l.* thick cloud

Ex. 20. 18. all the people saw the *l.*

Job 38. 35. canst thou send *l.*

Ps. 18. 14. he shot out *l.* and discomfited them
77. 18. *l.* lighted the world

Nah. 2. 4. the chariots run like the *l.*

Rev. 4. 5. proceeded *l.* thunderings
8. 5. voices, thunderings, *l.* 11. 12.

LIGHTS, *Gen.* 1. 14. let there be *l.* in the firmament of heaven

Luke 12. 35. let your loins be girded, your *l.* burning

Phil. 2. 15. ye shine as *l.* in the world

Jam. 1. 17. down from the Father of *l.*

LIKE, *Ex.* 15. 11. who is *l.* unto thee?
Deut. 33. 29; 1 *Kings* 8. 23; 2 *Chr.* 6. 14; *Ps.* 35. 10; 71. 19.

Num. 23. 10. let my last end be *l.* his

Deut. 18. 15. prophet of thy brethren *l.* unto me, *Acts* 3. 22; 7. 37.

2 *Sam.* 22. 34. my feet *l.* hinds' feet

Job 5. 26. to grave *l.* as a shock of corn cometh in its season
15. 10. drinketh iniquity *l.* water
37. 35. spreading *l.* a green bay tree
55. 6. O that I had wings *l.* a dove
77. 20. thou leddest thy people *l.* a flock, 78. 52.
102. 26. all wax old, *l.* a garment
103. 13. *l.* as a father pitieth
104. 2. who stretched out heavens *l.*
144. 4. man is *l.* to vanity
147. 16. snow *l.* wool, frost *l.* ashes

Prov. 25. 19. man is *l.* a broken tooth

Is. 11. 7. lion eat straw *l.* the ox
14. 14. I will be *l.* the Most High

Jer. 23. 29. my word *l.* fire and *l.* a hammer

Hos. 14. 8. I am *l.* a green fir tree

1 *Cor.* 16. 13. quit you *l.* men

Heb. 2. 17. be made *l.* unto his brethren

1 *John* 3. 2. appear we shall be *l.* him, for we shall

Jam. 1. 6. *l.* a wave of the sea
23. he is *l.* a man beholding his natural face
5. 17. Elias subject to *l.* passions

2 *Pet.* 1. 1. obtained *l.* precious faith

Rev. 1. 13. one *l.* the Son of man
18. 18. what city is *l.* to this great city

LIKE-MINDED, *Rom.* 15. 5. God grant you to be *l.-minded*

Phil. 2. 2. that ye be *l.-minded*; 20. I have no man *l.-minded*

LIKENESS, *Gen.* 1. 26. let no man make *l.*

Gen. 5. 3. and Adam begat a son in his own *l.*

Ps. 17. 15. I shall be satisfied with thy *l.*

Ezek. 1. 22. the *l.* of the firmament was as crystal
26. *l.* of a throne, 10. 1; 8. 2. lo, a *l.* as appearance of fire

Rom. 6. 5. planted him in the *l.* of his death, we shall be also in the resurrection
8. 3. his Son in *l.* of sinful flesh

Phil. 2. 7. and was made in the *l.* of men

LINE upon *l.* upon *l.* *Is.* 28. 10, 13.

Is. 28. 17. judgment will I lay to *l.*
34. 11. on it *l.* of confusion

2 *Cor.* 10. 16. boast in another man's *l.*

Ps. 16. 6. *l.* are fallen in pleasant places —This passage alludes to lands appointed by the measuring line or chain.

LINGER, *Gen.* 19. 16; 2 *Pet.* 2. 3.

LION, *Gen.* 49. 9; *Judg.* 14. 5, 18; *Job* 4. 10, 11. & 10. 16. & 28. 8; *Ps.* 7. 2. & 17. 12. & 10. 9. & 22. 13; *Is.* 38. 13.

Prov. 22. 13. there is a *l.* in way, 26. 13.
28. 1. righteous bold as a *l.*

Eccl. 9. 4. a living dog is better than a

dead *l.*
Is. 11. 6. calf and *l.* 7. & 65. 25.
35. 9. no *l.* shall be there nor
Ezek. 1. 10. face as a *l.* 10. 14; *Rev.* 4. 7.
Hos. 5. 14. and be as a young *l. Lam.*
3. 10.
Mic. 5. 8. remnant Jacob be as *l.*
2 *Tim.* 4. 17. delivered out of mouth
of *l.*
1 *Pet.* 5. 8. devil as a roaring *l.* seeking
Rev. 5. 5. the *l.* of the tribe of Judah
prevailed
LIPS, *Ex.* 6. 12, 30; *Prov.* 16. 10.
Ps. 12. 3. cut off flattering *l.*
4. our *l.* are our own
17. 1. not out of feigned *l.*
31. 18. lying *l.* 120. 2; *Prov.* 10. 18. &
12. 22. & 17. 4, 7; *Is.* 59. 3.
63. 5. I will praise with joyful *l.*
120. 2. deliver soul from lying *l.*
Prov. 7. 21. with flattering of her *l.*
10. 21. *l.* of righteous feed
12. 22. lying *l.* abomination to Lord
14. 23. the talk of the *l.* tendeth only
to penury
15. 7. the *l.* of the wise disperse
knowledge
16. 13. righteous *l.* are the delight of
20. 15. *l.* of knowledge precious jewel
26. 23. burning *l.* wicked heart
Songs 7. 9. *l.* of those asleep to
Is. 6. 5. man of unclean *l.* people of
unclean *l.*
Is. 28. 11. stammering *l.* will he speak
57. 19. create fruit of *l.* peace
Hos. 14. 2. render the calves of our *l.*
Heb. 13. 15.
Mal. 2. 7. priest's *l.* should keep knowledge
Matt. 15. 8. honoureth me with their *l.*
Mark 7. 6.
LIPS, my, *Ps.* 51. 15. open thou *my l.*
63. 3. *l.* shall praise thee, 71. 23.
66. 14. I will pay vows, which *my l.*
have uttered
119. 171. *my l.* shall utter thy praise
141. 3. keep the door of *my l.*
LIPS, thy, *Ps.* 17. 4. & 34. 13. & 45. 2.
Prov. 24. 28. deceive not with *thy l.*
27. 2. let another praise thee, and not
thy own l.
Songs 4. 11. *thy l.* drop as the honey-
comb
LITTLE, *Ezra* 9. 8; *Neh.* 9. 32.
Ps. 2. 12. when his wrath is kindled
but a *l.*
8. 5. a *l.* lower than the angels, *Heb.*
2. 7.
37. 16. *l.* that righteous hath
Prov. 6. 10. *l.* sleep a *l.* slumber, 24. 33.
10. 20. heart of wicked *l.* worth
15. 16. better is a *l.* with fear of the
Lord, 16. 8.
Is. 28. 10. here a *l.* and there a *l.* 13.
54. 8. in *l.* wrath I hid my face
Ezek. 11. 16. I will be a *l.* sanctuary
Ze h. 1. 15. I was *l.* displeased
Matt. 6. 30. of *l.* faith, 8. 26. & 14. 31. &
16. 8.
Luke 12. 32. fear not *l.* flock, it
19. 17. hast been faithful in *l.*
1 *Tim.* 4. 8. bodily exercise profiteth *l.*

Rev. 3. 8. hast *l.* strength and kept my
LIVE, *Gen.* 3. 22. & 17. 18.
Lev. 18. 5. if man do he shall *l. Neh.*
9; *Ezek.* 3. 21. & 18. 9. & 33. 13, 15,
16; *Rom.* 10. 5; *Gal.* 3. 12.
Deut. 32. 40. I. for ever, 1 *Kings* 1. 31;
Neh. 2. 3; *Ps.* 22. 26. & 49. 9; *Dan.*
2. 4. & 3. 9. & 5. 10. & 6. 21; *Zech.*
1. 5; *John* 6. 54, 58; *Rev.* 4. 9. & 5.
14. & 10. 6. & 15. 7.
Job 14. 14. if a man die shall he *l.* again
Ps. 55. 23. bloody men not *l.* out half
their days
63. 4. bless thee while I *l.* 146. 2.
118. 17. I shall not die but *l.*
Is. 26. 19. thy dead men shall *l.*
38. 16. by these things men *l.* and
make *l.*
55. 3. hear and your soul shall *l.*
Ezek. 16. 6. when thou wast in blood *l.*
18. 24. shall he *l.*; 32. turn yourselves
and *l.* 33. 11.
18. 32. turn yourselves and *l.* 33. 11.
37. 3. son of man, can these bones *l*
Amos 5. 4. seek me, and ye shall *l.* 6.
Hab. 2. 4. just shall *l.* by faith, *Rom.*
1. 17.
Matt. 4. 4. man not *l.* by bread, *Deut.*
8. 3.
Luke 20. 38. he is not a God of dead,
for all *l.* unto him
John 5. 25. dead hear voice of the Son
of God and *l.*
11. 25. believeth, though he were
dead, yet he shall *l.*
John 14. 19. because I *l.* ye shall *l.* also
Acts 17. 28. in whom ye *l.* move, and
Rom. 8. 13. if ye *l.* after the flesh ye
shall die
14. 8. whether we *l.* we *l.* unto the
Lord
1 *Cor.* 9. 14. preach gospel *l.* of
2 *Cor.* 5. 15. who *l.* should not *l.* to
themselves
6. 9. as dying and behold we *l.*
13. 11. be of one mind *l.* in peace
Gal. 2. 20. I *l.* yet not I but Christ *l.* in
5. 25. if we *l.* in S. walk in S.
Phil. 1. 21. to me to *l.* is Christ, to die,
is gain, 22.
1 *Thess.* 3. 8. we *l.* if we stand fast
2 *Tim.* 3. 12. all that *l.* godly
Tit. 2. 12. should *l.* soberly
Heb. 13. 18. will to *l.* honestly
1 *Pet.* 2. 24. should *l.* to righteousness
1 *John* 4. 9. might *l.* through him
Acts 23. 1. *l.* in good conscience
Jam. 5. 5. ye have *l.* in pleasure
Rev. 18. 7. and *l.* deliciously, *Luke* 7. 25.
20. 4. *l.* and reigned with Christ
LIVELY, *Ps.* 38. 19. enemies are *l.* and
strong
Acts 7. 38. receive the *l.* oracles
1 *Pet.* 1. 3. begotten to a *l.* hope
2. 5. ye as *l.* stones are built up
LIVES, 1 *John* 3. 16; *Rev.* 12. 11.
Acts 15. 26. men that have hazarded
their *l.* for our
1 *John* 3. 16. to lay down our *l.* for the
brethren
Rev. 12. 11. they loved not their *l.* to
the death

LIVEST, *Rev.* 3. 1. hast a name that thou *l.* and art dead

LIVETH, *Job.* 19. 25. I know that my Redeemer *l.*

Rom. 6. 10. in that he *l.* to God

14. 7. none *l.* to himself or

1 *Tim.* 5. 6. *l.* in pleasure dead while she *l.*

Heb. 7. 25. he ever *l.* to make intercession for them

Rev. 1. 18. I am he that *l.* and was dead

LIVING, *Job* 28. 13. nor found in the land of the *l.*

30. 23. house appointed for all *l.*

Ps. 143. 2. in thy sight shall no man *l.* be justified

Eccl. 7. 2. *l.* will lay it to heart

Is. 38. 19. the *l.* the *l.* he shall praise thee

Jer. 2. 13. Lord fountain of *l.* waters

Zech. 14. 8. *l.* waters shall go out from Jerusalem

Matt. 22. 32. God is not the God of the dead, but of the *l.* *Mark* 12. 27; *Luke* 20. 38.

Mark 12. 44. cast in all, even all her *l.*

Luke 24. 5. why seek ye *l.* among the dead

John 4. 10. he would have given thee *l.* water, 7. 38.

6. 51. I am the *l.* bread which

Rom. 12. 1. bodies *l.* sacrifice

14. 9. that be Lord of dead and *l.*

1 *Cor.* 15. 45. Adam made *l.* soul

Heb. 10. 20. boldness to enter by a new and *l.* way

1 *Pet.* 2. 4. coming as to *l.* stone

Rev. 7. 17. shall lead them to *l.* fountains of water

LOAD, *Ps.* 61. 19; *Is.* 46. 1.

LOATH, themselves for evils, *Ezek.* 6. 9. & 16. 5. & 20. 43. & 36. 31.

Jer. 14. 19. thy soul *l.* Zion

Zech. 11. 8. my soul *l.* them

Num. 21. 5. soul *l.* *Prov.* 27. 7.

Ps. 38. 7. *l.* disease

LOFTY eyes, *Ps.* 131. 1; *Prov.* 30. 13.

Is. 2. 11. *l.* looks humbled, 5. 15.

26. 5. the *l.* city he layeth low to the ground

57. 15. high and *l.* One that inhabiteth eternity

LOFTILY, *Ps.* 73. 8. are corrupt, they speak *l.*

LOINS, *Ex.* 12. 11. eat it, with *l.* girded

Is. 11. 5. righteousness girdle of *l.*

Ezek. 1. 27. from the appearances of his *l.* upward

23. 15. with girdles upon their *l.*

Dan. 5. 6. joints of his *l.* were loosed

Luke 12. 35. your *l.* girded about

Eph. 6. 14. *l.* girt about with truth

Heb. 7. 10. yet in the *l.* of his father

1 *Pet.* 1. 13. gird up the *l.* of your mind

LONG, (1) Of great extent in length, *Ezek.* 31. 5. (2) To love greatly, *Gen.* 34. 8. (3) To thirst, 2 *Sam.* 23. 15. (4) To desire very earnestly, *Job* 3. 21. Thus do, (1) Such as are greatly afflicted for death, *Job* 3. 21. (2) The father after the son, 1 *Sam.* 13. 39. (3) The absent for

his native place, *Gen.* 31. 30. (4) The godly after God's word, *Ps.* 119. 40, 131, 174. (5) The faithful teacher after his flock, *Phil.* 2. 26. (6) Saints after saints, *Rom.* 1. 11; *Phil.* 1. 8.

Ps. 91. 16; *Eccl.* 12. 5; *Matt.* 23. 14; *Luke* 18. 7; *Jam.* 5. 7.

Ex. 34. 6. Lord God *l.* suffering, *Num.* 14. 18; *Ps.* 86. 15; *Jer.* 15. 15; *Rom.* 2. 4. & 9. 22; 1 *Tim.* 1. 16; 1 *Pet.* 3. 20; 2 *Pet.* 3. 9, 15.

Gal. 5. 22. fruit of Spirit is *l.* suffering, *Eph.* 4. 2; *Col.* 1. 11. & 3. 12; 2 *Tim.* 3. 10. & 4. 2.

LONG, *Job* 3. 21. & 6. 8; *Rom.* 1. 11.

Ps. 63. 1. my flesh *l.* for thee

84. 2. my soul *l.* for courts of the Lord

119. 40. I have *l.* after precepts

131. I *l.* for commandments

174. I *l.* for thy salvation

20. soul breaks for *l.* it hath

107. 9. satisfieth the *l.* soul

LOOK, (1) To behold or see, *Deut.* 28. 32. (2) To consider or take particular notice of, *Lev.* 13. 5. (3) To expect or wait for, *Jer.* 13. 16; *Matt.* 11. 3. (4) To believe and trust in, *Is.* 45. 22.

LOOK, *Gen.* 13. 14; *Ex.* 10. 10.

Ps. 5. 3. direct my prayer and will *l.* up

123. 2. eyes of servants *l.* to masters

Prov. 4. 25. eyes *l.* right on and eye-lids

Eccl. 12. 3. that *l.* out at the windows be darkened

Is. 8. 17. wait for Lord and *l.* for him

45. 22. *l.* unto me and be saved

51. 1. *l.* to rock whence hewn

2 *l.* to Abraham your father

66. 2. to this man will I *l.* poor

Mic. 7. 7. I will *l.* for Lord, wait for G.

Luke 7. 19. or *l.* we for another, 20.

2 *Cor.* 4. 18. while we *l.* for things not

Phil. 2. 4. *l.* not every man on own things

3. 20. heaven whence we *l.* for the Saviour

Heb. 9. 28. them that *l.* for him

1 *Pet.* 1. 12. angels desire to *l.* into

2 *Pet.* 3. 14. since we *l.* for such things

LOOKED, *Gen.* 29. 32. Lord *l.* on my affliction, *Ex.* 2. 25. & 4. 31; *Deut.* 26. 7.

Gen. 19. 26. his wife *l.* back; 26. 8. *l.* out at a window

Ps. 14. 2. the Lord *l.* to see if any did understand

34. 5. they *l.* to him and were

Songs 1. 6. *l.* not upon me, sun hath *l.* upon me

Is. 5. 7. he *l.* for judgment and oppression

22. 11. not *l.* to the maker thereof

Is. 64. 3. terrible things which ye *l.* not

Jer. 8. 15. we *l.* for peace but, 14. 19.

Obad. 13. shouldst not have *l.*

Hag. 1. 9. ye *l.* for much and it

Luke 2. 38. that *l.* for redemption

22. 61. Lord *l.* on Peter and he remembered

Heb. 11. 10. *l.* for a ciy which hath foundations

1 *John* 1. 1. when we have *l.* on

LOOKETH, 1 *Sam.* 16. 7. man *l.* on

outward appearance, but the Lord *l.*
on the heart
Ps. 33. 13. Lord *l.* down from me, 14.
Prov. 14. 15. prudent *l.* well to goings,
31. 27.
Songs 2. 9. he *l.* forth at window, 6. 10.
Matt. 5. 28. whosoever *l.* on woman to
lust after her
24. 50. come in a day he *l.* not for
Jam. 1. 25. *l.* into perfect law of liberty
LOOKING, *Is.* 38. 14. mine eyes fail
with *l.*
Luke 9. 62. no man *l.* back is fit for
kingdom
John 1. 36. John *l.* on Jesus saith,
behold the Lamb
Tit. 2. 13. *l.* for blessed hope and
Heb. 10. 27. certain fearful *l.* for
12. 2. *l.* to Jesus the author and
finisher of faith
15. *l.* diligently lest any fail of the
grace of God
2 *Pet.* 3. 12. *l.* for and hasting unto day
of God
Jude 21. *l.* for mercy of God unto
eternal life
LOOKS, *Ps.* 18. 27. bring down high *l.*
LOOSE, *Deut.* 25. 9; *Josh.* 5. 15.
Ps. 146. 7. Lord *l.* the prisoners
102. 20. to *l.* them appointed to death
Eccl. 12. 6. before silver cord be *l.*
Is. 58. 6. fast chosen to *l.* the bands of
wickedness
Matt. 16. 19. thou *l.* on earth, *l.* in
heaven, 18. 18.
Acts 2. 24. having *l.* pains of death
1 *Cor.* 7. 27. married seek not to be *l.*
LORD ascribed to man, *Gen.* 18. 12. &
23. 11; *Is.* 26. 13; 1 *Cor.* 8. 5; 1 *Pet.*
5. 3; and in about 14 other places,
and to God, *Gen.* 28. 16; *Ex.* 5. 2;
1 *Cor.* 12. 5.
Ex. 34. 6. the L. Lord God merciful and
gracious
Deut. 4. 35. L. is God, 39; 1 *Kings* 18. 39.
6. 4. L. our God is one Lord
10. 17. L. of *l. Dan.* 2. 47; 1 *Tim.* 6.
15; *Rev.* 17. 14. & 19. 16.
Neh. 9. 6. art L. alone, *Is.* 37. 20.
Ps. 118. 27. God is the L. 100. 3.
Zech. 14. 9. one L. his name One
Mark 2. 28. Son of man is L. of the
sabbath
Acts 2. 36. made him L. and Christ
Rom. 10. 12. same L. over all, *Acts* 10.
36.
14. 9. L. of dead and of living
1 *Cor.* 2. 8. L. of glory
8. 6. one God and one L. Jesus Christ
15. 47. the L. from heaven
Eph. 4. 5. one L. one faith, one
Gen. 15. 6. believed in the L.
1 *Sam.* 2. 1. heart rejoice in L. *Ps.* 32.
11. & 33. 1. & 35. 9. & 97. 12. & 104.
34: *Is.* 41. 16. & 61. 10; *Joel* 2. 13;
Zech. 10. 7; *Phil.* 3. 1. & 4. 4.
2 *Kings* 18. 5. trust in L. *Ps.* 4. 5. & 11.
1. & 31. 6. & 32. 10. & 37. 3. & 115.
9, 10, 11. & 118. 8. & 125. 1; *Prov.*
3. 5. & 16. 20. & 28. 25. & 29.
25; *Is.* 26. 4; *Zeph.* 3. 2.
Ps. 31. 24. hope in the L. 130. 7. & 131. 3.

34. 2. soul make her boast in L.
37. 4. delight thyself in the L.
7. rest in the L.
Is. 45. 17. Israel be saved in L.
24. in L. have I righteousness and
strength
25. in L. seed of Israel justified and
shall glory
Rom. 16. 12. labour in L. 1. *Cor.* 15. 58.
Eph. 6. 10. be strong in the L. and
power of his might
1 *Thess.* 5. 12. are over you in L. *Col.* 4.
7, 17.
Rev. 14. 13. blessed are the dead which
die in the L.
LOSE, *Job* 31. 39. caused owners *l.* life
Prov. 23. 8. and *l.* thy sweet words
Eccl. 3. 6. there is a time to *l.*
Matt. 10. 39. he that findeth his life
shall *l.* it, 16. 25; *Mark* 8. 35;
Luke 9. 24.
16. 26. and *l.* his own soul, *Mark* 8.
36; *Luke* 9. 25.
Luke 15. 4. if he *l.* one sheep; 8. if she
l. one piece
17. 33. *l.* his life shall preserve it
2 *John* 8. look to yourselves, we *l.* not
those things
LOSETH, *Matt.* 10. 39. *l.* his life for my
sake
LOSS, *Is.* 47. 8. nor know *l.* of children
Acts 27. 21. have gained this *l.*
22. no *l.* of any man's life
Phil. 3. 7. gain I counted *l.* for Christ
8. I count all things but *l.* for
LOST, *Ps.* 119. 176. astray like *l.* sheep
Jer. 50. 6. my people *l.* sheep
Ezek. 19. 5. saw her hope was *l.*
34. 4. nor ye sought *l.*
Ezek. 37. 11. our hope is *l.* and
Matt. 5. 13. if salt have *l.* savour
10. 6. go to *l.* sheep of Israel, 15. 24;
Luke 15. 4.
18. 11. save that which was *l. Luke*
19. 10.
Luke 15. 32. thy brother was *l.* and is
found
John 6. 15. gather up fragments that
nothing be *l.*
17. 12. none of them is *l.* but the son
of perdition
John 18. 9. gavest me I have *l.* none
2 *Cor.* 4. 3. gospel hid to them that are *l.*
LOT, (1) Any thing cast or drawn in
order to determine any matter in
debate, *Prov.* 18. 18. (2) That which
falls out by lot to be one's proper
share, portion, or inheritance, *Josh.*
15. 1; 16. 1. (3) Habitations or
persons, *Ps.* 125. 3. (4) Punishment, *Is.* 17. 14. (5) Order, course,
or turn, *Luke* 1. 9. (6) Fellowship,
Acts 8. 21. (7) The object of one's
worship and trust, *Is.* 57. 6. Lots
were used, (1) To find out a person,
1 *Sam.* 14, 41; *Jonah* 1. 7. (2) To
divide lands, *Num.* 26. 55, 56. (3)
To choose a church officer, *Acts* 1.
26. (4) To order and regulate the
courses of men in office, 1 *Chr.* 24.
5; 25. 8. (5) To decide a controversy, *Ps.* 22. 8.

LOT, *Lev.* 16. 8, 9, 10; *Jonah* 1. 7.
Num. 26. 55. land shall be divided by
    l. Ezek. 48. 29.
    33. 54. he shall divide the land by *l.*
    for an inheritance, 36. 2; *Josh.* 31.
    6; *Ezek.* 47. 22.
1 *Sam.* 14. 41. God gave a perfect *l.* 42.
1 *Chr.* 24. 5. were divided by *l.*
    7. *l.* came forth to Jehoiarib
Ps. 16. 5. thou maintainest my *l.*
    22. 18. on my vesture they did cast *l.*
    125. 3. rod of the wicked not rest on
    l. of righteous
Prov. 1. 14. cast in thy *l.* among us
    16. 33. *l.* is cast into lap
    18. 18. *l.* causeth contentions to cease
Dan. 12. 13. shalt stand in thy *l.* at end
    of the days
Acts 1. 26. *l.* fell on Matthias and
    8. 21. hast neither *l.* nor part
LOUD, *Neh.* 12. 12. the singers sang *l.*
Ps. 33. 3. sing to him, play skilfully
    with a *l.* noise
Rev. 14. 18. angel cried with a *l.* cry
LOUD, joined with voice, *Rev.* 5. 12.
    many angels saying with a *l. voice,*
    woe, woe, 14. 7, 9, 15.
Rev. 12. 10. and I heard a *l. voice* saying
    in heaven
LOVE (1) A natural passion, inclining
    us to delight in an object, *Gen.* 29.
    20. (2) A gracious principle or habit
    wrought in the soul by God, which
    inclines us to delight in, esteem,
    and earnestly desire to enjoy an
    interest in God's favour, and com-
    munion with him as our chief good.
    (3) The effect of love, *John* 15. 13.
    (4) The person beloved, *Songs* 2. 2,
    7. (5) True friendship or kindness,
    Prov. 15. 17. LOVE is, Natural,
    which is either lawful, *Ps.* 34. 12;
    or, unlawful, *John* 12. 25; 2 *Tim.*
    3. 2. Conjugal Love, which is,
    Divine, that is God's love to his
    people, which is inexpressible, *John*
    3. 16. Inconceivable, *Eph.* 3. 19.
    Everlasting, *Jer.* 31. 3. Sovereign,
    Deut. 7. 8. Free and undeserved,
    Hosea, 14. 4. Immutable, *John*
    13. 1. Spiritual, as (1) The love of
    God towards his children, *John* 17.
    23; *Rom.* 5. 5, 8. (2) Their love to
    God, *Ps.* 116. 1; 1 *John* 4. 19. (3)
    Of Christ to his church, *Eph.* 3. 19;
    5. 2. (4) To some particular per-
    sons, *John* 2. 2; *Gal.* 2. 20. (5) The
    love of believers towards Christ,
    Songs 1. 4, 7; *John* 21. 15. (6) To
    one another, *John* 15. 17; *Col.* 1. 4.
LOVE, *Gen.* 27. 4; 2 *Sam.* 13. 15.
2 *Sam.* 1. 26. passing *l.* of women
Eccl. 9. 1. knows either *l.* or hatred by
Songs 2. 5. I am sick of *l.* 5. 8.
    7. 12. there I will give thee my *l.*
    8. 6. *l.* is strong as death, jealousy
    cruel as the grave
Is. 38. 17. hast in *l.* to my soul delivered
Jer. 2. 2. remember the *l.* of thy espou-
    sals
    31. 3. *l.* thee with an everlasting *l.*
Ezek. 16. 8. thy time was a time of *l.*

    33. 31. with mouth show *l.*
Hos. 11. 4. drew them with bands of *l.*
Matt. 24. 12. *l.* of many was cold
John 15. 9. continue in my *l.* 10.
    13. greater *l.* hath no man
Rom. 8. 35. who separate us from *l.* of
    Christ, 39.
    12. 9. let *l.* be without dissimulation
    13. 10. *l.* is the fulfilling of law
    15. 30. for Lord Jesus Christ's sake,
    and *l.* of the Spirit
2 *Cor.* 5. 14. *l.* of Christ constraineth us
Gal. 5. 6. faith worketh by *l.*
    13. by *l.* serve one another
    22. fruit of S. is *l.* joy, and peace
1 *Thess.* 1. 3. your labour of *l. Heb.* 6. 10.
    5. 8. breast-plate of faith and *l.*
2 *Thess.* 2. 10. received not the *l.* of the
    truth
Heb. 13. 1. brotherly *l.* continue
1 *John* 3. 1. what manner of *l.* Father
    4. 7. *l.* is of God
    8. dwell in *l.* God is *l.* 16.
    18. perfect *l.* casts out fear, perfect *l.*
Rev. 2. 4. thou hast left first *l.*
LOVE, his, *Ps.* 91. 14. hath set *his l.*
    upon me
Is. 63. 9. in *his l.* and in his pity he
    redeemed them
Zeph. 3. 17. he will rest in *his l.*
John 15. 10. and abide in *his l.*
Rom. 5. 8. God commended *his*
1 *John* 4. 12. *his l.* is perfected
LOVE, in, *Is.* 38. 17. hast *in l.* to my
    soul delivered it from the pit
Eph. 1. 4. without blame *in l.*
    3. 17. rooted and grounded *in l.*
    4. 2. forbearing one another *in l.*
    15. speaking truth *in l.* 16.
    5. 2. walk *in l.* as Christ hath *l.* us
Col. 2. 2. knit together *in l.* and
1 *Thess.* 3. 12. abound *in l.*
    5. 13. esteem highly *in l.*
1 *John* 4. 16. dwells *in l.* dwells in God
    18. no fear *in l.*
LOVE of GOD, *Luke* 11. 42. *l.* of God
    John 5. 42.
Tit. 3. 4. after the kindness and *l.* of
    God appeared
Rom. 5. 5. *l.* of God is shed abroad in
    our hearts
2 *Cor.* 13. 14. *l.* of God be with all
2 *Thess.* 3. 5. directs hearts into *l.* of God
John 2. 5. in him is *l.* perfected
    3. 16. perceive we *l.* of God
    17. how dwelleth *l.* of God in him
    4. 9. in this was manifest the *l.* of God
    toward us
    5. 3. this is *l.* of God that we keep com-
    mandments
Lev. 19. 18. thou shalt *l.* neighbour as
    thyself, 34; *Matt.* 19. 19. & 22. 39;
    Rom. 13. 9; *Gal.* 5. 14; *Jam.* 2. 8.
Deut. 6. 5. shall *l.* the Lord thy God
    with all thy heart, *Matt.* 22. 37;
    Luke 10. 27.
    10. 12. to fear the Lord and to *l.* him
Ps. 31. 23. O *l.* the Lord all saints
    97. 10. ye that *l.* the Lord hate evil
    145. 20. the Lord preserveth all them
    that *l.* him
Songs 1. 4. the upright *l.* thee

Mic. 6. 8. do justly and *l.* mercy
Zech. 8. 19. *l.* the truth and peace
Matt. 5. 44. *l.* your enemies, bless them
  that curse you
John 13. 34. *l.* one another 15. 12,
  17; *Rom.* 13. 8; 1 *John* 3. 11, 23. &
  4. 7, 11, 12; 1 *Pet.* 1. 22.
  14. 23. if a man *l.* me my Father will
  l. him
1 *Cor.* 16. 22. if any man *l.* not Lord
  Jesus Christ
Eph. 5. 25. husbands *l.* your wives, *Col.*
  3. 19.
2 *Tim.* 4. 8. *l*o them that *l.* his appearing
1 *Pet.* 1. 8. whom having not seen ye *l.*
  2. 17. *l.* the brotherhood, 3. 8.
1 *John* 2. 15. *l.* not the world
  4. 19. we *l.* him because he first *l.* us
Ps. 116. 1. I *l.* the Lord because, 18. 1.
  119. 97. how I *l.* thy law, 113, 119, 127,
  159, 163, 167. & 26. 8.
John 21. 15. *l.* thou me, knowest I *l.*
  thee, 16. 17.
2 *John* 1. whom I *l.* in the truth
Rev. 3. 19. as many as I *l.* I rebuke and
  chasten
LOVED, *Deut.* 7. 8. because Lord *l.* you,
  33. 3.
1 *Sam.* 18. 1. *l.* him as own soul, 20. 17.
2 *Sam.* 12. 24. Solomon and the Lord *l.*
  him
1 *Kings* 3. 3. Solomon *l.* the Lord
  10. 9. Lord *l.* Israel
Hos. 11. 1. Israel was a child then I *l.*
  him
Mark 10. 21. Jesus beholding *l.* him
Luke 7. 47. forgiven *l.* much
John 3. 16. God so *l.* the world that he
  gave only begotten Son
  19. men *l.* darkness rather than light
  11. 36. behold he *l.* him, 3. 5.
  12. 43. *l.* praise of men more
  13. 1. having *l.* his own he *l.* them
  unto the end
  23. one of his disciples whom Jesus *l.*
  14. 19, 26. & 20. 2. & 21. 7, 30.
  14. 21. *l.* me, beloved of my Father I
  will *l.* him
  28. if ye *l.* me ye would rejoice
  15. 9. as the Father *l.* me so have I
  l. you
  16. 27. Father *l.* you because ye *l.* me
  17. 23. I have *l.* them as thou hast *l.*
  26. that the *l.* wherewith thou hast
  l. them
Rom. 8. 37. conquerors through him
  that *l.* us
  9. 13. Jacob I *l.* Esau I hated, *Mal.*
  1. 2.
Gal. 2. 20. Son of God, who *l.* me and
Eph. 2. 4. *l.* wherewith he *l.* us
  5. 2. as Christ *l.* the church
  25. as Christ *l.* the church
2 *Thess.* 2. 16. God our Father hath *l.* us
2 *Tim.* 4. 10. having *l.* this present world
Heb. 1. 9. hast *l.* righteousness and hated
  iniquity, *Ps.* 45. 7.
2 *Pet.* 2. 15. *l.* unrighteousness
1 *John* 4. 10. not we *l.* God he *l.* us first
  Rev. 1. 5. that *l.* us and washed
  12. 11. for they *l.* not their lives

LOVETH, *Ps.* 11. 7. the Lord *l.* righteousness
  146. 8. Lord *l.* the righteous
Prov. 3. 12. whom Lord *l.* corrects, *Heb.*
  12. 6.
  17. 17. a friend *l.* at all times
  21. 17. who *l.* pleasure shall be
Songs 1. 7. whom my soul *l.* 3. 1, 4.
Matt. 10. 37. *l.* father or mother more
John 3. 35. Father *l.* the Son and given
  all things, 5. 20.
  16. 27. Father himself *l.* you
2 *Cor.* 9. 7. God *l.* a cheerful giver
3 *John* 9. *l.* to have pre-eminence
Rev. 22. 15. whosoever *l.* and maketh
  a lie
LOVELY, 2 *Sam.* 1. 23; *Songs* 5. 16;
  Ezek. 33. 32; *Phil.* 4. 8; Lover, *Ps.*
  88. 18; *Tit.* 1. 8; *Ps.* 38. 11; *Hos.*
  2. 5; 2 *Tim.* 3. 2, 4.
LOVING-KINDNESS, *Ps.* 25. 6. rem-
  member thy *l.-k.*
Ps. 36. 7. how excellent is thy *l.-k.*
  10. O continue thy *l.-k.* to such as
  63. 3. thy *l.-k.* is better than life
  103. 4. who crowneth thee with *l.-k.*
Is. 63. 7. I will mention *l.-k.* of the L.
  his *l.-k.*
Jer. 9. 24. I am Lord which exercise *l.-k.*
  31. 3. with *l.-k.* have I drawn
  32. 18. showest *l.-k.* to thousands
Hos. 2. 19. I will betroth thee in *l.-k.*
LOW, *Deut.* 28. 43; *Ezek.* 17. 24.
1 *Sam.* 2. 7. Lord brings *l.* and lifts up
Job 40. 12. look on proud, bring *l.*
Ps. 49. 2. high and *l.* rich and poor
  136. 23. remembered us in our *l.* estate
Prov. 29. 23. man's pride shall bring
  him *l.*
Is. 26. 5. lofty city he has laid *l.* 25. 12.
  32. 19. the city shall be *l.* in a *l.* place
Luke 1. 48. regarded *l.* estate of
  52. exalted them of *l.* degree, *Job* 5.
  11; *Ezek.* 21. 26; *Jam.* 1. 9, 10.
Luke 3. 5. every mountain be made *l.*
Rom. 12. 16. condescend to men of *l.*
  estate
Ps. 63. 9. *l.* parts of the earth, 139. 15;
  Is. 44. 23; *Eph.* 4. 9.
  138. 6. Lord hath respect to *l.*
Prov. 3. 34. giveth grace to the *l.*
Prov. 11. 2. with pride cometh shame
  with *l.* is wisdom
Matt. 11. 29. learn of me, for I am meek
  and *l.*
LOWLINESS, *Eph.* 4. 2; *Phil.* 2. 3.
LUCRE, signifies unlawful gain, 1 *Sam.*
  8. 3. The sons of Samuel walked
  not in the ways of their father, ' but
  turned aside after *lucre.*' The ministers of God must not be given to
  " filthy lucre;" 1 *Tim.* 3. 3, 8; *Tit.*
  1. 7; 1 *Pet.* 5. 2.
LUMP, *Is.* 38. 21; *Rom.* 9. 21. & 11. 16;
  1 *Cor.* 5. 6, 7; *Gal.* 5. 9.
LUST, unlawful carnal passions or
  desires; that original depravity of
  heart which inclines men to sin,
  Ex. 15. 9; *Ps.* 78. 18; *Jam.* 1. 14,
  15; 2 *Pet.* 1. 4.
Ps. 81. 12. gave up to hearts' *l.*
Matt. 5. 28. looks on woman to *l.* after

her
Rom. 7. 7. not known *l.* except
1 Cor. 10. 6. not *l.* after evil
Gal. 5. 16. shall not fulfil *l.* of flesh
1 Thess. 4. 5. *l.* of concupiscence
Jam. 1. 15. then when *l.* hath conceived
1 John 2. 16. *l.* of flesh, *l.* of eye
Mark 4. 19. *l.* of other things
John 8. 44. *l.* of your father ye
Rom. 6. 12. should obey it in *l.* thereof
   13. 14. for the flesh to fulfil *l.* thereof
Gal. 5. 17. flesh *l.* against Spirit, and
   Spirit *l.* against flesh
   24. crucified flesh with affections & *l.*
Eph. 2. 3. *l.* of our flesh and mind
1 Tim. 6. 9. foolish and hurtful *l.*
2 Tim. 2. 22. flee youthful *l.*
   3. 6. laden with sins, led away with
   divers *l.*
Tit. 2. 12. denying ungodliness worldly *l.*
   3. 3. serving divers *l.* and
Jam. 4. 3. consume it on *l.* 1.
1 Pet. 2. 11. abstain from fleshly *l.*
   4. 2. longer live to *l.* of men
2 Pet. 3. 3. walk after own *l.* Jude 16, 18.

MAD, Deut. 28. 34.
Eccl. 2. 2. I said of laughter, it is *m.*
Jer. 50. 38. and they are *m.* upon their
   idols
Hos. 9. 7. the spiritual man is *m.*
John 10. 20. hath a devil and is *m.*
Acts 26. 11. being exceedingly *m.* against
   them
   24. much learning makes *m.*
MADNESS, Deut. 28. 28; Eccl. 1. 17. &
   2. 12. & 9. 3. & 10. 13; Zech. 12. 4;
   Luke 6. 11; 2 Pet. 2. 16.
MADE, Ex. 2. 14; 2 Sam. 13. 6.
Ps. 104. 24. works in wisdom *m.*
   139. 14. I am wonderfully *m.*
Prov. 16. 4. Lord *m.* all things for him-
   self
John 1. 3. all things *m.* by him
Rom. 1. 3. *m.* of seed of David according
   to the flesh
   20. understood by things *m.*
1 Cor. 1. 30. Christ Jesus of God *m.* unto
   9. 22. *m.* all things to all men
Gal. 4. 4. *m.* of woman *m.* under
Phil. 2. 7. *m.* in likeness of men
MAGNIFY, Josh. 3. 7; 1 Chr. 29. 25.
Job 7. 17. what is man that thou shouldst
   m. him
   36. 24. remember to *m.* his work
Ps. 34. 3. *m.* the Lord with me, let us
   exalt his name
   69. 30. *m.* with thanksgiving
Is. 42. 21. *m.* the law and make it
   honourable
Luke 1. 46. my soul doth *m.* the Lord
Acts 10. 46. speak with tongues and *m.*
Rom. 11. 13. apostle of Gentiles, I *m.*
   my office
Gen. 19. 19. *m.* thy mercy
2 Sam. 7. 26. thy name be *m.* for
Ps. 35. 27. Lord be *m.* 40. 16. & 70. 4.
   138. 2. *m.* thy word above thy name
Acts 19. 17. name of the Lord was *m.*
Phil. 1. 20. Christ shall be *m.* in my
MAIMED, Lev. 22. 22. blind or *m.* not
   offer

Matt. 15. 30. those that were *m.*
   31. saw the *m.* to be whole
Luke 14. 13. makest a feast call the *m.*
MAINTAIN cause 1 Kings 8. 45, 49.
   Job 13. 15; Ps. 9. 4. & 140. 12.
Tit. 3. 8. careful to *m.* good works, 14.
Ps. 16. 5. thou *m.* my lot...
MAJESTY. The splendour of earthly
   princes; Esth. 1. 4. The infinite
   dignity and glory of God, Ps. 21. 5.
   It was seen in the Redeemer's trans-
   figuration, Matt. 17. 2; and in his
   ascension and exaltation, Heb. 1.
   3; Dan. 4. 30, 36, & 5. 18, 19; Job
   40. 10; Ps. 21. 5. & 45. 3, 4.
1 Chr. 29. 11. thine O Lord is the *m.*
   25. and bestowed upon him such
   royal *m.*
Job 37. 22. with God is terrible *m.*
   40. 10. deck thyself with *m.*
Ps. 21. 5. honour and *m.* hast thou laid
   on him
   29. 4. voice of God full of *m.*;
   45. 3. with thy glory and *m.*; 4. in
   thy *m.* ride
   93. 1. Lord is clothed with *m.*
   96. 6. honour and *m.* before him
   104. 1. clothed with honour and *m.*
   145. 5. glorious honour of *m.*
   12. glorious *m.* of his kingdom
Is. 2. 19. for glory of his *m.*
Heb. 1. 3. the right hand of the *m.* on
   high
Heb. 8. 1. throne of *m.* in heavens
2 Pet. 1. 16. eye-witnesses of his *m.*
Jude 25. to the only wise G. be glory *m.*
MAKE (1) To create, frame, or fashion,
   Gen. 1. 31; Ex. 32. 1; Is. 45. 9. (2)
   To choose, or bring that to be
   which was not so before, 1 Sam.
   12. 22. (3) To call one to a new
   vocation, and fit and qualify him
   for the same, Matt. 4. 19. (4) To
   ordain and appoint, Acts 26. 16.
   (5) To turn, Ps. 41. 3. (6) To build,
   Ezra. 5. 5. (7) To change one thing
   into another, John 2. 9.
MAKE, Gen. 1. 26. & 3. 6, 21; Deut. 32.
   39; 1 Cor. 6. 15; 1 Sam. 20. 38.
Ex. 5. 16. no straw given, they say to
   us, *m.* brick
   32. 10. *m.* thee a great nation
   33. 19. *m.* my goodness pass
Deut. 32. 39. I kill, and I *m.* alive,
   wound, and
2 Kings 7. 2. *m.* windows in heaven, 19.
Job 9. 30. I *m.* my hands never so clean
   34. 29. he giveth quietness, who then
   can *m.* trouble
Ps. 22. 9. thou didst *m.* me hope
   31. 16. *m.* thy face shine on thy
   servant, 119. 135.
   34. 32. *m.* her boast in the Lord
   39. 4. Lord, *m.* me to know mine end
   and days
   8. *m.* me not the reproach of
   51. 6. in hidden part shall *m.* me
   know wisdom
   8. *m.* me hear joy and gladness
   66. 2. *m.* his praise glorious
   90. 15. *m.* us glad according to
   139. 8. if I *m.* my bed in hell, there

6. 10. *m.* the heart of this people fat
13. 12. I will *m.* a man more precious than gold
25. 6. *m.* a feast of fat things
27. 5. he may *m.* peace with me
28. 9. *m.* to understand doctrine
42. 21. and *m.* the law honourable
45. 7. I *m.* peace and create evil
53. 10. shalt *m.* his soul an offering
54. 12. *m.* thy windows of agates
56. 7. I will *m.* them joyful in my house of prayer
62. 7. till *m.* Jerusalem a praise
Dan. 9. 24. seventy weeks are determined to *m.* reconciliation for iniquity
Hab. 2. 2. write the vision, and *m.* it plain on tables
3. 19. *m.* my feet like hinds' feet
Mal. 3. 17. when I *m.* up my jewels
Matt. 4. 19. *m.* you fishers of men
Matt. 5. 36. *m.* one hair white or black
23. 14. pretence *m.* long prayers, *Mark* 12. 40.
Luke 14. 18. consent began to *m.* excuse
John 8. 32. the truth shall *m.* you free
36. if the Son *m.* you free
14. 23. *m.* our abode with him
Rom. 3. 3. *m.* the faith of God without effect
31. *m.* void the law through
14. 19. follow things which *m.* for peace
2 *Cor.* 9. 8. and God is able to *m.* all grace abound
12. 17. did I *m.* gain by any of you
2 *Tim.* 3. 15. *m.* thee wise to salvation
4. 5. *m.* full proof of thy mercy
Heb. 2. 10. to *m.* the captain of their salvation perfect
7. 25. to *m.* intercession for them
Jam. 3. 18. is sown in peace of them that *m.* peace
2 *Pet.* 1. 10. *m.* your calling and election sure
Rev. 3. 12. I will *m.* a pillar in temple
21. 5. behold, I *m.* all things new
MAKE haste, *Ps.* 38. 22. *m.* haste to help me, O Lord, my salvation, 40. 13; 70. 1; 71. 12.
Is. 28. 16. believeth not *m.* haste
Luke 19. 5. Zaccheus *m. haste* and come
MAKE manifest, 1 *Cor.* 4. 5. will *m. manfest* the counsels of the heart
Eph. 5. 13. doth *m. manifest* is light
Col. 4. 4. may *m.* it *manifest* as I ought
MAKE ready, *Mark* 14. 15. there *m. ready* for us, *Luke* 22. 12.
Luke 1. 17. to *m. ready* a people prepared for the Lord
MAKER, *Job* 4. 17; man purer than M.
32. 22. my M. will soon take me
35. 10. but none says where is God my M.
36. 3. I will ascribe righteousness to my M.
Ps. 95. 6. kneel before God our M.
Prov. 14. 31. reproach M. 17. 5.
22. 2. rich and poor, Lord is M. of them all

Is. 17. 7. shall man look to M.
45. 9. woe to him that striveth with his M.
51. 13. forgettest the Lord thy M.
54. 5. thy M. thy husband God
Heb. 11. 10. whose builder and M. is G.
MAKETH, *Ps.* 23. 2. he *m.* to lie down in green pastures
Ps. 104. 3. *m.* the clouds his chariot
4. who *m.* his angels spirits, *Heb.* 1. 7.
Ps. 135. 7. he *m.* lightnings for rain
Prov. 10. 4. hand of the diligent *m.* rich
22. the blessing of the Lord it *m.* rich
18. 16. a man's gift *m.* room for him
Jer. 10. 13. *m.* lightnings with rain
17. 5. cursed be the man that *m.* flesh his arm
Matt. 5. 45. he *m.* his sun rise on evil
Mark 7. 37. he *m.* deaf to hear and
Rom. 5. 5. hope *m.* not ashamed
8. 26. Spirit *m.* intercession
11. 2. he *m.* intercession to God
1 *Cor.* 4. 7. who *m.* thee to differ
Eph. 4. 16. *m.* increase of the body
Rev. 21. 27. not whatsoever *m.* a lie 22. 15.
MAKING, *Mark* 7. 13. *m.* word of God of none effect
John 5. 18. himself equal with God
2 *Cor.* 6. 10. poor, yet *m.* many rich
Eph. 2. 15. man, so *m.* peace
5. 19. *m.* melody in your heart
2 *Pet.* 2. 6. *m.* them an ensample
Jude 22. compassion, *m.* a difference
MALEFACTOR, *John* 18. 30. if he were not a *m.* we would not
MALEFACTORS, *Luke* 23. 32. two *m.* led with him
Luke 23. 33. crucified him and the *m.*
39. one of the *m.* railed
MALE or female, *Gen.* 1. 27; *Num.* 5. 3; *Mal.* 1. 14; *Matt.* 19. 4; *Gal.* 3. 28.
MALICE. A fixed determination to revenge or injure another. It is a most hateful disposition in the sight of God, and forbidden in his holy word, *Col.* 3. 8; 1 *Pet.* 2. 1. and it is inimical to the spirit of Christianity, *Matt.* 5. 44. Malicious informers were odious in the judgment of the Mosaic law, *Lev.* 19. 16—18.
1 *Cor.* 14. 20. in *m.* be ye children
Eph. 4. 31. put away all *m.* *Col.* 3. 8; 1 *Pet.* 2. 1.
Tit. 3. 3. living in *m.* and envy
Rom. 1. 29. filled with all *m.* malignity, 1 *Pet.* 2. 16.
MAN, *Gen.* 1. 26, 27; 2 *Kings* 9. 11.
Job 4. 17. shall mortal *m.* be more just than God
5. 7. *m.* born to trouble, 14. 1.
7. 17. what is *m.* that thou shouldst magnify him
9. 2. shall *m.* be just with God
11. 12. vain *m.* would be wise
14. 1. *m.* that is born of a woman is of few days
15. 14. what *m.* that be clean
25. 6. *m.* that is a worm
28. 28. unto *m.* he said behold

Ps. 8. 4. what is *m.* that thou art mindful of him

10. 18. *m.* of earth no more oppress
25. 12. what *m.* feareth Lord, him
49. 12. *m.* in honour abideth
90. 3. turnest *m.* to destruction
104. 23. *m.* goeth to his work
118. 6. not fear what *m.* can do
144. 3. what is *m.* that thou takest knowledge

Prov. 20. 24. *m.* goings are of the Lord
Eccl. 6. 10. known that it is *m.*

7. 29. God made *m.* upright but
12. 5. *m.* goeth to his long home

Is. 2. 22. cease ye from *m.* whose
Jer. 17. 5. cursed be the *m.* that trusteth in *m.*
Zech. 13. 7. awake against the *m.* my fellow
Matt. 4. 4. *m.* shall not live by bread
John 7. 46. *m.* never spake like this *m.*
Rom. 6. 6. old *m.* crucified with Christ

7. 22. delight in law after inward *m.*

1 Cor. 2. 11. what *m.* knoweth the things of a *m.*

2. 14. natural *m.* receives not things of God
11. 8. *m.* not of woman but woman of *m.*
15. 47. first *m.* earthy, second *m.* is the Lord, 45.

2 Cor. 4. 16. outward *m.* perish, inward *m.* renewed
Eph. 4. 22. off the old *m.* corrupt

24. put on new *m.* renewed, *Col.* 3. 9, 10.

1 Pet. 3. 4. be hidden *m.* of the heart
Ex. 15. 3. Lord is a *m.* of war
Num. 23. 19. God not *m.* to lie
Is. 47. 3. I will not meet thee as *m.*

53. 3. *m.* of sorrow acquainted

Jer. 15. 10. born me *m.* of strife

31. 22. woman shall compass *m.*

Matt. 8. 9. for I am a *m.* under authority
16. 26. what shall *m.* give in exchange for his soul

John 3. 3. except a *m.* be born again, 5.
Acts 10. 26. I myself also am a *m.*
2 Cor. 12. 2. I knew a *m.* in Christ, 3.
Phil. 2. 8. in fashion as a *m.* he humbled himself
1 Tim. 2. 5. the *m.* Christ Jesus
Prov. 30. 2. if any *m. Matt.* 16. 24; *John* 6. 51. & 7. 17, 37; *Rom.* 8. 9; *2 Cor.* 5. 17; *Gal.* 1. 9; *Rev.* 22. 19.
Ps. 39. 5. every *m. Prov.* 19. 6; *Mic.* 4. 4. & 7. 2; *Gal.* 6. 4, 5; *Col.* 1. 28; *Heb.* 2. 9.
Is. 66. 2. this *m. Ps.* 87. 4; *Mic.* 5. 5; *Luke* 19. 14; *John* 7. 46; *Jam.* 1. 26.
Prov. 1. 5. a wise *m.* will hear

9. 8. rebuke *m.* he will love thee
14. 16. *m.* feareth and departeth from evil
17. 10. reproof enters into *m.*

Eccl. 2. 14. wise *m.* eyes are in his head

7. 7. oppression makes a wise *m.* mad
10. 2. *m.* heart at right hand

Jer. 9. 23. let not wise *m.* glory in his wisdom

Jam. 3. 13. who is wise *m.* and
Deut. 33. 1. *m.* of God, *Judg.* 13. 6, 8; *2 Kings* 1. 9, 13; *1 Tim.* 6. 11; *2 Tim.* 3. 11.

MANDRAKES, *Gen.* 30. 14; *Songs* 7. 13.

MANIFEST, easy to be known, clear, obvious, *2 Tim.* 3. 9; *Gal.* 5. 9. Spiritual communication, *John* 14. 21. To appear, be visible, *1 Tim.* 3. 16; *Eccl.* 3. 18; *1 Cor.* 15. 27.

Mark 4. 22. nothing hid shall be *m.*
John 2. 11. *m.* forth his glory and

17. 6. I have *m.* thy name to

1 Cor. 4. 5. make *m.* the counsels of the heart
Gal. 5. 19. works of flesh are *m.*
2 Thess. 1. 5. a *m.* token of righteous
1 Tim. 3. 16. God was *m.* in flesh
Heb. 4. 13. neither a creature that is not *m.* in his sight
1 John 3. 5. he was *m.* to take away sin, 8.

10. in this children of God *m.* and
4. 9. in this was *m.* love of God

Luke 8. 17. made *m. John* 3. 21; *1 Cor.* 3. 13; *2 Cor.* 4. 10. & 5. 11; *Eph.* 5. 13.

MANIFESTATION, *Rom.* 8. 19. *m.* of sons of God
1 Cor. 12. 7. *m.* of the Spirit
2 Cor. 4. 2. but by *m.* of truth

MANIFOLD mercies, *Neh.* 9. 19, 27; meaning, many, diverse, repeated, exhibited in various ways, or at divers times

Ps. 104. 24. how *m.* are thy works
Amos 5. 12. I know your *m.* transgresions
Luke 18. 30. *m.* more in this present time
Eph. 3. 10. be known the *m.* wisdom of God
1 Pet. 1. 6. in heaviness through *m.* temptations

4. 10. as good stewards of the *m.* grace of God

MANKIND, *Lev.* 18. 22. shall not lie with *m.* as with woman-kind
Lev. 20. 13. if a man lie with *m.* as with a woman
Job 12. 10. in whose hand is the breath of all *m.*
1 Tim. 1. 10. the law for them that defile *m.*
Jam. 3. 7. is tamed, and hath been tamed of *m.*

MANNA, *Ex.* 16. 15; *Num.* 11. 6; *Deut.* 8. 3, 16; *Josh.* 5. 12; *Neh.* 9. 20; *Ps.* 78. 24; *John* 6. 31, 49, 58.

Rev. 2. 17. to him that overcometh will I give hidden *m.*

To eat of hidden Manna, Rev. 2.
17. To partake of Christ and those comforts and blessings which flow from him. It is spoken in allusion to that bread wherewith God fed the Israelites, which was a type of Christ, who is the bread of eternal life, and was the true bread which came down from heaven to give life to the world, *John* 6. 32, 33, 35.

MANNER, *1 Sam.* 8. 9, 11; *Is.* 5. 17.

Ps. 107. 18. their soul abhorreth all *m.* of meat

144. 13. garner full, all *m.* of store

Is. 5. 17. lambs feed after their *m.*

Matt. 4. 23. and healing all *m.* of sickness, 10. 1.

    5. 11. say all *m.* of evil against

    8. 27. what *m.* of man is this, sea obey him, *Mark* 4. 41; *Luke* 8. 25.

Mark 13. 1. see what *m.* of stones

Luke 1. 66. what *m.* of child this be

    9. 55. ye know what *m.* of spirit ye

    11. 42. ye tithe all *m.* of herbs

    24. 17. what *m.* of communications

Acts 20. 18. ye know after what *m.* I have been with

    26. 4. *m.* of life from my youth

2 *Cor.* 7. 9. ye were made sorry after a godly *m.*

Heb. 10. 25. assembling as the *m.* of some is

Jam. 1. 24. what *m.* of man he was

1 *Pet.* 1. 11. what *m.* of time the Spirit of Christ

    15. holy in all *m.* of conversation

1 *John* 3. 1. *m.* of love the Father

Rev. 22. 2. tree of life, which bare twelve *m.* of fruits

MANNER, after the, 1 *Cor.* 11. 25. *after the* same *m.* also he took the cup

Gal. 2. 14. Jew, livest *after the m.* of Gentiles

MANNERS, *Lev.* 20. 23. shall not walk in the *m.* of the nation

2 *Kings* 17. 34. they do after the former *m.*

Acts 13. 18. forty years suffered their *m.*

1 *Cor.* 15. 33. evil communications corrupt good *m.*

Heb. 1. 1. God in divers *m.* spake

MANSIONS, *John* 14. 2. in my Father's house are many *m.*

MARBLE, *Songs* 5. 15. his legs are as pillars of *m.* set in sockets

Rev. 18. 12. the vessels of *m.* no man buyeth

MARCH, *Ps.* 68. 7. didst *m.* through the wilderness

Is. 27. 4. set briers, I would *m.* against them

MARCHED, *Ex.* 14. 10. Egyptians *m.* after them

MARCHEDST, *Judg.* 5. 4. when thou *m.* the earth trembled

MARK, *Gen.* 4. 15. the Lord set a *m.* upon Cain, lest any

Job 7. 20. why hast thou set me as a *m.* against thee, 16. 12.

Lam. 3. 12. set me as a *m.*

Ezek. 9. 4. set a *m.* on foreheads, *Rev.* 13. 16, 17. & 14. 9. & 19. 20.

Phil. 3. 14. I press toward the *m.* for

Rev. 20. 4. nor received his *m.* they lived with Christ

MARK, verb, *Ps.* 48. 13. *m.* well her bulwarks, consider her palaces

Ps. 37. 37. *m.* the perfect man

    130. 3. if thou shouldst *m.* iniquity, *Job* 10. 14; *Jer.* 2. 22.

Rom. 16. 17. *m.* them who cause divisions

Phil. 3. 17. *m.* them who walk so

MARKS, *Gal.* 6. 17. I bear in my body the *m.* of the Lord

MARRED, *Is.* 52. 14. his visage was so *m.* more than any man

MARKET, *Matt.* 20. 3. standing idle in the *m.*

Mark 12. 38. salutations in *m.* places

Luke 7. 32. sitting in the *m.* place

Acts. 16. 19. drew them into *m.* place

    17. 17. he disputed in the *m.*

MARRIAGE, (1) A civil contract, by which a man and a woman are joined together, which was instituted by God for the prevention of uncleanness, the propagation of mankind, and that the parties so contracting might be mutual helps and comforts to one another, *Gen.* 2. 18, 22, 23; *John* 2. 1; 1 *Cor.* 7. 2; *Heb.* 13. 4. (2) That marriage covenant which is between God and his Church, even the covenant of grace, wherein God graciously promises to be the God of his people, and to forgive and sanctify them through the merits of Jesus Christ and the influences of his Spirit, and so make them a willing people to himself, *Is.* 54. 5; *Jer.* 3. 14; *Hos.* 2. 19. 20. The union between husband and wife is so near, that thereby is represented the mystical union, the sacred and spiritual marriage of Christ with his Church, *Eph.* 5. 30, 31, 32.

MARRIAGE, *Gen.* 38. 8; *Deut.* 25. 5.

Ps. 78. 63. maidens, not given to *m.*

Is. 62. 5. man *m.* virgin, thy sons *m.* thee

Jer. 3. 14. I am *m.* to you saith the Lord

Matt. 22. 30. in the resurrection not given in *m.* but as the angels in heaven, *Mark* 12. 25; *Luke* 20. 35.

Luke 14. 20. I have *m.* a wife and cannot come

    17. 27. they drank, *m.* and were given in *m.*

John 2. 1. a *m.* in Cana of Galilee

1 *Cor.* 7. 9. better to *m.* than burn

1 *Cor.* 7. 38. giveth her in *m.* doeth well, giveth her not in *m.* doeth better

1 *Tim.* 4. 3. forbidding to *m.*

    5. 14. that younger women *m.*

Matt. 22. 2. king made *m.* for son

    25. 10. they that were ready went in with him to *m.*

Heb. 13. 4. *m.* is honourable in

Rev. 19. 7. *m.* of the Lord is come, 9.

MARROW to bones, *Prov.* 3. 8; *Job* 21. 24.

Ps. 63. 5. soul satisfied with *m.*

Is. 25. 6. feast of things full of *m.*

Heb. 4. 12. to the dividing asunder joints and *m.*

MARTYR. In the ordinary sense, a witness. Sometimes it refers to judicial witnesses. It is now applied to one who seals the truth of the gospel by his death on the scaffold, or at the stake, &c., *Acts* 22. 20; *Rev.* 2. 13; 17. 6.

MARVEL not, *Eccl.* 5. 8; *John* 5. 28;

Acts 3. 12; 1 *John* 3. 13.

Ps. 48. 5. they *m.* *Matt.* 8. 27. & 9. 8,
33. & 21. 20. & 22. 22; *Luke* 1. 63;
Acts 2. 7. & 4. 13.

Matt. 8. 10. Jesus *m.* *Mark* 6. 6.

MARVELLOUS, *Job* 5. 9. doth *m.* things

10. 16. thou showedst thyself *m.* upon
me

Ps. 17. 7. show me thy *m.* kindness,
31. 21.

98. 1. done *m.* things, *Mic.* 7. 15.

118. 23. it is *m.* in our eyes, *Matt.* 21.
42; *Mark* 12. 11.

1 *Pet.* 2. 9. called from darkness into *m.*
light

1 *Chr.* 16. 12. remember his *m.* works,
Ps. 105. 5. & 9. 1.

Ps. 139. 14. *m.* are thy works, *Rev.* 15. 3.

MASTER, 2 *Kings* 6. 5. alas, *m.* for it
was borrowed

Mal. 1. 6. I be *m.* where is my fear

Matt. 23. 10. one your *m.* even Christ

26. 49. hail *m.* and kissed, *Mark*
14. 45.

Mark 10. 17. *m.* what shall I do

13. 35. for ye know not when the
m. cometh

John 3. 10. art thou a *m.* of Israel
and knowest not

11. 28. the *m.* is come and calleth

13. 13. ye call me *m.* and say well

14. if then I your *m.* have washed
your feet

Rom. 14. 4. to his own *m.* stands

1 *Cor.* 3. 10. I as a *m.* builder

MASTERS, *Ps.* 123. 2. eyes of servants
look to *m.*

Eccl. 12. 11. *m.* of assemblies

Matt. 6. 24. no man can serve two *m.*
Luke 16. 13.

23. 8. neither be ye called *m.* one is
your master

Acts 16. 16. brought her *m.* much gain

Eph. 6. 5. servants be obedient to them
that are your *m.* *Col.* 3. 22; *Tit.* 2.
9; 1 *Pet.* 2. 18.

Col. 4. 1. *m.* give unto your servants

1 *Tim.* 6. 1. count their *m.* worthy of
all honour

Jam. 3. 1. brethren, be not many *m.*

MASTERY, 1 *Cor.* 9. 25. that striveth
for the *m.* is temperate

MASTERIES, 2 *Tim.* 2. 5. if a man also
strive for *m.* not crowned

MATTER, *Ex.* 18. 22. & 23. 7; 1 *Sam.*
10. 16; *Job* 19. 28. & 32. 18;
Dan. 7. 28; 2 *Cor.* 5. 8.

Ps. 45. 1. heart inditing a good *m.*

1 *Cor.* 6. 1. having a *m.* go to law

Jam. 8. 5. how great a *m.* a little fire

MATTER, this, *Acts* 8. 21. part nor lot
in *this m.*

MATTERS, *Job* 33. 13. account any of
his *m.*

Ps. 131. 1. exercise myself in *m.*

Matt. 23. 23. omitted weightier *m.*

1 *Pet.* 4. 15. busy body in other men's *m.*

MEAN what, *Deut.* 6. 20, 24; *Josh.* 4. 6,
21; *Ezek.* 17. 12; 37. 18; *Jonah* 1. 6.

Ex. 12. 26. *m.* by this service

Mark 9. 10. rising from dead should *m.*

Acts 17. 20. we should know what these

things *m.*

21. 13. what *m.* ye to weep and break
my heart

Gen. 50. 20. ye thought ill God *m.* good

MEAN, adjective, *Prov.* 22. 20. not
stand before *m.* men

Is. 5. 15. the *m.* man shall be brought
down

Acts 21. 39. citizen of no *m.* city

MEANS, 2 *Sam.* 14. 14. devise *m.* that
his banished

Ps. 49. 7. none can by any *m.* redeem
his brother

Rom. 11. 14. by any *m.* I provoke to
emulation

1 *Cor.* 9. 22. by all *m.* save some

Gal. 2. 2. lest by any *m.* I should run
in vain

Phil. 3. 11. if by any *m.* I attain to the
resurrection

2 *Thess.* 2. 3. let no man deceive you by
any *m.*

MEANEST, *Jonah* 1. 6. what *m.* thou,
O sleeper, arise, call on God

MEASURE, *Lev.* 19. 35; *Deut.* 25. 15.

Job 11. 9. *m.* longer than earth

Ps. 39. 4. know *m.* of my days

Is. 27. 8. in *m.* when shoots forth

Jer. 30. 11. correct thee in *m.* 46. 28.

Matt. 7. 2. with what *m.* ye mete

23. 32. fill up *m.* of fathers

John 3. 34. gives not Spirit by *m.* to him

Rom. 12. 3. given to every one *m.*

2 *Cor.* 1. 8. were pressed out of *m.*

12. 7. I should be exalted above *m.*

Eph. 4. 7. according to the *m.* of the
gift of Christ

13. to *m.* of stature of fulness of Christ

Rev. 11. 1. *m.* temple of God and

MEAT, *Job* 6. 7; *Ps.* 42. 3.

Ps. 44. 11. thou hast given us like sheep
for *m.*

69. 21. gave me gall for my *m.*

104. 27. give *m.* in due season, 145. 15.

111. 5. giveth *m.* to them that fear
him

Prov. 6. 8. provide *m.* in summer, 30. 25.

Hos. 11. 4. I laid *m.* unto them

Hab. 1. 16. portion fat and *m.* plenteous

3. 17. though fields yield no *m.*

Hag. 2. 12. *m.* shall it be holy

Mal. 1. 12. his *m.* is contemptible

Matt. 3. 4. *m.* locusts and wild honey

6. 25. life is more than *m.*

10. 10. workman is worthy of his *m.*

John 4. 32. I have *m.* to eat that

34. my *m.* is to do the will of Father

6. 27. labour not for *m.* that perisheth

55. my flesh *m.* indeed, blood

Acts 2. 46. eat their *m.* with gladness

Rom. 14. 15. destroy not with *m.*

17. the kingdom of God is not *m.* and

1 *Cor.* 6. 13. *m.* for the belly and the
belly for *m.*

8. 8. *m.* commends us not to God

10. 3. all did eat spiritual *m.*

MEDDLE. To provoke to war, *Deut.* 2.
5. To associate with, 2 *Kings* 14.
10; *Prov.* 17. 14. & 20. 3, 19. & 24.
21. & 26. 17.

MEDIATOR. A person that manages,
or transacts between two contend-

ing parties, in order to reconcile them, *Gal.* 3. 20. And is applied, (1) To Jesus Christ, who is the only peace-maker and intercessor between God and men, 1 *Tim.* 2. 5. (2) Moses, who came between the Lord and his people, to declare unto them his word, *Deut.* 5. 5.
Gal. 3. 19. ordained by angels hand of *m.*
20. a *m.* is not a *m.* of one
1 *Tim.* 2. 5. but one *m.* between God and men, Jesus
Heb. 8. 6. *m.* of a better covenant
9. 15. he is *m.* of the new testament
12. 24. Jesus the *m.* of the new covenant
MEDICINE, *Prov.* 17. 22; *Jer.* 30. 13. & 46. 11; *Ezek.* 47. 12.
MEDITATE, Isaac went to, *Gen.* 24. 63
Josh. 1. 8. *m.* in law day and night, *Ps.* 1. 2. & 119. 15, 23, 48, 78, 148.
Ps. 63. 6. *m.* on thee in night watches
77. 1 will *m.* of thy, 143. 5.
Is. 33. 18. your heart shall *m.*
Luke 21. 14. not *m.* before what ye shall answer
1 *Tim.* 4. 15. *m.* upon these things
MEDITATION, *Ps.* 5. 1. consider my *m.*
19. 14. let the *m.* of my heart be acceptable
49. 3. *m.* of my heart shall be of understanding
104. 34. my *m.* of him sweet
119. 97. it is my *m.* all the day
99. thy testimonies are my *m.*
MEEK, Moses was very, *Num.* 12. 3.
Ps. 22. 26. *m.* shall eat and be satisfied
25. 9. *m.* will he guide in
37. 11. *m.* shall inherit earth
76. 1 Lord rose to save all the *m.* of the earth
147. 6. Lord lifts up *m.* and casts down wicked
149. 4. Lord will beautify *m.* with salvation
Is. 11. 4. reprove, for *m.* of earth
29. 19. *m.* shall increase joy
61. 1. preach good tidings to *m.*
Amos 2. 7. turn aside way of *m.*
Zeph. 2. 3. seek the Lord all ye *m.* of the
Matt. 5. 5. blessed are the *m.* for
11. 29. I am *m.* and lowly
21. 5. thy King cometh *m.* and
1 *Pet.* 3. 4. ornament of a *m.* and quiet
MEEKNESS, *Ps.* 45. 4. ride prosperously because of *m.*
1 *Cor.* 4. 21. come in spirit of *m.*
2 *Cor.* 10. 1. beseech you by *m.* of Christ
Gal. 5. 23. *m.* temperance against
6. 1. restore him in spirit of *m.*
Eph. 4. 2. with lowliness and *m.*
Col. 3. 12. on *m.* long-suffering
1 *Tim.* 6. 11. follow after righteousness, holiness, love, patience, *m.*
2 *Tim.* 2. 25. in *m.* instructing those that oppose
Tit. 3. 2. showing *m.* to all men
Jam. 1. 21. receive with *m.* ingrafted word
3. 13. work with *m.* of wisdom
1 *Pet.* 3. 15. hope in you with *m.*
MEET help for him, *Gen.* 2. 18.

Job 34. 31. surely it is *m.* to be said unto God
Matt. 3. 8. fruits *m.* for repentance, *Acts* 26. 20.
1 *Cor.* 15. 9. not *m.* to be called an
Col. 1. 12. *m.* to be partakers of inheritance of the saints
2 *Tim.* 2. 21. vessel *m.* for master
Heb. 6. 7. *m.* for them by whom it is dressed
Prov. 22. 2. rich and poor *m.* together
Is. 47. 3. I will not *m.* thee as a man
64. 5. thou *m.* him that rejoiceth
Hos. 13. 8. I will *m.* thee as a bear robbed of whelps
Amos 4. 12. prepare to *m.* thy God
1 *Thess.* 4. 17. caught up to *m.* the Lord in the air
MELODY, *Is.* 23. 16. make sweet *m.* sing
Eph. 5. 19. making *m.* in your heart to the Lord
MELT, *Jer.* 9. 7. I will *m.* and try them
2 *Pet.* 3. 10. and the elements shall *m.* with heat, 12.
MEMBER body not one, 1 *Cor.* 12. 14.
Jam. 3. 5. tongue is a little *m.*
Ps. 139. 16. in book all my *m.* written
Matt. 5. 29. one of my *m.* perish
Rom. 6. 13. yield ye your *m.* as instruments
7. 23. another law in my *m.*
12. 5. and every one *m.* one of another
1 *Cor.* 6. 15. your bodies *m.* of Christ
12. 12. body is one and hath many *m.*
Eph. 4. 25. are *m.* one of another
5. 30. *m.* of his body, flesh, and bones
Col. 3. 5. mortify *m.* on earth
MEMORIAL, *Ex.* 3. 15. this is my *m.* unto all generations
13. 9. be for a *m.* between thy
17. 14. write this for *m.* in book
Josh. 4. 7. these stones shall be a *m.*
Ps. 9. 6. their *m.* is perished with them
135. 13. thy *m.* through all generations
Hos. 12. 5. Lord God of hosts, Lord is his *m.*
Matt. 26. 13. told for a *m.* of her, *Mark* 14. 9.
Acts 10. 4. prayers and alms are come up for a *m.*
MEMORY cut off, *Ps.* 109. 15.
Ps. 145. 7. utter *m.* of thy goodness
Prov. 10. 7. *m.* of just is blessed
Eccl. 9. 5. *m.* of them is forgotten
Is. 26. 14. made all their *m.* to perish
1 *Cor.* 15. 2. if keep in *m.* what I
MEN, *Gen.* 4. 26. then began *m.* to call on the name of the Lord
Gen. 32. 28. power with God and *m.* and hast prevailed
42. 11. we are true *m.* 31; 43. 16. bring *m.* home
2 *Kings* 6. 20. Lord open the eyes of these *m.* to see
Job 4. 13. sleep falleth on *m.* 33. 15.
Ps. 9. 20. know themselves to be but *m.*
17. 14. *m.* thy hand, *m.* of world
49. 18. *m.* will praise thee when thou doest well for thyself
62. 9. *m.* of low degree are vanity, *m.* of high degree are a lie

72. 17. *m.* shall be blessed in him

82. 7. shall die like *m.* and fall

Prov. 6. 30. *m.* do not despise a thief, if he steal

Eccl. 12. 3. strong *m.* shall bow themselves

Is. 31. 3. Egyptians are *m.* not God

46. 8. show yourselves *m.*

Hos. 6. 7. but they like *m.* have transgressed covenant

Matt. 5. 16. light so shine before *m.*

10. 32. confess me before *m. Luke* 12. 8.

33. deny me before *m. Luke* 12. 9.

Luke 2. 14. good will toward *m.*

5. 10. henceforth shalt catch *m.*

John 17. 6. manifested thy name to the *m.*

Acts 5. 4. not lied unto *m.* but unto G.

29. ought to obey God rather than *m.*

Rom. 1. 27. *m.* with *m.* working

12. 16. condescend to *m.* of low estate

1 *Cor.* 4. 9. made spectacle to angels and *m.*

Eph. 6. 6. *m.* pleasers, *Col.* 3. 22; 1 *Thess.* 2. 4.

2 *Tim.* 3. 2. *m.* be lovers of themselves

MEN, all, *Rom.* 5. 12. death passed upon all *m.*

Gal. 6. 10. do good to all *m.* especially to household of faith

Eph. 3. 9. to make all *m.* see what is the fellowship

1 *Thess.* 5. 14. be patient toward all *m.*

Tit. 2. 11. the grace of God hath appeared to all *m.*

Heb. 12. 14. follow peace with all *m.*

MENSTROUS, *Is.* 30. 22; *Lam.* 1. 17.

Ezek. 18. 6. nor come near *m.* woman

MENTION, *Ex.* 23. 13; *Job* 28. 18.

Ps. 71. 16. I will make *m.* of thy righteousness

Is. 26. 13. by thee only make *m.*

62. 6. ye that make *m.* of the Lord keep not silence

Rom. 1. 9. make *m.* of you in prayers, *Eph.* 1. 16; 1 *Thess.* 1. 2; *Philem.* 4.

MERCHANT. Those of Midian and Arabia were the most ancient, *Gen.* 37. 28. Chaldea was a land of traffic, *Rev.* 18. 11; *Hos.* 12. 7; *Matt.* 13. 45.

Is. 23. 18. *m.* holiness, *Matt.* 22. 5; *John* 2. 16; 2 *Pet.* 2. 3.

MERCY. (1) That essential perfection in God, whereby he pities and relieves the miseries of his creatures, *Ps.* 100. 5; *Tit.* 3. 5. (2) Grace, which flows from mercy as its fountain, *Jude* 2. (3) Eternal life and happiness in heaven, which is the chief fruit of mercy, 2 *Tim.* 1. 18. (4) All the blessings and benefits, whether bodily or spiritual, which proceed from the mercy of God, *Ps.* 106. 7; 119. 41. (5) That pity and compassion which one man shows towards another that is in misery, *Luke* 10. 37. (6) Clemency and bounty, *Prov.* 20. 28. (7) All duties of charity towards our neighbour, *Matt.* 9. 13. (8) Pretended

acts of mercy, *Prov.* 12. 10.

MERCY, *Gen.* 19. 19. & 39. 21.

Ex. 34. 7. keep *m.* for thousands, *Deut.* 7. 9; 1 *Kings* 8. 23; *Neh.* 1. 5. & 9. 32; *Dan.* 9. 4.

Num. 14. 18. L. is of great *m.*

Ps. 23. 6. goodness and *m.* follow

25. 10. all paths of the Lord are *m.* and truth

33. 18. hope in his *m.* 147. 11.

52. 8. trust in *m.* of God for ever

57. 3. God shall send forth *m.* and truth

66. 20. not turn away his *m.*

86. 5. plenteous in *m.* unto all that call on thee, 103. 8.

101. 1. I will sing of *m.* and judgment

103. 11. great is his *m.* 57. 10.

17. *m.* of the Lord from everlasting to

106. 1. his *m.* endureth for ever, 107. 1, & 118. 4, & 136. 1.—26; 1 *Chr.* 16. 34, 41; 2 *Chr.* 5. 13. & 7. 3, 6, & 20. 21; *Ezra* 3. 11; *Jer* 33. 11.

Prov. 16. 6. by *m.* and truth iniquity is purged

20. 28. *m.* and truth preserve the king

Is. 27. 11. he that made them will not have *m.* on them

Hos. 6. 6. desired *m.* not sacrifice

10. 12. reap in *m.*

12. 6. keep *m.* and judgment

14. 3. in thee fatherless find *m.*

Jonah 2. 8. forsake their own *m.*

Mic. 6. 8. God requires to love *m.*

7. 18. delighteth in *m.*

20. the *m.* to Abraham

Hab. 3. 2. in wrath remember *m.*

Luke 1. 50. his *m.* is on them that fear him

78. through tender *m.* of our God, day

Rom. 9. 23. on vessels of *m.*

15. he will have *m.* on whom he will have *m.*

11. 31. through your *m.* they obtain *m.*

15. 9. glorify God for his *m.*

2 *Cor.* 4. 1. receive *m.* we faint not

1 *Tim.* 1. 2. *m.* and peace, *Tit.* 1. 4; 2 *John* 3; *Jude* 2.

13. obtained *m.* because

2 *Tim.* 1. 18. may find *m.* in that day

Tit. 3. 5. according to his *m.* he saved us

Heb. 4. 16. may obtain *m.* and find

Jam. 2. 13. *m.* rejoiceth against judgment

3. 17. full of *m.* and good fruits

5. 11. Lord pitiful and of tender *m.*

Jude 21. looking for *m.* of Lord Jesus

MERCIES, *Gen.* 32. 10. not worthy of the least of thy *m.*

1 *Chr.* 21. 13. great are his *m.*

Ps. 69. 13. in the multitude of thy *m.* hear me, 16.

Is. 55. 3. the sure *m.* of David, *Acts* 13. 34.

Lam. 3. 22. Lord's *m.* we are not

Dan. 9. 9. to the Lord belongeth *m.* and forgiveness, 18.

Rom. 12. 1. I beseech by *m.* of God

2 *Cor.* 1. 3. Father of *m.* and God of all

Col. 3. 12. put on bowels of *m.*

Ps. 25. 6. tender *m.* 40. 11. & 51. 1. & 77. 9, & 79. 8, & 103. 4, & 119. 77, 156.

& 145. 9.

Prov. 12. 10. the tender *m.* of the wicked are cruel

Gen. 19. 19. thy *m. Num.* 14. 19; *Neh.* 13. 22; *Ps.* 5. 7, & 6. 4, & 13. 5, & 25. 7, & 31. 7, 16, & 33. 22, & 36. 5, & 44. 26, & 85. 7, & 86. 13, & 90. 14, & 94. 18, & 108. 4. & 57. 10, & 119. 64. & 143. 12.

MERCIFUL, *Ex.* 34. 6. Lord God *m.* and gracious, 2 *Chr.* 30. 9; *Neh.* 9. 17, 31; *Ps.* 103. 8; *Joel* 2. 13.

Ps. 18. 25. with *m.* show thyself *m.*
37. 26. he is ever *m.* and lends
117. 2. his *m.* kindness great

Prov. 11. 17. *m.* man doeth good, 12. 10.

Is. 57. 1. *m.* men are taken away

Jer. 3. 12. I am *m.* and will not keep

Matt. 5. 7. blessed are *m.* obtain m.

Luke 6. 36. be *m.* as your Father is *m.*

Heb. 2. 17. he might be a *m.* high-priest
8. 12. I will be *m.* to their unrighteousness

MERCY-SEAT, Or, Propituatory, was the covering of the ark of the covenant, or of the holy chest, in which the tables of the law were deposited: This cover was of gold, and at its two ends were fixed the two cherubims of the same metal, which by their two wings extended forward, and seemed to form a throne for the majesty of God, who in scripture is represented as sitting between the cherubims, *Ps.* 80. 1. and the ark itself was as it were his footstool. It was an eminent type of Christ, who by his atonement, covered our sins, and bore the curse for us; standing between God and the curse of the law for our sakes, that God might look on the law through Christ, as fulfilled by him on our behalf, *Gal.* 3. 10, 13. Hence Christ is called the Propitiation, *Rom.* 3. 25.

Ex. 25. 17. make a *m.-seat* of gold
22. commune from *m.-seat* between the cherubims, *Lev.* 16. 2; *Num.* 7. 89.
26. 34. shalt put the *m.-seat* upon the ark, 40. 20.

1 *Chr.* 28. 11. David gave Solomon pattern of *m.-seat*

MERRY, *Gen.* 43. 34. drank and were *m.* with him

Judg. 16. 25. hearts were *m.* call Samson

Prov. 15. 13. *m.* heart maketh cheerful countenance
17. 22. a *m.* heart doeth good like a medicine

Eccl. 8. 15. hath nothing better than to eat and be *m.*
9. 7. and drink thy wine with a *m.* heart

Is. 24. 7. vine languisheth, all the *m.*-hearted do sigh

Luke 12. 19. be *m.* 15. 23, 24, 29, 32.

Jam. 5. 13. is any *m.* let him sing psalms

Rev. 11. 10. rejoice over them, make *m.*

MESSAGE, *Judg.* 3. 20. I have a *m.* from God to thee

1 *John* 1. 5. this is the *m.* which we have heard, 3. 11.

MESSENGER, *Mal.* 2. 7. *m.* of the Lord of hosts

Mal. 3. 1. I will send *m.* of the covenant, *Matt.* 11. 10; *Mark* 1. 2; *Luke* 7. 27.

2 *Cor.* 12. 7. the *m.* of Satan to buffet

Phil. 2. 25. my companion in labour, but your *m.*

MESSENGERS, 2 *Chr.* 36. 16. mocked the *m.* of God

Luke 7. 24. *m.* of John were gone

2 *Cor.* 8. 23. the *m.* of the churches

MESSIAH, signifies, ANOINTED. It is applied by way of eminence, to that sovereign Deliverer, who was expected by the Jews, and whom they vainly expect even to this day. They used to anoint kings, highpriests, and sometimes prophets. Saul, David, Solomon, and Joash, received the royal unction: Aaron and his sons received the sacerdotal; and Elisha, the disciple of Elijah, received the prophetic unction, at least God ordered Elijah to give it, 1 *Kings* 19. 16. and therefore the name Messiah, or Anointed, is given to the kings, 1 *Sam.* 12. 3, 5; and also to the patriarchs or prophets, 1 *Chr.* 16. 22; *Ps.* 105. 15. But this name chiefly belongs to Jesus Christ, who was the object of the expectation of the saints.

Dan. 9. 25. from the commandment to build Jerusalem, unto *M.* the Prince shall be seven weeks
26. and after 62 weeks shall *M.* be cut off

John 1. 41. found *M.* which is Christ
4. 25. I know that *M.* cometh

METE, *Matt.* 7. 2. with what measure ye *m.* it shall be measured to you again, *Mark* 4. 24; *Luke* 6. 38.

METED, *Is.* 40. 12. *m.* out heaven with a span

MIDDLE, *Ezek.* 1. 16. wheel in the *m.* of a wheel

Eph. 2. 14. broken down the *m.* wall of partition

MIDNIGHT, *Ex.* 12. 29. at *m.* Lord smote first-born

Ps. 119. 62. at *m.* I will rise to give thanks

Mark 13. 35. whether he shall come at even, or *m.*

Acts 16. 25. and at *m.* Paul and Silas
20. 7. and Paul continued his speech till *m.*

MIDST, *Ps.* 22. 14. & 46. 5. & 110. 2; *Prov.* 4. 21; *Is.* 4. 4, & 41. 18; *Ezek.* 43. 7, 9. & 46. 10; *Joel* 2. 27; *Zeph.* 3. 5, 12, 15, 17; *Phil.* 2. 15; *Rev.* 1. 13, & 4. 6.

Rev. 5. 6. Lamb in *m.* of throne 7. 17.

MIGHT, *Gen.* 49. 3; *Num.* 14. 13.

Deut. 6. 5. love the Lord with all thy *m.*

2 *Kings* 23. 25. turn to the Lord with all

thy *m*.
2 *Chr*. 20. 12. no *m*. against this
Ps. 76. 5. none of the men of *m*. found
their hands
145. 6. speak of *m*. of thy acts
Eccl. 9. 10. do it with thy *m*.
Is. 40. 29. have no *m*. he increaseth
Zech. 4. 6. not by *m*. but by Spirit
Eph. 3. 16. strengthened with *m*. by his
Spirit
6. 10. strong in power of his *m*.
Col. 1. 11. strengthened with *m*.
MIGHTY, *Deut*. 7. 23. with *m*. destruc-
tion
10. 17. great God, a *m*. and terrible
Judg. 5. 23. to help of the Lord against
the *m*.
Ps. 24. 8. the Lord *m*. in battle
89. 19. help on one that is *m*.
Is. 5. 22. *m*. to drink wine, men of
63. 1. speak in righteousness *m*. to
save
Jer. 32. 19. *m*. in work, *Is*. 49. 26.
1 *Cor*. 1. 26. not many *m*. called
2 *Cor*. 10. 4. *m*. through God to pulling
down of strong holds
Ps. 93. 4. Lord *m*. *Matt*. 3. 11.
MIGHTILY, *Acts* 18.«28. *m*. convinced
the Jews
Acts 19. 20. so *m*. grew word of God
Col. 1. 29. which worketh in me *m*.
Rev. 18. 2. he cried *m*. saying, Babylon
is fallen
MILK, *Gen*. 18. 8. & 49. 12.
Job 10. 10. hast thou not poured me out
as *m*.
Songs 4. 11. honey and *m*. under thy
tongue
5. 1. drunk wine with my *m*.
Is. 55. 1. buy wine & *m*. without money
Joel 3. 18. the hills flow with *m*.
Heb. 5. 12. become such as have need
of *m*.
1 *Pet*. 2. 2. desire sincere *m*. of word
MILLSTONE, *Deut*. 24. 6. no man shall
take the *m*. to pledge
Job 41. 24. heart as hard as a piece of
the nether *m*.
Matt. 18. 6. better that a *m*. were hanged about his neck, *Mark* 9. 42;
Luke 17. 2.
Rev. 18. 21. an angel took up a stone
like a great *m*.
MILLSTONES, *Jer*. 25. 10. take away
sound of *m*.
MIND, (1) The understanding or judgment, whereby we distinguish
between good and evil, lawful and
unlawful, 2 *Cor*. 3. 14; *Tit*. 1. 15.
(2) The regenerated and renewed
part of man, *Rom*. 7. 25. (3) The
heart, *Gen*. 26. 35; *Deut*. 18. 6. (4)
The memory, *Ps*. 31. 12; *Is*. 46. 8.
(5) End, design, or intention, *Prov*.
21. 27. (6) Thought, or imagination, *Is*. 26. 3. (7) Wit or sound-
ness of mind, *Mark* 5. 15; *Luke* 8.
35. (8) The will, 1 *Pet*. 5. 2. (9)
Affection, *Acts* 17. 11.
MIND, *Gen*. 26. 35; *Lev*. 24. 12.
1 *Chr*. 28. 9. serve him with a willing *m*.
Neh. 4. 6. people had willing *m*.

Job 23. 13. he is of one *m*. and
Is. 26. 3. *m*. is stayed on thee
Luke 12. 29. not of doubtful *m*.
Acts 17. 11. receive word with readiness
of *m*.
20. 19. serve the Lord with all humility
of *m*.
Rom. 7. 25. with *m*. I serve law
8. 7. the carnal *m*. is enmity against
God
11. 34. who knows the *m*. of the Lord,
1 *Cor*. 2. 16.
12. 16. be of same *m*. one to another
1 *Cor*. 1. 10. joined together in *m*.
2 *Cor*. 8. 12. first a willing *m*. it
13. 11. be of one *m*. live in peace,
Phil. 1. 27, & 2. 2, & 4. 2; 1 *Pet*. 3. 8.
1 *Tim*. 1. 7. of faith and sound *m*.
Tit. 1. 15. their *m*. and conscience are
defiled
1 *Pet*. 5. 2. not for lucre but of a ready *m*.
MIND, verb, *Rom*. 8. 5. flesh *m*. things
of flesh
12. 16. *m*. not high things
Phil. 3. 16. *m*. the same things
19. who *m*. earthly things
MINDS, 2 *Cor*. 3. 14. their *m*. were
blinded
Phil. 4. 7. keep your hearts and *m*.
Heb. 10. 16. and in their *m*. I will write
12. 3. lest ye faint in your *m*.
2 *Pet*. 3. 1. stir up your pure *m*.
MINDED, *Rom*. 8. 6. to be carnally *m*.
is death, spiritually *m*. is peace
11. 20. be not high *m*. but fear
15. 5. the God of patience grant you
to be like *m*.
Tit. 2. 6. exhort to be sober *m*.
Jam. 1. 8. a double *m*. man, 4. 8.
Ps. 8. 4. what is man, that thou art
m. of him, and son of man visitest
him ? *Heb*. 2. 6.
Ps. 111. 5. ever *m*. of his covenant, 1
Chr. 16. 15.
115. 12. the Lord hath been *m*. of us,
8. 4.
2 *Tim*. 1. 4. being *m*. of thy tears
Heb. 11. 15. if been *m*. of that country
2 *Pet*. 3. 2. be *m*. of the words spoken
MINE, *Ps*. 18. 23. I kept myself from
m. iniquity
Ps. 50. 10. every beast of forest is *m*.
Songs 2. 16. my beloved is *m*.
Ezek. 18. 4. behold, all souls are *m*.
Mal. 3. 17. shall be *m*. saith the Lord
John 16. 15. all things that the Father
hath are *m*.
17. 10. all *m*. are thine, and thine
are *m*.
Rom. 12. 19. vengeance is *m*. I will
MINGLED, *Ex*. 9. 24. fire *m*. with the
hail
Ps. 102. 9. *m*. drink with weeping
Matt. 27. 34. gave vinegar *m*. with gall
Mark 15. 23. wine *m*. with myrrh
Luke 13. 1. whose blood Pilate had *m*.
Rev. 8. 7. hail and fire *m*. with blood
15. 2. a sea of glass *m*. with
MINISTER, *Josh*. 1. 1; *Luke* 4. 20.
Matt. 20. 26. let him be your *m*.
Acts 26. 16. to make thee a *m*. and a
Rom. 13. 4. he is the *m*. of God to

15. 8. Christ is a *m.* of circumcision
16. I be a *m.* of Jesus Christ to the Gentiles
Gal. 2. 17. is Christ the *m.* of sin
Eph. 3. 7. I made a *m.* according
1 *Tim.* 4. 6. shall be good *m.* of
Heb. 8. 2. a *m.* of the sanctuary
Ps. 103. 21. ye *m.* of his that do
104. 4. maketh his *m.* a flaming fire, *Heb.* 1, 7.
Is. 61. 6. men call you the *m.* of our G.
Joel. 1. 9. *m.* of the Lord mourn, 2. 17.
Luke 1. 2. from beginning *m.* of word
Rom. 13. 6. are G. *m.* attending
1 *Cor.* 3. 5. *m.* whom ye believed
4. 1. account of us as *m.* of Christ
2 *Cor.* 3. 6. made us able *m.* of new testament
6. 4. in all approve ourselves as *m.* of
11. 23. are *m.* of Christ, so am I
Rom. 15. 25. *m.* unto the saints, *Heb.* 6. 10.
27. *m.* to them in carnal things
1 *Cor.* 9. 13. who *m.* holy things
2 *Cor.* 9. 10. *m.* seed to sower
Eph. 4. 29. *m.* grace to hearers
1 *Pet.* 4. 11. if any man *m.* let
MINISTERED, *Matt.* 4. 11; *Luke* 8. 3; *Gal.* 3. 5; *Heb.* 6. 10; 2 *Pet.* 1. 11.
MINISTRATION, *Luke* 1. 23; *Acts* 6. 1, 2; 2 *Cor.* 3. 7, 8, & 9. 12, 13.
Heb. 1. 14. they all *m.* spirits
Rom. 15. 16. *m.* gospel of God, 12. 7.
Acts 6. 4. give ourselves to the *m.* of the
20. 24. I might finish my *m.* received of the Lord Jesus
2 *Cor.* 4. 1. we have *m.* faint not
5. 18. committed unto us the *m.* of reconciliation
6. 3. that the *m.* be not blamed
Col. 4. 17. take heed to *m.* thou hast re.
1 *Tim.* 1. 12. putting me into *m.*
2 *Tim.* 4. 5. make full proof of *m.*
Heb. 8. 6. hath obtained a more excellent *m.*
MIRACLE, *Ex.* 7. 9. Pharaoh speak, saying show a *m.*
Luke 23. 8. hoped to have seen some *m.*
MIRACLES, *Deut.* 11. 3. children not seen his *m.*
John 2. 11. this beginning of *m.* did Jesus in Cana
23. many believed when he saw the *m.* he did
3. 2. no man can do these *m.* except God be with him
6. 2. because they saw his *m.*
7. 31. will he do more *m.* than
9. 16. how can a sinner do such *m.*
Acts 2. 22. a man approved of God by *m.* and signs
6. 8. Stephen did great *m.* among the people
8. 13. wondered, beholding the *m.*
15. 12. declaring what *m.* God hath wrought
19. 11. God wrought special *m.* by hands of Paul
1 *Cor.* 12. 10. another working of *m.*
Heb. 2. 4. God bearing witness with *m.*
MIRTH. That which is vain, *Eccl.* 7. 4; *Prov.* 14. 13; *Eccl.* 2. 2; *Is.*

24. 8, 11; *Jer.* 7. 34. & 16. 9, & 25. 10; *Hos.* 2. 11; *Ezek.* 21. 10.
MISCHIEF sometimes signifies punishment, 2 *Kings* 7. 9; 16. 8. Falsehood, *Ps.* 7. 14. Vain and foolish things, *Ps.* 36. 4. Malice or vengeance, *Gen.* 42. 4, & 44. 29; *Ps.* 21. 11.
Job 15. 35. they conceive *m.* and, *Ps.* 7. 14.
Ps. 10. 14. thou beholdest *m.* and spite
28. 3. *m.* in their hearts, 10. 7.
36. 4. he deviseth *m.* on his bed
94. 20. frameth *m.* by a law
Prov. 10. 23. it is as sport to a fool to do *m.*
11. 27. seeks *m.* shall come to
24. 16. wicked shall fall into *m.* *Ps.* 7. 16.
Acts 13. 10. full of subtilty and *m.*
MISERY, *Job* 3. 20; *Lam.* 3. 19.
Judg. 10. 16. soul grieved for *m.* of Israel
Prov. 31. 7. drink and remember *m.* no more
Eccl. 8. 6. *m.* of man is great on
Rom. 3. 16. destruction and *m.* in all their ways
Job 16. 2. *m.* comforters are ye
1 *Cor.* 15. 19. of all men most *m.*
Rev. 3. 17. and knowest not that thou art wretched and *m.*
MITE, S, *Mark* 12. 42. a widow threw in two *m.* *Luke* 21. 2.
Luke 12. 59. till paid the last *m.*
MIXTURE, *Ps.* 75. 8. there is a cup, wine red, it is full of *m.*
John 19. 39. came Nicodemus, and brought a *m.* of myrrh and aloes
Rev. 14. 10. is poured out without *m.* into the cup
MOCK when fear cometh, *Prov.* 1. 26.
Job 21. 3. after I have spoken *m.* on
Prov. 14. 9. fools make *m.* at sin
Matt. 20. 19. shall deliver him to Gentiles to *m.* him
Mark 10. 34. *m.* him and scourge him
MOCKED, 1 *Kings* 18. 27. Elijah *m.*
2 *Chr.* 36. 16. they *m.* the messengers of God
MOCKER, *Prov.* 20. 1. wine is a *m.* and
Is. 28. 22. be not *m.* lest hands
Jude 18. there should be *m.* in the last
MOCKETH, *Prov.* 17. 5. whoso *m.* the poor
30. 17. eye that *m.* his father
Jer. 20. 7. every one *m.* me
MOCKING, *Gen.* 21. 9. Sarah saw son of Hagar *m.*
Acts 2. 13. others *m.* said, these men are full
MODERATION be known unto all. *Phil.* 4. 5.
MODEST apparel, 1 *Tim.* 2. 9.
MOMENT, *Ex.* 33. 5; *Is.* 27. 3.
Num. 16. 21. consume them in a *m.* 45.
Job 7. 18. try him every *m.*
26. 5. joy of hypocrite is but for a *m.*
Ps. 30. 5. his anger endureth but for a *m.*
Is. 26. 20. hide thee for a little *m.*
54. 7. for a small *m.* have I forsaken
1 *Cor.* 15. 52. in a *m.* twinkling of an
2 *Cor.* 4. 17. affliction but for a *m.*

MONEY, *Gen.* 23. 9. & 31. 15.
Eccl. 7. 12. wisdom is a defence, *m.* is a defence
   10. 19. *m.* answers all things
Is. 55. 1. he that no *m.* come
   2. why spend *m.* for that which is not bread
Mic. 3. 11. prophets divine for *m.*
Acts 8. 20. *m.* perish with thee
1 *Tim.* 6. 10. the love of *m.* is the root of all evil
MORNING, *Gen.* 19. 15. when the *m.* arose
Ex. 7. 15. get thee to Pharaoh in *m.*
   16. 7. in *m.* ye shall see glory of the L.
Lev. 6. 9. burning all night till the *m.*
2 *Sam.* 23. 4. and he shall be as the light of the *m.* when the sun riseth, even a *m.* without clouds
1 *Kings* 18. 26. called on Baal from *m.* to noon
Job 11. 17. shine forth and be as the *m.*
Ps. 5. 3. my voice shalt thou hear in the *m.* Lord, in the *m.* will I direct my prayer to thee
   30. 5. but joy cometh in the *m.*
   90. 5. in the *m.* they are like grass
   130. 6. than they that watch for *m.*
   143. 8. thy loving-kindness in the *m.*
Songs 6. 10. who is she looketh forth *m.*
Is. 14. 12. how art thou fallen, O Lucifer, son of the *m.*
   21. 12. watchman said, *m.* cometh
   58. 8. thy light breaketh forth as *m.*
Hos. 6. 3. his going forth is as the *m.*
   4. your goodness is as a *m.* cloud
MORNING, early in the, *Is.* 5. 11. woe to them that rise *early in the m.*
Matt. 20. 1. who went *early in the m.*
Mark 16. 2. *early in the m.* came to the sepulchre, *Luke* 24. 1.
Luke 21. 38. people came *early in the m.*
MORNING, every, *Ex.* 16. 21. gathered manna *every m.*
Job 7. 18. shouldst visit him *every m.*
Lam. 3. 23. Lord's mercies new *every m.*
MORNING, until the, 1 *Sam.* 3. 15. and Samuel lay *until the m.*
Prov. 7. 18. take our fill of love *until m.*
Is. 38. 13. I reckoned *until the m.*
MORNING star and stars, *Job* 38. 7. when *m.-stars* sang together
Rev. 2. 28. I will give him the *m. star*
   22. 16. I Jesus am the bright *m. star*
MORROW, *Ex.* 8. 23, & 16. 23.
Prov. 27. 1. boast not of *to-m.*
Is. 22. 13. *to-m.* we shall die, 1 *Cor.* 15. 32.
   56. 12. *to-m.* shall be as this day and more abundant
Matt. 6. 34. no thought for *to-m.*
Jam. 4. 14. know not what be on the *m.*
MORSEL, *Job* 31. 17. eaten my *m.* alone
Prov. 17. 1. better a dry *m.* and quietness
Heb. 12. 16. for one *m.* sold his birthright
MORSELS, *Ps.* 147. 17. casteth forth his ice like *m.*
MORTAL man be just, *Job* 4. 17.
Rom. 6. 12. not sin reign in *m.* body
   8. 11. raised Christ quicken your *m.*

bodies
1 *Cor.* 15. 53. this *m.* put on immortality
MORTALITY, 2 *Cor.* 5. 4. *m.* swallowed
MORTIFY, *Rom.* 8. 13. if ye *m.* deeds of the body
MOTH, *Job* 4. 19, & 27. 18; *Ps.* 39. 11; *Is.* 50. 9, & 51. 8; *Hos.* 5. 12; *Matt.* 6. 20; *Luke* 12. 33.
MOTHER, *Gen.* 3. 20, & 21. 21; *Judg.* 5. 7; 2 *Sam.* 20. 19; 1 *Kings* 3. 27; *Gal.* 4. 26.
Gen. 24. 60. *m.* of thousands of millions
Judg. 5. 28. the *m.* of Sisera looked out at a window
Job 17. 14. to the worm thou art my *m.*
Ps. 27. 10. father and *m.* forsake
   71. 6. took me out of my *m.* bowels, 139. 13.
Matt. 12. 49. behold my *m.* and my
   20. 20. *m.* of Zebedee's children
Gal. 4. 26. Jerusalem which is the *m.* of us all
Rev. 17. 5. the *m.* of harlots and
MOTHER, his, *Prov.* 10. 1. a foolish son is the heaviness of *his m.*
Prov. 15. 20. foolish man despiseth *his m.*
   29. 15. a child left bringeth *his m.* to shame
Is. 66. 13. as one whom *his m.* comforteth
Matt. 12. 46. *his m.* stood without *Mark* 3. 31; *Luke* 8. 19.
Luke 1. 15. filled with Holy Ghost from *his m.* womb
   7. 12. the only son of *his m.*
John 19. 25. *his m.* stood by the cross of Jesus
MOTHER, thy, *Matt.* 12. 47. behold *thy m.* and thy brethren, *Mark* 3. 32. *Luke* 8. 20; *John* 19. 27.
2 *Tim.* 1. 5. faith which dwelt in *thy m.* Eunice
MOTIONS, *Rom.* 7. 5.
MOUNT, *Gal.* 4. 24. one from *m.* Sinai, is Agar
   25. Agar is *m.* Sinai in Arabia
Heb. 12. 18. not come to the *m.* might be touched
MOUNT, in or into, *Gen.* 24. 14. *in the m.* of the Lord it shall be seen
Ex. 19. 12. Lord said to Moses, come *into m.*
   24. 18. Moses was *in the m.* forty days and forty nights. *Deut.* 9. 9; 10. 10.
   25. 40. look thou make them after their pattern showed thee *in the m.* 26. 30; 27. 8; *Heb.* 8. 5.
Deut. 32. 50. and die *in the m.* as Aaron died *in m.*
Acts 7. 38. angel spake *in m.* Sinai
2 *Pet.* 1. 18. when we were with him *in the holy m.*
MOUNTAIN, *Gen.* 19. 17. escape to the *m.*; 19. I cannot escape to *m.*
Ex. 19. 3. the Lord called of him out of the *m.* saying
   20. 18. all people saw the *m.* smoking
Deut. 3. 25. see that goodly *m.* and Lebanon
   4. 11. *m.* burnt with fire
Josh. 4. 12. give me this *m.* ; 17. 18. the

m. shall be thine
Judg. 1. 19. he drave out the inhabitants of the *m.*
2 *Kings* 6. 17. *m.* full of horses and
chariots
Ps. 30. 7. made my *m.* stand strong
Dan. 2. 35. stone became a great *m.*
45. the stone was cut out of the *m.*
without hands
Matt. 17. 20. faith, as a grain of mustard—say to this *m.* 21. 21.
Rev. 6. 14. every *m.* and island were
removed from
MOUNTAIN, high, *Matt.* 4. 8. the devil
taketh him up into an exceeding
high m. and showeth kingdoms of
the world, *Luke* 4. 5.
MOUNTAIN, in the, or in this, *Gen.* 19.
30. Lot went from Zoar and dwelt
in the *m.*
Is. 25. 6. in *this m.* shall the Lord make
a feast
7. he will destroy *in this m.* face of
John 4. 20. our fathers worshipped *in
this m.*
21. neither *in this m.* nor Jerusalem
worship the Father
MOUNTAINS, *Ps.* 46. 2. though the *m*
be carried into the midst of the sea
Ps. 76. 4. more glorious than *m.* of prey
90. 2. before *m.* were brought forth
125. 2. *m.* round about Jerusalem
144. 5. touch the *m.* shall smoke
Is. 40. 12. weighed the *m.* in scales
52. 7. how beautiful on the *m.*
54. 10. for the *m.* shall depart
Ezek. 34. 6. my sheep wandered through
all the *m.*
Amos 4. 13. he that formeth the *m.*
Nah. 1. 5. the *m.* quake at him
1 *Cor.* 13. 2. faith, I could remove *m.*
Rev. 16. 20. every island, and the *m*
were not found
Heb. 11. 38. they wandered in deserts
and in the *m.*
Ps. 72. 16. shall be an handful of corn
on top of the *m.*
MOURN, *Neh.* 8. 9; *Job* 5. 11.
Is. 61. to comfort all that *m.*
Matt. 5. 4. blessed they that m.
Jam. 4. 9. afflicted, *m.* and weep
Matt. 11. 17. we have *m.* and ye have
not lamented
Cor. 5. 2. have not rather *m.*
Eccl. 12. 5. *m.* go about streets
Is. 57. 18. and restore comforts unto
his *m.*
Ps. 30. 11. turned my *m.* into
Is. 22. 12. in that day the Lord called
to m.
61. 3. to give oil of joy for *m.*
Jer. 9. 17. call for the *m.* women
31. 13. turn their *m.* into joy
Joel. 2. 12. turn to me with *m.*
Jam. 4. 9. laughter be turned into *m.*
MOUTH of babes and sucklings, *Ps.* 8. 2.
Ps. 37. 30. the *m.* of the righteous speak-
eth wisdom
Prov. 10. 14. *m.* of foolish near destruc-
tion
31. *m.* of just brings wisdom
12. 6. *m.* of upright shall deliver them

14. 3. *m.* of fools is rod of pride
15. 2. *m.* of fools pours out
18. 7. a fool's *m.* is his destruction,
and snare of soul
22. 14. *m.* of a strange woman is a
deep pit
Lam. 3. 38. out of *m.* of most High
Matt. 12. 34. out of abundance of heart
m. speaketh
Luke 21. 15. I will give you a *m.* and
wisdom
Rom. 10. 10. with *m.* confession
15. 6. with one mind and *m.* glorify
God
Prov. 13. 3. keepeth his *m.* keeps
Lam. 3. 29. putteth *m.* in dust
Mal. 2. 7. they shall seek the law at
his *m.*
Ps. 17. 3. that my *m.* shall not transgress
39. 1. keep my *m.* with bridle
49. 3. my *m.* speak of wisdom
51. 15. my *m.* shall show forth thy
praise, 63. 5.
71. 15. my *m.* shall show forth thy
righteousness
Eph. 6. 19. I may open my *m.* boldly
Ps. 81. 10. open thy *m.* wide
103. 5. satisfies *m.* with good things
Prov. 31. 8. open *m.* for the dumb
Eccl. 5. 6. suffer not *m.* to cause thy
flesh to sin
MOVE, *Ex.* 11. 7; *Judg.* 13. 25.
Acts 17. 28. in him, we live, *m.*
20. 24. but none of these things *m.*
me, neither
Ps. 15. 5. shall never be *m.* 21. 7, & 46.
5, & 55. 22, & 62. 2, 6. & 66. 9. &
112. 6. & 121. 3; *Prov.* 12. 3.
Col. 1. 23. not *m.* from hope of gospel
1 *Thess.* 3. 3. no man be *m.* by these
afflictions
Heb. 12. 28. a kingdom which cannot
be *m.*
2 *Pet.* 1. 21. spake as *m.* by Holy Ghost
MOVEABLE. *Prov.* 5. 6.
MULTITUDE, *Gen.* 16. 10. & 28. 3; *Ex.*
12. 38, & 23. 2; *Num.* 11. 4.
Job 32. 7. *m.* of years shall teach wisdom
Ps. 5. 7. *m.* of mercies
10. *m.* of transgressions
33. 16. no king saved by the *m.* of an
host
51. 1. according to the *m.* of thy tender mercies, 69. 13, 16. & 106. 7, 45.
94. 19. in *m.* of thy thoughts
Prov. 10. 19. in *m.* of words there
wanteth not sin
11. 14. in *m.* of counsellors is safety,
15. 22, & 24. 6.
Eccl. 5. 3. the *m.* of business—by *m.*
of words
Jam. 5. 20. hide a *m.* of sins, 1 *Pet.* 4. 8.
MURDER, *Rom.* 1. 29; *Matt.* 15. 19;
Gal. 5. 21; *Rev.* 9. 21.
Job 24. 14. *m.* rising with light
John 8. 44. devil was a *m.* from the
beginning
Hos. 9. 13. bring forth children to the *m.*
1 *Pet.* 4. 15. none suffer as a *m.*
2 *John* 3. 15. who hateth his brother is
m. no *m.* hath eternal life abiding

in him
MURMUR, to complain, to be discontent
Deut. 1. 27; Ps. 106. 25; Ex. 16. 7.
John 6. 43. Jesus said, m. not among
yourselves
1 Cor. 10. 10. neither m. as sons
Ex. 15. 24. the people m. against Moses,
17. 3.
Matt. 20. 11. received a penny they m.
MURMURERS, Jude 16. these are m.
complainers
MURMURINGS, Ex. 16. 7. he heareth
your m.
Phil. 2. 14. do all things without m. and
disputings
MUSE, Ps. 39. 3. & 143. 5.
MUSTARD seed, Matt. 13. 31, & 17. 20.
MUZZLE, Deut. 25. 4; 1 Cor. 9. 9.
MYSTERY, of the kingdom, Mark 4. 11.
Rom. 11. 25. ignorant of this m.
    16. 25. according to the revelation of
    the m.
1 Cor. 2. 7. wisdom of God in a m.
    4. 1. stewards of the m. of God
    13. 2. prophecy and understand all m.
    14. 2. in spirit he speaketh m.
    15. 51. I show you a m. we shall not
    all sleep
Eph. 1. 9. make known the m. of his
    3. 4. my knowledge of m.
    9. the fellowship of the m.
    5. 32. this is a great m. concerning
    Christ
    6. 19. make known m. of gospel
Col. 1. 26. m. which hath been hid
    27. glory of this m. among the Gentile
    2. 2. to acknowledging m. of God
    4. 3. utterance to speak the m. of C.
2 Thess. 2. 7. m. of iniquity works
1 Tim. 3. 9. hold the m. of faith
    16. great is the m. of godliness
Rev. 1. 20. the m. of the seven stars
    thou sawest
    10. 7. m. of God shall be finished
    17. 5. m. of Babylon the great mother,
    7.

NAIL, Judg. 4. 21, & 5. 26.
Judg. 4. 22. the n. was in his temples
Ezra 9. 8. give a n. in holy place
Eccl. 12. 11. n. fastened by the master
    of assemblies
Is. 22. 23. as a n. in a sure place
Zech. 10. 4. out of him came n.
John 20. 25. put my finger into the
    print of the n.
NAILING, Col. 2. 14. he took it out of
    the way, n. it to his cross
NAKED, Gen. 2. 25, & 3. 7, 11.
Ex. 32. 25. the people were n.
2 Chr. 28. 19. made Judah n.
Job 1. 21. n. came I out of my mother's
Matt. 25. 36. I was n. ye clothed me,
1 Cor. 4. 11. hungry, thirsty, and n.
2 Cor. 5. 3. may not be found n.
Heb. 4. 13. all things are n. and
Rev. 3. 17. art miserable, poor, blind
    and n.
    16. 15. keep garments lest he walk n.
NAKEDNESS, Rom. 8. 35. shall n.
    separate us
2 Cor. 11. 27. fastings in cold and n.

Rev. 3. 18. shame of n. not appear
NAME, Ex. 34. 14; Lev. 18. 21.
Ps. 20. 1. let n. of God of Jacob defend
    109. 13. let their n. be blotted out
Prov. 10. 7. n. of wicked shall rot
    22. 1. a good n. rather to be chosen
Eccl. 7. 1. good n. is better than precious
    ointment
Is. 55. 13. shall be to the Lord for a sign
    and a n.
    56. 5. a n. better than that of sons and
    daughters
    62. 2. shalt be called by new n.
Jer. 13. 11. for a people, and a n.
Jer. 32. 20. made thee a n. this day
    33. 9. shall be to me a n. of joy, a
    praise and honour
Mic. 4. 5. we will in the n. of the Lord
Matt. 10. 41. a prophet in the n. of a
Luke 6. 22. cast out n. as evil
Acts 4. 12. none other n. under heaven
Rom. 2. 24. n. of God blasphemed
Eph. 1. 21. every n. that is n. Phil. 2. 9.
Col. 3. 17. do all in n. of the Lord Jesus
2 Tim. 2. 19. n. the n. of Christ depart
Heb. 1. 4. a more excellent n. than
1 Pet. 4. 14. if ye be reproached for the
    n. of Christ
1 John 3. 23. should believe on the n.
    of his Son
    5. 13. believe on n. of the son of God
Rev. 2. 17. n. written which no man
    3. 1. a n. that livest and art dead
    12. write on him n. of my God, and n.
    of the city of God
    14. 1. Father's n. on foreheads, 22. 4.
NAME, his, Ps. 76. 1. his n. is great in
    Israel
    72. 17. n. shall endure for ever
    106. 8. saved them for his n. sake
Prov. 30. 4. what is his n. and what
    son's n.
Is. 9. 6. his n. be called Wonderful
Zech. 14. 9. Lord shall be one, and his
    n. one
John 20. 31. have life through his n.
Rev. 3. 5. confess n. before my Father
    13. 17. number of his n. 15. 2.
NAME, my, Ex. 23. 21. my n. is in him
    3. 15. this is my n. for ever, and mem
    orial unto all
Judg. 13. 18. askest after my n. Gen
    32. 29.
Is. 48. 9. for n. sake I will defer ange
Ezek. 20. 9. wrought for my n. sake
    14. 22.
Mal. 1. 14. n. is dreadful among th
    heathen
    2. 2. lay to heart to give glory unto n
    n. saith the Lord
Matt. 10. 22. hated of all for my n. sak
John 14. 13. ask in my n. 15. 16, & 16. 2
    16. 24. asked nothing in my n.
Acts 9. 15. chosen vessel to bear my
Rev. 2. 3. for my n. hast laboured
    13. holdest fast my n.
    3. 8. not denied my n.
NAME, thy, 2 Chr. 14. 11. in thy n. we g
Ps. 8. 1. how excellent thy n. will p
    their trust in thee
    75. 1. thy n. is near, thy wondro
    works declare

138. 2. magnified word above all *thy n.*
Songs 1. 3. *thy n.* is as ointment
Is. 26. 8. desire of our soul is to *thy n.*
Is. 64. 7. none that calleth on *thy n.*
   stirreth up himself
Jer. 14. 7. do it for *thy n.* sake, 21; Dan.
   9. 19; Josh. 7. 9; Ps. 79. 9.
Mic. 6. 9. man of wisdom see *thy n.*
John 17. 12. I kept them in *thy n.* 26.
Ex. 23. 13. make no mention of the *n.*
   of other gods, Deut. 12. 3; Ps. 16. 4.
   28. 12. Aaron bear their *n.* before the
   Lord
Ps. 49. 11. call land after own *n.*
   147. 4. stars he calls by their *n.*
Luke 10. 20. rejoice, your *n.* are written
   in heaven
Rev. 3. 4. hast a few *n.* in Sardis
NARROW, 1 Kings 6. 4; Prov. 23. 27;
   Is. 28. 20, & 49. 19.
Matt. 7. 14. *n.* is the way that leadeth
   to life
NATION, Gen. 15. 14. & 21. 13.
Gen. 20. 4. wilt thou slay a righteous *n.*
Num. 14. 12. and will make of thee a
   great *n.*
2 Sam. 7. 23. what *n.* is like thy people
Ps. 33. 12. blessed is the *n.* whose God
   is the Lord
   147. 20. not dealt so with any *n.*
Is. 1. 4. ah, sinful *n.* people laden
   2. 4. *n.* shall not lift sword against *n.*
   49. 7. whom the *n.* abhorreth
   66. 8. shall a *n.* be born at once
Jer. 2. 11. a *n.* changed their gods
Matt. 24. 7. *n.* shall rise against *n.*
   Mark 13. 8.
Luke 7. 5. he loveth our *n.* and
Acts 10. 35. in every *n.* he that fears G.
Rom. 10. 19. by a foolish *n.* I will anger
   you
Phil. 2. 15. midst of a crooked *n.*
Pet. 2. 9. ye are an holy *n.* Ex. 19. 6.
Rev. 5. 9. redeemed out of every *n.*
NATIONS, Gen. 10. 32. & 17. 4, 6, 16.
Deut. 26. 19. high above all *n.* 28. 1.
Is. 9. 20. that the *n.* may know them-
   selves men
   113. 4. Lord is high above all *n.*
   2. 2. all *n.* shall flow unto it
   40. 17. all *n.* before him are as nothing
   55. 5. *n.* that know thee not
Jer. 4. 2. *n.* shall bless themselves in
Zech. 2. 11. many *n.* be joined to the
   Lord in that day
Hag. 25. 32. before him shall be
   gathered all *n.*
Acts 14. 16. suffered all *n.* to walk
Rev. 21. 24. *n.* of them that are saved
NATURE (1) The natural method and
   course of things established in the
   world by God its Creator, Rom. 1.
   26, 27. (2) Reason, or the light
   implanted in the mind, Rom. 2.
   14. (3) Birth, or natural descent,
   Gal. 2. 15. (4) Common sense, and
   the custom of all nations, 1 Cor.
   11. 14. (5) Substance, or essence,
   Heb. 2. 16. (6) Our corrupt and
   sinful estate by our birth, being
   naturally inclined to all sorts of
   evil, Eph. 2. 3. (7) Holy and divine

qualities and dispositions, which
express and resemble the perfections
of God, 2 Pet. 1. 4. (8) In truth
and very deed, Gal. 4. 8.
NATURE, Rom. 2. 27; Jam. 3. 6.
Rom. 1. 26. into that against *n.*
   2. 14. do by *n.* things contained
   11. 24. olive-tree wild by *n.* contrary
   to *n.*
1 Cor. 11. 14. doth not *n.* itself teach you
Gal. 2. 15. Jews by *n.* and not sinners
   of the Gentiles
   4. 8. served by *n.* are no gods
Eph. 2. 3. by *n.* children of wrath
Heb. 2. 16. took not *n.* of angels
2 Pet. 1. 4. partakers of divine *n.*
NATURAL, Deut. 34. 7. nor his *n.* force
Rom. 1. 26. did change the *n.* use
   27. *n.* use of the woman
   31. without *n.* affection, 2 Tim. 3. 3.
1 Cor. 2. 14. *n.* man receiveth not things
   of the Spirit of God
   15. 44. it is sown a *n.* body, there is
   a *n.* body
Jam. 1. 23. his *n.* face in a glass
2 Pet. 2. 12. *n.* brute beasts speak evil
NATURALLY, Phil. 2. 20. *n.* care for
   your state
Jude 10. not *n.* as brute beasts
NAUGHT, Gen. 29. 15; Deut. 13. 17.
Prov. 20. 14. it is *n.* it is *n.* saith the
   buyer
Is. 41. 12. shall be as a thing of *n.*
   49. 4. I have spent my strength for *n.*
   52. 3. sold yourselves for *n. Ps.* 44. 12.
Amos 6. 13. rejoice in thing of *n.*
Luke 23. 11. Herod and his men set him
   at *n.*
Rom. 14. 10. why set at *n.* thy brother
Jam. 1. 21. all superfluity of *n.*
NAY, Matt. 5. 37. but let your communication be yea, yea, *n. n.* more
   cometh of evil, Jam. 5. 12.
Luke 16. 30. *n.* father Abraham
2 Cor. 1. 17. with me there should be
   yea, yea, *n. n.*
   18. word was not yea and *n.*
   19. the Son of God Jesus Christ was
   not yea, *n.*
NEAR, nigh, at hand, Gen. 19. 20; Ps.
   22. 11. The name of God is said to
   be *n. Ps.* 119. 151, & 148. 14; Is. 55.
   6. & 57. 19; Jer. 12. 2.
NEARER, Rom. 13. 11. our salvation *n.*
   than when we believed
NECESSARY, Job 23. 12. I esteemed
   his word more than *n.* food
Acts 13. 46. was *n.* the word first be
   spoken to you
1 Cor. 12. 22. members feeble are *n.*
Phil. 2. 25. *n.* to send Epaphras
Heb. 9. 23. *n.* patterns should be
   purified with these
NECESSITY, Rom. 12. 13. distributing
   to the *n.*
Rom. 9. 16. for *n.* is laid upon me, yea,
   woe is to me
2 Cor. 9. 7. give, not grudgingly, or of *n.*
Philem. 14. not be as it were of *n.* but
   willingly
Heb. 8. 3. it is of *n.* this man have some

what to offer
9. 16. there must of *n.* be the death
of the testator
NECESSITIES, *Acts* 20. 34. hands
ministered to my *n.*
1 *Cor.* 12. 12. I take pleasure in *n.*
NECK, S, *Songs* 1. 10; *Is.* 48. 4; *Rom.*
16. 4.
2 *Kings* 17. 14. harden *n. Neh.* 9. 16,
17; *Jer.* 7. 26, & 19. 15.
Acts 15. 10. to put a yoke on the *n.* of
the disciples
NEED of all these, *Matt.* 6. 32.
9. 12. whole *n.* not a physician
Luke 15. 7. righteous *n.* no repentance
Eph. 4. 28. give to him that *n.*
2 *Tim.* 2. 15. *n.* not be ashamed
Heb. 4. 16. grace to help in the time of *n.*
1 *Pet.* 1. 6. if *n.* be ye are in heaviness
through temptations
1 *John* 2. 27. *n.* not that any teach you
Rev. 3. 17. having *n.* of nothing
21. 23. no *n.* of sun
22. 5. *n.* no candle
NEEDS, *Matt.* 18. 7. *n.* be offences come
John 4. 4. must *n.* go through Samaria
Acts 1. 16. this scripture must *n.* have
been fulfilled
17. 3. that Christ must *n.* have
suffered
1 *Cor.* 5. 10. *n.* go out of the world
2 *Cor.* 11. 30. if I must *n.* glory
NEEDFUL. *Luke* 10. 42. one thing is *n.*
NEEDY, *Ps.* 9. 18. *n.* not be forgotten
72. 12. he shall deliver the *n.* 13.
82. 3. do justice to the afflicted and
n. 4.
113. 7. lifts *n.* out of dunghill
Is. 14. 30. *n.* lie down in safety
Jer. 22. 16. he judgeth the cause of the
n. 5. 28.
NEGLECT to near, *Matt.* 18. 17.
1 *Tim.* 4. 14. *n.* not gift in thee
Heb. 2. 3. if we *n.* so great salvation
NEIGHBOUR, *Ex.* 3. 22. & 11. 2.
Ex. 20. 16. not bear false witness against
thy *n.*
Lev. 19. 13. shall not defraud *n.*
17. not hate *n.* in heart
18. love *n.* as thyself, *Matt.* 19. 19, &
22. 39; *Rom.* 13. 9; *Gal.* 5. 14;
Jam. 2. 8; *Matt.* 7. 12.
Ps. 15. 3. nor doth evil to his *n.*
Prov. 11. 9. an hypocrite with his mouth
destroyeth his *n.*
·27. 10. better is a *n.* near
Jer. 22. 13. useth his *n.* service without
wages
31. 34. teach no more every man his
n. Heb. 8. 11.
Zech. 8. 17. let none of you imagine evil
against his *n.*
Luke 10. 29. who is my *n.* 36.
Rom. 15. 2. every one please his *n.*
NEIGH. To make a noise like a horse.
An enticement to unchastity is so
called, *Jer.* 5. 8, & 8. 16, & 13. 27.
NEST, *Job* 29. 18; *Ps.* 84. 3; *Prov.* 27.
8; *Is.* 10. 14; *Hab.* 2. 9; *Matt.* 8. 20.
NET. Allusions are frequent to the
snare of the fowler, who artfully
spreads his nets to catch the birds,

Job 18. 8. & 19. 6; *Ps.* 9. 15, & 25.
15, & 31. 4, & 35. 7, 8, & 57. 6, & 66.
11; *Is.* 51. 20; *Hab.* 1. 15, 16; *Matt.*
13. 47; *Ps.* 141. 10; *Eccl.* 7. 26.
NEW things Lord make, *Num.* 16. 30.
Judg. 5. 8. they chose *n.* gods, *Deut.*
32. 17.
Eccl. 1. 9. no *n.* thing under the sun, 10
Is. 65. 17. *n.* heavens and *n.* earth, 66.
22; 2 *Pet.* 3. 13; *Rev.* 21. 1, 5.
Jer. 31. 22. created a *n.* thing on
Lam. 3. 23. his mercies are *n.* evening
and morning
Ezek. 11. 19. I will put a *n.* spirit within you
18. 31. make you a *n.* heart and a *n.*
spirit
36. 26. a *n.* heart I will give, and a *n.*
spirit put into you
Matt. 9. 16. putteth *n.* cloth on old
17. *n.* wine in old bottles
13. 52. out of treasure things *n.* & old
26. 28. this is my blood of the new
testament, *Mark* 14. 24; *Luke* 22.
20; 1 *Cor.* 11. 25.
29. until I drink it *n.* with you, *Mark*
14. 25.
Mark 1. 27. what *n.* doctrine, *Acts* 17. 29.
John 13. 34. *n.* commandment, 1 *John*
2. 7, 8.
Acts 17. 21. to hear some *n.* thing
1 *Cor.* 5. 7. ye may be a *n.* lump
2 *Cor.* 5. 17. it in Christ he is *n.* creature
Gal. 6. 15. circumcision nor uncircumcision, but a *n.* creature
Eph. 4. 24. put on *n.* man, *Col.* 3. 10.
Heb. 9. 15. Mediator of *n.* testament
10. 20. by a *n.* and living way
1 *Pet.* 2. 2. as *n.* born babes desire milk
1 *John* 2. 7. I write no *n.* command
8. a *n.* commandment I write unto
you
Rev. 2. 17. a *n.* name written, 3. 12; *Is.*
62. 12.
5. 9. they sung a *n.* song, 14. 3; *Ps.*
33. 3.
21. 1. I saw a *n.* heaven and a *n.* earth
5. he said, behold, I make all things *n.*
NEWNESS, *Rom.* 6. 4. walk in *n.* of life
7. 6. serve in *n.* of spirit, not
NEWS, *Prov.* 25. 25. good *n.* from far
country
NIGH, *Lev.* 25. 49; *Num.* 24. 17.
Deut. 4. 7. who hath God so *n.* then
30. 14. word is *n.* thee, *Rom.* 10. 8.
Ps. 34. 18. Lord is *n.* unto them of
broken heart
85. 9. salvation is *n.* them that
145. 18. the Lord is *n.* unto all them
that call
Matt. 15. 8. draweth *n.* with mouth, *I.*
29. 13.
Eph. 2. 13. *n.* by blood of Christ
17. peace to them are *n. Is.* 57. 19
Phil. 2. 27. sick, *n.* unto death
Heb. 6. 8. rejected is *n.* unto cursing
NIGHT, *Gen.* 1. 5, 14. & 26. 24.
Ex. 12. 42. this that *n.* of the Lord
Ps. 19. 2. and *n.* unto *n.* showeth knowledge
30. 5. weeping endure for à *n.*
139. 11. *n.* be light about me

Is. 21. 11. what of *n.* what of *n.*
Jer. 14. 8. as a wayfaring man to tarry for a *n.*
Luke 6. 12. continue all *n.* in prayer
12. 20. this *n.* thy soul required
John 9. 4. *n.* cometh when no man can work
Rom. 13. 12. *n.* is far spent, day
1 *Thess.* 5. 5. children not of *n.* nor of darkness
Rev. 21. 25. no *n.* there, 22. 5.
NIGHT, by, *Ps.* 134. 1. *by n.* stand in the, *Songs* 3. 1; *John* 3. 2, & 7. 50. & 19. 39.
Job 35. 10. giveth songs in the *n.*
Ps. 16. 7. instruct me in *n.* seasons
42. 8. in *n.* his song be with me
77. 6. call to remembrance my song in the *n.*
119. 55. remember thy name in *n.*
Is. 26. 9. soul desired thee in *n.*
Is. 30. 29. shall have a song as in *n.*
59. 10. stumble at noon-day as in *n.*
John 11. 10. if a man walk in *n.* 9. 4.
1 *Thess.* 5. 7. they that sleep in *n.* are drunk in *n.*
Ps. 63. 6. *n.* watches, 119. 148.
NOBLE, *Esth.* 6. 9; *Jer.* 2. 21; *Luke* 19. 12; *Acts* 17. 11; *Ex.* 24. 11; *Num.* 21. 18.
Neh. 3. 5. *n.* put not their necks to 13. 17. I contended with *n.* of Judah
Ps. 149. 8. bind *n.* with fetters
Prov. 8. 16. by me princes rule and *n.*
Eccl. 10. 17. blessed land when king is son of *n.*
1 *Cor.* 1. 26. not many *n.* called
NOISE, *Ex.* 20. 18. heard *n.* of trumpet
Ps. 42. 7. at the *n.* water-spouts
66. 1. make a joyful *n.* to God
93. 4. Lord mightier than *n.* of
Is. 9. 5. battle with confused *n.*
2 *Pet.* 3. 10. the heavens shall pass away with great *n.*
Rev. 6. 1. I heard the *n.* of thunder
NOISOME, *Ps.* 91. 3; *Rev.* 16. 2.
NOSE, *Prov.* 30. 33; *Is.* 65. 5.
Is. 2. 22. breath in *n.* *Lam.* 4. 20.
NOTHING, *Gen.* 11. 6; *Ex.* 9. 4. & 12. 10; *Num.* 6. 4. & 16. 26; *Josh.* 11. 15.
2 *Sam.* 24. 24. Lord which cost me *n.*
1 *Kings* 8. 9. *n.* in ark save tables
Neh. 8. 10. for whom *n.* is prepared
Job 6. 21. for now ye are *n.*
8. 9. know *n.* ; 26. 7. hangs earth on *n.*
34. 9. profits a man *n.*
Ps. 17. 3. tried me and shall find *n.*
39. 5. my age is *n.* before thee
49. 17. when dieth shall carry *n.* away
119. 165. peace *n.* offend them
Prov. 13. 4. the sluggard desireth and hath *n.*
7. maketh himself rich and hath *n.*
Is. 40. 17. nations *n.* less than *n.*
Jer. 10. 24. thou bring me to *n.*
Lam. 1. 12. is it *n.* to you, all ye
Hag. 2. 3. comparison of it as *n.*
Matt. 27. 12. he answered *n.* *Mark* 14. 69, 61; 15. 3, 4, 5.
19. have thou *n.* to do with that just man

34. when Pilate saw that he could prevail *n.*
Mark 6. 8. take *n.* for journey, *Luke* 9. 3.
Luke 1 37. with God *n.* is impossible
5. 5. have toiled all night and taken *n.* *John* 21. 3.
7. 42. they had *n.* to pay
11. 6. I have *n.* to set before him
John 6. 63. the Spirit quickeneth, the flesh profiteth *n.*
John 8. 28. I do *n.* of myself, but
14. 30. the prince of this world hath *n.* in me
15. 15. without me ye can do *n.*
1 *Cor.* 1. 19. bring to *n.* the understanding
13. 2. I am *n.* 2. *Cor.* 12. 11.
2 *Cor.* 6. 10. as having *n.*
1 *Tim.* 6. 7. brought *n.* into world
Jam. 1. 4. wanting *n.*
Phil. 4. 6. be careful for *n.*
NOTHING, in, *Phil.* 1. 20. *in n.* I shall be ashamed
Phil. 1. 28. *n.* terrified by your adversaries
NOTHING, of, *Rev.* 3. 17. I am rich, increased, and have need of *n.*
NOURISH. To feed or maintain, *Gen.* 47. 12. To educate or bring up, *Acts* 7. 21. To cause to grow, *Is.* 44. 14. To instruct, 1 *Tim.* 4. 6. To cherish and comfort, *Ruth* 4. 15.
NUMBER our days, *Ps.* 90 12.
Is. 65. 12. I will *n.* you to the sword
Rev. 7. 9. a multitude which no man could *n.*
Is. 53. 12. *n.* with transgressors
Dan. 5. 26. God hath *n.* thy kingdom
Hos. 1. 10. cannot be *n.* *Jer.* 33. 22.
Job 14. 16. thou *n.* my steps
Ps. 71. 15. not knowing *n.* of it
Rev. 13. 17. *n.* of his *n.* 18.

OATH is a solemn action, whereby we call upon God, the Searcher of hearts, to witness the truth of what we affirm, for the ending of strife or controversies, *Heb.* 6. 16.
OATH, *Gen.* 24. 8. & 26. 3, 28.
1 *Sam.* 14. 26. people feared the *o.*
2 *Sam.* 21. 7. Lord's *o.* was between
2 *Chr.* 15. 15. all Judah rejoiced at the *o.* of God
Eccl. 8. 2. keep commandment in regard of the *o.* God
9. 2. as he that feareth an *o.*
Ezek. 16. 59. despised *o.* 17. 18, 19.
Luke 1. 73. *o.* he sware to fathers
Heb. 6. 16. *o.* for confirmation
Jam. 5. 12. swear not by the earth nor by any other *o.*
OBEY, *Gen.* 27. 8; *Ex.* 5. 2.
Deut. 11. 27. a blessing if ye *o.* commandments
13. 4. walk after the Lord, and *o.* his
Josh. 24. 24. his voice will we *o.*
1 *Sam.* 12. 14. serve him and *o.* his voice
15. 22. to *o.* is better than sacrifice
Jer. 7. 23. *o.* my voice and I will be your God

Jer. 26. 13. amend ways and *o. Zech.* 6. 15.

Matt. 8. 27. is this, that winds and sea *o.* him? *Mark* 4. 41; *Luke* 8. 25.

Mark 1. 27. the unclean spirits *o.* him

Acts 5. 29. ought to *o.* God rather

Rom. 2. 8. contentious and *o.* not

6. 16. his servants ye are whom ye *o.*

17. *o.* from heart that doctrine

Eph. 6. 1. children *o.* parents in the Lord, *Col.* 3. 20.

Col. 3. 22. servants *o.* masters

2 *Thess.* 1. 8. that *o.* not gospel of

3. 14. if any man *o.* not in word

Tit. 3. 1. put in mind to *o.* magistrates

Heb. 5. 9. of salvation to all who *o.* him

13. 17. *o.* them that have rule

Jam. 3. 3. put bits in horses' mouths, that they may *o.*

1 *Pet.* 3. 1. if any *o.* not the word

6. Sarah *o.* Abraham, calling him lord

4. 17. end of them that *o.* not gospel

OBEYETH, *Is.* 50. 10. *o.* voice, *Jer.* 4. 3.

Jer. 7. 28. this nation *o.* not the Lord

11. 3. cursed be the man that *o.* not the words of

OBEYING, 1 *Pet.* 1. 22. purified in *o.* truth

OBEDIENCE, *Rom.* 1. 5. *o.* to faith among all

5. 19. by *o.* of one many were made righteous

6. 16. yield *o.* to righteousness

16. 19. your *o.* is come abroad unto all men

26. mystery known for the *o.* of faith

1 *Cor.* 14. 34. women commanded to be under *o.*

2 *Cor.* 7. 15. remember *o.* of you

10. 5. every thought to *o.* of Christ

6. revenge diso. when *o.* is fulfilled

Heb. 5. 8. learned *o.* by things

1 *Pet.* 1. 2. sanctification of spirit unto *o.*

OBEDIENT, *Ex.* 24. 7. will do and be *o.*

Num. 27. 20. children of Israel may be *o.*

Deut. 4. 30. be *o.* to his voice

Deut. 8. 20. perish because not *o.* to the Lord your God

2 *Sam.* 22. 45. strangers *o.* to me

Prov. 25. 12. so is a wise reprover upon an *o.* ear

Is. 1. 19. if ye be *o.* shall eat good

42. 24. were not *o.* to his law

Acts 6. 7. priests were *o.* to faith

Rom. 15. 18. to make Gentiles *o.* by word and deed

2 *Cor.* 2. 9. be *o.* in all things

Eph. 6. 5. servants be *o.* to masters

Phil. 2. 8. he became *o.* to death

Tit. 2. 5. women be *o.* to their husbands

9. servants to be *o.* to their masters

1 *Pet.* 1. 14. as *o.* children not fashioning

OBEISANCE, *Gen.* 37. 7. your sheaves made *o.* to my sheaf

Gen. 37. 9. the sun, moon, and eleven stars made *o.* to me

43. 28. made *o.* to Joseph

1 *Kings* 1. 16. Bath-sheba *o.* to David

2 *Chr.* 24. 17. princes of Judah made *o.* to the king

OBSERVE, *Ex.* 12. 17. & 34. 11.

Gen. 37. 11. his father *o.* saying

Ex. 12. 42. a night to be much *o.*

Ps. 107. 43. whose is wise and will *o.* these things

119. 34. *o.* it with whole heart

Prov. 23. 26. let thine eyes *o.* my ways

Jonah 2. 28. *o.* lying vanities forsake

Matt. 28. 20. teaching them to *o.*

Mark 6. 20. Herod feared John and *o.* him

10. 20. all things I *o.* from my youth

Gal. 4. 10. ye *o.* days and months

OBTAIN favour of the Lord, *Prov.* 8. 35.

Is. 35. 10. *o.* joy and gladness, 51. 11.

Luke 20. 35. worthy to *o.* that

1 *Cor.* 9. 24. run that ye may *o.*

1 *Thess.* 5. 9. but to *o.* salvation by.

2 *Tim.* 2. 10. may *o.* salvation which is in Christ Jesus

Heb. 4. 16. *o.* mercy and find grace

11. 35. might *o.* a better resurrection

Jam. 4. 2. ye desire and cannot *o.*

OBTAINED, *Hos.* 2. 23. had not *o.* mercy

Acts. 26. 22. having *o.* help of God

Rom. 11. 7. election hath *o.* it

Eph. 1. 11. in whom we *o.* inheritance

1 *Tim.* 1. 13. I *o.* mercy because, 16.

Heb. 1. 4. *o.* a more excellent name, 8. 6.

6. 15. patiently *o.* the promises

9. 12. *o.* eternal redemption for

Heb. 11. 2. elders *o.* good report, 39.

33. who *o.* promises, stopped

1 *Pet.* 2. 10. not *o.* mercy, but now have *o.*

2 *Pet.* 1. 1. that have *o.* like precious faith with us

OCCASION. A fit opportunity, *Gen.* 43. 18; *Judg.* 14. 4; 1 *Sam.* 10. 7. Ground of accusation, *Dan.* 6. 4, 5. Need, *Ezra* 7. 20. Reason, or because, 2 *Cor.* 8. 8.

2 *Sam.* 12. 14. give *o.* to enemies of the

Job 33. 10. findeth *o.* against me

Jer. 2. 24. in her *o.* who can turn her away

Dan. 6. 4. find no *o.* fault, 5.

Rom. 7. 8. sin taking *o.* by the commandment, 11.

14. 13. an *o.* to fall in his brother's

2 *Cor.* 11. 12. cut off *o.* from them

Gal. 5. 13. use not for an *o.* to the flesh

1 *Tim.* 5. 14. give no *o.* to adversary

1 *John* 2. 10. no *o.* of stumbling

OCCUPY, *Luke* 19. 13. servants, *o.* till I come

ODOUR, *John* 12. 3. house filled with *o.* of ointment

Phil. 4. 18. an *o.* of a sweet smell

Rev. 5. 8. having harps and golden vials full of *o.*

OFFENCE, 1 *Sam.* 25. 31; *Is.* 8. 14.

Eccl. 10. 4. yielding pacifieth great *o.*

Hos. 5. 15. acknowledge their *o.*

Matt. 16. 23. thou art an *o.* to me

18. 7. woe to world because of *o.*, *o.* must come, woe to him by whom *o.* cometh

Acts 24. 16. conscience void of *o.* toward God

Rom. 4. 25. delivered for our *o.*

5. 15. not as *o.* so gift, *o.* of one, 16.

17. if by one man's *o.* death came, 18.

9. 33. rock of *o.* 1 *Pet.* 2. 8; *Is.* 8. 14.

14. 20. is evil for him eateth with *o.*

16. 17. divisions and *o.* contrary

2 *Cor.* 6. 3. giving no *o.* in any thing

11. 7. committed *o.* in abasing
Gal. 5. 11. is the *o.* of the cross ceased
Phil. 1. 10. without *o.* till day of Christ
OFFEND, I will not any more, *Job* 34. 31
Ps. 73. 15. *o.* against generation of thy children
119. 165. nothing shall *o.* them
Jer. 2. 3. all that devour him *o.*
50. 7. we *o.* not because they have sinned
Hos. 4. 15. Israel play harlot let not Judah *o.*
Matt. 5. 29. right hand, eye *o.* 30.
13. 41. gather out of kingdom that *o.*
17. 27. lest we should *o.* give it
18. 6. shall *o.* one of these little
8. if hand, foot, eye *o. Mark* 9. 43—47.
1 *Cor.* 8. 13. if meat make my brother to *o.*
Jam. 2. 10. and *o.* in one point, he is guilty of all
3. 2. in many things we all *o.* not in word
OFFENDED, *Prov.* 18. 19. brother *o.* is harder
Matt. 11. 6. blessed who is not *o.*
26. 33. though all men be *o.* I will never be *o.*
Mark 4. 17. immediately are *o.*
Rom. 14. 21. *o.* or is made weak
2 *Cor.* 11. 29. who is *o.* and I burn not
OFFENDER, *Is.* 29. 21. make man *o.* for a word
Acts 25. 11. if I be an *o.* or have
OFFER, *Luke* 6. 29. cheek *o.* also the other
Heb. 9. 25. nor that he should *o.* himself often
13. 15. *o.* sacrifice of praise to God
1 *Pet.* 2. 5. by Jesus Christ to *o.* spiritual sacrifices
OFFER, *Gen.* 31. 54; *Lev.* 1. 3.
Ps. 50. 14. *o.* to God thanksgiving, 116. 17.
23. whoso *o.* praise glorifieth me
Matt. 5. 24. come and *o.* thy gift
Heb. 7. 27. needeth not to *o.* sacrifice, first for his own sins
OFFERED, *Mal.* 1. 11. incense be *o.* to my name
1 *Cor.* 8. 1. things *o.* to idols. 4. 7, 10; 10. 19, 28.
Phil. 2. 17. *o.* upon sacrifice and service
2 *Tim.* 4. 6. ready to be *o.* and the time
Heb. 5. 7. when he had *o.* up prayers and supplications
7. 27. this he did once when he *o.* up himself
Heb. 9. 14. *o.* him without spot
28. Christ once *o.* to bear the sins of many
11. 4. by faith Abel *o.* to God a more acceptable sacrifice
17. Abraham *o.* up Isaac
13. 15. let us *o.* the sacrifice of praise
Jam. 2. 21. Abraham justified by works when he *o.*
Rev. 8. 3. *o.* it with the prayers of
OFFERETH, *Ps.* 50. 23. *o.* praise glorifieth me
OFFERING, *Is.* 53. 10. make his soul an *o.* for sin
Rom. 15. 16. *o.* up of Gentiles

Eph. 5. 2. *o.* and sacrifice to God
Heb. 10. 5. sacrifice and *o.* thou wouldest not
14. by one *o.* hath perfected
Heb. 10. 18. where remission is, there is no more *o.* for sin
OFTEN reproved, hardeneth *Prov.* 29. 1.
Mal. 3. 16. spake *o.* one to another
Matt. 23. 37. how *o.* would I have gathered thy children
1 *Cor.* 11. 26. as *o.* as ye eat this
Phil. 3. 18. of whom I told you *o.*
Heb. 9. 25. needed not to offer himself *o.*
OIL, *Gen.* 28. 18; *Ex.* 25. 6.
Ps. 45. 7. with *o.* of gladness, *Heb.* 1. 9.
89. 20. with my holy *o.* have I anointed him
92. 10. anointed with fresh *o.* 23. 5.
104. 15. *o.* to make face shine
141. 5. an *o.* which shall not break
Is. 61. 3. *o.* of joy for mourning
Matt. 25. 3. foolish took no *o.*
4. the wise took *o.*
8. give us of your *o.* for our lamps
Luke 10. 34. pouring in *o.* and wine
OINTMENT, oil perfumed, used to anoint the head, &c. *Ps.* 133. 2; *Prov.* 27. 9, 16; *Eccl.* 10. 1; *Songs* 1. 3; *Is.* 1. 6; *Amos* 6. 6; *Matt.* 26. 7; *Luke* 7. 37.
OLD, *Gen.* 5. 32. & 18. 12, 13.
Ps. 37. 25. young and now am *o.*
71. 18. when I am *o.* and grey headed
Prov. 22 6. when *o.* he will not depart from it
Jer. 6. 16. ask for good *o.* paths
Acts 21. 16. Mnason an *o.* disciple
1 *Cor.* 5. 7. purge out *o.* leaven
2 *Cor.* 5. 17. *o.* things are past
2 *Pet.* 1. 9. purged from his *o.* sins
2. 5. if God spared not *o.* world
Rev. 12. 9. that *o.* serpent, called the devil and Satan
OLD AGE, *Gen.* 25. 8; *Judg.* 8. 32; *Job* 30. 2; *Ps.* 71. 9. & 92. 14; *Is.* 46. 4.
OLD MAN, *Rom.* 6. 6. *o.* man, *Eph.* 4. 22; *Col.* 3. 9.
Prov. 17. 6. *o.* men, 20. 29.
OLD, of, *Ps.* 25. 6. tender mercies ever of *o.*
Ps. 102. 25. of *o.* laid foundation of the earth
Prov. 8. 22. Lord possessed me before his works of *o.*
Is. 30. 33. for Tophet is ordained of *o.* he hath made
46. 9. remember the former things of *o.* I am God
Mal. 3. 4. be pleased as in the days of *o.*
2 *Pet.* 3. 5. the heavens were of *o.*
Jude 4. of *o.* ordained to condemnation
OLD time, *Deut.* 2. 20. giants dwelt there in *o. time* Zamzummims
Acts 15. 21. Moses of *o. time* hath in every city
1 *Pet.* 3. 5. in *o. time* holy women also adorned
2 *Pet.* 1. 21. the prophecy came not in *o. time* by man
OLIVE, *Ps.* 128. 3. thy children like *o.* plants round thy table
Hab. 3. 17. although the labour of the

o. shall fail

Zech. 4. 12. I said, what be these two *o*. branches

Jam. 3. 12. fig-tree bear *o*. berries

OLIVET, *2 Sam.* 15. 30. David went up mount *O*.

Acts 1. 12. they returned from the mount called *O*.

OLIVE-TREE, *Ps.* 52. 8. like a green *o - tree* in the house of God

Rom. 11. 17. the fatness of *o.-tree*

24. cut out of the *o.-tree*, grafted in a good *o.-tree*

ONCE, *Job* 33. 14. God speaks *o*. yea twice, man perceives not

Ps. 62. 11. God spoken *o*. twice

89. 35. *o*. have I sworn by my holiness

Rom. 6. 10. he died unto sin *o*.

Heb. 6. 4. *o*. enlightened and tasted

9. 26. *o*. in end of world appeared

1 Pet. 3. 18. Christ suffered *o*. for sins

Jude 3. faith *o*. delivered to saints

ONE, *Gen.* 2. 24; *Matt.* 19. 5.

Job 9. 3. he cannot answer him *o*. of a thousand

21. 23. *o*. dieth in his full strength at ease

23. 13. he is in *o*. mind, and who

Ps. 49. 16. be not afraid when *o*. is made rich

89. 19. laid help on *o*. mighty

137. 3. sing us *o*. of songs of Zion

Jer. 3. 14. *o*. of a city and two of a family

Zech. 14. 9. shall be *o*. Lord and his name *o*.

Matt. 18. 6. shall offend *o*. of these, *Mark* 9. 42; *Luke* 17. 2.

Matt. 19. 17. none good but *o*.

16. not hear. take *o*. or two more

23. 8. *o*. is your Master, even Christ

25. he that received *o*. 24.

45. did it not to *o*. of least

26. 40. could ye not watch *o*. hour, *Mark* 14. 37.

John 6. 70. *o*. of you is a devil; 7. 21. have done *o*. work

8. 9. went out *o*. by *o*. beginning at the eldest

10. 16. *o*. fold and *o*. shepherd

30. I and my Father are *o*.

11. 52. should gather in *o*. the children of God

Acts 17. 7. saying, that there is another king, *o*. Jesus

Rom. 5. 7. for scarcely for a righteous man will *o*. die

17. death reigned by *o*. shall reign in life by *o*. Jesus Christ

18. by the offence of *o*. so by right-eousness of *o*.

19. so by obedience of *o*. shall many be righteous

1 Cor. 8. 4. there is none other god but *o*. 6.

1 Cor. 9. 24. *o*. receiveth the prize

10. 17. are *o*. bread and *o*. body

2 Cor. 5. 14. if *o*. died for all

Gal. 3. 20. not a mediator of *o*. but God is one

Eph. 4. 5. *o*. faith, *o*. Lord, *o*. baptism; 6. *o*. God

Phil. 1. 27. stand fast with *o*. spirit

1 John 5. 7. these three are *o*.

Josh. 23. 14. not *o*. thing failed

Ps. 27. 4. *o*. thing have I desired, that I will seek after

Mark 10. 21. *o*. thing thou lackest

Luke 10. 42. *o*. thing is needful

Phil. 3. 13. *o*. thing I do, forgetting

OPEN thou my lips, *Ps.* 51. 15.

Ps. 81. 10. *o*. thy mouth wide

119. 18. *o*. thou mine eyes that

Prov. 31. 8. *o*. mouth for dumb

Songs 5. 2. *o*. to me, my sister, my spouse

Is. 22. 22. *o*. and shut, *Rev.* 3. 7.

42. 7. *o*. blind eyes, *Ps.* 146. 8.

Ezek. 16. 63. confounded never *o*.

Matt. 25. 11. Lord *o*. to us, *Luke* 13. 25.

Acts 26. 18. *o*. their eyes and turn

Col. 4. 3. would *o*. to us a door of utterance

Heb. 4. 13. all things are naked and *o*. to him

Rev. 5. 2. who is worthy to *o*. the book, 3. 9.

OPENED, *Gen.* 3. 7. eyes of both were *o*.

Is. 35. 5. eyes of blind shall be *o*.

53. 7. he *o*. not his mouth

Matt. 7. 7. knock and it shall be *o*. *Luke* 11. 9.

Luke 24. 45. then *o*. he their under-standing

Acts 14. 27. *o*. door of faith to the Gentiles

16. 14. Lydia, whose heart Lord *o*. is *o*. to us

1 Cor. 16. 9. a great door and effectual

2 Cor. 2. 12. door was *o*. to me

Heb. 4. 13. naked and *o*. to eyes

Rev. 4. 1. behold, a door was *o*. in heaven

11. 19. temple of God was *o*.

20. 12. the books were *o*.

OPENEST, *Ps.* 104. 28. *o*. thy hand

Ps. 145. 16. thou *o*. thine hand and satisfiest the desire

OPENETH *Is.* 53. 7. a lamb, *o*. not his mouth

John 10. 3. to him the porter *o*.

Rev. 3. 7. that hath key of David, that *o*. and no man shutteth, shutteth and no man *o*.

OPENLY, *Matt.* 6. 4. thy Father will reward thee *o*. 6. 18.

John 18. 20. Jesus said, I spake *o*. to the world

Acts 10. 40. him God raised up, and showed him *o*.

16. 37. beaten us *o*. uncondemned

Col. 2. 15. he made a show of them *o*.

OPERATION, *Ps.* 28. 5. regard not *o*. of his hands

Col. 2. 12. risen through the faith of the *o*. of God

OPPORTUNITY, a fit time or circum-stance, *Matt.* 26. 16; *Gal.* 6. 10; *Phil.* 4. 10; *Heb.* 11. 15.

OPPOSE, to resist, strive against *2 Tim.* 2. 25; *2 Thess.* 2. 4.

OPPRESS, *Ex.* 3. 9; *Judg.* 10. 12.

Ex. 22. 21. *o*. not a stranger, 23. 9.

Lev. 25. 14. *o*. not one another, 17.

Deut. 24. 14. nor *o*. hired servant

Job 10. 3. is it good that thou shouldest *o*.

Prov. 22. 22. neither *o.* afflicted
Zech. 7. 10. *o.* not the widow nor the fatherless
Mal. 3. 5. witness against those that *o.*
Jam. 2. 6. do not rich *o.* you
Ps. 9. 9. Lord will be a refuge for *o.*
10. 18. judge fatherless and *o.*
Eccl. 4. 1. tears of such as were *o.*
Is. 1. 17. relieve the *o.* 58. 6.
38. 14. I am *o.* undertake for me
53. 7. he was *o.* and afflicted
Ezek. 18. 7. hath not *o.* any
16. hath *o.* 12. & 22. 29.
Acts 10. 38. Jesus healed all *o.* of the
OPPRESSETH, *Prov.* 22. 16. & 14. 31. & 28. 3.
OPPRESSION, *Deut.* 26. 7. Lord looked on our *o.*
2 *Kings* 13. 4. Lord saw *o.* of Israel that it was great
Ps. 12. 5. for *o.* of poor and sighing of needy
62. 10. trust not in *o.* in robbery
Eccl. 7. 7. *o.* maketh a wise man mad
Is. 5. 7. but behold *o.*—a cry
33. 15. despiseth gain of *o.*
OPPRESSOR, *Ps.* 72. 4, & 54. 3, & 119. 121; *Prov.* 3. 31, & 28. 16; *Is.* 3. 12, & 14. 4, & 51. 13.
Heb. 2; *Heb.* 5. 12; 1 *Pet.* 4. 11.
ORACLES of God, *Acts* 7. 38; *Rom.* 3.
ORATION, *Acts* 12. 21. Herod made an *o.* to them
ORATOR, *Is.* 3. 3. Lord taketh away eloquent *o.*
Acts 24. 1. certain *o.* named Tertullus
ORDAINED, *Is.* 26. 12; *Tit.* 1. 5.
Ps. 8. 2. hast *o.* strength
132. 17. *o.* lamp for my anointed
Is. 30. 33. Tophet is *o.* of old; for the king it is prepared
Jer. 1. 5. *o.* thee a prophet to nations
Hab. 1. 12. *o.* them for judgment
Acts 13. 48. were *o.* to eternal life
14. 23. *o.* them elders in every church
17. 31. judge by that man whom he hath *o.*
Rom. 7. 10. commandment which was *o.* to life
13. 1. powers that be *o.* of God
1 *Cor.* 9. 14. Lord *o.* that they who preach
Gal. 3. 19. *o.* by angels in hand of a Mediator
Eph. 2. 10. which God before *o.* to
1 *Tim.* 2. 7. *o.* a preacher and a teacher of the Gentiles
Heb. 5. 1. *o.* for men in things pertaining to God
Jude 4. before *o.* to this condemnation
ORDER. Method; the established method of performing a thing, &c. *Gen.* 22. 9; *Job* 33. 5.
Job 23. 4. *o.* my cause before him, 13. 18.
Ps. 40. 5. he reckoned up in *o.*
50. 21. sins set them in *o.* before thee
119. 133. *o.* my steps in thy word
1 *Cor.* 14. 40. all done decently and in *o.*
Col. 2. 5. joying and beholding your *o.*
Tit. 1. 5. set in *o.* things wanting
ORDERED, 2 *Sam.* 23. 5. everlasting covenant *o.* in
Ps. 37. 23. a good man's steps *o.* by the

50. 23. that *o.* his conversation
ORDINANCE. (1) Any decree, statute, or law, made by civil governors, 1 *Pet.* 2. 13. (2) The laws, statutes, and commandments of God, *Lev.* 18. 4. (3) Appointment, decree, and determination, *Ps.* 119. 91. (4) Laws, directions, rites, institutions, and constitutions in the worship of God, *Heb.* 9. 1, 10.
ORDINANCE of God, *Is.* 58. 2; *Rom.* 13. 2.
1 *Pet.* 2. 13. submit to every *o.* of man for Lord's sake
Neh. 10. 32. made *o.* for us
Is. 58. 2. ask of me *o.* of justice
Jer. 31. 35. *o.* of the moon, and of stars, 36.
33. 25. appointed *o.* of heaven, *Job* 38. 33.
Ezek. 11. 20. keep my *o.* and do them, 43. 11; *Lev.* 18. 4, 30. & 22. 9; 1 *Cor.* 11. 2.
Luke 1. 6. walking in all *o.* of the Lord
Eph. 2. 15. law contained in *o.*
Col. 2. 14. hand-writing of *o.* was against
20. why are ye subject to *o.*
Heb. 9. 1. *o.* of divine service, 10.
ORNAMENTS, *Ex.* 33. 5; *Prov.* 1. 9, & 25. 12; *Is.* 49. 18, & 61. 10; *Jer.* 2. 32; *Ezek.* 16. 7, 11; 1 *Pet.* 3. 4.
OUGHT to do. signifies needful *Luke* 24. 26. Reasonable, *Luke* 13. 16. Matter and manner, *Rom.* 8. 26; 1 *Cor.* 8. 2. A duty, *Luke* 18. 1; *Act* 5. 29; 20. 35; *Eph.* 5. 28; *Matt.* 23. 23; *Jam.* 3. 10.
OURS, *Gen.* 26. 20; *Num.* 32. 32.
Mark 12. 7. inheritance shall be *o.* *Luke* 20. 14.
1 *Cor.* 1. 2. Christ our Lord both theirs and *o.*

Tit. 3. 14. let *o.* learn to maintain good
OUTCASTS of Israel. Spoken of the Israelites who had been led into captivity, *Ps.* 147. 2; *Is.* 56. 8.
Is. 11. 12. assemble the *o.*
16. 3. hide the *o.*
27. 13. *o.* in land of Egypt, *Jer.* 30. 17.
OUTER, *Ezek.* 46. 21. brought me into *o.* court
Matt. 8. 12. be cast into *o.* darkness, 22. 13; 25. 30.
OUTGOINGS, *Josh.* 17. 9; *Ps.* 65. 8.
OUTSIDE, *Ezek.* 40. 5; *Matt.* 23. 25.
OUTSTRETCHED arm, *Deut.* 26. 8; *Jer.* 21. 5, & 27. 5.
OUTRAGEOUS, *Prov.* 27. 4.
OUTWARD, 1 *Sam.* 16. 7; *Rom.* 2. 28;
2 *Cor.* 4. 16. though our *o.* man perish
2 *Cor.* 10. 1. do ye look on things after the *o.* appearance
1 *Pet.* 3. 3. not that *o.* adorning of plaiting hair
OUTWARDLY, *Matt.* 23. 28. ye *o.* appear righteous
Rom. 2. 28. not a Jew which is one *o.*
OVEN, *Ps.* 21. 9; *Hos.* 7. 4; *Mal.* 4. 1; *Matt.* 6. 30.
OVERCAME, *Rev.* 3. 21. even as I also *o.*
Rev. 12. 11. they *o.* him by blood of the
OVERCHARGE, to burden, 2 *Cor.* 2. 5.

To make heavy, *Luke* 21. 34.

OVERCOME, *Gen.* 49. 19; *Num.* 13. 30.

Songs 6. 5. thine eyes have o. me

John 16. 33. I have o. the world

Rom. 12. 21. not o. of evil, but o. evil with good

1 *John* 2. 13. have o. the wicked one, 14.

4. 4. of God ye have o. them

5. 4. o. the world

Rev. 17. 14. Lamb hath o. them

2. 7. to him that o. I will give to eat, 17.

11. o. shall not be hurt of the second death

2. 26. to him that o. I will give power

3. 5. he that o. shall be clothed in

12. him that o. I will make pillar in the temple of God

21. to him that o. I will grant to sit with me in my throne

21. 7. he that o. shall inherit all things

OVERFLOW, *Ps.* 69. 2. where the floods .o. me

Ps. 69. 15. let not water floods o. me

Is. 28. 17. waters o. the hiding-place

43. 2. and through the rivers they shall not o. thee

OVERFLOWED, *Ps.* 78. 20. he smote the rock and streams o.

OVERMUCH, more than is needful, *Eccl.* 7. 16; 2 *Cor.* 2. 7.

OVERPAST, *Ps.* 57. 1. make refuge until these calamities be o.

Is. 26. 20. hide thyself until indignation be o.

OVERSEER. One who holds office in civil life, *Gen.* 39. 4. Or in the church, *Neh.* 12. 42. "Over which the Holy Ghost hath made you overseers," *Acts* 20. 28; or inspectors, or bishops.

OVERSIGHT, *Gen.* 43. 12; 1 *Pet.* 5. 2.

OVERTAKE, *Ex.* 15. 9; *Amos* 9. 13; *Hos.* 2. 7; *Gal.* 6. 1; 1 *Thess.* 5. 4.

OVERTHROW, *Deut.* 12. 3, & 29. 23; *Job* 12. 19; *Ps.* 140. 4, 11; *Prov.* 13. 6. & 21. 12; *Amos* 4. 11; *Acts* 5. 39; 2 *Tim.* 2. 18.

OVERTURN, *Ezek.* 21. 27; *Job* 9. 5, & 12. 15, & 28. 9, & 34. 25.

OVERWHELMED, *Ps.* 55. 5, & 61. 2, & 77. 3, & 124. 4, & 142. 3, & 143. 4.

OVERWISE, not make thyself, *Eccl.* 7. 16.

OWL, *Job* 30. 29; *Ps.* 102. 6; *Is.* 13. 21, & 34. 11, 15, & 43. 20; *Mic.* 1. 8.

OWN, *Deut.* 24. 16; *Judg.* 7. 2.

John 1. 11. to his o. and his o. received him not

1 *Cor.* 6. 19. ye are not your o.

10. 24. no man seek his o. 13. 5.

Phil. 2. 4. look on o. things

21. all seek their o. not things of Jesus

OX knoweth owner, *Is.* 1. 3, & 11. 7; *Prov.* 7. 22, & 14. 4, & 15. 17.

OXEN, *Ps.* 144. 14; *Is.* 22. 13; *Matt.* 22. 4; *Luke* 14. 19; *John* 2. 14; 1 *Cor.* 9. 9.

PACIFY, *Esth.* 7. 10; *Prov.* 16. 14.

Ezek. 16. 63. when I am p. towards thee

Prov. 21. 14. gift in secret p. anger

Eccl. 10. 4. yielding p. great offences

PAIN, *Is.* 21. 3, & 26. 18, & 66. 7; *Jer.* 6. 24; *Mic.* 4. 10; *Rev.* 21. 4.

Ps. 116. 3. the p. of hell got hold upon

Acts 2. 24. loosed the p. of death

Ps. 55. 4. my heart is sore p. *Is.* 23. 5; *Jer.* 4. 19; *Joel* 2. 6.

Rev. 12. 2. travailing and p. to be

PAINFUL, *Ps.* 73. 16; 2 *Cor.* 11. 27.

PAINTED, 2 *Kings* 9. 30; *Jer.* 4. 30, & 22. 14; *Ezek.* 23. 40.

PALACE, 1 *Chr.* 29. 1, 19; *Ps.* 45. 8, 15; *Songs* 8. 9; *Is.* 25. 2; *Phil.* 1. 13.

PANT. Ardent desire after the waters of spiritual comfort, *Ps.* 42. 1. As the hart panteth, &c., *Amos* 2. 7; *Ps.* 38. 10, & 42. 1, & 119. 131; *Is.* 21. 4.

PARABLE, *Num.* 23. 7. Balaam took up his p.

Job 27. 1. Job continued his p. 29. 1.

Ps. 49. 4. incline mine ear to a p.

78. 2. open my mouth in a p.

Mic. 2. 4. take up a p. against you

Matt. 13. 18. the p. of the sower

24. another p. put he forth, 31, 33; 21. 33.

34. without a p. spake he not to them, *Mark* 4. 34.

36. the p. of the tares, 15. 15.

24. 32. learn a p. of the fig-tree, branch putteth forth leaves, *Mark* 13. 28; *Luke* 21. 29.

Mark 4. 10. they asked him of p. 7. 17; *Luke* 8. 9.

PARABLES, *Ezek.* 20. 49. doth he not speak p.

Matt. 13. 3. he spake many things to them in p. 13. 34; 22. 1; *Mark* 3. 23; 4. 2, 13, 33; 12. 1.

John 16. 25. no more speak in p.

PARADISE, *Luke* 23. 43. to-day shalt thou be with me in p.

2 *Cor.* 12. 4. how caught up into p.

Rev. 2. 7. in midst of the p. of God

PARCHED, *Is.* 35. 7. p. ground become a pool

PARCHMENTS, 2 *Tim.* 4. 13. bring especially the p.

PARDON iniquity, *Ex.* 34. 9.

Ex. 23. 21. he will not p. your transgressions

Num. 14. 19. p. the iniquity of this people, 20.

1 *Sam.* 15. 25. p. my sin; 2 *Kings* 5. 18.

2 *Kings* 24. 4. the Lord would not p.

2 *Chr.* 30. 18. good Lord p. every one

Neh. 9. 17. a God ready to p.

Job 7. 21. why dost not p. my transgressions

Ps. 25. 11. for thy name's sake p. mine

Is. 40. 2. that her iniquity is p.

55. 7. our God will abundantly p.

Jer. 5. 7. how shall I p. thee, 1.

33. 8. I will p. their iniquities

50. 20. I will p. whom I reserve

Lam. 3. 42. we have transgressed and thou hast not p.

PARDONETH, *Mic.* 7. 18. a God like to thee, that p. iniquity

PARDONS, *Neh.* 9. 17. thou art a God of p. slow to anger

PARENTS, *Luke* 2. 27, & 8. 56.
Matt. 10. 21. children shall rise up against their *p.*
Luke 18. 29. no man hath left *p.*
21. 16. shall be betrayed by *p.*
John 9. 2. who did sin, this man or his *p.*
Rom. 1. 30. disobedient to *p.* 2 *Tim.* 3. 2.
2 *Cor.* 12. 14. children not lay up for *p.* but *p.* for children

1 *Tim.* 5. 4. to requite their *p.*
PART, it shall be thy, *Ex.* 29. 26.
Num. 18. 20. I am thy *p.* and inherit.
Ps. 5. 9. their inward *p.* is very wicked
51. 6. in hidden *p.* make me to know
118. 7. Lord takes my *p.* with them
Mark 9. 40. he that is not against us, is on our *p.*
Luke 10. 42. chosen that good *p.*
John 13. 8. wash not hast no *p.*
Acts 8. 21. hast neither *p.* nor lot in this
2 *Cor.* 6. 15. what *p.* he that believeth with infidel
1 *Cor.* 13. 9. know in *p.* prophecy in *p.*
10. that which is in *p.* shall be done
Heb. 2. 14. took *p.* of the same
1 *Pet.* 4. 14. Spirit of God rests on you; on their *p.* he is evil spoken of, on your *p.* glorified
Rev. 20. 6. *p.* in the first resurrection
21. 8. liars have their *p.* in the lake
22. 19. God take away his *p.*
PARTS, *Job* 26. 14. *p.* of his ways, how
Ps. 2. 8. uttermost *p.* of earth for thy possession
139. 9. dwell in utmost *p.* of sea
John 19. 23. garments and made four *p.*
Eph. 4. 9. he descended first into lower *p.* of earth
PART, verb, *Ruth* 1. 17. if ought but death *p.* thee and me
Ps. 22. 18. *p.* my garments among
PARTED, *Matt.* 27. 35. they crucified him and *p.* his garments, *Mark* 15. 24; *Luke* 23. 34; *John* 19. 24.
Luke 24. 51. blessed them was *p.* from
PARTAKERS with adulterers; *Ps.* 50. 18.
Rom. 15. 27. *p.* of spiritual things
1 *Cor.* 9. 10. *p.* of this hope
13. are *p.* with the altar
10. 17. *p.* of that one bread
21. *p.* of the Lord's table
30. if I by grace be a *p.* why
Eph. 5. 7. be not *p.* with them
1 *Tim.* 5. 22. not *p.* of other men's sins
Heb. 3. 14. made *p.* of Christ
6. 4. made *p.* of Holy Ghost
12. 10. be *p.* of his holiness
1 *Pet.* 5. 1. a *p.* of glory revealed
2 *John* 11. is *p.* of his evil deeds
PARTIAL, *Mal.* 2. 9. but have been *p.* in law
Jam. 2. 4. are ye not *p.* in yourselves
PARTIALITY, 1 *Tim.* 5. 21. observe, do nothing by *p.*
Jam. 3. 17. without *p.* and hypocrisy
PARTITION, 1 *Kings* 6. 21. made a *p.* by chains of gold
Eph. 2. 14. broken down the middle wall of *p.*

PASS, *Ex.* 33. 19; *Ezek.* 20. 37; *Zeph.* 2. 2; *Zech.* 3. 4; 2 *Pet.* 3. 10.
Job 6. 15. as a stream of brooks they *p.* away
Prov. 22. 3. simple *p.* on, are punished
Matt. 5. 18. Till heaven and earth *p.*
26. 39. Father, let this cup *p.* from me
Mark 14. 35. the hour might *p.* from him
Luke 16. 26. they which would *p.* from it cannot; nor can they *p.* to us
Jam. 1. 10. as flower of the grass he shall *p.* away
1 *Pet.* 1. 17. *p.* time of sojourning
2 *Pet.* 3. 10. in which the heavens shall *p.* away
John 5. 24. is *p.* from death to life, 1 *John* 3. 14.
PASSED through, 1 *Cor.* 10. 1. fathers *p. through* the sea
Heb. 11. 29. by faith *p. through* Red Sea
PASSEST, *Is.* 43. 2. when thou *p.* through the waters
PASSETH, *Ps.* 78. 39. are a wind that *p.* away
Ps. 103. 16. for the wind *p.* over it, and it is gone
144. 4. days as a shadow *p.* away
Mic. 7. 18. *p.* by transgression
1 *Cor.* 7. 31. the fashion of this world *p.* away
Eph. 3. 19. love of Christ *p.* knowledge
Phil. 4. 7. peace of God which *p.* all understanding
1 *John* 2. 17. the world *p.* away and lust
PASSION, *Acts* 1. 3. to him he showed himself after *p.*
PASSIONS, *Acts* 14. 15. men of like *p.* with you
Jam. 5. 17. Elias subject to such like *p.*
PASSOVER, *Ex.* 12. 11; *Deut.* 16. 2; *Josh.* 5. 11; 2 *Chr.* 30. 15, & 35. 1, 11; *Heb.* 11. 28.
1 *Cor.* 5. 7. Christ our *p.* is sacrificed
PASTORS. Shepherds, or ministers of the gospel, whose business it is to feed the sheep of Christ, *Jer.* 3. 15; 10. 21; 23. 1, 2; *Eph.* 4. 11. Their counsels are to be obeyed. *Heb.* 13. 17. They are to be held in reputation and honour, *Phil.* 2. 29; and to be highly esteemed, 1 *Thess.* 5. 12, 13. The ground of this is, the resemblance they bear in their work and office to Jesus Christ, *Heb.* 13. 20; 1 *Pet.* 2. 25; 5. 4.
PASTURE. *Ps.* 74. 1. sheep of thy *p.* 79. 13, & 95. 7, & 23. 2, & 100. 3; *Is.* 30. 23, & 49. 9; *Ezek.* 34. 14, 18; *John* 10. 9.
PATH, *Num.* 22. 24; *Job* 28. 7.
Ps. 16. 11. wilt show me the *p.* of life
27. 11. lead me in a plain *p.*
119. 35. go in *p.* of thy commandments
139. 3. compassest my *p.* and my lying
Prov. 4. 18. *p.* of the just is as the shining light
26. ponder the *p.* of thy feet
5. 6. lest thou ponder *p.* of life

Is. 26. 7. dost weigh *p.* of just
Ps. 17. 4. keep me from *p.* of the des-
stroyer
    5. hold my goings in thy *p.*
    25. 4. teach me thy *p.*
    10. *p.* of Lord are mercy and truth
    65. 11. all thy *p.* drop fatness
Prov. 3. 17. all her *p.* are peace
Is. 59. 7. destruction are in their *p.*
    8. have made them crooked *p.*
Jer. 6. 16. ask for the old *p.* good way
Hos. 2. 6. shall not find her *p.*
Matt. 3. 3. made her *p.* straight
Heb. 12. 13. straight *p.* for your feet
PATIENCE with me, *Matt.* 18. 26, 29.
Luke 8. 15. bring forth fruit with *p.*
    21. 19. in your *p.* possess ye your souls
Rom. 5. 3. tribulation works *p.*, *experience*
    8. 25. if hope with *p.* wait for it
    15. 4. that through *p.* we might have
    5. God of *p.* grant you to be like-
minded
2 *Cor.* 6. 4. ministers of God in much *p.*
    12. 12. wrought among you in *p.*
Col. 1. 11. unto all *p.* and long-suffering
1 *Thess.* 1. 3. *p.* of hope in Lord Jesus
2 *Thess.* 1. 4. for your *p.* and faith
1 *Tim.* 6. 11. follow after love, *p.* meek-
2 *Tim.* 3. 10. long-suffering, charity, *p.*
Tit. 2. 2. sound in faith, charity, *p.*
Heb. 6. 12. through *p.* inherit the
promises
    10. 36. have need of *p.* that after
    12. 1. run with *p.* the race set before
Jam. 1. 3. trying of your faith worketh *p.*
    4. let *p.* have her perfect work
    5. 7. long *p.* for it till he receive
    10. prophets an example of *p.*
    11. ye have heard of *p.* of Job
2 *Pet.* 1. 6. to temperance *p.* to *p.*
godliness
Rev. 1. 9. brother in tribulation, kingdom, and *p.* of Jesus Christ
    2. 2. I know thy labour and *p.*
    19. I know thou hast *p.*
    13. 10. hast *p.* of saints, 14. 12.
PATIENT, *Eccl.* 7. 8. *p.* in spirit better
Rom. 2. 7. by *p.* continuance in well-
doing
    12. 12. *p.* in tribulation instant in
1 *Thess.* 5. 14. be *p.* toward all men
2 *Thess.* 3. into *p.* waiting for Christ
1 *Tim.* 3. 3. not greedy of, but *p.*
2 *Tim.* 2. 24. gentle unto all, apt to
teach *p.*
Jam. 5. 7. be *p.* therefore
    8. be ye also *p.* stablish your
PATIENTLY, *Ps.* 37. 7. wait *p.* for the
Lord, 40. 1.
Heb. 6. 15. after he had endured *p.*
1 *Pet.* 2. 20. buffeted, ye take it *p.*
PATRIMONY. The estate by a father
to his child, *Deut.* 18. 8.
PATTERN, *Tit.* 2. 7. a *p.* of good work
Heb. 8. 5. according to *p.* in mount
PATTERNS, *Heb.* 9. 23. necessary that
p. of things
PAVILION, S, 2 *Sam.* 22. 12. he made
darkness his *p. Ps.* 18. 11.
Ps. 27. 5. he shall hide me in *p.*
    31. 20. keep them secret in a *p.*

PAY, *Ps.* 22. 25. I will *p.* my vows, 66.
13; 116. 14, 18.
Matt. 17. 24. your master *p.* tribute
    18. 25. had not to *p.* he forgave him
    26. I will *p.* thee all, 29. 28. *p.* that
thou owest
    30. into prison, till he *p.* debt
Rom. 13. 6. this cause *p.* ye tribute
PAID, *Matt.* 5. 26. not come out thence
till thou *p.* the uttermost farthing,
Luke 12. 59.
Heb. 7. 9. Levi *p.* tithes in Abraham
PAYETH, *Ps.* 37. 21. the wicked
borroweth and *p.* not
PEACE. This word is used in the
scripture in different ways, as, (1)
There is peace or reconciliation
with God: (a) By satisfaction for
sins committed against him; this
is done by the sufferings and merits
of Christ, *Eph.* 2. 14. (b) There is
peace with ourselves or our own
consciences; this arises from a
sense of our reconciliation to God,
which is the gift of Christ, and
wrought in us by his Spirit, *Rom.*
14. 17; *Phil.* 4. 7. (2) Submission
to the will of God, *Job* 22. 21. (3)
Peace with men; (a) Mutual concord and agreement with Christian
brethren, *Ps.* 34. 14; *Gal.* 5. 22.
(b) Deliverance or safety from such
as are our enemies, *Prov.* 16. 7.
PEACE, *Lev.* 26. 6; *Num.* 6. 26.
Job 22. 21. acquaint thyself with God,
be at *p.*
Ps. 34. 14. seek *p.* and pursue it
    37. 37. the end of that man is *p.*
    85. 8. will speak *p.* to his people
    10. mercy and truth, righteousness
and *p.* kissed
    119. 165. great *p.* have they that have
thy law
    120. 6. him that hateth *p.*
    7. I am for *p.* they for war
    122. 6. pray for *p.* of Jerusalem
    125. 5. *p.* shall be upon Israel, 128. 6.
Prov. 16. 7. enemies be at *p.* with him
Is. 9. 6. everlasting Father, Prince of *p.*
    26. 3. keep them in perfect *p.*
    27. 5. may make *p.* with me, make *p.*
    45. 7. I make *p.* and create evil
    48. 18. thy *p.* been as a river
    22. no *p.* to the wicked, 57. 21.
    57. 19. I create fruit of thy lips *p. p.*
    59. 8. way of *p.* they know not, *Rom.*
3. 17.
    60. 17. make thy officers *p.* and
    66. 12. extend *p.* to her like a river
Jer. 6. 14. saying *p. p.* when is no *p.* 8.
11; 2 *Kings* 9. 18, 22; *Ezek.* 15. 10.
    8. 15. looked for *p.* but no good, 14. 19.
    29. 7. seek *p.* of the city in *p.* ye shall
have *p.*
    11. thoughts I think are thoughts of *p.*
Mic. 5. 5. this man shall be *p.*
Zech. 8. 19. love the truth and *p.*
Matt. 10. 34. I come not to send *p.*
Mark 9. 50. *p.* one with another
Luke 1. 79. guide feet to way of *p.*
    2. 14. on earth *p.* and good will
    29. now lettest thy servant depart in *p.*

19. 42. things that belong to *p*.
John 14. 27. *p*. I leave, my *p*. I give unto you
16. 33. in me ye might have *p*.
Rom. 5. 1. have *p*. with God through Lord Jesus Christ
8. 6. to be spiritually-minded is life and *p*.
14. 17. kingdom of God, righteousness *p*. and joy in Holy Ghost
15. 13. fill you with *p*. and joy
1 Cor. 7. 15. God called us to *p*.
2 Cor. 13. 11. live in *p*. and God of *p*. be with you
Gal. 5. 22. fruit of Spirit is love and *p*.
Eph. 2. 14. he is our *p*.
15. new man, so making *p*.
Phil. 4. 7. let the *p*. of God which, Col. 3. 15.
1 Thess. 5. 13. be at *p*. among yourselves
Heb. 12. 14. follow *p*. with all men
Jam. 3. 18. sown in *p*. of make *p*.
1 Pet. 3. 11. seek *p*. and ensue it
2 Pet. 3. 14. found of him in *p*.
PEACABLE, 1 Tim. 2. 2. lead a *p*. life
Heb. 12.1 11. yields *p*. fruit of righteousness
Jam. 3. 17. is first pure, then *p*.
PEACEABLY, Rom. 12. 18. live *p*. with all men
PEACE-MAKERS, Matt. 5. 9. blessed are *p*.-makers
PEARL, Matt. 13. 46. when he found one *p*. of great price
Rev. 21. 21. every gate was of one *p*.
PEARLS, Job 28. 18. no mention made of *p*.
Matt. 7. 6. neither cast ye your *p*. before swine
13. 45. merchant seeking goodly *p*.
1 Tim. 2. 9. not with gold, or *p*.
Rev. 17. 4. the woman was decked with gold and *p*.
18. 12. buyeth merchandise of *p*. 16.
21. 21. twelve gates were twelve *p*.
PECULIAR, Ex. 19. 5. shall be a *p*. treasure to me
Deut. 14. 2. *p*. people, 26. 18; Tit. 2. 14; 1 Pet. 2. 29.
Ps. 135. 4. Lord hath chosen Israel for his *p*. treasure
Eccl. 2. 8. *p*. treasure of kings of the provinces
Tit. 2. 14. purify to himself *p*. people
PEDIGREE, Heb. 7. 3. without father, mother, without *p*.
PEN, Judg. 5. 14. they that handle *p*.
Job 19. 24. graven with an iron *p*.
Ps. 45. 1. tongue *p*. of a ready writer
Is. 8. 1. write in it with a man's *p*.
Jer. 17. 1. the sin of Judah is written with a *p*. of iron
3 John 13. not with ink and *p*. write
PENCE, Matt. 18. 28. owed him a hundred *p*.
Mark 14. 5. sold for more than 300 *p*. John 12. 5.
Luke 7. 41. the one owed 500 *p*.
10. 35. on morrow he took out two *p*. and gave
PENNY, Matt. 20. 2. agreed with labourers for a *p*.

Matt. 20. 9. received every man a *p*.
22. 19. brought unto him a *p*.
PEOPLE, Gen. 27. 29.
Ex. 6. 7. take you for a *p*. you a God, Deut. 4. 20; 14. 2; 2 Sam. 7. 24; Jer. 13. 11.
Deut. 7. 6. Lord thy God hath chosen thee to be a special *p*.
33. 29. who is like to thee, O *p*. saved by Lord
1 Chr. 19. 13. behave valiantly for *p*.
Ps. 144. 15. happy is *p*. whose God is the Lord
148. 14. Israel a *p*. near to him
Is. 1. 4. *p*. laden with iniquity
10. 6. against *p*. of my wrath
27. 11. it is a *p*. of no understanding
65. 18. I create Jerusalem a rejoicing, and her *p*. a joy
Hos. 4. 9. like *p*. like priest
Ps. 73. 10. his *p*. return hither
100. 3. we are his *p*. and sheep of his pasture
Matt. 1. 21. Jesus shall save his *p*. from their sins
Luke 1. 17. to make ready a *p*.
Acts 15. 14. take out *p*. for his name
Rom. 11. 2. G. hath not cast away his *p*.
Tit. 2. 14. he might purify to himself a peculiar *p*.
Heb. 8. 10. a God, shall be to me a *p*.
1 Pet. 2. 9. peculiar *p*. to show forth
Rev. 5. 9. redeemed us out of every *p*.
PEOPLE, all, Is. 25. 6. Lord made to all *p*. a feast of fat things
Is. 25. 7. covering cast over all *p*.
56. 7. house of prayer for all *p*.
Mic. 4. 5. all *p*. will walk each in name of his god
Luke 2. 10. tidings of joy to all *p*.
PEOPLE of God, Heb. 4. 9. there remaineth a rest to the *p*. of God
Heb. 11. 25. choosing to suffer affliction with *p*. of God
PEOPLE, his, Ps. 14. 7. back captivity of his *p*. 53. 6.
Ps. 50. 4. that he may judge his *p*.
73. 10. his *p*. return and waters
85. 8. speak peace to his *p*. and
111. 9. he sent redemption to his *p*.
125. 2. so is the Lord round about his *p*. henceforth
149. 4. Lord taketh pleasure in his *p*. he will beautify
Matt. 1. 21. Jesus, he shall save his *p*. from their sins
Luke 1. 68. visited, and redeemed his *p*.
Rom. 11. 1. God cast away his *p*.
Heb. 10. 30. the Lord shall judge his *p*.
Rev. 21. 3. they shall be his *p*.
PEOPLE, my, Ps. 50. 7. hear, O my *p*. and I will
81. 11. my *p*. would not hearken, 8.
13. O that my *p*. had hearkened
Is. 1. 3. Israel know not, my *p*. doth not consider
Is. 19. 25. blessed be Egypt, my *p*. and
26. 20. come, my *p*. enter chambers
40. 1. comfort ye, comfort ye, my *p*.
63. 8. surely they are my *p*.
Jer. 4. 22. for my *p*. is foolish, they have not known me

Jer. 23. 22. ye shall be *my p.* and I will
be your God, 31. 32, & 24. 7, & 32.
38; *Ezek.* 11. 20. & 36. 28, & 37. 27;
Zech. 2. 11, & 8. 8, & 13. 9; *2 Cor.* 6. 16.
Hos. 1. 9. ye are not *my p.* 10, & 2. 23.
Rom. 9. 25. call them *my p.* which were
not *my p.*
2 Cor. 6. 16. their G. they shall be *my p.*
PEOPLE, the *Ps.* 2; 1. do *the p.*
imagine a vain thing
Ps. 67. 3. let *the p.* praise thee
89. 15. blessed is *the p.* that know the
joyful sound
95. 7. we are *the p.* of his pasture
98. 9. judge *the p.* with equity
Prov. 29. 18. is no vision, *the p.* perish
Is. 34. 5. upon *p.* of my curse
63. 6. tread *the p.* in mine anger
Ezek. 33. 31. come as *the p.* cometh
Matt. 4. 16. *the p.* that sat in darkness
saw light
John 11. 50. that one man should die
for *the p.*
Heb. 13. 12. sanctify *the p.* with his blood
Jude 5. the Lord having saved *the p.*
PERADVENTURE, *Gen.* 18. 24. *p.* there
be fifty righteous
Rom. 5. 7. *p.* for a good man some
would dare to die
2 Tim. 2. 25. *p.* God will give them
repentance
PERCEIVE, *Is.* 6. 19. and see but *p.* not
Luke 8. 46. I *p.* that virtue is gone out
of me
John 4. 19. I *p.* thou art a prophet
Acts 8. 23. I *p.* thou art in the gall
10. 34. I *p.* God is no respecter of
persons
1 John 3. 16. hereby *p.* we the love of
God
PERCEIVEST, *Luke* 6. 41. but *p.* not
beam in thine own eye
PERCEIVING, *Luke* 9. 47. Jesus *p.* the
thoughts of their heart
PERFECT, *Deut.* 25. 15; *Ps.* 18. 32.
Gen. 6. 9. Noah was a just man and *p.*
17. 1. walk before me and be thou *p.*
Deut. 18. 13. shalt be *p.* with the Lord
thy God
32. 4. his work *p.* just and right
2 Sam. 22. 31. his way is *p. Ps.* 18. 30.
Job 1. 1. man *p.* and upright, 8. & 2. 3.
Ps. 19. 7. law of Lord is *p.* converting
37. 37. mark the *p.* man
Ezek. 16. 14. *p.* through my comeliness
Matt. 5. 48. be *p.* as your Father in
heaven is *p.*
19. 21. if wilt be *p.* go sell all
1 Cor. 2. 6. wisdom among them that
are *p.*
2 Cor. 12. 9. my strength is made *p.* in
13. 11. be *p.* be of good comfort
Eph. 4. 13. to a *p.* man stature of
Phil. 3. 12. not as though already *p.*
15. as many as be *p.* minded
Col. 1. 28. present every man *p.* in Christ
Jesus
4. 12. stand *p.* and complete
2 Tim. 3. 17. man of God may be *p.*
Heb. 2. 10. Captain of salvation *p.* thro'
sufferings
7. 19. law made nothing *p.*

12. 23. spirits of just made *p.*
13. 21. make *p.* in every good
Jam. 1. 4. be *p.* and entire
1 Pet. 5. 10. make you *p.* stablish
1 John 4. 18. *p.* love casteth out fear
Rev. 3. 2. not found thy works *p.*
2 Cor. 7. 1. *p.* holiness in fear
Eph. 4. 12. for the *p.* of saints
Ps. 119. 96. seen an end of all *p.*
Luke 8. 14. bring no fruit to *p.*
2 Cor. 13. 9. we wish even your *p.*
Heb. 6. 1. let us go on unto *p.*
Col. 3. 14. bond of *p.*
PERFORM, *Gen.* 26. 3; *Ruth* 3. 13.
Job 5. 12. hands cannot *p.* their
Ps. 119. 106. I have sworn and I will *p.*
112. inclined my heart to *p.*
Is. 9. 7. zeal of the Lord of hosts shall
p. this
44. 28. shall *p.* all my pleasure
Mic. 7. 20. he will *p.* the truth to Jacob
Rom. 4. 21. promised, able to *p.*
7. 18. how to *p.* that which is good I
find not
Phil. 1. 6. he will *p.* it unto the day of
God
1 Kings 8. 20. Lord hath *p.* word
Neh. 9. 8. hast *p.* thy words, for
Is. 10. 12. when the Lord hath *p.* his
whole work
Jer. 51. 29. every purpose of the Lord
shall be *p.*
Ps. 57. 2. God that *p.* all things
Is. 44. 26. *p.* counsel of his messengers
PERIL, *Rom.* 8. 35. shall famine *p.* or
2 Cor. 11. 26. in *p.* of waters, in *p.* of
robbers, in *p.* by countrymen, &c.
2 Tim. 3. 1. last days *p.* times come
PERISH, (1) To die or lose life, *Jonah*
1. 6. (2) To be rooted out, *2 Kings*
9. 8. (3) To starve, *Luke* 15. 17. (4)
To be damned, *2 Cor.* 2. 15; *2 Pet.*
2. 12. (5) To be taken away, *Mic.*
7. 2. (6) To be deprived of being,
1 Cor. 15. 18.
PERISH, *Gen.* 41. 36; *Lev.* 26. 38.
Num. 17. 12. we die, we *p.* we *p.*
Esth. 4. 16. I will go in, and if I *p.* I *p.*
Job 29. 13. the blessing of him that was
ready to *p.*
Ps. 2. 12. ye *p.* from way if once
119. 92. have *p.* in mine affliction
Prov. 29. 18. where no vision is people *p.*
31. 6. give strong drink to him that
is ready to *p.*
Is. 27. 13. shall come ready to *p.*
Matt. 5. 29. that one of thy members
should *p.* 30.
Matt. 8. 25. Lord save us, we *p. Luke*
8. 24.
Luke 15. 17. have bread enough, and I
p. with hunger
John 3. 15. believeth should not *p.* 16.
1 Cor. 1. 18. preaching of cross is to
them that *p.* foolishness, but to us
saved, power of God
2 Cor. 2. 15. a savour of Christ in them
that *p.*
4. 16. but though our outward man
p. inward is renewed
2 Pet. 3. 9. not willing that any should
p. but that all

PERISH, shall, *Ps.* 1. 6. way of ungodly *shall p.*
Ps. 112. 10. desire of wicked *shall p.*
Prov. 10. 28. expectation of wicked *shall p.* 11. 7.
John 10. 28. sheep *shall* never *p.* nor any pluck them
Rom. 2. 12. sinned without law, *shall p.* without law
1 *Cor.* 8. 11. *shall* weak brother *p.*
Heb. 1. 11. *shall p.* but thou remainest
PERISHETH, *Jam.* 1. 11. and the grace of the fashion of it *p.*
1 *Pet.* 1. 7. trial of faith more precious than gold that *p.*
PERMIT if Lord, 1 *Cor.* 16. 7; *Heb.* 6. 3.
1 *Cor.* 7. 6. by permission not of commandment
PERNICIOUS ways, 2 *Pet.* 2. 2.
PERPETUAL. Everlasting, *Ps.* 9. 6. To the end of time, *Gen.* 9. 12; *Hab.* 3. 6.—during the continuance of the legal dispensation, *Ex.* 29. 9; *Jer.* 50. 5; 51. 39, 57.
PERPLEXED, *Is.* 22. 5; 2 *Cor.* 4. 8.
PERSECUTE, *Ps.* 7. 1, & 31. 15.
Job 19. 22. why do ye *p.* me as God, 28.
Ps. 10. 2. wicked doth *p.* poor
35. 6. let angel of Lord *p.* them
71. 11. *p.* and take him for none
83. 15. *p.* them with tempest
Lam. 3. 66. *p.* and destroy them in
Matt. 5. 11. blessed when men *p.*
44. pray for them that *p.* you
10. 23. when they *p.* you in this city
Rom. 12. 14. bless them who *p.* you, curse not
Ps. 10. 16. *p.* the poor and needy
119. 161. *p.* me without cause
143. 3. enemy hath *p.* my soul
John 15. 20. if they *p.* they will *p.*
Acts 9. 4. why *p.* thou me
22. 4. I *p.* this way to the death
26. 11. I *p.* them to strange cities, 16.
1 *Cor.* 4. 12. being *p.* we suffer it
15. 9. because I *p.* church of God
2 *Cor.* 4. 9. *p.* but not forsaken
Gal. 1. 13. beyond measure I *p.* church of God
4. 29. *p.* him born after the Spirit
1 *Thess.* 2. 15. hath *p.* us and please
1 *Tim.* 1. 13. who was a blasphemer, a *p.*
2 *Tim.* 3. 12. live godly, suffer *p.*
PERSON, *Lev.* 19. 15.
Mal. 1. 8. will he accept thy *p.*
Matt. 22. 16. regardest not *p.* of men
Acts 10. 34. God is no respecter of persons, *Deut.* 10. 17; *Gal.* 2. 6; *Eph.* 6. 9; *Col.* 3. 25; 1 *Pet.* 1. 17.
Heb. 1. 3. express image of his *p.*
12. 16. fornicator or profane as Esau
2 *Pet.* 3. 11. what manner of *p.* ought ye
Jude 16. having men's *p.* in admiration
PERSUADE we men, 2 *Cor.* 5. 11.
Gal. 1. 10. do I *p.* men or God
Acts 13. 43. *p.* them to continue
21. 14. when he would not be *p.*
26. 28. almost thou *p.* me to be a Christian
Rom. 8. 38. I am *p.* neither death
Heb. 6. 9. I am *p.* better things
11. 13. having seen were *p.* of

Gal. 5. 8. this *p.* cometh not of
PERTAIN, *Lev.* 7. 29; 1 *Cor.* 6. 3, 4; *Rom.* 9. 4; *Heb.* 2. 17, & 5. 1, & 9. 9; 2 *Pet.* 1. 3.
PERTAINING, *Acts* 1. 3.
PERVERSE, *Num.* 22. 32; *Deut.* 32. 5; *Job* 6. 30; *Prov.* 4. 24, & 12. 8, & 17. 20; *Is.* 19. 14; *Matt.* 17. 17.
Acts 20. 30. men arise, speaking *p.* things
Phil. 2. 15. blameless in the midst of a *p.* nation
1 *Tim.* 6. 5. *p.* disputings of men
PERVERT. To render corrupt, or to lead astray, *Is.* 47. 10; *Luke* 23. 2. Pervert judgment, *Deut.* 24. 17, & 16. 19; 1 *Sam.* 8. 3; *Job* 8. 3, & 34. 12; *Prov.* 17. 23, & 31. 5; *Mic.* 3. 9.
Job 33. 27. and *p.* that was right
Prov. 19. 3. foolishness of man *p.* his
Jer. 3. 21. they have *p.* their way
Luke 23. 2. found this fellow *p.* the
Acts 13. 10. not cease to *p.* ways
Gal. 1. 7. some would *p.* gospel of Christ
PESTILENCE, epidemic or contagious disorders, the plague, &c., 2 *Sam.* 24. 15; *Ps.* 78. 50, & 91. 3; *Jer.* 14. 12; *Ezek.* 5. 12; *Amos* 4. 10; *Hab.* 3. 5; *Matt.* 24. 7.
Acts 24. 5. found him *p.* fellow
PETITION, 1 *Sam.* 1. 17; *Esth.* 5. 6.
PETITIONS, *Ps.* 20. 5; 1 *John* 5. 15.
PHILOSOPHY, *Col.* 2. 8. beware, lest any man spoil you through *p.*
PHILOSOPHERS, *Acts* 17. 18. certain *p.* encountered him
PHYLACTERIES, *Matt.* 23. 5. made broad their *p.*
PHYSICIAN, *Jer.* 8. 22. is no balm in Gilead ? is there no *p.* there ?
Matt. 9. 12. they that be whole need not a *p.* but the sick, *Mark* 2. 17; *Luke* 5. 31.
Luke 4. 23. *p.* heal thyself
PHYSICIANS, *Gen.* 50. 2. Joseph commanded the *p.* to embalm his father; *p.* embalmed Israel
Job 13. 4. forgers of lies, *p.* of no value
Mark 5. 26. had suffered many things, of *p.* *Luke* 8. 43.
PIECE, 1 *Sam.* 2. 30. crouch to him for a *p.* of silver, that I may eat a *p.* of bread
PIECE of bread, *Prov.* 6. 26. & 28. 21; *Is.* 3. 15; *Ezek.* 13. 19.
Ps. 50. 22. tear you in *p.*
Mic. 3. 3. chop them in *p.*
Matt. 9. 16. no man puts *p.* of new cloth to old garment
Luke 14. 18. bought a *p.* of ground
PIERCE, *Num.* 24. 8; 2 *Kings* 18. 21.
Ps. 22. 16. they *p.* my hands and
Zech. 12. 10. look on him whom they *p.*
Luke 2. 35. sword shall *p.* through
1 *Tim.* 6. 10. *p.* them through with many sorrows
Rev. 1. 7. they also which *p.* him
Heb. 4. 12. *p.* to dividing asunder
PIETY, 1 *Tim.* 5. 4. learn to show *p.* at
PILGRIMAGE. Sojourning or wandering, *Gen.* 47. 9. not attained to years of *p.*

Ex. 6. 4. give them land of *p.*
Ps. 119. 54. songs in house of my *p.*
PILGRIMS, *Heb.* 11. 13. were strangers and *p.*
1 *Pet.* 2. 11. as *p.* abstain from
PILLAR of salt, *Gen.* 19. 26.
Ex. 13. 21. by day in *p.* of cloud, by night in *p.* of fire, *Num.* 12. 5. & 14. 14; *Deut.* 31. 15; *Neh.* 9. 12; *Ps.* 99. 7.
Is. 19. 19. a *p.* at border thereof
Jer. 1. 18. I will make thee iron *p.*
1 *Tim.* 3. 15. *p.* and ground of truth
Rev. 3. 12. him that overcometh I will make a *p.*
Job 9. 6. *p.* thereof to tremble
26, 11. *p.* of heaven tremble
Ps. 75. 3. I bear up the *p.* of it
Prov. 9. 1. hewn her seven *p.*
Songs 3. 6. *p.* of smoke
3. 10. made *p.* thereof silver
5. 15. *p.* of marble
Rev. 10. 1. *p.* of fire
PINE-TREE, *Is.* 41. 19. I will plant *p.* and box-tree together
Is. 60. 13. the *p.* and box-tree shall come to thee
PIPED, *Matt.* 11. 17. have *p.* unto you. *Luke* 7. 32.
1 *Cor.* 14. 7. how be known what is *p.*
PIPERS, *Rev.* 18. 22. voice of *p.* shall be heard no more
PIT, *Gen.* 14. 10, & 37. 20.
Ex. 21. 33. if man dig a *p.* 34.
Num. 16. 30. go down quick into *p.* 33.
Job 33. 24. deliver my soul from going to the *p.*
Ps. 9. 15. sunk into *p.* they digged
28. 1. go down to *p.* 30. 3; & 88. 4, & 143. 7; *Prov.* 1. 12; *Is.* 38. 18.
Ps. 40. 2. me out of horrible *p.*
55. 23. *p.* of destruction
119. 85. proud digged *p.* for me
Prov. 22. 14. mouth of strange woman is a deep *p.*
23. 27. is a narrow *p.*
28. 10. shall fall into his own *p. Eccl.* 10. 8.
Is. 38. 17. delivered it from *p.* of corruption
51. 1. hole of *p.* whence were digged
Jer. 14. 3. came to *p.* and found no water
Zech. 9. 11. prisoners out of *p.* no
Matt. 12. 11. if it fall into a *p.* on sabbath, *Luke* 14. 5.
Rev. 9. 1. key of the bottomless *p.* 20. 1.
PITCH, *Ex.* 2. 3. daubed it with *p.*
PITCH, *Num.* 1. 52. Israel shall *p.* every man by his tent
Is. 13. 20. neither shall the Arabian *p.* tent there
Jer. 6. 3. shepherd *p.* tents against her
PITCHED, *Heb.* 8. 2: true tabernacle which the Lord *p.*
PITCHER, *Gen.* 24. 14. let down *p.* that I may drink
Gen. 24. 15. Rebekah came with her *p.* 45.
Judg. 7. 16. empty *p.* lamps within *p.*
Eccl. 12. 6. *p.* be broken at the fountain
PITIFUL, *Jam.* 5. 11; 1 *Pet.* 3. 8.

PITY, *Deut.* 7. 16, & 13. 8, & 19. 13.
Job 6. 14. to him that is afflicted *p.* should be showed
19. 21. have *p.* on me, have *p.* O friend
Ps. 103. 13. as father *p.* children so the Lord *p.* them that fear him
Prov. 19. 17. hath *p.* on the poor lendeth to the Lord
Is. 63. 9. in *p.* he redeemed them
Ezek. 36. 21. I had *p.* for my holy name
Matt. 18. 33. as I had *p.* on thee
PLACE, *Ex.* 3. 5; *Deut.* 12. 5, 14.
Ps. 26. 8. *p.* where thy honour dwelleth
12. my foot standeth in an even *p.*
Ps. 32. 7. thou art my hiding-*p.* 119. 114.
90. 1. hast been my dwelling-*p.*
103. 16. the *p.* thereof shall know it no more
Prov. 15. 3. eyes of Lord are in every *p.*
Eccl. 3. 20. all go to one *p.* 6. 6.
Is. 49. 20. the *p.* is too strait for me
60. 1. I will make the *p.* of my feet glorious
Is. 66. 1. where is the *p.* of my rest
Dan. 2. 35. no *p.* was found for them
Hos. 5. 15. I will return to my *p.*
Matt. 28. 6. see the *p.* where the Lord lay, *Mark* 16. 16.
John 8. 37. word has no *p.* in you
11. 48. take away our *p.* and nation
7. 33. *p.* whereon thou standest, holy
49. or what is the *p.* of my rest
Rom. 12. 19. avenge not; give *p.* unto wrath
1 *Cor.* 4. 11. have no certain dwelling *p.*
11. 20. come together in one *p.*
2 *Cor.* 2. 14. the savour of his knowledge in every *p.*
Eph. 4. 27. neither give *p.* to devil
2 *Pet.* 1. 19. light that shines in dark *p.*
Rev. 12. 6. hath a *p.* prepared her of G.
Job 7. 10. neither shall his *p.* know him, 20. 9.
Ps. 37. 10. diligently consider *p.*
Is. 26. 21. Lord comes out of his *p. Mic.* 1. 3.
Acts 1. 25. Judas fell, might go to his own *p.*
Ps. 16. 6. the lines have fallen in pleasant *p.*
Is. 40. 4. rough *p.* shall be made plain
Eph. 1. 3. in heavenly *p.* 20, & 2. 6, & 3. 10.
Hab. 3. 19. high *p. Prov.* 8. 2, & 9. 14; *Hos.* 10. 8; *Amos* 4. 13; *Eph.* 6. 12.
PLAGUE, 1 *Kings* 8. 38. shall know every man the *p.* of his own heart
Ps. 91. 10. nor any *p.* come nigh
Mark 5. 29. she was healed of that *p.*
4. and be whole of thy *p.*
PLAGUED, *Ps.* 73. 5. nor are they *p.* like other men
Ps. 73. 14. all day *p.* and chastened
PLAGUES, *Gen.* 12. 17. Lord plagued Pharaoh with great *p.*
Hos. 13. 14. O death, I will be thy *p.* O grave
Mark 3. 10. touch him, as many had *p.*
Rev. 11. 6. power to smite earth with *p.*
16. 9. name of God, who hath power over these *p.*
18. 4. that ye receive not of her *p.*

22. 18. God add to him the *p.* written

PLAIN, *Gen.* 25. 27. Jacob was a *p.* man

Ps. 27. 11. and lead me in a *p.* path
Prov. 8. 9. *p.* to him that understandeth
15. 19. of righteous is made *p.*
Is. 40. 4. crooked made straight, and rough places *p.*
Hab. 2. 2. write vision, make it *p.*
Zech. 4. 7. Zerubbabel became *p.*
John 16. 29. now speakest thou *p.*
2 *Cor.* 3. 12. we use great *p.* of speech

PLAISTER, *Lev.* 14. 42; *Is.* 38. 21.

PLAIT, 1 *Pet.* 3. 3.

PLANT, *Gen.* 2. 5; *Job* 14. 9.

Ps. 128. 3. children like olive *p.* 144. 12.
Is. 53. 2. grow up as a tender *p.*
Jer. 2. 21. turned to degenerate *p.*
18. 9. concerning a kingdom to build and *p.* it
24. 6. *p.* them and not pluck up, 42. 10.
Ezek. 34. 29. raise a *p.* of renown

PLANTED, *Ps.* 1. 3. like a tree *p.* by
92. 13. that be *p.* in the house of the Lord
94. 9. he that *p.* ear shall he not
Is. 40. 24. yea they shall not be *p.*
Jer. 2. 21. I *p.* thee a noble vine
17. 8. as tree *p.* by water spreads
Matt. 15. 13. *p.* my heavenly Father hath not *p.*
21. 33. *p.* a vineyard and let it
Rom. 6. 5. *p.* together in likeness of
1 *Cor.* 3. 6. I *p.* Apollos watered

PLANTETH, 1 *Cor.* 3. 7. neither is he that *p.* any thing
1 *Cor.* 3. 8. he that *p.* and he that watereth
9. 7. who *p.* a vineyard and eateth not the fruit

PLANTING, *Is.* 60. 21. branch of my *p.* work of
Is. 61. 3. be called the *p.* of the Lord;

PLATTED, *Matt.* 27. 29. when they had *p.* a crown of thorns, they put it on his head, *Mark* 15. 17; *John* 19. 2.

PLATTER, *Matt.* 23. 25. clean outside of *p.* but within full of, *Luke* 11. 39.

PLAY, *Ex.* 32. 6. the people rose up to *p.* 1 *Cor.* 10. 7.
1 *Sam.* 16. 16. shall *p.* with his hand
17. provide a man, *p.* well
Ps. 33. 3. *p.* skilfully with a loud noise
Is. 11. 8. sucking child shall *p.* on hole of the asp
Ezek. 33. 32. can *p.* well on an instrument

PLAYED, 1 *Sam.* 18. 7. the women answered one another as they *p.*
1 *Sam.* 26. 21. I have *p.* fool, and have erred exceedingly

PLAYERS, *Ps.* 68. 25. the *p.* on instruments followed after
Ps. 87. 7. as well the singers as the *p.* on instruments

PLAYING, *Ps.* 68. 25. were the damsels *p.*
Zech. 8. 5. boys and girls *p.* in the streets thereof

PLEAD for Baal, *Judg.* 6. 31.
Job 13. 19. who is he that will *p.* with

me, 9. 19.
16. 21. O that one might *p.* for a man
23. 6. he *p.* against me with great power

Is. 1. 17. *p.* for the widow
43. 26. let us *p.* together
66. 16. by fire and sword Lord *p.* with flesh

Jer. 2. 9. I will yet *p.* with you and your children's children, 35.
29. wherefore will ye *p.* with me
12. 1. righteous art thou, Lord, when I *p.*
25. 31. Lord *p.* with all flesh, *Ezek.* 38. 22.

Hos. 2. 2. *p.* with your mother *p.*
Joel. 3. 2. I will *p.* with them for my

PLEASANT, *Gen.* 2. 9, & 3. 6; *Mic.* 2. 9.
2 *Sam.* 1. 23. Saul and Jonathan were *p.*
Ps. 16. 6. the lines have fallen to me in *p.* places
133. 1. how *p.* for brethren to dwell together
147. 1. for it is *p.* and praise is comely, 135. 3.

Prov. 2. 10. knowledge is *p.* to
5. 19. let her be as loving hind and *p.* roe
9. 17. bread eaten in secret is *p.*
Eccl. 11. 7. *p.* for eyes to behold
Songs 1. 16. behold, thou art fair, yea *p.*
4. 13. *p.* fruits, 16, & 7. 13.
7. 6. *p.* art thou for delights
Is. 5. 7. men of Judah his *p.* plant
Jer. 31. 20. is Ephraim my dear son, is he a *p.* child
Dan. 8. 9. *p.* land, *Jer* 3. 19; *Zech.* 7. 14.

Prov. 3. 17. ways are ways of *p.*

PLEASE, 2 *Sam.* 7. 29; *Job* 6. 9.
Ps. 69. 31. this shall *p.* the Lord better
Prov. 16. 7. when man's ways *p.* the L.
Is. 55. 11. accomplish that I *p.*
56. 4. choose things that *p.* me
Rom. 8. 8. are in flesh cannot *p.* God
15. 1. strong ought not to *p.*
2. every one *p.* his neighbour
1 *Cor.* 7. 32. how to *p.* the Lord
33. how he may *p.* his wife
10. 33. as I *p.* men in all things
Gal. 1. 10. if seek to *p.* men not servant of Christ

1 *Thess.* 4. 1. how to walk to *p.* God
Heb. 11. 6. without faith impossible to *p.* God

PLEASED, *Ps.* 51. 19. be *p.* with sacrifices
115. 3. L. do whatsoever he *p.* 135. 6.
Eccl. 7. 26. whoso *p.* God shall escape from her
8. 3. he doeth whatsoever *p.* him
Is. 42. 21. Lord is well *p.* for his right-eousness' sake
Is. 53. 10. it *p.* the Lord to bruise him
Mic. 6. 7. will the Lord be *p.*
Matt. 3. 17. beloved Son in whom well *p.* 17. 5.
Rom. 15. 3. Christ *p.* not himself
Col. 1. 19. *p.* the Father that in him all fulness
Heb. 13. 16. with such sacrifice God is

well *p.*
Phil. 4. 18. sacrifice well *p.* to God
Col. 1. 10. worthy of the Lord unto all *p.*
   3. 20. obey parents is w. *p.* to the Lord
1 *Thess.* 2. 4. not as *p.* men, *Eph.* 6. 6;
Heb. 13. 21. in you that well *p.*
1 *John* 3. 22. do things that are *p.* in his sight
PLEASURE, *Gen.* 18. 12. shall I have *p.*
1 *Chr.* 29. 17. *p.* in uprightness
Ps. 5. 4. not a God that hath *p.* in wickedness
   35. 27. hath *p.* in prosperity of his servants
   51. 18. in thy good *p.* to Zion
   102. 14. servants take *p.* in her
   103. 21. ministers that do his *p.*
   111. 2. sought out of, have *p.*
   147. 11. Lord takes *p.* in them that fear him, 149. 4.
Prov. 21. 17. loveth *p.* shall be poor
Eccl. 5. 4. he hath no *p.* in fools
   12. 1. shall say I have no *p.* in them
Is. 44. 28. shall perform all my *p.*
   53. 10. *p.* of the Lord shall prosper in his hand
   58. 13. not finding thy own *p.*
Ezek. 18. 23. have no *p.* in death, 33. 11.
Mal. 1. 10. I have no *p.* in you
Luke 12. 32. fear not, it is Father's good *p.* to give the kingdom
2 *Cor.* 12. 10. take *p.* in infirmities
Eph. 1. 5. according to the good *p.* of his will
Phil. 2. 13. to will and to do of good *p.*
2 *Thess.* 1. 11. fulfil all good *p.* of his goodness
Heb. 10. 38. my soul shall have no *p.* in
   12. 10. chastened us after their own *p.*
Rev. 4. 11. for thy *p.* are created
PLEASURES, *Ps.* 16. 11. right hand are *p.* for ever
Ps. 36. 8. drink of river of thy *p.*
Is. 47. 8. hear this, thou that art given to *p.*
Luke 8. 14. choked with *p.* of life
2 *Tim.* 3. 4. lovers of *p.* more than
Tit. 3. 3. serving divers lusts and *p.*
Heb. 11. 25. the *p.* of sin for a season
PLEDGE, *Deut.* 24. 6. no man shall take the nether or upper millstone to *p.*
Deut. 24. 17. nor take a widow's raiment to *p.*
Job 24. 3. take the widow's ox for a *p.*
PLENTEOUS, *Ps.* 86. 5. *p.* in mercy to all who call, 15.
Ps. 103. 8. Lord is merciful, *p.* in mercy
   130. 7. with him is *p.* redemption
Is. 30. 23. bread shall be *p.* in that day
Hab. 1. 16. their meat *p.*
Matt. 9. 37. the harvest truly is *p.*
PLENTIFUL, *Ps.* 68. 9. thou didst send a *p.* rain
PLENTIFULLY, *Ps.* 31. 23. and *p.* rewardeth the proud doer
Luke 12. 16. ground of a rich man brought forth *p.*
PLENTY, *Gen.* 27. 28. God give thee *p.* of corn and wine
Gen. 41. 29. seven years of great *p.*
PLOUGH, *Deut.* 22. 10; *Prov.* 20. 4.

Judg. 14. 18. except ye *p.* with my heifer ye had not
Job 4. 8. they that *p.* iniquity and sow wickedness
Ps. 129. 3. ploughers *p.* on my back
Is. 28. 24. doth ploughman *p.* all day
Jer. 26. 18. Zion shall be *p.* as a field, *Mic.* 3. 12.
Hos. 10. 13. have *p.* wickedness
Luke 9. 62. no man put hand to *p.*
1 *Cor.* 9. 10. *p.* should *p.* in hope
PLOUGHMAN, *Amos* 9. 13; *Is.* 61. 5.
PLOUGHSHARES, *Is.* 2. 4; *Joel* 3. 10; *Mic.* 4. 3.
PLUCK out, *Ps.* 25. 15, & 52. 5, & 74. 11;
   Amos 4. 11; *Zech.* 3. 2; *Matt.* 5. 29, & 18. 9; *John* 10. 28, 29; *Gal.* 4. 15.
2 *Chr.* 7. 20. *p.* up, *Jer.* 12. 17, & 18. 7, & 31. 28, 40; *Dan.* 11. 4; *Jude* 12.
Ezra 9. 3. *p.* off. *Job* 29. 17; *Is.* 50. 6; *Ezek.* 23. 34; *Mic.* 3. 2.
PLUMMET, *Is.* 28. 17. lay righteousness to the *p.*
Zech. 4. 10. *p.* in land of Zerubbabel
PLUNGE, *Job* 9. 31. *p.* me in the ditch and my
POETS, *Acts* 17. 28. certain of your own *p.* said
POINT, *Gen.* 25. 32. behold, I am at the *p.* to die
Jer. 17. 1. is written with the *p.* of a diamond
John 4. 47. was at the *p.* of death
Jam. 2. 10. offend in one *p.* is guilty
POINTS, *Heb.* 4. 15. in all *p.* tempted like as we
POISON, *Deut.* 32. 24, 33; *Job* 6. 4, & 20. 16; *Ps.* 58. 4; 140. 3; *Rom.* 3. 13; *Jam.* 3. 8.
POLLUTE, *Num.* 18. 32; *Ezek.* 7. 21; *Mic.* 2. 10; *Zeph.* 3. 1; *Mal.* 1. 7, 12.
POLLUTIONS, *Acts* 15. 20; 2 *Pet.* 2. 20.
PONDER path of feet, *Prov.* 4. 26.
Prov. 5. 21. he *p.* all his goings, 6.
   21. 2. Lord *p.* the hearts, 24. 12.
Luke 2. 19. *p.* them in her heart
POOR may eat. *Ex.* 23. 11.
Ex. 30. 15. *p.* shall not give less
Lev. 19. 15. shalt not respect the person of the *p.*
Deut. 15. 4. when no *p.*
   11. *p.* shall never cease
1 *Sam.* 2. 7. Lord maketh *p.* and maketh rich
   8. raiseth *p.* out of the dust, *Ps.* 1.
Job 5. 16. *p.* hath hope and iniquity
   36. 15. deliver *p.* in affliction
Ps. 10. 14. *p.* committeth himself unto thee
   68. 10. prepared of thy goodness for the *p.*
   69. 33. Lord hears the *p.* and despiseth not
   72. 2. he shall judge thy *p.* 4. 13.
   132. 15. I will satisfy her *p.* with bread
   140. 12. the Lord will maintain the right of the *p.*
Prov. 13. 7. maketh himself *p.*
   14. 20. the *p.* is hated of his neighbour
   31. oppresseth the *p.* reproacheth his Maker

19. 4. *p.* is separated from his neighbour
7. all brethren of *p.* hate him
22. 2. rich and *p.* meet together
22. rob not *p.* because he is *p.*
30. 9. not poverty lest I be *p.* and
Is. 14. 32. *p.* of his people shall
29. 19. *p.* among men rejoice
41. 17. when *p.* and needy seek
58. 7. bring *p.* that are cast out to thy house
66. 2. that is *p.* and of a contrite spirit
Jer. 5. 4. surely these are *p.* foolish
Amos 2. 6. sold *p.* for a pair of shoes, 8. 6.
Zeph. 3. 12. leave an afflicted and *p.*
Zech. 11. 11. *p.* of flock waited
Matt. 5. 3. blessed are *p.* in spirit
11. 5. the *p.* have the gospel preached to them
Matt. 26. 11. have the *p.* always with you, *John* 12. 8.
Luke 6. 20. blessed be ye *p.* for
14. 13. called *p.* maimed, halt
2 *Cor.* 6. 10. as *p.* yet making many rich
8. 9. was rich, for your sakes he became *p.*
9. 9. he hath given to the *p. Ps.* 112. 9.
Gal. 2. 10. we should remember *p.*
Jam. 2. 5. God hath chosen the *p.* of this world
Rev. 3. 17. knowest not that art *p.*
PORTER, 2 *Sam.* 18. 26. watchman called to the *p.* and said
1 *Chr.* 9. 21. Zechariah was *p.* of door of tabernacle
Mark 13. 34. commanded *p.* to watch
John 10. 3. to him the *p.* openeth
PORTERS, 1 *Chr.* 15. 18. and Obed-edom, and Jehiel the *p.*
1 *Chr.* 23. 5. four thousand were *p.*
26. 1. the division of the *p.* 12. 19.
2 *Chr.* 8. 14. the *p.* by their courses at every gate
35. 15. and the *p.* waited at every gate
PORTION, *Deut.* 21. 17, & 33. 21.
Deut. 32. 9. Lord's *p.* is his people
2 *Kings* 2. 9. let a double *p.* of thy spirit be upon me
Job 20. 29. this is *p.* of wicked
24. 18. their *p.* is cursed in earth
26. 14. how little a *p.* is heard, 27. 13.
31. 2. *p.* of God is from above
Ps. 11. 6. this shall be the *p.* of their cup
Ps. 16. 5. the Lord is the *p.* of mine inheritance
17. 14. have their *p.* in this life
63. 10. shall be a *p.* for foxes
73. 26. God is my *p.* for ever
119. 57. thou art my *p.* O Lord
142. 5. my *p.* in land of living
Eccl. 11. 2. give *p.* to seven and to eight
Is. 53. 12. I will divide him a *p.* with the great
61. 7. shall rejoice in their *p.*
Jer. 10. 16. *p.* of Jacob not like them, 51. 19.
12. 10. trodden my *p.* under foot
Lam. 3. 24. the Lord is my *p.* saith my
Hab. 1. 16. by them their *p.* is fat
Zech. 2. 12. the Lord shall inherit Judah

his *p.*
Man. 24. 51. appoint him his *p.*
Luke 12. 42. give their *p.* in due season
46. appoint his *p.* with unbelievers
15. 12. give *p.* of goods that falleth
Neh. 8. 10. send *p. Esth.* 9. 19, 22.
POSSESS, *Gen.* 22. 17; *Judg.* 11. 24.
Num. 13. 30. let us go up and *p.* it, we are able to overcome it, *Deut.* 1. 21.
Job 7. 3. to *p.* months of vanity
13. 26. makest me to *p.* iniquities of my youth
Luke 21. 19. in your patience *p.* ye your souls
1 *Thess.* 4. 4. how to *p.* his vessel
POSSESSED, *Ps.* 139. 13. hast *p.* my reins
Prov. 8. 22. Lord *p.* me in the beginning
Is. 63. 18. people of thy holiness *p.* it but a little
Dan. 7. 22. saints *p.* kingdom, 18.
1 *Cor.* 7. 30. as though they *p.* not
POSSESSING, 2 *Cor.* 6. 10. having nothing yet *p.* all things
POSSESSION, *Gen.* 17. 8. I will give land of Canaan for everlasting *p.* and be their God, 48. 4.
Lev. 14. 34. Canaan I gave for a *p.*
Ps. 2. 8. the uttermost parts of earth for thy *p.*
Eph. 1. 14. redemption of purchased *p.*
POSSESSIONS, *Matt.* 19. 22. for he had great *p. Mark* 10. 22.
Acts 2. 45. and sold their *p.*
POSSESSOR, *Gen.* 14. 19. high God, *p.* of heaven and earth
POSSIBLE all things with God, *Matt.* 19. 26.
Matt. 24. 24. if *p.* deceive very elect
Mark 9. 23. all things *p.* to them that believe
14. 36. Father; all things *p.* to thee
Luke 18. 27. impossible with men, *p.* with God
Acts 20. 16. if *p.* be at Jerusalem
Rom. 12. 18. if *p.* as much as in you lies
Heb. 10. 4. not *p.* blood of bulls
POSTERITY. The generation following, *Gen.* 45. 7; *Ps.* 49. 13; 109. 13.
POSTS, *Judg.* 16. 3. Samson took the two *p.*
Is. 6. 4. the *p.* of the door moved
POT, *Ex.* 16. 33; *Ps.* 68. 13, & 81. 6; *Jer.* 1. 13; *Zech.* 14. 21.
POTENTATE, 1 *Tim.* 6. 15. who is the blessed and only *P.*
POTSHERD, *Job* 2. 8. took a *p.* to scrape himself
Ps. 22. 15. my strength is dried up like a *p.*
Is. 45. 9. let the *p.* strive with *p.*
POTTAGE, *Gen.* 25. 29. Jacob sod *p.* and Esau
Gen. 25. 30. feed me with *p.*
POTTER, *Ps.* 2. 9. dash in pieces like a *p.* vessel
Jer. 18. 2. go down to the *p.* house
Lam. 4. 2. work of the hands of the *p.*
Matt. 27. 10. gave them for the *p.* field
POUND, *Luke* 19. 13; *John* 19. 39.
POUR, *Job* 36. 27; *Lev.* 14. 18, 41.
Ps. 62. 8. *p.* your hearts before him,

Lum. 2. 19.

79. 6. *p.* thy wrath on heathen, 69. 24; *Jer.* 10. 25; *Zeph.* 3. 8.

Prov. 1. 23. I will *p.* out my spirit unto you

Is. 44. 3. *p.* water upon him that is thirsty

Joel 2. 28. *p.* my Spirit on all flesh

POURED, *Job* 10. 10. *p.* me out as milk

30. 16. my soul is *p.* out in me, *Ps.* 42. 4.

Ps. 45. 2. grace is *p.* into thy lips

Songs 1. 3. thy name is as ointment *p.* forth

Is. 26. 16. *p.* out a prayer when

32. 15. till Spirit be *p.* on us

53. 12. *p.* his soul unto death

Jer. 7. 20. my fury shall be *p.* out, 42. 18, & 44. 6; *Is.* 42. 25; *Ezek.* 7. 8, & 14. 19, & 20. 8, 13, 21, & 30. 15.

Rev. 16. 1.—17. *p.* vials of God's wrath

POURETH, *Job* 12. 21. *p.* contempt on princes, *Ps.* 107. 40.

16. 20. my eye *p.* out tears to God

POVERTY, *Gen.* 45. 11; *Prov.* 11. 24.

Prov. 6. 11. so shall thy *p.* come, 24. 34.

10. 15. destruction of poor is *p.*

20. 13. love not sleep, lest thou come to *p.*

23. 21. drunkard and glutton shall come to *p.*

30. 8. give me neither *p.* nor riches

2 *Cor.* 8. 2. their deep *p.* abounded

9. ye through his *p.* might be rich

Rev. 2. 9. I know thy *p.* but art

POWDER, *Ex.* 32. 20; *Deut.* 28. 24; 2 *Kings* 23. 15; *Songs* 3. 6; *Matt.* 21. 44.

POWER with God as prince, *Gen.* 32. 28.

Gen. 49. 3. excellency of dignity and *p.*

Lev. 26. 19. break pride of your *p.*

Deut. 8. 18. gives thee *p.* to get

32. 36. when seeth their *p.* is gone

2 *Sam.* 22. 33. God is my strength and *p.*

1 *Chr.* 29. 11. thine the *p.* and glory

Ezra 8. 22. his *p.* and wrath against

Job 26. 2. hast thou helped him that is without *p.*

14. thunder of his *p.* who can understand

Ps. 49. 15. redeem my soul from the *p.* of the grave

Ps. 62. 11. *p.* belongs to God, also mercy

65. 6. mountains girded with *p.*

66. 7. he ruleth by his *p.* for ever

90. 11. knoweth the *p.* of thy anger

Prov. 3. 27. when it is in the *p.* of thy hand

Prov. 18. 21. death and life are in the *p.* of the tongue

Eccl. 8. 4. word of king there is *p.*

8. no man has *p.* over spirit to retain

Is. 40. 29. givest *p.* to faint and weak

Jer. 10. 12. made the earth by his *p.* 51. 15.

Hos. 12. 3. by his strength he had *p.* with God, 4.

Mic. 3. 8. I am full of *p.* by the Spirit of the Lord

Hab. 1. 11. imputing his *p.* to God

3. 4. there was hiding of his *p.*

Zech. 4. 6. not by might nor by *p.*

Matt. 9. 6. hath *p.* on earth to forgive

8. glorified God who had given *p.*

22. 29. not knowing scripture nor *p.* of God

26. 64. sitting on right hand with *p.* *Mark* 14. 62.

28. 18. all *p.* is given to me in

Mark 9. 1. kingdom of God come with *p.*

Luke 1. 35. *p.* of the highest come upon

4. 32. his word was with *p.*

5. 17. *p.* of Lord present to heal

12. 5. fear him that hath *p.* to cast into hell

22. 53. this is your hour and the *p.* of darkness

24. 49. endued with *p.* from on high

John 1. 12. to them gave he *p.* to become sons of God

10. 18. *p.* to lay it down and *p.* to take

17. 2. given him *p.* over all

19. 10. *p.* to crucify, *p.* to release, no *p.* 11.

Acts 26. 18. turn them from *p.* of Satan to God

Rom. 1. 16. gospel is *p.* of God unto salvation

20. eternal *p.* and Godhead, 4.

9. 22. to make his *p.* known

13. 1. higher *p.* there is no *p.* but of God, 2.

1 *Cor.* 1. 24. Christ *p.* of God and wisdom of God, 18.

2. 4. in demonstration of spirit and *p.*

4. 19. know not speech but *p.*

5. 4. gathered together with *p.* of Lord

6. 12. not be brought under *p.*

9. 4. have we not *p.* to eat and

2 *Cor.* 4. 7. excellency of *p.* may be of G.

8. 3. to their *p.* yea, beyond their *p.*

13. 10. according to *p.* Lord gave

Eph. 1. 19. the exceeding greatness of his *p.*

2. 2. prince of *p.* of air works

6. 12. against principalities and *p.* 1.

21; *Col.* 1. 13, & 2. 10, 15; 1 *Pet.* 3. 22.

Phil. 3. 10. may know *p.* of his resurrection

Col. 1. 11. according to his glorious *p.*

13. delivered from *p.* of darkness

1 *Thess.* 1. 5. not in word but *p.*

2 *Thess.* 1. 9. from glory of his *p.*

11. pleasure works of faith with *p.*

2 *Tim.* 1. 7. spirit of *p.* and love

3. 5. form of godliness denying *p.*

Heb. 1. 3. uphold all things by word of his *p.*

2. 14. destroy him that had *p.* of death

6. 5. word of God and *p.* of world

1 *Pet.* 1. 5. kept by the *p.* of God through faith to salvation

2 *Pet.* 1. 3. divine *p.* hath given

Rev. 2. 26. I give *p.* over nations

4. 11. worthy to receive *p.* 5. 13, & 7. 12, & 19. 1; 1 *Tim.* 6. 16; *Jude* 25.

11. 3. give *p.* to my two witnesses

17. taken to thee thy great *p.*

12. 10. kingdom of our God and *p.* of

16. 9. that had *p.* over these plagues

Ex. 15. 6. in *p.* Job 37. 23; *Nah.* 1. 3; 1 *Cor.* 4. 20, & 15. 43; *Eph.* 6. 10.

Ps. 63. 2. thy *p.* 110. 3 , & 145. 11.

POWERFUL, *Ps.* 29. 4; *Heb.* 4. 12.

2 Cor. 10. 10. letters, say they, are p.
Heb. 4. 12. word quick, p. and sharper
PRAISE. (1) A confession and due acknowledgement of the great and wonderful excellences and perfections that are in God, Ps. 138. 1; Rev. 19. 5. (2) A speaking forth and commending the good qualifications that are in others, Prov. 27. 2. (3) The object, matter, and ground of praise, Deut. 10. 20; Ps. 118. 14. (4) Commendation, encouragement and protection, Rom. 13. 3; 1 Pet. 2. 14. (5) Great and praiseworthy actions, Ps. 106. 2.

PRAISE, Judg. 5. 3; Ps. 7. 17.
Deut. 10. 21. he is thy p. and thy God
Neh. 9. 5. is exalted above all blessing and p.
Ps. 22. 25. my p. shall be of thee
    33. 1. p. is comely for upright, 147. 1.
    34. 1. his p. continually be in my
    50. 23. whoso offereth p. glorifies me
    65. 1. p. waiteth for thee in Zion
    100. 4. enter his courts with p.
    106. 2. who can show forth all his p.
    109. 1. hold not thy peace God of my p.
    119. 171. lips shall utter p.
    147. 1. p. is comely
    149. 1. sing his p. in the congregation
Prov. 27. 21. so is a man to his p.
Is. 60. 18. call walls Salvation, and thy gates P.
    62. 7. Jerusalem a p. in earth
Jer. 13. 11. for a p. and a glory
    17. 14. thou art my p.
Jer. 17. 26. bringing sacrifices of p.
Hab. 3. 3. earth was full of his p.
John 12. 43. loved p. of men more than p. of God
Rom. 2. 29. whose p. is not of man but of God
1 Cor. 4. 5. every man have p. of God
2 Cor. 8. 18. whose p. is in the gospel throughout the churches
Eph. 1. 6. to p. of glory of his grace, 12.
Phil. 4. 8. if there be any p. think
Heb. 13. 15. offer to God sacrifice of p. continually
1 Pet. 2. 14. for the p. of them that do well
1 Pet. 4. 11. to whom be p. dominion

PRAISE, verb, Ps. 30. 9. shall dust p. thee, 12.
    42. 5. I shall p. him for help, 11, & 42. 4.
    44. 8. p. thy name for ever
    49. 18. men will p. thee, when thou doest well for thyself
    63. 3. my lips shall p. thee
    71. 14. p. thee more and more
    76. 10. surely the wrath of men shall p. thee
    88. 10. shall dead arise and p.
    115. 17. the dead p. not the Lord
    119. 164. seven times a-day do I p. thee
    138. 2. I will p. thy name for thy loving-kindness
    145. 10. all thy works p. thee
    147. 12. p. the Lord, Jerusalem. p. thy God, O Zion

Prov. 27. 2. let another p. thee
    31. 31. her works p. in her gates
Is. 38. 18. the grave cannot p. living p. thee, 19.
Dan. 2. 23. I thank and p. thee
Joel 2. 26. eat and be satisfied, and p. the Lord
Rev. 19. 5. p. our God, ye servants
PRAISE, I will or will I, Ps. 43. 4. on the harp will I p. thee, O God
Ps. 9. 1. I will p. thee, 111. 1, & 138. 1, & 35. 18, & 52. 9, & 56. 4, & 118. 21, & 119. 7, & 139. 14.
Ps. 71. 22. I will also p. thee with the psaltery
Is. 12. 1. I will p. thee, though thou wast angry
PRAISED, 2 Sam. 22. 4. worthy to be p.
1 Chr. 16. 25. greatly to be p. Ps. 48. 1, & 96. 4, & 145. 3, & 72, 15.
PRAISES, Ex. 15. 11. like thee, fearful in p.
Ps. 9. 11. sing p. to the Lord
    27. 6. I will sing, yea I will sing p. to God, 47. 6; 68. 32; 75. 9; 108. 3.
    146. 2. I will sing p. to my God while I have being
    147. 1. good to sing p. to God
Is. 60. 6. show forth the p. of the Lord
Acts 16. 25. Paul and Silas prayed and sung p. to God
1 Pet. 2. 9. show forth the p. of him who called you
PRAISING, 2 Chr. 5. 13; Ezra 3. 11; Ps. 84. 4; Luke 2. 13, 20; Acts 2. 46.
PRATING, Prov. 10. 8, 10; 3 John 10.
PRAY for thee and thou live, Gen. 20. 7.
1 Sam. 7. 5. I will p. for you to the Lord, 12. 19, 23.
2 Sam. 7. 27. found in his heart to p. this p. unto thee
Job 21. 15. what profit if we p. to
    42. 8. Job shall p. for you, him
Ps. 5. 2. my God, to thee will I p.
    55. 17. evening and morning, and noon, will I p.
    122. 6. p. for peace of Jerusalem
Jer. 7. 16. p. not for this people, 11, 14, & 14. 11.
Zech. 8. 22. seek the Lord and p. before the Lord of hosts
Matt. 5. 44. p. for them that despitefully
Matt. 26. 41. watch and p. enter not
Mark 11. 24. what ye desire when p.
    13. 33. watch and p. know not
Luke 11. 1. teach us to p. as John
    18. 1. men ought always to p.
    21. 36. watch and p. always
John 16. 26. I will p. the Father for you, 14. 16.
    17. 9. I p. for them, I p. not for the world
    20. neither p. I for these alone
Acts 8. 22. p. God if perhaps
    24. p. ye the Lord for me
    10. 9. Peter went on the house-top to p.
Rom. 8. 26. know not what p. for
1 Cor. 14. 15. I will p. with the spirit, 14.
2 Cor. 5. 20. we p. you in Christ's stead
Col. 1. 9. not cease to p. for you
1 Thess. 5. 17. p. without ceasing

25. p. for us, 2 Thess. 3. 1; Heb. 13. 18.
1 Tim. 2. 8. I will that men p.
Jam. 5. 13. is any afflicted, let p.
  16. p. for one another, Eph. 6. 18.
Luke 22. 32. I have p. for thee
  44. in agony p. more earnestly
Acts 9. 11. behold he p.
  10. 2. gave alms and p. to God
  20. 36. Paul p. with them all
Jam. 5. 17. he p. earnestly that it might
  not rain
PRAYER. Is an offering up of our
  desires to God for things lawful and
  needful, with an humble confidence
  to obtain them through the alone
  mediation of Christ, to the praise
  of the mercy, truth, and power of
  God, Matt. 6. 6; John 16. 23, 24,
  26. It is either mental or vocal,
  ejaculatory, or occasional, either
  private or public; for ourselves, or
  others; for the procuring of good
  things, or the removing, or prevent-
  ing of things evil, 1 Tim. 2. 1, 2.
  As God is the only object of prayer,
  Ps. 50. 15. and as we must pray for
  others, as well as for ourselves,
  Jam. 5. 16, so we are to pray fervently, Col. 4. 12, sincerely, Ps. 17.
  1. constantly, Col. 4. 2. with faith,
  Jam. 5. 15. and not without repentance, Ps. 66. 18; Jer. 36. 7. and by
  the help of the Holy Spirit, Rom.
  8. 26.
PRAYER, 2 Sam. 7. 27. found in his
  heart to p. this p.
1 Kings 8. 28. have respect to p. of
  38. what p. and supplication
  45. hear their p.
2 Chr. 30. 27. their p. came up to God
Neh. 1. 6. mayest hear the p. of thy servant
  4. 9. we made our p. to God
Job 15. 4. restrainest p. before God
Ps. 65. 2. thou that hearest p. to thee
  shall all come
  102. 17. he will regard p. of destitute,
  and not despise their p.
  109. 4. I give myself to p.
Prov. 15. 8. p. of the upright is his
  delight
  29. he heareth p. of righteous
  28. 9. his p. shall be abomination, Ps.
  109. 7.
Is. 26. 16. poured out a p. when
  56. 7. joyful in house of p. for all people
Jer. 7. 16. lift up cry nor p. for
Lam. 3. 44. our p. should not pass
Dan. 9. 3. by p. and supplication
Matt. 17. 21. not out but by p. and fast-
Acts 3. 1. to temple at hour of p.
  6. 4. we will give ourselves continually to p.
  12. 5. p. made without ceasing
  16. 13. where p. was wont to be made
1 Cor. 7. 5. give ourselves to fasting
  and p.
2 Cor. 1. 11. helping together by p. for us
Eph. 6. 18. p. always with all p.
Phil. 4. 6. in every thing by p. and
  supplication
1 Tim. 4. 5. sanctified by word and p.

Jam. 5. 15. p. of faith save sick
  16. fervent p. of righteous
1 Pet. 4. 7. watch unto p. Col. 4. 2.
Luke 6. 12. continued in p. Acts 1. 14;
  Rom. 12. 12.
Job 16. 17. my p. Ps. 5. 3, & 6. 9, & 17.
  1, & 35. 13, & 66. 20, & 88. 2; Lam.
  3. 8; Jonah 2. 7.
  22. 27. thy p. Is. 37. 4; Luke 1. 13;
  Acts 10. 31.
PRAYERS, Ps. 72. 20. p. of David ended
Is. 1. 15. make many p. I not hear
Matt. 23. 14. for pretence make long p.
Acts 10. 4. thy p. and alms are
1 Tim. 2. 1. first p. intercessions
1 Pet. 3. 7. that your p. be not hindered
  12. his ears are open to their p.
Rev. 5. 8. are the p. of saints, 8. 3.
PRAYING, Dan. 9. 20; 1 Cor. 11. 4.
1 Thess. 3. 10. night and day p.
Jude 20. building up p. in Holy Ghost
PREACH at Jerusalem, Neh. 6. 7.
Is. 61. 1. anointed me to p. good tidings
Jonah 3. 2. p. the p. I bid thee
Matt. 4. 17. Jesus began to p. the king-
  dom of heaven
  10. 7. p. kingdom of heaven is at hand
  27. hear in the ear p. on house-tops
Mark 1. 4. p. baptism of repentance
Luke 4. 18. to p. deliverance to captives
  9. 60. go thou p. kingdom of God
Acts 10. 42. commanded us to p.
  15. 21. hath in every city them that
  p. him
Rom. 10. 8. word of faith we p.
  15. how shall they p. except sent
1 Cor. 1. 23. we p. Christ crucified
  15. 11. so we p. and believed
2 Cor. 4. 5. we p. not ourselves but
  Christ Jesus our Lord
Phil. 1. 15. some p. Christ of envy
Col. 1. 28. whom we p. warning every
2 Tim. 4. 2. p. the word, instant
Ps. 40. 9. I have p. righteousness
Mark 2. 2. he p. word unto them
  6. 12. he p. men should repent
  16. 20. p. everywhere word, 15.
Luke 4. 44. he p. in synagogues of Galilee
  24. 27. remission of sins be p. in his
  name
Acts 8. 5. Philip p. Christ unto them, 40.
  9. 20. Saul p. Christ in synagogues
Acts 13. 38. through this man is p. to
1 Cor. 9. 27. I have p. to others
  15. 2. if Christ be p. that he rose
2 Cor. 11. 4. p. another Jesus whom we
  have not p.
Gal. 1. 8. other gospel than that we
  have p. to you
  23. now p. the faith he once destroyed
Eph. 2. 17. p. peace to you afar off, and
  to them nigh
Phil. 1. 18. Christ is p. and I therein do
  rejoice
Col. 1. 23. which was p. to every creature
1 Tim. 3. 16. God was manifest in flesh,
  p. to Gentiles, believed on
Heb. 4. 2. word p. did not profit
1 Pet. 3. 19. p. to spirits in prison
PREACHER, Eccl. 1. 1, 2, 12, & 12, 8, 9.
Rom. 10. 14. how shall they hear without a p.

1 *Tim.* 2. 7. I am ordained a *p.* 2 *Tim.*
   1. 11.
2 *Pet.* 2. 5. saved Noah a *p.* of
PREACHING, *Matt.* 3. 1. in those days
   came John *p.*
Mark 1. 14. Jesus came into Galilee *p.*
Acts 8. 4. they went every where *p.* the
   word
   12. *p.* the things concerning the kingdom of God
   10. 36. *p.* peace by Jesus Christ
   11. 19. *p.* word to none but Jews
   20. 9. as Paul was long *p.* Eutychus
1 *Cor.* 1. 18. *p.* of cross to them is
   foolishness
   21. by foolishness of *p.* to save them
   2. 4. my *p.* was not with enticing
   15. 14. then is our *p.* vain
PRECEPT, *Neh.* 9. 14; *Jer.* 35. 18.
Ps. 119. 4. command us to keep thy *p.*
   diligently
   15. I will meditate in thy *p.* 78.
   27. understand way of thy *p.*
   40. I have longed after thy *p.*
   45. for I seek thy *p.*
   56. I kept thy *p.* 63. 69, 134.
   87. I forsook not thy *p.* 93.
   94. I have sought thy *p.*
   104. through *p.* get understanding
   110. I erred not from thy *p.*
   128. I esteem thy *p.*
   141. I do not forget thy *p*
   159. how I love thy *p.*
   173. I have chosen thy *p.*
Is. 28. 10. for *p.* must be upon *p.*
   29. 13. fear taught by *p.* of men
PRECIOUS things of heaven, &c., *Deut.*
   33. 13, 14, 15, 16.
1 *Sam.* 3. 1. word of Lord was *p.* in those
   days
   26. 21. my soul *p.* in thine eyes
2 *Kings* 1. 13. let my life be *p.* in
Ps. 49. 8. redemption of soul is *p.*
   72. 14. *p.* shall their blood be
   116. 15. *p.* in sight of the Lord death
   of saints
   126. 6. weeping bearing *p.* seed
   139. 17. *p.* are thoughts to me
Eccl. 7. 1. a good name better than *p.*
   ointment
Is. 13. 12. man more *p.* than fine gold
   28. 16. foundation-stone a *p.* corner-
   stone
Is. 43. 4. thou wast *p.* in my sight
Jer. 15. 19. take forth *p.* from vile
Lam. 4. 2. the *p.* sons of Zion as earthen
   pitchers
Jam. 5. 7. husbandman wait for *p.* fruit
1 *Pet.* 1. 7. trial more *p.* than gold
   19. redeemed with *p.* blood of Christ
   2. 4. stone chosen of God and *p.* 6.
   7. to them who believe he is *p.*
2 *Pet.* 1. 1. obtained like *p.* faith
   4. great and *p.* promises
PREDESTINATED, *Eph.* 1. 5. *p.* us to
   the adoption of sons
Eph. 1. 11. *p.* according to the purpose
PRE-EMINENCE, *Eccl.* 3. 19. man no
   p. above a beast
Col. 1. 18. in all things he might have *p.*
3 *John* 9. Diotrephes loveth the *p.*
PREFER, *Ps.* 137. 6. if I *p.* not Jerusalem above

PREFERRED, ING, *Dan.* 6. 3. Daniel
   p. above presidents
Rom. 12. 10. in honour *p.* one another
1 *Tim.* 5. 21. without *p.* one before
PREJUDICE, 1 *Tim.* 5. 21. observe
   things without *p.*
PREMEDITATE, *Mark* 13. 11. neither
   p. nor whatsoever is given
PREPARATION, *Prov.* 16. 1. *p.* of heart
Matt. 27. 62. the next day that followed
   the day of *p. Mark* 15. 42; *Luke* 23.
   54; *John* 19. 14, 31, 42.
Eph. 6. 15. shod with the *p.* of the
   gospel of peace
PREPARE, *Ex.* 15. 2, & 16. 5.
1 *Sam.* 7. 3. *p.* your hearts to the Lord
1 *Chr.* 29. 18. *p.* their hearts to
2 *Chr.* 35. 6. *p.* your brethren
Job 11. 13. if thou *p.* thy heart
Ps. 10. 17. thou wilt *p.* their heart
   61. 7. O *p.* mercy and truth
Prov. 24. 27. *p.* thy work without
Is. 40. 3. *p.* ye the way of the Lord
Amos 4. 12. *p.* to meet thy God, O Israel
Mic. 3. 5. they '*p.* war against him
Matt. 11. 10. shall *p.* thy way before
Luke 3. 4. saying, *p.* ye the way of the
   Lord, 7. 27.
John 14. 2. I go to *p.* a place for you
1 *Cor.* 14. 8. *p.* himself to the battle
PREPARED, 2 *Chr.* 19. 3. hast *p.* thy
   27. 6. he *p.* his ways before the Lord
   29. 36. God hath *p.* the people
   30. 19. pardon every one that *p.* his
   heart to seek God
Ezra 7. 10. Ezra had *p.* his heart to seek
   the law of the Lord
Neh. 8. 10. for whom nothing is *p.*
Ps. 23. 5. thou *p.* a table before me
   65. 9. thou *p.* them corn
   68. 10. *p.* goodness for poor

Ps. 147. 8. who *p.* rain for earth
Is. 64. 4. what God hath *p.* for, 1 *Cor.*
   2. 9.
Hos. 6. 3. his going forth is *p.* as morn.
Matt. 20. 23. given to for whom *p.*
   22. 4. I have *p.* my dinner, my
   25. 34. inherit kingdom *p.* for
Luke 1. 17. ready people *p.* for the Lord
   12. 47. knew not his lord's will and *p.*
   not himself
Rom. 9. 23. vessels of mercy *p.*
2 *Tim.* 2. 21. *p.* to every good work
Heb. 10. 5. a body hast thou *p.* me
   11. 7. *p.* ark to save house
   16. called their God, for he hath *p.* for
   them a city
Rev. 12. 6. into wilderness a place *p.* of
   God
   21. 2. new Jerusalem *p.* as a bride for
PREPARING, 1 *Pet.* 3. 20. Noah, while
   the ark was *p.*
PRESBYTERY, 1 *Tim.* 4. 14. laying on
   hands of *p.*
PRESENCE, *Gen.* 3. 8. hid themselves
   from *p.* of the Lord
Gen. 4. 16. Cain went out from the *p.* of
   the Lord, *Job* 1. 12, & 2. 7; *Ps.* 114.
   7; *Jer.* 4. 26; *Jonah* 1. 3, 10; *Zeph.*
   1. 7; *Jude* 24.
Job 23. 15. am troubled at his *p.*
Ps. 16. 11. in *p.* is fulness of joy

31. 20. hide them in secret of thy *p.*
51. 11. cast me not away from *p.*
95. 2. come before his *p.* with thanksgiving
97. 5. the hills melted like wax at the
   p. of God
100. 2. came before his *p.* with singing
114. 7. tremble earth at *p.* of the Lord
139. 7. whither shall I flee from thy *p.*
140. 13. upright dwell in thy *p.*
Is. 63. 9. the angel of his *p.* saved them
Jer. 5. 22. ye not tremble at my *p.*
Luke 13. 26. eaten and drunken in thy *p.*
Acts 3. 19. times of refreshment from *p.*
   of the Lord
1 *Cor.* 1. 29. no flesh glory in his *p.*
2 *Cor.* 10. 1. who in *p.* am base among
2 *Thess.* 1. 9. everlasting destruction
   from *p.* of the Lord
Jude 24. present you faultless before *p.*
   of his glory
Rev. 14. 10. *p.* of holy angels and the L.
PRESENCE, in the, *Luke* 1. 19. I am
   Gabriel, that stand *in the p.* of God
Luke 15. 10. there is joy *in the p.* of the
   angels of God
1 *Thess.* 2. 19. are not even ye *in the p.*
   of our Lord Jesus
PRESENT, noun, *Gen.* 32. 13. a *p.* from
   Esau his brother
Gen. 43. 11. Israel said, carry down the
   man a *p.*
1 *Sam.* 9. 7. not a *p.* for man of God
1 *Kings* 10. 25. brought every man his *p.*
PRESENT help in trouble, *Ps.* 46. 1.
Acts 10. 33. all here *p.* before God
Rom. 7. 18. to will is *p.* with me
   21. evil is *p.* with me
   8. 18. sufferings of this *p.* time
   38. nor things *p.* able to separate
1 *Cor.* 3. 22. things *p.* or things to come,
   all are yours
1 *Cor.* 5. 3. absent in body, but *p.* in
2 *Cor.* 5. 8. to be *p.* with the Lord
   9. whether *p.* or absent we be
Gal. 1. 4. deliver us from *p.* world
2 *Tim.* 4. 10. having loved this *p.* world
2 *Pet.* 1. 12. be established in the *p.*
PRESENT, *Rom.* 12. 1. *p.* body a living
   sacrifice
2 *Cor.* 11. 2. *p.* you as a chaste virgin to
Eph. 5. 27. he might *p.* it to himself a
   glorious church
Col. 1. 22. to *p.* you holy and
   28. *p.* every man perfect in Christ J.
Jude 24. *p.* you faultless before the Lord
PRESENTS, 1 *Sam.* 10. 27. they brought
   him no *p.*
Ps. 68. 29. kings shall bring *p.*
   72. 10. kings of Tarshish and the isles
   shall bring *p.*
PRESERVE. To reserve, save, or keep
   alive, *Gen.* 45. 7; *Ps.* 12. 7; to keep
   safe or defend, *Ps.* 16. 1.
Ps. 25. 21. integrity and truth *p.* me
   32. 7. thou *p.* me from trouble
   41. 2. I will *p.* and keep him
   61. 7. prepare mercy to *p.* him
   64. 1. *p.* my life from fear of enemies
   79. 11. *p.* those appointed to die
   86. 2. *p.* my soul for I am holy
   121. 7. the Lord shall *p.* thee from evil
   140. 1. *p.* me from violent men

Prov. 2. 11. discretion shall *p.* thee
Luke 17. 33. whosoever will lose his life
   shall *p.* it
2 *Tim.* 4. 18. will *p.* me to his heavenly
   kingdom
PRESERVED, ETH, *Josh.* 24. 17. *p.* us
   in all the way
2 *Sam.* 8. 6. the Lord *p.* David whither-
   soever he went
Job 10. 12. thy visitation has *p.* my spirit
Ps. 97. 10. he *p.* soul of his saints
   116. 6. Lord *p.* simple
   145. 20. Lord *p.* all that love him
   146. 9. the Lord *p.* the strangers
Prov. 2. 8. he *p.* way of his saints
1 *Thess.* 5. 23. soul and body be *p.*
   blameless
Jude 1. *p.* in Christ Jesus and called
PRESERVER, *Job* 7. 20. what shall I do
   O thou *P.* of men
PRESERVEST, *Ps.* 36. 6. O Lord, thou
   p. man and beast
PRESS. To throng or crowd, thrust,
   weigh down, *Luke* 8. 45; 19. 3.—
   To urge, *Gen.* 19. 3; 40. 11; *Judg.*
   16. 16.
Ps. 38. 2. thy hand *p.* me sore
Amos 2. 13. I am *p.* as a cart is *p.*
Luke 6. 38. good measure *p.* down and
   16. 16. kingdom of God every man *p.*
   into it
Acts 18. 5. Paul was *p.* in spirit
2 *Cor.* 1. 8. we were *p.* above
Phil. 3. 14. I *p.* towards mark for
PRESSES, *Prov.* 3. 10. thy *p.* shall
   burst with new wine
Is. 16. 10. treaders shall tread out new
   wine in their *p.*
PRESUMPTIOUS, *Ps.* 19. 13; 2 *Pet.* 2.
   10; *Num.* 15. 30; *Deut.* 17. 13.
PRETENCE for a, *Matt.* 23. 14; *Phil.*
   1. 18.
PREVAIL, *Gen.* 7. 20; *Judg.* 16. 5.
Gen. 32. 28. power with men and God
   hast *p.*
Ex. 17. 11. Moses held up his hand,
   Israel *p.*
1 *Sam.* 2. 9. by strength shall no man *p.*
Job 14. 20. thou *p.* for ever
Ps. 9. 19. O Lord, and let not man *p.*
   65. 3. iniquities *p.* against me
Eccl. 4. 12. if one *p.* against him
Hos. 12. 4. power over angel and *p.*
Matt. 16. 18. gates of hell shall not *p.*
   against it
Acts 19. 20. word of God grew mightily
   and *p.*
PREVENT, *Job* 3. 12; *Ps.* 59. 10, & 79.
   8, & 88. 13, & 119. 148; *Amos* 9.
   10; 1 *Thess.* 4. 15.
PREVENTED, 2 *Sam.* 22. 6, 19; *Job* 30.
   27, & 41. 11; *Ps.* 18. 5, 18, & 21. 3,
   & 119. 147; *Is.* 21. 14; *Matt.* 17. 25.
PREY, *Gen.* 49. 9, 27; *Esth.* 9. 15, 16.
Ps. 124. 6. not given us as a *p.* to their
   teeth
Is. 49. 24. shall *p.* be taken from
   mighty, 25.
   59. 15. he that departeth from evil,
   maketh himself a *p.*
Jer. 21. 9. life for a *p.* 38. 2, & 39. 18, &
   45. 5.
Ezek. 34. 22. my flock shall no more be

a *p.*
PRICE, *Lev.* 25. 16: *Deut.* 23. 18.
Job 28. 13. man knows not *p.* of it
Ps. 44. 12. not increase wealth by *p.*
Prov. 17. 16. wherefore is a *p.* in hand
of a fool to get wisdom
Is. 55. 1. buy wine and milk without
money and *p.*
Matt. 13. 46. pearl of great *p.*
Acts 5. 2. kept back part of *p.*
1 *Cor.* 6. 20. bought with a *p.* 7. 23.
1 *Pet.* 3, 4. in sight of God great *p.*
PRICKED, *Ps.* 73. 21; *Acts* 2. 37.
PRICKS, *Num.* 33. 55. those that
remain be *p.* in your eyes
Acts 9. 5. it is hard to kick against the
p. 26. 14.
PRIDE of heart, 2 *Chr.* 32. 26; *Ps.* 10. 4.
Job 33. 17. may hide *p.* from man
Ps. 10. 2. wicked in his *p.* doth persecute
31. 20. hide from *p.* of man
73. 6. *p.* compasseth them about
Prov. 8. 13. *p.* and arrogance I hate
11. 2. when *p.* cometh shame
13. 10. by *p.* cometh contention
16. 18. *p.* before destruction
29. 23. man's *p.* bring him low
Is. 9. 9. say in *p.* of their hearts
23. 9. Lord purposed to stain *p.* of
28. 1. woe to the crown of *p.* to the
drunkards, 3.
Jer. 13. 17. weep in secret for your *p.*
Ezek. 7. 10. rod hath blossomed, *p.* hath
budded
16. 49. the iniquity of sister Sodom, *p.*
fulness
Dan. 4. 37. walk in *p.* able to abase
Hos. 5. 5. *p.* of Israel testify to face
Obad. 3. *p.* of thy heart deceiveth
Mork 7. 22. blasphemy, *p.* foolish
1 *Tim.* 3. 6. lest, lifted up with *p.* he fall
1 *John* 2. 16. lust of eyes, *p.* of life
PRIEST, *Gen.* 14. 18; *Ex.* 2. 16; *Lev.* 6.
20, 26, & 5. 6, & 6. 7, & 12. 8.
Is. 24. 2. as with people. with *p.*
28. 7. *p.* and prophet have erred
Jer. 23. 11. prophet and *p.* are profane
Ezek. 7. 26. law perish from *p.*
Hos. 4. 4. those that strive with the *p.*
9. like people, like *p.*
Mal. 2. 7. *p.* lips keep knowledge
Heb. 5. 6. a *p.* for ever, 7. 17, 21.
Lev. 21. 10. high-*p.*- *Heb.* 2. 17. & 3. 1. &
4. 14, 15, & 5. 1, 10, & 6. 20 & 7.
26. 8, 1, 3, & 9. 11, & 10. 21.
Ps. 132. 9. let thy *p.* be clothed
16. I will clothe her *p.* with salvation
Is. 61. 6. shall be named *p.* of the Lord
Jer. 5. 31. *p.* bear rule by their means,
31. 14. satisfy soul of *p.* with fatness
Ezek. 22. 26. *p.* have violated law
Joel. 1. 9. *p.* the Lord's ministers mourn
2. 17.
Mic. 3. 11. *p.* teach for hire, and
Matt. 12. 5. *p.* in temple profane the
sabbath
Acts 6 7. company of *p.* obedient
Rev. 1. 6. kings and *p.* to God, 5. 10, &
20. 6.
Ex. 40. 15. everlasting *p.*-hood
Heb. 7. 24. he hath an unchangeable *p.*
1 *Pet.* 2. 5. ye are an holy *p.*

9. ye are a royal *p.*
PRINCE, *Gen.* 23. 6, & 34. 2.
Gen. 32. 28. as a *p.* hast power with God
Ex. 2. 14. made thee a *p.* over us
2 *Sam.* 3. 38. a *p.* and great man fallen
this day in Israel
Job 31. 37. as a *p.* I would go near unto
Is. 9. 6. everlasting Father, *P.* of peace
Ezek. 34. 24. my servant David a *p.*
among them, 37. 25, & 44. 3, & 45.
7, & 46. 10, 16; *Dan.* 9. 25.
Dan. 10. 21. Michael your *p.*
12. 1. the great *p.*
Hos. 3. 4. many days without a *p.*
John 12. 31. now the *p.* of this world be
14. 30. *p.* of this world cometh
16. 11. because *p.* of this world is
Acts 3. 15. ye killed the *P.* of life
5. 31. to be a *P.* and a Saviour
Eph. 2. 2. according to the *p.* of the
power of air
Rev. 1. 5. *p.* of kings of the earth
Job 12. 19. leadeth *p.* away spoiled
21. pours contempt on *p.* 107. 40.
34. 18. fit to say to *p.* ye are ungodly
19. accepts not person of *p.*
Ps. 45. 16. children make *p.* in earth
76. 12. he will cut off spirit of *p.*
82. 7. ye shall fall like one of *p.*
118. 9. to put confidence in *p.*
119. 23. *p.* did speak against me
161. *p.* have persecuted me without
146. 3. put not trust in *p.*
Prov. 8. 15. by me *p.* decree justice, 16.
17. 26. not good to strike *p.* for
28. 2. for the transgression of a land
many are *p.* of it
31. 4. not for *p.* to drink strong
Eccl. 10. 7. I have seen *p.* walking upon
Is. 3. 4. children to be their *p.*
Hos. 7. 5. *p.* have made the king sick
with wine
8. 4. made *p.* and I knew it not
Matt. 20. 25. *p.* of Gentiles exercise
1 *Cor.* 2. 6. wisdom of the *p.* of this world
8. none of the *p.* of this world knew
PRINCIPAL, *Ex.* 30. 23; *Lev.* 6. 5; 2
Kings 25. 19.
Prov. 4. 7. wisdom is the *p.* thing
Is. 16. 8. broken down the *p.* plants
Jer. 25. 35. nor the *p.* of flock escape
Acts 25. 23. the *p.* of the city entered
PRINCIPALITIES, *Rom.* 8. 38. angels
p. and powers be able to separate
Eph. 1. 21. far above all *p.*
Eph. 3. 10. to *p.* might be known wisdom
6. 12. we wrestle against *p.* and
against powers
Col. 1. 16. *p.* were created by him
2. 10. head of all *p.* and power
15. having spoiled *p.* he made
Tit. 3. 1. to be subject to *p.*
PRINCIPLES, *Heb.* 5. 12. one teach you
the first *p.*
Hed. 6. 1. leaving the *p.* of the doctrine
PRISON, *Gen.* 39. 20; *Eccl.* 4. 14.
Ps. 142. 7. bring my soul out of *p.* to
praise thy name
Is. 42. 7. bring out *p.* from *p.*
53. 8. he was taken from *p.* and judg-
61. 1. opening of *p.* to bound
Matt. 4. 12. Jesus heard that John was
cast into *p.*

5. 25. thou be cast into *p*.

14. 3. Herod put him in *p*. for Herodias' sake

18. 30. cast him into *p*. till he should pay the debt

25. 36. I was in *p*. and ye came

Acts 5. 18. apostles in common *p*.

19. angel opened *p*. doors

12. 4. Peter was put in *p*.

16. 23. Paul and Silas were cast into *p*.

26. 10. many saints I shut in *p*.

1 Pet. 3. 19. preached unto the spirits in *p*.

Rev. 2. 10. devil cast some into *p*.

20. 7. Satan be loosed out of *p*.

PRISONS, *Luke* 21. 12; *2 Cor*. 11. 23.

PRISONER, S, *Ps.* 79. 11. sighing of *p*. come

102. 20. Lord to hear the groaning of the *p*.

Is. 42. 7. bring out the *p*. from the

49. 9. say to the *p*. go forth

Matt. 27. 15. wont to release a *p*.

Eph. 4. 1. I *p*. of the Lord beseech you, 3. 1.

Job 3. 18. there *p*. rest together

Ps. 69. 33. Lord despiseth not his *p*.

146. 7. giveth food, Lord looseth *p*.

Zech. 9. 11. sent forth *p*. out of pit

12. turn to strong hold ye *p*. of hope

PRIVATE, *Gal.* 2. 2; signifies such as arises out of man's mind, *2 Pet.* 1. 20. " No prophecy of the scripture is of any private interpretation "— not of the prophet's own invention; but the holy prophets of God spake their prophecies, being inspired by the Holy Ghost. Apart from others, *Matt.* 24. 3; *Mark* 6. 32.

PRIVILY, *Ps.* 10. 8; & 11. 2, & 101. 5; *Acts* 16. 37; *Gal.* 2. 4; *2 Pet.* 2. 1.

PRIVY, *Deut.* 23. 1; *Acts* 5. 2.

PROCEED, *2 Sam.* 7. 12.

Job 40. 5. twice spoken I will *p*. no further-

Is. 29. 14. I will *p*. to do a marvellous

51. 4. a law shall *p*. from me

Jer. 9. 3. they *p*. from evil to evil

Matt. 15. 19. out of the heart *p*. murders

Luke 4. 22. gracious words that *p*. out of his mouth

John 8. 42. I *p*. forth and came from G.

Eph. 4. 29. no corrupt communication *p*. out of his mouth

2 Tim. 3. 9. shall *p*. no further

Gen. 24. 50. thing *p*. from the Lord

Deut. 8. 3. by every word that *p*. out

1 Sam. 24. 13. wickedness *p*. from the

Lam. 3. 38. out of the mouth of the Lord *p*. not evil

John 15. 26. Spirit or Holy Ghost *p*. from the Father

Jam. 3. 10. out of mouth *p*.

Rev. 11. 5. fire *p*. out of mouth

PROCLAIM. To declare, publish, or make known, *Lev.* 23. 2; *Deut.* 20. 10.

Ex. 33. 19. I will *p*. name of the Lord,

Prov. 20. 6. most men will *p*. his

12. 23. fools *p*. foolishness

Is. 61. 1. to *p*. liberty to captives

2. to *p*. the acceptable year of the Lord. The proclaiming of perfect liberty to the bound, and the year

of acceptance with Jehovah, alludes to the proclaiming of the year of jubilee by sound of trumpet, *Lev.* 25. 9. &c.

PROCURED, *Jer.* 2. 17; 4. 18.

PROFANE not the name of the Lord, *Lev.* 18. 21, & 19. 12, & 20. 3, & 21. 6, & 22. 2, 32.

Neh. 13. 17. *p*. sabbath *Matt.* 12. 5.

Ps. 89. 39. thou hast *p*. his crown

Ezek. 22. 8. hast *p*. my sabbaths

26. put no difference between holy and *p*.

Amos 2. 7. to *p*. my holy name

Mal. 1. 12. ye have *p*. it in that ye say

2. 10. by *p*. the covenant of fathers

11. Judah hath *p*. holiness of the Lord

1 Tim. 1. 9. for unholy and *p*. for

4. 7. refuse *p*. and old wives' fables

6. 20. avoid *p*. babblings

Heb. 12. 16. fornication or *p*. person as

PROFESS, *Deut.* 26. 3; *Tit.* 1. 16.

PROFESSION, *1 Tim.* 6. 12, 13; *Heb.* 3. 1, & 4. 14, & 10. 23.

PROFIT, *Prov.* 14. 23; *Eccl.* 7. 11; *Jer.* 16. 19; *2 Tim.* 2. 14; *Heb.* 12. 10.

1 Sam. 12. 21. not *p*. *Job* 33. 27, & 34. 9; *Prov.* 10. 2, & 11. 4; *Is.* 30. 5, & 44. 9, 10, & 57. 12; *Jer.* 2. 8, 11, & 7. 8, & 23. 32; *John* 6. 63; *1 Cor.* 13. 3; *Gal.* 5. 2; *Heb.* 4. 2; *Jam.* 2. 14.

PROFITABLE, *Job* 22. 2; *Eccl.* 10. 10; *Acts* 20. 20; *1 Tim.* 4. 8; *2 Tim.* 3. 16; *Tit.* 3. 8; *Philem.* 11.

PROLONG days. Spoken of life and days; *Deut.* 4. 26, 40; 5. 16, 33; 6. 2; 11. 9; 17. 20; 22. 7; 30. 18; 32. 47; *Prov.* 10. 27; 28. 16; *Eccl.* 8. 12; *Is.* 53. 10.

PROMISE, *Num.* 14. 34; *Neh.* 5. 12.

Ps. 77. 8. doth his *p*. fail for ever

105. 42. remembered his holy *p*.

Luke 24. 49. I send the *p*. of my Father upon you

Acts 1. 4. wait for *p*. of the Father

3. 39. *p*. is to you and to your children

Rom. 4. 16. that *p*. might be sure

9. 8. children of *p*. 9; *Gal.* 4. 28.

Eph. 1. 13. Holy Spirit of *p*.

2. 12. covenant of *p*.

6. 2. is first commandment with *p*.

1 Tim. 4. 8. *p*. of life, *2 Tim.* 1. 1.

Heb. 4. 1. lest a *p*. being left us

6. 17. heirs of *p*. 11. 9.

9. 15. might receive the *p*. of eternal

2 Pet. 3. 4. where is the *p*. of his coming

1 John 2. 25. *p*. that he *p*. us eternal life, *Luke* 1. 72; *Rom.* 1. 2. & 4. 21; *Tit.* 1. 2; *Heb.* 10. 23, & 11. 11.

Rom. 9. 4. to whom pertain *p*.

15. 8. confirm the *p*. made unto the fathers

2 Cor. 1. 20. all *p*. are yea and amen

7. 1. having these *p*. let us

Gal. 3. 21. is the law against *p*.

Heb. 6. 12. inherit the *p*.

8. 6. established on better *p*.

11. 13. not received *p*. 17. 33.

2 Pet. 1. 4. exceeding great & precious *p*.

PROMOTION. Advance to greater dignity, *Num.* 22. 17. Exaltation *Prov.* 4. 8. To restore to former honour, *Ps.* 75. 6; *Prov.* 3. 35; *Dar.* 3. 30.

PROOF, by many, *Acts* 1. 3; 2 *Cor.* 2. 9. & 8. 24.
PROPER, 1 *Chr.* 29. 3; *Heb.* 11. 23
PROPHECY, 1 *Cor.* 12. 10; 1 *Tim.* 4. 14 & 1. 18; 2 *Pet.* 1. 19. 20; *Rev.* 1. 3 & 11. 6, & 19. 10, & 22. 7, 10, 18, 19
PROPHESY, 1 *Kings* 22. 8. doth not *p* good, 18.
Is. 30. 10. speak smooth. *p.* deceits
Jer. 14. 4. *p.* lies in my name
Joel 2. 28. sons and daughters *p.*
Amos 2. 12. saying *p.* not
3. 8. who can but *p.*
1 *Cor.* 13. 9. we *p.* in part
14. 1. but rather that ye *p.*
14. 31. all may be *p.* one by one
39. covet to *p.* forbid not
Rev. 10. 11. must *p.* again before
PROPHESIED, *Num.* 11. 25. they *p.* not cease
Jer. 23. 21. I have not spoken to them, yet they *p.*
Matt. 7. 22. have *p.* in thy name
11. 13. law and prophets *p.* until John
John 11. 51. *p.* that Jesus should die
1 *Pet.* 1. 10. prophets *p.* of grace
Jude 14. Enoch also *p.* of these
PROPHESYING, *Ezra* 6. 14; 1 *Cor.* 11. 4, & 14. 6, 22; 1 *Thess.* 5. 20.
PROPHET, 1 *Sam.* 22. 5; 1 *Kings* 1. 32; 13. 11; 18. 36.
Gen. 20. 7. pray, for he is a *p.*
Ex. 7. 1. Aaron thy brother shall be *p.*
Deut. 18. 15. will raise up a *p.* 18.
2 *Kings* 5. 13. if *p.* had bid thee
Ps. 74. 9. there is no more any *p.*
Ezek. 33. 33. know that a *p.* hath been
Hos. 9. 7. the *p.* a fool, spiritual man is
12. 13. by a *p.* was he preserved
Amos 7. 14. I was no *p.* nor *p.* son
Matt. 10. 41. receiveth *p.* in name of a *p.*
11. 9. see a *p.* and more than a
13. 57. a *p.* is not without honour,
Luke 7. 28. is not a greater *p.*
13. 33. cannot be a *p.* perish
24. 19. was a *p.* mighty in deed
John 7. 40. truth this is the *p.* 1. 21.
52. search, out of Galilee ariseth no *p.*
Acts 3. 22. a *p.* shall the Lord raise, 7.
Tit. 1. 12. even a *p.* of their own
2 *Pet.* 2. 16. ass forbade sadness of the *p.*
Num. 11. 29. all the Lord's people *p.*
1 *Sam.* 10. 12. is Saul among *p.* 19. 24.
Ps. 105. 15. do my *p.* no harm
Jer. 5. 13. *p.* shall become wind
23. 26. they are *p.* of deceit of
Lam. 2. 14. thy *p.* have seen vain things
Hos. 6. 5. I hewed them by *p.*
Mic. 3. 11. *p.* divine for money
Zeph. 3. 4. *p.* are treacherous persons
Zech. 1. 5. the *p.* do they live for ever
Matt. 5. 17. not destroy law or *p.*
7. 12. this is the law and *p.*
13. 17. many *p.* desired to see
22. 40. hang all the law and the *p.*
23. 34. I send you *p.* wise men
Luke 1. 70. spake by mouth of holy *p.* *Acts* 3. 18.
6. 23. so did their fathers to *p.*
16. 29. they have Moses and the *p.* 31.
24. 25. to believe all that *p.* have spoken, 24. 27.
John 8. 52. Abraham is dead and the *p.*

are dead
Acts 3. 25. ye are children of the *p.*
10. 43. to him give all the *p.* witness
13. 27. knew not voice of *p.*
26. 27. believest thou the *p.* 22.
Rom. 1. 2. promised by his *p.* in holy
Rom. 3. 21. witnessed by law and *p.*
1 *Cor.* 12. 28. God set some in the church apostles, *p.* 29; *Eph.* 2. 20, & 4. 11.
14. 32. spirits of *p.* are subject to the *p.*
1 *Thess.* 2. 15. who killed their *p.*
Heb. 1. 1. God spake to fathers by *p.*
Jam. 5. 10. take *p.* for an example of suffering
1 *Pet.* 1. 10. of which salvation the *p.*
Rev. 18. 20. rejoice over her holy apostles and *p.*
22. 6. Lord God of holy *p.* hath sent
9. fellow-servant and of brethren *p.*
PROPORTION of faith, *Rom.* 12. 6.
PROSPER, *Gen.* 24. 40; *Neh.* 1. 11.
Gen. 39. 3. Lord made all to *p.* in his hand, 23.
Deut. 29. 9. may *p.* in all, *Josh.* 1. 7.
2 *Chr.* 20. 20. believe his prophets so shall ye *p.*
Job 12. 6. tabernacle of robbers *p.*
Ps. 1. 3. whatsoever he doeth shall *p.*
122. 6. they shall *p.* that love
Prov. 28. 13. covers sins not *p.*
Is. 53. 10. pleasure of the Lord shall *p.*
54. 17. no weapon that is formed against thee shall *p*
55. 11. it shall *p.* in the thing whereto the wicked *p.*
Jer. 12. 1. wherefore doth the way of the wicked *p.*
23. 5. a king shall reign and *p.*
1 *Cor.* 16. 2. lay by him as God hath *p.*
3 *John* 2. be in health even as soul *p.*
PROSPERITY, 1 *Kings* 10. 7. wisdom and *p.* exceed
Job 36. 11. spend their days in *p.*
Ps. 30. 6. in my *p.* I said, I shall never be moved
73. 3. when I saw *p.* of wicked
Ps. 118. 25. save now, O Lord, send *p.*
122. 7. *p.* be within thy palaces, 35. 27.
Prov. 1. 32. *p.* of fools destroy them
Eccl. 7. 14. in day of *p.* be joyful
Jer. 22. 21. I spake to thee in *p.*
PROSPEROUS, *Gen.* 24. 21. journey *p.* *Josh.* 1. 8; *Ps.* 45. 4; *Rom.* 1. 10.
PROTEST. To declare solemnly, *Gen.* 43. 3; 1 *Sam.* 8. 9; *Jer.* 11. 7; *Zech.* 3. 6; 1 *Cor.* 15. 31.
PROUD, *Job* 9. 13, & 26. 12, & 38. 11, & 40. 11, 12; *Ps.* 12. 3.
Ps. 40. 4. respecting not *p.* nor
101. 5. a *p.* heart will I not suffer
138. 6. *p.* he knoweth afar off
Prov. 6. 17. *p.* look and lying tongue
21. 4. high look and a *p.* heart, 28. 25.
Eccl. 7. 8. lowly better than *p.* in spirit
Mal. 3. 15. we call *p.* happy, 4. 1.
Luke 1. 51. scattered the *p.* in the imagination
1 *Tim.* 6. 4. is *p.* knowing nothing
Jam. 4. 6. God resisteth *p.* 1 *Pet.* 5. 5.
PROUDLY, *Ex.* 18. 11. wherein they dealt *p.*
1 *Sam.* 2. 3. talk no more so *p.*
Neh. 9. 10. knewest that they dealt *p.*
Ps. 17. 10. they speak *p.* 31. 18.
Is. 3. 5. child shall behave *p.*

PROVE them. To put to the test;—to
sift by some affliction, *Deut.* 8. 2;
—to make manifest, *Acts* 9. 22;—
to know by experience, *Rom.* 12. 2.
Ex. 20. 20. God is come to *p.* you
Deut. 13. 3. Lord *p.* you, 8. 2, 16.
33. 8. holy one whom thou didst *p.* at
Massah
1 *Kings* 10. 1. she came to *p.* him
Job 9. 20. my mouth *p.* me perverse
Ps. 17. 3. thou hast *p.* my heart
26. 2. examine me O Lord and *p.* me,
66. 10. thou O God hast *p.* us
95. 9. they *p.* me and saw my work,
Heb. 3. 9.
Mal. 3. 10. *p.* me now herewith
Rom. 12. 2. *p.* what is the will of God
2 *Cor.* 8. 8. to *p.* sincerity of your love
13. 5. *p.* your own selves
Gal. 6. 4. let every man *p.* his own work
1 *Thess.* 5. 21. *p.* all things hold
PROVING, *Acts* 9. 22; *Eph.* 5. 10.
PROVERB and a by-word, *Deut.* 28. 37;
1 *Kings* 9. 7; *Jer.* 24. 9; *Ezek.* 14. 8.
Ps. 69. 11. I became a *p.* to them
Eccl. 12. 9. he set in order many *p.* 1
Kings 4. 32; *Prov.* 1. 1, & 10. 1.
Is. 14. 4. take up *p.* against, *Luke* 4. 23.
John 16. 25. spoken in *p.*
29. thou speakest no *p.*
2 *Pet.* 2. 22. happened according to *p.*
PROVIDE, *Ex.* 18. 21; *Acts* 23. 24.
Gen. 22. 8. God will *p.* himself a lamb
for a burnt offering
30. 30. when I *p.* for my own
Job 38. 41. who *p.* for the raven his food
Ps. 78. 20. can he *p.* flesh for his people
Prov. 6. 8. *p.* her meat in summer
Matt. 10. 9. *p.* neither silver nor gold
Luke 12. 33. *p.* bags not wax old
Rom. 12. 17. *p.* things honest in the
sight of all
2 *Cor.* 8. 21. *p.* honest things not only
1 *Tim.* 5. 8. if any *p.* not for his own
PROVOKE him not, *Ex.* 23. 21.
Num. 14. 11. how long will ye *p.*
Deut. 31. 20. *p.* me and break covenant
Job 12. 6. they that *p.* God are secure
Ps. 78. 40. how oft did they *p.* him
Is. 3. 8. to *p.* eyes of his glory
65. 3. a people that *p.* me to anger
Jer. 7. 19. do they *p.* themselves
44. 8. ye *p.* me to wrath with
Luke 11. 53. to *p.* him to speak
Rom. 10. 19. *p.* you to jealousy, 11.
11, 14.
1 *Cor.* 10. 22. do we *p.* Lord to jealousy
Eph. 6. 4. fathers *p.* not your children
Heb. 3. 16. some when they heard did *p.*
10. 24. *p.* to love and good works
Num. 16. 30. these have *p.* the Lord
14. 23. neither any which *p.* me
Deut. 9. 8. we *p.* the Lord to wrath, 22.
1 *Sam.* 1. 6. her adversary *p.* her
1 *Kings* 14. 22. *p.* him to jealousy
2 *Kings* 23. 26. Manasseh had *p.* him
1 *Chr.* 21. 1. Satan *p.* David to number
Ezra 5. 12. our fathers had *p.* the God
of heaven
Ps. 78. 56. and *p.* the most high God
106. 7. *p.* him at the sea
33. because they *p.* his Spirit he spake

43. *p.* him with their counsel
Zech. 8. 14. when your fathers *p.* me to
1 *Cor.* 13. 5. not easily *p.* thinks no evil
2 *Cor.* 9. 2. your zeal hath *p.* very many
PROVOKING, *Deut.* 32. 19; 1 *Kings* 14.
15, & 16. 7; *Ps.* 78. 17; *Gal.* 5. 26.
PRUDENT, 1 *Sam.* 16. 18.
Prov. 12. 16. a *p.* man covers shame
23. *p.* man conceals knowledge
13. 16. every *p.* man deals with knowledge
14. 8. wisdom of the *p.* is to understand his way
15. *p.* man looks to his going
18. *p.* are crowned with knowledge
15. 5. that regards reproof is *p.*
16. 21. wise in heart is called *p.*
18. 15. the heart of the *p.* getteth
knowledge
19. 14. a *p.* wife is from the Lord
22. 3. a *p.* man foreseeth the evil, 27. 12.
Is. 5. 21. woe unto wise and *p.* in their
52. 13. my servant shall deal *p.*
Jer. 49. 7. counsel perished from *p.*
Hos. 14. 9. *p.* and he shall know
Amos 5. 13. *p.* keep silence in that
Matt. 11. 25. hide these things from wise
and *p.*
1 *Cor.* 1. 19. nothing understanding of *p.*
2 *Chr.* 2. 12. *p.* understanding, wisdom
Prov. 8. 12; *Eph.* 1. 8.
PSALM, 1 *Chr.* 16. 7; *Ps.* 81. 2, & 98. 5;
Acts 13. 33; 1 *Cor.* 14. 26.
1 *Chr.* 16. 9. sing *p.* unto him
Ps. 95. 2. make a joyful noise unto him
with *p.*
105. 2. sing *p.* talk of wonderful works
Acts 1. 20. it is written in the book of *p.*
Eph. 5. 19. speak to yourselves in *p.* and
hymns
Col. 3. 16. admonish one another in *p.*
and hymns
Jam. 5. 13. is any merry, let him sing *p.*
PUBLICAN, *Matt.* 18. 17; *Luke* 18. 13.
Matt. 5. 46. do not even the *p.* the
same, 47.
11. 19. friend of *p.* and sinners
21. 31. *p.* go into kingdom of God
before you
32. *p.* and harlots believed him
Luke 3. 12. *p.* to be baptized
7. 23. the *p.* justified God
PUBLISH the name of the Lord *Deut.*
32. 3.
2 *Sam.* 1. 20. *p.* it not in streets
Ps. 26. 7. *p.* it with voice of thanksgiving
Is. 52. 7. *p.* peace that *p.* salvation
Jer. 4. 15. a voice *p.* affliction
Mark 13. 10. gospel must be *p.*
Acts 13. 49. word of the Lord was *p.*
PUFFED up, 1 *Cor.* 4. 6, 19, & 5. 2; 2
Cor. 8. 1, & 13. 4; *Col.* 2. 18.
PULL, ED, *Matt.* 7. 4. *p.* out mote out of
Luke 12. 18. I will *p.* down my barns
14. 5. not *p.* him out on sabbath
Acts 23. 10. Paul been *p.* in pieces
PULLING, 2 *Cor.* 10. 4. *p.* down of
strong holds
Jude 23. others save with fear, *p.* them
out of fire
PUNISH seven times, *Lev.* 26. 18, 24
Ezra 9. 13. hast *p.* us less than iniquities

deserve
Prov. 17. 26. to *p.* the just is not
Is. 10. 12. *p.* the fruit of king of Assyria
 13. 11. I will *p.* world for evil
Jer. 9. 25. *p.* all circumcised with
Hos. 4. 14. I will not *p.* your daughters
 12. 2. I will *p.* Jacob according to his
2 *Thess.* 1. 9. shall be *p.* with everlasting
 destruction
2 *Pet.* 2. 9. unto the day of judgment
 to be *p.*
PUNISHMENT, *Gen.* 4. 13. my *p.* is
 greater than I can bear
Lev. 26. 41. accept of the *p.* of their
 iniquity, 43.
Job 31. 3. a strange *p.* to workers
Lam. 3. 39. a man for *p.* of sins
Amos 1. 3. not turn away *p.* thereof, 13.
Matt. 25. 46. go away into ever. *p.*
2 *Cor.* 2. 6. to such is this *p.*
Heb. 10. 29. how much sorer *p.*
1 *Pet.* 2. 14. by him for *p.* of evil
PURCHASED, *Ps.* 74. 2; *Acts* 8. 20, &
 20. 28; *Eph.* 1. 14; 1 *Tim.* 3. 13.
PURE, *Ex* 27. 20, & 30. 23, 34.
2 *Sam.* 22. 27. with *p.* show thyself *p.*
Job 4. 17. shall a man be more *p.* than
 his Maker
 25. 5. stars not *p.* in his sight
Ps. 12. 6. words of the Lord are *p.*
 19. 8. commandment of the Lord is *p.*
 24. 4. clean hands and *p.* heart
Prov. 15. 26. words of *p.* pleasant
 20. 9. heart clean *p.* from sin
 30. 5. every word of God is *p.*
 12. generation *p.* in own eyes
Zeph. 3. 9. turn to people a *p.* language
Acts 20. 26. I am *p.* from the blood of all
Rom. 14. 20. all things indeed are *p.*
Phil. 4. 8. whatsoever things are *p.*
1 *Tim.* 3. 9. the mystery of faith in a *p.*
 5. 22. of other men's sins keep *p.*
Tit. 1. 15. to *p.* all things are *p.*
Heb. 10. 22. washed with *p.* water
Jam. 1. 27. *p.* religion undefiled
 3. 17. wisdom from above is *p.*
2 *Pet.* 3. 1. stir up your *p.* minds
1 *John* 3. 3. *p.* himself as he is *p.*
Is. 1. 25. *p.* purge away thy dross
PURENESS, *Job* 22. 30; 2 *Cor.* 6. 6.
PURGE me with hyssop, alludes to
 Levitical purifyings, *Ps.* 51. 7.
Ps. 65. 3. transgressions thou shalt *p.*
 79. 9. *p.* away our sins for thy name's
Prov. 16. 6. by mercy and truth iniquity
 is *p.*
Is. 6. 7. iniquity is taken and sin *p.*
 27. 9. the iniquity of Jacob be *p.*
Ezek. 24. 13. because I *p.* and thou not
 p. shalt not be *p.* from, 1 *Sam.* 3. 14.
Mal. 3. 3. he shall purify and *p.* as gold
Matt. 3. 12. thoroughly *p.* his floor
John 15. 2. he *p.* it to bring forth
1 *Cor.* 5. 7. *p.* out the old leaven
2 *Tim.* 2. 21. if man *p.* himself
Heb. 1. 3. by himself *p.* our sins
 9. 14. *p.* your conscience from dead
2 *Pet.* 1. 9. forget he was *p.* from
PURIFIER, *Mal.* 3. 3. sit as a refiner,
 p. of silver
PURIFY sons of Levi, *Mal.* 3. 3.
Ps. 12. 6. silver *p.* seven times
Dan. 12. 10. many shall be *p.*

Acts 15. 9. *p.* their hearts by faith
Tit. 2. 14. *p.* to himself a peculiar people
Heb. 9. 13. sanctifieth to the *p.* of flesh
Jam. 4. 8. *p.* your hearts ye double-
1 *Pet.* 1. 22. have *p.* your souls in
1 *John* 3. 3. *p.* himself as he is *p.*
Mal. 3. 3. sit as a *p.* of silver
PURITY, 1 *Tim.* 4. 12, & 5. 2.
Hab. 1. 13. *p.* eyes than to behold evil
PURPOSE, *Jer.* 6. 20, & 49. 30.
Job 33. 17. withdraw man from *p.*
Prov. 20. 18. *p.* is established by counsel
Eccl. 3. 1. time to every *p.* 8. 6.
Is. 14. 26. this is *p.* 14. 27.
Jer. 51. 29. *p.* of the Lord shall stand
Acts 11. 23. with *p.* of heart cleave to
 the Lord
Rom. 8. 28. called according to his *p.*
Eph. 1. 11. according to *p.* of him
 1. 9. mystery be *p.* in himself

Eph. 3. 11. eternal *p.* he *p.* in Christ J.
2 *Tim.* 1. 9. according to his own *p.*
1 *John* 3. 8. for this *p.* Son of God was
 manifested
PURSUE, *Gen.* 35. 5; *Deut.* 28. 22.
Ex. 15. 9. enemy said I will *p.*
Job 13. 25. wilt thou *p.* dry stubble
Ps. 34. 14. seek peace and *p.* it
Prov. 11. 19. he that *p.* evil *p.* it
 28. 1. wicked flee when none *p.*
PUT, *Gen.* 2. 8, & 3. 15, 22.
Job 4. 18. *p.* no trust in servants
Ps. 4. 7. *p.* gladness in my heart
 8. 7. *p.* all things under his feet
Songs 5. 3. *p.* off coat how *p.* it on
 42. 1. I will *p.* my spirit on him
 53. 10. to bruise him, *p.* him to grief
 63. 11. *p.* his holy Spirit in him
Jer. 31. 33. *p.* law in their inward parts
 32. 40. *p.* my fear in their hearts
Ezek. 11. 19. I will *p.* a new spirit within
 36. 27. will *p.* my Spirit within you
Luke 1. 52. *p.* down mighty from
Eph. 4. 22. *p.* off old man. *Col.* 3. 9.
2 *Pet.* 1. 14. I must *p.* off this my tab.
Rom. 13. 12. *p.* on armour of light
 14. *p.* on Lord Jesus Christ
Eph. 4. 25. *p.* on the new man, *Col.* 3. 13.
 6. 11. *p.* on the whole armour of God
Job 15. 15. *p.* no trust in his saints
Lam. 3. 29. he *p.* mouth in dust
Eph. 4. 25. *p.* away lying, speak
Col. 2. 11. in *p.* off body of sins
1 *Thess.* 5. 8. *p.* on breast-plate of faith
 and love
2 *Tim.* 1. 6. by *p.* on of hands

QUEEN, 1 *Kings* 10. 1. & 15. 13; *Ps.* 45.
 9; *Songs* 6. 8; *Jer.* 44. 17, 25; *Rev.*
 18. 7.
Matt. 12. 42. *q.* of south rise in judgment
Is. 49. 23. *q.* thy nursing mothers
QUENCH. A figurative expression,
 borrowed from the practice of extin-
 guishing fire, by throwing water
 upon it. The Apostle applies it to
 the influences of the Holy Spirit,
 when he says, "Quench not the
 Spirit;" 2 *Sam.* 14. 7; 1 *Thess.* 5. 19.
2 *Sam.* 21. 17. *q.* not light of Israel
Songs 8. 7. waters cannot *q.* love
Is. 42. 3. smoking flax he will not *q.*
Mark 9. 43. fire never *q.* 44. 46, 48.

Eph. 6. 16. *q.* fiery darts of the wicked
1 *Thess.* 5. 19. *q.* not the Spirit
QUESTION. An inquiry; or, a proposition in order to obtain an answer to it, *Mark* 12. 34; 1 *Cor.* 10. 25.
QUESTIONS, 1 *Kings* 10. 1; *Luke* 2. 46; 1 *Tim.* 1. 4, & 6. 4; 2 *Tim.* 2. 23.
QUICK, QUICKEN. To give life to the dead, *Rom.* 4. 17. To raise up and cheer such as languish, *Ps.* 119. 25. To raise the spiritually dead to spiritual life, *Num.* 16. 30; *Ps.* 55. 15; *Eph.* 2. 1, 5; *Rom.* 8. 11.
Ps. 124. 3. swallowed us up *q.*
Is. 11. 3. of *q.* understanding
Acts 10. 42. judge of *q.* and dead
2 *Tim.* 4. 1. shall judge *q.* and dead
80. 18. *q.* us and we will call on thy
119. 25. *q.* thou me according to thy
37. *q.* me in thy way
50. for thy word hath *q.* me
John 5. 21. Father *q.* them, Son *q.* whom
6. 63. it is the Spirit that *q.*
Rom. 8. 11. *q.* your mortal bodies
1 *Cor.* 15. 45. last Adam made a *q.* spirit
Eph. 2. 1. you hath he *q.* who were
1 *Pet.* 3. 18. but *q.* by the Spirit
QUICKLY, *Ex.* 32. 8; *Deut.* 11. 17.
Eccl. 4. 12. threefold cord not *q.* broken
Matt. 5. 25. agree with adversary *q.*
Rev. 3. 11. behold I come *q.* 22. 7, 8, 20.
QUIET, QUIETNESS. Opposed to disorderly motion or conduct, to turbulency, to contention, *Judg.* 18. 7; *Job* 3. 13, 26.
Ps. 131. 2. *q.* myself as a child
Is. 7. 4. heed and be *q.* fear not
33. 20. see Jerusalem a *q.* habitation
1 *Thess.* 4. 11. study to be *q.* and
1 *Tim.* 2. 2. lead a *q.* peaceable life
1 *Pet.* 3. 4. of a meek and *q.* spirit
QUIETNESS, 1 *Chr.* 22. 9; *Job* 20. 20.
Job 34. 29. when he giveth *q.* who
Prov. 17. 1. better is a dry morsel and *q.*
Eccl. 4. 6. better is handful with *q.*
Is. 30. 15. in *q.* and confidence shall be
32. 17. effect of righteousness *q.* and
QUIT like men, 1 *Sam.* 4. 9; 1 *Cor.* 16. 13.
QUIVER. A case for arrows, *Gen.* 27. 3; *Job* 39. 23. It signifies divine protection, *Is.* 49. 2.
Ps. 127. 5. *q* full of them, not ashamed
Is. 49. 2. in his *q.* hath he hid me

RACE, *Ps.* 19. 5. a strong man to run a *r.*
Eccl. 9. 11. *r.* is not to the swift
1 *Cor.* 9. 24. run in a *r.* run all
Heb. 12. 1. patience, *r.* set before us
RAGE, 2 *Kings* 5. 12; 2 *Chr.* 16. 10.
2 *Chr.* 28. 9. slain them in a *r.*
Ps. 2. 1. why do heathen *r.* and
46. 6. heathens *r.* the kingdoms were
Prov. 6. 34. jealousy is *r.* of a man
14. 16. fool *r.* and is confident
20. 1. wine, a mocker, strong drink *r.*
29. 9. whether he *r.* or laugh
Jude 13. *r.* waves of sea foaming
RAGS, *Prov.* 23. 21; *Is.* 64. 6.
RAILER, or drunkard, 1 *Cor.* 5. 11.
RAILING, 1 *Tim.* 6. 4; 1 *Pet.* 3. 9.
2 *Pet.* 2 11. *r.* accusation, *Jude* 9.

RAIMENT to put on, *Gen.* 28. 20.
Ex. 21. 10. food and *r.* not diminished
Deut. 8. 4. *r.* waxed not old nor
24. 17. not take widow's *r.* to
Zech. 3. 4. clothe with change of *r.*
Matt. 6. 25. body more than *r.* 28.
11. 8. man clothed in soft *r.*
17. his *r.* was white as light
1 *Tim.* 6. 8. having food and *r.*
Rev. 3. 5. clothed in food and *r.* 4. 4.
RAIN in due season, *Lev.* 26. 4; *Deut.* 32. 2. my doctrine shall drop as *r.*
1 *Kings* 8. 36. no *r.* because they sinned
Job 5. 10. who giveth *r.* on earth
28. 26. he made a decree for *r.*
Ps. 68. 9. didst send a plentiful *r.*
72. 6. shall come down like *r.*
27. 15. continual dropping in *r.*
Eccl. 12. 2. clouds return after *r.*
Songs 2: 11. winter past, *r.* is over
Is. 4. 6. covert from storm and from *r.*
55. 10. *r.* cometh down from heaven
Jer. 5. 24. fear the Lord who giveth *r.*
Amos 4. 7. withholding *r.* from you
Zech. 10. 1. ask of the Lord *r.* in time of
14. 18. family of Egypt have no *r.* 17.
Matt. 5. 45. sendeth *r.* on the just and on the unjust
Heb. 6. 7. earth drinketh in *r.*
Jam. 5. 18. prayed again, and heaven gave *r.*
Ps. 11. 6. on the wicked shall *r.* snares
78. 27. *r.* down manna on them
Hos. 10. 12. *r.* righteousness on you
Amos 4. 7. to *r.* on one city, and
RAINBOW, *Rev.* 4. 3. *r.* round about the throne
Rev. 10. 1. angel, *r.* was upon his head
RAISE, *Deut.* 18. 15, 18; 2 *Sam.* 12. 11.
Ex. 9. 16. I *r.* thee up to show my power
Ps. 113. 7. he *r.* up poor out of
145. 14. *r.* up those bowed down
Hos. 6. 2. third day he will *r.* us
Amos 9, 11. *r.* up tabernacle of David
Matt. 11. 5. deaf hear, dead are *r.*
Luke 1. 69. *r.* a horn of salvation
John 6. 40. *r.* him up at last day
Rom. 4. 25. *r.* for our justification
6. 4. Christ was *r.* by glory of Father,
1 *Cor.* 6. 14. God *r.* up the Lord, and will also *r.* us
2 *Cor.* 4. 14. *r.* up the Lord Jesus, *r.* us up also by Jesus
Eph. 2. 6. *r.* us together with him
RANSOM of life, *Ex.* 21. 30.
Ex. 30. 12. give man a *r.* for soul
Job 33. 24. I have found a *r.*
36. 18. a *r.* cannot deliver thee
Ps. 49. 7. give to God a *r.* for him
Prov. 6. 35. he will not regard any
13. 8. *r.* of man's life are riches
21. 18. wicked *r.* for righteous
Is. 43. 3. I gave Egypt for thy *r.*
Hos. 13. 14. *r.* them from grave
Matt. 20. 28. give his life a *r.* for many
1 *Tim.* 2. 6. give himself a *r.* for all
RANSOMED, *Is.* 35. 10, & 51. 10; *Jer.* 31. 11.
RASH, hasty, *Eccl.* 5. 2; *Is.* 32. 4; *Acts* 19. 36.
RAVISHED, *Prov.* 5. 19; *Songs* 4. 9.
REACH, *Gen.* 11. 4; *John* 20. 27.
Ps. 36. 5. faithfulness *r.* to heaven

Phil. 3. 13. r. forth to those things
READ in audience of, *Ex.* 24. 7.
Deut. 17. 19. shall r. therein all the days
Neh. 13. 1. r. in books of Moses
Luke 4. 16. custom, stood up to r.
Acts 15. 21. r. in synagogue every
     sabbath day
2 *Cor.* 3. 2. known and r. of all
1 *Thess.* 5. 27. this epistle be r. *Col.* 4. 16.
Acts 8. 30. understandest what thou r.
Rev. 1. 3. blessed is he that r.
READING, *Neh.* 8. 8; 1 *Tim.* 4. 13.
READY. Fully prepared, *Matt.* 22. 4.
     —Prepared and fitted for death,
     Matt. 24. 44.
Neh. 9. 17. r. to pardon
Ps. 45. 1. tongue is pen of a r. writer
     86. 5. Lord good and r. to forgive
Eccl. 5. 1. be more r. to hear than
Matt. 24. 44. be ye r. also, *Luke* 12. 40.
Mark 14. 38. spirit is r. flesh weak   •
Acts 21. 13. r. not to be bound only, but
1 *Tim.* 6. 18. r. to distribute
2 *Tim.* 4. 6. am now r. to be offered
Tit. 3. 1. r. to every good work
1 *Pet.* 5. 2. willingly, of a r. mind
Rev. 3. 2. strengthen things that are r.
     to die
READINESS, *Acts* 17. 11; 2 *Cor.* 10. 6.
REAP, *Lev.* 19. 9. when ye r.
John 4. 36. he r. receiveth wages
1 *Cor.* 9. 11. great things if we r. your
Gal. 6. 9. in due season we shall r. if we
Rev. 14. 16. earth was r. 15.
Matt . 13. 39. r. are angels, 30.
REASON, *Prov.* 26. 16; *Dan.* 4. 36.
Is. 41. 21. bring forth strong r.
1 *Pet.* 3. 15. a r. of hope in you
Acts 24. 25. he r. of righteousness
Rom. 12. 1. your r. service
REBEL not against the Lord, *Num.* 14.
     9; *Josh.* 22. 19.
Neh. 9. 26. they r. against thee
Job 24. 13. r. against the light
Is. 1. 20. if ye refuse and r. ye
Is. 63. 10. r. vexed his Holy Spirit
1 *Sam.* 15. 23. r. is as witchcraft
Num. 20. 10. hear now, ye r.
Ezek. 20. 38. I will purge out the r.
Deut. 9. 7. been r. against the Lord, 24.
Ps. 68. 18. received gifts for men, for r.
Is. 30. 9. this is r. people children
     50. 5. I was not r. nor returned
     65. 2. spread out my hands to a r.
     people, 1. 23.
Jer. 4. 17. she been r. against me
Ezek. 2. 3, 5, 8, r. house, 3. 9, 26, & 12.
     5 .23. hath a r. heart
     2. 3. & 17. 12. & 24. 3.
REBUKE neighbour, *Lev.* 19. 17.
Ps. 6. 1. r. me not in anger nor
     39. 11. with r. dost correct
Prov. 9. 8. r. a wise son he will love
     13. 1. scorner heareth not r.
     27. 5. open r. better than secret love
     28. 23. he that r. afterwards shall find
Amos 5. 10. hate him that r. in
Zech. 3. 2. Lord said to Satan, the Lord
Matt. 16. 22. Peter began to r. him
Luke 17. 3. thy brother trespass against
     thee r. him
Phil. 2. 15. sons of God without r.

1 *Tim.* 5. 1. r. not an elder, but
     20. them that sin r. before all
Tit. 1. 13. r. them sharply
     2. 15. r. with all authority
Heb. 12. 5. not faint when r. of
RECEIVE good, r. evil, *Job* 2. 10.
Ps. 6. 9. Lord will r. my prayer
     49. 15. God will redeem, he shall r.
     73. 24. afterward r. me to glory
Hos. 14. 2. take away iniquity, r. us
Matt. 10. 41. r. a prophet's reward
     18. 5. r. one such little child in
     21. 22. ask, believing. ye shall r.
Mark 4. 16. word r. with gladness
     11. 24. believe that ye r. ye shall r.
Luke 16. 9. may r. you into everlasting
     habitations
John 3. 27. can r. nothing except
     5. 44. r. honour one of another
     16. 24. ask and ye shall r. that
Acts 2. 38. r. gift of the Holy Ghost
     7. 59. Lord Jesus r. my spirit
     10. 43. that believeth shall r.
     20. 35. more blessed to give than to r.
     26. 18. may r. forgiveness and
Rom. 14. 1. him weak in faith r.
1 *Cor.* 3. 8. every man r. his own
2 *Cor.* 5. 10. r. things done in his body
     6. 1. r. not grace of God in vain
Gal. 3. 14. r. promise of Spirit
     4. 5. might r. adoption of sons
Eph. 6. 8. same shall be r. of the Lord
Jam. 1. 21. r. meekness ingrafted word
1 *Pet.* 5. 4. ye shall r. a crown of glory
1 *John* 3. 22. whatsoever we ask we r.
2 *John* 8. but that we r. reward
Ps. 68. 18. hast r. gifts for men
Jer. 2. 30. r. not correction, *Zeph.* 3. 2.
Matt. 10. 8. freely ye r. freely give
Luke 6. 24. have r. consolation
     16. 25. hast r. thy good things and
     Lazarus evil
John 1. 11. own r. him not
     12. as many as r. him
Acts 8. 17. they r. Holy Ghost
     17. 11. in that they r. the word
     20. 24. I r. of the Lord, 1 *Cor.* 11. 23.
Rom. 5. 11. C. by whom r. atonement
     8. 15. have r. spirit of adoption
     15. 7. r. ye one another, as C. r. us
1 *Tim.* 3. 16. r. into glory, *Mark* 16. 19.
Heb. 11. 13. not having r. promises
Matt. 7. 8. every one that asketh r.
     10. 40. he that r. you, r. me, r. him
     13. 20. hears word and r. it with joy
John 3. 32. no man r. his testimony
     12. 48. rejecteth me r. not my words
1 *Cor.* 2. 14. natural man r. not things
Phil. 4. 15. giving and r. but ye
Heb. 12. 28. we r. a kingdom
1 *Pet.* 1. 9. r. end of your faith
RECKONED, *Ps.* 40. 5; *Is.* 38. 13; *Luke*
     22. 37; *Rom.* 4. 4, 9, 10, & 8. 18.
RECOMPENCE, *Prov.* 12. 14; *Is.* 35. 4.
Deut. 32. 35. to me belongs r. *Heb.* 10. 30.
Job 15. 31. vanity shall be his r.
Is. 34. 8. year of r. for controversy
     66. 6. render r. to enemies, 59. 18.
Hos. 9. 7. the days of r. are come
Luke 14. 12. a r. be made thee, 14.
Heb. 2. 2. disobedience received just r.
     10. 35. confidence has great r.
Num. 5. 8. be r. to the Lord, even to

Prov. 11. 31. righteous shall be *r.*
20. 22. say not I will *r.* evil
Jer. 18. 20. evil be *r.* for good
25. 14. I will *r.* your iniquity, 16. 18.
Luke 14. 14. they cannot *r.* thee
Rom. 11. 35. it be *r.* to them again
12. 17. *r.* no man evil for evil

RECONCILE with blood, *Lev.* 6. 30.
Matt. 5. 24. be *r.* to thy brother
Rom. 5. 10. enemies we were *r.*
2 *Cor.* 5. 18. hath *r.* us to himself
19. God in Christ *r.* world
20. be ye *r.* to God
Eph. 2. 16. *r.* both to God in the body
Col. 1. 20. by him to *r.* all things to
himself, 21.
Lev. 8. 15. to make *r.* 2 *Chr.* 29. 24; *Ezek.*
45. 15, 17; *Dan.* 9. 24; *Heb.* 2. 17.
2 *Cor.* 5. 18. to us ministry of *r.*
19. to us the word of *r.*

RECORD my name, *Ex.* 20. 24.
Deut. 30. 19. take heaven and earth to
r. 31. 28.
Job 16. 19. my witness in heaven *r.* on
John 1. 32. bear *r.* 8. 13, 14, & 12. 17, &
19. 35; *Rom.* 10. 2.
2 *Cor.* 1. 23. I call God a *r. Phil.* 1. 8.
1 *John* 5. 7. three that bear *r.* in
11. this is the *r.* that God hath given
us eternal life, 13.
Rev. 1. 2. bare *r.* of word of God, and

RECOVER strength, *Ps.* 39. 13.
Jer. 8. 22. why is not health of—*r.*
Hos. 2. 9. I will *r.* my wool and flax
Luke 4. 18. *r.* of sight to blind
2 *Tim.* 2. 26. may *r.* themselves

RED, *Ps.* 75. 8; *Is.* 1. 18. & 27. 2, & 63.
2; *Zech.* 1. 8, & 6. 2; *Rev.* 6. 4, &
12. 3.

REDEEM with outstretched arm *Ex.* 6. 6.
2 *Sam.* 7. 23. whom God went to *r.*
Job 5. 20. he shall *r.* thee from death
Ps. 34. 22. *r.* soul of his servants
42. 26. *r.* for mercies' sake
49. 7. none can *r.* his brother
15. God will *r.* my soul from
103. 4. who *r.* thy life from destruction, 72. 14.
Hos. 13. 14. *r.* them from death
Tit. 2. 14. might *r.* us from all iniquity
Gen. 48. 16. angel which *r.* me
Ex. 15. 13. people which hast *r.*
2 *Sam.* 4. 9. hath *r.* my soul out
Ps. 136. 24. *r.* us from our enemies, 31. 5.
Is. 1. 27. Zion shall be *r.* with judgment
51. 11. *r.* of the Lord shall return
52. 3. be *r.* without money, 9.
63. 9. in love and pity he *r.* them, 4.
Luke 1. 68. visited and *r.* his people
24. 21. he should have *r.* Israel
Gal. 3. 13. Christ hath *r.* us from curse
1 *Pet.* 1. 18. not *r.* us with corruptible
Rev. 5. 9. hast *r.* us to God by
14. 4. were *r.* from among them
Eph. 5. 16. *r.* time, *Col.* 4. 5.
Job 19. 25. I know my *R.* liveth
Ps. 19. 14. my strength and my *R.*
78. 35. that high God was their *R.*
Prov. 23. 11. their *R.'s* mighty
Is. 63. 16. our Father and our *R.* 48. 17.
Jer. 50. 34. their *R.* is strong, *Is.* 49. 26.

REDEMPTION, *Lev.* 25. 24;
Ps. 49 8. *r.* of soul is precious

111. 9. he sent *r.* to his people
130. 7. with him is plenteous *r.*
Luke 2. 38. looked for *r* in Jerusalem
21. 28. your *r.* draweth nigh
Rom. 3. 24. through *r.* in Christ Jesus
1 *Cor.* 1. 30. Christ Jesus made wisdom,
righteousness, sanctification, *r.*
Eph. 1. 7. in whom we have *r. Col.* 1. 14.
14. earnest till *r.* of purchased possess.
Eph. 4. 30. sealed unto the day of *r.*
Heb. 9. 12. having obtained eternal *r.*

REFINE, *Is.* 25. 6, & 48. 10; *Zech.* 13. 9;
Mal. 3. 2, 3.

REFORMATION, *Heb.* 9. 10.

REFRAIN, *Prov.* 1. 15; 1 *Pet.* 3. 10.
Prov. 10. 19. that *r.* his lips is wise

REFRESH, REFRESHING, *Ex.* 23. 12;
1 *Kings* 13. 7; *Is.* 28. 12; *Acts* 3.
19; 1 *Cor.* 16. 18.

REFUGE, *Num.* 35. 13; *Josh.* 20. 3.
Deut. 33. 27. eternal God is thy *r.*
Ps. 9. 9. Lord will be a *r.* for oppressed,
14. 6; *Is.* 4. 6, & 25. 4.
Ps. 18. 2. God my *r.* 57. 1, & 59. 16, &
62. 7, & 71. 7, & 142. 5; *Jer.* 16. 19.
46. 1. God is our *r.* 7. 11. & 62. 8.
Is. 28. 15. made lies our *r.* 17.
Heb. 6. 18. fled for *r.* to lay hold

REFUSE, *Lam.* 3. 45; *Amos* 8. 6.
Neh. 9. 17. *r.* to obey, neither
Ps. 77. 2. my soul *r.* to be comforted
118. 22. stone which builders *r.*
Prov. 1. 24. I have called, and ye *r.*
Jer. 5. 3. *r.* to receive instruction
8. 5. they *r.* to return
11. 10. *r.* to hear my words
15. 18. *r.* to be healed
31. 15. *r.* to be comforted
Hos. 11. 5. Assyrian his king because
they *r.* to return
1 *Tim.* 4. 4. nothing to be *r.* if received
7. *r.* profane old wives' fables
Heb. 12. 25. *r.* not him that speaketh

REGARD not works of Lord, *Ps.* 28. 5.
Ps. 66. 18. if I *r.* iniquity in my heart
102. 17. *r.* prayer of destitute
Is. 5. 12. *r.* not the work of the Lord
Prov. 1. 24. no man *r.*
Ps. 106. 44. he *r.* their affliction
Luke 1. 48. *r.* estate of his handmaiden
Heb. 8. 9. not in my covenant I *r.* them
Deut. 10. 17. *r.* not persons
Job 34. 19. nor *r.* the rich more than the
Prov. 12. 10. righteous *r.* life of
13. 18. *r.* reproof be honoured
15. 5. that *r.* reproof is prudent
Eccl. 5. 8. higher than highest *r.*
Matt. 22. 16. *r.* not the persons of men
Rom. 14. 6. he that *r.* a day *r.* it unto

REIGN, *Gen.* 37. 8; *Lev.* 26. 17.
Ex. 15. 18. Lord shall *r.* for ever
1 *Chr.* 29. 12. thou *r.* over all
Ps. 93. 1. Lord *r.* 97. 1, & 99. 1.
Prov. 8. 15. by me kings *r.* and
Is. 32. 1. a king shall *r.* in righteousness
52. 7. say unto Zion, thy God *r.*
Jer. 23. 5. King *r.* and prosper
Luke 19. 14. not this man to *r.*
Rom. 5. 14. death *r.* from Adam to Moses
17. shall *r.* in life by one Jesus Christ
Rom. 5. 21. as sin *r.* to death, grace *r.* to
1 *Cor.* 4. 8. would to God ye did *r.*
2 *Tim.* 2. 12. if we suffer shall *r.* with

Rev. 5. 10. we shall *r.* on earth
19. 6. Lord God Omnipotent *r.*
20. 4. lived and *r.* with C. 1000 years
22. 5. they shall *r.* for ever
REINS, *Job* 16. 13, & 19. 27.
Ps. 7. 9. God trieth hearts and *r.* 26. 2;
  Jer. 17. 10, & 20. 12; *Rev.* 2. 23.
16. 7. my *r.* instruct me in
73. 21. I was pricked in my *r.*
139. 13. thou hast possessed my *r.*
Prov. 25. 16. my *r.* shall rejoice
Jer. 12. 2. art far from their *r.*
REJECT, *Mark* 6. 26; *Gal.* 4. 14.
1 *Sam.* 8. 7. not *r.* thee, but they *r.* me
Is. 53. 3. despised and *r.* of men
Jer. 2. 37. Lord *r.* thy confidence
6. 19. they have *r.* my law
8. 9. *r.* the word of the Lord
30. Lord *r.* them, 7. 29, & 14. 19; 2
  Kings 17. 15; *Lam.* 5. 22.
Hos. 4. 4. hast *r.* knowledge I will *r.*
Mark 7. 9. ye *r.* commandments
Luke 7. 30. alway *r.* counsel of God
John 12. 48. that *r.* me and receiveth no
Tit. 3. 10. after first and second admo-
  nition *r.*
Heb. 12. 17. would blessing was *r.*
REJOICE, *Ex.* 18. 9; *Deut.* 12. 7.
Deut. 28. 63. Lord will *r.* over you to
1 *Sam.* 2. 1. I *r.* in thy salvation
2 *Chr.* 6. 41. let thy saints *r.* in goodness
20. 27. Lord made them to *r.* over
Neh. 12. 43. God made them *r.*
Ps. 2. 11. serve Lord with fear, *r.* with
5. 11. let all put trust in thee *r.*
9. 14. *r.* in thy salvation, 13. 5.
51. 8. bones thou hast broken *r.*
63. 7. in shadow of wings I will *r.*
65. 8. morning and evening to *r.*
68. 3. let righteous *r.* before God
85. 6. thy people may *r.* in thee
86. 4. *r.* soul of thy servants
104. 31. Lord shall *r.* in his works
119. 162. I *r.* at thy word
Prov. 5. 18. *r.* with wife of youth
24. 17. *r.* not when enemy falleth
Eccl. 11. 9. *r.* O young man
Is. 29. 19. poor among men *r.*
62. 5. thy God shall *r.* over thee
65. 13. my servants shall *r.*
Jer. 32. 41. I will *r.* over them
Luke 6. 23. *r.* ye in that day
10. 20. *r.* that names written
John 5. 35. for a season to *r.* in his light
14. 28. if ye loved me ye would *r.*
Rom. 5. 2. *r.* in hope of glory
12. 15. *r.* with them that do *r.*
1 *Cor.* 7. 30. that *r.* as though they *r.* not
Phil. 3. 3. *r.* in Christ Jesus and have
Col. 1. 24. *r.* in my sufferings for
1 *Thess.* 5. 16. *r.* evermore
Jam. 1. 9. let brother of low degree *r.*
1 *Pet.* 1. 8. *r.* with joy unspeakable
Ps. 33. 1. *r.* in the Lord, 97. 12; *Is.* 41.
  16; *Hab.* 3. 18; *Zech.* 10. 7; *Phil.*
  3. 1, & 4. 4.
119. 14. I have *r.* in way of
Luke 1. 47. my spirit *r.* in God my S.
10. 21. Jesus *r.* in spirit and
John 8. 56. Abraham *r.* to see my
1 *Cor.* 7. 30. as though they *r.* not
Ps. 16. 9. my heart glad glory *r.*
Prov. 13. 9. light of righteous *r.*

15. 30. light of eyes *r.* heart
Is. 62. 5. as the bridegroom *r.* over his
1 *Cor.* 13. 6. *r.* not in iniquity, but *r.* in
Jam. 2. 13. mercy *r.* against judgment
Ps. 19. 8. statutes of the Lord *r.* heart
119. 111. they are *r.* of my heart
Prov. 8. 31. *r.* in habitable part of earth
Jer. 15. 16. word found *r.* of heart
Acts 5. 41. *r.* they are counted worthy
Acts 8. 39. eunuch went on his way *r.*
Rom. 12. 12. *r.* in hope, 5. 2.
2 *Cor.* 1. 12. our *r.* is this, testimony of
6. 10. sorrowful, yet always *r.*
Gal. 6. 4. have *r.* in himself alone
Heb. 3. 6. *r.* of hope, firm to the end
RELIEVE, to succour; providential and
  gracious regards, *Lev.* 25. 35; *Is.* 1.
  17; *Ps.* 146. 9; *Acts* 11. 29; 1 *Tim.*
  5. 16.
REMAINDER, 1 *Thess.* 4. 15; *Rev.* 3. 3;
  Eccl. 2. 9; *Lam.* 5. 19; *John* 1. 33.
John 9. 41. therefore your sin *r.*
2 *Cor.* 9. 9. his righteousness *r.* for ever
Heb. 4. 9. *r.* a rest for the people of G.
10. 26. there *r.* no more sacrifice
1 *John* 3. 9. his seed *r.* in him
Ps. 76. 10. *r.* of his wrath restrain
REMEDY, 2 *Chr.* 36. 16; *Prov.* 6. 15, &
  29. 1.
REMEMBER, *Gen.* 40. 23; *Neh.* 1. 8.
Ex. 13. 3, *r.* this day come out of Egypt
Deut. 5. 15. *r.* thou wast a servant
7. 18. shalt well *r.* what the Lord did
8. 18. thou shalt *r.* the Lord thy God
9. 7. *r.* and forget not how provokedst
32. 7. *r.* days of old, consider
Ps. 20. 7. we will *r.* name of the Lord
22. 27. shall *r.* and turn to the Lord
Ps. 25. 6. *r.* thy mercies
7. *r.* not sins of my youth
79. 8. *r.* not against us former iniquities, *Is.* 64. 5; *Jer.* 14. 10; *Hos.* 8. 13.
89. 47. *r.* how short my time is
119. 49. *r.* word to thy servant
132. 1. *r.* David and all his afflictions
Eccl. 12. 1. *r.* thy Creator in the days of

Songs 1. 4. we will *r.* thy love
Is. 43. 25. I will not *r.* thy sins
46. 8. *r.* and show yourselves men
Jer. 31. 20. I do earnestly *r.* him
Ezek. 16. 61. shall *r.* thy ways
36. 31. shall *r.* your evil way
Hab. 3. 2. make known in wrath *r.*
Luke 1. 72. *r.* his holy covenant
16. 25. *r.* that thou in lifetime
17. 32. *r.* Lot's wife, *Gen.* 19. 29.
Gal. 2. 10. we should *r.* the poor
Col. 4. 18. *r.* my bonds
Heb. 8. 12. iniquity I will *r.* no more
Neh. 13. 14. *r.* me, 22. 31; *Ps.* 25. 7.
Ps. 63. 6. I *r.* thee, 143. 5.
Jer. 2. 2. I *r.* kindness of youth
Ps. 77. 11. *r.* the works of the Lord
Jer. 31. 34. *r.* their sins no more
Gen. 8. 1. God *r.* Noah
19. 29. God *r.* Abraham
30. 22. God *r.* Rachel, 1 *Sam.* 1. 19.
Num. 10. 9. shall be *r.* before the Lord
Ps. 77. 3. I *r.* God and was troubled
78. 39. he *r.* they were flesh
98. 3. he hath *r.* mercy and truth
103. 14. he *r.* we are dust
119. 52. I *r.* thy judgments

53. I have r. thy name in night
136. 23. who r. us in our low estate
137. 1. we wept when we r. Zion
Lam. 1. 7. she r. not her last end
Matt. 26. 75. Peter r. words of Jesus
Luke 24. 8. they r. his words
REMEMBRANCE, Lam. 3. 19; 1 Thess.
1. 3.
1 Kings 17. 18. call my sin to r.
Ps. 6. 5. in death no r. of thee
Is. 26. 8. the r. of thee
43. 26. put me in r.
Lam. 3. 20. soul hath them in r.
Mal. 3. 16. book of r. was written
John 14. 26. bring all things to r.
Acts 10. 31. thy alms are had in r.,
2 Tim. 1. 6. put in r. 2. 14; 2 Pet. 1. 12.
REMIT sins they shall, John 20. 23.
Matt. 26. 28. r. of sins, Mark 1. 4; Luke
1. 77, & 3. 3, & 24. 47; Acts 2. 28, &
10. 43; Rom. 3. 25; Heb. 9. 22, &
10. 18.
REMNANT, Lev. 2. 3; Deut. 3. 11.
2 Kings 19. 4. lift up prayer for r.
Ezra 9. 8. leave us a r. to escape
Is. 1. 9. except Lord left us a small r.
10. 21. a r. shall return, 22.
Jer. 15. 11. it be well with thy r.
23. 3. I will gather r. of my flock
Rom. 9. 27. a r. shall be saved, 11. 5.
REMOVE thy stroke from, Ps. 39. 10.
Ps. 103. 12. so far r. our iniquity
119. 22. r. from me reproach and
29. r. from me the way of lying
Prov. 4. 27. r. thy foot from evil
10. 30. righteousness never be r.
23. 10. r. not old landmarks
31. 8. r. far from me vanity and
Eccl. 11. 10. r. sorrows from thy heart
Is. 30. 7. teachers not be r. into
Matt. 17. 20. r. hence and it shall r.
Luke 22. 42. r. this cup from me
Gal. 1. 6. so soon r. from him
Rev. 2. 5. I will r. thy candlestick
REND. To tear in pieces, Ps. 7. 2. The
rending of garments denoted the
greatest grief, Gen. 37. 29, 34; Ezra
9. 3. The high-priest rent his
clothes, Matt. 26. 65. Also the
apostles, when the people offered
to pay them divine honours, Acts
14. 14. To rend the heart is to
grieve for sin, Joel 2. 13; Jer. 4. 30.
RENDER vengeance, Deut. 32. 41, 43.
2 Chr. 6. 30. r. to every man according
32. 25. Hezekiah r. not again
Job 33. 26. r. to man his righteousness
Ps. 116. 12. what shall I r. to the Lord
Prov. 26. 16. that can r. a reason
Hos. 14. 2. r. calves of our lips
Matt. 22. 21. r. to Caesar the things
Rom. 13. 7. r. all their dues
1 Thess. 5. 15. none r. evil for evil, 3. 9.
RENEW a right spirit, Ps. 51. 10.
Ps. 103. 5. youth is r. like eagles
104. 30. thou r. face of the earth
Is. 40. 31. wait on the Lord, r. strength
2 Cor. 4. 16. inward man is r.
Eph. 4. 23. be r. in spirit of mind
Col. 3. 10. r. in knowledge after
Heb. 6. 6. to r. them again unto repent.
RENEWING, Rom. 12. 2; Tit. 3. 5.

RENOUNCED, hidden, 2 Cor. 4. 2.
RENOWN, denotes men of celebrity,
Gen. 6. 4; Num. 1. 16. Christ is
called a 'plant of renown,' Ezek.
34. 29, & 39. 13.
RENOWNED, Is. 14. 20; Ezek. 23. 10.
REPAIR. To mend or rebuild; 2 Chr.
29. 3; Is. 61. 4. Repairer of
breaches, Is. 58. 12.
REPAY, Job 21. 31, & 41. 11.
Deut. 7. 10. r. him to his face
Rom. 12. 19. vengeance is mine, I will r.
Prov. 13. 21. righteous good shall be r.
REPENT of this evil, Ex. 32. 12.
Num. 23. 19. son of man should r.
Deut. 32. 36. Lord shall r. himself for
1 Sam. 15. 29. God is not a man that r.
1 Kings 8. 47. and make supplication
Job 42. 6. I r. in dust and ashes
Ps. 90. 13. let it r. thee concerning thy
135. 14. he will r. himself concerning
Jer. 18. 8. will r. of evil I thought to do
Ezek. 14. 6. r. and turn 18. 30.
Joel 2. 14. if he will r. and leave a
Jonah 3. 19. tell if God turn and r.
Matt. 3. 2. r. for the kingdom of heaven
Mark 1. 15. r. and believe gospel
6. 12. preached men should r.
Luke 13. 3. except ye r. ye perish
16. 30. if one from dead they will r.
17. 3. if he r. forgive him, 4.
Acts 2. 38. r. and be baptized
3. 19. r. and be converted, that
8. 22. r. of this thy wickedness
17. 30. commands all men to r.
26. 20. should r. and turn to God
Rev. 2. 5. remember whence fallen and r.
16. r. or I will come unto thee
21. I gave her space to r. she r. not
3. 19. I love, be zealous and r.
Gen. 6. 6. it r. the Lord, 7; Ex. 32. 14;
Judg. 2. 18; 1 Sam. 15. 11; 2 Sam.
24. 16; Joel 2. 13
Matt. 21. 29. afterwards he r. and
27. 3. Judas r. himself and brought
Luke 15. 7. over one sinner that r.
REPENTANCE, Jer. 15. 6; Hos. 11. 8.
Hos. 13. 14. r. hid from mine eyes
Matt. 3. 8. fruits meet for r. Luke 3. 8.
11. I baptize with water unto r.
9. 13. not righteous but sinners to r.
Mark 1. 4. baptism of r. Luke 3. 3.
Luke 15. 7. just persons need no r.
24. 47. r. and remission be granted
Acts 5. 31. give r. to Israel and
11. 18. God to Gentiles granted r.
13. 24. preached baptism of r. to all
20. 21. r. towards God and faith
Rom. 2. 4. goodness of God leads to r.
11. 29. calling of God are without r.
2 Cor. 7. 10. godly sorrow works r.
Heb. 6. 1. not lay foundation of r.
12. 17. found no place of r.
2 Pet. 3. 9. but that all should come to r.
REPLIEST against God, Rom. 9. 20.
REPORT signifies rumour 1 Sam. 2. 24;
a true one; 1 Kings 10. 6; a false
one, Ex. 23. 1; the message of salvation, Is. 53. 1. Gen. 37. 2; Num.
13. 32, & 14. 37; Neh. 6. 13.
Ex. 23. 1. not raise a false r.
Prov. 15. 30. good r. makes fat

Is. 53. 1. who hath believed our *r.* *John*
   12. 38; *Rom.* 10. 16.
2 *Cor.* 6. 8. by evil *r.* and good *r.*
1 *Tim.* 3. 7. good *r.* of them
Heb. 11. 2. obtained a good *r.* 39.
REPROACH. Derision or scorn, *Neh.* 2.
   17; 5. 9. Shame, infamy, or disgrace, *Prov.* 6. 33. Censure, or
   reflection, *Is.* 51. 7. *Josh.* 5. 9;
   Neh. 1. 3; *Ps.* 69. 7; *Prov.* 18. 3;
   Is. 54. 4; *Jer.* 31. 19; *Heb.* 13. 13;
   Gen. 30. 23; *Luke* 1. 25.
2 *Cor.* 12. 10. pleasure in *r.*
Job 27. 6. my heart not *r.* me
Ps. 15. 3. a *r.* against his neighbour
   69. 9. *r.* of them that *r.* thee are fallen
   20. *r.* broken my heart, 119. 22.
Prov. 14. 31. *r.* his Maker, 17. 5.
   34. sin is a *r.* to any people
Is. 51. 7. fear not *r.* of men nor
Joel 2. 17. give not heritage to *r.*
Heb. 11. 26. esteem *r.* of Christ greater
   riches, 13. 13.
1 *Pet.* 4. 14. if *r.* for name of Christ
REPROOF, astonished at, *Job* 26. 11.
Prov. 1. 23. turn thou at my *r.*
   25. would none of my *r.* 30.
   10. 17. he that refuseth *r.* erreth
   12. 1. he that hateth *r.* is brutish
   13. 18. regards *r.* be honoured
   15. 5. that regards *r.* is prudent
   10. he that hateth *r.* shall die
   32. heareth *r.* get understanding
   17. 10. *r.* enters more into wise
   29. 15. rod and *r.* give wisdom
2 *Tim.* 3. 16. profitable for *r.*
REPROOFS, *Ps.* 38. 14; *Prov.* 6. 23.
REPROVE, *Ps.* 50. 21. I will *r.* thee
   141. 5. let him *r.* me, and it
Prov. 9. 8. he that *r.* a scorner
   29. 1. he that being *r.* hardens
Is. 29. 21. hateth him that *r.* in gate
Hos. 4. 4. let no man *r.* another
John 3. 20. his deeds should be *r.*
   16. 8. *r.* world of sin righteousness
Eph. 5. 11. works of darkness *r.*
   13. all things *r.* are made manifest by
REPROVER, *Prov.* 25. 12; *Ezek.* 3. 26.
REPUTATION. Spoken of persons high-
   ly esteemed, *Eccl.* 10. 1; *Acts* 5. 34;
   Phil. 2. 7, 29; *Gal.* 2. 2.
REQUEST, *Rom.* 1. 10. making *r.* for a
   prosperous journey
Phil. 1. 4. making *r.* with joy
   4. 6. let your *r.* be made known to
   God
REQUIRE, *Gen.* 9. 5, & 42. 22; *Ezek.* 3.
   18. 20, & 33. 8.
Deut. 10. 12. what the Lord *r.* *Mic.* 6. 8.
   18. 19. if not hearken I will *r.* it
Prov. 30. 7. two things I *r.* of thee
Is. 1. 12. who *r.* this at your hand
Luke 12. 20. thy soul be *r.* of thee
   48. of him much shall be *r.*
1 *Cor.* 4. 2. *r.* of stewards to be faithful
REQUITE, *Gen.* 50. 15; 2 *Sam.* 16. 12;
Deut. 32. 6. do ye thus *r.* the Lord
1 *Tim.* 5. 4. learn to *r.* parents
2 *Chr.* 6. 23. by *r.* the wicked
RESEMBLE, ED, *Judg.* 8. 10. each *r.*
   children of a king
Luke 13. 18. shall I *r.* kingdom of God
RESERVE, *Jer.* 50. 20; 2 *Pet.* 2. 9.

Job 21. 30. wicked is *r.* to-day of
Jer. 3. 5. will *r.* his anger for ever
   5. 24. *r.* appointed weeks of harvest
Neh. 1. 2. he *r.* wrath for enemies
1 *Pet.* 1. 4. inheritance *r.* for you
Jude 6. *r.* in everlasting chains to judg.
RESIDE, *Zeph.* 2. 9; *Mal.* 2. 15.
RESIST not evil, *Matt.* 5. 39.
Zech. 3. 1. Satan at right hand to *r.* him
Acts 7. 51. ye alway *r.* the Holy Ghost
Rom. 9. 19. who hath *r.* his will
   13. 2. that *r.* receive damnation
2 *Tim.* 3. 8. so do these *r.* truth
Heb. 12. 4. not yet *r.* to blood
Jam. 4. 6. God *r.* the proud, 1 *Pet.* 5. 5.
   4. 7. *r.* the devil and he will flee
1 *Pet.* 5. 9. whom *r.* steadfast in
RESPECT the Lord hath to Abel, *Gen.*
   4. 4; *Ex.* 2. 25; 2 *Kings* 13. 23.
Deut. 1. 17. not *r.* persons, 16. 19.
2 *Chr.* 19. 7. nor *r.* of persons with God,
   Rom. 2. 11; *Eph.* 6. 9; *Col.* 3. 25;
   Acts 10. 34; *Job* 37. 24; 1 *Pet.* 1. 17.
Ps. 119. 6. I have *r.* to all thy
   138. 6. hath *r.* unto the lowly
Prov. 24. 23. not good to have *r.* of per-
   son, 28. 21; *Jam.* 2. 1, 3, 9.
Heb. 11. 26. *r.* to recompense of reward
REST, *Ex.* 16. 23, & 33. 14; *Deut.* 12. 9.
Ps. 95. 11. not enter into *r. Heb.* 3. 11.
   116. 7. return to thy *r.* O my
   132. 14. my *r.* here I will dwell
Is. 11. 10. his *r.* shall be glorious
   28. 12. this is *r.* and refreshing
   30. 15. in return, and *r.* be saved
   62. 7. give him no *r.* till he
Jer. 6. 16. find *r.* for your souls
Mic. 2. 10. this not your *r.* polluted
Matt. 11. 28. I will give *r.* to souls, 29.
Acts 9. 31. then had churches *r.*
Heb. 4. 9. *r.* for people of God
   10. entered into his *r.*
   11. to enter into that *r.*
Ps. 16. 9. my flesh *r.* in hope
   37. 7. *r.* in the Lord, and wait
Is. 57. 2. *r.* on their beds each
   20. wicked like troubled sea cannot *r.*
Zeph. 3. 17. he shall *r.* in his love
Rev. 14. 13. dead in the Lord *r.* from
Rom. 2. 17. Jew, and *r.* in the law
Eccl. 7. 9. anger *r.* in the bosom of fools
1 *Pet.* 4. 14. Spirit of God and glory *r.*
   upon you
RESTITUTION, *Acts* 3. 21. times of *r.*
   of all things
RESTORE, 2 *Sam.* 12. 6. he shall *r.* the
   lamb fourfold
Ps. 51. 12. *r.* joy of thy salvation
Matt. 17. 11. Elias *r.* all things
Luke 19. 8. have taken any thing, I *r.*
Gal. 6. 1. *r.* such in the spirit of meek-
RESTORER, *Is.* 58. 12. called *r.* of
   paths to dwell in
RESTORETH, *Ps.* 23. 3. he *r.* my soul
RESTRAIN, 1 *Sam.* 3. 13; *Job* 15. 4;
   Ps. 76. 10; *Is.* 63. 15.
RESTRAINEST, *Job* 15. 4. yea, thou *r.*
   prayer before God
RESURRECTION, *Matt* 22. 23, 28, 30;
   Acts 23. 8; 1 *Cor.* 15. 21; *Heb.* 6. 2.
Luke 20. 36. being children of *r.*
John 5. 29. *r.* of life, evil to *r.* of dam-

11. 25. I am the *r*. and the life
Acts 17. 18. preached Jesus and the *r*.
24. 15. shall be a *r*. of the dead
Rom. 6. 5. in likeness of his *r*.
Phil. 3. 10. the power of his *r*.
2 *Tim*. 2. 18. saying that the *r*. is past
Heb. 11. 35. obtain a better *r*.
Rev. 20. 5. this is the first *r*.
RETAIN, *Job* 2. 9; *Prov*. 3. 18, & 11. 16;
Eccl. 8. 8;
RETAINED, *John* 20. 23. whose sins ye
retain, they *r*.
Philem. 13. whom I have *r*.
Mic. 7. 18. *r*. not his anger for ever
RETURN to ground, *Gen*. 3. 19.
Job 1. 21. naked shall *r*. thither
Ps. 35. 13. my prayer *r*. into mine own
73. 10. his people *r*. hither
90. 3. *r*. ye children of men
116. 7. *r*. to thy rest, O my soul
Eccl. 12. 7. dust shall *r*. to the earth,
Is. 10. 21. remnant *r*. to God
21. 12. if inquire, *r*. come
35. 10. ransomed of Lord shall *r*. 51. 11.
55. 11. word shall not *r*. void
Jer. 3. 12. *r*. backsliding Israel, 14. 22.
4. 1. if thou wilt *r*. *r*. unto me
15. 19. let them *r*. to thee, *r*. not thou
Hos. 2. 7. *r*. to my first husband
7. 16. they *r*. but not to the Most High
11. 9. I will not *r*. to destroy
Amos 4. 6. ye *r*. not to me, 8. 9, 11.
Mal. 3. 7. *r*. to me and I will *r*. to you
18. ye shall *r*. and discern
1 *Pet*. 2. 25. are now *r*. to Shepherd
Jer. 5. 3. they refused to *r*. 8. 5.
Deut. 30. 2. *r*. to the Lord, 1 *Sam*. 7. 3;
Is. 55. 7; *Hos*. 5. 3, & 6. 1.
REVEAL, *Prov*. 11. 13; *Dan*. 2. 19.
Deut. 29. 29. things which are *r*.
Job 20. 27. heaven *r*. his iniquity
Prov. 20. 19. tale-bearer *r*. secrets
Is. 22. 14. it was *r*. in my ears
53. 1. to whom is arm of the Lord *r*.
Amos 3. 7. he *r*. secrets to his servants
Matt. 10. 26. covered not be *r*.
11. 25. hast *r*. them to babes
16. 17. flesh and blood hath not *r*.
Rom. 1. 18. righteousness of God *r*.
8. 18. glory shall be *r*. in us
1 *Cor*. 2. 10. God hath *r*. it to us
Gal. 1. 16. pleased God to *r*. his Son in
Phil. 3. 15. God *r*. even this to you
2 *Thess*. 1. 7. Lord Jesus shall be *r*.
2. 3. falling away and man of sin be *r*.
REVELATION, *Rom*. 2. 5. of righteous judgment
Gal. 1. 12. by the *r*. of Jesus Christ
2. 2. and I went up by *r*. and communicated
Eph. 1. 17. give Spirit of wisdom and *r*.
3. 3. by *r*. made known to me
1 *Pet*. 1. 13. grace at the *r*. of Jesus
Christ
Rev. 1. 1. the *r*. of Jesus Christ
REVELATIONS, 2 *Cor*. 12. 1. visions
and *r*. of the Lord
2 *Cor*. 12. 7. exalted through abundance
of *r*.
REVENGE. To return injury for injury, or the infliction of pain on
another in consequence of an

injury received from him, further
than the just ends of reparation or
punishment require, *Jer*. 15. 15; 2
Cor. 7. 11, & 10. 6; *Nah*. 1. 2.
Ps. 79. 10. by *r*. blood of servants
Num. 35. 19. a *r*. to execute wrath,
Rom. 13. 26.
REVERENCE my sanctuary, *Lev*. 19. 30.
Ps. 89. 7. to be had in *r*. of all
Eph. 5. 33. wife see that she *r*. husband
Heb. 12. 28. serve God acceptably with *r*.
Ps. 111. 9. holy and *r*. his name
REVILE. To curse or rail, *Ex*. 22. 28;
Matt. 5. 11; 1 *Cor*. 4. 12
1 *Pet*. 2. 23. when *r*. *r*. not again
1 *Cor*. 6. 10. nor *r*. shall inherit kingdom
REVILEST, *Acts* 23. 4. *r*. thou God's
high priest
REVILING, *Is*. 51. 7; *Zeph*. 2. 8.
REVIVE. To invigorate, *Neh*. 4. 2.
To become strong, *Judg*. 15. 19.
To restore to one's former con-
dition, *Ps*. 85. 6. To give comfort
in trouble, *Ps*. 138. 7.
Is. 57. 15. *r*. spirit of humble, *r*. heart
Hos. 6. 2. after two days he will *r*. us
14. 7. under his shadow *r*. as
Hab. 3. 2. *r*. thy work in midst
Rom. 7. 9. sin *r*. and I died
14. 9. Christ rose and *r*. that
REVOLT more and more, *Is*. 1. 5.
Is. 31. 6. children of Israel deeply *r*.
REWARD, *Gen*. 15. 1. exceeding great *r*.
Deut. 10. 17. takes not *r*. *Ps*. 15. 5.
Ps. 19. 11. in keeping them is great *r*.
58. 11. there is a *r*. for righteous
Prov. 11. 18. soweth righteous, sure *r*.
Is. 3. 11. woe to wicked, *r*. of his hands
be given him
Is. 5. 23. to justify wicked for *r*.
Mic. 7. 3. judge asketh for a *r*.
Matt. 5. 12. great is your *r*. in
6. 2. hypocrites have their *r*.
10. 41. receive a prophet's *r*.
Rom. 4. 4. *r*. is not reckoned of
1 *Cor*. 3. 8. receive his own *r*.
Col. 2. 18. none beguile you of *r*.
3. 24. *r*. the *r*. of inheritance
1 *Tim*. 5. 18. labourer is worthy of *r*.
Heb. 2. 2. received just recompense of *r*.
11. 26. had respect to recompense of *r*.
2 *John* 8. may receive a full *r*.
Rev. 22. 12. my *r*. is with me
Ps. 31. 23. plentifully *r*. proud
103. 10. nor *r*. us according to iniquity
Is. 3. 9. have *r*. evil to themselves
Matt. 6. 4. Father shall *r*. thee openly
RICH, *Gen*. 13. 2, & 14. 23; *Ex*. 30. 15.
Prov. 10. 4. hand of diligent maketh *r*.
22. blessing of Lord maketh *r*.
13. 7. makes himself *r*. yet hath
14. 20. *r*. man has many friends
18. 11. *r*. man's wealth strong city
22. 2. *r*. and poor meet together
23. 4. labour not to be *r*. cease
28. 11. *r*. man is wise in his conceit
20. hasteth to be *r*. falls in snare
Jer. 9. 23. let not *r*. man glory in his *r*.
Matt. 19. 23. a *r*. man hardly enter
Luke 1. 53. *r*. hath sent empty away
6. 24. woe to you *r*. have received you
16. 1. certain *r*. man which had

18. 23. sorrowful, was very *r.*
2 *Cor.* 6. 10. making many *r.*
  8. 9. Jesus though he was *r.* became
Eph. 2. 4. God who is *r.* in mercy
1 *Tim.* 6. 9. that will be *r.* fall
  17. charge *r.* in this world
  18. *r.* in good works
Jam. 2. 5. poor in this world *r.* in faith
Rev. 2. 9. poverty, but thou art *r.*
  3. 17. sayest I am *r.*
  18. that thou mayest be *r.*
Ps. 39. 6. he heaps up *r.* and
  49. 6. boast in multitude of *r.*
  52. 7. trusted in abundance of his *r.*
  62. 10. if *r.* increase set not
  104. 24. earth is full of thy *r.*
  112. 3. wealth and *r.* be in house
Prov. 3. 16. in her left hand *r.*
  11. 4. *r.* profit not in day of wrath
  28. he trusts in his *r.* shall fall
  13. 8. ransom of man's life are his *r.*
  23. 5. *r.* make themselves wings
  27. 24. *r.* are not for ever
  30. 8. give me neither poverty nor *r.*
Jer. 17. 11. so that he gets *r.* and
Matt. 13. 22. deceitfulness of *r.* choke
Luke 16. 11. commit to your trust true *r.*
Rom. 2. 4. despisest thou the *r.* of his
Rom. 9. 23. make known *r.* of glory
  11. 12. fall of them be *r.* of Gentiles
2 *Cor.* 8. 2. to *r.* of liberality
Eph. 1. 7. according to *r.* of grace
  2. 7. show exceeding *r.* of grace
Phil. 4. 19. according to his *r.* in glory
Col. 2. 2. *r.* of the full assurance, 1. 27.
1 *Tim.* 6. 17. nor trust in *r.*
Heb. 11. 26. reproach of Christ greater *r.*
Jam. 5. 2. your *r.* are corrupted
Col. 3. 16. word of God dwell *r.*
RIDE. Figuratively, honour and triumph, *Is.* 58. 14. Divine protection *Deut.* 33. 26; *Ps.* 18. 10, & 45. 4, & 66. 12, & 68. 4, 33; *Hab.* 3. 8.
RIGHT, *Num.* 27. 7; *Deut.* 21. 17.
Gen. 18. 25. Judge of earth do *r.*
Ezra 8. 21. seek of him a *r.* way
Job 34. 23. not lay on man more than *r.*
Ps. 19. 8. statutes of the Lord are *r.*
  51. 10. renew a *r.* spirit within
  119. 128. I esteem all thy precepts *r.*
Prov. 4. 11. I led thee in *r.* paths
  25. let thine eyes look *r.* on before
  8. 9. all *r.* to them that find knowledge
  12. 5. thoughts of the righteous are *r.*
  14. 12. way which seemeth *r.*
  21. 2. way of man is *r.* in eyes, 12. 25.
Is. 30. 10. prophesy not to us *r.*
Ezek. 18. 5. man be just do lawful and *r.*
Hos. 14. 19. ways of Lord are *r.*
Amos 3. 10. know not to do *r.*
Mark 5. 15. in his *r.* mind
Luke 12. 57. judge not what is *r.*
Acts 4. 19. whether *r.* in sight of
  8. 21. heart is not *r.* in sight of
  13. 10. cease to pervert *r.* ways
Eph. 6. 1. obey parents, this is *r.*
2 *Pet.* 2. 15. forsaken the *r.* way
Rev. 22. 14. have *r.* to tree of life
2 *Tim.* 2. 15. *r.* dividing word of
RIGHTEOUS before me, *Gen.* 7. 1, 18. will destroy *r.* with wicked, 20. 4.
Num. 23. 10. let me die the death of *r.*

Job 4. 7. where were *r.* cut off
  17. 9. *r.* shall hold on his way
Ps. 1. 6. Lord knoweth way of *r.*
  5. 12. will bless *r.* with favour
  32. 11. rejoice in the Lord, ye *r.* 33. 1.
  34. 17. *r.* cry, the Lord heareth and
  19. many are afflictions of *r.* but Lord
  37. 25. I have not seen *r.* forsaken
  29. *r.* shall inherit the land
  55. 22. never suffer *r.* to be
  58. 11. there is reward for *r.*
  64. 10. *r.* shall be glad in the Lord
  68. 3. let *r.* be glad before God
  92. 12. *r.* shall flourish like palm
  97. 11. light sown for *r.* 112. 4.
  112. 6. *r.* in everlasting remembrance
  141. 5. let *r.* smite me and
Prov. 3. 32. his secret is with *r.*
  10. 3. not suffer soul of *r.* to famish
  16. labour of *r.* tendeth to life
  21. lips of *r.* feed many
Prov. 10. 24. desire of *r.* shall be granted
  25. *r.* is an everlasting foundation
  28. hope of *r.* shall be gladness
  30. *r.* shall never be moved
  28. *r.* shall flourish as a branch
  30. fruit of *r.* is a tree of life
  12. 3. root of *r.* not be moved
  5. thoughts of the *r.* are right
  7. but house of *r.* shall stand
  10. *r.* man regards life of beast
  12. 26. *r.* is more excellent than his neighbour
  13. 9. lamp of *r.* rejoiceth but
  14. 32. *r.* hath hope in his death
  15. 6. in house of *r.* is treasure
  19. way of the *r.* is made plain
  29. Lord heareth prayer of *r.*
  18. 10. *r.* runs into it and is safe
  28. 1. *r.* are bold as a lion
Eccl. 7. 16. be not *r.* overmuch
  9. 2. one event to *r.* and wicked
Is. 3. 10. say to *r.* it shall be well
  57. 1. *r.* perisheth, and no man
  60. 21. thy people be all *r.*
Mal. 3. 18. discern between the *r.* and
Matt. 9. 13. not come to call the *r.*
  10. 41. receive a *r.* man's reward
  25. 46. these go punishment, *r.* into
Luke 1. 6. both were *r.* before God
  18. 9. they were *r.* and despised
Rom. 3. 10. none *r.* no not one
  5. 7. scarcely for a *r.* man will one die
  19. obedience of one many made *r.*
2 *Thess.* 1. 5. is a *r.* thing with God
1 *Tim.* 1. 9. law not made for *r.*
Jam. 5. 16. prayer of *r.* availeth
1 *Pet.* 4. 18. if *r.* scarcely saved
1 *John* 3. 7. that doth righteousness is *r.*
Rev. 22. 11. he that is *r.* let him be *r.*
Tit. 2. 12. live soberly *r.*
RIGHTEOUSNESS, *Deut.* 6. 25. be our *r.*
  33. 19. offer a sacrifice of *r.* *Ps.* 4. 5.
Job 29. 14. I put on *r.* it clothed
Ps. 15. 2. he that worketh *r.*
  85. 10. *r.* and peace have kissed
  97. 2. *r.* and judgment are the habita.
Prov. 10. 2. *r.* deliphereth from death
  11. 6. *r.* of upright shall deliver
  19. *r.* tendeth to life, so pursue
  12. 28. in way of *r.* is life
  13. 6. *r.* keeps upright in way

14. 34. r. exalteth a nation, but
16. 8. better is a little with r.
12. his throne established by r.
31. hoary head is a crown of glory, if found in way of r.
Is. 11. 5. r. be girdle of loins
Is. 26. 9. inhabitants of world learn r.
28. 17. judgment to the line, r. to the
32. 17. work of r. be peace
45. 24. in Lord have I r. and
46. 12. far from r.; 13. I bring near r.
54. 17. their r. is of me, saith the L.
61. 3. trees of r. planting of the Lord
10. covered me with robe of r.
62. 1. the r. go forth as brightness
64. 5. meetest him that works r.
Jer. 23. 6. be called the L. our r. 33. 16.
Dan. 4. 27. break off sins by r.
9. 7. r. belongeth to thee, to us confu.
24. bring in everlasting r.
Dan. 12. 3. that turn many to r. as
Zeph. 2. 3. seek r. seek meekness
Mal. 4. 2. Sun of r. arise with
Matt. 3. 15. becometh us to fulfil all r.
5. 6. hunger and thirst after r.
20. except your r. exceed the r. of
Luke 1. 75. in holiness and r. before
John 16. 8. reprove world of sin, r. and
Acts 10. 35. works r. is accepted
13. 10. thou enemy of all r.
24. 25. reasoned of r. temperance
Rom. 1. 17. therein is r. of God
3. 22. even r. of God by faith
4. 6. to whom God imputeth r.
11. seal of the r. of faith, 13.
5. 18. by r. of one, the free gift came
21. grace reign through r. to eternal
6. 13. members instruments of r.
18. became servants of r. to
8. 4. that r. of law be fulfilled
9. 30. Gentiles who followed not after r. have attained to r. even r. o
10. 3. ignorant of r. of God, establish own r. not submitted to r. of God
5. the r. of law, r. which is of faith
10. with heart, man believeth to r.
14. 17. kingdom of God is r. peace, joy
1 Cor. 1. 30. Christ Jesus made to us r.
15. 34. awake to r. and sin not
2 Cor. 5. 21. made r. of God in him
6. 7. by the armour of r.
14. what fellowship hath r.
Gal. 2. 21. if r. come by the law Christ
Eph. 6. 14. having breastplate of r.
Phil. 1. 11. filled with fruits of r.
3. 6. touching the r. of the law
9. not our own r. but the r. of God
1 Tim. 6. 11. follow r. 2 Tim. 2. 22.
Tit. 3. 5. not by works of r. have done
Heb. 12. 11. yields fruit of r.
Jam. 1. 20. wrath of man works not r.
3. 18. fruit of r. sown in peace
1 Pet. 3. 14. if ye suffer for r.
2 Pet. 1. 1. through r. of God our Saviour
3. 13. heaven and earth dwelleth r.
1 John 2. 29. every one that doeth r. is
3 7. he that doeth r. is r.
Rev. 19. 8. fine linen r. of saints
Gen. 15. 6. counted to him for r. Ps. 106. 31; Rom. 4. 3, 5, 9, 22; Gal. 3. 6.
1 Kings 8. 22. his r. Job 33. 26; Ps. 50. 6; Ezek. 3. 20; Matt. 6. 33; Rom.

3. 25; 2 Cor. 9. 9.
Ps. 17. 15. in r. Hos. 10. 12; Acts 17. 31; Ps. 96. 13, & 98. 9; Eph. 4. 24; Rev. 19. 11.
Deut. 9. 4. thy r. Job 35. 8; Ps. 35. 28, & 40. 10, & 51. 14, & 89. 16, & 119. 142; Is. 57. 12.
Is. 64. 6. all our r. Ezek. 33. 13; Dan. 9. 18.
RIGOUR, Ex. 1. 13; Lev. 25. 43, 53
RIOT, Tit. 1. 6; 1 Pet. 4. 4.
RIOTING, Pet. 2. 13; Rom. 13. 13.
RIOTOUS, Prov. 23. 20, & 28. 7; Luke 15. 13.
RIPE fruit, Ex. 22. 29; Num. 18. 13; Mic. 7. 1.
Jer. 24. 2. r. figs, Hos. 9. 10; Nah. 3. 12.
Gen. 40. 10. r. grapes, Num. 13. 20; Is. 18. 5.
Joel 3. 13. harvest r. Rev. 14. 15.
RISE, Songs 3. 2; Is. 14. 21, & 24. 20, & 26. 14, & 33. 10, & 43. 17, & 54. 17, & 58. 10; 1 Thess. 4. 16.
RISING, Prov. 30. 31; Luke 2. 34.
RIVER, Ex. 1. 22. & 4. 9; Job 40. 23; Ps. 36. 8, & 46. 4. & 65. 9; Is. 48. 18, & 66. 12; Rev. 22. 1, 2.
RIVERS, Job 20. 17, & 29. 6; Ps. 119. 136; Prov. 5. 16, & 21. 1; Is. 32. 2, & 33. 21; Mic. 6. 7; John 7. 38.
ROAR, Is. 42. 13; Jer. 25. 30; Hos. 11. 10; Joel. 3. 16; Amos 1. 2.
ROB, Lev. 19. 13; Prov. 22. 22.
Mal. 3. 8. will a man r. God
9. ye have r. me
Is. 42. 22. a people r. and spoiled
2 Cor. 11. 8. I r. other churches
Job 5. 5. r. swalloweth up, 18. 9.
John 10. 1. climbs up as a thief and a r.
ROBBERY, Ps. 62. 10; Prov. 21. 7; Is. 61. 8; Amos 3. 10; Phil. 2 6.
ROCK, Ex. 17. 6; Num. 20. 8, 11; Deut. 32. 4, 13, 15, 18, 30, 31, 37.
Ps. 18. 2. Lord my r. and fortress, 92. 15.
18. 31. who is a r. save our God, 46.
31. 3. thou my r. and fortress, 2.
61. 2. lead me to r. higher than
62. 2. he only my r. and salvation, 6.
71. 3. strong habitation r. and fortress
89. 26. Father and r. of my salvation
94. 22. God is the r. of my refuge
Matt. 7. 24. man built house on r.
16. 18. on this r. I will build
1 Cor. 10. 4. R. followed; that R. was
Rev. 6. 16. said to r. fall on us
ROD, Ex. 4. 4, 20; Num. 17. 2, 8.
Ps. 23. 4. thy r. and staff comfort
125. 3. r. of wicked rest not on
Prov. 13. 24. he that spareth r. hateth
22. 15. r. of correction drive it
23. 14. shall beat him with r.
29. 15. r. and reproof give wisdom
Is. 10. 5. r. of my anger, staff
Ezek. 20. 37. cause pass under r. Lev. 27. 32.
Mic. 6. 9. hear ye the r. and
7. 14. feed people with thy r.
Rev. 12. 5. rule with r. of iron, 19. 15.
ROLL, Zech. 5. 1. and behold, a flying r. 2.
ROLLED, Matt. 27. 60. he r. a great stone to the door

28. 2. angel r. back the stone
Mark 16. 4. the stone was r. away
Luke 24. 2. found the stone r. away
ROOM, *Ps.* 31. 8. set feet in a large r.
Mal. 3. 10. not be r. enough to
Luke 2. 7. no r. for them in the inn
12. 17. no r. where to bestow
14. 8. sit not down in highest r.
22. and yet there is r.
Acts 1. 13. went up to an upper r.
ROOMS, *Matt.* 23. 6. love uppermost r.
Luke 14. 7. they chose out the chief r.
ROOT. This word denotes stability, *Col.*
2. 7. The cause of a thing, 1 *Tim.*
6. 10. Strength, *Is.* 14. 30. A
particular sin, *Heb.* 12. 15. Foun-
dation, *Job* 28. 9. Parents, *Dan.*
11. 7. Christ, *Is.* 11. 10; *Rev.* 5.
5. *Job* 5. 3, & 31. 12; *Ps.* 52. 5.
Deut. 29. 18. r. that beareth gall
Job 19. 28. seeing the r. of the matter is
Prov. 12. 3. r. of righteous shall not be
moved
Is. 11. 10. be a r. of Jesse his r.
37. 31. take r. downward, 27. 6.
Matt. 3. 10. axe is laid to r. of tree
13. 6. because no r. withered
Luke 17. 6. be plucked up by r.
Rom. 11. 16. if r. be holy so are branches
1 *Tim.* 6. 10. love of money is the r. of
Heb. 12. 15. lest r. of bitterness
Matt. 15. 13. not planted be r. up
Eph. 3. 17. being r. and grounded
Col. 2. 7. r. and built up in him
ROSE noun, *Songs* 2. 1. am r. of Sharon
Is. 35. 1. desert blossom as the r.
ROSE, verb, *Rom.* 14. 9. Christ both
died and r.
1 *Cor.* 15. 4. and r. again the third day
2 *Cor.* 5. 15. live to him who died and r.
1 *Thess.* 4. 14. believe that Jesus died
and r.
Rev. 19. 3. smoke r. up for ever
ROT. To be offensive, *Prov.* 10. 7; *Is.*
40. 20.
RUDDY, *Songs* 5. 10; *Lam.* 4. 7.
RULE, *Esth.* 9. 1; *Prov.* 17. 2, & 19. 10.
Prov. 25. 28. has no r. over his own
Gal. 6. 16. walk according to r.
Phil. 3. 16. let us walk by same r.
Heb. 13. 7. them have r. over you, 17.
2 *Sam.* 23. 3. r. over men must be just,
r. in the fear of God
Ps. 103. 19. kingdom r. over all
Prov. 16. 32. mighty he that r. his spirit
Hos. 11. 12. Judah r. with God is faithful
Col. 3. 15. peace of God r. in hearts
1 *Tim.* 3. 5. to r. his own house
5. 17. elders that r. be counted worthy
of honour
Rev. 12. 5. child to r. all nations
Mic. 5. 2. is to be r. in Israel
Matt. 25. 21. I will make thee r. over
many things
Acts 23. 5. not speak evil of the r. of thy
people
Rom. 13. 3. r. not a terror to good
Eph. 6. 12. r. of darkness of this world
RUN, *Gen.* 49. 22; *Lev.* 15. 3; 1 *Sam.*
8. 11; *Ps.* 19. 5; *Eccl.* 1. 7; *Heb.*
6. 20.
2 *Chr.* 16. 9. eyes of Lord r. to and fro

Ps. 119. 32. r. way of commandments
Songs 1. 4. draw me, r. after thee
Is. 40. 31. r. and not be weary
Dan. 12. 4. many r. to and fro
1 *Cor.* 9. 24. let us so r. that we may
Gal. 2. 2. or had r. in vain
5. 7. ye did r. well
Heb. 12. 1. let us r. with patience
1 *Pet.* 4. 4. r. not to excess of riot
Ps. 23. 5. my cup r. over
Prov. 18. 10. righteous r. into it and is
Rom. 9. 16. it is not of him that r.

SABBATH holy. *Ex.* 16. 23, 29, & 20. 8.
—11. & 31. 14; *Acts* 13. 42, & 18. 4.
Lev. 23. 3. seventh day is the s.
Neh. 9. 14. madest known thy s.
13. 18. bring wrath profaning s.
Is. 56. 2. keepeth the s. from polluting
58. 13. call the s. a delight the holy of
the Lord
Matt. 12. 5. priests profane s.
28. 1. in end of s. as it began to dawn
Lev. 19. 3. my s. 30. & 26. 2; *Is.* 56. 4;
Ezek. 20. 12, 13, & 22. 8, 26, & 23. 38, &
44. 24, & 46. 3.
Deut. 5. 12. s. day, *Neh.* 13. 22; *Jer.* 17.
21; *Acts* 15. 21; *Col.* 2. 16.
SACKCLOTH, *Gen.* 37. 34; *Job* 16. 15;
Ps. 30. 11, & 35. 13; *Is.* 22. 12; *Rev.*
11. 3.
SACRIFICE, *Gen.* 31. 54; *Ex.* 8. 25.
1 *Sam.* 2. 29. wherefore kick ye at my s.
3. 14. Eli's house not purged with s.
1 *Sam.* 15. 22. to obey is better than s.
Ps. 4. 5. offer s. of righteousness
40. 6. s. and offering not desire
50. 5. made a covenant with me by s.
51. 16. desirest not s. else I
17. s. of God are a broken spirit
107. 22. Lord offer s. of thanks, 116. 17.
141. 2. lifting up hands as evening s.
Prov. 15. 8. s. of wicked is abomination
to the Lord, 27.
21. 3. justice more acceptable than s.
Eccl. 5. 1. than to give s. of fools
Dan. 8. 11. daily s. taken away
9. 27. s. and obligation to cease
11. 31. take away daily s. 12. 11.
Hos. 6. 6. desired mercy not s.
Mark 9. 49. every s. be salted
Rom. 12. 1. present bodies living s.
1 *Cor.* 5. 7. Christ our passover is s. for
Eph. 5. 2. s. to God for a sweet-smelling
Phil. 2. 17. offered on s. of faith
4. 18. sweet s. acceptable to God
Heb. 9. 26. put away sin by the s. of
13. 15. let us offer s. of praise
16. with such s. God is pleased
1 *Pet.* 2. 5. priesthood to offer spiritual s.
SACRILEGE, *Rom.* 2. 22. that abhor-
rest idols, dost thou commit s.
SAD, 1 *Sam.* 1. 18; *Ezek.* 13. 22; *Mark*
10. 22.
SADLY, *Gen.* 40. 7. why look ye so s. to-
day
SADNESS, *Eccl.* 7. 3. by s. of counten-
ance heart is made better
SAFE, 2 *Sam.* 18. 29. is young man
Absalom s.
Ps. 119. 117. hold me up, I shall be s.
Prov. 18. 10. righteous run into it, are s.

29. 25. whoso trusteth in the Lord shall be s.

Luke 15. 27. because received him s.

SAFELY, *Prov.* 1. 33. whoso hearkeneth to me shall dwell s.

Prov. 31. 11. heart of her husband doth s. trust in her

Hos. 2. 18. make them to lie down s.

SAFETY. External peace, *Lev.* 25. 18, 19; *Ezek.* 34. 25. Without fear, *Ps.* 78. 53. False confidence, 1 *Thess.* 5. 3. Well-grounded hope *Job* 5. 4, 11, & 11. 18; *Ps.* 4. 8, & 12. 5, & 33. 17; *Prov.* 11. 14, & 21. 31.

SAINT, S. Believers in Christ Jesus, 1 *Cor.* 1. 2; *Phil.* 1. 1; *Col.* 1. 2, 12. The literal import of the term is *holy ones*, and such as were redeemed by the blood of Christ, *Ps.* 52. 9, & 79. 2, & 89. 5; *Rev.* 13. 10; 14. 12.

Deut. 33. 2. come with 10,000 of his s.

3. all his s. are in thy hand

1 *Sam.* 2. 9. he keeps feet of his s.

2 *Chr.* 6. 41. s. rejoice in goodness

Job 15. 15. he puts no trust in s.

Ps. 16. 3. goodness extends to s. on earth

37. 28. Lord forsaketh not his s.

50. 5. gather my s. together

97. 10. Lord preserveth souls of s.

106. 16. envied Aaron s. of the Lord

116. 15. precious in sight of the Lord is the death of his s.

149. 9. this honour have all s.

Prov. 2. 8. preserveth way of s.

Dan. 7. 18. s. shall take kingdom, 22. 27.

Hos. 11. 12. Judah ruleth and is faithful with the s.

Zech. 14. 5. God come, s. with thee

Rom. 1. 7. called to be s 1 *Cor.* 1. 2; 2 *Cor.* 1. 1; *Eph.* 1. 1; *Col.* 1. 2, & 12, 8, 27. intercession for the s. *Eph.* 6. 18.

12. 13. necessity to s. 2 *Cor.* 9. 12.

15. 25. minister to s. 26. 31; 1 *Cor.* 16. 1; 2 *Cor.* 8. 4, & 9. 1; *Heb.* 6. 10.

1 *Cor.* 6. 2. s. shall judge the world

Eph. 3. 8. than the least of all s.

4. 12. perfecting s. for work

1 *Thess.* 3. 13. coming of Lord with all s.

2 *Thess.* 1. 10. to be glorified in s.

Jude 14. Lord cometh with 10,000 s.

Rev. 5. 8. prayers of s. 8. 3, 4.

11. 18. reward of the s.

13. 7. war with thy s.

14. 12. patience of s.; 15. 3. King of s.

16. 6. blood of s. 17. 6, & 18. 24.

19. 8. righteousness of the s.

20. 9. compassed camp of s.

SALVATION, *Ps.* 14. 7, & 53. 6.

Ex. 14. 13. see s. of the L., 2 *Chr.* 20. 17.

Ps. 3. 8. s. belongs only to the Lord

37. 39. s. of righteous is of the Lord

50. 23. I will show him the s. of God,

68. 20. our God is the God of s. 65. 5.

85. 9. s. is nigh them that fear

98. 2. made known his s.

3. have seen s. of our God

132. 16. I clothe priests with s.

149. 4. Lord will beautify meek with s.

Is. 26. 1. s. will God appoint

25. 9. we rejoice in his s. 12. 3.

33. 6. be the strength of thy s.

45. 17. Israel saved in the Lord with everlasting s.

46. 13. I will place s. in Zion

52. 7. that publisheth s.

10. ends of the earth see the s.

59. 16. own arm brought s. 63. 5.

17. helmet of s. *Eph.* 6. 17.

60. 18. call thy walls S. gates Praise

61. 10. with garments of s.

62. 1. s. thereof as a lamp

Jer. 3. 23. in vain is s. in the Lord

Lam. 3. 26. wait for s. of the Lord

Jonah 2. 9. s. is of the Lord

Hab. 3. 8. ride on chariots of s.

Zech. 9. 9. king comes having s.

Luke 19. 9. s. come to this house

John 4. 22. we know s. is of the Jews

Acts 4. 12. neither s. in any other

13. 26. to you is word of s. sent

47. be for s. unto ends of the earth

Rom. 1. 16. power of God to s.

11. 11. through fall s. is come

13. 11. now is our s. nearer

2 *Cor.* 1. 6. your consolation and s.

6. 2. in the day of s. have I

Eph. 1. 13. gospel of s.

6. 17. take the helmet of s.

Phil. 2. 12. work out s. with fear

1 *Thess.* 5. 8. the hope of s.

9. to obtain s. by Lord Jesus Christ

2 *Thess.* 2. 13. God chosen you to s.

2 *Tim.* 2. 10. to obtain s. with eternal glory

3. able to make wise to s.

Tit. 2. 11. grace of God bringeth s.

Heb. 1. 14. shall be heirs of s.

2. 3. we escape if neglect so great s.

10. captain of our s. perfect

5. 9. became author of eternal s.

6. 9. better things accompany s.

9. 28. second time without sin unto s.

1 *Pet.* 1. 5. through faith unto s.

9. end of faith s. of souls

Jude 3. write you of common s.

Rev. 7. 10. s. to our God, 12. 10, & 19. 1.

Ex. 15. 2. God is become my s. *Job* 13. 16; *Ps.* 18. 2, & 25. 5, & 27. 1, & 38. 22, & 51. 14, & 62. 7, & 88. 1, & 118. 14; *Is.* 12. 2; *Mic.* 7. 7; *Hab.* 3. 18.

Ps. 89. 26. the rock of my s.

140. 7. strength of my s.

2 *Sam.* 23. 5. covenant is all my s. and desire

Is. 46. 13. my s. shall not tarry, 49. 6, & 51. 5, 6, 8, & 56. 1.

Gen. 49. 18. thy s. 1 *Sam.* 2. 1; *Ps.* 9. 14, & 13. 5, & 20. 5, & 18. 35, & 21. 1. 5, & 35. 3, & 40. 10, 16, & 51. 12, & 69. 13, 29, & 70. 4, & 71. 15, & 85. 7, & 106. 4, & 119. 41, 81, 123, 166, 174; *Is.* 17. 10, & 62. 11; *Luke* 2. 30.

SAME, *Job* 4. 8. they that sow wickedness reap the s.

Ps. 102. 27. thou art the s. thy years

Matt. 5. 46. do not even publicans the s.

26. 23. dippeth, the s. shall betray me

Luke 6. 38. s. measure ye meet withal

Eph. 4. 10. descended, is the s. that

Phil. 3. 16. let us walk by the s. rule

2 *Tim.* 2. 2. the s. commit thou to faithful men

Heb. 1. 12. thou art the s. thy years

2. 14. himself took part of the s.
Heb. 11. 9. heirs of the s. promise
13. 8. Jesus Christ, s. yesterday, to-day
Rev. 3. 5. s. shall be clothed in white
SANCTIFICATION, 1 *Cor.* 1. 30. who
of God is made to us s.
1 *Thess.* 4. 3. will of God, even your s.
4. how to possess his vessel in s.
2 *Thess.* 2. 13. through s. of the Spirit,
1 *Pet.* 1. 2.
SANCTIFY, to prepare or set apart
persons and things to a holy use,
Ex. 19. 23. God *sanctified* Christ
when he set him apart to his
mediatory office, and furnished him
with gifts and graces for the discharge of it, *John* 10. 36. Christ
sanctified himself by his solemn
prayer, he surrendered himself to,
and prepared himself for suffering,
and by his suffering, he prepared
himself to be our effectual Saviour,
John 17. 19.
SANCTIFY, *Ex.* 13. 2. & 19. 10.
Ex. 31. 13. Lord which s. you, *Lev.* 20. 8.
Lev. 20. 7. s. yourselves, be holy
Num. 20. 12. believed not to s. me
Is. 8. 13. s. Lord of hosts himself
Ezek. 38. 23. I will s. myself, 44. 19.
Joel. 1. 14. s. a fast, s. congregation, 2.
15, 16.
John 17. 17. s. them through thy truth
19. for their sakes I s. myself, that
they may be s.
Eph. 5. 26. might s. and cleanse it
1 *Thess.* 5. 23. s. you wholly in
Heb. 13. 12. might s. people
1 *Pet.* 3. 15. s. Lord God in your hearts
SANCTIFIED, *Gen.* 2. 3. blessed the
seventh day and s. it
Deut. 32. 51. ye s. me not in midst
Job 1. 5. Job sent and s. them
Is. 13. 3. commanded my s. ones
Jer. 1. 5. I s. thee and ordained thee a
Matt. 23. 17. temple that s. the gold
John 10. 36. him whom Father has s.
17. 19. might be s. through thy truth
Acts 20. 32. inherit. among s. 26. 18.
Rom. 15. 16. s. by the Holy Ghost
1 *Cor.* 1. 2. s. in Christ Jesus
6. 11. but ye are s. in the Lord Jesus
7. 14. the unbelieving husband is s. by
the wife
1 *Tim.* 4. 5. s. by word and prayer
2 *Tim.* 2. 21. s. to master's use
Heb. 2. 11. who s. and they s. are all of
one
10. 10. by the which will we are s.
through Jesus
10. 14. perfected for ever them s. 10.
29. blood of the covenant wherewith
he was s.
Jude 1. to them that are s. by God the
Father and preserved in
SANCTUARY. A holy house—denoting
the tabernacle, *Ex.* 25. 8; *Heb.* 9.
1 2,. The word sometimes signifies
" the holiest of all," in which the
God of Israel dwelt by the Shechi-
nah, or visible symbol of his presence, a bright effulgent cloud upon
the mercy-seat, between the cher-

ubims of glory, *Lev.* 4. 6. It also
denoted the temple. Sanctuary
also means a refuge, defence, or
protection, *Is.* 8. 14. *Ps.* 63. 24.
SANCTUARY, *Ps.* 20. 2. send thee help
from s.
63. 2. I have seen thee in the s.
77. 13. thy way, O God, is in the s.
96. 6. strength and beauty are in his s.
Is. 60. 13. beautify the place of my s.
Dan. 9. 17. cause thy face to shine upon
thy s.
SAND, *Gen.* 22. 17. multiply seed as s.
Job 6. 3. be heavier than the s.
Ps. 139. 18. more in number than the s.
Matt. 7. 26. foolish man built house on s.
SANDALS, *Mark* 6. 9. be shod with s.
Acts 12. 8. angel said, bind thy s.
SANG, *Job* 38. 7. morning stars s. to-
gether
Acts 16. 25. Paul and Silas s. praises to
SAPPHIRE, *Ex.* 24. 10. a paved work
of s. stone
Ex. 28. 18. the second row a s.
Ezek. 1. 26. throne, as appearance of s.
Rev. 21. 19. second foundation was s.
SAPPHIRES, *Is.* 54. 11. lay thy foun-
dations with s.
SARDINE, *Rev.* 4. 3. to look upon like
a s. stone
SARDIUS, *Ex.* 28. 17. first row shall be
a s.
Rev. 21. 20. sixth foundation was a s.
SARDONYX, *Rev.* 21. 20. fifth found-
ation was a s.
SAT, *Ps.* 26. 4. not s. with vain persons
Luke 7. 15. he that was dead s. up
10. 39. Mary s. at Jesus' feet
Acts 2. 3. cloven tongues s. upon each
Rev. 4. 3. he that s. on the throne was
like a jasper
14. 14. one s. like the Son of man
SAT down, *Ps.* 137. 1. we s. *down,* yea,
we wept
Songs 2. 3. I s. *down* under shadow
Heb. 1. 3. s. *down* on the right hand of
God, 10. 12.
SATAN provoked David, 1 *Chr.* 21. 1.
Job 1. 6. S. came among them, 2. 1.
Ps. 109. 6. S. stand at right hand
Matt. 4. 10. get thee hence S. 16. 23.
Luke 10. 18. I beheld S. as lightning
22. 31. S. desired to have you
Acts 26. 18. from power of S. to God
Rom. 16. 20. God bruise S. under feet
1 *Cor.* 5. 5. to deliver such unto S.
7. 5. that S. tempt you not for incon-
tinency
2 *Cor.* 2. 11. S. get advantage of us
11. 14. S. is transformed into an angel
of light
2 *Cor.* 12. 7. messenger of S. to buffet me
1 *Tim.* 1. 20. I delivered to S. that
Rev. 2. 9. the synagogue of S.
24. not known the depths of S.
SATISFY. Signifies to refresh, *Job* 38.
27. To relieve the poor, *Ps.* 132.
15. To fulfil, *Ps.* 145. 16; *Prov.*
6. 30.
Ps. 90. 14. s. us early with mercy
91. 16. with long life I will s. him
103. 5. who s. thy mouth with good

107. 9. he s. the longing soul
132. 15. I will s. poor with bread
Prov. 5. 19. let her breasts s. thee
Is. 55. 2. labour for that which s. not
SATISFIED, *Ps.* 17. 15. be s. with thy likeness
Jer. 31. 14. my people be s. with
Ps. 22. 26. meek shall eat and be s.
36. 8. s. with fatness of house
63. 5. soul s. as with marrow and fat.
65. 4. s. with goodness of house
Prov. 14. 14. a good man shall be s. from himself
30. 15. three things never s.
Eccl. 5. 10. loveth silver not be s.
Is. 53. 11. see the travail of his soul and be s.
66. 11. be s. with breasts of consola.
SATISFACTION, *Num.* 35. 31, 32.
SATISFIEST, *Ps.* 145. 16. s. the desire of every thing
SATISFIETH, *Ps.* 103. 5. s. mouth with good things
Is. 55. 2. labour for that which s. not
SAVE your lives, *Gen.* 45. 7.
Gen. 50. 20. good to s. much people
Ps. 18. 27. wilt s. afflicted people
28. 9. s. thy people, 37. 40, & 60. 5.
69. 35. God will s. Zion
72. 4. s. children of needy
76. 9. s. meek of the earth
109. 31. poor s. him
118. 25. s. now, send prosperity
Is. 35. 4. come and s. you
45. 20. cannot s. 59. 1; *Jer.* 14. 9.
49. 25. I will s. thy children
Ezek. 18. 27. he s. his soul, 3. 18.
36. 29. I will s. from all uncleanness, 37. 25.
Hos. 1. 7. I will s. them by the Lord
Zeph. 3. 17. the Lord will s.
19. I will s. her that halteth
Zech. 8. 7. I s. my people, 9. 16, & 10. 6.
Matt. 1. 21. s. his people from sins
16. 25. whosoever will s. his life shall lose it
18. 11. Son of man is come to s. lost, *Luke* 19. 10.
Mark 3. 4. lawful to s. life or to kill
John 12. 47. I came not to judge but to s. the world
Acts 2. 40. s. ourselves from
1 *Cor.* 1. 21. by foolishness of preaching to s.
9. 22. that I might s. some
1 *Tim.* 1. 15. world to s. sinners
4. 16. both s. thyself and those
Heb. 7. 25. able to s. to uttermost
Jam. 1. 21. word able to s. your souls
5. 15. prayer of faithful s. sick
20. converts a sinner shall s. a soul
Jude 23. others s. with fear
Ps. 6. 4. s. me, 55. 16, & 57. 3. & 119. 94; *Jer.* 17. 14; *John* 12. 27.
Is. 25. 9. s. us, 33. 22. & 38. 20; *Hos.* 14. 3; *Matt.* 8. 25; 1 *Pet.* 3. 21.
Is. 45. 22. look to me and be s.
Jer. 8. 20. summer ended we not s.
Matt. 19. 25. who can be s. *Luke* 18. 26.
Luke 7. 50. thy faith hath s. thee
23. 35. he s. others
John 3. 17. world through him s. 5. 34.

Acts 2. 47. added to church such as be s.
4. 12. name where by must be s.
16. 30. what must I do to be s.
Rom. 8. 24. we are s. by hope
10. 1. prayer for Israel that they might be s.
1 *Cor.* 1. 18. to us who are s.
Eph. 2. 5. by grace ye are s.
1 *Tim.* 2. 4. will have all men s.
Tit. 3. 5. according to his mercy he s. us
1 *Pet.* 4. 18. if righteous scarcely be s.
Rev. 21. 24. nations of them are s.
Ps. 80. 3. shall be s. 7. 19; *Is.* 45. 17, & 64. 5; *Jer.* 23. 6, & 30. 7; *Matt.* 10. 22, & 24. 13; *Mark* 16. 16; *Acts* 16. 31; *Rom.* 5. 10; 11. 26; 1 *Tim.* 2. 15.
SAVIOUR, 2 *Sam.* 22. 3. God is my refuge, my S.
2 *Kings* 13. 5. Lord gave Israel a S. *Neh.* 9. 27.
Is. 43. 3. I am thy S. 49. 26. & 60. 16.
11. besides me no S. *Hos.* 13. 4.
45. 15. G. of Israel the S. 21; *Jer.* 14. 8.
Obad. 21. S. come on mout Zion
Luke 1. 47.-spirit rejoiced in God my S.
2. 11. to you is born a S. who is Christ
Acts 5. 31. exalted to be a Prince and S.
Eph. 5. 23. Christ Head and S. of body
1 *Tim.* 4. 10. who is S. of all
1. 1. God our S. *Tit.* 1. 4, & 2. 10, 13, 3. 4, 6; 2 *Pet.* 1. 1, 11; *Jude* 25.
2 *Pet.* 2. 20. knowledge of Lord and S. Jesus Christ
3. 18. grow in grace and knowledge of our Lord and S. Christ
1 *John* 4. 14. the Father sent the Son to be the S.
Jude 25. only wise God, our S. be glory
SAVOUR sweet, *Gen.* 8. 21; *Ex.* 29. 18; *Lev.* 1. 9, & 2. 9, & 3. 16.
Songs 1. 3. because of s. of thy good
2 *Cor.* 2. 14. make manifest s. of
15. were to God a sweet s. of Christ
16. to one the s. of death, and to the other s. of life
Eph. 5. 2. a sacrifice to God for a sweet-smelling s.
Matt. 16. 23. s. not things of God
SCALES, *Is.* 40. 12. weighed mountains in s.
Acts 9. 18. fell from his eyes as s.
SCARCELY, *Rom.* 5. 7; 1 *Pet.* 4. 18.
SCAREST, *Job* 7. 14. thou s. me with dreams
SCARLET, *Is.* 1. 18. come now, though your sins be as s.
Matt. 27. 28. put on Jesus a s. robe
Heb. 9. 19. took water and s. wool
Rev. 18. 16. great city clothed with s.
SCATTER them, *Gen.* 49. 7.
Num. 10. 35. let enemies be s.
Ps. 68. 30. s. people that delight in war
Luke 1. 51. s. proud in imagination of
SCATTERED, *Zech.* 13. 7. awake, O sword, smite the shepherd, and the sheep shall be s.
Matt. 9. 36. s. as sheep having no shepherd
John 11. 52. gather in children s.
16. 32. hour cometh ye shall be s.
Acts 8. 4. s. everywhere preaching
Jam. 1. 1. twelve tribes s. abroad

1 *Pet.* 1. 1. strangers *s.* through Pontus
SCATTERETH, *Ps.* 147. 16. *s.* hoar-
    frost like ashes
Prov. 11. 24. *s.* and yet increaseth
Matt. 12. 30. gathereth not with me *s.*
    abroad
SCENT, *Job* 14. 9. through *s.* of water
    bud
Hos. 14. 7. the *s.* as wine of Lebanon
SCEPTRE shall not depart from Judah,
    Gen. 49. 10.
Num. 24. 17. a *s.* rise out of Israel
Ps. 45. 6. the *s.* of thy kingdom is a
    right *s. Heb.* 8. 1.
Zech. 10. 11. the *s.* of Egypt shall depart
SCHOLAR, 1 *Chr.* 25. 8; *Mal.* 2. 12.
SCHOOLMASTER, *Gal.* 3. 24. law our
    s. to bring to Christ
Gal. 3. 25. after faith, we are no longer
    under a *s.*
SCOFFERS. Persons who try to turn all
    religion into ridicule, with a design
    to depreciate truth and represent
    it as contemptible, *Hab.* 1. 10; 2
    Pet. 3. 3.
SCORN, ER, *Job* 16. 20; *Ps.* 44. 13.
Prov. 9. 12. if thou *s.* bear it
    1. 22. *s.* delight in *s.*
    3. 34. he *s.* the *s.* but giveth
    9. 8. reprove not *s.* lest he hate
    13. 1. *s.* heareth not rebuke
    14. 6. a *s.* seeketh wisdom and find-
    eth it not
    15. 12. *s.* loveth not one that reproves
    19. 29. judg. are prepared for *s.*
SCORNFUL, *Ps.* 1. 1; *Prov.* 29. 8; *Is.*
    28. 14.
SCOURGE of tongue, *Job* 5. 21.
Is. 28. 15. overflowing *s.* 18, & 10. 26.
Matt. 10. 17. *s.* you in their synagogues
Matt. 20. 19. they shall *s.* him, *Mark* 10.
    34: *Luke* 18. 33.
Acts 22. 25. lawful to *s.* a Roman
SCOURGED, *Matt.* 27. 26. had *s.* Jesus,
    he delivered him to be crucified,
    Mark 15. 15; *John* 19. 1.
SCOURGETH, *Heb.* 12. 6. the Lord *s.*
    every man whom he receiveth
SCOURGINGS, *Heb.* 11. 36. others had
    trial of *s.*
SCRIP, 1 *Sam.* 17. 40. David put smooth
    stones in a *s.*
Matt. 10. 10. provide *s.* for journey
Luke 22. 35. sent without *s.* lacked ye
SCRIPTURE of truth, *Dan.* 10. 21.
Matt. 22. 29. err. not knowing *s.*
John 5. 39. search the *s. Acts* 17. 11.
Rom. 15. 4. through comfort of *s.* might
2 *Tim.* 3. 15. from a child known *s.*
    16. *s.* is given by inspiration
2 *Pet.* 1. 20. no prophecy of the *s.* is of
    any private interpretation
    3. 16. wrest as do other *s.* to own
SEA, *Ps.* 33. 7, & 72. 8; *Prov.* 8. 29; *Is.*
    48. 18, & 57. 20; *Zech.* 9. 10; *Rev.*
    4. 6, & 10. 2, 6, & 15. 2, & 18. 21,
    & 20. 13, & 21. 1.
SEAL set on heart, *Songs* 8. 6.
John 3. 33. set to *s.* that God is true
Rom. 4. 11. *s.* of righteousness
    Cor. 9. 2. *s.* of my apostleship
Tim. 2. 19. have this *s.* Lord knows

Rev. 7. 2. having *s.* of living God
SEALED, *Job* 4. 17. transgression is *s.*
Songs 4. 12. a spring shut up, fountain *s.*
John 6. 27. him hath God the Father *s.*
2 *Cor.* 1. 22. who hath *s.* us and
Eph. 1. 13. ye *s.* with Holy Spirit, 4. 30.
Rev. 5. 1. a book *s.* with seven *s.*
    Rev. 7. 3. were *s.* 144,000 of tribes, 4.
SEARCH a resting-place, *Num.* 10. 33.
1 *Chr.* 28. 9. Lord *s.* all hearts
Job 10. 6. thou *s.* after my sin
Ps. 139. 23. *s.* me, O God, and know my
Prov. 2. 4. *s.* for her as treasures
    18. 17. neighbour, comes and *s.*
    25. 27. for men to *s.* own glory
Jer. 17. 10. I the Lord *s.* the heart
    29. 13. when ye *s.* for me with
Lam. 3. 40. let us *s.* and try ways
Zeph. 1. 12. *s.* Jerusalem with candles
Acts 17. 11. *s.* scriptures daily
1 *Cor.* 2. 10. Spirit *s.* all things
Rev. 2. 23. I am he that *s.* the reins
Judg. 5. 16. great *s.* of heart
SEASON. Short space of time, *Heb.* 11.
    25. Opportunity to do any par-
    ticular work, *Acts* 1. 7. The
    revolutions of time, *Gen.* 1. 14; 40.
    4; *Ex.* 13. 10.
Ps. 1. 3. bring forth fruit in his *s.*
Eccl. 3. 1. to every thing a *s.*
Is. 50. 4. to speak word in *s.*
Luke 4. 13. departed from him for a *s.*
John 5. 35. willing for a *s.* to rejoice
    in his light
Acts 1. 7. to know times and *s.*
    14. 17. gave rain from heaven and
    fruitful *s.*
1 *Thess.* 5. 1. of times and *s.* I have no
2 *Tim.* 4. 2. instant in *s.* out of *s.*
Heb. 11. 25. enjoy pleasures of sin for *s.*
1 *Pet.* 1. 6. a *s.* ye are in heaviness
Col. 4. 6. speech be *s.* with salt
SEAT, S, *Job* 23. 3. I might come even
    to his *s.*
Ps. 1. 1. nor sitteth in *s.* of scornful
Matt. 23. 6. love chief *s.* in synagogues
Luke 11. 43. love the uppermost *s.* 20. 46.
Rev. 2. 13. dwellest where Satan's *s.* is
    4. 4. four-and-twenty *s.* upon the *s.*
    24 elders
SECRET. In private, *Ps.* 64. 4. The
    meaning of a dream, *Dan.* 4. 9.
    That which belongs to God only,
    Deut. 29. 29. The knowledge of
    salvation, *Ps.* 25. 14; *John* 15. 15.
    Divine mysteries, *Matt.* 13. 34.
    Gen. 49. 6; *Job* 40. 13.
Job 11. 6. he would show thee the *s.* of
    wisdom
    29. 4. *s.* of God upon my tabernacle
Ps. 25. 14. *s.* of Lord with them
    27. 5. in *s.* of tabernacle he
    31. 20. hide in *s.* of thy presence
    44. 21. he knows *s.* of hearts
    139. 15. when I was made in *s.*
Prov. 3. 32. *s.* is with righteous
    9. 17. bread eaten in *s.* pleasant
    11. 13. tale-bearer reveals *s.* 20. 19.
Prov. 25. 9. discover not a *s.* to another
Dan. 2. 28. a God that revealeth *s.*
Amos 3. 7. reveals *s.* to servants
Matt. 6. 4. alms in *s.* Father seeth in *s.*

John 18. 20. in *s.* I sa͏̇d nothing
19. 38. but *s.* for fear of Jews
Rom. 2. 16. when G. shall judge the *s.* of men
SECT, *Acts* 26. 5. after straitest *s.* of our religion
Acts 28. 22. this *s.* is everywhere spoken against
SEDUCE. To decoy or draw away a person from that which is right, by temptation and deception, *Ezek.* 13. 10; *Mark* 13. 22.
SEDUCERS, 2 *Tim.* 3. 13; 1 *Tim.* 4. 1.
SEE, *Ps.* 34. 8; *Matt.* 5. 8; *John* 16. 22; 1 *John* 3. 2; *Rev.* 1. 7, & 22. 4.
Matt. 6. 1. to be *s.* of men, 23. 5.
13. 17. desired to *s.* and not *s.*
John 1. 18. no man has *s.* God at
20. 29. hast *s.* and believed, not *s.*
2 *Cor.* 4. 18. look not at things *s.* things not *s.*
1 *Tim.* 6. 16. in light no man *s.*
Heb. 11. 1. evidence of things not *s.*
1 *Pet.* 1. 8. having not *s.* ye love
1 *John* 1. 1. that which ye have *s.*
4. 12. no man hath *s.* God at
Job 10. 4. *s.* thou as man *s.*
John 12. 45. he that *s.* me *s.* him that
14. 9. he that *s.* me hath *s.* Father
17. world *s.* him not, nor knows
SEED, *Gen.* 38. 9.
Ps. 126. 6. bearing precious *s.*
Eccl. 11. 6. in morning sow thy *s.*
Is. 55. 10. give *s.* to sower and
Matt. 13. 38. good *s.* are children of the kingdom
Luke 8. 11. *s.* is the word of God
1 *Pet.* 1. 23. born again not of corrup. *s.*
1 *John* 3. 9. for his *s.* remaineth in
Prov. 11. 21. *s.* of righteous shall be
Is. 1. 4. sinful nation, *s.* of evil-doers
14. 20. *s.* of evil-doers never
45. 25. *s.* of Israel be justified
53. 10. see his *s.* and be satisfied
Mal. 2. 15. shall seek a godly *s.*
Rom. 9. 8. children of promise counted for *s.*
29. Lord of sabbaoth hath left a *s.*
Gal. 3. 16. not to *s.* but to thy *s.*
SEEK, *Ezra* 8. 21; *Job* 5. 8; *Ps.* 10. 15.
Deut. 4. 29. if thou *s.* him with all thy heart, 1 *Chr.* 28. 9; 2 *Chr.* 15. 2; *Jer.* 29. 13.
2 *Chr.* 19. 3. prepared heart to *s.* God, 30. 19.
Ezra 8. 22. them for good that *s.*
Ps. 9. 10. not forsaken them that *s.*
Ps. 27. 4. one thing I desire, and will *s.*
63. 1. God, early will I *s.* thee
69. 32. hearts live that *s.* God
119. 176. *s.* thy servant
Prov. 8. 17. *s.* me early shall find
Songs 3. 2. *s.* whom soul loveth
Is. 36. 9. with spirit will I *s.* thee
45. 19. I said not *s.* me in vain
Jer. 29. 13. *s.* me and find me
Lam. 3. 25. Lord is good to soul that *s.*
Amos 5. 4. *s.* me and live, 5. 8.
Mal. 2. 7. *s.* law at his mouth
Matt. 6. 33. *s.* first kingdom of God
7. 7. *s.* and ye shall find
Luke 13. 24. will *s.* to enter in

19. 10. to *s.* and save which was lost, *Matt.* 18. 12.
John 4. 23. Father *s.* such to worship
8. 21. ye shall *s.* and not find
Rom. 2. 7. *s.* glory, honour, &c.
1 *Cor.* 10. 24. let no man *s.* own
13. 5. charity *s.* not her own
Phil. 2. 21. all *s.* their own, not
Col. 3. 1. *s.* things above
1 *Pet.* 3. 11. let him *s.* peace and
5. 8. *s.* whom he may devour
SEEM *Gen.* 27. 12; *Deut.* 25. 3.
1 *Cor.* 11. 16. if any *s.* contentious
Heb. 4. 1. *s.* to come short of it
Jam. 1. 26. if *s.* to be religious
Luke 8. 18. that he *s.* to have
1 *Cor.* 3. 18. *s.* wise in this world
Heb. 12. 11. no chastening *s.* to be joyous, but grievous
SELL me thy birth right, *Gen.* 25. 31.
Prov. 23. 23. buy truth and *s.* it not
Matt. 13. 44. he *s.* all and buyeth
19. 21. go *s.* all that thou hast
25. 9. go rather to them that *s.* and
SENATORS, *Ps.* 105. 22.
SEND thee help from the sanctuary, *Ps.* 20. 2.
Ps. 43. 3. *s.* out thy light and truth
57. 3. *s.* from heaven and save
Matt. 9. 38. *s.* forth labourers into
John 14. 26. Father will *s.* in my name, 16. 7.
2 *Thess.* 2. 11. *s.* them strong delusions
SENSE, *Neh.* 8. 8; *Heb.* 5. 14.
SENSUAL, *Jam.* 3. 15; *Jude* 19.
SENTENCE, signifies opinion, *Acts* 15. 19. A full persuasion, 2 *Cor.* 1. 9. *Deut.* 17. 9; *Dan.* 5. 12.
Prov. 16. 10. divine *s.* in lips of
Eccl. 8. 11. because *s.* is not executed speedily
2 *Cor.* 1. 9. had *s.* of death in
SEPARATE, *Gen.* 13. 9; *Ex.* 33. 16.
Gen. 49. 26. head of him *s.* from brethren, *Deut.* 33. 16.
Deut. 29. 21. Lord shall *s.* him to
Is. 59. 2. your iniquities have *s.*
Acts 13. 2. *s.* me Paul and Barnabas
19. 9. he departed and *s.* his disciples
Rom. 8. 35. who shall *s.* us from love of Christ, 39.
2 *Cor.* 6. 17. come out, be ye *s.*
Gal. 1. 15. who *s.* me from mother
Heb. 7. 26. holy, harmless, and *s.* from sinners
SERPENT, *Gen.* 3. 1, 13, & 49. 17.
Num. 21. 6. Lord sent fiery *s.* 8. 9.
Prov. 23. 32. biteth like a *s.* and
Eccl. 10. 11. *s.* will bite without
Matt. 7. 10. ask fish will he give *s.*
10. 16. be wise as *s.* harmless as
John 3. 14. as Moses lifted up *s.*
2 *Cor.* 11. 3. as *s.* beguiled Eve
Rev. 12. 9. old *s.* called devil
SERVANT, *Prov.* 29. 19. *s.* will not be corrected
Is. 24. 2. with *s.* so with master
42. 1. behold my *s.* 49. 3, & 42. 19
Matt. 20. 27. be chief let him be *s.*
25. 21. well done thou good and faithful *s.* 23.
John 8. 34. committeth sin is *s.* of

13. 16. *s.* not greater than L. 15. 20.
1 *Cor.* 7. 21. art called being a *s.*
9. 19. I made myself *s.* to all
Gal. 1. 10. if pleased men not *s.* of
Phil. 2. 7. took on him form of a *s.*
2 *Tim.* 2. 24. *s.* of Lord must not
Ezra 5. 11. *s.* of the God of heaven. *Dan.*
3. 26; *Acts* 16. 17; 1 *Pet.* 2. 16;
Rev. 7. 3.
Rom. 6. 16. yield *s.* to obey
17. ye were the *s.* of sin
Phil. 1. 1. *s.* of Jesus Christ
2 *Pet.* 2. 19. *s.* of corruption
SERVE the Lord with all thy heart,
Deut. 10. 12, 20, & 11. 13; *Josh.* 22.
5; 1 *Sam.* 12. 20.
Deut. 13. 4. shall *s.* him and cleave to
Josh. 24. 14. *s.* him in sincerity
15. choose this day whom you will *s.*
for I and my house will *s.* the Lord
1 *Sam.* 12. 24. *s.* him in truth with
1 *Chr.* 28. 9. *s.* him with a perfect heart
Job 21. 15. what Almighty that we *s.*
Is. 43. 24. made me to *s.* with
Matt. 6. 24. no man can *s.* two masters;
ye cannot *s.* God and mammon
Luke 1. 74. *s.* him in holiness
12. 37. come forth and *s.* them
John 12. 26. if any *s.* me him will my
Father honour
Acts 6. 2. leave word of God and *s.*
27. 23. whose I am and whom I *s.*
Rom. 1. 9. *s.* in gospel
6. 6. we should not *s.* sin
7. 6. *s.* in newness of life
Rom. 25. *s.* law of God
Col. 3. 24. ye *s.* the Lord Christ
Gal. 5. 13. by love *s.* one another
1 *Thess.* 1. 9. to *s.* living and true God,
Heb. 9. 14.
Heb. 12. 28. may *s.* God acceptably
Rev. 7. 15. *s.* him day and night
22. 3. his servants shall *s.* him
SERVICE, *Rom.* 12. 1. reasonable *s.*
SERVING. *Acts* 20. 19. *s.* Lord with
26. 7. twelve tribes instantly *s.* God
Rom. 12. 11. fervent in spirit *s.* Lord
Tit. 3. 3. foolish, disobedient, *s.* divers
SET, *Ps.* 2. 6, & 4. 3, & 12. 5, & 16. 8, &
54. 3, & 75. 7, & 113. 8; *Prov.* 1. 25;
Songs 8. 6; *Rom.* 3. 25; *Col.* 3. 2.
SETTLE, *Luke* 21. 14; 1 *Pet.* 5. 10.
Col. 1. 23. continued in faith *s.*
SEVERITY and goodness, *Rom.* 11. 22.
SHADE, *Lord* is thy, *Ps.* 121. 5.
SHADOW our days are a, 1 *Chr.* 29. 15;
Eccl. 8. 13, & 6. 12; *Job* 8. 9; *Ps.*
102. 11, & 109. 23, & 144. 4.
Ps. 17. 8. under *s.* of thy wings, 36. 7, &
57. 1, & 63. 7, & 91. 1.
Songs 2. 3. I sat under his *s.* with great
delight
17. until day break and *s.* flee, 4. 6.
Is. 4. 6. for a *s.* from, 25. 4, & 32. 2.
49. 2. in *s.* of his hand hath he
Jer. 6. 4. *s.* of evening stretched
Acts 5. 15. *s.* of Peter might over-
shadow them
Col. 2. 17. *s.* of things to come *Heb.* 10. 1.
Jam. 1. 17. no variableness or *s.* of a
SHAKE heaven and earth, *Hag.* 2. 6, 21.
Hag. 11. 7. will *s.* all nations and desire

Matt. 10. 14. *s.* of dust off your feet
11. 7. to see reed *s.* with the wind
Luke 6. 38. good measure *s.*
2 *Thess.* 2. 2. not soon *s.* in mind
Heb. 12. 26, 27. shook—shake—shaken
SHAKING, *Ps.* 44. 14; *Is.* 17. 6, & 24.
13, & 30. 32; *Ezek.* 37. 7, & 38. 19.
SHAME, 1 *Sam.* 20. 34; 2 *Sam.* 13. 13.
Ex. 32. 25. made naked to their *s.*
Ps. 119. 31. put me not to *s.* 69. 7.
Prov. 3. 35. *s.* shall be the promotion of
fools, 9. 7, & 10. 5, & 11. 2, & 13. 5,
18, & 14. 35, & 17. 2, & 19. 26, & 18.
13, & 25. 8.
Is. 50. 6. hide not face from *s.*
Dan. 12. 2. awake some to *s.* and
Hos. 4. 7. change glory into *s.*
Zeph. 3. 5. unjust knoweth no *s.*
Acts 5. 41. worthy to suffer *s.* for
Phil. 3. 19. glory is in their *s.*
Heb. 12. 2. endured the cross despising
the *s.*
Rev. 3. 18. *s.* of thy nakedness
1 *Tim.* 2. 9. *s.* facedness

SHAPE, *Luke* 3. 22. bodily *s.* like dove
John 5. 37. his voice, nor seen his *s.*
SHAPEN, *Ps.* 51. 5. *s.* in iniquity
SHARP instrument, *Is.* 41. 15, & 49. 2;
SHARPENETH, *Job* 16. 9; *Prov.* 27. 17.
SHARPER, *Mic.* 7. 4; *Heb.* 4. 12.
SHARPLY, *Judg.* 8. 1; *Tit.* 1. 13.
2 *Cor.* 13. 10. should use *s.*
SHED for many for remission, *Matt.* 26.
28.
Rom. 5. 5. love of God is *s.* abroad
Tit. 3. 6. Holy Ghost he *s.* on us
SHEEP, *Ps.* 49. 14, & 74. 1, & 78. 52.
Ps. 44. 22. as *s.* for the slaughter, *Rom.*
8. 36.
79. 13. *s.* of pasture, 95. 7, & 100. 3.
119. 176. astray like lost *s.*
Is. 53. 6. all we like *s.* are gone
Jer. 23. 1. woe be unto the pastors that
scatter the *s.*
50. 6. my people hath been lost *s.*
Zech. 13. 7. smite shepherd and *s.*
Matt. 7. 15. beware of false prophets in
s. clothing
Matt. 9. 36. as *s.* having no shepherd
10. 6. to lost *s.* of Israel, 15. 24.
15. 24. sent unto the lost *s.* of Israel
18. 12. an hundred *s.* and one be gone
25. 32. dividing *s.* from goats, *s.* on
right hand, 33.
John 10. 2.—27. shepherd of the *s.*
21. 16. feed my lambs, feed my *s.* 17.
1 *Pet.* 2. 25. as *s.* going astray
SHEEP-FOLD, *John* 10. 1. entereth not
s. by the door
SHELTER, *Job* 24. 8. they embrace the
rock for want of a *s.*
Ps. 61. 3. been *s.* for me and a tower
SHEPHERD, *Gen.* 46. 34, & 49. 24.
Num. 27. 17. as sheep that have no *s.*
1 *Kings* 22. 17; *Mark* 6. 34.
Ps. 23. 1. the Lord is my *s.*
80. 1. *S.* of Israel
Songs 1. 8. feed kids beside *s.* tents
Ezek. 34. 2. prophesy against *s.* woe be
to the *s.*
Zech. 13. 7. awake sword against my *s.*

John 10. 14. I am the good s. a good s.
giveth
16. one fold one s. Eccl. 12. 91.
Heb. 13. 20. that great S. of sheep
1 Pet. 2. 25. returned to S. of souls
5. 4. chief S. shall appear
SHEPHERDS, Luke 2. 8. in the same
country s. in field
Luke 2. 18. things told them by the s.
20. the s. returned glorifying and
SHEW, Ps. 39. 6; Luke 20. 47; Col. 2. 23.
Ps. 4. 6. who will s. us any good
16. 11. wilt s. me path of life
25. 14. Lord will s. them covenant
Ps. 511. 15. and my mouth shall s. forth
thy praise
91. 16. will s. him my salvation
92. 15. to s. that Lord is upright
John 5. 20. Father loves Son and s. him
1 Cor. 11. 26. do s. Lord's death till
Tit. 2. 7. s. thyself a pattern of
1 Pet. 2. 9. should s. forth praises
Rev. 22. 6. angel to s. to servant
SHIELD and exceeding great reward,
Gen. 15. 1.
Deut. 33. 29. saved by Lord s. of
Ps. 3. 3. Lord is a s. for me, 5. 12, & 28.
7, & 119. 114. & 144. 2.
18. 35. given me s. of salvation
84. 11. God is a sun and s. 91. 4.
115. 9. their help and s. 10. 11.
Prov. 30. 5. a s. to put trust in
Eph. 6. 16. take s. of faith
SHINE, Job 22. 28, & 36. 32, & 37. 15.
Num. 6. 25. Lord make face to s.
Job 10. 3. why s. on wicked
Ps. 31. 16. make face to s. on 67. 1, &
80. 3, 7, 19, & 119. 135.
67. 1. cause his face to s. upon us
80. 1. dwellest between cherubims, s.
forth
Eccl. 8. 1. wisdom makes face s.
Dan. 12. 3. wise s. as firmament
Matt. 5. 16. light so s. before men
13. 43. righteous s. forth as sun
17. 2. his face did s. as sun
2 Cor. 4. 6. God who commanded the
light to s.
Phil. 2. 15. among whom ye s. as
Rev. 21. 23. no need of sun nor moon
to s.
SHINED, Ps. 50. 2. out of Zion perfection of beauty God hath s.
Is. 9. 2. upon them hath the light s.
SHINETH, Prov. 4. 18. as shining light
that s. more
John 1. 5. the light s. in darkness, and
2 Pet. 1. 19. light that s. in dark place
1 John 2. 8. the true light now s.
Rev. 1. 16. countenance was as sun s.
SHINING, Prov. 4. 18. path of just is
as s. light
John 5. 35. burning and a s. light
Acts 26. 13. a light above the brightness
of sun s.
SHIPWRECK, 2 Cor. 11. 25. thrice I
suffered s.
1 Tim. 1. 19. some concerning faith
have made s.
SHORT. A small space of time. Job 20.
5; 1 Cor. 7. 29; 1 Thess. 2. 17.

Weakness, inability, Num. 11. 23;
Is. 50. 2; 69. 1.
Num. 11. 23. Lord's hand waxed s.
Ps. 89. 47. remember how s. my time is
Rom. 3. 23. come s. of glory of God
SHORTENED, Ps. 102. 23. he s. my
days, 89. 45.
SHORTENED, Prov. 10. 27. the years
of the wicked shall be s.
Is. 50. 2. is my hand s. 59. 1.
59. 1. Lord's hand is not s.
Matt. 24. 22. except days be s.
SHORTER, Is. 28. 20. the bed is s. than
that a man
SHORTLY, Rom. 16. 20. God of peace
bruise Satan under your feet s.
2 Pet. 1. 14. s. I must put off tabernacle
SHOULDER, Is. 9. 4. broken the staff
of his s.
6. government be upon his s.
22. 22. key of David lay on his s.
SHOUT. The voice of an enemy in
war, Jer. 50. 15; 51. 14. The voice
of lamentation; Lam. 3. 8. Of
impious flattery, Acts 12. 22. Of
joy, Ex. 32. 18. Num. 23. 21; Is.
12. 6, & 42. 11, & 44. 23; Zeph. 3.
14; Zech. 9. 9.
Ps. 47. 5. God is gone up with a s.
1 Thess. 4. 16. Lord descend with s.
SHUT, Is. 45. 1. gates shall not be s.
Is. 52. 15. kings shall s. their mouths
Dan. 6. 22. God hath s. lions' mouths
Rev. 21. 25. gates shall not be s. by day
SHUT up or left, Deut. 32. 36.
Ps. 77. 9. hath he s. up tender mercies
Matt. 23. 13. s. up kingdom of heaven
Acts 26. 10. many did I s. up in prison
Gal. 3. 23. s. up to the faith
SHUTTETH, 1 John 3. 17. s. up bowels
Rev. 3. 7. he openeth and no man s. Is.
22. 22.
SICK, 2 Kings 20. 1. was Hezekiah s.
unto death, 2 Chr. 32. 24; Is. 38. 1.
Prov. 13. 12. hope deferred maketh s.
Songs 5. 8. tell him I am s. of love
Is. 1. 5. whole head is s. and heart
33. 24. inhabitant not say, I am s.
38. 9. Hezekiah had been s. and
Matt. 4. 24. brought to him s. people
8. 16. healed all that were s. 14. 14.
9. 12. need no physician, but they
that are s. Mark 2. 17; Luke 5. 31.
25. 36. I was s. and ye visited me
John 11. 1. Lazarus of Bethany was s. 2.
Jam. 5. 14. is any s. call elders
15. prayer of faith shall save s.
SICKLY, 1 Cor. 11. 30. for this cause
many s.
SICKNESS, 2 Chr. 21. 19. bowels fell
out by reason of s.
Ps. 41. 3. make bed in s.
Ex. 23. 25. I will take away s.
Matt. 8. 17. himself bare our s.
SICKLE, Deut. 23. 25. not move s. unto
SIDE, John 19. 34. with spear pierced s.
John 20. 20. he showed his hands and s.
25. except I thrust hand into s.
Rev. 22. 2. on either s. of river was
SIDE, every, 2 Cor. 4. 8. are troubled on
every s. 7. 5.

SIFT, *Is.* 30. 28; *Amos* 9. 9; *Luke* 22. 31.
SIGHT, *Acts* 1. 9. received him out of *s.*
2 *Cor.* 5. 7. we walk by faith, not *s.*
SIGHT of GOD, *Acts* 8. 21. heart not right in *s. of God*
1 *Tim.* 2. 3. acceptable in *s. of God*
6. 13. I give thee charge in *s. of God*
1 *Pet.* 3. 4. in *s. of God* of great price
SILENCE, *Ps.* 31. 18, & 32. 3,{& 35. 22, & 50. 3, 21, & 83. 1, & 94. 17; *Jer.* 8. 14; *Amos* 5. 13, & 8. 3; 1 *Cor.* 14. 34; 1 *Tim.* 2. 11, 12; 1 *Pet.* 2. 15; *Rev.* 8. 1.
SILENT, in darkness, 1 *Sam.* 2. 9.
Ps. 28. 1. be not *s.* to me, 30. 12.
Zech. 2. 13. be *s.* all flesh before
SILLY, *Job* 5. 2; 2 *Tim.* 3. 6.
SIMPLE, *Prov.* 1. 4, 22, 32, & 7. 7, & 8. 5, & 9. 4, 13, & 19. 25, & 21. 11.
Ps. 19. 7. testimony of the Lord maketh wise the *s.*
116. 16. Lord preserveth the *s.*
119. 139. giveth understanding to *s.*
Prov. 14. 15. *s.* believeth every word, 22. 3. *s.* pass on and are, 27. 12.
Rom. 16. 19. *s.* concerning evil, 18.
SIN lieth at door, *Gen.* 4. 7.
Ps. 4. 4. stand in awe and *s.* not
32. 1. blessed whose *s.* covered
5. I acknowledge my *s.* to thee
38. 18. I will be sorry for my *s.*
51. 3. my *s.* is ever before me
5. in *s.* did my mother conceive
119. 11. I might not *s.* against thee
Prov. 14. 34. *s.* is a reproach to
Is. 30. 1. that they may add *s.* to *s.*
53. 10. an offering for *s.*
12. he bare the *s.* of many
John 1. 29. taketh away *s.* of
5. 14. *s.* no more, lest worse
Rom. 5. 12. by one man *s.* entered
6. 14. *s.* not have dominion
7. 9. *s.* revived and I died, 8. 11.
13. *s.* it might appear *s.*
14. sold under *s.*
17. *s.* that dwelleth in me
25. law of *s.* and death, 8. 2.
1 *Cor.* 15. 34. awake and *s.* not
2 *Cor.* 5. 21. made him *s.* for us who knew no *s.*
Eph. 4. 26. be angry and *s.* not
Jam. 1. 15. *s.* and *s.* when it is finished bringeth forth
1 *Pet.* 2. 22. who did no *s.*
1 *John* 1. 8. any say we have no *s.*
2. 1. if any man *s.* we have an advocate
3. 9. he cannot *s.* because seed
5. 16. there is a *s.* unto death
SINS, *Ps.* 19. 13. from presumptuous *s.*
Ezek. 33. 16. none of his *s.* shall
Dan. 9. 24. to make an end of *s.*
1 *Tim.* 5. 22. be not partakers of other men's *s.*
2 *Tim.* 3. 6. silly women laden with *s.*
1 *John* 2. 2. propitiation for *s.* of the
Ps. 65. 5. my *s.* 51. 9; *Is.* 38. 17.
79. 9. our *s.* 90. 8, & 103. 10; *Is.* 59. 12; *Dan.* 9. 16; *Gal.* 1. 4; 1 *Cor.* 15. 3; *Heb.* 1. 3; 1 *Pet.* 2. 24; *Rev.* 1. 5.
Matt. 1. 21. their *s.* *Rom.* 11. 27; *Heb.* 8. 12, & 10. 17; *Num.* 16. 26.

Is. 59. 2. your *s.* *Jer.* 5. 25; *John* 8. 21; 1 *Cor.* 15. 17; *Josh.* 24. 19.
SINNED, *Ex.* 32. 33. who hath *s.* I will
Job 1. 22. in all this Job *s.* not
Lam. 1. 8. Jerusalem grievously *s.*
5. 7. our fathers *s.* and are not
Rom. 2. 12. many *s.* without law
3. 23. all have *s.* and come short of
1 *John* 1. 10. say we have not *s.*
Ex. 9. 27. I have *s.* *Num.* 22. 34; *Josh.* 7. 20; 1 *Sam.* 15. 24, 30; 2 *Sam.* 12. 13, & 24. 10; *Job* 7. 20, & 33. 27; *Ps.* 41. 4, & 51. 4; *Mic.* 7. 9; *Matt.* 27. 4; *Luke* 15. 18, 21.
Judg. 10. 10. we have *s.* 1 *Sam.* 7. 6; *Ps.* 106. 6; *Is.* 42. 24, & 64. 5; *Jer.* 3. 25, & 8. 14, & 14. 7, 20; *Lam.* 5. 16; *Dan.* 9. 5, 8, 11, 15.
Prov. 8. 36. *s.* against me wrongs
Eccl. 7. 20. there is no man that doeth good and *s.* not
Ezek. 18. 4. soul that *s.* shall die
1 *John* 5. 18. is born of God *s.* not
SINNER, *Eccl.* 7. 26. *s.* shall be taken
9. 18. one *s.* destroyeth much
Is. 65. 20. *s.* 100 years old accursed
Luke 15. 7. joy in heaven over one *s.* that repenteth
18. 13. God be merciful to me a *s.*
Jam. 5. 20. convorteth a *s.* from
1 *Pet.* 4. 18. where shall *s.* appear
SINNERS, *Gen.* 13. 13. *s.* before the L.
Ps. 1. 1. nor stands in way of *s.*
25. 8. Lord will teach *s.* in way
51. 13. *s.* be converted to thee
Is. 33. 14. *s.* in Zion are afraid
Matt. 9. 13. come to call *s.* to repent
Luke 13. 2. *s.* above Galileans, 4.
John 9. 31. God heareth not *s.*
Rom. 5. 8. while we were yet *s.*
15. by one man's disobedience many are made *s.*
1 *Tim.* 1. 15. Christ came to save *s.*
Heb. 7. 26. holy, separate from *s.*
12. 3. endureth such contradiction of *s.*
Jam. 4. 8. cleanse hands ye *s.*
Jude 15. ungodly *s.* have spoken
SINFUL, *Num.* 32. 14; *Is.* 1. 4; *Luke* 5. 8; *Rom.* 7. 13, & 8. 3.
SINCERE, *Phil.* 1. 1C, 16; 1 *Pet.* 2. 2.
Josh. 24. 14. serve him in *s.*
1 *Cor.* 5. 8. unleavened bread of *s.*
2 *Cor.* 1. 12. in godly *s.* we had our conversation
2. 17. as of *s.* in sight of God
8. 8. to prove *s.* of your love
Eph. 6. 24. grace be with all who love our Lord Jesus Christ in *s.*
Tit. 2. 7. showing gravity, *s.*
SING to the Lord, *Ex.* 15. 21; 1 *Chr.* 16. 23; *Ps.* 30. 4, & 68. 32, & 81. 1, & 95. 1, & 96. 1, 2, & 98. 1, & 147. 7, & 149. 1; *Is.* 12. 5, & 52. 9; *Eph.* 5. 19.
Ex. 15. 1. I will *s.* *Judg.* 5. 3; *Ps.* 13. 6, & 57. 7, 9, & 59. 16, 17, & 101. 1, & 104. 33, & 144. 9; *Is.* 5. 1; 1 *Cor.* 14. 15
Job 29. 13. *s.* for joy, *Is.* 65. 14.
Ps. 9. 11. *s.* praises, 18. 49, & 27. 6, & 30. 12, &47. 6, & 68. 4, & 75. 9, & 108. 1, 3, & 135. 3, & 147. 1, & 149. 3, & 146. 2, & 92. 1.

145. 7. *s.* of thy righteousness
Prov. 29. 6. the righteous shall *s.* and
Is. 35. 6. shall tongue of dumb *s.*
1 *Cor.* 14. 15. I will *s.* with spirit
Jam. 5. 13. merry, let him *s.*

SINGLE eye, *Matt.* 6. 22; *Luke* 11. 34.
Acts 2. 46. *s.* of heart, *Eph.* 6. 5; *Col.*
   3. 22.

SINK, *Ps.* 69. 2, 14; *Luke* 9. 44.

SIT, *Ps.* 110. 1. *s.* thou at my right hand
Lam. 1. 1. how doth city *s.* solitary
Matt. 8. 11. shall *s.* down with Abraham
   19. 28. Son of man shall *s.* on throne
      of his glory, ye shall *s.* on 12
      thrones, *Luke* 22. 30.
   20. 21. sons may *s.* on thy right hand
   22. 44. *s.* on my right hand till I make
      thy enemies, *Mark* 12. 36; *Luke*
      20. 42; *Heb.* 1. 13.
   26. 36. *s.* ye here while I pray
Luke 13. 29. *s.* down in kingdom of G.
Eph. 2. 6. made us *s.* in heavenly
Rev. 3. 21. grant to *s.* with me in
   18. 7. saith in heart, I *s.* a queen

SITUATION pleasant, 2 *Kings* 2. 19;
   Ps. 48. 2.

SKIN for skin, *Job* 2. 4, & 10. 11, & 19.
   26; *Jer.* 13. 23; *Heb.* 11. 37.

SKIP, *Ps.* 29. 6, & 114. 4; *Songs* 2. 8.

SLACK, to delay, 2 *Kings* 4. 24; to be
   indolent, *Prov.* 10. 4; *Zeph.* 3. 16.
   See *Deut.* 7. 10; *Hab.* 1. 4; 2,
   3. 9.

SLAY, *Job* 13. 15; *Ps.* 139. 19; *Lev.* 19. 17.
Eph. 2. 16. having *s.* enmity
Rev. 5. 9. wast *s.* hast redeemed
   6. 9. souls of *s.* for word of God
   13. 8. Lamb *s.* from foundation of the
      world

SLEEP deep, *Gen.* 2. 21, & 15. 12;
   1 *Sam.* 26. 12; *Job* 4. 13; *Ps.* 76. 6;
   Prov. 19. 15; *Is.* 29. 10.
Ps. 90. 5. they are as a *s.* in the morning
   127. 2. he giveth his beloved *s.*
   132. 4. not give *s.* to mine eyes
Prov. 3. 24. thy *s.* shall be sweet
   6. 4. give not *s.* to thine eyes nor
   10. yet a little *s.* a little slumber,
      24. 33.
   20. 13. love not *s.* lest come to
Eccl. 5. 12. *s.* of labouring man is sweet
Jer. 31. 26. my *s.* was sweet to
   51. 39. *s.* a perpetual *s.* 57.
Luke 9. 32. were heavy with *s.*
Rom. 13. 11. high time to awake out of *s.*
Esth. 6. 1. that night king not *s.*
Ps. 3. 5. laid me down and *s.* 4. 8.
   76. 5. they have *s.* their *s.*
Eccl. 5. 12. abundance of the rich not
   suffer to *s.*
Songs 5. 2. I *s.* my heart waketh
1 *Cor.* 11. 30. for this cause many *s.*
   15. 20. become the first-fruits of them
      that *s.*
   51. we shall not all *s.* but
Eph. 5. 14. awake thou that *s.*
1 *Thess.* 4. 14. *s.* in Jesus will God bring
   5. 6. let us not *s.* as others
   7. they that *s. s.* in the night
   10. whether we *s.* or wake we should
      live with him

SLEIGHT of men. A mode of tricking

and deceiving, *Eph.* 4. 14.

SLIDE, *Deut.* 32. 25; *Ps.* 26. 1, & 37.
   31; *Jer.* 8. 5; *Hos.* 4. 16.

SLIGHTLY, *Jer.* 6. 14, & 8. 11.

SLIP, *Ps.* 17. 5, & 18. 36, & 38. 16, & 94.
   18; *Heb.* 2. 1.

SLIPPERY, *Ps.* 35. 6, & 73. 18; *Jer.* 23.
   12.

SLOTHFUL be under tribute, *Prov.* 12.
   24.
Prov. 12. 27. *s.* roasteth not that took
   in hunting
Prov. 15. 19. way of *s.* is an hedge
   18. 9. *s.* is brother to great waster
   19. 15. *s.* casteth into deep sleep
   24. *s.* man hideth hand in his bosom,
      26. 15.
   21. 25. desire of *s.* killeth him
   22. 13. *s.* saith there is a lion, 26. 13.
   24. 30. I went by field of the *s.*
   26. 14. as door on hinges, so is *s.* upon
Rom. 12. 11. not *s.* in business

Heb. 6. 12. be not *s.* but followers

SLOW to anger, *Neh.* 9. 17.
Luke 24. 25. fools to believe
Jam. 1. 19. *s.* to speak, *s.* to wrath

SLUGGARD go to ant, *Prov.* 6. 6.
Prov. 6. 9. how long sleep, O *s.* when
   13. 4. soul of *s.* desireth and hath
   20. 4. *s.* will not plough by reason of
   26. 16. *s.* wiser in own conceit

SLUMBER, *Ps.* 132. 4; *Rom.* 11. 8.
Ps. 121. 3. that keepeth will not *s.*
Matt. 25. 5. they all *s.* and slept
2 *Pet.* 2. 3. their damnation *s.* not

SMITE thee shall L. *Deut.* 28. 22.
Ps. 141. 5. let righteous *s.* me
Jer. 18. 18. *s.* him with tongue
Matt. 5. 39. *s.* thee on right cheek
Is. 53. 4. esteem him *s.* of God
Hos. 6. 1. he hath *s.* and he will bind us

SMOKE, *Gen.* 19. 28; *Ex.* 19. 18.
Deut. 29. 20. anger of the Lord shall *s.*
Ps. 74. 1. why doth thine anger *s.*
   102. 3. as *s. Prov.* 10. 26; *Is.* 65. 5.
Is. 42. 3. *s.* flax, *Matt.* 12. 20.

SMOOTH, *Gen.* 27. 11, 16; *Is.* 30. 10.
SMOOTHER, *Ps.* 55. 21; *Prov.* 5. 3.
SNARE, *Ex.* 23. 33; *Judg.* 2. 3.
Ps. 11. 6. on wicked he will rain *s.*
   18. 5. *s.* of death prevented me
   69. 22. let their table become a *s.*
   91. 3. deliver from *s.* of fowler
   119. 110. wicked laid a *s.* for me
   124. 7. *s.* is broken, we escape
Prov. 13. 14. to depart from the *s.* of
   29. 25. fear of man bringeth a *s.*
1 *Tim.* 6. 9. will be rich fall into *s.*
2 *Tim.* 2. 26. recover themselves out of
   the *s.* of devil

SNARED, *Ps.* 9. 16; *Prov.* 6. 2, & 12. 13.
   Eccl. 9. 12; *Is.* 8. 15, & 28. 13, & 42. 22.

SNOW as *Job* 9. 30; *Ps.* 51. 7, & 68. 14;
   Is. 1. 18; *Dan.* 7. 9; *Matt.* 28. 3;
   Rev. 1. 14.

SNUFFED, *Mal.* 1. 13; *Jer.* 2. 24.

SOBER for your sake, 2 *Cor.* 5. 13.
1 *Thess.* 5. 6. watch and be *s.* 8.
1 *Tim.* 3. 2. a bishop must be vigilant, *s.*
   11. wives not slanderers *s.* in all
Tit. 1. 8. *s.* just, holy, temperate
   2. 2. aged man be *s.* grave

4. teach young women to be *s.*
1 *Pet.* 1. 13. gird up loins, be *s.*
    4. 7. be *s.* and watch unto prayer
    5. 8. be *s.* be vigilant
SOBERLY, *Rom.* 12. 3. not think highly but *s.*
Tit. 2. 12. teaching us to live *s.*
Acts 26. 25. speak words of *s.*
SOBRIETY, 1 *Tim.* 2. 9, 15.
SOFT my heart God maketh, *Job* 23. 16.
Prov. 15. 1. *s.* answer turneth wrath
Prov. 25. 15. *s.* tongue breaketh the
Matt. 11. 8. clothed in *s.* raiment
SOJOURN, *Gen.* 12. 10; *Ps.* 120. 5.
Lev. 25. 23. *s.* with me, 1 *Chr.* 29. 15;
    Ps. 39. 12.
SOJOURNED, *Heb.* 11. 9. by faith *s.* in land of
SOJOURNERS, *Ps.* 39. 12. stranger, a *s.* as all
SOJOURNING, *Ex.* 12. 40; 1 *Pet.* 1. 17.
SOLD thyself to work ill, 1 *Kings* 21. 20.
2 *Kings* 17. 17. *s.* themselves to do evil in the sight of the Lord
Rom. 7. 14. carnal *s.* under sin
SOLDIER, 2 *Tim.* 2. 3. hardness as good *s.* of Christ
2 *Tim.* 2. 4. who hath chosen him to be a *s.*
SON, 2 *Sam.* 18. 33, & 19. 4.
Ps. 2. 12. kiss ye *S.* lest be angry
    116. 16. I am *s.* of handmaid
Prov. 10. 1. wise *s.* makes a glad father
    15. 20.
Mal. 3. 17. as man spareth own *s.*
Matt. 11. 27. no man knows *S.* but F.
    17. 5. this is my beloved *S.* 3. 17.
Luke 10. 6. if *s.* of peace be there
John 1. 18. only begotten *S.* 3. 16; 3. 18.
    5. 21. *S.* quickens whom he will
    23. honour *S.* as honour Father, 26.
    8. 35. the *S.* abideth for ever
    36. *S.* shall make you free
    17. 12. lost none but the *s.* of perdition
Rom. 8. 3. sent his own *S.* 32.
Gal. 4. 7. if *s.* then an heir of God
2 *Thess.* 2. 3. man of sin *s.* of
Heb. 5. 8. though *s.* learned obedience
1 *John* 2. 22. denieth *S.* denieth Father
    5. 11. life is in his *S.*
    12. he that hath *S.* hath life
Matt. 21. 37. his *s. Acts* 3. 13; *Rom.* 1.
    8, 9, & 5. 10, & 8. 29, 32; 1 *Cor.* 1. 9;
    Gal. 1. 16, & 4. 4, 6; 1 *Thess.* 1. 10;
    Heb. 1. 2; 1 *John* 1. 7, & 3. 23, & 4.
    9, 10, 14, & 5. 9, 10, 11, 20.
Luke 15. 19. thy *s. John* 17. 1. 19, 26.
Dan. 3. 25. the *S.* of God, *Matt.* 4. 3, &
    16. 16, and 41 other places
Num. 23. 19. *s.* of man, *Job* 25. 6; *Ps.*
    8. 4, & 80. 17, & 144. 3; *Dan.* 7. 13.
Ps. 144. 12. our *s.* be as plants
Songs 2. 3. my beloved among *s.*
Is. 60. 10. *s.* of strangers 61. 5, & 62. 8.
Mal. 3. 3. purify *s.* of Levi
    6. *s.* of Jacob not consumed
Mark 3. 17. Boanerges *s,* of thunder
1 *Cor.* 4. 14. my beloved *s.* I warn
Gal. 4. 6. because *S.* of God sent forth Spirit of his *S.*
Heb. 2. 10. bring many *s.* to glory
    12. 7. God deals with you as *s.*

Heb. 12. 8. bastards and not *s.*
Gen. 6. 2. *s.* of God, *Job* 1. 6, & 2. 1, &
    38. 7; *Hos.* 1. 10; *John* 1. 12; *Rom.*
    8. 14, 19; *Phil.* 2. 15; 1 *John* 3. 1, 2
SONG unto the Lord, *Ex.* 15. 1.
Ex. 15. 2. God is my *s. Ps.* 118. 14.
Job 30. 9. I am their *s. Ps.* 69. 12.
    35. 10. giveth *s.* in night, *Ps.* 42. 8, &
    77. 6; *Is.* 30. 29.
Ps. 32. 7. with *s.* of deliverance
    33. 3. sing a new *s.* 40. 3, & 96. 1, &
    144. 9, & 149. 1; *Is.* 42. 10; *Rev.* 5. 9.
    119. 54. been *s.* in house of
    137. 3. required a *s.* one of the *s.* of Zion
Ezek. 33. 32. as a very lovely *s.*
Eph. 5. 19. speak in spiritual *s.*
Rev. 14. 3. no man could learn *s.*
    15. 3. sing *s.* of Moses and of the Lamb
SOON as they be born, *Ps.* 58. 3.
Ps. 106. 13. they *s.* forgot his mighty
Prov. 14. 17. *s.* angry: not *s.* angry, *Tit.*
    1. 7.
Gal. 1. 6. *s.* removed to another
2 *Thess.* 2. 2. be not *s.* shaken in
SORES, *Is.* 1. 6. bruises and putrifying *s.*
SORROW, labour and, *Ps.* 90. 10.
Prov. 15. 13. by *s.* of heart the spirit is
Eccl. 1. 18. knowledge increaseth *s.*
    7. 3. *s.* better than laughter
Is. 35. 10. *s.* and sighing flee away 51. 11
Lam. 1. 12. is any *s.* like to my *s.*
John 16. 6. *s.* filled your hearts
    20. your *s.* be turned into joy
2 *Cor.* 2. 7. with overmuch *s.*
    7. 10. godly *s.* worketh repentance to salvation, *s.* of world death, 9.
Phil. 2. 27. should have *s.* upon *s.*
1 *Thess.* 4. 13. *s.* not as others who have
Rev. 21. 4. no death neither *s.*
Ps. 18. 3. *s.* of hell compassed
Is. 53. 3. a man of *s.*
    4. he hath carried our *s.*
1 *Tim.* 6. 10. pierced through with *s.*
SORROWED, 2 *Cor.* 7. 9; *Jer.* 31. 12.
Prov. 14. 13. in laughter heart is *s.*
Jer. 31. 25. replenished *s.* soul *Ps.* 69. 29.
Matt. 19. 22. man went away *s.*
    26. 22. my soul is exceeding *s.* even unto death, 37. 38.
2 *Cor.* 6. 10. *s.* yet alway rejoicing
SORROWING, *Luke* 2. 48; *Acts* 20. 38.
SORRY, *Ps.* 38. 18; 2 *Cor.* 2. 2. & 7. 8.
SORT godly, 2 *Cor.* 7. 11; 3 *John* 6.
SOUGHT the L., *Ex.* 33. 7; 2 *Chr.* 14. 7.
Ps. 34. 4. I *s.* the Lord and he heard me
    111. 2. *s.* out of all that take pleasure
    119. 10. with whole heart I *s.*
Eccl. 7. 29. *s.* out many inventions
Is. 65. 1. I am *s.* found of them that *s.*
    62. 12. be called *s.* out city not
Rom. 9. 32. *s.* it not by faith
Heb. 12. 17. he *s.* it carefully
1 *Chr.* 15. 3. *s.* him, 2 *Chr.* 14. 7, & 15.
    4; *Ps.* 78. 34; *Songs* 3. 1, 2.
2 *Chr.* 16. 12. *s.* not the Lord, *Zeph.* 1. 6.
SOUL abhor my judgments, *Lev.* 26. 15.
Gen. 2. 7. man became a living *s.*
Deut. 11. 13. serve him with all your *s.*
    13. 3. love the Lord with all *s. Josh.*
    22. 5; 1 *Kings* 2. 4; *Mark* 12. 33.
1 *Sam.* 18. 1. *s.* of Jonathan knit to *s.* of
1 *Chr.* 22. 19. set your *s.* to seek

Job 16. 4. if your *s.* in my *s.* stead
Ps. 19. 7. law of the Lord is perfect, converting the *s.*
    34. 22. Lord redeems *s.* of his
    49. 8. redemption of *s.* precious
    107. 9. he filleth the hungry *s.* with
Prov. 10. 3. not suffer *s.* of the righteous to famish
    19. 2. *s.* be without knowledge
    27. 7. full *s.* loatheth honeycomb
Is. 55. 2. let *s.* delight in fatness
    3. hear, and your *s.* shall live
    58. 10. I will satisfy afflicted *s.*
Matt. 10. 28. are not able to kill *s.*
Rom. 13. 1. every *s.* be subject
1 *Thess.* 5. 23. spirit *s.* and body be
Heb. 4. 12. to the dividing of *s.*
    10. 39. believe to saving of *s.*
Ex. 30. 12. ransom for his *s.*
2 *Kings* 23. 25. turned to the Lord with all his *s.*
Job 27. 8. when God taketh away *s.*
Hab. 2. 4. *s.* lifted up *s.* not right
Matt. 16. 26. lose his *s.* what give in exchange for his *s.*
Ps. 16. 10. not leave my *s.* in hell
    31. 7. thou hast known my *s.* in
    35. 3. say to my *s.* I am thy salvation
    9. my *s.* joyful in the Lord rejoice
    42. 5. why art thou cast down, O my *s.* 11, & 43. 5.
    62. 1. my *s.* waiteth upon God, 5.
    63. 1. my *s.* thirsteth for thee
    5. my *s.* shall be satisfied as
    8. my *s.* followeth hard after thee
Is. 26. 9. with my *s.* have I desired thee
    61. 10. my *s.* shall be joyful
Luke 1. 46. my *s.* doth magnify
John 12. 27. now is my *s.* troubled
Ps. 33. 20. our *s.* 44. 25, & 66. 9, & 123. 4, & 124. 4; *Is.* 26. 8.
Deut. 13. 5. own *s.* 1 *Sam.* 18. 1 & 20. 17; *Ps.* 22. 29; *Prov.* 8. 36, & 11. 17, & 15. 32, & 19. 8, 16, & 6. 32, & 20. 2, & 29. 24; *Mark* 8. 36.
    4. 9. with all thy *s.* 6. 5, & 10. 12, & 30. 6; *Matt.* 22. 37.
Ezek. 3. 19. delivered thy *s.* 21, & 33. 9.
Luke 12. 20. thy *s.* be required
3 *John* 2. as thy *s.* prospereth
Ps. 72. 13. save *s.* of needy, 97. 10.
Prov. 11. 30. winneth *s.* is wise
Is. 57. 16. spirit fail and *s.* which I have
Ezek. 14. 14. but deliver own *s.*
    18. 4. all *s.* are mine, *s.* of the father and *s.* of the son
Luke 21. 19. your *s.* *Josh.* 23. 14; *Jer.* 6. 16, & 26. 19; *Matt.* 11. 29; *Heb.* 13. 17; 1 *Pet.* 1. 9, 22, & 2. 25.
1 *Pet.* 3. 20. wherein few, i.e., *s.* were
    4. 19. commit keeping of our *s.*
2 *Pet.* 2. 14. beguiling unstable *s.*
Rev. 6. 9. *s.* of them slain that were beheaded, 20. 4.

SOUND dreadful, *Job* 15. 21.
Ps. 47. 5. God gone up with *s.* of
    89. 15. people know joyful *s.*
    119. 80. my heart be *s.* in thy statutes
Prov. 2. 7. *s.* wisdom, 3. 21, & 8. 14.
Eccl. 12. 4. *s.* of grinding is low
    6. 5. woe to chant to *s.* of viol
Rom. 10. 18. their *s.* went into all

1 *Tim.* 1. 10. contrary to *s.* doctrine, 2
    Tim. 4. 3.
2 *Tim.* 1. 7. of a *s.* mind
    13. the form of *s.* words
Tit. 1. 9. by *s.* doctrine, and *s.* in faith
    2. 8. *s.* speech cannot be condemned
SOW washed to wallowing, 2 *Pet.* 2. 22.
SOW wickedness, reap same, *Job* 4. 8.
Ps. 126. 5. *s.* in tears, reap in joy
Eccl. 11. 4. observeth wind shall not *s.*
Is. 32. 20. blessed that *s.* beside all
Jer. 4. 3. fallow ground *s.* not among
    31. 27. I will *s.* with seed of man
Hos. 10. 12. *s.* in righteousness
Mic. 6. 15. shall *s.* and not reap
Matt. 13. 3. sower went out to *s.*
Luke 12. 24. ravens neither *s.* nor
    19. 22. reaping what I did not *s.*
Ps. 97. 11. light is *s.* for righteous
Hos. 8. 7. *s.* wind and reap whirlwind
1 *Cor.* 9. 11. have *s.* to you spiritual
    15. 42. *s.* in corruption, in weakness
2 *Cor.* 9. 10. multiply your seed *s.*
Jam. 3. 18. fruit of righteousness *s.* in
Prov. 11. 18. *s.* righteousness be sure
    22. 8. *s.* iniquity reap vanity
John 4. 37. one *s.* another reapeth
2 *Cor.* 9. 6. *s.* sparingly, *s.* bountifully
Gal. 6. 7. what a man *s.* that he will
    8. *s.* to flesh, reap corruption
Is. 55. 10. seed to *s.* 2 *Cor.* 9. 10.

SPARE all the place, *Gen.* 18. 26.
Neh. 13. 22. *s.* according to thy mercy
Ps. 39. 13. *s.* me that I may recover
Prov. 13. 24. he that *s.* his rod hateth
    19. 18. let not thy soul *s.* for his
Joel 2. 17. *s.* thy people give not
Mal. 3. 17. I will *s.* them as man *s.* his
Rom. 8. 32. *s.* not his own son
    11. 21. if God *s.* not natural branches
2 *Pet.* 2. 4. God *s.* not angels that
SPARKS, *Job* 5. 7; *Is.* 50. 11.
SPARROW, *Ps.* 102. 7; *Matt.* 10. 29.
SPEAK against Moses, *Num.* 12. 8.
Gen. 18. 27. taken on me to *s.* to the L.
Ex. 4. 14. Aaron thy brother can *s.*
    34. 35. went in to *s.* to the Lord
1 *Sam.* 3. 9. *s.* Lord thy servant heareth
Ps. 85. 8. I will hear what the Lord *s.*
Is. 8. 20. if *s.* not according to
    50. 4. knoweth how to *s.* word
Jer. 18. 7. at what instant I *s.* 9.
Hab. 2. 3. at end it shall *s.* and not lie
Matt. 10. 19. how or that ye *s.*
    12. 32. who *s.* against Son of
    34. how *s.* good, out of abundance of
Luke 6. 26. when all *s.* well of
John 3. 11. we *s.* that we know
Acts 4. 20. cannot but *s.* things
1 *Cor.* 1. 10. all *s.* the same thing
    2. 6. we *s.* wisdom among them that
Tit. 3. 2. to *s.* evil of man
Heb. 11. 4. he being dead yet *s.*
    12. 24. *s.* better things than
    25. refuse not him that *s.* from
1 *Pet.* 2. 12. *s.* against you as evil
Jam. 1. 19. swift to hear, slow to *s.*
2 *Pet.* 2. 10. *s.* evil of dignities, *Jude* 8.
Jude 10. *s.* evil of things they not
Is. 45. 19. *Is.* 63. 1; *John* 4. 26, & 7. 17, 8, 26, 28, 38, & 12. 60; *Rom.* 3. 5, & 6. 19; 1 *Tim.* 2. 7.

65. 24. while they are *s.* I will hear
Dan. 9. 26. while I was *s.* and
Matt. 6. 7. be heard for much *s.*
Eph. 4. 15. *s.* the truth in love
    31. evil *s.* be put away from you
1 *Tim.* 4. 2. *s.* lies in hypocrisy *Ps.* 58. 3.
SPECTACLE to angels, 1 *Cor.* 4. 9.
SPEECH, *Gen.* 11. 1. earth of one *s.*
Deut. 32. 2. my *s.* shall distil as
Matt. 26. 73. thy *s.* betrayeth thee
1 *Cor.* 2. 1. came not with excellency of *s.*
2 *Cor.* 3. 12. great plainness of *s.*
    10. 10. bodily presence weak, *s.* con.
Col. 4. 6. *s.* be always with grace
Tit. 2. 8. sound *s.* cannot be condemned
Jude 15. of all their hard *s.*
Rom. 16. 18. by fair *s.* deceive
SPEECHLESS, *Matt.* 22. 12. he was *s.*
Luke 1. 22. Zacharias remained *s.*
Acts 9. 7. men with him stood *s.*
SPEED, *Gen.* 24. 12; 2 *John* 10. 11.
SPEEDILY, *Ezra* 7. 21, 26; *Ps.* 31. 2;
    79. 8; *Eccl.* 8. 11; *Luke* 18. 8.
SPEND days in wealth, *Job* 21. 13.
Ps. 90. 9. *s.* days as a tale that is
Is. 49. 4. have *s.* my strength for
    55. 2. why *s.* money for that which is
Rom. 13. 12. night is far *s.* day is
2 *Cor.* 12. 15. I would *s.* and be *s.*
SPICES, *Songs* 4. 10, 14, 16, & 8. 14.
SPIDER, *Prov.* 30. 28; *Job* 8. 14; *Is.* 59.
    5.
SPIKENARD, *Songs* 1. 12, & 4. 13, 14.
SPIRIT made willing, *Ex.* 35. 21.
Num. 11. 17. take of *s.* on thee, 2 *Kings*
    2. 9.
    14. 24. Caleb had another *s.*
Ezra 1. 5. chose *s.* God raised to go
Neh. 9. 20. good *s.* to instruct
Job 26. 13. by his *s.* he garnished heaven
    32. 8. there is a *s.* in man
    18. the *s.* within me
Ps. 31. 2. into thine hand I commit my *s.*
    32. 2. in whose *s.* there is no guile
    51. 10. renew right *s.* within me
    11. take not away holy *s.*
    12. uphold me with thy free *s.*
    17. a broken and contrite *s.* 34. 18;
    Prov. 15. 13, & 17. 22.
    76. 12. cut off *s.*. of princes
    78. 8. whose *s.* is not steadfast
    104. 30. sendest forth thy *S. Job* 34. 14.
    139. 7. should I go from thy *S.*
    142. 3. my *s.* overwhelmed, 143. 4.
    143. 7. my *s.* faileth
    10. thy *s.* is good
Prov. 14. 29. hasty of *s.* exalteth
Prov. 16. 18. haughty *s.* before a fall
    32. better that ruleth his own *s.*
    18. 14. wounded *s.* who can
    20. 27. *s.* of man is candle of the Lord
Eccl. 3. 21. who knoweth *s.* of a man
    8. 8. power over *s.* to retain it
    11. 5. thou knowest not way of *s.*
    12. 7. *s.* shall return to God
Is. 32. 15. till *s.* be poured from
    34. 16. his *s.* gathered them
    57. 16. *s.* shall fail before me
    61. 3. garment of praise for *s.* of heav.
Mic. 2. 11. walk in *s.* and falsehood
Zech. 12. 1. formeth *s.* of man within
    10. pour out *s.* of grace and supplica.

Mal. 2. 15. take heed to your *s.*
Matt. 22. 43. how then doth David in *s.*
    call him Lord
    26. 41. *s.* is willing, flesh weak
Luke 1. 80. waxed strong in *s.*
    2. 37. came by *s.* into temple
    8. 55. her *s.* came again and
    9. 55. ye know not what manner of *s.*
    ye are of
    24. 39. a *s.* hath not flesh and
John 3. 5. born of water and of *s.*
    6. that which is born of *S.* is *s.*
    34. God giveth not *s.* bv measure
    4. 24. God is a *S.* worship in *s.* and
    6. 63. *s.* quickeneth, words, *s.* and the
Acts 6. 10 not able to resist *s.*
    16. 7. the *S.* suffered them not
    17. 16. Paul's *s.* was stirred in
    18. 5. Paul was pressed in *s.*
Rom. 8. 1. not after flesh, but after *s.* 4.
    2. *s.* of life in Christ Jesus made me
    9. if any have not the *S.* of Christ, he
    is none of his
    13. if ye through *s.* mortify deeds of
    15. *s.* of bondage, *s.* of adoption
    16. the *s.* itself beareth witness
    26. *S.* helpeth our infirmities
1 *Cor.* 2. 10. the *S.* searcheth all
    5. 3. but present in *s.*
    6. 17. joined unto the Lord in one *s.*
2 *Co* . 3. 6. not of letter but of *s.* for *s.*
    17. where the *S.* of the Lord is there
    7. 1. from filthiness of flesh and *s.*
Gal. 3. 3. begun in *S.* are ye now
    4. 6. sent forth *S.* of his Son
    5. 17. flesh lusteth against *S.* and *S.*
    18. if led by *S.* not under law
    22. fruit of the *S.* is love ioy and peace
    25. if live in *S.* let us walk in *S.*
    6. 18. grace be with your *s.* 2 *Tim.* 4. 22.
Eph. 1. 13. sealed with Holy *S.*
    4. 4. is one body and one *s.*
    23. renewed in *s.* of your mind
    5. 9. fruit of *S.* in all goodness
    18. not drunk but filled with *S.*
    6. 18. praying always in *S. Jude* 19.
Col. 2. 5. I am with you in the *S.*
1 *Thess.* 5. 23. *s.* soul and body
Heb. 4. 12. dividing asunder of soul & *s.*
    9. 14. through eternal *S.* offered
Jam. 4. 5. *s.* that dwelleth in us
1 *Pet.* 3. 4. of a meek and quiet *s.*
    18. put to death in flesh, but quick-
    ened in *S.*
1 *John* 4. 1. believe not every *s.* try the *s.*
Jude 19. sensual, not having *S.*
Rev. 1. 10. I was in the *S.* on the Lord's
    11. 11. *S.* of life from God
    14. 13. yea, saith *S.* that they may rest
    22. 17. *S.* and bride say come
Gen. 6. 3. my *s. Job* 10. 12; *Ps.* 31. 5. &
    77. 6; *Is.* 38. 16; *Ezek.* 36. 27;
    Zech. 4. 6; *Luke* 1. 47. & 23. 46;
    Acts 7. 59; *Rom.* 1. 9; 1 *Cor.* 14. 14.
Gen. 1. 2. *S.* of God *Ex.* 1. 3; 2 *Chr.*
    15. 1; *Job* 33. 4; *Ezek.* 11. 24; *Matt.*
    3. 16, & 12. 28; *Rom.* 8. 9, 14, & 15.
    19; 1 *Cor.* 2. 11, 14, & 3. 16, & 6.
    11, & 12. 3; 2 *Cor.* 3. 3; *Eph.* 4. 30;
    1 *Pet.* 4. 14; 1 *John* 4. 2.
Is. 11. 2. *s.* of wisdom, *Eph.* 1. 17.
Zech. 13. 2. unclean *s. Matt.* 12. 43.

Ps. 104. 4. maketh his angels *s.*
Prov. 16. 2. Lord weigheth the *s.*
Matt. 10. 1. unclean *s. Acts* 5. 16. & 8.
    7; *Rev.* 16. 13, 14.
Luke 10. 20. rejoice not that *s.* are sub-
    ject unto you
1 *Cor.* 14. 32. *s.* of prophets subject
Heb. 12. 23. to the *s.* of just men made
1 *Pet.* 3. 19. preached to *s.* in prison
1 *John* 4. 1. try *s.* for many false
SPIRITUAL, *Hos.* 9. 7. spiritual man
Rom. 1. 11. impart some *s.* gift
    7. 14. law is *s.* but I am carnal
    15. 27. partakers of *s.* things
1 *Cor.* 2. 13. comparing *s.* things with *s.*
    15. he that is *s.* judgeth all
    3. 1. not speak to you as *s.* but babes
    9. 14. if we have sown to you *s.* things
    10. 3. did all eat *s.* meat
    15. 44. it is raised a *s.* body
Gal. 6. 1. ye who are *s.* restore
Eph. 1. 3. with all *s.* blessings
    5. 19. speaking in psalms and *s.* songs
    6. 12. wrestle against *s.* wickedness
Col. 1. 9. filled with all *s.* understand
1 *Pet.* 2. 5. built *s.* house *s.* sacrifices
Rom. 8. 6. to be *s.* minded is life
1 *Cor.* 2. 14. of *S.* of God are *s.* discerned
Rev. 11. 8. *s.* is called Sodom and
SPITE, *Ps.* 10. 14; *Matt.* 22. 6.
SPITTING, *Is.* 50. 6; *Luke* 18. 32.
SPOIL, *Gen.* 49. 27; *Ps.* 68. 12.
Ex. 12. 36. they *s.* the Egyptians
Ps. 119. 162. as one that findeth great *s.*
Is. 53. 12. divide *s.* with strong
Matt. 12. 29. he will *s.* his house
Col. 2. 8. lest any *s.* you through philos.
    15. having *s.* principalities
Heb. 10. 34. took joyfully the *s.* of your
SPOT without, *Num.* 19. 2, & 28. 3, 9;
    Job 11. 15; 1 *Tim.* 6. 14; *Heb.* 9.
    14; 1 *Pet.* 1. 19; 2 *Pet.* 3. 14.
Deut. 32. 5. their *s.* not *s.* of
Songs 4. 7. there is no *s.* in thee
Eph. 5. 27. not having *s.* nor
SPOTS, *Jer.* 13. 23; *Jude* 23.
SPREAD, *Job* 9. 8; *Is.* 25. 11, & 37. 14;
    Jer. 4. 3; *Lam.* 1. 17; *Ezek.* 13. 8.
SPRING, *Ps.* 85. 11; *Matt.* 13. 5, 7.
SPRINGING, *Ps.* 65. 10; *John* 4. 14;
    Heb. 12. 15.
Ps. 87. 7. all my *s.* are in thee
SPRINKLE, *Lev.* 14. 7, & 16. 14.
Is. 52. 15. shall he *s.* many nations
Ezek. 36. 25. I will *s.* clean water upon
Heb. 10. 22. hearts *s.* from evil
    12. 24. come to blood of *s.*
1 *Pet.* 1. 2. through *s.* of blood of Jesus
SPUE out of my mouth, *Rev.* 3. 16; *Hab.*
    2. 16; *Lev.* 18. 28; *Jer.* 25. 27.
SPY, *Num.* 12. 16; *Gal.* 2. 4.
STABILITY of times, *Is.* 33. 6.
STAFF, *Gen.* 32. 10; *Zech.* 11. 10.
Ps. 23. 4. thy rod and *s.* comfort
Is. 3. 1. take away the *s.* of bread
    9. 4. broken *s.* of burden, 14. 5.
    10. 5. the *s.* in their hand is mine
STAGGER, *Ps.* 107. 27; *Rom.* 4. 20.
STAIN, *Is.* 23. 9, & 63. 3.
STAKES, *Is.* 33. 20, & 54. 2.
STAMMER, *Is.* 28. 11, & 33. 19, & 32. 4.
STAND. To wait with humble depend-

ance upon God, *Ex.* 14. 13; 2 *Chr.*
    20. 17. Deeply to contemplate
    the works of God, *Job* 37. 14. To
    be established; *Is.* 32. 8; *Rom.* 5.
    2. *Ezek.* 29. 7; *Ex.* 9. 11.
Job 19. 25. shall *s.* on earth at
Ps. 76. 7. who *s.* in thy sight if once
    130. 3. if mark iniquities O Lord, who
    shall *s.*
Is. 46. 10. my counsel shall *s. Prov.*
    19. 21.
Mal. 3. 2. who *s.* when he appears
Matt. 12. 25. divided against itself, shall
    not *s.*
Rom. 5. 2. grace wherein ye *s.*
    14. 4. God is able to make him *s.*
2 *Cor.* 1. 24. by faith ye *s. Rom.* 11. 20.
Eph. 6. 13. having done all to *s.*
    14. *s.* therefore having
1 *Pet.* 5. 12. grace of God wherein ye *s.*
Rev. 3. 20. I *s.* at door and knock
1 *Cor.* 16. 13. *s.* fast in the faith
Gal. 5. 1. *s.* fast in the liberty
Phil. 1. 27. *s.* fast in one spirit
    4. 1. *s.* fast in the Lord
1 *Thess.* 3. 8. we live if ye *s.* fast in Lord
2 *Thess.* 2. 15. *s.* fast and hold
Ps. 1. 5. *s.* in 4, & 24. 3.
Ex. 14. 13. *s.* still see salvation, 2 *Chr.*
    20. 17; *Josh.* 10. 12; *Zech.* 11. 16.
STANDETH, *Ps.* 1. 1, & 26. 12, & 33. 11;
    Prov. 8. 2; *Song* 2. 9; *Is.* 3. 13.
Ps. 119. 161. my heart *s.* in awe
Rom. 14. 4. to own master *s.* or
1 *Cor.* 10. 12. him that thinketh he *s.*
2 *Tim.* 2. 19. foundation of God *s.* sure
Jam. 5. 9. behold the judge *s.* before
STAR, *Num.* 24. 17; *Matt.* 2. 2.
Judg. 5. 20. *s.* in courses fought
Job 25. 5. *s.* not pure in his sight
    38. 7. when the morning *s.* sang
Dan. 12. 3. shine as *s.* together
Jude 13. wandering *s.* to whom is
Rev. 12. 1. crown of twelve *s.* ·
STATURE, *Matt.* 6. 27; *Eph.* 4. 13.
STATUTES, and laws, *Neh.* 9. 14.
Ps. 19. 8. *s.* of the Lord are right
Ezek. 20. 25. *s.* not good
    33. 15. *s.* of life
Mic. 6. 16. *s.* of Omri works of
Ex. 15. 26. his *s. Deut.* 6. 17; 2 *Kings*
    17. 15; *Ps.* 18. 22, & 105. 45.
1 *Chr.* 29. 19. thy *s. Ps.* 119. 12, 16, 23,
    26, 33, 54, 64, 68, 71, 117.
STAY, *Ps.* 18. 18; *Song* 2. 5; *Is.* 10. 20.
    & 26. 3, & 27. 8, & 48. 2, & 50. 10.
STEAD, *Gen.* 4. 25, & 22. 13.
Gen. 30. 2. am I in God's *s.* who
Job 16. 4. your soul in my soul, *s.*
Prov. 11. 8. wicked cometh in his *s.*
2 *Cor.* 5. 20. we pray you in C's stead
STEAL, *Ex.* 20. 15; *Lev.* 19. 11.
Prov. 6. 30. if he *s.* to satisfy his soul
    30. 9. lest I be poor and *s.*
Jer. 23. 30. against prophets that *s.* my
Matt. 6. 19. thieves break through and *s.*
Eph. 4. 28. that stole *s.* no more
Prov. 9. 17. stolen waters sweet
STEDFAST, *Job* 11. 15; *Dan.* 6. 26.
Ps. 78. 8. spirit was *s.* with God, 37.
Acts 2. 42. *s.* in the apostles' doctrine
1 *Cor.* 15. 58. be *s.* unmovable

Heb. 3. 14. if we hold confidence *s.* unto
1 *Pet.* 5. 9. whom resist *s.* in faith
STEDFASTNESS, *Col.* 2. 5; 2 *Pet.* 3. 17.
STEPS. Signifies the footsteps of God,
  Job 23. 11; *Ps.* 85. 13. The ex-
  ample of Christ, 1 *Pet.* 2. 21. The
  ways of men, *Job* 31. 4; *Prov.* 4. 12.
  Holy pursuits, *Ex.* 20. 26; *Ps.* 18.
  36; 37. 31; 56. 6.
Ps. 37. 23. *s.* of good men ordered
  31. none of his *s.* shall slide
  44. 18. neither our *s.* declined
  119. 133. order my *s.* in thy word
Prov. 16. 9. but the L. directeth his *s.*
Jer. 10. 23. not in man to direct his *s.*
Rom. 4. 12. walk in *s.* of that faith
1 *Pet.* 2. 31. should follow his *s.*
STEWARD, *Luke* 12. 42. & 16. 2; 1 *Cor.*
  4. 1; *Tit.* 1. 7; 1 *Pet.* 4. 10.
STIFF neck, *Deut.* 31. 27; *Jer.* 17. 23.
Ex. 32. 9. *s.* necked people, 33. 3, 5. &
  34. 9; *Deut.* 9. 6. 13. & 10. 16.
Acts 7. 51. *s.* necked, ye always resist
2 *Chr.* 36. 13. he *s.* his neck
STILL, *Ex.* 15. 16; *Ps.* 8. 2. & 139. 18.
Ps. 4. 4. be *s. Jer.* 47. 6; *Mark* 4. 39.
  46. 10. be *s.* and know that I am
  83. 1. keep not silence, be not *s.*
Is. 30. 7. their strength is to sit *s.*
Rev. 22. 11. unjust *s.* filthy *s.* holy *s.*
Ps. 65. 7. stilleth noise, 89. 9.
STING, 1 *Cor.* 15. 55, 56; *Rev.* 9. 10.
Prov. 23. 32. it *s.* like an adder
STINK, *Ps.* 38. 5; *Is.* 3. 24.
STIR up. To provoke, *Prov.* 15. 1.
  To disquiet, *Song* 2. 7. To exhort
  2 *Pet.* 1. 13. *Num.* 34. 9; *Job*
  17. 8.
Ps. 35. 23. *s.* up thyself, 80. 2.
  78. 38. did not *s.* up his wrath
Song 2. 7. ye *s.* not up, 3. 5. & 8. 4.
2 *Tim.* 1. 6. *s.* up gift of God in thee
2 *Pet.* 1. 13. meet to *s.* you up
STOCK, S, *Acts* 13. 26. children of the
  s. of Abraham
Acts 16. 24. who made their feet fast in
  the *s.*
Phil. 3. 5. of the *s.* of Israel, an Hebrew
GAZING-STOCK, *Nah.* 3. 6. set thee as
  a gazing-*s.*
Heb. 10. 33. ye were made a gazing-*s.*
STOLE, 2 *Sam.* 15. 6. Absalom *s.* the
  hearts
Matt. 28. 13. disciples *s.* him while we
  slept
Eph. 4. 28. him that *s.* steal no more
STOLEN. *Prov.* 9. 17. *s.* waters are
  sweet, bread eaten in secret
STOMACH, 1 *Tim.* 5. 23. but use a little
  wine for thy *s.* sake
STONE of Israel, *Gen.* 49. 24.
Ps. 118. 22. *s.* which the builders
Is. 8. 14. a *s.* of stumbling, *Rom.* 9. 32.
  28. 16. a tried *s.* a precious corner *s.*
Dan. 2. 34. a *s.* was cut out of mountain
Hab. 2. 11. *s.* shall cry out of wall
Zech. 3. 9. on one *s.* shall be seven
Matt. 7. 9. bread will he give him a *s.*
1 *Pet.* 2. 4. as unto a living *s.*
  6. in Sion a chief corner *s.*
Gen. 11. 3. had brick for *s.* and slime for
  mortar

Josh. 24. 27. this *s.* shall be a witness
1 *Sam.* 7. 12. Samuel set up a *s.* and
  called it Eben-ezer
Ps. 91. 12. lest thou dash thy foot
  against a *s. Matt.* 4. 6; *Luke* 4. 11.
Zech. 4. 7. shall bring forth the head *s.*
Matt. 21. 44. whosoever shall fall on
  this *s.* shall be broken, but on, *Luke*
  20. 18.
  24. 2. shall not be left one *s.* upon
  another, *Mark* 13. 2; *Luke* 19. 44;
  21. 6.
  27. 66. sealing the *s.*; 28. 2. angel
  rolled back *s.*
  20. 17. *s.* builders rejected, is become
  head of the corner, *Acts* 4. 11; 1
  Pet. 2. 7.
John 1. 42. Cephas, by interpretation,
  a *s.*
  8. 7. without sin, first cast *s.* at her
Zech. 12. 3. Jerusalem a burdensome *s.*
STONE, hewn, *Luke* 23. 53. laid it in
  sepulchre that was *hewn* in *s.*
STONE, precious, *Is.* 28. 16. 1 lay in
  Zion a *precious* corner *s.* 1 *Pet.* 2. 6.
Rev. 21. 11. light like to a *s.* most *p.*
STONE, white, *Rev.* 2. 17. I will give
  him a *white s.*
STONE, verb, *Luke* 20. 6. the people
  will *s.* us
John 10. 31. Jews took up stones to *s.*
  him
STONED, *Acts* 7. 58. they *s.* Stephen,
  calling, 59.
Acts 14. 19. having *s.* Paul, drew him
2 *Cor.* 11. 25. once was I *s.*
Heb. 11. 37. were *s.* sawn asunder
STONES, *Is.* 54. 11. lay thy *s.* with fair
  colours
Is. 60. 17. bring for *s.* iron
Matt. 3. 9. able of these *s.* to raise up
  4. 3. these *s.* be made bread
Mark 13. 1. what manner of *s.* are here
Luke 19. 40. *s.* would immediately cry
John 8. 59. they took up *s.* to cast at
  him, 10. 31.
1 *Pet.* 2. 5. ye as lively *s.* are built up
Ps. 141. 12. daughters may be as
  corner *s.*
STONY, *Ezek.* 11. 19; *Matt.* 13. 5.
STOOP, *Job* 9. 13; *Prov.* 12. 25; *Mark*
  1. 7; *Luke* 24. 12.
STOP, 2 *Cor.* 11. 10. no man shall *s.* me
  of this boasting
STOPPED, *Gen.* 8. 2. and the windows
  of heaven were *s.*
Ps. 63. 11. mouth that lies be *s.*
Acts 7. 57. *s.* ears, and ran upon him
Rom. 3. 19. every mouth may be *s.*
Heb. 11. 33. through faith *s.* mouths of
  lions
STORE. Provision, *Gen.* 41. 36. That
  which has been reserved, *Lev.* 25.
  22. Abundance, 1 *Kings* 10. 10;
  1 *Chr.* 29. 16; 2 *Chr.* 11. 11; 1 *Cor.*
  16. 2; 1 *Tim.* 6. 19.
STOREHOUSE, *Luke* 12. 24; *Ps.* 33. 7.
STORM. The judgments of God against
  the wicked, *Ps.* 55. 8. & 83. 15; *Is.*
  29. 6; *Ezek.* 13. 13; *Job* 18. 21.
Ps. 107. 29. he makes *s.* a calm
  148. 8. *s.* wind fulfilling his word

Is. 4. 6. covert from *s.* and
    25. 4. refuge from the *s.*
Nah. 1. 3. Lord hath his way in *s.*
Mark 4. 37. there arose a great *s.*
STOUT-hearted, *Ps.* 76. 5; *Is.* 46. 12.
Is. 10. 12. punish fruit of *s.* heart
Dan. 7. 20. look more *s.* than his
Mal. 3. 13. words have been *s.* against
Is. 9. 9. say in pride and *s.* of heart
STRAIGHT, *Josh.* 6. 5; *Jer.* 31. 9.
Ps. 5. 8. make thy ways *s.* before
Eccl. 7. 13. who can make *s.* crooked
Is. 40. 3. make *s.* the highway
    4. crooked shall be made *s.* 42. 16. &
       45. 2; *Matt.* 3. 3; *Luke* 3. 4, 5.
Heb. 12. 13. makes *s.* paths for feet
STRAIT, 2 *Sam.* 24. 14; *Job* 20. 22, &
    36. 16; *Is.* 49. 20; *Phil.* 1. 23.
Matt. 7. 13. enter in at *s.* gate, 14.
Job 18. 7. steps is *Prov.* 4. 12.
Mic. 2. 7. is the spirit of L. *s.*
Luke 12. 50. how I am *s.* till it be
2 *Cor.* 6. 12. not *s.* in-us ye are *s.* in
STRANGE, *Ezr.* 21. 8, & 30. 9; *Lev.*
    10. 1; *Ps.* 81. 9; *Jer.* 2. 21; *Luke*
    5. 26; *Heb.* 11. 9.
Is. 28. 21. his *s.* work, his *s.* act
Hos. 8. 12. law counted a *s.* thing
Zeph. 1. 8. clothed with *s.* apparel
Heb. 13. 9. carried about with *s.* doctrin.
1 *Pet.* 4. 9. think it *s.* ye run not
Judg. 11. 2. *s.* women, *Prov.* 2. 16, & 5.
    3, 20, & 6. 24, & 20. 16, & 23. 17, &
    27. 13; *Ezra* 10. 2, 11.
STRANGER, *Gen.* 23. 4. stranger and
    sojourner, *Ps.* 39. 12. & 119. 19; 1
    Chr. 29. 15.
Prov. 14. 10. *s.* not intermeddle
Jer. 14. 8. why should be as a *s.*
Matt. 25. 35. I was a *s.* and ye took me
Luke 17. 18. give God glory save this *s.*
John 10. 5. *s.* will they not follow
Ps. 105. 12. when is a *s.* in
    146. 9. Lord preserveth *s.* he relieveth
Eph. 2. 12. *s.* from the covenants of
    19. are no more *s.* and foreigners
Heb. 11. 13. confessed they were *s.* on
    13. 2. not forget to entertain *s.*
1 *Pet.* 2. 11. beseech you as *s.* and
STRANGLED, *Acts* 15. 20, 29.
Job 7. 15. soul chooseth *s.*
STREAM, *Job* 6. 15; *Ps.* 124. 4; *Is.* 30.
    33, & 66. 12; *Dan.* 7. 10; *Amos* 5.
    24; *Luke* 6. 48.
STREAMS, *Ps.* 46. 4, & 126. 4; *Song* 4.
    15; *Is.* 30. 25, & 33. 21, & 35. 6.
STREET, *Gen.* 9. 22. his voice not heard
    in *s. Matt.* 12. 19.
Acts 9. 11. the *s.* called Straight
Rev. 21. 21. *s.* of the city was pure gold
    22. 2. in midst of the *s.* was the tree
       of life
STREETS, *Prov.* 1. 20; *Song* 3. 2.
Ps. 144. 14. be no complaining in our *s.*
Matt. 6. 2. do not sound a trumpet
    before thee in *s.*
    5. love to pray in corners of *s.*
Luke 14. 21. go into *s.* and lanes of the
       city
STRENGTH, *Gen.* 49. 24; *Ex.* 13. 3.
Ex. 15. 2. Lord is my *s.* and song, *Ps.* 18.
    2, & 28. 7; *Is.* 12. 2.

Judg. 5. 21. hast trodden down *s.*
1 *Sam.* 2. 9. by *s.* shall no man
    15. 29. *S.* of Israel will not lie
Job 9. 19. if I speak of *s.* lo, he is strong
    12. 13. with him is wisdom and *s.* 16.
Ps. 18. 32. girded me with *s.* 39.
    27. 1. Lord is the *s.* of my life
    29. 11. will give *s.* to my people
    39. 13. that I may recover *s.*
    46. 1. God is our refuge and *s.* 81. 1.
    68. 34. ascribe *s.* to God
    35. God is he that giveth *s.*
    73. 26. God is the *s.* of my heart, 43. 2.
    84. 5. blessed whose *s.* is in thee
    7. they go from *s.* to *s.* every
    138. 3. *s.* me with *s.* in soul
Eccl. 9. 16. wisdom better than *s.*
Is. 25. 4. *s.* to poor, *s.* to needy
    26. 4. in L. Jehovah is everlasting *s.*
    40. 29. no might increaseth *s.*
    45. 24. in L. I have righteousness & *s.*
Luke 1. 51. showed *s.* with his arm
Rom. 5. 6. when yet without *s.* Christ
1 *Cor.* 15. 56. *s.* of sin is the law
Rev. 3. 8. open door hast a little *s.*
    5. 12. worthy Lamb to receive *s.*
    12. 10. now is come salvation and *s.*
1 *Chr.* 16. 11. his *s. Ps.* 33. 17; *Is.* 63.
    1; *Hos.* 7. 9, & 12. 3.
Gen. 49. 24. in *s. Job* 9. 4, & 36. 5; *Ps.*
    71. 16, & 103. 20.
    49. 3. my *s. Ex.* 15. 2; 2 *Sam.* 22, 33;
    Job 6. 12; *Ps.* 18. 1, 2, & 19. 14,
    & 28. 7, & 38. 10, & 43. 2, & 59. 17,
    & 62. 7, & 71. 9, & 90. 10, & 102. 23,
    & 118. 14, & 144. 1; *Is.* 12. 2, & 27.
    5, & 49. 4, 5; *Jer.* 16. 19.
Ps. 37. 39. their *s.* 89. 17; *Prov.* 20. 29;
    Is. 30. 7, & 40. 31.
Neh. 8. 10. your *s. Is.* 23. 14, & 30. 15.
Ps. 20. 2. Lord *s.* thee out of Zion
    27. 14. wait on Lord he shall *s.* your
    31. 24. be of good courage he shall *s.*
    41. 3. Lord will *s.* him on bed of
    119. 28. *s.* me according to thy
Is. 35. 3. *s.* ye the weak hands
    41. 10. I will *s.* thee
    54. 2. and *s.* thy stakes
Dan. 11. 1. I stood to confirm and *s.*
Zech. 10. 12. I will *s.* them in the Lord
Luke 22. 32. when converted *s.* thy
1 *Pet.* 5. 10. stablish *s.* settle you
Rev. 3. 2. watchful and *s.* things
Ezek. 34. 4. diseased have ye not *s.*
Eph. 3. 16. *s.* with might, *Col.* 1. 11.
2 *Tim.* 4. 17. L. stood with me and *s.*
Ps. 138. 3. thou *s.* me with *s.* in my
Phil. 4. 13. through Christ which *s.* me
STRETCH thy hands, *Job* 11. 13.
Gen. 22. 10. *s.* forth hand to slay
1 *Kings* 17. 21. *s.* himself upon the child
Prov. 31. 20. she *s.* out her hand to the
Is. 5. 25. his hand is *s.* out still, 9. 12.
    & 10. 4.
    40. 22. *s.* out the heavens as a curtain,
    42. 5, & 44. 24, & 45. 12, & 51. 13.
Amos 6. 4. *s.* themselves on couches
Matt. 12. 13. *s.* forth thy hand—and he
John 21. 18. shall *s.* forth hands
Rom. 10. 21. all day long I have *s.* forth
STRIFE between me, *Gen.* 12. 7, 8.
Ps. 80. 6. thou makest us a *s.* to our

Prov. 10. 12. pride stirreth up`s.
Prov. 16. 28. froward man soweth *s.*
 20. 3. it is honour to leave off *s.*
 26. 20. where no tale-bearer *s.* ceaseth
 30. 33. forcing of wrath brings *s.*
Luke 22. 24. was a *s.* among the
Rom. 13. 13. not in *s.* and envying
1 *Cor.* 3. 3. among you *s.* and envving
Gal. 5. 20. wrath *s.* seditions
Phil. 1. 15. preach Christ of *s.* and
 2. 3. nothing be done through *s.*
1 *Tim.* 6. 4. whereof cometh *s.* of words
2 *Tim.* 2. 23. genders *s.* 2 *Cor.* 12. 20.
Jam. 3. 14. envying and *s.* 16.
STRICKEN, *Is.* 1. 5. why be *s.* any more
 53. 4. did esteem him *s.* of God
STRIKE, 2 *Kings* 5. 11. and *s.* his hand
 over place
Job 17. 3. who will *s.* hands with me
Ps. 110. 5. shall *s.* through kings
Prov. 7. 23. dart *s.* through his liver
 17. 26. not good to *s.* princes
Hos. 14. 5. *s.* forth his roots as Lebanon
Mark 14. 65. to *s.* Jesus with palms of
STRIKER, 1 *Tim.* 3. 3. a bishop must
 be sober, no *s. Tit.* 1. 7.
STRIPES. Spoken of the Christian min-
 istry, *Rom.* 15. 20. Prayer, *Rom.*
 15. 30. Contending against God,
 Is. 45. 9. Against his ministers,
 Hos. 4. 4. Against the righteous,
 Ps. 35. 1; 1 *Pet.* 2. 24; *Prov.* 17. 10,
 & 20. 30; *Luke* 12. 47, 48.
Acts 16. 33. same hour & washed their *s.*
2 *Cor.* 6. 5. in *s.* in imprisonments, in
 tumults
 11. 23. in *s.* above measure, in prisons
 24. five times received 1 forty *s.*
STRIPPED, *Job* 19. 9. *s.* me of my glory
 and crown
Matt. 27. 28. they *s.* Jesus, put on him
 scarlet robe
Luke 10. 30. thieves, which *s.* him of
 his raiment
STRIVE, *Ex.* 21. 18, 22; *Job* 33. 13.
Gen. 6. 3. my Spirit not alway *s.*
Prov. 3. 30. *s.* not without cause
Is. 45. 9. woe unto him that *s.* with his
Matt. 12. 19. he shall not *s.* nor
Luke 13. 24. *s.* to enter strait gate
2 *Tim.* 2. 24. servant of the Lord must
 not *s.*
Phil. 1. 27. *s.* together for faith
Heb. 12. 4. blood *s.* against sin
STRIVETH, 1 *Cor.* 9. 25. every man
 that *s.* for mastery
STRONG this day as, *Josh.* 14. 11.
Ps. 24. 8. L. is *s.* and mighty in battle
 30. 7. my mountain to stand *s.*
 31. 2. be thou my *s.* rock for
 71. 7. thou art mv *s.* refuge. 3.
Prov. 10. 15. rich man's wealth is his *s.*
 city
 11. 16. *s.* men retain riches
 14. 26. in fear of Lord *s.* confidence
 18. 10. name of Lord is as a *s.* tower
Eccl. 9. 11. battle not to *s.*
 12. 3. *s.* men bow themselves
Song 38. 6. love is *s.* as death
Is. 35. 4. be *s.* fear not, behold
Jer. 50. 34. their redeemer is *s.*

Luke 11. 21. *s.* man armed keep house
Rom. 4. 20. *s.* in faith giving glory
 15. 1. *s.* ought to bear infirmities
2 *Cor.* 12. 10. when weak, then am I *s.*
Heb. 11. 34. of weakness made *s.*
Is. 35. 4. be *s. Hag.* 2. 4; 1 *Cor.* 16. 13;
 Eph. 6. 10; 2 *Tim.* 2. 1.
1 *Cor.* 1. 25. *s.* than, 10. 22.
STRUCK, *Matt.* 26. 51. *s.* a servant of
 high-priest's
Luke 22. 64. *s.* Jesus on the face, *John*
 18. 22.
STUBBLE, the stalks left in a field of
 grain which has been reaped. Stubble is of little value; of no strength
 or force; is easily scattered by the
 wind; and easily burnt. *Job* 13.
 25; 21. 18; 41. 29; *Joel* 2. 5. To
 it wicked men are compared, *Ps.*
 83. 14; *Is.* 40. 24; *Mal.* 4. 1. False
 doctrines are as stubble, of no
 worth; of no force to convince or
 comfort men's consciences, and
 cannot abide the trial of God's
 word, 1 *Cor.* 3. 12.
STUBBORN. Spoken of sin, *Judg.* 2. 19.
 Of the harlot. *Prov.* 7. 11. Of
 a stubborn, gluttonous, rebellious son, *Deut.* 21. 18; *Ps.* 78. 8.
STUBBORNNESS, 1 *Sam.* 15. 23;
 Deut. 9. 27.
STUDY, *Eccl.* 12. 12; 1 *Thess.* 4. 11; 2
 Tim. 2. 15; *Prov.* 15. 28, & 24. 2.
STUMBLE, foot shall not, *Prov.* 3. 23.
Is. 5. 27. none be weary or *s.*
 28. 7. err in vision, *s.* in judgment
Mal. 2. 8. many to *s.* with law
John 11. 9. walk in day he *s.* not
Rom. 9. 32. they *s.* at that *s.* 1 *Pet.* 2. 8.
 14. 21. whereby thy brother *s.*
STUMBLING, *Is.* 8. 14; 1 *John* 2. 10.
Lev. 19. 14. *s.*-block, *Is.* 8. 14, & 57. 14;
 Jer. 6. 21; *Ezek.* 3. 20, & 7. 19, &
 14. 3, 4. 7; *Rom.* 9. 32, 33. & 11. 9,
 & 14. 13; 1 *Cor.* 1. 23, & 8. 9; *Rev.*
 2. 14.
SUBDUE our iniquities, *Mic.* 7. 19.
Ps. 81. 14. I should soon have *s.* their
 enemies
Phil. 3. 21. able to *s.* all things
Heb. 11. 33. through faith *s.* kingdoms
SUBJECT devils, *Luke* 10. 17, 20.
Rom. 8. 7. not *s.* to law of God
 20. made *s.* to vanity
 13. 1. *s.* unto the higher power 5.
1 *Cor.* 14. 32. *s.* to the prophets
 15. 28. Son himself be *s.* to him
Eph. 5. 24. as Church is *s.* to Christ
Tit. 3. 1. to be *s.* to principalities
Heb. 2. 15. all life-time *s.* to bondage
Jam. 5. 17. Elias was a man *s.* to like
1 *Pet.* 2. 18. servants be *s.* to
 3. 22. angels, authorities, *s.* to him
 5. 5. all be *s.* to one another
SUBJECTION, 1 *Cor.* 9. 27; 1 *Tim.* 2.
 11, & 3. 4; *Heb.* 2. 5, 8, & 12. 9; 1
 Pet. 3. 1, 5.
SUBMIT, *Gen.* 16. 9; *Ps.* 18. 44, & 66.
 3, & 68. 30, & 81. 15.
1 *Cor.* 16. 16. *s.* yourselves, *Eph.* 5. 21,
 22; *Col.* 3. 18; *Heb.* 13. 17; *Jam.*
 4. 7; 1 *Pet.* 2. 13, & 5. 5.

n. 10. 3. have not *s.* to righteousness
SUBSCRIBE, *Is.* 44. 5; *Jer.* 32. 44.
SUBSTANCE, *Gen.* 7. 4, & 15. 14.
Deut. 33. 11. bless Lord, his *s.* and
Ps. 139. 15. my *s.* was not hid from thee
Prov. 3. 9. honour Lord with thy *s.*
8. 21. those that love me to inherit *s.*
Luke 8. 3. ministered of their *s.*
Heb. 10. 34. in heaven more enduring *s.*
11. 1. faith is *s.* of things hoped
SUBTLE, *Gen.* 3. 1; *Prov.* 7. 10.
SUBTLETY, *Acts* 13. 10; 2 *Cor.* 11. 3;
Prov. 1. 4.
SUBVERT, *Lam.* 3. 36; *Tit.* 1. 11. & 3.
11.
Acts 15. 24. *s.* souls, 2 *Tim.* 2. 14.
SUCK, *Gen.* 21. 7; *Deut.* 32. 13.
Job 20. 16. *s.* poison of asps and
Is. 60. 16. *s.* milk of Gentiles, *s.* breasts
of kings
Matt. 24. 19. woe to them that give *s.*
in those days
Luke 11. 27. blessed paps thou hast *s.*
23. 29. blessed paps that never gave *s.*
Is. 11. 8. *s.* child, 49. 15.
Ps. 8. 2. sucklings, *Lam.* 2. 11, & 4. 4.
SUDDEN, *Prov.* 3. 25; 1 *Thess.* 5. 3.
SUFFER, *Ex.* 12. 23; *Deut.* 18. 14.
Ps. 55. 22. never *s.* righteous to be
89. 33. nor *s.* faithfulness to fail
121. 3. not *s.* foot to be moved
Prov. 10. 3. L. not *s.* soul of righteous
to famish
Matt. 16. 21. must *s.* many things
17. 17. how long shall I *s.* you
19. 14. *s.* little children to come
Rom. 8. 17. if we *s.* with'him we
1 *Cor.* 4. 12. being persecuted we *s.* it
10. 13. God will not *s.* you to be
Phil. 1. 29. also to *s.* for his sake
2 *Tim.* 2. 12. if we *s.* we shall reign
Heb. 11. 25. choosing rather to *s.*
13. 3. remember them that *s.*
22. *s.* word of exhortation
19. them that *s.* according to the will
Acts 16. 19. *s.* all nations to walk
16. 7. the Spirit *s.* them not
Phil. 3. 8. 1 *s.* loss of all things
Heb. 5. 8. learned obedience by things
he *s.*
1 *Pet.* 2. 21. *s.* for us, leaving us
3. 18. Christ *s.* once for sin, just for
5. 10. after ye have *s.* a while
SUFFERETH, *Matt.* 11. 12; 1 *Cor.* 13. 4.
SUFFERINGS, *Rom.* 8. 18; 2 *Cor.* 1. 5,
6; *Phil.* 3. 10; *Col.* 1. 24; *Heb.* 2.
10; 1 *Pet.* 1. 11, & 4. 13, & 5. 1.
SUFFICE, 1 *Pet.* 4. 3; *John* 14. 8.
SUFFICIENT to day is evil, *Matt.* 6. 24.
1 *Cor.* 2. 16. who is *s.* for these
3. 5. not *s.* of ourselves our
2 *Cor.* 12. 9. my grace is *s.* for thee
SUFFICIENCY, *Job* 20. 22; 2 *Cor.* 9. 8.
SUM, *Ps.* 139. 17; *Ezek.* 28. 12; *Heb.* 8. 1.
SUMMER and winter not cease, *Gen.*
8. 22.
Ps. 74. 17. hast made *s.* and winter
Prov. 6. 8. provideth her meat in *s.*
10. 5. gathereth in *s.* is a wise son
Is. 18. 6. fowls shall *s.* and winter on
Jer. 8. 22. harvest past, *s.* ended
Zech. 14. 8. living waters in *s.* and

SUMPTUOUSLY fared, *Luke* 16. 19.
SUN stand still, *Josh.* 10. 12.
Ps. 19. 4. he set a tabernacle for *s.*
74. 16. prepared the light and *s.*
104. 19. *s.* knoweth his going
121. 6. *s.* not smite by day, *Is.* 49. 10.
136. 8. *s.* to rule by day, *Gen.* 1. 16.
Eccl. 12. 2. *s.* or stars darkened
Song 1. 6. *s.* hath looked on me
6. 10. fair as moon, clear as *s.*
Is. 30. 26. light of *s.* be sevenfold
38. 8. *s.* returned ten degrees
60. 19. *s.* be no more thy light
20. thy *s.* no more go down
Jer. 31. 35. giveth *s.* for light by day
Mal. 4. 2. unto you that fear shall *S.* of
righteousness arise
Matt. 5. 45. his *s.* to rise on evil
13. 43. righteous shall shine as *s.* in
1 *Cor.* 15. 41: one glory of *s.*
Eph. 4. 26. let not *s.* go down on
Rev. 10. 1. his face as the *s.* 1. 16;
Matt. 17. 2.
7. 16. nor *s.* light on them, nor
21. 23. had no need of *s.* 22. 5.
SUP, *Luke* 17. 8; *Rev.* 3. 20.
SUPERSCRIPTION. It was a custom
among the Romans to write the
crime for which any man suffered
death, on a tablet, and carry it before him to execution; and as of
other kinds of death, so in particular
of those that were crucified.
Matt. 22. 20. Jesus saith unto them,
whose is this image and *s.?* *Mark*
12. 16; *Luke* 20. 24.
Mark 15. 26. the *s.* of his accusation,
Luke 28. 38.
SUPERSTITION. The practice of
religious rites unauthorized by
Divine revelation, and such as result
from unnecessary fear or dread of
an imagined invisible power, *Acts*
25. 19, & 17. 22.
SUPPER, *Luke* 14. 12. makest a dinner
or *s.*
Luke 14. 16. certain man made a great *s.*
24. none of those were bidden shall
taste of my *s.*
22. 20. cup after *s.* saying, this cup
John 12. 2. there they made Jesus a *s.*
Martha served
1 *Cor.* 11. 20. not to eat the Lord's *s.*
Rev. 19. 9. to the marriage *s.*
17. to *s.* of the great God
SUPPLICATION. Earnest entreaties
for averting impending calamities,
and for the bestowal of blessings
needed, 1 *Kings* 8. 28, & 9. 3; *Job*
8. 5, & 9. 15; *Ps.* 6. 9, & 30. 8 & 55.
1, & 142. 1, & 119. 170; *Dan.* 6. 11,
& 9. 20; *Hos.* 12. 4; *Zech.* 12. 10;
Eph. 6. 18; *Phil.* 4. 6; 1 *Tim.* 2. 1,
& 5. 5; *Heb.* 5. 7.
SUPPLY of Spirit of Jesus Christ, *Phil.*
1. 19.
Phil. 4. 19. my God shall *s.* all
SUPPLIETH, 2 *Cor.* 9. 12; *Eph.* 4. 16.
SUPPORT weak, *Acts* 20. 34; 1 *Thess.*
5. 14.
SUPPOSE, *Luke* 7. 43. I *s.* that he to
Luke 13. 1. *s.* Galileans were sinners

John 21. 25. I *s*. the world could not contain the books

Acts 2. 15. not drunken as ye *s*.

2 *Cor*. 11. 5. I *s*. not behind chiefest

SUPPOSED, *Mark* 6. 49. they *s*. it had been a spirit

Luke 3. 23. Jesus being, as was *s*. the son of Joseph

Phil. 2. 25. I *s*. it necessary to send to you Epaphroditus

SUPPOSING, *John* 20. 15. she *s*. him to be gardener

Acts 14. 19. Paul out, *s*. had been dead

16. 27. jailor *s*. prisoners had fled

Phil. 1. 16. *s*. to add affliction to my

1 *Tim*. 6. 5. *s*. gain is godliness

SUPREME, 1 *Pet*. 2. 13. submit, whether it be to the king as *s*.

SURE, *Gen*. 23. 17; 1 *Sam*. 25. 38.

2 *Sam*. 23. 5. covenant ordained in all things and *s*.

Neh. 9. 38. made a *s*. covenant

Ps. 19. 7. testimony of Lord is *s*.

93. 5. thy testimonies are very *s*.

111. 7. all his commands are *s*.

Prov. 11. 15. hateth suretyship is *s*.

18. to soweth righteousness shall be a *s*. reward

Is. 22. 23. fasten in a *s*. place, 25.

28. 16. for a *s*. foundation

32. 18. *s*. dwellings

33. 16. thy water shall be *s*.

55. 3. *s*. mercies of David, *Acts* 13. 34.

John 6. 69. we believe and are *s*.

16. 30. *s*. thou knowest all things

Rom. 2. 2. *s*. the judgment of G. is true

4. 16. promise might be *s*.

2 *Tim*. 2. 19. foundation of G. standeth *s*.

Heb. 6. 19. hope we have as anchor *s*. and steadfast

2 *Pet*. 1. 10. calling and election *s*.

19. a more *s*. word of prophecy

SURETY, one who becomes bound for another. Sins are called *debts*, *Matt*. 6. 12. and Jesus Christ is called the Surety, *Heb*. 7. 22. Christ fulfilled the law by the holiness of his life, and underwent the penalty when he offered up himself a sacrifice to satisfy divine justice. The Scripture forbids *suretyship*, or engagement for the payment of another person's debt, *Prov*. 11. 15; 22. 26.

Gen. 44. 32. for thy servant became *s*. for the lad

Ps. 119. 122. be *s*. for thy servant

Prov. 6. 1. if thou be *s*. for friend

Heb. 7. 22. Jesus made *s*. of better

SURFEITING, *Luke* 21. 34. hearts overcharged with *s*.

SURMISING, 1 *Tim*. 6. 4. envy, strife, evil *s*.

SURPRISED hypocrites, *Is*. 33. 14.

SUSTAIN, *Ps*. 55. 22; *Prov*. 18. 14.

SUSTAINED, *Ps*. 3. 5; *Is*. 59. 16.

SWALLOW, *Ps*. 84. 3; *Jer*. 8. 7.

Ex. 15. 12. earth *s*. them, *Num*. 16. 32.

Ps. 124. 3. they had *s*. us up quick

Is. 25. 8. *s*. up death in victory, 2 *Cor*. 5. 4.

Matt. 23. 24. strain at gnat and *s*. a

SWEAR, *Num*. 30. 2; *Deut*. 6. 13.

Is. 45. 23. to me every tongue *s*.

65. 16. *s*. by the God of truth

Jer. 4. 2. *s*. Lord liveth in truth, 12. 16.

Zeph. 1. 5. *s*. by L., and *s*. by Malcham

Matt. 5. 34. *s*. not at all, *Jam*. 5. 12.

Ps. 15. 4. *s*. to his own hurt

Eccl. 9. 2. that *s*. as he that fears

Zech. 5. 3. that *s*. shall be cut off

Jer. 23. 10. because of *s*. land mourneth

Hos. 4. 2. by *s*. and lying they

10. 4. *s*. falsely in making a

Mal. 3. 5. be a witness against false *s*.

SWEET, *Job* 20. 12; *Ps*. 55. 14.

Ps. 104. 34. meditation of him shall be *s*.

119. 103. how *s*. are thy words

Prov. 3. 24. sleep shall be *s*. *Jer*. 31. 26.

9. 17. stolen waters *s*. 20. 27.

13. 19. desire accomplished is *s*.

27. 7. to hungry every bitter is *s*.

Eccl. 5. 12. sleep of labouring man is *s*.

11. 7. light is *s*. and to behold

Song 2. 3. his fruit was *s*. to my

14. *s*. is thy voice, and countenance

Is. 5. 20. put bitter for *s*. and

Phil. 4. 18. odour of a *s*. smell

Rev. 10. 9. mouth *s*. as honey

SWEETER, *Ps*. 19. 10. *s*. than honey

SWEETNESS, *Judg*. 14. 14; *Prov*. 16. 21, & 27. 9.

SWELLING, *Ps*. 46. 3. mountains shake with *s*.

2 *Pet*. 2. 18. speak great *s*. words of vanity

Jude 16. and their mouth speaking great *s*. words

SWEPT, *Matt*. 12. 44. return to my house, he findeth it empty, *s*. and garnished, *Luke* 11. 25.

SWERVED, 1 *Tim*. 1. 6. having *s*. have turned aside

SWIFT, *Deut*. 28. 49; *Job* 9. 26.

Eccl. 9. 11. race is not to *s*. nor

Rom. 3. 15. feet *s*. to shed blood, *Prov*. 6. 18.

Jam. 1. 19. *s*. to hear, slow to

2 *Pet*. 2. 1. bring on them *s*. destruction

Job 7. 6. days *s*. than shuttle, 9. 25.

SWIFTLY, *Ps*. 147. 15. *Joel* 3. 4.

SWIM, 2 *Kings* 6. 6; *Ps*. 6. 6; *Ezek*. 47. 5; *Acts* 27. 42, 43.

SWINE, *Prov*. 11. 22. jewel of gold in *s*. snout

Is. 65. 4. which eat *s*. flesh

66. 17. eating *s*. flesh, and abomination, and the mouse

Matt. 8. 31. suffer us to go into the herd of *s*. *Mark* 5. 12.

Luke 15. 15. sent into field to feed *s*.

SWORD, *Ex*. 32. 27; *Lev*. 26. 25.

Gen. 3. 24. cherubim and flaming *s*.

Deut. 33. 29. *s*. of thy excellency

Judg. 7. 20. *s*. of the Lord and of Gideon

2 *Sam*. 12. 10. *s*. shall never depart

Ps. 17. 13. wicked which is thy *s*.

149. 6. a two-edged *s*. in hands

Song 3. 8. has his *s*. upon his thigh

Jer. 9. 16. send a *s*. after them

Jer. 15. 2. such as for *s*. to *s*. 43. 11.

Ezek. 21. 13. what if *s*. contemn

Zech. 11. 17. *s*. be on his arm

13. 7 awake O *s*. against my shepherd

Matt. 10. 34. not to send peace, but a *s*.

Luke 2. 35. a *s*. shall pierce through

Rom. 13. 4. beareth not s. in vain
Eph. 6. 17. s. of Spirit which is word of
Heb. 4. 12. word of God sharper than a
two-edged s.
Rev. 1. 16. sharp two-edged s. 19. 15.
SWORDS, Ps. 55. 21, & 59. 7; Prov. 30.
14; Is. 2. 4; Ezek. 32. 27; Joel 3. 10.
SWORN by myself have I, Gen. 22. 16.
Ps. 24. 4. not s. deceitfully
119. 106. I have s. and I will perform
SYNAGOGUE, Ps. 74. 8; Matt. 6. 5, &
23. 6; Luke 7. 5; John 9. 22, & 18.
20; Acts 15. 21; Rev. 2. 9, & 3. 9.

TABERNACLE, Ex. 26. 1, & 29. 43.
Job 5. 24. thy t. shall be in peace
Ps. 15. 1. who shall abide in thy t.
27. 5. in secret of his t. hide
Prov. 14. 11. t. of upright flourish
Is. 33. 20. t. shall not be taken down
Amos 9. 11. raise t. of David Acts 15. 16.
2 Cor. 5. 1. if earthly house of t.
4. we that are in this t. groan
Heb. 8. 2. minister of the true t.
2 Pet. 1. 13. I am in this t.
14. I must put off this t.
Rev. 21. 3. t. of God is with men
Job 12. 6. t. of robbers prosper
Ps. 84. 1. how amiable are thy t.
118. 15. salvation in t. of righteous.
Heb. 11. 9. dwell in t. with Isaac
TABLE, Ex. 25. 23; Job 36. 16.
Ps. 23. 5. preparest a t. before me
69. 22. their t. become a snare
128. 3. olive plants round thy t.
Prov. 3. 3. write them on the t. of thy
Song 1. 12. while king sits at t.
Jer. 17. 1. sin graven on t. of heart
Mal. 1. 7. t. of Lord is contemptible
Matt. 15. 27. fall from master's t.
1 Cor. 10. 21. partakers of Lord's t. and
TABLES, Deut. 10. 4, 5; Heb. 9. 4; 2
Chr. 4. 8, 19; Is. 28. 8.
Hab. 2. 2. make it plain on t.
Acts 6. 2. word of God and serve t.
2 Cor. 3. 3. not in t. of stone, but in
TAKE you for a people, Ex. 6. 7.
Ex. 20. 7. not t. name of Lord in vain
34. 9. t. us for thy inheritance
Ps. 27. 10. when—Lord will t. me up
51. 11. t. not Holy S. from me
116. 13. I will t. cup of salvation
119. 43. t. not word of truth
Hos. 14. 2. t. with your words and say t.
Matt. 16. 24. t. up his cross and follow
Matt. 18. 16. t. with thee one or two
23. t. account of his servants
20. 14. t. that thine is, and go
26. 26. t. eat this is my body, 1 Cor.
11. 14.
Luke 12. 19. t. thy ease, eat, drink
Eph. 6. 13. t. whole armour of God, 17.
Rev. 3. 11. no man t. thy crown
Ex. 23. 25. t. away, Josh. 7. 13; 2 Sam.
24. 10; 1 Chr. 17. 13; Job 7. 21, &
32. 22, & 36. 18; Ps. 58. 9; Is. 58.
9; Jer. 15. 15; Hos. 1. 6, & 4. 11, &
14. 2; Amos 4. 2; Mal. 2. 3; Luke
17. 31; John 1. 29; 1 John 3. 5;
Rev. 22. 19.
Deut. 4. 9. t. heed, 11. 16, & 27. 9; 2
Chr. 19. 6; Ps. 39. 1; Is. 7. 4; Mal.
2. 15; Matt. 6. 1, & 16. 6, & 18. 10,

& 24. 4; Mark 4. 24, & 13. 33, Luke
8. 18, & 12. 15; 1 Cor. 10. 12; Col.
4. 17; Heb. 3. 12; 2 Pet. 1. 19.
32. 41. t. hold, Ps. 69. 24; Is. 27. 5, &
56. 4. & 64. 7; Zech. 1. 6.
TAKEN, Ps. 83. 3. t. crafty counsel against
119. 111. testimonies have I t. as my
Is. 53. 8. he was t. from prison and
Lam. 4. 20. anointed of the Lord t. in
Matt. 21. 43. kingdom of God t. from
24. 40. one be t. the other left
Mark 4. 25. shall be t. even that which
Acts 1. 9. t. up to heaven, 11. 22.
2 Tim. 2. 26. t. captive by him
Is. 6. 7. iniquity is t. away
16. 10. gladness is t. away
57. 1. merciful men t. away
Luke 10. 42. part not be t. from her
2 Cor. 3. 16. vail t. away when return
Ps. 40. 12. iniquity t. hold of me
119. 143. trouble and anguish have t.
hold of me
Prov. 1. 19. t. away, John 1. 29, & 10.
18, & 15. 2.
John 16. 22. no man t. from you
TAKING, Ps. 119. 9. by t. heed thereto
Matt. 6. 27. who by t. thought can
Rom. 7. 8. sin t. occasion by, 11.
Eph. 6. 16. above all t. the shield of
TALE, Ps. 90. 9; Luke 24. 11.
TALEBEARER, Lev. 19. 16; Prov. 11.
13, & 18. 8, & 20. 19, & 26. 20, 22.
TALK of them when sittest, Deut. 6. 7.
1 Sam. 2. 3. t. no more so exceeding
Job 13. 7. t. deceitfully for God
Ps. 37. 30. tongue t. of judgment
71. 24. tongue t. of righteous
77. 12. meditate of works and t. of
105. 2. t. ye of all his wondrous
145. 11. shall speak of glory—t. of thy
Jer. 12. 1. let me t. with thee of
John 14. 30. not t. much with you
Eph. 5. 4. filthiness, nor foolish t.
Tit. 1. 10. unruly and vain t.
TAME, Mark 5. 4; Jam. 3. 7, 8.
TARRY, 1 Chr. 19. 5; 2 Kings 14. 10.
Ps. 101. 7. liar not t. in my sight
Prov. 23. 30. that t. long at wine
Is. 46. 13. my salvation shall not t.
Jer. 14. 8. aside to t. for a night
Hab. 2. 3. though t. wait come, not t.
Matt. 26. 38. t. here and watch
John 21. 22. that he t. till I come
1 Cor. 11. 33. t. one for another
Ps. 68. 12. she that t. at home
Matt. 25. 5. while bridegroom t. they
Luke 2. 43. child Jesus t. behind in
Acts 22. 16. why t. thou ? arise
Ps. 40. 17. make no t. 70. 5.
TASTE. Experimental religion, Ex.
16. 31; 1 Sam. 14. 43; Ps. 34. 8; 1
Pet. 2. 3.
Job 6. 6. is there any t. in the white of
Ps. 34. 8. O t. and see Lord is good
119. 103. sweet are thy words unto t.
Song 2. 3. fruit was sweet to my t.
Jer. 48. 11. his t. remained in him
Matt. 16. 28. shall not t. of death
Luke 14. 24. none bidden t. of my supper
John 8. 52. keep my saying, never t.
Col. 2. 21. touch not, t. not
Heb. 2. 9. should t. death for
6. 4. t. of the heavenly gift

5. *t.* good word of God
1 *Pet.* 2. 3. if have *t.* that the Lord is
TATTLERS, 1 *Tim.* 5. 13.
TAUGHT, 2 *Chr.* 30. 22. *t.* good knowledge of Lord
Ps. 71. 17. thou hast *t.* me from
   119. 171. hast *t.* me thy statutes
Eccl. 12. 9. *t.* people knowledge
Is. 29. 13. fear of me *t.* by precept of men
   54. 13. thy children be *t.* of the Lord
John 6. 45. shall be all *t.* of God
Acts 20. 20. *t.* you publicly and
Gal. 6. 6. let him *t.* communicate
1 *Thess.* 4. 9. yourselves are *t.* of God
TEACH. To cause to learn, or instruct,
   Ex. 4. 12; *Lev.* 10. 11; *Ps.* 119. 26.
Deut. 4. 9. *t.* them thy sons, 6. 7.
   33. 10. they shall *t.* Jacob thy
1 *Sam.* 12. 23. *t.* you good way, 1 *Kings*
   8. 36.
2 *Chr.* 17. 7. *t.* in cities of Judah
Job 21. 22. shall any *t.* God
Ps. 25. 8. *t.* sinners in way
   9. the meek will he *t.* his way
   34. 11. I will *t.* you the fear of Lord
   51. 13. I will *t.* transgressors
   90. 12. *t.* us to number our days
Is. 2. 3. he will *t.* us of his ways, *Mic.* 4. 2.
Jer. 31. 34. *t.* no more every man
Matt. 28. 19. go and *t.* all nations
John 9. 34. in sins dost thou *t.* us
John 14. 26. Holy Ghost shall *t.* you all
1 *Cor.* 4. 17. as I *t.* every where
1 *Tim.* 2. 12. I suffer not a woman to *t.*
   3. 2. given to hospitality, apt to *t.*
2 *Tim.* 2. 2. faithful men able to *t.*
Heb. 5. 12. *t.* need one to *t.* you
1 *John* 2. 27. need not that any man *t.*
Job 34. 32. what I see not *t.* me
Ps. 25. 4. *t.* me thy paths, 5.
   27. 11. *t.* me thy way, 86. 11.
   119. 12. *t.* me thy statutes, 26. 64, 68.
   66. 7. me good judgment
   108. *t.* me thy judgments
   143. 10. *t.* me to do thy will
TEACHEST, *Ps.* 94. 12. *t.* him out of thy
Matt. 22. 16. *t.* way of God in truth
Rom. 2. 21. *t.* another *t.* not thyself
TEACHETH, *Job* 36. 22. who *t.* like him
   35. 11. *t.* us more than beasts
Ps. 18. 34. *t.* my hands to war, 144. 1.
   94. 10. he that *t.* man knowledge
Is. 48. 17. thy G. *t.* thee to profit
1 *Cor.* 2. 13. words man's wisdom *t.*
1 *John* 2. 27. anointing *t.* you all
TEACHER, *Hab.* 2. 18; *John* 3. 2; *Rom.*
   2. 20; 1 *Tim.* 2. 7; 2 *Tim.* 1. 11.
TEACHERS, *Ps.* 119. 99; *Is.* 30. 20.
2 *Tim.* 4. 3. heap up to themselves *t.*
Tit. 2. 3. be *t.* of good things
Heb. 5. 12. ought to be *t.* of others
TEACHING, 2 *Chr.* 15. 3. without *t.*
   priest
Matt. 15. 9. *t.* for doctrines commandments of men
   28. 20. *t.* them to observe all things
Col. 1. 28. *t.* every man wisdom
   3. 16. *t.* admonishing one another
Tit. 2. 12. *t.* us that, denying
TEARS, *Job* 16. 20; *Ps.* 6. 6; *Is.* 38. 5.
Ps. 56. 8. put my *t.* in thy bottle, 39. 12.
   80. 5. feed them with bread of *t.*
   126. 5. sow in *t.* reap in joy

Is. 25. 8. wipe all *t.* from off faces
Jer. 9. 1. my eyes a fountain of *t.*
Luke 7. 38. wash his feet with *t.*
Acts 20. 19. with many *t.* and, 31.
2 *Cor.* 2. 4. wrote you with many *t.*
2 *Tim.* 1. 4. mindful of thy *t.*
Heb. 5. 7. strong cry and *t.* to him
   12. 17. sought it carefully with *t.*
Rev. 7. 17. wipe away all *t.* from their
TEETH white with milk, *Gen.* 49. 12.
Job 4. 10. *t.* broken, *Ps.* 3. 7, & 58. 6.
Song 4. 2. *t.* like flock of sheep, 6. 6.
Jer. 31. 29. children's *t.* set on edge
Amos 4. 6. cleanness of *t.* in all
Matt. 8. 12. weeping and gnashing of
   t. 22. 13, & 24. 51, & 25. 30.
TELL it not in Gath. 2. *Sam.* 1. 20.
Ps. 48. 13. *t.* it to the generation
   56. 8. thou *t.* all my wanderings
Prov. 30. 4. name if thou canst *t.*
Matt. 8. 4. see thou *t.* no man
   18. 15. *t.* him his fault
   17. *t.* it to the church
John 3. 8. canst not *t.* whence it
   4. 25. Messiah *t.* us all things
   8. 14. cannot *t.* whence I come
2 *Cor.* 12. 2. in or out of body I cannot *t.*
Gal. 4. 16. am I an enemy because I *t.*
Phil. 3. 18. have told now *t.* you
TEMPERANCE, *Acts* 24. 25; *Gal.* 5. 23;
   2 *Pet.* 1. 6.
TEMPERATE, 1 *Cor.* 9. 25; *Tit.* 1. 8,
   & 2. 2.
TEMPLE, 1 *Sam.* 1. 9; 1 *Kings* 6. 5.
Ps. 29. 9. in his *t.* every one speak
Jer. 7. 4. the *t.* of the Lord, the *t.* of the
Mal. 3. 1. Lord suddenly come to his *t.*
Matt. 12. 6. one greater than *t.* is
John 2. 19. destroy this *t.* and in three
   21. he spake of *t.* of his body
Acts 7. 48. Most High dwelleth not in *t.*
1 *Cor.* 3. 16. ye are *t.* of God if, 7.
   6. 19. your bodies are *t.* of Holy Ghost
   9. 13. live of things of *t.*
2 *Cor.* 6. 16. what agreement *t.* of God,
   with idols ? ye are *t.* of God
Rev. 7. 15. serve him day and night in *t.*
   11. 19. *t.* of God was opened in
   21. 22. I saw no *t.* Lord God and
TEMPLES, *Song* 4. 2. thy *t.* 6. 7.
TEMPT Abraham, God did, *Gen.* 22. 1.
Ex. 17. 2. wherefore do ye *t.* Lord
Deut. 6. 16. not to *t.* the Lord your God
Mal. 3. 15. that *t.* God are delivered
Matt. 4. 7. thou shalt not *t.* the Lord
   22. 18. why *t.* ye me
1 *Cor.* 7. 5. that Satan *t.* not for
   10. 9. neither let us *t.* Christ as
Ex. 17. 7. because they *t.* the Lord
Ps. 78. 18. *t.* God in their heart
   41. turned back and *t.* God
   95. 9. when your fathers *t.* me, *Heb.*
   3. 9.
Matt. 4. 1. wilderness to be *t.* of devil
1 *Cor.* 10. 13. not suffer you to be *t.*
Gal. 6. 1. lest thou also be *t.*
Heb. 2. 18. being *t.* able to succour
   4. 15. in all points *t.* as we are
   11. 37. sawn asunder were *t.*
Jam. 1. 13. no man say when *t.* I am *t.*
   of God; God *t.* no man, nor can be
   t. with evil
   14. man is *t.* when led away

TEMPTATION, *Ps.* 95. 8. as in day of *t.*
Matt. 6. 13. lead us not into *t.*
1 *Cor.* 10. 13. no *t.* taken you but common, will make a way to
1 *Tim.* 6. 9. be rich fall into *t.*
Heb. 3. 8. day of *t.* in wilderness
Jam. 1. 12. blessed that endureth *t.*
Rev. 3. 10. keep thee from hour of *t.*
TEMPTATIONS, *Deut.* 4. 34, & 7. 19; *Luke* 22. 28; *Acts* 20. 19; *Jam.* 1. 2; 1 *Pet.* 1. 6; 2 *Pet.* 2. 9.
TEMPTER, *Matt.* 4. 3; 1 *Thess.* 3. 5.
TENDER. Spoken of a branch, *Matt.* 24. 32; *Job* 14. 7. Calf, *Gen.* 18. 7. Of love, *Dan.* 1. 9. Of the heart, 2 *Kings* 22. 19; *Eph.* 4. 32.
Luke 1. 78. *t.* mercy, *Jam.* 5. 11.
TENDETH, *Prov.* 10 16, & 11. 19, & 19. 23, & 11. 24, & 14. 23, & 21. 5.
TENTS of Shem, dwell in, *Gen.* 9. 27.
Num. 24. 5. goodly thy *t.* O Jacob
1 *Kings* 12. 16. to your *t.* O Israel
Ps. 84. 10. than dwell in *t.* of wicked.
120. 5. dwell in *t.* of Kedar
Song 1. 8. kids beside she herd's *t.*
TERRESTRIAL, earthly 1 *Cor.* 15. 40.
TERRIBLE, *Ex.* 34. 10; *Deut.* 1 19.
Deut. 7. 21. a mighty God and *t.* 10. 17; *Neh.* 1. 5, & 4. 14, & 9. 32; *Jer.* 20. 11. 10 21. done *t.* things, 2 *Sam.* 7. 23.
Job 37. 22. with God is *t.* majesty
Ps. 45. 4. right hand teach *t.* things
65. 5. by *t.* things in righteousness
66. 3. how *t.* in working, 5.
99. 3. praise great and *t.* name
Song 6. 4. *t.* as army with banners
Is. 64. 3. didst *t.* things we looked
Heb. 12. 21. so *t.* was the sight
TERRIBLENESS, 1 *Chr.* 17. 21; *Jer.* 49. 16.
TERRIFY, *Job* 7. 14; *Phil.* 1. 28.
TERROR, *Gen.* 35. 5; *Deut.* 32. 25.
Job 31. 23. destruction from G. was a *t.* 33. 18. thy heart meditate *t.*
Jer. 17. 17. be not a *t.* to me in
20. 4. a *t.* to thyself and, *Ezek.* 26: 21.
Rom. 13. 3. rulers not *t.* to good
2 *Cor.* 5. 11. knowing *t.* of Lord
1 *Pet.* 3. 14. not afraid of their *t.*
TERRORS, *Job* 6. 4, & 18. 11, 14, & 27. 20; *Ps.* 55. 4, & 73. 19.
TESTAMENT, *Matt.* 28. 28; *Luke* 22. 20; 1 *Cor.* 11. 25; 2 *Cor.* 3. 6, 14; *Gal.* 3. 15; *Heb.* 7. 22, & 9. 15, 16, 17, 20; *Rev.* 11. 19.
Heb. 9. 16. death of the Testator
17. while the *t.* liveth
TESTIFY. To bear witness, to vouch, or affirm, *John* 3. 11. *Deut.* 8. 19. & 32. 46; *Neh.* 9. 26, 34; *Ps.* 50. 7.
Num. 35. 30. one witness not *t.*
Is. 59. 12. our sins *t.* against, *Jer.* 14. 7.
John 3. 11. *t.* what we have seen
5. 39. search scriptures they *t.* of me
Acts 20. 24. *t.* gospel of grace
1 *John* 4. 14. have seen and *t.* that
TESTIFIED, *Neh.* 13. 15; *Acts* 23. 11; 1 *Tim.* 2. 6; 1 *John* 5. 9.
TESTIFYING, *Heb.* 11. 4; 1 *Pet.* 5. 12.
TESTIMONY, 2 *Kings* 11. 12. gave him the *t.*
Ps. 78. 5. he established a *t.* in Jacob

Is. 8. 16. bind up *t.* seal law
20. to law and *t.* if they speak
Matt. 10. 18. for a *t.* against them
John 3. 32. no man receiveth *t.*
Acts 14. 3. gave *t.* unto the word
2 *Cor.* 1. 12. *t.* of our conscience
Heb. 11. 5. before translation had this *t.*
Rev. 1. 9. *t.* of Jesus Christ, 12. 17.
11. 7. when they have finished *t.*
TESTIMONIES, *Ps.* 25. 10. keep his *t.* 119. 2.
93. 5. thy *t.* 119. 14, 24, 31, 46, 59, 95, 111, 129, 144.
THANK, 1 *Chr.* 16; 4. 29, 13; *Matt.* 11. 25; *Luke* 6. 32, 33, & 17. 9, & 18. 11; *John* 11. 41; *Rom.* 1. 8, & 7. 25; 1 *Cor.* 1. 4; 1 *Thess.* 2. 13; 1 *Tim.* 1. 12.
Ps. 100. 4. be *t.* *Acts* 24. 3; *Rom.* 1. 21.
1 *Pet.* 2. 19. this is *t.*-worthy
Dan. 6. 10. gave *t.* *Matt.* 26. 27; *Mark* 8. 6; *Luke* 22. 19; *Rom.* 14. 6.
2 *Cor.* 9. 15. *t.* to God for his unspeakable gift, 2. 14, & 8. 16; 1 *Cor.* 15. 57.
Eph. 5. 4. giving of *t.* 20; 1 *Tim.* 2. 1.
1 *Thess.* 3. 9. what *t.* can we render to
THANKSGIVING, *Lev.* 7. 12; *Neh.* 11. 17; *Ps.* 26. 7, & 50. 14, & 100. 4, & 107. 22, & 116. 17; *Is.* 51. 3; *Phil.* 4. 6; 1 *Tim.* 4. 3; *Rev.* 4. 9.
THINE is day, night, *Ps.* 74. 16.
Ps. 119. 94. I am *t.* O save me
Is. 63. 19. we are *t.* thou never
John 17. 6. *t.* they were and thou gavest
10. mine are *t.* and *t.* are mine
THINK on me, *Neh.* 5. 19.
Jer. 29. 11. I know thoughts I *t.* toward
Rom. 12. 3. not *t.* more highly
1 *Cor.* 8. 2. *t.* that he knows any
Gal. 6. 3. *t.* himself something is
Eph. 3. 20. above all we ask or *t.*
Phil. 4. 8. *t.* on these things
THOUGHT, *Gen.* 50. 20. ye *t.* evil
Ps. 48. 9. we *t.* of thy loving kindness
50. 21. thou *t.* I was like thyself
73. 16. when I *t.* to know this
119. 59. I *t.* on my ways and
Mal. 3. 16. for them that *t.* on his
Mark 14. 72. *t.* thereon he wept
1 *Cor.* 13. 11. I *t.* as a child, spake
Phil. 2. 6. *t.* it no robbery to be equal
Ps. 139. 2. understandest my *t.*
Matt. 6. 25. take not *t.* for life
34. take no *t.* for the morrow
Mark 13. 11. take no *t.* beforehand
2 *Cor.* 10. 5. bring every *t.* into
Gen. 6. 5. imagination of *t.* of heart
Ps. 10. 4. God is not in all his *t.*
Ps. 40 5. many are thy *t.* to us-ward
94. 11. Lord knoweth *t.* of men
19. in multitude of my *t.* within
119. 113. I hate vain *t.* but they
139. 17. how precious are thy *t.*
23. try me and know my *t.*
Is. 55. 7. unrighteous man forsake *t.*
8. my *t.* are not your *t.* 9.
66. 18. I know their works and *t.*
Jer. 29. 11. *t.* I think toward you, *t.* of
Matt. 15. 19. out of heart proceed evil *t.*
Luke 2. 35. *t.* of hearts revealed
24. 38. why do *t.* arise in your hearts
Rom. 2. 15. their *t.* accuse or excuse
Heb. 4. 12. discerner of *t.* and intents
THIRST. Great affliction, *Deut.* 28.

48; 29. 19; *Is*. 41. 17. An
earnest desire for Christ, and his
salvation, *Is*. 55. 1.
Ps. 42. 2. my soul *t*. for God
63. 1. soul *t*. for thee, 143. 6.
Is. 49. 10. they shall not hunger nor *t*.
55. 1. every one that *t*. come
Matt. 5. 6. blessed which hunger and *t*.
John 4. 14. shall never *t*. 6. 35.
7. 37. if any *t*. let him come
Rom. 12. 20. if he *t*. give him drink
Rev. 7. 16. hunger nor *t*. any more

THORNS in your sides, *Num*. 33. 55;
Judg. 2. 3; *Gen*. 3. 18.
Josh. 23. 13. be *t*. in your eyes
Jer. 4. 3. sow not among *t*.
12. 13. sown wheat, but shall reap *t*.
Hos. 2. 6. hedge up way with *t*.
Matt. 7. 16. do men gather grapes of *t*.
13. 7. some fell among *t*. and *t*. 22.
Heb. 6. 8. that which bears *t*.

THREATENING, *Eph*. 6. 9; *Acts*. 4.
29, & 9. 1; 1 *Pet*. 2. 23.
THREE, 2 *Sam*. 24. 12; *Prov*. 30. 15,
18, 21, 29; *Amos* 1. 3, 13, & 2. 1; 1
Cor. 14. 27; 1 *John* 5. 7, 8; *Rev*.
16. 13.
THRESH, *Is*. 25. 10; 41. 15; *Jer*. 51.
33; *Mic*. 4. 13; *Hab*. 3. 12; 1 *Cor*.
9. 10.
Lev. 26. 5. *t*. reach to vintage
THROAT is open sepulchre, *Ps*. 5. 9.
Ps. 69. 3. my *t*. is dried, eyes fail
Prov. 25. 2. put a knife to thy *t*.
Jer. 2. 25. withhold *t*. from thirst
THRONE, is in heaven, *Ps*. 11. 4.
Ps. 94. 20. *t*. of iniquity have fellow.
Prov. 25. 5. *t*. is established in
Is. 66. 1. heaven is my *t*. and
Jer. 14. 21. do not disgrace the *t*. of thy
Lam. 5. 19. thy *t*. remains from
Dan. 7. 9. the *t*. were cast down
Matt. 19. 28. when Son of man sit on *t*.
ye also shall sit on twelve *t*.
25. 31. sit on *t*. of his glory
Col. 1. 16. whether they be *t*. or
Heb. 4. 16. come boldly to *t*. of grace
Rev. 3. 21. in my *t*. my Father in his *t*.
20. 11. a great white *t*. and he
22. 3. *t*. of God, and Lord shall be in
Ps. 97. 2. his *t*. 103. 19; *Prov*. 20. 28;
Dan. 7. 9; *Zech*. 6. 13.
Ps. 45. 6. thy *t*. 89. 4; *Heb*. 1. 8.
Is. 22. 23. glorious *t*. *Jer*. 17. 12.
THRUST, *Ex*. 11. 1; *Job* 32. 13; *Luke*
13. 28; *John* 20. 25; *Acts* 16. 37.
THUNDER, *Job* 26. 14, & 40. 9; *Ps*. 29.
3, & 81. 7; *Mark* 3. 17.
THUNDERINGS, *Rev*. 4. 5, & 8. 5, &
10. 3; 11. 19; 16. 18; 19. 6.
TIDINGS evil, *Ex*. 33. 4; *Ps*. 112. 7.
Luke 1. 19. show thee glad *t*. 8. 1; *Acts*
13. 32; *Rom*. 10. 15.
TIME mayest be found, *Ps*. 32. 6.
Ps. 37. 19. ashamed in evil *t*.
41. 1. in *t*. of trouble
69. 13. acceptable *t*. *Is*. 49. 8; 2 *Cor*.
6. 2.
89: 47. remember how short my *t*. is
Eccl. 3. 1.—8. a *t*. to every purpose—to
be born—die—plant—pluck up—
kill—heal, &c.
9. 11. *t*. and chance happen

Ezek. 16. 8. thy *t*. was a *t*. of love
Dan. 7. 25. a *t*. times and dividing of *t*.
12. 7. for a *t*. times and half
Luke 19. 44. knewest not *t*. of thy
John 7. 6. my *t*. is not yet come
Acts 47. 21. spent *t*. in nothing else
Rom. 13. 11. high *t*. to awake out of
1 *Cor*. 7. 29. *t*. is short
2 *Cor*. 6. 2. accepted *t*. day of salvation
Eph. 5. 16. redeem *t*. *Col*. 4. 5.
1 *Pet*. 1. 17. pass *t*. of sojourning
Rev. 10. 6. *t*. shall be no longer
12. 12. great wrath has short *t*.
14. for a *t*. times and half a *t*.

TIMES, *Ps*. 31. 15. my *t*. are in thy hand
Luke 21. 24. till *t*. of Gentiles be fulfilled
Acts 1. 7. not for you to know *t*.
3. 19. the *t*. of refreshing shall come
17. 26. determined *t*. before
1 *Tim*. 4. 1. in latter *t*. some depart
2 *Tim*. 3. 1. in last days perilous *t*.
Ps. 34. 1. bless Lord at all *t*.
62. 8. trust in Lord all *t*. ye people
Prov. 5. 19. her breasts satisfy thee at
all *t*.
17. 17. a friend loveth at all *t*.

TIN, *Num*. 31. 22; *Is*. 1. 25; *Ezek*. 22. 18.
TITHES, *Gen*. 14. 20; *Mal*. 3. 8; *Amos*
4. 4; *Matt*. 23. 23; *Luke* 18. 12.
TOGETHER, *Ps*. 2. 2; *Prov*. 22. 2.
Rom. 8. 28. things work *t*. for good
1 *Cor*. 3. 9. labourers *t*. with God
2 *Cor*. 6. 1. workers *t*. with him
Eph. 2. 5. quickened us *t*. with Christ
6. raised us up *t*. made us sit *t*. in C.
TOKEN, *Ps*. 86. 17. show me a *t*. for
Phil. 1. 28. evident *t*. of perdition
2 *Thess*. 1. 5. *t*. of righteous judgment
Job 21. 29. ye not know their *t*.
Ps. 65. 8. afraid at thy *t*. 135. 9.
Is. 44. 25. frustrateth *t*. of liars
TONGUE, *Ex*. 11. 7; *Josh*. 10. 21.
Job 5. 21. hide from scourge of *t*.
20. 12. hide wickedness under *t*.
Ps. 34. 13. keep thy *t*. from evil
Prov. 10. 20. *t*. of just as silver
12. 18. the *t*. of wise is health, 31. 26.
19. a lying *t*. but for a moment
15. 4. wholesome *t*. is tree of life
18. 21. death and life are in the *t*.
21. 23. keepeth *t*. keepeth soul
25. 15. soft *t*. breaketh bones
Is. 30. 27. his *t*. as a devouring fire
50. 4. Lord given me *t*. of learned
Jer. 9. 5. taught *t*. to speak lies
18. 18. let us smite him with *t*.
Jam. 1. 26. bridleth not *t*.
3. 8. *t*. can no man tame, 5.
1 *Pet*. 3. 10. refrain *t*. from evil
1 *John* 3. 18. let us not love in *t*. but in
Ps. 35. 28. my *t*. 39. 1, & 45. 1, & 51. 14,
& 71. 24, & 119. 172, & 137. 6, &
139. 4; *Acts* 2. 26.
TONGUES, *Ps*. 31. 20, & 55. 9; *Mark*
16. 17; *Acts* 19. 6; 1 *Cor*. 12. 10, 28,
& 14. 39.
TOOK me out of womb, *Ps*. 22. 9.
Phil. 2. 7. *t*. upon him the form of a
Heb. 10. 34. *t*. joyfully the spoiling of
TOPHET, *Is*. 80. 33; *Jer*. 7. 31, 32.
TORCH, *Zech*. 12. 6; *Nah*. 2. 3, 4.
TORMENT us before the time, *Matt*.
8. 29.

Luke 16. 23. to this place of *t.*
Rev. 18. 7. so much *t.* and sorrow
Luke 16. 24. I am *t.* in this flame
    25. comforted and thou art *t.*
Heb. 11. 37. destitute, afflicted, *t.*
Rev. 14. 11. smoke of *t.* ascendeth
TORN, *Hos.* 6. 1; *Mal.* 1. 13; *Mark* 1. 26;
TOSS, *Is.* 22. 18; *Jer.* 5. 22; *Jam.* 1. 6.
Ps. 109. 23. I am *t.* up and down
Prov. 21. 6. treasure by a lying tongue
    is a vanity *t.* to and fro
TOUCH not anointed, *Ps.* 105. 15.
Job 5. 19. in seven no evil *t.* thee
Matt. 9. 21. may but *t.* his garment
    14. 36. only *t.* hem of garment
Mark 10. 13. children that he should *t.*
Luke 11. 46. yourselves *t.* not burdens
John 20. 17. *t.* me not, for I am not yet
1 Cor. 7. 1. not to *t.* a woman
Col. 2. 21. *t.* not, taste not
1 Sam. 10. 26. hearts God hath *t.*
Job 19. 21. hand of God hath *t.* me
Zech. 2. 8. he that *t.* you *t.* apple of his
Luke 8. 45. who *t.* me
    46. *t.* me for virtue is gone out
1 John 5. 18. wicked one *t.* him not
TOWER high God is, *Ps.* 18. 2. & 144. 2.
Ps. 61. 3. strong *t. Prov.* 18. 10.
Song 4. 4. *t.* of David
    7. 4. *t.* of ivory of Lebanon
Is. 5. 2. built a *t. Matt.* 21. 33.
TRADITION, *Matt.* 15. 3; *Gal.* 1. 14;
    Col. 2. 8; 2 *Thess.* 2. 15, & 3. 6; 1
    Pet. 1. 18.
TRAIN, *Prov.* 22. 6; *Is.* 6. 1.
TRAITOR, *Luke* 6. 16; 2 *Tim.* 3. 4.
TRAMPLE, *Is.* 63. 3; *Matt.* 7. 6.
TRANQUILITY, *Dan.* 4. 27.
TRANSFORMED, *Rom.* 12. 2; 2 *Cor.*
    11. 14, 15.
TRANSGRESS commandments of the
    Lord, *Num.* 14. 41.
1 Sam. 2. 24. ye make Lord's people to *t.*
Neh. 1. 8. if ye *t.* I will scatter you
Ps. 17. 3. that mouth shall not *t.*
    25. 3. ashamed that *t.* without
Prov. 28. 21. for a piece of bread man *t.*
Matt. 15. 2. why do disciples *t.*
    3. why *t.* commandments of God by
Deut. 26. 13. not *t.* thy commandments
Josh. 7. 11. have *t.* my covenant
Is. 43. 27. teachers *t.* against me
Jer. 2. 8. pastors also *t.* against me
Ezek. 2. 3. they and their fathers have *t.*
Dan. 9. 11. Israel have *t.* thy law
Hos. 6. 7. they like men have *t.*
Hab. 2. 5. he *t.* by wine
1 John 3. 4. that committeth sin *t.* law
TRANSGRESSION, *Ex.* 34. 7. forgiving
    iniquity, *t.* and sin
Job 13. 23. make me know my *t.*
Ps. 19. 13. innocent from great *t.*
    32. 1. blessed whose *t.* forgiven
    89. 32. visit their *t.* with rods
    107. 17. fools because of *t.* are afflicted
Prov. 17. 9. he that covereth *t.* seeketh
Is. 53. 8. for *t.* of my people was
    58. 1. show my people their *t.*
Dan. 9. 24. to finish *t.* and make an end
Mic. 3. 8. declare to Jacob his *t.*
    6. 7. give first-born for my *t.*
Rom. 4. 15. where no law is no *t.*

1 John 3. 4. sin is the *t.* of law
Ex. 23. 21. not pardon *t.*
Lev. 16. 21. all their *t.* in all their sins
Job 31. 33. I covered my *t.*
    36. 9. showeth them their *t.*
Ps. 25. 7. remember not my *t.* against
    32. 5. I will confess my *t.*
    39. 8. deliver me from all my *t.*
    51. 1. blot out my *t.*
    3. I acknowledge my *t.*
    65. 3. our *t.* thou shalt purge
    103. 12. so far removed our *t.*
Is. 43. 25. he that blotteth out thy *t.*
    44. 22. out as thick cloud thy *t.*
    53. 5. he was wounded for our *t.*
Ezek. 18. 31. cast away all our *t.*
Gal. 3. 19. law added because of *t.*
Heb. 9. 15. for the redemption of *t.*
Ps. 51. 13. teach *t.* thy way
    119. 158. I beheld the *t.* and was
Prov. 13. 15. way of *t.* is hard
Is. 53. 12. he was numbered with the *t.*
TRAVAIL, *Is.* 53. 11; *Gal.* 4. 19, 27.
Job 15. 20. wicked *t.* with pain
Ps. 7. 14. he *t.* with iniquity
Is. 66. 7. before she *t.* she brought forth
Is. 13. 8; 21. 3; 42. 14. *t.* woman, *Hos.*
    13. 13; *Jer.* 31. 8; *Rev.* 12. 2.
TRAVEL, *Eccl.* 1. 13, & 2. 23, 26, & 4. 4,
    6, 8, & 5. 14; 2 *Thess.* 3. 8.
TRAVELLETH, *Josh.* 15. 20; *Prov.* 6.
    11, & 24. 34.
TRAVELLING, *Is.* 21. 13, & 63. 1.
TREACHEROUS. *Is.* 21. 2, & 24. 16.
Jer. 9. 2. assembly of *t.* men
TREACHEROUSLY, *Is.* 21. 2, & 24. 16,
    & 33. 1.
Is. 48. 8. thou wouldst deal *t.*
Jer. 3. 20. as wife *t.* departs from
    12. 1. are all happy that deal *t.*
Hos. 5. 7. dealt *t.* against the Lord. 6. 7.
Mal. 2. 15. let none deal *t.*
TREAD down wicked in place, *Job* 40. 12.
Ps. 7. 5. let him *t.* down my life
    44. 5. through thy name we *t.* down
Is. 1. 12. required this to *t.* my
    63. 3. *t.* them in my anger that
Hos. 10. 11. Ephraim loveth to *t.* out
Rev. 11. 2. holy city shall *t.* under
Deut. 25. 4. not muzzle ox that *t.* out
    the corn, 2 *Cor.* 9. 9; 1 *Tim.* 5. 18.
TREADING, *Is.* 22. 5; *Amos* 5. 11.
TREASURE, *Prov.* 15. 6, & 21. 20.
Deut. 28. 12. Lord opens his good *t.*
Ex. 19. 5. peculiar *t. Ps.* 135. 4.
Ps. 17. 14. fillest with thy hidden *t.*
Is. 33. 6. fear of the Lord is his *t.*
Matt. 6. 21. where your *t.* is there is
    12. 35. good man out of good *t.*
    13. 52. forth out of his good *t.*
    19. 21. shall have *t.* in heaven
Luke 12. 21. layeth up *t.* for himself
2 Cor. 4. 7. have *t.* in earthen vessels
Deut. 32. 34. sealed among my *t.*
Prov. 2. 4. searched for as hidden *t.*
    10. 2. *t.* of wicked profiteth nothing
    21. 6. getting *t.* by lying tongue
Matt. 6. 19. lay not up *t.* on earth
    20. lay up for yourselves *t.* in heaven
Col. 2. 3. in whom are hid all the *t.* of
Heb. 11. 26. greater riches than *t.* of
Rom. 2. 5. *t.* up wrath
TREE, *Gen.* 2. 16, 17, & 3. 22.

Ps. 1. 3. like *t.* planted by rivers
37. 35. spread himself like bay *t.*
52. 8. I am like green olive *t.*
Prov. 3. 18. she is a *t.* of life to
11. 30. fruit of righteousness is *t.*
Is. 6. 13. be eaten as teil *t.*
56. 3. eunuch say I am a dry *t.*
Jer. 17. 8. as a *t.* planted by waters
Matt. 3. 10. *t.* that bringeth not forth
7. 17. good *t.* bringeth forth good
12. 33. make *t.* good; *t.* known by
1 *Pet.* 2. 24. in his own body on *t.*
Rev. 2. 7. give to eat of *t.* of life
22. 2. *t.* of life which bear 12 mann
14. may have right to *t.* of life
Ps. 104. 16. *t.* of Lord are full of sap
Is. 61. 3. called *t.* of righteousness
Ezek. 47. 12. by river *t.* for meat
Mark 8. 24. see men as *t.* walking
Jude 12. *t.* whose fruit withered
TREMBLE at commandment of God
Ezra 10. 3.
Ps. 99. 1. Lord reigns, let people *t.*
Eccl. 12. 3. keepers of house *t.*
Jer. 5. 22. will ye not *t.* at my presence
10. 10. at his wrath earth *t.*
Dan. 6. 26. men *t.* and fear before
Jam. 2. 19. devils believe and *t.*
1 *Sam.* 4. 13. heart *t.* for ark of God
Ezra 9. 4. every one that *t.* at word of
Acts 24. 25. Felix *t.* and answered
TREMBLETH, *Job* 37. 1; *Ps.* 119. 120;
Is. 66. 2.
Deut. 28. 65. L. shall give thee a *t.* heart
Ps. 2. 11. serve God, rejoice with *t.*
Hos. 13. 1. Ephraim spake *t.*
Zech. 12. 2. make Jerusalem a cup of *t.*
1 *Cor.* 2. 3. in fear and in much *t.*
Eph. 6. 5. with fear and *t.* in singleness
Phil. 2. 12. work out salvation with *t.*
TRESPASS. To miss the mark, or to
err from right rule. To commit
any sin against God or man, *Lev.*
26. 40; *Ezra* 9. 6; 1 *Kings* 8. 31;
Matt. 18. 15; *Luke* 17. 3.
TRESPASSES, *Ezra* 9. 15; *Ezek.* 39. 26.
Ps. 68. 21. goeth on still in his *t.*
Matt. 6. 14. forgive men their *t.*
18. 35. if forgive not every one his *t.*
2 *Cor.* 5. 19. not imputing their *t.*
Eph. 2. 1. dead in *t.* and sins
Col. 2. 13. hath forgiven you all *t.*
TRIAL, *Job* 9. 23; *Ezek.* 21. 13; 2 *Cor.*
8. 2; *Heb.* 11. 36; 1 *Pet.* 1. 7, & 4. 12.
TRIBES, *Num.* 24. 2.
Ps. 105. 37. not one feeble among their *t.*
122. 4. whither *t.* go up to the *t.* of
Hab. 3. 9. according to oaths of *t.*
Matt. 24. 30. *t.* of earth mourn
Acts 26. 7. unto which promise our 12. *t.*
TRIBULATION when thou art in, *Deut.*
4. 30.
Judg. 10. 14. deliver you in *t.*
1 *Sam.* 26. 24. deliver me out of all *t.*
Matt. 13. 21. when *t.* or persecution
24. 21. then shall be great *t.*
29. immediately after *t. Mark* 13. 34.
John 16. 33. in world shall have *t.*
Acts 14. 22. through much *t.* enter
Rom. 2. 9. *t.* and anguish on every soul
5. 3. *t.* works patience, experience
8. 35. separate us from Christ, shall *t.*
12. 12. in hope patient in *t.*

2 *Cor.* 1. 4. comfort us in all *t.*
7. 4. exceeding joyful in all *t.*
1 *Thess.* 3. 4. we should suffer *t.*
2 *Thess.* 1. 6. accompany *t.* to them
Rev. 1. 9. brother and companion in *t.*
2. 9. 1 know thy works in *t.*
10. we shall have *t.* ten days
22. cast into great *t.* except they
7. 14. have come out of great *t.*
Rom. 5. 3. glory in *t.*
1 *Sam.* 10. 19. saved you out of great *t.*
Eph. 3. 13. faint not at my *t.*
2 *Thess.* 1. 4. patience in all *t.*
TRIBUTE, *Gen.* 49. 15; *Num.* 31. 28.
Prov. 12. 24. slothful be under *t.*
Matt. 17. 24. doth not your master pay *t.*
22. 17. it is lawful to give *t.* to
Rom. 13. 7. *t.* to whom *t.* is due
TRIMMED *Matt.* 25. 7; *Jer.* 2. 33.
TRIUMPH, 2 *Sam.* 1. 20; *Ps.* 25. 2.
Ps. 92. 4. I will *t.* in works of hands .
106. 47. give thanks *t.* in praise
2 *Cor.* 2. 14. causeth us to *t.* in Christ
Ex. 10. 1. Lord hath *t.* gloriously, 21.
TRIUMPHING, *Job* 20. 5; *Col.* 2. 15.
TRODDEN down strength, *Judg.* 5. 21.
Ps. 119. 118. *t.* down all that err
Is. 63. 3. I have *t.* wine-press alone
2 *Luke* 1. 24. Jerusalem shall be *t.* down
Heb. 10. 29. *t.* under foot Son of God
TROUBLE. Outward afflictions, 2 *Chr.*
15. 4; *Ps.* 60. 11; *Neh.* 9. 32.
Job 5. 6. neither doth *t.* spring
7. man is born to *t.* as sparks
14. 1. few days and full of *t.*
Ps. 9. 9. Lord is a refuge in times of *t.*
22. 11. *t.* is near and none to help
27. 5. in time of *t.* he will hide
37. 39. strength in time of *t.*
46. 1. God is a present help in *t.*
60. 11. giveth us help in *t.*
91. 15. I will be with him in *t.*
119. 143. *t.* and anguish take hold
143. 11. bring my soul out of *t.*
Prov. 11. 8. righteous delivered out of *t.*
12. 13. just shall come out of *t.*
Is. 26. 16. Lord, in *t.* they have visited
33. 2. our salvation in time of *t.*
Jer. 8. 15. looked for health, behold *t.*
14. 8. hope and S. thereof in *t.*
19. time of healing and behold *t.*
30. 7. even time of Jacob's *t.*
Dan. 12. 1. shall be a time of *t.*
1 *Cor.* 7. 28. such shall have *t.* in the
Ps. 88. 3. my soul is full of *t.*
25. 17. *t.* of my heart enlarged
34. 17. deliver them out of all their *t.*
71. 20. showed me great *t.*
TROUBLED, *Ex.* 14. 24. Lord *t.* host of
Ps. 30. 7. didst hide thy face and I was *t.*
77. 3. I remembered God and was *t.*
Is. 57. 20. wicked are like the *t.* sea
John 12. 27. now is my soul *t.*
14. 1. let not your hearts be *t.*
2 *Cor.* 4. 8. we are *t.* on every side, 7. 5.
2 *Thess.* 1. 7. to you who are *t.* rest
TROUBLETH, *Job* 23. 16. Almighty *t.*
1 *Kings* 18. 17. art thou he that *t.* Israel
Prov. 11. 17. *t.* his own flesh
29. he that *t.* his own house
Luke 8. 15. this widow *t.* me
Gal. 5. 10. he that *t.* you shall bear
TROUBLING, *Job* 5. 17; *John* 5. 4.

TRUE, *Gen.* 43. 11;   2 *Sam.* 7. 28.
Ps. 19. 9. judgments of Lord *t.* *Neh.* 9. 13.
   119. 160. thy word is *t.* from
Prov. 14. 25. *t.* witness, *Jer.* 42. 5.
Ezek. 18. 8. *t.* judgment, *Zech.* 7. 9.
Matt. 22. 16. we know thou art *t.*
Luke 16. 11. *t.* riches
John 1. 9. was the *t.* light
   4. 23. *t.* worshippers
   6. 32. *t.* bread from heaven
   7. 28. he that sent me is *t.*
   8. 14. my record is *t.*
   15. 1. I am the *t.* vine
2 *Cor.* 1. 18. as God is *t.* our word
   6. 8. as deceivers and yet *t.*
Phil. 4. 8. whatsoever things are *t.*
1 *John* 5. 20. know him that is *t.*
Rev. 3. 7. saith he that is *t.*
   15. *t.* witness
   19. was called faithful and *t.*
TRUMP, 1 *Cor.* 15. 52; 1 *Thess.* 4. 16.
TRUMPET, *Ex.* 19. 16; *Ps.* 81. 3.
Is. 27. 13. great *t.* shall be blown
   58. 1. lift up thy voice like a *t.*
Matt. 6. 2. do not sound a *t.* when
TRUMPETS, *Num.* 10. 2; *Josh.* 6. 4;
   Ps. 98. 6; *Rev.* 8. 13.
TRUST put in him, 1 *Chr.* 5. 20.
Job 4. 18. put not *t.* in servants, 15. 15.
   8. 14. his *t.* is a spider's web
Ps. 4. 5. put your *t.* in the Lord
   9. 10. know thy name put their *t.* in
   40. 4. blessed is man makes Lord his *t.*
   71. 5. thou art my *t.* from my
   141. 8. in thee is my *t.*
Prov. 22. 19. thy *t.* may be in the Lord
1 *Tim.* 6. 20. keep that committed to *t.*
Job 13. 15. though he slay me yet will I *t.*
Ps. 37. 3. *t.* in Lord and do good
   40. because they *t.* in him
   55. 23. bloody not live—I will *t.* in
   62. 8. *t.* in him at all times
   115. 9.—11. *t.* in the Lord O Israel
   118. 8. better to *t.* in Lord than put
   119. 42. for I *t.* in thy word
   125. 1. they that *t.* in the Lord shall
Prov. 3. 5. *t.* in the Lord with all thy
Is. 26. 4. *t.* in the Lord for ever
   50. 10. let him *t.* in name of the Lord
Jer. 7. 4. *t.* not in lying words
   8. 4. *t.* not in brother, friend, *Mic.* 7. 5.
Mark 10. 24. hard for them that *t.* in
2 *Cor.* 1. 9. should not *t.* in ourselves
Phil. 3. 4. whereof to *t.* in flesh
Ps. 22. 4. our fathers *t.* in thee
   28. 7. my heart *t.* in him but
   52. 7. *t.* in abundance of his riches
Luke 18. 9. certain which *t.* in themsel.
Eph. 1. 12. who first *t.* in Christ, 13.
Ps. 32. 10. that *t.* in the Lord mercy
   34. 8. blessed man that *t.* in him
   57. 1. my soul *t.* in thee
   84. 12. blessed is the man that *t.* in
   86. 2. save servants that *t.* in thee
Jer. 17. 5. cursed be man that *t.* in man
   7. blessed is man that *t.* in the Lord
1 *Tim.* 5. 5. widow indeed *t.* in God
Ps. 112. 7. heart fixed *t.* in the Lord
TRUTH, *Gen.* 24. 27; *Ex.* 18. 21.
Ex. 34. 6. abundant in goodness and *t.*
Deut. 32. 4. a God of *t.* without
Ps. 15. 2. speaketh *t.* in his heart

   25. 10. paths of Lord are mercy and *t.*
   51. 6. desirest *t.* in inward parts
   91. 4. his *t.* is thy shield and
   117. 2. his *t.* endures for ever
   119. 30. I have chosen way of *t.*
   142. thy law is the *t.*
   151. thy commandments are *t.*
Prov. 12. 19. lips of *t.* be established
   16. 6. by mercy and *t.* iniquity is
   23. 22. buy *t.* and sell it not
Is. 59. 14. *t.* is fallen in streets
   9. 3. they are not valiant in *t.*
Dan. 4. 37. all whose works are *t.*
Zech. 8. 16. speak every man *t.* to his
Mal. 2. 6. law of *t.* in his mouth
John 1. 14. full of grace and *t.* 17.
   8. 32. know the *t.* and the *t.* shall
   14. 6. I am the way, *t.* and life
   17. the Spirit of *t.*
   16. 13. he will guide into all *t.*
   17. 19. sanctify them through *t.*
   18. 37. bear witness to *t.*
   38. what is *t.*
Acts 26. 25. words of *t.* and soberness
Rom. 1. 18. hold *t.* in unrighteousness
   25. change *t.* of God into a lie
   2. 2. judgment of G. is according to *t.*
   20. hast form of *t.* in the law
1 *Cor.* 5. 8. unleavened bread of sincerity and *t.*
2 *Cor.* 13. 8. nothing against *t.* but for *t.*
Gal. 3. 1. should not obey *t.* 5. 7.
Eph. 4. 15. speaking *t.* in love, 25.
   21. taught by him as *t.* in Jesus
   5. 9. fruit of the Saviour is in *t.*
   6. 14. loins girt about with *t.*
2 *Thess.* 2. 10. received not love of *t.*
1 *Tim.* 3. 15. pillar and ground of *t.*
   6. corrupt, destitute of *t.*
2 *Tim.* 2. 18. concerning the *t.* have
   25. to the acknowledging of *t.*
   3. 7. never able to come to the knowledge of *t.*
   8. resist *t.* reprobates concerning the
   4. 4. turn away their ears from *t.*
Jam. 3. 14. glory not nor lie against *t.*
1 *Pet.* 1. 22. purified your souls in obeying the *t.*
2 *Pet.* 1. 12. established in present *t.*
1 *John* 1. 8. *t.* not in us
   5. 6. the Spirit is *t.*
Josh. 24. 14. in *t.* 1 *Sam.* 12. 24; *Ps.*
   145. 18; *Jer.* 4. 2; *John* 4. 24; 1
   Thess. 2. 13; 1 *John* 3. 18; 2 *John* 4.
Ps. 25. 5. thy *t.* 26. 3, & 43, 3. & 108. 4;
   John 17. 17.
TRY, *Judg.* 7. 4; *Job* 12. 11; *Jer.* 6. 27.
2 *Chr.* 32. 31. God left him to *t.* him
Job 7. 18. *t.* them in every moment
Ps. 11. 4. his eyelids *t.* children
   26. 2. *t.* my reins and heart
   139. 23. *t.* me and know my heart
Jer. 9. 7. I will melt and *t.* them
   17. 10. Lord search heart and *t.* reins
Lam. 3. 40. let us search and *t.* our
Dan. 11. 35. shall fail to *t.* them
Zech. 13. 9. I will *t.* them as gold
1 *Cor.* 3. 13. fire shall *t.* every man's
1 *Pet.* 4. 12. fiery trial is to *t.* you
1 *John* 4. 1. *t.* spirits for many false
Rev. 3. 10. to *t.* them that dwell
2 *Sam.* 22. 31. word of Lord is *t.* *Ps.*
   18. 30.

Ps. 12. 6. word of the Lord as silver *t.*
17. 3. thou hast *t,* me
66. 10. *t.* us as silver is *t.*
105. 19. until word of the Lord *t.* me
Jer. 12. 3. *t,* my heart toward thee
Dan. 12. 10. many shall be purified & *t.*
Heb. 11. 27. Abraham when he was *t.*
Jam. 1. 12. when he is *t.* he shall rece.
1 *Pet.* 1. 7. though it be *t.* with fire
Rev. 2. 2. hast *t.* them, found liars
10. into prison, that they may be *t.*
Rev. 3. 18. buy of me gold *t.* in fire
TRIEST, 1 *Chr.* 29. 17. know thou *t.*
Jer. 11. 20. thou *t.* reins and heart
20. 12. that *t.* righteous and seest
Ps. 7. 9. righteous God *t.* reins
11. 5. his eyes see, Lord *t.* righteous
Prov. 17. 3. pot for silver, Lord *t.* the
1 *Thess.* 2. 4. God who *t.* our hearts
Jam. 1. 3. *t.* of our faith worketh
TUMULT, *Ps.* 65. 7; 2 *Cor.* 12. 20.
TURN, from their sin, 1 *Kings* 8. 35.
2 *Kings* 17. 13. *t.* from evil ways
Job 23. 13. who can *t.* him
Prov. 1. 23. *t.* you at my reproof
Song 2. 17. *t.* my beloved
Is. 31. 6. *t.* to him from whom
Jer. 18. 8. if *t.* from their evil I will
31. 18. *t.* me and I shall be *t.*
Lam. 5. 21. *t.* us unto thee O Lord
Ezek. 3. 19. *t.* not from his wickedness
18. 30. *t.* yourselves from transgress.
31. *t.* yourselves and live, 33. 9, 11, &
14. 6; *Hos.* 12. 6; *Joel* 2. 12; *Zech.*
9. 12.
Zech. 1. 3. *t.* to me and I will *t.* to you
Mal. 4. 6. *t.* hearts of fathers to
Acts 26. 18. to *t.* them from darkness to
20. repent, *t.* to God. do works
2 *Pet.* 2. 21. to *t.* from holy command.
Chr. 30. 6. *t.* again, *Ps.* 60. 1, & 80. 3,
7, 19, & 85. 8; *Lam.* 3. 40; *Mic.* 7.
19; *Zech.* 10. 9; *Gal.* 4. 9.
Sam. 12. 20. *t.* aside, *Ps.* 44. *Is.* 30.
11; *Lam.* 3. 35; *Amos* 2. 7, & 5. 12.
s. 119. 37. *t.* away, *Song* 6. 5; *Is.*
58. 13; 2 *Tim.* 3. 5; *Heb.* 12. 25.
Deut. 4. 20. *t.* to the Lord, 30. 10; 2 *Chr.*
15. 4; *Ps.* 22. 27; *Lam.* 3. 40; *Hos.*
14. 2; *Joel* 2. 13; *Luke* 1. 16; 2 *Cor.*
3. 16.
URNED, *Ps.* 9. 17. wicked be *t.* into
30. 11. *t.* my mourning into dancing
119. 5. *t.* my feet to testimonies
53 6. *t.* every one to his own
63. 10. *t.* to be their enemy
r. 2. 27. *t.* their back to me, 32. 33.
8. 6. every one *t.* to own course
31. 18. *t.* me and I shall be *t.*
os. 7. 8. Ephraim is cake not *t.*
11. 8. my heart is *t.* within me
hn 16. 20. your sorrow shall be *t.* into
Thess. 1. 9. *t.* from idols to God
m. 4. 9. laughter be *t.* into mourning
Pet. 2. 22. dog is *t.* to his vomit
ut. 9. 12. *t.* aside, *Ps.* 78. 57; *Is.* 44.
20; 1 *Tim.* 1. 6. & 5. 15.
Kings 11. 3. *t.* away, *Ps.* 66. 20, & 78.
38; *Is.* 5. 25, & 9. 12, & 10. 4; *Jer.*
5. 25.
.44. 18. *t.* back, 78. 9, 41; *Is.* 42.
17; *Jer.* 4. 8; *Zeph.* 1. 6.
RNEST, *Job* 15. 13; *Ps.* 9. 3.

Ps. 146. 9. way of wicked *t.* upside
Prov. 15. 1. soft answer *t.* wrath
21. 1. Lord *t.* king's heart as rivers
Is. 9. 13. people *t.* not to him that
Jer. 14. 8. *t.* aside to tarry for a
Jam. 1. 17. with whom no shadow of *t.*
Jude 4. *t.* the grace of God into
TUTORS, *Gal.* 4. 2.
TWAIN, *Matt.* 5. 41, & 19. 5; *Eph.* 2. 15.
TWICE, *Gen.* 41. 32; *Ex.* 16. 22; *Num.*
20. 11; 1 *Kings* 11. 9; *Job* 33. 14, &
40. 5; *Ps.* 62. 11; *Mark* 14. 30.
Luke 18. 12. *t.* dead, *Jude* 12.
TWINKLINC, 1 *Cor.* 15. 52.

UNACCUSTOMED, *Jer.* 31. 18.
UNADVISEDLY, *Ps.* 106. 33.
UNAWARES, *Deut.* 4. 42; *Ps.* 35. 8;
Luke 21. 34; *Heb.* 13. 2; *Jude* 4.
UNBELIEVERS, *Luke* 12. 46; 2 *Cor.*
6. 14.
UNBELIEVING, *Acts* 14. 2; 1 *Cor.* 7.
14, 15; *Tit.* 1. 15; *Rev.* 21. 8.
Matt. 13. 58. did not many mighty
works because of their **UNBELIEF,**
17. 20.
Mark 6. 6. marvelled because of their *u.*
9. 24. I believe, help thou my *u.*
16. 14. upbraided them with *u.*
Rom. 4. 20. staggered not through *u.*
11. 20. because of *u.* they were broken
32. concluded them all in *u.*
1 *Tim.* 1. 13. I did it ignorantly in *u.*
Heb. 3. 12. lest there be in you an evil
heart of *u.*
19. not enter in because of *u.*
UNBLAMEABLE, *Col.* 1. 22; 1 *Thess.*
3. 13.
1 *Thess.* 2. 10. *u.* behaved ourselves
UNCERTAIN, 1 *Cor.* 14. 8; 1 *Tim.* 6. 17.
UNCIRCUMCISED, *Ex.* 6. 12, 30; *Jer.*
6. 10, & 9. 25, 26; *Acts* 7. 51.
UNCIRCUMCISION, *Rom.* 2. 25, 26,
27, & 3. 30, & 4. 10; 1 *Cor.* 7. 18,
19; *Gal.* 2. 7, & 5. 6, & 6. 15; *Col.*
2. 13, & 3. 11.
UNCLEAN, *Lev.* 5. 11, 13, 15; *Num.*
19. 13.
Lev. 10. 10. put difference between *u.*
Is. 6. 5. I am a man of *u.* lips
Lam. 4. 15. depart ye, it is *u.*
Ezek. 22. 26. not difference between *u.*
44. 23. to discern *u.* and clean
Hag. 2. 13. if one *u.* by dead body
Acts 10. 28. not call any common or *u.*
Rom. 14. 14. nothing *u.* of itself
1 *Cor.* 7. 14. else were your children *u.*
Eph. 5. 5. nor *u.* person hate any
UNCLEANNESS, *Num.* 5. 19; *Ezra*
9. 11.
Zech. 13. 1. opened for sin and *u.*
Matt. 23. 27. are within full of *u.*
Rom. 6. 19. members servants to *u.*
Eph. 4. 19. work all *u.* with greediness
5. 3. *u.* let it not once be named
1 *Thess.* 4. 7. not called us to *u.*
Ezek. 36. 39. save you from all *u.*
UNDEFILED in way, *Ps.* 119. 1.
Song 5. 2. my dove, my *u.* 6. 9.
Heb. 7. 26. holy, harmless, *u.*
13. 4. marriage is honourable, bed *u.*
Jam. 1. 27. pure religion *u.*
1 *Pet.* 1. 4. inheritance, incorruptible *u.*
UNDER their God, *Hos.* 4. 12.

Rom. 3. 9. all *u.* sin, 7. 14; *Gal.* 3. 22.
Rom. 6. 14. *u.* law, 15; 1 *Cor.* 9. 20;
    Gal. 3. 23, & 4. 4.
1 *Cor.* 9. 27. I keep *u.* my body
Gal. 3. 10. works of law *u.* curse
UNDERSTAND not speech, *Gen.* 11. 7.
Neh. 8. 7. caused people to *u.* 17.
Ps. 19. 12. who can *u.* his errors
    107. 43. shall *u.* loving-kindness of
    119. 100. I *u.* more than ancients
Prov. 2. 5. *u.* wisdom
    14. 8. *u.* his way, 20. 24.
    19. 25. *u.* knowledge
    28. 5. seek Lord *u.* all things
Is. 32. 4. heart of rash shall *u.*
Dan. 12. 10. wise shall *u.* wicked
1 *Cor.* 13. 2. and *u.* all mysteries
Ps. 139. 2. thou *u.* my thoughts
Acts 8. 30. *u.* thou what thou readest
1 *Cor.* 28. 9. *u.* all imaginations
Ps. 49. 20. in honour and *u.* not
Prov. 8. 9. plain to him *u.* 14. 6.
Jer. 9. 24. glory in that he *u.* me
Matt. 13. 29. heareth word *u.* it not
Rom. 3. 11. none that *u.* and seeks after
Ex. 31. 3. wisdom and *u.*
Deut. 4. 6. your wisdom and *u.*
1 *Kings* 3. 11. asked for thyself *u.*
    4. 29. God gave Solomon wisdom & *u.*
    7. 14. filled with wisdom and *u.*
1 *Chr.* 12. 32. men that had *u.* of
2 *Chr.* 26. 5. had *u.* in visions of
Job 12. 13. he hath counsel and *u.*
    20. he taketh away *u.* of aged
    17. 4. hid their hearts from *u.*
    28. 12. where is the place of *u.*
    28. to depart from evil is *u.*
    32. 8. Almighty gives them *u.*
    38. 36. hath given *u.* to heart
    39. 17. imparted to her *u.*
Ps. 47. 7. sing praises with *u.*
    49. 3. meditation of heart shall be of *u.*
    119. 34. give me *u.* and I shall
    99. more *u.* than my teacher
    104. through precepts I get *u.*
    130. it gives *u.* to the simple
    147. 5. his *u.* is infinite
Prov. 2. 2. apply thy heart to *u.*
    3. 5. lean not to thine own *u.*
    13. happy man that getteth *u.*
    4·5.with thy getting get *u.* 7.
    8. 1. doth not *u.*
    14. I am *u.* I have strength
    9. 6. go in the way of *u.*
    10. knowledge of holy *u.*
    11. 4. *u.* shall keep thee
    29. slow of wrath of great *u.*
    16. 22. *u.* is a well spring of life
    19. 8. keepeth *u.* shall find good
    21. 30. no *u.* nor counsel against *L.*
    23. 23. buy truth and buy *u.*
    24. 3. by *u.* a house established
    30. 2. I have not *u.* of man
Eccl. 9. 11. nor riches to men of *u.*—
Is. 11. 2. spirit of wisdom and *u.*
    3. make him of quick *u.* in
    27. 11. it is a people of no *u.*
    40. 28. is no searching of his *u.*
Jer. 51. 15. stretch out heaven by his *u.*
Matt. 15. 16. are ye also without *u.*
Mark 12. 33. love him with all *u.*
Luke 2. 47. astonished with his *u.*
    24. 45. then opened he their *u.*
Rom. 1. 31. without *u.* unthankful

1 *Cor.* 1. 19. brings to nothing *u.*
    14. 14. my *u.* unfruitful
    15. I will pray with the *u.*
    20. in malice children, in *u.* be
Eph. 1. 18. eyes of *u.* enlightened
    4. 18. having *u.* darkened
Phil. 4. 7. peace of God passeth *u.*
Col. 1. 9. filled with spiritual *u.*
    2. 2. riches of full assurance of *u.*
2 *Tim.* 2. 7. give thee *u.* in all
Ps. 111. 10. good *u. Prov.* 3. 4, & 13. 15.
Prov. 1. 5. a man of *u.* 10. 23, & 11. 12,
    & 15. 21, & 17. 27.
UNDERSTOOD, *Deut.* 32. 29. they
Ps. 73. 17. then *u.* I their end
Dan. 9. 2. *u.* by books number
Matt. 13. 51. have ye *u.* all these
John 12. 16. these things *u.* not his
1 *Cor.* 13. 11. when a child I *u.* as child
2 *Pet.* 3. 16. things hard to be *u.*
UNDERTAKE for me, *Is.* 38. 14.
UNDONE, *Is.* 6. 5; *Matt.* 23. 23.
UNEQUAL your ways, *Ezek.* 18. 25.
2 *Cor.* 6. 14. be not *u.* yoked together
UNFAITHFUL, *Prov.* 25. 19; *Ps.* 78. 57.
UNFEIGNED. Upright, sincere, and
    without dissimulation, 2 *Cor.* 6. 6;
    1 *Tim.* 1. 5; 2 *Tim.* 1. 5; 1 *Pet.* 1. 22.
UNFRUITFUL, *Matt.* 13. 22; 1 *Cor.*
    14. 14; *Eph.* 5. 11; *Tit.* 3. 14; 2 *Pet.*
    1. 8.
UNGODLY men, 2 *Sam.* 22. 5.
2 *Chr.* 19. 2. shouldst help the *u.*
Job 16. 11. hath delivered me to *u.*
    34. 18. to say to princes, ye *u.*
Ps. 1. 1. walk not in counsel of *u.*
    4. the *u.* are not so
    5. *u.* not stand in judgment
    6. way of *u.* men shall perish
    8. 7. hast broken teeth of the *u.*
    43. 1. plead my cause against the *u.*
    73. 12. these are *u.* that prosper
Prov. 16. 27. *u.* man diggeth up evil
    19. 28. an *u.* witness scorneth judg
Rom. 4. 5. God that justifieth the *u.*
    5, 6. Christ died for the *u.*
1 *Tim.* 1. 9. law not for righteous but *u*
1 *Pet.* 4. 18. where shall *u.* appear
2 *Pet.* 2. 5. flood on world of *u.*
    6. to them afterward live *u.*
    3. 7. judgment & perdition of *u.* men
Jude 4. *u.* men turn grace of God
    15. convince *u.* of their *u.* deeds
    18. scoffers walk after *u.* lusts
Rom. 1. 18. wrath revealed against *u.*
    11. 26. turn away *u.* from Jacob
2 *Tim.* 2. 16. increase to more *u.*
Tit. 2. 12. that denying *u.* and worldl
UNHOLY, *Lev.* 10. 10; 1 *Tim.* 1. 9;
    Tim. 3. 2; *Heb.* 10. 29.
UNITE, *Ps.* 86. 11; *Gen.* 49. 6.
Ps. 133. 1. brethren to dwell in *u.*
Eph. 4. 3. endeavour to keep *u.*
    13. till we all come to *u.* of faith
UNJUST deliver from, *Ps.* 43. 1.
Prov. 14. 7. hope of *u.* perisheth
    28. 8. by usury and *u.* gain increase
    29. 27. *u.* man is an abomination
Zeph. 3. 5. *u.* knoweth no shame
Matt. 5. 45. rain on just and *u.*
Luke 16. 8. L. commended *u.* stewa
    10. *u.* in least *u.* in much
    18. 6. hear what *u.* judge saith
    11. I am not as extortioners, *u.*

Acts 24. 15. resurrection of just and *u.*
1 *Cor.* 14. 2. to law before *u.* 6.
1 *Pet.* 3. 18. suffered just for *u.*
2 *Pet.* 2. 9. reserve *u.* for the day of
Rev. 22. 11. *u.* let him be *u.* still
Ps. 82. 2. will ye judge *u.*
Is. 26. 10. in uprightness will he deal *u.*
UNKNOWN God, *Acts* 17. 23; *Gal.* 1. 22.
1 *Cor.* 14. 2. speak in *u.* tongue, 4. 27.
2 *Cor.* 6. 9. *u.* and yet well known
UNLAWFUL, *Acts* 10. 28; 2 *Pet.* 2. 8.
UNLEARNED, *Acts* 4. 13; 1 *Cor.* 14.
    16, 23, 24; 2 *Tim.* 2. 23; 2 *Pet.* 3. 16.
UNLEAVENED, *Ex.* 12. 39; 1 *Cor.* 5. 7.
UNMERCIFUL, *Rom.* 1. 31.
UNMINDFUL, *Deut.* 32. 18.
UNMOVEABLE, 1 *Cor.* 15. 58.
UNPERFECT, *Ps.* 139. 16.
UNPREPARED, 2 *Cor.* 9. 4.
UNPROFITABLE talk, *Job* 15. 3.
Matt. 25. 30. cast *u.* servant into outer
Luke 17. 10. we are *u.* servants
Rom. 3. 12. altogether become *u.*
Tit. 3. 9. they are *u.* and vain
Philem. 11. was to thee *u.* but now
Heb. 13. 17. with grief is *u.* for you
UNPUNISHED, *Prov.* 11. 21, & 16. 5, &
    17. 5, & 19. 5, 9; *Jer.* 25. 29, & 30.
    11, & 46. 28, & 49. 12.
UNQUENCHABLE, *Matt.* 3. 12; *Luke*
    3. 17.
UNREASONABLE, *Acts* 25. 27; 2
    Thess. 3. 2.
UNREBUKEABLE, 1 *Tim.* 6. 14.
UNREPROVEABLE, *Col.* 1. 22.
UNRIGHTEOUS decrees, *Is.* 10. 1.
Is. 55. 7. the *u.* man his thoughts
Luke 6. 11. not been faithful in the *u.*
Rom. 3. 5. is God *u.* who taketh
1 *Cor.* 6. 9. *u.* shall not inherit kingdom
Heb. 6. 10. God is not *u.* to forget
Lev. 19. 15. do no *u.*
Ps. 92. 15. Lord is upright, no *u.* in
Jer. 22. 13. buildeth his house by *u.*
Luke 16. 9. friends of mammon of *u.*
John 7. 18. is true no *u.* in him
Rom. 1. 18. who hold truth in *u.*
    2. 8. obey not truth, but obey *u.*
    6. 13. members instruments of *u.*
9. 14. is there *u.* with God
Cor. 6. 14. what fellowship hath right-
    eousness with *u.*
Thess. 2. 10. deceivableness of *u.*
    12. but had pleasure in *u.*
Heb. 8. 12. I will be merciful to their *u.*
Pet. 2. 15. Balaam loved wages of *u.*
John 1. 9. cleanse us from all *u.*
    5. 17. all *u.* is sin, not to
UNRULY, 1 *Thess.* 5. 14; *Tit.* 1. 6, 10;
    Jam. 3. 8.
UNSAVOURY, *Job* 6. 6; *Jer.* 23. 13.
UNSEARCHABLE things doth, *Job* 5. 9.
    145. 3. his greatness is *u.*
Prov. 25. 3. heart of kings is *u.*
Rom. 11. 33. *u.* are his judgments
Eph. 3. 8. preach *u.* riches of Christ
UNSEEMLY, *Rom.* 1. 27; 1 *Cor.* 13. 5.
UNSKILFUL in word of righteousness,
    Heb. 5. 13.
UNSPEAKABLE, 2 *Cor.* 9. 15. & 12. 4;
    1 *Pet.* 1. 8.
UNSPOTTED, *Jam.* 1. 27.
UNSTABLE. Wavering, continually
    distracted, *Gen.* 49. 4; *Jam.* 1. 8.

2 *Pet.* 2. 14. beguiling *u.* souls
    3. 16. unlearned and *u.* wrest
UNTHANKFUL. The unthankful are
    persons without grace, or graceful-
    ness; who think they have a right
    to the services of all men, yet feel
    no obligation, and have no gratitude,
    Luke 6. 35; 2 *Tim.* 3. 2.
UNTOWARD generation, *Acts* 2. 40.
UNWASHEN, *Matt.* 15. 20; *Mark* 7. 2, 5.
UNWISE, *Deut.* 32. 6; *Hos.* 13. 13;
    Rom. 11. 14; *Eph.* 5. 17.
UNWORTHY, *Acts* 13. 46; 1 *Cor.* 6. 2.
1 *Cor.* 11. 27. eateth and drinketh *u.* 29.
UPBRAID, *Judg.* 8. 15; *Matt.* 11. 20;
    Mark 16. 14; *Jam.* 1. 5.
UPHOLD me with free Spirit, *Ps.* 51. 12.
Ps. 119. 116. *u.* me according to thy
Prov. 29. 23. honour *u.* humble
Is. 41. 10. I will *u.* thee with
    42. 1. my servant whom I *u.*
    63. 5. my fury it *u.* me
Ps. 37. 17. Lord *u.* the righteous
    41. 12. *u.* me in my integrity
    63. 8. thy right hand *u.* me
    145. 14. Lord *u.* all that fall
Heb. 1. 3. *u.* all by word of
UPRIGHT. A correct moral deport-
    ment, *Job* 1. 1.
Ps. 7. 10. *u.* in heart
    11. 7. pleasant countenance behold *u.*
    18. 23. I was *u.* before him
    25. with *u.* show thyself *u.*
    19. 13. I shall be *u.* and innocent
    25. 8. good and *u.* is the Lord
    37. 37. behold *u.* end of that
    112. 2. generation of *u.* shall be
    4. to the *u.* light ariseth in darkness
    140. 13. *u.* dwell in thy presence
Prov. 2. 21. *u.* shall dwell in land
    10. 29. Lord is strength to the *u.*
    11. 3. integrity of *u.* shall deliver
    20. *u.* in way are his delight
    12. 6. mouth of *u.* shall deliver
    13. 6. righteousness keepeth *u.*
    14. 11. tabernacle of *u.* shall flourish
    15. 8. prayer of *u.* are his delight
    28. 10. *u.* shall have good things in
Eccl. 7. 29. God made man *u.* but
Song 1. 4. the *u.* love thee
Ps. 15. 2. that walketh *u.* 84. 11; *Prov.* 2.
    7, & 10. 9, & 15. 21, & 28. 18; *Mic.*
    2. 7; *Gal.* 2. 14.
    58. 1. judge *u.* 75. 2.
Is. 33. 15. speaketh *u.* *Amos* 5. 10.
Deut. 9. 5. not for *u.* of heart
1 *Chr.* 29. 17. hast pleasure in *u.*
Job 33. 23. show to man his *u.*
Ps. 25. 21. let integrity and *u.* preserve
    143. 10. lead me to land of *u.*
Is. 26. 7. way of just is *u.*
    10. in land of *u.* he will deal unjustly
URIM and Thummim, *Ex.* 28. 30; *Lev.*
    8. 8; *Num.* 27. 21; *Deut.* 33. 8; 1
    Sam. 28. 6; *Ezra* 2. 63; *Neh.* 7. 65.
USE, *Rom.* 1. 26; *Eph.* 4. 29; *Heb.*
    5. 14.
1 *Cor.* 7. 31. *u.* this world as not abusing
Gal. 5. 13. *u.* not liberty for cloak
1 *Tim.* 1. 8. law is good if a man *u.* it
Tit. 3. 14. good works for necessary *u.*
Ps. 119. 132. as thou *u.* to do unto
1 *Cor.* 9. 15. I have *u.* none of these
USING, *Col.* 2. 22; 1 *Pet.* 2. 16.

USURP, 1 *Tim.* 2. 12.
USURY, *Ex.* 22. 25; *Lev.* 25. 36, 37;
Deut. 23. 19, 20; *Neh.* 5. 7, 10; *Ps.*
15. 5; *Prov.* 28. 8; *Is.* 24. 2; *Jer.*
15. 10; *Ezek.* 18. 8, 13, 17, & 22. 12;
Matt. 25. 27; *Luke* 19. 23.
UTTER, *Ps.* 78. 2, & 94. 4.
Ps. 106. 2. who can *u.* the mighty acts
2 *Cor.* 12. 4. not lawful for me to *u.*
Rom. 8. 26. groanings cannot be *u.*
Heb. 5. 11. things hard to be *u.*
UTTERANCE, *Acts* 2. 4. as Spirit gave
them *u.*
Eph. 6. 19. that *u.* may be given
Col. 4. 3. God would open door of *u.*
UTTERLY, *Deut.* 7. 2; *Ps.* 89. 33, &
119. 8, 43; *Song* 8. 7; *Jer.* 14. 19.

VAIL, *Gen.* 24. 65; *Song* 5. 7.
Is. 25. 7. destroy *v.* spread over all
Matt. 27. 51. *v.* was rent from top to
2 *Cor.* 3. 13. Moses put a *v.* over his
15. *v.* is on their heart
Heb. 6. 19. entered within the *v.*
10. 20. through *v.* that is his
VAIN, *Ex.* 5. 9, & 20. 7.
Deut. 32. 47. not *v.* thing for you
1 *Sam.* 12. 21. turn ye not after *v.* things
Job 11. 12. *v.* man would be wise
Ps. 19. 6. man walks in *v.* show
60. 11. *v.* is help of man, 108. 12.
119. 113. I hate *v.* thoughts
127. 2. it is *v.* to rise up early
Jer. 4. 14. how long *v.* thoughts
Mal. 2. 14. said it is *v.* to serve God
Matt. 6. 7. use not *v.* repetitions
Rom. 1. 21. *v.* in their imaginations
1 *Cor.* 3. 20. thoughts of wise are *v.*
Eph. 5. 6. deceive with *v.* words
Col. 2. 8. spoil you through *v.* philos.
Jam. 1. 26. man's religion is *v.*
1 *Pet.* 1. 18. from your *v.* conversation
Ps. 73. 13. cleansed heart in *v.*
89. 47. why made all men in *v.*
127. 1. labour in *v.* waketh in *v.*
Is. 45. 19. I said not, seek me in *v.*
49. 4. laboured in *v.* spent strength
Jer. 3. 23 in *v.* is salvation hoped for
Matt. 15. 9. in *v.* do they worship
Rom. 13. 4. beareth not sword in *v.*
1 *Cor.* 15. 58. labour is not in *v.*
2 *Cor.* 6. 1. receive not grace of G. in *v.*
Phil. 2. 16. not run in *v.* nor laboured
Jam. 4. 5. think you Scrip. saith in *v.*
VALIANT, *Song* 3. 7; *Is.* 10. 13.
Jer. 9. 3. they are not *v.* for truth
Heb. 11. 34. through faith waxed *v.* in
VALIANTLY, *Ps.* 60. 12, & 108. 13, &
118. 15, 16; *Num.* 24. 18.
VANITY, they followed, 2 *Kings* 17. 15.
Job 7. 3. to possess months of *v.*
16. for my days are *v.*
Ps. 12. 2. speak *v.* every one to his
24. 4. not lift up his soul to *v.*
39. 5. man at best altogether *v.*
11. surely every man is *v.*
62. 9. men of low degree are *v.*
94. 11. man's thoughts are *v.*
119. 37. turn from beholding *v.*
144. 4. man like to *v.* his days
8. whose mouth speaketh *v.* 11.
Prov. 22. 8. soweth iniquity shall reap *v.*
Eccl. 1. 2. *v.* of *v.* all is *v.* 14, & 3. 19, &
2. 1, & 4. 8, & 12. 8.

11. 10. childhood and youth are *v.*
Is. 5. 18. draw iniquity with cords of *v.*
40. 17. less than nothing and *v.*
41. 29. all *v.* wind and confusion
Hab. 2. 13. weary themselves from *v.*
Rom. 8. 20. made subject to *v.*
Eph. 4. 17. walk in *v.* of their mind
2 *Pet.* 2. 18. swelling words of *v.*
Ps. 31. 6. hate them regard lying *v.*
Jer. 10. 8. stock is a doctrine of *v.*
14. 22. can *v.* of Gentiles cause rain
Jonah 2. 8. that observe lying *v.* forsake
Acts 14. 15. turn from these *v.* to
VAPOUR. A watery exhalation raised
up by heat into the atmosphere,
Job 36. 27; *Ps.* 135. 7. Human life
is compared to a vapour, because
it is fleeting, uncertain, and soon
extinct, *Jer.* 10. 13; *Jam.* 4. 14.
See *Hos.* 6. 4.
VARIABLENESS. Subject to change,
Jam. 1. 17.
VARIANCE, disagreement, contention,
Matt. 10. 35; *Gal.* 5. 20.
VAUNT, *Judg.* 7. 2; 1 *Cor.* 13. 4.
VEHEMENT, *Song* 8. 6; 2 *Cor.* 7. 11.
VENGEANCE taken, *Gen.* 4. 15.
Deut. 32. 35. to me belongeth *v.* 41. 43;
Ps. 94. 1; *Rom.* 12. 19; *Heb.* 10. 30.
Ps. 58. 10. rejoice when he sees *v.*
99. 8. tookest *v.* of their inventions
Is. 34. 8. day of Lord's *v.* 61. 2; *Jer.* 51.
6, 11.
Jer. 11. 20. let us see thy *v.* 20. 12.
Luke 21. 22. these be days of *v. Is.* 63. 4.
2 *Thess.* 1. 8. in flaming fire take *v.*
Jude 7. suffering *v.* of eternal fire
VERILY. A term of affirmation, 2
Kings 4. 14. Of confidence and
assurance, *Ps.* 37. 3. Of asseveration, *Ps.* 73. 13. Of the greatest
certainty, *Gen.* 42. 21; *Jer.* 15. 11.
v. is often used by Christ, as well as
verily, verily, *John* 1. 51, & 3. 3, 5,
11, & 5. 19, 24, 25, & 6. 26.
VERITY, *Ps.* 111. 7; 1 *Tim.* 2. 7.
VERY. Truth, *Prov.* 17. 9; *Matt.* 24.
24; *John* 7. 26, & 14. 11; 1 *Thess.*
5. 23.
VESSEL, *Ps.* 2. 9; 32. 12; *Jer.* 18. 4.
Jer. 22. 28. *v.* wherein is no pleasure
48. 11. not been emptied from *v.* to *v.*
Acts 9. 15. a chosen *v.* to me
Rom. 9. 21. one *v.* to honour, and
22. *v.* of wrath fitted to destruction
23. riches of glory on *v.* of
2 *Cor.* 4. 7. treasure in earthen *v.*
1 *Thess.* 4. 4. possess his *v.* in sanctifica.
2 *Tim.* 2. 21. be a *v.* to honour
1 *Pet.* 3. 7. to wife as weaker *v.*
VEXED, *Job* 27. 2; *Ps.* 6. 2, 3, 10.
Is. 63. 10. rebelled and *v.* Holy Spirit
2 *Pet.* 2. 7. Lot *v.* with conversation
VIAL, *Rev.* 5. 8, & 16. 1, & 21. 9.
VICTORY thine, O Lord, 1 *Chr.* 29. 11.
Ps. 98. 1. hand and arm gotten him *v.*
Is. 25. 8. swallow up death in *v.*
Matt. 12. 20. send judgment unto *v.*
1 *Cor.* 15. 55. swallowed up in *v.*
55. O death, where is thy sting, O
grave where is thy *v.*
57. thanks to God who giveth *v.*
1 *John* 5. 4. this is *v.* that overcomer
VIGILANT. Watchful: ' Be vigilant

—be always watchful; never be off your guard; your enemies are alert, they are never off theirs. A believer's watchfulness is somewhat like that of a soldier on guard. A sentinel posted on the walls, when he discovers an hostile party advancing, does not attempt to make head against them himself, but informs his commanding officer of the enemy's approach, and leaves him to take the proper measures to repel the foe; so the Christian does not attempt to fight temptations in his own strength, his watchfulness lies in observing their approach, and in telling God of it by prayer, 1 *Tim.* 3. 2; 1 *Pet.* 5. 8.

VILE thy brother, *Deut.* 25. 3.
1 *Sam.* 3. 13. sons made themselves *v.*
2 *Sam.* 6. 22. I will yet be more *v.*
Job 40. 4. I am *v.* what shall I answer
Ps. 15. 4. in whose eyes *v.* person
Is. 32. 6. *v.* persons will speak
Jer. 15. 19. take precious from *v.*
Rom. 1. 26. gave them up to *v.* affections
Phil. 3. 21. who shall change *v.* body

VINE, 1 *Kings* 4. 25; *Mic.* 4. 4.
Deut. 32. 32. their *v.* is the *v.* of Sodom
Ps. 128. 3. wife as a fruitful *v.*

Jer. 2. 21. I had planted thee a noble *v.*
Hos. 10. 1. Israel is an empty *v.*
14. 7. revive and grow as *v.*
Matt. 26. 29. not drink of fruit of the *v.*
John 15. 1. I am the true *v.*
5. I am the *v.* ye are branches

VINEYARD, *Ps.* 80. 15; *Prov.* 24. 30.
Song 1. 6; *Is.* 5. 1, 7; *Matt.* 20. 1. & 21. 33; *Luke* 13. 6; 1 *Cor.* 9. 7; *Song* 8. 11, 12.

VIOLENCE. It denotes great sins, *Gen.* 6. 11; *Ps.* 11. 5; 55. 9. The fury of an enemy, *Jer.* 6. 7; 20. 8. The punishment of oppressors, *Prov.* 13. 2; *Lev.* 6. 2; 2 *Sam.* 22. 3.
Gen. 6. 11. the earth was filled with *v.*
Ps. 72. 14. redeem soul from *v.*
73. 6. *v.* covers them as garment
Hab. 1. 2. cry out to thee of *v.*
Matt. 11. 12. kingdom of heav. suffers *v.*
Luke 3. 14. do *v.* to no man
Heb. 11. 34. quenched *v.* of fire

VIRTUE, *Mark* 5. 30; *Luke* 6. 19.
Phil. 4. 8. if there be any *v.* think on
1 *Pet.* 1. 3. called us to glory and *v.*
5. add to faith *v.* and to *v.* knowledge
Prov. 12. 4. woman, 31. 10.

VISAGE, *Is.* 52. 14; *Lam.* 4. 8.

VISIBLE and INVISIBLE, *Col.* 1. 16.

VISION. The act of seeing. Also a "supernatural appearance," by which God revealed his will, *Acts* 9. 10, 12; 2 *Cor.* 12. 1. The vision was often in sleep, and sometimes by a temporary trance, *Is.* 1. 1.; 1 *Sam.* 3. 1; *Ps.* 89. 19; *Matt.* 17. 9; *Acts* 10. 19, & 16. 9.
Prov. 29. 18. where there is no *v.* people perish
Hab. 2. 2. write the *v.*
3. *v.* for an appointed time
Ezek. 13. 16. see *v.* of peace for
Ezek. 12. 10. I have multiplied *v.*

Joel 2. 28. young men see *v. Acts* 2. 17.
2 *Cor.* 12. 1. I will come to *v.* and

VISIT you, *Gen.* 50. 24, 25; *Ex.* 13. 19.
Job 7. 18. *v.* him every morning
Ps. 106. 4. *v.* me with salvation
Jer. 5. 9. shall I not *v.* for these
Lam. 4. 22. *v.* iniquity, *Jer.* 14. 10, & 23. 2; *Hos.* 2. 13, & 8. 13.
Acts 7. 23. *v.* his brethren, 15. 36.
15. 14. pleased God to *v.* Gentiles
Jam. 1. 27. to *v.* the fatherless and

VISITED, *Ex.* 3. 16. I have *v.* you and
Ps. 17. 3. thou hast *v.* me
Is. 26. 16. in trouble they *v.* thee
Matt. 25. 36. sick and in prison ye *v.* me
Luke 1. 68. *v.* and redeemed his people
78. day-spring from on high hath *v.* us

VISITEST, *Ps.* 8. 4, & 65. 9; *Heb.* 2. 6.
Ex. 20. 5. *v.* iniquity of fathers on children, 34. 7; *Num.* 14. 18; *Deut.* 5. 9.

VOICE is *v.* of Jacob, *Gen.* 27. 22.
Gen. 4. 10. *v.* of thy brother's blood
Ex. 5. 2. who is the Lord that I should obey his *v.*
Ps. 5. 3. my *v.* shalt thou hear in
18. 13. Highest gave his *v.* hail
42. 4. went to house of God with *v.* of
95. 7. if ye will hear his *v.*
103. 20. hearken to *v.* of his word
Eccl. 12. 4. rise up at *v.* of bird
Song 2. 14. let me hear thy *v.* 8. 13.
Is. 30. 19. gracious at *v.* of thy cry
50. 10. obeyeth *v.* of his servant
Ezek. 33. 32. song of one that hath a pleasant *v.*
John 5. 25. dead shall hear *v.* 28.
10. 3. sheep hear his *v.* 16. 27.
Gal. 4. 20. I desire to change my *v.*
1 *Thess.* 4. 16. descend with *v.* of archa.
Rev. 3. 20. if any man hear my *v.*

VOICES, *Acts* 13. 27; *Rev.* 4. 5, & 11. 19.

VOID of counsel, *Deut.* 32. 28.
Ps. 89. 39. made *v.* covenant of
119. 126. they have made *v.* thy law
Is. 55. 11. my word not return *v.*
Acts 24. 16. conscience *v.* of offence
Rom. 3. 31. do we make *v.* the law
1 *Cor.* 9. 15. make my glorying *v.*

VOLUME, *Ps.* 40. 7; *Heb.* 10. 7.

VOMIT, *Job* 20. 15; *Prov.* 23. 8, & 26. 11; *Is.* 19. 14; 2 *Pet.* 2. 22.

VOW Jacob vowed, *Gen.* 28. 20, & 31. 13; *Num.* 6. 2. & 21. 2, & 30. 2; 1 *Sam.* 1. 11; 2 *Sam.* 15. 7, 8.
Ps. 65. 1. to thee shall *v.* be performed
76. 11. *v.* and pay to the Lord
Eccl. 5. 4. a *v.* defer not to pay, 5.
Is. 19. 21. shall *v.* a *v.* to the Lord
Jonah 2. 9. I will pay that I have *v.*
Job 22. 27. shall pay thy *v.*
Ps. 22. 25. I will pay my *v.* before
50. 14. pay thy *v.* to most High
56. 12. thy *v.* O God are on me
61. 5. hast heard my *v.*
8. that I may perform my *v.*
Prov. 20. 25. after *v.* make inquiry
31. 2. son of my *v.* 1 *Sam.* 1. 11.
Jonah 1. 16. offered sacrifice & made *v.*

WAGES, *Jer.* 19. 13; *Ezek.* 29. 18.
Jer. 22. 13. neighbour's serv. without *w.*
Hag. 1. 16. earneth *w.* to put into
Mal. 3. 5. oppress hireling in his *w.*
Luke 3. 14. be content with your *w.*

Rom. 6. 23. *w.* of sin is death
WAIT till my change come, *Job* 14. 14
Ps. 25. 5. on thee I *w.* all day
   27. 14. *w.* on Lord, *w.* I say on Lord
   37. 34. *w.* on Lord and keep his
   62. 5. *w.* thou only on God
   104. 27. these *w.* on thee that
   130. 5. I *w.* for Lord, my soul doth *w.*
   145. 15. eyes of all *w.* on thee
Prov. 20. 22. *w.* on the Lord and he
Is. 8. 17. I will *w.* on the Lord that
   30. 18. will the Lord *w.* that he may be
   gracious; blessed are they that *w.*
   for him
   40. 31. *w.* on the Lord shall renew.
Lam. 3. 25. good to them that *w.*
   26. *w.* for salvation of the Lord
Hos. 12. 6. *w.* on God continually
Mic. 7. 7. I will *w.* for the God of my
Hab. 2. 3. *w.* for it, it will surely
Zeph. 3. 8. *w.* on me till I rise to
Luke 12. 36. men that *w.* for the Lord
Gal. 5. 5. through Spirit *w.* for hope
1 *Thess.* 1. 10. *w.* for his Spirit from
WAITED, *Gen.* 49. 18. I *w.* for thy
Ps. 40. 1. I *w.* patiently for the Lord
Is. 25. 9. our God we have *w.* for
   26. 8. way of thy judgments we *w.* for
   33. 2. be gracious to us, we *w.* for
Zech. 11. 11. poor of flock that *w.*
Mark 15. 43. *w.* for kingdom of God
1 *Pet.* 3. 20. long-suffering of God *w.*
WAITETH, *Ps.* 33. 20. our soul *w.* for
   the Lord, 40. 1.
Ps. 65. 1. praise *w.* for thee in Zion
   130. 6. my soul *w.* for the Lord
Prov. 8. 34. *w.* at posts of my doors
Is. 64. 4. prepared for him that *w.* for
Luke 2. 25. *w.* for the consolation of
Rom. 8. 23. *w.* for the adoption
1 *Cor.* 1. 7. *w.* for coming of our Lord
2 *Thess.* 3. 5. to a patient *w.* for Christ
WAKETH, *Ps.* 127. 1; *Song* 5. 2.
Ps. 77. 4. holdest mine eyes *w.*
WAKENETH, *Is.* 50. 4; *Joel* 3. 12.
WALK in my law, *Ex.* 16. 4.
Gen. 24. 40. the Lord before whom I *w.*
   17. 1. *w.* before me, and be perfect
Lev. 26. 12. I will *w.* among you
   21. if ye *w.* contrary—I *w.* contrary
Deut. 5. 33. *w.* in the ways of the Lord,
   8. 6, & 10. 12, & 11. 22, & 13. 5, &
   28. 9.
   13. 4. shall *w.* after Lord your God
Ps. 23. 4. though I *w.* through valley
   84. 11. no good thing from them that
   w. uprightly
   116. 9. I will *w.* before the Lord
   119. 3. do no iniquity they *w.* in this
Is. 2. 3. we will *w.* in his paths
   5. walk in the light of the Lord
   40. 31. shall *w.* and not faint
   50. 11. *w.* in light of your fire
Jer. 23. 14. they commit adultery and *w.*
Dan. 4. 37. those that *w.* in pride he is
Hos. 14. 9. just shall *w.* in them
Mic. 6. 8. *w.* humbly with thy God
Amos 3. 3. can two *w.* together
Zech. 10. 12. *w.* up and down in his
Luke 13. 33. I must *w.* to-day and
John 8. 12. followeth me shall not *w.* in
   11. 9. *w.* in day he stumbleth not
Rom. 4. 12. *w.* in steps of that faith
   6. 4. *w.* in newness of life

   8. 1. *w.* not after the flesh, but after
2 *Cor.* 5. 7. we *w.* by faith, not
   10. 3. though *w.* in flesh, not after
Gal. 6. 16. as many as *w.* according to
   this rule
Eph. 2. 10. good works that *w.* in
   4. 1. *w.* worthy of vocation
   5. 15. *w.* circumspectly, not as
Phil. 3. 17. mark them who *w.* so
Col. 1. 10. that ye might *w.* worthy
1 *Thess.* 4. 12. would *w.* worthy of God
   4. 1. how he ought to *w.* and please
1 *John* 1. 7. is we *w.* in the light
   2. 6. ought so to *w.* as he *w.*
3 *John* 4. that my children *w.* in truth
Rev. 3. 4. *w.* with me in white
   16. 15. lest he *w.* naked and see
   21. 24. nations of saved *w.* in light
Eccl. 11. 9. *w.* in way of thy heart
Is. 30. 21. this is the way, *w.* in it
John 12. 35. *w.* in light while ye have
Rom. 13. 13. let us *w.* honestly
Gal. 5. 16. *w.* in Spirit and not fulfil
   25. if live in Spirit let us *w.* in Spirit
Eph. 5. 2. *w.* in love as Christ loved us
   8. in Lord *w.* as children of light
Phil. 3. 16. let us *w.* by same rule
Col. 2. 6. received Christ, so *w.* in him
   4. 5. *w.* in wisdom towards them
WALKED, *Gen.* 6. 9. Noah *w.* with G.
Gen. 5. 22. Enoch *w.* with God and was
Ps. 55. 14. *w.* unto house of God in
   81. 12. *w.* after own counsel
   13. O that Israel had *w.* in my ways
Is. 9. 2. people that *w.* in darkness
2 *Cor.* 10. 2. as if we *w.* according to
   12. 18. *w.* we not in same spirit
Gal. 2. 14. they *w.* not uprightly
Eph. 2. 2. in time past we *w.* *Col.* 3. 7.
1. *Pet.* 4. 3. we *w.* in lasciviousness
WALKEST, *Ex.* 42. 2. when thou *w.*
   through fire
Rom. 14. 15. now *w.* thou not charitably
WALKETH, *Ps.* 15. 2. he that *w.* upri.
Ps. 39. 6. every man *w.* in vain show
Prov. 10. 9. *w.* uprightly, *w.* surely
   13. 20. *w.* with wise shall be
Is. 50. 10. *w.* in darkness and hath no
Jer. 10. 23. not in man that *w.* to direc
Mic. 2. 7. words do good to him that *w*
2 *Thess.* 3. 6. from every brother tha *w.*
1 *Pet.* 5. 8. *w.* about seeking whom
Rev. 2. 1. *w.* in midst of seven golden
WALKING, *Gen.* 3. 8. voice of Lord *w*
   in garden
Is. 57. 2. *w.* in his own uprightness
Jer. 6. 28. grievous revolters *w.* with
Mic. 2. 11. if a man *w.* in Spirit and
Luke 1. 6. *w.* in all commandments of L
Acts 9. 31. *w.* in fear of Lord and
2 *Cor.* 4. 2. not *w.* in craftiness
2 *Pet.* 3. 3. *w.* after own lusts, *Jude* 16
2 *John* 4. I found thy children *w.* in
WALL, *Ps.* 62. 3; *Prov.* 18. 11; *Son*
   2. 9. & 8. 9, 10; *Is.* 26. 1, & 60. 18
WANDER, *Num.* 14. 33; *Ps.* 119. 10
WANDERED, *Lam.* 4. 14; *Heb.* 11. 37
WANDERETH, *Prov.* 21. 16, & 27. 8
WANDERING, 1 *Tim.* 5. 13; *Jude* 13
Ps. 56. 8. thou tellest my *w.*
WANT. Extreme wretchedness, *Jo*
   30. 3; *Prov.* 15. 25; *Amos* 4. 6
   Luke 15. 14. *Deut.* 28. 48; *Job* 31. 1
Ps. 23. 1. the Lord is my shepherd,

shall not *w.*
34. 9. no *w.* to them that fear
Prov. 6. 11. thy *w.* as armed men, 24. 34.
2 *Cor.* 8. 14. a supply for your *w.*
Phil. 4. 11. not that I speak in respect of *w.*
Jam. 1. 4. entire *w.* nothing
WANTONNESS, Lasciviousness, carnal lusts, *Rom.* 13. 13; 2 *Pet.* 2. 18.
WAR, *Ex.* 13. 17, & 17. 16; *Ps.* 27. 3.
Job 10. 17. changes and *w.* are against
Ps. 18. 34. he teacheth my hands to *w.*
120. 7. I am for peace, they are for *w.*
Prov. 20. 18. with good advice make *w.*
Eccl. 8. 8. no discharge in this *w.*
Is. 2. 4. not learn *w.* any more, *Mic.* 4. 3.
Mic. 3. 5. they prepare *w.* against
2 *Cor.* 10. 3. do not *w.* after flesh
1 *Tim.* 1. 18. mightest *w.* a good
2 *Tim.* 2. 4. no man that *w.* entangleth
1 *Pet.* 2. 11. fleshly lusts *w.* against
Rev. 11. 7. beast shall make *w.* against
12. 7. there was *w.* in heaven
17. 14. these make *w.* with the Lord
19. 11. in righteousness doth judge make *w.*
Num. 21. 14. in book of *w.* of the Lord
Is. 46. 9. maketh *w.* to cease to
Matt. 24. 6. hear of *w.* and rumours of
Jam. 4. 1. whence come *w.* and
WARRING, *Is.* 37. 8; *Rom.* 7. 23.
WARFARE, *Is.* 40. 2; 1 *Cor.* 9. 7; 2 *Cor.* 10. 4; 1 *Tim.* 1. 18.
WARN, 2 *Chr.* 19. 10; *Acts* 10. 22.
Ps. 19. 11. by them is thy servant *w.*
Ezek. 3. 19. if thou *w.* wicked he turn not
33. 3. blow a trumpet and *w.* the
Matt. 3. 7. who hath *w.* you to flee
Acts 20. 31. I ceased not to *w.*
1 *Cor.* 4. 14. as my beloved sons I *w.*
1 *Thess.* 5. 14. brethren *w.* them that
Heb. 11. 7. Noah being *w.* of God
Jer. 6. 10. to whom I give *w.*
Col. 1. 28. teaching every man, *w.* every
WASH, *Lev.* 6. 27, & 14. 8, & 15. 16.
Job 9. 30. if I *w.* myself in snow
Ps. 26. 6. will *w.* my hands in innocency
51. 2. *w.* me throughly from mine
7. *w.* me, and I shall be whiter then
Is. 1. 16. *w.* you, make you clean
Jer. 2. 22. though thou *w.* with nitre
4. 14. *w.* thy heart from wicked
Luke 7. 38. *w.* his feet with tears
John 13. 5. he began to *w.* the disciples'
8. if I *w.* thee not thou hast no part
10. needed not save to *w.* feet
14. ought to *w.* one another's feet
Acts 22. 16. be baptized and *w.* away
Job 29. 6. I *w.* steps with butter
Song 5. 3. I *w.* my feet, how shall I
Is. 4. 4. *w.* away filth of daughters
Ezek. 16. 4. neither wast thou *w.* in
9. I thoroughly *w.* away thy blood
1 *Cor.* 6. 11. ye are *w.* justified
Heb. 10. 22. bodies *w.* with water
Rev. 1. 5. *w.* us from our sins in his
7. 14. *w.* robes and made white in
WASHING, *Eph.* 5. 26; *Tit.* 3. 5.
WASTE, *Ps.* 80. 13; *Matt.* 26. 8.
WASTED, *Luke* 15. 13, & 16. 1; *Gal.* 1. 13.
WASTETH, *Job* 14. 10; *Prov.* 19. 26.
WASTER, *Prov.* 18. 9; *Is.* 54. 16.
Is. 59. 7. *w.* and destruction, 60. 18.

WATCH, *Neh.* 4. 9; *Job* 7. 12.
Job 14. 16. dost thou not *w.* over my sin
Ps. 102. 7. I *w.* and am as a sparrow
141. 3. set a *w.* before my mouth
Je 1.44. 27. I will *w.* over them
Matt. 24. 42. *w.* for ye know not, 25. 13.
26. 41. *w.* and pray that ye enter not
Mark 13. 33. *w.* and pray, 37.
1 *Cor.* 16. 13. *w.* we stand fast in the
Col. 4. 2. *w.* in same with thanksgiving
1 *Thess.* 5. 6. let us *w.* and be sober
2 *Tim.* 4. 5. *w.* thou in all things
Heb. 13. 17. they *w.* for your souls
1 *Pet.* 4. 7. be sober *w.* unto prayer
Rev. 3. 3. if shalt not *w.* I will come
Matt. 24. 43. he would have *w.*
Ps. 37. 32. wicked *w.* righteous
Ezek. 7. 6. the end *w.* for thee
Rev. 16. 15. blessed is he that *w.*
WATCHES, *Ps.* 63. 6, & 119. 48; *Lam.* 2. 19.
Rev. 3. 2. be *w.* strengthen the things
Prov. 8. 34. *w.* daily at my gates
Luke 12. 37. blessed servants the Lord shall find *w.*
Eph. 6. 18. praying always *w.* with all
2 *Cor.* 6. 5. in *w.* 11. 27.
WATCHMAN, *Is.* 21. 11; *Ezek.* 3. 17, 33. 7.
WATCHMEN, *Song* 3. 3. & 5. 7; *Is.* 52. 8. & 56. 10. & 62. 6; *Jer.* 31. 6.
WATER, *Gen.* 49. 4; *Ex.* 12. 9, & 17. 6.
2 *Sam.* 14. 14. we are as *w.* spilt
Job 15. 16. drinketh up iniquity like *w.*
Ps. 22. 14. am poured out like *w.*
Is. 12. 3. draw *w.* out of the wells of
27. 3. I will *w.* it every moment
30. 20. through the Lord give you *w.*
41. 17. poor seek *w.* and find none
58. 11. shalt be like a spring of *w.*
Lam. 1. 16. mine eye runneth with *w.*
Ezek. 36. 25. sprinkle clean *w.* on
Amos 8. 11. not thirst for *w.* but
Matt. 3. 11. I baptize you with *w.*
10. 42. cup of cold *w.* in name of a
Luke 16. 24. dip tip of finger in *w.*
John 3. 5. except man be born of *w.*
23. baptized because of much *w.* there
4. 14. be in him a well of *w.*
7. 38. flow rivers of running *w.*
19. 34. came out *w.* and blood
Acts 8. 34. both went down into *w.*
10. 47. can any forbid *w.* that
Eph. 5. 26. cleanse it with washing of *w.*
1 *John* 5. 6. came by *w.* and blood
8. three bear witness, spirit, *w.* and
Jude 12. clouds without *w.* carried
Rev. 7. 17. lead them to living fountains of *w.*
21. 6. fountain of *w.* of life, 22. 1.
22. 17. let him take the *w.* of life
Ps. 23. 2. leadeth me beside still *w.*
69. 1. *w.* are come into my soul, 2.
124. 4. *w.* had overwhelmed us
Prov. 5. 15. draw *w.* out of thine own
9. 17. stolen *w.* are sweet
Eccl. 11. 1. cast bread on *w.* shalt
Song 4. 15. fountain of gardens, well of living *w.*
Is. 32. 20. that sow beside all *w.*
33. 16. bread given him his *w.* shall
35. 6. in the wilderness *w.* break out
54. 9. this is as the *w.* of Noah
55. 1. come ye to *w.* buy wine

Jer. 2. 13. fountain of living *w.* 17. 13.
  9. 1. O that my head were *w.*
Hab. 2. 14. knowledge of the Lord as *w.*
  cover the sea, *Is.* 11. 9.
Zech. 14. 8. living *w.* go out of Jerusalem
Rev. 1. 14. many *w.* 14. 2, & 17. 1, 15,
  & 19. 6.
Prov. 11. 25. watereth shall be *w.*
Is. 58. 11. soul like *w.* garden
1 *Cor.* 3. 6. I planted, Apollos *w.* 7.
Ps. 42. 7. at noise of thy *w.*-spouts
WAX, *Ex.* 32. 10, 11, 22; *Ps.* 22. 14. &
  68. 2, & 97. 5; *Matt.* 24. 12; *Luke*
  12. 33; 1 *Tim.* 5. 11; 2 *Tim.* 3. 13.
WAY, *Ex.* 13. 21, & 23. 20, & 32. 8.
1 *Sam.* 12. 23. teach you good & right *w.*
1 *Kings* 2. 2. I go *w.* of all earth
Ezra 8. 21. seek of him a right *w.*
Ps. 1. 6. Lord knoweth the *w.* of the
  2. 12. lest ye perish from *w.*
  49. 13. this their *w.* is their folly
  67. 2. that thy *w.* may be known
  78. 50. made a *w.* to his anger
  119. 30. I have chosen the *w.* of truth
  32. *w.* of thy commandments
  104. I hate every false *w.*
Prov. 2. 8. Lord preserveth the *w.* of his
  10. 29. *w.* of the Lord is strength
  14. 12. a *w.* seems right to man, 16. 25.
  15. 9. *w.* of wicked is an abomination
  24. *w.* of life is above to wise
Eccl. 11. 5. knoweth not *w.* of Spirit
Is. 26. 7. *w.* of just is upright, 8.
  30. 21. this is *w.* walk ye in it
  35. 8. an high *w.* and *w.* called *w.* of
  40. 3. prepare *w.* of the Lord, *Luke* 3. 4.
  43. 19. make *w.* in wilderness, 16.
  59. 8. *w.* of peace they know not
Jer. 6. 16. where is good *w.* and walk
  10. 23. *w.* of man not in himself
  21. 8. set before you *w.* of life and *w.*
  32. 39. give one heart, one *w.*
  50. 5. ask *w.* to Zion with faces
Amos 2. 7. turn aside *w.* of meek
Mal. 3. 1. shall prepare the *w.* before
Matt. 7. 13. broad is *w.* to destruction
  14. narrow is the *w.* that leadeth unto
  22. 16. teachest *w.* of God in truth
John 1. 23. make straight *w.* of Lord
  14. 4. the *w.* ye know
  6. I am the *w.* truth and life
Acts 16. 17. servants of God show us *w.*
  18. 25. instructed in *w.* of Lord, 26.
1 *Cor.* 10. 13. with temptation make *w.*
  12. 31. I will show unto you a more
  excellent *w.*
2 *Pet.* 2. 2. *w.* of truth evil spoken
1 *Kings* 19. 32. bring his *w.* upon his
Job 17. 9. righteous shall hold on his *w.*
Ps. 18. 30. as for God, his *w.* is perfect
  37. 23. Lord delighteth in his *w.*
  34. wait on Lord, keep his *w.*
  119. 9. young man cleanse his *w.*
Prov. 14. 8. prudent to understand *w.*
  16. 9. man's heart deviseth his *w.*
Is. 55. 7. let wicked forsake his *w.* and
Ps. 25. 8. teach sinners in the *w.*
  119. 14. I rejoiced in the *w.* of thy
  139. 24. lead me in *w.* everlasting
Is. 26. 8. in *w.* of thy judgments we
Matt. 5. 25. agree with adversary while
  in the *w.*
  21. 32. John came in *w.* of righteous.
Luke 1. 79. guide feet in *w.* of peace

Job 40. 19. he is chief of *w.* of God
Ps. 84. 5. in whose heart are the *w.* of
Prov. 3. 17. her *w.* are *w.* of pleasant.
  5. 21. *w.* of man are before the Lord
  16. 2. the *w.* of a man are clean in his
  7. when a man's *w.* pleasoth Lord
Jer. 7. 3. amend your *w.* and doings
Lam. 1. 4. *w.* of Zion do mourn
  3. 4. let us search and try our *w.*
Deut. 32. 4. his *w. Ps.* 145. 17; *Is.* 2. 3;
  Mic. 4. 2; *Rom.* 11. 33.
Ps. 119. 5. my *w.* 26. 59, 168, & 39. 1;
  Prov. 23. 26; *Is.* 55. 8, & 49. 11.
Prov. 14. 14. own *w.* *Is.* 53. 6, & 58. 13.
  & 66. 3; *Ezek.* 36. 31, 32.
Job 21. 14. thy *w. Ps.* 25. 4. & 91. 11;
  Prov. 3. 6, & 4. 26;. *Is.* 63. 17; *Ezek.*
  16. 62; *Dan.* 5. 23; *Rev.* 15. 3.
WAYFARING, *Is.* 35. 8; *Jer.* 14. 8.
WEAK, 2 *Chr.* 15. 7; *Job* 4. 3.
Is. 35. 3. strengthen ye *w.* hands
Ezek. 16. 30. how *w.* is thy heart
Matt. 26. 41. spirit is willing but flesh *w.*
Rom. 4. 19. Abraham being not *w.* in
  14. 1. that is *w.* in faith receive
1 *Cor.* 4. 10. we are *w.* ye strong
  9. 22. to the *w.* I became as *w.*
  11. 30. for this cause many are *w.*
2 *Cor.* 11. 29. who is *w.* and I am not *w.*
  12. •10. when I am *w.* then am I
1 *Thess.* 5. 14. support the *w.*
WEAKEN, *Is.* 14. 12; *Ps.* 102. 23; *Job*
  12. 21.
WEAKER, 2 *Sam.* 3. 1; 1 *Pet.* 3. 7.
WEAKNESS, 1 *Cor.* 1. 25, & 2. 3, & 15.
  43; 2 *Cor.* 12. 9, & 13. 4; *Heb.* 11. 43.
WEALTH, *Gen.* 34. 29; *Deut.* 8. 17.
Deut. 8. 18. L. giveth power to get *w.*
Job 21. 13. spend their days in *w.*
Ps. 49. 6. that trust in their *w.*
  10. die and leave their *w.*
  112. 3. *w.* and riches in his house
Prov. 10. 15. rich man's *w.* is his strong
  13. 11. *w.* got by vanity shall be
  22. *w.* of sinners is laid up for
  19. 4. *w.* maketh many friends
1 *Cor.* 10. 24. seek every man another's
  w.
WEANED, *Ps.* 131. 2; *Is.* 11. 8, & 28. 9.
WEAPON, *Is.* 13. 5, & 54. 17; 2 *Cor.* 10. 4.
WEAR, *Deut.* 22. 5, 11; *Dan.* 7. 25;
  Matt. 11. 8; *Jam.* 2. 3; 1 *Pet.* 3. 3.
WEARY of my life, *Gen.* 27. 46.
Job 3. 17. there *w.* be at rest
  10. 1. my soul is *w.* of life, *Jer.* 4. 31.
Prov. 3. 11. neither be *w.* of his
Is. 7. 13. *w.* men will ye *w.* my God
  40. 28. Lord fainteth not neither is *w.*
  31. they that wait upon the Lord shall
  run and not be *w.*
Is. 43. 22. been *w.* of me, O Israel
  50. 4. speak word in season to *w.*
Jer. 6. 11. *w.* withholding in, 20. 9.
  9. 5. *w.* themselves to commit iniquity
  15. 6. I am *w.* with repenting
  31. •25. I have satiated every *w.* soul
Gal. 6. 9. not *w.* in well-doing, 2 *Thess.*
  3. 13.
WEARIED, *Is.* 43. 24, & 57. 10; *Jer.*
  12. 5; *Ezek.* 24. 12; *Mic.* 6. 3;
  Mal. 2. 17; *John* 4. 6; *Heb.* 12. 3.
WEARINESS, *Eccl.* 12. 12; *Mal.* 1. 13.
Job 7. 3. *w.* nights appointed
WEB, *Job* 8. 14; *Is.* 59. 5, 6.

WEDDING, *Matt.* 22. 8, 3, 11; *Luke* 14. 8.

WEEK, *Dan.* 9. 27; *Matt* 28. 1; *Luke* 18. 12; *Acts* 20. 7; 1 *Cor.* 16. 2.

WEEKS, *Jer.* 5. 24; *Dan.* 9. 24.—26, & 10. 2.

WEEP, *Job* 30. 25; *Is.* 30. 19, & 33. 7; *Jer.* 9. 1, & 13. 17.

Luke 6. 23. blessed are ye that *w.*
23. 28. *w.* not for me, but *w.* for
Acts 21. 13. what mean ye to *w.*
Rom. 12. 15. *w.* with them that *w.*
1 *Cor.* 7. 30. as they that *w.* as though
Jam. 5. 1. rich men *w.* and howl

WEEPETH, *Ps.* 126. 6; *Lam.* 1. 2.

1 *Sam.* 1. 8. why *w. John* 20. 13, 15.
Ps. 30. 5. *w.* may endure for a night
Is. 22. 12. Lord call to *w.* mourning
Jer. 31. 9. come with *w.* and supplica.
Joel 2. 12. turn to me with *w.*
Mal. 2. 13. covering altar of L. with *w.*
Matt. 8. 12. *w.* and gnashing of teeth, 22. 13. & 24. 51. & 25. 30.

WEIGH the paths of the just, *Is.* 26. 7.
Job 31. 6. let me be *w.* in even balances
Prov. 16. 2. Lord *w.* the spirits
Dan. 5. 27. thou art *w.* in balances
Prov. 11. 1. just *w.* his delight
16. 11. just *w.* and balances are his
2 *Cor.* 4. 17. more exceeding & eternal *w.*
Heb. 12. 1. laying aside every *w.*
Lev. 19. 36. just balances, just *w.*
Deut. 25. 13. divers *w. Prov.* 20. 10, 23.
Matt. 23. 23. omitted *w.* matters

WELL, *Ps.* 84. 6; *Prov.* 5. 15. & 10. 11; *Song* 4. 15; *Is.* 12. 3; *John* 4. 14; 2 *Pet.* 2. 17.

Gen. 4. 7. if doest *w.* be accepted
Ex. 1. 20. dealt *w.* with midwives
Ps. 119. 65. dealt *w.* with thy servant; 128. 2. it shall be *w.* with thee
Eccl. 8. 12. shall be *w.* with them that;
Is. 3. 10. say to righteous it shall be *w.*
Rom. 2. 7. *w.* doing, *Gal.* 6. 9: 2 *Thess.* 3. 13; 1 *Pet.* 2. 15, & 3. 17. & 4. 19.

WENT, *Ps.* 42. 4, & 119. 67; *Matt.* 21. 30.

WEPT, *Neh.* 1. 4; *Ps.* 69. 10;

Matt. 26. 75; *Luke* 19. 41; *John* 11. 35.

WHEAT, *Ps.* 81. 16; *Prov.* 27. 22; *Song* 7. 2.

Jer. 12. 13. sown *w.* reap thorns
23. 28. what is chaff to the *w.*
Amos 8. 5. sabbath gone, set forth *w.*
Matt. 3. 12. gather *w.* into garner
Luke 22. 31. may sift you as *w.*
John 12. 24. except corn of *w.* fall into

WHEEL, *Ps.* 83. 13; *Prov.* 20. 26.
Ezek. 1. 16. *w.* in the midst of *w.* 10. 10.
10. 13. was cried to them, O *w.*

WHEELS, *Ex.* 14. 25; *Judg.* 5. 28; *Ezek.* 1. 16, & 10. 19; *Dan.* 7. 9; *Nah.* 3. 2.

WHET, *Deut.* 32. 41; *Ps.* 7. 12, & 64. 3.

WHISPERER separateth, *Prov.* 16. 28.

WHIT, *John* 7. 23, & 13. 10; 2 *Cor.* 11. 5.

WHITE, *Lev.* 13. 3, 4; *Num.* 12. 10.
Job 6. 6. any taste in *w.* of an egg
Ps. 68. 14. *w.* as snow, *Dan.* 7. 9.
Eccl. 9. 8. garments be always *w.*
Song 5. 10. my beloved is *w.* and ruddy
Is. 1. 18. sins shall be *w.* as snow
Dan. 11. 35. fall to make them *w.*
14. 10. purified and made *w.*
Matt. 17. 2. his raiment was *w.* as the

Rev. 2. 7. give him a *w.* stone
3. 4. walk with me in *w.* raiment, 5. 18, & 4. 4, & 7. 9, 13, & 15. 6, & 19. 8, 14.

WHITED, *Matt.* 23. 27; *Acts* 23. 3.

WHITER, *Ps.* 51. 7; *Lam.* 4. 7.

WHOLE. To be sound *Josh.* 5. 8; *Ps.* 9. 1, & 119. 10; *Is.* 54. 5; *Mic.* 4. 13; *Zech.* 4. 14; *Matt.* 16. 26; *Mark* 5. 28; *Eph.* 6. 11; 1 *John* 2. 2, & 5. 19.

Job 5. 18. he woundeth, and his hands make *w.*
Matt. 9. 12. *w.* need not a physician
Mark 5. 34. thy faith hath made *w.* 10. 52; *Luke* 8. 48, & 17. 19.
John 5. 4. made *w.* of whatsoever
6. wilt thou be made *w.*
14. art made *w.*
Acts 9. 34. Jesus Christ maketh thee *w.*

WHOLLY, *Jer.* 46. 28; 1 *Thess.* 5. 23; 1 *Tim.* 4. 15.

WHOLESOME, *Prov.* 15. 4; 1 *Tim.* 6. 3.

WHORE. Idolatrous worship, 1 *Chr.* 5. 25; *Ezek.* 16. & 23. The popish church, *Rev.* 17. 1. *Lev.* 19. 29, & 21. 7, 9; *Deut.* 22. 21, & 23. 17, 18; *Prov.* 23. 27; *Ezek.* 16. 28; *Rev.* 17. 1, 16.

WHOREDOM, *Jer.* 3. 9; *Ezek.* 16. 33; *Hos.* 2. 2, & 4. 11, 12, & 5. 3, 4.

WHOREMONGER, *Eph.* 5. 5; 1 *Tim.* 1. 10; *Heb.* 13. 4; *Rev.* 21. 8, & 22. 15.

WICKED, *Ex.* 23. 7; *Deut.* 15. 9, & 25. 1.
Gen. 18. 25. wilt destroy righte. with *w.*
1 *Sam.* 2. 9. *w.* shall be silent in
Job 21. 30. *w.* is reserved to the day of
34. 18. say to a king, thou art *w.*
Ps. 7. 11. G. is angry with *w.* every day
9. 17. *w.* be turned into hell
11. 6. on *w.* he will rain snares
58. 3. *w.* estranged from whom
119. 155. salvation far from *w.*
145. 20. all the *w.* shall be destroyed
Prov. 11. 5. the *w.* shall fall by his own
21. *w.* not be unpunished, 31.
21. 12. God overthrows the *w.*
28. 1. *w.* flee when none pursueth
Eccl. 7. 17. be not overmuch *w.*
Is. 55. 7. let *w.* forsake his way
57. 20. *w.* like troubled sea
Jer. 17. 9. heart is desperately *w.*
25. 31. he will give *w.* to sword
Ezek. 3. 18. warn the *w.* from *w.* way
Dan. 12. 10. *w.* shall do *w.*
Gen. 19. 7. do not so *w. Neh.* 9. 33.
1 *Sam.* 12. 25. if ye still do *w.*
Job 13. 7. will ye speak *w.* for God
Ps. 18. 21. *w.* departed from God
Gen. 6. 5. God saw *w.* was great
39. 9. how can I do this great *w.*
1 *Sam.* 24. 13. *w.* proceedeth from *w.*
Job 4. 8. that sow *w.* reap same
Ps. 7. 9. let *w.* of *w.* come to end
45. 7. lovest righteousness & hatest *w.*
Prov. 8. 7. *w.* is an abomination to me
10. 2. treasures of *w.* profit nothing
13. 6. *w.* overthroweth sinners
Eccl. 8. 8. neither shall *w.* deliver those
Is. 9. 18. *w.* burneth as fire, shall devour
Jer. 2. 19. own *w.* shall correct thee
4. 14. O Jerusalem wash thy heart from *w.*
14. 20. we acknowledge our *w.*
Hos. 10. 13. ye have plowed *w.*

Acts 8. 22. repent of this thy *w.*
1 *John* 5. 19. whole world lieth in *w.*
WIDE, *Deut.* 15. 8, 11; *Ps.* 35. 21, & 81.
    10; *Prov.* 13. 3; *Matt.* 7. 13.
WIDOW, *Mark* 12. 42; 1 *Tim.* 5. 5;
    Deut. 10. 18; *Ps.* 146. 9; *Luke* 18.
    3, 5.
WIDOWS, *Ps.* 68. 5; *Jer.* 49. 11; *Matt.*
    23. 14; 1 *Tim.* 5. 3; *Jam.* 1. 27.
WIFE, *Ex.* 20. 17; *Lev.* 21. 13.
Prov. 5. 18. rejoice with *w.* of youth
    18. 22. that findeth a *w.* findeth a
    19. 14. a prudent *w.* is from the Lord
Eccl. 9. 9. live joyfully with the *w.* of
Hos. 12. 12. Israel served for *w.* and
Mal. 2. 15. none deal treacherously
    against *w.* of his youth
Luke 17. 32. remember Lot's *w.*
Eph. 5. 33. every man love his *w.* as
Rev. 19. 7. *w.* made herself ready

    21. 9. show thee the bride, Lamb's *w.*
WIVES, 1 *Cor.* 7. 29; *Eph.* 5. 25, 28, 33;
    Col. 3. 18, 19; 1 *Tim.* 3. 11, 1 *Pet.*
    3. 1, 7.
WILDERNESS, *Deut.* 32. 10; *Prov.* 21.
    19; *Song* 3. 6. & 8. 5; *Is.* 35. 1. 6, &
    41. 18, 19, & 42. 11, & 43. 19, 20.
WILL, *Lev.* 1. 3, & 19. 5, & 22. 19.
Deut. 33. 16. good *w.* of him that dwelt
Matt. 7. 21. doeth *w.* of my Father
Luke 2. 14. good *w.* towards men
John 1. 13. not of the *w.* of man
    4. 34. my meat is to do the *w.* of him
    6. 40. this is *w.* of him that sent
Acts 21. 14. we ceased, saying, *w.* of L.
Eph. 5. 17. understand what the *w.* of
    6. 7. with good *w.* doing service
Acts 22. 14. his *w. John* 7. 17; *Rom.* 2.
    18; *Eph.* 1. 5, 9; *Col.* 1. 9; 2 *Tim.*
    2. 26; *Heb.* 13. 21; 1 *John* 5. 14;
    Rev. 17. 17.
Luke 22. 42. my *w. Acts* 13. 22.
John 5. 30. own *w.* 6. 38; *Eph.* 1. 11;
    Heb. 2. 4; *Jam.* 1. 18.
Ps. 40. 8. thy *w.* 143. 10; *Matt.* 6. 10, &
    26. 42; *Heb.* 10. 7, 9.
Ezra 7. 18. *w.* of God, *Mark* 3. 35; *Rom.*
    1. 10, & 8. 27, & 12. 2; 1 *Cor.* 11;
    2 *Cor.* 8. 5; *Gal.* 1. 4; *Eph.* 1. 1, & 6.
    6; *Col.* 1. 1, & 4. 12; 1 *Thess.* 4. 3;
    Heb. 10. 36; 1 *Pet.* 4. 2, 19; 1 *John*
    2. 17.
Matt. 26. 39. not as I *w.* but as
John 16. 7. ask what ye *w.* and it shall
    17. 24. I *w.* that those thou hast given
Rom. 7. 18. to *w.* is present with me
    9. 18. on whom he *w.* have mercy
Rev. 22. 17. whosoever *w.* let him
Rom. 9. 16. not of him that run or *w.*
Heb. 10. 26. if we sin *w.* after
Ex. 35. 5. whosoever is of *w.* heart
    22. as many as were *w.*-hearted
1 *Chr.* 28. 9. with perfect heart and *w.*
Ps. 110. 3. people shall be *w.* in
Is. 1. 19. if ye be *w.* and obedient
Matt. 26. 41. spirit *w.* flesh weak
Luke 22. 42. if thou be *w.* remove this
John 5. 35. *w.* for a season to rejoice
2 *Cor.* 5. 8. *w.* rather to be absent
1 *Tim.* 6. 18. *w.* to communicate
Heb. 13. 18. *w.* in all things to live
2 *Pet.* 3. 9. not *w.* any perish
Judg. 5. 2. *w.* offered themselves, 9.

1 *Chr.* 29. 9. with perfect heart offered *w.*
Lam. 3. 33. Lord doth not afflict *w.*
Hos. 5. 11. he *w.* walked after the
1 *Pet.* 5. 2. not by constraint, but *w.*
Col. 2. 23. wisdom in *w.* worship
    Rev. 12. 6.
WILLOWS, *Lev.* 23. 40; *Is.* 44. 4.
WIN, *Phil.* 3. 8.
WINNETH, *Prov.* 11. 30.
WIND, *Job* 7. 7, & 30. 15; *Ps.* 103. 16.
Prov. 11. 29. inherit the *w.*
    27. 16. hideth the *w.*
    30. 4. gathered the *w. Ps.* 135. 7.
Eccl. 11. 4. he that observeth the *w.*
Is. 26. 18. have brought forth *w.*
    27. 8. he stayeth his rough *w.*
Jer. 5. 13. prophets shall become *w.*
    10. 13. brings forth *w.* out of his
Hos. 8. 7. have sown the *w.*
    12. 1. feedeth on the *w.*
John 3. 8. *w.* blows where it listeth
Eph. 4. 14. carried about with every *w.*
WHIRLWIND, 2 *Kings* 2. 11; *Prov.* 1.
    27, & 10. 25; *Is.* 66. 15; *Hos.* 8. 7,
    & 13. 3; *Nah.* 1. 3; *Hab.* 3. 14;
    Zech. 7. 14, & 9. 14.
WINDS, *Ezek.* 37. 9; *Matt.* 8. 27; *Luke*
    8. 25.
WINDOWS. The clouds, *Gen.* 7. 11.
    The eyes, *Eccl.* 12. 3; *Song* 2. 9;
    Is. 60. 8; *Jer.* 9. 21.
WINE maketh glad heart, *Ps.* 104. 15.
Prov. 20 1. *w.* is a mocker, and
    21. 17. loveth *w.* and oil not
    23. 30. tarry long at *w.* seek mixed *w.*
    31. look not upon *w.* when red
    31. 6. give *w.* unto those that be of
Song 1. 2. thy love is better than *w.* 4.
Is. 5. 11. continue till *w.* inflame
    12. pipe and *w.* are in their feasts
    25. 6. *w.* on lees well refined
    28. 7. have erred through *w.*
    56. 1. buy *w.* and milk, *Song* 5. 1.
Hos. 2. 9. take away my *w.* in season
    3. 1. love flagons of *w.*
    4. 11. *w.* and new *w.* take away
Hab. 2. 5. he transgresseth by *w.*
Eph. 5. 18. be not drunk with *w.*
1 *Tim.* 3. 3. not given to *w.* 8; *Tit.* 1.
    7, 8.
    5. 23. use a little *w.* for thy stomach's
    sake
Prov. 23. 20. *w.*-bibber, *Matt.* 11. 19.
WINGS of God of Israel, *Ruth* 2. 12.
Ps. 17. 8. hide me under shadow of thy
    w. 36. 7, & 57. 1, & 61. 4, & 91. 4.
    18. 10. fly on *w.* of the wind, 2 *Sam.*
    22. 11.
Prov. 23. 5. riches make themselves *w.*
Is. 6. 2. each had six *w.* with
Mal. 4. 2. each had six *w.* with
WINK, *Job* 15. 12; *Ps.* 35. 19; *Prov.*
    6. 13, & 10. 10; *Acts* 17. 30.
WINTER, *Song* 2. 11; *Zech.* 14. 8.
WIPE, 2 *Kings* 21. 13; *Neh.* 13. 14;
    Prov. 6. 33; *Is.* 25. 8; *Rev.* 7. 17,
    & 21. 4.
WISE, *Gen.* 41. 39; *Ex.* 23. 8; *Deut.*
    16. 19.

Deut. 4. 6. this great nation is a *w.*
    32. 29. O that they were *w.*
Job 5. 13. he taketh the *w.* in their own
    11. 12. vain man would be *w.*

32. 9. great men not always *w.*
Ps. 2. 10. be *w.* O kings
19. 1. making *w.* the simple
107. 43. whoso is *w.* and will observe
Prov. 3. 7. be not *w.* in own eyes
35. *w.* shall inherit glory
9. 12. if thou be *w.* be *w.* for thyself
13. 20. walketh with *w.* shall be *w.*
26. 12. seest thou a man *w.* in his
Eccl. 7. 4. heart of *w.* is in house
9. 1. the *w.* and their works are in
Is. 5. 21. woe to *w.* in own eyes
Jer. 4. 22. they are *w.* to do evil
Dan. 12. 3. *w.* shall shine as stars
Hos. 14. 9. who is *w.* and he shall
Matt. 10. 16. be ye *w.* as serpents
11. 25. hid these things from *w.* and
Rom. 1. 22. professing themselves *w.*
16. 19. *w.* to that which is good
1 *Cor.* 3. 18. seemeth to be *w.* in this
4. 10. but ye are *w.* in Christ
Eph. 5. 15. not as fools, but as *w.*
2 *Tim.* 3. 15. able to make thee *w.*
Matt. 10. 42. shall in no *w.* lose his
Luke 18. 17. shall in no *w.* enter
John 6. 37. him that cometh I will in
no *w.* cast out
Rev. 24. 27. in no *w.* enter into it.
WISDOM, *Deut.* 4. 6. this is your *w.*
1 *Kings* 4. 29. God gave Solomon *w.*
Job 28. 28. fear of Lord that is *w.*
Prov. 4. 5. get *w.* get understanding
7. *w.* is the principal thing
16. 16. better get *w.* than gold
19. 8. getteth *w.* loveth his own soul
23. 4. cease from thine own *w.*
23. buy truth, and instruction
Eccl. 1. 18. for in much *w.* is much grief
8. 1. a man's *w.* maketh his face to
Matt. 11. 19. *w.* is justified of her child.
1 *Cor.* 1. 17. not with *w.* of words
24. Christ the *w.* of God, *Luke* 11. 49.
30. who of God is made to us *w.*
2. 6. we speak *w.* among them
3. 19. *w.* of this world is foolishness
2 *Cor.* 1. 12. not with fleshly *w.*
Col. 1. 9. might be filled with *w.*
4. 5. walk in *w.* toward them
Jam. 1. 5. if any lack *w.* let him ask it
3. 15. *w.* from above is pure
Rev. 5. 12. worthy is Lamb to receive *w.*
13. 18. here is *w.* let him, 17. 9.
Ps. 111. 10. of *w.* Prov. 9. 10, & 10. 21;
Mic. 6. 9; *Col.* 2. 3; *Jam.* 3. 13.
WISELY, *Ps.* 64. 9. & 101. 2; *Eccl.* 7. 10.
WISER, 1 *Kings* 4. 31; *Job* 35. 11; *Ps.*
119. 98; *Luke* 16. 8; 1 *Cor.* 1. 25.
WITCH, *Ex.* 22. 18; *Deut.* 18. 10.
WITCHCRAFT, 1 *Sam.* 15. 23; *Gal.*
5. 20.
WITHDRAW, *Job* 9. 13, & 33. 17;
Prov. 25. 17; *Song* 5. 6; 2 *Thess.* 3. 6;
1 *Tim.* 6. 5.
WITHHOLD not thy mercies, *Ps.* 40. 11.
Ps. 84. 11. no good thing will he *w.* from
Prov. 3. 27. *w.* not good from them
23. 13. *w.* not correction from that
WITHHELD, *Gen.* 20. 6, & 22. 12; *Job*
31. 16.
WITHHOLDEN, *Job* 42. 2; *Jer.* 5. 25.
WITHHOLDETH, *Prov.* 11. 24, 26; 2
Thess. 2. 6.
WITHIN, *Ps.* 40. 8, & 45. 13; *Matt.* 3.

9, & 23. 26; *Mark* 7. 21; 2 *Cor.* 7.
5; *Rev.* 5. 1.
WITHOUT, *Prov.* 1. 20, & 24. 27; 1 *Cor.*
5. 12; 2 *Cor.* 7. 5; *Col.* 4. 5; *Rev.*
22. 15.
WITHSTAND, *Eccl.* 4. 12; *Eph.* 6. 13.
Acts 11. 17. what was I, that I could *w.*
WITHSTOOD, *Gal.* 2. 11; 2 *Tim.* 4. 15.
WITNESS, *Gen.* 31. 44, 48; *Lev.* 5. 1.
Num. 35. 30. one *w.* not testify against
any, *Deut.* 17. 6, & 19. 15; 2 *Cor.* 13. 1.
Judg. 11. 10. Lord be *w.* 1 *Sam.* 12. 5;
Jer. 42. 5, & 29. 23; *Mic.* 1. 2; *Mal.*
2. 14.
Job 16. 19. my *w.* is in heaven
Ps. 89. 37. faithful *w.* in heaven
Prov. 14. 5. faithful *w.* will not lie
25. a true *w.* delivereth souls
24. 28. not *w.* against neighbour
Is. 55. 4. I have given him for a *w.* to
Mal. 3. 5. I will be a swift *w.* against
John 3. 11. ye receive not our *w.*
5. 36. greater *w.*
37. Father borne *w.* of me
Acts 14. 17. left not himself without a *w.*
1 *John* 5. 10. he that believeth hath *w.*
Rev. 1. 5. is the faithful *w.*
20. 4. beheaded for *w.* of Jesus
Deut. 17. 6. two or three *w.* 19. 15; 2
Cor. 13. 1; *Matt.* 18. 16; *Heb.* 10.
28; 1 *Tim.* 5. 19; *Num.* 35. 30.
Josh. 24. 22. *w.* against yourselves—we
Is. 43. 10. ye my *w.* saith Lord
1 *Thess.* 2. 10. ye are *w.* and God also
1 *Tim.* 6. 12. before many *w.* 13.
Heb. 12. 1. so great a cloud of *w.*
Rev. 11. 3. power to my two *w.*
WIZARDS. See *Witch. Lev.* 19. 31,
& 20. 6; *Is.* 8. 19.
WOLF, *Is.* 11. 6. & 65. 25; *Jer.* 5. 6.
WOLVES, *Ezek.* 22. 27; *Hab.* 1. 8; *Zeph.*
3. 3; *Mat.* 7. 15, & 10. 16; *Acts* 20. 29.
WOMAN, *Gen.* 2. 23, & 3. 15; *Lev.* 18.
22, 23, & 20. 13; *Num.* 30. 3.
Ps. 48. 6. pain as of *w.* in travail, *Is.* 13.
8, & 21. 3, & 26. 17, & 42. 14, & 66.
7; *Jer.* 4. 31, & 6. 24, & 13. 21, &
22. 23, & 30. 6, & 31. 8, & 48. 41, &
49. 22, 24. & 50. 43.
Prov. 11. 16. a gracious *w.* retaineth
12. 4. a virtuous *w.* is a crown to her
14. 1. wise *w.* buildeth her house
31. 10. virtuous *w.* who can find
30. *w.* that fears Lord be praised
Eccl. 7. 28. a *w.* among all those have I
Is. 49. 15. can a *w.* forget her child
54. 6. called thee as *w.* forsaken
Jer. 31. 22. a *w.* compass a man
Matt. 5. 28. whosoever looketh on a *w.*
15. 28. O *w.* great is thy faith
26. 13. that this *w.* hath done
John 2. 4. *w.* what have I to do with
8. 3. a *w.* taken in adultery
19. 26. *w.* behold thy son
Rom. 1. 27. leaveth natural use of *w.*
1 *Cor.* 11. 7. *w.* is glory of man
Gal. 4. 4. God sent forth his son made
of a *w.*
1 *Tim.* 2. 12. suffer not *w.* to teach
14. *w.* being deceived was in the
Rev. 12. 1. *w.* clothed with sun, 6. 16.
17. 18. *w.* thou saw a great city
WOMEN, *Judg.* 5. 24. blessed above *w.*

Prov. 31. 3. give not thy strength unto *w.*
Song 1. 8. O thou fairest among *w.*
Is. 3. 12. children oppresseth *w.* rule
     32. 11. tremble ye *w.* at ease
Jer. 9. 17. call for mourning *w.*
Lam. 4. 10. *w.* had sodden their own
Matt. 11. 11. among them born of *w.*
Luke 1. 28. blessed art thou among *w.*
Rom. 1. 26. *w.* did leave natural use
1 *Cor.* 14. 34. let *w.* keep silence
1 *Tim.* 2. 9. *w.* adorn themselves
     11. let *w.* learn silence with
     5. 14. that younger *w.* marry
2 *Tim.* 3. 6. lead captive silly *w.*
1 *Pet.* 3. 5. after this manner the holy
     w. also
Rev. 14. 4. not defiled with *w.*
WOMB, *Gen.* 25. 23, & 29. 31.
Gen. 49. 25. blessings of the *w.* and
1 *Sam.* 1. 5. Lord hath shut her *w.*
Ps. 22. 9. took me out of the *w.*
     10. I was cast upon thee from *w.*
     127. 3. fruit of *w.* is his reward
     139. 13. covered me in my mother's *w.*
Eccl. 11. 5. how bones grow in *w.*
Is. 44. 2. Lord formed thee from *w.*
     66. 9. cause to bring forth and shut *w.*
Hos. 9. 14. give miscarrying *w.*
Luke 1. 42. blessed is fruit of *w.*
     11. 27. blessed *w.* that bare thee
     23. 29. blessed are the *w.* that never
WONDER. Any thing which causes sur-
     prise by its strangeness, *Deut.* 13.
     1, & 28. 46; *Ps.* 71. 7; *Is.* 29. 14;
     Rev. 12. 1.
Acts 13. 41. ye despisers *w.* and perish,
     Hab. 1. 5.
WONDERS, *Ex.* 3. 20, & 7. 3, & 15. 11.
1 *Chr.* 16. 12. remember his *w. Ps.* 105. 5.
Job 9. 10. God doeth *w. Ps.* 77. 11, 14.
Ps. 78. 11. they forgat his *w. Neh.* 9. 17.
     88. 10. wilt thou show *w.* to dead
     136. 4. who alone doeth great *w.*
Dan. 12. 6. how long to end of *w.*
Joel 2. 30. I will show *w.* in the heavens
John 4. 48. except ye see signs and *w.*
2 *Thess.* 2. 9. with power, signs, and *w.*
Rev. 13. 13. he doth great *w.* fire
Zech. 3. 8. men *w.* at
Is. 59. 16. I *w.* there was no
Luke 4. 22. *w.* at gracious words
Rev. 13. 3. all the world *w.* after the
     17. 6. I *w.* with great admiration
WONDROUSLY, *Judg.* 13. 19; *Joel* 2. 16.
WONDERFUL, *Deut.* 28. 59. plagues *w.*
Job 42. 3. uttering things too *w.*
Ps. 119. 129. the testimonies are *w.*
     139. 6. such knowledge is too *w.* for
Prov. 30. 18. be three things too *w.* for
Is. 9. 6. his name shall be called W.
     25. 1. done *w.* things
     28. 29. *w.* in counsel
Jer. 5. 30. a *w.* thing is committed
Job 37. 14. *w.* works, *Ps.* 26. 7, & 75. 1,
     & 105. 2, & 119. 27, & 145, 5, &
     71. 17, & 78. 32, & 106. 22.
Ps. 72. 18. *w.* things, 86. 10, & 119. 18.
WONDERFULLY, *Ps.* 139. 14; *Lam.* 1. 9.
WOOD, hay, stubble, 1 *Cor.* 3. 12.
2 *Tim.* 2. 20. also vessels of *w.* and of
WORD, *Num.* 23. 5; *Deut.* 4. 2.
Deut. 8. 3. by every *w.* man live
     30. 14. the *w.* is very nigh unto thee

Ps. 68. 11. the Lord gave the *w.* and
     119. 49. remember *w.* to servant
Prov. 15. 23. *w.* spake in due season
     25. 11. *w.* fitly spoken is like
Is. 29. 21. man offender for a *w.*
     30. 21. bear a *w.* behind thee
     44. 26. confirm *w.* of his servants
     50. 4. to speak a *w.* in season
Jer. 5. 13. prophets *w.* not in them
     44. 16. the *w.* thou hast spoken we
Matt. 8. 8. speak the *w.* only and my
     12. 36. every idle *w.* men speak
Luke 4. 36. what a *w.* is this for
     24. 19. mighty in deed and in *w.*
John 1. 1. in the beginning was the W.
     and the W. was with God, and
     the W. was God
     14. the W. was made flesh and dwelt
     15. 3. through *w.* I have spoken
Acts 13. 15. if ye have any *w.* of exhor.
     26. to you is *w.* of salvation sent
     17. 11. received the *w.* with all
     20. 32. to God and to *w.* of grace
1 *Cor.* 4. 20. kingdom of God not in *w.*
Gal. 6. 6. taught in *w.* communicate
Eph. 5. 26. washing of water by *w.*
Col. 3. 16. let the *w.* of Christ dwell
     17. whatsoever ye do in *w.* or deed
1 *Thess.* 1. 5. our gospel came not into
     you in *w.* only
2 *Thess.* 2. 17. stablish you in every *w.*
     3. 14. if any obey not our *w.*
1 *Tim.* 5. 17. labour in *w.* and doctrine
2 *Tim.* 4. 2. preach *w.* be instant in
Tit. 1. 9. holding fast faithful *w.*
Heb. 4. 2. *w.* preached did not profit
     1. 13. unskilful in the *w.* of righteous
     13. 22. suffer *w.* of exhortation
Jam. 1. 21. receive with meekness *w.*
     22. be ye doers of the *w.*
     3. 2. offend not in *w.*
1 *Pet.* 3. 1. if any obey not the *w.*
2 *Pet.* 1. 19. sure *w.* of prophecy
1 *John* 1. 1. hands have handled *w.* of
     5. 7. Father, W. and Holy Ghost,
     these three are one
Rev. 3. 10. kept *w.* of my patience
     12. 11. overcome by *w.* of their
WORD, his, *Ps.* 130. 5. in *his w.* do I
     hope, 119. 81.
     147. 19. showeth *his w.* to Jacob
Jer. 20. 9. *his w.* was in my heart as a
John 5. 38. ye have not *his w.* abiding
Acts 2. 41. gladly received *his w.* and
John 8. 37. my *w.* 43; *Rev.* 3. 8.
Is. 8. 20. this *w. Rom.* 9. 9.
Ps. 119. 11. *thy w.* have I hid in my
     50. *thy w.* have quickened me
     105. *thy w.* is a lamp to my feet
     140. *thy w.* is very pure
     160. *thy w.* is true from beginning
     138. 2. magnified *thy w.* above all thy
Jer. 15. 16. *thy w.* was unto me joy and
John 17. 6. I kept *thy w.*
     17. *thy w.* is truth
Prov. 30. 5. *w.* of God, *Is.* 40. 8; *Mark*
     7. 13; *Rom.* 10. 17; 1 *Thess.* 2. 13;
Heb. 4. 12, & 6. 5; 1 *Pet.* 1. 23; *Rev.* 19. 31.
2 *Kings* 20. 19. *w.* of the Lord, *Ps.* 18.
     30, & 33. 4; 2 *Thess.* 3. 1; 1 *Pet.*
     1. 25.
Ps. 119. 43. *w.* of truth, 2 *Cor.* 6. 7;
     Eph. 1. 13; *Col.* 1. 5; 2 *Tim.* 2. 15;

Jam. 1. 18.

WORDS, *Job* 23. 12. esteem *w.* of his
Prov. 15. 26. *w.* of pure are pleasant *w.*
   19. 7. he pursueth them with *w.*
   22. 17. bow down thine ear and hear
     w. of the wise
Eccl. 10. 12. *w.* of wise gracious
   12. 10. find out acceptable *w.*
   11. *w.* of wise are as goads
Jer. 7. 4. trust ye not in lying *w.*
   44. 28. whose *w.* shall stand
Dan. 7. 25. speak great *w.* against the
Hos. 6. 5. slain them by *w.* of mouth
   14. 2. take with you *w.* and
Zech. 1. 13. good *w.* comfortable *w.*
Matt. 26. 44. Prayed saying the same *w.*
Luke 4. 22. gracious *w.* proceedeth
John 6. 63. the *w.* I speak are spirit and
   68. thou hast *w.* of eternal life
   17. 8. I have given them *w.* thou
Acts 7. 22. Moses mighty in *w.*
   15. 24. troubled you with *w.* 18. 15.
   20. 35. remember *w.* of Lord Jesus
   26. 25. speak *w.* of truth and
1 *Cor.* 2. 4. not with enticing *w.*
2 *Tim.* 1. 13. hold fast the form of *w.*
   2. 14. strive not about *w.* to no
Rev. 1. 3. hear *w.* of this prophecy
Ps. 50. 17. my *w. Is.* 51. 16, & 59. 21;
   Jer. 5. 14; *Mic.* 2. 7; *Mark* 8. 38.
   & 13. 31; *John* 5. 47, & 15. 7.
1 *Thess.* 4. 18. these *w. Rev.* 21. 5.
Ps. 119. 193. thy *w.* 130. 139; *Prov.* 23.
   8; *Eccl.* 5. 2; *Ex.* 33. 31; *Matt.*
   12. 37.

WORK, *Gen.* 2. 3; *Ex.* 20. 10, & 31. 14.
Deut. 31. 1. accept *w.* of his hands
Job 1. 10. blessed *w.* of his hands
   10. 3. wilt despise the *w.* of thine
   14. 15. desire to *w.* of thy hands
   36. 9. he shows them their *w.*
Ps. 8. 3. heavens *w.* of thy fingers
9. 16. wicked is snared in the *w.* of his
19. 1. firmament showeth his handy *w.*
101. 3. I hate the *w.* of them that
143. 5. muse on *w.* of thy hand
Eccl. 8. 14. according to *w.* of wicked
   17. I beheld all the *w.* of God
   12. 14. God shall bring every *w.* into
Is. 10. 12. performed his whole *w.*
   28. 21. do his strange *w.*
   29. 16. shall the *w.* say of him that
   45. 11. concerning *w.* of my hands
   49. 4. my *w.* is with my God
Jer. 10. 15. vanity and *w.* of errors
   18. 3. the potter wrought a *w.* on the
Hab. 1. 5. I will *w.* a *w.* in those days
Mark 6. 5. could do no mighty *w.*
John 17. 4. I have finished the *w.* thou
Acts 5. 38. if this *w.* be of men
   13. 2. *w.* whereto I called them
Rom. 2. 15. show *w.* of law written
   11. 6. otherwise *w.* is no more *w.*
1 *Cor.* 3. 13. every man's *w.* be made
   9. 1. are you not my *w.* in the Lord
Eph. 4. 12. *w.* of ministry edifying
2 *Thess.* 1. 11. *w.* of faith with power
   2. 17. stablish you in every good word
     and *w.*
2 *Tim.* 4. 5. do *w.* of evangelist
Jam. 1. 4. patience have her perfect *w.*
   25. doer of the *w.* be blessed
1 *Pet.* 1. 17. judgeth according to every

man's *w.*
Ps. 104. 23. his *w.* 62. 12, & 111. 3; *Prov.*
   24. 29; *Is.* 40. 10; *Job* 36. 24.
   90. 16. thy *w.* 92. 4; *Prov.* 24. 27;
   Jer. 31. 16; *Hab.* 3. 2.
Ex. 32. 16. *w.* of God, *Ps.* 64. 9; *Eccl.* 7.
   13, & 8. 17; *John* 6. 29; *Rom.* 14. 20.
Ps. 28. 5. *w.* of the Lord, *Is.* 5. 12; *Jer.*
   48. 10; 1 *Cor.* 15. 58, & 16. 10.
   17. 4. concerning *w.* of men
   92. 4. triumph in *w.* of thy hands
   111. 7. *w.* of his hands are verity
   138. 8. forsake not *w.* of thine own
Prov. 31. 31. let her own *w.* praise her
Is. 26. 12. wrought all our *w.* in us
Dan. 4. 37. all whose *w.* are truth
John 5. 20. show him greater *w.*
   10. 32. for which of those *w.* do ye
   38. believe the *w.* that the Father is
   14. 11. believe me for *w.* sake
   12. greater *w.* shall he do, I go unto
Acts 26. 20. *w.* meet for repentance
Rom. 3. 27. by what law ? of *w.* nay, but
   4. 6. G. imputes righteous, without *w.*
   9. 11. not of *w.* but him that
   32. sought as by *w.* of the law
   11. 6. then it is no more of *w.*
   13. 12. cast off the *w.* of darkness
Gal. 2. 16. by *w.* of the law no flesh
   3. 2. received ye Spirit by *w.* of the
   10. as many as are of *w.* of law are
   5. 19. *w.* of flesh are manifest
Eph. 2. 9. not to *w.*
   10. created unto good *w.*
   5. 11. unfruitful *w.* of darkness
Col. 1. 21. enemies in mind by wicked *w.*
1 *Thess.* 5. 13. in love for *w.* sake
2 *Tim.* 1. 9. not according to *w.*
Tit. 1. 16. in *w.* they deny him
   3. 5. not by *w.* of righteousness
Heb. 6. 1. repentance from dead *w.* and
   9. 14. purge conscience from dead *w.*
Jam. 2. 14. have not *w.* can faith save
   20. faith without *w.* is dead, 17. 26.
   21. justified by *w.* 24. 25.
   22. by *w.* faith was made perfect
1 *John* 3. 8. Son of God destroy *w.* of
Rev. 9. 20. I repented not of the *w.*
   18. 6. according to her *w.* 20.
Ps. 33. 4. his *w.* 78. 11, & 103. 22, & 104.
   31, & 106. 13, & 107. 22, & 145. 9, 17;
   Dan. 9. 14; *Acts* 15. 18; *Heb.* 4. 10.
   106. 35. their *w. Is.* 66. 18; *Jonah* 3.
   10; *Matt.* 13. 3, 5; 2 *Cor.* 11. 15;
   Rev. 14. 13, & 20. 12, 13.
Deut. 15. 10. thy *w. Ps.* 66. 3, & 73. 28, &
   92. 5, & 104. 24, & 143. 5; *Prov.* 16.
   3; *Eccl.* 9. 7; *Rev.* 2. 2.
Ps. 40. 5. wonderful *w.* 78. 4, & 107. 8,
   & 111. 4; *Matt.* 7. 22; *Acts* 2. 11.
Job 37. 14. *w.* of God, *Ps.* 66. 5, & 78. 7;
   Eccl. 11. 5; *John* 6. 28, & 9. 3.
Ps. 46. 8. *w.* of the Lord. 111. 2.
1 *Sam.* 14. 6. may be that Lord will *w.*
Ps. 119. 126. time for thee, Lord, to *w.*
Is. 43. 13. I will *w.* and who let it
Matt. 7. 23. depart from me, ye that *w.*
John 6. 28. might *w.* the *w.* of God
   9. 4. I must *w.* the *w.* of him that
Phil. 2. 12. *w.* out your own salvation
1 *Thess.* 4. 11. *w.* with own hands
2 *Thess.* 2. 7. mystery of iniquity doth *w.*
   3. 10. if any *w.* not neither should he
WORKETH, *Prov.* 11. 18. wicked *w.*

deceitful work

Is. 64. 5. him that *w.* righteousness
John 5. 17. Father *w.* hitherto and I *w.*
Acts 10. 35. he that *w.* righteousness is
Rom. 4. 4. him that *w.* his reward
1 *Cor.* 12. 6. God who *w.* all in all
2 *Cor.* 4. 17. *w.* for us a far more exceed
Gal. 5. 6. faith which *w.* by love
Eph. 2. 2. spirit that now *w.* in children
Phil. 2. 13. it is God that *w.* in you both
WORKING, *Is.* 28. 29. excellent in *w.*
Mark 16. 20. Lord *w.* with them
Rom. 7. 13. sin *w.* death in me by that
1 *Cor.* 4. 12. *w.* with our own hands
    9. 6. not power to forbear *w.*
Eph. 1. 19. according to the *w.* of mighty
    3. 7. effectual *w.* of his power
    4. 28. *w.* with hands the things that
Phil. 3. 21. according to *w.* whereby
2 *Thess.* 3. 11. *w.* not at all but
Heb. 13. 21. *w.* in you that which is
WORKERS, 2 *Cor.* 6. 1, & 11. 13; *Phil.*
    3. 2.
Job 31. 3. *w.* of iniquity, 34, 8, 22; *Ps.*
    5. 5, & 6. 8, & 28. 3, & 125. 5, & 141.
    9; *Prov.* 10. 29, & 21. 15.
WORKMAN, *Matt.* 10. 10; 2 *Tim.* 2. 15.
WORKMANSHIP, *Ex.* 31. 3; *Eph.* 2. 10.
WORLD, 1 *Sam.* 2. 8; 1 *Chr.* 16. 30.
Ps. 17. 14. from men of *w.* which
    24. 1. the *w.* is the Lord's, 9. 8.
    50. 12. *w.* is mine, and fulness of it
Eccl. 3. 11. set *w.* in their heart
Is. 26. 9. inhabitants of the *w.* will
Jer. 10. 12. established *w.* by his
Matt. 16. 26. what profit if gain whole *w.*
    18. 7. woe unto the *w.* because of
    24. 3. what shall be end of *w.*
Mark 16. 15. go into all *w.* and preach
Luke 20. 35. worthy to obtain that *w.*
John 1. 10. *w.* made by him, and the
    29. Lamb of G. taketh away sin of *w.*
    3. 16. God so loved the *w.* he gave
    17. that the *w.* through him might
    7. 7. *w.* cannot hate you, but me
    12. 47. not judge *w.* but save *w.*
    14. 17. whom *w.* cannot receive
    19. *w.* seeth me no more, but
    15. 18. if the *w.* hate you
    16. 28. I leave the *w.* and go to the
John 17. 9. I pray not for the *w.* but
    16. are not of the *w.* as I am not
    23. *w.* may know thou hast sent
Rom. 3. 19. *w.* become guilty before G.
1 *Cor.* 1. 21. *w.* by wisdom knew not G.
Gal. 6. 14. *w.* is crucified to me, and I
Col. 1. 6. preaching as in all the *w.*
Tit. 1. 2. promised before *w.* began
Heb. 2. 5. *w.* to come, 6. 5.
    11. 38. of whom the *w.* was not
1 *John* 2. 2. propitiation for sins of *w.*
    15. love not *w.* nor things in *w.*
    16. all in *w.* is lust, lust of eyes
    17. *w.* passeth away and lust of it
    3. 1. sons of God *w.* knoweth us not
    4. 5. they are of *w.* speak of *w.* and
    5. 19. *w.* lieth in wickedness
Rev. 3. 10. temptation shall come upon
    all the *w.*
    13. 3. *w.* wondered after beast
Matt. 12. 32. this *w.* *John* 8. 23, & 18.
    36; *Rom.* 12. 2; 1 *Tim.* 6. 7.
Heb. 1. 2. *w.* made, 11. 3.
WORM. Denotes extreme degrada-

tion, *Job* 24. 20. A mean contemptible person, *Ps.* 22. 6. Corruptible, *Ex.* 16. 20; *Is.* 51. 8.

Job 25. 6. man that is a *w.* is a *w.*
Ps. 22. 6. I am a *w.* and no man
Is. 41. 14. fear not thou *w.* Jacob
    66. 24. *w.* shall not die, *Mark* 9. 44, 48.
Job 19. 26. *w.* destroy this body, *Acts*
    12. 23.
WORMWOOD, *Deut.* 29. 18; *Prov.* 5.
    4; *Lam.* 3. 15, 19; *Amos* 5. 7;
    Rev. 8. 11.
WORSE, *Matt.* 12. 45; *John* 5. 14; 1
    Cor. 8. 8, & 11. 17; 2 *Tim.* 3. 13; 2
    Pet. 2. 20.
WORSHIP Lord in beauty of holiness,
    1 *Chr.* 16. 29; *Ps.* 29. 2, & 66. 4, &
    96. 9, & 45. 11, & 95. 6, & 99. 5;
    Matt. 4. 10.
Ps. 97. 7. *w.* him, all ye gods
Matt. '15. 9. in vain do they *w.* me
John 4. 24. they that *w.* him must *w.*
Acts 17. 23. whom ye ignorantly *w.*
    24. 14. so *w.* I God of my fathers
Phil. 3. 3. circumcision, which *w.* God
Rev. 3. 9. come and *w.* before thy feet
    13. 12. earth to *w.* the first beast
    19. 10. to *w.* God, 22. 9.
WORSHIPPED, *Ex.* 4. 31, & 32. 8;
    Jer. 1. 16; 1 *Chr.* 29. 20; *Rom.* 1.
    25; 2 *Thess.* 2. 4; *Rev.* 5. 14, & 7.
    11. & 11. 16. & 13. 4.
WORTHY, *Job* 24. 25; *Prov.* 10. 20.
Gen. 32. 10. I am not *w.* of the least
Matt. 10. 10. workmen is *w.* of meat
    13. if house be *w.* let peace rest
    37. loveth father or mother more
    than me is not *w.* of me
    22. 8. that were bidden were not *w.*
Luke 3. 8. bring fruits *w.* of repentance
    7. 4. he was *w.* for whom he should
    10. 7. labourer is *w.* of his hire
    15. 19. no more *w.* to be called thy
    20. 35. accounted *w.* to obtain resur.
    21. 36. *w.* to escape all things
Acts 5. 41. *w.* to suffer shame for
Rom. 8. 18. not *w.* to be compared
Eph. 4. 1. walk *w.* of the Lord fruitful
1 *Thess.* 2. 12. 'walk *w.* of God who hath
2 *Thess.* 1. 5. be counted *w.* of kingdom
    11. God would count you *w.* of this
1 *Tim.* 1. 15. *w.* of all acceptation, 4. 9.
    5. 17. elders *w.* of double honour
    18. labourer is *w.* of reward
    6. 1. masters *w.* of all honour
Heb. 3. 3. counted *w.* of more glory
    10. 29. shall be thought *w.*
    11. 38. of whom world was not *w.*
Rev. 3. 4. in white, for they are *w.*
    5. 12. *w.* is Lamb slain to receive
    16. 6. blood to drink, for they are *w.*
WOULD God, *Ex.* 16. 3; *Num.* 11. 29;
    Acts 26. 29; 1 *Cor.* 4. 8; 2 *Cor.* 11. 1.
Neh. 9. 30. *w.* not, *Is.* 30. 15; *Matt.* 18.
    30, & 23. 30, 37; *Rom.* 11. 25.
Ps. 81. 11. Israel *w.* none of me
Prov. 1. 25. *w.* none of my reproof
    30. they *w.* none of my counsel
Matt. 7. 12. whatsoever ye *w.* that
Rom. 7. 15. what I *w.* that I do not
Gal. 5. 17. cannot do things ye *w.*
Rev. 3. 15. I *w.* thou wert cold or
WOUND, *Ex.* 21. 25; *Prov.* 6. 33; *Jer.*
    10. 19, & 15. 18, & 30. 12, 14; *Mic.*

1. 9.
WOUNDS, ...
30. 17.
Deut. 32. 39. I w. a...
1 *Cor.* 8. 12. w. their...
Rev. 13. 3. deadly w. was...
WOUNDED, *Ps.* 69. 26,
  Song 5. 7.

Prov. 18. 14. but a w. spirit w...
Is. 53. 5. was w. for our transgres...
Job 5. 18. he w. and his hands mak...
WRATH, *Gen.* 49. 7; *Ex.* 32. 10, 11.
Num. 16. 46. w. gone out from Lord
Deut. 32. 27. feared w. of enemy
Neh. 13. 18. bring more w. on Israel
Job 5. 2. w. killeth foolish man
Ps. 76. 10. the w. of man shall praise
  thee, the remainder of w. shalt
  thou restrain
Prov. 16. 14. w. of king as messenger
Is. 54. 8. in a little w. I hid my face
Hab. 3. 2. in w. remember mercy
Matt. 3. 7. flee from w. to come
Rom. 2. 5. treasure up w. against the
  5. 9. saved from w. through him
  12. 19. rather give place unto w.
  13. 5. not only for w. but conscience
Eph. 2. 3. by nature children of w.
  4. 26. let not sun go down upon w.
1 *Thess.* 1. 10. delivered from the w. t
  5. 9. is come upon them
  5. 9. not appointed us to w.
1 *Tim.* 2. 8. holy hands without w.
Heb. 11. 27. not fearing w. of king
Jam. 1. 19. every man be slow to w.
  20. w. of man worketh not the
Rev. 6. 16. from w. of the Lamb
  12. 12. having great w. because
  14. 8. wine of the w. of her fornica
Ezra 8. 22. his w. *Ps.* 2. 5, 12, & 78. 38;
  Jer. 7. 29. & 10. 10; *Rev.* 6. 17.
Num. 25. 11. my w. *Ps.* 95. 11; *Is.* 10
  6, & 60. 10; *Ezek.* 7. 14; *Hos.* 5. 10.
Ps. 38. 1. thy w. 85. 3, & 88. 7, 16, & 89.
  46, & 90. 9, 11, & 102. 10.

WREST, *Ex.* 23. 2; 2 *Pet.* 3. 16.
WRESTLE, *Gen.* 32. 24, 25; *Eph.* 6. 12.
WRETCHED, *Rom.* 7. 24; *Rev.* 3. 17.
WRINKLE, *Job* 16. 8; *Eph.* 5. 27.
WRITE, *Ex.* 34. 1, 27; *Deut.* 27. 3; *Is.*
  30. 8; *Jer.* 30. 2; *Hab.* 2. 2.
Deut. 6. 9. w. them upon the posts of
Prov. 3. 3. w. them upon table of thine
Jer. 31. 33. I will w. it in their hearts

WRITTEN, *Ps.* 69. 28. not be w. with
  102. 18. this shall be w. for the
Prov. 22. 20. have not I w. thee excel.
Eccl. 12. 10. that which was w. was
Dan. 12. 1. deliverer found w. in book
1 *Cor.* 10. 11. are w. for our admonition
2 *Cor.* 3. 2. epistle w. in our hearts
  3. w. not with ink, but with Spirit
Heb. 12. 23. w. in heaven, *Luke* 10. 20.
WRONG, *Ps.* 105. 14; *Jer.* 22. 3, 13.
Matt. 20. 13. I do thee no w. didst
1 *Cor.* 6. 7. do ye not rather take w.
Col. 3. 25. he that doeth w. shall receive
WRONGED, 2 *Cor.* 7. 2; *Phile.* 18.
Prov. 8. 36. w. his own soul

WROTH, *Ps.* 89. 38; *Is.* 54. 9, & 57. 17.
WROUGHT, 1 *Sam.* 6. 6, & 14. 45.
Ps. 139. 15. curiously w. in the lowest
  ...6. 12. w. all our works for us
  9. I w. for my name's sake
Job's works are w. in God
Ps. ... me all manner of
YIELD ...
Ps. 67. 6. ...w. us for same
Rom. 6. 13. in Christ
  ...ments of un...tiles
  selves to God
  16. y. members as...
Heb. 12. 11. y. peaceab...
YOKE, *Deut.* 28. 48; 1 *Kin...*
Is. 9. 4. broken y. of his burd...
  10. 27. y. shall be destroyed because
Lam. 1. 14. y. of my transgression is
  3. 27. good for a man to bear the y.
Matt. 11. 29. take my y. upon you
Gal. 5. 1. y. of bondage, *Acts* 15. 10.
2 *Cor.* 6. 14. be not unequally y,
YOU only have I known of, *Amos* 3. 2.
Luke 10. 16. he that heareth y. heareth
  13. 28. y. yourselves thrust out
2 *Cor.* 12. 14. seek not yours but y.
Eph. 2. 1. y. hath he quickened
Col. 1. 21. y. sometime alienated
Luke 6. 20. for y. is the kingdom of God
1 *Cor.* 3. 22. all are y. and ye are C's.
YOUNG have I been, now old, *Ps.*
  37. 25.
Is. 40. 11. gently lead those with y.
1 *Tim.* 5. 1. entreat the y. men as
  14. I will that y. women marry
1 *Pet.* 5. 5. ye y. submit yourselves
YOUTH, every imagination is evil from,
  Gen. 8. 21.
1 *Kings* 18. 12. fear Lord from my y.
Job 13. 26. makest me to possess the
  iniquities of my y.
Ps. 25. 7. remember not sins of my y.
  103. 5. y. is renewed as eagles
Eccl. 11. 9. rejoice, O young man, in y.
  10. childhood and y. are vanity
Jer. 2. 2. I remember the kindness of y.
1 *Tim.* 4. 12. no man despise thy y.
YOUTHS, *Prov.* 7. 7; *Is.* 40. 30.
YOUTHFUL, 2 *Tim.* 2. 20. flee y. lusts

ZEAL, for the Lord, 2 *Kings* 10. 16.
Ps. 69. 9. the z. of my house hath
  119. 139. z. hath consumed me
Is. 9. 7. the z. of the Lord will perform
  59. 17. I was clad with z. as a
Rom. 10. 2. z. of God, but not according
2 *Cor.* 7. 11. what z. what revenge
Phil. 3. 6. concerning z. persecuting the
Num. 25. 13. he was z. for his God
Acts 22. 3. I was z. towards God
Tit. 2. 14. people z. of good works
Rev. 3. 19. I rebuke, be z. and repent
Gal. 4. 18. good to be z. affected in a

...rew monarchy was divided between the kings of Judah and Israel.

...ore the
...viii.

...s of the Patriarchs ...n the days of Noah; ... to the escape from the ...dian bondage, Ex. xv.

III. *The journeyings of Israel to Canaan;* accounts of which are given Exodus xv. to xl.; and further particulars in Numbers, and other books.

IV. *The government of the Judges ;* beginning with Judges iii., and ending 1 Sam. viii.

V. *The monarchy of the Hebrews,* beginning 1 Sam. ix., and 1 *Kings* xi.; after which the He-

VI. *The kings of Judah and Israel,* beginning with 1 Kings xii., and ending 2 Kings xxiv; of these there are also other accounts in the Chronicles and the Prophets.

VII. *The captivity in Babylon,* recorded in 2 Kings xxiv., xxv.; and in Chronicles, and various prophets.

VIII. *The restoration of the Jews after their captivity,* recorded in Ezra.

IX. *The times of Christ and his apostles* beginning with Matthew, and ending with Acts, and embracing all the Epistles.

CURIOUS CALCULATION

OLD TESTAMENT		NEW TESTAMENT	
Books	39	Books	27
Chapters	929	Chapters	260
Verses	23,214	Verses	7,959
Words	592,439	Words	181,258
Letters	2,728,100	Letters	838,380
Middle chapter	*Job* 29.	Middle book	2 *Thessalonians*
Shortest verse	1*Chr*.1.25.	Middle verse	*Acts* 17. 17.
The alphabet is contained in *Ezra* 7. 21.		Shortest verse	*John* 11. 35.
Two chapters are alike, 2 *Kings* 19; *Is.* 37.			

TOTAL.—Books in the whole Scriptures, 66. Chapters, 1,189. Verses, 31,173. Words, 773,697. Letters, 3,566,480. Middle chapter and least, *Ps.* 117. Middle verse, *Ps.* 118. 8. This calculation occupied three years. It is more curious than useful.

NAMES AND TITLES OF CHRIST

1 *Cor.* 15. 45.	Adam	*Rev.* 3. 14.	Beginning of the Creation of God
Rev. 3. 14.	Amen		
— 1. 8.	Alpha and Omega	1 *Pet.* 2. 25.	Bishop of souls
— 22. 13.	,,	*Jer.* 23. 5.	Branch
1 *John* 2. 1.	Advocate	*Zech.* 3. 8 ;	,,
Dan. 7. 22.	Ancient of days	— 6. 12.	,,
Heb. 3. 1.	Apostle of our profession	*John* 6. 35;	Bread of life
		— 3. 29.	Bridegroom
— 12. 2.	Author and Finisher of faith	*Josh.* 5. 14.	Captain of the Lord's host

Heb. 2. 10.	Captain of salvation	Is. 40. 5.	
Luke 9. 20.	Christ of God	Acts 10. 46.	
— 2. 25.	Consolation of Israel	Rom. 10. 12.	
Eph. 2. 20.	Chief corner-stone	Jer. 23. 6.	Lord (Jehovah our) righteousness
1 Pet. 2. 6.	,,		
Is. 9. 6.	Counsellor	1 Tim. 2. 5.	Mediator
Jer. 30. 9.	David	Heb. 7. 1.	Melchizedek
Ezek. 34. 23.	,,	Mal. 3. 7;	Messenger of the covenant
Job 9. 33.	Daysman	— 3. 1.	
Luke 1. 78.	Dayspring	Dan. 9. 25.	Messiah
Rom. 11. 26.	Deliverer	John 1. 41.	,,
Hag. 2. 7.	Desire of all nations	Is. 9. 6.	Mighty God
John 10. 7.	Door	— 63. 1.	Mighty to save
Is. 42. 1.	Elect of God	Rev. 2. 28.	Morning star
— 7. 14.	Emmanuel	— 22. 16.	,,
Matt. 1. 23.	,,	——— 6.	Offspring of David
Is. 9. 6.	Everlasting Father	John 1. 14.	Only-begotten
Rev. 1. 5.	Faithful Witness	1 Cor. 5. 7.	Passover
— 3. 14.	,,	Ezek. 34. 29.	Plant of renown
— 1. 5.	First begotten of the dead	1 Tim. 6. 15.	Potentate
— 1. 17.	First and last	Heb. 4. 14.	Priest
— 2. 8.		— 7. 26.	,,
Zech. 16. 1.	Fountain opened for sin and uncleanness	Rev. 1. 5.	Prince of the kings of the earth
Matt. 11. 19.	Friend of sinners	Acts 3. 15.	——— life
Is. 40. 5.	Glory of God	Is. 9. 6.	——— peace
— 9.	GOD	1 Tim. 2. 6.	Ransom
John 20. 28.	,,	Is. 59. 20.	Redeemer
Zech. 13. 7.	God's Fellow	Mal. 3. 3.	Refiner and Purifier
Matt. 2. 6.	Governor	John 11. 25.	Resurrection and Life
Heb. 1. 2.	Heir of all things	1 Cor. 10. 4.	Rock
Col. 1. 18.	Head of the church	Rev. 22. 16.	Root and Offspring of David
Heb. 3. 1.	High priest	Mic. 5. 2.	Ruler in Israel
— 7. 1.	,,	2 Pet. 2. 20.	Saviour
Ps. 16. 10.	Holy One	— 3. 18.	,,
Mark 1. 24.	——— of God	Is. 42. 1.	Servant
Is. 41. 14.	——— of Israel	John 10. 11, 14.	Shepherd
1 Tim. 1. 1.	Hope	Gen. 49. 10.	Shiloh
Ps. 18. 2.	Horn of salvation	Mark 14. 61, 62.	Son of the Blessed
Luke 1. 69.		Luke 1. 35.	——— God
John 8. 58.	I AM ,,	——— 32.	——— the Highest
Matt. 1. 21.	Jesus	John 5. 27.	——— Man
Acts 7. 52.	Just One	Num. 24. 17.	Star
Ps. 2. 6.	King	Gen. 49. 24.	Stone of Israel
Matt. 21. 5.	,,	Mal. 4. 2.	Sun of Righteousness.
John 1. 49.	——— of Israel	Heb. 7. 22.	Surety
Rev. 15. 3.	——— of saints	1 John 5. 20.	True God
1 Tim. 6. 15.	——— of kings	John 15. 1.	True vine
Rev. 17. 14.	,,	— 14. 6.	Truth
John 1. 29. 36.	Lamb of God	———	Way
Is. 55. 4.	Leader & Commander.	Is. 54. 5.	Witness
John 14. 6.	Life	— 9. 6.	Wonderful
Col. 3. 4.	,,	John 1. 1.	Word
John 8. 12.	Light of the world	Rev. 19. 13.	——— of God
Rev. 5. 5.	Lion of tribe of Judah	1 John 1. 1.	——— of life

NAMES AND TITLES OF THE HOLY SPIRIT.

John 3. 6.	The Spirit	Rom. 8. 15.	Spirit of Adoption
1 Tim. 4. 1.	,,	Gal. 4, 5, 6.	
Gen. 1. 2.	The Spirit of God	Is. 11. 2.	,, ———— Counsel
— 41. 38.	,,	2 Cor. 4. 13.	———— Faith
Eph. 4. 30.	The Holy Spirit of God	1 Pet. 4. 14.	———— Glory
Rev. 1. 4.	The 7 Spirits of God	Zech. 12. 10.	———— Grace
Is. 11. 2.	The Spirit of the Lord	Heb. 10. 29.	,, ,,
Acts 5. 9.	,,	Rom. 1. 4.	———— Holiness
2 Cor. 3. 17.	,,	Is. 4. 4.	———— Judgment
Heb. 9. 14.	The Eternal Spirit	— 28. 6.	,, ,,
Matt. 10. 20.	The Spirit of the Father	— 9. 2.	———— Knowledge
Is. 6. 8.	The Voice of the Lord	Rom. 8. 2.	———— Life
Job 33. 4.	The Breath of the Al-	Rev. 11. 11.	,, ,,
	mighty	Rom. 15. 30.	———— Love
Luke 1. 35.	The Power of the high-	2 Tim. 1. 7.	,, ,,
	est	Is. 11. 2.	———— Might
Ps. 51. 12.	Free Spirit	Eph. 1. 13.	———— Promise
Neh. 9. 20.	Good Spirit	Rev. 19. 10.	———— Prophecy
Ps. 143. 10.	,,	Eph. 1. 17.	———— Revelation
Rom. 8. 9.	Spirit of Christ	John 14. 17.	———— Truth
1 Pet. 1. 11.	,,	— 15. 26, &c.	,, ,,
Gal. 4. 6.	———— of the Son	Is. 11. 2.	———— Understanding
John 14. 16, 26;	The Comforter	— —	———— Wisdom
— 15. 26.	,,	Eph. 1. 17.	,, ,,

CHARACTERISTICS OF THE BOOKS OF THE OLD TESTAMENT

GENESIS.—Creation—Old World—Patriarchs. Called the *Book of the Generation*, or the Production of all things.

EXODUS.—The departure of the Jews from Egypt—Giving of the Law—Tabernacle.

LEVITICUS.—Ceremonial Law, its Sacrifices and Services.

NUMBERS.—Marshalling the Israelites—Journeyings in the Wilderness to the Promised Land.

DEUTERONOMY.—Repetition of the Laws, or the *Second Law*.

JOSHUA.—Conquest of Canaan, the Promised Land.

JUDGES.—Rulers who had the government before the Kings.

RUTH.—History of a pious Moabitess.

1 SAMUEL.—Life of Samuel—Reign of Saul—His death.

2 SAMUEL.—Reign of David, a period of about forty years.

1 KINGS.—Reign of Solomon—Revolt of the Ten Tribes.

2 KINGS.—Kings of Judah and Israel—The Prophets, Elisha and Elijah—Destruction of the city and temple by Nebuchadnezzar, king of Babylon.

1 CHRONICLES.—Genealogies of the Tribes—Repetitions and additions concerning David's reign. and that of other kings.

2 CHRONICLES.—Additions to the reign of Solomon and the kings of Judah and Israel. These two books may be considered as an epitome of all Sacred History from the origin of the Jewish nation, to their return from the first captivity.

BIBLE INFORMATION

EZRA.—Return of the Jews from captivity—Rebuilding of the Temple

NEHEMIAH.—Sanballat and Tobiah obstruct the Rebuilding of the Wall—Nehemiah overcomes them, and restores Jerusalem from its ruin to a state of dignity. A register of the persons who returned from Babylon.

ESTHER.—A pious Jewess, who by her personal beauty and virtuous character, obtained the favour of King Ahasuerus, and was made queen of Persia.

JOB.—Trials and deliverances of a pious Edomite. The Christian's Pattern of Patience under the reverses of fortune.

PSALMS.—Poems for worship, written chiefly by David. The great book of Christian direction and experience.

PROVERBS.—Wise sayings, composed chiefly by Solomon.

ECCLESIASTES.—A Treatise on the Vanity of the World.

SOLOMON'S SONG.—An allegorical Poem respecting the Church.

ISAIAH.—Predictions concerning Christ and the future extension of his glorious kingdom.

JEREMIAH.—Predictions of the weeping prophet concerning the Captivity of the Jews and the final destruction of their enemies.

LAMENTATIONS.—A Dirge or Elegy for fallen Jerusalem.

EZEKIEL.—Prophecies during the Babylonish Captivity to admonish and comfort the Jews.

DANIEL.—Incidents at the end of the Babylonish Captivity, and Predictions respecting Christ's sacrifice, and the extension and prosperity of his kingdom.

TWELVE MINOR PROPHETS
(So called from the Books being short)

HOSEA.—Prophecies respecting *Jews*, Messiah, and latter days, and the reproof of Israel for their sins.

JOEL.—	,,	,,	*Chaldean* invasion, and Gospel times
AMOS.—	,,	,,	The calamities which should visit Syria, Philistia, Edom, Ammon, Moab, Judah, and Israel, for their idolatry and sins.
OBADIAH.—			Predictions of *Edom's* destruction.
JONAH.—	,,	,,	The Missionary to *Nineveh*.
MICAH.—	,,	,,	*Israel* and *Judah's* Idolatry and Punishment. The ruin of monarchies.
NAHUM.—	,,	,,	Prophecies against Nineveh—the destruction of the Assyrian empire.
HABAKKUK.—		,,	*Chaldea's* Ruin. The Majesty of God
ZEPHANIAH.—		,,	*Judah's* Captivity, and future glory of the Church.

HAGGAI.—Prophecies respecting The Jews reproved for neglect of God's house.—The rebuilding of the *Temple*.

ZECHARIAH.— ,,   ,,   Same as Haggai; and Messiah.

MALACHI.—The calling of the *Gentiles*, and Christ's coming.

NEW TESTAMENT

MATTHEW.—Memoir of Christ incorporating Mark.

MARK.—A brief Memoir of Christ.

LUKE.—Supplying especially striking incidents, and discourses by Christ.

JOHN.—Supplying discourses not given by the other Evangelists.

ACTS.—Foundation and History of Christ's Church.

ROMANS.—On the doctrine of man's fall, his Redemption and Justification by Christ.

1 CORINTHIANS.—Important truths, as the Gospel, Christian Resurrection, also the correction of schisms, errors, and disorders.

2 CORINTHIANS.—A vindication of the apostle Paul and the doctrines of the Gospel—Abolition of the law by Christ.

GALATIANS.—*On Justification by Faith*, and not by Rites.

EPHESIANS.—The fulness and freeness of *Divine Grace*.

PHILIPPIANS.—*Christian kindness* commended, and Christian love reciprocated.

COLOSSIANS.—The Church warned against *Errors*, and Exhorted to *Duties*.

1 THESSALONIANS.—To confirm in *the faith* and in *holy conversation*.

2 THESSALONIANS.—Correcting an error respecting Christ's speedy *coming* to judgment.

1 TIMOTHY.—The Minister's Directory—Duties of Pastors and Churches.

2 TIMOTHY.—Encouragement in the work of the *Ministry*.

TITUS.—The Minister's Book of Practice and Consolation.

PHILEMON.—Letter to a converted Master to receive a *converted runaway Servant*.

HEBREWS.—Christ the Substance of the Ceremonial Law.

JAMES.—*Good Works* united with genuine *Faith*.

1 PETER.—Exhortations to *Christian Practice*.

2 PETER.—Exhortations, Warnings, and Predictions.

1 JOHN.—On the *Person of Christ*, and *Christian Love* and Practice.

2 JOHN.—A Pious Lady cautioned against *False Teachers*.

3 JOHN.—Gaius commended for his *Hospitality*.

JUDE.—Cautions against *Deceivers*.

REVELATION.—*Destinies of the Church* predicted, as afflicted, redeemed, saved, and glorified.

Scripture Chronologies

Patriarch's Name.	Age at Birth of his Son	Age at Death	Year of Birth A.M.	B.C.	Year of Death. A.M.	B.C.
Adam	130	930	--	4288	930	3358
Seth	105	912	130	4158	1042	3246
Enos	90	905	235	4063	1140	3148
Cainan	70	910	325	3963	1235	3053
Mahalaleel ...	65	895	395	3893	1290	2998
Jared	162	962	460	3828	1322	2966
Enoch	65	365*	622	3666	987*	3301*
Methuselah ...	187	969	687	3601	1656	2632
Lamech	182	777	874	3414	1651	2637
Noah	502	950	1056	3232	2006	2282
Shem	100	600	1558	2730	2158	2130
Arphaxad	35	438	1658	2630	2096	2192
Salah	30	433	1693	2595	2126	2162
Eber	34	464	1723	2505	2187	2101
Peleg	30	239	1757	2531	1996	2292
Reu	32	239	1787	2501	2026	2262
Serug	30	230	1819	2469	2049	2239
Nahor	29	148	1849	2439	1997	2291
Terah	70	205	1878	2410	2083	2205
Abraham ...	100	175	1948	2340	2123	2165
Isaac	60	180	2048	2240	2228	2060
Jacob	50	147	2108	2180	2255	2033
Joseph	—	110	2158	2130	2268	2020
Moses	—	120	2588	1700	2708	1580
David	—	70	3206	1082	3276	1012

*Enoch was " translated " without seeing death.

Biblical Emblems and their Meanings

Water, The Word in cleansing (Psa. cxix. 9; Eph. v. 26; Heb. x. 22).

Light, The Word for illumination, guidance (Psa. cxix. 105, 130; xliii 3).

Lamp, The Word as daily companion in walk (Ps. cxix. 105; Prov. vi. 23).

Mirror, The Word shewing what man is (Jas. i. 25); and Christ (2 Cor. iii. 18).

Laver, Means whereby God keeps His people clean (Eph. v. 26. R.V.).

Milk, The Word in its adaptation to young believers (1 Pet. ii. 2).

Strong Meat, Deep things of God for mature believers (Heb. v. 12-14).

Hammer, Power of the Word to break the sinner's heart (Jer. xxiii. 29).

Fire, Testing, trial (Mal. iii. 2; 1 Pet. i. 7); Divine wrath (Rev. xx. 9).

Dew, Reviving and refreshing of the Spirit (Hos. xiv. 5; Psa. cx. 3).

Rain, Abundant blessing, causing fruit (Isa. lv. 10, 11; Heb. vi. 7).

Leaven, Silent diffusion of evil (Matt. xiii. 33; xvi. 1; 1 Cor. v. 6; Gal. v. 9).

Leprosy, Sin in the nature, breaking forth in corrupt life (Lev. xiii.).

Anchor, The Christian's hope, security (Heb. vi. 19; Acts xxvii. 29, 30).

Seal, Authority, preservation, possession (Dan. vi. 17; Matt. xxvii. 66).

Shield, Defence, shelter (Psa. v. 12; xci. 4; Prov. xxxv.; Eph. vi. 16.).

Sword, Warfare, the Word as given by the Spirit (2 Sam. xii. 10; Eph. i. 13).

Girdle, Preparation, readiness, service (Acts xii. 8; Judges xviii. 11).

Crown (*Stephanos*, victor's crown), reward for service (Jas. i. 12; 1 Pet. v. 4).

Bible Customs, with their References

Anointing the Head, at banquets, for honour (Mark xiv. 3; Ps. xxiii. 5).

Washing Hands, freedom from ceremonial or moral guilt (Ps. xxvi. 6).

Washing Feet, done by a slave, for comfort, refreshment (John xiii. 5).

Eating, with the hand, hence the need of cleanliness (Mark vii. 5).

Binding and Loosing, bidding and forbidding (Matt. xvi. 19).

Wine in Bottles, bottles were " wineskins " (R.V.) (Matt. ix. 17).

Lamps and Lampstands—not Candlesticks, for house use (Luke xi. 23).

Lanterns, used for walking, at night, held close to feet (Ps. cxix. 105).

Grinding Corn, two women, on ground, with two stones (Matt. xxiv. 41).

Treading Corn, by oxen, dragging a log of wood (2 Sam. xxiv. 22).

Salutations, a ceremony of many parts, taking a long time (Luke x. 4).

Sitting at Meat, reclining on couches, feet exposed behind (Luke vii. 38).

Yoke, crossbar to which animals drawing plough were tied (Phil. iv. 3).

Marriage, after dark, bride led home, met by torchbearers, (Matt. xxv. 1, 12).

Landmarks, single stones set up, easily removed, hence Deut. xxvii. 17.

Beds, Mattress, or thick rug, could be rolled up and carried (Mark ii. 9).

Housetop, flat, reached by outer stair, easily uncovered (Matt. ix. 2).

Tombs, outside cities, hewn in rocks and caves (John xix. 41).

Symbols in the Book of Daniel

Metal.	Kingdom.	Symbol.	Character.
Gold.	Babylonian.	The Lion.	Despotic.
Silver.	Persian.	The Bear.	United.
Brass.	Grecian.	The Leopard.	Military.
Iron (and Clay).	Roman.	The Wild Beast.	Democratic.

The Four Gospels:

THEIR SUBJECTS, SYMBOLS, AND KEYWORDS

Matthew, Christ the King; Symbol, The Man; Keyword, " Kingdom."
Mark, Christ the Servant; Symbol, The Lion; Keyword," Immediately."
Luke, Christ, Perfect Man; Symbol, The Ox; Keyword, "A certain Man."
John, Christ, Son of God; Symbol, Eagle; Keywords, " Life," " Love."

Symbols in the Book of Revelation

Golden Lampshades, The Seven Churches, actually & representatively.
Stars, Spiritual representatives, probably the leaders of these churches.
Crowned Elders, The Redeemed, glorified in heaven, as worshippers.
Living Creatures (not beasts), Saints as administrators in government.
Lion, Majesty, power, kingly rule. Symbol of Power.
Calf, Service endurance, dependence. Symbol of Subjection.
Man, Intelligence, human nature, compassion. Symbol of Sympathy.
Eagle, Strength, heavenly vision. Symbol of Omniscience.
Horse, Conquest, strength for warfare. Symbol of War.
Sword, Slaughter, power for judgment. Symbol of Judgment.
Seven Seals, Widespread judgment, chiefly on apostate Christendom.
Seven Trumpets, Judgments on Christendom, Israel and Roman Earth.
Seven Vials, The wrath of God upon the guilty world.
Man-child, Christ personally. His saints associated with Him.
Dragon, Satan in his character as usurper and destroyer.
Serpent, The Devil in his subtlety and deceivings.
Harvest, Discerning and separating judgment of God.
Vintage, Unsparing judgment upon the ungodly.
Babylon, The False Church as fully developed in sin.
New Jerusalem, The True Church with Christ in resurrection glory.

Notes, Suggested by the Foregoing Dates

Adam lived contemporary with eight generations of his descendants.
Adam and Enoch would converse with Methuselah for 243 years.
Seth was contemporary with all the Antediluvians except Noah.
Enoch's Translation was 55 years before the death of Seth.
Methuselah would converse with Noah for 600 years.
Noah lived and walked with six generations of his forefathers.
Noah lived contemporary with ten generations of his sons.
Noah would hold converse with Abram for over 56 years.
Terah and his family were linked in their faith with Noah.
Haran, refusing to go forth at Babel, died in the presence of his father.
Peleg was the first to claim possession of earth and rule by the sword.
Abram was 99 years old when God confirmed His promise to him in Ur.
Shem outlived Abraham 35 years, and died the year of Joseph's birth.
Abram's sojourn in Egypt gave him Hagar, the mother of Ishmael.
Isaac died in the first of Egypt's seven years of plenty.
Rachel died and **Benjamin** was born, in the year that Joseph was sold.
Jacob and his sons came into Egypt when Joseph was eighty years old.
Israel's bondage to Pharaoh began in the year of Joseph's death.
Levi to Moses, there were four generations, extending over 430 years.
From Joshua's death to the death of **Jair** was 301 years (Judg. xi. 26).
To the **480 years** in 1 King's v. 1, add 131 years of servitude (1 Sam. viii).

Length of Human Life in Various Periad

Antediluvian times, average length, 900 years. Methuselah lived 969.
From the Deluge to Babel, reduced by a half. Heber lived **464** yrs.
Babel to Moses, was again shortened. Reu, the longest life, age **239.**
Moses to David, the average length of life was (Ps. xc. 10), 70 years.
The Lord Jesus was cut off in the midst of His days (Ps. cii. 24) at 33 years.
Human Life in the **Millennium** will reach the full measure, **1,000** yrs.

The Ages

WITH THEIR CHARACTERISTICS AND REPRESENTATIVES

Innocence, Represented in *Adam*, as created and placed in Eden.
Lawlessness, Manifested in *Cain*, who slew his brother.
Government, Committed to *Noah*, with power of capital punishment.
Promise, Bestowed on *Abraham*, and his seed, through whom Christ came
Law, Given through *Moses*, to the earthly people at Sinai.
Grace, Exhibited in *Jesus* as Man, in Life and in Death. Now it reigns.
Glory, To be revealed in *Christ* as King and Priest on His Throne.
Eternity, " The Ages of Ages," in which " God is All in All."